BRISTOL
FIGHTER

BRISTOL FIGHTER

FRANK BARNWELL'S UBIQUITOUS MULTIROLE MASTERPIECE

Ray Sturtivant, Gordon Page
James J Halley & Philip Jarrett

Air-Britain

Published in the United Kingdom by
Air-Britain

Air-Britain
Sales Department:
Unit 1A, Munday Works Industrial Estate,
Morley Road, Tonbridge, Kent TN9 1RA

For details of the books and magazines we publish,
and how to join Air-Britain, please visit us at
www.air-britain.com

ISBN 978-0-85130-536-3

Printed in Poland
www.lfbookservices.co.uk

Origination by Sue Bushell
Cover Origination by Lee Howard

Find us on Facebook

CONTENTS

INTRODUCTION

The first powered flight in the United Kingdom took place in 1908. In the next few years many others followed and in 1912 the Royal Flying Corps (RFC) was established. In 1915, only seven years after the first flight, a requirement was issued for a two-seat biplane to undertake the RFC's main requirement, reconnaissance. In a very few years the miscellaneous collections of wood and fabric had evolved into the classical form of the two-seat biplane that lasted for decades before being overtaken by monoplane designs.

The Bristol Company's response to the requirement was a workmanlike design that quickly found favour with the War Office and RFC. The initial production batch was designated the F.2A, but the type was more commonly known as the Bristol Fighter. In the RFC it was nicknamed the 'Biff', but it was also identified later as the 'Brisfit'. The F.2B version was produced in large numbers and saw service during the First World War with the RFC and, from 1 April 1918, the Royal Air Force (RAF), in France, Italy, Greece, Egypt, Palestine and, post-war, in India. At a time when aircraft types usually remained in service for only a few years before being overtaken by new designs, it served the RAF until the early 1930s.

One of the problems encountered while writing the history of the RFC and RAF in 1914-1918 was the large-scale destruction of files thought to be of 'no historical interest'. A selection of Air Ministry files was made soon after the end of the First World War for use in writing the official history of the war. As a result, most of the records are for operational units. Relatively few provide details of the aircraft used by training units, the official history depending heavily on the records of the 6th Brigade, which administered the training units and which contained sufficient general information for

the chapter on training to be compiled. The activities of individual training units were, in general, scrapped. The same applies to the large number of storage and repair units. Consequently, for example, aircraft suddenly appear in India without any reference as to how they got there.

Operational units submitted daily records of 'work performed', and from these we have compiled the table of individual aircraft histories insofar as they could be found. Wing and Brigade records were also kept, and sometimes fill the gaps in the squadron files. The transfer of aircraft from squadron to repair unit was usually recorded in the squadron files, although some did not record details of their aircraft. These records died out after the end of hostilities and the Forms 540 and 541 that provided details during the Second World War were not introduced until the late 1930s. Some squadrons used these to transfer information from their existing records, but not many detailed their aircraft. The allocation of aircraft in the tables was often extracted from pilots' log books, and accident records also pinpoint a particular aircraft at a specific unit when an accident took place; however, accident records are incomplete for the 1920s and early 1930s. One drawback of the cards used at this time was that there was no place for the location of the accident to be recorded.

After the First World War many Bristol Fighters were sold to overseas air forces or converted to civilian use. Airworthiness and registration requirements meant that these were documented to a greater extent than the military aircraft.

In recording the members of crews involved, we have retained full initials on each occasion to avoid confusion between the many similar names. The *Air Force List* has been used to check these, but by 1918

the number of officers in the RAF was considerable and it was not always possible to verify which 'Smith' was the one involved.

In some cases, the aircraft serial numbers were misrecorded and this usually applied to the prefix letter, but typing errors could result in an aircraft destroyed in France in 1918 appearing in documents in India or the Middle East in the 1920s. We have tried to reconcile these as far as possible.

Background

This book has had a long and troubled gestation. It was due to be published in 2009 and had reached an advanced stage of preparation, but completion was halted by the deaths of its initial authors and also by the loss or corruption of disks, particularly those containing the images; thus it languished in a semi-prepared state more than a decade. When the present contributing editor took it on, consequently, the illustrations had to be re-sourced and a great deal of additional or updated information had to be incorporated in the light of more recent research. The book also underwent a complete redesign to bring it into line with Air-Britain's latest styling. This laborious process had its benefits, however, as considerably more images have been amassed, many hitherto unpublished, and it has been possible to include valuable additional contributions, both textural and pictorial, from generous researchers around the world who made their expertise freely available. Consequently, the resulting book might reasonably be described as a second, revised and greatly expanded, edition of the unpublished first edition.

Philip Jarrett,
Honorary Companion RAeS
Contributing Editor
Dorking, 2019

Left: **F.2B Coupe H1460 and seven other Bristol Fighters of Kenley-based 24 Sqn practising for the RAF Pageant in July 1921.**
(Philip Jarrett)

Bristol F.2B J8432 with two others of 2 Sqn at Manston in formation about 1929. *(Philip Jarrett)*

ACKNOWLEDGEMENTS

Among the many people worldwide who have helped with information and illustrations for this book are Lennart Andersen, Guy Black, Trevor Boughton, the late Chaz Bowyer, Daniel Brackx, the late Jack Bruce, Geoffrey Bussey, Phil Butler, Dugald Cameron, Bob Casari, the late Frank Cheesman, Patrick J. Cummins, Howard J. Curtis, Ted D'Arcy, John Davis, Mick Davis, Nigel Dingley, Barry Dowsett, Yves Duwelz, Malcolm Fillmore, Juanita Franzi, Brian Gardner, Dan Hagedorn, Tim Hall, Eric Harlin, the late John Havers, John Heaven, Trevor Henshaw, Dave Howley, Colin Huston, David Jackson, Tomek Kopalski, Georges Lecomte, the late Stuart Leslie, Ricardo Lezon, Michael Magnussen, Bernard Martin, Errol Martyn, Tim Mason, Wojtek Matusiak, Rob Millinship, the late Tony Morris, Piotr Mrozowski, Michael Napier, Geoff Negus, the late Mike O'Connor, Bob Ogden, Frank Olynyk, Graham Orphan, Colin Owers, Richard Paver, Chris Salter, Wojtek Sankowski, Paul Smiddy, Stuart W.R. Smith and Martin Farley of Denzil Print, Ken Smy, Nick and Amanda Stroud, Stuart Tucker, Mark Tuffield, Mark Wagner, Colin Waugh, Piotr Wisniewski, Cross and Cockade International, the present and former staff of the RAF Museum especially Peter Elliott, Simon Moody and Andrew Renwick, members of the Farnborough Air Sciences Trust Association, the staff of the Liddle Collection (Brotherton Library), Matias Laitinen, Keeper, Head of Collections, Finnish Aviation Museum; Museums in Akershus/Norway; Romsdalsmuseet photo archive, Norway; and Gail van Tonder at the South African Air Force Museum.

PHOTOGRAPHY

The photographs in this volume have been garnered over a period of many years from a wide variety of sources, and vary in quality owing to the standards of photography 100 years ago. Although some are manufacturer's photographs, produced on full-plate or half-plate cameras, many come from small amateur contemporary prints of variable quality that have suffered from poor fixing or the ravages of time. Amateur photography was often of inferior quality, and air-to-air photography a rarity. The Defence of the Realm Act 1914 prohibited private photography on military bases (though, mercifully for latter-day researchers, this was sometimes ignored!), with the result that relatively few images from the war period exist. It was decided to let the photographs 'speak for themselves' (as seen in the image opposite), without the excessive retouching that often detracts from their authenticity, apart from removing scratches, marks and creases.

GLOSSARY OF TERMS AND ABBREVIATIONS

A&AEE	Aeroplane and Armament Experimental Establishment
AAP	Aircraft Acceptance Park
ADC	Aircraft Disposal Company Ltd
AEE(H)	Aeroplane Experimental Establishment (Home)
AEF	American Expeditionary Force
AFC	Australian Flying Corps
ALG	Advanced Landing Ground
ARD	Aircraft Repair Depot
ASD	Aeroplane Supply Depot
CFS	Central Flying School
C of A	Certificate of Airworthiness
C of R	Certificate of Registration
CSL	Centralne Składy Lotnicze (Central Aircraft Depot)
CWL	Centralne Warsztaty Lotnicze (Central Aircraft Works)
CWOL	Initials of original title of CWL, above
DC	Dual Control
DGMA	Director-General of Military Aeronautics
EW	Eskadra Wywiadowcza (Reconnaissance Squadron)
FAM	Fuerza Aérea Mexicana
FMA	Fábrica Militar de Aviones
FTS	Flying Training School
HAD	Home Aircraft Depot
HD	Home Defence
HE	High-Explosive
LG	Landing Ground
LSSiB	Lotnicza Szkola Strzelania i Bombardowania (Air School of Gunnery and Bombardment)
MAEE	Marine Aircraft Experimental Establishment
NAF	National Aircraft Factory
NAF	Naval Aircraft Factory (USA)
NWFP	North West Frontier Province
NZAF	New Zealand Air Force
NZPAF	New Zealand Permanent Air Force
OSL	Oficerska Szkola Lotnicza (Air Officers' School)
(O)SoAG	(Observers) School of Aerial Gunnery
OSOL	Oficerska Szkola Obserwatorów Lotniczych (Officers' School for Air Observers)
PL	Pułk Lotniczy (Air Regiment)
RAE	Royal Aircraft Establishment
RAF	Royal Air Force
RFC	Royal Flying Corps
RL	Royal Laboratory
RNAS	Royal Naval Air Service
RNZAF	Royal New Zealand Air Force
RPL	Ruchomy Park Lotniczy (Mobile Aircraft Park)
RS	Reserve Squadron
SABCA	Société Anonyme Belge de Constructions Aéronautiques
SL	Szkola Lotnicza (Flying School)
SoAC	School of Army Co-operation
SoAF	School of Aerial Fighting
SoAF&G	School of Aerial Fighting and Gunnery
SoAG	School of Aerial Gunnery
SOC	Struck Off Charge
SOL	Szkola Obserwatorów Lotniczych (School of Aircraft Maintenance)
SPL	Szkola Podchorazych Lotnictwa (Aviation Cadet Officers' School)
Sqn	Squadron
SWRT	Short Wave Radio Telephony
TDS	Training Depot Station
TS	Training Squadron
USAS	United States Air Service
USN	United States Navy
WCZL	Warsztaty Centralnych Zakladów Lotniczych (Workshops of the Central Aircraft Works)
WO	Written Off
WSP	Wyzsza Szkola Pilotów (Advanced Pilots' School)

Bristol F.2A prototype A3303 at the Central Flying School, Upavon, fitted with a two-bladed propeller and without wing-root endplates. *(C&C)*

Chapter 1

THE F.2A

As the First World War progressed, more specialised aircraft were required to suit current needs and to replace types such as the Royal Aircraft Factory B.E.2, which had undertaken a variety of tasks, and would continue do so until after the Armistice, especially in the training role.

In the autumn of 1915 Royal Flying Corps (RFC) Headquarters issued a requirement for a two-seat aircraft to undertake corps reconnaissance and artillery spotting as well as fighting patrols. There were two responses to this in March 1916. One was the R.E.8, designed by the Royal Aircraft Factory as a direct replacement for its B.E.2, which was basically a pre-war design. The other was from the British & Colonial Aeroplane Co Ltd (Bristol) for a proposed design designated Bristol R.2A. Both were accepted for further development and prototypes were ordered.

The R.2A, designed under the leadership of Bristol's chief designer, Capt Frank Barnwell, was to have been a relatively light biplane powered by a 120hp Beardmore water cooled in-line engine and having 40ft 8in equal-span two-bay staggered wings. The two-man crew was seated in tandem, the pilot having a fixed forward-firing synchronised Lewis machine-gun mounted on the starboard upper fuselage longeron. His observer sat immediately behind him, the fuselage tapering in depth towards the tailplane. This gave him quite a good field of

fire, especially as more than a third of the vertical tail surfaces were below tailplane level. He had dual controls and was provided with a wireless set, a camera and a message-launching tube. He also had a Lewis machine-gun, mounted on an Etévé rotating-ring mounting. To use this, he had to fold his seat up and stand on the fuselage floor. To minimise the extent to which the upper wing obscured the pilot's field of view, the fuselage was positioned in a mid-gap so that, his eyes being close to the upper-wing level, he had the smallest possible blind spot.

It soon became apparent that the aircraft would be underpowered, and in May 1916 a 150hp Hispano-Suiza was substituted, with a proposed change of designation to R.2B. The design now had unequal-span wings with strut-braced extensions, the lower wing being attached directly to the lower longerons, and partial Warren girder lift bracing intended to simplify rigging when in the field. This in turn gave way to a redesign capable of accommodating the new 190hp Rolls-Royce Mark I vee-twelve engine as an alternative. Barnwell accordingly revised both the cowling and the fuselage, incorporating new fuel and oil tank installations.

An example of the Vickers machine-gun was obtained from the RFC Machine Gun School at Hythe in Kent, where Leslie G. Frise, a member of the company's design staff, had been sent on a two-week course to

be taught its operation. Installing this weapon in place of the pilot's Lewis gun required further consideration, the designers eventually settling for a mounting on the fuselage centreline. This necessitated a tunnel in the upper forward petrol tank. The cocking handle was now immediately in front of the pilot, where it would have the benefit of warm air from the engine to prevent stoppages due to the mechanism's oil freezing at high altitudes.

Captain Frank Sowter Barnwell, OBE, AFC, BSc, the British and Colonial Aeroplane Company's chief designer at the time the Bristol Fighter was created, had joined the company as a draughtsman in April 1911. *(Bristol)*

Predecessors

The configuration adopted for the Bristol Fighter, a two-bay biplane with its fuselage positioned in mid-gap, had been used in two earlier aeroplanes produced by the British & Colonial Aeroplane Co. Two Bristol Gordon England G.E.2s (upper left) were built for the Military Aeroplane Competition of 1912. This is the 70hp Daimler-engined version; the other one had a 100hp Gnome. The G.E.3 of 1912 (lower left) was a large long-range biplane to meet a Turkish Government requirement. In these instances, the fuselage was positioned in mid-gap to allow greater ground clearance for the propeller, rather than to minimise the upper wing's obstruction of the pilot's view.

Other two-bay biplane predecessors were the Bristol-Coanda biplanes (below) designed by Rumanian Henri Coanda, the most successful of which was the Gnome-engined T.B.8, a number of which served with the RNAS in the early war years.

The design had reverted to two-bay wings of equal span, with the crew sitting closer together and the fuselage once more in mid-gap. The observer's seat was now mounted on slides so that he could move it backwards and forwards to face either way, and his view was improved by the downward curve of the upper longerons being increased to run down to a horizontal knife edge on the rear spar of the variable-incidence tailplane. He again had an Etévé gun mounting, and his new position allowed him a better view while using the wireless set. He could also warn the pilot of the approach of enemy aircraft from the rear by thumping him on the back. The variable-incidence tailplane enabled the aircraft to be flown 'hands-off' over quite a wide speed range, making it less tiring to fly and allowing the pilot to concentrate on other essential tasks. The dual control was no longer standard equipment, but in the event of an emergency a small lever could be inserted into a socket, giving the observer a degree of control over the elevator, and hand grips fitted to the rudder cables where they passed through his cockpit would hopefully have enabled him to minimise the effect of a crash landing if the pilot was incapacitated.

In July 1916, only four months after the initial responses to the specification, the intended role had evolved from purely reconnaissance to that of fighter-reconnaissance. Thus, a fresh designation was required and, as the F.2A, it was considered sufficiently acceptable for an order to be placed. Accordingly, Contract No.87/A/552 was placed for 52 aircraft, the airframe serial numbers A3303 to A3304 being allocated on 28 August 1916. Of these, the first two would serve as prototypes, fitted respectively with a Rolls-Royce and an Hispano-Suiza engine. Construction began in July 1916. In the event Hispano-Suiza engines were unavailable, so Rolls-Royce Falcons were to be fitted. As the aircraft was primarily a fighter it became referred to as the Bristol Fighter.

The Rolls-Royce-engined prototype, A3303, had two long vertical radiators, one each side on the fuselage flanks, short exhaust manifolds with forward outlets and a four-bladed left-handed propeller. As completed, A3303 did not have the proposed decking on the rear fuselage, nor was a gun mounting fitted to the observer's cockpit. The wing panels were apparently B.E.2c components, which would have been readily available as British & Colonial had received several subcontracts for this type. Both prototypes had uncovered lower wing centre sections, the lower wing panels being attached to a cross-braced steel-tube anchorage frame. Initially, A3303 had endplates fitted to the roots of the lower wing panels.

The first flight was made on 9 September 1916 by Capt C.A. Hooper, commanding officer of the Bristol Aircraft Acceptance Park at Filton. Failure to climb higher than an indicated 6,000ft on this flight resulted in rigging checks and alterations to incidence and stagger, but this had no apparent effect. Harold Barnwell, Vickers's chief test pilot, made another flight with similar results,

A head-on view of F.2A prototype A3303 at the Central Flying School, Upavon, around September-October 1916. (C&C)

Right: **This study of A3303 at Upavon for its official performance and handling trials in September 1916 shows the aircraft essentially as originally completed, with tall flank radiators and lacking a proper mounting for the observer's Lewis gun, the weapon being mounted temporarily on the starboard upper longeron. The high and exposed position of the pilot is evident.** *(Philip Jarrett)*

although he believed he had climbed to a much higher altitude. Further consideration led to the altimeter being changed, as a consequence of which it was discovered that the aircraft was actually capable of reaching a much more satisfactory 10,000ft in 15min.

This apparent problem having been overcome, on 21 September A3303 was flown to the Central Flying School (CFS) at Upavon to undertake Service trials. Here testing revealed that actual performance was much greater than estimated, though

modifications were necessary. The radiator arrangement excessively obscured the pilot's forward view, especially during landing, and this was resolved by designing an entirely

new installation comprising a single circular frontal radiator fitted with shutters to control cooling. Modifications to the manifolds provided a rear outlet for the gases, and a two-bladed left-handed propeller was later fitted. The endplates on the lower wing roots were removed. With this work completed, the aircraft had been returned to Upavon by 16 October and was given a generally favourable report, though with reservations about a reportedly indifferent performance, a number of minor modifications being called for. Three days later it was flown across the Channel to No.2 Aircraft Depot at Candas. After a brief stay to be test-flown under Service conditions it returned to England on 22 October. Further modifications were made, including the fitting a Scarff ring gun mounting on the rear cockpit, and by February 1917 it was with the Experimental Armament Squadron at Orfordness (more correctly Orford Ness) in East Suffolk.

Some account of A3303's time at Orfordness was recorded by Sqn Ldr F.D. Holder in *Cross & Cockade Great Britain Journal* Vol 8 No 2 of 1977. As a lieutenant, Holder was posted there on 31 December 1916 as a test pilot. He served with Lt Oxland on 'A' Flight, commanded by Capt G. Collett. This Flight was equipped with reconnaissance and fighter/bomber types. Holder recalls that the Rumanian engineer Constantinesco came to Orford to demonstrate his interrupter gear for firing through the propeller arc. He says: 'It was fitted by Collett to the prototype Bristol Fighter A3303. This had a Rolls-Royce 190hp Falcon engine … with a two-bladed propeller which made the firing that much easier. The idea was successful in test and proved of great value.'

'A' Flight was then detailed to undertake tests of oxygen apparatus and the use of electrically heated clothing, both of which had to be tested in the Bristol Fighter in order to attain the required altitudes. Holder says: 'The main trouble about the Bristol Fighter was that its petrol was carried in four

Left: **Three-quarter-front port, starboard side, and three-quarter rear port views of Bristol F.2A A3303 at Filton in 1916.** *(C&C and Philip Jarrett)*

Right: **This starboard three-quarter view of A3303 at Filton in 1916 shows the lower wing root endplates to advantage.** *(C&C)*

tanks and it was essential to get the pressure up in the next tank before the change over. All the petrol had to be poured into the tanks from two-gallon cans through chamois leather to eliminate water.'

When Collett and Oxland departed, Holder was left in acting command of 'A' Flight, and in February 1917 he flew over to Martlesham Heath to collect the 'expert on oxygen apparatus'. He says: 'I enjoyed the power and speed of the Bristol Fighter and the height to which we climbed much more quickly than anything I had met before. At about ceiling height I looked back to see how the experiment was progressing and was so interested that I lost control and fell several thousand feet before correcting my first spin. We then climbed up again and the expert said on landing that he thought the sudden change was a wonderful way of testing atmosphere pressure.' In addition to F.2A A3303, Holder also flew F.2Bs A7181, A7183 and B1181 during his time at Orfordness, but he does not specify which aircraft were used for which tests.

During its time at Orfordness A3303, piloted by Lt Holder, was used in attempted interceptions of daylight Gotha bomber raids. The first occasion was on 4 July 1917, when Holder and Lt H.L. Billington took off at 07:30 in the hope of intercepting a raid on Harwich and Felixstowe and landed at 08:45; one of 103 sorties flown by defending

aircraft. On 7 July the Germans sent a force of 24 Gothas to attack London in daylight. A total of 108 sorties was flown by defending aircraft. They included A3303, piloted by Lt F.D. Holder, with Lt F.W. Musson as observer, who took off from Orfordness at 09:50. Spotting the enemy formation east of Southend in Essex, Holder chased it for thirty minutes, but by then he was low on fuel and not perceptibly gaining on his prey, so he fired off a 30-round burst at long range, his observer also firing one drum from his Lewis gun. They landed safely at Southend on the last of their fuel at 12:05. On 22 July, as one of 122 sorties in response to another daylight Gotha raid against Harwich and Felixstowe, Holder took off in A3303 at 08:20, accompanied by Sgt S. Ashby, returning at 10:15. As part of a 139-sortie response to a daylight Gotha raid targeting Southend on 12 August, Holder

and Lt Wallace flew from 17:45 to 18:45, and on 22 August Holder and Capt B.M. Jones took off from Orfordness in A3303 at 10:30 and returned at 12:00; one of 138 defensive sorties against a daylight Gotha raid targeting Margate, Ramsgate and Dover. Nothing further is known of this aircraft, which was presumably scrapped.

Meanwhile, the second prototype, A3304, had flown at Filton on 25 October 1916. From the outset its 150hp Hispano-Suiza engine had shutters fitted behind a circular frontal radiator. The wings were again of B.E.2 type, with an open lower centre-section frame and sloping longerons. As in A3303, endplates were fitted to the inboard ends of the lower wing panels, but the tailskid was mounted on the rudder, instead of the pylon-type skid support of the first machine. Several modifications were then made. The pilot's view was improved by

Above left: **The fuselage-flank radiators and the lower wing inboard endplates of the first F.2A in its early form are conspicuous here.** *(Philip Jarrett)*

Above: **By the time this picture was taken, A3303's engine cowling had been painted and fairings had been added to its radiators.** *(Philip Jarrett)*

Left: **The first F.2A, A3303, at Filton after being given a single radiator in its nose, a four-blade propeller, redesigned engine cowlings and exhaust manifolds having rear outlets.** *(Bristol)*

Above: **F.2A prototype A3303 with the Aeroplane Experimental Squadron at Orfordness, July-August 1916. Used for five flights attempts to intercept German Gotha bombers, it has navigation lights on the lower wingtips but lacks radiator shutters.** *(C&C)*

Right: **Another view of A3303 at Orfordness, here fitted with a synchronising disc for its fixed Vickers gun. Lieutenant H.L. Billington is on the left, and Capt R.W Oxland is on the right.** *(C&C)*

sloping the upper longerons downwards from the level of the pilot's cockpit towards the level of the engine bearers, and his seat was armoured, as in A3303. Tapering the top decking forward enabled a large upper tank to be fitted, as well as an ammunition box for the pilot's Vickers gun. In addition, a lower centre-section had been fashioned by building out the wing-attachment frame. Like its companion, A3304 was sent to the CFS at Upavon, where performance trials were performed on 4 and 6 December. There is no known surviving record of the fate of this second prototype. Official trials were passed with ease, performance figures being better than projected.

Rolls-Royce 190hp Mk.II engines had been specified for the 50 production aircraft of the initial order, but in the event the majority appear to have been fitted with the Mk.I, driving a laminated wooden propeller. An open structure was retained for the lower centre-section, and the wingtips were now of blunt outline, which would be adopted as standard for future orders. The pilot's seat now had no armour. A large proportion of this batch was delivered to 38 Reserve Squadron (RS) at Rendcomb in

A modified Scarff No.2 gun mounting fitted to the prototype F.2A, A3303, at the Experimental Armament Squadron at Orfordness in 1917. The mounting was modified to enable the ring to be driven by bungee-operated gearing on top of the fuselage. The device was apparently intended to enable the pilot to centre the gun automatically for elevated firing. The gunsight mounted on the trailing edge of the upper centre-section is at an angle of 45 degrees seen from the pilot's cockpit. *(C&C)*

The same device as in the image to the left, but with a yoked pair of Lewis guns.

Left: **The second F.2A prototype, A3304, at Filton shortly after completion, October 1916, in its initial form with the straight and horizontal fuselage upper longerons in front of the cockpit. It had a 150hp Hispano-Suiza engine, and its tailskid was built into the base of the rudder.** *(Philip Jarrett)*

Gloucestershire, starting with A3305 on 20 December 1916, for familiarisation by the pilots and observers, and others went either to this school or to 48 Sqn for service in due course with the British Expeditionary Force (BEF) in France. Deliveries of the F.2A ended in March 1917.

Formed at Netheravon on 15 April 1916, 48 Sqn had worked-up on such types as the Avro 504A and the Royal Aircraft Factory R.E.7, B.E.2c, B.E.8a and B.E.12. On 8 June 1916 it moved to Rendcomb, six miles north of Cirencester and conveniently only some 35 miles from the manufacturer's aerodrome at Filton, north of Bristol. Re-equipment with the F.2A began early in 1917 under the command of Maj A.C. Wright, and by the time the unit went to France, on 8 March, the squadron was fully equipped. Later deliveries from this batch appear to have been made direct to the squadron's new base at La Bellevue, and it became part of 13th (Army) Wing in the 4th Brigade, RFC, now under the command of Maj A. Vere Bettington. The F.2A crews anticipated that their new mounts would stand a far better chance against the Albatros D.III formations and 'circuses' than would have been the case with the originally intended B.E.12s, and hopefully would enable them to achieve local air superiority. Unfortunately, many squadron records have not survived, often making it difficult to identify individual serial numbers.

April 1917

To achieve maximum surprise the F.2A, and also the then-new Airco D.H.4, were kept back until four weeks later, when, on 4 April, an air offensive began in support of the battle of Arras, flying over the British front line which ran from Givenchy-en-Gohelle southwards to Croiselles. The key objective of the attack was to capture the strongly held vantage point at Vimy Ridge, a task give to the First Army with its major Canadian component, the remainder of the attack being the responsibility of the Third Army.

This was 48 Sqn's opportunity, and it went into action on the second day, when six aircraft departed for reconnaissance led by Capt W. Leefe Robinson VC, who had earned this ultimate award for shooting down the German Schütte-Lanz airship SL11 on the night of 2/3 September 1916 in a B.E.2c of 39 (Home Defence) Sqn based at Sutton's Farm. Sadly, however, 48

Left: **Three views of Hispano-engined A3304 after being fitted with a Scarff ring gun mounting on the observer's cockpit. The lower wing-root endplates have now been done away with, and there is a faired centre-section between the lower wing panels.** *(Philip Jarrett)*

Right: **Bristol F.2A A3343 displays shutterless radiators and the redesigned mainplanes of production F.2As, which had revised wingtip planform, straight upper longerons, and the open lower wing centre-section. This machine was one of the six aircraft of 48 Sqn that took part in the unit's unfortunate first operational patrol, on 5 April 1917, when it was brought down by the guns of Manfred von Richthofen's Albatros D.III, thus becoming his 39th combat victory. Fortunately the crew of A3343, Lts A.T. Adams and D.J. Stewart, survived and were able to set their aircraft alight before becoming prisoners of war.** *(Philip Jarrett)*

Sqn's Bristol Fighters had the misfortune to find themselves beset by five Albatros D.IIIs of Jagdstaffel l, led by Baron Manfred von Richthofen, and lost four of its aircraft near Douai that day. Captain A.M. Wilkinson and Lt L.W. Allen, in an unspecified aircraft, claimed to have sent an Albatros D.III down out of control, as did Lt P. Pike and Lt H.B. Griffith in A3325, while 2nd Lt O.W. Berry and his observer fought a two-seater then drove down a single-seater. However, A3320, A3337, A3340 and A3343 are mentioned in other records. Captain Leefe Robinson and 2nd Lt E.D. Warburton managed to send down one of the enemy out of control before they were shot down themselves by Vzfw S. Festner. Lieutenant L.H.A. Cooper and 2nd Lt A. Boldison were claimed by Ltn K. Simon of Jasta 11. Richthofen himself claimed both A3340 (2nd Lt A.N. Leckler and 2nd Lt H.D.K. George) and A3343 (Lt A.T. Adams and 2nd Lt D.J. Stewart) as his 35th and 36th victories respectively. The British pilots had fought as best they could in what was then the orthodox manner, manoeuvring to try to give the observer as much opportunity as possible to get favourable shots at the enemy, but this had proved disastrous.

This major setback on the Bristol Fighter's first significant foray caused great dismay. Clearly, lessons had to be learnt as to the best way of employing this new type. Mistakenly, the Germans decided that the F.2A/B would not be the major new foe they had feared. Richthofen declared that his Albatroses were unquestionably superior both in speed and climbing power, and events during the

remainder of that month appeared to support this view. However, on the 6th Lt F.P. Holliday, with Capt A.H.W. Wall as observer, sent an enemy aircraft down out of control northeast of Arras, while 2nd Lt W.T. Price and 2nd Lt M.A. Benjamin dealt similarly with another near Douai, both F.2A serials being unrecorded. Next day, though, in combat northeast of Arras, Lt J.W. Warren in A3317 forced-landed near Saulty with engine failure, observer 2nd Lt G.C. Burnand being killed. This steady attrition continued; A3330 was shot down in combat east of Arras and fell near Rémy, its pilot, 2nd Lt O.W. Berry, being killed and 2nd Lt F.B. Goodison being taken prisoner, only to die later of his wounds.

On 8 April 48 Sqn drove down six enemy aircraft, two of them out of control, one of these being an Albatros near Rémy shared between 2nd Lt G.N. Brockhurst and 2nd Lt C.B. Boughton (observer) and 2nd Lt A.G. Riley and 2nd Lt L.G. Hall (observer). Other pilots involved were 2nd Lt R.E. Adeney, Capt D.M. Tidmarsh and 2nd Lt O.W. Berry, with observers 2nd Lt L.G. Lovell, 2nd Lt C.B. Holland and Lt F.B. Goodison. On the next day, the 9th, two 48 Sqn aircraft attacked five enemy aircraft near Arras and 2nd Lt J.H.T. Letts and Lt H.G. Collins in A3315 sent two Albatros D.IIIs down out of control, but Collins was hit and killed by return fire. Captain A.M.

Wilkinson with Lt L.W. Allen were also involved in this action. Also that day Capt A.M. Wilkinson and Lt H.B. Griffith sent an Albatros two-seater out of control near Lens.

On the 10th an enemy aircraft sent down out of control at Rémy was claimed jointly by 2nd Lts Brockhurst and Boughton in A3323 and Capt Tidmarsh and 2nd Lt Holland in A3338. On 11 April four F.2Bs were in combat with four Albatros D.IIIs of Jasta 11 near Fampoux. Two of the enemy were destroyed, after which 2nd Lt A.G. Riley and 2nd Lt L.G. Hall in an unspecified machine landed safely, but none of the others returned. When A3318 came down behind enemy lines its pilot, 2nd Lt R.E. Adeney, was taken prisoner briefly before dying of his wounds, and 2nd Lt L.G. Lovell was killed, their aircraft possibly having been shot down by Ltn J.E. Schafer. Leutnant Lothar von Richthofen claimed A3323, 2nd Lt G.N. Brockhurst and 2nd Lt C.B. Boughton, both of whom were wounded, being taken prisoner, while Capt D.M. Tidmarsh and 2nd Lt C.B. Holland were taken prisoner when A3338 was claimed by Ltn K. Wolff. That same day A3353 was written off after it hit a tree while landing and then caught fire, 2nd Lt A.B. Anstey being concussed and AM2 Rutherford escaping unhurt. Next day two enemy aircraft were sent down out of control, being shared by Capt A.M. Wilkinson and Lt L.W. Allen with 2nd Lt W.O.B. Winkler and 2nd Lt E.S. Moore. On the 13th, 2nd Lt H.D. Davies and 2nd Lt R.S.L. Worsley were taken prisoner when A3322 was brought down near Vitry-en-Artois by anti-aircraft fire, their aircraft being captured intact. On the same day in the same area 2nd Lt J.W. Warren and Lt H.B. Griffith sent an Albatros down out of control, as did Capt A.M. Wilkinson and Lt L.W. Allen, who also destroyed another enemy aircraft.

By now the British offensive had breached the German lines, and on the 16th the French launched a big attack in the south, but this soon collapsed and British forces had to apply fresh pressure on the enemy to relieve them. On the 22nd Capt Wilkinson and Lt Allen sent an enemy aircraft down

Brought down by anti-aircraft fire at Vitry on 13 April 1917, F.2A A3322 '5' of 38 Sqn was captured intact by the Germans. Its occupants, 2nd Lt H.D. Davies and 2nd Lt R.S.L. Worsley, were taken prisoner. *(via Philip Jarrett)*

F.2B A7147 '5' of 11 Sqn comes in for close scrutiny after being captured on 18 August 1918. Its crew, 2nd Lt G.A. Rose and Cpl H.G. Bassenger (above), were taken prisoners of war. (Trevor Henshaw)

out of control. On the 23rd hard-pressed 48 Sqn lost A3321, which had to be written off after suffering engine failure and crashing in an attempted forced landing on a road bordering the aerodrome, 2nd Lt W.T. Price and 2nd Lt M.A. Benjamin both being unhurt. However, on that day a patrol led by Lt F.P. Holliday and Capt A.H.W. Wall sent two Albatros D.IIIs down out of control near Vitry-en-Artois and drove down another, others involved being pilots Lt W.T. Price, Lt R.B. Hay and 2nd Lt

W.O.B. Winkler with observers 2nd Lt E.S. Moore, Lt V.W.G. Nutkins and Lt M.A. Benjamin. Holliday, and Wall claimed another Albatros D.III in the same area. A casualty that day was observer Lt L.E. Porter, who was wounded when his aircraft was hit by anti-aircraft fire.

On the 24th Lt F.P. Holliday and Capt A.H.W. Wall destroyed an enemy aircraft and sent down a two-seater out of control near Cagnicourt, and three Albatros D.IIIs were sent down out of control in the same

area by Lt Holliday and Capt Wall, with Lt W.O.B. Winkler and 2nd Lt E.S. Moore, and also Lt R.B. Hay and his unnamed observer. On the 25th Lt W.T. Price and Lt M.A. Benjamin destroyed an enemy aircraft east of Arras, but A3336 was written off when it stalled on take-off, without injury to either 2nd Lt E.G. Roberts or AM2 A. Trusson. Tragically that same day 2nd Lt W.J. Clifford and 2nd Lt H.L. Tomkies were killed when A3352 failed to return from patrol east of Arras, the victory being credited to Ltn K. Schafer of Jasta 11. On the 27th Lt R.B. Hay and Lt V.W.G. Nutkins in A3327, together with 2nd Lt W.T. Price and Lt M.A. Benjamin in another F.2B, shot down a two-seater which crashed into the River Scarpe near Vitry-en-Artois. On the last day of the month the squadron was involved in a number of combats, Lt F.W. Game and Lt C.A. Malcolmson driving down an enemy aircraft out of control, while Lt T.P. Middleton and Lt C.G. Claye, who flew together six times that day, sent another down out of control. So ended 'Bloody April', as it became known in the RFC, other squadrons also having suffered heavy losses.

May 1917

In May the first F.2Bs reached 48 Sqn, and the F.2As were gradually phased out. Quite a number of engagements took place on 2 May; 2nd Lt T.P. Middleton and 2nd Lt C.G. Claye in A3325, with 2nd Lt H.C. Farnes and 2nd Lt Davis in A3349, drove down an Albatros two-seater completely out of control east of Adinfer Wood. In one very large engagement 2nd Lt W.O.B. Winkler and 2nd Lt E.S. Moore in A3348 sent two Albatros D.IIIs down out of control and destroyed another between Brebières and Biache. Lieutenant O.F.J. Scholte and AM2 F.W. Dame in A3347 shot an Albatros D.III down in flames and drove another down out of control between Biache and Vitry, and yet another was driven down out of control by Lt L.G. Harrison and Lt H.L.E. Richards, both of whom were wounded by return fire.

On the 4th Capt J.H.T. Letts and 2nd Lt L. Speller in A3347 shared a two-seater destroyed at Pelves with 2nd Lt H. Smither and AM2 V. Reed. On the 10th, 2nd Lt

Above: Seen with its full peripheral engine cowling, Bristol F.2A A3312 was allocated to the Expeditionary Force while it was at Filton on 27 March 1917, but this was cancelled while it was with DAE2a Repair Section. It was at the Southern Aircraft Repair Depot at Farnborough on 19 May, when it was again assigned to the EF. It was short-lived, however, for after going to 11 Sqn as a practice machine it crashed on 28 June at Bellevue, being struck off charge that day. (Philip Jarrett)

Below: One of only 50 production F.2As, A3346 was allotted to 48 Sqn, and was with the unit by March 1917. Its stay was short, however, as it is recorded as being wrecked during a practice flight on the 23rd of that month when it suffered an engine failure and crashed near Bellevue Aerodrome. Although it was repaired and reissued to 48 Sqn by 1 June, it was flown back to England on the 13th. A Vickers FB5 Gunbus is visible behind on the left. (the late Ken Molson)

T.P. Middleton and 2nd Lt C.A. Malcolmson in A3350 destroyed an Albatros D.III between Brebières and Douai, and on the same day 2nd Lt G.E. Hawksley and 2nd Lt L. Speller in A3349 were both wounded when they were shot up and their aircraft's radiator damaged during an offensive patrol east of Arras, having to make a forced landing. On the 11th 2nd Lt H. Smither and AM2 Rutherford in A3350 sent an Albatros D.III down out of control between Biache and Dury, sharing it with Capt J.H.T. Letts and Lt J. Jameson in F.2B A7104. During an offensive patrol A3347 was damaged in combat, pilot 2nd Lt J.A.W. Binnie being unhurt but 2nd Lt F.M. Magenais being wounded.

Lieutenant H.M. Fraser and Pte J.H. Muscott sent down an enemy aircraft out of control with a broken tail on the 20th, but A3341 was shot down in combat east of Arras, 2nd Lt J.A.W. Armstrong being unhurt but 2nd Lt G. Baines dying of his wounds on 3 June. On the 24th Capt J.H.T. Letts and Lt L.W. Allen sent a two-seater down out of control near Vitry-en-Artois, Allen being wounded. By this time 48 Sqn had very few F.2As still on strength.

June 1917

Towards the end of May 11 Sqn had begun to exchange its Royal Aircraft Factory F.E.2bs for a mixture of Bristol F.2As and F.2Bs. It was based with 48 Sqn at La Bellevue, both units being in the 13th (Army) Wing. The first F.2A to arrive was A3325, a former 48 Sqn aircraft, on 8 June. The only F.2A casualty before total re-equipment with F.2Bs appears to have been A3312, which was lost in action on 28 June, 2nd Lt G.N. Hunstone being killed and his observer, 2nd Lt H.D. Duncan, being injured.

Postscript

In a letter to Capt Louis Strange after his posting to the CFS, Maj Bettington, CO of 48 Sqn, wrote from France on 13 May 1917:

Regarding the Bristol, she is a topping fighting two-seater, the best here not

Germans pose for their photographs with F.2B A7130 '3' of 11 Sqn after it was brought down near Bullecourt on 19 September 1917, probably by Untoff. F. Gille of Jasta 12. Both crewmembers, 2nd Lt N.J. Taylor and Lt G.M. Mumford, were wounded and taken prisoner. Part of the aircraft's name, 'Otazell', is visible between the two Germans on the left, and on either side of the fuselage roundel are the two sloping bars of the squadron markings used from 26 August 1917 to 22 March 1918. *(Trevor Henshaw)*

excepting the D.H. as she is much handier than that and communication between pilot and passenger in the Bristol is splendid whereas D.H.4 is not. ... She is faster than the Hun two-seater but cannot touch the latest Albatros Scout for speed. Where she does score tremendously is in her power to dive, in this she is alone among English or Allied machines. Many Huns who have dived on the tail of one, missed and gone on diving, have been dived after, overtaken and destroyed. They are dived plumb vertically for thousands of feet until the noise is like that of a million sabres cleaving the air. The indicated speed on a Clift or Ogilvie Indicator is then generally 60 to 90mph the second time round the dial. The indicator reads normally to 130mph, then a space, so probably the speed is considerably over 230mph. ... She loops well ... she will do a fine spinning nose dive (if held in but will come out soon if left alone). ... She stands an enormous amount of punishment in the way of

being shot about and several have been very hard hit and come home, to be written off charge as beyond repair. ... The Norman sight for the Lewis seems to be awfully good: observers have done well with it and many a Boche diving on the tail of a Bristol, possibly mistaking it for a wretched Quirk [B.E.2], has been badly stung; up to now observers have got about as many Huns as the pilots have done with their front guns.

The last recorded loss of an F.2A in battle was on 20 May, when A3341 was shot down. By the end of that month the squadron had completely re-equipped with the F.2B and the surviving F.2As had been withdrawn to Depot. The F.2As A3312, A3315, A3325, A3327 and A3329 were used initially by 11 Sqn at Le Bellevue in addition to new F.2Bs when the unit's F.E.2bs were replaced in June 1917, but during June and July all the remaining F.2As in France were ferried home across the Channel to be used for training purposes.

Seen on a winter's day, A3307, the third production F.2A, has had its Scarff ring removed, and was probably being used for pilot training at Rendcomb when this photograph was taken. Delivered in December 1916, it was with 38 TS at Rendcomb by 23 November 1917, with 62 Sqn at the same location by 7 January 1918, and with 38 RS there from 20 January 1918 until about 23 February. *(Philip Jarrett)*

Although they were soon succeeded by F.2Bs in front-line units, F.2As soldiered on as trainers. This one, A3328, was photographed at Port Meadow in Oxfordshire in 1919. *(Philip Jarrett)*

Newly completed Arab-engined F.2B F5110 in the Harris & Sheldon workshops in 1918. The company's business was shop fitting and manufacturing shop fittings, so it had the skilled woodworkers required to build aircraft. *(Geoff Negus)*

Chapter 2
F.2B PRODUCTION AND DEVELOPMENT

The various modifications carried out on the second prototype F.2A, A3304, were incorporated in all production Bristol Fighters from A7101 onwards, and the company considered the improvements to be sufficient for the revised aircraft to be redesignated Bristol F.2B. This designation covered all wartime production, irrespective of the engine fitted, though the post-war retrospective type numbering system would refer to those fitted with Rolls-Royce Falcon engine as being Type 14, those with the Sunbeam Arab or B.H.P. Pumas as Type

15, those with a 200hp Hispano-Suiza 8B as Type 16 and those with a 300hp Hispano-Suiza 8Fb as Type 17.

The first 150 aircraft (A7101 to A7250) retained the 190hp Rolls-Royce Mark I engine (later named Falcon I) in a relatively close-fitting cowling through which the water-conducting pipes of the cooling system partly protruded, and these were referred to as Type F.2B series I. The first delivery from this batch was made on 13 April 1917. When the 220hp Rolls-Royce Mark II (Falcon II) became available it was

installed from about A7221, a modified engine cowling being fitted which enclosed all the water pipes. The 275hp Falcon III came soon afterwards, its first installation being in A7177, which then became the F.2B series 2 prototype, delivered at the beginning of July 1917. A second installation was made in A7183, which was delivered to the Testing Squadron at Martlesham Heath on 25 July for performance tests with this engine, passing on 10 August to the Experimental Armament Squadron at Orfordness.

The last 50 machines in this batch, ordered under Contract No.87/A/552 (Additional) and serialled A7251 to A7300, with manufacturer's sequence numbers 2069 to 2268, were completed to series 2B standard with the Falcon II. It is not clear whether this designation also applied to all later wartime production with the Falcon III engine. Both batches were assembled at the Bristol Tramway Company works at Brislington, southwest of Bristol, as the Filton factory was tied up with B.E.2c, B.E.2d and B.E.2e production, of which nearly 950 were eventually built by the company. Deliveries of the first batch of F.2As began on 20 December 1916, when A3305 was delivered to No.38 RS at Rendcomb, the fiftieth machine being despatched on 23 March 1917.

In the summer of 1917 changes were made in the design of the horizontal tail

Bristol F.2B A7183, fitted with a Falcon III engine, at the Armament Experimental Station, Orfordness, in February 1918. *(C&C)*

surfaces. Some aircraft had F.2B tailplanes modified in July 1917 to take F.2A elevators. These new tail surfaces were slightly smaller than those of the F.2A and early F.2B but were of a higher aspect ratio. On 10 August 1917 Gen Brooke-Popham informed IV Brigade that '... the first Bristol Fighter machine to be fitted with the new type tailplanes will be No. 1240', obviously meaning B1240.

Quantity deliveries of Falcon IIIs began to arrive in late 1917, and many of these were fitted to the next production batch of 250 aircraft, B1101 to B1350 (sequence numbers 2269 to 2518). These were built by the parent company under an extension to the original Contract No.87/A/552 (Addl) and delivered between 18 July 1917 and 18 February 1918. However, supplies of the Falcon III were still limited, so some aircraft in this batch had to be fitted with the Falcon II and a few with the Falcon I. Deliveries from this order to the RFC started in August 1917 and continued through to February 1918. The majority went to France, but quite a number were retained for use by training units at home.

In July 1917 the War Office decided that the Bristol F.2B would become the standard aircraft type for all fighter-reconnaissance squadrons. Its qualities were now becoming recognised, and indeed it was to become one of the outstanding aeroplanes of 1917 and 1918. This would inevitably entail a substantial expansion of production by subcontractors, as the sudden surge in orders would be beyond the capabilities of the parent company. In that same month the firm of Harris & Sheldon at Stafford Street, Birmingham, received an order under Contract No. A.S.20379 for 200 aircraft, to be numbered C1951 to C2150, but in the event this order was soon cancelled and the serials reallocated to 200 Airco D.H.6s built by another company. However, British & Colonial received three further orders in September. The first of these was for 300 aircraft under new Contract No.A.S.17573/17, to be numbered C751 to C1050, which could be built on a second production line at Filton, as B.E.2e production there had ended by then. These followed immediately after the previous order, with deliveries between March and June 1918. Another 200 were meanwhile ordered under two contracts, Nos. A.S.17573 and A.S.8871/17, to be numbered C4601 to C4800, and these were delivered in due course between November 1917 and May 1918, the production line at Brislington running concurrently with that for B1101 to B1350, built at Filton. The third order that month was for 100 aircraft under contracts No.87/A/552 (Addl) and A.S.22909/1/17, to be numbered C4801 to

An alternative to the Falcon was needed when the F.2B was selected to replace the Armstrong Whitworth F.K.8 reconnaissance aircraft, and the first choice was the 200hp Hispano-Suiza. Trials of the installation were undertaken at Martlesham Heath using B1201, which went there on 31 December 1917. It was transferred to Farnborough on 28 February 1918. *(Philip Jarrett)*

C4900, and these were delivered between 17 October 1917 and 2 March 1918.

The increasing demand for F.2Bs would evidently be too great for the Bristol factories, which were already working to their limit, so from October 1917 large contracts were let to firms outside the aircraft industry, including Angus Sanderson & Co and Sir W.G. Armstrong Whitworth & Co Ltd, both of Newcastle-on-Tyne; the Austin Motor Co Ltd and Harris &

Sheldon, both of Birmingham; the Gloucestershire Aircraft Co Ltd of Cheltenham; Marshall Sons & Co Ltd of Gainsborough; National Aircraft Factory No. 3 (managed by the Cunard Shipping Co Ltd) at Aintree (see later); and the Standard Motor Co Ltd of Coventry. Each of these received orders for between 100 and 600 airframes, and contracts placed or under consideration by the end of the war amounted to 4,285 aircraft, but there were

Above: **F.2B B1200 at AES Martlesham Heath in September 1918 for performance tests of its 200hp Wolseley Viper engine.** *(Philip Jarrett)*

Right: **F.2B B1206 was flown at Martlesham Heath from January 1918 for performance tests with its 230hp Siddeley Puma engine.** *(C&C)*

From May 1918 F.2B B1220 'B' was with the Wireless Experimental Establishment at Biggin Hill, fitted with a wireless transmitter. Note the generator impeller mounted near the starboard lower wing root. *(Philip Jarrett)*

wholesale cancellations following the Armistice of 11 November 1918. All except those from Aintree were to be fitted with liquid-cooled vee-eight Sunbeam Arab engines. Production by outside contractors was finally halted on 26 November 1918, but the parent company was allowed to continue with deliveries of all machines contracted for and started at that date. Production under wartime contracts continued until September 1919, the final figures being 2,081 at Filton, 1,045 at Brislington and 1,621 by other contractors; a total of 4,747 Bristol Fighters completed.

Engine supply was a continuing problem. Rolls-Royce was unable to produce Falcons in quantity fast enough to power all the Bristol Fighters being ordered. As an alternative, consideration was given to a 200hp geared version of the Hispano-Suiza 8B, which was being produced by the French motor industry and also in England by Wolseley Motors Ltd at Birmingham. As this had less power, the Falcon III was reserved for fighter-reconnaissance squadrons and the alternative engines were to be supplied to corps-reconnaissance units. However, both alternative engines

had been rushed into production prematurely and were beset by teething troubles. Wolseley-built and French Brasier-built Hispano-Suizas were found to suffer crankshaft failure after an average of only four hours' life. The French-built engines suffered from problems with hardening of the gears and propeller shaft, but the depots in England were overwhelmed with engines requiring overhaul, and so desperate was the situation that many of these were passed into service still with faulty gears. Those built by Mayen were found to have greater reliability, but these were all earmarked for the Royal Aircraft Factory S.E.5a programme. By the end of 1917 only 81 out of the promised 1,800 Sunbeam Arabs had been accepted owing to severe vibration problems, and even these gave endless trouble when installed.

As an alternative, a 300hp direct-drive Hispano-Suiza 8Fb engine was mooted, with the advantage that it would not suffer from reduction-gear problems, and the Arab installation was modified for the purpose. The 8Fb had been promised for July 1918 and a batch of 350 F.2Bs was proposed, but there were engine production delays, and in

any event the engines were all required for a Martinsyde F.4 production programme, though in fact further engine delays meant that very few had materialised before the war's end. Consequently, re-equipment of R.E.8 squadrons with F.2Bs, planned to take place in April 1918, had to be postponed until September. In the meantime, large numbers had to be stockpiled in UK storage, and only Rolls-Royce-powered machines reached the front to participate in the fighting. By the time of the Armistice around 900 Rolls-powered F.2Bs had reached the RAF, plus 720 with other engines.

Meanwhile, the failure of both 200 and 300hp Hispano-Suiza engines to materialise led to the 230hp six-cylinder in-line B.H.P. Puma being chosen as an alternative. But its installation presented problems, including moving the front gun from its successful central position, and supplies of the Puma also became delayed owing to foundry difficulties. However, the Arab-engined version did give useful service in France with five long-range corps-reconnaissance units. British & Colonial completed only E3253 to E5258 and H1690 to H1707 with Pumas, all of these remaining in storage at the Aircraft Acceptance Park. Fortunately, production of the original Falcon-engined version steadily continued and it gave sterling service with six squadrons in France as well as two in Palestine and five on home-defence duties. Trials were carried out in September 1918 with C4654 powered by a high-compression 290hp Siddeley Puma, but this gave little improvement in performance.

The different engine and radiator installations led to variations in the external appearance of the nose of the F.2B. Little change was needed for the Falcon, the installation requiring only minor variation throughout, though some late ones had enlarged radiators of squarer shape. The 200hp Hispano-Suiza 8B had an almost circular radiator that was slightly taller than it was wide, with the oil tank mounted

Factory-fresh F.2B C823 was from a batch of 300 built by the parent company. Powered by a Falcon III, it was tested at Filton on 5 April 1918 and was with 141 (Home Defence) Sqn at Biggin Hill by May of that year. Lt L.P. Kelsey was injured when it crashed on landing during night flying for searchlight practice on 18 August. *(BAE Systems)*

Sunbeam Arab-engined F.2B C906, photographed at Filton in 1918, has been fitted experimentally with an S.E.5a radiator. *(Philip Jarrett)*

externally below the cowling. The Sunbeam Arab initially had a somewhat similar radiator to that of the Hispano-Suiza, though of larger area and more rectangular in outline, but this very rough-running engine proved too flexible for its tubular engine mounting, which resulted in the bottom of the cowling being made horizontal and square. For a time this mounting was used with an S.E.5a radiator, which then required an increase in its area to suit the 300hp Hispano-Suiza, resulting in a raised top cowling forming an arched shape. The cowling sloped down towards the top of the radiator, but the resulting length of the gun blast-tube was deemed too short for the Vickers gun. Other changes were made, but eventually an improved standard mounting and radiator appeared, able to accommodate either the Arab or the 300hp Hispano-Suiza, being fitted on the production lines in 1918. The Puma installation, designed by the Royal Aircraft Establishment (RAE) at Farnborough, was somewhat similar to that of the D.H.9, having a similar underslung radiator. A few F.2Bs were fitted with the air-cooled vee-twelve 200hp R.A.F. 4d engine, mostly for test purposes at Farnborough, but this gave the nose an ugly appearance. (See also chapter 17.)

The parent company steadily increased its output of Bristol Fighters quarter by quarter, but was handicapped by the limited supplies of Falcons, which lagged further and further behind airframe production. Compounding the problem was the lack of any comparable engine from any other engine manufacturer. To make matters worse, Maj-Gen W. Sefton Brancker, Comptroller-General of Equipment, recommended at a meeting of the Progress and Allocation Committee on 13 September 1917 that the Falcon engine '… should be taken out of Bristol Fighters and put into Martinsyde Scouts', after being impressed by the performance of the Martinsyde R.G. and the outstanding

potential of the brilliant Martinsyde F.3, both of which had the Falcon III. He went on to enquire how the trial of a Bristol Fighter with a Hispano-Suiza engine was progressing. General D. le G. Pitcher responded that there had been difficulty in obtaining a 200hp Hispano-Suiza for the Bristol and that it was intended to try fitting it with a 200hp Sunbeam Arab. Two Arab engines were available by 2 October, so it was decided that one of these should go to the Royal Aircraft Factory at Farnborough for installation in an S.E.5a and the other to British & Colonial for a Bristol Fighter.

It was officially anticipated that, of the 70 Bristol Fighters planned to be delivered in October, 30 would be fitted with the Hispano-Suiza engine, and 36 more in November. On 3 October it was decided that 62 Sqn's aircraft would be Hispano-powered Bristols, while the other four Bristol squadrons then in France would have Falcon engines. However, the supply of Hispano engines was also now running into difficulties. By 17 October British &

Colonial had six airframes adapted to take Hispano-Suiza engines, but only five engines, none with their radiators. By the time 62 Sqn was intended to receive its first aircraft, on 20 October, no Hispano-powered F.2Bs had yet been flown A pragmatic approach was then adopted, and on 18 October the decision was reached that 62 Sqn's Bristols would all be Falcon powered. It was decided that such Hispano-Suiza engines as were available should be installed in aircraft and turned over to the Technical Department for testing.

Despite the contretemps, intimation was given to RFC Headquarters in France that Arab-engined Bristol Fighters would soon be forthcoming. This elicited a sharp response on 24 December from Brig Gen R. Brooke-Popham to Sir William Weir at the Air Board Office in London:

I am sending to you a copy of a letter which has been sent to DGMA [Director-General of Military Aeronautics]. General Trenchard wishes me to point out that

This photograph of Siddeley R.T.1 B6625, probably at London Colney, is of interest because F.2B C4800 is conspicuous in the background. The R.T.1 was a potential replacement of the Armstrong Whitworth F.K.8 and Royal Aircraft Factory R.E.8 in the corps reconnaissance role but was not adopted because the Arab-powered Bristol Fighter was eventually selected to fulfil that duty. *(Philip Jarrett)*

this is a very urgent matter. People at home do not appear to realise that we cannot start replacing squadrons with an untried engine in the middle of a battle. However carefully an engine is tried out in England or on a test bench, there are always more troubles developing as soon as it is taken into use in service conditions and it takes at least two months, generally more, to discover all these troubles. Unless, therefore, we can get some machines here at once with this Sunbeam Arab engine, the sole result will be that shall have the first squadrons that are replaced by Bristol Fighters out of action at a very critical period. [*vide* TNA File AIR.1/6A/4/50]

There were further delays at Bristol even after the first Hispano engine arrived, owing to the necessity to redesign the radiator, and it was not until the second week of December 1917 that Martlesham Heath began to anticipate delivery of B1200 fitted with the Hispano-Suiza. Delivery of this aircraft was delayed by labour troubles at

Filton, a relatively uncommon occurrence at the company, and when it finally departed for Martlesham on 5 January 1918 it suffered engine trouble and forced-landed at Woodford in Essex. In the event, B1201 arrived instead at Martlesham with the same engine on 31 December, and underwent performance trials with this engine, and later tests of a top-wing gravity tank, after which the engine was removed and transferred to Sopwith Dolphin C3778.

The RFC in France had in fact already received one Hispano-engined machine in the shape of B1119, which was tested by the Repair Park element of No.1 Aeroplane Supply Depot (ASD) at St Omer on 3 and 6 December. On 16 December it forced-landed at Ardres in the hands of Lt Russell and was dismantled, but was repaired by the new year, undertaking another test flight on 2 January 1918. It was flown back to England on 24 January and subsequently used by the CFS at Upavon.

Meanwhile, consideration had been given to other alternative engines. Despite an earlier decision that the 200hp R.A.F. 4d

engine would not be fitted to the Bristol Fighter, one was installed in A7260 around September 1917, and another was later fitted to B1202, though this combination was never developed. Another contemporary installation was that of the 230hp BHP engine, initially in B7781, a rebuilt airframe from Farnborough, which undertook simple performance trials at No.1 ASD on 10 and 13 January 1918 before returning to England on 2 February. It was unusual in having a frontal radiator, a gravity tank above the centre section and an externally mounted Vickers gun. Extensive modifications were made in France, the gun being enclosed within the cowling, the large exhaust manifold being turned upwards to discharge above the wing, and two new tanks being fitted within the centre section, replacing the external gravity tank.

On 27 January BHP-powered B1206 arrived at Martlesham Heath for trials. By mid-February it had been fitted with the engine from Sopwith Rhino X7, and after several weeks' testing it departed on 3 April for Hendon to become a station aircraft. The BHP-powered Bristol Fighter had been envisaged as a possible escort for bombers, but the engine gave it a poor performance, the pilot's vital forward view was much obstructed by the upright engine and exhaust manifold, and its manoeuvrability was impaired. On 26 February 1918 Maj-Gen Sefton Brancker wrote to RFC Headquarters to the effect that the combination was therefore not considered good enough for use as an escort fighter and would not be going into production.

This Arab-engined F.2B, thought to be D7907, has the installation and radiator originally designed for the 300hp Hispano-Suiza but adopted for the Arab-powered variant. Although it has brackets for long Falcon-type exhaust pipes on its fuselage sides, the engine has stub exhausts. Delivered to Martlesham Heath during the week ending 13 July 1918, it was short-lived, being wrecked on 3 September in a forced landing brought about by engine failure and written-off four days later. *(IWM)*

It had been recognised that the Bristol F.2B with the 200hp Hispano-Suiza would have inferior performance to the Falcon-powered version, and the variant was consequently to be issued as a replacement for the R.E.8 and Armstrong Whitworth F.K.8 in the corps-reconnaissance squadrons. However, late in 1917 the Hispano-Suiza was still unsatisfactory, being scarce and giving trouble, and in any event would be badly needed to power the S.E.5a and Dolphin, both by now in large-scale production. A War Office letter dated 19 December 1917 announced a change of power unit for the Bristol Fighter, stating that the standard engine for the corps-reconnaissance version would now be the unfamiliar Sunbeam Arab. However, this surprise decision was not welcomed by RFC Headquarters, which quickly pointed out that the RFC in the Field had no experience of it whatsoever and requested that a specimen aircraft fitted this engine should be sent to France for trials.

Accordingly, an Arab engine was sent to France and two Bristol Fighters were hurriedly fitted with Arabs at the Western Aircraft Repair Depot, Yate, though why the somewhat belated haste was necessary at this stage is not apparent, for the first Arab had been delivered in May 1917. An initial decision to install it in the Bristol F.2B had been taken on 7 August, but the Hispano-Suiza was being tried instead. Two Arab engines had been received by British & Colonial at Filton on 1 and 2 October 1917, but no steps appear to have been taken subsequently to fit them in F.2B airframes. RFC Headquarters was by now understandably concerned; forward planning having called for the re-equipment of corps squadrons with Bristol Fighters to start in March 1918.

From July 1918 B1200 was tested at Farnborough with its 200hp Hispano-Suiza engine replaced by a Wolseley Viper of similar power. Initially it was flown with an S.E.5 propeller and results were disappointing, but they improved when an RAE 30018 propeller was fitted in early August. The following month it was sent to Martlesham Heath for performance tests, but nothing further transpired with the fitment of this engine.

The first Arab-powered Bristols were B8914 and B8915, the first two of around 30 F.2B rebuilds from spares and salvage by No.3 (Western) Aircraft Repair Depot (ARD) at Yate in Gloucestershire, only some eight miles from Filton. The first, B8914, had reached France by 25 January 1918, and on 28 January went to 11 Sqn for evaluation. Headquarters called for weekly reports on

Arab-engined Bristol Fighters under construction at Harris & Sheldon of Birmingham in 1918. *(Geoff Negus)*

the aircraft, but it was detached to 12 Sqn, an R.E.8 unit, on 3 February 1918. During the delivery flight from 11 to 12 Sqn five exhaust stubs fell off, an omen of the troubles that lay ahead. On the same day, a Falcon-powered F.2B was attached to 15 Sqn, being one of several aircraft withdrawn from the four Bristol Fighter squadrons for this purpose. Two were allotted to 35 Sqn on 4 February. Aircraft B8915 went to Martlesham Heath for trials on 8 February

1918, and was joined there on 1 March by B1204, which had a geared Arab I.

So hastily had B8914 and B8915 been modified that their Rolls-Royce engine bearers and Falcon radiators were retained. Six more F.2Bs, this time from the firm's production line, C4657 to C4659 and C4662 to C4664, were fitted with Arab engines by No.3 (Western) ARD and then allotted to the RFC in France in February 1918. These also retained Rolls-Royce engine

From a batch of 100 Arab-powered F.2Bs ordered from Harris & Sheldon of Birmingham in 1918, F5097 eventually found its way to 8 Sqn in 1919. *(C&C)*

Puma-engined F.2B H6058 was one of the last of a batch of 600 to emerge from the Austin Motor Company factory, only about 125 being completed before production was stopped. All are believed to have gone into storage before eventual scrapping. Any aerodynamic advantage that might have been gained by streamlining the nose was undoubtedly lost by fitting the under-nose radiator. *(Philip Jarrett)*

bearers and had an alarmingly unsatisfactory radiator installation. Apparently C4663 went to 12 Sqn also, and that unit experienced many problems with the Arab engine. Eventually vibration was established as the cause of many of the difficulties, and this was confirmed by Martlesham Heath, where B1204 and B8915 were extensively tested with the Arab.

These problems led to protracted development of the Arab, its radiators and its mountings, until a suitable installation designed by F.W. Lanchester was evolved by July 1918. (Further details regarding trials with Arab installations will be found in chapter 17.) This meant that the RFC was unable to re-equip any of its corps squadrons in March 1918 as had been intended, and in mid-June there was a possibility that the Arab Bristol would be abandoned. This did not happen, but the war was nearly over by the time the Royal Air Force (RAF) began to receive Arab Bristols in quantity. Before the RFC merged with the Royal Naval Air Service (RNAS) to form the RAF on 1 April 1918, further large contracts for Bristol Fighters were given to several contractors, the Arab engine being the specified power unit in most cases. With only one or two exceptions, Bristol-built F.2Bs had the Rolls-Royce Falcon.

The Bristol F.2B has always been represented as an aircraft of great structural strength, but early in 1918 much trouble was experienced with buckling compression struts in the lower mainplanes. These had apparently been modified at some time during the production of the type, and while the F.2A had solid spruce struts the F.2B had built-up compression members of ash and plywood. Once this problem had been identified, new F.2Bs were fitted with solid spruce compression struts, local reinforcement then being fitted to those aircraft already in service with built-up struts. Initially, ash strips were glued and screwed on externally, but a permanent scheme was also devised, and by 10 February strengthening was required on the second, third and fourth compression ribs.

Two more squadrons, 62 and 88, were to have flown the F.2B in France, but only 62 Sqn had arrived before the RFC merged into the new RAF on 1 April 1918. The aircraft acquitted itself well, also equipping 67 and 111 Sqns in Palestine and 'Z' Flight attached to 34 Sqn in Italy, this flight providing the nucleus for a new 139 Sqn. In addition, F.2Bs were used from September 1917 for Home Defence work against German airships and Gotha and giant bombers by 39 Sqn and, later, four more squadrons.

National Aircraft Factory No.3

One of four such establishments set up by the Ministry of Munitions of War in late 1917, National Aircraft Factory (NAF) No.3 was built at Aintree, Liverpool. The Ministry had come into existence under David Lloyd George as a response to public criticism of a shortage of munitions supply for the Western Front, especially artillery shells. Once a network of 'National' factories had been set up, attention turned to building more aircraft for the RFC, and its successor the RAF, as existing factories were having difficulty meeting demand. (The name was originally to have been 'National Aeroplane Factory', but in surviving contemporary correspondence both 'Aeroplane' and 'Aircraft' are used.)

Several other 'National' factories already existed in the Merseyside area. A prime reason for selecting Aintree was a nearby Lancashire & Yorkshire Railway station which would help to provide transport for the workforce, and a spur could be built to cater for incoming material. In February 1917 the Ministry's Aeroplane Construction Department began discussions with the Cunard Steamship Co Ltd, enquiring whether its Furnishing Department could assist with aeroplane manufacture. This department was primarily concerned with fitting-out passenger accommodation in steamships ordered by the shipping line, and installing cabins and public areas into hulls supplied by Cammell Laird, Harland & Wolff and other shipbuilders, as well as maintaining and refitting them once in service.

A copy of the preliminary plans for NAF No.1 at Waddon (Croydon) was supplied to Cunard early in September 1917 as a basis on which to start construction, even though no decision had yet been made as to the type of aircraft to be built, and construction started on 4 October. A nucleus Aeroplane Department was set up in the company's headquarters at Liverpool Pier Head, staff being seconded from the Engineering and Furnishing Departments. The original

Left: **Bristol F.2B A7260, seen here with the Testing Squadron at Martlesham Heath in 1917, was one of several of the type to have a 200hp R.A.F. 4a engine fitted experimentally and tested at RAE Farnborough. In this picture the engine has stub exhausts.** *(C&C)*

intention had evidently been to build the de Havilland D.H.9, but this was soon changed, a contract being placed on 22 November for 500 Bristol Fighters, serialled D2126 to D2625, to be powered by the 200hp Hispano-Suiza 8B rather than the more usual Rolls-Royce Falcon or Sunbeam Arab. Aircraft deliveries were scheduled to begin in May 1918, and in order to meet this deadline Cunard ordered 50 fuselages to be built under subcontract by a Liverpool organ maker, Rushworth & Dreaper, and a further 50 by Birkenhead coachbuilder W. Watson & Co, each aircraft being priced at £3,250. Waring & Gillow, the furniture firm, also appears to have built some fuselages at its Fleet Street works in Liverpool.

In the event, production got off to a slow start and only about a dozen aircraft were nearing completion by mid/late June, with flight-testing from early July. Delays in delivery of Hispanos resulted in some aircraft being delivered without engines, and the remainder were mostly fitted with the Arab. Many of those actually built were packed and sent by rail from the factory's spur line. The delivery arrangement also necessitated the preparation of an aerodrome at Aintree, and this was laid out immediately north of the factory itself, becoming the first recognised aerodrome in Liverpool. The alternative, of requisitioning part of Aintree Racecourse, had been rejected in March 1918. The factory site was bounded by the Leeds and Liverpool Canal to the north, Ormskirk Road to the west and the racecourse to the east.

The Cunard company experienced continuous problems with the Ministry of Munitions, which had asked the company to dismiss Capt Calder, the factory's superintendent. Cunard took the line that they had a contract to manage the factory and were prepared to do so only on their own terms, without Ministry interference. Minutes of a Board of Directors' meeting on 11 September record a decision that Sir Alfred Booth, chairman of the company, and his general manager, were to travel to London immediately after the meeting to see Alexander Duckham, Controller of National Aeroplane Factories. However, a stalemate was reached, and at the end of work on 17 October the factory was handed over to the Ministry. By the time of the Armistice in November 1918 only 126 aircraft had been completed, and the contract was cancelled on 1 January 1919, the last completed airframe, D2250, being flown on 4 January. On 3 January the factory was restyled No.4 National Aircraft (Salvage) Depot, to help deal with the large number of redundant airframes and was closed down later in the year.

Shortly before the outbreak of the Second World War a study was produced on the

Right: **A newly arrived F.2B attracts attention at an RFC station.**

Another study of A7260, now at RAE Farnborough, showing the enormous air scoop above the engine. It now has a long exhaust manifold, with two heating pipes coming from the front end.

A typical R.A.F. 4d installation in a Bristol Fighter, as tested at the RAE.

practicability of having a new programme of national aircraft factories set up. Now held by The National Archive in document file AVIA.10/306, it reads (*inter alia*):

Production at the factories began much later than had been anticipated, and once the production stage had been reached the rate of progress fell far short of what had been allowed for. It is possible that had the war continued into late 1919 or 1920 the national aircraft factories would have justified themselves in the matter of output, cost of production, and general efficiency. That is as may be. What is certain is that the factories were slow and costly to get started, and what is more than probable is that the same amount of money expended upon the expansion of existing private concerns would have brought quicker and larger returns. It would be unwise to make too much play

with figures, which can be dangerous symbols, but it may be said that each aeroplane made by the Government in its own factories cost an unreasonably higher sum than similar aircraft bought from private manufacturers. Each Bristol Fighter produced at Aintree, for example, would appear to have cost at least £5,000, whereas the contemporary contract price, with private makers, was about £1,350. If, in addition, the amount expended on capital account is apportioned between the aeroplanes as produced in the factory, the figure of £5,000 would be doubled.

An accompanying table indicated that £692,900 was the capital expenditure incurred to March 1919, with production expenditure accounting for an additional £627,697. Labour strength in November was 1,580 men and 1,054 women.

An aside: the Bristol M.R.1

Although the M.R.1 two-seat fighter-reconnaissance biplane resembled the F.2B in its general configuration, it was not directly related to its contemporary. First drafted in July 1916, the M.R.1 was conceived in the belief that a severe shortage of timber suitable for aircraft production might arise if war continued. To that end, it was to have a metal semi-monocoque fuselage primarily constructed from duralumin and small amounts of mild steel and comprising four sections bolted together. The fuselage units featured a double-skin construction, with a smooth outer skin riveted to an inner skin that was corrugated longitudinally. The front section consisted of a semi-monocoque open channel with channel-section struts at each frame, bracing the top longitudinals to the centre of the bottom frame member. It carried the engine bulkhead bearers and the tanks and upper and lower centre-section struts. The next section, of similar construction, contained the pilot's cockpit and the fixed Vickers gun and its ammunition box. The third section, a self-contained parallel-sided monocoque structure, incorporated the observer's cockpit with its Scarff ring for a Lewis gun, and bolted on to the back of this was the tapered fourth section, a monocoque boom to which the empennage was attached. The third section could be omitted, and, combined with wings of less area, the aircraft then became a single-

seater. Design and construction of the unstaggered, fabric-covered all-metal wings was subcontracted to the Steel Wing Company of Gloucester, and they incorporated rolled high-tensile steel strip. The tail surfaces were also fabric covered.

Owing to delay in the production of the wings, the first M.R.1, A5177, which had 150hp Hispano-Suiza engine, was initially fitted with a set of conventional wooden wings with ailerons on the upper wing only. It was intended to fit metal wings built on the Mayrow system, but it is not known if this was done before the aircraft underwent strength tests at RAE Farnborough in May 1918. It may well have met its end by being broken during these tests. The second machine, A5178 (later renumbered A58623 for some unknown reason), eventually received its 42ft 2in-span metal wings, with shorter-

span ailerons on both upper and lower surfaces, in late 1918, and was successfully flown under the power of a 200hp Wolseley Viper engine. It was frequently flown at Filton after the Armistice, but on 19 April 1919, on its delivery flight to Farnborough, Capt Barnwell crashed into a pine tree at the aerodrome's North Gate. Although Barnwell escaped injury, the M.R.1 was badly damaged and had to be written off. The M.R.1's disposable load amounted to more than 40 per cent of its all-up weight, and despite its low-powered engine the manufacturer's performance figures were good, but as J.M. Bruce states, 'not good enough to meet the combat needs of 1918'. Moreover, the successful F.2B could be manufactured easily by the many woodworking companies sub-contracted to aeroplane production at the time.

Right: **The second M.R.1, A5178, in its later markings as A58623, showing the ailerons on both upper and lower wings.** *(Bristol)*

Although it is a very poor image, this snapshot is of interest, as it depicts the AID flight section at Farnborough in April 1919, with a variety of aircraft lined up outside the hangars on the left. Barely discernible further to the right, close to the path, is the wreckage of the second M.R.1. *(Philip Jarrett)*

Seen here shortly after being brought down in hostile territory, presentation F.2B *Newfoundland No.4*, A7181 'H' of 22 Sqn, was lost in action during an offensive patrol on 11 October 1917, Lt R.I.V. Hill and 2nd Lt R.S. Gilbert being made PoWs. *(C&C)*

Chapter 3

THE F.2B ENTERS SERVICE

The F.2B first went into service with 48 Sqn at Le Bellevue, where it began to replace the unit's F.2As in May 1917. At the time this squadron was serving with the 13th (Army) Wing in the 4th Brigade, being commanded by Maj A.V. Bettington.

May 1917

On the morning of 9 May Lt F.P. Holliday and Capt A.H. Wall in A7108, with 2nd Lt W.T. Price and 2nd Lt E.S. Moore in A7110, destroyed an LVG two-seater between Vitry and Noyelles. Early in the evening a 48 Sqn patrol encountered eight Albatros D.IIIs near Vitry-en-Artois. Three of these were sent down out of control by Lt Holliday and Capt Wall, again in A7108. Second Lieutenant Price, now with Lt C.G. Claye but again in A7110, destroyed one and sent another down out of control, but was then shot down northeast of Fampoux by Ltn Lothar von Richthofen and had to force-land within British lines, Claye having been wounded.

Two days later Capt J.H.T. Letts and Lt J. Jameson in A7104 sent an Albatros D.III down out of control between Biache and Dury, shared with 2nd Lt H. Smither and AM2 Rutherford in F.2A A3350. Later, while on an offensive patrol, A7101 was shot down in flames over Fresnes, Capt A.T.

Cull and AM1 A. Trusson being killed. An hour later, however, Capt F.P. Holliday and Capt A.H.W. Wall in A7108 destroyed an Albatros D.III and sent another down out of control southwest of Izel-lès-Esquerchin. That same day Lt W.O.B. Winkler and 2nd Lt E.S. Moore on an offensive patrol in A7111 were shot down near Gavrelle, both being taken prisoner.

On the 12th, Capt J.H.T. Letts and Lt J. Jameson in A7106 sent an Albatros D.III down out of control at Beaumont, and later in the day another was similarly dealt with at Izel-lès-Esquerchin. On the 20th, Capt R. Raymond-Barker and Lt R.N.W. Jeff in A7112 sent down two Albatros D.IIIs at Brebières, one of these being shared with 2nd Lt H.J. Pratt and 2nd Lt H. Owen in A7108. Another enemy aircraft was sent down out of control that day by Lt H.M. Fraser and Pte J.H. Muscott in an unspecified F.2A or F.2B during escort duty.

On the evening of the 26th Capt Raymond-Barker and Lt Jeff, again in A7112, destroyed an Albatros D.III east of Brebières, while Lt P. Pike and Lt J.H. Robertson in an unspecified aircraft sent an Albatros D.III out of control southwest of Douai. Near Cantin Palleul, south of Douai, Capt J.H.T. Letts and Lt C.A. Malcolmson

in A7106, and 2nd Lt H. Smither and Lt J. Jameson in A7109, each sent an Albatros D.III down out of control, three others being similarly dealt with, two by Lt J.W. Warren and Lt M.A. Benjamin in A7119, southwest of Douai, and the other by Lt H.M. Fraser and Lt A.R.H. Noss in A7117, southeast of Douai. Next day Lt T.P. Middleton and 2nd Lt A.W. Merchant in A7119 destroyed an Albatros D.III and sent a two-seater down southwest of Douai. However, A7108 was damaged in action, 2nd Lt J.A.W. Armstrong being unhurt but his observer, 2nd Lt G. Baines, was badly wounded and died seven days later.

June 1917

An unspecified F.2B of 48 Sqn was shot up during an offensive patrol on 2 June, observer 2nd Lt G. Rogers being wounded. Next morning Lt T.P. Middleton and 2nd Lt A.W. Merchant in A7112 destroyed an Albatros D.III at Plouvain, and in the evening Capt F.P. Holliday and Capt A.H.W. Wall in A7112 opened fire at about 20 yards' range on an Albatros D.III and saw its tail fall off as it went down out of control east of Douai. Early on the 5th, Capt J.H.T. Letts and Lt J. Jameson in A7106 sent a two-seater down out of control between Riencourt and Cagnicourt, another being similarly dispatched east of Bullecourt immediately afterwards by Capt R. Raymond-Barker and Sgt Nicholson in A7112. Combats were few for the next few days, but in the evening of 14 June Capt F.P. Holliday and Capt A.H.W. Wall in A7108 destroyed an Albatros D.III and sent another down out of control at Arleux.

Things livened up for the squadron on the following day. While on patrol alone in the evening, Capt Holliday and Capt Wall in A7108 encountered seven Albatros D.IIIs. Decoying them up towards a formation of their own 48 Sqn F.2Bs approaching from the north, they sent one down out of control at Etaing, and another was similarly dealt with by 2nd Lt H.J. Pratt and 2nd Lt H. Owen in A7116 and Lt H.M. Fraser and Lt M.A. Benjamin in A7117. A third was sent down out of control southwest of Douai by 2nd Lt J.A.W. Binnie and Cpl V. Reed in A7123 and Capt B.E. Baker and Lt H. Munro in A7149. A fourth was destroyed in flames at Etaing by Lt R.B. Hay and Lt V.W.G. Nutkins in A7146. Half-an-hour later 2nd Lt J.A.W. Binnie and Cpl V. Reed sent yet another down in flames north of Vitry-en-Artois.

Next morning, 16 June, 2nd Lt R.L. Curtiss and 2nd Lt L.W. Allen in A7107 destroyed an Albatros D.III at Fresnes-lès-Montauban, then later that morning 2nd Lt H.J. Pratt and 2nd Lt H. Owen in A7116 sent another down out of control at Estrée.

Another 13th Wing unit to receive the Bristol Fighter was 11 Sqn, which was based with 48 Sqn at La Bellevue and had replaced its F.E.2bs with F.2Bs and a few F.2As at the end of May. Its crews initially found that they could not bring the enemy to battle unless they flew in pairs or singly; enemy pilots would not attack if more than three of the squadron's machines were flying together. Its crews then began to make full use of their new mounts, shooting down many German

aircraft before the end of the year. Engaged in photographic reconnaissance, initially without interference, the squadron's first success was probably that on 17 June, when 2nd Lt F.J. Foster and Lt D.G. Davidson, flying A7141, sent an Albatros two-seater down out of control at Sailly-en-Ostrevert.

On the 18th Lt T.P. Middleton and 2nd Lt A.W. Merchant of 48 Sqn in A7102 destroyed an Albatros D.V south of Rumaucourt. Two days later, while Lt A.E. McKeever and 2nd Lt H.D. Duncan of 11 Sqn in A7125 were undertaking artillery observation, Duncan fired on an Albatros two-seater, which spiralled down at Inchy. They were able to land safely after being hit by anti-aircraft fire. The same crew scored hits on an Albatros scout east of Arras the following day, when A7125 of 48 Sqn was damaged in combat, its pilot, 2nd Lt W.D. Bostock, being unhurt but observer 2nd Lt H.R. Price being badly wounded. On the 21st A7139 of 11 Sqn was shot down between Bailleul and Oppy, pilot 2nd Lt D.C.H. MacBrayne being killed and Sgt W. Mollison taken prisoner. Fighter A7144 of the same unit, flown by Lt McKeever and 2nd Lt Duncan, sent an Albatros down out of control from 8,000ft at Villers. In this same aircraft two days later, they scored hits on an Albatros scout east of Arras. On the 24th 2nd Lt H.P. Lale and 2nd Lt R.N.W Jeff of 48 Sqn in A7119 sent an Albatros D.III down out of control at Douai.

An 11 Sqn patrol on 26 June encountered ten Albatros scouts. Two of them attacked Lt A.E. McKeever and 2nd Lt E. Oake in A7144, who then proceeded to destroy an Albatros D.V at 12,500ft before sending the other down out of control from 7,000ft between Etaing and Dury. Lieutenant G.H. Hooper and Capt F.J. Carr in A7140 destroyed an Albatros D.III in the latter area. East of Cambrai, 2nd Lt P.C. Ross and AM2 Woodward in A7154 engaged four

D.IIIs, destroying one and sending another down out of control, despite Ross being seriously wounded. He managed to land safely, only to die of his wounds. Next day 2nd Lt A.J.P. Hytch and 2nd Lt L.H. McRobert of 11 Sqn in A7124 engaged a two-seater south of Monchy, but Lt T.E. Wylde, piloting another aircraft of the same unit, died of his wounds after his aircraft was hit by anti-aircraft fire during an offensive patrol. On the 28th Lt C.G.O. MacAndrew and Lt A.M. West of 11 Sqn in A7127 drove down two Albatros D.Vs out of control near Frèsnes. Finally that month, Lt O.J.F. Scholte and 2nd Lt A.W. Merchant in A7118 of 48 Sqn sent an Albatros D.III down out of control at Brebières.

July 1917

By early July, a number of 48 Sqn pilots had concluded that a complete change of tactics was necessary. They started to fly the F.2B as if it were a single-seat fighter, the task of the observer now being to protect the aircraft's tail. This change took full advantage of the aircraft's manoeuvrability and structural strength, proving it to be far more effective, and the Bristol Fighter soon began to show its real worth.

In early July preparations were being made for the Battle of Ypres, in which the RFC was to play a significant part. The German Air Force was also being prepared for the coming offensive in Flanders, its composition now including a new fighter wing, Jagdgeschwader 1 (JG1), under the command of Baron Manfred von Richthofen. In the event, British plans went awry when, at 7pm on 10 July, the German Army made a surprise attack. Next day 48 Sqn was moved to a frontier aerodrome at Bray Dunes on the coast, transferring there to the 14th (Army) Wing, still within the 4th Brigade. Major H.S. Shield took over as CO. The squadron was quickly in action at its new location and would distinguish itself during the Battles of Ypres at little cost.

On 2 July 2nd Lt T.W. Abbott and 2nd Lt M. Nicholson of 11 Sqn sent an enemy aircraft down out of control near Boiry-Notre-Dame. Next morning a 48 Sqn patrol met four scouts and a two-seater near Quéant. Second Lieutenant H.W. Elliott and 2nd Lt J.W. Ferguson sent an Albatros D.V down in flames, 2nd Lt R.L. Curtiss and 2nd Lt D.P. Fitzgerald-Uniacke in A7149 sent a two-seater down in flames, and an Albatros D.V was sent down out of control by 2nd Lt A. Riley and 2nd Lt W. O'Toole in A7153. Later in the day Capt F.P. Holliday and Capt A.H.W. Wall in A7108 drove an Albatros D.III down out of control at Haucourt. In the evening of the 5th, 2nd Lt R.L. Curtiss and 2nd Lt D.P. Fitzgerald-Uniacke in A7153 sent a single-seater down out of control at Bapaume. On the morning of the 6th two aircraft failed to

Bristol F.2B A7163 of 22 Sqn, flown in combat by Sgt J.M. Bainbridge on 18 August 1917, displays vertical white squadron identification stripes either side of the fuselage roundel. This was one of 22 Sqn's early arrivals, allocated to the RFC in France in June 1917. On 17 March 1918, having reached the end of its operational career it was flown back to England, and this photograph, possibly taken at Dover, was taken by Capt J.T.B. McCudden. (via C.C. Cole)

return from an offensive patrol, Lt H.C. Farnes and Cpl J.T. Park in A7109 and 2nd Lt H. Smither and 2nd Lt H.C. Clarke all being killed, the latter victory being credited to Ltn Wisseman of Jasta 3. Later that morning a patrol from the same squadron encountered six enemy aircraft east of Cambrai. An Albatros D.V was destroyed by Lt O.J.F. Scholte and Lt A.E. Merchant in A7118, and an Albatros D.V was driven down out of control by Capt J.T. Milne and 2nd Lt K.E. Tanner in A7129. That evening 2nd Lt A.J.P. Hytch and 2nd Lt L.H. McRobert of 11 Sqn in A7124 encountered an Albatros D.V at Dury.

On the 7th, 2nd Lt H.W. Elliott and 2nd Lt J.W. Ferguson of 48 Sqn in A7146 drove down an enemy aircraft out of control at Vitry-en-Artois, while Capt J.T. Milne and Lt A.D. Light in A7129 shot down an Albatros D.V into a wood south of Vitry-en-Artois. Lieutenant H. Scandrett and Cpl S.A. Mee of 11 Sqn in A7147 sent an Albatros D.V down out of control northwest of Cambrai, and later Lt A.E. McKeever and 2nd Lt L.A. Powell in A7144 destroyed an Albatros D.V at 7,000ft just south of Vitry, then sent two more down out of control in the Vitry-Monchy area. On the 8th Capt R. Raymond-Barker and Pte J. Mason sent an enemy scout down out of control from 5,000ft to see it crash at Arras St Quentin, but while attacking another machine at 6,000ft their engine failed and a forced landing was made at Marchies. Shortly after this, 2nd Lt A.J.P Hytch and 2nd Lt L.H. McRobert in A7124 sent an Albatros D.V down out of control at Montigny.

Number 11 Sqn had three successes on the 10th: 2nd Lt F.J. Foster and 2nd Lt H.J. Day fired 50 rounds into an enemy aircraft they encountered near Lécluse and saw it crash; Capt E.H.G. Sharples and Cpl H.G. Bassenger shot down another enemy aircraft near Gouelzin; and Lt A.E. McKeever and 2nd Lt W. de C. Dodd in A7140 sent an Albatros scout down out of control from 13,000ft at Sailly.

On the 12th more fighting took place in the air than on any day since war broke out three years earlier, the Bristols of 48 Sqn being busy throughout the day. In the morning Capt J.T. Milne and 2nd Lt K.E. Tanner in A7129 forced an Albatros scout to land southwest of Ghistelles. That evening, flying in the same aircraft, they destroyed an Albatros D.V at Leffinghe, while Lt R.B. Hay and Lt V.W.G. Nutkins sent an Albatros D.III down out of control at Ghistelles. Although 2nd Lt G. Colledge and Sgt H. Lindfield in A7112 drove down an Albatros scout out of control at Ghistelles, their own aircraft was damaged by enemy fire. Second Lieutenant H.J. Pratt and 2nd Lt H. Owen in A7116 drove down an Albatros scout at Westende. Similarly, 11 Sqn was active, 2nd Lt R.F.S. Mauduit and

The warmly clad crew of an 11 Sqn F.2B run up its Falcon before take-off. The squadron markings, comprising sloping white bars on either side of the fuselage roundels, were used between 26 August 1917 and 22 March 1918. Flight leader's pennants hang beneath the outer trailing edges of the lower wings. *(Philip Jarrett)*

Lt E.R. Dibbs sending an Albatros D.V down out of control at Pelves, but Capt C.E. Robertson and Sgt J.F. Carr were both killed, reportedly having been shot down in flames by anti-aircraft fire.

Air activity was still above normal next day, the 13th. An offensive patrol of 48 Sqn attacked eight Albatros scouts, and a D.V was driven down in flames at Slype by 2nd Lt J. Binnie and Cpl B. Reid in A7151, while Lt O.J.F. Scholte and Lt A.D. Light in A7155 drove down an Albatros D.V out of control nearby, and Lt R.D. Coath and 2nd Lt A.W. Merchant in A7106 claimed an Albatros D.III out of control, and 2nd Lt G. Colledge and Sgt A.S.C. Lindfield an Albatros D.V. Also active that day was 11 Sqn, Lt J.C.L. Barnett and Lt A. Firth sending down an Albatros out of control at Moeuvre. Two enemy aircraft were sent down from 14,000ft completely out of control, one an Albatros two-seater at Haynecourt. Lieutenant G.F. Manning and 2nd Lt P. LaT. Foster claimed a 'Nieuport-type' out of control between Cagnicourt and Pronville, but observer Cpl S. Brett was killed when his aircraft was shot up in combat during an offensive patrol.

Both F.2B squadrons were active again on the 17th. That morning A7166 of 48 Sqn was lost when it had to land on the beach at Nieuport, Lt R.B. Hay dying of his wounds and observer Lt O.J. Partington being taken prisoner. A German two-seater was forced to land at Lombartzyde Bains by 2nd Lt R.L. Curtiss and 2nd Lt D.P. Fitzgerald-Uniacke of the same unit in A7151. Also that morning an 11 Sqn patrol met a number of scouts and two-seaters, Capt R. Raymond-Barker and 2nd Lt J.E. Price in A7168 sending an Albatros down in flames from 9,000ft just northwest of Inches and then damaging an Albatros two-seater west of Villers, while 2nd Lt M.S. West and 2nd Lt F.A Adams in A7138 sent a two-seater down out of control at Sandemont. In the evening Lt H. Scandrett and Cpl J.W. Ross

in A7156 of 11 Sqn sent an Albatros D.V down out of control five miles east of Bullecourt, and 2nd Lt West and Adams, again in A7138, attacked an Albatros D.V which broke up and crashed at Bourlon Wood.

On the 20th, 2nd Lt M.S. West and 2nd Lt F.A. Adams of 11 Sqn in A7138 shot down an Albatros D.V which crashed northwest of Blécour, and 2nd Lt R.F.S. Mauduit and Lt E.R. Dibbs sent another down out of control at Novelles, while Lt A.W. Gardner and Lt E.R. Dibbs in A7128 dealt similarly with another enemy aircraft near Quéant. On the following day three aircraft of 48 Sqn sent an Albatros D.III down out of control at Slype, the respective Fighter crews being Capt B.E. Baker and Lt G.R. Spencer in A7107, Lt R. Dodds and Lt T.C.S. Tuffield in A7151 and Lt R.D. Coath and 2nd Lt K.E. Tanner in A7164. Meanwhile, 2nd Lt H.W. Elliott and 2nd Lt J.W. Ferguson in A7151 dealt with an Albatros D.V in similar fashion.

Reports were received on the 22nd that Gotha bombers were carrying out a daylight raid on Harwich, and aircraft of 48 Sqn went up to intercept them on their return. About eight miles off Ostend they sighted a formation of five bombers at a low altitude, and A7146, crewed by Capt B.E. Baker and Lt G.R. Spencer, promptly dived down from 16,000ft to 3,000ft, sending one of the Gothas down to ditch in shallows a mile off Ostend. They shared this success with Lt R.D. Coath and 2nd Lt A.W. Merchant in A7164. Four hours later the Gotha's tail could still be seen above the surface. Later in the day 2nd Lt H.P. Lale and 2nd Lt G.R. Waters in A7117 sent an Albatros D.III down out of control two miles east of Ostend.

On the 24th A7170 of 48 Sqn, piloted by Capt B. Baker, was hit by anti-aircraft fire, slightly wounding observer Lt G.R. Spencer. During a photographic reconnaissance next day New Zealander Lt K.R. Park in A7176

F.2B A7115, with 48 Sqn in France during 1917, displays two vertical white unit identification stripes aft of its fuselage roundel. *(C&C)*

of 48 Sqn, with 2nd Lt A.W. Merchant as his observer, sent an Albatros D.III down out of control over the sea near Ravensyde. This was the first of 20 victories recorded by Park while he was with 48 Sqn. He was destined to win fame during the Second World War for commanding No.11 (Fighter) Group RAF in the southeast of England during the Dunkirk evacuation and the Battle of Britain, and eventually became Air Chief Marshal Sir Keith Park. Also that day, 2nd Lt J.A.W. Armstrong and 2nd Lt P.N. Shone of 48 Sqn sent an Albatros scout down in flames over the sea northeast of Nieuport.

A further 48 Sqn victory on the 27th was claimed by Capt B.E. Baker and Lt G.R. Spencer in A7170, who sent down an Albatros D.V out of control, it then being set on fire by a 6(N) Sqn Sopwith Camel, N6358, flown by Flt Sub Lt J.H. Forman, to crash into the sea in flames northeast of Nieuport. Also, Capt F.P. Holliday and Lt W. O'Toole of 48 Sqn in A7108 sent a DFW two-seater down out of control, probably in flames, in the Lombartzyde-Westende area. However, A7134 of 11 Sqn failed to return from an offensive patrol, having been last seen over Vis-en-Artois apparently under control; 2nd Lt J. Chapman and Lt W.R. Mackay were both taken prisoner.

On the 28th Capt B.E. Baker and Lt G.R. Spencer in A7170, in company with 2nd Lt J.A.W. Binnie and Cpl V. Reed in A7123, drove down an Albatros D.V between Ghistelles and Zevecote, it then being shot down in flames by a Camel which was seen to attack it from astern at low altitude. Around the same time, 2nd Lt R.L. Curtiss and 2nd Lt D.P. Fitzgerald-Uniacke of 48 Sqn in A7121 sent down an Albatros D.III which they said 'fell like a falling leaf'.

From late July, 22 Sqn gradually relinquished its F.E.2bs for F.2Bs, being then based at Izel-le-Hameau in 13th Wing, 3rd Brigade, and commanded by Maj L.W. Learmount. At the time the new F.2Bs arrived, preparations were under way for what was to be the Third Battle of Ypres, but most squadron pilots were newly arrived in France, and even an experienced crew had to adjust to reversal of the positions of pilot and gunner from those to which they had become accustomed in their old mounts. In addition, the Bristols gave them a greater ceiling, which called for more stamina in the thinner air at 15,000-18,000ft, as well as having new engines, guns and other equipment. On the 29th Capt C.M. Clement and 2nd Lt L.G. Davies in A7174, leading a 22 Sqn patrol, chased four two-seaters, one of which turned to fight while the others continued east. They shot it down in flames at Tortequesne, assisted by 2nd Lt E.A.H. Ward and Lt G.G. Bell in another F.2B.

August 1917

August 1917 proved to be one of the wettest Augusts in living memory, so a further offensive was ruled out for the time being. No flying was possible on the first three days of the month, and very little on the 4th. Next day, Lt H. Scandrett and Lt F.A. Herron of 11 Sqn in A7156 sent an Albatros scout down out of control between Quéant and Pronville in the evening. Shortly afterwards, Lt A.E. McKeever and 2nd Lt L.A. Powell in A7159 sent another down out of control in the Quéant area, then shot down in flames another that came out of clouds, and after several indecisive combats sent yet another down out of control.

On the 7th A7114, crewed by Capt R. Raymond-Barker and 2nd Lt H.J. Day of 11 Sqn, was damaged in combat; Day died next day of his wounds. In the evening A7168 of the same unit, crewed by 2nd Lt M.S. West and 2nd Lt F. Adams, was also damaged during a patrol, Adams being wounded. Next day Lt H. Scandrett and Lt F.A. Herron of 11 Sqn dived down on six Albatros scouts and succeeded in sending a D.V down out of control. On 9 August Capt C.M. Clement and 2nd Lt L.G. Davies of 22 Sqn in A7174 shot down a two-seater in flames at Tortequesne. Lieutenant G.C. MacAndrew and Lt H.C. McKinney of 11 Sqn in A7143 shot down an Albatros D.V, which broke up at Quiéry-la-Motte, and sent another down out of control. In the evening Lt A.E. McKeever and T.W. Morse of 11 Sqn in A7159 sent an Aviatik two-seater down out of control at Vis-en-Artois.

On the 10th, Capt C.M. Clement and Pte D.W. Clement of 22 Sqn in A7172 sent down an Albatros D.V out of control at Aubigny-au-Bac. That day, 20 Sqn received its first F.2B to begin replacement of its F.E.2ds, which it had been flying for the previous fifteen months. Then based at Ste Marie Cappel as part of the 11th Wing, 2nd Brigade, it was fully re-equipped by 21 September.

During the next week German aircraft were especially aggressive against Allied troops, kite balloons and front-line trenches. On the 11th Capt C.M. Clement and Pte D.W. Clement of 22 Sqn sent an Albatros scout down out of control and, during an encounter with six Albatros scouts, Sgt C.L. Randall with Sgt G.E. Lambeth in A7201 and Lt E.A.H. Ward with Lt K.W. Holmes in A7179 each sent an Albatros scout down in flames northeast of Douai. However, these squadron successes were achieved at the expense of several casualties. After being in combat during the morning with five enemy aircraft over Arleux, A7169 failed to return, being credited by the Germans to Obltn A. Rt von Tutschek of Jasta 12. Captain P.W. Chambers and AM2 W. Richman were wounded and taken prisoner, Chambers dying soon afterwards, these being 22 Sqn's first casualties. Also lost that day was A7177 of 48 Sqn, which was hit by anti-aircraft fire during a photographic mission in the Ostend area and had to land east of the lines, 2nd Lt G. Colledge and 2nd Lt R.N.W. Jeff being captured. In the evening, A7179 of 22 Sqn was lost in combat with six enemy aircraft northeast of Douai, both Lt E.A.H. Ward and Lt K.W. Holmes being killed, this too being credited to von Tutschek. Lieutenant R.N. Treadwell was seriously wounded when his aircraft was shot up, and died of his wounds on 9 September.

While escorting D.H.4 bombers on the 12th, 48 Sqn engaged four Albatros scouts, three of which dived at Lt R.D. Coath and AM2 W. Walkère in A7164. The latter opened fire on one, which then turned completely over and fell out of control. Another Albatros then got on their tail and was also shot down out of control by Walker, bursting into flames before crashing. In the same engagement Lt K.R. Park and 2nd Lt A.R.H. Noss in A7164 sent down another D.III out of control. Also very busy that evening was 22 Sqn. An offensive patrol engaged seven Albatros scouts, and Capt C.M. Clement and Lt R.B. Carter in A7172 engaged the leader and sent his Albatros D.V down out of control, and another in flames at Biache-St-Vaast. Towards the end of the patrol an enemy scout followed the patrol and got fairly close to the rearmost aircraft, but Capt Clement dived under the F.2B to zoom up and attack the enemy machine, which then dived away, only to be followed by Clement, who continued firing until it burst into flames and crashed. Next, a bright red scout attempted to get between the Bristols and the lines, coming straight for the formation before veering off at right angles. Clement, with Lt J.C. Bush and AM1 A.G. Whitehouse in A7174 and Lt M.W. Turner and 2nd Lt C.R. Edson in A7189, fired at it and saw it fall out of control in the Lens-Douai area. They then saw some S.E.5s involved in a dogfight and joined in the fray, Lt J. Bush (A7174) and Lt M.W. Turner (A7189) sending one enemy aircraft down out of control at Lens.

On 14 August 22 Sqn moved to Boisdinghem. That afternoon 2nd Lt R.F.S. Mauduit and Pte J. Mason in A7124 of 11 Sqn sent an Albatros D.V down out of control at Brebières. Early next morning, however, A7140 of 11 Sqn side-slipped and crashed at Wagnonlieu advanced landing ground (ALG), injuring both 2nd Lt F.H. Thorndike and 2nd Lt H.M. Drake.

Thorndyke died in hospital two days later. Despite cloudy weather, air activity intensified over Ypres on 16 August. Crews of 48 Sqn dived on a two-seater but lost sight of it and found themselves surrounded by Albatros scouts, with others flying lower down. Lieutenant K.R. Park and 2nd Lt A.R.H. Noss of 48 Sqn in A7182 sent a DFW two-seater down out of control at Slype, and later 2nd Lt R.L. Curtiss and 2nd Lt D.P. Fitzgerald-Uniacke in A7151 sent an Albatros D.V down in flames at St Pierre Capelle, and another down out of control in the same area shortly thereafter. That day 2nd Lt D.K. Best of 22 Sqn was killed when A7208 crashed, his observer, Lt J. Stevenson, being injured.

A 48 Sqn patrol fought several enemy formations on the 17th. In one large scrap in the Slype area 2nd Lt K.R. Park and 2nd Lt A.R.H. Noss in A7124 saw three aircraft attacking a Camel and dived at them but were promptly attacked themselves by two more from astern. Noss emptied a drum into one, which fell out of control, then another enemy aircraft dived past them, so they followed it down and destroyed it. Seven more then attacked the patrol, but one was hit by the observer's first burst and turned on its back, falling out of control. The pilot's front gun had by then jammed; he turned west but was attacked from behind by one of three Albatros scouts, and that too was sent down completely out of control. Second Lieutenant A.C. Simpson and 2nd Lt L.H. Tanner in A7150, in conjunction with Capt J.H. Letts and Lt J. Jameson in A7219, then attacked an Albatros scout, which fell in pieces east of Nieuport. Another enemy aircraft was shot down near Ostend by Sgt W. Roebuck and AM2 W. Walker in A7115. Earlier that day the engine of A7210 had been shot up in combat. Despite wounds 2nd Lt H.S. Gough landed it safely, but observer Capt L.F. Reincke had been killed. Offensive patrols by 20 Sqn engaged several enemy formations at various times: 2nd Lt O.H.D. Vickers and Lt J.A. Hone drove down four, and Lt H.G.E. Luchford and 2nd Lt J. Tennant drove down out of control one of eight Albatros two-seaters near Menin. Two enemy scouts escorting a photographic aircraft were attacked by 11 Sqn, one being driven off and the other, an Albatros, crashing in flames just southwest of Douai.

While escorting Martinsyde G.100 Elephants of 27 Sqn on the 17th, 2nd Lt A.H. Gilbert and AM2 S. Boxall in A7204 of 22 Sqn sent down in flames at Handzaeme one of two Albatros D.Vs attempting to interfere with RFC bombing aircraft. In another encounter Lt J.H. Butler and Flt Sgt W. Organ sent an aircraft down out of control. However, while acting as escort to Cortemarck, A7162 was shot down in flames near Handzaeme, Lt R. Cornford and 2nd Lt S.E. Raper both being killed.

Also lost was A7201, which was forced down during an offensive patrol, 2nd Lt R.S. Phelan being wounded and taken prisoner and Lt J.L. Macfarlane, a South African whose real name was E.E. White, dying nine days later. In another similarly engaged aircraft, Lt M.W. Turner was wounded and 2nd Lt C.R. Edson died of his wounds. Lt J.C. Bush and Lt W.W. Chapman in A7174 sent an Albatros D.V down out of control at Staden.

The weather continued wet on the 18th. Near Douai during the early morning an 11 Sqn formation came across a formation of Albatros scouts, which fought back ferociously but were all eventually driven down. One was engaged by 2nd Lt C.G.O. McAndrew and Pte L.S.D. Long and crashed, and two more were sent down out of control, one by Lt A.J.P. Hytch and Lt L.H. McRobert in A7124 and the other by Capt G.H. Hooper and Lt H. Kent, the latter crew also driving down another. Yet another, driven down by Capt J.C.L. Barnett and Cpl J. Mason, was seen to force-land in a field. However, 11 Sqn lost three aircraft that day; 2nd Lt L.O. Harel and Capt W.H. Walker (a Canadian) were both killed in A7191, and 2nd Lt T.W. Abbott and 2nd Lt M. Nicholson died in A7126, while 2nd Lt G.A. Rose and Cpl H.G. Bassenger in A7147 were taken prisoner.

On the 19th 20 Sqn engaged six Albatros scouts near Menin, one being destroyed by 2nd Lt C.B. Simpson and Lt R.F. Hill, and another driven down out of control by 2nd Lt G.L. Boles and LCpl W. Harrop. During the morning A7160 of 22 Sqn was hit by anti-aircraft fire and had to land at 5 Sqn's aerodrome at Ascq. Its occupants, Capt H. Patch and 2nd Lt L.M. Quelch, were fortunately unhurt. However, A7172, last seen in combat in the evening at Langemarck, was also hit by anti-aircraft fire and is believed to have gone down in flames near Arras, Capt C.M. Clement and Lt R.B. Carter both being killed. Clement had made 14 victory claims.

Also active that day was 48 Sqn. In the morning two Albatros scouts were sent down out of control at Ostend, a D.III by Capt B.E. Baker and Lt H. Munro in A7179, and the other, a D.V, by 2nd Lt J.A.W. Binnie and Cpl V. Reed. However, A7171 was shot down by anti-aircraft fire, 2nd Lt R. Dutton being killed and 2nd Lt H.R. Hart-Davies being wounded and taken prisoner. In the evening, 2nd Lt H.P. Lale and 2nd Lt G.R. Waters of 48 Sqn sent an Albatros D.V down out of control five miles south of Nieuport. Next day Capt J.T. Milne and 2nd Lt W. O'Toole in A7216 shot down an Albatros D.V of MFJa1 and sent another down out of control at Ghistelles, while 2nd Lt R.L. Curtiss and 2nd Lt D.P. Fitzgerald-Uniacke in A7224 sent an Albatros D.V down out of control in the same area.

On the 21st Lt K.R. Park and 2nd Lt W. O'Toole of 48 Sqn in A7216 sent two Albatros scouts down out of control east of Westende. Later that day Capt J.T. Milne and 2nd Lt W. O'Toole in the same aircraft destroyed an Albatros D.V, and Lt R.D. Coath and Lt A.D. Light in A7213 shot down an Albatros D.V in flames in the same area. During a hostile aircraft patrol on the 22nd, A7219 of 48 Sqn was badly shot up some 30 miles off Nieuport when it was hit by return fire while chasing a Gotha bomber out to sea. Observer 2nd Lt H. R. Power was killed, and as he slumped Capt H.R. Letts was hit by the aircraft's Lewis gun, but managed to land safely. On the same date, observer 2nd Lt J.H.R. Price, in A7125 of 48 Sqn, was wounded during a combat.

In the morning of the 22nd Lt A.E. McKeever and Lt T.W. Morse in A7168 forced an Aviatik two-seater to land at Biache. Some time later five aircraft of 48 Sqn engaged 20 enemy aircraft over Ghistelles Aerodrome, an Albatros D.V being sent down in flames by 2nd Lt J.A.W. Binnie and Cpl V. Reed in A7229, and an Albatros D.III by Lt R.E. Dodds and 2nd Lt T.C.S. Tuffield in A7222. Shortly afterwards Lt R.D. Coath and Lt A.D. Light in A7213 of 48 Sqn sent an Albatros D.V down out of control some three miles southwest of Ostend, then dealt similarly with another between Slype and Westende. Flying the accompanying aircraft, A7224, 2nd Lt R.L. Curtiss and 2nd Lt D.P. Fitzgerald-Uniacke destroyed an Albatros D.V at Ostend, followed by another down out of control. That evening Lt A.E. McKeever and 2nd Lt L.F. Ebbutt in A7159 of 11 Sqn shot down an Albatros scout which broke up in the air at 5,000ft between Auby and Douai, and 2nd Lt H.E.T. Crocker and AM2 H. Lindfield in A7153 of 48 Sqn sent an Albatros scout out of control south of Ghistelles. Observer AM2 S.C. Boxall of 22 Sqn was wounded that day during an offensive patrol.

In the morning of the 23rd part of a formation of six 22 Sqn aircraft was attacked

by five enemy aircraft, 2nd Lt H.G. Tambling and Flt Sgt W. Organ in A7204 being shot down and taken prisoner. Sergeant C.L. Randell and AM1 J.V. Hurley were both killed when B1102 was shot down in flames, this being the first loss of an aircraft from the second production batch. However, one Albatros scout was sent down out of control between Terhand and Gheluwe, shared by Capt J.L. Williamson and Lt H.D. McGrath in A7161, Sgt J.H. Hamer and AM1 S.W.T. Otley in A7149, and Capt J. McKelvie and P. Brookes in A7223. While returning from patrol in the evening, A7175 of 11 Sqn crashed and was completely burnt out near the aerodrome, 2nd Lt F.J. Foster and Lt D.G. Davidson both perishing in the fire.

Very little aerial work took place between the 24th and the end of the month owing to poor weather, though some artillery and reconnaissance squadrons performed their unglamorous but essential task whenever possible. Just after noon on the 25th an offensive patrol of 48 Sqn attacked four scouts near Westkerke, and in the ensuing fight two Albatros D.Vs were sent down out of control by Capt J.T. Milne and 2nd Lt W. O'Toole in A7216 and 2nd Lt H.J. Pratt and 2nd Lt H. Owen in A7217. That evening a 48 Sqn patrol came across 25 enemy aircraft south of Slype. Two Albatros scouts were shot down, one by 2nd Lt J.A.W. Armstrong and Lt P.N. Shone, the other by Lt K.R. Park and Lt A.R.H. Noss in A7213.

Low clouds limited activity on the 26th, but in the morning 2nd Lt J.A.W. Binnie and Cpl V. Reed in A7220 of 48 Sqn destroyed one Albatros D.V and sent another down, both west of Middelkerke. On the last day of the month 2nd Lt H.J. Pratt and 2nd Lt H. Owen of 48 Sqn in A7217 sent an Albatros D.V down out of control at Zarren.

September 1917

By early September troops on both sides of the lines were exhausted, having fought to a standstill during one of the wettest Augusts

on record, and operations paused during replenishment and regrouping. However, the air offensive continued, despite persistent bad weather. During this month 48 Sqn began to fly at night, attempting to intercept German bombers attacking Dunkerque. On the 2nd, Lt H.W. Elliott and 2nd Lt J.W. Ferguson in B1108 of 48 Sqn destroyed an Albatros D.V, which crashed near Beerst, and around the same time Lt K.R. Park and 2nd Lt A.D. Light in A7170, with 2nd Lt R.L. Curtiss and 2nd Lt D.P. Fitzgerald-Uniacke in A7224, both 48 Sqn crews, sent another down out of control five miles east of Dixmude. A third was then disposed of in the same way by the crew of A7170.

On the 3rd four F.E.2ds of 20 Sqn were attacked by about twelve enemy aircraft, but four F.2Bs of 20 Sqn soon joined in, 2nd Lt R.M. Makepeace and Lt M.W. Waddington in A7214 sending an Albatros D.V down in flames between Menin and Wervicq. Also that day Lt R.E. Dodds, a Canadian, and 2nd Lt T.C.S. Tuffield, in A7222 of 48 Sqn, were attacked by two scouts, one of which, an Albatros D.V, was sent down out of control. The other, an Albatros D.III, attacked from behind but was outmanoeuvred and shot down in flames at Kayem, east of Dixmude.

The Bristol Fighters of 22 Sqn were also very active. Three of a formation of ten enemy aircraft dived on Lt R.S.P. Boby and 2nd Lt A.T. Smith in A7265 (probably an error for A7205), an Albatros Scout being driven down out of control between Passchendaele and Roulers, while Sgt J.H. Hamer and Sgt G.E. Lambeth in A7207 drove down an Albatros D.V near Roulers. However, Lt G.R. Carmichael in A7120 had to force-land at Ypres during an offensive patrol because his observer, 2nd Lt S. Cleobury, was wounded.

On 4 September A7156 of 11 Sqn was lost when it was sent down in flames in combat with three enemy aircraft southeast of Havrincourt, 2nd Lt J.F. Wightman and AM2 J. Heedy both being killed. During that day aircraft of 48 Sqn sent three Albatros scouts down out of control. The first was a D.V despatched at Ghistelles by Capt J.H.T. Letts and 2nd Lt J. Frost in A7219, the next one fell to 2nd Lt W.D. Bostock and 2nd Lt V. St B. Collins in A7224 between Middelkerke and Ostend, and the third was brought down at Ostend by Sgt W.H. Roebuck and AM2 W. Walker in A7217.

On the 5th, Bristol Fighters of 48 Sqn were attacked by Albatros scouts north of Ostend, and one of the attackers was shot down into the sea by 2nd Lt K.R. Park and AM2 H. Lindfield in A7182. When an offensive patrol of 22 Sqn engaged seven enemy aircraft east of Houthulst Forest, Lt J.C. Bush and Lt W.W. Chapman in A7185 shot down an Albatros D.V in flames, while

Second Lieutenant F.R. Hunt was injured on 4 September 1917 when F.2B A7212 of 82 Sqn overturned when the pilot failed to flatten out while landing at Waddington and flew into the ground. The squadron markings appear to be two narrow vertical white lines just forward of the tail surfaces. *(Philip Jarrett)*

This captured F.2B could well be B1125 of 20 Sqn, which was reported missing on 8 October 1917, along with its crew, Lt W.D. Chambers and 2nd Lt F.H. Berry, and was subsequently used by *Jasta* 5 as a communications aircraft. *(Philip Jarrett)*

Lt H.J. McKenzie and Lt S.L. McLenaghan in B1104 sent another down out of control. Later that day 2nd Lt R. de L. Stedman and 2nd Lt H.E. Jones in B1105 of 22 Sqn sent down an Albatros scout apparently out of control west of Staden. Elsewhere, 20 Sqn was involved in a conflict west of Lille late in the morning, and 2nd Lt R.M. Makepeace and Lt M.W. Waddington in A7203 sent an Albatros D.V down out of control, while 2nd Lt W.R. Campbell and AM W. Harrop in A7214 shot off part of the tail of an Albatros scout, Harrop being wounded in the leg during the encounter. Further success came to 48 Sqn during the day when 2nd Lt R.L. Curtiss and 2nd Lt D.P. Fitzgerald-Uniacke in A7170 sent a DFW down in a vertical dive at Middelkerke and then, around midday, Lt O.J.F. Scholte and 2nd Lt G.R. Horsfall in A7221 sent an Albatros D.V down out of control at Mariakerke. An Albatros D.V which was harassing British artillery machines was sent down in flames three miles out to sea between Middelkerke and Westende Bains when 2nd Lt R.L. Curtiss and 2nd Lt H. Munro in A7155 attacked it.

Next morning, aircraft of 22 Sqn encountered several Albatroses near Zonnebeke, and both Capt R. Stuart-Wortley and 2nd Lt P.V. Burton in A7118 and Sgt J.H. Hamer and Sgt G.E. Lambeth in A7207 sent one down out of control. A little later Sgt J.M. Bainbridge and AM2 F. Scott had a similar success northeast of Houthulst Forest, though Scott was wounded.

Heavy ground mist and low clouds then prevented much aerial work until 9 September, when a limited amount of flying was resumed. In the early afternoon, Lt H.G.E. Luchford and Lt R.F. Hill of 20 Sqn sent an Albatros scout down out of control at Becelaere. Later, though, Sgt J.H. Hamer

and Sgt G.E. Lambeth in A7207 of 22 Sqn were killed when their aircraft was shot down in flames near Wambrechies during an escort patrol. Bristol Fighter A7189 of the same squadron had to force-land when the gunner, AM1 S.W.T. Otley was wounded, but it overturned and the pilot, 2nd Lt E.O. Peel, suffered shock. Three Albatros scouts were sent down out of control near Middelkerke by 48 Sqn, one each by Capt J.T. Milne and Lt A.D. Light in A7216, 2nd Lt K.R. Park and AM2 H. Lindfield in A7220, and 2nd Lt E.G.H.C. Williams and AM2 B. Jackman in A7213.

On 10 September 22 Sqn moved to Estrée Blanche as part of 9th Wing, GHQ Brigade. Bristol Fighters of 11 Sqn engaged eight Albatros scouts at 11,000ft over Dury, and one was shot down out of control by Lt R.F.S. Mauduit and Lt C.C. Dennis and another shared by the rest of the squadron, including 2nd Lt C.G.O. McAndrew with Lt H.C. McKinney and Capt G.H. Hooper with 2nd Lt L.A. Powell.

Enemy aircraft were much in evidence on the 11th, large scout formations attacking British reconnaissance, bombing and photographic machines. Near Menin about 25 Albatros scouts engaged six Bristol Fighters of 20 Sqn busy with photography during the afternoon. They responded vigorously to disperse the enemy formation, 2nd Lt F.F. Babbage and 2nd Lt R.C. Purvis in A7193 sending one down in flames, as did Lt R.K. Kirkman and 2nd Lt J.P. Flynn in A7234. Two more were sent down out of control by Lt H.G.E. Luchford and Lt R.F. Hill in A7215 and 2nd Lt R.M. Makepeace and Lt M.W. Waddington in A7214. A second 20 Sqn photographic formation was attacked by an enemy scout, which was sent down out of control by 2nd Lt A.G.V. Taylor and 2nd Lt G.A. Brooke. In addition, 2nd Lt J.A.W. Binnie and 2nd Lt T.C.S.

Tuffield of 48 Sqn in A7220 sent down a DFW near Dixmude, and 2nd Lt E.G.H.C. Williams and AM2 H. Lindfield in A7216 claimed an Albatros D.V near Ostend. However, the squadron lost an aircraft that morning, it being last seen at 16,000ft south of Nieuport while escorting D.H.4s of 5 (Naval) Sqn; Sgt W.H. Roebuck and 2nd Lt H.T. Batson were both killed. The squadron escorted many such raids. Another loss was B1105 of 22 Sqn, last seen in a spin at 2,000ft over Schapp Baillie after being engaged by an enemy aircraft. Both 2nd Lt R. de L. Stedman and 2nd Lt H.E. Jones were wounded, Jones succumbing a month later. However, Sgt J.M. Bainbridge and 2nd Lt G.F. Dell in B1112 of 11 Sqn sent a D.V down out of control at Houthulst Forest in the morning.

Over Cagnicourt on the evening of 12 September, six aircraft of 11 Sqn met six Albatros scouts. Four were driven off and the other two were shot down out of control, one each by Capt G.H. Hooper with 2nd Lt L.A. Powell and 2nd Lt M.S. West with Lt F.A. Herron. Another enemy aircraft was sent down out of control at 7,000ft over Havrincourt, this being credited jointly to Capt E.H.G. Sharples with 2nd Lt S. Sutcliffe as observer and 2nd Lt H. Scandrett with Capt C. Watson. On the night of the 12th/13th Lt O.J.F. Scholte and Lt G.R. Horsfall of 48 Sqn went up after enemy aircraft that were bombing Dunkirk and managed to fire 40 rounds at close range into one as it was returning to its own lines, but the pilot's gun then jammed and the enemy could be seen diving away, possibly having been hit, as its exhaust ceased to be visible after it was attacked.

Continuing bad weather interfered once more, but on the 14th a photographic formation of 20 Sqn engaged three Albatros scouts and three DFW two-seaters near

Lille. One of the DFWs was sent down out of control by 2nd Lt H.F. Tomlin and 2nd Lt R.S.V. Morris in A7203, though their aircraft was hit by return fire. Also engaged in similar work that day was a formation of 48 Sqn aircraft, which was attacked by three enemy aircraft, an Albatros D.V being shot down over Ghistelles by 2nd Lt R.L. Curtiss and 2nd Lt D.P. Fitzgerald-Uniacke in A7224 and the other two being driven down. Later, 2nd Lt H.P. Lale and 2nd Lt G.R. Waters of 48 Sqn sent an Albatros D.V down out of control at Slype, while Lt K.R. Park and Lt H. Owen in A7227 sent an Albatros D.III down in flames and an Albatros D.Va was sent down to crash in Allied lines north of Dixmude.

On 15 September 48 Sqn moved inland to Leffrinckhouke, still with the 14th Wing. Twice during 1917 a 48 Sqn Bristol Fighter was taken up with the back seat occupied by King Albert of Belgium, who wanted to see the battlefield for himself. On the evening of the 15th aircraft of 48 Sqn encountered seven Albatros scouts east of Dixmude. Three of them attacked 2nd Lt H.H. Hartley and 2nd Lt E.C. Birch in A7213, but one, an Albatros D.V that passed their tail, was destroyed by machine-gun fire and fell several thousand feet in pieces. Lower down, Capt J.H.T. Letts and 2nd Lt J. Frost in B1117 saw the enemy aircraft destroyed but had become detached from the rest of the formation. On attempting to attack a two-seater the front gun jammed, but the pilot managed to free the blockage and, diving in front of the enemy, put in a burst which sent it down out of control. It then righted itself and headed west, but they got in a final burst and saw it crash northeast of Dixmude. Meanwhile, 2nd Lt E.G.H.C. Williams and

2nd Lt J.C. Boughton in A7216 of the same squadron sent an Albatros scout down out of control in the same area.

There was more unfavourable weather on the 16th, and enemy activity was slight on the 17th, but in the early morning Lt W.M. Yool and Pte D.W. Clement in A7185 of 22 Sqn were shot up during an offensive patrol, crashing owing to dense mist when they forced-landed at Coyecque. Later in the morning a two-seater was sent down out of control at Leke by 2nd Lt R.L. Curtiss and 2nd Lt D.P. Fitzgerald-Uniacke in A7224 of 48 Sqn in company with Sgt J. Oldham OK and AM2 W. Walker, but the latter aircraft was itself shot down in this combat, Walker being injured.

On the 19th, 2nd Lt N.J. Taylor and Lt G.M. Mumford in A7130 of 11 Sqn were shot down near Bullecourt, to be taken prisoner, both having been wounded. Later that morning 2nd Lt A.J.P. Hytch and 2nd Lt L.H. McRobert damaged a single-seater, which probably went down out of control from 13,000ft south of Cambrai. While taking photographs, 2nd Lts A.G.V. Taylor and H. Dandy in A7246 of 20 Sqn were suddenly attacked by eight enemy aircraft. Although the observer was badly wounded in the leg, he managed to maintain fire on an Albatros D.V, which fell in flames, and then he sent two more down out of control in the Becelaere-Polygon Wood area.

Despite relentlessly terrible weather with low clouds, strong winds and rain, the Second and Fifth Armies launched a third main battle on 20th September, and 20 and 22 Sqns participated in the fighter-reconnaissance role. There were no F.2B losses on the 20th, but next day all Bristol Fighter squadrons were very active. Aircraft

A7234 of 20 Sqn was last seen between Menin and Wervicq, 2nd Lt C.H. Woods (Canadian) and 2nd Lt T.A. McLean both being killed. However, Lt R.K. Kirkman and 2nd Lt J.P. Flynn in A7141 of the same squadron sent an Albatros D.V down smoking in a vertical dive over Becelaere, and later that day, in the same area, Lt H.G.E. Luchford and Lt R.F. Hill in A7248 sent another down out of control. Two aircraft of 22 Sqn were lost during an offensive patrol when 2nd Lt S.M. Spurway and AM1 H. Friend in A7149 collided at 10,000ft with 2nd Lt A.H. Gilbert and AM2 C. Loveland in A7233, pieces of both aircraft falling 2,000 yards east of Ypres. Also lost that day was A7224 of 48 Sqn, which was involved in combat with 15 enemy aircraft. After it had been chased down in a spin by five of the enemy, the observer, 2nd Lt D.P. Fitzgerald-Uniacke, was seen trying to reach the controls before it crashed ten miles northeast of Roulers. Both he and the pilot, 2nd Lt R.L. Curtiss, were wounded and taken prisoner, but Curtiss then died.

The weather on the 22nd was fine but visibility was poor, morning clouds interfering with the work of the RFC squadrons. Two aircraft of 11 Sqn sent enemy aircraft down out of control in the morning. First, 2nd Lt E.D. Perney and 2nd Lt C.H. Jordan in A7167 attacked an Albatros scout at 12,000ft over Estrées and saw it turn completely over and fall out of control into the clouds. Later, 2nd Lt J.H. Wallace and Capt J.A. Revill in A7143 sent an Aviatik two-seater down out of control at 8,000ft over Bullecourt. Mixed fortunes befell 22 Sqn; 2nd Lt E.A. Bell and 2nd Lt R.E. Nowell in A7205 were both killed

On 17 October 1917 F.2B A7209 'E' of 11 Sqn was shot down during combat over La Sensée canal. Second Lieutenants S.E. Stanley and E.L. Fosse were taken prisoner, but Stanley succumbed to his wounds two days later. *(C&C)*

when they were attacked by enemy aircraft and shot down in flames near Hollebeke, but Capt J. McKelvie and 2nd Lt G. Nelson-Smith in A7223 sent an Albatros scout down out of control between Houthulst Forest and Ledeghem. Then Capt R. Stuart-Wortley and 2nd Lt P.V. Burton in A7118 destroyed two Albatros D.Vs over Houthulst Forest, shooting the propeller off the second one, and an hour later sent an Albatros scout down out of control in the same area.

The weather on the 23rd enabled enemy aircraft to be active most of the day. During a fight near Vitry-en-Artois between four machines of 11 Sqn and a formation of enemy aircraft, Lt A.E. McKeever and 2nd Lt L.A. Powell in A7159 sent two Albatros D.Vs down out of control, while Sgt T.F. Stephenson and AM1 S.H. Platel in A7209 dealt similarly with another at 14,000ft. Second Lieutenant J.H. Wallace and Capt J.A. Revill in A7220 of 48 Sqn did the same with a DFW, and Lt S. Sibley and 2nd Lt P. Shone accounted for yet another enemy aircraft. Captain J.E. Johnston and Lt J.A. Hone in A7141 of 20 Sqn destroyed an Albatros D.V north of Houthem.

The fine weather continued on 25 September and there was quite a lot of aerial activity. Lieutenant A.E. McKeever and Lt W. de C. Dodd in A7157 of 11 Sqn shot down an Albatros two-seater at 9,000ft over Le Catelat, watching it break up in the air, but in the same engagement A7124 was hit and then broke up at 1,000ft, killing Lt G.L. Miall-Smith and 2nd Lt C.C. Dennis. In the evening 20 Sqn had an encounter with a number of Albatros D.Vs near Becelaere in which Sgt F. Hopper and Capt L.W. Burbidge in B1111 and Lt J.P. Dalley and Sgt W.J. Benger in A7255 sent one down out of control, and 2nd Lt N.V. Harrison and Lt V.R.S. White in B1126 sent another down out of control. A third was shot down at Gheluvelt by Lt H.G.E. Luchford and 2nd Lt R.F. Hill in B1122.

On the 27th a formation of 20 Sqn aircraft left on photographic reconnaissance but were engaged by several Albatros D.Vs near Moorslede. Second Lieutenant F. Babbage and 2nd Lt R.C. Purvis in A7255 sent one down out of control, while 2nd Lt F. Durrand and Sgt W.J. Benger in A7245 and Lt J.P. Dalley and Lt O.A. Rowan in A7248 each sent one down in flames, the latter F.2B being damaged by return fire. In the evening 2nd Lt W.D. Bostock and 2nd Lt V. St B. Collins in A7266 of 48 Sqn shot down two Albatros scouts at Pervyse, but A7150 was shot down in flames in the same area, Sgt H. Clark being killed and observer Bmdr E.A. Nash dying of wounds.

Next day an offensive patrol by 20 Sqn was engaged by 25 Albatros scouts between Menin and Wervicq. In the ensuing melee Lt H.G.E. Luchford MC and 2nd Lt R.F. Hill in A7255 destroyed two D.Vs, one in

Seen shortly after being shot down on 17 October 1917 and captured intact, A7231 of 11 Sqn was crewed by 2nd Lts E. Scholtz and H.C. Wookey, who were taken prisoner. *(Philip Jarrett)*

flames. On the debit side, the squadron lost two aircraft engaged on photo-reconnaissance; Capt J.S. Campbell and Driver G. Tester in A7210 and 2nd Lt H.F. Tomlin and 2nd Lt H.T. Noble in A7241 all being killed. Over Bugnicourt, F.2Bs of 11 Sqn and Airco D.H.5s of 41 Sqn met nine Albatros scouts, and although the enemy fought back well, they were completely beaten. Having sent one down out of control, Lt A.E. McKeever and AM2 A.W. Hewitt of 11 Sqn dived on another, which they destroyed. They followed this by diving on three more, one of which one went down in flames while the other two fled. Diving at an Albatros, 2nd Lt S.E. Stanley and 2nd Lt H.A. LeFeuvre in another F.2B found another on their tail, but the pilot dealt successfully with the first and the gunner with the second, both enemy aircraft going down out of control. Another scout was sent down apparently out of control by 2nd Lt J.H. Wallace and AM1 W.T. Long of the same squadron. A 48 Sqn patrol attacked some Albatros scouts, Capt J.T. Milne and 2nd Lt L.H. Tanner in B1124 sending down a D.V out of control over Slype. On 29 September B1124, now crewed by 2nd Lt F.L. Smith and 2nd Lt J. Frost, was hit in the engine by anti-aircraft fire over Zeebrugge. With the engine failing they headed towards Holland, flying over Aardenburg before making a forced landing at Zuidzande. They were interned. Later on the 29th, 2nd Lt C. Pern and 2nd Lt P.J. Cayley in A7167 of 11 Sqn sent a Halberstadt-type two-seater down completely out of control at 9,000ft northwest of Cambrai.

On the last day of the month an 11 Sqn patrol and another of 41 Sqn D.H.5s met an enemy formation, and in the resulting battle nine enemy aircraft were shot down over Etaing without loss of any of the British crews. One Albatros was sent down out of control by 2nd Lt C. Pern and 2nd Lt P.J. Cayley in A7167, two more by Lt H. Scandrett and Lt G. Watson in A7231, and

another two by 2nd Lt A.R. Browne and 2nd Lt C.H. Jordan in A7145, Browne being wounded. Upon returning from an offensive patrol, A7119 of 22 Sqn crashed on the aerodrome, 2nd Lt H.G. Robinson having been wounded, but observer 2nd Lt F.J.B. Hammersley escaped unhurt. Later in the day Capt J. McKelvie and 2nd Lt G.F. Dell in B1121 of 22 Sqn destroyed an enemy scout southwest of Roulers while escorting D.H.4s of 55 Sqn, which were hard-pressed while fighting their way back over the lines.

October 1917

On 1 October Lt H.G.E. Luchford and 2nd Lt R.F. Hill in B1122 of 20 Sqn destroyed an Albatros D.V southeast of Roulers, and later a 20 Sqn patrol dived at six enemy aircraft and Lt J.C. Bush and Lt W.W. Chapman in B1114 sent an Albatros scout down out of control over Westroosebeke. Lieutenant A.E. McKeever and Lt G.H. Kent in A7121 of 11 Sqn fired 25 rounds into a two-seater which crashed out of control at Brebières. However, both 2nd Lt H. Scandrett and 2nd Lt C. Watson were wounded in combat during an offensive patrol.

The next day 11 Sqn lost A7138, 2nd Lt J.M. McKenna and 2nd Lt S. Sutcliffe being killed. They were last seen during a combat that took place between Douai and Cambrai, after sending an Albatros scout down out of control. However, Lt A.E. McKeever and 2nd Lt L.A. Powell of the same squadron sent an Albatros D.V down in flames and 2nd Lt L.A. Rivers and 2nd Lt E.L. Fosse sent another down out of control. In the late morning Lt J.P. Dalley and Lt O.A. Rowan of 20 Sqn in A7193 sent an Albatros D.V down out of control at Moorslede, while Sgt F. Hopper and Capt L.W. Burbidge in A7164 sent down two more Albatros scouts at Adizeele, but then had to leave the fight as their elevator controls had been shot away and the guns had jammed. Later, 2nd Lt G.D. Jooste and

While on the strength of 48 Sqn, B1134 was the mount of Capt N.C. Millman and Lt T.C.S. Tuffield when they sent down an Albatros D.V out of control east of St Georges on 11 November 1917. The aircraft is seen here as '19' of 35 Sqn, pre-22 March 1918, when it was a Corps Reconnaissance unit attached to the Cavalry Corps. Another view appears on page 42. *(SAAF Museum)*

Capt J.E. Johnston in B1113 of 20 Sqn drove one of four Albatros scouts down out of control at Roulers. Elsewhere, Lt J.C. Bush and AM1 A.G.J. Whitehouse in B1115 of 22 Sqn attacked a two-seater which crashed north of Courtrai after the observer fired into it. Work was limited again on the 3rd by unsettled weather, but during an offensive patrol by 20 Sqn six enemy scouts were engaged, an Albatros D.V being driven down out of control at Wervicq by Lt A.G.V. Taylor and Sgt W.J. Benger in A7141.

A certain amount of work was possible on the 5th despite continuing unsettled and stormy weather, and in a fight between aircraft of 20 Sqn and some Albatros scouts near Becelaere, Capt E.H. Johnston and Lt J.A. Hone shot down an Albatros scout completely out of control. However, Capt D.D. Walrond-Skinner and Pte F.F. Johns in B1133 of the same squadron both became prisoners of war after a combat north of Dadizeele. Some sorties were possible on the morning of the 7th, Lts J.C. Bush and W.W. Chapman of 20 Sqn both being killed in A7280, which was last seen over Kruiseik while on escort patrol.

Rain hampered preparations for another Allied attack scheduled for 5.20am on the 9th, which was intended to broaden a salient between the Yser and Houthulst Forest. Another aircraft was lost by 20 Sqn that day when B1125 descended in enemy territory following engine failure, both Lt W.D. Chambers and 2nd Lt F.H. Berry being taken prisoner, and B1135 of the same unit had to force-land after being shot up by flak, though Lt J.C. Kirkpatrick and AM J. McMechan were both unhurt.

The attack was proving unsuccessful, but aerial activity continued, and on 10 October Lt W.G. Meggitt and AM1 A. Whitehouse in B1123 of 20 Sqn destroyed an Albatros D.V at Moorslede. The next day aircraft of 20 Sqn met about 16 enemy aircraft, and Lt H.G.E. Luchford and Sgt W.J. Benger in

B1122 sent an Albatros D.V down in flames and another down out of control over Moorslede. An Albatros D.III was also driven down out of control by Sgt F. Johnson and Lt N.M. Sanders in B1130. On the 12th Lt W.G. Meggitt and Capt F.A. Durrad in A7223 of 22 Sqn took part in a combat with six enemy aircraft, the observer sending an Albatros D.V down out of control and smoking near Gheluwe, though their own aircraft suffered damage in the encounter. However, Lt R.I.V. Hill and 2nd Lt R.S. Gilbert of the same unit failed to return from an offensive patrol, being taken prisoner and their aircraft being captured intact. In addition, 11 Sqn lost A7127 when it was shot down in combat near Ham; 2nd Lt A.E. Turvey and AM2 W. Hewitt were taken prisoner, Hewitt having been wounded.

Yet another attack started on the 12th but was aborted in the afternoon because incessant rain caused the valleys to the west of the main ridge to become totally bogged. Aerial activity continued, but no Bristol Fighters were lost that day. The rain continued to hamper aerial activity for over a week. On 14 October Lt N.V. Harrison and 2nd Lt J.P.F. Adams in B1137 of 20 Sqn were on reconnaissance when their formation was jumped by about ten Albatros scouts from the fringe of a cloud. After being chased back to the lines and badly shot up by three of the enemy they crashed at 6 Sqn's aerodrome, Adams being killed.

Two Bristol Fighters were lost on the 15th. Lieutenant H.S. Wellby and AM2 W. Nichol in A7255 were both taken prisoner after being chased by several enemy aircraft at 7,000ft over Maldeghem during an offensive patrol, their F.2B going down under control but smoking. During a combat over Wervicq 2nd Lt J.P. Dalley and Lt L.H. Gould A7269 of 20 Sqn were both killed, but Lt J.C. Kirkpatrick and 2nd Lt N. Couve in A7193 of the same squadron sent an Albatros D.V down out of control.

Limited aerial activity continued despite the unfavourable weather. On 16 October two Albatros D.Vs were destroyed between Brebières and Douai by Lt A.E. McKeever and 2nd Lt L.A. Powell in A7159 when aircraft of 11 Sqn engaged on photographic reconnaissance attacked enemy two-seaters accompanied by an escort of six Albatros scouts.

On the 17th the crew of A7231 of 11 Sqn, 2nd Lt E. Scholtz and 2nd Lt H.C. Wookey, were doubly unfortunate. Shot down in combat during a photographic reconnaissance sortie, they were reported to have come down in a controlled glide over Cambrai, both them and their aircraft being captured. They were evidently dropping propaganda leaflets at the time, as they were sentenced to ten years' penal servitude 'for dropping enemy proclamations', but were later transferred to a prisoner-of-war camp. Later photographs of their aircraft in German markings show it with the inscription '*Nicht Schiessen! … Gute Leute*' (Do Not Shoot! … Good People) writ large across the wing surfaces.

An offensive patrol of 20 Sqn met nine Albatros scouts near Zonnebeke, three of which dived on the tail of 2nd Lt D. French and Gnr E. Veale in B1114. Veale sent one D.V down out of control, which then crashed. Another was sent down out of control by Lt R.M. Makepeace and Lt M.W. Waddington in A7255, who sent a third down out of control soon afterwards. Captain A.G.V. Taylor and Sgt W.J. Benger were taken prisoner when A7271 failed to return, last being seen in combat near Zonnebeke. The observer died of his wounds. Bristol Fighter A7193 of 20 Sqn was damaged in action, pilot Lt J.C. Kirkpatrick being unhurt but observer Lt S.J. Veacock dying of wounds. Flying A7141, 2nd Lt W. Durrand and 2nd Lt A.E. Woodbridge destroyed a DFW two-seater which crashed two miles north of Bousbecque, near Menin. When three aircraft of 20 Sqn on photographic reconnaissance were attacked by eight enemy aircraft near Dadizeele, 2nd Lt G.D. Jooste and Capt J.E. Johnston in A7256 sent down an enemy aircraft in flames, and another was shot down by Lt H.G.E. Luchford and Lt V.R.S. White in B1138. An offensive patrol by 11 Sqn was set upon by 20 Albatros scouts, two of which were sent down out of control near Cambrai by Lt R.F.S. Mauduit and 2nd Lt L.H. McRobert in A7275, and another by 2nd Lt S.E. Stanley and 2nd Lt E.L. Fosse in A7209. However, the latter aircraft failed to return, last being seen in vertical dive during combat over La Sensée canal. The pilot died of wounds two days later. Also that day Capt R.N.M. Stuart-Wortley and Lt H.D. McGrath in A7268 of 22 Sqn destroyed an Albatros D.III near Ypres.

On the following day, the 18th, an offensive patrol of 22 Sqn engaged several enemy formations. Captain H.G.E. Luchford and Lt V.R.S. White in B1138 attacked three Albatros D.Vs they saw diving on an R.E.8. Two escaped by diving down steeply, but the Bristol crew fired 200 rounds into the other at a range of 20 yards and it crashed between Houthem and Tenbrielen. Shortly afterwards they fired another 200 rounds at point-blank range into a DFW two-seater, which crashed near Dadizeele. Late that day another 20 Sqn patrol engaged six or seven enemy aircraft, sending down an Albatros D.V which crashed beside an anti-aircraft battery at Gheluvelt. However, 22 Sqn had mixed fortunes during an offensive patrol that morning. Although Lt M.W. Turner and Lt L.G. Kettlewell in A7243 sent an Albatros scout down out of control at Ardoye, and 2nd Lt H.G. Robinson and Lt F.J.B. Hammersley in A7243 sent another spinning down northeast of Roulers, three crews failed to return following an encounter over Ardoye. Second Lieutenant B.B. Berry and 2nd Lt C.H. Bartlett in A7125 were both taken prisoner, 2nd Lt C.E. Ferguson and 2nd Lt A.D. Lennox in A7247 were both killed, and in A7264 Capt H. Patch died next day of his wounds and Pte R. Spensley was killed.

Owing to thick mist and clouds there was little air activity the next day. During an offensive patrol on the 20th A7245 of 20 Sqn was written off after its engine and controls were shot up in combat over Dadizeele, both 2nd Lt R.B. Slade and Lt G.B. Booth being injured, but 2nd Lt J.L. Boles and Lt O.A. Rowan in A7240 sent an enemy aircraft down out of control at Dadizeele. In the afternoon four aircraft of 11 Sqn engaged seven Albatros scouts, one of which was sent down in flames northwest of Cambrai by 2nd Lt A.E. McKeever and Lt H.G. Kent in A7153. Two others were driven down out of control in the same area by Sgt T.F. Stephenson and AM1 S.H. Platel in A7235.

Two studies showing A7231 at different stages after German markings had been applied, along with the plea 'Nicht Schiessen! ... Gute Leute' (Do Not Shoot! ... Good People) in a bid to prevent attack by over-zealous fellow German pilots. (Philip Jarrett)

Another aircraft to land in enemy territory was A7157 of 11 Sqn, which suffered engine failure on the 21st, Sgt C.J. Butler and AM1 W.T. Long both being captured, and observer 2nd Lt H.L. Walter was wounded in combat during an offensive patrol. However, when four of the squadron's aircraft engaged two two-seaters escorted by ten scouts, Lt R.F.S. Mauduit and Cpl J. Mason, incorrectly recorded as being in 'A7124', destroyed two Albatros scouts and drove another down out of control. The crew of B1138, Capt H.G.E. Luchford and Lt V.R.S. White, were on patrol with eight other aircraft of 20 Sqn when they engaged seven enemy scouts and two two-seaters. They poured 250 rounds into one of the two-seaters, which fell out of control and crashed between Dadizeele and Menin. Meanwhile, Lts Davies and Tubbs each fired more than 200 rounds into an aircraft which crashed in the Belgian trenches. In the morning of that day, 2nd Lt R.H.P. Nixon and 2nd Lt J.T. Johnson sent down an Albatros scout out of control east of Éterpigny, the observer being wounded, and

in the early afternoon Capt B.E. Baker and Lt E.F. Dixon in A7170 sent an Albatros D.III down out of control at Ostend, and Lt R.P. Dodds and 2nd Lt H.A. Cooper in B1134 dealt similarly with a two-seater at Clemskerke.

The ground offensive resumed on the 22nd, once more in heavy rain initially. While some progress was made, air activity was restricted, and rain and mist continued next day. Six enemy aircraft met a 48 Sqn patrol in the 24th, and an Albatros scout dived on the tail of 2nd Lt H.F. Jenkins and AM1 E.J. Dunford in A7155 only to be sent down in flames south of Dixmude, though Jenkins was hit by return fire. However, Capt J.T. Milne DFC and Lt S. Wright of 48 Sqn were killed when B1117 was shot down at Merckem. Heavy rain and a violent gale persisted over the next two days, but on the ground preparations were in progress for what was to be the final infantry assault of the campaign in Flanders, set to begin on the 30th, with Passchendaele as the target.

On the morning of the 27th 2nd Lt S.A. Oades and 2nd Lt H.V.R. Hill in A7281

F.2B A7131 of 11 Sqn during the winter of 1917/18. (RAF Museum P.7679)

sent a Rumpler down out of control north of Roulers, while Lt R.S.P Boby and 2nd Lt A.T. Smith in B1121 sent another enemy aircraft down out of control between Houthulst Forest and Roulers. An hour later Lt R.D. Coath and 2nd Lt K.F. Jones in A7128 of 11 Sqn drove an Albatros D.V down out of control at Ribecourt. In the afternoon, aircraft of 20 Sqn on reconnaissance met ten enemy machines over Comines, and 2nd Lt W. Durrand and 2nd Lt A.E. Woodbridge in A7198 sent down an Albatros D.V and saw it crash next to a British anti-aircraft-gun position southwest of Roulers, while 2nd Lt D.M. McGoun and 2nd Lt N. Couve in A7250 sent an Albatros D.III down out of control at Roulers. Later that day four Bristol Fighters of 11 Sqn engaged five Albatros scouts at 500 yards' range, Lt R.D. Coath and 2nd Lt K.F. Jones in A7128 drove one down out of control at Ribecourt, and 2nd Lt F. Babbage and Gnr J. McMechan of 20 Sqn drove an Albatros D.V down out of control at Moorslede.

In the late afternoon of the 29th an offensive patrol of 48 Sqn northeast of Dixmude met a large enemy formation at 16,500ft. Upon firing a burst into an Albatros scout at a range of 150 yards, 2nd Lt E.G.H.G. Williams and 2nd Lt G.W. Croft in A7216 saw it burst into flames and then crash, this victory being shared with 2nd Lt L.A. Payne and 2nd Lt V. Bourdillon. An Albatros D.III was sent down in flames by 2nd Lt H.H. Hartley and 2nd Lt E.C. Birch of the same patrol.

The weather was still unfavourable on the 30th, but Sgt T.F. Stephenson and AM1 S.H. Platel of 11 Sqn in A7235 destroyed two Albatros D.Vs at Fresse, Platel being wounded by return fire. While flying in a formation, 2nd Lt W. Beaver and Pte C.M. Snoulton of 20 Sqn became lost in cloud and were attacked by two enemy aircraft, Snoulton being wounded.

On the last day of the month eight Bristol Fighters of 11 Sqn met 11 enemy scouts over Fresse and a general engagement ensued at close range. Second Lieutenant A.E. McKeever and 2nd Lt L.A. Powell in A7153 put a burst of 50 rounds into an Albatros at five yards' range and saw it go down out of control, then Powell fired at another at 75 yards and saw it dive into the ground and burst into flames. Then a third, attacked at 50 yards' range, turned over and fell out of control, but was not seen to crash owing to clouds. Soon afterwards, Capt B.E. Baker and Lt E.F. Dixon in A7170 of 48 Sqn sent a Pfalz D.III down out of control northeast of Dixmude. Earlier that day Capt A.A. Knight and Lt A.P. Wornum in A7285 of 20 Sqn had driven an Albatros Scout down out of control at Gheluvelt. During an offensive patrol in the late afternoon B1109 was shot down by an enemy aircraft near Fresnies, 2nd Lt S.W. Randall being killed and 2nd Lt W. de C. Dodd briefly being taken prisoner before dying of wounds. Two Albatros D.Vs were destroyed at Fresse by Sgt T.F. Stephenson and AM1 S.H. Platel of 11 Sqn in A7235, but the F.2B then crashed when it landed on barbed wire, Platel having been wounded.

November 1917

Poor weather in early November meant that air activity was very restricted, but the advance on the ground was maintained, Passchendaele being taking by Canadian forces on the 6th after bitter fighting. That day another Bristol Fighter was lost, both 2nd Lt C.B. Simpson and 2nd Lt J.H.W. Duggan being killed in B1139 of 20 Sqn, which was possibly hit by anti-aircraft fire. In B1117, another 20 Sqn aircraft, 2nd Lt E.S. Brander and AM A. Townsend were both wounded during combat.

Two days later both 20 and 22 Sqns were active. Early in the day 2nd Lt B. Starfield

and Lt A. Hutchinson of 20 Sqn in A7255 shot down an enemy aircraft, which was seen by ground observers to crash northeast of Ypres. Later, Lt J.C. Kirkpatrick and Lt G.A. Brooke in A7193 of the same unit sent an enemy aircraft down in flames at Staden, and shortly afterwards Capt W. Durrand and 2nd Lt A.E. Woodbridge in A7253 drove an Albatros D.V down out of control northeast of Houthulst Forest. In the afternoon, a 22 Sqn formation fought eight enemy scouts they encountered near Moorslede. Seeing an Albatros attacking a Bristol, Lt H.J. McKenzie and Lt S.L. McClenaghan in A7230 dived on it, and another was sent down out of control by Capt J.H. Butler and S/Lt H.K. Johnstone RN in A7251. However, 2nd Lt H.G. Robinson and Lt F.J.B Hammersley were both taken prisoner when B1123 was shot down north of Moorslede. During an offensive patrol, 2nd Lt E.C. Bromley and 2nd Lt A.H. Middleton in B1120 forced-landed after combat but were both unhurt. Next, A7118 of 20 Sqn forced-landed during an offensive patrol after suffering engine trouble while over the lines; Lt J.C. Kirkpatrick was unhurt when it came down on ground that had been shelled, but his observer, 2nd Lt N. Couve, was injured.

On the 10th the ground advance during the third Battle of Ypres finally came to a halt, a gain of only four or five miles of ground being small reward for terrible loss of life. Low cloud and rain still prevailed, but on the 11th Capt A.E. McKeever and Lt L.V. Pogson in A7288 of 11 Sqn attacked and destroyed one of a pair of DFW two-seaters at Brebières. In a fight with six scouts, Capt N.C. Millman and Lt T.C.S. Tuffield in B1134 of 48 Sqn drove an Albatros D.V down out of control east of St Georges. Later, a 48 Sqn patrol encountered a formation of four large bombers with an escort of 30 scouts, and in a fight with 15 scouts Capt B.E. Baker and AM2 B. Jackman in A7170 sent down two Albatros D.IIIs out of control northeast of Dixmude.

On the 12th a 20 Sqn patrol of five Bristols was attacked by seven scouts. Captain A.A. Knight and Lt A.P. Wornum in A7285 drove an Albatros D.V down out of control, and 2nd Lt J.L. Boles and 2nd Lt F.B. Wallis in A7253 dispatched another in similar fashion. Captain N.C. Millman and Lt T.C.S. Tuffield in B1134 of 20 Sqn forced an Albatros D.III to land. Later, 2nd Lt B. Starfield and Lt A. Hutchinson in A7193 sent an Albatros scout down out of control, followed by another Albatros D.III an hour later between Wervicq and Gheluwe. During the afternoon 2nd Lt J.R. Mees and AM2 B. Jackman in B1115 of 48 Sqn sent an Albatros D.III down out of control at Dixmude, but the crew of A7155 of the same unit became lost on a patrol and crashed while landing after it had become dark. The pilot, 2nd Lt J.W.D. Needham, was killed and Lt J.S.M. Evans was injured.

The weather continued to be unfavourable for aerial work for much of the next few days, though 20 Sqn managed some flying in the mid-afternoon of the 13th, Lt R.K. Kirkman and Capt L.W. Burbidge in A7253 sending down an Albatros D.V out of control at Becelaere, and 2nd Lt W. Beaver and 2nd Lt C.J. Agelasto destroying another which crashed southeast of Houthulst Forest. Around the same time, three aircraft of 48 Sqn had successful encounters near Ostend, each sending down an Albatros scout; 2nd Lt H.H. Hartley and 2nd Lt E.C. Birch were in A7254, 2nd Lt E.G.H.C. Williams and AM2 T.W. Jones in A7216, and Lt W.A. Michael and AM2 H. Lindfield in A7227. On the 15th, 2nd Lt R.M. Makepeace and 2nd Lt W.T.V. Harmer of 20 Sqn in A7193 dealt similarly with an Albatros D.V at Moorslede.

Flying activity continued as weather permitted, the next Bristol Fighter loss being A7282 of 48 Sqn on the 18th, which was shot down in flames during an offensive patrol to Dixmude. The pilot, 2nd Lt W.S. McLaren, died next day of his wound, and his observer, 2nd Lt D.W. Hardie, was killed. Of the six enemy aircraft that had attacked them, Lt J.B.H. Cordes and AM1 E.J. Dunford in A7295 destroyed an Albatros D.III which crashed between Nieuport and Dixmude, and Capt A.W. Field and 2nd Lt G.R. Horsfall sent down another out of control west of Dixmude. Elsewhere, two 20 Sqn observers, 2nd Lt F.B. Wallis and 2nd Lt L.H. Phelps, were wounded.

On the 20th an infantry advance signalled the start of the battle of Cambrai, nearly 400 tanks affording cover as the foot soldiers progressed over four miles in fog. In the air, the only Bristol Fighter lost was A7292 of 11 Sqn, shot down by ground fire while on reconnaissance, pilot Sgt T.F. Stephenson

Although F.2B A7239 of 22 Sqn was wrecked on a test flight on 29 September 1917, when it crashed on landing, it was reconstructed and returned to the unit, but was wrecked again during gunnery practice on 18 January 1918 when its engine failed on take-off and the pilot tried to return to the aerodrome, stalled and crashed. *(SAAF Museum)*

being killed and observer Lt T.W. Morse being wounded and taken prisoner. One other squadron casualty that day was observer 2nd Lt P.J. Cayley, who was wounded during a combat patrol. That same day A7277 of 48 Sqn was engaged in combat, Capt A.W. Field escaping unhurt but 2nd Lt G.R Horsfall being killed.

Further poor weather the next day restricted flying, but activity resumed on the 23rd, and 2nd Lt E.D. Perney and 2nd Lt E.J. Blackledge of 11 Sqn were both killed when B1116 was lost the next day, last being seen over Cambrai soon after noon while on reconnaissance. In the afternoon 2nd Lt L.A. Rivers and Lt L.V.J. Pogson in A7167 of 11 Sqn drove an Albatros Scout down out of control east of Cambrai, this being the squadron's 100th victory. That same day Lt R.D. Coath of 11 Sqn was wounded while engaged on reconnaissance.

The weather continued to restrict air activity at times during the remainder of the month, but some flying was occasionally possible. On the 27th 2nd Lt T. Colvill-Jones and Capt L.R. Speakman in B1122 of 20 Sqn sent an Albatros D.III down out of control at Westroosebeke. Two days later a 48 Sqn patrol met nine enemy scouts, Capt B.E. Baker and AM2 B. Jackman in A7170 sending an Albatros D.III down out of control between Dixmude and Houthulst Forest, and later another was made to land on the Allied side of the lines between Armesvelde and Zarren, to be captured. After leaving their patrol, 2nd Lt W.G. Pudney and 2nd Lt G.S.L. Hayward of 22 Sqn were attacked by five enemy aircraft, the observer successfully shooting down a two-seater which was seen to crash near Lambersart, northwest of Lille. Meanwhile, 2nd Lt W. Beaver and AM1 G. Thomas of 20 Sqn had the engine of their aircraft, C4817, seize in combat during the morning, but made a successful forced landing without injury near Steenworde. Later, 2nd

Lt D. French and Lt A.D. Keith in A7164 of 20 Sqn sent an enemy two-seater down out of control, but 2nd Lt E.V. Clark and 2nd Lt G. Noon in A7253 of the same unit were killed in combat during an offensive patrol, having last been seen near Westroosebeke.

On 30 November 1917 Capt A.E. McKeever, a Canadian with 22 Sqn, was returning in A7288 from a line patrol deep into enemy territory with 2nd Lt A.E. Powell when they were attacked south of Cambrai by seven Albatros D.Vs and two two-seaters; the pilot and observer each destroyed two of the D.Vs. The first was engaged at only 15 yards and burst into flames when it crashed. The next two were accounted for by Powell, and the fourth was shot down by the pilot after overshooting the Bristol. Powell's gun had a stoppage during the fighting and McKeever then fought the enemy down to within 20ft of the ground, then as the enemy was still attacking he pretended to land, this deception enabling him to zoom up by giving his engine a burst, then get away before the remaining enemy realised his intention. McKeever, who already had an MC and bar, was awarded the DFC for this magnificent demonstration of the F.2B's fighting ability when handled by an experienced and determined crew. He had now notched up a total of 18 enemy aircraft destroyed and 13 out of control to become the highest scorer of any Bristol Fighter pilot. He never returned to the front, and in November 1918 he formed 1 Sqn, Canadian Air Force, at Upper Heyford, equipped with Sopwith Dolphins.

December 1917

By the beginning of December the early gains of the tank offensive had been lost to counterattacks. Ground fighting was subsiding, and mist and low cloud continued to restrict air activity, as did the shorter

Probably serving with a training unit in the UK, this F.2B '2' has had the face of Bruce Bairnsfather's famous 'Old Bill' character painted on its radiator shutters, and the greeting "'ullo!" applied on the bottom of the front of the cowling.

days. Squalls and very strong winds prevented much flying on the 2nd, though three aircraft of 20 Sqn dived on an Albatros two-seater they came across southeast of Passchendaele during an offensive patrol, 2nd Lt W.P. Beaver and AM M.B. Mather in B883 shooting it down. At about the same time A7270 was shot down in combat, Capt H.G.E. Luchford being killed and Capt J.E. Johnston being taken prisoner, injured. On reconnaissance that day the engine of A7167 of 11 Sqn was hit by flak and the aircraft crashed, though without injury to either 2nd Lt L.A. Rivers or Pte J.W. Scott. Next day, a 20 Sqn patrol met eight enemy aircraft over Wervicq, and an Albatros D.V was sent down out of control by Sgt F.P. Johnson and 2nd Lt S.H.P. Masding in A7214. However, A7141 of the same squadron failed to return, having been last seen in combat north of Hollebeke; 2nd Lt W. Bevan and Lt F.B. Gloster were both killed. Another aircraft lost that day was B1153 of 22 Sqn, last seen going down over Poperinghe, apparently with engine trouble. It was later reported that 2nd Lt A.F. Goodchap and 2nd Lt A.H. Middleton were prisoners of war.

The weather was fine on the 4th, though fine ground mist prevented aircraft from working freely, but the next day brought an improvement. The Bristol Fighters of 20 Sqn encountered some Albatroses near Dadizeele and a two-seater was destroyed by Lt J.C. Kirkpatrick and 2nd Lt W.T.V. Harmer in A7299, another was sent down out of control by 2nd Lt W.P. Beaver and AM M.B. Mather in B883, and a D.V was similarly dealt with by Sgt F. Johnson and Capt J.H. Hedley in A7144. Also that morning, A7143 of 11 Sqn failed to return from photographic reconnaissance, Sgt M.H. Everix and Lt H. Whitworth being captured. While performing similar duties near Cambrai, A7266 of the same squadron

was shot up in combat but landed safely; 2nd Lt H.R. Child and Lt A. Reeve were unhurt. Likewise, A7250 of 20 Sqn, on a similar task, was shot up by an enemy aircraft and forced-landed in a shelled area, Sgt F. Hopper being wounded and observer Capt R.H. Warden shaken. Soon afterwards, Lt R.K. Kirkman and Capt L.W. Burbidge in A7298 of 20 Sqn sent an Albatros D.V down out of control at Ostnieuwkerke. In the early evening, 2nd Lt S.A. Oades and AM2 J.H. Jones in B1164 of 20 Sqn sent a two-seater down in flames north of Roulers, while Sgt J.M. Bainbridge and Sgt J. Johnston in B1112 of 22 Sqn sent down another two-seater which crashed northwest of Roulers.

The following day, the 6th, 48 Sqn withdrew to Lièttres to come under GHQ Reserve. That day, 2nd Lt S.A. Oades and AM2 J.H. Jones of 22 Sqn in B1164 destroyed a two-seater at Haubourdin, while 2nd Lt W.G. Pudney and 2nd Lt G.S.L. Hayward in A7279 of the same unit sent another two-seater down apparently out of control at Bailleul. Bad weather then intervened again, the next reasonably good flying day being the 10th, when Sgt F. Johnson and Capt J.H. Hedley in A7144 of 20 Sqn destroyed an Albatros D.V which crashed east of Staden, but A7299 of the same squadron was lost to flak while on an offensive sortie, Lt J.C. Kirkpatrick being killed and 2nd Lt W.T.V. Harmer injured.

On the 18th 48 Sqn moved again, now joining the 22nd Wing at Villers-Bretonneux to come under the 5th Brigade. On the 22nd a 20 Sqn patrol engaged seven enemy aircraft over Moorslede, Sgt F. Johnson and Capt J.H. Hedley in A7144 shooting down an Albatros D.V out of control and then engaging two others. Hedley fired 80 rounds into one at close range, and it crashed and burst into flames, and the other crashed and burnt at Roulers.

Then 2nd Lt R.M. Makepeace and Lt G.A. Brooke in A7255 found a D.V on their tail and dived and fired back, the enemy going into a vertical dive before crashing at Roulers.

The final F.2B loss of the year was that of C4801 on the 28th, Lt D.G. Barnett and AM2 G.L. Sims being shot down over Nieppe Forest during a bomber escort mission. The wreckage was later found, but Barnett died of his wounds.

Squadron identification markings
The introduction of the Bristol Fighter into service occurred at a time when standardised identification markings were under consideration for all squadrons in France. An earlier such system, confined to the B.E.2c squadrons, had been authorised by RFC Headquarters in France on 23 April 1916 and consisted of assorted distinctive bars, circles and squares to be painted on the fuselage sides, each B.E.2c squadron having a different set of symbols. On 26 August 1917 this system was standardised and fresh white markings were promulgated for squadrons of all types in France, those for the Bristol Fighter units being as follows:

11 Squadron – inward sloping diagonal white stripes fore and aft of the fuselage roundel.

20 Squadron – two vertical white bands aft of fuselage roundel.

22 Squadron – a vertical white band each side of the fuselage roundel.

48 Squadron – two vertical white bands aft of the fuselage roundel.

In October 1917 the markings for 20 Sqn were changed to a single white vertical band forward of the fuselage roundels. A further promulgation on 23 December 1917 led to numerous changes and additions to the previous listing. An addition to those for the Bristol Fighter squadrons was one for the imminent arrival of 62 Sqn, to consist of three vertical white bands, one in front of and two behind the fuselage roundels. One change was to 22 Sqn, whose aircraft would now bear a single vertical white band forward of the fuselage roundels, another just behind, and a third just in front of the tailplane. At a later date 48 Sqn changed to a horizontal white zigzag aft of the fuselage roundels.

These markings continued on F.2Bs until 22 March 1918, when it was decided to discontinue squadron markings with the exception of single-seat fighters, the remainder, including the Bristol Fighter units, ceasing to use them. The system remained in use just on single-seat fighters until the Armistice.

After being delivered to 48 Sqn at Rendcomb in March 1917, F.2AA3329 went to France with the squadron on the 8th of that month but crashed on take-off on 8 April 1917 with 2nd Lts R.E. Adeney and H.L. Tomkins aboard. Rebuilt, it subsequently served with 11 Sqn and 38 TS at Rendcomb. This photograph was taken at East Boldrfe, Hampshire, on 19 July 1917. *(C&C)*

Chapter 4

THE STRUGGLE CONTINUES

By the beginning of 1918 the outlook for the Allies was unpromising. Their efforts during the latter half of the previous year on the Western Front had been in vain. Enormous losses had been incurred, and time was needed to allow newly recruited troops to be trained and made battle-ready. Colossal bombardments preceding a battle had proved counter-productive, as they gave the enemy full warning of an impending attack. Events had shown that it was likely to be more fruitful to rely on tanks to open up enemy defences, supported by new ground-strafing aircraft.

However, other factors now came into play. Fighting on the Russian Front had ceased altogether after the Communist revolution, and had eased on the Italian Front, releasing more than a million German troops to be transported to support their comrades on the Western Front. Moreover, the German aircraft industry had got into its stride, and in just eight months the nation's air force had doubled in size. Both sides had newer designs of aircraft. American troops would soon be on their way in their thousands, and Germany would inevitably aim to mount a big new offensive before they could arrive and be blooded. The RFC planned for numerous new operational squadrons, but in most cases it would take months for them to be fully equipped with the aircraft they would take to France, and the crews would need to be

sufficiently trained in modern aerial warfare if they were to play an active part on arrival.

January 1918

The year started with a victory on New Year's Day, when 2nd Lt J.S. Chick and Lt H.R. Kinkead in C4846 of 11 Sqn, attacked by an Albatros D.V while taking photographs, drove it down out of control at Crèvecoeur. Seasonal low cloud and thick mist prevented much flying during the next day, but there was an improvement on the 3rd, when 2nd Lt W. Beaver and 2nd Lt H.E. Easton in B883 of 20 Sqn sent down an Albatros two-seater which attacked them while they were on photographic work, seeing it crash and burst into flames northeast of Moorslede. A little while later Capt N.C. Millman and 2nd Lt H.A. Cooper in B1187 of 48 Sqn sent an Albatros two-seater down out of control at Le Catelet, and then Capt K.R. Park and Lt J.H. Robertson in A7229 of the same unit were attacked by six enemy aircraft while photographing, but managed to send an Albatros D.III down out of control at St Quentin before evading the others, even though their engine had been hit. An LVG two-seater was also sent down out of control by 2nd Lt L.A. Payne and his observer in another 48 Sqn aircraft, while observer 2nd Lt L. Lambe, also of this squadron, was wounded. Also that day, Lt T. Colvill-Jones and 2nd Lt H.G. Crowe in B1122 of 20

Sqn sent a two-seater down in flames north of Moorslede.

On the 4th, 20 Sqn had several of encounters, Lt G.D. Jooste and Lt S.H.P. Masding in one aircraft destroying an Albatros D.V during the morning. Later, 2nd Lt R.M. Makepeace and Capt J.H. Hedley, on a photographic mission in the same area, were attacked by five scouts and sent another Albatros D.V down out of control. Low clouds and mist returned next day. The weather improved on the 6th, and 2nd Lt S.A. Oades and Lt D.N.G. Brampton in A7300 of 22 Sqn sent an Albatros D.V down out of control north of Roulers. Later, 2nd Lt W. Beaver and 2nd Lt H.E. Easton in B883 of 20 Sqn despatched an Albatros two-seater similarly at Houthulst Forest. Second Lieutenant R.H. Nixon and 2nd Lt E.H. Church in A7226 of 11 Sqn drove an Albatros D.III down out of control near Estourmel, but their own aircraft was hit by return fire and the observer wounded. Also wounded was 2nd Lt N.E. Gwyer of 11 Sqn, when his aircraft was in engaged combat during an offensive patrol. The weather then clamped down again, including snowstorms on the 8th.

Lieutenant R. Dodds and 2nd Lt W. Hart in B1182 of 48 Sqn were taking photographs on the 9th when they were attacked by three enemy aircraft. They succeeded in sending down a Rumpler two-seater out of control, then shortly afterwards they engaged three scouts, sending down an Albatros D.III out of control at Warlencourt. At around the same time Capt A.W. Field and 2nd Lt W.S. Smith were both killed when C4816 of 48 Sqn was hit while on a counter-battery photographic mission; its wings were shot away and it fell out of control at Estrées.

The next fine day was the 13th, when a great deal of flying was possible. During an offensive patrol 2nd Lt T. Colvill-Jones and 2nd Lt H.G. Crowe in B1122 of 20 Sqn spotted a two-seater, 150 rounds being sufficient to send it crashing north of Moorslede. Elsewhere, A7174 of 11 Sqn was hit by anti-aircraft fire while on an offensive patrol, being last seen over Douai going east with smoke issuing from the engine, after which it crashed; 2nd Lt H.V. Biddington was taken prisoner and observer 2nd Lt J.H. Corbet was killed. This was the squadron's first Bristol Fighter operational loss of the year.

The weather then clamped down again until the 19th, when visibility was good with only high clouds, and 20 Sqn took advantage of the opportunity. Captain N.V. Harrison and Lt T.C. Noel in C4617 sent an Albatros D.V down in a slow spin southwest of Roulers, and later Capt T. Colvill-Jones and Lt L.H. Phelps in B1122 sent an Albatros D.V down out of control east of Moorslede. However, 2nd Lt B. Starfield and Lt A. Hutchinson were both killed in A7193 while on an offensive patrol to Roulers, being last seen near Wytschaete.

After more bad weather 22 Sqn joined the 10th Wing, 1st Brigade, at Auchel on 22 January. This turned out to be a busy day for flying, with 20 Sqn again active. During the morning, a patrol of 11 Bristols was attacked by about 20 Albatros scouts. Second Lieutenant D.G. Cooke and 2nd Lt H.G.

Crowe in A7256 sent an Albatros D.V down out of control, then dived on another, which was seen going down issuing smoke before crashing south of Moorslede. Flying in B1156, Capt R.K. Kirkman and AM2 J. McMechan shot a D.V. down out of control nearby, and Sgt H.O. Smith and 2nd Lt C.J. Agelasto in B883 shot down a D.V which crashed between Dadizeele and Moorslede. However, C4825, which had left on an offensive patrol to St Julien, failed to return, having come down in enemy territory, 2nd Lt A.R. Paul and AM2 A. Mann both dying of their wounds.

Over the next few days the weather improved, and on the 25th an offensive patrol of 20 Sqn Bristols engaged 12 Albatros scouts. In the ensuing fight Capt R.K. Kirkman and Lt D. Keith in B1156 drove down a D.V over Kortemark, and it was seen by 60 Sqn pilots to be falling with its wings folded back. Another Albatros was fired at by 2nd Lt D.M. McGoun and 2nd Lt C.J. Agelasto in C4836, and went down out of control. Another pilot confirmed that it crashed near Stadenberg. Lieutenant D. Leigh-Pemberton and Lt N.W. Taylor in A7214 sent another down out of control at Houthulst, and Sgt F.P. Johnson and 2nd Lt D.H. Prosser in C4604 shot down one which crashed at Staden. In the same area, Lt D.J. Weston and Lt W. Noble in B1177 shot at one which broke up, then sent yet another down out of control. One squadron aircraft was lost, however, Sgt H.O. Smith and 2nd Lt H.S. Clemons being taken prisoner with wounds when B883 was hit by flak and had to force-land northeast of Passchendaele, near Houthulst Forest.

Also active on the 25th was 22 Sqn, 14 Albatros scouts being sighted southwest of Lille, while, on an offensive patrol, Capt

R.S.P. Boby and 2nd Lt B.C.M. Ward in A7259 and Lt W.L. Wells and Lt H.F. Moore in A7286 each sent down an Albatros D.III out of control. Unfortunately, on that day 2nd Lt D.S. Smallwood and Sgt T. Kavanagh were both killed when their lower port wing collapsed during gunnery practice. Another Albatros D.III was sent down out of control northeast of St Quentin by Lt H.W. Elliott and Lt R.S. Herring of 48 Sqn in B1187.

More flying was possible on the 28th, all four squadrons being busy that day. Lieutenant J.S. Chick and Lt A. Reeve in A7131 of 11 Sqn drove down a DFW two-seater north of Bourlon Wood, but the squadron suffered two losses; 2nd Lt S. Reay and AM2 A. Patterson were both killed when A7288 was shot down northwest of Cambrai during an offensive patrol, the pilot jumping to his death, and 2nd Lt J.L. Milne-Henderson and 2nd Lt E.A. Cunningham in B1189 on a similar task were also killed after experiencing engine problems over Douai. Captain T. Colvill-Jones and Lt L.H. Phelps in B1122 of 20 Sqn sent an Albatros two-seater down out of control northwest of Westroosebeke, while 2nd Lt F.C. Ransley and 2nd Lt R.S. Herring in B1193 of 48 Sqn similarly sent down a Rumpler two-seater at Beaurevoir. Captain R.N.M. Stuart-Wortley and 2nd Lt D.W. Kent-Jones in C4835 of 22 Sqn had an indecisive combat over Hénin-Liétard with a two-seater, the observer of which appeared to have been hit. They then shot down an Albatros D.V which crashed in flames near Douvrin.

The first of the new squadrons had arrived during the month in the shape of 62 Sqn, which had been equipped in the UK, initially at Filton and later at Rendcomb,

F.2B B1112 during its detachment to 16 Sqn, an R.E.8-equipped unit, at Complain l'Abbé around February-May 1918, piloted by Capt C. Jones, still displays its former 22 Sqn markings and code letter. *(C&C)*

before sailing from Southampton on 21 January 1918 to join the Expeditionary Force. After disembarking at Le Havre, the squadron went next day to Lièttres, the ground crew going on to St Omer on the 23rd, and the aircraft flying across the Channel on the 29th. On the 30th the now-complete squadron took up residence at Serny as part of 9th (Headquarters) Wing.

On that date Lt R.G. Bennett and AM2 B. Matthews in C4604 of 20 Sqn sent an Albatros scout down out of control west of Ghistelles, while 2nd Lt D.M. McGoun and 2nd Lt C.J. Agelasto in C4826 shot down another which crashed into a wood just west of Zedelghem. Elsewhere, 2nd Lt S.A. Oades and 2nd Lt S.W. Bunting in B1164 of 22 Sqn shot down a two-seater. Its starboard wing crumpled up and it crashed north of La Bassée. However, C4832 of the same squadron was shot down in flames by an enemy aircraft, New Zealander 2nd Lt G.G. Johnstone being killed and 3AM R.A. Duff dying of his injuries.

February 1918

Effective reconnaissance had been rendered difficult throughout January by the appalling weather, but by early February it was becoming obvious that the Germans had taken advantage of the lull to make a massive build-up of troops and equipment. Construction work included new aerodromes, and it was apparent that the intention was to attack opposite the Cambrai salient, with Amiens as the main objective. Royal Flying Corps activity continued to be on a limited scale for the first half of the month, with correspondingly low aircraft losses throughout February. German air activity was being kept deliberately low-key to conceal the enemy's concentrations, and in response the Allies sought out and bombed their aerodromes in advance of the forthcoming battle.

The unfavourable weather continued through much of the month, full aerial activity being possibly only on occasional days. On 2 February 22 Sqn moved with the 10th Wing 1st Brigade to Treizennes. On the 3rd, 2nd Lt W.P. Beaver and 2nd Lt H.E. Easton in B1156 of 20 Sqn dived on an Albatros D.V, which fell out of control then burst into flames just before crashing on the Roulers-Menin road. Next morning 2nd Lt T. Colvill-Jones and Capt J.H. Hedley in B1122 of 20 Sqn dived on an enemy kite balloon, which crumpled on the ground, and shortly after this they attacked an Albatros D.V which crashed between Roulers and Menin.

In the afternoon, a 20 Sqn offensive patrol engaged 20 Albatros scouts between Menin and Roulers and a general melee ensued. Lieutenant R.D. Leigh-Pemberton and Capt N.W. Taylor in C4614 fired at an Albatros which burst into flames, and Lt D.J. Weston and Lt W. Noble sent a D.V

down out of control. Lieutenant R.G. Bennett and AM1 M.B. Mather in C4604 fired 200 rounds into a third Albatros, which fell out of control, but they were then attacked by three scouts. Mather fired a drum into one of them and it went down in flames, breaking up in the air. An Albatros D.V was sent down out of control by 2nd Lt D.G. Cooke and 2nd Lt C.J. Agelasto in C4605, then 2nd Lt E. Lindup and 2nd Lt N.S. Dougall in B1191 dealt similarly with another D.V, which fell to a burst from the rear gun, while 2nd Lt W. Beaver and 2nd Lt H.E. Easton in C4826 sent yet another D.V down to crash at Roulers. About half-an-hour later 2nd Lt L.P. Roberts and Lt M.F. Farquharton-Roberts in C4617 of 20 Sqn sent an Albatros down out of control over Houthulst Forest. During the day 2nd Lt A.M. Beamer of 22 Sqn was killed when the wings of A7279 collapsed during a practice flight.

On the 5th, 2nd Lt W.P. Beaver and 2nd Lt H.E. Easton in B1156 of 20 Sqn sent two Albatros D.Vs down out of control at Roulers, while Lt D.G. Cooke and 2nd Lt C.J. Agelasto in C4605 dispatched two more the same way at Staden. However, A7255 had its radiator shot through by machine-gun fire and crashed at Crombeke, fortunately without injury to either Lt D.G. Campbell or 2nd Lt W.H. Nash. There was very little flying for the next few days, but on the 7th, 2nd Lt C.G. Napier and 2nd Lt J.M.J. Moore of 48 Sqn attacked an LVG two-seater near Le Catelet. On the 9th an Albatros D.III was driven down out of control south of Guise by 2nd Lt H.H. Hartley and 2nd Lt R.S. Herring in C4628 of 48 Sqn, but that same day B1210 of the same squadron suffered engine failure during a photographic patrol and overturned in a ploughed field near the aerodrome, 2nd Lt F.R. Hunt being injured and Lt J.E.M. Evans dying of his injuries while en route to hospital.

The poor weather persisted, though a little flying was possible of the 14th, when Capt S.J. Sibley and Lt O.G.S. Crawford in B1254 of 48 Sqn were hit by flak while on a special low reconnaissance, being last seen flying east

over St Quentin; they were later reported as prisoners of war. Bristol F.2B losses during February were low, mainly due to the lack of flying opportunities, but on the 16th A7229 of 48 Sqn was shot down in flames during a photographic mission, Sgt E.F. Hardeman and 2nd Lt G.W. Croft both being killed. That day, 2nd Lt W. Beaver and 2nd Lt H.E. Easton in C4826 of 20 Sqn sent a two-seater down out of control at Menin.

On 17 February, which was also a better day for flying, 2nd Lt S.A. Oades and 2nd Lt S.W. Bunting in B1152 of 22 Sqn fired 100 rounds into an Albatros D.V at close range and it crashed north of Douai, while Capt J McKelvie and Sgt C. Hagan in C4828 sent another Albatros scout down to crash west of Douai. Recently arrived 62 Sqn notched up a victory that day when Capt G. Hughes, an Australian, and Capt H. Claye in C4630 sent down a two-seater which broke up and crashed near Armentières. A 20 Sqn formation of 12 aircraft encountered 16 enemy aircraft, Lt E. Lindup and Cpl M. Mather in C4641 firing 100 rounds into a Pfalz D.III which crashed in flames at Westroosebeke. Sergeant F. Johnson and Capt J.H. Hedley in B1177 destroyed a Pfalz D.III and sent another down out of control near Moorslede. A Pfalz was driven down out of control at Moorslede by 2nd Lt D.M. McGoun and Lt S.H.P Masding in C4826, and Lt R.G. Bennett and Cpl F. Archer in C4604 dealt similarly with another scout. However, 2nd Lt L.P. Roberts and 2nd Lt W. Noble, on an offensive patrol in B1209, sent another scout out of control northwest of Menin but then crashed during a forced landing at Woesten, the observer being concussed.

Next day, three aircraft of 22 Sqn met four enemy scouts near Seclin, 2nd Lt S.H. Wallage and Sgt J.H. Jones in C4808 sending a two-seater down out of control while Lt W.L. Wells and Lt H.E. Moore in A7251 sent down another, which crashed. Elsewhere, 2nd Lt S.A. Oades and 2nd Lt S.W. Bunting in B1152 of 22 Sqn sent an Albatros D.V down out of control east of La Bassée. There were no successes the next day, but Lt D.G. Campbell and Lt J.H.

Bristol F.2B Fighter A7220 of 48 Sqn, displaying the unit markings authorised by 26 August 1917, is prepared for an operation in France. This aircraft was credited with several victories and claims in 1917 but was shot down by an enemy aircraft during an offensive patrol on 21 February 1918. *(Philip Jarrett)*

This F.2B, C4814 'D' of 11 Sqn, spent only a brief period in France, being returned to the UK on 12 December 1917. *(Philip Jarrett)*

Stream in C4837 of 20 Sqn were shot down in flames during an offensive patrol.

On the 21st eight aircraft of 20 Sqn came across a two-seater and Lt R.G. Bennett and Cpl E. Veale in C4604 dived down and gave it a burst of 50 rounds from the front gun at about 200 yards' range, then saw it sideslip and crash southwest of Comines. Captain G.F. Hughes and Capt H. Claye of 62 Sqn, again in C4630, were leading a formation at 13,000ft when they saw a large two-seater flying south over Armentières at about 7,000ft. Diving down to within 200ft of the enemy machine and then zooming up within 50 yards of its tail, Hughes fired 50 rounds from his front gun. The aircraft turned east, then broke into pieces in the air. Elsewhere, 2nd Lt C.D.B. Stiles and Lt W.G.S. Gregson in A7220 of 48 Sqn were shot down by an enemy aircraft during an offensive patrol, crashing some 2,000 yards east of Savy. Gregson was wounded.

The only other fine day this month was the 22nd. On this day Sgt E.J. Elton and Sgt J.C. Hagen in B1152 of 22 Sqn were attacked east of Lens by ten Albatros scouts. Hagen fired a long burst into one which was diving down on to his tail, and the pilot collapsed over the fuselage before his aircraft crashed. They then dived down on another one, and a burst from short range caused it to collapse in mid-air and fall in pieces. Elsewhere, 2nd Lt S.A. Oades and 2nd Lt S.W. Bunting in B1168 of 22 Sqn attacked one of five scouts and sent this Albatros D.V down in flames near Douai. Also on this day, 2nd Lt L.A. Payne and Lt G.H.H. Scutt in A7298 of 48 Sqn sent an LVG down in flames.

March 1918

March proved to be a very busy month. Plans were in hand to deploy RFC squadrons according to where the anticipated German attack could be expected. At a meeting on the 2nd the proposed order of battle included 11 Sqn as part of 13th (Army) Wing in the 3rd Brigade in support of the

Third Army, 48 Sqn in the 22nd (Army) Wing in the 5th Brigade, while 62 Sqn would provide some of the air support for the 5th Army.

Poor weather restricted aerial activity at the beginning of the month, though Capt N.C. Millman and 2nd Lt H.A. Cooper in B1190 of 48 Sqn sent a two-seater down out of control at Joncourt on the morning of the 1st, and dealt similarly with an Albatros D.III south of St Quentin shortly afterwards. On the afternoon of the 5th, 2nd Lt S.A. Oades was slightly wounded and 2nd Lt S.W. Bunting in B1168 of 22 Sqn attacked a two-seater, a burst of fire resulting in its starboard wing folding back, whereupon it went down in a spinning dive. Soon afterwards they attacked a scout which turned over and went down completely out of control east of Lens. However, their machine-gun continued firing after the combat and shot away one blade of the propeller, the aircraft crashing in the subsequent forced landing, both crew members having been wounded. That same day Lt R.H. Little and Lt L.N. Jones in B1265 of 48 Sqn destroyed a Pfalz D.III between La Fère and Hanegicourt, their own aircraft being shot up and the observer wounded. In the late morning 2nd Lt G.W. Bulmer and 2nd Lt S.J. Hunter in C4810 of 22 Sqn destroyed a Pfalz D.III east of La Bassée. In the afternoon, 2nd Lt H.F. Davison and 2nd Lt J.L. Morgan in B1152 of 22 Sqn sent an Albatros D.V down out of control near Lille, while Sgt E.J. Elton and 2nd Lt G.S.L. Hayward in B1162 of 22 Sqn sent another Albatros D.V out of control at Douai and destroyed a third, which crashed between the railway and road running toward Dechy, southeast of Douai, this machine falling victim to the Bristol Fighter's observer.

On 8 March 62 Sqn moved to Cachy, and on this day there was quite a lot of aviation activity. While escorting R.E.8s, 2nd Lt H.F. Davison and 2nd Lt J.L. Morgan in B1152 of 22 Sqn sent two

Albatros D.Vs down out of control southwest of Lille, and later claimed a Pfalz D.III, a wing of which broke off in the air. It crashed at Douai. Sergeant E.J. Elton and Sgt S. Belding in B1162 of 22 Sqn destroyed an Albatros D.V which crashed southwest of Lille. This was an especially busy day for 48 Sqn. Early in the day 2nd Lt C.G. Napier and 2nd Lt J.M.J. Moore in B1187 sent a DFW down in flames at St Quentin, Lt J. Baird and 2nd Lt F. Keith in C4628 drove a Pfalz D.III down out of control at Caudry, and 2nd Lt L.A. Payne and Lt G.H.H. Scutt in A7298 sent two Albatros D.Vs down out of control at Mont d'Origny. Mid-morning, Lt R. Dodds and Lt D. Wishart-Orr sent two Pfalz D.IIIs down in flames, while Lt W.A. McMichael and Lt E.G. Humphrey in B1251 sent down an Albatros D.III out of control, both in the La Fère region. In the Bohain-Busigny area, Capt N.C. Millman and 2nd Lt H.A. Cooper in B1190 sent an Albatros D.V down out of control, following this with a second one late in the day; 2nd Lt E.J. Smethan-Jones and 2nd Lt G. Dixon in B1269 sent down an Albatros D.III out of control; Capt N.C. Millman and 2nd Lt H.A. Cooper in B1190 sent an Albatros D.V down out of control and a second one later in the day; and 2nd Lt H.H. Hartley and 2nd Lt J.H. Robertson in A7114 drove two Albatros D.Vs down out of control and destroyed another, but they were hit by return fire and the observer died of his wounds. Elsewhere, Lt J.E. Drummond and 2nd Lt N. Sillars in B1265 of 48 Sqn sent an Albatros D.III out of control northeast of Laon, while Lt R. Dodds and Lt D. Wishart-Orr in C4606 claimed a Rumpler two-seater down out of control northeast of Bellecourt.

On 9 March 53 aircraft participated in a large-scale bombing raid on enemy aerodromes, the pilots having practised low-level bombing techniques beforehand. The raids were timed to take place while the enemy were preparing for their afternoon activities, so as to catch them on the ground and inflict the maximum damage. One of several squadrons to attack Busigny and Escaufort aerodromes was 48 Sqn, which dropped 32 25lb bombs from around 400ft, obtaining direct hits on hangars, two of which were set on fire. Returning at low height, the pilots engaged ground targets en route. Elsewhere, Lt D.G. Cooke and 2nd Lt J.J. Scaramanga in C4605 of 20 Sqn sent an Albatros D.V down out of control south of Comines, and 2nd Lt L.H.T. Capel and Cpl M.B. Mather in B1191 sent two Albatros scouts down out of control south of Menin. Second Lieutenant D.W. Beard and Sgt H.W. Scarnell in C4846 of 11 Sqn drove a Pfalz D.III down out of control at Douai, and 2nd Lt D.C.M. Brooks and Lt H.R. Kincaid in A7153 dealt similarly with another in the Scarpe Valley. During a special-duty flight, Maj L.W. Learmount, the squadron CO, and 2nd Lt C.J. McGrane in C4835 of 22 Sqn shot up an enemy artillery-spotting aircraft, which was driven east and forced to land at Bas Maisnil. They then strafed trenches, but the pilot was wounded by ground fire. Although he lost blood, he managed to land his aircraft safely.

On the next day 62 Sqn was busy. Captain G.F. Hughes and Capt H. Claye in C4630 sent an Albatros D.V down in flames and another out of control, Lt C.W. Robinson and Lt C.D. Wells sent two enemy aircraft down out of control, and two more were similarly dealt with by 2nd Lt C. Allen and Lt J.M. Hay, and Lt M.H. Cleary and Lt N.T. Watson respectively. Around midday on the 11th, 2nd Lt E.J. Smethan-Jones and Lt A.C. Cooper in B1269 of 48 Sqn sent down an Albatros D.III out of control southeast of St Quentin. In the same area, 2nd Lt H.H. Hartley and 2nd Lt J.H. Robertson in A7114 sent down a Fokker Dr.I out of control, but they had been hit by return fire and the observer died of his wounds. In addition, A7227 of 48 Sqn was damaged in combat during an offensive patrol, but 2nd Lt W.L. Thomas and Cpl J.H. Bowler landed safely. In the afternoon, 2nd Lt S.H. Wallage and Sgt J.H. Jones in A7286 of 22 Sqn sent two Albatros D.Vs down out of control at Lomme and Ligny respectively, while Sgt E.J. Elton and 2nd Lt G.S.L. Hayward in B1152 destroyed an Albatros D.V which crashed at Faches, and another went down out of control at Lille. Two successes were claimed by 62 Sqn; Capt G.F. Hughes and Capt H. Claye in C4630 sent down a Fokker Dr.I out of control, and another was sent down by 2nd Lt S.W. Symons and Sgt W.N. Holmes and burst into flames near the ground.

On 12 March 62 Sqn suffered its first losses since it had moved down to the Fifth Army area five days earlier, one of several squadrons of the 9th (Headquarters) Wing to operate on the boundary between the Third and Fifth Armies, where the coming offensive, and therefore the hottest action, was expected. While co-operating with D.H.4 bombers of 25 and 27 Sqns they had just two successes that day, Lt G.E. Gibbons and 2nd Lt S.A.W. Knights in B1302 sending a Fokker Dr.I down out of control northeast of Nauroy, and another enemy aircraft being similarly dealt with by Lt P.R. Hampton and Lt L.G. Lane. However, the squadron suffered four losses in late morning, all at about the same time, east of Cambrai. An offensive patrol met a large enemy formation led by Rttm Manfred von Richthofen, and in the ensuing melee B1251 was shot down in flames by von Richthofen of JG1, 2nd Lt L.C.F. Clutterbuck and 2nd Lt H.J. Sparks being wounded and subsequently becoming prisoners of war. A similar fate befell 2nd Lt C.B. Fenton and Lt H.B.P. Boyce in B1250 at the hands of Ltn Lothar von Richthofen of Jasta 11, who also shot down B1247 in

flames, killing Capt D.S. Kennedy and Lt H.G. Gill. The fourth machine to go down in flames was C4824, shot down by Ltn Werner Steinhauser of Jasta 1, resulting in Lt J.A.A. Ferguson and Sgt L.S.D. Long being wounded and then captured.

In the Cambrai area 11 Sqn fared better that day. Captain A.P. Maclean and Lt F.H. Cantlon in C4844 sent either an Albatros D.III or Fokker Dr.I down in flames and another out of control, an Albatros D.V was destroyed by 2nd Lt J.P. Seabrook and 2nd Lt C. Wrigglesworth in A7153, and Capt C.C. Haynes and Lt J.L. Smith in A7281 drove a Fokker Dr.I or Albatros scout down out of control. Flying in C4847, 2nd Lt J.S. Chick and 2nd Lt P. Douglas sent a two-seater down out of control and then dealt similarly with four Fokker Dr.Is at Caudry. Elsewhere, Lt H.W. Sellars and Lt C.C. Robson in C4673 of 11 Sqn forced an Albatros two-seater to land near Doignies, the captured aircraft later being allotted serial number G.149. Around noon 2nd Lt N. Roberts and Cpl W. Lawder in C4603 of 48 Sqn attacked two Fokker Dr.Is, destroying one and sending the other down out of control northeast of St Quentin. During an offensive patrol, 2nd Lt C.A. Hore and Cpl J. Cruikshank in A7290 of 48 Sqn sent two more Dr.Is down out of control at Catelat, but their own aircraft was damaged and they had to force-land in a field. Pilot Hore was unhurt, but his observer had been killed.

Next day, the 13th, again co-operating with D.H.4 bombers of 25 and 27 Sqns, 62 Sqn once more encountered a large formation led by von Richthofen in the same place as the previous day, this time losing two aircraft, both of which came down behind enemy lines, three crew members being wounded and one killed. Bristol Fighter B1207 was shot down at Marcoing by Ltn Heins of Jasta 56. Its pilot, 2nd Lt C. Allen, was killed but Lt N.T. Watson survived. Leutnant F. Schleiff, also of Jasta 56, claimed B1268, manned by 2nd Lt N.B. Wells and Lt G.R. Crammon, which came down at La Terrière. This time,

however, the encounter was less one-sided, for 2nd Lt W.E. Staton and Lt H.E. Merritt in C4619 claimed a Fokker Dr.I and an Albatros D.V down out of control, Lt A.R. James and Lt J.M. Hay an Albatros D.V out of control, and Capt H.L. Symons and Sgt W.N. Holmes in C4609 claimed another D.V. In a general engagement, Capt G.F. Hughes and Capt H. Claye in C4630 shot down a Fokker Dr.I which was seen by other pilots to crash; they then attacked one of three more that were diving on their tail, and it went down vertically with its top wing falling away in pieces. The pilot attacked at least six more Albatros scouts and Dr.Is, by which time his observer's gun was out of action, so he turned for home, outdistancing all of the enemy aircraft and crossing the lines at 3,000ft. One of the Fokker Dr.Is was flown by Ltn Lothar von Richthofen, which crashed, this success being shared with Capt A.H. Orlebar in 73 Sqn Camel B7282. Lothar von Richthofen was the younger brother of Manfred; his injuries from the crash put him in hospital for several weeks.

Also involved in fighting that day were aircraft of 22 Sqn. Late in the afternoon 2nd Lt H.F. Davison and 2nd Lt J.L. Morgan in B1152 shot down a Pfalz D.III which crashed in flames near Annoeullin, Lt F.G.C. Weare and 2nd Lt S.J. Hunter in C4631 sent down an Albatros D.V, which spun and its right wing came off, whereupon it crashed between Seclin and Houplin. Flying in A7286, Lt W.L. Wells and 2nd Lt P.S. Williams destroyed a Pfalz D.III which crashed west of Emmerin, and an Albatros D.V which crashed southwest of Lille. Sergeant E.J. Elton and 2nd Lt G.S.L. Hayward in B1162 claimed an Albatros D.V and a Pfalz D.III destroyed south-southwest of Lille, while 2nd Lt G.L. Ormerod and Sgt A. Burton in B1171 sent down another Pfalz D.III out of control nearby. Other squadrons active that day included 20 Sqn, Lt E. Lindup and Cpl F. Archer in B1191 driving down a Pfalz D.III out of control near Houthem, and Lt D. Latimer and 2nd Lt J.J. Scaramanga in

F.2B A3343 went to 48 Sqn but was lost in action during an offensive patrol on 5 April 1917, falling to the guns of Oblt Manfred von Richthofen of Jasta 11, his 36th victory. Lieutenant A.T. Adams and 2 Lt D.J. Stewart were taken prisoner but managed to burn their aircraft first. *(Philip Jarrett)*

This F.2B, 'F' of 22 Sqn (probably B1162), was one of the mounts of NCO pilot Sgt Ernest John Elton, who modified it himself by making an overwing mounting for a forward-firing Lewis gun to augment the observer's guns. The additional weapon could be fixed to fire forwards over the propeller disc or, as seen here, could be manhandled by the pilot to direct fire in the sphere above the upper wing. This photograph was published in the August 1935 issue of Popular Flying magazine, illustrating an article by Elton, who was the RFC's most successful NCO pilot, he and his observers claiming 14 enemy aircraft destroyed and two out of control in 32 days flying Bristol Fighters, ten with the front gun six with the rear. It is stated that this experimental installation 'was not altogether successful so it was subsequently abandoned'. Elton remarks that, after an inconclusive 15-minute combat with a Pfalz in late March 1918: 'I was just about done. A Bristol Fighter is not an easy machine to throw about for fifteen minutes.' A very similar installation, made on the F.2B flown by Capt W.F.J. Harvey of the same unit, is illustrated in the next chapter.

C4615 dealing likewise with an Albatros D.V between Comines and Wervicq. The unit's only casualty was observer 2nd Lt D.E. Stevens, killed in another machine. Crews of 11 Sqn sent three Albatros scouts down out of control, these falling to Lt H.W. Sellars and Lt C.C. Robson in C4673 at Oisy, Capt C.C. Haynes and Lt D.S. Allison in A7281 east of Avoignt, and 2nd Lt J.S. Chick and 2nd Lt P. Douglas in C4847 south of Cambrai. One other casualty that day was observer 2nd Lt E.G. Humphrey of 48 Sqn, who was wounded.

Low clouds, mist and rain prevented flying on the morning of 14 March, but conditions improved in the afternoon, when 19 aircraft of 24, 48 and 84 Sqns mounted an attack on Mont-d'Origny Aerodrome. Sixteen bombs were dropped from between 1,000 and 2,000ft by crews of 48 Sqn, who also fired over 8,600 rounds at troops on the road, billets and lorries. However, C4846 was lost at Estrées when its pilot, 2nd Lt H.H. Hartley, was killed by a bullet in the heart while flying at 100ft, 2nd Lt G. Dixon being injured. One other casualty that day was 62 Sqn observer Sgt J. Lake, who was wounded.

Better weather the next day gave 11 Sqn an opportunity to score a few more successes during the morning in the Rumilly area. Second Lieutenant J.S. Chick and Lt P. Douglas in A7153 sent an Albatros Scout down out of control and another down in flames; 2nd Lt D.W. Beard and Sgt H.W. Scarnell in C4846 destroyed one Albatros D.V and sent two more down out of control at Rumilly, and soon afterwards a Pfalz D.III out of control at Douai; and Lt H.W. Sellars and Lt C.C. Robson in C4673 and Capt L.R. Wren and Lt E.C. Gilroy in

C4845 sent an Albatros scout or two-seater down out of control apiece. That afternoon Lt A.R. James and Lt J.M. Hay in B1267 of 62 Sqn drove an Albatros down out of control five miles southeast of Cambrai.

On 16 March 22 Sqn was busy again. A Pfalz D.III was sent down out of control at Beaumont by 2nd Lt W.F.J. Harvey and Sgt A. Burton in A7161, and they then accounted for another at Oignies. Sergeant E.J. Elton and Lt R. Critchley in B1162 sent down an Albatros D.V in flames and claimed another out of control, whose pilot fell out before it crashed at Carvin. Lieutenant W.L. Wells and 2nd Lt G.S.L. Hayward in C4808 attacked three Pfalz D.IIIs, sending two down out of control at Oignies, whereupon the third immediately turned upside down and fell several thousand feet out of control before crashing near Beaumont. Another was sent down in flames by 2nd Lt H.L. Christie and Sgt S. Belding in C4835, crashing in a wood at Carvin. Three Pfalz D.IIIs were attacked by Lt F.G.C. Weare and 2nd Lt S.J. Hunter in B1152, and one fell completely out of control and crashed southwest of Esquerchin. Two more Pfalz D.IIIs fell out control at Hénin-Liétard to the guns of 2nd Lt G.W. Bulmer and 2nd Lt P.S. Williams in C4810. Also achieving success that day was 48 Sqn, 2nd Lt C.G. Napier and 2nd Lt J.M.J. Moore in B1187 sending an Albatros D.III down early in the day, and Lt P. Burrows and 2nd Lt R.S. Herring, in B1181, then claiming an Albatros D.V and a DFW two-seater, both out of control between Bellicourt and Bellenglise.

Thick cloud set in between the 17th and 20th, limiting reconnaissance flights. Other

activities were possible at times but met with mixed fortunes. On the 17th, Capt W.H. Park and 2nd Lt J.H. Greenwood in B1283 of 11 Sqn engaged the leading aircraft of four Albatros scouts, and it was sent down to crash and burn on the ground at Dury. Lieutenant G.E. Gibbons and 2nd Lt S.A.W. Knights in B1302 of 62 Sqn sent an Albatros scout down out of control northeast of Cambrai, but C4632 of the same squadron had its engine hit by anti-aircraft fire during an offensive patrol, and overturned when it forced-landed in a shell hole. Fortunately its occupants, 2nd Lt S.W. Symons and Sgt W.N. Holmes, escaped injury. Also badly damaged by flak was B1231 of 48 Sqn on an offensive patrol over at St Quentin, neither 2nd Lt N. Roberts nor Cpl T. Ramsden being hurt in the subsequent forced landing. A similar fate befell B1181 of 48 Sqn, which also overturned, in this case while landing on soft ground upon return from an offensive patrol. Again the crew, 2nd Lt A.C.G. Brown and Lt D. Wishart-Orr, were unharmed.

There was a considerable amount of activity by enemy aircraft on 18 March, resulting in intense fighting throughout the day, and the Bristol Fighter squadrons had several successes for only a single loss. Several Albatros D.Vs were engaged by 22 Sqn over Carvin. When Sgt E.J. Elton and Lt R. Critchley in B1162 attacked one its tailplane came off and then its top wing also parted company before it crashed. Another was sent down in flames by 2nd Lt W.F.J. Harvey and 2nd Lt J.L. Morgan in C4808, and both Capt F.G.C. Weare and 2nd Lt G.S.L. Hayward in C4631 and 2nd Lt H.L. Christie and Sgt R. Pritchard sent one down out of control. Lieutenant H.W. Sellars and Lt C.C. Robson in C4673 of 11 Sqn sent an Albatros scout down out of control north of St Quentin, but C4844 of 11 Sqn was shot down between Fresnoy-le-Grand and Bohain. Captain A.P. Maclean was wounded and then taken prisoner, but died soon after capture, while Lt F.H. Cantlon was killed.

After a two-day lull with air activity limited by rain and low cloud, the enemy artillery opened up early on the 21st with a massive and continuous barrage, after which German troops poured 20 miles through the British, French and Portuguese positions, helped by continuing thick fog. Despite being badly hampered by the weather the RFC did everything it could, no Bristol Fighters being lost that first day. Also on that day, 22 Sqn moved with the 10th Wing, 1st Brigade, to Serny, but it was briefly detached two days later to the 13th Wing, 1st Brigade, at Vert Galand, returning to Serny on 10 April.

On the first day of the enemy advance, the 21st, Lt H.W. Sellars and Lt C.C. Robson in C4673 of 11 Sqn attacked an enemy aircraft undertaking artillery observation, and three bursts were sufficient to send it spinning down out of control with its engine smoking, to crash on the British side of the lines north of the Bapaume-Cambrai road. Shortly afterwards they were attacked by three Albatros, and two bursts of fire into the nearest one caused it to burst into flames and crash north of Morchie. During an offensive patrol 2nd Lt A.D. Shannon and Sgt B.J. Maisey in B1256 of 11 Sqn sent an Albatros two-seater down out of control southeast of Cambrai, then had to force-land due to mist.

On that same day 62 Sqn had further successes. In an engagement near Cambrai between a patrol of Bristol Fighters and a formation of triplanes and scouts, Lt W.E. Staton and Lt J.R. Gordon in C4619 engaged a Fokker Dr.I at very close range and their tracers were seen to hit the pilot before it went down in a vertical dive and burst into flames. Captain T.L. Purdom and 2nd Lt P.V.G. Chambers in B1216 attacked an Albatros D.V whose top wing broke off, and sent another down out of control. Second Lieutenant H.N. Arthur and 2nd Lt J. Bruce Norton in B1281 sent an Albatros down out of control northwest of Cambrai. Also that day, 2nd Lt E.R. Stock and observer Cpl J.H. Bowler B1269 sent an LVG two-seater down out of control east of Epehy, but force-landed after being hit by return fire. Stock was unhurt but Bowler was wounded. Capt T.L. Purdom and 2nd Lt P.V.G. Chambers, now in C4629, attacked an Albatros D.V which broke up north of Cambrai. Also involved in combats was 48 Sqn. Second Lieutenant L.A. Payne and Lt G.H.H. Scutt drove down an LVG two-seater out of control, while Capt W.L. Wells and Cpl W. Beales in C4707 destroyed a Pfalz D.III, which crashed at the crossroads just beside a brickfield southwest of Honnecourt. During an offensive patrol in B1187 of 48 Sqn, 2nd Lt C.G. Napier and 2nd Lt J.M.J. Moore had their petrol tank shot through by machine-gun fire near St Quentin, the aircraft being wrecked in the ensuing forced landing without injury to the occupants.

Thick mist again prevented flying for most of the morning on the 22nd, after which there was considerable aerial activity. Captain T.P. Colvill-Jones and 2nd Lt J.A. Galbraith in C4964 of 48 Sqn shot down an Albatros scout which crashed in a field about a mile southeast of Monchy Legache. Second Lieutenant A.C.G. Brown was wounded when 2nd Lt G.C. Bartlett in C4606 of 48 Sqn attacked one of five enemy aircraft circling another Bristol Fighter, then dived on the nearest one, firing short bursts. These caused its pilot to put its nose down, only to fly into the ground, and another was sent down out of control two miles southeast of Flez. Two 48 Sqn aircraft were lost that day. During an offensive patrol B1301 was shot down, crashing on the British side of the lines southeast of Flez; 2nd Lt A.C. Hore and Lt S.R. Parker were both wounded, and their aircraft could not be

salved. During another offensive patrol B1255 was badly shot up near St Quentin, 2nd Lt N.H. Muirden and 2nd Lt E.S. Herring returning safely. As the aerodrome was about to be evacuated, the aircraft was set alight before the unit departed for its new base to prevent its capture during the impending retreat. Elsewhere, 11 Sqn shot down three Albatros scouts in an engagement near Quéant, these falling to 2nd Lt D.W. Beard and 2nd Lt H.M. Stewart in C4846 (a D.V), 2nd Lt J.P. Seabrook and Lt A. Reeve in B1194 (a D.V), and Capt H.R. Child and Lt J.P.Y. Dickey in B1307.

On 23 March 22 Sqn was briefly detached to the 13th Wing, 1st Brigade, at Vert Galand. This was to be another hectic day for the hard-pressed RFC squadrons. Two aircraft of 22 Sqn on an offensive patrol failed to return in the morning, Capt P. Thompson being killed and Lt D.W. Kent-Jones being taken prisoner in B1171, which was last seen near Cambrai. Second Lieutenant H.L. Christie and 2nd Lt N.T. Berrington in C4827 were more fortunate when their engine was damaged in combat and they forced-landed in a shelled area at Ham, escaping unscathed although their aircraft was destroyed. Later that morning 2nd Lt G.W. Bulmer and 2nd Lt P.S. Williams in A7251 of 22 Sqn shot down an Albatros D.V which crashed at Bussy, while Capt D.M. McGoun and 2nd Lt F.N. Harrison sent another down out of control and smoking at Auchy-en-Artois, and 2nd Lt W.P. Beaver and 2nd Lt H.E. Easton in B1114 of 20 Sqn attacked one of six Albatros Scouts which crashed in a fight from Menin to south of Ronzcq. Captain R.K. Kirkman and Capt J.H. Hedley in B1156 of 20 Sqn drove down an Albatros scout out of control east of Wervicq and another east of Menin. Captain W.L. Wells and Cpl W. Beales in C4707 of 48 Sqn destroyed an LVG two-seater in a fight from northwest of Ham to north of Dury, and in the afternoon repeated this with another east of Matigny, as well as a Pfalz D.III. In

mid-afternoon Capt T.L. Purdom and 2nd Lt P.V.G. Chambers in B1305 of 62 Sqn sent an Albatros scout down out of control south of Havrincourt Wood.

Another move was that of 62 Sqn to Remaisnil on the 24th. On that day 35 Sqn lost the two Bristol Fighters which had recently been attached for corps work, its main equipment being Armstrong Whitworth F.K.8s. The squadron was in the process of moving from Chipilly to Poulainville, but on take-off A7221 taxied into a shell-hole, fortunately without injury to either Capt G. McPherson or Lt C. Kniverton, but the aircraft had to be burnt to prevent it falling into enemy hands. Then, on arrival at the new aerodrome, B1134 ran into a ridge on landing and overturned, and had to be burned; 2nd Lt A.S. Hanna and 2nd Lt R.A. Burnard were unhurt. A week later C4849 and B1347 arrived as replacements. Another F.K.8 unit with two Bristol Fighters attached for similar purposes was 10 Sqn at Droglandt, which lost one that day when Lt R.O. Williams and Lt S.S. Birbeck in A7214 overran the aerodrome on landing and hit a road, wrecking the undercarriage. They were unhurt, but the aircraft was later declared a write-off by the Depot.

Low ground-attack work was a major preoccupation at this time, with RFC aircraft heavily involved in strafing the advancing enemy infantry, guns blazing and blasting enemy batteries with 20lb Cooper and 112lb Hales bombs as they flew almost at ground level in support of the hard-pressed Third and Fifth Armies. Ground targets were available in abundance, and in the Bristol Fighter squadrons 48 Sqn was in the thick of the ground-attack work, with 11, 22 and 62 Sqns operating at any altitude where there was fighting to be done. Bristol Fighter losses were small during this phase.

On 24 March Capt F.G.C. Weare and 2nd Lt G.S.L. Hayward in C4828 of 22 Sqn shot down an Albatros D.V which crashed near Cherisy, and then fired a short burst at another which crashed at Vis-en-Artois.

After being allotted to 22 Sqn in November 1917, B1153 was lost while on an offensive patrol on 3 December, last seen going down over Poperinghe, apparently with engine trouble; 2nd Lt A.F. Goodchap and 2nd Lt A.H. Middleton were taken prisoner. *(IWM MH3313 via Philip Jarrett)*

After armament trials at Orfordness in late 1917, C4808, powered by a Falcon II, went to 22 Sqn in France, where it was used by several crews to down a number of enemy aircraft. On 18 February 1918 2nd Lt Wallage and Sgt J.H. Jones claimed a two-seater out of control; on 16 March a Pfalz D.III out of control and an Albatros D.V destroyed were claimed by Lts W.L. Wells and G.S.L. Hayward; two days later another Albatros D.V was claimed destroyed by 2nd Lts W.F.J Harvey and J.L. Morgan; and on 2 April a Fokker Dr.1 was destroyed by 2nd Lt G.H. Traunweiser and Sgt S. Belding. However, on 15 April Traunweiser and Belding were killed when C4808 was brought down by British infantry fire. *(Philip Jarrett)*

Flying A7286 of 22 Sqn, 2nd Lt W.F.J. Harvey and 2nd Lt H.F. Moore shot down another Albatros D.V, which was seen to crash, and a second was sent down out of control southeast of Arras. Captain T. Colvill-Jones and Lt D. Wishart-Orr in C4864 of 48 Sqn shot down an LVG two-seater which crashed east of Ham. While engaged on a low offensive patrol, C4710 of the same squadron was shot down by ground fire west of Foucaucourt and had to be destroyed, as it was impossible to salve owing to heavy traffic and the proximity of the enemy; Capt C.R. Steele and 2nd Lt E.H. Stanes were both unharmed.

Still on 24 March, 62 Sqn was also very busy. Second Lieutenant M.H. Cleary and 2nd Lt V.G. Stanton in C4709 sent down an Albatros D.V out of control and smoking east of Péronne, and later 2nd Lt S.W. Symons and Sgt W.N. Holmes destroyed another ten miles northeast of Péronne. Observer 2nd Lt F. Keith in another F.2B was wounded, while Lt A.R. James and Lt J.M. Hay were both killed when B1267 failed to return from trench strafing between Péronne and Ham. Capt T.L. Purdom and 2nd Lt P.V.G. Chambers in B1305 were attacking ground troops when their petrol tank was hit, and the engine stopped. They were then attacked by six aircraft, so dived towards the west, the observer getting a good burst at an Albatros scout a hundred feet above them. It burst into flames near Péronne. They evidently landed safely, as did B1122 of 20 Sqn, which was damaged by enemy fire but successfully forced-landed, 2nd Lt L. Campbell and Lt A. Mills being unhurt.

By the morning of the 25th the ground situation was very grave, the enemy having reached the River Ancre on the Third Army Front and preparing to take Albert. Aircraft of the 1st, 3rd and 5th Brigades flew numerous low-level sorties, attacking troop concentrations, convoys and other targets. During a low-flying patrol in Bristol Fighter A7248 of 62 Sqn, 2nd Lt V.K. Hilton and Cpl J. Borwein had the engine cut out over Albert and had to burn and abandon the aircraft after their forced landing. Observer Lt D. Wishart-Orr was wounded in a 48 Sqn aircraft. However, 22 Sqn had several successes early that day against Albatros D.Vs. Two were sent down out of control by 2nd Lt H.F. Davison and 2nd Lt J.L. Morgan in A7243, one north of Havrincourt Wood and the other northeast of Bapaume. Flying A7286, 2nd Lt W.F.J. Harvey and 2nd Lt H.F. Moore shot one down with a long burst when its left wing folded back above St Ledger, while Capt D.M. McGoun and 2nd Lt F.N. Harrison in C4828 destroyed one nearby and sent another down out of control and smoking east of St Ledger.

The 26th was a crucial day for air operations, with a wholesale redeployment on to ground-attack work. The River Somme had become the front between the opposing sides, with the heaviest fighting right up to Albert, which fell that day in which 62 Sqn was heavily involved with mixed fortunes. Early in the day 2nd Lt J.M. Goller and 2nd Lt E.C.W. Deacon in A7298 were trench strafing when they had to forced-land owing to engine trouble, their aircraft being abandoned under shellfire. Around noon 2nd Lt H.N. Arthur and 2nd Lt J. Bruce-Norton left on a low-flying patrol in B1305, but the engine was damaged by ground fire and they too had to forced-land, abandoning their aircraft near Mailly-Maillet owing to the proximity of the enemy. On the credit side, two crews, 2nd Lt D.A. Savage and 2nd Lt L.M. Thompson, and Lt W.E. Staton and Lt J.R. Gordon, each sent an aircraft down out of control, while Capt T.L. Purdom and 2nd Lt P.V.G. Chambers in B1216 of 62 Sqn attacked an enemy aircraft which then crashed, before sending another falling out of control. During a mid-afternoon offensive patrol B1196 of 20 Sqn crashed near Albert and had to be abandoned owing to the advancing enemy. Its pilot, Lt D. Leigh-Pemberton, was wounded, but his observer, Capt N.W. Taylor, was unhurt. Early in the afternoon three 22 Sqn crews dived on a formation of five Pfalz D.IIIs east of Albert. Sergeant E.J. Elton and Lt R. Critchley in B1162 sent one down to crash, while 2nd Lt H.F. Davison and 2nd Lt J.L. Morgan in A7243 shot another down from 4,000ft, following it down to see it burst into flames when hit the ground. Captain F.G.C. Weare and 2nd Lt G.S.L. Hayward in B1217 destroyed a third and sent another down out of control. Another casualty that day was observer 2nd Lt R.S. Herring of 48 Sqn, who was wounded.

The situation on the ground had stabilised somewhat on the 27th, though Proyart fell that day. After a lengthy spell at La Bellevue, 11 Sqn withdrew to Fienvillers, and on this same day they lost B1332, which failed to return from a reconnaissance sortie between Albert and the Somme, Capt H.R. Child and Lt A. Reeve being killed. Aircraft C4843 of the same squadron was damaged by gunfire, without injury to 2nd Lt R. Fitton and 2nd Lt R.A. West. When 2nd Lt A.R. Knowles and Lt A.E. Matthews in C4862 of 11 Sqn were attacked by six enemy aircraft, they engaged the leader, an Albatros two-seater, and sent it down out of control to crash on the outskirts of Meaulte, southwest of Albert. Soon afterwards they encountered two others and sent one down in flames, seeing it burning on the ground near Morlancourt. Also engaged in low bombing was 20 Sqn, and Capt R.K. Kirkman and Capt J.H. Hedley were taken prisoner when B1156 failed to return from an attack in the Albert area. However, Lt R.G. Bennett and Lt T.C. Noel in C4641 of 20 Sqn shot down an Albatros scout which crashed in the River Somme, west of Cappy. 2nd Lt H.F. Davison and 2nd Lt J.L. Morgan in B1164 of 22 Sqn sent one of four Fokker Dr.Is down to crash into railway sidings southeast of Albert and sent another down out of control southeast of the town. Elsewhere, 2nd Lt F.C. Ransley and 2nd Lt J.M.J. Moore in C4628 of 48 Sqn shot down an LVG two-seater which crashed between Morlancourt and Bois de Tailles. Second Lieutenant C.D.G. Napier and 2nd Lt J.M.J. Moore in C4886 of 48 Sqn destroyed a two-seater and drove down a Pfalz D.III out of control southwest of Roye, by the River Avre. Observer 2nd Lt H.J. Finnemore of the same squadron died of wounds in another aircraft. Two aircraft of 62 Sqn scored successes, Sgt F. Johnson and Sgt C.C. Brammer sending an enemy aircraft down out of control and Lt H.M.C. Nangle and 2nd Lt S. Parry meting out the same fate to two more as well as attacking a third, but observer 2nd Lt V.K. Hilton was wounded in another aircraft.

On the 28th the Germans launched fresh attacks at Arras, roughly on the boundary between the British First and Third Armies, but an elastic defence held firm, though more was likely to come. Albatros D.V squadrons were heavily involved, and 62 Sqn suffered several losses while performing the dangerous task of low-level strafing. Early in the day B1281's port aileron and controls were shot away during a low-flying patrol, causing it to crash on landing. Both 2nd Lt H.N. Arthur and Cpl J. Borwein were wounded. Two others which left at noon to undertake strafing were also lost; B1211 was shot down east of Villers-Bretonneux, 2nd Lt M.H. Cleary being killed and 2nd Lt V.G. Stanton dying next day of his wounds. Second Lieutenant E.T. Morrow and Lt H.E. Merritt in C4613 were unharmed when their aircraft was badly hit by ground machine-gun fire, also east of Villers-Bretonneux, forcing them to land close to the lines under shellfire. Captain T.L. Purdom and 2nd Lt P.V.G. Chambers in C4629 of 62 Sqn sent an aircraft down out of control at Sailly, but two observers, 2nd Lt S.W. Symons and AM1 A. Boxall, were wounded in other squadron aircraft.

There were also casualties in 48 Sqn that day. Early in the day Capt T. Colvill-Jones and 2nd Lt W. Hart were unhurt when A7277 was badly damaged by ground fire during an offensive patrol, as were Lt J.E. Drummond and 2nd Lt J.J. Mackenzie in B1265. Later that morning B1273 had its radiator and fuel tank shot through and 2nd Lt E.R. Stock and 2nd Lt W.D. Davidson were forced to land at Allonville but escaped unhurt. Also 2nd Lt E.G. Humphrey was wounded in action, dying next day of his wounds. An enemy scout was sent down out of control by Capt W.L. Wells and Cpl W. Beales in C4701, but both were wounded, Beales dying next day. Two aircraft of 20 Sqn had successes in the morning. Lieutenant E. Lindup and 2nd Lt H.G. Crowe in B1191 sent a Fokker Dr.I down out of control at Albert, and Lt R.G.

Bennett and Lt J.D. Boyd in C4641 dealt similarly with another scout, possibly a Pfalz D.III, near La Boiselle.

On the 29th the Allies withdrew to a new front designated the 'Amiens Defence Lines', producing a measure of stability from Mezières to Ignaugourt and Hamel. Bad weather helped to make it the lightest day for air casualties since the German offensive began, and no further Bristol Fighters were lost by the RFC in France. On that day 62 Sqn moved to Planques, and three crews of 22 Sqn had successes during a general engagement in the afternoon. Second Lieutenant H.F. Davison and 2nd Lt J.L. Morgan in A7243 sent down an LVG two-seater which crashed in a wood southeast of Hangard, near Rosières, and a little while later a Rumpler C went down out of control east of Bervillers. Sergeant E.J. Elton and Lt R. Critchley in B1162 destroyed three Rumpler or Albatros two-seaters southeast of Hangard and at Lihons and forced another to land and then turn on its nose when its pilot attempted to take off again. Flying at 900ft in B1126 (possibly an error for B1128), 2nd Lt E.J. Smethan-Jones and 2nd Lt J.C. Fitton destroyed an Albatros D.III or D.V east of Villers-Bretonneux to just east of Bayonvillers. One success was enjoyed by 22 Sqn that day, Capt F.G.C. Weare and 2nd Lt G.S.L. Hayward in B1164 driving an Albatros D.V down out of control at Guillancourt. The same squadron had another victory next day, when Lt W.F.J. Harvey and 2nd Lt H.F. Moore in C4894 fired 150 rounds into a kite balloon which went down in flames northeast of Albert. The claimants' view was obscured by an immediate cloud of smoke, but there was no sign of the balloon by the time it cleared. By then the worst of the crisis seemed to be over for the Allies, at least for the time being.

Probably photographed in transit at Hounslow, C4827, seen here in pristine condition, went to 22 Sqn on 5 December 1917, but was lost in action during an offensive patrol on 23 March 1918 after its Falcon II engine was damaged in combat with an enemy aircraft and it was forced-landed and abandoned in a shelled area near Ham. Its crew, 2nd Lt H.L. Christie and 2nd Lt N.T. Berrington, both escaped 'OK'. *(Stuart Tucker)*

Previously a 48 Sqn machine, F.2B B1134 '19' is seen soon after it was taken over by 35 Sqn on 4 February 1918. It carries that unit's identification marking, a horizontal white line along its fuselage flanks. *(C&C)*

Chapter 5

THE TIDE BEGINS TO TURN

April 1918

On 1 April the Royal Air Force came into existence, combining both the RFC and the RNAS, the number 200 being added to the unit numbers of the RNAS squadrons to avoid confusion with their former RFC counterparts. In France, the first month of the RAF's existence proved to be somewhat less busy than had been the last month of its predecessors, partly due to weather restrictions, though the first two days were fine, with good visibility.

Although 59 Sqn's main equipment was the R.E.8, it had several F.2Bs on strength from around April 1918 at Vert Galand, where it formed part of the 12th Wing, 3rd Brigade.

The first Bristol Fighter loss for the new Service came in the morning of 1 April, when C4615 of 20 Sqn caught fire after being hit by flak and came down near Pypegaale, Lt R.B.T. Hedges and Lt A.C. Horlock both being injured. In the late afternoon two aircraft of 62 Sqn each sent an Albatros D.V down out of control at Bouchoir, one by 2nd Lt H.C.M. Nangle and 2nd Lt T.C. Cooper in C791 and the other sent down smoking by Lt W.E. Staton and Lt J.R. Gordon in C4619. Another Albatros Scout was similarly dealt with at Quesnil by 2nd Lt C.E. Glover and Cpl W. Beales in C4701. However, A7240 of 20 Sqn crashed at Wulverghem after being hit by anti-aircraft fire, but without harm to Maj J.A. Dennistoun and 2nd Lt H.G. Crowe.

The most fruitful Bristol Fighter activity on 2 April appears to have been in the early evening, 22 Sqn having several successes. The first was that of 2nd Lt G.N. Traunweiser and Sgt S. Belding in C4808, in which the observer fired a drum into a Fokker Dr.I which crashed west of Vauvillers. In the same area 2nd Lt J.E. Gurdon and 2nd Lt A.J.H. Thornton in B1162 sent two Dr.Is down out of control, while Capt F.G.C. Weare and 2nd Lt G.S.L. Hayward in B1164 destroyed an Albatros D.V and sent another down in flames. One loss, however, was that of A7286, which was shot down in flames south of Albert, 2nd Lt F. Williams and 2nd Lt R. Critchley being killed. Three aircraft were lost by 48 Sqn that day, all on an evening offensive patrol to Villers-Bretonneux. Both 2nd Lt K.W. Pope and 2nd Lt W.J. Battle were wounded when B1269 was damaged in combat, but 2nd Lt C.E. Glover and Cpl W. Beales in C4701 were unhurt. However, C4707 was shot down in combat close to the front-line trenches and was unrecoverable, pilot 2nd Lt C.D.B. Stiles being wounded and 2nd Lt F.F. Walker dying of wounds some days later. Both 2nd Lt A.R. Knowles and Lt A.E. Matthews of 11 Sqn were killed when C4862 failed to return from an offensive patrol; but Lt H.W. Sellars and Lt C.C. Robson in C4673 sent a Fokker Dr.I down out of control southeast of Albert.

The Germans continued their pressure, but poor weather prevented much aviation

activity. Despite the continuing low cloud and rain, some offensive patrols were carried out on the 4th. Captain T. Colvill-Jones and 2nd Lt W. Hart in C4831 of 48 Sqn sent two long bursts into an Albatros scout which went down steeply, emitting smoke, and crashed southeast of Villers-Bretonneux. Earlier, 2nd Lt G.D. Jooste and Lt S.H.P. Masding in A7294 of 20 Sqn had sent another Albatros Scout down out of control.

Some flying became possible on the 6th, and 2nd Lt C.D.G. Napier and 2nd Lt J.M.J. Moore in C4753 of 48 Sqn were both unhurt when their aircraft was badly shot up in combat during a low reconnaissance. In the afternoon, C4864 of 48 Sqn failed to return from an offensive patrol, 2nd Lt B.G.A. Bell and 2nd Lt C.G. Bartlett being killed in a combat with three Fokker Dr.Is over Lamotte. However, Lt J.E. Drummond and 2nd Lt H.F. Lumb in B1299 of 48 Sqn sent down a Dr.I which crashed in flames in the same area, Drummond being wounded when his aircraft was shot up. Later, Lt V. Voss and Lt C.J.R. Gibson in B1271 of 48 Sqn drove a Fokker Dr.I down out of control south of Christ. Also in action that day was 22 Sqn, 2nd Lt B.C. Budd and 2nd Lt H.J. Weaver in C4810 sending an enemy aircraft down out of control at Cambrai, though C4631 was damaged in action, Capt H.F. Davison being unhurt but observer 2nd Lt B.C.M. Ward wounded.

On 7 April Lt H.A. Hay and Sgt P.A. Sherlock in C4861 of 11 Sqn sent an

Albatros two-seater down out of control at Grévillers. The poor weather continued, but on the 9th B1221 of 20 Sqn was shot up in combat before becoming lost in thick fog and crashing into sandhills near Wimereux; Lt R.H. Harmer was injured and observer Lt N. Peters badly shaken.

On 10 April 22 Sqn, which had been briefly detached to the 13th Wing, 1st Brigade, at Vert Galand, returned to Serny. Weather conditions improved during the afternoon of the 11th, and 20 Sqn took advantage of this, with mixed fortunes. Lieutenant L.H.T. Capel and Cpl E.A. Deighton in C4616 sent down a two-seater which crashed south of Armentières, but B1275 was shot up by ground fire near Neuve Eglise and was forced-landed within range of enemy shellfire, where it was unsalvable, Maj J.A. Dennistoun was wounded and Lt J.J. Scaramanga badly shaken. When B1257 failed to return from a low patrol to Neuf Berquin, Lt A.L. Pemberton and Cpl F. Archer were taken prisoner but were later interned in Switzerland for repatriation.

The German effort on the ground slackened on 12 April, but the weather improved considerably that day, a record number of flying hours being logged by the RAF squadrons. In the morning Capt D.M. McGoun and 2nd Lt F.N. Harrison in B1253 of 22 Sqn dived on a two-seater and sent it down with a 100-round burst, watching it side-slipping and smoking before crashing among buildings in a small village near Laventie. Later, Capt F.G.C. Weare and 2nd Lt G.S. Hayward in B1253 of 22 Sqn met a formation of five Pfalz D.IIIs, Weare sending down two, which crashed in a green field just southwest of Sailly-sur-la-Lys, and the observer another, which crashed in a field just north of this. During the afternoon 62 Sqn had a string of victories. Capt G.F. Hughes and Capt H. Claye in C4630 sent an Albatros D.V down out of control over Bois du Biez, then an hour later they dived on an LVG two-seater near Seclin, but the pilot misjudged the dive so the observer fired a double drum over the top plane, followed by 50 rounds from the pilot at close range, the LVG then going down to crash in flames. Sergeant F. Johnson and Sgt W.N. Holmes in B1336 sent down two Albatros D.Vs, one crashing near Allènes and the other a mile north of Chémy. Lieutenant D.A. Savage and 2nd Lt L.M. Thompson in B1234 sent a Pfalz D.III down out of control east of Estaires, and an hour later an Albatros D.V down out of control near Aubers. Two Albatros scouts were sent down out of control by 2nd Lt L. Campbell and 2nd Lt W. Hodgkinson in B1339 of 62

Sqn, a D.V east of Estaires and the other half-an-hour later near Lille. Elsewhere, 2nd Lt C.H. Arnison and Lt S. Parry in C4859 sent an Albatros Scout down out of control near La Bassée, and 2nd Lt G.M. Hemsworth and 2nd Lt A.J. Todd in B1343 dealt similarly with another over Bois du Biez. One other success that day was by 2nd Lt F.C. Ransley and 2nd Lt C.W. Davies in C4886 of 48 Sqn, who destroyed a Pfalz D.III which crashed on the southwest edge of Moreuil Woods. There were no Bristol Fighter losses that day, but C4605 of 20 Sqn left on an offensive patrol and was badly shot up, fortunately without harm to either Lt D.G. Cooke or Lt H.G. Crowe.

On 13 April 20 Sqn moved from Ste Marie Cappel back to Boisdinghem, still in the 11th Wing. Poor weather was again restricting flying, but on the 13th C776 of 22 Sqn was hit by machine-gun fire, Capt H.F. Davison being wounded but observer Lt G. Thomson unhurt. On the 15th C4606 of 48 Sqn was shot up near Chaulnes by machine-gun fire on low reconnaissance, 2nd Lt A.C.G. Brown and 2nd Lt W. Hart being unhurt, but C4808 of 22 Sqn, on a similar task was, was fired on and brought down by British infantry and completely wrecked in a shelled area, 2nd Lt G.N. Traunweiser and Sgt S. Belding both being killed. Second Lieutenant W.S. Hill-Tout and 2nd Lt P.S. Williams of 22 Sqn, on an offensive patrol, were also shot up but escaped injury.

On the 16th 11 Sqn moved from Fienvillers back to Remaisnil, where it was to remain for the next three months. Next day, Capt T.P. Middleton and Capt F. Godfrey in C4699 of 20 Sqn destroyed an Albatros D.V and drove another down out of control southeast of Hazebrouck. Further ground battles took place later in the month, when flying conditions eased, the 21st being a particularly fine day with 62 Sqn notching up several more victories during the morning. Captain T.L. Purdom and 2nd Lt P.G. Chambers in B1216 fired 100 rounds into an Albatros D.V which turned over and spiralled down to crash southeast of Estaires. Two Pfalz D.IIIs were sent down out of control by 2nd Lt G.M. Yuille and Lt E.W. Collis in C4633, one between Estaires and

Lille at 10:00, then another later by the observer over Bois de Ploegsteert. Second Lieutenant C.H. Arnison and Lt S. Parry in C4859 also sent two Pfalz D.IIIs down out of control, one by the pilot, the other by the observer, again between Estaires and Lille. Then Lt D.A. Savage and 2nd Lt L.M. Thompson in B1234 destroyed an Albatros D.V and a Pfalz D.III west of Lille, but then were themselves hit by anti-aircraft fire, both being injured when they had to force-land and their machine was wrecked. Two Albatros scouts were sent down out of control north of Wervicq by 20 Sqn, one by Capt D.G. Cooke and Lt H.G. Crowe in C4749 and the other, a D.V, by Lt D. Latimer and Lt T.C. Noel in B1232.

On the 22nd 22 Sqn sent three Albatros D.Vs down out of control east of Merville, two falling to Capt F.G.C. Weare and 2nd Lt G.S.L. Hayward in B1253, and the third to Lt S.F.H. Thompson and 2nd Lt C.G. Gass in B1136. Captain G.F. Hughes and Capt H. Claye in C4630 of 62 Sqn were credited with sending down two 'Fokker D.VIs' out of control over Nieppe Forest. (This type, similar to a D.VII but with a rotary engine, had started to arrive in April 1918, but D.VI may be a typing error for D.VII.) Next day, Capt T. Colvill-Jones and 2nd Lt J.M.J. Moore in B1126 of 20 Sqn drove down a Pfalz D.III out of control west of Bray. On the 24th, 2nd Lt T.G. Jackson and Lt A.E. Ansell were both unhurt when A7114 of 62 Sqn was shot up at Villers-Bretonneux by enemy machine-gun fire while returning from a patrol, as were 2nd Lt F.C. Ransley and 2nd Lt C.W. Davies in C4886 of 48 Sqn while returning from an offensive patrol. None of these four was injured, unlike 2nd Lt W.L. Thomas, who was wounded by rifle fire in another 48 Sqn aircraft.

A further operational Bristol Fighter squadron arrived on 25 April, when 88 Sqn joined the 65th Wing, 7th Brigade, at Bergues-Capelle, moving to Petite Synthe on the 27th. It had equipped with F.2Bs in July 1917 at Gosport, moving to Harling Road on 2 August and then, on 2 April 1918, to Kenley. From there it had left for France on 14 April and was established at St Omer two days later.

Right: **Bristol F.2B C917 first served with 35 Sqn and then with 9 Sqn, being safely force-landed on 7 September 1918. It then went to 'O' Flight, where an accident on 7 January 1919 rendered it unfit for further service.** *(C&C)*

The 25th was a reasonably good flying day, and in the evening 2nd Lt W. Beaver and Cpl M. Mather in C817 of 20 Sqn were on a long-range reconnaissance when they attacked five scouts which promptly turned and flew east. Approaching to within 300 yards of an Albatros D.V, they fired a 100-round burst and saw it go down out of control, hit the ground and burst into flames just north of Ploegsteert Wood. Elsewhere, Lt R.H. Little and Cpl W. Beales in C814 of 48 Sqn destroyed a Rumpler two-seater one mile east of Harbonnières. That was the last Bristol Fighter success of the month, but there was another loss that day; B1126 of 20 Sqn was last seen diving on enemy aircraft at 8,000ft over Wiencourt, and it was later reported that both Capt Colvill-Jones and AM1 F. Finney had become prisoners of war. Colvill-Jones died in captivity a month later.

May 1918
In May the excellent Fokker D.VII biplane entered service in numbers, it becoming an even better machine during the summer when its engine was upgraded from the 160hp Mercedes to the 185hp BMW. Used in great numbers, by September 1918 800 were serving with 48 *Jagdstaffeln*. Bristol Fighter losses remained comparatively low as the fighting continued.

The weather this month was generally considerably improved, and combined with the lighter evenings led to an increasing amount of aerial activity. By the 3rd the weather had improved, and enemy aircraft activity was apparent, with large formations in the evenings especially. That morning, Capt T.P. Middleton and Capt F. Godfrey in C4699 were leading 11 Bristol Fighters on an offensive patrol when they encountered 12 enemy scouts and promptly dived on them. Following an Albatros D.V down to 2,000ft, they fired 100 rounds and saw it turn on its back and crash southeast of Ploegsteert Wood. Later, 2nd Lt W. Beaver and Capt N.W. Taylor in C817 sent another one down to crash near Gheluvelt. Then 62 Sqn became involved in a general engagement, Lt H.C.M. Nangle and 2nd Lt T.C. Cooper in B1245 sending a Fokker Dr.I down out of control at Armentières. Captain T.L. Purdom and 2nd Lt P.G. Chambers in B1216 drove an Albatros D.V down out of control south of Armentières, and an Albatros two-seater crashed north of Merville. Lieutenant E.T. Morrow and Lt H.E. Merritt in C796 sent down an Albatros D.V which crashed, and another broke up south of Armentières. A Pfalz D.III was sent down by Lt W.E. Staton and Lt J.R. Gordon in C4619, and crashed and burst into flames east of Armentières, and they then claimed a two-seater which crashed a mile southeast of Ploegsteert Wood. Captain G.E. Gibbons and Lt S.A.W. Knights in C779 dived on three scouts, climbed to rejoin their

formation, then dived again, only to find there were 24 scouts coming up from below. Firing 100 rounds into an Albatros D.V which went down in flames, Gibbons dived and fired 70 rounds into another before flying over it to avoid a collision. His observer then followed up with two drums from the twin rear guns, and after a slow roll the Albatros crashed on the Lille-Carvin road. Soon afterwards they sent a Fokker Dr.I down out of control north of Armentières. Second Lieutenant C.H. Arnison and Lt S. Parry in C4859 sent two Albatros D.Vs down out of control and another in flames east of Armentières, but their own aircraft had been shot up, Parry being killed. In C4709 Capt H. Rees-Jones and 2nd Lt J. Bruce-Norton shot down an Albatros scout, which burst into flames south of Armentières, then sent another down out of control, but their own controls were damaged in combat and they crashed in a forced landing, both escaping injury. One loss that day was C4744 of 62 Sqn, which failed to return from an offensive patrol, Lt P.R. Hampton and Lt L.C. Lane being wounded and taken prisoner. During the evening Capt D.G. Cooke and Lt H.G. Crowe in C4749 of 20 Sqn sent a Fokker Dr.I down in flames southeast of Hollebeke, and an Albatros D.V out of control southeast of Ypres. Bristol Fighter C4818 of 22 Sqn had its petrol tank shot through in combat and crash-landed at Wormhoudt without harm to Lt F.E. Boulton and AM W.H. Foster. Both 2nd Lt A.C.G. Brown and Cpl A.W. Sainsbury in C814 of 48 Sqn failed to return from reconnaissance, being wounded and taken prisoner; Brown died three days later.

On the 4th, Lt H.A. Hay and Sgt P.A. Sherlock in C4861 of 11 Sqn were attacked by six scouts while on reconnaissance and sent the leading Pfalz D.III down in flames near Marquion. Lieutenant L.R. Fitton in C4839 of 11 Sqn was wounded in another aircraft. In the morning of the 6th 2nd Lt G.W. Bulmer and 2nd Lt H.E. Elsworth in C4888 of 22 Sqn drove down a Pfalz D.III out of control near Fresnoy. In the evening 2nd Lt W.S. Hill-Tout and 2nd Lt A.G.H. Williamson in C4706 of 22 Sqn destroyed an Albatros D.V near Fresnoy, while 2nd Lt E.C. Bromley and 2nd Lt J.H. Umney in C4747 sent an Albatros scout down out of control, believed to have crashed at Roeux, east of Arras.

On 7 May two crews of 22 Sqn, 2nd Lt A.C. Atkey and 2nd Lt C.G. Gass in B1164, and 2nd Lt J.E. Gurdon and Lt A.J.H. Thornton in B1253, provided eloquent testimony and remarkable justification for the confidence F.2B crews had in their mounts when, in a thirty-minute fight which was to go down in the annals of First World War aviation legends, they set upon seven Fokker D.VIIs at 15,000ft near Hénin-Liétard. Each pilot shot down a

D.VII in flames, and as they pulled out of the dive their observers each accounted for two more. At that point, another formation of enemy fighters appeared, increasing the opposition to about 20 machines. Exhaustion of their observers' ammunition eventually obliged the two pilots to break off the engagement, but by that time they had shot down four more D.VIIs, and only seven then remained on the scene. No damage had been incurred to the British aircraft, nor injury to any of their occupants.

The weather was now set fine, and 22 Sqn had further successes next day. In the morning 2nd Lt E.C. Bromley and 2nd Lt J.H. Umney in C4747 sent down two two-seaters which crashed southeast of Arras. Then 2nd Lt G.W. Bulmer and 2nd Lt P.S. Williams in C4888 dived on a Pfalz D.III which broke up and crashed near Brebières, while Lt S.F.H. Thompson and Sgt L. Kendrick in B1162 attacked a two-seater on artillery observation, seeing the observer collapse into the cockpit before a burst from Kendrick sent it down in flames to crash southeast of Arras. In the evening 2nd Lt S.H. Wallage and Lt G. Thomson in C795 engaged a formation of scouts, sending a Pfalz D.III to crash north of La Bassée and driving another down southeast of La Bassée. At about the same time 2nd Lt J.E. Gurdon and 2nd Lt C.G. Gass in B1253 fired 100 rounds into a DFW two-seater which went down steeply and crashed in a field south of the road at Cuincy, northwest of Douai.

Also busy that day was 20 Sqn. In the morning Capt T.P. Middleton and Capt F. Godfrey in C4699 dived on an Albatros D.V, but the front gun jammed. However, a further 80 rounds from the observer sent it down to crash southeast of Bailleul. A little later the observer fired 200 rounds into a Fokker Dr.I which hit the ground east of Dranoutre. Lieutenant D. Latimer and Lt T.C. Noel in C856 sent an Albatros D.V down in flames southeast of Wervicq, then in the evening in the same machine they shot down a Dr.I in flames and two more were sent down out of control between Comines and Wervicq. In that same area, Capt D.G. Cooke and Lt H.G. Crowe in C4749 shot down another Dr.I, while Lt V.E. Groom and 2nd Lt E. Hardcastle in C4764 sent a further one down in flames northwest of Wervicq. A further Dr.I was claimed in the evening by Lt G.K. Runciman and 2nd Lt A.J. Todd in B1343, who sent it down out of control and smoking at Wytschaete.

The 9th was another fine day with plenty of aerial activity, 22 Sqn again being in the thick of it. In the morning 2nd Lt J.E. Gurdon and 2nd Lt A.J.H. Thornton in B1164 sent a scout down out of control and smoking southeast of Lille, while in the same area Capt A.C. Atkey and Lt C.G. Gass in B1253 sent one of a formation of seven scouts down in flames and two out of control. That evening, B1164, now crewed by Lt S.F.H. Thompson and Sgt L. Kendrick, sent a Pfalz D.III down out of control a mile north of Douai, the observer being slightly wounded by return fire. Also in the evening in the same area, 2nd Lt L.W. King and 2nd Lt H.E. Elsworth in C840 sent another down out of control, smoking; 2nd Lt E.C. Bromley and 2nd Lt J.H. Umney in C4747 also sent one down; 2nd Lt J.E. Gurdon and 2nd Lt A.P. Bollins in B1162 shot one down in flames and two more out of control, and Capt A.C. Atkey and Lt C.G. Gass in B1253 dived on a formation of eight enemy aircraft, sending one down in flames and another out of control and emitting smoke.

Another busy unit on the 9th was 11 Sqn. In a general engagement just after midday between Albert and Combles, 2nd Lt D.W. Beard and Sgt V.H. Davis in C807 fired two bursts into a Pfalz D.III to send it down out of control, Lt E.S. Coler and 2nd Lt C.W. Gladman in C792 downed three more, while Lt J.S. Chick and Lt E.C. Gilroy in C4845 despatched two Albatros D.Vs out of control. Two other enemy aircraft were sent down out of control by squadron aircraft crewed respectively by Lt R.F. Mullins and Lt N.F. Brace and Lt D.C.M. Brooks and Lt H.R. Kincaid.

Another very active unit was 20 Sqn. In the early afternoon, 2nd Lt W. Beaver and Capt N.W. Taylor in C817 dived down several thousand feet and brought down an Albatros scout, which spun down and crashed near the canal east of Warneton, while Lt W.M. Thomson and 2nd Lt G.H. Kemp in C4851 destroyed an Albatros D.V west of Comines. In the late afternoon Lt L.M. Price and Lt A. Mills shot down a Fokker Dr.I west of Lille, and Lt D.E. Smith and Prob F.J. Ralph sent another down in flames near the canal southwest of Menin. Not to be outdone, 2nd Lt T.G. Jackson and Lt A.E. Ansell in A7128 shot down a Pfalz D.III and sent another down out of control early in the evening at Vauvillers, while Capt C.D.G. Napier and Sgt W. Beales in C4750 drove down three Fokker Dr.Is out of control between Wiencourt and Méricourt. Victories came for 62 Sqn when 2nd Lt C.H. Arnison and Lt H.E. Merritt in C4859 destroyed a Pfalz D.III south of Herlies and sent another down out of control northeast of La Bassée.

In the afternoon of 10 May Lt R.H. Little and Lt H.F. Lumb in C841 of 48 Sqn sent one of a formation of Fokker Dr.Is down in flames near Suzanne and another out of control at Méricourt, while Lt N. Roberts and 2nd Lt W.F. Hanna in C805 sent a Dr.I down out of control east of Caffy and, later, a Rumpler two-seater out of control between Combles and Péronne. However, Lt N.G. Stransom and Pte C.V. Taylor were both killed when B1299 of 48 Sqn failed to return from an offensive patrol, last being seen in a

spin after combat near Méricourt. Elsewhere, Capt G.F. Hughes and Capt H. Claye in C4630 of 62 Sqn sent a Rumpler two-seater down out of control at Albert. During an offensive patrol C4851 of 20 Sqn was damaged by enemy fire and forced-landed near Hazebrouck; Lt D.E. Smith was unhurt, but observer Prob F.J. Ralph was slightly wounded. Little flying was possible for the next few days owing to mist and low cloud, but on the 12th 2nd Lt C.E. Tylor and 2nd Lt A.P. Bollins were both taken prisoner when B1162 of 22 Sqn failed to return from an offensive patrol. It was believed to have been shot down by flak after it was last seen between Armentières and Merville, the pilot having been wounded.

Some flying was possible in the evening of the 14th, when a 20 Sqn patrol encountered a formation of eight Albatros D.Vs between Wervicq and Zillebeke. Lieutenant D. Latimer and Lt T.C. Noel, who were leading in C856, sent one down with a burst of 80 rounds and another was forced down to be captured. Meanwhile, Lt V.E. Groom and 2nd Lt E. Hardcastle in C4764 kept firing at another down to 3,000ft then saw it crash three miles east of Zillebeke Lake. They were then set upon by a two-seater into which the observer fired a whole drum, and it crashed southwest of Polygon Wood. One other squadron victory that day was claimed by Lt E. Boulton and Prob H.G. Holman in B1232, who sent a Pfalz D.III down to crash northwest of Lille.

On 15 May, a much better day, Lt D. Latimer and Lt T.C. Noel in C856 of 20 Sqn sent a Pfalz D.III down out of control northwest of Lille and later dived on a Fokker Dr.I accompanied by six Albatros scouts between Comines and Ypres, seeing it break up after firing 100 rounds into it. Lieutenant E. Boulton and Prob H.G. Holman in B1232 fired at another Pfalz until within 30 yards' range, sending it spinning down vertically to crash northwest of Lille, while Lt R.G. Bennett and 2nd Lt P.G. Jones sent down two Albatros D.Vs out of control at Wervicq. In a 48 Sqn aircraft, possibly C4745, 2nd Lt E.R. Stock and 2nd Lt W.D. Davidson singled out one of a large formation of triplanes and scouts, sending one down with a 150-round burst. It dived steeply then burst into flames as it crashed, and another scout was then despatched in the same manner. Two aircraft of 48 Sqn were lost that day; Capt C.D.G. Napier and Sgt P. Murphy were killed when B1337 was shot down in flames during an offensive patrol, as were 2nd Lt C.E. Glover and 2nd Lt J.C. Fitton in C855, last seen near Lamotte in a spin with two enemy aircraft on its tail. Two other casualties that day were pilot Lt W.A. McMichael, wounded in one squadron aircraft, and observer 2nd Lt H.F. Lumb wounded in another.

Other F.2B activities on the 15th included an Albatros D.V destroyed at Ghistelles by

Lt R.J. Cullen and 2nd Lt E.H. Ward in C780 of 88 Sqn. A DFW two-seater was shot down near Pozières by Capt T.L. Purdom and 2nd Lt P.G. Chambers in B1216 of 62 Sqn at about the same time as another two-seater was destroyed between Albert and Ayette, south of Pye, by 2nd Lt C.H. Arnison and Lt C.D. Wells in C4859. Captain A.C. Atkey and Lt C.G. Gass in B1253 of 22 Sqn sent two Pfalz D.IIIs out of control northwest of Lille, while 2nd Lt S.H. Wallage and Lt G. Thomson in C795 dealt likewise with two DFW two-seaters near La Bassée. Also very active in the evening was 11 Sqn. Lieutenant J.S. Chick and Lt E. Gilroy in C797 were leading a patrol when they sighted about 20 enemy scouts southeast of Albert and led the formation in to attack. They first dived on a Fokker Dr.I which crashed, following this with a Pfalz D.III which crashed on a house, then sent another Dr.I down out of control. Captain J.P. Seabrook and 2nd Lt C. Wrigglesworth in C867 sent another Pfalz D.III down out of control, Lt H.W. Sellars and Lt C.C. Robson in C845 with Capt J.V. Aspinall and Lt P.V. de la Cour in C4882 sent a Dr.I down out of control but were then shot down themselves, all the occupants being killed except Lt Robson, who was taken prisoner.

The fine weather continued for the next few days. On the 16th Lieutenant D.C.M. Brooks and Lt H.R. Kincaid of 11 Sqn fired 50 rounds into a two-seater which spun down to crash northwest of Mametz, while Capt J.P. Seabrook and 2nd Lt C. Wrigglesworth in C867 destroyed a two-seater east of Cambrai. Lieutenant D.J. Weston and Sgt E.A. Deighton in C4763 of 20 Sqn destroyed an Albatros D.V, which crashed on the canal bank at Wervicq after being hit by 80 rounds from the observer as it tried to get under their tail, but Lt F.E. Boulton and Prob H.G. Holman were both wounded and taken prisoner when B1232 failed to return from an offensive patrol. In a general engagement between 22 Sqn and a formation of scouts, Lt S.F.H. Thompson and Sgt R.M. Fletcher sent down a Pfalz D.III which crashed after its starboard wing failed, and another out of control at Douai, while 2nd Lt E.C. Bromley and 2nd Lt J.H. Umney destroyed two more. An enemy kite balloon one mile northeast of Neuf Berquin was the target of 2nd Lt G.W. Bulmer and 2nd Lt P.S. Williams in C4888 of 22 Sqn, and it crumpled up under their fire. The crews of 62 Sqn were less fortunate that day. Shot up during an offensive patrol, C886 was forced-landed safely at Picquigny, both Lt J.A. Chubb and 2nd Lt E. Dumville being unhurt. After being damaged in combat, C4859 crash-landed within Allied lines and was abandoned under shellfire at Corbie, pilot 2nd Lt C.H. Arnison having been wounded and Lt C.D. Wells killed.

During an offensive patrol on the 17th, Lt W.M. Thomson and 2nd Lt G.H. Kemp in

This series of images depicts Bristol F.2Bs of 62 Sqn with the BEF in France.
The original captions from the album containing the prints are quoted.

Above: '**Hughes taking empty drums out of his machine.**' This aircraft, 'J' might well be C4630, the machine shot down on 19 May 1918. *(Philip Jarrett)*

Left: '**Hughes and another observer**' alongside the same aircraft. Note twin Lewis guns. *(Philip Jarrett)*

Below: '**Tuning up before a show.**' *(Philip Jarrett)*

'A Bristol Fighter,' 'W' of 62 Sqn. *(Philip Jarrett)*

Above: 'Starting a Bristol Fighter.' The aircraft having its propeller swung by a three-man chain is C4746 'N', which was wrecked while stationary on 26 May 1918, when B1314 ran into it as it was landing. It was eventually reconstructed and re-serialled H7174. Visible on the left is the tail of C4630 'J'. *(Philip Jarrett)*

Right: 'Going over a Bristol Fighter before a show.' Here is the celebrated C4630 'J', which was credited with a good tally of victories before it was brought down. Its top engine cowling has been removed and its rear fuselage fabric is loose along the top longeron. *(Philip Jarrett)*

Left: 'Waiting to do a show.' Note the decorated wheel covers of F.2B 'D' in the background. *(Philip Jarrett)*

Below: 'A Bristol Fighter ready for a show.' Yet another shot of C4630 'J', showing its individual letter on the top centre section as well as on both sides of the nose. *(Philip Jarrett)*

Shot down by Ltn Delling of Jasta 34 near Corbie on 19 May 1918, F.2B C4630 'J' is seen on a German aerodrome. Its occupants, Lt Clarke and Capt Claye, were taken prisoner. *(Philip Jarrett)*

C859 of 20 Sqn singled out an Albatros D.V in a formation of enemy scouts and a 200-round burst sent it down in a vertical dive to crash between Armentières and Lille. They then sent down another out of control near Armentières, while Capt D.G. Cooke and 2nd Lt E. Hardcastle in another F.2B sent an Albatros D.V down out of control nearby. While returning from escort duty, 2nd Lt G.W. Bulmer and 2nd Lt P.S. Williams in C4888 of 22 Sqn sighted a two-seater flying through clouds and promptly dived on it; 150 rounds sent it spinning down to crash southeast of Douai. Captain A. Hepburn and 2nd Lt G.W. Lambert in C821 of 88 Sqn sent an Albatros D.V down out of control east of Middelkerke, while Capt T.L. Purdom and 2nd Lt P.G. Chambers in B1216 of 62 Sqn drove down a Fokker D.VII out of control at Armentières and then a Rumpler two-seater in a vertical dive at Warneton.

On 18 May 88 Sqn suffered its first losses in combat, Lt L.G.S. Gadpaille and 2nd Lt S. Griffin being killed when C783 was shot down in a combat near Ypres, last seen in a spinning nosedive near Langemarck. After Lt R.J. Cullen and 2nd Lt E.H. Ward in C780 had sent down an Albatros D.III out of control near Zandevoorde, their engine cut out at 7,000ft. Cullen glided westwards and forced-landed on a road near Busseboom and hit telegraph poles, but neither of the crew was injured. The aircraft was subsequently rebuilt and renumbered. Captain E.C. Johnston and 2nd Lt J. Rudkin in C4867 of 88 Sqn sent an Albatros D.V down in flames, followed by another out of control north of Langemarck, and in a general engagement Lt C.W.B. Martin and 2nd Lt H.R. Goss were attacked by a scout and Goss sent it down in flames. Lieutenant T.E. Duffy and Lt F.A. Lewis drove another enemy aircraft down out of control.

Flying in C856, Lt D. Latimer and Lt T.C. Noel of 20 Sqn dived on a Pfalz D.III at the rear of a formation of six scouts and fired 100 rounds; they saw it crash in Comines. Later that day they sent another Pfalz D.III down out of control northeast of Nieppe Forest, and one more at Merville. Lieutenant P.T. Iaccaci and AM1 A. Newlands sent a Fokker Dr.I down out of control southwest of Nieppe, but B1279 crashed after being damaged by enemy fire near Vlamertinghe, Lt T.W. Williamson escaping unhurt but Cpl W.A. Foster being wounded. Later in the morning, Lt W.M. Thomson and 2nd Lt G.H. Kemp in C859 of 20 Sqn sent a Pfalz D.III down out of control south of Merville, and Lt J.H. Colbert and Lt R.W. Turner in B1168 destroyed another north of Neuf-Berquin. That evening, Capt K.R. Park and 2nd Lt G.J. Maynard in C808 of 48 Sqn sent a Pfalz D.III down out of control at Bray.

On the 19th 62 Sqn suffered badly, three aircraft and crews all being shot down mid-morning in combat near Corbie during an offensive patrol. Lieutenant H.A. Clarke and Capt H. Claye in C4630 were both taken prisoner; Lt H.C. Hunter became a wounded prisoner of war and Sgt J. Lake was killed in C796; and 2nd Lt F. Atkinson and Sgt C.C. Brammer in C4751 were both taken prisoner, though Atkinson died of his wounds. Although Lt D.A. Savage and Lt E.W. Collis in B1336 sent an Albatros D.V down out of control at Bray, they were themselves attacked while diving on enemy aircraft and badly shot about, but managed to force-land some 3,000 yards behind the front line near Corbie. Although the undercarriage was torn off by barbed wire, both were unhurt. More successfully, Capt T.L. Purdom and Sgt W.N. Holmes in B1216 of 62 Sqn sent a Fokker D.VII down out of control northwest of Douai in the evening.

Further success was enjoyed by 20 Sqn that day. When an offensive patrol attacked about 20 enemy aircraft in a general engagement between Armentières and Merville, Lt D.J. Weston and Sgt E.A. Deighton in C4763 first sent an Albatros D.V down out of control south of Calonne, then a Pfalz D.III out of control and smoking at Armentières, followed by another in flames at Merville. Another crashed after a vertical dive north of Frelinghem and, finally, yet another crashed south of Vieux Berquin. A Pfalz D.III was sent down smoking by Lt A.T. Iaccaci and AM1 A. Newlands in C859, and crashed south of Vieux Berquin, while Lt V.E. Groom and 2nd Lt E. Hardcastle in C4764 sent an Albatros D.V out of control south of Calonne, and Capt D.G. Cooke and Lt S.H.P. Masding in C4749 sent a D.VII down in flames at Estaires, followed by another which attacked them from behind only to receive 30 rounds in return and crash in flames at Laventie. The same day Lt W.M. Thomson and Lt G.H. Kemp in C843 sent down a Pfalz D.III which crashed on a house at Estaires, while Lt P.T. Iaccaci and Sgt W. Sansome in C4604 fired on a Fokker Dr.I, which crashed near Merville. Elsewhere, Capt A.C. Atkey and 2nd Lt C.G. Gass in C4747 of 22 Sqn sent down an Albatros two-seater which crashed south of Douai during the morning, and that evening they sent down two LVG two-seaters out of control, one of them smoking, west of Lille. Lieutenant L.A. Payne and Lt C.J.R. Gibson in C793 of 48 Sqn sent an Albatros D.V down out of control east of Proyart, and late in the day Capt F.J. Cunninghame and 2nd Lt H. Knowles in C950 sent down a Pfalz D.III out of control southeast of Foucaucourt. Captain R.C. StJ. Dix in another 48 Sqn aircraft was wounded by ground machine-gun fire.

The fine weather was still holding on the 20th, when Lt D. Latimer and Lt T.C. Noel in C856 of 20 Sqn became separated from their formation and were attacked by three Albatros D.Vs. They shot one down in flames and another out of control northeast of Merville. Linking up with two of the formation, they were then joined by an Albatros. Realising his mistake, the pilot dived down, pursued by the formation, but overturned on landing at Coucou Airfield. Also busy that day was 22 Sqn. In the morning Capt A.C. Atkey and 2nd Lt C.G. Gass in C4747 sent down three Halberstadt two-seaters out of control between Lille and Armentières, and in late afternoon 2nd Lt W.F.J. Harvey and Lt G. Thomson in B1209 sent two enemy kite balloons down in flames near Bailleul. In the evening Capt W.J. Mostyn and Sgt J.H. Jones in C901 shot down a Pfalz D.III which crashed northwest of Estaires, while 2nd Lt C.H. Dunster and 2nd Lt J.H. Umney in C4747 had their engine damaged in combat and crashed on landing, both being unhurt.

Bristol Fighter squadrons were active again next day. In the morning Lt W.M. Thomson and Lt G.H. Kemp in C843 of 20 Sqn shot down an Albatros D.V which crashed near Warneton. Later Capt W.J. Mostyn and Sgt J.H. Jones in C901 of 22 Sqn sent two LVG two-seaters down out of control southwest of Vitry, while nearby Lt S.F.H. Thompson and Sgt R.M. Fletcher in B1213 shot down one Pfalz D.III which crashed and another out of control. In the evening Lt J.E. Drummond and Lt C.C. Walmsley in C805 of 48 Sqn destroyed a Fokker Dr.I south of Combles, and 2nd Lt H.A. Oaks and 2nd Lt C.S. Bissett in C883 sent one down out of control between Carnoy and Méricourt, and another which crashed a mile east of Méricourt. However, two 88 Sqn aircraft came to grief on an offensive patrol, failing to return from a fight with enemy aircraft over the sea near Ostende; Lt C.G. Scobie and 2nd Lt F.J.D. Hudson in B1341, and Lt K.O. Millar and 2nd Lt S. Davidson in C839 were killed.

On the 22nd a 22 Sqn patrol attacked ten enemy scouts near Cambrai, 2nd Lt S.H. Wallage and 2nd Lt A.P. Stoyle in C795 sending down a Albatros D.V which crashed near Hancourt and another out of control by a burst from the observer. Nearby, Lt S.F.H. Thompson and Sgt R.M. Fletcher in B1213 destroyed another. South of Arras, Capt A.C. Atkey and Lt C.G. Gass in B1253 shot down an Albatros D.V, while Capt W.J. Mostyn and Sgt J.H. Jones in C901, and 2nd Lt E.C. Bromley and 2nd Lt J.H. Umney in A7243, sent down an Albatros scout apiece. In the Merville area during the evening Capt A.C. Atkey and Lt C.G. Gass in B1253 sent a DFW two-seater down out of control, as did Capt W.F.J. Harvey and Lt G. Thomson in C776, while 2nd Lt I.O. Stead and Sgt C. Williams in C4706 sent a Pfalz D.III down out of control. Early that day Capt T.P. Middleton and Lt A. Mills in C856 of 20 Sqn sent down an LVG two-seater which crashed between Wytschaete and St Eloi, then in the evening they sent an Albatros D.V down out of control at Warneton, another being similarly dealt with by Lt W.M. Thomson and Lt G.H. Kemp in C856. Three victories

were claimed by 62 Sqn in the morning, Capt W.E. Staton and Lt J.R. Gordon in C874 and Capt G.E. Gibbons and Lt S.A.W. Knights in C919 each sending down an LVG two-seater to crash near Laventie, while Lt W.K. Swayze and Lt W.E. Hall in C4633 destroyed another two miles northwest of Merville.

The weather finally broke on the 23rd, but a little flying was possible two days later, when Lt S.F.H. Thompson and Sgt R.M. Fletcher in B1213 of 22 Sqn sent down a Albatros D.V in flames west of Carvin. The 26th was cloudy, but 22 Sqn took advantage of some bright intervals, 2nd Lt W.F.J. Harvey and Lt G. Thomson in C842 sending a Pfalz D.III down out of control, its pilot believed killed, between Armentières and Lille. Later in the day the squadron had further successes near Armentières, 2nd Lt W.F.J. Harvey and Lt G. Thomson, again in C842, sending down an Albatros scout which crashed in a small field, and 2nd Lt S.H. Wallage and 2nd Lt A.P. Stoyle in C795 sending down an Albatros D.V southeast of Armentières, while 2nd Lt H.H. Beddow and Sgt J. Goodman in B1209 and Capt W.J. Mostyn and Sgt J.H. Jones in C901 sent a D.V down out of control. An aircraft of 29 Sqn was hit by anti-aircraft fire, wounding observer 2nd Lt W. Jacklin.

On the 27th the enemy mounted a surprise assault on the French front on the River Aisne, quickly tearing a hole in the Franco-British front to advance 12 miles by nightfall. Near-complete aerial superiority was achieved by a secret reinforcement, 12 German fighter units having been moved to the front. While on an offensive patrol, Capt W. Beaver and Sgt E.A. Deighton in C889 of 20 Sqn dived down on eight enemy aircraft, and Beaver sent down an Albatros D.V which crashed in flames northeast of Armentières. They then dived on several Fokker Dr.Is, four of which got on their tail. Deighton put about fifty rounds into one at close range and it went down out of control; a further 200 rounds then resulted in another crashing northeast of Perenchies, after which, being out of ammunition and badly shot about, they managed with great difficulty to shake off their remaining pursuers and return home. While returning from an offensive patrol in B1114, Lt A.T. Iaccaci and AM A. Newlands of 20 Sqn were attacked by eight Pfalz D.IIIs. In a running fight they sent one down in a vertical dive, smoking, its crash being confirmed by French anti-aircraft troops 3km southwest of Neuve Eglise. In the evening Capt A.C. Atkey and Lt C.G. Gass in B1253 of 22 Sqn joined with 40 Sqn's S.E.5as in a combat northeast of Lens, sending a Pfalz D.III down to crash at Meurchin and another two down out of control. An Albatros D.V was shot down out of control south of Albert by Lt L.A.

Payne and Lt C.J.R. Gibson in C877 of 48 Sqn, the observer being hit by return fire. While on an offensive patrol, B1193 of 48 Sqn was damaged by enemy fire and forced to land at Clairmarais South aerodrome; Sgt A. Stansfield was unhurt but observer Prob J. Tulloch was wounded.

The weather was fine on the 28th, though cloud persisted and limited visibility. The last F.2B loss of the month was C4763 of 20 Sqn, which failed to return from an offensive patrol, last seen during the morning near Neuf-Berquin; Lt R.G. Bennett and Lt G.T.C. Salter were both killed. Also during the morning, three aircraft of 22 Sqn had successes near La Bassée; 2nd Lt G.V Wheatley and Sgt C. Williams in C842 sent down a two-seater out of control after it was fired upon by Williams; 2nd Lt W.F.J. Harvey and Lt G. Thomson in C4631 shot down two more two-seaters, one of which was claimed by the observer, and 2nd Lt C.W.M. Thompson and Sgt H.C. Hunt in C4894 sent one more down out of control. In the evening, Capt G.E. Gibbons and Lt S.A.W. Knights in C919 of 62 Sqn sent a Fokker D.VII down in flames west of Lille, followed by a Rumpler two-seater out of control between La Creche and Steenwerck and then another D.VII in flames between Menin and Armentières.

In the evening of the 29th, aircraft of 20 Sqn were in combat near Bac-St-Maur. Lieutenant W.M. Thomson and Lt G.H. Kemp in C843 sent an Albatros D.V down out of control, as did Capt T.P. Middleton and Lt A. Mills in C951, while Lt T.C. Traill and 2nd Lt P.G. Jones in C856 sent a Fokker Dr.I down out of control west of Armentières but then crashed near the aerodrome after suffering combat damage. Captain W. Beaver and Sgt E.A. Deighton in C889 shot down another Dr.I which crashed near the river. Shortly afterwards Capt W.E. Staton and Lt J.R. Gordon in C874 of 62 Sqn sent an LVG two-seater down out of control at Aubigny.

On the 30th the fine weather continued. In the morning 2nd Lt W.B. Yuille and 2nd Lt W.D. Davidson were killed when C871 of 48 Sqn was shot down in flames near Bois de Senécat during an offensive patrol. In the afternoon Capt W.E. Staton and Lt J.R. Gordon in C874 of 62 Sqn sent a two-seater down out of control between Arras and Cambrai. Then, in the evening, Capt T.P. Middleton and Lt A. Mills in C951 of 20 Sqn were leading a patrol which attacked nine enemy aircraft. Middleton fired at a D.V at close range and saw it crash in the canal northwest of Lille. He then side-slipped on to one of seven Pfalz D.IIIs so that Mills could get in a burst. Its starboard upper wing came off and it crashed near Wez Macquart. In the same combat Lt D.J. Weston and Lt W. Noble in C979 shot down another Pfalz D.III which crashed near Lille Citadel. In the evening 2nd Lt

E.C. Bromley and 2nd Lt J.H. Umney in C961 of 22 Sqn sent down a Pfalz D.III out of control south of Armentières, while Capt A.C. Atkey and Lt C.G. Gass in B1253 shot down a Pfalz D.III in flames and another out of control in the same area, the latter falling to the observer.

Aircraft of 20 Sqn aircraft were involved in a number of combats on the morning of the 31st. A Pfalz D.III was shot down by Lt P.T. Iaccaci and AM1 A. Newlands in B1122 and crashed in flames just east of Merville. They then claimed an Albatros scout which crashed on the canal bank south of Merville. Captain T.P. Middleton and Lt A. Mills in C951 shot down a Pfalz D.III which crashed between Armentières and Estaires, while Lt D.J. Weston and Lt W. Noble in C4699 sent an Albatros D.V down out of control at Estaires. Lieutenant A.T. Iaccaci and Sgt D. Malpas in C4672 sent an Albatros D.V out of control in a vertical dive southwest of Armentières, and Lt L.H.T. Capel and Prob F.J. Ralph in C4604 shot down an Albatros D.V which crashed just north of Laventie. Also that morning, 2nd Lt O. StC. Harris and Sgt G. Shannon were wounded when A7256 was badly damaged by enemy aircraft fire during an offensive patrol. The squadron was again in action during an evening patrol, when Lt E. Lindup and Sgt E.A. Deighton in C850 sent a Pfalz D.III in a vertical dive to break up south of Armentières. Lieutenant W.M. Thomson and Lt G.H. Kemp in C843 sent down a Pfalz D.III which crashed at Bois Grenier and an Albatros D.V which went down out of control at Armentières. An Albatros D.V was driven down out of control northwest of Armentières by Lt P.T. Iaccaci and AM1 S.W. Melbourne in C4699.

Aircraft of 22 Sqn were also active. In the early morning Lt J.H. Colbert and 2nd Lt B.W. Wilson in B1168 shot down a Pfalz D.III which crashed just east of Estaires and, later, Lt L.W. King and 2nd Lt J. McDonald in C4835 sent down an Albatros D.V which crashed and burnt at Neuve Chapelle. Captain A.C. Atkey and Lt C.G. Gass in B1253 sent down two Pfalz D.IIIs out of control at Armentières, while 2nd Lt C.H. Dunster and Sgt J.H. Jones in A7243 drove another down out of control and then another broke up. During the evening a patrol encountered more Pfalz D.IIIs in the Armentières area, and Lt J.H. Colbert and Lt A. Mills in B1168 sent one down in flames, Lt F.G. Gibbons and Sgt J.H. Jones in A7243 sent another down out of control, and 2nd Lt E.C. Bromley and 2nd Lt J.H. Umney in C961 sent down a third, which crashed near Lavantie.

By the end of the month the Germans had reached Soissons and were heading for the River Marne. However, at this point the first of the American reinforcements arrived on the scene, enabling the advance to be halted at Château Thierry.

June 1918

Early on 1 June Lt W.M. Thomson and Lt G.H. Kemp of 20 Sqn in C843 became cut off from their patrol and were attacked by four enemy aircraft, but Thomson turned and fired 200 rounds into a Pfalz D.III which crashed at Bois Grenier. Kemp then fired at an Albatros D.V at close range, sending it down out of control over Armentières. Another Albatros then attacked from above, killing Kemp. Thomson spun down to 2,000ft when, still unable to shake off his attacker, he turned and fired at it and drove it away. He then departed the scene and managed to reach the British lines. Another 20 Sqn success at about this time was that of Lt V.E. Groom and 2nd Lt E. Hardcastle in C4764, who shot down a Pfalz D.III which dived into the ground north of Comines, and another crashed after going down out of control. Captain D. Latimer and Lt T.C. Noel in C892 shot down another Pfalz D.III, which crashed into railway sidings. However, Lt T.C. Traill and 2nd Lt P.G. Jones in C4749 of 20 Sqn forced-landed at Poperinghe when the front petrol tank was shot up during an offensive patrol. Later in the morning Lt A.T. Iaccaci and Sgt W. O'Neill became separated from their formation and were attacked by three Pfalz D.IIIs, one of which they sent down out of control 'like a falling leaf' north of Merville.

Elsewhere that morning, 2nd Lt C.H. Dunster and Sgt J.H. Jones in C842 of 22 Sqn sent an observation balloon down in flames at Neuf-Berquin, while Capt H. Rees-Jones and 2nd Lt C. Wealthall in C959 of 62 Sqn shot down a Fokker Dr.I which crashed just east of Montdidier. In the evening Lt F.C. Ransley and 2nd Lt G. Dixon in C786 of 48 Sqn sent an Albatros D.V down in flames and another out of control north of Lamotte. Two aircraft of 22 Sqn were in combat near Erquinghem, Lt F.G. Gibbons and 2nd Lt J.H. Umney in C961 destroying two Pfalz D.IIIs, and Lt S.F.H. Thompson and Sgt R.M. Fletcher in C929 scoring an Albatros two-seater and an Albatros D.V, the latter being hit by the observer.

The fine weather held, and 2 June was a very busy day for the RAF, with numerous successes. Among the Bristol Fighter units, 22 Sqn had an eventful morning, especially in the Lens area. Captain A.C. Atkey and Lt C.G. Gass in B1253 sent two two-seaters down out of control, and 2nd Lt E.C. Bromley and 2nd Lt J.H. Umney in C9612 claimed two more, while Lt F.G. Gibbons and Sgt J.H. Jones in C901 dealt similarly with a Pfalz D.III. Lieutenant S.F.H. Thompson and Sgt R.M. Fletcher in C929 accounted for one more, as well as sending yet another down in flames. Both an Albatros D.V and a two-seater were sent down out of control southeast of La Bassée by Lt L.W. King and 2nd Lt J. McDonald in C4835. A

little later Lt F.G. Gibbons and 2nd Lt J.H. Umney in C961 sent another Pfalz D.III down out of control northeast of Lens.

In the evening 88 Sqn had a busy time near Ostende, Capt A. Hepburn and AM2 T. Proctor in C821 sending down an Albatros D.V in flames and another out of control, Lt E.P. Pownall and Sgt H.E. Hinchliffe claiming an Albatros Scout out of control, and Lt W.G. Westwood and 2nd Lt W. Tinsley an Albatros D.V. Another D.V was sent down out of control by Lt J.P. Findlay and 2nd Lt G.W. Lambert in C777 or C785, but they were hit by return fire, the observer being wounded. Around the same time 62 Sqn had a successful encounter with some Fokker Dr.Is, Capt W.E. Staton and Lt J.R. Gordon sending one down to crash just south of Pozières, as did 2nd Lt D.A. Savage and Sgt W.N. Holmes in C953, who also sent another down out of control.

On 3 June 62 Sqn, then still at Planques, was temporarily attached to the 81st Wing, still in the 9th Brigade, until the 21st of the month. There was little aviation activity for the two days, but further American troops which arrived in early June helped to stop the German advance at Belleau Wood on the 4th. On the 5th, Lt E.C. Bromley and 2nd Lt C.G. Gass in C961 were leading a 22 Sqn offensive patrol south of Laventie when they sighted a Halberstadt two-seater, but on their approach it fired a green light. Wisely suspecting a trap, Bromley waited, and then six Albatros scouts appeared, followed by six more which, diving out of the sun, appeared to mistake the first six for British aircraft. In the ensuing melee C961's crew shot down the Halberstadt which had been acting as bait, as well as sending an Albatros D.V down out of control. Another was disposed of by Capt J.E. Gurdon and Sgt J.H. Hall in A7243, falling to the observer's gunfire, while Lt S.F.H. Thompson and Sgt R.M. Fletcher in C929 destroyed two more south of Laventie. The enemy aircraft continuing to fight among themselves, their aircraft recognition evidently leaving something to be desired, and several were seen to go down out of control. In a further offensive patrol during the evening, Lt F.G. Gibbons and Sgt R.M. Fletcher sent a Pfalz D.III down out of control near La Bassée, and Capt J.E. Gurdon and Sgt J.H. Hall in A7243 sent another down in flames at Fromilly, their own aircraft being damaged by enemy fire and Hall being slightly wounded. Aircraft B1253 failed to return, having been seen going down under control towards Lestrem; Lt C.H. Dunster was wounded and taken prisoner, and Sgt L.A.F. Young was killed.

Also that evening, Lt J.E.W. Sugden and Sgt W. O'Neill in B1114 and Lt E.A. Magee and Prob R.J. Gregory in C817 of 20 Sqn were all taken prisoner, having last been seen near Armentières. More success was achieved by 62 Sqn, Lt G.K. Runciman and

2nd Lt A.J. Todd in B1343 sending down a Pfalz D.III which crashed northwest of Douai, and Capt W.E. Staton and Lt J.R. Gordon in C874 sending down another in flames in the same area and a third which crashed at crossroads. Late in the evening, Lt K.B. Conn and 2nd Lt B. Digby-Worsley in C787 of 88 Sqn destroyed two Albatros D.Vs at Messines.

On the 8th the weather was fair but there was very little enemy air activity. During the day C882 of 88 Sqn had a longeron shot through by flak near Ostende but returned safely, Lt R.J. Cullen and 2nd Lt F.A. Lewis being uninjured. In the evening a number of Pfalz D.IIIs were encountered, Lt A.T. Iaccaci and Cpl A. Newlands C892 of 20 Sqn sending down one which crashed near the railway northeast of Wervicq, while Capt T.P. Middleton and Capt F. Godfrey in C951 sent down two more which crashed southeast of Comines. Another was sent down out of control southeast of Bray by Capt W.E. Staton and Lt J.R. Gordon in C874 of 62 Sqn.

On the 9th the Germans mounted another offensive, this time towards the River Marne, but despite intense aerial activity during the next few days the Bristol Fighter squadrons again suffered few losses. On the first day of the attack 20 Sqn destroyed two Pfalz D.IIIs; Lt W.M. Thomson and Prob F.J. Ralph in C843 sent one down between Comines and Houthem, while Capt D. Latimer and Lt T.C. Noel in C892 sent the other down a

spin, the port wings coming off. A little later Lt W.K. Swayze and 2nd Lt E.M. Nicholas in B1238 of 62 Sqn sent two more down in flames northwest of Cambrai. On the 10th a 48 Sqn evening patrol shot down an Albatros D.V at Roye. Two days later Capt T.P. Middleton and Capt F. Godfrey in C951 of 20 Sqn sent down another Albatros D.V which crashed and burst into flames east of Zillebeke Lake. On the morning of the 12th Lt P.T. Iaccaci and Lt W. Noble in B1122 of 20 Sqn and Capt W. Beaver and Sgt E.A. Deighton in C889 sent an Albatros D.V down out of control northwest of Armentières. On the 14th, Lt F.C. Ransley and Lt W. Lauder of 48 Sqn sent an LVG two-seater down out of control east of Albert, but 2nd Lt B.M. Battey and Sgt H.F. Watson in C932 of the same squadron had their propeller damaged and then overturned while making a forced landing in a wheat field.

A singular loss during a reconnaissance on 15th June was that of C920, which had been attached to 4 Sqn only the previous day. It was badly shot up by three enemy aircraft between Merville and Neuf-Berquin while on reconnaissance. However, the wreckage was recovered and later rebuilt with a fresh serial number, and the machine was replaced in turn by C1036 and E2570. The weather on the 16th was variable with some rain, but a fair amount of flying was achieved. In the morning a 62 Sqn formation on an offensive patrol met some

enemy scouts near Montdidier, 2nd Lt G.M. Yuille and Lt H.E. Merritt in C919 sending a Pfalz D.III down out of control, but Lt J.M. Goller and 2nd Lt M. Ross-Jenkins in C788 failed to return, both later reported killed. In the evening Lt D.E. Smith and Prob F.J. Ralph in C859 of 20 Sqn shot down a Pfalz D.III which crashed just south of Comines. Next morning a 20 Sqn patrol engaged a formation of Pfalz D.IIIs or Fokker D.VIIs and accounted for several of the enemy without loss to themselves. Lieutenant A.T. Iaccaci and AM A. Newlands in C892 sent one down to crash near Houthem, as did Lt L.M. Price and 2nd Lt E. Hardcastle in C4672, northwest of Armentières. Sometime later that morning both Lt P.T. Iaccaci and Lt W. Noble in B1122 destroyed a Pfalz D.III near Menin, while Lt L.H.T. Capel and Sgt E.A. Deighton in C4604 sent one Pfalz D. III down out of control and another which crashed northeast of Gheluvelt. A D.VII which went down out of control at Boesinghe was shared by Lt W.M. Thomson and Prob F.J. Ralph in C843 and Capt D. Latimer and Lt T.C. Noel in C987. Also that day, C914 of 48 Sqn had its engine shot up by flak during an offensive patrol and Lt R.H. Davies and 2nd Lt G. Rider forced-landed at Querieu without injury.

Some flying was possible on the 18th; C776 of 22 Sqn crashed during an offensive patrol after its fuel tank and radiator were shot up in combat, neither Capt W.F.J.

A custom-made improvised overwing Lewis gun mounting on F.2B E2466 of 22 Sqn at Agincourt (Maisoncelle) in 1918. This was done for Capt W.F.J. Harvey, who is in the pilot's seat in this picture, with Capt D.E. Waight in the rear with twin Lewis guns on his Scarff ring. This four-gun installation was flown only once, as the overwing installation had an adverse effect on the compass in the centre-section trailing edge, and the twin rear guns could not be swung effectively at heights above 8,000ft owing to the effects of anoxia on the rear gunner. *(C&C)*

Harvey nor Lt A.P. Stoyle being hurt. On the evening of the 19th Lt J.E. Gurdon and Lt J.J. Scaramanga in C989 of 22 Sqn dived on a formation of D.VIIs, fired at one at close range and caused it to sideslip steeply and collide with the centre section of another Fokker below it, both going down locked together southeast of Armentières. Poor weather then intervened, but some flying was possible on the 23rd. In the morning Lt L.H.T. Capel and Sgt E.A. Deighton in C4604 of 20 Sqn sent a Pfalz D.III down in a vertical dive before it broke up to crash near Laventie. After the petrol tank of B1122 was shot through during an offensive patrol, Lt H.C. McCreary and Sgt J.D. Summers of 20 Sqn force-landed at Tilques. In an encounter near La Bassée by 22 Sqn, Lt J.E. Gurdon and 2nd Lt J. McDonald in C989 sent two D.VIIs down out of control, while Lt S.F.H. Thompson and Sgt R.M. Fletcher in C929 sent two Pfalz D.IIIs down out of control, though their own aircraft was badly shot up.

Although the poor weather continued, flying was possible at times. In encounters by 62 Sqn on the morning of the 24th, Lt L.W. Hudson and Lt H.E. Merritt in A7215 shot down an LVG two-seater which crashed near Harnes. Lieutenant T.H. Broadley and Sgt F.R. Bower in B1273 sent a Pfalz D.III down out of control in a vertical dive between Lille and Carvin. As Bower was wounded in the arm Broadley landed at the dummy aerodrome at Senlecques to obtain help for him, but unfortunately crashed. Both Lt F. Williams and 2nd Lt E. Dumville were killed in D8028 during combat with an enemy aircraft over Lille, while C976 of 20 Sqn had its controls damaged by flak and crashed near Boisdinghem Hospital, without injury to the pilot, Lt A.B.D. Campbell.

During the morning of the 25th 48 Sqn was very busy and suffered mixed fortunes in an encounter with enemy scouts in the Foucaucourt region. Although 2nd Lt N. Roberts and 2nd Lt C.C. Walmesley in C983 sent down a D.VII, as did Lt F.C. Ransley and 2nd Lt C.W. Davies in C786, Lt F. Cabburn and Sgt W.E. Lawder were killed when C789 went down out of control

in flames. A similar fate befell 2nd Lt N.H. Muirden and 2nd Lt E. Roberts in C4719, both being taken prisoner. Muirden died of his wounds some weeks later. However, 2nd Lt H.A. Oaks and 2nd Lt G.J. Maynard in C883 were credited with a D.VII which went down out of control, falling from side to side, between Foucaucourt and Rosières. Observer 2nd Lt J.W. Whitmarsh was wounded in another 48 Sqn aircraft. A little later Capt K.R. Park and 2nd Lt H. Knowles in C940 sent a Rumpler two-seater down out of control over the River Luce at Wiencourt, quickly followed by a DFW two-seater which crashed half a mile north of Bayonvillers. Elsewhere that morning, Lt J.P. West and Sgt E. Antcliffe in C4880 of 88 Sqn shot down a D.VII in flames between Thorout and Breskene, while in the evening Capt D. Latimer and Lt T.C. Noel of 20 Sqn in C987 drove down a two-seater at Bailleul. Next day, C818 of 48 Sqn left soon after dawn on reconnaissance but was hit by anti-aircraft fire over the target, Villers-Bretonneux, Lt J.E. Doe and 2nd Lt A.J. Elvin both becoming prisoners of war. In the evening Lt P.T. Iaccaci and 2nd Lt F.J. Ralph in D8090 of 20 Sqn became separated from their formation and were attacked by five Pfalz D.III, one of which they sent down out of control at Armentières.

On the 27th 48 Sqn in particular took advantage of the arrival of better weather, though with mixed fortunes. In the Lamotte area that evening, Lt N. Roberts and 2nd Lt W.F. Hanna in C943 destroyed a D.VII, 2nd Lt F.C. Ransley and 2nd Lt C.W. Davies in C8908 sent another down in flames, and Lt R.H. Little and 2nd Lt E. Vickers in C841 sent a third down out of control. However, during an offensive patrol near Villers-Bretonneux, 1st Lt J.M. Goad and Sgt C. Norton were both killed when they were shot down in flames during combat. Lieutenant E.A. Foord and Sgt L. James in C989 suffered the same fate and were killed. Southeast of Armentières that evening, Lt J.E. Gurdon and Lt J.J. Scaramanga in C989 of 22 Sqn claimed a Fokker Dr.I down out of control after it was fired on by the observer. In the morning of the 28th Lt F.G. Gibbons and Lt V.StB.

Collins in C989 of 22 Sqn sent down a Fokker Dr.I which broke up north of Estaires. That evening, Lt A. Williamson and Pte E. Hoare in C4720 of 88 Sqn sent two Halberstadt two-seaters down in flames over Houthoulst Forest, a third being similarly dealt with by Lt K.B. Conn and 2nd Lt B.H. Smyth in C787. However, C4880 of 88 Sqn failed to return, possibly being the British aircraft shot down in flames near Clerkem; Lt J.P. West and Pte2 A.J. Loton were killed.

In the Ghistelles area on the 29th 88 Sqn was again in action, engaging in a fight in which several D.VIIs were sent down. The crews involved were Lt W.A. Wheeler and Lt T.S. Chilton in C774, Lt K.B. Conn and 2nd Lt B.H. Smyth in C787, Capt K.R. Simpson and Sgt C. Hill in C983 and Lt R.J. Cullen and 2nd Lt H.H. Ward in D8022. Two of the Bristols were damaged by return fire, C983 overturning during a force landing and D8022 having to force-land 300 yards inside the British lines, from where it could not be salvaged owing to enemy shellfire. Its pilot was wounded in the leg.

Early on the 30th a 20 Sqn patrol attacked two enemy formations, one of nine aircraft and the other of seven. Of these, Capt T.P. Middleton and Capt F. Godfrey sent down a Fokker Dr.I and a Pfalz D.III, both of which crashed east of Comines, Lt A.T. Iaccaci and AM A. Newlands in C892 shot down a Pfalz D.III which crashed near a canal west of Halluin, and Capt D. Latimer and Lt T.C. Noel in C987 sent down another which went down in a spin before breaking up over Comines. A Pfalz D.III crashed between Wervicq and Comines after being attacked by Lt D.J. Weston and Lt W. Noble in B1307, who then sent two more down out of control. After driving an Albatros D.V down out of control north of Comines, Lt T.C. Traill and 2nd Lt P.G. Jones in C938 forced-landed at St Monelin-Metz with the petrol tank shot through. Captain H.P. Lale and 2nd Lt E. Hardcastle were credited with a D.VII which crashed near Menin, supposedly in 'A8716', but as this was a B.E.2e serial the aircraft's correct identity is surmised to have been D7816.

Photographed at Nivelles, F6142 'B' of 62 Sqn was a rebuild of B1328. It joined 62 Sqn in late September 1918. *(Eric Harlin)*

Chapter 6

THE BATTLE TO VICTORY

As it turned out, the war was now about to enter its final phase.

July 1918

Bristol Fighter losses continued to be quite light in the early part of July. The first was that of C4849 of 35 Sqn, which was wrecked when it force-landed at Coisy after being attacked and shot up on the 1st, Lt A. McGregor being wounded and Lt R.J. Fitzgerald killed. Three Bristol squadrons were in action that evening, including 88 Sqn, which was in combat with Fokker D.VIIs near Westroosebeke. Captain E.C. Johnston and 2nd Lt J. Rudkin in C4867 sent one down in flames, and Lt K.B. Conn and 2nd Lt B. Digby-Worsley in C787 sent two down, one in flames and the other out of control. Lieutenant C. Foster and Pte E. Hoare in C4720 sent yet another down, and Lt J.E. Gurdon and Lt J.J. Scaramanga in C989 of 22 Sqn shot down a Pfalz D.III at Armentières, while Capt D. Latimer and Lt T.C. Noel of 20 Sqn sent a Dr.I down at Menin and Lt F.G. Harlock and Prob A.S. Draisey in C873 of 20 Sqn drove a D.VII down at Tourcoing.

During a combat near Gheluvelt on the morning of the 2nd, Lt D.J. Weston and Lt W. Noble in B1168 and Lt E.W. Sweeney and Prob C.G. Boothroyd in C843 each sent down a D.VII to crash, while Lt T.C. Traill and 2nd Lt P.G. Jones in B1344 sent down a third in flames, though Jones was killed by return fire. Lieutenant D.E. Smith and Prob J. Hills in C859, also of 20 Sqn, sent down a Pfalz D.III southeast of Ypres.

However, two squadron aircraft failed to return, Lt H.C. McCreary and Sgt W.H. Barter in D8090 and Lt B.T. Davidson and Sgt J. Helsby in C850 being last seen over Halluin; all four were killed. Also in action that morning was 48 Sqn, in a fight with Pfalz D.IIIs in the Soyecourt area. Captain J.E. Drummond and 2nd Lt J.A. Galbraith in C926, 2nd Lt N.Y.P. Lewis and 2nd Lt H. Buckner, Capt H.A. Oaks and Lt G.J. Maynard in C883 and Lt E.D. Shaw and Sgt T.W. Smith in another aircraft were all involved in sending down two of the enemy, but C883 crashed on landing back at base. In the evening, Capt F.J. Cunninghame and 2nd Lt H. Knowles in C950 of 48 Sqn sent a Pfalz D.III down southeast of Foucaucourt, as did Capt E.N. Griffiths and Lt A.E. Ansell in D8061, but C808 had its fuel tank shot up in combat, Lt E.D. Shaw and Sgt T.W. Smith returning safely and uninjured.

The weather on the 3rd was poor, but in the evening of the next day Lt P.T. Iaccaci and 2nd Lt R.W. Turner in C951 of 20 Sqn sent down an Albatros D.V which crashed and burst into flames and then another, both just west of Veldhoek, then a third which crashed near the railway northeast of Zillebeke Lake. Elsewhere, the radiator of C842 of 22 Sqn was shot through but neither Lt I.O. Stead nor 2nd Lt W.A. Cowie was hurt, a forced landing being made near Berbere. On the morning of the 5th 2nd Lt B.S. Hillis and Sgt S.J. Pratt in C791 of 62 Sqn were killed when their aircraft was shot down at Guillemont while

on reconnaissance. During the morning of the 7th 2nd Lt H.W. Elliott and 2nd Lt J.W. Ferguson in A7146 of 48 Sqn sent down an enemy aircraft at Vitry-en-Artois, and later Capt C.R. Steele and Lt A.E. Ansell in D7909 shot down a Pfalz D.III, which turned on its back and then burst into flames upon crashing on to the Amiens-St Quentin road. After their radiator was shot through, 2nd Lt B.E. Sharwood-Smith and Sgt E. Collinson in B1135 of 48 Sqn had to make a forced landing south of Amiens; both were unhurt.

During an offensive patrol early on the 8th, aircraft of 62 Sqn engaged some Fokker Dr.Is northwest of Carvin. Captain W.E. Staton and Sgt W.N. Holmes in D7899 destroyed one, while Lt L. Campbell and 2nd Lt P. Pilkington in B1339 sent another down, but C1002 was last seen in a dive under control with three enemy aircraft on its tail; Lt J.A. Chubb and Sgt J. Borwein were taken prisoner. Next morning, Lt J.E. Gurdon DFC and Lt J.J. Scaramanga in C989 of 22 Sqn shot down a DFW two-seater north of La Bassée, while Capt G.W. Bulmer and 2nd Lt J. McDonald in C4888 sent another two-seater down in flames north of Bois de Phalempin, and Lt T.W. Martin and Sgt J.H. Hall in D7896 sent down two Albatros D.Vs, one of which crashed north of La Bassée and the other west of Steenwerck. In the evening, however, B1113 of 48 Sqn left on reconnaissance and was probably shot down in combat with three Pfalz D.IIIs, 1st Lt E.D. Shaw, United States Air Service (USAS), and Sgt T.W.

Lieutenant W.E. Staton and Lt J.R. Gordon with F.2B C4619 'R' of 62 Sqn on 1 April 1918, the day on which they sent an Albatros D.V down out of control and smoking at Bouchoir. The aircraft carries the squadron identification markings of three vertical white bands. (C&C)

Smith being killed. On that day 11 Sqn moved from Remaisnil to Le Quesnoy.

On 9th July 'L' Flight was formed by restyling the Artillery Flight to become one of five new Long-Range Artillery Flights, each given an identifying letter instead of a number. Earlier, five of the Corps squadrons in France each had one or two Bristol Fighters on strength from March 1918, numbers 10 and 35 (Armstrong Whitworth F.K.8) and 16 (R.E.8) each having two, while 12 and 15 (R.E.8) had one apiece. No Corps squadron was ever re-equipped throughout with Bristol Fighters. Subsequent lettered flights equipped with the Arab-engined F.2B were lettered 'M', 'N', 'O' and 'P'.

On the 10th nine aircraft of 22 Sqn encountered between 15 and 20 Fokker Dr.Is and Pfalz D.IIIs, and Lt J.E. Gurdon DFC and Lt J.J. Scaramanga in C1003 dived on a Pfalz D.III which went down in flames. Then two others which got on to their tail were both sent down in the Armentières-Lille area, but their own aircraft was damaged in the combat, Gurdon being wounded and Scaramanga dying of his wounds. Meanwhile, Lt F.C. Stanton and

Lt C.J. Tolman in D8089 had dived on another Pfalz D.III, which crashed. Five more then got on to their tail, and Stanton sent two down out of control, followed by a DFW two-seater south of Merville. Capt W.F.J. Harvey and Lt G. Thomson in C1040 sent down a Fokker Dr.I which crashed southeast of Lille, and another followed, both succumbing to the observer's fire. Lieutenant T.W. Martin and Capt D.E. Waight in D7896 fired a long burst at a Pfalz D.III which crashed near Lille, and Lt F.G. Gibbons and Lt V.StB. Collins in C989 sent down in the same area one of three Fokker Dr.Is which got on to their tail. That same day Lt H.M. Dickinson was killed, and Lt M.H.K. Kane taken prisoner when C795 of 22 Sqn failed to return from an offensive patrol, having been last seen over Merville. Elsewhere that day, Lt P.T. Iaccaci and 2nd Lt R.W. Turner in D7915 of 20 Sqn sent down two Fokker D.VIIs east of Zillebeke Lake.

The weather then clamped down again, but on the 13th Lt C.F. Hurst and Lt S.G. Birch had to force-land when C4835 of 22 Sqn was hit by flak on an offensive patrol to Lillers. On the 14th Capt D. Latimer and Lt

T.C. Noel in C987 of 20 Sqn sent down two D.VIIs southeast of Ypres, one of these being shared with the patrol they were leading. Then on the 15th came the German Army's last offensive in the west, this time against the French Army around Reims, but once again RAF losses remained reasonably light. The British agreed to provide air co-operation, and on the 17th 62 Sqn, then still at Planques, was attached to the 54th Wing, 9th Brigade, and on the 19th 88 Sqn moved from Petite Synthe to Drionville.

On the 17th, Lt G.F. Anderson and 2nd Lt H.R. Goss of 88 Sqn shot down a Halberstadt two-seater, then two days later Lt W.M. Thomson and Sgt J.D.C. Summers of 20 Sqn in C843 claimed a Fokker Dr.I destroyed south of Gheluvelt. Around the same time Capt D. Latimer and Lt T.C. Noel in C987 sent down a D.VII which crashed north of Comines. On the ground the German troops which had been moving towards Reims were stopped in their tracks by an Allied counterattack on the 18th, spearheaded by French and American troops with some involvement by British troops. A brief bombardment was followed by a devastating assault which included 225 tanks, taking the German Army completely by surprise. Few enemy aircraft were seen at this time, but on the morning of the 20th Capt W.F.J. Harvey and Lt G. Thomson in C989 of 22 Sqn sent down two D.VIIs which crashed, and another that went down south of Lille. Lieutenant D.C.M. Brooks and 2nd Lt Spinks of 11 Sqn sent a Pfalz D.III down at Monchy. On the evening of the 21st C974 of 48 Sqn failed to return from an offensive patrol to La Motte, being last seen going east over the lines; 2nd Lt B.M. Battey USAS and 2nd Lt J. Gondre were later reported to have been taken prisoner.

Fine weather continued, and early on the 22nd Capt A. Morrison and Sgt R. Allan of 11 Sqn in C867 sent a Pfalz D.III down between Bray and Morlancourt. However, Lt W.E. Coulson and 2nd Lt W.H.E. Labett were both captured when F5810 of 62 Sqn failed to return from an offensive patrol after being seen diving on three enemy triplanes near Laventie. In the evening Lt L.R. Brereton and 2nd Lt G.R. La Cecilia were both wounded during an artillery observation and photographic mission when D8087 of 52 Sqn was hit by anti-aircraft fire over Bapaume, though the pilot managed to land safely. In an encounter over Foucaucourt during an offensive patrol on the 24th, Capt H.A. Oaks and 2nd Lt C.W. Davies in F6094 of 48 Sqn sent two D.VIIs down, but 2nd Lt

Major Keith Park stands in front of F.2B C814 '12' of 48 Sqn in 1918. (C&C)

S.N. Waddy and Sgt W.J. Shuker were both killed when D7902 was shot down in flames. That evening 20 Sqn fought several D.VIIs, Lt L.M. Price and Lt A. Mills in C4672 sending one down which broke up north of Comines, while Lt J.H. Colbert and Lt R.W. Turner in D7951 and Lt G.E. Randall and Lt G.V. Learmond in D8086 each sent one down to crash near Wervicq. However, Sgt H.D. Alridge and Sgt M.S. Samson in C4604 were taken prisoner, their aircraft last being seen north of Armentières.

On the 25th, 20 Sqn encountered about 20 enemy aircraft while returning from a bombing raid on Menin. In the ensuing fight Lt D.E. Smith and Prob J. Hills in C4672 sent down a D.VII which crashed and another that went down near Comines. One was destroyed at Gheluvelt by Lt W.M. Thomson and Sgt J.D.C. Summers in C843, who shared another which went down in flames with other aircraft in the patrol. One of the other aircraft involved in this was C4718, flown by Capt H.P. Lale and 2nd Lt F.J. Ralph, who sent down another D.VII to crash just north of Comines. Later that morning Capt K.R. Park and 2nd Lt H. Knowles in C940 of 48 Sqn sent a Rumpler two-seater down over the River Luce at Wiencourt, followed by a DFW two-seater which crashed north of Bayonvillers. Next day Lt S.F.H. Thompson and Lt C.G. Gass in D7896 of 22 Sqn sent a Fokker Dr.I down at Laventie. On the 28th C821 of 88 Sqn was hit by anti-aircraft fire during an attack on Wavrin Aerodrome; pilot Capt A. Hepburn was unhurt but observer Lt C.B. Marshall was wounded.

The fine weather continued, and in the evening of the 29th Capt A. Hepburn and Sgt E. Antcliffe in C821 and Lt W.G. Westwood and 2nd Lt W. Tinsley in D7942, both of of 88 Sqn, each sent a D.VII down, while Lt J.P. Findlay and 2nd Lt R.E. Hasell in E2474 sent a third down in flames, all near Bois-Grenier. That evening 20 Sqn also encountered several D.VIIs; Capt T.P. Middleton and Capt F. Godfrey in C951 sent down one which crashed near Geluwe, and Capt T.C. Traill and Lt R. Gordon-Bennett in D7951 sent another down nearby. Shortly afterwards, Lt J.H. Colbert and Lt R.W. Turner in D7951 shot down a D.VII and Sgt Mech J.J. Cowell and Cpl C.W. Hill in E2471 disposed of another, both northwest of Wervicq.

On 30th July 22 Sqn moved from Serny to Maisoncelle. In further encounters that morning Lt H.R. Little and Lt F.W. Addison in C852 of 88 Sqn sent down an enemy aircraft out of control, followed by another which crashed at Don, while Capt C. Findlay and 2nd Lt B. Digby-Worsley in C4601 of 11 Sqn sent a Pfalz D.III down at Richebourg.

Presentation F.2B D7939 'P', named *Toronto*, was flown by 20 Sqn until 15 September 1918, when it was brought down by anti-aircraft fire near Epehy, 2nd Lt A.B.D. Campbell and Sgt T.A. Stac both being captured. *(C&C)*

Sunbeam Arab-engined C927 'A1' of 'M' Flight was used for long-range artillery spotting during October and November 1918. *(C&C)*

In the evening 20 Sqn was involved in an encounter with some D.VIIs near Bailleul in which Lt P.T. Iaccaci and 2nd Lt H.L. Edwards in D7915 sent down one which crashed, Lt J.M. Purcell and 2nd Lt J. Hills in D7897 sent down another, and Lt V.E. Groom and 2nd Lt E. Hardcastle in D7939 shot two more down in flames. Two aircraft were lost; Lt G.H. Zellers and Sgt J.D. Cormack in C904 and Sgt Mech J.J. Cowell and Cpl C.W. Hill in E2471 were killed when both aircraft were shot down in flames.

During the morning of the last day of the month, aircraft of 88 Sqn were involved in several encounters. The first success fell to Lt G.F. Anderson and Lt T.S. Chilton in D8062, who sent a Pfalz D.III down at Fromelles. Another Pfalz D.III was then despatched in flames south of Merville by Lt W.G. Westwood and 2nd Lt W. Tinsley in D7942. Around the same time, Lt G.R. Poole and Sgt C. Hill in D8064 sent a D.VII down in flames between Estaires and Merville, as did Capt A. Hepburn and Sgt E. Antcliffe in C821 in the Zelobes/Béthune area two hours later. That evening, C859 of 20 Sqn failed to return from an offensive patrol, last being seen southeast of Merville; Lt W.H. Shell and Sgt J.D. Summers were taken prisoner.

August 1918

On 2 August 88 Sqn moved again, this time to Serny, where it remained for nearly three months. By now the tide was beginning to turn against the Germans. Their Army was in a parlous state, and the losses suffered by their air force meant that it was no longer able to mount massed large-scale attacks. Germany now faced a numerous and ever-growing foe that would pose an even greater threat to its battered armies. For the remainder of the war 62 Sqn was primarily used to escort the D.H.9 bombers of 27, 49, 98 and 107 Sqns, a job the Bristol Fighter pilots hated. They also worked on an *ad hoc* basis with the S.E.5as of 1 and 32 Sqns and the Sopwith Camels of 73 Sqn.

The weather was good throughout much of August, so much flying was possible. On the 1st, aircraft 11 Sqn aircraft helped to escort a large bombing raid on Epinoy aerodrome, no casualties being incurred by the unit. Also on that date Lt G.E. Gibbons and 2nd Lt T. Elliott in E2457 of 62 Sqn sent an enemy aircraft down. The following day B1168 of 20 Sqn was shot up during an offensive patrol and force-landed south of Aire with a holed petrol tank, both Lt J.J. Quinn and Prob K. Penrose having been wounded.

Two views of presentation F.2B E2233 'B4' *Alresford Rural District* of 12 Sqn, then based at Estourmel, after Lt J.B. Purefoy's crash on 15 November 1918. *(Philip Jarrett)*

also on a low patrol and having forced down a D.VII which was captured northeast of Lamotte, had their engine hit by ground fire. They were unhurt when they force-landed in a shell hole. In the afternoon Capt C.R. Steele and 2nd Lt E. Vickers in D7909 sent a DFW two-seater down out of control south of Estrées, but later Lt J.C. Nuttall and 2nd Lt B.C. Pearson were both taken prisoner when C786 failed to return from another low offensive patrol, Pearson being wounded. Other casualties that day were Lt H.R. Little and 1/Pte W.J. Spaulding in C870 of 88 Sqn; both were wounded by anti-aircraft fire during an offensive patrol. Other successes that day were a Fokker Dr.I, which broke up, and another sent down out of control at Provin by Capt E.C. Johnston and 2nd Lt J. Rudkin in E2458 of 88 Sqn, and another enemy aircraft was sent down out of control by Lt L. Campbell and 2nd Lt W. Hodgkinson of 62 Sqn.

The 9th was another busy day for the RAF, but Bristol Fighter squadrons had few successes or casualties. In the morning Lt R.K. Harrison and 2nd Lt L.W. King of 11 Sqn in C878 drove a D.VII down out of control between Bray and Péronne, as did Lt J.P. Seabrook and Lt C. Wigglesworth in another aircraft of this squadron. However, Sgt R.S. Hutt and Sgt R.A. Watson in C931 were on escort duty with 57 Sqn when their fuel tank was hit by fire from an enemy aircraft and the pilot was overcome by the fumes. Both were unhurt when C391 crashed in corn near St Just.

In a general engagement with a formation of 12 D.VIIs near Péronne on 10 August, two aircraft of 22 Sqn had successes. Captain J.E. Gurdon DFC and 2nd Lt C.G. Gass in E2454 sent down two aircraft which crashed, as did Lt L.W. King and Lt V.StB. Collins in D7894, the pilots and observers in each aircraft each accounting for one D.VII. Flying in a 62 Sqn aircraft, Lt E.T. Morrow and 2nd Lt L.M. Thompson sent two enemy aircraft down during the day, and 2nd Lt H. Gale and 2nd Lt E. Vickers of 48 Sqn in F5811 sent a D.VII down out of control between Rosières and Chaulnes. When the upper wing centre section of A7226 of 11 Sqn was hit by flak, Lt B.S.B. Thomas and 2nd Lt C.E. Spinks were unhurt when they ran into barbed wire in the ensuing forced landing at Monchy-au-Bois.

On the morning of the 11th an 88 Sqn patrol engaged a formation of 25 D.VIIs and a fierce fight ensued. Captain C. Findlay and 2nd Lt B. Digby-Worsley in C4601 sent two D.VIIs down out of control at Cléry, as did Lt W.A. Wheeler and Lt G.N. Howard between Rancourt and Suzanne. In this same area, Lt A.R. Stedman and AM T. Proctor in C852 sent two more down, one

On the 3rd, 61 Sqn sent three enemy aircraft down, the crews involved being Lt G.E. Gibbons and 2nd Lt T. Elliott in E2457, Lt W.K. Swayze and 2nd Lt W.E. Hall in D7945 and 2nd Lt L. Campbell and 2nd Lt W. Hodgkinson in an unidentified F.2B. Early in the day Capt H.A. Oaks and 2nd Lt H. Knowles in F6094 of 48 Sqn sent down an Albatros two-seater which crashed at Aveluy on the Allied side of the lines. Rain then intervened for a while but, on the morning of the 6th, Lt A. Williamson and Pte E. Hoare of 88 Sqn in C4720 drove down a D.VII near Ploegsteert, and Capt C. Findlay and 2nd Lt B. Digby-Worsley in C4601 sent another down in flames nearby. On the 7th, 62 Sqn moved from Planques to Croisette.

Early on the 8th the Battle of Amiens opened with a deafening artillery barrage by more than 2,000 guns. The RAF was heavily involved in the fighting that followed, suffering far more casualties that day than on any other day in the entire war. A 22 Sqn patrol was escorting 18 D.H.4s on a bombing raid to Somain when it engaged ten enemy aircraft that attempted to attack the bombers in the Vitry area. Captain W.J.F. Harvey and Capt D.E. Waight in the leading aircraft, E2466, sent down a Pfalz D.III which crashed near the railway, and another in flames, the latter being shared with E2454. Another was sent down out of

control by Lt O.StC. Harris and 2nd Lt S.G. Birch in C978, and Lt H.H. Beddow and 2nd Lt W.A. Cowie in D7908 did likewise. Another was sent down in a vertical dive and smoking south of Douai by Lt L.W. King and Lt V.StB. Collins in D7894. Lieutenant S.F.H. Thompson and Sgt R.M. Fletcher in E2477 destroyed a Fokker Dr.I near Dechy when its tailplane collapsed. Near the railway just outside Brebières Lt T.H. Newsome and Sgt H.C. Hunt in C4706 shot down a D.VII, and then the observer sent a Pfalz D.III down in flames. Captain J.E. Gurdon and 2nd Lt C.G. Gass in E2454 drove an Albatros D.V down out of control at Douai, followed by a Pfalz D.III in flames near Vitry, the latter shared with E2466.

A busy but unhappy day was had by 48 Sqn. Early in the morning 2nd Lt B.E. Sharwood-Smith and 2nd Lt J.N. Kier in C876 left on a low-level offensive patrol, but their aircraft caught fire due to a machine gun bullet in the rear tank. Although they both managed to get out unharmed, the aircraft was destroyed. A little while later, on a similar patrol, 2nd Lt B.J. McCutcheon and 2nd Lt V.S. Gray in D8061 were both killed. Captain C.R. Steele and 2nd Lt E. Vickers in F5811 then destroyed a DFW two-seater between Rosières and Chaulnes, but another aircraft was lost when Lt C. Imeretinsky and Lt A. Urinowski in C947,

F.2B E2479 'T' of 62 Sqn after coming down under control near Cambrai in the early afternoon of 1 September 1918. Its crew, 2nd Lt L.B. Raymond and 2nd Lt D.S. Hamilton, became prisoners of war. The decorated wheel covers are noteworthy. *(Trevor Henshaw)*

of which crashed and the other was last seen out of control. Lieutenant A. Williamson and Pte E. Hoare in C787 shot one down in flames at Combles, while Lt G.R. Poole and Sgt E. Antcliffe in C821 sent down two, one of which crashed while the other went down out of control. Two D.VIIs were also accounted for by Capt E.C. Johnston and 2nd Lt J. Rudkin in E2458; one crashed and the other went down out of control at Rancourt. In the evening Lt W.G. Westwood and 2nd Lt W. Tinsley in D7942 drove a D.VII down out of control near Barleux, as did Capt K.R. Simpson and Sgt C. Hill in D8064. Captain C. Findlay and 2nd Lt B. Digby-Worsley in C4601 disposed of two more in flames, and another went down out of control at Méricourt, while Lt A. Williamson and Pte E. Hoare in E2183 sent yet another down out of control at Herbécourt. In attacks on observation balloons by 20 Sqn, Lt E.W. Sweeney and 2nd Lt C.G. Boothroyd in C987 burned one on the ground south of Heule, and Capt H.P. Lale and 2nd Lt J. Hills in E2467 sent one down in flames west of Courtrai.

In other combats that day Lt C.W.M. Thompson and 2nd Lt J. Amos of 22 Sqn in C1035 sent a D.VII down out of control southeast of Arras, and Capt W.J.F. Harvey and Capt D.E. Waight did likewise in E2466 near Armentières. An Albatros was shot down near Péronne by Lt H.A. Hay and 2nd Lt E.J. Norris of 11 Sqn in E2476. Lieutenant R.H. Davis and 2nd Lt E.G. Locke in D8057 of 48 Sqn sent a D.VII

down out of control at Péronne, but 2nd Lt H. Knowles, the observer in another 48 Sqn aircraft, was hit during combat and died of this wounds.

By the 12th the enemy was in retreat on the ground and was losing the battle in the air, though still fighting bravely. Flying in D7942, Lt W.G. Westwood and 2nd Lt W. Tinsley of 88 Sqn sent a Fokker D.VII down out of control at La Chapellette. Lieutenant A.B. Cort and 2nd Lt J.N. Mitchell of 62 Sqn were both killed in E2468 when it was shot down in flames north of Péronne, both crew members falling out when it turned on its back. Two enemy aircraft were sent down out of control by Lt W.K. Swayze and 2nd Lt W.E. Hall of 62 Sqn in D7945.

The 13th was another heavy day for the Bristol Fighters. Near Péronne, while escorting a bombing raid, Lt E.S. Coler and 2nd Lt C.W. Gladman of 11 Sqn in D7912 saw about 20 enemy scouts, so Coler dived down and fired a burst at close range into a D.VII, which went down in flames. His gun then suffered a stoppage while he was attacking a second, so he pulled out of his dive because he was being attacked from the rear. Gladman took the opportunity to get in a burst at an enemy aircraft, which went down in a spin. By then Coler had freed the stoppage, and he fired at another D.VII which crossed in front of him at close range. This too went down in flames. Gladman was wounded in the shoulder shortly after this, but by manoeuvring his gun with his left

arm he managed to send a further one down in flames.

During the morning Lt C.W.M. Thompson and 2nd Lt J. Amos in C1035 of 22 Sqn sent a Pfalz D.III down out of control, while Lt H.H. Beddow and 2nd Lt T.J. Birmingham in E2499 despatched two more at Auberchicourt. Some time later a 22 Sqn patrol on escort duty attacked a large formation of Fokker D.VIIs and Pfalz D.IIIs. Lieutenant S.F.H. Thompson and Sgt R.M. Fletcher of 22 Sqn in E2477 shot down a Fokker Dr.I, a Fokker D.VII was sent down out of control southeast of Douai and another D.VII crashed in the Bois de Loison. While on escort duty, Lt F.C. Stanton and 2nd Lt C.J. Tolman in E2500 of 22 Sqn shot down a D.VII which crashed southwest of Auberchicourt, and another was sent down in flames by the observer and crashed south of Sancourt. Captain W.J.F. Harvey and Capt D.E. Waight in E2466 of 22 Sqn shot down a Rumpler C, following this with a Pfalz D.III down out of control two miles northwest of Cambrai. While escorting D.H.4s of 18 Sqn, Capt J.E. Gurdon DFC and 2nd Lt C.G. Gass of 22 Sqn in E2454 sent a D.VII down out of control near Auberchicourt.

Other squadrons also claimed enemy aircraft. Captain C.R. Steele and Lt J.B. Jameson in C940 of 48 Sqn claimed a D.VII destroyed and two others sent down out of control east of Roye at 17:00. Another 48 Sqn crew, 2nd Lt O. O'Connor and 2nd Lt G.K. Hodgetts in E2480, sent a D.VII

Bristol F.2B E2529 on loan to the 3rd Sqn, Australian Flying Corps, around September-October 1918. *(Colin Owers)*

down out of control east of Ham at 19:55, but in another 48 Sqn aircraft observer Capt M.S. Anthony was wounded.

Lieutenant F.G. Harlock and 2nd Lt A.S. Draisey in C4718 of 20 Sqn were lagging behind the formation when they were attacked by a D.VII. It was shot down by the observer and seen to crash near Quesnoy at 19:05. In another 20 Sqn aircraft, D8086, Capt S. Dalrymple and Lt G.V. Learmond shot down two Albatros scouts, and Capt G.E. Gibbons and 2nd Lt T. Elliott in E2457 of 62 Sqn claimed a two-seater destroyed near Bullecourt at 10:25.

Captain W.E. Staton and 2nd Lt L.E. Mitchell in D7899 of 62 Sqn claimed an unidentified enemy aircraft which crashed near Récourt at 17:05, and Capt E.C. Johnston and 2nd Lt J. Rudkin in D8064 of 88 Sqn sent a D.VII down out of control near Provin at 16:10.

On the 14th Lt W.A. Wheeler and Sgt C. Hill in C774 of 88 Sqn sent a D.VII down out of control near Wavrin at 10:00, while Lt A. Williamson and Pte E. Hoare in E2183 sent another D.VII down out of control near Dompierre at 17:45. Another 88 Sqn aircraft, C852, left on offensive patrol at 16:55 and was last seen in combat at 17:45, going down vertically near the Amiens-St Quentin road; Lt A.R. Stedman and 2nd Lt G.R. Howard both became prisoners. In return, Capt D. Latimer and Sgt A. Newlands in D7993 of 20 Sqn shot down two Pfalz D.IIIs which crashed near Dadizeele, and Lt G.E. Randall and Lt G.V. Learmond in D8086 sent a Pfalz D.III down out of control in the same area. Also involved in the combat near Dadizeele was C987 of 20 Sqn, which was posted as missing; Lt D.E. Smith was killed and Lt J. Hills was taken prisoner. Captain H.P. Lale and 2nd Lt F.J. Ralph in E2467 of 20 Sqn sent a D.VII down out of control near Dadizeele at 18:30, and Lt W.M. Thomson and Lt M.A. Mckenzie in E2154 of 20 Sqn also shot down a D.VII, which crashed east of Dadizeele, and a two-seater was sent down

out of control in the Courtrai-Menin-Dadizeele area.

At 07:10 Lt E.S. Coler and 2nd Lt C.W. Gladman in D7912 of 11 Sqn left on escort duty. Their machine was damaged by an enemy aircraft and force-landed at Vert Galand; both occupants were wounded. At 10:50 Capt W.J.F. Harvey and Capt D.E. Waight in E2466 of 22 Sqn sent a two-seater down out of control one mile southwest of Lille, and at 17:45 Lt C. Foster and Lt B.H. Smyth in E2153 of 88 Sqn shot down a D.VII in flames at Dompierre.

By next day, the fighting at Amiens was drawing to a close. The next F.2B losses did not occur until the 19th, when C926 and D8027 of 48 Sqn crashed after becoming locked together 10,000ft above Péronne, killing 2nd Lt E.S. Glasse and 2nd Lt C.N. Woodend in C926, and Lt R.H. Davis and 2nd Lt E.G. Locke in D8027. On 15 August Lt W.M. Thomson MC and Lt M.A. McKenzie of 20 Sqn in E2154 shot down a D.VII which crashed at Beselare at 07:10, and at 07:35 Lt W.H. Markham and 2nd Lt E.S. Harvey in E2155, also of 20 Sqn, shot a kite balloon down in flames west of Comines. Markham was wounded but Harvey was unhurt. Captain W.E. Staton and 2nd Lt L.E. Mitchell of 62 Sqn in D7899 sent a D.VII down out of control near Bullecourt at 10:30.

The next day 22 Sqn went on an offensive patrol to Lille, and Lt I.O. Stead and 2nd Lt W.A. Cowie in B1330 sent a Pfalz D.III down out of control south-southeast of Lille at 10:35. Lieutenant H.H. Beddow and 2nd Lt T.J. Birmingham in D7908 shot down a Fokker D.VII and a Pfalz D.III, both of which were seen to crash near Lille at 10:30. Flying in E2466, Capt W.J.F. Harvey and Capt D.E. Waight sent down a Pfalz D.III which crashed between Fretin and Lesquin, south-southeast of Lille, at 10:35. A two-seater was shot down near Fresnoy at 10:30 by Lt C.E. Hurst and Sgt H.C. Hunt in F5824.

Enemy aircraft were also found by 11 Sqn. A two-seater was shot down by Lt N.B. Scott and 2nd Lt H.N. Power in C775 and crashed at Vaux, while Lt N.B. Scott and 2nd Lt L.W. King in C775 shot down an Albatros scout which crashed southeast of Cambrai at 10:30, and a D.VII was sent down out of control near Douai at 10:45.

Next day, E2183 of 88 Sqn was damaged in action; Lt A. Williamson was unhurt but Pte E. Hoare was wounded. At 10:30 Capt E.C. Johnston and 2nd Lt J. Rudkin in C4867 of 88 Sqn sent a D.VII down out of control near Oignies, shared with E2216, flown by Lt K.B. Conn and 2nd Lt B.H. Smyth, who also saw another D.VII go down out of control. A D.VII was driven down by at Oignies by Lt A. Williamson and Pte T. Proctor in E2153 at 10:20.

Successful offensive patrols were flown by 20 and 22 Sqns on the 21st. With 22 Sqn, Lt T.W. Martin and Sgt G. Shannon in C1040 sent a Fokker D.VII down out of control north of Cambrai at 19:45; Lt L.W. King and Lt V.StB. Collins in E2454 sent a D.VII down out of control in the Albert-Cambrai area at 19:45; and Capt W.J.F. Harvey and Capt D.E. Waight in E2466 sent a two-seater down out of control near Ervillers at 14:10.

Fifteen enemy aircraft intercepted by 20 Sqn near Menin were soon increased to 25 as others arrived to join the fray. Three Pfalz D.IIIs claimed by Lt D. Latimer and Sgt A Newlands in D7993 crashed at Menin, Dadizeele and Gheluwe between 19:10 and 19:15, one being shared with E2158, flown by Lt J.H. Colbert and 2nd Lt H.L. Edwards, and E2467, flown by Capt H.P. Lale and 2nd Lt F.J. Ralph. The former duo shot down a D.VII near the Roulers-Menin road just north of Menin, and the latter pair claimed a Pfalz D.III which broke up and crashed northeast of Gheluwe, a D.VII which crashed west of the Menin-Roulers railway, and an Albatros sent down out of control.

By now the Allies were on the advance, and Albert was recaptured on the 22nd after heavy fighting. While escorting a formation of 27 Sqn aircraft raiding Cambrai, F.2Bs of 62 Sqn met enemy fighters and B1216 sent a Pfalz down out of control at Pronville before having its port aileron shot away. Although it was followed back to the lines by four enemy aircraft, Lt C. Allday and 2nd Lt L. Millar were both unhurt. Flying in C895, Capt E.T. Morrow and 2nd Lt L.M. Thompson sent a D.VII down out of control and smoking, and another broke up near Pronville. But their petrol tank was hit, and the aircraft caught fire. The observer fought the flames on descent to a forced landing at Ficheux, but C895 was completely destroyed. Morrow was wounded in the leg. At 07:40 Lt S.A.R. Solomon and 2nd Lt L. Egan in C953 sent down a D.VII out of control near Pronville, but the F.2B was badly shot up in the combat. The crew force landed at Dainville, Solomon being wounded in the leg. The aircraft went off to be rebuilt. Captain W.E. Staton and 2nd Lt L.E. Mitchell in D7899 shot down a D.VII in flames at Pronville at 0945; in D7948 Lt A.W. Blowes and 2nd Lt H.S. Hind sent two Pfalz D.IIIs down out of control near Pronville at 07:45. A D.VII was shot down by Lt R.O. Schallaire and 2nd Lt R. Lowe in E2182 and crashed at Bourlon-Inchy at 07:40. Captain G.E.G. Gibbons MC and 2nd Lt T. Elliott in E2457 saw one of their victims, a D.VII, crash west of Pronville, and another went down in flames near Aubercourt at 07:40.

Lieutenant H.H. Beddow and 2nd Lt T.J. Birmingham of 22 Sqn in D7908 sent a Halberstadt C down out of control and emitting smoke northeast of Bailleul at 19:10, shared with E2466 (Capt W.J.F. Harvey and Capt D.E. Waight) and F5820 (Lt I.O. Stead and 2nd Lt W.A. Cowie).

An offensive patrol sent out by 20 Sqn in the morning of the 22nd ran into Fokker D.VIIs near Comines, and Lt G.E. Randall and Sgt A. Newlands in E2158 were attacked by four of them, one of which was shot down by the observer and crashed east of Comines at 08:40. However, D7993 was shot down near Westroosebeke by Ltn Nebgen of Jasta7; Capt D. Latimer was taken prisoner and Lt T.C. Noel was killed. A D.VII was shot down in flames over Bapaume at 07:40 by C.R. Smythe and Lt W.T. Barnes of 11 Sqn in D7981.

On the 23rd the Battle of Bapaume began along a 33-mile front with an early morning assault. Rebuild F.2B F6158 of 62 Sqn was badly shot up in combat between Denain and Douai; Lt J.K. Stewart and 2nd Lt E.M. Buckley were unhurt. When B1330 of 22 Sqn was shot down by flak near Arras at 07:30, Lt J.S. Tarbolton was slightly wounded but Sgt T. Hooton was unhurt.

On the 24th, 48 Sqn was the victim of the most effective air attack on a British airfield

Above and below: **Two studies of presentation F.2B F4306 *Burgate* of 'L' Flight in the 1st Wing.** *(Philip Jarrett)*

of the entire war. Seven aircraft from Schlachtstaffel 16 bombed Bertangles and set five hangars on fire. Nine Bristol Fighters were destroyed in them, as well as S.E.5a E4012 of 84 Sqn. Fifteen of 48 Sqn's pilots and observers were wounded, two of whom, 2nd Lt A. Urinowski and Lt J.B. Jameson, later died. The wounded were: Lt T. Beck, Lt H. Hood, Lt C.G. Imeretinsky, 2nd Lt J.N.B. Kier, Lt F.D. Kilby, Lt M.F.J. Mahony, 2nd Lt H.Y. Lewis, Capt H.A. Oaks, Capt C.R. Steele, 2nd Lt D.T. Turnbull, Lt E. Vickers, 2nd Lt E.G. Weller and 2nd Lt S.H. Whipple (USAS). The official history, typically, makes no mention of non-commissioned personnel casualties. The Bristol Fighters destroyed are given as C886, C940, C4629, D7909, E2472, E2480, F5811, F6094 and F6118. The squadron moved to Boisdinghem to re-equip and was back in action two days later.

On the 25th, F.2Bs of 22 Sqn were escorting de Havillands to Péronne. At 18:30 Lt O.StC. Harris and 2nd Lt J.H. Umney MC in C978 sent a Pfalz D.III down out of control and smoking after the observer emptied a Lewis gun drum into it. A Pfalz D.III shot down by Lt C.E. Hurst and Sgt H.C. Hunt in C1035 crashed west of Péronne. They also claimed a Fokker D.VII which crashed near Maricourt and a Pfalz D.III sent down out of control. At 18:30 Lt L.N. Caple and 2nd Lt S.G. Birch in F5824 sent a D.VII spinning down out of control.

On the 25th, D8088 of 11 Sqn, flown by Capt A. Morrison and Sgt R. Allan, sent a D.VII down out of control in Havrincourt Wood at 07:40, as did Lt F.C.B. Greene and 2nd Lt L.K. Ward at the same time.

On the 26th 20 Sqn finally left Boisdinghem, joining the 22nd Wing, 5th Brigade, at Vignacourt. At this time RAF activity was restricted by low cloud.

The 27th was another busy day for 22 Sqn. An offensive patrol found numerous enemy fighters, and Lt T.H. Newsome and Lt C. Partington in C4706 shot down a kite balloon in flames at Hénin-Liétard-Quierry-La-Motte at 17:30. Lieutenant H.H. Beddow and 2nd Lt T.J. Birmingham in D7908 sent a D.VII down out of control near Vitry at 06:30, and Lt F.G. Gibbons and Lt J. McDonald in E2454 shot a D.VII down out of control near Douai at 13:45. Captain S.F.H. Thompson and Sgt R.M. Fletcher in E2477 sent two D.VIIs down out of control, while Lt F.C. Stanton and 2nd Lt C.J. Tolman in E2500 shot down another Fokker D.VII, both southeast of Senlemont at 14:00. In the same encounter and location, Lt L.W. King and Lt V.StB. Collins and Lt T.W. Martin and Sgt J.H. Hall both shot down a D.VII out of control. However, Lt F.M. Sellars became a prisoner of war and 2nd Lt T.B. Collis was killed in E2514, which was last seen going down under control southeast of Arras. It was claimed by Ltn H. Frommherz of Jasta 27,

Bristol F.2B F4438 of 'P' Flight in late 1918 or early 1919. *(Philip Jarrett)*

who kept its tail fabric as a trophy. Heavy fighting continued, but by now the Germans were being steadily pushed back despite their best efforts.

An early patrol by 88 Sqn on 29 August resulted in Capt A. Hepburn and 2nd Lt H.G. Eldon in C821 sending a D.VII down out of control east of Lille 08:30, and Lt W.A. Wheeler and 2nd Lt W. Tinsley in D8064 claimed another Fokker D.VII down out of control at Engles, east of Lille. A D.VII was sent down out of control in Bourlon Wood at 18:30 by Lt C.R. Smythe and Lt W.T. Barnes of 11 Sqn in D7981, but 2nd Lt E.W.S. Sharpe was wounded in the encounter. At 05:40 E2453 of 22 Sqn left on an offensive patrol and failed to return. It was last seen going south over the Arras-Cambrai road, apparently under control; Lt J.J. Borrowman and 2nd Lt J. Amos were both killed.

Next day, Capt E.S. Coler and 2nd Lt B.E.J.D. Tuke of 11 Sqn in E2215 destroyed a Pfalz D.XII and a Fokker D.VII northwest of Havrincourt at 18:40. An enemy aircraft was sent down out of control near Douai by Lt O.StC. Harris and 2nd Lt S.G. Birch in C978 of 22 Sqn. Although D7981 of 11 Sqn was damaged by flak over Bourlon Wood, Lt C.R. Smythe and Lt W.T. Barnes were unhurt.

On the last day of August E2469 of 48 Sqn was hit by flak and forced to land in bad country at Elverdinghe at 20:00; 2nd Lt J.B. Cowan and Sgt R.L.G. White were unhurt. At 17:10 22 Sqn found some D.VIIs, and Lt C.E. Hurst and Sgt H.C. Hunt in F5824 sent a D.VII down out of control southeast of Vitry, and Lt I.O. Stead and Capt D.E. Waight in F5820 shot down a D.VII near Douai, both at 17:10.

September 1918

On the first day of September 62 Sqn lost E2479 when it failed to return from an offensive patrol. It was last seen going down under control near Cambrai at 13:40; 2nd Lt L.B. Raymond became a PoW and 2nd Lt D.S. Hamilton was killed. Bristol Fighter C843 of 20 Sqn crashed at Villers Carbonel at 15:33 under shellfire and was wrecked, but Lt F.E. Finch and Prob E.S. Harvey escaped unhurt. While returning from escorting a raid on Solesmes D7948, flown by Lt A.W. Blowes and 2nd Lt H.S. Hind, was attacked by a D.VII which the observer sent down out of control northeast of Cambrai at 13:30. At the same time Lt C. Allday and 2nd Lt T. Elliott in E2218 shot down a D.VII in flames east of Cambrai. While on an offensive patrol E2494 became involved in a general combat east of Cambrai

and its controls were shot through. It was force-landed near Monchy-aux-Bois; Lt L.W. Hudson was unhurt, but 2nd Lt J. Hall was wounded. Finally, Lt G.K. Runciman and Sgt H.H. Inglis in E2497 were returning from escorting a raid on Solesmes when they were attacked by three D.VIIs, one of which was sent down out of control by the observer northeast of Cambrai at 13:30.

Captain A. Hepburn and 2nd Lt H.G. Eldon of 88 Sqn in C821 shot down a D.VII which crashed and burned east of Beselere at 19:10. At 11:00 Lt G.L. Barritt and 2nd Lt R.H.G. Boys in E2521 of 'L' Flight left for a photographic mission and were attacked by enemy aircraft over the Canal de la Sensée. The F.2B was seen to go down out of control and both men were taken prisoner.

Next day, the British Armies fired no fewer than 943,857 shells on the retreating German forces. Number 22 Sqn was very active, attacking enemy troops and flying offensive patrols, and Lt F.G. Gibbons and Sgt G. Shannon in D7894 encountered 15 enemy aircraft engaged in trench strafing. The pilot shot down a D.VII, and another was sent down out of control by the observer near Haynecourt at 11:15. Joining in general combat with S.E.5as and Camels over the Arras-Cambrai road, Lt H.H. Beddow and 2nd Lt T.J. Birmingham in D7908 shot down a D.VII, while Capt S.F.H. Thompson and Sgt R.M. Fletcher in E2477 shot down a D.VII near Haynecourt at 11:15. There were two losses. Captain B.L. Dowling and Lt V.StB. Collins in D7990 were last seen east of Cambrai during an offensive patrol; both were killed. After E2516 had its petrol tank shot through and its observer, 2nd Lt W.A. Cowie, was wounded in the leg, a D.VII attempted to follow them but was shot down by Cowie over the Arras-Cambrai road. The pilot, Lt I.O. Stead, who was unhurt, force-landed in a shelled area.

In 48 Sqn, which was equally busy, 2nd Lt J.B. Cowan and 2nd Lt T.L. Jones in C943 shot down a D.VII in flames west of Lille at 19:30, and sent down another out of control east of Menin at 19:45, their own

Arab-engined Bristol F.2Bs of 'L' Flight lined up in alphabetical order, from 'A' to 'E', in 1918. Third from the left is C9873 'C', built by the Gloucestershire Aircraft Co, which passed to 8 Sqn post-war. The curious shape of this photograph is due to it being positioned diagonally across the front of a 1918 Christmas card sent from the unit. *(Philip Jarrett)*

aircraft being damaged in combat. In E2527 Lt H.A. Cole and 2nd Lt J.W. London sent a D.VII down out of control 'falling like a leaf' over Menin. At 18:10 E2214 left on an offensive patrol but failed to return, probably having been shot down east of Lille at 19:15; 2nd Lt O. O'Connor and 2nd Lt J.J. Ambler were both captured. Also having left at 18:10, E2455 was last seen east of Lille at 19:15; 2nd Lt I.M.B. McCulloch became a PoW and 2nd Lt L.P. Perry was killed. A D.VII was sent down out of control by 2nd Lt W.S. Rycroft and 2nd Lt H.C. Wood in E2492, having been hit by the observer north of Menin at 19:30.

On the 3rd the German Army evacuated Lens. Air activity continued apace, the RAF engaging German fighter cover for the troops and playing a significant role in the advancing Allied armies. The main advance was then temporarily halted to enable the forces to regroup after the enormous progress by then achieved. The RAF fighter squadrons were ordered to stop low flying and bombing, and switch mainly to providing cover and protecting the corps machines. There was inevitably some tough fighting ahead as the enemy pulled back to the main Hindenburg Line, manned by its best and most formidable troops.

On 3 September 20 Sqn mounted an offensive patrol and caught German fighters over Havrincourt Wood at 17:45. A D.VII or Pfalz D.III was shot down by Lt P.T. Iaccaci and Lt A. Mills in E2470 and broke up. In the confusion, the Fokker D.VII or a Pfalz D.III claimed by Lt G.E. Randall and Lt G.V. Learmond in E2249 could have been the same aircraft. Lieutenant C. Oberst and Lt R. Gordon-Bennett in D7915 hit a Pfalz D.III which broke up, and another went down out of control. Last seen in combat over Havrincourt Wood, Lt W.F. Washington and 2nd Lt K. Penrose in

B1344 were killed. After sending a D.VII down out of control south of Havrincourt Wood, Capt H.P. Lale and 2nd Lt F.J. Ralph in E2181 failed to return. Lale was unhurt but Ralph was killed.

Captain G.E. Gibbons and 2nd Lt T. Elliott in E2457 of 62 Sqn sent two D.VIIs down out of control north of Cambrai at 18:45, and Capt W.E. Staton MC DFC and 2nd Lt L.E. Mitchell in D7899, while escorting 27 Sqn's D.H.9s, shot down a D.VII southeast of Marquion at 18:30. Lieutenant C.W.M. Thompson and 2nd Lt G. McCormack of 22 Sqn in F5820 shot down a Pfalz Scout west of Marquion.

On 4 September offensive patrols and escorts for bombers kept many F.2Bs in the air throughout the day. Two D.VIIs were accounted for by 11 Sqn; Lt C.R. Smythe and 2nd Lt W.T. Barnes in B8941 shot down a D.VII in flames south of St Hilaire at 10:45, and at the same time Lt E.N. Underwood and 2nd Lt G.S. Turner in D7906 sent a D.VII down out of control east of Cambrai. In the morning 88 Sqn sent out an offensive patrol which found several German fighters. Flying in E2153, Lt K.B. Conn and 2nd Lt B.H. Smyth sent a D.VII down out of control at Seclin; Lt K.B. Conn and Sgt C.M. Maxwell in E2216 accounted for a Fokker Dr.I down out of control at Provin; Lt C. Findlay and 2nd Lt G.T. Gauntlett in C4601 sent two D.VIIs down out of control south of Don; and Lt C. Foster and 2nd Lt B.H. Smyth in E2153 sent a Fokker Dr.I down out of control at Provin. A D.VII was shot down in flames at Seclin by Capt E.C. Johnston and 2nd Lt W.J.N. Grant in C4867, and they sent another down out of control at Phalempin, plus a Dr.I down out of control at Provin. Their F.2B was badly shot up by enemy fire. In the evening Lt K.B. Conn and 2nd Lt B. Digby-Worsley in E2216 sent a Fokker

Dr.I down out of control near Armentières at 18:45.

Aircraft of 62 Sqn were out at the same time as those of 88 Sqn, and just after crossing the lines they were attacked by about 25 Fokker D.VIIs. Captain W.E. Staton and 2nd Lt L.E. Mitchell in D7899 sent a D.VII down out of control at Marquette at 09:30. In a combat north of Cambrai Lt W.K. Swayze and 2nd Lt W.E. Hall in D7945 suffered engine failure, being attacked and forced to land. Both men were captured. Lieutenant R.O. Schallaire and 2nd Lt R. Lowe in E2182 brought down a D.VII three miles north of Cambrai, while Capt G.E. Gibbons and 2nd Lt T. Elliott in E2457 shot down a D.VII near Abancourt and sent another down out of control and falling upside down.

During the day 11 Sqn was also operating in the same area; Lt A.D. Shannon and 2nd Lt C.E. Spinks in C955 sent a D.VII down east of Cambrai at 10:45, and Lt C.B. Seymour and Lt W.J. Gillespie in F5814 sent another down over the Douai-Cambrai road at 13:30. In the evening Capt A. Morrison and Sgt R. Allen in D8088 shot down a D.VII which crashed at Baralle, north of Hamel, at 18:15, while Lt L. Arnott and Sgt C.W. Cooke in F6131 shot down another D.VII at Auberchicourt. Lieutenant G.F. Manning and 2nd Lt P.A. Clayson of 48 Sqn in E2511 shot down a Fokker D.VII which crashed north of Armentières at 09:40; Clayson was wounded.

On 5 September offensive patrols helped to keep German fighters away from the bombers and corps machines. In 88 Sqn, Capt A. Hepburn and 2nd Lt H.G. Eldon in C821 sent a D.VII down out of control north of Douai, and another crashed in flames near Armentières. A D.VII shot down by Lt V. Voss and Sgt C. Hill in D7942 crashed near Armentières, and Lt K.B.

The pilot of F.2B B1152 'C' of 22 Sqn runs up his engine against the chocks in readiness for a patrol from Villeneuve-des-Vertues on 1 April 1918, the day the RAF came into being. The overpainted vertical white squadron identification bands on either side of the roundel can just be discerned.

Conn; 2nd Lt B. Digby-Worsley in E2216 sent another D.VII down out of control northeast of Armentières; and Lt C. Findlay and 2nd Lt G.T. Gauntlett in C4601 disposed of a D.VII east of Perenchies.

While 48 Sqn was out on offensive patrol around noon, Capt H.A. Oaks and Lt T. Beck in D7984 shot down a D.VII in flames and sent another down out of control between Courtrai and Roulers at 12:40, but 2nd Lt R. Beesley and 2nd Lt A.M. Miller in E2495 failed to return.

In the afternoon 20 Sqn went on patrol and Capt H.P. Lale and Lt H.L. Edwards in E2467 fired on a D.VII and saw it break up southeast of Cambrai at 15:20. Flying in E2249, Lt G.E. Randall and Lt G.V Learmond sent a D.VII down smoking in the same position, and 2nd Lt R.B. Campbell and 2nd Lt C.G. Russell in E2512 did likewise.

In the evening 22 Sqn was out and found D.VIIs near Douai. Lieutenant F.G. Gibbons and Sgt G. Shannon in E2454 sent a D.VII down out of control, as did Lt H.H. Beddow and Lt W.V. Tyrrell in D7908. Another D.VII was sent down out of control by Lt C.W.M. Thompson and 2nd Lt G. McCormack in F5820, and Capt S.F.H. Thompson and Sgt R.M. Fletcher in E2477 shot down a D.VII in flames.

There was no let-up on the following day, and F.2B squadrons formed part of the intensive air cover provided over the front by British fighters. Around 08:45, D.VIIs were intercepted and Capt A.T. Iaccaci and Sgt A Newlands in E2213 sent one down out of control between Cambrai and St Quentin, while another crashed northeast of St Quentin, close to a wood near the St Quentin Canal. A D.VII was sent down out of control by 2nd Lt A.B.D. Campbell and 2nd Lt D.M. Calderwood in D7939, and Capt H.P. Lale and 2nd Lt H.L. Edwards in E2181 shot two D.VIIs down in flames near St Quentin. Also hunting in the Cambrai area was 22 Sqn, and Lt L.N. Caple and 2nd Lt S.C. Barrow in E2303 sent a D.VII down out of control. However, F5820 was shot down by flak and crashed; Lt L.C. Rowney was unhurt but Sgt J. Goodman was injured.

At 08:45 Lt C.B. Seymour and 2nd Lt E.G. Bugg of 11 Sqn left for a reconnaissance of the Le Cateau area in C4745. Last seen being chased by several enemy aircraft over Cambrai, heading west, it failed to return. The occupants were wounded and taken prisoner. Another F.2B that failed to return was D7906, Lt E.N. Underwood and 2nd Lt C.M. Coleman both being killed. A few hours later, at 10:30, Capt H.A. Hay and Lt A.H. Craig in C937 shot down a D.VII and sent another down out of control west of Cambrai, and Capt E.S. Coler and Lt D.F. Conyngham in E2215 did the same. A D.VII was sent down out of control east of Douai at 18:45 by Lt J.P. Findlay and 2nd Lt W. Tinsley of 88 Sqn in E2474, and Capt A.

Hepburn and 2nd Lt H.G. Eldon in C821 shot down a D.VII out of control and saw part of its top wing coming loose. An F.2B was lost when E2492 of 48 Sqn was damaged by flak and force landed near Poperinghe at 19:15; 2nd Lt W.S. Rycroft was injured but 2nd Lt H.C. Wood was unhurt.

The 7th was a quieter day, only Capt H.P. Lale and 2nd Lt H.L. Edwards in E2181 of 20 Sqn finding a Fokker D.VII, which crashed northeast of St Quentin at 18:10. There were no losses until 12 September, when E2527 of 48 Sqn became lost in a thunderstorm at 18:30 and failed to return, the only RAF loss that day; Lt H.A. Cole and 2nd Lt C.R. Gage both became prisoners of war. Rain and low cloud hampered operations until the 15th, when the F.2Bs went out in force again. Captain E.S. Coler and Lt E.J. Corbett in E2215 of 11 Sqn destroyed two D.VIIs two miles west of Esnes at 12:00, but both were wounded in the combat. During that day 20 Sqn was heavily involved. Flying in C951, Lt A.R. Strachan and 2nd Lt D.M. Calderwood shot down a D.VII which crashed near Omissy and sent another down out of control. At 10:20 Lt A.B.D. Campbell and Sgt A.J. Winch in F5816 left to bomb Busigny, and sent a D.VII down out of control northeast of St Quentin; their aircraft was damaged in combat and they force-landed, the observer being injured. A D.VII shot down by Lt W.M. Thomson and 2nd Lt H.L. Edwards in E2154 crashed at Omissy, and they sent another down out of control at 11:20. Lieutenant A.T. Iaccaci and Sgt A Newlands in E2213 shot down a D.VII which crashed and burned south of Lesdins at 11:15 and, five minutes later, a D.VII which crashed south of Morcourt. Captain T.P. Middleton and Lt A. Mills in E2470 shot down a Hannover C-type which crashed near Harly at 17:50, while Lt N.S. Boulton and Lt G.W. Pearce in E2493 sent a D.VII down out of control northeast of St Quentin at 11:10. After E2512 was last seen near St Quentin, Lt F.E. Finch and 2nd Lt C.G. Russell were captured, the pilot being wounded. A final loss for the squadron that day was D7939, which was brought down by flak near Epehy. Both 2nd Lt A.B.D. Campbell and Sgt T.A. Stac were taken prisoner.

At 17:30 Lt G.F. Anderson and 2nd Lt T.S. Chilton of 88 Sqn in E2451 sent a D.VII down out of control east of Seclin. When E2525 of 62 Sqn was shot down near Cambrai at 16:30, Lt T.H. Broadley and 2nd Lt R.H. Dillaway were killed. Pfalz D.XII 2486/18 (later renumbered G/HQ/6), which crashed near Récourt on the Allied side of lines at 17:05, was shared by Lt L. Campbell and 2nd Lt L. Egan and Capt W.E. Staton and 2nd Lt L.E. Mitchell. An unidentified enemy aircraft was sent down out of control at Marquion at 17:05 by 2nd Lt P.S. Manley and Sgt G.F. Hines.

Air activity was back to normal on the 16th. Two aircraft sent on reconnaissance by 11 Sqn failed to return; C878 left at 07:00 and was shot down at Fontaine at 08:45, killing 2nd Lt L. Arnott and 2nd Lt G.L. Bryars, while C946 was shot down near Quievy at 08:50 wounding Lt J.C. Stanley. He and 2nd Lt E.J. Norris were taken prisoner.

Offensive patrols were also sent out by 11 Sqn. Although D8088 was damaged by flak between Cambrai and Le Cateau, Capt A. Morrison and Sgt R. Allan were unhurt. Captain E.S. Coler and Lt E.J. Corbett in E2215 shot down a Pfalz D.XII and a Fokker D.VII east of Cambrai, but their radiator was hit and they force-landed at Beugny, neither being injured. In D7978 Lt B.S.B. Thomas and Lt W.T. Barnes shot down a D.VII which crashed north of Cambrai at 18:50, and another which crashed south of Cambrai at 19:00.

Enemy fighters were found by 20 Sqn at around 08:15. Three D.VIIs were claimed in the St Quentin area by Lt W.M. Thomson and 2nd Lt H.L. Edwards in E2154, one being shared with Lt A.R. Strachan and 2nd Lt D.M. Calderwood in C951. A D.VII was sent down out of control west of Lesdin by Lt N.S. Boulton and Sgt J. Dodds in E2467, and Lt A.T. Iaccaci and Sgt A. Newlands in E2213 shot down a D.VII which also crashed west of Lesdin.

An early patrol by 22 Sqn resulted in no claims, but F5824 (Lt T.D. Smith and 2nd Lt S.C. Barrow) and C978 (Lt L.N. Caple and Lt G.S. Routhier) were damaged in combat. During an offensive patrol in the afternoon Lt T.W. Martin and Sgt M Jones in D8089 shot down a D.VII which crashed near Quesnoy Wood at 15:30. However, their aileron cables were shot away and the observer, although wounded, climbed out on to the lower wing to steady the machine. Also damaged by ground fire, it force-landed at 11 Sqn's airfield at Le Quesnoy. Lieutenant F.G. Gibbons and Sgt G. Shannon in E2454 sent a D.VII down out of control in Quesnoy Wood, and 2nd Lt W. Kellow and 2nd Lt H.A. Felton were both killed when E2519 went down near Cambrai.

When 62 Sqn was engaged near Douai, 2nd Lt P.S. Manley and Sgt G.F. Hines sent a D.VII down out of control. Another D.VII was destroyed, but the F.2B involved was shot up, 2nd Lt C.H. Moss being wounded and 2nd Lt R. Lowe escaping injury. When E2244 was shot down in combat ten miles northeast of Douai, 2nd Lt R.N. Stone and 2nd Lt N.F. Adams were both taken prisoner. Also out hunting was 88 Sqn; Lt K.B. Conn and 2nd Lt B. Digby-Worsley in E2216 shot down two D.VIIs northeast of Harbourdin, and Lt H.E. Johnston and 2nd Lt E.S. Harvey in C4718 forced a D.VII down out of control at St Quentin, but their aircraft was damaged and they force-landed at Vignacourt.

The aircraft flown by Lt Ashlin of 11 Sqn, '4' has an improvised overwing mounting for a forward-firing Lewis gun that is reminiscent of the type used on the S.E.5a fighter, but somewhat taller.
(Eric Harlin)

On 17 September 59 Sqn moved from Vert Galand to Beugnâtre with a mixture of R.E.8s and F.2Bs. On that day Lt C.W.M. Thompson and Lt G. McCormack in C1035 shot down in flames a D.VII which crashed southwest of Douai 18:30, and another D.VII was shot down by the observer just north of the railway triangle at Brebières. When Lt F. Jeffreys and Lt F.W. Addison of 88 Sqn in D8062 were attacked by six Fokkers during a photographic sortie near Treizennes they shot down a D.VII in flames and another broke up in the air near Lomelet. Second Lieutenant R.A. Boxall and 2nd Lt L. Millar of 62 Sqn in E2218 force-landed and crashed into a shell hole at Rémy, but 2nd Lt P.S. Manley and Sgt G.F. Hines of the same unit sent a D.VII down out of control. A D.VII shot down by Lt B.S.B. Thomas and Lt W.T. Barnes of 11 Sqn in D7978 crashed just east of Wasnes.

On the following day there was little activity, but C951 of 20 Sqn was damaged in combat at 17:30, Lt A.R. Strachan and Lt B.W. Wilson being unhurt.

On the 19th 11 Sqn moved from Le Quesnoy to Vert Galand. The previous day an attack had begun on the outlying fortifications of the Hindenburg Line, preparatory to the main assault with tanks and full air cover, though the latter was restricted by poor weather for much of that week.

Next day, 20 Sqn was busy covering the offensive, sending out an offensive patrol in mid-morning. Two D.VIIs were sent down out of control over St Quentin by Lt S.L. Walters and Lt T. Kirkpatrick in E2337, while Capt T.P. Middleton and Lt A. Mills in E2246 accounted for two more; a D.VII crashed near Rouvroy and another crashed near Neuville light railway. Flying in E2258, Lt F.G. Harlock and 2nd Lt A.S. Draisey shot down a D.VII which crashed near Mesnil, then sent another down in flames at St Quentin. Lieutenant N.S. Boulton and Sgt E.G. Mitchell in E2493 shot down a D.VII which crashed northeast of St Quentin, and Lt M. McCall and Lt C.G. Boothroyd in D7915 shot down a D.VII which crashed east of the river at Longchamps, then sent another down out of control. However, E2158 was shot down in flames, killing Lt A.R. Strachan and 2nd Lt D.M. Calderwood.

Also out on a sweep was 88 Sqn. Two D.VIIs were claimed destroyed over Quesnoy by Lt G.R. Poole and Sgt C. Hill in C922, one of them being shared with E2533 (Capt E.C. Johnston and 2nd Lt H.R. Goss) and E2216 (Lt K.B. Conn and 2nd Lt B. Digby-Worsley). The last-mentioned team also claimed a D.VII sent

down out of control. Two F.2Bs were lost; D8064 had engine trouble and crashed into a shell hole, but Capt K.R. Simpson and 2nd Lt F.A. Lewis were unhurt. When a bullet pierced E2183's water jacket the engine seized up and the F.2B crash-landed at Strazeele; Lt A. Williamson and 2nd Lt A.C. Craig were also unhurt.

Having left on an offensive patrol at 09:20, Lt M.F.J.R. Mahony and 2nd Lt C.N. Kier of 48 Sqn in E2260 failed to return after a combat over Roubaix at 11:00. Their aircraft came down intact and they were captured. The victory was claimed by Ltn Carl Degelow of Jasta 40.

The 22nd was less hectic. Captain E.C. Johnston and 2nd Lt W.J.N. Grant in E2533 of 88 Sqn shot an LVG down out of control. Next day an evening patrol by 20 Sqn became involved in a dogfight with D.VIIs near St Quentin, and Lt N.S. Boulton and 2nd Lt H.L. Edwards in E2213 attacked a D.VII which broke up, sent another down in flames, and a third fell out of control. A D.VII shot down by Lt A.D. Keirnander and Lt C.G. Boothroyd in E2340 crashed and burned two miles north of St Quentin. Lieutenant E.A. Britton and Sgt R.S. Dodds in E2467 shot down a D.VII which crashed west of Rouvroy and sent another down out of control, but their own aircraft was damaged and the observer wounded. When E2562 was shot down in flames near Villers Outreux, Lt J. Nicholson and 2nd Lt B.W. Wilson were killed.

By now the Allies were preparing for an attack on the Hindenburg Line, and RAF offensive patrols were meeting larger and increasingly aggressive enemy formations.

On 24 September there was widespread activity by the Bristol Fighter squadrons. While performing photo reconnaissance over Bellevue, E2363 of 62 Sqn was damaged by flak; 2nd Lt C. Johnson was unhurt but Sgt C.H. Hampson was wounded. At 09:00 Sgt E. Campbell and Sgt H.O. Taylor in C797 sent a Fokker D.VII down in flames southeast of Havrincourt Wood.

In the afternoon 20 Sqn ran into many enemy fighters. At 16:00 Capt G.H. Hooper and 2nd Lt H.L. Edwards in E2536 shot a D.VII down southeast of Cambrai. Lieutenant G.E. Randal and Lt J. Hackett in E2470 attacked a D.VII which crashed south of Cléry, and another went down out of control west of Busigny. In the same area, Capt T.C. Traill and Lt R. Gordon-Bennett in E2252 also sent a D.VII down out of control. Although E2181 was damaged in combat with enemy fighters, 2nd Lt H.E. Johnstone and 2nd Lt E.C. Harvey were unhurt.

Four enemy aircraft were claimed near Cambrai by 22 Sqn. Lieutenant L.C. Rowney and Lt W.V. Tyrrell in F5823 shot down a D.VII which crashed between Mesnières and Crevecourt, and another went down out of control. Captain S.F.H. Thompson and Sgt R.M. Fletcher in E2477 sent a D.VII down out of control, and Lt C.W.M. Thompson and Lt G. McCormack were wounded in C1035 while on escort duty but sent a D.VII down out of control over Cambrai.

While escorting bombers, 62 Sqn became involved with about 30 enemy aircraft near Cambrai. Although Capt W.E. Staton and

2nd Lt L.E. Mitchell in D7899 shot a D.VII down out of control east of Cambrai, they were shot up in return and the pilot wounded. After E2457 had its radiator damaged, 2nd Lt L. Hudson and 2nd Lt A. Palmer force landed at Écouvres aerodrome. Last seen near Cambrai, Lt N.N. Coope and 2nd Lt H.S. Mantle in E2515 were wounded and captured. The same fate befell 2nd Lt L. Hudson and 2nd Lt A. Palmer in E2457. Although 2nd Lt P.S. Manley and Sgt G.F. Hines shot down a D.VII in flames east of Cambrai, it had been an expensive day for the squadron.

At 10:10 a D.VII which had been attacking D.H.9s at Harbourdin was shot down in flames by Capt A. Hepburn and 2nd Lt H.G. Eldon of 88 Sqn in C821.

The 25th found 20 and 22 Sqns engaged by many D.VIIs. In the evening 20 Sqn sent out a patrol. Captain T.C. Traill and Lt R. Gordon-Bennett in E2252 shot a D.VII down in flames northeast of St Quentin, but Gordon-Bennett was wounded. Another D.VII was sent down smoking and out of control in the same location by Lt S.L. Walters and Lt T. Kirkpatrick in E2337. Two D.VIIs were accounted for by Lt F.G. Harlock and 2nd Lt A.S. Draisey in E2340; one crashed near Magny and the other near Lehancourt. Lieutenant M. McCall and 2nd Lt C.G. Boothroyd in E2568 shot down a D.VII in flames at Estrées. Three D.VIIs were claimed northeast of St Quentin by Capt G.H. Hooper and 2nd Lt H.L. Edwards in E2536.

With 22 Sqn, Lt C.W.M. Thompson and Lt L.R. James in C1035 sent a D.VII down in a vertical dive and out of control over Bourlon Wood, near Fontaine. Lieutenant F.G. Gibbons and 2nd Lt J.A. Oliver in E2477 sent a D.VII down smoking, to crash just north of Bourlon Wood.

The following day, 26 September, was quieter. While returning from escort duty, Lt C.W.M. Thompson and Lt W.V. Tyrrell of 22 Sqn in C1035 joined in a combat between 203 Sqn Camels and D.VIIs. The F.2B crew sent two D.VIIs down out of control over the Arras-Cambrai road, one falling to the pilot and the other to the

observer. Having left on an offensive patrol at 12:33, E2155 of 20 Sqn failed to return after being seen in combat northwest of St Quentin; 2nd Lt L.G. Smith and 2nd Lt E.S. Harvey both died of wounds after capture. At 11:55 E2163 of 'L' Flight left on a photoreconnaissance sortie, but was shot up in combat north of Bourlon Wood and crash-landed; 2nd Lt C.A. Harrison and Lt J.A. Parkinson both became prisoners. Crewed by 2nd Lt W.S. Rycroft and 2nd Lt H.C. Wood, E2282 of 48 Sqn engaged eight D.VIIs and one was shot down in flames E of Menin at 11:40. However, both of the F.2B's occupants were wounded and the engine was hit, and the aircraft was force landed.

The assault by the ground forces finally came on 27 September along a 13-mile front between Ecourt St Quentin and Gouzeaucourt. The Bristol Fighters suffered heavily that day.

In mid-morning 20 Sqn sent out a patrol, and Lt A.T. Iaccaci and Sgt A. Newlands in E2213 shot down a Fokker D.VII which crashed south of Fontaine, then sent another down out of control. A D.VII which crashed west of Bernot was claimed by Lt M. McCall and 2nd Lt C.G. Boothroyd in E2470, and Lt F.G. Harlock and 2nd Lt A.S. Draisey in E2338 hit a D.VII which crashed northeast of Marcy. After leaving on an operational patrol at 09:30, E2568 and was last seen in combat northeast of St Quentin; Lt F.E. Turner and Lt C.E. Clarke were both killed.

A patrol was sent out just after dawn by 22 Sqn, and Capt S.F.H. Thompson and 2nd Lt C.J. Tolman in E2477 shot down a Halberstadt C which crashed just north of Noyelles at 07:20. A D.VII which crashed between Oisy-le-Verger and Bois de Quesnoy was shared between Lt L.C. Rowney and Lt W.V. Tyrrell in E2517 and Lt C.W.M. Thompson and Lt L.R. James in F5820. Lieutenant J.R. Drummond and 2nd Lt C.H. Wilcox in E2243 sent a D.VII down out of control, also at Oisy-le-Verger, while Lt F.G. Gibbons and Sgt G. Shannon in F6040 sent a D.VII down out of control in the Sensée Canal at Cambrai. During an afternoon patrol E2477 was lost, last being

seen heading east over Cambrai; Capt S.F.H. Thompson and 2nd Lt C.J. Tolman were both killed. Likewise, D8089 was last seen going east over Cambrai, and Lt I.F. Smith and 2nd Lt B.G. Shum became PoWs. A similar fate befell E2243, Lt J.R. Drummond being killed and 2nd Lt C.H. Wilcox captured. Although D7894 was shot up in combat during an evening patrol, 2nd Lt T.D. Smith and Lt B. Caillard escaped injury.

At 08:15 C944 of 62 Sqn left on an offensive patrol and was shot down east of Douai; 2nd Lt P.S. Manley and Sgt G.F. Hines were captured. Lieutenant G.F. Anderson and 2nd Lt T.S. Chilton in E2451 of 88 Sqn sent a D.VII down out of control at Lambersart at 07:55, and Lt C. Foster and Sgt T. Proctor in E2153, also of 88 Sqn, left at 12:55 on a special mission and were last seen in combat near Abancourt. Both were killed. Another 88 Sqn aircraft, E2533, crewed by Capt E.C. Johnston and 2nd Lt H.R. Goss, sent a D.VII down out of control at Abancourt.

Next day the final Allied campaign in Flanders began, with an attack by French, Belgian and British troops between Dixmude and St Eloi. The RAF units operating with the 11th (Army) Wing included the Bristol Fighters of 48 Sqn. Lieutenant F.G. Gibbons and Sgt G. Shannon of 22 Sqn in D7894 shot down two D.VIIs at Haynecourt at 11:15, and E2263 was attacked by a mixed formation, a Pfalz D.XII being shot down by the observer just east of Bugnicourt at 17:55. When Capt F.J. Cunninghame and 2nd Lt R.A. Brunton MC in E2532 of 48 Sqn attacked the rear machine of a formation of six D.VIIs southeast of Roulers at 14:45, the Fokker's upper starboard wing crumpled up.

On the 29th 11 Sqn went on a dawn patrol to Cambrai. Lieutenant T. Peacock and Lt G.W.A. Kelty in C937 shot a D.VII down in flames and sent another down out of control southeast of Cambrai at 08:45, but F5814 was shot down, killing 2nd Lt T.T. Smith and Lt J.L. Bromley.

During an offensive patrol in the morning 20 Sqn found a gaggle of D.VIIs, and Lt S.L. Walters and Lt T. Kirkpatrick in E2337 sent one down to crash near Laveqies. Captain T.C. Traill and Capt L.W. Burbidge in E2370 attacked a D.VII which broke up north of St Quentin, and Lt M. McCall and 2nd Lt C.G. Boothroyd in E2470 brought down a D.VII which crashed near Lehancourt, northeast of St Quentin. Captain G.H. Hooper MC and 2nd Lt H.L. Edwards in E2536 sent a D.VII down out of control, followed by two more that crashed northeast of St Quentin. Four of 20 Sqn's F.2Bs failed to return: E2561 was last seen going west over the lines, and

Another 11 Sqn aircraft, E2586 '6', has a similar overwing Lewis installation. This aircraft joined the Squadron early in October 1918.
(Eric Harlin)

Lt N.S. Boulton and Lt C.H. Case were killed; E2517 was last seen in combat with D.VIIs east of Cambrai and Lt C.W. Thompson and Lt L. James both became PoWs; E2155 was shot down northwest of St Quentin and 2nd Lt L.G. Smith and 2nd Lt E.S. Harvey were captured but died of wounds received; and E2266 was engaged by D.VIIs east of Cambrai and Lt E. Adams USAS and Sgt G.H. Bissell were both killed. Adams was in the USAS and was with the RAF for operational experience. A final loss was E2509 of 62 Sqn, which was hit by flak and broke up in the air over Dury, killing Lt R.R. O'Reilly and 2nd Lt L.E. Mitchell.

Further flying during the month was heavily restricted by rain, and no claims or losses are recorded.

October 1918

By 1 October improved weather conditions enabled a great increase in aerial activity. The war was moving into its final phase, with advances right along the front. On that day Lt C.R. Smythe and 2nd Lt W.T. Barnes of 11 Sqn in E2573 shot down a Fokker D.VII in flames and sent another down out of control south of Le Cateau at 08:20. But more F.2Bs were written off. After shooting down a D.VII, Sgt Mech A. Cridlan and 2nd Lt W. Connor of 11 Sqn crashed south of Le Cateau at 08:30, their aircraft, E2366, damaged by AA fire. They were unhurt. At 09:00 E2250 of 10 Sqn left on a photo-reconnaissance flight and was damaged in a combat with sixteen D.VIIs over Courtrai; both Lt A.W. Bennett and 2nd Lt G.H.E. Kime were wounded. Captain W. Buckingham and Lt T. Beck in E2265 of 48 Sqn were shot down near Thielt. Both were taken prisoner, and Beck later died of his wounds. Although E2531 of 48 Sqn was badly shot up, Lt E.C. Shirley and Sgt R.L.G. White were both unhurt.

Next day, Capt E.C. Johnston and Sgt C.M. Maxwell of 88 Sqn in E2533 shot down two D.VIIs in flames and sent another down out of control at Wavrin-Berclaw. At the same time Lt C. Findlay and Lt. I.W.F. Agabeg in E2412 sent two D.VIIs down out of control at La Bassée.

On the 3rd Lt J.W. Coons and Sgt Mech F.S. New were killed when A7153 of 11 Sqn on reconnaissance collided with C4753 at about 9,000ft near Doullens around 07:00; 2nd Lt T.C. Sutcliffe was wounded and 2nd Lt N.J. Dalgleish died of wounds. Lieutenant C.R. Smythe and 2nd Lt W.T. Barnes in B8941 shot down a D.VII which dived vertically northeast of Cambrai at 18:00.

In the morning, a 20 Sqn patrol found D.VIIs near Méricourt, and Lt E.A. Britton and Sgt R.S. Dodds in E2252 attacked a D.VII, whereupon its starboard wings folded back; it crashed near Fontaine. Captain H.P. Lale and Lt G.V. Learmond in E2588 sent a D.VII down out of control

east of Méricourt, and Lt F.G. Harlock and 2nd Lt J.F. Kidd in E2338 shot down a D.VII which also crashed near Méricourt.

While 22 Sqn was escorting D.H.4s it was attacked by eight D.VIIs. One was sent down out of control northeast of Cambrai by Lt T.H. Newsome and 2nd Lt R.S. Walshe in E2263. When Capt S. Collier and 2nd Lt J.V. Scottern in E2269 fired on a D.VII northeast of Cambrai it broke up, its starboard wing folding back and the tail detaching.

A patrol was sent to Ingelmunster by 48 Sqn, and Capt F.J. Cunninghame and Lt R.A. Brunton in E2507 shot down a D.VII in flames at Ingelmunster and another crashed north of Lendelede. But E2498 was shot down at Ingelmunster and Lt J.A. Sykes and Sgt S. Kitchin were killed, as were 2nd Lt J.B. Cowan and Lt L.N. Jones in E2523. Also active in the area was 88 Sqn, and Lieutenant K.B. Conn and Lt A.B. Radford in E2216 and Capt E.C. Johnson and Lt I.W.F. Agabeg in E2533 each shot down a D.VII which crashed at Meurchin. Bristol F.2B D7946 of 'N' Flight was reported lost in combat at Estomnel, but further details have not been recorded.

On 4 October 2nd Lt D.R. Phillips and 2nd Lt W. Connor of 11 Sqn were killed when C937 collided near Bapaume with D7978; Lt B.S.B. Thomas MC and 2nd Lt C.E. Spinks were also killed. Sergeant J. Moffat and AM S. Julian in E2511 of 48 Sqn shot down a D.VII which crashed and burned east of Armentières; the pilot was seen to jump out before the aircraft hit the ground. Flying in E2522 of 48 Sqn, 2nd Lt T.G. Farnborough and 2nd Lt R. Pickering shot down a D.VII near Wambrechies then force-landed in mist; they were unhurt. Lieutenant J.P. Findlay and 2nd Lt R.E. Hasell of 88 Sqn in E2474 destroyed a D.VII and a Halberstadt one mile southeast of Lille, while Lt G.F. Anderson and 2nd Lt T.S. Chilton in E2451, also of 88 Sqn, sent a D.VII down out of control.

Enemy aircraft proved elusive for the next few days, but on 7 October 88 Sqn encountered some, and Lt J. Baird and 2nd Lt F.A. Lewis in D7942 sent a D.VII down out of control at Haubourdin and Lt C. Findlay and Lt I.W.F. Agabeg in E2412 claimed another D.VII down out of control

at Annapes. At 09:50 E2591 of 11 Sqn left on reconnaissance of the Cambrai area and failed to return; Sgt Mech A. Cridlan and Sgt Mech G.E. Fuller were both killed. Next day, Capt A. Hepburn and 2nd Lt H.G. Eldon in C821 of 88 Sqn shot down a D.VII southwest of Cambrai at 12:45, but E2420 of 20 Sqn failed to return from an offensive patrol; Lt F.W. Ely and 2nd Lt J.G. McBride were both killed.

On the 9th 48 Sqn sent out a morning patrol. Lieutenant T.G. Farnborough and Sgt C.F. Perkin in E2281 shot down a D.VII north of Courtrai at 10:45, while Capt F.J. Phillips and 2nd Lt J.W. London in E2608 accounted for another D.VII between Heule and Courtrai at 10:55. In the afternoon 2nd Lt H. Thomas and 2nd Lt F.H.V. Coomer in E2510 engaged a D.VII which broke up over Courtrai at 16:30. After a bomber escort flight, E2528 of 62 Sqn failed to return. It was last seen going down southeast of Cambrai at about 08:00; Lt J.E. Sitch and 2nd Lt D.S. Fox were both captured. Another of 62 Sqn's aircraft to be lost was E2256, crewed by Capt L. Campbell and 2nd Lt W. Hodgkinson. After they had shot down a D.VII at Preseau their F.2B was last seen going down over the Forêt de Mormal with two enemy fighters on its tail. Both men were killed. A D.VII shot down by Lt A. Hepburn and 2nd Lt H.G. Eldon of 88 Sqn in C821 crashed at Seclin at 08:45.

The ranks of enemy fighters were beginning to thin, and it was not until the 13th that Lt L.N. Caple and 2nd Lt G.S. Routhier in E2560 of 22 Sqn, while escorting D.H.4s, met a D.VII which the observer sent down out of control northeast of Cambrai. The following day B8941 of 11 Sqn left on reconnaissance to Le Cateau but failed to return; Sgt Mech R. McCondach and 2nd Lt C.E. Wainwright were both killed. While Lt R.D.C. Blake and Lt L.E. Tremayne in C1013 of 'P' Flight were escorting a photographic aircraft a D.VII interfered; it was driven down near Lille. Lt W.G. Westwood and 2nd Lt A. Trantor of 88 Sqn also sent a D.VII down out of control east of Lille, and Capt F.J. Cunninghame and 2nd Lt T.C. Jones of 48 Sqn in E2507 sent another D.VII down out of control west of Thielt. Unfortunately,

The nearest aircraft in this 11 Sqn line-up is F4399, which was delivered to the unit on 30 May 1919. *(Eric Harlin)*

they then crashed on landing while trying to avoid a crashed aircraft in the centre of the aerodrome.

On the 18th 88 Sqn found some D.VIIs near Tournai, and two crews, Lt F. Jeffreys and 2nd Lt Woods in E2459 and Lt R.H. Hanmer and 2nd Lt A. Trantor in E2481, each sent down a D.VII out of control at Tournai at 12:45. Although E2579 was damaged by ground fire, Capt A. Hepburn and 2nd Lt D. Vavasour were unhurt.

Keeping enemy fighters from interfering with the corps reconnaissance and light bomber squadrons that ranged over the battle area remained the Bristol Fighters' main task. The numbers of enemy aircraft encountered had by now declined considerably. One reason was the attacks on enemy airfields. Often, instead of being bombed and strafed by a flight of aircraft, each one was now the target for a complete wing of fighters and bombers.

On the 20th Sgt N. Hunt and Sgt C.F. Levett in E2415 of 48 Sqn sent a D.VII down out of control southwest of Audenarde at 10:20. Next day, Lt T.G. Rae and Lt H.G. Lewis in E2433, also of 48 Sqn, sent another D.VII down out of control at Poteghem at 12:20. The squadron seemed adept at finding targets. The Sgt Hunt and Sgt Levett team, this time in E2511, shot down another D.VII which crashed into a wood near Peldenhoek at 10:20.

The 23rd saw more activity. In the afternoon, the F.2Bs of 20 Sqn bombed Aulnoye railway junction but were jumped by D.VIIs. Lieutenant A.C.T. Perkins and 2nd Lt D.M. Lapraik in E2377 shot down a D.VII which crashed west of Aulnoye at 15:10. Captain T.C. Traill and Capt L.W. Burbidge in E2403 shot down another D.VII which crashed east of Aulnoye, but they then collided in the haze with E2590, losing part of their upper starboard wing and crash-landing, Burbidge being injured.

Last seen in combat low over Aulnoye, E2470 failed to return; Lt H.L. Pennal and Sgt G. Aitken were both killed. Flying in E2588, Lt R.B. Tapp and 2nd Lt W.H. Welsh attacked a D.VII which broke up over the Forêt of Mormal. After bombing Aulnoye junction, Capt H.P. Lale and 2nd Lt C.G. Boothroyd in E2407 were attacked by D.VIIs and turned on them; one crashed southwest of Noyelles and another east of Preux.

During an evening sweep 88 Sqn claimed five D.VIIs. Lieutenant K.B. Conn and 2nd Lt D.A. Vavasour in E2216 shot down a D.VII at Beclers at 17:10; Lt H.C. Foley and Sgt C.M. Maxwell in E2220 sent a D.VII down out of control at Beclers; Lt G.F. Anderson and 2nd Lt C.M.W. Elliott in E2451 shot down a D.VII out of control in the Bois D'Allemont, and another in flames at Beclers; and Lt W.A. Wheeler and 2nd Lt W.B. Clarke in E2458 shot down another D.VII in flames at Lenze.

When D2652 of 'P' Flight was hit by flak and crashed in-between the lines on 25 October, Lt J.T. Brown and 2nd Lt Gutheridge both escaped unhurt. While undertaking low-level photography of the retreating enemy columns, E2534 of 48 Sqn was hit by anti-aircraft fire at Deerlyck and force-landed at 14:45; 2nd Lt G. Thornton-Norris and Sgt R.L.G. White were both unhurt.

On the 26th Lt T.G. Farnborough and 2nd Lt F.G. Smith, flying E2413 in a 48 Sqn patrol, shared a D.VII which crashed near Flobecq with Capt F.J. Phillips and 2nd Lt J.W. London in E2608. However, E2532 was last seen at 13:30; 2nd Lt H. Thomas and 2nd Lt F.H.V. Coomer were both captured, the latter being wounded. During a low-level patrol on the 27th E2609 was last seen over the River Scheldt; 2nd Lt W. Saunders and 2nd Lt H.G. Lewis both became PoWs.

On the 28th Capt M.W. Turner and Lt L.G. Kettlewell of 22 Sqn in E2466 found a two-seater attacking an S.E.5a and shot the enemy aircraft down northeast of Valenciennes at 12:25. Captain F.J. Phillips and 2nd Lt J.W. London of 48 Sqn in E2608 found an LVG west of Cellas at 10:00 and shared it with Lt B.E. Sharwood-Smith and Sgt C.F. Perkin in E2281. A D.VII was sent down out of control at Leuze-Ath by Capt A. Hepburn and Lt C.B. Marshall of 88 Sqn in C821.

Bristol F.2Bs F5815 of 'N' Flight, crewed by 2nd Lt H.P. Illsley and 2nd Lt G. Crowther, and F6101, manned by 2nd Lt E.L. Barrington and Sgt N. Sandison, combined to send a D.VII down out of control at Le Quesnoy, but the Flight lost D7919 when Lt J. Thomson and 2nd Lt A.F. Perry were both killed on artillery observation duty. On the 29th E2367 of 48 Sqn, was brought down by flak at 15:00 near Deerlyke, but Lt I.O. Gaze and 2nd Lt C.W. Newstead escaped injury.

On 30 October German fighters were up in force. When 20 Sqn found enemy fighters near Aulnoye, Capt H.P. Lale and 2nd Lt C.G. Boothroyd in E2407 shot down two D.VIIs which crashed south of Avesnes, and 2nd Lt A. McHardy and Lt W.A. Rodger in E2419 sent a D.VII down out of control four miles southeast of Aulnoye Junction. Engine trouble forced 2nd Lt R.B. Tapp and 2nd Lt W.H. Welsh in E2603 to leave formation. They were initially followed by seven enemy aircraft, but all but one withdrew. The observer was able to fire a full drum at it, and it crashed south of Avesnes, near La Croix. When F6040 of 22 Sqn was damaged by gunfire during a dawn patrol, Lt O.H. Williamson and Capt G.B. Crawford both escaped unhurt. At 13:30 Sgt N. Hunt and Sgt C.F. Levett in E2413 of 48 Sqn sent a D.VII down out of control southwest of Audenarde, and at 15:45 Lt T.G. Farnborough and Lt E. Watson of the same unit in E2596 shot down a D.VII in flames near Meldon.

Then 88 Sqn encountered a large number of D.VIIs during a dawn patrol over Caumont. A D.VII claimed by Lt V. Voss and Sgt E. Antcliffe in C922 crashed at Caumont, and Lt A.H. Berg and 2nd Lt W.J.N. Grant in E2412 shot another down in flames. Lieutenant G.F. Anderson and 2nd Lt C.M.W. Elliott in E2451 sent a D.VII down in flames and another down out of control but had to force-land within 400 yards of an enemy outpost under shellfire; both were wounded. Flying in E2458, Lt W.A. Wheeler and 2nd Lt W.B. Clarke sent a D.VII down out of control, and Lt J.G. Fleming and Sgt W.J. Spaulding in E2474 two D.VIIs down out of control. Yet another D.VII down out of control was claimed by Lt G.L. Des Lauriers and 2nd Lt F.A. Lewis in E2481, while Lt J. Baird and Sgt C. Hill in E2506 saw their D.VII crash. Lieutenant

Bristol F.2B E2152 'E' of 62 Sqn at Nivelles. This machine was taken on charge by the squadron on 5 September 1918. *(Eric Harlin)*

Believed to have been in transit when photographed at Elsham, Arab-engined F.2B F5087 was from a batch of 100 ordered from Harris & Sheldon of Birmingham, the last 20 of which were cancelled. *(Philip Jarrett)*

K.B. Conn and 2nd Lt K.C.W. Craig in E2612 sent one D.VII down in flames and another to crash near Caumont, Capt K.R. Simpson and 2nd Lt A. Trantor in E2339 shot down two D.VIIs in flames at Péruwelz and north of Warchin, and Capt C. Findlay and Lt I.W.F. Agabeg in E2533 claimed two D.VII in flames at Havinnes. On the last day of the month 2nd Lt E.L. Barrington and Sgt N. Sandison in F6101 of 'N' Flight met a D.VII which they shot down in flames north of Le Quesnoy at 11:25.

November 1918

By the beginning of November the weather had taken another turn, restricting air activities yet again. This afforded some advantage to the demoralised German infantry trudging back to the Fatherland. Those who were more optimistic considered the possibility of falling back to a defensive position, possibly as far as the Rhine, but the German General Staff had a more realistic scenario. Asked by the still-deluded Emperor what they would be doing next, they told him that Germany had to ask for an armistice. In the meantime, he could abdicate. This he did, fleeing to the Netherlands, where he lived out the rest of his life. The politicians started to arrange for talks with the Allies.

By this time, the Bristol Fighter in its standard fighter-reconnaissance form with the Rolls-Royce Falcon engine had won undying fame. After a slow start, its great strength and manoeuvrability had been appreciated and exploited by its pilots, making it one of the most effective weapons in the RFC and RAF armoury. By the time of the Armistice 48 Sqn alone had destroyed 148 enemy aircraft.

The squadrons favoured offensive patrols to seek out any enemy aircraft. They were the hunters, and any enemy aircraft found were attacked. The combination of pilot and gunner made it very difficult for Germans fighters to shoot them down. Earlier, crews had only a few hours' experience on an operational type before joining a squadron on the Western Front, but the establishment of Training Depot Stations equipped with specific types meant that pilots had much greater experience when they arrived in France. A course at a Fighting School provided them with training in tactics.

The observers doubled as rear gunners, and gunnery schools taught them how to handle their machine guns and protect their tails. The wide variety of ranks of gunners ran from captains to privates,

and they learned to work as a team with their pilots.

On 1 November 2nd Lt P. Segrave and Lt J.F. Kidd were both killed when F6116 of 20 Sqn failed to return; it was last seen in a steep dive over the Forêt de Mormal. Lieutenant P.J. Long and 2nd Lt R. Lowe of 62 Sqn sent a Fokker D.VII down out of control. On the 3rd a midday patrol of 20 Sqn found some D.VIIs, whereupon Lt R.E. Johnston and 2nd Lt W.N. Dawkes in E2338 sent a D.VII down out of control in the Forêt de Mormal at 13:30, Lt H.J. Gye and Lt P.B. de Moyse-Bucknall did the same in F4436, and Lt G.E. Randall and Lt G.V. Learmond in E2429 shot down a D.VII one mile southwest of Berlaimont.

On 4 November the F.2B squadrons found a larger number of targets. In 22 Sqn, Lt S.H. Wallage and Capt D.E. Waight in E2454 sent a Pfalz D.XII down out of control northwest of Bavay, while Capt M.W. Turner and Lt B. Caillard in E2466 sent another Pfalz down out of control and smoking at the same time.

In the afternoon 48 Sqn engaged D.VIIs over Lessines. Sergeant N. Hunt and Sgt/Maj C.J. O'Toole in E2511 shot down a D.VII which crashed in flames northwest of Lessines, Lt T.G. Farnborough and 2nd Lt R. Evans in E2596 shot another down in flames at Enerbeck, and Capt L.A. Payne MC and 2nd Lt R.L. Ford in F6041 sent a D.VII down out of control and smoking at Lessines-Gramont. On the debit side, three of the squadron's F.2Bs were lost over Lessines: Lt I. Glaze and 2nd Lt C. Newstead in E2583; 2nd Lt J. McNamara and 2nd Lt J. Pugh in E2592; and Capt A. Harcourt-Vernon and 2nd Lt D. Lee in E2625. All became prisoners for a brief period.

After engaging in combat with enemy aircraft southwest of Mons at 08:50, Lt F. Sumsion and Capt W.G. Walford of 62 Sqn in E2513 were last seen going down with a broken wing. Lieutenant F.C.D. Scott and 2nd Lt C. Rigby were both killed after their

machine, D7948, was seen going down under control, pursued by two D.VIIs. A dawn patrol by 88 Sqn resulted in Lt J. Baird and Lt A.B. Radford in D7942 shooting down a D.VII at Renaix at 09:15. In the early afternoon, another sweep found more enemy aircraft, and Lt C.E. Lacoste and Lt I.W.F. Agabeg in E2412 attacked a D.VII which crashed west of Faucaumont at 13:00. Captain A. Hepburn and 2nd Lt A. Trantor in E2610 shot down two Pfalz D.XIIs at Mainvault-Faucaumont, while Lt K.B. Conn and 2nd Lt K.C.W. Craig in E2612 accounted for another D.VII at Foucaumont.

Next day, D7884 of 'P' Flight was hit by flak during a photoreconnaissance, but 2nd Lt J.T. Brown and 2nd Lt H.V. Irving were both unhurt. On the 6th, Capt L.H. Jones and Lt V. Lockey in C1013 of 'P' Flight were on an artillery patrol when their petrol tank was ripped open by ground fire. They force-landed but the aircraft burst into flames and was destroyed. On the 9th Lt G.E. Randall and Lt G.V. Learmond in E2429 of 20 Sqn sent a D.VII down out of control southeast of Beaumont at 11:30.

On 10 November 20 Sqn ended its wartime career by finding enemy fighters near Charleroi. A D.VII was shot down by Lt H.W. Heslop and 2nd Lt J. Hackett in E2338 and crashed southwest of Charleroi, and Capt G.H. Hooper MC and Lt M.A. McKenzie in E2407 sent another down out of control. An Albatros attacked by 2nd Lt F.H. Solomon and 2nd Lt A.D. Sinclair in E2423 crashed in a wood south of Charleroi at 11:30, while Lt G.E. Randall and Lt G.V. Learmond in E2429 attacked a D.VII which crashed west of Loverval, and the observer then sent another down in flames.

Sadly, two F.2Bs failed to return from this encounter. Lieutenant E.A.C. Britton was taken prisoner and Sgt R.S. Dodds killed in F4421, and Lt A.W. McHardy and Lt W.A. Rodgers were both killed in F6195, only 24 hours before the guns fell silent.

The officers of 139 Sqn in Italy on 11 November 1918, Armistice Day. The unit had been formed from two combined Flights on 3 July 1918. *(Eric Harlin)*

Chapter 7

THE FIGHTING IN ITALY

On 24 October 1917, nine Austrian and six German divisions launched a heavy offensive against Britain's Italian allies, who had been at war with the Austro-Hungarian Empire for two-and-a-half years, along a 375-mile front between Switzerland and the Adriatic Sea. Helped by misty conditions, the enemy very quickly broke through the lightly defended stretch of the front at Caporetto. By 10 November they had advanced some 50 to 80 miles and had reached the banks of the River Piave, but they then called a halt due to lack of readily available reserves. In the meantime, the British and French governments agreed to send divisions and air support from the Western Front as soon as possible. The latter included the Camels of 28 Sqn and the R.E.8s of 34 Sqn, which left on 7 November, and by the end of that month they were based at forward airfields. Crews found themselves operating in wild and mountainous terrain that was vastly different from the Western Front, necessitating totally different flying techniques. The first sortie over the Italian Front was flown on 29 November by a 34 Sqn aircraft. These were soon supplemented by the Camels of 45 and 66 Sqns and the R.E.8s of 42 Sqn, based alongside Italian squadrons. Although air superiority had been established by February 1918, the use of the R.E.8s for long-range reconnaissance was limited because of their vulnerability to fierce attacks by enemy scouts, an escort of Camels being necessary.

On 14 March 42 Sqn left to return to the Western Front, but that month an un-numbered Flight of Bristol Fighters arrived from home and was attached to 28 Sqn to take over the task of escorting R.E.8s, though the latter had operated for four months without a single machine being lost to enemy action. Soon afterwards the Flight was reattached to 34 Sqn, and now adopted the title 'Z' Flight. On 3 April B1185, crewed by Lt W.L. Vorster and Lt C.leG. Amy, was reported missing from a reconnaissance, but was later recovered and removed to 7 Aircraft Park to be repaired. The following day B1214, piloted by Lt T.C. Lowe, successfully attacked an Albatros D.V, which was sent down out of control near Stirgus, though the F.2B's observer, Lt H.V.N. Bankes, was wounded. On the 24th the first F.2B loss was recorded. The machine was reported to have been seen coming of clouds in a spin to the east of the front line, and 2nd Lt P.G. Ratliff and Lt H.V.N. Bankes were captured.

Weather conditions for much of April and May limited aviation activity across the mountains, but such reconnaissance sorties as were possible indicated that the Valsugana area was the likely objective for an enemy spring offensive. It was proposed to pre-empt this with an Allied offensive, but before this was ready there was evidence to suggest that the Austrians intended to resume their attacks in the Piave area, with a simultaneous attack in the mountains. Attempts to reconnoitre this front were encountering stiff air defences, and on 3 May C4756 was damaged by anti-aircraft fire near Nove during a reconnaissance flight. Fortunately Lt T.C. Lowe and 2nd Lt T. Newey were both unhurt and their aircraft was repairable. Eight days later,

however, Lt J.B. Guthrie and Lt H.V. Thornton in C4755 were both killed during a reconnaissance, last being seen in combat with four enemy aircraft at 16,000ft above Levico. Credit for the victory was given to Oblt Frank Linke-Crawford, CO of Austrian fighter squadron Flik 60. On the last day in May Lt M.O. Ramsay and 2nd Lt R. Walker in B1230 left on a photo-reconnaissance mission, but their engine seized and the aircraft forced-landed at Musestre. Both occupants were unhurt.

On 2 June 2nd Lt E.M. Brown and 2nd Lt H. Milburn in C4700 claimed to have shot down out of control one of five Albatros D.IIIs over Borgo. Seven days later six Albatros D.IIIs attacked a patrol of three F.2Bs near Trento. Of these, 2nd Lt A.E. Ryan and 2nd Lt T. Newry in C4758 shot down one of the enemy aircraft in flames, and Lt G. Robertson and 2nd Lt H Milburn in C4757 sent another down out of control. Lieutenant E.M. Brown and 2nd Lt C.A. Gordon in C4700 were taken prisoner after being shot down at 2,000ft over Trento. Earlier that day C913 crashed on landing at Villaverla after an early morning reconnaissance, Capt T.C. Lowe and 2nd Lt A.S. Withers both being wounded. The following day, the 10th, Lt W.L. Vorster and Lt R. Murdoch were both wounded when C916 was hit by anti-aircraft fire.

The long-awaited enemy offensive finally began on 15 June with a short but heavy bombardment along the whole front between the Adriatic and the Asiago Plateau. Royal Air Force and Italian aircraft flew continuously to help stem the flow of enemy troops attempting to cross the River Piave over bridges and by water in all manner of river craft, including rafts. The slaughter they inflicted significantly slowed the enemy, who were assisted in the mountains by fog and low clouds, though 'Z' Flight suffered loss and damage in the air. Bristol Fighter C4757, crewed by Lt C.E.G. Gill and Lt T. Newey, was damaged by gunfire over Piave, while C4758 was shot down and its wreckage then shelled, Lt G.H. Wood and Lt C.LeG. Amy both escaping unharmed. Two days of heavy rain followed, wreaking havoc as the swollen and swirling river washed away temporary pontoons to isolate troops on either side of the river. By the 20th the Austrian troops were being steadily pushed back by an Italian counteroffensive. Next day, C4761 crashed near the aerodrome at Villaverla; 2nd Lt A.E. Ryan was unhurt, but 2nd Lt Davies was injured. By the 24th the enemy had completed his withdrawal across the Piave, though at a cost of 20,000 troops captured, in addition to numerous guns and other vital equipment. The RAF had played a vital part in this action, though one more F.2B was lost that month, when C993 received a direct hit from anti-aircraft fire near Sao Paolo on the 28th and went down in flames over the River Piave west of Oderzo, killing Lt F.S. Williams and Lt D. Thomas.

On 1 July C991 crashed during escort duty, Lt R.R. Evans and Lt M.I. Hough evidently being unhurt. In the meantime, reinforcements in the shape of a second F.2B Flight had arrived in Italy, and on 3 July the two flights were combined to form

Above: **F.2B D8063 of 139 Sqn at Villaverla, Italy, piloted by Maj W. George Barker DSO MC DFC, the squadron's commander, who was taking HRH the Prince of Wales for a joyride.** *(Public Archives of Canada)*

Below: **HRH Prince Edward of Wales (later HM King Edward VIII) in the observer's cockpit of F.2B D8084 'S' of 139 Sqn. Despite assertions to the contrary, his pilot on this occasion was not Maj Barker.** *(Philip Jarrett)*

Below: **Serving with 139 Sqn at Villaverla in September 1918, D8084, piloted by Capt S. Dalrymple, displays a dozen white bands around its rear fuselage, two spanwise stripes along its upper wing, white wheel covers and a Charlie Chaplin caricature on its engine cowling. It was in this machine that Capt Dalrymple and 2nd Lt Baldwin achieved several victories.** *(Eric Harlin)*

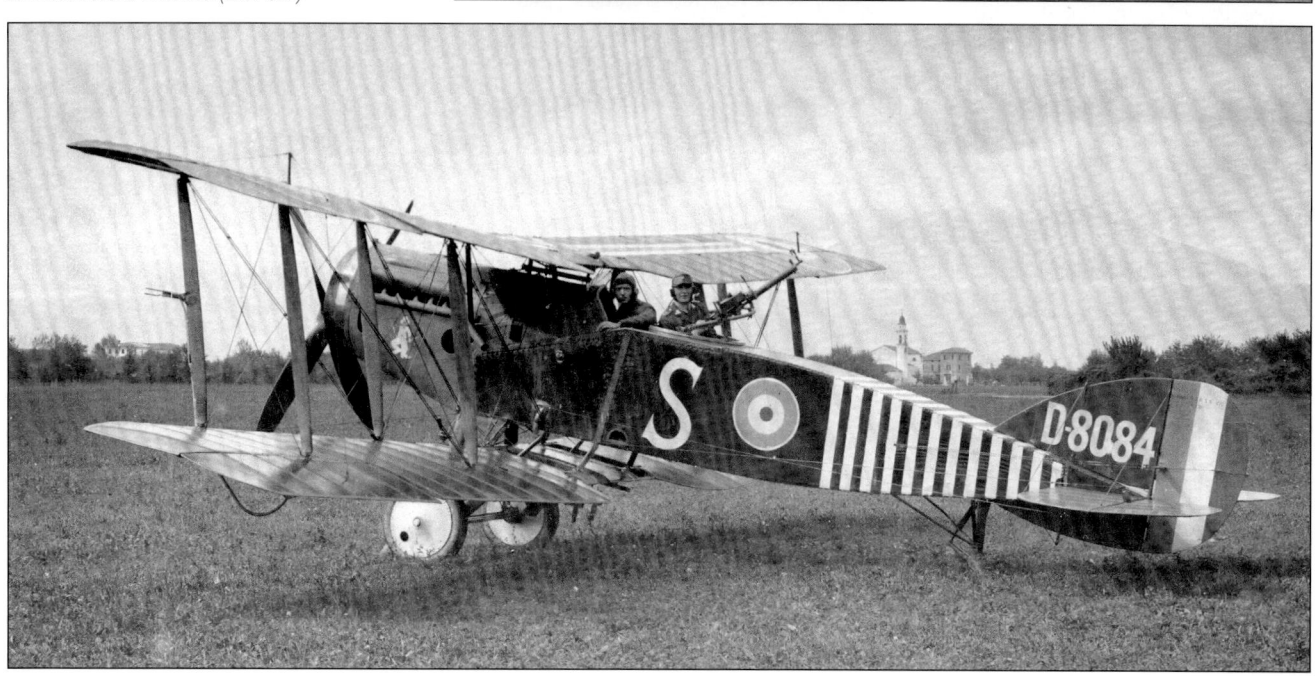

Left: **D8084 'T' of 139 Sqn in unhappier circumstances, possibly the crash that resulted after its propeller was shot through while the guns were being tested on 25 September 1918.** (Philip Jarrett)

three scouts, this being his first confirmed victory. On the 20th he was leading two F.2Bs in his Camel when he shot down two Albatros D.IIIs near Motta Airfield, a third being claimed by Lt G.W. Curtis and Sgt H.G. Frow in F.2B C997; it was seen to crash into a wood near Motta. On the 22nd Lt H.D. Walters and Lt W.T. Davies in C997 destroyed an Albatros D.V, seeing it crash 300 yards south of Godega Airfield, but on that same day Lt W.L. Vorster, a South African, and Sgt H.G. Frow were killed when C4759 was shot down over Trento by Obltn Roman Schmidt of Flik 30J. Lieutenant V.D. Fernald, an American, and 2nd Lt W. Watkins in C4762 were last seen over Belluno; both were killed when their F.2B was shot down by Friedrich Navratil of Flik 3J. On 27 July Lt A.J. David and 2nd Lt R.W. Ellis were both injured when the engine of D8060 cut as they returned from a reconnaissance flight and they forced-landed on the aerodrome. On the 29th C990 was shot up in combat over Nove and crashed in the ensuing forced landing; Lt A.E. Ryan was wounded but Lt C.LeG. Amy was unhurt. Next day Lt W.C. Simon and Lt W.W. Smith in C999 sent down two Albatros D. IIIs in flames near Motta, as well as two LVG two-seaters and a scout all out of control between Torre di Mosta and Caorle; Smith

a new unit, 139 Sqn, still stationed at Villaverla as part of the 14th Wing in the 7th Brigade, initially under the command of Capt A.A. Harcourt-Vernon. The following day the new squadron scored its first victories when three F.2Bs attacked four Albatroses during a reconnaissance sortie. Lieutenant H.C.W. Walters and Lt C. Beagle in C916 destroyed an Albatros D.III near Asolo, and Lt W.C. Simon, an American, and Lt W.W. Smith, both in C999, sent another down out of control at Levico. On the 11th, during an offensive patrol, the crew of C4756 became lost in clouds then ran out of petrol and had to force-land; 2nd Lt J.B. Isaacs was unhurt but 2nd Lt F.F. Crump was slightly injured.

The new squadron's prospects were greatly enhanced when, on 14 July, Maj W.G. Barker DSO MC DFC took over command, on promotion from 66 Sqn, from which he brought his favourite Camel, B6313. The next day four aircraft took off early for a reconnaissance, but B1185 developed engine trouble and crashed on return to the aerodrome at Villaverla. The others continued, and attacked eight Albatros D.IIIs at 16,000ft over Mattarello; Lt H.C.W. Walters with 2nd Lt W.W. Smith in C997 sent one down smoking to crash at Cortesono, and Lt W.C. Simon with AM J.C. Ings in

C999 shot down another, which crashed at Migazzone. Lieutenant G.W. Curtis with 2nd Lt H. Bladen sent another down out of control, it being last seen at 3,000ft, but their own aircraft was badly damaged by return fire. On the 17th Lt Walters with 2nd Lt W.W. Smith in C994 sent down another Albatros D.III, which crashed into a wood on the outskirts of Nemo. On the 18th the CO took off in his Camel, in company with Lt H.C. Walters and Lt W.T. Davies in a Bristol Fighter. Barker shot down one of two LVGs they spotted over Asiago being escorted by

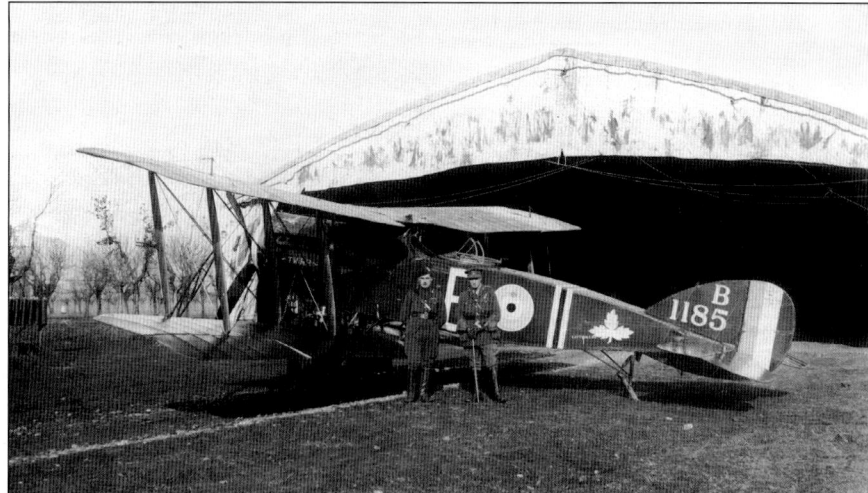

Above: **Believed to have been flown by a Canadian pilot because of the maple leaf insignia on its rear fuselage, B1185 'B' or 'E' of 139 Sqn had previously served in 28 Sqn before going to 'Z' Flight of 34 Sqn, later renumbered 139 Sqn. The name 'TWIRP' is inscribed beneath the exhaust pipe.** (Eric Harlin)

Left: **Aircraft and personnel of 139 Sqn lined up at Villaverla in mid-1918. The aircraft carry the unit's initial marking of two vertical white bars aft of the fuselage roundel. The nearest machine, D8063 'D', arrived on the squadron on 26 July 1918.** (Philip Jarrett)

On 23 August 1918 Fw. Navratil, OC of Flik 3J, gained his ninth victory when he forced D7966 'A' of 139 Sqn, crewed by Lts C.E.G. Gill and T. Newey, to land at Gardolo, as seen here. The F.2B's crew were taken prisoner, and D7966 joined the Austro-Hungarian Air Force as 00.83. *(Philip Jarrett and C&C)*

was wounded. On the same day, while on reconnaissance, C916 crashed at Sacca after combat southwest of Porto Gurnado. Pilot Lt H.C.W. Walters was wounded but observer 2nd Lt W.F. Davies was unhurt.

On 1 August, while providing an escort for 66 Sqn, both Lt M.O. Ramsay and 2nd Lt F.F. Crump were injured when D8081 was forced down and had to land on an Italian aerodrome south of Pietro-in-Gu. The squadron's F.2Bs distinguished themselves against odds on 8 August when four machines left at 07:00 on a bombing mission, led by Capt S. Dalrymple and observer 2nd Lt H.O. Baldwin in D8084. In the Trento area they had to beat off an onslaught by 20 enemy fighters. They attacked an Austrian Albatros D.V over Trento, but its pilot spun down to 6,000ft before recovering control, then promptly fled the scene. They then engaged the Albatroses of Karl Linner and Johann Pinkasly of Flak 9J, who turned out to be on protection patrol above local Austrian airfields being visited by Emperor Carl. Both were shot down in flames, one at Levico and the other at Caldonazzo. On the 10th Lt W.C. Simon with Sgt M. Akam in D8075 shot down one of a pair of Albatros D.Vs they attacked at 18,000ft over Caldonazzo, and saw it crash into a nearby wood.

On 16 August Capt S. Dalrymple led four aircraft on a bombing raid against Levico Airfield, but D8069 was seen to go down in flames over Treviso, having fallen to the fire of Obltn Navratil, CO of Flik 3J. Lieutenant C.R.H. Jackson and Lt W.F. Keepin were both killed, and their aircraft was captured and repaired, subsequently being flown in the Austro-Hungarian Air Force as 00.80. On the 22nd two F.2Bs which left on reconnaissance at 07:00 both fell into enemy hands; D7966, crewed by Lt C.E.G. Gill and Lt T. Newey, was forced to land at Gardolo by Fw. Navratil, OC of Flik 3J, his ninth victory, and D8075, crewed by Lt

N.E. Gwyer and 2nd Lt T.R. Hilton on their first flight, was landed in error at Austrian-held Casara Airfield. All four members of the two crews were taken prisoner, and their aircraft were taken over by the Austro-Hungarian Air Force and renumbered 00.83 and 00.75 respectively. Next day C4760, crewed by 2nd Lt J.B. Isaacs and Capt M.G. Cahill-Byrne, sent a DFW Aviatik down in flames northeast of Trento, and another was seen to crash near Madrano, 15km northeast of Trento. Sorties during the last week in August and the early part of September mainly comprised photographic and reconnaissance work, with little contact with the enemy air force.

On 1 September C992, crewed by Lt A.N. Martyn and 2nd Lt G.L. Kaye, was badly shot up and forced to land. On the 13th, however, things livened up. On that day four F.2Bs led by Capt Dalrymple spotted ten Albatros scouts at about 15,000ft over Trento and promptly set upon them. Dalrymple was flying D8084, with Lt G.O. Beagle as his observer, and after sending one Albatros D.V down in flames they were attacked by another, into which Beagle emptied three drums of ammunition before having the satisfaction of seeing it engulfed in flames as it fell. Meanwhile, Lt G.W. Curtis and AM J.C. Ings in D8078 sent an Albatros D.III down in flames and two more out of control in the same area. On the 14th 2nd Lt J.B. Isaacs and Lt L.O. Abraham in C4760 attacked an Albatros D.III at close range over Levico

and saw it break up. In the same action D7975 was damaged in combat, but Lt H.V. Jellicoe and Sgt F.H. Shanks were unhurt. The following day, D8078 was hit by anti-aircraft fire. The pilot, Lt G.R.B. Playfair, was wounded, but his observer, AM J.C. Ings, was unhurt.

Activities during the remainder of the month mainly consisted of low-level bombing raids on several Austrian aerodromes in the Levico and Fonzaso areas and their adjacent railway stations, to limit aerial activities by the opposing air force, as well as strafing Austrian troop locations. On the 20th Lt E. Exton was unhurt when D7972 crashed during a test flight, though his observer, AM3 R.W. Hare, was injured. Only four days earlier this aircraft had given local flights to HRH the Prince of Wales, later to become His Majesty King Edward VIII. Five days later Lt W.C. Simon and AM Gay were unhurt when D8084 crashed after its propeller was shot through while the guns were being tested. On the 26th Lt H.V. Jellicoe and Lt W. Mackay in D7960 shot down an Albatros which crashed just south of Lavis, though it was not officially confirmed because the crash was not independently witnessed by another crew. That same day B1214 of 34 Sqn force-landed at Piovene after its engine failed during a photo reconnaissance, Capt P. Grosset and Capt A.C. Rankin being unhurt. At the end of the month Maj Barker left for England on repatriation, and Capt Dalrymple took temporary command.

Right: **A very hazy image of F.2B D8078 'X' of 139 Sqn, which was hit by anti-aircraft fire on 15 September 1918 while crewed by Lt G.R.B. Playfair, who was wounded, and AM J.C. Ings, who was unharmed. It subsequently went to 34 Sqn.** *(Philip Jarrett)*

Captain L.F. Hursthouse of 139 Sqn poses with visiting Capt Wilson of 28 Sqn in front of F.2B E2285 'A', with the black-and-white rear fuselage banding well shown. *(Philip Jarrett)*

Barker was subsequently awarded the Victoria Cross after an amazing series of victories in a Snipe on 27 October with 201 Sqn on the Western Front.

From the beginning of October, the RAF began to concentrate on bombing and strafing attacks against enemy airfields, especially the training fields at Pergine and Campoformido, southwest of Udine, and Egna, south of Bolza. Pergine was successfully bombed by 139 Sqn on the 7th, and the next day, during a bombing and reconnaissance mission, four F.2Bs were attacked over Borgo by nine Albatroses. The lead aircraft, D7957, piloted by Capt S.H. Holland, came under heavy fire, observer 2nd Lt R.G. Fullager being wounded, and the pilot's gun jammed. Although he was in pain, Fullager continued firing at one Albatros D.III and saw it spin vertically into the ground. On the 10th 139 Sqn moved to Grossa, northwest of Padua, as part of a realignment of RAF forces in readiness for a planned final offensive against the Austro-Hungarian armies. However, bad weather over the next few days prevented any photo-reconnaissance work. On the 12th an attempt at reconnaissance in C994 came to nought when the engine cut out and Lt H.V. Jellicoe and Sgt F.H. Shanks had to forced-land near Piave. Once the weather improved the squadron instigated an intense programme of photo-reconnaissance, its photographic section providing some 8,000 prints between 22 and 24 October for use by army commanders. On the 24th Maj H.H. Kitchener, nephew of Field Marshal Lord Kitchener, took over command of 139 Sqn. While travelling from 34 Sqn to 139 Sqn, C4754 ran into mist and crashed at Lendenara; Lt R.F.S. Johnson was injured, but AM2 R.S. Hudson was unhurt. On 26 October 139 Sqn moved again, to San Luca.

On 27 October the planned offensive began and the RAF squadrons, including 139 Sqn, carried out offensive patrols. Lieutenant A.A. Bartram and 2nd Lt C.A. Sander in D7969 claimed a scout sent down out of control at Cimaldormo. Next day 2nd Lt A.A. Bartram and 2nd Lt C.A. Sander left on reconnaissance in D7960 but had to forced-land, unhurt, at Borghetto, and 2nd Lt J.R. Dean in C997 crashed while taxying into a hangar. With RAF aircraft undertaking zero-height bombing, bombing infantry positions, striking at retreating troop columns and destroying transports, the enemy was in full retreat by the 30th. On that date the CO, Major Kitchener, in D8048, was shot up and had to force-land at Conegliano. His observer, Lt H.H. Dowse, was wounded in the leg but sadly fell victim in hospital to the raging influenza epidemic of that time, dying of pneumonia 11 days later. Among other events that day, 2nd Lt J.B. Isaacs and Capt M.G.McL. Cahill-Byrne were shot down during a bombing mission but managed to set fire to their aircraft before being captured. Also on a bombing mission, Capt L.F. Hursthouse in D7969 was shot through the chest by ground fire, but managed to make a crash-landing at Treviso Aerodrome, observer 2nd Lt W.W. Smith being unhurt. Finally, neither Lt G.W. Curtiss nor 2nd Lt R.G. Fullager was hurt when E2292 taxied into a concealed ditch after a perfect landing.

The squadron's final casualty through enemy action came on 1 November, when 2nd Lt H. Baldwin, the observer in E2187, was wounded. To keep pace with the rapid Allied advance, 139 Sqn moved forward next day to Arcade, just south of the River Piave. The RAF was keeping up its relentless attacks, even though it was by now apparent that the enemy cause was hopeless. The official cessation of hostilities on this front came on the 4th. By then the crews of 139 Sqn had amassed at total of over 1,450 operational hours, during which they had released more than five-and-a-half tons of bombs. In aerial combat they had claimed 25 enemy aircraft destroyed and seven out of control, two others shot down being to the credit of the earlier 'Z' Flight, for the loss of only 12 of their own aircraft in combat.

Losses had not entirely ceased, however. On the 11th (Armistice Day) 139 Sqn moved back to Grossa. There were two more accidents in the month, both on the 22nd. Lieutenant A. Bell and Lt Herner crashed at Garda in E2186, and in D8072 Lt Jones was unhurt but Lt Mortimer suffered injuries. On 7 December, Lt J.A. Carr and AM Brown were unhurt when E2188 crashed after its engine failed on a practice flight, as were Lt T.B. Service and Lt J.G. Acheson on the 21st, when D7963 crashed on landing. On 7 January E2291 crashed during a test flight after a losing oil pressure, without harm to either Capt G.W. Curtiss or 2nd Lt T.W. Smith.

There were two further incidents in the New Year. On 11 January Lt T.B Service and Lt J.G. Acheson in D7954 ran into low clouds over mountains, but made a safe forced landing at Borgo, south of Lorenzo, after running out of fuel. Five days later Sgt Bromley and Lt Griffiths in E2270 crashed near Sienna, their aircraft being destroyed by fire. On 30 January 1919 139 Sqn moved to Caldero Aircraft Park, discarding all of its aircraft and being reduced to a cadre, which then left for the UK. The personnel arrived at Blandford Camp in Dorset on the 25th, the unit being officially disbanded on 7 March 1919.

Bristol F.2B D7969 'A' of 139 Sqn after a forced landing on 28 Sqn's aerodrome after being hit by ground fire on 30 October 1918. The sideways application of the 'A' on the upper wing centre section is curious. *(IWM Q70797)*

Bristol F.2B C4626 with 1 Sqn AFC, and sporting a brace of Lewis guns on the observer's Scarff ring. This was a presentation aircraft, named *Australia No.16, New South Wales No.7. The Women's Battleplane*, but appears to have lost its inscription. It had a chain of victories to its credit. *(Eric Harlin)*

Chapter 8

OPERATIONS AGAINST THE TURKS

When Turkey declared war against Britain and France on 5 November 1914 it put the Suez Canal in danger, this being an essential line of communication. The RFC sent a small defence force to Egypt, and it arrived at Alexandria on 17 November. Based in the Suez Canal Zone at Ismailia, it initially comprised three Maurice Farmans shipped from England, two Henry Farmans from Heliopolis, plus a B.E.2a and two Maurice Farmans from India, the latter three arriving without engines. In addition, seven French seaplanes were placed at the disposal of this small detachment. The RFC gradually increased its strength in the area as its influence spread, and on 1 August 1917 a

flight of 14 Sqn, based at Deir-el-Balah, provided the nucleus of a new 111 Sqn, to be equipped with Bristol Fighters and commanded by Maj A. Shekleton. Operational flying started only nine days later, the full establishment of three flights being attained by the end of September with a motley collection of aircraft comprising six F.2Bs, five Vickers FB.19s, four D.H.2s, two Bristol monoplanes and a Bristol Scout D.

The first real opportunity for the RFC to carry the war to the enemy came with the arrival from England on 26 August of four F.2Bs, A7184, A7186, A7188 and A7190. The first of these to reach 111 Sqn was A7188, on 15 September. This small batch

was followed by six more from England on 11 September and another two on 29 October, other small shipments following as machines became available. In October ten S.E.5as were also added to the squadron strength. Five Bristols were serviceable by the 7th, and on that day the first offensive patrol took place. On 8 October A7184 was badly shot about in a fight with a Rumpler C, Lt R.B. Sutherland and Lt W. J. Bethune both being unhurt. On the same day 2nd Lt R.C. Steele and Lt J.J. Lloyd-Williams in A7194 forced down an Albatros D.III in the Allied lines near Shellah-Sharia, this being the first German fighter captured on the Sinai-Palestine The pilot was taken prisoner and

Above: An early shot of A7194 with 1 Sqn AFC, taken when its fin was still painted in PC10 and its serial number was white. *(C&C)*

Right: Another 1 Sqn AFC aircraft was A7188, seen here at Ramleh about October 1918, which appears to have an all-white fuselage. *(C&C)*

A different view of A7188. This was the first of two F.2Bs that subsequently served with 'X' Flight, based at El Gueira in 1918. *(Philip Jarrett)*

his aircraft was so little damaged that squadron mechanics soon had it flying again.

On 11 October a new 40th (Army) Wing formed at Deir-el-Balah, to control 111 Sqn and 67 Sqn at Weli Sheikh Nuran, as well as 'X' Aircraft Park at Abbassia. On the 15th 2nd Lt R.C. Steele and Lt J.J. Lloyd-Williams in A7194 attacked three Albatros D.IIIs as they crossed Allied lines. Steele promptly put the engine of one of them out of action, then held his fire when it seemed likely from the pilot's hand signals that he wished to surrender, but it soon became apparent that his intention was to glide towards the Turkish lines. Lloyd-Williams quickly put a stop to that by loosing off another burst of fire, resulting in the death of the enemy pilot after one of the wings fell off. Steele was subsequently awarded a DSO for this action and Lloyd-Williams an MC. On the 30th A7194 was again in action when Capt A.H. Peck and Capt J.J. Lloyd-Williams caused a two-seater to land northwest of Khalasa, the aircraft and crew being captured.

On 6 November a Rumpler two-seater was forced to land, and then destroyed, at Um Dabkal, and on the 8th an Albatros D.III was shot down at Huleikat, both of these victories being achieved by Capts Peck and Lloyd-Williams in A7194. On the 8th

Lt N.C. Riddell and 2nd Lt A. Simmons in A7198 shot down an enemy aircraft five miles south of Bireh, Jerusalem. On the 24th Lt W.A. Horan, a South African, was wounded in combat in an F.2B, as were Cpl W. Richards and AM2 P.L. Smith in A7184 on the 29th. On the latter date Lt A.H.W. Fleming and 2nd Lt C. Gilham in A7198 sent an Albatros down out of control at Tul Keram, southwest of Samaria, the F.2B's observer being wounded by return fire.

On 12 December Capt R.M. Drummond and AM2 F.J. Knowles as gunner in A7202 were escorting a reconnaissance patrol by two two-seaters of 67 (Australian) Sqn when three Albatros scouts appeared near Tul Keram. Drummond immediately went after the three enemy aircraft and sent one spinning down to crash nearby. A burst of fire into one of the remaining two caused it to break up in mid-air, and the other pilot escaped only to fly into the side of a hill near Wadi Auja while apparently attempting a hasty landing. Two days later the same crew and aircraft destroyed an Albatros D.V north of Beisan. Then, on the 17th, Lt C.R. Davidson and 2nd Lt L.A. Simmons in A7192 forced an Albatros two-seater to land north of Bireh, whereupon they machine-gunned it. Five days later they forced a two-seater to land northeast of Nablus and then

destroyed it. On the 28th Davidson, still flying A7192 but now with AM2 F.J. Knowles as gunner, forced another two-seater to land in field in the Nablus Valley, where it was destroyed. By now the Bristol Fighters and their crews were being transferred one at a time to 67 (Australian) Sqn to replace that unit's assortment of R.E.8s, B.E.2cs and Martinsyde G.102s. On 29 December, just after A7202 had been transferred, it was crewed by Lt C.R. Davidson and 2nd Lt A. Simmons when they sent an Albatros D.III down out of control some eight miles southwest of Samaria.

In January 1918 the first of three Nieuport scouts arrived, the intention now being for 111 to become a solely single-seater squadron. On the 3rd a combined force of sixteen RFC aircraft, including eight F.2Bs from 67 Sqn, dropped some 1,200lb of high-explosive bombs on enemy targets at El Afule. On the return flight two Albatros D.Vs attacked the formation near El Afule Aerodrome. Lieutenant R.A. Austin and Lt L.W. Sutherland of 67 Sqn in B1128 climbed above them and shot one down to crash near the line railway between El Afule and Jenin. On the 9th Lt C.R. Davidson and Capt J.J. Lloyd-Williams in A7192 of 111 Sqn were shot up in combat, Davidson being wounded in the right leg. On 14 January, 67 (Australian) Sqn, now based at El Mejdel, reverted to its original title of 1st Sqn, Australian Flying Corps (AFC), its crews now looking forward to flying the Bristol Fighter with its greatly superior capabilities to their former mounts, though some of these were still being flown by 111 Sqn at that time.

On 17 January A7192 and A7194 of 111 Sqn were on a reconnaissance patrol at 11,000ft south of Nablus when their crews sighted five Albatros D.IIIs some 500ft below them, and a further three enemy aircraft a further 1,000ft below them, all of them seemingly reluctant to attack. Diving on the lower Albatroses, Lt L.M.S. Potts and Lt F. Hancock in A7194 fired 30 rounds into the rearmost aircraft and saw it turn on its back and then drop away out of control over El Lubban. The enemy pilots evidently

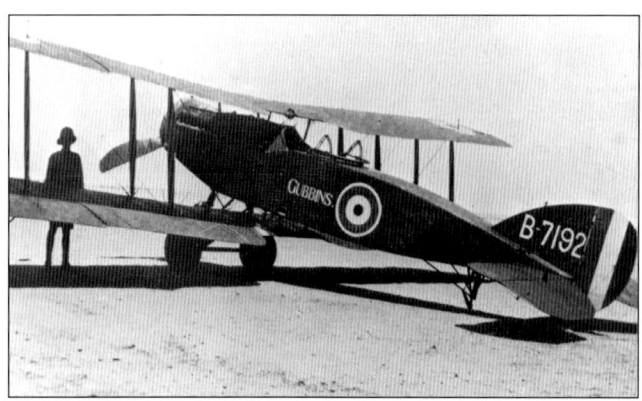

At one stage A7192 had its serial number incorrectly applied as B7192. It was named *Gubbins* at the time. *(C&C)*

F.2B A7192 displays a similar finish to that of A7188. *(Philip Jarrett)*

Right: **Captain D.W. Rutherford stands alongside F.2B B1146 of 1 Sqn AFC at El Medjel in April 1918. A presentation aircraft, it carries the inscription:** *New South Wales No. 1 "The White Belltrees".* (via *Philip Jarrett*)

had great respect for the F.2B's capabilities, and this proved to be justified when Lt A.L. Fleming and Cpl F.J. Knowles in A7192 shot down a Rumpler which crashed near Kalkalieh, northwest of Nablus. The following day Lt R.B. Sutherland and Lt P.B. Butters in A7192 shot down an Albatros D.III near Nablus, while Lt D.B. Aitken and Lt L.A.J. Barbe in A7196, together with Lt A.L. Fleming and Cpl F.J. Knowles in A7198, shot down an Albatros two-seater between Jaffa and Arsuf. Two days later Lt R.B. Sutherland and Lt P.B. Butters, again in A7192, shot down an Albatros D.III near Ramin. The same day, however, the engine of A7202 was hit by a 20mm shell, fired from either Tul Keram or Kalkilieh, and forced to glide down and land within 100 yards of the Turkish lines; 2nd Lt A.A. Poole and Lt F.W. Hancock were taken prisoner. The following month the transfer of Bristol Fighters from 111 Sqn to what was now the 1st Sqn, AFC, was completed.

Although the city of Jerusalem had been captured by Gen Allenby's forces on 9 December 1917, Jerusalem and Jaffa remained within range of Turkish artillery, so a further offensive aimed at Jericho was planned, which it was hoped would drive Turkish forces back across the River Jordan. It was intended to launch it on 19 February, and in the preceding weeks the RFC concentrated its efforts on photographing the Turkish lines and their reserve areas. Likewise, 1st Sqn AFC photographed some 624 square miles of enemy territory by the end of January alone, interspersing this with several bombing raids on Turkish gun emplacements and railway junctions. Once the attack started, the Allied forces pushed steadily forward and by 2 February had reached Jericho, but no Bristol Fighters appear to have been lost, or to have brought down any enemy aircraft, during February.

Aerial attacks continued, the F.2Bs going deep into Turkish-held territory but seeing very few enemy aircraft. On 5 March two F.2Bs were set upon by five Albatroses, but Lt E.S. Headlam and Lt E.B.S. Beaton in A7198 sent an Albatros D.III down out of control southeast of Jiljulieh, and Lt C.N. Watt and Lt T.C. Macauley in the other Bristol also attacked the enemy. On the 9th the squadron, operating with the newly formed 142 Sqn, caused serious damage and inflicted many casualties when they dropped

150 bombs on Turkish positions on the Lubban-Nablus road. On 19 March Capt R.A. Austin and Lt O.M. Lee landed at El Kutrani to help the crew of Martinsyde G.102 A3960 of 142 Sqn, which had forced-landed with engine trouble, but their own aircraft broke a wheel. They had time to set fire to the Bristol before being

captured. General Allenby's troops advanced again on 21 March, with the intention of moving towards Amman across the River Jordan. At this time RFC squadrons introduced the technique of trailing a weighted hook beneath the fuselage to pick up handwritten messages from the ground, held in containers in the centre of a cord

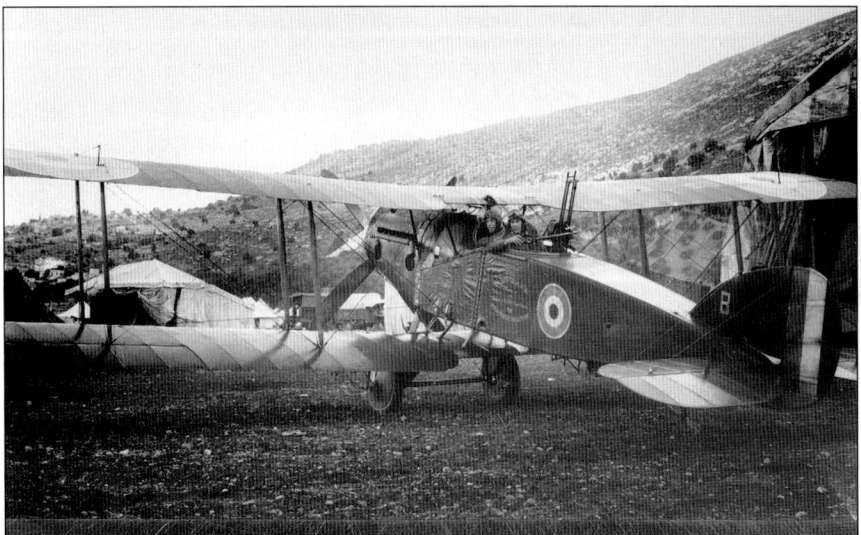

Above right: **Another presentation aircraft serving with 1 Sqn AFC was B1223,** *New South Wales No.16, The Upper Hunter Battleplane,* **which shared an Albatros D.III with C4626 on 3 August 1918, when it was crewed by Lt P.J. McGuiness and Lt H. Fysh.** (*Philip Jarrett*)

Right: **An enlarged detail of the previous picture, showing the inscription.** (*Philip Jarrett*)

F.2B C4625 was with 1 Sqn AFC by 21 March 1918. It was wrecked and struck off charge on 3 April 1918. *(C&C)*

stretched between a pair of poles. This practice was used regularly in the 1920s by RAF Bristol Fighter army co-operation squadrons. On 27 March Lt J.M. Walker and Lt G. Finlay in B1140 and Capt D.W. Rutherford and 2nd Lt J. McElligott in B1146 each forced an AEG two-seater to land at Kissir, near Amman, then destroyed

it. Shortly afterwards Lt E.S. Headlam and Lt W.A. Kirk in A7198 repeated this tactic with another AEG near Amman.

By early April the attempted advance had failed. The Allied forces had withdrawn to their previous position, and strong Turkish opposition frustrated further efforts. To make matters worse, some of the most

experienced divisions had been sent to France to help counteract the German spring offensive, to be replaced in Palestine and Mesopotamia by inexperienced Indian Army troops and cavalry. As a consequence, the 1st Sqn AFC was reduced to undertaking daily reconnaissance flights east of the River Jordan and across the Dead Sea, during which its aircraft were increasingly met by enemy machines. On 15 April Lt G.C. Peters and Lt J.H. Traill in C4623 sent an Albatros D.III down out of control two miles southeast of Kalkilieh, and this was repeated soon afterwards by Lt R.S. Adair and Lt R.A. Camm in C4624, who forced another to land in the same area. On the 28th Lt E.P. Kenny and Lt F.C. Hawley in C4626 met three Albatros D.Vs, one of which they sent down out of control south of Nablus.

On 1 May two aircraft departed at dawn for a reconnaissance sortie and to drop leaflets to the Arabs at Beni Sakr. While they were flying near Amman B1146, crewed by Capt D.W. Rutherford and 2nd Lt J. McElligott, was hit by ground machine-gun fire, and forced to land with both petrol tanks ruptured. The crew set fire to their aircraft to prevent it falling into enemy hands. Lieutenant F.W. Haig and Lt R.T. Challinor in A7196 immediately landed alongside the burning wreckage in an attempt to rescue their compatriots, but a wheel collapsed on take-off, and after setting fire to the second machine all four occupants

Two studies of C4732 of 111 Sqn undergoing engine maintenance in late 1918 or early 1919, possibly at Qantara. *(Philip Jarrett)*

were taken prisoner by Circassian cavalry. Two days later Lt J.K. Curwen-Walker crashed while on escort patrol in A7198, and on the same day Capt A.R. Brown and Lt G. Finlay in B1149 and Lt G.V. Oxenham and Lt H.A. Letch in B1225 forced a two-seater to land near Suweileh and then shot it up. On 7 May Capt Ross M. Smith and Lt E.A. Mustard in B1229 and Lt A.V. Tonkin and Lt R.A. Camm in B1276 sent a two-seater down in flames southeast of Jenin Aerodrome, and soon afterwards the latter crew sent an Albatros D.Va out of control at Tul Keram. On the 9th Lt G.C. Peters and Lt G. Finlay in C4623 forced a Rumpler to land on Jenin Aerodrome. On 16 May Capt Ross Smith carried Lt Col T.E. Lawrence ('Lawrence of Arabia'), who was acting as the British adviser to Sherif Nazir, the Arab leader, to visit Arabs at Mecca following Lawrence's visit to Gen Allenby's headquarters to discuss Arab co-operation. On the 22nd two Bristol Fighters at 11,000ft spotted two Albatros D.Vas, and their respective gunners attacked them from beneath without response. Captain Smith and Lt W.A. Kirk in B1229 sent one down out of control three miles north of Nablus, while Lt E.P. Kenny and Lt W.J.A. Alexander in C4624 saw the other fall away near Beir Chucate. Next day, two F.2Bs patrolling south of Nablus came across four Albatros D.Vas at 12,000ft near Huwara, and Lt C.S. Paul and Lt W.J.A. Weir in C4627 sent one out of control and forced another to land to be destroyed on the ground at Nablus. Lieutenant A.V. Tonkin and Lt R.A. Camm in B1276 sent down another which might have got away. On the 29th Lt E.C. Stooke and Lt W.J.A. Weir in B1280, along with Lt G.C. Peters and Lt J.H. Traill in C4623, sent a Rumpler two-seater down in flames northeast of Nablus.

An entry for June in a captured official diary reads: 'The enemy, who possesses in his Bristol Fighter an exceptionally fine machine, has made himself lately very redoubtable. Nearly always flying in twos, the Bristol Fighters present an extraordinary fighting force, and their harassing of our activities becomes more and more felt.' The strength of the F.2B as a fighting machine was no doubt enhanced in the Australian squadron by their daring, offensive-minded crews with their tactical flexibility. The German crews were somewhat handicapped by a tendency to fight using tactics which were rigidly laid down, with little scope for individual initiative when meeting unexpected situations. Although the F.2B crews often faced numerically superior odds, this never deterred them and they almost invariably prevailed. At the end of May a German report provided to the Turkish

Another 1 Sqn aircraft, A718? Displays a similar scheme to that applied to A7194. *(Philip Jarrett)*

Command stated: 'As long as the English use two-seaters which are superior to our machines in climbing capacity, successful activity on our part is very much in question, owing to the impossibility of the single-seater even attempting to make an attack on higher-flying and better-climbing two-seaters, and owing to our inability during the attack of the enemy to take over the attack ourselves'.

During most of June and the early part of July the F.2B crews enthusiastically undertook ground-strafing attacks on enemy troops, transport, camel trains and airfields. Casualties continued to be rare, but on 4 June Lt A.V. Tonkin and Lt R.A. Camm attacked a Rumpler out of the sun over Jerusalem. They manoeuvred beneath it while the German crew were still unaware of their attackers, and Camm aimed his twin Lewis guns and opened fire, but one gun jammed. When Tonkin aimed his Vickers gun the same thing occurred. By this time the enemy were alerted, and the gunner fired a burst into the F.2B's Rolls-Royce Falcon engine. Tonkin was sprayed with hot water, and as he turned away Camm was wounded seriously in the wrist by another burst from the German gunner. Tonkin landed the F.2B at the nearest field hospital at Bireh, and Camm was later invalided home to Australia.

On the 8th Capt A.R. Brown and Lt H.A. Letch in A7200 forced a two-seater to land between Kissir and Kastal, some six miles southeast of Amman, and then shot it up. Three days later Capt Ross Smith and Lt W.A. Kirk in B1229, with Lt E.G.C. Stooke and Lt L.P. Kreig in B1276, forced a Rumpler C.IV to land eight miles north of Tul Keram, then machine-gunned it. Early on the 13th Lt C.S. Paul and Lt W.J.A. Weir in C4627 shot down a Rumpler eight miles north of Nablus, then on the 19th, Capt R.M. Smith and Lt W.A. Kirk in B1229 forced two more Rumplers to land northwest of Damie and then machine-gunned them. An Albatros D.Va was the target on the 23rd, when Capt S.W. Addison and Lt W.H. Fysh in A7237 sent it down out of control five miles southeast of Bireh. A sad loss on the 26th was the death in combat with an Albatros two-seater at 18,000ft over Ramleh of Lt A.W.K. Farquhar in the back seat of C4623, piloted by Lt A.W. Murphy, who was unhurt. Next day, Capt A.R. Brown and Lt G. Finlay in B1149 forced an AEG two-seater to land ten miles south of Kutrani and then machine-gunned it, a second AEG also being sent down smoking and forced to land. On the same date Lt G.V. Oxenham and Lt L.H. Smith were in combat with some AEGs when they were hit by ground fire. Oxenham, who was mortally

The crew of B1146, Capt Ross Smith (right) and Lt E.A. Mustard, indulge in some pre-flight planning. *(Philip Jarrett)*

Captain R. Williams, Gen Harry Chauvel, Col Newton and Capt W.S. Addison prepare to depart in a pair of 1 Sqn AFC F.2Bs. one of which was A7198, seen here. *(Philip Jarrett)*

Major S.W. Addison (left) and Lt W. Hudson Fysh (later Sir Hudson) DFC in front of F.2B A7200 of 1 Sqn AFC in Palestine in 1918. The aircraft was nicknamed 'The Yellow Peril'.

wounded, managed to bring the aircraft down to crash behind enemy lines in the Hills of Lebanon, Smith being taken prisoner. An Albatros D.Va was shot down east of Amman on the 28th by Lt R.S. Adair and Lt C.J. Vyner in A7200, and another east of the railway station. Yet another was destroyed in the same area by Lt S.A. Nunan and Lt G. Finlay in B1149.

Enemy aircraft were appearing more frequently by mid-July, but they were promptly dealt with and nearly always shot down or driven off. On the 16th Capt A.R. Brown and Lt G Finlay in B1284, with Lt G.C. Peters in B1278, drove down an Albatros D.Va near Tul Keam, and an hour later Lt A.V. Tonkin and Lt A.V. McCann in B1276 similarly despatched an Albatros D.V. The next day Capt Ross Smith and Lt W.A. Kirk in B1229 forced down two Albatros D.Vs, the first west of Huwarra and the second a few minutes later at Wadi Auja. Both were destroyed, but then they themselves had to force-land near Bireh, north of Jerusalem, but their aircraft was recovered. On the same day Lt D.R. Dowling and Lt E.A. Mulford in A7190 drove down a two-seater some three miles east of Amman, while Lt G.W. Sheppard and Lt L.P. Kreig in C4840 did the same to another four miles south of Amman. On the

22nd Lt A.V. Tonkin and Lt L.W. Sutherland in B1276 sent a Rumpler down to crash south of Beit Lid, and two days later another was destroyed near Tanturah by Lt G.C. Peters and Lt J.H. Traill, along with Lt J.M. Walker and Lt H.A. Letch in B1222. On the 28th Capt A.R. Brown and Lt G. Finlay in B1284 forced a Rumpler to land near Upper Wadi Farah; it was then shot up by Lt C.S. Paul and Lt W.J.A. Weir in C4627. Finally, on the 30th, Lt E.P. Kenny and Lt L.W. Sutherland in C4626 forced down a DFW at Wadi Aujah then shot it up on the ground.

August continued in similar vein. On 3 August, in an epic 40-minute engagement, Lt E.P. Kenny and Lt L.W. Sutherland in C4626 forced an Albatros two-seater to land northwest of Afuleh at 11:30 and then destroyed it. They then sent another of the same type down out of control at 11:45, and destroyed a third Albatros two miles northeast of Ez Buba at 12:10, this one being shared with Lt P.J. McGuiness and Lt W.H. Fysh in B1223. On the 5th Lt R.S. Adair and Lt E.A. Mulford in A7200 forced an Albatros D.Va to land five miles east of Amman. On the 13th B1276 crashed and was burnt out. Next day Lt P.J. McGuiness and Lt W.H. Fysh in C4623, with Lt W.C. Thompson and Lt M.D. Lees in A7192,

forced a Fokker biplane to land at Jenin. On the 16th Lt C.S. Paul and Lt W.J.A. Weir in C4627 destroyed a Rumpler two-seater at Kefr Kaddum. Six days later Capt A.R. Brown and Lt G. Finlay in B1284 forced down an LVG C.V in the Allied lines near the 57th Balloon Station, where it was captured. The same day Lt J.M. Walker and Lt H.A. Letch in B1222 were killed in combat with another LVG C.V when return fire ruptured their fuel tank, which exploded. They went down in flames southwest of Samail, the observer jumping to his death while the pilot was blown out of his cockpit by the blast. On the 24th two crews engaged a total of eight enemy aircraft; Lt G.C. Peters and Lt J.H. Traill in B1278 destroyed an LVG two-seater and one of the new Pfalz D.IIIs east of Hanutah, while Lt P.J. McGuiness and Lt H.B. Fletcher in C4623 sent down a Pfalz D.III in flames and another, forced to land, was then destroyed on the ground at Kalkilieh. On the 28th Lt G.W. Sheppard and Lt C.J. Viner in C4840 forced an LVG to land near Jenin, and another was driven down by Lt E.S. Slade and Lt E.B.S. Neaton in C4623. Next day, Handley Page O/400 C9681 was attached to the squadron, the sole example of its type to reach the theatre. On the last day of the month Lt P.J. McGuiness and Lt H. Fysh in C4623 forced an LVG C to land at Rantieh, where it was captured, another being destroyed east of Kalkilieh.

By the beginning of September Gen Allenby had completed preparations for a fresh offensive, planned for the 19th. The 1st Sqn AFC was selected to provide overall strategic bombing and reconnaissance and was also tasked with being general 'supervisors' of the battle area. Meanwhile,

F.2B B1148 of 1 Sqn AFC in front of a Bessonneau hangar, with R.E.8s A4405 and A4408 for company. *(Philip Jarrett)*

Bristol F2B A7200 of 1 Sqn AFC with its lower engine cowling dropped for maintenance.

the Australian F.2Bs were fully engaged. On the 14th Lt P.J. McGuiness and Lt H. Fysh in C4623, with Lt D.R. Dowling and Lt E.A. Mulford in B1223, forced a Rumpler C to land east of Jenin, then machine-gunned it. Next day, Lt A.W. Murphy and Lt F.C. Hawley, while on reconnaissance in A7188, shot a two-seater down in flames near Amman.

By this time, after months of tremendous air fighting, the RAF had achieved complete air superiority. In particular, every enemy aircraft shot down over Palestine in the preceding two months had been claimed by the Australian crews. The Germans had some excellent machines and fought bravely, but their efforts had been totally frustrated. The 1st Sqn AFC records for one week reported, regarding enemy reconnaissance flights, '… hostile aeroplanes had crossed our lines one hundred times – mainly on the tip-and-run principle. They came at high altitudes (16,000 to 18,000ft), from which accurate observation was impossible.' Two months later such visits were down to only 18 a week. One great consequence of this was the ability of Allenby's armies and the RAF to complete their preparations almost completely unobserved by the enemy. In particular they were able to give the impression that the coming offensive would be across the River Jordan, whereas in fact it would come from the opposite corners of Palestine, leaving the enemy totally unprepared and his main forces in the wrong place.

On the 19th, the first day of the Battle of Nablus (generally referred to as the Battle of the Field of Armageddon, this being the biblical name for what was now Megiddo), Capt Ross Smith, piloting the O/400 loaded with 16 112lb bombs, wrecked the enemy's vital central telephone exchange at El Afule and also the nearby rail junction. That evening he took off again, this time dropping his bomb load on Jenin and its adjacent aerodrome. During the day B1225 was hit by ground fire while carrying out low bombing, and came down near Tul Keram; Lt D.R. Dowling and Lt E.A. Mulford were both wounded and taken prisoner. When B1287 was hit by ground fire during a low shoot, Lt A.V. Tonkin and Lt L.S. Climie had to force-land were also taken prisoner, but fortunately were rescued later in the day by Australian light cavalry. Lieutenant H.S.R. Maughan and Lt L.W. Sutherland in B1229 were escorting a bombing operation when a 144 Sqn D.H.9 had to force-land, and they landed near Jenin Aerodrome to rescue the occupants. Some

approaching Bedouin tribesmen were held off by fire from the aircraft's rear gun. The enemy airfield at El Afule was captured that day, becoming useful as an advanced landing ground for RAF reconnaissance aircraft.

Two days later Capt A.R. Brown and Lt G. Findlay in B1284, with Lt S.A. Nunan and Lt F.C. Conrick in B1285, carried out a morning reconnaissance, and soon radioed back that the enemy was in retreat. Turkish transport was attempting to escape along the vulnerable Balat-Ferwah-Shibleh-Jordan road, running along Wadi Beidan, a valley with a sheer precipice on one side and steep hills on the other. The two aircraft promptly bombed and machine-gunned the troops from just above their heads, causing many casualties. Throughout the next day further RAF aircraft kept up a continuous attack, first blocking escape at the head of the column, then raining death and destruction on the thousands of congested Turkish troops in a horrifying massacre. By the end of the day the crews were appalled by their mass killing. Over the next two days, in what became known as the Nine Miles of Dead, the Australian squadron alone fired 30,000 machine-gun rounds and dropped three tons of bombs, as much as all the other squadrons combined. The onslaught continued as survivors of the Seventh and Eighth Turkish Armies attempted to continue their headlong retreat, but by now they were virtually destroyed as an organised

force. The official history of Australia in the First World War says of the Australian airmen's part in this episode: 'The victory could not have been complete without them. They prepared it during the weeks beforehand. They consummated it in the critical days. The worst scenes of destruction were their work. Many thousands of Turks believed the Bristol Fighter to be a direct instrument of Allah.'

The 1st Sqn AFC was then asked to provide assistance to the northern Arab army, working under the inspiration of T.E. Lawrence. Three F.2Bs, B1229, B1278 and B1286, were despatched to the main Arab encampment at Um es Surab to deal mainly with German aircraft based at Der'a which had been attacking the Arab forces. Accompanied by the O/400, they arrived early on 22 September. At 10:00 Capt R.M. Smith and Lt E.A. Mustard in B1229, with Lt E.S. Headlam and Lt W.H. Lilly in B1286, shot down a DFW at Mafrak, where it was machine-gunned on the ground and set on fire. Forty-five minutes later they attacked and sent down three Pfalz D.IIIs in the same area, Smith and Mustard being credited with the destruction of two of them on the ground.

At 17:00 Lt G.C. Peters and Lt J.H. Traill in B1278 sent a DFW down smoking eight miles north of Der'a and then destroyed it on the ground with Lewis-gun fire, killing the German crew. That night the Handley

Another presentation F.2B was B1285, *Australia No.7, New South Wales No.6. The White Edenglassie.* This F.2B joined 1 Sqn AFC in late August 1918.
(Eric Harlin)

Above: **Two Bristol Fighters of 67 (Australian) Sqn, later 1 Sqn Australian Flying Corps at El Medjel, Palestine, in 1918. The nearest machine, A7194, had previously served with 111 Sqn. The colour is authentic but has deteriorated over the years.**

Below: **F.2Bs of 1 Sqn AFC lined up. The second aircraft is A7194, depicted above. There is a B.E.12a at the far end.**

The pilot and observer/gunner of A7194 make some pre-flight preparations. The aircraft's cowlings and wheel covers are gloss black, and a polished conical spun metal spinner is affixed to the propeller boss.

Page completed the damage by dropping nearly a ton of bombs on the now-shattered airfield, effectively putting it out of action for the remainder of the war. Early next morning, the 23rd, 16 bombs were dropped across Der'a Airfield by C4626 and C4627, setting a hangar on fire and destroying or damaging several DFWs. The crews of the 1st Sqn were busy that morning, attacking troop columns on the road between Es Salt and Amman, during which they dropped 48 bombs and fired 7,000 rounds. They then turned their attention on Amman, where they unloosed nearly three tons of bombs as well as firing 15,000 rounds by the time dusk fell. Lieutenant E.P. Kenny and Lt L.W. Sutherland in C4626 then forced an DFW to land north of the aerodrome and machine-gunned it on the ground. Bombing and strafing continued for the next few days, wherever targets could be found in the open. On the 28th, during a raid by four F.2Bs on Damascus Aerodrome, Kenny and Sutherland, again in C4626, forced a DFW to land on the aerodrome and then machine-gunned it. Next day the Germans departed. On the last day of the month Lts Maughan and Weir happened upon a scattering of around 4,000 infantry and cavalry along the north bank of the River Zabirani, but they were easy targets, too exhausted and cowed to put up any resistance, and the F.2B crew decided not to waste any more ammunition on them in their sorry state.

The next day, 1 October, British cavalry entered Damascus to find it bereft of enemy troops, who had left behind quantities of stores and equipment. RAF units moved forward with the advancing troops, and two days later the 1st Sqn AFC moved from Ramleh to Haifa, where one Flight had already been detached on 25 September. Long-range reconnaissance sorties were undertaken from there to search for remaining pockets of enemy troops. A further move was made on the 15th to Homs in Syria. On the 19th Capt Ross Smith and Lt A.V. McCann in B1229, with Lt E.S. Headlam and Lt W.H. Lilly in B1295, found a solitary DFW C.V at 18,000ft and forced it to land 25 miles southwest of Aleppo. After accepting the surrender of the crew, they destroyed it with Very pistol cartridges, leaving the airmen to their own devices. This was the first German

A line-up of 1 Sqn AFC aircraft seen from inside a Bessonneau hangar. From left to right: a Bristol Fighter, two Martinsyde G.102s and a B.E.12a. The motley assortment of clothing is noteworthy, as is the tented accommodation in the distance.

Above: **From what can be discerned on the original print, this is believed to be F.2B C9933, photographed in featureless Egyptian terrain during the First World War.** *(Philip Jarrett)*

Right: **An unfortunately unidentifiable F.2B in Mesopotamia in 1917.** *(Philip Jarrett)*

aircraft seen since the attacks on Der'a Aerodrome nearly a month earlier. Four days later, during a squadron attack on Muslimie railway junction near Aleppo, Lt S.H. Harper and Lt W.H. Lilly in C4626 chased two DFW C.Vs down to a nearby aerodrome at Babannit, where four more could be seen preparing to take off. They forced one of the pair to land before shooting it up, and then bombed and strafed all six, none of the enemy crews making any further attempt to take to the sky.

Eight days later an Armistice was declared in this theatre, ending the war against Turkey. The F.2Bs of 1st Sqn AFC had contributed in good measure to ensuring the success of Allenby's offensive in September 1918, their efforts in the arid wastes of the Palestine desert earning them the following tribute in *The War in the Air* (Vol. VI, page 207): '… it would hardly be an exaggeration to say that the Bristol Fighters of the Australians kept the sky clear.' Captain Ross Smith and his observer Lt. E. A. Mustard had flown B1229 throughout the campaign, destroying 17 enemy aircraft between them and twice rescuing the crews of stranded machines.

On 22 November the Australian squadron moved back to Ramleh, a detachment being sent to Rayak three days later. In February 1919 the whole unit assembled at Kantara in the Suez Canal Zone of Egypt, six of its aircraft having been handed over to 111 Sqn

there. Before this, as a last tribute to the squadron's dead and with the CO's permission, C4626 circled Ramleh Aerodrome, dipping a wing in salute before scattering a handful of Palestine poppies. The squadron sailed for Australia aboard the SS *Port Sydney* on 5 March. Meanwhile, 111 Sqn had moved on 6 February to Ramleh, where on 1 February 1920 it was redesignated 14 Sqn, and as such remained in the Middle East and Mediterranean for nearly a quarter of a century.

At Akaba in the Wadi Araba in September 1917 a special unit, 'X' Flight, RAF, had been formed to work with Lawrence in the desert. It was initially equipped with B.E.2es, B.E.12s and a D.H.2, and later also with Martinsyde G.102 Elephants. Towards the end of its existence, at its Advanced Landing Ground at El Gueira in August/ September 1918, 'X' Flight received a Bristol Fighter, A7188, from the Palestine Front to replace the Martinsydes. It was piloted by Lt A.W. Murphy, with Lt F.C.

Hawley as his observer, who flew from Ramleh to join Lawrence. On 15 September Murphy and Hawley had a long combat with a Rumpler, which stalled and crashed in flames. Unfortunately, their F.2B also suffered damage and was declared unfit for further use. It was returned to Palestine and replaced by another of the type, A7184. When 'X' Flight was disbanded on 23 October 1918, the F.2B, along with two B.E.12s and a B.E.2e, was flown to Egypt.

In late 1919 Ross Smith, with his brother Keith as navigator, distinguished himself by flying a Vickers Vimy 11,000 miles from England to Australia. As the first aviators to accomplish this, they laid the foundations for future long-distance flights of this nature. They were awarded a prize of £A10,000 by the Australian Government for being the first Australians to complete this feat within 30 days and before the end of 1919. They reached Darwin from Hounslow on 10 December, having taken 28 days.

A side view of first prototype F.2A A3303 at Orfordness, where it was flown on home-defence night flights against raiding German bombers. The wingtip navigation lights are in evidence, and brackets for Holt flares are visible beneath the lower wing leading edges. The propeller blades are protected by fabric sleeves. *(Philip Jarrett)*

Chapter 9

HOME DEFENCE

During 1915 and 1916 the Germans made a number of bombing attacks on the British mainland, the majority at night by airships. A few daylight attacks were hit-and-run ventures by one or two aeroplanes or floatplanes at or near the limit of their range. The most notable of these was probably a daylight attack on central London on 28 November 1916 by an LVG C.IV captained by Ltn Walther Ilges and piloted by Deck-Offizier Paul Brandt. Flying from their base at Mariakerke, they dropped six bombs and,

after crossing the coast near Hastings, almost made it home, only to suffer engine failure and be captured after they force-landed near Ostend.

By early 1917 the Germans were building new twin-engine Gotha bombers with sufficient range to enable daylight attacks to be made in force. On 25 May, 21 Gothas flew across the Channel and reached Folkestone, where their bombs killed 95 people and injured another 195, some of these in a nearby army camp at Shorncliffe.

Of the 77 Home Defence (HD) sorties flown from 18 RNAS and RFC aerodromes, the only aircraft to attack the enemy formation was the prototype Sopwith Pup (3691) from Dover.

At around this time the Air Board had several non-operational units in the southeast, notably Training Squadrons. These were to be issued with aircraft suitable for home defence and, accordingly, 35 Training Squadron (TS) at Northolt received six Bristol Fighters, initially A7103, A7121, A7135 and A7135, shortly followed by A7173 and A7180.

On 5 June Sheerness was the target for a force of 22 Gothas, and 35 TS sent up three F.2Bs at around 7pm, but Lt Walmsley in A7136 had to force-land near Barnet with engine trouble, and Capt C.W.E. Cole-Hamilton in A7135 and Lt Child in A7122 were unable to make contact with the enemy bombers. Then, on 13 June, 18 Gothas out of 20 despatched targeted London. Two F.2Bs of 35 TS at Northolt happened to be taking off on patrol only four minutes before the air raid warning was sounded at

Presentation F.2B B1145, inscribed *Presented by Maharaja Bahadur Sir Rameswar Singh of Darbhanga No.3*, served for a time coded '5' with 39 (HD) Sqn at North Weald. *(IWM Q69255)*

11:21. 2nd Lt J. Chapman in A7135, with 2nd Lt F.G.C. Weare as observer, flew east along the north of the River Thames, while Capt C.W.E. Cole-Hamilton with Capt C.H.C. Keevil in A7136 went south of the river. When they had climbed to 10,000ft, both pilots sighted the enemy formation over Hackney in east London but needed to gain more height and thus were unable to prevent bombs being dropped. By the time they had closed the gap the Gothas were heading home and were now east of Ilford, Essex. Cole-Hamilton succeeded in getting 600ft below a group of three stragglers and fired 98 rounds at the rearmost Gotha, after which Keevil fired off further rounds from his Lewis gun as they turned away. As the formation approached Southend they made a further attack on the same group, but this time came under fire from the rearmost flanking machine, which had dropped back, and were themselves hit. Keevil managed to return 157 rounds before he was killed by a bullet in the neck. Unable to continue the fight because his Vickers gun was now jammed, Cole-Hamilton returned to Northolt at 1pm. Chapman, meanwhile, had attempted to attack the same three Gothas, but having flown further north and

Right: A line-up of F.2Bs of 141 (HD) Sqn at Biggin Hill in September 1918, displaying an assortment of striped fuselages. The nearest aircraft is F4368. *(Philip Jarrett)*

Below: A line-up of three F.2Bs of 39 (HD) Sqn at North Weald. The nearest two aircraft, B1330 '2' and C4650 '1', bear horizontal lines along their fuselages which are the same colour as their identification numbers, while the other has a black triangle outlined in white. B1330 was another presentation aircraft and is inscribed *Presented by Maharaja Bahadur Sir Rameswar Singh of Darbhanga No.5.* During February and March 1918 three patrols in search of night-flying German bombers were flown in C4650 by Capt J.M. Clark and Lt L. Speller. *(C&C)*

with his aircraft climbing badly, he was unable to gain sufficient height to do more than have his observer fire off a few optimistic bursts at an ineffective range before he, too, had to return home.

This was followed by a night raid on London on 16/17 June in which the Northolt F.2Bs were not involved, and then a daylight raid on Harwich and Folkestone on 4 July. The only Bristol Fighter to be involved was A7136, crewed this time by Capt A.C. Wright and Capt H.H. Bagnall, but without success. A further daylight raid on London was made on 7 July, but HD

Above: **Major Brian E. Baker, CO of 141 (HD) Sqn, in front of his F.2B, E2604, at Biggin Hill in 1918. The red rooster painted on the aircraft's fin signified the unit's assertion that it was the 'Cock-of-the-Walk' squadron.** *(Philip Jarrett)*

Left: **A crashed F.2B night fighter shows the overpainted white sections of its upper wing roundels, which rendered it less visible to raiding German pilots and gunners.** *(Philip Jarrett)*

in A7117, both from No 8 Aircraft Acceptance Park (AAP) at Lympne, to which their aircraft had been flown that day after service in France with 48 Sqn. During a daylight Gotha raid on 22 August Holder went up again from Orfordness, as did 2nd Lt J.G. Dainty in A7106 and 2nd Lt S.J. Riley in A7116 from No 8 AAP at Lympne. A further daylight attack was made on 22 August, this time against Margate, Ramsgate and Dover. Holder again went up in A3303, as did 2nd Lt J.G. Dainty in A7106 and 2nd Lt S.J Riley in A7116.

The Bristol Fighter was evidently one of the few types that could stand much chance of gaining sufficient height and have sufficient speed on arrival to be a serious threat to the attackers, having already proved its fighter abilities in France. However, it was not ideal for this work, its stationary water-cooled engine needing longer to warm up than rotary engines. It was a difficult machine to land on small aerodromes and landing grounds during the night because of its long nose. Nonetheless a decision was made to re-equip three of the HD squadrons with the type.

For this role, the aircraft were painted matt dull green overall to render them less visible to the enemy, with all white stripes and rings in the national insignia obscured. Powered by Rolls-Royce engines, they were equipped with a sight set to face forward at an elevation of 45 degrees from the pilot's eye, enabling the rear gunner to fire over the pilot's head while the latter was aiming the aircraft, and the trajectory would remain straight at a speed of 100mph. When the pilot had manoeuvred into position by lining up the sight, he signalled the gunner to start firing. This method of gun positioning came about as a result of tests at Orfordness early in 1918, when a 39 (HD) Sqn Bristol Fighter, piloted by Lt C.P. Donnison with Lt Fox as gunner, scored 99 hits on a towed target out of 194 rounds fired from a distance of 400-450 yards. In the event only 39 Sqn initially became wholly equipped with Bristol Fighters. With headquarters at Woodford Green in Essex, it had flights based at North Weald, Sutton's Farm (Hornchurch) and Hainault Farm; the unit's new mounts started to arrive in September 1917. To help with night work, Sgt A.E. Hutton had earlier devised a special illuminated gunsight. This was replaced in December by the Neame sight, which worked in a similar manner.

On the night of 5/6 December 'A' Flight of 39 Sqn sent up two Bristol fighters during an attack on London by 16 Gothas and two *Riesenflugzeug* (giant aircraft). At 04:59 2nd

efforts were largely ineffectual despite the large number of sorties flown each time, including two from Northolt, one of which was A7135 crewed by Capt G.D. Hill and Capt R. Stuart-Wortley. Also flown was prototype F.2A A3303 from the Experimental Armament Squadron at Orfordness, crewed by Lt F.D. Holder and Lt F.W. Musson. Holder attempted to chase the Gotha formation east of Southend, and

after a difficult chase of 30 miles got in a 30-round burst at some distance before having to return owing to shortage of fuel. Holder went up again on 22 July during a daylight raid on Harwich and Felixstowe, this time with Sgt S. Ashby as observer.

On 12 August, during a daylight raid on Southend, Holder was once more airborne among the defending aircraft, as were Lt R.S. Slingsby in A7106 and Lt R.S. Carroll

Crews of 141 (HD) Sqn overwhelm one of their F.2Bs at Biggin Hill in 1918. Maj B.E. Barker, the CO, stands seventh from right. *(Philip Jarrett)*

Inscribed *Presented by Maharaja Bahadur Sir Rameswar Singh of Darbhanga No.2. The Lord of Chelmsford*, F.2B B1262 '8' of 39 (HD) Sqn was photographed in 1918. It has wingtip lights on its lower wings and a ring-sight angled upwards at 45 degrees on the trailing edge of the upper wing centre-section to enable the pilot to sight the target for his gunner in the rear cockpit. The horizontal coloured bar along the rear fuselage has been overpainted.

Lt C.P. Donnison and Lt W.N. Fraser in A7249 took off, followed six minutes later by C4823, crewed by Lt C.J. Chabot and Lt V.A. Lanos, but neither had any success. In a further London raid by 13 Gothas and one giant after dusk on 18/19 December, four sorties were flown from North Weald (known at that time as North Weald Bassett), and two more went up in a similar raid on 22/23 December, again without success.

Several HD squadrons received Bristol Fighters during 1918. The first seems to have been 141 Sqn at Biggin Hill, which became the second to be wholly equipped with the type in March 1918; these were in place of the intended Sopwith Dolphins, this type having proved disappointingly unsuccessful in the role. A small number went the following month to 36 Sqn at Newcastle and detached flights based at Hylton (Usworth), Ashington and Seaton Carew. At Emswell 75 Sqn had a few from May, as did 33 Sqn in June, with flights at Brattlesby (Scampton), Kirton-in-Lindsey and Elsham. It was proposed to re-equip 51 Sqn at Marham with 24 F.2Bs in June 1918, to become a third wholly equipped squadron, but this did not materialise. The only other HD squadron to receive a small number appears to have been 76 Sqn at Ripon. The F.2B had a tendency to 'float' during its approach, giving it a reputation for being difficult to land at night, but despite this it remained in service with HD squadrons for the remainder of the war.

On the night of 28/29 January 1918 39 Sqn sent up ten Bristol Fighters from North Weald during a raid by seven Gothas and a giant, and this time Lt J.G. Goodyear and AM1 W.T. Merchant in F.2B C4639 sighted a giant while patrolling between Suttons' Farm and Sawbridgeworth. As the pilot fired a long burst from his Vickers gun from astern the bomber, his aircraft was flung aside by the slipstream from the giant's propellers. A further attempt met with similar results as he came under attack from the giant's defensive guns. An attempt to turn in to give the rear gunner a chance to bring his Lewis guns to bear was thwarted when the F.2B's main petrol tank was shattered by enemy defensive fire, and Merchant was wounded. The engine cut shortly after this, but with the North Weald flarepath in sight to the southeast he was able to land successfully. Merchant was taken to hospital but proved to have only a minor arm wound. The following night just three giants reached the capital, the 80 defending sorties including eight by Bristol Fighters, again from North Weald.

After a short lull, four giants attacked targets in London and Dover on the night of 16/17 February, and seven Bristol Fighters

One of only two F.2Bs of Home Defence units to be credited with confirmed aerial victories over England, C4636 'A6' of 39 (HD) Sqn, flown by Lt A.J. Arkell with AM A.T.C. Stagg as gunner, shot down a Gotha bomber on the night of 19/20 May 1918. The raider crashed off Roman Road, East Ham, London, and burst into flames. Although C4636 was hit by return fire, its crew were unharmed and landed safely. *(via Philip Jarrett)*

On the night of 5/6 December 1917 C4823, seen here shortly after completion, was one of two F.2Bs of 39 (HD) Sqn at North Weald sent up in an attempt to intercept a raid on London by German Gothas and *Riesenflugzeug*. Unfortunately its crew, Lts C.J. Chabot and V.A. Lanos, had no success. *(Philip Jarrett)*

F.2B A7183 and others of its kind of 39 (HD) Sqn on the airfield at North Weald. This aircraft had previously been with the Testing Squadron at Martlesham Heath for performance tests with the Falcon engine, and also at Orfordness. (J. Goldsworthy)

Close-up of a 39 (HD) Sqn F.2B at North Weald, with a mounting for Lewis guns on the upper centre section. The propellers have protective fabric sleeves. (J. Goldsworthy)

All dressed up and ready to go. Crew members of 39 (HD) Sqn. (J. Goldsworthy)

A close-up of the Scarff ring and Lewis gun of a 39 (HD) Sqn F.2B. (J. Goldsworthy)

from North Weald were among the 60 sorties which went up. Captain J.M. Clarke in C4650 was mistakenly fired on by Capt O.V. Thomas in C4815, fortunately without harm. A solitary giant over London the following night resulted in seven North Weald Bristols being sent up. Many of the fighters were fired on by their own anti-aircraft defences after being caught by searchlights, including a near miss on Lt C.P. Donnison in C4635. An enquiry of the

gunners revealed that they had mistaken the sound of two Rolls-Royce engines as being very similar to that of one Gotha. Five more giants attacked London on the night of 7/8 March, and North Weald despatched eight Bristols, three of which had to be diverted to land at Hainault Farm owing to a heavy mist at their own base, and another had to make a forced landing.

There were no further raids on London until the night of 19/20 May, when 28

Gothas and three giants were met by 88 defending sorties. These now included two Bristol Fighter-equipped squadrons, 39 Sqn putting up eight from North Weald and 141 Sqn seven from Biggin Hill. This time their efforts rewarded. At 22:56 Lt A.J. Arkell and AM1 A.T.C. Stagg took off from North Weald in C4636 of 39 Sqn, marked 'A-6' and named *Devil in the Dusk*. At 00:05, after flying at 11,000ft for just over an hour and near the southern extremity of the patrol line, he spotted a Gotha's twin exhaust flames 1,000ft below. The enemy aircraft had already received the attention of Capt D.V. Armstrong of 78 Sqn in Sopwith Camel C6713. Promptly diving down, Arkell went beneath its tail and started to close from 500 yards so that Stagg could fire half a drum upwards, before he zoomed up to give another long burst from his own forward Vickers gun. As he levelled off to give Stagg another opportunity, the enemy aircraft began to dive, making flat turns so that both its own gunners had a chance to fire. Arkell responded with several further bursts, then moved close under its tail so that Stagg could get in two more bursts before they zoomed up to get in another quick Vickers burst, now having expended a total of 350 rounds. By this time he saw that he was down to 3,000ft, so he again got underneath, and Stagg's final burst succeeded in setting fire to the Gotha's starboard engine. After spinning round for about one-and-a-half turns it crashed just off Roman Road, East Ham, where it burst

A trio of 39 (HD) Sqn F.2Bs lined up outside the North Weald hangars. The nearest aircraft is probably C4636 'A6', and the furthest has an indecipherable 'C' serial. (J. Goldsworthy)

Right: **Bristol F.2Bs of 39 (HD) Sqn viewed from inside a hangar. Flying the nearest machine, C4815, Capt O.V. Thomas made three unsuccessful attempts to intercept Gotha bombers, on the nights of 18 December 1917 and 29/30 January and 16/17 February 1918.** *(J. Goldsworthy)*

into flames, none of the crew surviving. On return to base one of several bullet holes in C4636 was found only a few inches from Arkell's seat.

That night it was also 141 Sqn's turn for some success. Major F. Sowrey, CO of 143 Sqn, had taken off from Detling at 23:30 in S.E.5a C1804, and fifteen minutes later he spotted a bomber northeast of Maidstone, firing at it unsuccessfully before losing sight of it. Fifteen minutes later he sighted an outbound Gotha in the same position and again fired unsuccessfully before losing it. This second machine changed direction to evade Sowrey's attention, but after flying west for only five minutes was picked up over South Ash by Lt E.E. Turner, who had taken off from Biggin Hill at 23:05 with Lt H.B. Barwise in Bristol Fighter C851. Turner took up position behind and below the Gotha, waiting until it filled the 45-degree Neame sight on his upper wing, then his observer delivered a burst of explosive and incendiary RTS[1] ammunition into its port engine. The enemy bomber now went down into a flat turn, but two further bursts from Barwise hit the fuselage and starboard wings before his gun jammed. The Bristol's engine then began to give trouble, and by the time it had picked up the duo had lost sight of their prey, Turner not having fired any shots from his Vickers gun. At 01:25 he landed at Detling before returning to Biggin Hill, unaware that, in the meantime, the Gotha had crashed between Frinsted and Harrietsham at 00:45. Its pilot had attempted unsuccessfully to land at Harrietsham Aerodrome, and only one of the three crew members survived. It transpired that the Gotha pilot had been wounded by Maj Sowrey. After some investigation Turner was credited with the victory.

In due course medals were awarded for this action, which proved to have taken place during the last night attack on London. Arkell gained the Military Cross, Stagg the Military Medal and Turner and Barwise the Distinguished Flying Cross, at that time a new decoration.

The HD organisation remained in existence for a short time after the war had ended, but the only other German raid was by four naval Zeppelins on the Midlands during the night of 5/6 August 1918.

---

1 RTS stood for Richard Threlfall and Son, Sir Richard Threlfall being the leading chemical engineer who had designed the highly sensitive bullet, which exploded on striking aircraft fabric.

Above: **Some of 39 (HD) Sqn's F.2Bs were heavily armed; this one has twin elevating Lewis guns on the upper wing centre section in addition to the observer's twin Lewises. All four guns could be aligned forwards and upwards at 45 degrees to direct maximum firepower against German intruders flying overhead.** *(J. Goldsworthy)*

This study of an F.2B of 39 (HD) Sqn at North Weald poses a problem. The aircraft's serial number clearly appears to be B1356, but this serial was allocated to a SPAD 7 built by Mann Egerton. *(Epping Forest District Council Museum Service)*

88

This line-up of F.2Bs at 35 TS at Port Meadow, Oxfordshire, includes C4804 and, in the distance, C4830. Note the chequerboard nose markings. *(Eric Harlin)*

Chapter 10

TRAINING AND SUPPORT UNITS

The Bristol Fighter was used for training purposes from the outset. The first two production aircraft, A3305 and A3306, were delivered on 20 December 1916 to 38 RS at Rendcomb, some five miles north of Cirencester in Gloucestershire and only a 35-mile flight from the manufacturer's Filton Aerodrome, near Bristol. Also situated at Rendcomb was 48 Sqn, which began to re-equip with F.2As early in the new year, taking these to France on 8 March 1917. On 31 May 1917 38 RS was redesignated 38 TS, as were all such units on that date.

The first major accident involving a training Bristol Fighter appears to have occurred on 23 January 1917, when A3309 crashed during a delivery flight to 38 RS. While 2nd Lt B.F. Parsons was still some 13-14 miles short of his destination a failing

engine obliged him to attempt a forced landing at Charlton Park, near Malmesbury in Gloucestershire, but as he turned downwind, he lost speed and crashed. Both he and 2nd Lt C.B. Fenton survived the crash, but sadly Parsons died of his injuries later that day.

The second such unit to receive Bristol Fighters appears to have been 35 RS at Northolt, which was allotted its first example, F.2A A3332, on 28 April 1917 and also had several F.2Bs. Its 'C' Flight was equipped soon afterwards with R.E.8s and it also still had numbers of B.E.2es for a time. This unit, redesignated 35 TS on 31 May, moved to Port Meadow in Oxford, on 16 December, being absorbed into No 44 Training Depot Station (TDS) there on 5 August 1918, still with F.2Bs.

The F.2B went on to fly with numerous training and support units until it was finally withdrawn from RAF service over 20 years later. The only other Training Squadron which appears to have received Bristol Fighters during 1917 was 59 TS, based at Yatesbury in Wiltshire. This entailed a delivery flight of only some 30 miles east of Filton, probably starting in August 1917. The unit's official establishment at this time is unknown, but all were F.2Bs, these carrying white individual fuselage identification numbers aft of the fuselage roundel, ranging from '1' (A7218) to at least '19' (C4775). Some also bore individual names, an example being *TIGER*, carried by A7238/'6'. Number 38 TS continued to fly F.2Bs during subsequent moves, to Beaulieu on 30 October, Netheravon on 4 November,

Although F.2B A7195 was initially allotted to the BEF, it was re-allotted to training in July 1917 and flown to 82 Sqn at Waddington. It subsequently served with No 1 School of Air Fighting at Ayr, and at one stage it had a striped nose and interplane struts. *(Philip Jarrett)*

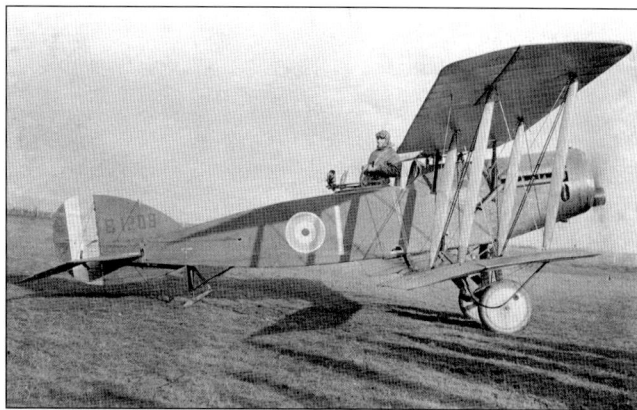

Above: **Two views of F.2B B1208, which went to No 1 (Auxiliary) School of Aerial Gunnery at Hythe in December 1917.** *(Philip Jarrett)*

Lilbourne on 6 December and finally, on 1 February 1918, to Rendcomb, where it eventually lost its identity on 15 August 1918 to became part of the new 24 TDS at Collinstown near Dublin.

Training Bristol Fighters became more common during 1918. In January they were received by 8 TS at Netheravon, and around the same time by 24 TS there. They were also used by 7 (Training) Sqn, AFC, which formed as such at Yatesbury on 14 January. Quite a number of Training Squadrons received Bristol Fighters during that year, but the only other one to have very many was 71 TS at Port Meadow. This unit, like its fellow 35 TS, was absorbed into the new 44 TDS there on 5 August 1918. A small number were flown from 1 April 1918 by 189 (Night) TS, this type of unit being involved in training selected pilots in methods of stalking and attacking Zeppelins and Gotha bombers at night from bases in the UK.

From July 1917 a new type of unit began to appear, the aforementioned TDS. This generally incorporated all the Training Squadrons into RAF stations. The process of amalgamation was gradual and continued throughout 1918. Those known to have flown a sizeable number of Bristol Fighters were 33 TDS at Witney, 37 TDS at Yatesbury, 44 TDS at Port Meadow and 45 TDS at Rendcomb. In Egypt, where similar units existed in the form of 16, 17 and 19 TDSs at Amriya, El Firdan and El Rimal respectively. All had Bristol Fighters on strength.

Other wartime units to use the Bristol Fighter in some numbers included No 1 School of Aerial Fighting at Ayr, the Aeroplane Experimental Station at Martlesham Heath, the Armament Experimental Station at Orfordness, the Artillery and Infantry Co-operation School at Hursley Park, Winchester, No 2 Fighting School at Marske, the Royal Aircraft Establishment (RAE) at Farnborough, the RAF and Army Co-operation School at Worthy Down and the Wireless Experimental Establishment at Biggin Hill.

The declaration of an Armistice in November 1918 brought a steady rundown of the RAF, and this took its toll on the

Above: **F.2B B1218 was with 62 Sqn at Rendcomb by late December 1917, but by February 1918 it was with No.38 TS at the same station.** *(Philip Jarrett)*

Above: **Flying Officer Walter Longton used dual F.2B C4666 as his personal mount at Port Meadow, Oxford, in the spring months of 1919.**

Bristol F.2B C4695
'76' of No.2
Fighting School at
Marske in 1918
displays a
distinctive
chequered nose.
(Philip Jarrett)

training units during the following 12 months. By the early 1920s the training units equipped with Bristol Fighters in any numbers were reduced to the Armament and Gunnery School at Eastchurch, the School of Army Co-operation at Stonehenge (later Old Sarum), the CFS at Upavon, the Electrical and Wireless School flying from Worthy Down and later Cranwell, the School of Photography Flight at Farnborough, the RAF College at Cranwell and No 1 School of Technical Training at Halton. In addition to these, there was a new type of all-in flying training unit, the Flying Training School (FTS), F.2Bs being used in some numbers by Nos 1 at Netheravon, 2 at Duxford (later Digby), 4 at Abu Sueir in Egypt and 5 at Shotwick, the last being renamed Sealand in 1924.

By the early 1930s the Bristol Fighter had become obsolescent, being replaced by Armstrong Whitworth Atlases in the Army Co-operation squadrons and was accordingly disappearing from training and support units. Among the last to use it were the Cambridge and Oxford University Air Squadrons at Duxford and Upper Heyford respectively. Some were employed on communications work, and a small number lingered on with the RAE at Farnborough for trials purposes, but even these had been scrapped by 1937. The lucky ones were civilianised, and details of these will be found in Appendix 7.

Many people had been killed in Bristol Fighter accidents of various kinds during the quarter-century it had remained in use, but on the whole it was regarded as a safe and reliable machine to the end.

Left and below: **One of the F.2Bs used by the Wireless Experimental Establishment at Biggin Hill was C4611 '1'.** *(Philip Jarrett)*

Above: **Arab-engined F.2B C9889, built by the Gloucestershire Aircraft Co Ltd, displays the white triangle that identifies it as a machine serving with No.36 TDS at Yatesbury. It was also used by No.37 TDS at the same location.** *(Philip Jarrett)*

Above right: **Named** *Panther,* **A7218 '1' was photographed while with No 59 TS at Yatesbury in 1918.** *(C&C)*

Right: **A sister aircraft to 'Panther' in No 59 TS at Yatesbury was A7238 '6', which was named** *Tiger,* **although its name is not visible here.** *(RAF Museum)*

These four photographs, dated 25 September 1918, depict the wreck of C988, a Bristol-built Arab-engined F.2B that was serving with No.5 TDS at Easton on the Hill in East Northamptonshire. On 24 September 2nd Lts H. Marsden and R.A. McAvity were flying from Farnborough to Stamford when the engine failed over Dunstable. In the attempted forced landing the aircraft side-slipped, the pilot was unable to straighten it out, and both officers were injured in the ensuing crash. As is often the case with crash pictures, an interesting detail is revealed; namely that C988 had its serial number painted in large numerals along the underside of its rear fuselage. Evidently, the aircraft's starboard side hit the ground first. *(Philip Jarrett)*

Major J.T.B.
McCudden took this
photograph of a
striped-nose F.2B
trainer at Turnberry.
(via C.C.H. Cole)

Left: **This is F.2B B1107** *Falkland*, **after nosing over at Yatesbury in August 1917 while serving with No 59 TS.** *(C&C)*

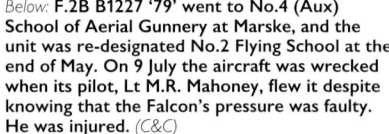

Below: **F.2B B1227 '79' went to No.4 (Aux) School of Aerial Gunnery at Marske, and the unit was re-designated No.2 Flying School at the end of May. On 9 July the aircraft was wrecked when its pilot, Lt M.R. Mahoney, flew it despite knowing that the Falcon's pressure was faulty. He was injured.** *(C&C)*

Above: **F.2B, C1009 '85' of No.2 School of Aerial Fighting and Gunnery at Marske, North Yorkshire, draws a crowd after overturning** *(left)*. **Ground crew set about restoring it to its normal posture** *(right)*.
(C&C and Eric Harlin)

Left and below: **Some aircraft at home stations acquired elaborate colour schemes, but 'piscine' F.2B B1288, with its painted scales, was one of the most extravagantly decorated examples. It served at No.1 (Obs) School of Aerial Gunnery at Hythe until it was wrecked in a fatal flying accident on 23 October 1918, probably due to jammed controls.** *(Philip Jarrett)*

With its Scarff ring removed from the rear cockpit, F4375 served as a personal transport for Gen Groves at the Air Council Inspection Squadron at Kenley in 1919. It later went to Egypt and India, was reconditioned to 'J' Type back in the UK, and then went to No. 2FTS at Digby. *(Philip Jarrett)*

A red-and-blue striped F.2B, believed to be '84', at No.2 School of Aerial Fighting and Gunnery at Marske. *(Eric Harlin)*

Above: **Almost certainly photographed at a training unit in the UK, Arab-engined F.2B C9840 was allocated to the South-West Area. The date of its inversion is unknown.** *(Ken Smy/SAAF Museum)*

Above: **An anonymous F.2B in use with a training unit in the Bournemouth area.** *(Philip Jarrett)*

Left: **The history of H1591 is not recorded, but this photograph of it, after what appears to have been a heavy landing on rough ground, was probably taken at a UK training unit.** *(Ken Smy/SAAF Museum)*

Above and right: **F.2B C4800 served with 29 TS at Hendon. Lt J.J. Doughty-Davis is standing by its nose in the second picture.** *(Eric Harlin)*

Below: **Another shot of C4800, this time with short exhaust pipes.** *(Philip Jarrett)*

Above left and right: **It is recorded that F.2B C4812 was 'wrecked' at 35 TS, Port Meadow, on 30 January 1918, when it hit a ridge on the aerodrome and stood on its nose, injuring 2nd Lt H.F. Robinson. However, these pictures of C4812 after colliding with Avro 504J B4276 in the snow are captioned as being taken at the CFS in February 1918, so, if the caption is correct, perhaps the F.2B was repaired after its first mishap.** *(Philip Jarrett)*

Above, left, and below: **C4879, known as *The Crocodile*, was covered in a chequerboard scheme apart from the cowling, which bore the teeth which earned the aircraft its name. It was on the strength of No.7 Training Squadron at No.33 TDS, Witney, in Oxfordshire, and subsequently went to Netheravon Flying School, and is believed to have been flown by the Wing Examining Officer in the Salisbury Plain district. It was wrecked in a fatal accident at Netheravon on 18 August 1919, when Flt Cdt H.S. Morris stalled on a gliding turn and spun in. The accident shown here was evidently earlier and somewhat less disastrous.** *(The late Peter F.G. Wright and Eric Harlin)*

F.2B E2580 'C' of 62 Sqn, with 'roundeled' wheel covers, at Nivelles early in 1919. It subsequently went to Mesopotamia and Hinaidi. In the background on the left is F430?, evidently a presentation aircraft, but the inscription is indecipherable. *(Eric Harlin)*

Chapter 11

THE F.2B STILL IN SERVICE

With the signing of the Armistice on 11 November 1918 it became necessary to slim down the RAF and reduce the number of types in service to those deemed necessary to meet anticipated peacetime needs. Among the few wartime aircraft to be retained was the Bristol Fighter, although it would no longer serve as a fighter, but became the standard army co-operation type.

In the closing stages of the war the Bristol Fighter squadrons had moved steadily forward with the advancing armies, and after the Armistice they went into Germany itself. Number 11 Sqn had moved from Vert Galand to Mory on 15 October, Bettoncourt on 1 November, Aulnoye on

18 November, Nivelles on 19 December and finally Spich in Germany on 20 May 1919. It finally discarded its aircraft and returned home to the UK on 3 September.

Meanwhile, 88 Sqn at Serny had moved to Floringhem on 21 October, then three days later to Ascq, to Gondecourt on the 26th and Bersée on the 28th. It joined the 51st Wing, 9th Brigade at Aulnoye on 18 November, then moved to Dour on 13 December, Burdinne on the 14th and Nivelles in Belgium on the 18th. Finally, in May 1919 it went to Hangelar, near Bonn, in Germany, to disband there on 10 August 1919, its aircraft being taken over by 12 Sqn at Heumar.

Having moved to La Bellevue on 26 September, 62 Sqn went to Villers-lès-Cagnicourt on 29 October, and after the Armistice to Aulnoye on 18 November, Bouge in Belgium on 14 December and Nivelles on the 20th, remaining there until it joined the Army of the Rhine at Spich in Germany on 2 May 1919, disbanding there on 31 July 1919.

On 22 October 1918 22 Sqn moved from Maisoncelle to Izel-le-Hameau, and then to Aniche on 26 October. On 18 November it transferred to the 51st Wing, 9th Brigade, based initially at Aulnoye, then to Witheries on 22 November and Nivelles in Belgium on 20 December. After a spell at Spich in

A collection of early post-war Bristol products ranged in front of the imposing Pullman civil transport triplane at Filton in 1920. From left to right: the first Puma Tourer, G-EAIZ; the F.2C Badger fighter; the Babe private single-seater; a civilianised M.1C scout; and an F.2B from a batch of 700 ordered on 12 April 1918. *(Bristol)*

A splendid view of the RAF Pageant at Hendon in 1920, with Avro 504s overflying a fascinating assortment of aircraft. Prominent in the centre foreground is F.2B E2505, which was probably based at Kenley with 24 Sqn at this time, and there are another three F.2Bs immediately behind its neighbour, D.H.9A F1611. Several J-serialled F.2Bs are among the massed aeroplanes on the left. Besides a great many 504s, machines of particular interest include Parnall Puffin N137, Westland Weasel F2914 and an early Siddeley Siskin. *(Philip Jarrett)*

Germany from 21 May 1919 its aircraft were withdrawn and it left for Ford on 1 September 1919.

Number 20 Sqn moved from Vignacourt to Suzanne on 16 September, Proyart on the 24th, Moislains on 7 October, Clary/Iris Farm in 89th Wing, 5th Brigade on the 25th, then to 22nd Wing, 5th Brigade, on 16 November. Further moves took it on 3 December to Ossogne. On 30 May 1919 it sailed from Marseilles for India, where it would again fly Bristol Fighters.

On 17 September 59 Sqn moved from Vert Galand to Beugnâtre, then on 14 October to Caudry, where on 16 November it transferred to the 15th Wing, 5th Brigade. With this formation it went to Gerpinnes on 29 November, still with some F.2Bs

until at least January 1919. Stationed at Béthencourt, 11 Sqn finally left the 13th Wing on 10 November 1918 briefly to join the newly-formed 90th (Army) Wing in the 3rd Brigade, but only seven days later it went to Aulnoye to become part of the 51st Wing in the 9th Brigade. After further moves to Bonneville and Nivelles it went on 21 May to Spich. It transferred to the 11th Wing, 2nd Brigade, on 24 July, before being reduced to a cadre and sent home on 3 September without aircraft, being disbanded at Scopwick (later renamed Digby) on the last day of the year.

On 23 October 1918, 48 Sqn finally left the 22nd Wing to join the 11th Wing at Reckem North, under the 2nd Brigade, moving to Nivelles in Belgium on 27

December, then to Bickendorf in Germany on 19 December. On 26 May 1919 it left there for India, its role being changed from fighter-reconnaissance to army co-operation.

Having replaced its F.K.8s with Arab-powered F.2Bs at Le Bellevue in December 1918, 8 Sqn formed part of the 12th Wing, 3rd Brigade. On 17 January 1919 it transferred from there to the 89th Wing. On 11 May it went to Sart in Belgium, being reduced to a cadre there in July, and its aircraft were withdrawn before it returned home to Duxford on 28 July, disbanding there on 20 January 1920.

Re-equipped from R.E.8s in December 1918 at Clavier (Belgium), 12 Sqn was part of the 11th Wing, 2nd Brigade. It moved to Düren in Germany on 19 December, then to Heumar on 5 May 1919 and finally to Bickendorf on 17 November 1920. It was disbanded there on 27 July 1922, being the last RAF squadron to leave Germany.

At Hangelar in Germany, 5 Sqn, a unit in the 2nd Wing, 2nd Brigade, re-equipped with F.2Bs from R.E.8s and remained there until 8 September 1919, when it returned to Bicester in the UK after discarding its aircraft, disbanding there on 20 January 1920.

A group of F.2Bs at Manston in 1918. The two central aircraft have the enlarged radiator; the nearest is Falcon III-powered D8074 '20', which went to No.3 School of Aerial Fighting and Gunnery at Bircham Newton on 24 June 1918. The aircraft immediately behind it is numbered '29'. Four of the F.2Bs have white radiator surrounds and shutters and white wheel discs, and two of those on the left have four-bladed propellers. *(Philip Jarrett)*

Right: **This anonymous F.2B at Frieston features the enlarged radiator fitted to several F.2Bs in the late-war and post-war periods, when it was believed that the standard radiator would be inadequate for the Falcon III.** *(Philip Jarrett)*

Below right: **Another anonymous F.2B with the larger radiator; a normal Falcon-engined aircraft under maintenance in the right background allows comparison.** *(Philip Jarrett)*

At the time of the Armistice 48 Sqn was at Reckem North in the 11th Wing, 2nd Brigade. On 27 November it moved to Nivelles in Belgium, then on 19 December to Bickendorf in Germany. From there it left for India on 26 May 1919, its role being changed at that time from fighter-reconnaissance to army co-operation.

Two other squadrons in Belgium and Germany had some Bristol Fighters on strength from February 1919. At Gerpinnes in Belgium 6 Sqn had them in addition to its R.E.8s. The unit moved to Sart on 19 March but left its aircraft behind when it embarked for Iraq on 14-15 April, re-equipping with R.E.8s on arrival at Baghdad on 18 July 1919. Another predominantly R.E.8 unit, 9 Sqn, had moved from Prémont to Tarcienne on 29 November 1918, then to Cognelée in Germany on 11 December and to Ludendorf on 3 January 1919, before returning to the UK as a cadre on 31 July 1919.

Peacetime usage

Although most of the RAF's First World War aircraft types were declared obsolete in 1919, the sturdy, reliable and versatile Bristol Fighter was one of the few to be retained. It was to remain in first-line service as a reliable workhorse, both at home and abroad, for most of the 1920s, and in smaller numbers was still to be seen in the early 1930s.

Aircraft being sent overseas post-war were initially despatched to the Packing Depot at Sealand, near Chester, where they were packed in individual crates ready for shipment as components. Those destined for the Middle East would then be shipped to the Aircraft Depot at Aboukir in Egypt, those for Iraq to a similar establishment at Hinaidi, and those for India to one at Drigh Road, near Karachi. On arrival they would be re-erected and test flown in readiness for issue to a local unit.

In the interwar years Bristol Fighters were used in a large number of experiments with wings of various aspect ratio, different aerofoil section and modified control surfaces, evaporative cooling systems, and Handley Page slots (See chapter 17). This last device prolonged the F.2B's Service life by a few years, and the ultimate service version had slots, long-travel undercarriage suspension, and a balanced rudder.

With regard to the dual-control version, in a report on a Bristol Fighter tested at the RAE Farnborough in 1920, attention was drawn to the unsatisfactory movement of the control column. On comparison with a standard aeroplane there was found to be 15 degrees less movement on the elevators, and the trouble appeared to be due to the dual control fitted by the British & Colonial Aeroplane Co, which was described as being of the "Badger" type. The aeroplane in question was moved to Croydon for inspection.

Full details of post-war orders are given in chapter 16.

The F.2Bs of B Flight of 12 Sqn at Heumar in Germany, probably April or early May 1920. Aircraft 'C2' on the extreme left, was F4435; in the centre row, front to rear, are F4855 'B4', D8059 'B5', and possibly F4661 'B6'; on the right are F4414 'B2', H1566 'B1' and possibly F4402 'B3'. *(Philip Jarrett)*

Above: **This collection of faded images is believed to feature the F.2Bs of 12 Sqn at Heumar in the early post-war years.** *(Philip Jarrett)*

Above: **A closer look at F4661 'B6' of 12 Sqn at Heumar in 1920. Note the Flight letter on the Bessonneau hangar in the background.** *(Philip Jarrett)*

Below: **While serving with No.1 (Observers) School of Aerial Gunnery at New Romney D8020 '23' was wrecked while landing on rough ground, injuring Lt T.H. Jackson.** *(via the late P.H.T Green)*

Customers abroad

Other nations were quick to adopt the type for their air service, and the post-war years saw considerable numbers of variously-powered Bristol Fighters bound for destinations in Spain, Argentina, Belgium, Mexico, Norway, Sweden, Greece, Bulgaria and the Irish Free State. (See chapter 18.)

In 1923 the use of the terms 'corps reconnaissance squadron' and 'close co-operation squadron' was discontinued by the RAF. All were now to be Army Co-operation squadrons, and the roles of their aircraft were described as close reconnaissance, artillery reconnaissance or photographic reconnaissance, according to the work upon which they were engaged.

Bristol Fighters served in Ireland until 1922 and on the Rhine until July 1922, when the last squadron (12) left Germany. In April 1927 2 Sqn sailed for China aboard HMS *Hermes* to support the Shanghai Defence Force, a formation set up locally to protect European settlements in China. It was based on arrival at the local racecourse. It arrived back at Manston six months later after a more permanent RAF base at been set up at Kai Tak, Hong Kong, and re-equipped with Armstrong Whitworth Atlases from the end of 1929.

Unarmed F.2B Mk.1s of 24 Sqn climbing over English countryside, circa 1919-20. The nearest machine is F4341, and two of the aircraft behind it are H1426 and H1400.

A movie 'still' depicting H1434 of the Inland Area Communication Flight 'rehearsing for Aerial Pageant' in 1920. *(Philip Jarrett)*

Post-war home-based squadrons

In April 1920 4 Sqn was re-established at Farnborough with a detached flight at Stonehenge. One flight was detached to Ireland from August 1920 until January 1922. In August of that year the whole squadron was shipped to Turkey during the Chanak crisis, returning home to Farnborough in September 1923. During the General Strike in 1926 4 Sqn was detached to Turnhouse for a time, then in October 1929 it was re-equipped at Farnborough with Armstrong Whitworth Atlases.

Re-formed at Kenley on 1 April 1924 as an Army Co-operation unit by renaming the Signal Co-operation Flight, 13 Sqn moved to Andover three months later. It re-equipped there with the Armstrong Whitworth Atlas from August 1927.

A component of the Aeroplane and Armament Experimental Establishment (A&AEE) at Martlesham Heath, 15 Sqn had two Bristol Fighters on strength from May 1924, its main equipment being the D.H.9A.

Re-formed in April 1924 as 16 (Army Co-operation) Sqn, 16 Sqn was fully equipped with Bristol Fighters at Old Sarum. It worked there with the School of Army Co-operation, re-equipping with the Armstrong Whitworth Atlas from January 1931.

At Duxford 19 Sqn had two Bristol Fighters on strength around May-June 1924, its main equipment being the Sopwith Snipe and Avro 504K.

Re-formed on 24 July 1923 within the A&AEE at Martlesham Heath for testing aircraft types, 22 Sqn had two Bristol Fighters on strength for a time.

For communications work, 24 Sqn re-formed at Kenley on 1 February 1920 from 1 Communication Squadron and the Air

Council Inspection Squadron. It moved to Northolt in February 1927 and had some Bristol Fighters on strength until it re-equipped with de Havilland Moths in June 1928.

At home, the F.2B was superseded in the squadrons by the Armstrong Whitworth Atlas from August 1927. It was finally supplanted overseas in 1932, when 6 Sqn received Fairey Gordons.

Above right: **In the immediate post-war period Bristol Fighters performed a variety of tasks. This one, photographed at Biggin Hill in 1919, was employed during a newspaper strike.** *(Philip Jarrett)*

Right: **Captain A.M. West delivers films by air in F4767, March 1919. This aircraft was with 2 Sqn at Fermoy by September 1920.** *(Philip Jarrett)*

The contents of the large chest being manhandled into C1037 are unknown, as are the location and unit involved.

The undercarriage of F4525 of the RAF and Army Co-operation School at Worthy Down collapsed after the aircraft stalled at 10ft while landing early in 1919. Both the unidentified pilot and Flt Cdt J.G. Gradidge were unhurt. *(J.M. Gradidge)*

Above: **Bristol Fighter F4569 In Mk.IV configuration while serving in the army co-operation role with 16 Sqn at Old Sarum. The squadron retained its Bristol Fighters until January 1931, when they were replaced by Armstrong Whitworth Atlases.** *(Philip Jarrett)*

The following four pages present a series of images depicting Bristol F.2Bs of 2 Squadron during the time it was based at Manston, Kent.

Above: **The F.2Bs of 2 (Army Co-operation) Sqn at Manston in 1924. Visible serials are, left to right: F4585, F457, F4546, F44??, F469?, C4741, F4490, F4956, F4717, F47?4.** *(Philip Jarrett)*

Right: **An aerial view of Manston, with a pair of F.2Bs in the foreground, an Avro 504 above and right, and a Vickers Virginia on the far left.** *(Philip Jarrett)*

Below: **Bristol F.2B C4741 of 2 Sqn aloft.** *(Philip Jarrett)*

Below: **Here is C4741 at Manston in 1924, after being reconditioned to J Type and looking in pristine condition.** *(Philip Jarrett)*

Above left: **A familiar photograph of Manston-based Mk.II F4717 of 'C' Flight, 2 Sqn. Three coloured bands encircled the rear fuselage. The outer bands were red, and the colour of the central band denoted the respective Flight to which the aeroplane belonged: white for 'A' Flight, yellow for 'B' Flight and blue for 'C' Flight.** *(Philip Jarrett)*

Above right: **Another 2 Sqn F.2B was J7686, which joined the unit in 1925.** *(Philip Jarrett)*

Left: **F.2B F4965 served in 2 Sqn during 1924-25.** *(Philip Jarrett)*

Above: **Another 2 Sqn F.2B from the same batch was F4967, photographed here at Colchester.** *(Philip Jarrett)*

Left: **An intimate air-to-air study of F4965.** *(Philip Jarrett)*

Right: **This 2 Sqn F.2B, J6662, was from the first post-war production order. It was not normal practice for the pilot to stand.** *(Philip Jarrett)*

Right: **Another flying shot of J6662, this time with the crew demonstrating 'Look, no hands!'. The squadron's motto, 'Hereward', meant 'Guardian of the Army'.** *(Philip Jarrett)*

Below: **Two views of F4484 of 2 Sqn after it stalled on a turn and crashed on 6 August 1924.** *(Philip Jarrett)*

Right: **F.4546 of 2 Sqn crashed and overturned while night flying at Worthy Down on 2 September 1925, but Flt Lt Culley and FO Reedman were both 'OK'. It was repaired. The Klaxon horn attached beneath the lower wing centre section, used for signalling, is well shown here.** *(Philip Jarrett)*

Left: **The identity of this 2 Sqn F.2B, J7??7, has not been confirmed, and the date and cause of this accident are unknown.** *(Philip Jarrett)*

Above: **These F.2Bs are said to be aircraft of 2 Sqn at the RAF Pageant at Hendon in 1923. The dark-coloured F.2B in the background on the extreme right is C4776, the aircraft that was tested with a much-modified fin and rudder at the RAE in 1925.** *(Philip Jarrett)*

Left: **J6663 of 2 Sqn over typically British patchwork countryside. After reconditioning to J Type this aircraft served in India.** *(Philip Jarrett)*

Right: **Three J Type F.2Bs of 2 Sqn over their Manston base, with Margate and Cliftonville in the distance. Front to rear: C757, B1325 and J6662.** *(Philip Jarrett)*

Top: **This 2 Sqn F.2B, F4500, carries the squadron number in a triangle on its fin.** (Philip Jarrett)

Above: **This view of F.2B J7620 of 2 Sqn in an unfortunate predicament is believed to have been taken in the Shanghai region.** (Philip Jarrett)

Right: **An evocative shot of J7665 of 2 Sqn over Shanghai City in 1927.** (Philip Jarrett)

When this picture was taken, H1423 was probably with 16 Sqn, attached to the School of Army Co-operation at Old Sarum, Wiltshire, in the mid-1920s. It has the hinged board hanging from the lower port wing trailing edge that enabled ground troops to identify it as a Contact Patrol aircraft, a signalling Klaxon horn beneath the lower wing centre section, alongside the starboard wheel, and an RL Bomb Tube protruding from the fuselage under the rear cockpit. After being reconditioned to 'J' Type H1423 caught fire on the ground on 29 July 1926, owing to the accidental firing of a Very pistol. Repaired, it served with No.2 FTS at Digby. *(Philip Jarrett)*

Left: Originally delivered engineless to store, F.2B J8291 was taken on charge on 23 December 1926. After being reconditioned to Mk.IV it was again taken on charge on 14 December 1928 and served with 16 Sqn at Old Sarum during 1929-30. It is seen here as 'L' of that unit, in Mk.IV configuration with slats in the upper wing leading edge, and with all the necessary paraphernalia for its role, including the message hook. *(Philip Jarrett)*

Above left: **F.2B F4445 'B' of 12 Sqn at Heumar in Germany during the winter of 1919/20.** *(RAF Museum)*

Above: **F.2B C4800 in the early post-war era, possibly with No.3 Communications Squadron at Hounslow.** *(C&C)*

Left: **F.2B E2428 'Y' of 11 Sqn upside-down in a cabbage patch in 1919; probably the occasion on which it was wrecked on 4 July 1919.** *(Eric Harlin)*

Affectionately known as 'The Old Biff 1928', C4680 is seen in a hangar at Upavon about 1928/29, while it was with the Central Flying School. *(RAF Museum)*

Above and left: **Arab-engined F.2B C9837 'B4' of 8 Sqn at Sart after colliding with a tree and a fence on 18 July 1919.** *(Philip Jarrett)*

Believed to have been photographed at Witney in 1920, this is F4867 of 20 Sqn, perhaps after a wheel collapse. *(Eric Harlin)*

Above: **An aerial view of the aerodrome at Bickendorf in 1919, with Bristol Fighters nearest and Sopwith Snipes lined up neatly in the distance. The right-hand aircraft of the three nearest the camera is a Fokker D.VII.**

Left: **Photographed at Bickendorf in 1919, this is F4440 '2' of 18 Sqn,** *Presented by Maharaja Bahadur Sir Rameswar Singh of Darbhanga No.1 The Lord Hardinge.* *(Philip Jarrett)*

Left: **Another Bickendorf-based presentation F.2B in 1919 was F4664** *Tyldesley,* **which later went to India.** *(Philip Jarrett)*

Above left: **An F.2B numbered '9' warms up at snowbound Bickendorf in 1919. There is a Sopwith Dolphin in the background.** *(Philip Jarrett)*

Above right: **Running-up the engine of an Arab-powered F.2B at Bickendorf.** *(Philip Jarrett)*

Right: **It was at Bickendorf that this unfortunate mishap befell F4400 '9' in 1919.** *(Philip Jarrett)*

Below: **Nearest the camera in this line-up of 12 Sqn F.2Bs at Bickendorf are F4468 and E2427.** *(Philip Jarrett)*

Another of 12 Sqn's F.2Bs at Bickendorf was F4425 '1-7'. *(Andy Thomas)*

Another Bickendorf resident in 1919 was H7292 '3'. This machine began life as E2254, but when reconstructed was given the compromised serial F6407, already allocated to a Sopwith Camel, so was reserialled H7292. *(Philip Jarrett)*

Above left: **This F.2B at Bickendorf in 1919, C4???, has been adapted as a communications machine, with a large windshield around the pilot's cockpit and a smaller one for the rear cockpit, from which the Scarff ring has been removed. A pennant marking has been added aft of the fuselage roundel.** *(Philip Jarrett)*

Above right: **The Cadet College at Cranwell always maintained its aeroplanes in top condition, as this study of F4549, with its gleaming cowling, shows.**

Right: **Another Cranwell machine, C4740 'D1', which went to the College in July 1923, stands in front of the D Flight hangar. It has a rather large and unconventional windscreen in front of its rear cockpit, which retains its Scarff ring. In 1925 C4740 was reconditioned to J Type DC standard, so this photograph must have been taken during the earlier period.** *(Philip Jarrett)*

Left: **During reconditioning in 1925/26 this F.2B, F4845, was the first to be fitted with Uniflex cable for wireless. In 1929/30 it was reconditioned to Mk. IV standard as seen here, with leading-edge slats on the upper wing and the enlarged fin and horn-balanced rudder.** *(Philip Jarrett)*

Below left and right: **How F4651 ended up in this sad state does not appear to have been recorded, but it was probably serving with No.1 FTS at Netheravon at the time. It had previously served in Ireland and Egypt.** *(Philip Jarrett)*

At the RAF's No.1 School of Technical Training at Halton Camp in Buckinghamshire, the camp's photographer, Mr W.H. 'Daddy' Christmas, took this picture of the line-up of the team entered for the 1923 relay race at the RAF Aerial Pageant at Hendon. Each of the teams, from various RAF stations, entered three machines, an Avro 504K, a Bristol Fighter and a Sopwith Snipe, and also had reserve aircraft. Nearest here is F.2B J6680 *Bonzolean*, and next to it is the reserve F.2B, F4845. Halton won the race in 1923. *(Philip Jarrett)*

Above left: A 'Daddy' Christmas shot of F.2B J6680 *Bonzolean* having its Falcon run up at Halton in 1923. The number 6 denoted the team's entry number. *(Philip Jarrett)*

Above right: Halton's reserve F.2B for the 1923 relay race, F4845. *(Philip Jarrett)*

Right: Another of Halton's well-maintained F.2Bs, J65??. *(Philip Jarrett)*

Below: Another Halton resident captured by Mr Christmas's camera was H1488, which had been brought up to Mk.III standard and went there in 1925. Note the RL tube protruding beneath the rear cockpit. *(Philip Jarrett)*

Above left: **F.2B F4619 looks well cared for in this view, probably taken while it was serving with the RAF Cadet College at Cranwell.** *(Philip Jarrett)*

Above right: **This snap of J6760 was taken over the paling fence barrier at Croydon Airport in 1923 by a young Don Brown, later of Miles Aircraft fame.** *(Philip Jarrett)*

Left: **Supposedly with 25 Sqn when this picture was taken, F4396 was reconditioned to J Type and was then involved in an aerial collision while flying in formation with D8035 near Peshawar, India, on 20 March 1928, while serving with 20 Sqn.** *(Philip Jarrett)*

Below left: **Bristol F.2B E2624 'A4' of 4 Sqn at Farnborough makes a low pass with message hook lowered in the early 1920s.** *(Philip Jarrett)*

Below right: **Although the location of this shot of F4870 is not known, it was probably photographed at the Air Pilotage School at Andover in 1919.** *(Philip Jarrett)*

Left: **Seen here in the snow at Port Meadow, Oxfordshire, in February 1919, F4766 appears again in a later chapter of this book, when it was serving in India in the late 1920s as 'H' of 5 Sqn.** *(Philip Jarrett)*

Right: **On 2 May 1924 Pt Off E. Martin, flying F.2B F4485 of No.2 FTS at Duxford, collided with Avro 504K F8945 of the same unit a mile from the aerodrome and died in the ensuing crash. The Avro suffered relatively little damage.** *(Philip Jarrett)*

Below: **While serving with No.2 FTS at Duxford, Cambridgeshire, F.2B F4323 '3' ended up like this in a ploughed field, presumably as the result of a forced landing.**
(Philip Jarrett)

Right: **F.2B J6751 is here seen with 100 Sqn at Spittlegate in 1922, still in its old camouflage finish.** *(Philip Jarrett)*

Below: **By March 1924 J6751, now re-covered or repainted, had gone to No.2 FTS at Duxford, where it is seen here after what appears to have been a rather heavy landing.** *(Philip Jarrett)*

Left: **A scenic study of F4381 'K' of 16 Sqn over the patchwork Wiltshire countryside. Reconditioned to J Type in 1924, this aircraft then went to 16 Sqn, and during its time there it was again reconditioned, to Mk.III standard.** *(Philip Jarrett)*

Another 16 Sqn F.2B was J7691 'N', seen here with a camera gun mounted on the upper wing centre section. *(Philip Jarrett)*

The Old Sarum Hucks starter, based on the chassis of a Ford Model T. *(Philip Jarrett)*

An aerial view of Old Sarum aerodrome, home of the School of Army Co-operation and 16 Sqn. *(Philip Jarrett)*

Bristol F.2B F4796 after landing at Collinstown in January 1919, and thereby becoming the first of its kind to join 106 Sqn in Ireland. *(The late G.S. Leslie)*

Chapter 12

THE BRISTOL FIGHTER IN IRELAND

At the end of 1918 there were two RAF corps reconnaissance squadrons in Ireland using Bristol Fighters, 105 and 106 Sqns. Both had been based at Andover, equipped with R.E.8s, 105 Sqn arriving at Omagh on 19 May 1918 and 106 Sqn at Fermoy the following day. Their task was to support the Army in its internal security tasks by carrying out reconnaissance and communication flights. In December 1918 105 Sqn re-equipped with Bristol Fighters, and 106 Sqn did likewise the following month. On 1 March 1919 they were joined by another Bristol Fighter unit, 141 Sqn, which flew across from Biggin Hill to be based at Tallaght. At around the same time 117 and 149 Sqns arrived, but neither had Bristol Fighters.

These five squadrons were administered by the 11th (Irish) Group, formed on 22 September 1918 with its headquarters at 9 Merrion Square, Dublin, until 1 November 1919, when it moved to Baldonnel.

Aircraft initially arrived by ship, but by 1919 it was considered that enough experience had been gained and that aircraft and engines were by now sufficiently reliable for aircraft to be flown direct to Baldonnel from Shotwick, near Chester.

Right: **The highly decorated F.2B flown by Flt Lt W.H. de W. Waller, H1441, at Fermoy, Ireland, in 1920, possibly with 106 Sqn.** *(via Philip Jarrett)*

On 9 April 1919, as part of a night-flying exercise, three Bristol Fighters of 141 Sqn, which had previously been a night fighter squadron, flew across Dublin at night from the sea in a westerly direction. They had their navigation lights on and dropped flares while over the city. On 26 May 12 Bristol Fighters of the same squadron, led by Maj Brian Baker DSO, MC, DFC and Croix de Guerre, flew over the capital in battle formation, performing various manoeuvres, the object reportedly being to announce a new military newspaper venture. At this time, the squadron's three flight commanders had their aircraft painted in patriotic colours. 'A' Flight Commander's aircraft was all red, 'B' Flight's was all white with black trim and the name *Daphne*, and 'C' Flight's was bright blue. They flew around Dublin in formation, and appeared at garden fêtes and shows.

On 15 June news came through that Alcock and Brown had landed their Vickers Vimy near Clifden, County Galway, after making the first transatlantic flight, but had done so on boggy land and nosed in. A Bristol Fighter of 105 Sqn flew down from Oranmore to assist, only to suffer the same fate.

Another jazzy F.2B serving in Ireland was F4380, which is recorded as serving with 105 Sqn at Omagh, 11 Grp at Collinstown/Tallaght and 106 Sqn at Fermoy.

On 8 August, the RAF held an Irish Aerial Derby at Tallaght. The route was from there to the Curragh, then to Gormanston and back over Dublin to Tallaght, a distance of 102½ miles. Only 21 of the 24 aircraft entered actually started, including four Bristol Fighters. The race was won by an Avro 504.

In the latter half of 1919 the RAF in Ireland was reorganised under the 'Defence of Ireland Scheme'. The 11th (Irish) Group moved to Baldonnel on 1 November, then on 1 February 1920 a major reorganisation of its squadrons took place. At Oranmore 105 Sqn was reorganised to become a new 2 Sqn comprising 'A', 'B' and 'C' Flights. Number 100 Sqn arrived at Baldonnel from St Inglevert in France and absorbed 141 Sqn on arrival, there being now four Flights, 'A', 'B', 'C' and 'D', one of which was equipped with Bristol Fighters and the other three

with D.H.9As initially, but later with Bristol Fighters. Under the scheme, 2 Sqn had one flight based at Oranmore to carry out patrols in the Fermoy area; the other two flights went to Fermoy, one to patrol the immediate area and the other to undertake a similar task in the Cork area. To carry out patrols in the Athlone area 100 Sqn detached its Bristol Fighter Flight to Castlebar, the other three Flights patrolling the Dublin, Curragh and Ulster areas with their D.H.9As. Changes were made later as circumstances necessitated.

Three coloured bands were carried around the rear fuselages of 2 Sqn's aircraft, 'A' Flight's being red/white/red, 'B' Flight's white/yellow/white and 'C' Flight's red/blue/red.

By this time the political situation had taken a turn for the worse, and the services of the RAF were in great demand by the

Army. In addition to reconnaissance sorties and communications work, they carried mail and undertook patrols, looking for illegal drilling in remote places by the IRA, as well as attempting to deter demonstrations by their presence. The aircraft were unarmed, except during periods of heightened tension, but their use was strictly controlled and in fact there is no surviving evidence that the RAF in Ireland ever fired a single shot. They were particularly useful in affording protection for armoured cars on the road. Mail carrying was also a vital task, as there were very few proper roads in Ireland at that time.

About April 1920 the 11th (Irish) Group was scaled down to become 11th (Irish) Wing, still at 9 Merrion Square, Dublin. Then, in August 1920, reinforcements arrived in the shape of 'A' Flight of 4 Sqn, detached from Farnborough to Aldergrove, and moving on 4 May 1921 to Baldonnel. In June 1921 100 Sqn flew its D.H.9As to Shotwick, and during that month Bristol Fighter replacements arrived from there, the squadron sending up an aerial escort to meet each incoming flight.

A truce came into effect on 11 July 1921, and Bristol Fighter flights were much reduced thereafter. The following month the total flying hours were only 76hr 20min, of which more than 56hr were flown in connection with practising for and carrying out an air display on 30 August, when Lord

While dropping mail on barracks on 17 November 1920, F.2B H1590 of 2 Sqn at Fermoy struck a wireless mast. Its pilot, Fg Off C.F. Briggs, was seriously injured, but Fg Off K.W. MacKichan is believed to have escaped injury. (C&C)

Photographed while serving with 2 Sqn at Oranmore in 1921, F.2B J6694 was destined to return to the unit six years later as a J Type, this time in Shanghai. *(Philip Jarrett)*

FitzAlan, Viceroy of Ireland, visited Baldonnel. Fourteen aircraft participated, carrying out various manoeuvres.

On 6 December 1921, a treaty was signed providing for the creation of an Irish Free State, to comprise the 26 counties of Southern Ireland but excluding the six counties of Ulster in the north. The treaty was ratified on 7 January 1922, but this was quickly followed by a civil war in the South.

As a result of the handing over of responsibility, 'A' Flt of 4 Sqn left from Baldonnel to return to Farnborough on 18 January 1922, followed by 100 Sqn, which departed Baldonnel for Spittlegate 11 days later. Finally, on 13 February, 2 Sqn left for Digby, though it subsequently had spells in Northern Ireland, based at Aldergrove. Two aircraft suffered accidents during this evacuation; J6698 of 4 Sqn forced-landed at Rhos-on-Sea, North Wales, on 20 January following engine failure, and J6706 of 100 Sqn forced-landed at Dysert, near Rhyl in North Wales on 29 January owing to fuel starvation.

An Advance Party of the 11th (Irish) Wing left for Spittlegate on 27 January, followed on 17 February by the Main Party, the unit now becoming 11 Group, RAF. To administer the remnants during their withdrawal, a new RAF Ireland was formed on 17 February to replace 11th (Irish) Wing at Baldonnel. To cover the final withdrawal the RAF formed an Irish Flight of four F.2Bs at Baldonnel in April 1922, transferring it on 1 May to Collinstown, near Dublin (now Dublin Airport). Also in May, RAF Ireland moved to Island Bridge Barracks, Dublin, then north to Templepatrick, County Antrim, in September, and finally to Aldergrove in October, where it disbanded in February 1923. In the meantime the Irish Flight disbanded at Collinstown on 31 October 1922, the station being handed over to the Irish Free State government the following day.

The Irish Army Air Corps

In early 1922 a National Army was formed following the acceptance by the Irish delegation of an Anglo-Irish Treaty and the setting up of the Irish Free State. In May of that year the former RAF airfield at Baldonnel, seven miles southwest of Dublin, was taken over. Within two months this became the base of an Irish Air Service comprising one flying unit, 1 Sqn, consisting of 'A' Flight for flying training and 'B' Flight for operational flying.

Meanwhile a civil war had erupted in June 1922 between the National Army,

supporting the Provisional Government, and the Irregulars, supporting the Anti-Treaty faction, the National Army being mainly engaged on combat operations against Republican forces in the south and southwest regions of Ireland. By October the conflict was mainly confined to the southwest of Ireland, comprising Counties Cork and Kerry, and in the same month a detachment from the Air Service was deployed to the former RAF airfield at Fermoy, County Cork, equipped with Bristol Fighters and Martinsyde F.4 Buzzards.

Eight F.2B Fighters were delivered to Baldonnel Aerodrome between July and November that year. Two were taken over from the Irish Flight of the RAF, and the remaining six were acquired from RAF stocks in England through the Aircraft Disposal Co Ltd. Roman numerals were initially allotted as serial numbers, the prefix letters 'BF' being added later.

The fuselage and upper surfaces of the wings and tailplanes of the initial batch of eight F.2B Fighters had an overall matt khaki-green finish, while the under surfaces of the wings and tailplane were clear-doped. Chord-wise green, white and orange stripes were displayed on the upper surfaces of the top wings and under surfaces of the lower

wings, and vertical stripes were applied on both sides of the rudder. Each aircraft's serial number was displayed in white on the upper part of the fuselage centre section.

The first Bristol Fighter, ex-H1251, was delivered to Baldonnel Aerodrome on 4 July 1922 by Maj Gen MacSweeney, and as 'II' entered service with 'B' Flight, 1 Sqn. Green, white and orange roundels were painted on the tail and wings of this aircraft, these later being replaced by tricolour stripes. The second aircraft, ex-E2411, delivered on 14 July 1922 by Capt Russell, was allocated serial number BI and is considered to be the first to enter service with the Irish Air Service, joining 'B' Flight, 1 Sqn.

The first serious accident occurred on 17 July 1922, when III, ex-H1485, crash-landed near Naas, County Kildare, and overturned, damaging the undercarriage, wings, fin, propeller and parts of the fuselage. The crew survived. The fourth aircraft, IV, ex-E1958, arrived at Baldonnel on 19 September only to be so badly damaged on landing that it had to be scrapped. It was followed on 13 and 14 October by V and VI, respectively ex-D7886 and D7865. These also joined 'B' Flight, 1 Sqn. The final pair, ex-D7882 and D7885, arrived on 22 November to

F.2B J6763 of the Irish Flight at Collinstown overturned after making a forced landing in Phoenix Park, Dublin, on 21 October 1922. *(via Philip Jarrett)*

Irish Bristol Fighters: Individual Histories

The first delivery consisted of eight ex-RAF Bristol Fighters supplied in 1922 to the Irish Army Air Corps at Baldonnel. Of these, the first and third aircraft were taken over from the RAF in Ireland, while the remainder were supplied through the ADC. They comprised:

BI   (Ex-E2411). Delivered from the Irish Flight to Baldonnel Aerodrome by Capt Russell 5.7.22. To 'B' Flight, 1 Sqn. Forced-landed near Limerick after being refuelled with 'ordinary motor spirit' 8.22; crashed and WO 14.2.24.

II.   (Ex-H1251) Later BFII. Purchased from the ADC and delivered to Baldonnel Aerodrome by Maj Gen MacSweeney, 3hrs flying time, 4.7.22. To 'B' Flight, 1 Sqn. Bomb racks fitted 21.7.22; Lewis gun mounted 13.8.22. To Fermoy 2.10.22 (Flt Sgt Crossley and Sgt R. Spittle). Fitted with engine from No.IV 1.11.22. Retd Baldonnel 4.2.23 (J.C. Fitzmaurice and Lt B. McSweeney). No further flying until 1.10.23. Engine cut; forced-landed, Baldonnel, 6.12.23. Crashed at Castlebaggott near Baldonnel 23.1.24 (Lt R.T. Nevin died of injuries 24.1.24). Total flying time 37hrs 15min; awaiting Board of Survey 9.4.27.

III.   (Ex-H1485) Later BFIII. To 2 Sqn and the Irish Flight. Delivered to Baldonnel Aerodrome 10.7.22; To 'B' Flight, 1 Sqn; Crashed and WO at Naas, County Kildare, 17.7.22.

IV.   (Ex-E1958). Delivered by ADC to Baldonnel Aerodrome but crashed and WO on delivery 16.9.22.

V.   (Ex-D7865) Later BFV. Delivered by ADC to Baldonnel Aerodrome, 14.10.22. To 'B' Flight, 1 Sqn. Engine failure over Dublin; crashed at Crumlin, County Dublin and written off 6.8.24 (Lt C. Russell & Lt Cumiskey both unhurt).

VI.   (Ex-D7886) Later BFVI. Delivered by ADC to Baldonnel Aerodrome 13.10.22. To 'B' Flight, 1 Sqn. Crashed during military exercises at the Curragh, County Kildare and WO 22.9.25 (Cmdt Thos Moloney killed and Sgt Tracy seriously injured).

VII.   (Ex-D7882) Later BFVII and then No.7; Delivered by ADC to Baldonnel Aerodrome 22.11.22. To 'B' Flight, 1 Sqn. Withdrawn from use 27.4.32; scrapped June 1935 following an Air Corps survey of obsolete engines and aircraft held in storage.

VIII.   (Ex-D7785) Later BFVIII. Delivered by ADC to Baldonnel Aerodrome 22.11.22. To 'B' Flight, 1 Sqn; Crashed near Baldonnel Aerodrome and WO, 3.8.28 (Lt A. Russell and Lt C. Russell both unhurt).

A second delivery of six new Bristol Fighters Mk.II (s/nos 6858 to 6863) was supplied direct from the maker in 1925 as replacements for the crashed aircraft of the first batch, and numbered 17 to 22. All were flown by 'B' Flight of 1 Sqn for training purposes:

17.   Delivered to Baldonnel Aerodrome, 24.10.25. To 'B' Flight, 1 Sqn. Crashed during military exercises at Hempstown, County Wicklow, and WO 21.9.26 (2nd Lt Timothy Prenderville and Lt Ed. O'Reilly both killed)

18.   Delivered to Baldonnel Aerodrome, 24.10.25. To 'B' Flight, 1 Sqn. Withdrawn from use 4.35; scrapped 6.35 following an Air Corps survey of obsolete aircraft and engines held in storage.

19.   Delivered to Baldonnel Aerodrome, 10.11.25. To 'B' Flight, 1 Sqn. Withdrawn from use 5.35; scrapped 6.35 following an Air Corps survey of obsolete aircraft and engines held in storage.

20.   Delivered to Baldonnel Aerodrome, 4.11.25. To 'B' Flight, 1 Sqn. Withdrawn from use 10.31.

21.   Delivered to Baldonnel Aerodrome, 18.11.25; To 'B' Flight, 1 Sqn. Withdrawn from use July 1930.

22.   Delivery test flight at Filton by Uwins on 5.11.25. Delivered to Baldonnel Aerodrome, 9.11.25. To 'B' Flight, 1 Sqn. Withdrawn from use 5.35; scrapped 6.35 following an Air Corps survey of obsolete aircraft and engines held in storage.

Left: **A manufacturer's pre-delivery photo of F.2B '19' for the Irish Army Air Corps.** *(Bristol)*

complete the delivery, also joining 'B' Flight, as VII and VIII respectively.

The Irish Bristol Fighters were engaged on combat missions in support of the National Army against the Republican forces throughout the Civil War, from July 1922 to May 1924. They undertook reconnaissance flights, patrolling over the country's railway system and dropping propaganda leaflets over territory occupied by Republican forces. Soon after being delivered, the first machine, BI, carried out reconnaissance flights over southwest Ireland, refuelling at a temporary airstrip near the city of Limerick. On 21 August 1922, however, this aircraft suffered engine failure and forced-landed, damaging the leading edge of one wing and the propeller, but the pilot and observer were uninjured. On investigation it was found that it had been refuelled with ordinary motor spirit instead of aviation fuel, but the damage was not serious, and it was returned to service after repair by Air Service personnel.

From October 1922 an Air Service detachment was deployed to the former RAF airfield at Fermoy to carry out combat operations against Republican forces in the southwest. At least three Bristol Fighters, BI, BFVII and BFVIII, are known to have operated from this airfield throughout the civil war. Two months later a small Air

Service detachment arrived in Tralee, County Kerry, to start operations with Bristol Fighter BI from a former RAF reserve airfield on the outskirts of the town. Reconnaissance flights over the southwest were carried out from this airfield by a single aircraft, usually a Bristol Fighter, until the detachment was withdrawn to the airfield at Fermoy in October 1923. In April 1924, following the end of the civil war, the Air Service detachment was withdrawn from the airfield at Fermoy to Baldonnel Aerodrome.

During 1924 three Bristol Fighters were written-off in crashes. The first was BFII, which crashed near Baldonnel Aerodrome on 23 January, killing the pilot. Shortly afterwards, on 14 February 1924, BI was written-off in a crash, then on 6 August BFV crashed at Crumlin, County Dublin, following engine failure, the pilot and observer being uninjured. By the time the Irish Army Air Corps was formed in October 1924 only three F.2B Fighters, BFVI, BFVII and BFVIII, remained in service, all with 'B' Flight, 1 Sqn. One of these was lost when, on 22 September 1925, BFVI crashed during Army manoeuvres in The Curragh, County Kildare, killing the pilot and observer.

To make good these losses the Irish Free State Government ordered six new Bristol

Above: **A line-up of F.2Bs of the Irish Army Air Corps at Baldonnel. All are in standard aluminium and grey finish apart from one camouflaged aircraft just visible at the far end on the right.** *(Philip Jarrett)*

Fighter Mk.II replacements for the Air Corps in 1925, these having Bristol sequence numbers 6858 to 6863 inclusive. The first two (c/ns 6858 and 6859) were delivered to Baldonnel Aerodrome on 24 October 1925, followed by four more (c/ns 6861, 6863, 6860 and 6862) on 4, 9, 10 and 18 November respectively. The Corps' numbering system had now changed to Arabic numerals and they became 17 to 22, by sequence number, and all entered service with 'B' Flight, 1 Sqn, these being the first new aircraft to be delivered to the Air Corps. Over the next five years these aircraft were used for advanced flying training, aerial survey flights for the Archaeological Research Commission, and participation in military exercises held by the Defence Forces.

The fuselage and wings of the batch of Mk. IIs had an overall aluminium dope finish, and the engine cowlings were grey. The tricoloured stripes were displayed in the same positions as on the F.2B Fighters. Each aircraft's serial number was displayed in black on the rear fuselage, just in front of the tailplane.

In February 1926 the first search-and-rescue mission was undertaken by the Air Corps, using three Bristol Fighters and two de Havilland D.H.9s, operating off the west coast of Ireland from the former RAF airfield at Oranmore. Starting on 20 February the five aircraft were engaged on aerial searches over the next four days for a missing trawler in the coastal sea areas off Counties Galway and Mayo. Because of the appalling weather conditions over the search area the vessel was not located by the crews of the Air Corps aircraft.

One of the new Mk.IIs, 17, was written-off on 21 September 1926 when it crashed at Hempstown, County Wicklow, killing the pilot and observer, while participating in military exercises held by the Defence Forces. When BFVIII was written off in a crash near Baldonnel Aerodrome on 3 August 1928, the crew escaped without injury.

Above: **Falcon-engined Bristol Fighter '18' of the Irish Army Air Corps, which served with the force from October 1925 to April 1935.** *(Philip Jarrett)*

The remaining aircraft were gradually withdrawn from use or scrapped between 1930 and 1935. The first Mk.II (21) was 'withdrawn from use' in July 1930, followed by the second (20) in October 1931. The sole remaining F.2B Fighter, now numbered 7, was withdrawn in April 1934 and the remaining three Mk.IIs (18, 19 and 22) were withdrawn in April and May 1935. In June 1935, following a survey of obsolescent aircraft held in storage by the Air Corps, these four aircraft were valued as scrap and sold or destroyed.

In 1937 the Irish Free State became known as Eire, and retained that name until 1948, when it changed again to become the Republic of Ireland. Baldonnel Aerodrome was renamed Casement Aerodrome in 1965, and this name has been retained to date.

Flying officers of the Irish Army Air Corps' Bristol Fighter Flight at Baldonnel. *(Philip Jarrett)*

Eleven F.2Bs of 14 Sqn, some displaying chequerboard fins. The nearest machine is F493?. *(Eric Harlin)*

Chapter 13

POST-WAR OPERATIONS IN THE MIDDLE EAST

After the First World War Britain had huge responsibilities, not only to the various countries around the world in what was then the British Empire, but also to several mandated territories for which it took over responsibility. By the end of 1919 it had been decided that the majority of RAF squadrons would be based overseas, Egypt being a key area for guarding supply lines to the East and especially for protecting the Suez Canal.

At the time of the Armistice there were only two F.2B units in the Middle East, one of these being the 1st Sqn, AFC, at Ramleh in Palestine. This unit had been formed at El Mejdel on 6 February 1918 by redesignating 67 (AFC) Sqn RAF and re-equipping it with Bristol Fighters that same month, initially with machines taken over from 111 Sqn. On 23 April it moved to Ramleh, then to Haifa on 3 October, returning to Ramleh on 22 November. Moving to Kantara in the Egyptian Canal Zone on 8 February 1919, it sailed home to Australia in the SS *Port Sydney* on 5 March 1919. Before departing, the unit passed on its F.2Bs to 111 Sqn at Ramleh.

Number 111 Sqn had received its first F.2B at Deir-el-Belah on 25 September 1917, and they supplemented its S.E.5as. It passed the F.2Bs on to the Australian squadron in February 1918, but in January 1919 it received six more, probably all from the Australian squadron. It moved to Ramleh on 6 February 1919. However, a month later there was a nationalist uprising in Egypt, but with the departure of 111 Sqn there were no RAF squadrons in Egypt at that time, so several lettered provisional squadrons were formed from locally available training resources, none of which were equipped with Bristol Fighters.

On 1 February 1920 111 Sqn was redesignated 14 Sqn. On that same date, 208 Sqn re-formed with Bristol Fighters at Ismailia, but in September it was hastily sent to Turkey to join the Constantinople Wing.

Palestine and Trans-Jordan
On 6 February 1919 the Bristol Fighters of 111 Sqn arrived in Palestine from Egypt to set up base at Ramleh, one detached flight being sent to Aleppo and another to Damascus in Syria. On 1 February it was renumbered 14 Sqn.

On 14 June 1920 New Zealander Fg Off N. Fitzgerald-Eager and AC1 P.W.J. Thacker of 14 Sqn went missing in E2293

A handwritten note on the back of this picture of E2293 of 111 Sqn reads: 'Bristol Fighter. Left Ramleh June 16th 1920. Found as in photo on Sinai Desert near Nekhl about 20th Aug 1920. Found by JCC.' The actual departure date from Ramleh is recorded as 14 June; as recounted here, the occupants met a tragic end after forced-landing, one dying from exposure on 21 June and the other being killed. *(Philip Jarrett)*

Bristol Fighters of Sqn on the deck of HMS *Argus* on 11 October 1922. An original print of this picture is captioned: 'Before the landing at Khelia [*sic*]. B Fighters lining up for gun practice on port side No.1 rear empennage'. *(Philip Jarrett)*

The F.2Bs of 4 Sqn are prepared for take-off from HMS *Argus* on 11 October 1922. *(Philip Jarrett)*

between Ramleh and Ismailia. The pilot had flown off course and forced-landed in the Sinai Desert, 30 miles west of Nekhl, Palestine. Fitzgerald-Eager died of exposure on 21 June, and Thacker was killed. On 1 August 1920 Fg Off R.D.C. Palmer and Fg Off H. Hutchinson in H1462 of 6 Sqn spun in from 3,000ft during a reconnaissance flight from Baghdad; both were killed.

On 14 April 1921 H1533 of 14 Sqn suffered engine failure, stalled and crashed at Ramleh; Fg Off P.J. Cox was killed and Fg Off C. Pilkington was seriously injured.

On 15 April 1921 H1633 of 14 Sqn had engine failure, and crashed near Jerusalem, killing Fg Off Cox, the squadron's adjutant.

As a result of the March 1921 Cairo Conference on the future of the Middle East, HRH Emir Abdullah was made Head of State of the newly established Emirate of Transjordan. On 10 and 11 April 14 Sqn provided four F.2Bs to fly Col T.E. Lawrence to Amman to see Abdullah. On 17 April the squadron's commander, Sqn Ldr W.L. Welsh, flew Lawrence to Amman in H1526 to attend Abdullah's inauguration, and during the following ten days Welsh transported Lawrence around the new Emirate.

On 18 April 1921 E2288 of 14 Sqn crash-landed after a petrol pipe broke and the throttle jammed; Plt Off B.W.T Hare and Plt Off J.C. Bulteel both escaped unhurt. On 12 July 1921 H1643 of 14 Sqn forced-landed on rough ground at Bir Salem, near Ramleh; Fg Off J.H. Huxley DSO was unhurt, and Ihsan Ali Khan, his passenger, slightly injured.

On 30 September 1921 Fg Off W. Elliott DFC and Mr Vernon were both injured when H1504 of 14 Sqn suffered engine failure on take-off from LG1 at Jerusalem.

In July 1922 a Flight was sent to Amman in Trans-Jordan to assist an element of the Transjordanian Army in bringing the Kura District into submission to the Government. Operating from an advanced landing ground at Mafraq on the Hejaz Railway, two days of intensive bombing forced the local Sheikh to surrender after the ground forces had brought the territory under control.

On 17 January 1925 14 Sqn lost an unidentified aircraft at Ramleh; Fg Off R.R.H. Bruce died of his injuries and LAC A. Sutton was seriously injured. On the same day 208 Sqn lost an aircraft at Ismailia, Fg Off J.A. McLaren MC being killed.

A Flight of 14 Sqn remained until 15 February 1926, when it was joined by the remainder of the squadron, now flying D.H.9As. On 28 August 1930 Flt Lt S.C. Strafford was injured when JR6635 flew into high ground and overturned while landing at Kolundia LG, near Jerusalem.

The Chanak Crisis

After signing the Armistice Turkey was virtually reinvented. Reorganising its resurgent armies, the government began to assert itself, and then in 1922, under Kemal Attaturk, started to recover lands which had been occupied by France and Italy, and to make war against Greece. With political confusion reigning in the region, the former allies were in a difficult position because they still retained forces on the shores of the Dardanelles to ensure that it remained open as an international waterway. The Turkish actions resulted in two serious threats to British interests in that region. First, numbers of Turkish troops crossed a neutral demarcation line in the Dardanelles, especially at Chanak, and refused to withdraw. Secondly, troops began to concentrate in the Mosul area with the apparent intention of supporting anti-Mandate and anti-Treaty agitation boiling up in Iraq. The small British garrison in the Dardanelles zone was quickly strengthened, and air reinforcements arrived from the UK, included the Bristol Fighters of 4 Sqn,

which reached Kilia Bay aboard the seaplane carrier HMS *Ark Royal* on 8 October. To enable the F.2Bs to get ashore they had to be transferred to the aircraft carrier HMS *Argus*, from whose deck they were flown ashore three days later to Kilia Airfield, the pilots having had no previous experience of deck take-offs. Here the squadron joined the Constantinople Wing, which had formed on 28 September, also administering 25, 207 and 208 Sqns as well as a flight of 56 Sqn.

Also equipped with F.2Bs, 208 Sqn had already arrived from Egypt in the SS *Podesta* and SS *Khartoum* on 25 September, disembarking five days later to San Stefano, where the aircraft were quickly reassembled. Operational flights began on 5 October, mainly comprising daily reconnaissance sorties to keep the British cavalry commanders informed of enemy troop movements, together with W/T work and some practice bomb-dropping.

Although 4 Sqn also attempted to provide strategic and tactical support for the Army, in the first two weeks it had to contend with extremely hot weather and violent dust storms, and then the onset of winter made things even more difficult. When the rainy season arrived the airfield soon became a sea of mud, making normal flying activities virtually impossible. At the end of October fierce gales wrecked hangars and tents, and further rain caused extensive flooding. A 60yd × 10yd makeshift runway was constructed, consisting of wire netting stretched over canvas and then pegged down, but the F.2Bs still sank up to six inches in it. Finally, 4 Sqn gave up and moved instead to Kilid-el-Bahr on 11 December.

In April 1923 a number of interesting trials were carried out by 208 Sqn in conjunction with the Royal Navy. These included one on 10 April, when a Bristol Fighter dropped a 112lb bomb aimed at a torpedo fired without warning from HMS *Seraphis*. The bomb was dropped after the missile had run about 3,000 yards from the ship, and landed ahead and a little to the left of the torpedo, its explosion causing the torpedo to veer 45 degrees to port; then it leaked oil and smoke as it continued slowly.

The crisis ended in August 1923, and on the 11th of that month the Bristol Fighters of 208 Sqn performed at an 'At Home' flying display at San Stefano. The Constantinople Wing disbanded on 1 October 1923, 4 Sqn having embarked in HMS *Ark Royal* for the UK on 4 September and 208 Sqn being shipped back to Egypt on 23 September.

Left: **The last of 4 Sqn's Bristol Fighters takes off from HMS *Argus* on 11 October 1922.** *(via Tim Mason)*

Right: **Five F.2Bs of C Flight, 208 Sqn, run-up their Falcons in Turkey on 21 November 1922, during the Chanak Crisis. The one on the far left is still doped with PC.10.** *(Eric Harlin)*

Below: **F.2B J6789 of 208 Sqn at San Stefano, Turkey, in 1923.** *(RAF Museum)*

Right: **An unfortunately double-exposed shot of another 208 Sqn F.2B at San Stefano, H1623.**

Below: **Bristol F2b D8096 of 208 Sqn at San Stefano in 1923. This aircraft is still flying today, with the Shuttleworth Collection at Old Warden.** *(Philip Jarrett)*

Above: **Another study of D8096 at San Stefano.** *(Philip Jarrett)*

Left: **Flying Officer Bob Aldridge runs up D8096's Falcon at San Stefano in 1923. Note the message hook.** *(Philip Jarrett)*

The ground crew of D8096 indulges in a bit of tomfoolery with their charge. *(Philip Jarrett)*

The F.2Bs of 4 Sqn at Kilid Bahr, Gallipoli, in January 1923 for the Chanak incident. The nearest aircraft is J6704, and the tail of J6715 'A' is on the right. *(Philip Jarrett)*

Left: **Bristol F.2Bs H1623, H1501 and H1678 of 208 Sqn at San Stefano in 1922.** *(Philip Jarrett)*

Right: **An aerial view of San Stefano on 11 August 1923, the day of the pre-departure flying display, with Bristol Fighters lined up outside their Bessonneau hangars.** *(Philip Jarrett)*

Bristol Fighters H1455, H1494, D8098, H1456 and D8096 of 208 Sqn over San Stefano on 11 August 1923, when they held a flying display before leaving for the UK. *(Tim Mason via Philip Jarrett)*

Another 208 Sqn formation over San Stefano on 11 August 1923. *(Tim Mason via Philip Jarrett)*

This rebuilt F.2B, HR16??, was serving with 4 Sqn when it ended up in this undignified position. The squadron, identified by a Roman IV aft of the fuselage roundel and in a star on the fin, was equipped with the F.2B from April 1920 to October 1929. The aircraft could be HR1677, but that aircraft's known history does not list 4 Sqn as one of its users. *(Philip Jarrett)*

This snapshot of a pair of anonymous F.2Bs in front of four Vickers Vernons is captioned 'Air Mail at Ligia(?), Transjordania'. The second F.2B has a four-blade propeller and a chequered tail. *(Philip Jarrett)*

Having served at Cranwell and Spittlegate, J-Type F.2B F4511 had joined 6 Sqn in Egypt by May 1930. It is seen here with a Leitner-Watts metal propeller and baggage panniers beneath the lower wings. The purpose and contents of the small parcels attached to the bottoms of the outermost front interplane struts are unknown. *(Philip Jarrett)*

Egypt

On 26 September 1923 208 Sqn returned to Ismailia from Turkey to resume normal duties. On 14 April 1921, during aerial co-operation with cavalry, D7831 of 208 Sqn collided with E2298 of the same unit and crashed near Bilbeis, killing Fg Off E.B. Jones and Fg Off W.A. Armstrong. The other F.2B also crashed, killing Flt Lt G.M. Clarke AFC and Plt Off F.J. Smith MC MM. On 29 April 1922 H1647 of No 4 FTS overshot on landing at Heliopolis; Fg Off E.G. O'Gorman was killed.

When F4582 of 208 Sqn was forced-landed on soft ground and overturned near Shile, on the Ismid Peninsula, on 24 November 1922, following engine failure, it was abandoned and burned. On 9 April 1923 J6606 of 14 Sqn spun into the ground from 300ft at Heliopolis, killing Fg Off C. Bousfield.

A crash recovery team with a day's work ahead of them. The picture is captioned as being taken at the RAF Egypt School of Aeronautics in 1918. *(Philip Jarrett)*

On 27 October 1927 208 Sqn moved from Ismailia to Heliopolis, where in May 1930 it re-equipped with Armstrong Whitworth Atlases. On 18 October 1926 C802 of 208 Sqn crashed and caught fire at Moascar, killing Fg Off V.B. Bingham-Hall and Plt Off W. Higgins. On 22 May 1929 J6596 of 208 Sqn burst into flames while being refuelled; LAC Mills was seriously injured.

On 25 October 1929 the Bristol Fighters of 6 Sqn arrived at Ismailia from Iraq. New F.2B Mk.IIIAs were received in April 1931, then some Fairey Gordons the next month, the last F.2B being given up in June 1932.

Below: **Photographed on 24 March 1924, these are the F.2Bs of 208 Sqn's Khartoum Flight. Nearest is H1492 with the encircled club of the unit's A Flight on its fin, with Sgt W. Lawrence (left) and Fg Off Millen. Immediately behind on the left is J6685.** *(SAAF Museum)*

Above: **Still finished in PC10 dope, E2295 went to the Middle East in late 1918, eventually going to No.17 TDS. By September 1920 it was with 208 Sqn.** *(Philip Jarrett)*

Above right: **Seen here with 14 Sqn in Egypt, H1526 was returned to the UK in 1921, reconditioned, and then went to 4 Sqn at Farnborough.** *(Philip Jarrett)*

Right: **F.2Bs of 14 Sqn lined up, with the two nearest aircraft displaying quartered wheel covers.** *(Philip Jarrett)*

Right: **F.2B F4435 of 208 Sqn at Ismailia flying in the Suez Canal area in the mid-1920s. It is equipped with a message hook and is carrying some screw pickets beneath the lower wing.** *(Philip Jarrett)*

Below: **F.2B C762 of 208 Sqn comes in to land past a Vickers Vimy in Egypt in 1925.** *(Philip Jarrett)*

The pilot of D7802 '11' of 208 Sqn poses his F.2B for the camera. The rudder carries a six-pointed star emblem with a letter or number in its centre. *(RAF Museum)*

Squadron Leader Welsh of 14 Sqn and his passenger, Col T.E. Lawrence, in F.2B H1526 at Amman on 17 April 1921. Note the squadron badge on the fuselage side. *(US Library of Congress Matson Photograph Collection LC-DIG-matpc-02318)*

The F.2Bs of 14 Sqn lined up on the aerodrome at Amman in 1925 and displaying diamonds, hearts and clubs on their fins, with FR4583 nearest and FR4712 next in line. The card-suit Flight identification emblems were also used by 208 Sqn. *(Philip Jarrett)*

A group of Arab dignitaries pose with 14 Sqn F.2Bs providing a backdrop. *(US Library of Congress Matson Photograph Collection LC-DIG-matpc-00015)*

F.2B F4612 of 14 Sqn at Ramleh, Palestine, around 1922-23, after crashing while carrying Col T.E. Lawrence. On the fuselage side is the squadron's winged badge. *(RAF Museum)*

Above: **A nice study of dual-control F.2B Mk.II H1398 of No.4 FTS at Abu Sueir about 1929-31, fitted with a Leitner-Watts adjustable-pitch metal propeller and apparently in an all-white scheme.** *(Philip Jarrett)*

Below: Bristol F.2B H1651 of 14 Sqn in the Middle East keeps company with a couple of armoured cars at Ramleh in 1922. Note the chequered fin. *(Philip Jarrett)*

Displaying a spade motif on its fin, this is H1502 of 14 Sqn at Ramleh, Palestine, in 1924. (Philip Jarrett)

F.2Bs J6648 and J6593 of 14 Sqn at the opening of Jerusalem Aerodrome in May 1924. An encircled spade motif has been applied to J6648's fin. (Philip Jarrett)

A nice 'through-the-bracing-wires' air-to-air shot of F.2B C764 of 14 Sqn. (Philip Jarrett)

F.2B H1496 served in Egypt with No.4 FTS and 208 Sqn. Whether the punctured tyres were the cause or the result of this nose-over is unknown. (Philip Jarrett)

Above: Another 4 FTS F.2B that suffered a mishap was J6617, which crashed and overturned in 1923/24. (Philip Jarrett)

Right: A locally modified aircraft, rebuilt F.2B JR6788 had its Scarff ring removed and a fairing added to the rear fuselage top-decking, possibly for it to serve as a communications hack. The club emblem on the fin denoted an aircraft of A Flight, 208 Sqn. It was flying over the Suez Canal area when this photograph was taken. (Philip Jarrett)

Left: This pristine F.2B was obviously regarded as the personal property of the Aircraft Depot at Aboukir; hence the inscription and the doctored roundel. It also seems that even the Scarff ring has been painted white. *(Philip Jarrett)*

Right: A low pass by C802 of 14 Sqn, which carries a spare wheel and has the heart Flight emblem on its fin. The squadron's badge has been painted on the radiator shutters. This aircraft ended its life in a fatal crash at Moascar on 18 October 1926, while serving with 208 Sqn. *(Philip Jarrett)*

Left: This view of 208 Sqn F.2B F4731 reveals the club Flight emblem painted beneath both lower wings and on the fin. After reconditioning to J Type, it went to 6 Sqn in Iraq, but caught fire at 100ft on 9 December 1924 and was wrecked. *(Philip Jarrett)*

Left: The F.2Bs of 208 Sqn 'on parade', with at least the first two machines displaying chequered fins. *(Philip Jarrett)*

This rebuilt F.2B in the FR4??? serial range, picketed down in the Middle East, appears to have suffered fire damage. It has a diamond on its fin, which links it to either 14 or 208 Sqn, and a two-blade metal propeller. (Philip Jarrett)

According to the inscription on the reverse of this photo of C4655 at Aboukir in May 1929, it was known by its pilot as 'My old barrer'. It had served in 42 Sqn in 1918. (Philip Jarrett)

Left: Refuelling a bombed-up, metal-propellered J-Type F.2B of 14 or 208 Sqn bearing the club emblem of 'A' Flight on its fin and beneath its starboard wing. It has a High-Altitude Mk.IA bomb sight alongside the rear cockpit and a tubular canister mounted on top of the lower wing root. The slats in the upper wing leading edges are deployed. (Philip Jarrett)

Right: The personnel of 208 Sqn with ten of their F.2Bs at Heliopolis in March 1928. Visible serial numbers are: J7640, FR4349, D8055, DR7890, J6798, FR4583 and ER2533. (Philip Jarrett)

Left: A classic shot of JR6785 of the 'diamond' Flight of 208 Sqn in 1929, carrying a pair of panniers beneath its lower wing. It has wingtip and central lamps on its upper wing, and flare brackets beneath the lower wingtips. (Philip Jarrett)

Above: **This F.2B at Aboukir, F4392, carries a winged 'B' insignia incorporating the number '2'. As both this aircraft and DR7802 (see page 304) were allocated to the Aircraft Depot at Aboukir in 1926, it seems possible that the markings related to a unit at that station.** *(Philip Jarrett)*

Left: **At Heliopolis on 6 February 1926 J6664 entered into a spin on turning into wind and crashed, killing Fg Off A.C. Tremellon and injuring his passenger, Flt Lt G.P. Simpson.**

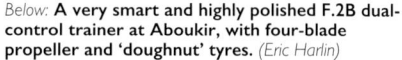

Below: **A very smart and highly polished F.2B dual-control trainer at Aboukir, with four-blade propeller and 'doughnut' tyres.** *(Eric Harlin)*

Right: **F.2B JR6789 of A Flight, 208 Sqn, over Lake Timsah, Ismailia, on 24 March 1927, displaying the Flight's club emblem on its upper centre section and fin.** *(Philip Jarrett)*

Left: **Apart from 2 Sqn at Manston in 1926, the units with which J7657 served are not recorded, but this picture is believed to have been taken in the Middle East, evidently post-June 1930, after it had been converted to Mk.IV standard with the enlarged fin and rudder and auto-slotted upper wings.** *(Philip Jarrett)*

Iraq and Kurdistan

In April 1919 6 Sqn, which had served on the Western Front with R.E.8s, was sent out to the British Mandate of Mesopotamia. Sailing from Marseilles in the SS *Malwa*, SS *Clan Stuart* and SS *Syria*, it assembled at Basrah in July and on 6 September became established at Baghdad, again with R.E.8s, until these were superseded by Bristol Fighters in July 1920.

In April 1920 Mesopotamia was renamed Iraq. On 1 August 1920 H1462 of 6 Sqn spun in from 3,000ft during a reconnaissance from Baghdad, Fg Offs R.D.C. Palmer and H. Hutchinson both being killed. While ferrying, D7867 of 6 Sqn crashed in the desert at Tank, on 9 December 1920, while its pilot was landing to ascertain his location; Fg Off R.N. Essell was killed but the fate of his passenger, Mr C.C. Garbett, was not recorded. On 1 May 1922 D8037 collided with H1453, both of 6 Sqn, and both crashed at Baghdad West without injury to the crews. On 16 May 1922 D7845 of 6 Sqn suffered engine failure on take-off, crashed at Baghdad West and was destroyed by fire; Fg Off L.C. Hooton MC and AC2 G.W. Butler were both killed.

At Sulaymaniyah on 31 May 1922 D7844 from HQ Iraq crashed after engine failure

on take-off and caught fire. Flight Lieutenant F.N. Hudson MC died of injuries on 6 June and Flt Lt E. Drudge MBE was seriously injured. On 8 August 1922 Fg Off V.C. Cordingly of 6 Sqn was unhurt when he stalled D7838 during a night landing.

Relations were strained with Turkey, which was dissatisfied with the existing boundary between the two countries, and on 9 October 1922 6 Sqn was moved to Hinaidi. On 1 October 1922 AVM Sir John Salmond arrived to become General Officer Commanding for both military and air forces in the theatre, also holding the temporary Army rank of major-general. On that same date RAF Iraq was restyled Iraq Command. By this time Turkey had troops concentrated on the frontier and was menacing the Mosul and Kurdistan regions of Iraq, but the presence of an RAF Wing, including 6 Sqn, which had moved to Mosul on 19 May 1924, forestalled an attempt to seize Mosul.

In March and April 1923 the RAF was called upon to take part in a combined ground and air operation to repel an uprising in Kurdistan supported by Turkish troops. In addition to reconnaissance and bombing, they supplied rations, stores and

clothing to columns on the march, as well as evacuating sick and wounded from inaccessible positions. By the end of April the Turkish troops had been driven back across the frontier into Persia. On 8 March 1923 D7832 of 6 Sqn crashed on landing at Kirkuk, seriously injuring Fg Off H. J. Bradley, but his observer, Sgt R.A. Long, was unhurt. In the summer of 1923 the fanatical Sheikh Mahmud, who had been a source of trouble for some time, declared himself King of Kurdistan and then continued to make trouble over the next two years. He declared a Jihad, or Holy War, so in June 1924 a force of 42 aircraft from six squadrons, including 6 Sqn based at Kingerban, carried out two days of continuous bombing on Sulaymaniyah in which 26 tons of bombs were dropped without the loss of any aircraft. The inhabitants had been forewarned by proclamations, so there were no casualties, and the town was reoccupied in July.

The situation again became critical in the autumn of 1924 but was met by a fresh concentration of British air and ground forces at Mosul. Although there was some local fighting, effective air action helped to keep the situation in hand. Early on 14 September 6 Sqn moved to Zakho in response to a message that Turkish forces were about to cross the border and seize that town. Bristol Fighters patrolled along the River Hazil, and at 08:08 reported to Baghdad by wireless that 300 Turkish cavalry had been seen crossing the River Borana near Biespon, only six miles from Zakho, and asked for instructions. Seven

Left: **Three F.2Bs of 6 Sqn make a reconnaissance flight, with the snow-covered 11,500ft-high Gara Dagh mountain providing a dramatic backdrop. The lead aircraft is C923, and the others are F4580 and E2629.** *(Philip Jarrett)*

Left: **F.2B H1438, said to have been photographed while with 20 Sqn in India in the early 1920s. It was at Cranwell by July 1922, and after reconditioning to J Type in 1925 eventually went to Iraq and then to 6 Sqn in Egypt, where it was wrecked when it struck a ridge and overturned on landing at Imshash in Egypt on 11 August 1930. Well shown here are the tubular bearers beneath the rear cockpit on which lead discs weighing 17½lb each were threaded to serve as ballast for flights with the rear cockpit unoccupied.** *(Philip Jarrett)*

Above: **Twelve F.2Bs of 6 Sqn ranged at Mosul, Iraq, in 1924. The nearest machine is E2424, and second in line is F4890.** *(Philip Jarrett)*

Left: **Bristol Fighter F4278 of 6 Sqn after a forced landing. This aircraft was reconditioned to J Type in 1924-25.** *(Philip Jarrett)*

Right: **Seen here with 6 Sqn in the early 1920s, F4727 was reconstructed as FR4727 in 1923, and after reconditioning at Bristol's in 1925 eventually went to the Home Communication Flight at Northolt.** *(RAF Museum)*

minutes later they received instructions to attack. They did so at 08:31, and nine minutes later were able to report that the Turkish cavalry was in full retreat. No aircraft were lost, but while bombing and machine-gunning ground troops F4731 was hit by ground fire; Fg Off D.W.F. Bonham-Carter was wounded but managed to return before crashing near Zakho. The remainder of the formation landed safely at Zakho, and after refuelling and rearming set off again to attack a group of 150 horsemen at Birkar. On return, F4731 of 6 Sqn crashed at Zakho LG; Fg Off T.J. Desmond was seriously injured and LAC C.E. Edge was also injured. The situation evidently having settled down, at least for the time being, 6 Sqn returned to Mosul on 1 November 1924.

On 4 May 1925 an aircraft of 6 Sqn crashed at Khaniutman. Although Flt Lt W.A.B. Saville was only slightly injured, his passenger, Lt J.E. Griffiths of the Iraq Levies, was killed. At Heliopolis an F.2B of No 4 FTS crashed during training on 6 February 1926, killing Fg Off A.C. Tremellon and seriously injuring Flt Lt G.P. Simpson.

At Ankara, the Turkish capital, in June 1926 an amicable agreement was at last reached between the British, Turkish and Iraqi Governments, settling the entire frontier problem. The presence of 6 Sqn at Mosul was no longer needed, and it returned to Hinaidi on 20 October 1926. Pilot

Above: **Displaying a pennant on its fin and an indecipherable emblem on its fuselage, this is H1453 of 6 Sqn at Baghdad West, Iraq, about 1921.** *(C&C)*

Officer L.E.R. Fisher MC was killed when an F.2B of 6 Sqn crashed near Mosul, and his passenger, Lt. S.G. Haserick of the King's Own Yorkshire Light Infantry, died later of his injuries. On 8 June 1928 Sgt A.J. Garner and Sgt W.F. Fletcher were both killed when one of 6 Sqn's F.2Bs spun into

the ground near Mosul. On 4 July 1928 another of 6 Sqn's F.2Bs hit telegraph wires across the Mosul Bridge and crashed in the Tigris; Fg Off A.B. Kay died of his injuries and LAC A.H. Bolton was slightly injured. On 23 October 1929 6 Sqn left Iraq for Egypt.

It is believed that this rather smart chequer-tailed F.2B, D7??? 'C4', was photographed in the Middle East, but details are lacking. *(Philip Jarrett)*

This study of F.2B J6647 of 20 Sqn flying over the Khyber Pass on 9 December 1925 gives a vivid impression of typical terrain over which operations were flown. The aircraft has flight commander's pennants attached to its rudder and lower wingtips. *(Philip Jarrett)*

Chapter 14

OPERATIONS IN INDIA

At the beginning of the twentieth century India was part of the British Empire. Most areas of the subcontinent had by then largely accepted British rule, at least for the time being, but a notable exception was the large mountainous area on the border with neighbouring Afghanistan. On 9 November 1901 the Viceroy of India, Lord Curzon, named this region the North West Frontier Province (NWFP). In 1947, on gaining independence, the area was to become known as West Pakistan, its fellow Muslim region in north-eastern India then becoming East Pakistan. When East Pakistan seceded

from the union in 1971, they became Pakistan and Bangladesh respectively.

In 1901 the NWFP had an overall population of around ten million tribesmen, consisting of numerous districts with varying loyalties, being collectively referred to as Pathans. These were fighting men by tradition, each having a rifle of some description, being brought up as marksmen and gaining experience as formidable and merciless hill and mountain guerrilla fighters. They regarded the British as invaders, and the Province was a constant source of rebellion, sometimes escalating

into pitched battles involving thousands of men.

During the First World War the British Army, largely preoccupied with fighting Germany and its allies on the Western Front and in the Middle East, had still to maintain a sizeable force in India, and in 1915 the RFC was called upon to provide assistance. Initially this was in the form of 31 Sqn, 'A' Flight of which was formed at Farnborough on 11 October 1915, equipped with five B.E.2cs from the resident No 1 Reserve Aeroplane School. After working up, the Flight sailed from Liverpool on 27 November, arriving on Boxing Day at Bombay, from where they travelled to Nowshera in the NWFP. Shortly after its arrival 'B' Flight formed at Fort Rowner, Gosport, with six B.E.2cs acquired from the resident 22 Sqn. This unit duly embarked on 4 February, eventually arriving on 1 March at Risalpur, also in the NWFP, to be joined there for a short time by 'A' Flt, which detached the following month to Murree. Then, on 10 May, 'C' Flt formed at Gosport, from units of the Home Defence Brigade, embarking 13 days later and arriving at Bombay on 17 June to complete

Left: **Photographed with 20 Sqn in India in 1919, F4446 has twin Lewis guns on the Scarff ring.** *(Philip Jarrett)*

Above: **After being reconditioned to J Type, F.2B F4463 served with 5, 31 and 20 Sqns in India during 1924-1930. It was with 31 Sqn when this photograph was taken. It was wrecked at Peshawar on 18 March 1930 when it was taxied into stationary Westland Wapiti J9396.** *(Philip Jarrett)*

the squadron complement. As well as Murree and Risalpur the squadron, which later also received some B.E.2es, used various other airfields and landing grounds in the region, including Ambala, Bannu, Cawnpore, Dardoni, Dera-Ghazi-Khan, Dera Ismail, Duki, Khanpur, Lahore, Quetta, Shabkadar, Sibi, Sora Rogha and Tank (pronounced 'Tonk').

In March 1918 31 Sqn joined the newly formed 52nd (Corps) Wing, which had its headquarters at Peshawar. In June 1919 the squadron's now-obsolete B.E.2s were replaced by the redoubtable Bristol Fighter. That same month 31 Sqn was joined in the Wing by three further Bristol Fighter-equipped squadrons. One was 20 Sqn, which had been flying the type in France since August 1917 and had sailed from Marseilles on 30 May to arrive at Risalpur on 16 June and take up residence next month at Parachinar.

The second was 114 Sqn at Ambala, which had formed from two flights of 31 Sqn in September 1917, re-equipping from B.E.2cs and B.E.2es in October 1919. The unit was redesignated 28 Sqn on 1 April 1920 under a post-war restructuring. On the same date the 52nd Wing became No 3 (Indian) Wing, only to be further

This F.2B, F4637 'A' of 48 Sqn, photographed at Quetta, India, in December 1919, was the personal mount of the A Flight commander, Flt Lt L. Hollinghurst, DFC, standing second from right. *(Philip Jarrett)*

redesignated No 1 (Indian) Wing in July 1920.

To complete the trio, 48 Sqn arrived from Germany on 22 June 1919, taking up residence initially at Quetta on 12 July. Likewise redesignated under the post-war renumbering of many squadrons, it became 5 Sqn on 1 February 1920, this renumbering of existing squadrons in India taking place against the wishes of the Chief of the Air Staff, Hugh Trenchard.

Detailed movements in India of all four of these squadrons are given in Appendix 9. On 27 March 1924 28 Sqn was further redesignated 28 (Army Co-operation) Sqn,

the other Bristol Fighter squadrons in India being similarly retitled around the same time. In due course the aircraft of the four army co-operation squadrons were visually distinguished for identification purposes by a single coloured band around the rear fuselage, blue in the case of 5 Sqn, red for 20 Sqn, green for 28 Sqn and black for 31 Sqn.

From September 1920 new and replacement aircraft were despatched by the Packing Depot at Sealand, near Chester, a task previously undertaken by No 6 Stores Depot at Ascot. After being packed in individual crates as components they were shipped out to Karachi, to be reassembled

and test flown from February 1921 by the Aircraft Depot at nearby Drigh Road.

One other unit in India with some Bristol Fighters on strength for a time was HQ RAF India Communication Flight, which formed in October 1928. This used Willingdon, near Delhi, in the winter months, but moved each year to Lahore to be nearer the main headquarters, which moved from Delhi to Simla during the summer season. Bristol Fighters were still use with the Flight in February 1931.

Frontier operations

Initial operations over the frontier by F.2Bs were sporadic until the full force had been assembled. On 12 March 1919 2nd Lt C.A. Allen and 2nd Lt W. Kennedy were both killed during a reconnaissance flight, and on 20 July 1919 Lt F.V. Devonshire was killed on a reconnaissance of the Charra region. On 30 July 1919 F4626 of 20 Sqn was fired on while bombing Badarna and Capt G.S.W. Eastwood was wounded. Another aircraft of 20 Sqn was brought down by ground fire and Plt Off H.J. Gye and Plt Off L. Jones were wounded. The wreck was burnt by tribesmen.

Bristol Fighters were used in 1920 when, in a strange incident, Afghanistan invaded India. It arose because the Chief of Afghan Intelligence, who was also the Afghan Postmaster in Peshawar, reported to his ruler that India was in a state of near collapse. It appeared that large numbers of Indians were deserting from the Indian Army, and British troops were being sent home. Unfortunately, the word 'demobilisation' does not seem to have been included in his vocabulary. In Kabul this seemed an ideal opportunity to occupy India.

The news that Afghan troops were flooding over the frontier took the Indian Government by surprise. Orders went out that the invaders had to be expelled. Traditionally, this entailed infantry columns marching towards the enemy, supported by supply wagons and mountain guns dismantled and carried on mules. The First World War had changed all that. While army engineers improved the roads leading to Afghanistan, lorries conveyed troops and supplies forward, escorted by armoured cars. The artillery, mainly 18-pounders that had played such a large part as field artillery in France, was towed.

Right: **Noteworthy features in this 1920 view of F.2B F4611 'D' of 48 Sqn are the hinged oblong board hanging from the trailing edge of the lower port wing, immediately inboard of the aileron, and the streamer attached to the rudder. These were used during the latter part of the First World War as a means of enabling ground troops to identify a Contact Patrol aircraft, and it seems that the practice was continued into the interwar years.** *(Norman Franks)*

Below right: **Here is F4611 'D' of 48 Sqn again, this time creating a dust storm as its Falcon is run-up preparatory to take-off. On 16 August 1922, after the unit had been redesignated 5 Sqn, this F.2B crashed on take-off at Pislim and was wrecked.** *(Norman Franks)*

In the air, the elderly B.E.s had been replaced by Bristol Fighters, and tactics perfected by the RAF in support of troops were applied to India. Communication between ground and air forces was maintained by radio, and any attempt by the Afghans to hold defensive positions would bring down bombing and strafing raids on their positions.

The final bizarre occurrence came when the bomber force decided on some strategic bombing. Its entire strength, the one and only Handley Page V/1500 in India, flew to Kabul and dropped bombs on a selection of forts. This brought an immediate reaction. Messages came through to Peshawar that the whole incident was a regrettable mistake. Afghanistan was only trying to help to keep order in India, and the Afghan forces withdrew. Unfortunately the local tribes had been persuaded to join in, and it was some months before their natural warlike activities had been curbed, Bristol Fighters maintaining watch on the movements of groups of rebels and, if necessary, going to the relief of Indian Army forts or convoys if they were attacked.

The hazardous nature of flying over the mountains was shown when Fg Off J.S. Dearlove in F4866 of 48 Sqn became lost in failing light and mist on 20 February 1920 while flying over the Torkham Pass. He flew into the ground while making a forced landing 23 miles northwest of Barkham and was injured. On 20 March Fg Off W. Deane DFC and Fg Off G.R. Bissett DFC were killed when F4447 of 20 Sqn was hit by ground fire over Sherrani and crashed.

On 13 April H1524 of 20 Sqn was brought down near Datta Khal; Flt Lt P.E. Bishop and Plt Off McCormack were both captured but were released later on payment of a ransom. Three days later, F4627 of 5 Sqn crashed at Loralai LG during a training flight, killing Fg Off R. Pugh.

On 7 May 1920 operations against the tribes gave way to an uneasy peace when tribal leaders accepted terms they had been

Above right: **Another 48 Sqn F.2B in 1920 was H1530 'A'. Presumably the dog being held over the rear fuselage was a squadron mascot. This aircraft was wrecked on 10 March 1922 when it crashed during a high-altitude landing at Quetta.** *(Norman Franks)*

Right: **With rugged terrain forming a backdrop, this is F.2B H1456 of Quetta-based 5 Sqn, photographed in 1920.** *(Philip Jarrett)*

Left: **A line-up of F.2Bs of 5 Sqn, probably at Kohat around 1925, with the squadron number on their fins. The nearest machine is probably F4766 'H'.** *(Philip Jarrett)*

Above: **On 20 March 1928 F.2B D8035 'M' of 20 Sqn collided with F4396 while turning in formation over Peshawar and was badly damaged in the resulting crash-landing. Fortunately Fg Off G.W.P. Irwin was unhurt, and the aircraft was rebuilt.** *(Philip Jarrett)*

Below: **This photograph was taken to show the damage inflicted on the upper starboard mainplane leading edge of F.2B F4396 'B' of 20 Sqn on 20 March 1928 when it collided with D8035. It also provides some nice detail of the type's general features.** *(Philip Jarrett)*

Left: **Well-presented F.2B F4916 'N' of 20 Sqn in 1927/28 displays the squadron number on its fin and has coloured (red?) wheel discs. A spare wheel is attached beneath the rear cockpit.** *(Philip Jarrett)*

offered. By 1 June there were 40 Bristol Fighters serviceable in India, plus 27 other types, mainly D.H.9As. Three months later only 20 Sqn was operating in direct support of forward army garrisons in Waziristan. Operating conditions were difficult, both on the ground and in the air, the now ageing and patched-up wartime-built aircraft and engines usually being maintained in the open and subject to sudden sand and dust storms. Pilots operated as best they could in thin mountain air, with consequent overheating of engines, temperatures ranging from freezing point to 120° Fahrenheit. For survival, it was essential that pilots quickly learned to navigate through passes, or nullahs, between towering rocks often several thousands of feet high. Spares were in short supply owing to budget cuts at home, exacerbated by the fact that the RAF in India came under the Army Vote and consequently received very few supplies. It was not uncommon for F.2Bs to have to take off for an operation with a full war load without tyres on their wheels. On 19 January 1921 H1658 of 20 Sqn went missing while carrying mail and radio parts to Wana. It had force-landed in Afghanistan, and Fg Off L.H.I. Bell and Fg Off C.R. Smythe were returned to India a month later. On 3 March 1922 E2442 of 28 Sqn and H1548 of 20 Sqn collided over Atari, killing Fg Off J. Buckley and AC2 Richardson of 28 Sqn and Flt Lt J.B. Fox and Sgt Hemmings of 20 Sqn.

On 6 April 1922 an army garrison at Wana Fort was threatened by a large group of tribesmen. Four RAF squadrons were available for immediate operations in support of army garrisons and positions in an area approximately the size of Scotland, but of the 30 aircraft supposedly available, only seven F.2Bs and five other aircraft were anything like serviceable. By the end of that month only 38 F.2Bs and 11 other aircraft were declared fit for operations. The situation was such that Air Vice-Marshal Salmond, who was sent out to investigate, reported to the Viceroy of India in August that the RAF in India was virtually ineffective in its present state. In the short term a welcome but inadequate supply of spares began to arrive from depots and stores, but it took a further six years for his recommendation for two further squadrons to be implemented.

On 12 December 1922 activities were stepped up in the Razmak region, 28 Sqn being sent forward to the LG near Fort Dardoni. For the next five months

Right: **F.2B F4430 in flight while serving with 210 Sqn in 1931.** *(H.1185)*

operations were carried out daily, despite the freezing conditions experienced in this hilly territory throughout the winter. On 24 January 1923 one of six F.2Bs from 28 Sqn, all armed with 12 20/25lb Cooper bombs and three boxes of Baby Incendiaries, had to break off an attack on villages to the side of Bakri Ounga when one of its incendiaries dropped out of the bottom of the box and ignited several others. The observer, Fg Off L.H. Ridley, was able to throw several of them overboard, being badly burned in the process, but one escaped and rolled underneath the rear petrol tank. The pilot, Fg Off R.M. Foster DFC, hastily made a forced landing among rocks in the valley bottom, but the aircraft then overturned before bursting into flames and exploding. The two crew members were soon captured by Manzir Khan tribesmen, who treated them very badly and took most of their clothing. They were eventually released without further harm on 12 February.

Soon after this, on 17 March, 28 Sqn moved to another landing ground at Tank, before returning to a more hospitable airfield at Peshawar on 19 April, the squadron headquarters being based there for the rest of that year and the whole of 1924, with small detachments being sent out as required.

The crews were in constant danger with having to operate over this mountainous and inhospitable region in aircraft subject to poor serviceability, and faced with ever-changing weather and the stark possibility of being subjected to torture or death should they be forced down over country offering no opportunity for a successful forced landing.

An F.2B of 28 Sqn was lost when it stalled off a turn and crashed two miles south-west of Peshawar; Fg Off F.G. Whitmore and LAC G.A. Taylor were both killed. On 25 January 1924 Fg Off J.N. Jacques was injured and LAC A.V. Stevens killed when D8039 of 20 Sqn had engine failure and hit telephone lines in a forced landing four miles from Quetta. On 16 May D7821 of 20 Sqn stalled after take-off from Quetta

Above: **An unusual angle on F.2B J6656 'G' of 28 Sqn, flying near Ambala, India, in 1931. For some reason only the first two digits of its serial number are carried on the rear fuselage.** *(RAF Museum)*

and Fg Off E.C. Usher-Somers and Lt Mackenzie of the RFA were killed.

On 28 July 1924 events took a calamitous turn when three F.2Bs of 28 Sqn and one of 5 Sqn were caught in heavy fog that suddenly closed in from the hills during one of several raids near Razmak. Flying Officer I.C. Anderson and AC K.H. Taylor of 28 Sqn were killed when F4286 flew into a hillside, and another crashed at Duncan's Piquet, killing Fg Off E. Bell and badly

injuring AC1 P. Slack. who died next day. The third crashed at Idak, fortunately without injury to the two crewmembers. The 5 Sqn aircraft crashed in the Shawali Algad, both Sqn Ldr A.J. Capel and LAC A. Bell being taken prisoner but later released.

During the three months to October of that year tribes in southern Waziristan, especially the Mahsuds, attacked several Government and Service outposts. These forays were mostly quelled, except for the

F.2B J6601 of 5 Sqn in India in 1928, with the squadron number on its fin, red wheel covers, and a spare wheel.. *(RAF Museum)*

Displaying its serial number on both fin and rudder, this is F.2B F4403 'C' of 5 Sqn in India around 1920-22. *(Philip Jarrett)*

Left: **The engineless F4621 'J' of 28 Sqn, Ambala, at the engine test house in 1928. Note the tailskid dolly, using aircraft wheels, and the camera gun on the upper centre section.** *(Eric Harlin)*

Lower left: **Another 28 Sqn F.2B, 'D' at Ambala in 1928, with the squadron number on its fin, flashy 'whitewall' tyres, painted auxiliary radiator and hinged contact-patrol boards dangling from the lower wing trailing edge.** *(Eric Harlin)*

Abdur Rahman Khel tribe, which persisted in its attacks on army posts at Gomal, Manzai and Spli Toi. The Government of India then agreed to a trial of independent air action on the North-West Frontier, to try to bring to submission the remaining sections of the tribes in Waziristan. Accordingly, Wg Cdr R.C.M. Pink, who commanded No 2 (Indian) Wing at Risalpur, was tasked with organising conclusive air operations against the tribe, and he made the old fort at Tank his headquarters, having six squadrons of D.H.9As and F.2Bs at his disposal. The D.H.9As of 27 Sqn and 60 Sqns moved forward for operations on 3 March 1925, using the old fort at Miranshah as headquarters, and 5 Sqn, with ten F.2Bs available, operated from Tank. Six days later operations commenced with D.H.9As bombing villages with 112lb and 230lb bombs while the F.2Bs machine-gunned surrounding caves and other hill hideouts. Owing to the height of the surrounding mountains the aircraft generally flew only partly loaded at 9,000ft above sea level, being then some 3,000ft above the actual targets. Several villages were set ablaze and a watchtower destroyed.

Discussions with the whole of the Abdur Rahman Khel tribe initially offered the prospect of some tribal sections meeting the Government's demands, but nothing came of promises that were made, and on 18 March the F.2Bs of 5 Sqn were reinforced by the arrival of one flight of 20 Sqn F.2Bs at Miranshah. Operations were then stepped up; the now normal bombing and strafing sorties being supplemented by intermittent bombing attacks at odd times of day to keep the tribesmen unsettled during daylight hours. This evidently gave them the illusion that night time was safe from bombing, until an F.2B of 31 Sqn, equipped for night flying, flew from Ambala to Tank on 30 March and five days later made a night attack in which a notorious Faridai leader named Tormarchai was killed. The remainder of 31 Sqn soon followed, to be based at Tank. The F.2Bs of 5 Sqn then detached to Miranshah together with one flight of 20 Sqn. Thereafter operations continued apace by night and day, until at

Upper left: **F.2B J6674 'K' of 31 Sqn is restrained during a ground run of its engine in 1923.** *(RAF Museum)*

Left: **Running-up the engine of J6752 'K' at Peshawar in 1927. It has the wide red band of 20 Sqn around its rear fuselage, the leading-edge slats in the upper wingtips are deployed, and it carries a load of small bombs. The fin of Westland Wapiti IIA K1306 is visible behind.** *(Philip Jarrett)*

the end of April the tribes agreed to begin talks at Jandola, resulting in terms being agreed on 1 May. Not only was this achieved in less than two months and at small cost, but it had the effect of persuading several tribal sections outside the actual area of operations, who were also at issue with the Government, to come in voluntarily and submit to the terms imposed.

This result was achieved after only 54 days of actual operations involving 2,720hrs of flying. Pink, who was universally respected, was given accelerated promotion to group captain, and the brief campaign became known as 'Pink's War'. All 46 officers and 214 other ranks serving under his command during this period in No 2 (Indian) Wing were awarded the silver India General Service Medal with a clasp inscribed 'Waziristan 1925'.

On 20 May, a F.2B of 31 Sqn crashed on landing at Sialkot, killing Fg Off A. Findlay and Capt G. Rich of the Indian Army.

The success of this independent campaign changed the attitude of the Army and civil hierarchy regarding the RAF in India. They now had to accept the reality of the great potential of air power in India, especially in respect of control of the air in the northwest of the country. This was reflected in a much-needed improvement in general supply and maintenance facilities for the aircraft and other equipment, which had long been sought, hitherto unavailingly. The change of attitude soon had its effect, and 5 Sqn's F.2Bs, for instance, were able to average 266 flying hours during 1926, the annual total for the whole squadron being 3,194hrs. Apart from the occasional necessity for further anti-tribal operations, the F.2B crews were now able to concentrate mainly on their intended army co-operation role, including much time spent on photo-reconnaissance of the overall territory to enable more detailed and accurate maps to be produced.

On 5 March 1926 a F.2B of the Aircraft Depot at Karachi crashed, Fg Off C.P.M.B. Callard being killed and LAC A. Barron later dying of his injuries. Another 28 Sqn machine crashed at Quetta on 31 March, Fg Off R.E.J. Wilson and LAC A.J. Burgess dying of their injuries. One of 5 Sqn's aircraft was lost on 6 July when it crashed at Razmak, Fg Off C.C. Harris being killed and LAC C.C. Avery dying of his injuries. On 1 August J6640 of 31 Sqn crashed on take-off at Multan; Fg Off J.C. Marcy was seriously injured and LAC P.W.E. Crunden died later. On 15 August, when an F.2B of 20 Sqn crashed at Dalbandin in Baluchistan, Wg Cdr J.S. Archer CBE was seriously

Above: **A lone F.2B coded 'F' dwarfed by mountainous Indian terrain.** *(Philip Jarrett)*

injured and LAC W.S. Bolam died of his injuries. On 14 September Plt Off D.C. Sherman of 31 Sqn was killed at Lahore, and on 21 September a 5 Sqn aircraft crashed in the Indus at Attock and sank, Fg Off D. Robinson being injured and AC1 P. Jones killed. On 5 October pilot Fg Off P.H. Nicholls died of serious burns following the crash of F.2B J6631 of 20 Sqn at Peshawar on 1 October when the aircraft hit an obstruction on take-off, crashed and

caught fire. His passenger, LAC George Cairns, received only slight injuries. Finally, on 29 December, Flt Lt A.N. Macneal and LAC C.A. Overy died of their injuries when one of 5 Sqn's aircraft crashed at Ambala. Such regular casualties were part of the gruelling flying regime in India.

Improvements could now be made in air-to-ground communication, especially with scattered and remote army ground formations, and pick-up hooks under the

Left: **Another F.2B in monsoon conditions, this is J7684 'F' of 20 Sqn. Behind on the right is 'G', probably F4881.** *(Philip Jarrett)*

fuselage enabled messages to be retrieved. During 1927 experiments with W/T and R/T equipment produced mixed results, it being considered best to have just one or two squadron F.2Bs specially fitted with R/T sets fitted in the rear cockpit. In June of that year F.2Bs of 5 and 20 Sqns and D.H.9As of 27 and 60 Sqns were called upon to undertake operations against tribes in the Beshawar district who were heading towards Peshawar. Night bombing attacks using airburst flares to identify targets were made by 5 Sqn, and the tribal threat soon ceased.

The necessity for further operations came with inter-tribal disorder in Afghanistan at the end of 1928, the Shiamwari tribe in Eastern Afghanistan openly rebelling against King Amanullah. Besieging Dakka, they occupied positions between Kabul and the Khyber Pass, cutting road and telegraph communications. The rebellion began to spread, cutting off the British Legation in Kabul, and on 14 December 1928 rebel leader Kabibullah Khan advanced on Kabul, his forces becoming established on the Asmai Heights, with the result that the Legation was now also cut off from the rest of the city. As shells and bullets were falling on the Legation the British Commissioner, Sir Francis Humphreys, requested that the women and children should be urgently evacuated by air.

An evacuation began on 23 December, and by the time it ended on 25 February 1929 some 586 passengers of various nationalities had been rescued. During this period the RAF flew 28,160 miles on this duty, flying over mountains averaging 10,000ft in height, and this during one of the severest winters on record, with no opportunity for a successful forced landing in the rough terrain.

On 5 March 1930 Fg Off J.W. Hawke and LAC E.R. Charlesworth were both killed when F4414 of 20 Sqn hit a telegraph wire while in the circuit at Jhelum. On the 14th Flt Lt J.C.H. Tavendale and LAC H.J. Chapell of 20 Sqn were both killed at Ali Masjid, near Peshawar. The final operational loss appears to have occurred when J6650 of 20 Sqn was hit by rifle fire on 17 June 1930

Two F.2Bs of 20 Sqn at Wana in Waziristan in May 1926. Their identities are probably J6616 'C' and H1601 'A'. *(Philip Jarrett)*

An anonymous F.2B with a four-bladed propeller in India in the 1920s. The group in front are enjoying mugs of tea, presumably provided by the lady with the picnic basket. *(Philip Jarrett)*

Two views of four 20 Sqn F.2Bs at Peshawar. The nearest two machines in the three-quarter-rear view are J6647 'D' and J6782 'C'. *(Philip Jarrett)*

Above: **A mechanic clambers over H1513 'L' of 48 Sqn in India in 1919.** *(Philip Jarrett)*

Right: **Bristol F.2B 'V' of 20 Sqn kicks up the dust as it takes off from Miranshah in 1932.** *(Philip Jarrett)*

and crash-landed at Basawal, Afghanistan; Fg Off R.W.A. Alexander was wounded but AC1 C.R. Wiltshire was unhurt, and both were returned to India soon afterwards.

Thereafter the RAF units in India were able to resume more normal activities. In March 1930 the D.H.9A squadrons began re-equipping with the new Westland Wapiti, and in February 1931 31 Sqn became the first Bristol Fighter squadron to receive this type. It was followed in September by 28 Sqn, then 5 Sqn in October and finally 20 Sqn in November, the completion of this process being marked on 13 March 1932, when 20 Sqn flew a final formation flight, some 15 years after the F.2B had first entered service.

F.2B H1530 'A' of 48 Sqn in India in 1919 appears to have white centres to its wheel discs. *(Philip Jarrett)*

Above: **At the front of this trio of F.2Bs of 5 Sqn at Quetta in 1922 is H1530 'A', which was with the unit when it was previously designated 48 Sqn. Next in line is F4403 'C'.** *(Philip Jarrett)*

Left: **A brace of Biffs; the pilots of F4555 'E' and F4921 'F' of 20 Sqn pose their charges for the camera.** *(Philip Jarrett)*

Below left: **Indian soldiers stand guard on three 20 Sqn F.2Bs, the foremost machine having the unit's number on its fin.** *(Philip Jarrett)*

Above: **Tropical kit is conspicuous in this study of J6630, which joined 28 Sqn in 1924. The oft-carried spare wheel beneath the fuselage is well shown.** *(Philip Jarrett)*

Left: **F.2B J6758 looking poorly after an encounter with a barbed-wire entanglement. This might well be the accident that wrecked it while it was with 31 Sqn in India, having previously served in Egypt.** *(Philip Jarrett)*

Right: **An anonymous F.2B of 20 Sqn aloft over India.** *(Philip Jarrett)*

Below: **The F.2Bs of 20 Sqn running-up at Peshawar on 11 May 1930, just before taking off to bomb a tribe in the hills near Shabqadar, now in Pakistan. De Havilland D.H.9As are ranged behind them.** *(Philip Jarrett)*

Right and below: **Four F.2Bs of A Flight of 5 Sqn lined up in alphabetical order at Quetta. Serial numbers, flight letters and names are: H1565 'A'** *Silver Star,* **F4746 'B'** *Wembley,* **E2421 'C'** *Palace* **and F4592 'D'** *White City.* *(Philip Jarrett)*

Left: **An F.2B serving with a squadron based in India in the action of collecting a message.** *(Philip Jarrett)*

Right: **Although H1554 looks tired and worn in this study taken in 1923, when it was with 28 Sqn, it continued in service in India for at least another three years.** *(Philip Jarrett)*

Left: **Bristol Fighters F4947 'G' and J6647 'F' of 20 Sqn over the Peshawar Valley circa 1924-25.** *(Philip Jarrett)*

Above: **F.2B F4643 of 31 Sqn, complete with message hook, photographed on 1 June 1928.** *(Philip Jarrett)*

Below: **An unusual 'parting shot' of F9616 'M' of 5 Sqn, a rebuild that served with the squadron during 1926-28.** *(Philip Jarrett)*

Above: **F.2B J6783 of 20 Sqn after what seems to have been a heavy landing at Fort Sandeman (now known as Zhob, and in the Balochistan Province of Pakistan).** *(Philip Jarrett)*

Above: **An intimate aerial close-up of pilot Fg Off Fresson and gunner LAC France in F4839 of 31 Sqn during a close formation flight over Delhi.** *(Philip Jarrett)*

Left: **Seen en route from Tank to Jelal Khel during 'Pink's War' in 1925, this is E2421 'C' of 5 Sqn, showing the letter code on its upper centre section as well as on the fuselage flanks.** *(Philip Jarrett)*

Right: **The original print of this picture is captioned as a Bristol Fighter of 20 Sqn (H1461) at '8,000ft over Bannu Boundary', Bannu being a city in the Bannu District in southern Khyber Pakhtunkhwa in what is now Pakistan. The aircraft, H1461 'F', is recorded as having served in 5 Sqn and 31 Sqn.** *(Philip Jarrett)*

Two F.2Bs of 31 Sqn, H1461 'F' and H1457 'E', leave Peshawar in 1930 with their underwing panniers loaded and other personal kit carried beneath their fuselages. *(Philip Jarrett)*

Above: **F.2B J6774 'C' of 20 Sqn, photographed in 1930, is equipped with a pair of camera guns. This aircraft was also used by 5 Sqn.** *(Philip Jarrett)*

Left: **Flying Officer Ford of 32 Sqn takes off on a reconnaissance from Fort Dardoni, North West Frontier Province, in J6782 'O' in 1923.** *(Philip Jarrett)*

F.2B J6641 'T' of 28 Sqn on the North West Frontier in the 1930s. *(Philip Jarrett)*

Above: **Four F.2Bs of 28 Sqn lined up and displaying their white-wall tyres.** *(Philip Jarrett)*

Right: **Some of 28 Sqn's F.2Bs, with 'B' in the foreground. The aircraft having its uncowled engine run is possibly J6621 'D'.** *(Philip Jarrett)*

When E2605 'C' of 28 Sqn landed on rough ground at Akora on the North West Frontier on 7 July 1924, its starboard wheel collapsed. After repair, the aircraft went to 20 Sqn that August. *(Philip Jarrett)*

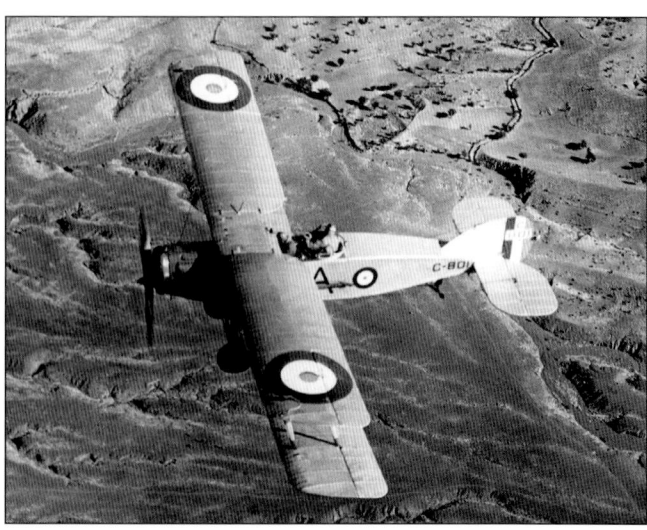

A close-up of a 28 Sqn F.2B 'A' as it is run-up against the chocks at
Secunderabad in preparation for a reconnaissance on 17 January 1931, showing
the tropical radiator, desert tyres, generator impeller and extra coolant outlet.
(Philip Jarrett)

Flight Lieutenant A.C. Sanderson DFC of 5 Sqn flying C801 'A' in 1927.
Sanderson eventually became Air Marshal Sir Clifford, KBE, CB, DFC.
(Philip Jarrett)

Left: Another air-to-air shot of C801
'A' of 5 Sqn. *(Philip Jarrett)*

Below: In June 1923 J6715 was 'A1' of
4 Sqn in Gallipoli during the
Chanak incident, but here it is as
'R' of 5 Sqn at Quetta in 1925.
(Philip Jarrett)

Two studies of 5 Sqn F.2Bs picketed down and swathed in protective covers at Hindu Bagh in India (now Muslim Bagh, Pakistan). The aircraft in the picture with the ambulance in the background is 'R' (but not J6715), and the nearest aircraft in the picture showing the tents and aerial mast is F4766 'H', with a J-serialled F.2B next in line. *(Philip Jarrett)*

"'Write off' in Razmak. No one injured' is the caption pencilled on the back of this picture of inverted F.2B F4665 'G', but no date is given. It was with 31 Sqn in 1926, and was 'K' of 20 Sqn in 1930, so it was probably not written off in this incident. *(Philip Jarrett)*

A very unusual ground-to-air angle on F.2B 'H' of 5 Sqn as it climbs away under the control of its sola topee'd pilot, revealing its Flight letter on the upper wing centre-section and showing the rib tapes to advantage. *(Philip Jarrett)*

A pair of 5 Sqn F.2Bs over mountainous terrain in 1927; D8035 'A' and F4320 'D'. *(Philip Jarrett)*

A pair of 20 Sqn F.2Bs, F4958 'A' and F 4562 'C' of A Flight, are prepared for flight at Sialkot. Quite a large crowd of onlookers is visible in the background. *(Philip Jarrett)*

Two shots of 5 Sqn F.2Bs which have been positioned among trees at Sialkot to render them less visible. Aircraft 'P' is J767?. *(Philip Jarrett)*

Left: **This line-up of 20 Sqn F.2Bs Mk.II in India includes J6781 'B' and J6647 'D', both part of the first post-war production order.** *(Philip Jarrett)*

Taken on 31 May 1926, the day of its demise, J7682 of Quetta-based 20 Sqn was written off because of this accident. *(Philip Jarrett)*

On 14 May 1930 tragedy struck 20 Sqn when F4562, crewed by Flt Lt Tavendale and LAC Chapell, crashed at Ali Masjid in the Khyber Pass near Peshawar, killing both occupants. In the view showing the aircraft's tail a shield is visible on the fin, showing a castle with a motto beneath it. *(Philip Jarrett)*

F.2B F4670, probably of 5 Sqn, draws attention at Karachi in the 1930s. *(Philip Jarrett)*

Left: **Four F.2Bs of 31 Sqn lined up at Karachi in the 1930s, with H1457 'E' on the right.** *(Philip Jarrett)*

Above: **Forced-landed F.2B F4908 'L' of 20 Sqn attracts a large audience as mechanics tend to its engine.** *(Philip Jarrett)*

Left: **A lonely 5 Sqn F.2B 'C' in a mountainous Indian setting.** *(Philip Jarrett)*

Right: **A Flight of 5 Sqn F.2Bs airborne from Risalpur, circa 1925.** *(Philip Jarrett)*

Left: A 'B' Flight group with E2501, with F4958 'F' in the background. The photographs of the F2Bs of 5 Sqn on this page were taken on Proclamation Day, 1 January 1928.

Below: F.2B E2501 'R' of B Flight, 5 Sqn, with Flight leader's streamers on outer interplane struts and rudder.

F.2B H1461 'F' of 5 Sqn lacks the squadron number on its fin but carries its serial number on both fuselage and rudder.

Someone in 48 Sqn evidently liked to play the daredevil (or the fool), as testified by this collection of images of him clambering over H1530 'A' in flight during the1920s. *(Trevor Henshaw and Philip Jarrett)*

Liberty-engined USAO-1s in assembly in the Curtiss factory at Buffalo on 20 July 1918. The optimistic overhead sign on the right proclaims: '175 Bristols must be finished during July. Boys, we've simply got to do it!'. A smaller poster proclaims, in part, 'big production will win the war' and 'every minute counts'. *(Curtiss)*

Chapter 15

AMERICAN PRODUCTION

The USAO-1 observation aircraft

When the United States of America joined the Allied powers after declaring war on Germany on 6 April 1917, it was realised that, while the country had a large capability for producing effective military aircraft, there were no suitable indigenous designs. Accordingly, the Bolling Commission was sent to Europe to select aircraft considered suitable for mass production in the USA. Among the types chosen was the Bristol Fighter, which was selected for use solely as a corps reconnaissance or observation aircraft. Consequently, a recommendation was forthcoming in August 1917, and the designation USAO-1 was adopted for the planned American production, though in practice it was generally still referred to as the Bristol Fighter.

Aircraft production was to be on a typically ambitious scale, with a planned 'Procurement Program' setting an optimistic target of 7,375 aircraft initially, building up to 20,475 in 12 months, many to be of British design. Of these, the first production order for the Bristol Fighter was entrusted towards the end of 1917 to the Curtiss Aeroplane and Motor Corporation of Buffalo, New York. The original proposal

was that the American-built version be fitted with 300hp geared Hispano-Suiza engines built under licence by the Wright-Martin Corporation, and 4,000 engines were ordered in October 1917.

An incomplete set of working drawings and the derelict airframe of A7207, lacking engine and equipment, had arrived in Washington, D.C., from England on 5 September. Even though the US Air Service had never before prepared production drawings, the head of its new Plane Design Section, Col Virginius E. Clark, deemed it

his department's responsibility to do so. In initiating this work he elected to replace the Hispano-Suiza engine with the much heavier 12-cylinder Liberty, because of an anticipated long delay in getting the Hispano into production in the USA, the cancellation of the medium-powered 8-cylinder Liberty, and the similar power output of the prototype 12-cylinder Liberty (330hp) to that of the Rolls-Royce Falcon III (275hp) intended for the latest British-built fighter version of the F.2B. Moreover, the Liberty, which was just entering

The third USAO-1 observation aircraft, 34233, with a radiator on the leading edge of the upper wing centre section.

A Curtiss-built USAO-1 with a Liberty engine, photographed on 3 March 1918. Faulty construction resulted in several crashes which led to cancellation of the production contract.

USAO-1 specification	
Type	Observation
Crew	Pilot and observer/gunner
Powerplant	400hp Liberty 12
Weight empty	2,281lb
Weight loaded	3,538lb
Wing span	39ft 4in (11.98m)
Length	27ft 1in (8.25m)
Height	10ft 1½in (3.09m)
Wing area	415.8ft^2 (38.65m^2)
Maximum speed at sea level	125mph (200km/h)
Climb to 10,000ft	7.05min
Absolute ceiling	25,000ft
Endurance	2hrs
Armament	2 fixed forward-firing Marlin and 2 moveable Lewis machine guns

production, was the only engine of sufficient power that might be available in time to meet USA0-1 delivery schedules set for January 1918. As a result of Clark's decision, the contract for the Hispano-Suizas was cancelled in November 1917.

Clark delivered his 'practically completed' drawings based on the English models to Curtiss in November 1918, but after that he was neither consulted by nor permitted to keep in touch with the American manufacturer or consulted by the authorities.

Designed solely as an observation aircraft to serve in the photographic reconnaissance or artillery-fire control roles, the USAO-1 was to be sufficiently fast and adequately armed to be able to defend itself in air-to-air combat. It was to have one fixed forward-firing machine gun and one moveable machine gun on a Scarff ring mounting on the rear cockpit. The radiator was relocated beneath the engine. No bombs were to be carried. Its estimated all-up weight was optimistically put at 1,790lb, and it was expected to cruise at 85 to 90mph and to be able to attain 138mph.

A contract for 1,000 USAO-1s was awarded to the Curtiss Airplane and Motor Company on 3 November 1917. Two months later, in January 1918, this was doubled to 2,000 aircraft, serialled 34232-36231, and deliveries from the company's Buffalo factory were expected to take place from February to July, an impossible requirement. As the Plane Design Section could do little more than deliver the drawings, Curtiss had to take responsibility for control of the design.

However, construction of 25 USAO-1s with flank radiators had already been approved on 2 February 1918. Things had not gone smoothly. Although the company made a great deal about draughtsman's errors in January1918, its own drawings proved just as bad, requiring several aircraft had to be built to correct and prove the Curtiss drawings, and changes were made to the engine support structure. Consequently, barely any progress at all was made with the first three production aircraft during the first eight days of February.

When the first USAO-1 was rolled out in February it was considerably heavier than estimated, had been given flank radiators to speed production, and was of questionable strength. Also in February, however, the American Expeditionary Force (AEF) in France submitted requirements calling for the aircraft to carry four machine guns, bombs and other equipment. Not only did this further increase its weight by 525lb to 3,671lb, but it also turned the aircraft into a light day bomber. On 1 March Mr J.E. Perrin, one-time chief engineer of the Lozier Automobile Co who had been engaged to assist in the preliminary design (though he knew nothing about flying), estimated that fully equipped production machines would weigh 'well over 3,700lb'.

Subsequently, when the AEF compared the performance of the American bomber built to its requirements with that of the fighter variant of the British F.2B, which carried only 185lb of equipment, it recommended that it should not go into production. As the USAO-1 was designed for the observation role, its poor performance as a fighter or bomber should hardly have been surprising.

Completion of the first, 34236, was delayed by poor workmanship until 1

Another shot of the Curtiss assembly shop at Buffalo on 20 July 1918, with patriotic Allied flags prominently displayed. (Curtiss)

March. On its maiden flight it proved to be easy to control, but suffered damage on landing owing to the poor state of the airfield outside Buffalo. Both Curtiss and the Signal Corps still believed that there were basic deficiencies in the airframe, and the company requested that the wings be modified, which meant that half of the 1,402 manufacturing drawings had to undergo revision. Moreover, the company had no experimental department to resolve problems, and its muddy flying field lacked electricity to heat the hangars during a very cold winter or to power tools. On 11 March Maj E.J. Hall, a co-designer of the Liberty engine, was put in charge of production and arrived at Buffalo with the first set of equipment.

A USAO-1 averaged 113mph during an official speed trial later in March, but after less than two hours of flying it was destroyed by fire while on the ground on 24 March. With the poor facilities and only a few aircraft available for testing, the correction of deficiencies and type evaluation proceeded slowly. After carrying out a stress analysis and duly modifying the design to meet the required safety factor, Curtiss approved the manufacture of components for another 375 USAO-1s.

Early in April a third aircraft, 34233, was delivered to the Department of Military Aeronautics at Wilbur Wright Field near Dayton, Ohio. This machine had a radiator in the upper wing centre section, now the desired position. At this stage 25 fuselages were in final assembly, ten of which had engines installed. Minor changes were introduced to increase the factor of safety further. During April the type successfully underwent a structural test.

The Air Service's Operations Section now laid planes for two USAO-1 squadrons to be trained by British officers on Long Island, New York. The squadrons were then to leave for France. However, during a demonstration flight at Wilbur Wright Field on 7 May, the propwash from the 400hp Liberty engine caused the stitching attaching the fabric to the upper surface of 34233's top port wing to fail. Although the panel tore off when Curtiss pilot J. Ralph Doolittle was halfway through his third loop, he was able to bring off a crash landing from which he escaped with minor injuries. His passenger, Lt W.M. Oler, was unhurt.

Following this and other failures, Curtiss added wing ribs and veneer along the leading edge in the region affected by propwash. The training at Long Island was postponed, and deliveries were rescheduled to proceed from May to early 1919, but although ten USAO-1s were transported to Wright Field late in May they did not have the modified wing and did not undergo performance tests.

Nonetheless, a demonstration at the Curtiss airfield before several officials was arranged for 10 June. Ignoring the fact that

Ranks of USAO-1 fuselages in the Curtiss shipping department on 20 July 1918. *(Curtiss)*

the aircraft's wing fabric was clearly loose, pilot Lt P. Radar took off, carrying Lt R. Conner as his passenger. As he performed am Immelmann turn the fabric peeled away from the upper port wing panel and the aircraft dived in to ground from 500ft. Its petrol tank ruptured on impact and both crewmembers died in the ensuing inferno, the tragedy being witnessed by the invited officials.

The crash was wrongly attributed to failure of the airframe, and another structural test was made at McCook Field. But on 15 July Lt Sharp crashed after the engine of his USAO-1 failed and he stalled the aircraft, both Sharp and his crewman, Lt Hale, being killed.

Although both fatal crashes were due to pilot error, an investigating board concluded that the USAO-1 was unsafe, that its wing loading of 8.5lb/sq ft was too high, and that, because of its sluggish handling qualities, it was unsuited to its intended observation role, and recommended that production cease. This despite the facts that it had never suffered a structural failure, the required factor of safety could be met, and the problem of the detaching wing fabric had been resolved. There was no suggestion that the aircraft was over-powered, but, production delays and the availability of the USB-1 (see below), in addition to the accidents, led to the cancellation of the contract on 20 July 1920, when 26 or 27[1] USAO-1s had been completed and hundreds more were in manufacture. Of the 26, only eight had flown, the other 18 being in their delivery crates at Wilbur Wright Field. Instructions were issued that all airframes be returned to Curtiss so that components in common with the USB-1 could be reused.

The Bristol Fighter/USAO-1 programme proved a costly disaster, some $6,500,000 having been expended for no useful outcome. The whole sad story is summarised thus by US Historian Bob Casari:

The Bristol fighter was rushed into production early because it was imagined that the AEF would need it almost immediately. The USA found out very quickly that you don't rush into production before fully testing prototypes. We had no experience in mass production of aircraft, and our Allies became their own worst enemies as far as getting an American Air Force in Europe. They furnished incomplete drawings, junk sample airplanes of old models, not the version we intended to build, and rarely provided timely answers to questions. ...

The reasons that building the US Bristol failed are many, including being completely ignorant of almost every step in getting a redesigned aeroplane into production. Inexperience, and virtually no assistance from the foreign designing firms, is not the poor management the three government investigations concluded was the principal reason for its failure.

The USB-1 and USB-2 trainers

A month before the USAO-1 made its maiden flight, the Technical Section of the US Air Service had submitted a request on 7 February 1918 for a trainer variant to be developed. However, owing to the perceived deficiencies of the USAO-1 caused by the redesign for production in the USA, it was specified that the trainer should closely follow the original British F.2B design. The specified engine was the eight-cylinder 270hp Liberty or the 300hp Hispano-Suiza.

The two prototypes, one with each type of engine, were to use British-built airframes. As only one British F.2B, A7206, was available in the USA at the time, on 20 March a second was requested from the UK.

---

1 The 27th was probably the Curtiss CB, or Liberty Battler, which was built under the same contract. Four of the serial numbers initially allocated to USAO-1s, 34632 to 34635, were reallocated to Liberty Battlers, but the first prototype crashed before delivery, killing J. Ralph Doolittle, and the others were cancelled.

The airframe of British-built F.2B A7206 was fitted with a 300hp Hispano-Suiza H to produce the single prototype of the USB-1 observation aeroplane, P-30. (Philip Jarrett)

Meanwhile, owing to its poor condition, A7206 had to be rebuilt at McCook Field. It was completed on 29 April and had the first and untested US-built Hispano-Suiza H, which had been assembled by Wright-Martin. Designated USB-1, the aircraft was given the McCook Field identity P-30; it had no US serial number. Evaluation was delayed until June by the aircraft suffering damage in May and by problems with the engine. On 27 June P-30 arrived at Wright Field for trials. On 4 July Maj Ocker took it 25,000ft during an altitude test, and the speed tests were flown four days later by Capt R.W. Schroeder, who attained a maximum ground speed of only 114.6mph. Despite its troublesome engine, the aircraft made several more flights before being returned to McCook Field on 23 July, by which time a second Hispano had arrived. In an effort to enhance performance the armament was limited to a single fixed synchronised forward-firing 0.30 Marlin machine-gun and a 0.303 Lewis on the rear-cockpit Scarff ring.

In July, with the cancellation of the USAO-1, the USB-1 replaced it in the production programme as an observation aircraft. Quantity deliveries of the Hispano were not due until early 1919, so the Liberty-engined version, the USB-2, was set to go into combat first, and production of the engine was planned. Demand for both types was now of much greater priority, so the Airplane Engineering Department (AED) at McCook Field set about producing standardised drawings for them, incorporating a high percentage of interchangeable parts. The station's Factory Department was charged with building four prototypes of each version, the USB-1s being serialled 40046-40049, and the USB-2s 40050-40053.

Although there was a large quantity of new Bristol Fighter airframes in storage in England, owing to the non-availability of engines, the example requested by the USA did not arrive at McCook Field until 25 June. Moreover, rather than being a new aircraft, it was a used aircraft, C949, minus engine and with its wings in poor condition. However, the 8-cylinder Liberty had been cancelled in 1917 on the AEF's advice, so the only examples available were experimental engines built before the cancellation. One of these was therefore installed in the rebuilt C949, which was completed as the USB-2 about 1 August and given McCook Field number P-37. Again, it had no US serial. Both aircraft continued to undergo tests until the USB-2 was damaged early in September and had to spend a month under repair.

(A third British-built F.2B, C4729, is also recorded as having been sent to the USA on an unknown date, but its use in the USA is unknown.)

That same month, Curtiss was granted approval to prepare its own drawings and to build three prototype USB-1s, 40096-40098, to verify the drawings' accuracy. Consequently, the eight aircraft ordered from McCook Field were cancelled. But, having studied the USB-1 test results, the AEF proposed that, unless performance could be improved, production be cancelled. As this would mean that a year of work on the type would have been wasted, it was recommended that John D. Ryan, the head of the Bureau of Aircraft Production and the Assistant Secretary of War, approach the AEF in Europe on the matter. He received no response, so on 1 November Curtiss was awarded a contract to build 2,000 USB-1s, to be serialled 49545-62444.

As far as the USB-2 was concerned, the installation of Liberty 8 engine No.5 in P-37 for evaluation was at first due to be finished on 25 July, but the date was deferred to 5 August. This aircraft was flying in the latter half of August, and was at Wright Field on 6 September, which is also the date that it was reported to have been written off in a crash. Unfortunately, vibration problems that seriously damaged the prototype led to cancellation of production. Nonetheless, the performance tests were completed after the Armistice. The end of the war also brought cancellation of the USB-1 order, though the type would otherwise have gone into service. By late 1918 the aged P-30's airframe was deemed unsafe to fly, and on 19 February 1919 it was removed from service and then transferred to Wright Field, where it was discarded.

The XB-1, XB-2 and XB-1A
In the spring of 1918, under the direction of engineer Jean A. Roché, the AED at McCook Field embarked on further development of the USB-1 and USB-2. The aim was to employ the German technique of building semi-monocoque aircraft fuselages skinned with moulded wood veneer, as used in the Albatros and Pfalz fighters of the later war period, and thereby save weight and increase structural strength.

Intended for corps observation duties, the new aircraft, designated USXB-1 and USXB-2, and were to combine the flying surfaces, tail unit and undercarriage of the

A side view of USB-1 P-30, with twin Lewis guns on its rear-cockpit Scarff ring. (Philip Jarrett)

The USB-2 prototype, P-37, powered by a 270hp Liberty 8, was the sole example of the type. It crashed at Wright Field in September 1918 before any performance tests had been undertaken.

USB-1 with the new fuselage. The engine for the USXB-1 was to be the Wright-built 300hp Hispano-Suiza H, while the USXB-2 was to have the 8-cylinder 270hp Liberty. Both versions were to be armed with two synchronised forward-firing Marlin machine guns and twin moveable Lewis guns on a rear cockpit ring mounting.

It was also planned to build two new aircraft with each engine, and fitted with an entirely new plywood fuselage, to be known as the B-3 and B-4.

In June one of two veneer fuselages built at McCook Field was sand-loaded to a factor of safety of 5, and the other was incorporated in the first USXB-1. In addition, an order for two more experimental fuselages was placed with the Davis-Putman Company of Michigan, and another from the Widman Company, also in Michigan. These underwent structural tests in July.

During the summer of 1918, the new types were redesignated XB-1 and XB-2. It was planned to produce two examples of each type, the Marlin guns now being replaced by twin 0.30 Brownings. In September the plans to produce the XB-2 with the Liberty engine were cancelled, probably because of the vibration problems with this engine in the USB-2. Nonetheless, the prototypes were to be completed and to undergo evaluation. By the end of October the first XB-1 was 75 per cent complete and, in addition, an XB-1A Two-Seater Observation aircraft with twin fixed Browning guns, of 800lb greater all-up weight and with a new laminated-wood monocoque fuselage and the 300hp Wright Hispano engine was schemed. However, the first XB-1 was still unfinished at the time of the Armistice, owing to assembly problems and Roché being ill, and only the fuselages

for the pair of XB-2s had been completed. Further progress was halted on 28 February 1919, when the hangar housing the almost complete XB-1 and the XB-2 under assembly was damaged during a severe storm. The XB-1's fuselage was destroyed, and that of the XB-2 badly damaged, resulting in the cessation of work on both types.

In March assembly was begun of an XB-1A, incorporating many components from the damaged XB-1. This machine, serialled 40125 and powered by a 300hp Wright-built Hispano-Suiza H, made its maiden flight on 3 July, when it exhibited good handling characteristics but suffered from an overheating engine. Its evaluation at McCook Field as P-90 continued into the autumn.

During 1920 and 1921 the AED built three more XB-1As, serialled 64300, 94107 and 94108. The four AED machines served

Two views of the first XB-1A, 40125/McCook Field P-90, incorporated many components from the damaged and unflown XB-1. On its first flight, on 3 July 1919, its 300hp Hispano-Suiza H suffered from overheating. *(Philip Jarrett)*

One of 40 XB-1As built by Dayton-Wright, 64172 briefly entered service with the Army as the Type X Corps Observation aircraft. *(Colin Owers)*

The second Dayton-Wright-built XB-1A, 64156, with a Curtiss D-12 engine and a large under-nose radiator, serving as a test aircraft.

An in-flight study of an XB-1A.

XB-1A specification	
Engine	300hp Wright type H
Wing span	39ft 5in
Wing area	405.6ft^2
Gap	5ft 5in
Dihedral	3°
Chord	5ft 6in
Stagger	1ft 6in
Aerofoil section	modified RAF 15
Height	9ft 9in
Length	25ft 6in
Area, ailerons	52ft^2
Area elevators	11.5ft^2
Area tailplane	22.5 ft^2
Area fin	10.3 ft^2
Area rudder	7.2 ft^2
Max fuselage cross-section	8.3 ft^2
Weight (empty, with water)	2,155lb
Weight (loaded)	3,791lb
Wing loading	7.38 lb/ft^2
Power loading	9.98lb/hp
Oil capacity	1.2gal
Petrol capacity	54gal
Minimum speed	59mph
Maximum speed at sea level	129.5mph
Endurance at 10,000ft (full throttle inc climb)	2.4hr
Armament	Two fixed synchronised 0.30cal Browning machine guns and two moveable 0.30cal Lewis machine guns

as test aircraft at McCook for several years, being allocated the McCook identities P-90 (40125), P-150 (94107), P-151 (94108) and P-180 (64300). The last of these was test-flown with the new 350hp Packard 1A-1237 on 11 August 1921 but proved to have an inferior performance to that of Hispano-powered P-90. This aircraft continued in service until it was 'surveyed' (struck off charge) on 17 September 1923.

Forty production XB-1As with the Hispano H and minor modifications (64155-64194) were built for the US Army

Air Service by Dayton-Wright in 1920-21, plus two for the US Navy in 1921 which were initially allocated the Army serial numbers 64371 and 64372 but were renumbered A-5974 and A-5975 (see below). Five production XB-1As, 64155, 64158, 64160, 64161 64177, were also tested at McCook Field. Brief details are given below:

P-171 (64155)   Surveyed 30.6.21.
P-179 (64158)   Wrecked by Lt Harris
                23.6.22.

P-181 (64160)   Shipped to Fairfield,
                Ohio, 5.3.23.
P-182 (64161)   Crashed on airfield,
                1.7.21. Surveyed 30.9.22.
P-205 (64177)   Transferred to Fairfield,
                Ohio, 11.7.22.

In addition, 64156 became a testbed for the Curtiss D-12, later produced in Britain under licence as the Fairey Felix and fitted to the initial version of the Fairey Fox day bomber.

In USAAS service the XB-1A, the only US Bristol Fighter derivative to go into

service, was officially described as the Type X Corps Observation aircraft. However, it served only briefly, being unliked and suffering engine vibration.

The US Navy's dalliance with the USXB-1A

A lesser-known aspect of the USA's involvement with the Bristol Fighter is the fact that the US Navy (USN) considered operating the XB-1A with its ship-plane units. These were the aircraft carried by capital ships and launched from platforms erected over the main gun armament.

On 27 September 1920 the Chief of Naval Operations (CNO) wrote to the Bureau of Construction and Repair, saying that it appeared 'very desirable to thoroughly test (the) USXB-1A type airplane as developed by the Army', and requesting the loan of one for testing at Anacostia or, if that was not possible, at McCook Field.

In October 1920 it was decided that the flotation gear required to be fitted to the aircraft need not be in an operating condition, as it was only needed 'to provide head resistance in comparative tests' on the XB-1A at McCook Field. Comparison was to be made with the Loening M-8-0 at the same weights, 'to determine whether the USXB-1A type would be suitable for shipboard work as a two-seat gun machine equipped with emergency flotation gear'.

The following month two XB-1A biplanes were requested to be tried at Guantanamo, Cuba, by the Atlantic Fleet Air Detachment 'this winter', so that comparative data could be obtained.[2] It was noted that shipboard maintenance of the XB-1A posed serious problems, but there was little to choose between the Loening M-8-0 and the XB-1A regarding take-off from a turret. In response to their requests

Above: **The large centre-section fuel tank on the upper wing is evident in this shot of Dayton-Wright XB-1A A.S.64180.**

2 NA RG72 Bureau of Aeronautics General Correspondence initiated in the Bureau of Construction & Repair 1917-25, Box 383, File O-ZA-34. To NAF from Taylor, 2.10.20.

the USN was informed that there was only one, possibly two, of the aircraft in existence. Although Dayton-Wright had received an order to build 40, no deliveries had been made to date.

On December 20 Maj V.E. Clark, Chief Engineer Aviation Service, wrote that he wanted it on record that he did not recommend the XB-1A and would not do so, on account of its powerplant installation. Notwithstanding Clark's misgivings, two

XB-1As, previously Army 64371 and 64372, were received from the Army by the Navy Aircraft Factory (NAF). These were given the respective Bureau Nos. A-5974 and A-5975 in November 1921. The aircraft were delivered without ordnance and were to have hydrovanes on the undercarriage and air bags in the fuselage installed by the NAF. What had taken place in the interim is not known, but it appears that interest in the project waxed and waned.

Left and above: **Dayton-Wright XB-1A P-182 (64161) after crashing on 1 July 1921.** *(Philip Jarrett)*

One of the four XB-1As built at McCook Field, A.S.94108, McCook Field No. P-151, has a pitot tube mounted on a rod extending from its interplane struts, a wind-driven generator and underwing bomb racks. *(Colin Owers)*

Tested at McCook Field as P-205, XB-1A 64177 was given a rather crudely built belly fairing that filled the gap between the fuselage and the lower wing centre-section.

Left: Although it was modelled on the Bristol Fighter, the Airplane Engineering Division's USAC-1 of 1918 was larger and had the experimental 12-C Liberty engine, which failed to give its expected power and gave the aircraft very poor performance.

An Inter-Divisional Memo dated 16 June 1922 noted: 'Interest in this project seems to have died down and work had been held up on account of more urgent work'. It was recommended that the project be dropped unless more interest was shown. A definite decision was required. As no work had been undertaken on installing the emergency flotation gear, the change was cancelled as 'the project is of no interest at this time'. The machines were to be stored at the Philadelphia Navy Yard.

In September 1923 the Bureau of Aeronautics offered to sell to the Army the following aircraft for $1 each:[3]

10 Thomas-Morse MB-3 fighters at Quantico.
1 Thomas-Morse MB-7 at the NAF.
2 USXB-1A biplanes at the NAF.

The War Department accepted this offer, and the following month XB-1 biplanes were to be shipped to Fairfield Air Intermediate Depot, Fairfield, Ohio. The offer for the XB-1A biplanes was withdrawn on November 20, 'provided there was no objection on the part of the Air Service', the Bureau understanding that the Army had no immediate use for the aircraft. The Army agreed and the XB-1As be omitted from the 'sale'.

The reason for their withdrawal dated back to August 1923, when the CO of the Naval Reserve Aviation Unit at Squantum, Massachusetts, saw and inspected A-5975 while he was en route from Washington to Boston. 'At that time the ship in general seemed to be in excellent condition. The

fabric particularly was remarked upon as being free of tears, quite taut and in excellent condition.' A request was made for the aircraft for the use of the Reserve Unit. 'It is intended to use this plane only under good weather conditions, in connection with instruction in aircraft radio and bombing and gunnery.' In January 1924 the condition of A-5975 and its Hispano-Suiza engine, No. SE13656/656, was described. The wing panels had been in storage since 22 December 1921, and the fabric had deteriorated over time. It was therefore recommended that they be re-covered, re-doped and repainted. However, a pencilled note to the file reads: 'This fabric is in good condition'.

That same month it was requested that A-5975 be prepared for flight. The Bureau noted that the aircraft would be subject to a limited amount of usage and therefore, if it were desirable to go ahead and accept the aircraft, the amount of reconditioning work the Bureau would accept was limited to $500. While A-5975 was costed at $3,550 for reconditioning, A-5974 could be restored to flying condition for $350 by using parts from A-5975. Authority was given for A-5975 to be surveyed and its components to be used to recondition A-5974. On 5 June 1924 the NAF notified the Bureau that A-5974 had been set up and was ready for its delivery flight to Squantum. This was not to be, and the order to ship A-5974 was cancelled.[4]

Nevertheless, the saga of these aircraft continued, as in the following year another attempt was made to use them at Hampton Roads for Reserve Training. A pencilled memo, signed 'C', reads: 'Dillon – Can you

use the plane. We have plenty of engines – you might be able to use the plane and another one we have at HRds. Reconditioning them there, using for advanced training.' The reply, signed 'D' states: 'Sure I can use it. Prefer to recondition them at HR in order to save overhead can use them for gunnery planes.'

'Since the USXB-1A airplanes are rather old and were not adopted as a service type, the Bureau feels that definite recommended action should be submitted after inspection' (by the NAF) before final disposition.

The Aircraft Record Cards for the two biplanes note that both were stricken from the List of Naval Aircraft on 30 November 1925. Under normal circumstances they would have been destroyed, but the cards also appear to indicate that both were shipped to the Naval Academy in January 1926. They were mere curiosities by this time, and what possible use they would have been to the Academy cannot be guessed.

No photographs of these aircraft in Naval service have been discovered to date. The 'Characteristics Weights and Performances' Chart issued by the Bureau of Aeronautics and dated January 1924 lists the Bristol Fighter powered by a 300hp Hispano engine, the Bristol Scout powered by an 80hp Le Rhone rotary engine, and the Bristol USB-2 powered by a 280hp Liberty, but no USXB-1A.

---

3 NA RG72 Bureau of Aeronautics General Correspondence initiated in the Bureau of Construction & Repair 1917-25, Box 383, File O-ZA-34. Memo. 30.06.22.

4 Lt George Pond USNRF-5, CO, Naval Reserve Aviation Unit, Squantum, to Bu of Aeronautics. 28.03.24. NARA RG72 Bureau of Aeronautics, General correspondence initiated in Bureau of Construction & Repair 1917-1925. Box 28, File 2-O.

The crowd at Mousehold Aerodrome, Norwich, on 30 May 1928 views F.2B Mk.III DC J8430 of 24 Sqn Northolt, as HRH The Prince of Wales (later King Edward VIII) climbs into the rear cockpit for the return flight to London. The Prince flew this aircraft between April and July 1928. It carries a chevron on the fin. *(Philip Jarrett)*

Chapter 16

POST-WAR PRODUCTION AND SERVICE

On 6 March 1920, primarily for financial reasons, Bristols began trading as the Bristol Aeroplane Co Ltd.

The advent of the Mk.II

Early in 1920 the Directorate of Research (DoR) reported in its 11th report, issued in February 1920 and covering work during January, that:

In view of the possibility of a new contract being placed for Bristol Fighters (Falcon III), the complete aeroplane drawings

have been checked; desirable modifications, which had not hitherto been introduced owing to the termination of contracts, have been incorporated and the whole set brought thoroughly up-to-date. By this means it is hoped that no further modifications will be needed during the production stage. The new aeroplanes will be fitted with self-sealing petrol tanks, including the new top centre section tank and parachute, while provision will be made for tropical radiators.

Additional Petrol Capacity

The preliminary drawings have been checked and a set has been supplied to Messrs. British and Colonial Aeroplane Co. The firm estimates that the aeroplane will be completed within one month of its delivery to them. The final drawings are ready for issue with the exception of one or two unimportant arrangements.

In its 14th report, issued in May 1920 and covering work during April, the DoR added that:

These close-ups of J8430 at Mousehold on 30 May 1928 provide some good detail of the aircraft, especially the oversize windshield on the rear cockpit. *(Philip Jarrett)*

Above: **Three views of Mk.II J6586 during trials at Martlesham Heath.** *(Philip Jarrett)*

Above: **This F.2B, J6586, was the first Mk.II and the first machine of Bristol's first post-war contract. As part of an improved cooling system its radiator had narrower and more numerous shutters, and the aircraft was provided with internal equipment to cater for service in desert areas. After spending 2½ years at Martlesham undergoing performance trials and testing assorted devices, J6586 was reconditioned and fitted with dual controls.** *(Bristol)*

To embody further improvements on [the Bristol Fighter] in view of another contract being placed, drawings are being prepared of the twin oil tank mounting, centre plane covering, bottom portion of engine cowling, and mounting for ring and bead, also Aldis sights. The fuselage fittings are being re-designed in order to introduce wiring plates to replace the eyebolt system of bracing.

The production drawings of an auxiliary radiator for use during the English summer have been completed.

Drawings are being made to assist in the preparation of diagrams for indicating the method of installing electric lighting equipment.

It was also reported that:

Preliminary tests of the underslung tropical radiator on this aeroplane have been somewhat disappointing, the improvement in the cooling only being from 25 to 30 percent increase as compared with the nose-piece radiator alone, whereas 50 percent increase is required to meet extreme tropical conditions.

In a subsequent test the auxiliary radiator was lowered, further outlet louvres were made in the cowling, and flight tests repeated to determine what further improvements could be effected by these means. The tests have not been entirely completed, but with these modifications the system, though not perfect, is considered adequate.

The first post-war order for Bristol Fighters, placed on 24 June 1920 under contract No 211474/20, was for 215 F.2B Mk.II or 'J' Type, fitted with 275hp Falcon III engines. Of increased all-up weight, they were to be numbered J6586 to J6800 (sequence numbers 5893 to 6107), these being delivered from December 1920. The first aircraft of this batch, J6586, was to serve as a prototype.

In the DoR's 21st report, issued in December 1920 and covering the work during November, it was reported that:

The first aeroplane of the new contract has been completed and will shortly be despatched to AEE (Home) for type trials. All essential drawings have been finished and supplied to the Bristol Aeroplane Co Ltd for completion of the contract. A decision regarding the type of

F.2B J6612 was flown by the Instrument Design Establishment at Biggin Hill in 1921. At Farnborough on 6 July that year AC2 F.C. Ashcroft was killed while swinging its propeller. It was wrecked on 11 September 1922 when it stalled from 20ft at Biggin Hill while serving with the Signal Co-operation Flight and its undercarriage collapsed. *(RAF Museum)*

Above: **When E2431 stalled while landing and crashed at the RAF (Cadet) College, Cranwell, on 31 July 1923, an aircraftman's careless error was revealed. While the aircraft's serial number was rendered correctly beneath its starboard lower wing, it had been painted in reverse, as '1342E', beneath the port wing.** *(Philip Jarrett)*

Above: **F.2B F4549 of 13 Sqn at Andover crashed at Worthy Down some time during 1925.** *(The late Peter Green)*

axle fairing to be fitted is delayed pending the results of flying tests. The Mark II Vickers gun will not be fitted on these aircraft.

The oil pressure pipe will be made in one piece, since, owing to the high pressures sometimes obtained, a flexible rubber joint in this pipe is considered undesirable.

Investigation has been made into a Service complaint regarding restrictions in the delivery pipe from the rear petrol tank. This delivery pipe, which is sweated to the plate over the sump, occasionally becomes detached, the broken solder causing a restriction in the flow owing to the end of the pipe resting on the plate. In the case of new contract aircraft this objection will be overcome by increasing the diameter of the delivery pipe from ⁵⁄₁₆in to ½in and projecting the pipe through the plate to a distance of ½in.

A new method of making the joints in the radiators for this aeroplane has been devised with a view to overcoming minor troubles which have occurred in the past.

On 15 January 1921 J6586 was delivered to the Aeroplane Experimental Establishment (Home) (AEE(H)) at Martlesham Heath for performance tests. In its 23rd report, issued in February 1921 and covering the work of January 1921, the DoR reported:

The first aeroplane of the new contract has been delivered to Martlesham for type trials, and delivery of subsequent aircraft under this contract has commenced. The Leitner-Watts metal propeller will be tested on this aircraft.

A modification to the tail skid shoe has been put in hand, in which the shoe is a

manganese steel casting of ample proportions, to increase its durability.

The RAE standard pattern petrol filter will in future be fitted instead of the AGS type, as the former has now given satisfactory results on test.

The design of the 40-gallon auxiliary petrol tank for attachment to the bomb ribs under the bottom centre section has been completed and the necessary parts are in process of manufacture for its installation.

Electrical equipment has been inspected and attention drawn to certain installation

details where a high standard of work is necessary.

New arrangement drawings of water piping and auxiliary radiator mounting have been completed.

In May, following the performance tests, J6586 underwent tests with a tropical radiator and then, two months later, with the Leitner-Watts metal propeller and, in December of that year, tests of new navigation lights. In addition to the tropical cooling system J6586 was also tested with a wide range of desert equipment, making it

When J6671 was wrecked in this crash at the Air Gunnery School at Eastchurch on 16 January 1923, when its engine failed during a turn while landing and the aircraft side-slipped in, it still had the bands around the fuselage that had been applied when it served with 2 Sqn in Ireland.

Above: **This Mk.III from the first production batch, J8251, underwent tests at Martlesham Heath in October 1926. Note the message hook and the RL tube beneath the rear cockpit.** *(Philip Jarrett)*

Left: **Represented here by H1488, this is a typical Mk.III F.2B. In March 1925 this aircraft was converted to 'J' Type.** *(Philip Jarrett)*

suitable for use in maintaining law and order in Iraq, Baluchistan and the North West Frontier of India. This prototype was later reconditioned by Bristol and subsequently saw service with the Electrical and Wireless School flight at Worthy Down in 1925-26. Meanwhile, the last aircraft of this batch, J6800, had also been sent to the AEE(H) at Martlesham Heath, on 2 January 1922, for long-range trials.

There were still large numbers of serviceable F.2Bs in service or storage, and in 1923 the company received an order for the reconditioning of F.2Bs, authorised under Air Ministry file number 470523/23 to the earlier specification number 22/21, of which no details now survive. This was followed by a further contract under files 308228/21 and 470523/23 to Specification 35/23, then in 1925 to Specification 4/25 (Item 14) under file Nos 579343/25 and 766664/27. Finally, there followed a series of orders under blanket Specification 1/27, these being 1/27 (Item III) for Mk.IIIs under file Nos 743864/27 and 926733/29, 1/27 (Item XX) for Mk.Is under field No 794417/27 and lastly 1/27 (Item XXI) for Mk.IVs under files Nos 743864/27 and 927127/29. Other Specifications were 41/23 for the fitment of slotted wings, possibly related to H1417 (modified to Mk.II and later became the prototype Mk.IV), which was fitted with interconnected slot and aileron controls on a square-tipped upper wing.

Several resulting orders were placed in quick succession to these, the first being for

This experimental fin and rudder, tested on C4776 at the RAE in 1925, resulted in a marked improvement in the type's rudder control and led to the new enlarged fin and balanced rudder that distinguished the F.2B Mk.IV. See pages 175–176. *(RAE)*

F.2B H1417, a Mk.III rebuild, after modification in March 1926 to serve as the prototype Mk.IV, with slot-and aileron controls fitted to a square-tipped upper wing. *(Bristol)*

60 standard F.2Bs given fresh sequence numbers 6162-6221 but retaining their original serial numbers, of which no record has survived. Serial numbers are known, however, for subsequent orders, the next being for 130 aircraft to 'J' Type (Mk.II) standard, with sequence numbers 6243-6372, being delivered between June and December 1923. These aircraft were electrically bonded throughout and fitted up for wireless. An engine was fitted to each machine but removed before despatch, and the Scarff gun ring was moved back. They were followed by a similar order for 75 aircraft, sequence numbers 6385-6459, delivered from February to June 1924. Ten of these were fitted with dual controls. This was immediately followed by a contract for 50 aircraft to 'J' Type standard, sequence numbers 6460-6509 (Order No 6764), of which the first 16 were supplied from July 1924 fitted with engines screened and bonded for short-wave radio telephony (SWRT). Fifteen of this batch were fitted with dual controls.

The next 19 were supplied without engines, but screened and bonded for SWRT, with ballast weights, a new type pistol case and R/L bomb cases for eight and four bombs. Bristol Fighter F4689 (s/n 6481) was the first machine to be fitted with a new type of rudder lamp bracket, while F4916 (s/n 6485) had a batten for two terminal blocks in the rear fuselage. The next 15 (s/n 6495-6509) were fitted with

dual controls, but were not screened and bonded for SWRT, and nor were ballast weights or CC firing gear fitted. No lighting cables were fitted in the fuselage, but the wings were fitted with lighting and Holt flare cables. This contract was completed in October 1924.

The next order was for 100 more between November 1924 and February 1925, being given company Order No 6827, with fresh sequence numbers between 6529 and 6628. Of these the first aircraft, 6529 (F4836) was the first to have three-eighth-inch copper bonding strip and silencer exhaust pipes,

Right: **Comparative shots of Mk.IV F4587 taken on July 9, 1931, showing the wing slats in the upper wingtips retracted and deployed. Characteristic features of this final version of the classic F.2B were a strengthened undercarriage, oleo tailskid and the enlarged fin with a horn-balanced rudder. The message hook is also conspicuous. This machine went on to the civil register as G-AFHJ.**

Like all of Cranwell's F.2Bs, F4619 is looking in good condition. The rods under the rear cockpit to take the ballast weights are shown to good advantage. *(Philip Jarrett)*

F.2B E1908 of 9 Sqn was based at Ludendorf in Germany when it ended up on its nose after crashing on 14 June 1919. *(C&C)*

6539 (H1598) was the first with a new type of swivelling arm, 6559 (H1632) was the first to have a new type of fire bulkhead and tie rods for CPX bracing, and 6560 (F4385) was the first with fibre between the incidence wires and ash strips on the gunner's seat rail. Delay was incurred on this contract by old- and new-type tailplane and elevator hinges.

This order was immediately followed by a further contract for 80 reconditioned aircraft to 'J' type, given Order No 7120 and sequence numbers 6629-6708, deliveries taking place between February and May 1925.

Next came an order for 84 Mk.IIs to Air Ministry Specification 3/25, to be given serial numbers J7616-J7699 (Order No 8005, sequence numbers 6721-6804) and similarly fitted with the Falcon III. Built from spares, deliveries started on 20 May 1925 and were completed on 2 September 1925.

Another order for 50 reconditioned F.2Bs to 'J' type followed (Order No 8092, sequence numbers 6806-6855), of which 24 were fitted as dual-control aircraft, and another six were fitted with engines and 'sent to the aerodrome [i.e. Filton] re-rigged for flight test'.

A further order for 54 F.2Bs reconditioned to 'J' type, all but one with dual controls, was next (Order No 8302, sequence numbers 6864-6917), to be followed by Order No 8673 for yet another 40 reconditioned to 'J' type, sequence numbers 6940-6951, built to Specification 4/25, Appendix A Serial No 140. These had:

Lewis gun stowage as H1420, divided doors in Vickers gun mtg. Adjustable mtg for Vickers gun. HA drift sight mtg fitted & bottom plane modified to suit. New exhaust pipe on Starbd side also new brackets. Voltage control box fitted. Stick & clips for RL Bomb Tube. Oil thermometer fitted also map & photo boards, writing pad, message picking up gear, cockpit & engine covers. Wireless as H1420 as far as possible. Fixed aerial omitted. Hand starter mag to Modn 570, not as H1420.'

Transferred to this batch, and thus bringing the total to 41 machines, was H1390.

Another batch of 30 reconditioned F.2Bs (Order No 9789, sequence numbers 7090-7119), which included nine dual-control aircraft, was followed by Order No 42 (Contract 742470/27) for 30 more, 22 to Mk.III standard and 8 to dual control. Then came Order No 161 for another 20, 12 of which were reconditioned to 'J' type, and 8 as dual-control machines. Order No 315, Contract No 793687/27 covered 12 reconditioned F.2Bs, 9 to 'J' type which were sent to the packing depot at RAF Ascot during June and July 1928, and three to dual control that went to Home Aircraft Depot, Henlow, in September 1928.

Bristol Fighter Mk.III

By this time, some modernisation had become necessary to meet changed needs, and a redesign fitted with an oleo tailplane resulted in the Mk.III, the changes being deemed to justify the new Type Number 96. Production aircraft H1420 had been reconditioned and modified by the maker with increased loading in addition to all the Mk.II modifications as integral features to act as a mock-up or prototype, with new sequence number 6669. It was despatched for extended trials to the School of Army Co-operation at Old Sarum on 21 August 1925. Five months later, on 9 January 1926, it came back for further modifications, returning to Old Sarum on 4 March until again going back to the manufacturer on 23 July 1926.

The trials and resulting modifications had proved satisfactory, and in September 1926 an order was placed to Specification 8/26 under contract number 709172/26 for 50 Mk.IIIs, to be serialled J8242-J8291 (Order No 9433, sequence numbers 7040-7089). The first 20 (J8242-J8261), with the exception of J8251, and the last 19 (J8273-J8291) were supplied from October 1926 without engines, the other 12 having the trusty Falcon III fitted at the factory, and this contract was completed by the end of 1926. The final production order was for a further 30 of this type, all fitted with dual controls for training purposes instead of armament and designated Mk.IIIDC. Supplied under Specification 30/26 to contract No 73811/26, they were numbered J8429-J8458 (Order No 9279, sequence numbers 6988-7017) and delivered between January and June 1927, again fitted with Falcon IIIs. One of these, J8430, was subsequently converted by 29 Sqn into a special two-seater for His Royal Highness the Prince of Wales (later King Edward VIII), for whom it was flown and maintained by 24 (Communications) Sqn at Northolt.

About September 1927 Bristol received F.2B Mk.III F4618 from RAF Northolt for

Bristol F.2B FR4744 of 6 Sqn at Ismailia, Egypt, in April 1932, with the type's replacement represented by Fairey Gordon K1730, nearest. On the left is the airship mooring tower erected at the station for the anticipated England-to-India airship service that never materialised. *(Philip Jarrett)*

modification under contract o/o 269. It was fitted with a 'new type undercarriage', with the chassis vee tubes set back 3in at the base. Shock absorber rings were used, and balsa wood fairings were attached to the vee struts. A new type tailskid was also fitted, with compression rubbers instead of springs. It had new attachment fittings on the fuselage, with lugs in the centre of the longeron for the tailskid struts; extension piece AD5230/1 was lengthened by ¾in to accommodate the skid struts on the new fittings. A new wooden crossmember was fitted in the fuselage, and new anchorage of

the skid check cables was installed, with new shock absorbers made up of 3 rings each. The aircraft was sent to the aerodrome for rigging and test on 29 September 1927.

The final mark

As late as 1924-25 the Stability and Control Panel of the Aeronautical Research Committee had concluded that the standard Bristol Fighter was 'considerably under-ruddered from the point of view of stopping an incipient spin following an accidental stall'. Consequently a larger horn-balanced rudder and modified fin, similar to those of

Despite having been 'wrecked' in the early 1920s, D8033 was reconditioned to a J Type DC F.2B in 1925, and again, to a Mk.III DC, two years later. Seen here at an unknown location, it carries ballast weights on the rods below the rear cockpit and has protective covers over its nose and cockpits. *(Philip Jarrett)*

Below and right: **Before and after pictures of J-Type F.2B DC F4939 'B6' at Cranwell. It was at the College by October 1926 and survived until 4 February 1929, when it was wrecked in the landing accident shown in the second picture.** *(RAF Museum and Philip Jarrett)*

Above: **The red fuselage band on J-type F4725 identifies it as belonging to the School of Army Co-operation at Old Sarum, with which it served during 1924-25. The Scarff ring has been removed. It was then reconditioned as a DC.** *(Eric Harlin)*

Left: **On 16 May 1930 F.2B DC H1634 of No.5 FTS at Sealand was wrecked in a collision over the airfield with de Havilland Moth J9927, the two aircraft falling close together.** *(Air-Britain)*

on the F.2B resulting from engine failure on take-off, leading to a stall and incipient spin.

Flight tests showed that rudder control was 'very definitely improved', enabling the aeroplane to be brought out of a spin very much more quickly. While the rudder of a standard F.2B was practically ineffective below 50mph, the new rudder enabled control to be maintained down to stalling speed, and under those conditions it was 'just adequate' to cope with the yawing moment of the ailerons. Due to the rudder's extra height, the aeroplane's natural turning tendency was increased, and 'somewhat heavier' rudder bar loads were required in straight flight. Although it was thought that this might prove tiring on long flights, the rudder bar forces were much more in keeping with those on the other controls.

It was then decided to modify the upper fin to neutralise the turning tendency, but instead of setting over the fin, which would have entailed considerable structural modifications, a cambered surface was built from ribs and three-ply and fastened with doped fabric and bolts to the port side of the fin. The initial camber was slightly too great, but a surface of reduced camber proved satisfactory.

As a result of these modifications the aircraft's turning tendencies were so slight under all conditions that they could be detected only by removing the feet from the rudder bar. The aeroplane could be looped with the feet off the rudder bar. However, as the two-blade P.3033 propeller was standard in the RAF, further experiments were made

Photographed at the time of the 1929 UK Air Exercise, F.2B Mk.IV J8290 of 13 Sqn has temporary rear-fuselage markings identifying it as an 'enemy' aircraft. *(Philip Jarrett)*

the de Havilland D.H.9A, were made at the RAE and fitted to the otherwise standard C4776, which had been delivered to France in 1918 but had not been used operationally and went to the RAE in April 1921. While the area of the new fin was only slightly greater than that of the standard unit, the area of the rudder was increased by 80 per cent, from 7.2sq ft to 13sq ft. The small lower fin was unchanged. The experiments were carried out using a four-blade P.3045

propeller, 'the type used on most of the RAE aeroplanes on aerodynamic experiments'.

It had not been expected that the modification would be preferred at first, 'as any change in a popular aeroplane is usually unconsciously resented'. But it was hoped that the resulting increase in control, especially near stalling, would be appreciated, and that adoption of the modification by the RAF would bring a reduction in the number of fatal accidents with this fitted, and even less camber proved satisfactory.

All who had flown C4776 now liked it 'very much', the firmness of rudder control at the stall being especially noticeable. The modification was considered a great improvement over the standard Bristol Fighter, and it was recommended that the new fin and rudder be put into Service use.

This led to the incorporation of an enlarged fin and balanced rudder, of somewhat different form to those of C4776, on the Bristol F.2B Mk IV. Whether C4776 retained its new tail feathers is unknown, but it remained at the RAE until June 1933. With hindsight it seems curious that, if the F.2B's rudder had been so unsatisfactory for so long, nothing had been done much earlier to rectify the problem.

(In contradiction to the foregoing, pilots who fly the Shuttleworth Collection's Bristol Fighter nowadays find no fault at all with the smaller unbalanced rudder. However, they are very aware of its adverse yaw in a turn, which is marked. Put simply, this means that, when the pilot applies aileron and rolls into a turn, the nose swings out in the opposite direction even before rudder is applied. The solution is to apply rudder in the direction of the turn first, and then apply a little aileron to keep the turn going.)

The Mk.IV, Bristol Type Number 96A, was the final variant. It was fitted with Handley Page slots to Specification 41/23 and dual control to Specification 30/26, as well as having the larger fin and horn-balanced rudder, and a strengthened undercarriage. The engine was still the reliable Rolls-Royce Falcon III. Aircraft H1417, a Mk.III rebuild, was modified in March 1926 to serve as the prototype, initially with slot-and aileron controls fitted to a square-tipped upper wing. No contract was placed to produce new Mk.IVs, but several Service aircraft were reconditioned to this standard.

During 1928-1930 all the RAF's Mk.IIIs were converted either to Mk.III dual-control machines or to Mk.IVs with a still higher gross weight, strengthened longerons and undercarriage, Handley Page auto slots and the enlarged fin and horn-balanced rudder. Order No 468, Contract No 79687/27, was for 17 Bristol Fighters, 're-condition where necessary and convert to Mk.IV', all minus engines, completed during September and October 1928. They included H1420, which was fitted with a 'large type rudder and cambered fin'. Ten more were converted from Mk.IIIs to Mk.IVs under Contract No 856629/28, Order No 641, completed in October 1928, and during December another ten Mk.IIIs were so converted, less engines, under Order No 713. In April and May 1929 another ten Mk.III conversions were completed under Order No 928, and in June of that year seven Mk.IIIs were made into dual-control machines. August

Three F.2Bs at Bicester in 1930, with an Avro 504N behind. On the left is Mk.IV DC J8256, which was on the Andover Communication Flight at this time, with coloured vertical stripes on its radiator shutters, and in the centre is Mk.III DC D8033 of the Andover Station Flight, with chequered shutters. Both machines have ballast weights on the rods beneath their rear cockpits. *(Philip Jarrett)*

1929 saw Order No 1112, for ten Mk.IIIs converted into Mk.III dual-control aircraft, seven minus engines. Order No 1143 is recorded as '10 Bristol Fighters reconditioned to Mk.IV and Mk.III Dual', but a total of 22 aircraft are listed, and the dual-control ones are not identified. The despatch dates range from 31 January to 25 August 1930.

Finally, Order No 1167 covered the repair of ten F.2Bs, including at least two dual-control aircraft.

In late 1929 or early 1930 Bristol Fighter H1526 was received on Contract Loan for modifications to be made under Order No 1278. This aircraft had been reconditioned to 'J' type as part of Order No 8092 in 1925 (sequence number 6809), and had then served with 4 Sqn at Farnborough until it was 'wrecked' on 1 February 1927, when it collided with a stationary aircraft while landing. It had then been returned to the manufacturer and again 'reconditioned' as part of Order No 161. It was ready on 2 March 1928, and back with 4 Sqn by August of that year. In October 1929 4 Sqn had re-equipped with the Armstrong Whitworth Atlas, so H1526 was probably out of use. The modifications now required were as follows:

Mod F.2B/627 – Pilot's seat parachute installation
Mod F.2B/629 – Rear petrol tank and mounting
Mod F.2B/630 – Fuselage and fuselage covering
Mod F.2B/631 – Petrol and air pressure systems

Comparative weights were to be taken before and after modification, and following the modifications the company was required to carry out test flights for a maximum of five hours 'in order to try out the "mods" generally and to ascertain their effect on performance'. The modified aircraft was sent to the aerodrome on 14 February 1930, and

subsequently dispatched. The reason for this work, and H1526's subsequent history, are obscure.

Large numbers of Bristol Fighters were shipped overseas during the 1920s, many of the survivors of these being reconditioned and rebuilt in Aircraft Depots at Aboukir in Egypt, Hinaidi in Iraq and Drigh Road (Karachi) in India. Details of activities in these theatres are covered in separate chapters.

At home, the four Army Co-operation Squadrons were equipped for a time with Bristol Fighters, these being 2 Sqn, which settled at Manston in 1927, 4 Sqn at Farnborough, 13 Sqn at Andover and 16 Sqn at Old Sarum. At the annual RAF Display at Hendon they became well-known for demonstrating their message pick-up hook technique. Other units to use the type in some numbers included the School of Army Co-operation at Old Sarum, the Inland Area Communication Flight at Northolt (this later became the Home Communication Flight, which moved to Hendon), the CFS at Upavon, the Electrical and Wireless School flight at Flowerdown (later moved to Cranwell), the Army and Gunnery School at Eastchurch on the Isle of Sheppey, the Andover Communication Flight, the Air Pilotage School, also at Andover, and the A&AEE at Martlesham Heath.

In July 1928 Mk.IVs were issued to the Oxford and Cambridge University Air Squadrons, flying from Duxford and Upper Heyford respectively, until they were replaced by Armstrong Whitworth Atlases. The type was finally superseded in 1931. Most were then scrapped, but a few were released for sale and came on to the Civil Register. Details of the latter are given in Appendix 7.

The 3,576th and last new Bristol Fighter to be built at Bristol for the Air Ministry was 7122, one of two Mk.IIIs delivered to the Royal New Zealand Air Force (RNZAF) in July 1927 together with a dual-control trainer, 7120.

Instructional airframes

A rather careworn Bristol Fighter in use as an instructional airframe for Halton cadets forms the subject of this 1920s RAF recruiting postcard appealing for fitters.

Cranwell cadets at work on the fuselage frame of F.2B M207. The aircraft's identity is stencilled on a wooden panel between the heads of the two central cadets. On the left is the tail of D.H.9A E9679.

In the early days of the adoption of the special 'M' suffixed or prefixed numbers for non-flying instructional airframes, the abbreviation 'Instr' was also applied, as seen here on F.2B 213M at Halton.

Attentive Halton cadets listen to an instructor seated in the cockpit of a dual-control F.2B relegated to earthbound service.

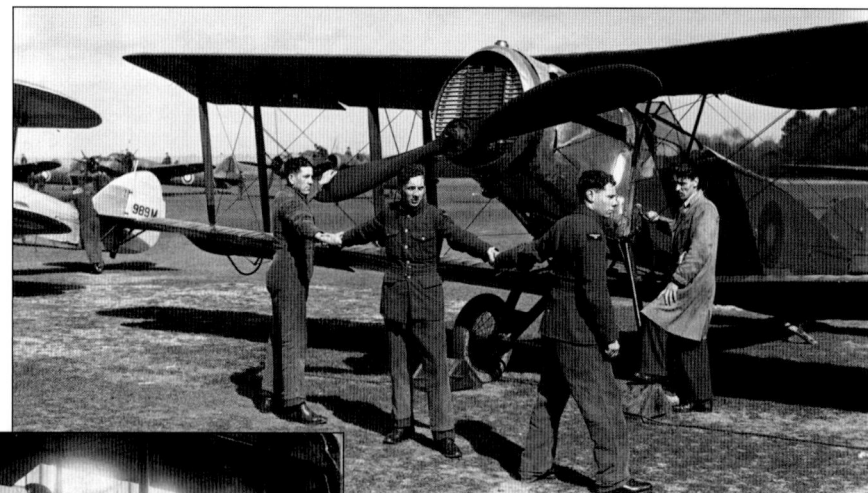

Right: Halton cadets learn how to swing a propeller, using an instructional F.2B still in use in the late 1930s, and wearing its old colour scheme. The tail of Hawker Audax I 989M, previously K3057, is on the left, and Bristol Blenheims are lined up in the background.

Left: The sad state of this worn and engineless Bristol Fighter, with its badly wrinkled fuselage fabric, and the fact that the 'erks' were clearly allowed to clamber all over it, leaves no doubt that it is being used as an instructional airframe. The original undated postcard bears the imprint of photographers Bennett & Son of Ramsgate, Kent, so it seems reasonable to posit that the picture was taken at what was then the School of Technical Training (Men) at nearby RAF Manston.
(Philip Jarrett)

One of two Siddeley Puma-engined F.2Bs to undergo tests at Martlesham Heath in 1918, C4655 went to Farnborough in 1920, where it was given an enlarged fin and rudder. *(C&C)*

Chapter 17

TRIAL AND TEST AIRCRAFT

Apart from the normal handling and performance trials, Bristol Fighters were used for a range of experimental modifications and installations well into the interwar period. While the following overview does not pretend to be complete, it gives some impression of the wide variety of work carried out using the type, not just specifically related to the Bristol Fighter, but for other research work as well.

As recounted in Chapter 1, in 1917 the F.2A prototype, A3303, was used for trials of the Constantinesco interrupter gear at the Experimental Station at Orfordness. The F.2Bs A7181, A7183 and B1181 were also used for trials carried out there with oxygen apparatus and electrically heated flying clothing. Another F.2B at Orfordness was B1308, which was apparently being used for spinning trials in 1918. On 14 April that year it was destroyed in a flying accident in which Lt Benedict Henry Melvill 'Toddy' Jones and AM1 H.H. Palmert were killed. Although it is recorded that the aeroplane 'lost speed on a turn and spun in', Paddy Heazell, in his book *Most Secret: The Hidden History of Orford Ness*, states: 'It was thought that somehow his observer inadvertently caused the controls to become jammed', but

goes on to say that this explanation 'may well have been put about to soften the blow to Benedict's elder brother', the Cambridge University don and pilot/scientist Capt Bennett Melvill Jones, who commanded the research section at Orfordness 'concerned with tactics and enemy aircraft' and ended the war with the rank of lieutenant colonel. (According to test pilot Sqn Ldr F.D. Holder, however, Jones 'dealt with machine guns and sights'.) 'Within the family,' Heazell continues, 'the real truth of the matter could not be disguised. "Toddy" was working on a theory about the impact of

airflow over tailplane surfaces on a spinning aircraft, as proposed by his elder brother. Clearly, the theory was flawed. Bennett [who in 1919 became Francis Mond Professor of Aeronautical Engineering at Cambridge] always felt that he was ultimately responsible for the terrible crash that killed his brother.' The actual circumstances of the accident will probably now remain undetermined, but the reported propensity of the F.2B to enter a spin in the event of an accidental stall, due to it being 'under-ruddered' (see Chapter 16), cannot be discounted.

Photographed by Howard Earl, a draughtsman at the Marine Aircraft Experimental Establishment at Grain, this is believed to be C4900, the F.2B used for comparative trials of mineral and castor oils as engine lubricants. *(Philip Jarrett)*

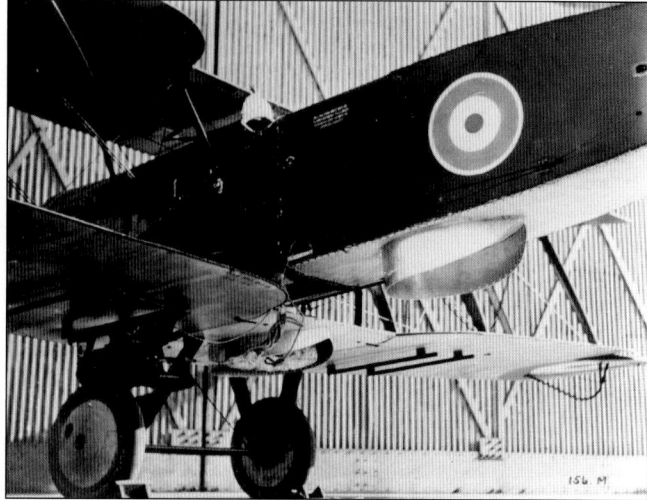

Photographed at Grain on 21 September 1918, this Bristol Fighter has been fitted with two fairings to house a static-line parachutes. The parachute intended for the pilot was stowed under the lower wing centre-section, while that for the observer was housed beneath the fuselage. Only the pilot's parachute is fitted in this instance, and it is connected with a deactivated 112lb bomb beneath the wing to provide the necessary weight for a trial drop.

As mentioned in Chapter 2, Siddeley Puma engine installations were tested in several Bristol Fighters. The first, which retained the Falcon radiator, was in B1206, which was tested at Martlesham Heath in January 1918. It was intended that this variant would be used as an escort fighter, but its performance was so poor that the idea was abandoned in February. However, problems with the Arab engine demanded that alternatives be investigated, and a different Puma installation was designed by the RAE, incorporating suggestions contained in the Martlesham report on B1206. Two Puma-powered F.2Bs with this installation, C4654 and C4655, underwent trials. Further details appear below.

Trials during September-December 1918

In the 63rd Report of the Controller of the Technical Department, covering the fortnight ending 18 September 1918, it was reported that the design of the installation of the Siddeley-Deasy (ex-BHP) Puma engine in the Bristol Fighter had now been decided, and that the engine was to be fitted to machines originally designed for Rolls-Royce engines, using the existing engine bearer tubes. To overcome nose-heaviness it had been decided to fit an underslung radiator. The first installation was being carried out at the RAE, and production drawings were to be available 'in about 14 days' time'.

Work was almost completed upon an F.2B fitted with the new type of engine mounting for the Sunbeam Arab, and the aircraft was then to be sent to Martlesham Heath for trials.

An improved method of fixing the F.2B's aileron control pulleys had been introduced, guards now being fitted to the pulleys to prevent any possibility of the cable running off.

An examination of F.2B C9863 had revealed that the AID inspection tab on the port side rudder control cable had been sweated on too near the fairlead fixed to the third compression strut from the fuselage rear end. Consequently, when hard right rudder was applied, the tab displaced the

An F.2B, almost certainly D7910, photographed on 9 November 1918 during buoyancy trials at the Marine Aircraft Experimental Station on the Isle of Grain. *(C&C)*

Right: These before-and-after post-war shots show C4721 at the Marine Aircraft Experimental Establishment at Grain, though what it was used for there is not known. On 15 November 1924 it was wrecked when it made a sharp turn at 150ft after take-off and dived into the ground, killing Flt Lt W.R. Curtis and Sqn Ldr S.M. Cleverly. (Philip Jarrett)

fibre brush fairlead, and during take-off the tab fouled the retaining clip, and the pilot had to exert such force to centralise the rudder that the strut broke. Fortunately this occurred on the ground, 'otherwise there might have been an accident'. This serious matter was raised with the AID.

Trials of the Sopwith Bulldog contact patrol and ground-attack aircraft had entailed 'a considerable number of mock fights between the Bulldog and Bristol Fighter' at the RAE. It was found that the manoeuvrability of the two types was 'very much the same', but that the Bulldog was 'remarkably light on controls'. However, while the Bulldog was considered good for attacking ground targets with its front guns, the view and positions of the pilot and observer were better in the Bristol Fighter.

Aircraft listed as under test at Martlesham Heath included two Bristol Fighters. One was D7968, with an American Willys Overland direct-drive Sunbeam Arab installed for running trials. The other, C4654 with a high-compression Siddeley Puma, was undergoing performance tests with propeller A.B.7931.

The RAE had then received D7968 from Martlesham Heath, but its engine had to be removed after running for 3hr 30min owing to trouble developing in the gear housing. When the engine was dismantled and examined it was found that three teeth on the crankshaft main gear wheel were broken, and the remainder were damaged. In addition, the teeth on the airscrew gear wheel were badly burred. Both gears showed signs of running hot, several teeth on each wheel being slightly 'blued' at the tips. The airscrew gear wheel had seized badly on its shaft, rendering the shaft useless.

In addition, the base of the port block of cylinders was cracked at the forward end, and a small crack had developed between a holding-down-bolt hole and the outside of the base at the rear end of the starboard block of cylinders. The head of one of the set pins which secured the rear roller bearing housing of the airscrew shaft had sheared off and was found in the sump. As it was undamaged, it was considered 'hardly possible' that it could have caused the breakage of the gear wheel teeth. One piston ring in No 3a cylinder was broken about half an inch from its end.

Above right: One of the RAE's workhorses was Bristol F.2B F4675, this photograph of it in the mud at Farnborough having been taken on 26 March 1919. It had arrived there in January of that year. (RAE)

Right: Here is F4675 again, this time in an RAE photograph dated 25 January 1923. It has evidently been spruced up in the intervening years, and now has a four-blade propeller. It also appears to have a new fin and rudder, possibly fitted in connection with rudder-surface trials. (RAE)

During the 1920s the RAE used C4654 for a variety of trials. It is seen here being used for trials of meteorological instruments. The pipework beneath the upper starboard wing was connected to an air sampler in the rear cockpit and might have be related to trials in 1926 with a Jaumotte meteorograph and instruments for measuring upper air humidity. An instrument, possibly a thermometer, is affixed to the rear inner interplane strut. It apparently has a magnifying cursor that can be moved up and down the instrument by means of cords from the rear cockpit to enable the occupant to take readings in flight. An impeller-driven Rotherham pump is affixed to the starboard front undercarriage leg. Of incidental interest are the two aircraft in the background: a Vickers Vimy on the right, and, beneath the F.2B's nose, Gloster Gamecock II J8804, a modified aircraft that was purchased by the Air Ministry in 1928 and underwent a series of trials. *(RAE via C&C)*

Above: **By 26 July 1918 B1201 had had a 200hp R.A.F. 4d installed, as seen in this picture, taken at RAE Farnborough on 22 February 1923. It was also flown with three-bay wings.** *(RAE via C&C)*

Left: **Falcon-engined F.2B F4360 at the RAE with the single-bay 4.69 aspect ratio wings. These were also tested on A7860, which had a R.A.F. 4d engine.**

The clearances on the roller bearings of the airscrew shaft appeared excessive. The port magneto's distributor cover was cracked as a result of the screw securing the lead from the hand magneto coming loose and fouling the brush holder, which was also damaged.

It was noted that on English Arab engines it was usual to provide a small trough for the lubrication of the bevel wheels driving the diagonal shafts, but that this engine lacked the trough, though one for the forward gears was fitted.

At the test depot of the Marine Aircraft Experimental Station on the Isle of Grain, Bristol Fighter C4900, with a Falcon III, was engaged on comparative trials of mineral and castor oils. These trials had been initiated because a shortage of castor oil was anticipated in the spring of 1919, because the majority of aero engines were lubricated with it and the Allies were being supplied with castor from British stocks. Consequently it was advised that castor oil should be used only when a mineral oil could not be used, i.e. in rotary engines.

In the 64th Report, covering the fortnight ending 2 October 1918, it was reported that, as a result of trials at Martlesham Heath, the cowling for the Sunbeam Arab-engined Bristol Fighter was being redesigned. It had been found that the temperature of both oil and water was

Above and right: **Two views of F.2B J6790 at Martlesham Heath during trials of its oleo undercarriage. After a busy Service life it went on to the civil register as G-ACCG.** *(IWM)*

considerably lowered by making additional louvres in the cowling.

Drawings had been completed showing the required modification of controls to permit the fitting of air bags to the F.2B for flotation tests, and drawings of a strengthened mounting for the Arab engine had been submitted for approval.

No fewer than eight Bristol Fighters were now recorded as being under test at Martlesham Heath:

C9883, with modified Sunbeam Coatalen Arab engine No.53793 and L.2 mounting, had undergone running tests with an H.C.7 carburettor, but after 32hr running it was found that the base of the starboard block of cylinders was cracked at the propeller end. A new block of cylinders was fitted, using 'stopped' bolts at the front end, but after 4hr running the paper washer between the block and the crankcase started to come out at the front end of the starboard block. When a new washer was fitted it was found that one front holding-down bolt on the port block of cylinders had broken off flush with the base flange. It was being replaced by a 'stopped' bolt.

The modified H.C.7 carburettor had a lower rate of flow compared with the Zenith, and in the air the engine cut out repeatedly. Modifications increased the flow, but in the air the engine again cut out, However, this was found to be due to the radiator shutters, which, when fully opened, allowed full air stream through the radiator to the intake. With the shutters closed the engine ran satisfactorily as regards the carburettor. A comparative climb and speed trial with standard and Liberty engine-type air intakes revealed a slightly worse rate of climb, slightly slower speeds and increased consumption with the Liberty intake.

It was also noted that the Liberty-type intake did not permit the Vickers gun to be fitted in its usual central position on the standard Bristol Fighter.

Above: **Although the addition of a 40gal tank attached beneath J6800's lower centre section doubled the type's range, it might have proved extremely hazardous in the event of a forced or hard landing.** *(C&C)*

D7968 for tests with an Arab with gears 31-41 with propeller A.B.6626. A modified engine was having its gears installed.

D7971, with a modified Arab engine and a Martlesham mounting, was to be written off and the mounting to be fitted to another machine.

D7965, with an ungeared Arab, had been flown to the RAE to have the engine put on a brake. It was then to be returned to have another ungeared Arab installed.

E2306 and **E2400**, both Arab powered F.2Bs, were at Filton but were expected shortly for trials of a new type of mounting.

C4654, with a high-compression Siddeley Puma, had returned from Hendon on 22 September for full performance tests with the boosted engine. A special camshaft had now been fitted and tests were proceeding.

B1200, with a Wolseley Viper, had arrived on 22 September for performance tests, but these had been held up by a damaged radiator, now being replaced.

On the Isle of Grain, C4900 had developed engine trouble and the Falcon was being overhauled.

Grain's Experimental Construction Department had conducted flotation trials using Arab-engined Bristol Fighter D7910.

Right: **A previous owner of this photograph thoughtfully added notes to explain how J6753 ended up like this at Martlesham on 11 August 1922, following a flight to test parachutes (see page 186). The carriers for the parachutes beneath the lower wing are well shown.** *(Philip Jarrett)*

Fitted with a hydrovane and fuselage bags of a total buoyancy of 1,110lb, the aircraft, carrying two-thirds fuel, one man, a sandbag and the flotation gear, weighed an estimated 2,458lb. Floated off the slipway to ascertain the duration of the aircraft's buoyancy, D7910 was in the water for 30min and 'sank steadily' throughout the whole period. It was concluded that the fuselage bags alone did not provide sufficient buoyancy, and that the aircraft would not float for much more than two hours in calm water. It was planned to let the machine overboard from HMS *Slinger* to ascertain the time it would take to sink completely, before making any alterations to the flotation gear. Modifications were put in hand.

By the 66th Report, covering the fortnight ending on 30 October, A Bristol Fighter fitted with a BHP engine by the RAE had been flown and found satisfactory. Preliminary drawings had been issued to contractors, and working drawings were to be available very shortly.

Work was proceeding at the British & Colonial works upon fitting two F.2Bs with the modified form of Bristol 'box' engine mounting. One aircraft was to have an Arab, and the other a 300hp Hispano.

A direct pumping system, incorporating a Vickers centrifugal pump and a Weyman hand pump, had been devised for use with the F.2B's Imber fuel tanks.

Propellers with the new 25/47 gearing were being designed for the Bristol Fighter with the Sunbeam Arab engine.

At Martlesham Heath the following F.2Bs were continuing their trials:

C9883 with the modified Arab with the L.2 Liberty mounting and standard and Liberty air intakes and the H.C.7 carburettor. The trials were 'not altogether satisfactory' but showed that there was no appreciable difference between the two intakes regarding performance and consumption.

D7968 was undergoing running tests of its Arab engine, and being used for comparative trials of lightened and unlightened gun rings.

D7965, which had been fitted with ungeared Arab No.19,100 after its return from the RAE, had completed its performance trials with propeller No.A.B.6629. It was flown with a military load of 545lb, comprising pilot and passenger (360lb), Vickers and Lewis guns (51lb) and deadweight (134lb). This brought the aircraft's total loaded weight to 2,765lb. In climbing trials 2,000ft was reached in 3.3min, 5,000ft in 9.2min,

Falcon-engined F.2B F4728 at the RAE in 1923, fitted with three-bay wings with an aspect ratio of 9.73 to examine the angle of incidence near stalling speed.

10,000ft in 24.6min, and 13,000ft in 43.4min. Speeds attained were 97mph ay 6,500ft, 91.5mph at 10,000ft and 85.5mph at 13,000ft. The engine was to be kept running in this aircraft.

E2306, another Arab-powered machine, was undergoing 'satisfactory' general running tests of the new type British & Colonial engine mounting.

E2400, with either an Arab or a 300hp Hispano, was expected shortly from Filton for tests of the new-type mounting.

At the Isle of Grain, comparative trials of mineral and castor oils had resumed on C4900, and modified flotation gear was being fitted to D7910.

In the report for the fortnight ending 27 November, the RAE provided details of the fitting of stay wires to the fin of C4655, a Puma-powered F.2B, to overcome vibration problems. Vibration 'throughout the tail system' had occurred on the aircraft's first test flight, and was at its maximum at the top of the fin post above the fuselage, where it was so pronounced that it was 'not considered satisfactory' to fly the aircraft without modification. Stay wires from the top and bottom of the fin were anchored to attachment lugs on a mild steel plate with fitted to a vertical strut in the rear fuselage, which replaced the original aluminium plate that served as a guide for the variable-incidence tailplane mechanism. Subsequent test flights showed that the vibration was eliminated.

Bristol F.2B J6721 at the RAE in the late 1920s/early 1930s, fitted with steel RAF 34-section bi-convex wings with condensers along the leading edges, part of an evaporative cooling system for the Falcon engine. It has an adjustable-pitch Leitner-Watts two-bladed metal propeller. (C&C)

It is known that F.2B F4819 was used for testing metal propellers at Martlesham Heath, but it is not known whether it is the aircraft featured here. Quite a few F.2Bs at home and abroad were fitted with two-blade Leitner-Watts metal propellers, but this four-blader, reputedly of Air Ministry design and possibly having adjustable pitch, appears to have been unique. *(C&C)*

A port side view of the Falcon engine in F.2B F4573 taken at the RAE on 8 July 1924 to show screening and bonding. *(Philip Jarrett)*

In addition to depicting the screening and bonding, this view of the starboard side of F4573's Falcon also shows the large oil tank that flanked the engine on this side. *(Philip Jarrett)*

The port side of the Falcon engine of F4883, the other F.2B used for screening and bonding trials, also taken at the RAE on 8 July 1924. *(Philip Jarrett)*

The starboard side of F4883's Falcon. *(Philip Jarrett)*

At Martlesham Heath two Bristol Fighters were now undergoing performance tests. Arab-engined C9883, with the modified engine and L.2 mounting, had undergone running tests and carburation tests with an exhaust heated manifold jacket, but running tests of D7968, with the 31-41 geared Arab and propeller A.B.7804, had been held up by engine trouble. After running for 20hr 10min with these gears fitted, play developed in the propeller shaft and a front holding-down bolt of the starboard block of cylinders broke. A slight movement noticed after two hours' running had gradually worsened. Pilots reported that, regarding noise and vibration, the running of these gears was the same as the standard gearing up to 1,600-1,650rpm, but that above this speed and up to 2,000rpm the 31-41 gears were noisier and the vibration was thought to be greater. The gears did not appear to offer any advantage over the Arab's standard gear ratio.

Engine and mounting tests were also being carried out on D7968, as well as on Arab-powered E2306.

At Grain, the buoyancy trials using D7910 had been resumed. The flotation gear now consisted of four bags of progressively decreasing volume arranged in line in the rear fuselage, with a hand pump fitted in the fuselage tail so that the bags could be fully inflated and the petrol blown out of the main tank.

The aircraft was taken out to sea off the Thames Estuary in HMS *Slinger*, and lowered into the water. It had been loaded to 2,593lb, and the petrol tank was half full, the weight being distributed so as to be equivalent to the pilot and observer sitting on the tail end of the fuselage. At the time of the trial there was a moderate breeze and a slight swell. After 25 minutes D7910 was largely submerged apart from its rear fuselage, but then floated thus for 2½ hours, giving 'every appearance of floating indefinitely'. The petrol in the tank was pumped out, whereupon the aircraft's attitude reverted to that after the first 12 minutes. It was then left floating for another 2½ hours without any alteration in position. It was concluded that the Bristol Fighter needed no flotation gear beyond the bags fitted for the trial, and that emptying of the tank would be of use on any type of machine whose fuselage bags were insufficient to support it alone. Following these trials, D7910 was deleted.

The report for the week ending 1 January 1919 stated that the British & Colonial company had fitted a 300hp Hispano engine to one of the Bristol Fighters with a modified form of box-type engine mounting, and that it was shortly to be sent to Martlesham for test.

At Martlesham Heath, Arab-powered C9883 with a modified engine and 'M.H.' mounting was undergoing running tests, and also carburation tests with the exhaust heated manifold jacket. Its H.C.7 carburettor was also under continuing examination. Instructions had been issued for the 31-41 gears from Arab-powered D7968 to be retained, and for the engine to be returned to store for overhaul. General running tests of the new type B and C mounting and Arab engine in E2306 were continuing satisfactorily. Bristol Fighter E2400, with an Arab or a 300hp Hispano, was expected from Filton for tests of a new-type mounting, and general running tests with a new type of Arab mounting were in progress using F.2B F4631.

At the Isle of Grain, the comparative trials of mineral and castor oils using C4900 had been completed, and its Falcon III engine was undergoing overhaul and inspection.

Subsequent trials

Falcon III-engined Bristol Fighter F4864 was at Martlesham Heath from October 1920, and in November was being prepared for consumption trials, which were to be done at 3,000, 6,500, 10,000, 12,500 and 15,000ft. The engine was then to be put on the test bed. The aircraft was subsequently used for parachute work, which ended in a crash circa June 1921. It was replaced in this work by H1436, which was still being used in March 1926. Another machine used for parachute work was H1559, converted for dual control, which also served in assessment of the new F16 type of fuel, of higher specific gravity than the usual fuel.

Bristol Fighter F4819 was used to test metal propellers, and from mid-1921 to mid-1922 the same machine flew 40 hours testing a new Reid gyro turn instrument.

During 1921-22 J6753 was used at the Aeroplane Experimental Establishment at Martlesham Heath for radiator and parachute trials. Following a parachute test on 11 August 1922 it overturned on landing and was wrecked when the starboard wheel came off.

Late in 1922 Martlesham received C4654 from the RAE, fitted with the latest development in engine silencers. Miscellaneous trials were carried out by F4949 until it crashed at King's Lynn, Norfolk, on 28 January 1925. Meanwhile, serving with 15 Sqn on armament work were F4724 (1924-28), F4745 (1927-28) and H1490 (1927).

On 20 January 1921 J6586, the first of the new Bristol Fighters, arrived and underwent full type trials. It was subsequently tested with both wood and metal two- and three-bladed propellers. The type's new lighting was evaluated in night flights by J6689, and radiator suitability tests were undertaken using J6753. A supplementary 40gal tank tested on J6800 in 1922 proved a success. An oleo undercarriage intended for service in the East took the shocks of more than 100 landings and gave smooth taxying when tested on J6790. Bristol Fighter Mk II J7643 served on armament trials with 15 Sqn from March 1927 to October 1928, being used for the first British firing of the 0.5in Browning gun.

In the 1920s a Bristol Fighter, along with other aircraft types, was used by the RAF in experiments with air-launching model gliders strut-mounted above the upper wing centre section, for use as unguided aerial targets for gunnery training.

Among many propellers tested on Bristol Fighters was a metal four-blader with adjustable pitch.

Time-expired Bristol Fighter airframes, stripped of all usable items, were used as catapult dummies during trials of launch structures on capital ships, a test being made aboard the seaplane carrier HMS *Ark Royal* on 27 March 1930. A photograph dated 25 March 1931 shows the airframe being launched tail-first and upside-down, which suggests that it was simply being disposed of, having reached the end of its useful life.

Royal Aircraft Establishment

Numerous Bristol Fighters were used for trials at the RAE, Farnborough, during the interwar years. Some of the more outstanding examples follow.

Nose-heaviness of Puma Bristol Fighters

In 1920 it was reported that Puma-engined F.2Bs with underslung radiators that had been converted by various firms in accordance with RAE drawings were dangerously nose heavy. To investigate this, the RAE undertook comparative trials using C4655, which had been converted at the RAE and found 'fairly satisfactory', and Austin-built H6055. The only external differences between the two aircraft were:

1. C4655 had a Douglas starter at the side of the observer's cockpit, the load carried being reduced to allow for this.
2. The radiator of C4655 had vertical shutters, whereas those of H6055 were horizontal.
3. During the experiments C4655 was fitted with a larger fin and rudder (see below), but the load carried was adjusted so that the position of the centre of gravity was unaffected.

In addition, while H6055 had a stagger of 17° 8', that of C4655 was 17° 22', which meant that H6055's centre of gravity was 0.05ft further forward than that of C4655. Furthermore, the range of tailplane setting for H6055 was from −1.8 to −4.8, while that of C4655 was from −1.5 to −4.1, and the range of tail setting and the more negative values obtained on H6055 were expected to compensate completely for the further forward centre of gravity.

Although it was found that the Austin machine was slightly more nose heavy than C4655 owing to a slightly more forward centre of gravity, it could not be described as 'dangerously so, when the proper load is carried'. The difference in the control forces required was attributed to two causes. Firstly, the further-forward centre of gravity of H6055, and, secondly, the fact that the horizontal radiator shutters, when open, imparted a nose-down moment to the aeroplane.

The experiments also showed that the Bristol Fighter was neutrally stable with fixed elevators and engine on, but definitely stable when gliding. With free elevators it was slightly unstable with engine on, but stable when gliding.

An offshoot experiment

During the course of the above experiments it was noticed that the Puma-engined F.2B 'had a strong tendency to yaw off its course, and this tendency, if unchecked, eventually resulted in the aeroplane dropping one wing and going down in a steep turn'. It was known that one accident due to this type of instability had been discussed by the Accident Committee. The standard Rolls-Royce-engined F.2B did not suffer from this defect, 'though a slight tendency of the same nature' was observable.

It was stated that the Puma F.2B's modified nose would counteract to some extent the stabilising effect of the fin, and 'the nature of the instability suggested that an improvement could be secured by a suitable increase in fin area'. Consequently an experimental fin and rudder were fitted to C4655, giving an increase of 80 per cent in fin area and 40 per cent in rudder area compared with the standard F.2B, but maintaining the general shape of these surfaces on the standard aeroplane.

The modified aeroplane was test-flown, including spins, by several pilots, namely Sqn Ldr Roderic Hill, Fg Off E.R.C. Scholefield, Fg Off S.T.B. Cripps and Flt Lt J. Noakes, to assess the general controllability with the larger fin and rudder. The general conclusion, reported in October 1920, was that the rudder control was 'greatly improved, particularly at low speeds, and that the aeroplane showed no objectionable features'. Scholefield, for example, found it 'very nice to fly and most manoeuvrable, though very heavy laterally and somewhat

heavy on the rudder', while Cripps said it was 'nice to fly but very heavy on the elevators and ailerons, and about normal on the rudder'. On the other hand, the control had become heavy, and it was suggested that the rudder might be improved by providing a suitable amount of balance area, as Bristol had already done with the Seely Puma.

Examination of the effect upon the control of an aeroplane having its load distributed along its wings

In 1922 three Bristol Fighters were used at the RAE in this trial, which assessed the effect of distribution of load on an aeroplane's stability, control and rate of banking. The first experiment tested the effect of carrying the normal fuel supply under the inner pairs of struts. Two F.2Bs were fitted in turn with a pair of tanks holding 16gal each under the lower wings beneath the inner interplane struts. The first, unidentified, F.2B, which had a 300hp Hispano-Suiza, was crashed during the experiment, and the tanks were transferred to the second, H1560, which had a standard Rolls-Royce Falcon. The tanks were filled with water representing a load of about 44gal, the type's usual fuel capacity. The procedure was as follows:

The aeroplane's petrol tanks were drained of all but a few gallons so that it would still be reasonably light with the added weight, and a locker which could hold 300lb of lead was fitted near the centre of gravity. The aeroplane was then flown five times in succession by the same pilot, either with lead in the locker and the wing tanks empty, or with no lead in the locker and the wing tanks full of water. The pilot was not told in which form the aircraft was for each flight, and had to report any differences he observed. These were then compared with the actual load distribution.

It was found that in most cases the pilots were able to tell in which position the load was located, but 'the difference in feel was so slight that an interval of over an hour between flights made detection extremely difficult'. The four pilots involved were Fg Off T.A. Langford Sainsbury, Fg Off E.R.C. Scholefield, Flt Lt J. Noakes and Sqn Ldr R.M. Hill.

Next, three pilots, Sqn Ldr Hill, Flt Lt D. Grinnell-Milne and Fg Off Scholefield, flew consecutively a standard F.2B, H1561, and the experimental machine, H1560, this time carrying two steel weights of 169lb each attached to the lower planes beneath the outer interplane struts. Both machines were

loaded as nearly as possible to the same gross weight. From their reports it was clear that H1560's manoeuvrability was 'seriously affected by this very large increase in the moment of inertia although it has not been made unsafe'. With hindsight, of particular interest is Sqn Ldr Hill's statement that: 'The chief deterioration in control occurred in yaw at low speeds. The Bristol Fighter rudder is in any case poor at low speeds, and this poverty of control was, in the weighted Bristol, increased. A flat swing developed more rapidly, and was considerably more difficult to check cleanly.' The inadequacy of the F.2B's rudder was evidently well known among pilots, but, surprisingly, nothing was done to address the problem until a new fin and rudder was tested on C4776 in 1925, resulting in the belated adoption of enlarged vertical tail surfaces in the Mk.IV.

Comparison of data and aspect ratios

At the RAE during 1922-23 several Bristol Fighters were used in experiments to investigate the correspondence of wind tunnel measurements of the lift and drag of a thin-wing biplane with measurements obtained in flight, and also to investigate the influence of aspect ratio upon performance. For the full-scale aspect of this examination measurements were made on three Bristol Fighters with RAF 15-section wings having three different aspect ratios. For the greater part of the experiments the aeroplanes differed from the standard Bristol Fighter in having R.A.F. 4d engines instead of the standard Rolls-Royce Falcon. The three principal aircraft involved are listed in the table at the bottom of the page.

However, the determination of incidence near stalling for the aspect ratios 4.69 and 9.73, which was the last part of the experiment, was made using two Falcon-engined aircraft which had considerably higher drag:

Serial	Engine	Aspect ratio
F4360	R-R Falcon	4.69
F4728	R-R Falcon	9.73
(The standard F.2B spanned 39ft 3in and had an aspect ratio of 7.596)		

Although the wing areas, gaps and wingtip shapes of the three principal aircraft were approximately the same, the stagger had to be altered to keep the centre of gravity relative to the mean chord within reasonable

Serial	Engine	Aspect ratio	Chord (ft)	Span (ft)	Gap (ft)	Stagger	Wing area (sq ft)
A7860	R.A.F. 4d	4.69 & 7.72	7.0	30.95	5.38	15° 41′	407½
A7260	R.A.F. 4d	7.72	5.5	39.45	5.32	17° 53′	403½
B1201	R.A.F. 4d	9.73	4.75	44.13	5.45	25° 3′	400

A frame from a film made during the pioneering aerial refuelling trials undertaken at the RAE during February-March 1924, showing Bristol Fighter A7260 acting as the 'tanker' for F4675, the 'receiver', beneath it. *(Farnborough Air Sciences Trust Association)*

limits. Consequently the bracing for the three wings were very different, the aircraft being one-, two-, and three-bay machines. The top centre section of the wings of the smallest aspect ratio had to have the cutaway enlarged after construction because the trailing edge was just in front of the pilot's head, making the aircraft dangerous 'even in a minor crash'. The resultant aeroplanes 'were considered to represent what the Bristol Fighter would have been like if the designer had decided to use the particular aspect ratio'.

The experiments comprised glides with the propeller stationary at various speeds, with the pilots making regular readings of height, temperature and airspeed. At the lower end of the speed range the aeroplane was flown at as large an incidence [i.e. angle of attack] as possible, which in some cases was beyond stalling incidence. The maximum speed was in the region of the machine's level speed, about 120mph, and the glides were made over a height range of about 5,000ft.

The flight trials and wind tunnel tests showed that the aspect ratios 4.69 and 7.72 were equally good for speed, while the low aspect ratio was markedly inferior and its stalling speed was higher. The aspect ratio 9.73 was inferior to the standard throughout, owing to the greater drag of the interplane bracing, and did not show the reduction of drag at climbing incidences that might have been expected.

When the wind tunnel and flight test results were compared, it was concluded that a test of a complete model gave a more accurate prediction of the performance of a full-scale aeroplane than could be obtained by applying corrections for aspect ratio to a somewhat similar machine.

Refuelling in flight

In a letter dated 16 January 1924 the Air Ministry asked the RAE to carry out experiments to ascertain the best method of

refuelling one aeroplane from another while in flight. Having decided that Bristol Fighters were the types best suited to the task, the trials began on 7 February, using Bristol Fighters A7260, which was to act as the 'tanker', and F4675, the 'receiver'. The object of the initial flights was to determine the best means of establishing a connection. Flying steadily at a set speed, the upper 'tanker' machine trailed a 100ft length of weighted copper wireless aerial while the lower 'receiver' aircraft was manoeuvred into position. In early attempts the pilot of the receiver approached at an angle to prevent the weight striking his aircraft's propeller. This proved very difficult, only about one in three attempts succeeding, and it was found that an approach from below was better, allowing the receiver pilot to watch both the tanker and the weight.

As the receiver approached at a low relative speed, the man in the receiver's rear cockpit could catch the weight easily, but the weight would pass rapidly out of reach if the approach were too fast. It was fairly easy to maintain connection if the lower aircraft moved forward to allow for relative movement.

Tests using a shorter length of line were hampered by frequent breakages of the copper wire, so it was replaced by a steel cable. In case of an emergency, the occupant in the tanker's rear cockpit was provided with a pair of wire cutters.

The cable was then replaced by a 60ft hosepipe of ¾in inside diameter, and an attempt was made to transfer water from the tanker's standard rear fuel tank, which had been fitted with a drain cock for the purpose. The hose was attached in such a way that the pipe's weight and air loads were not transmitted to the drain cock when the hose was let out through a hole in the floor of the rear cockpit. A quick-release coupling for a weight and a hook was attached to the free end of the hose. Because F4675 was carrying other experimental apparatus, a tank to take

the water could not be fitted, so the hose was attached and the water was discharged overboard.

The tanker was flown steadily at 70mph while the hose was deployed, and the receiver approached from below. Once the occupant in the rear cockpit caught the hose, the tanker was flown up and forwards while the weight was removed and the hose was secured using the hook. The receiver crewman then signalled the tanker and a total of 17gal of water was transferred in 2min 20sec. The hose was then unhooked and the receiver was flown slowly away from the tanker, its crewman holding the hose as long as possible to take up slack and prevent it from striking the aircraft.

As additional oil would also be required on long flights, and would be difficult to transfer by pipeline, a test to transfer a two-gallon cylindrical drum let down on a wire was made and proved successful.

When the last trials were completed, on 4 March 1924, 11 trials had been made by several RAE pilots; two on 7 February, two on 11 February, one on 26 February, two on 27 February, and four on 4 March. The flights were brief, lasting from 10 minutes to half an hour. During the final trials on 4 March the procedure was observed from a third F.2B, J6776.

In the resulting report it was stated that specially equipped aircraft would be required if further trials were to be made, as the investigation had reached its limit with the simple devices used thus far, and the Bristol Fighters were already equipped for other experiments. It would also be necessary to investigate other matters, such as refuelling in turbulent conditions or between aircraft of different types and speeds, and the possible difficulties that might arise with large multi-engined aircraft that lacked manoeuvrability.

These were the first aerial refuelling experiments with aeroplanes to be carried out in the UK, and it was not until 1930 that trials were resumed at the RAE.

In this connection it should be mentioned that, in 1932, civil-registered Bristol Fighter G-ABXA was modified as a tanker and used for the in-flight refuelling of The Honourable Mrs Victor Bruce's Saro Windhover, G-ABJP, during her unsuccessful attempts to set a new world endurance record. (See chapter 19.)

Testing ailerons

In 1924 an unidentified Bristol Fighter was used for comparative flight trials of three different types of aileron; the standard F.2B type, the Handley Page balanced aileron and the Bristol Frise. These were fitted in turn,

Above: **An unofficial photograph of the anonymous F.2B with the 'evaporation coil' installation.** *(Eric Harlin)*

Left: **An unidentified Bristol Fighter with a triangular 'evaporation coil' fitted on its upper wing centre section. This picture was taken at the RAE on 24 January 1928.** *(Philip Jarrett)*

Wireless work

In 1922 the RAE created the Wireless and Photographic Department by transferring staff and equipment from the Instrument Deign Establishment at Biggin Hill, which had been set up in 1920. Throughout the remainder of the decade the Department (renamed the Experimental Wireless Department in 1928) made extensive use of Bristol Fighters in the testing of wireless equipment. In this connection, Bristol Fighters F4573 and F4883 had their engines fitted with screening and bonding in 1924 to counter electromagnetic interference from the engine during wireless operation, and in 1928 H1420 was equipped with a Morse key in the pilot's cockpit and a battery box in the rear cockpit.

'Harp'-type aerial

In December 1926 an uncovered Bristol Fighter fuselage frame was used by the Experimental Wireless Department for the trial installation of the 'harp'-type wireless aerial. This device was incorporated into the message hook used by army co-operation aircraft, and was deployed for use by lowering the hook, when the reason behind its name immediately became apparent. Up to this time it had been necessary for the pilot or observer to reel out a long aerial wire with a bob weight beneath the aircraft when it was required to send or receive messages by Morse code or wireless. If the operator failed to wind in the aerial after use, the trailing aerial could prove hazardous to other aircraft, or to persons or structures on the ground and the aircraft itself during the subsequent approach and landing. The 'harp'-type aerial enabled the same length of wire to be deployed in the triangular space created between the fuselage underside and the lowered message-hook boom. It was not adopted, however.

and for each type flights were made with and without loads on the wingtips, in the form of two tanks of 15gal capacity, one under each pair of outer struts, which could be filled with water or other liquid. They were fitted with release valves operated from the observer's cockpit, to enable them to be emptied in flight. The aeroplane was flown straight, with no bank and the engine switched off, but with the propeller not stopped, at speeds of 55, 70 and 90mph, with both tanks full, one tank empty and both tanks empty. In each case, measurements were made of aileron angle, rudder angle and lateral force on the control column. The differences in rolling and yawing moments proved very small.

Evaporation coil

Two photographs are known depicting an as yet unidentified Falcon-powered Bristol Fighter at RAE Farnborough with a triangular 'evaporation coil' mounted on the upper wing centre section. The precise function of this device is unknown, but it seems to have entailed a means of condensing boiled-off water vapour from the water-cooled engine and returning it to the cooling system, rather than letting it disperse in the

atmosphere. One of these pictures is dated 24 January 1928.

Steel wings and evaporative cooling

Bristol Fighter J6721 was flown from Stag Lane to Farnborough on 16 November 1926, and remained there until 1934. During this time it was tested with steel bi-convex wings of RAF 34 section with condensers along the leading edges for an evaporative cooling system for the aircraft's Falcon engine, which drove an adjustable-pitch Leitner-Watts two-bladed propeller.

The 'Harp'-type aerial, incorporated into the message hook, is seen here in its retracted position in a trial installation on an uncovered F.2B fuselage at the RAE on 24 December 1926. *(Philip Jarrett)*

The 'Harp'-type aerial being deployed by lowering the message hook. *(Philip Jarrett)*

The 'Harp'-type aerial fully deployed. *(Philip Jarrett)*

Bristol Fighters flown at the RAE included the following:

A7860 At Farnborough by 1.20 to 25.6.20, fitted with a 200hp R.A.F. 4d engine and single-bay wings of 4.69 aspect ratio.

B1201 Arriving from Martlesham Heath on 28.2.18 with a 200hp Hispano-Suiza engine, it undertook tests with this and later a 200hp R.A.F. 4d engine. Flown with both standard two-bay wings and with experimental three-bay wings of 9.73 aspect ratio (see above), it was transferred to the Instrument Design Establishment at Biggin Hill on 17.1.22, returning to Farnborough on 9.3.22 until at least 12.23.

C810 After being reconditioned to 'J' type (Mk.II) standard, it went to Farnborough on 4.1.26 in connection with Davis landing light development until being crashed on 9.11.27.

C4654 Originally fitted with a BHP engine. It was flown for some time at Martlesham Heath until going to Farnborough. In 1921 it was tested with silencing exhaust pipes, possibly of the ejector type. By 7.7.22 it had been fitted with a Falcon III. Returning to Martlesham for a time, it went back to Farnborough on 4.4.23 for tests to improve the type's engine cooling in hot climates, being flown with numerous louvres on the top, sides, and underside of its engine cowling. It was subsequently used for meteorological instrument research before finally being sent to the Home Aircraft Depot (HAD) at Henlow on 7.9.27. (See page 182.)

C4655 Fitted with a Siddeley Puma engine, it went to Martlesham on 14.8.18 and was in use at Farnborough from 1.20 for various trials, being fitted with an enlarged fin and rudder in 1920. It went to HAD Henlow on 13.9.27.

Bristol F.2B H1420 with its generator impeller driven by a motor for ground-based wireless tests at the RAE, 19 December 1928. *(Philip Jarrett)*

The Morse key installation in H1420's front cockpit, for operation by the pilot's right hand. *(Philip Jarrett)*

The battery installation and cabling in H1420's rear cockpit. *(Philip Jarrett)*

A Bristol Fighter airframe being fired from an F111H-type Hinged Structure catapult during trials aboard the seaplane carrier HMS *Ark Royal* on 27 March 1930. *(Philip Jarrett)*

The starboard side of H1420's forward fuselage, showing the cable connection between the front and rear cockpits. *(Philip Jarrett)*

Dated 25 March 1931, this shows the catapult dummy airframe being launched tail-first and upside-down, which suggests that it was simply being disposed of, having reached the end of its useful life. *(Philip Jarrett)*

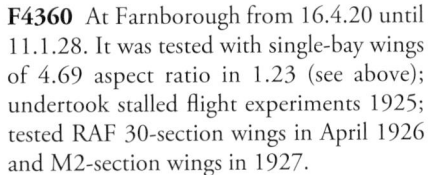

C4776 At Farnborough from 21.4.21 for fin and rudder trials (see Chapter 16). It departed on 8.6.33.

F4329 At Farnborough by 1.20 as a standard machine for comparison tests. It undertook stalling tests in 1925 and was also used for trials with R.A.F.30-section wings. To HAD Henlow 12.9.27.

F4360 At Farnborough from 16.4.20 until 11.1.28. It was tested with single-bay wings of 4.69 aspect ratio in 1.23 (see above); undertook stalled flight experiments 1925; tested RAF 30-section wings in April 1926 and M2-section wings in 1927.

F4573 Used for wireless experiments, July 1924. (See page 185.)

F4587 At Farnborough from 15.1.30, going to Handley Page 24.9.31. Returned to RAE Farnborough 9.12.31 for rudder and spinning trials. Left for 24 Sqn Hendon on 19.1.37 to be stored for display purposes, later becoming registered G-AFHJ.

F4675 At Farnborough from 2.1.19, being tested with Handley Page slotted wings and

Although it is not mentioned in this chapter, F.2B H1450 spent much of its time with experimental establishments after its return from Iraq in 1925. In 1926 it was flown at Gosport by officers of the Directorate of Scientific Research and Technical Development, and then spent its time at RAE Farnborough and Yeovil until 1932. As seen here it is equipped with two impeller-driven generators, one on the forward starboard fuselage flank and the other on the lower port wing root, there is a tall (aerial?) mast attached to its fin, and the rear cockpit has no Scarff ring. The wingtips of an Armstrong Whitworth Siskin fighter are visible on the left. *(Philip Jarrett)*

being used for rudder surface trials. Went to A&AEE Martlesham Heath 20.11.28.

F4728 At Farnborough from 21.4.20. Tested with three-bay wings of 9.73 aspect ratio (see above), and later with RAF 32-section wings. Undertook stalling experiments in 1925 but crashed after take-off at Farnborough on 12.9.25.

F4819 At Farnborough 10:20, fitted with Mk.V Gyro before going to A&AEE Martlesham Heath for metal propeller tests.

F4883 Used for wireless experiments, July 1924. (See page 185.)

F4886 At Farnborough from 19.10.26 for tests with R.A.F.30-section wings, being last flown there on 26.8.27.

H1417 Converted to become the Mk.IV prototype, it was flown at Farnborough between 23.3.27 and 3.5.27.

H1420 Used for wireless experiments, December 1928. (See page 190.)

H1561 To Farnborough from Martlesham Heath 6.3.22, being modified to test the Calthorp Al parachute. Last flown 5.9.28.

H1689 Delivered 7.19 as a dual-control long-range communications aircraft for use by the Director of Civil Aviation, it went from Croydon to Farnborough 21.11.19 until 27.12.19, being then flown for some time 24 Sqn at Kenley for the use of the Directorate of Research.

H6055 An Austin-built Puma-powered F.2B used in comparative controllability trials with C4655

J6689 Used by the Instrument Design Establishment at Biggin Hill until going to Farnborough on 8.5.22; damaged on 16.10.23 while testing landing lights at night. It was transferred to A&AEE Martlesham Heath on 2.10.24 for night-flying trials, returning to Farnborough on 9.10.24. It departed again for Martlesham Heath on 24.10.30.

J6790 Following trials of its oleo undercarriage at Martlesham (see above) this aircraft was detached from A&AEE Martlesham Heath to Farnborough on 28.1.24 for parachute tests, returning to Martlesham Heath 5.2.24. It eventually became G-ACCG.

J6800 During January and February 1922 this F.2B underwent tests at Martlesham Heath with a 40gal supplementary fuel tank beneath its lower wing centre-section. Although this doubled the aircraft's endurance, it was not adopted for Service use. (See page 183.)

J8263 Fitted with Handley Page slots. Went to Farnborough on 8.2.28, then to A&AEE Martlesham Heath on 24.4.28.

Surviving Farnborough logbooks listing daily flights can be found in the AVIA 1 series at The National Archives, Kew. The earlier ones include many entries for Bristol Fighters.

This Spanish Bristol Fighter numbered 50 is believed to be in service with the Escuela de Bombardo y Tiro at Los Alcázares. *(Archivo Histórico del Ejército del Aire)*

Chapter 18

OVERSEAS MILITARY USE

Bristol Fighters were supplied in small quantities to many foreign air forces. A large proportion were sold in 1920-23 from war disposal stocks held by ADC and had 300 h.p. Hispano-Suizas. In Belgium the Société Anonyme Belge de Constructions Aéronautiques (SABCA) acquired a manufacturing licence after 16 new aircraft (sequence numbers 6223 to 6238) had been purchased, fitted with Frise ailerons and oleo undercarriages. Twelve similar new Fighters (Nos.6510 to 6521) were supplied to Spain between July and October 1924, plus a further ten with further revised control surfaces and oleo undercarriage. Ten aircraft (Nos.7222 to 7231) were shipped to Mexico in 1927.

Abyssinia
New Zealander Eric Griffiths had learnt to fly while working as a mechanic with a joy-riding outfit, and had then given flying instruction on de Havilland Moths and Avro Avians in China and acted as a ferry pilot. He then returned to New Zealand to gain his commercial pilot's licence. In 1935, when the Italo-Ethiopian dispute was fermenting, Griffiths realised that, in the event of an Italian invasion, the Ethiopians had few aircraft and trained pilots, so in June he visited the Ethiopian Legation in London and proposed that he organise a

volunteer air arm for them, equipped with Bristol Fighters that had been declared obsolete by the RAF and were now being offered for sale. The Ethiopians approved his plan, asking him to engage pilots to fly the aircraft to Addis Ababa. Griffiths began recruiting 15 ex-service pilots plus mechanics, but one of them informed the Air Ministry of his plans before he had informed the Foreign Office in accordance with the request of the Ethiopian authorities. Griffiths wrote to the Foreign Office on 4 July 1935, outlining his 'Scheme for a Private British Military Aviation Mission to Abyssinia', his plan being to disguise the force as a 'self contained aerial film expedition, proceeding to Egypt and the Sudan, with the ostensible object of making a historical film of the war activities of Col Lawrence, and the Australian Flying Corps'. Unfortunately for Griffiths, the UK Government informed him that it would not approve his proposal, as its purpose 'would contravene the regulations prescribed by the Arms Export Prohibition Order of 1931', so he was forced to abandon the scheme.

Afghanistan
Two aircraft were supplied in August 1924, ex-E2600 and F4733. They were stated to have come from the Government of India

but were actually from RAF stocks held by the Aircraft Park, India, at Lahore in the North West Frontier Province.

Argentina
Both military and civil aviation in Argentina underwent a complete transformation in the early 1920s, both in equipment and training. This development was attributed to the end of the war in Europe. The greatest contributing factor was that Argentina obtained new equipment and valuable help from foreign missions that visited the country, both from Europe and the USA. In addition, the return to their homeland of several pilots who had served in the war, and the arrival of others attracted by peacetime prospects, had a considerable influence.

The Escuela de Aviación Militar (Military Aviation School) worked until 31 January 1922, when it became the Grupo 1 de Aviación, the first operational aviation unit of the Ejército Argentino (Argentine Army). Shortly thereafter the unit changed its name and became the Grupo 1 de Observación, comprising the Propósitos Generales (General Purposes), Escuadrilla de Caza (Fighter Squadron), Observación (Observation), Bombardeo (Bomber), and Sección Aerofotográfica (aerial photography) section) units. This became the nucleus of the later operational units that reached the

Built by the Gloucestershire Aircraft Company, Arab-engined F.2B H945 shows the rather stylized characters used by this manufacturer when applying serial numbers. This picture was taken in Argentina, and H945 is believed to be possibly the first of its type to be acquired by that country. *(Archivo General de la Nación, via Ricardo Lezon)*

level of Regimientos Aéreos (Air Regiments) in 1936.

New equipment was acquired to perform these specific missions, the aircraft being assigned to operational units based at El Palomar, Buenos Aires and Paraná, Entre Rios. This improvement was completed with complementary equipment such as aero engines, weaponry, photographic cameras, radios, vehicles, aviation medicine, simulators and campaign equipment (canvas hangars, laboratories, illumination, etc).

The first British combat aircraft to serve with Servicio de Aviación de Ejército (SAE) was the Bristol F.2B (Type 96). This aircraft was presented at El Palomar on 22 December 1920 by Handley Page's representative in Buenos Aires, Mr Alberto Hind. The aircraft had arrived in Buenos Aires as part of the Handley Page mission.

Also included was a Martinsyde F.4 Buzzard, which was offered as a fighter to the SAE but finally sold to Uruguayan army. It is not clear if the Bristol was handed over to the army when, in April 1921, Briton Capt Stuart Stewart flew it to Montevideo to display it to Uruguayan Army Aviation. On 26 April, accompanied by Uruguayan Gerardo Dotti, a mechanic at the Uruguayan Army Aviation School, he carried out the first night crossing of the Rio de La Plata (River Plate), landing at San Isidro Aerodrome on the outskirt of Buenos Aires.

From photographic evidence it seems that the F.2B might have been H945, a Sunbeam Arab-engined aircraft built by the Gloucestershire Aircraft Company, and the only Arab-powered example to go to Argentina. It also seems very likely that the troublesome Arab engine was soon replaced by a 300hp Hispano-Suiza, the engine fitted to subsequent F.2Bs delivered to Argentina. After the F.2B had been evaluated for a year the authorities decided to acquire twelve more F.2Bs Mk.III from the Aircraft Disposal Company (ADC), an associate company of Handley Page. An Intelligence Report dated 9 December 1921 stated that the Army was authorised to buy 12 Bristols from Handley Page (i.e. ADC), complete with armament, photographic equipment and wireless equipment, amounting to 183,200 Pesos, presumably as a result of the popular subscriptions. These were war surplus aircraft purchased through its Armament Commission in Europe from ADC and had arrived by November 1922.

Left: **Bristol F.2B No.9 in Argentine military colours.** *(Dirección Estudios Históricos Fuerza Aérea Argentina)*

Below: **An Argentine military pilot poses with F.2B No.14.** *(Dirección Estudios Históricos Fuerza Aérea Argentina)*

A trio of Bristol F.2Bs aloft; No.28 leading Nos.22 and 13. *(Ricardo Lezon)*

Bristol F.2Bs 2, 4, 5 and 13 of the Escuadrilla de Observación about to set off on their long-distance flight to north-east Argentina on 23 November 1922. The aircraft on the right, No.2, was one of the longer-lived Argentine F.2Bs. *(Dirección Estudios Históricos Fuerza Aérea Argentina)*

A hangar full of Argentine F.2Bs and Bréguet 19s, including F.2Bs 23 and 26. The tail of Bréguet 23 is in the right foreground, and Bréguets 14,15 and 16 are behind the Bristols. *(Ricardo Lezon)*

To these thirteen F.2Bs three more were added, thanks to popular subscription by the townships of Flores and Avellaneda. The next year, another 12 F.2Bs were ordered. This brought the total number of F.2Bs Mk.III acquired by Argentina to 28, comprising the first one donated by Handley Page/ADC, 12 in the first order from ADC, three purchased by public subscription, and a further 12 from ADC in 1921.

The aircraft were given the individual identification numbers 1 to 28 and were allocated to Grupo 1 de Aviación, by that time the first and only tactical unit of Aviación de Ejército.

The F.2Bs (Type 17) were powered by liquid-cooled 300hp Hispano Suiza 8Fb vee-8 engines. Armament consisted of a centrally mounted forward-firing Vickers 0.303in machine gun synchronized by Constantinesco CC interrupter gear, and a Scarff-ring mounted 0.303in Lewis machine gun for the observer. In the offensive role the F.2B could carry two 50kg bombs under each wing. Eight machines were equipped to carry ten 12kg bombs on underwing racks.

On 9 June 1921, Sargento Primero (1st Sgt) Luis Barrufaldi reached 7,400m (24,275ft) over El Palomar Aerodrome. According to Escuela Militar de Palomar headquarters records, Jefe de Pilotos (Chief of Pilots) Capitán (Capt) Parodi ordered him to take Bristol No.1 (presumably the HP-donated aircraft) on 3 June. Barrufaldi found it easy to reach 5,000m, favoured by the excellent atmospheric conditions, but it was difficult to reach 6,800m, so he decided to land and report it.

On 9 June he tried again. Equipped with warm clothes and an oxygen tube, Barrufaldi and mechanic Luis Fossatti took off at 10:40. He reached 5,000m easily and then reached 6,000m, at which height the Bristol stalled. After recovering, he reached 6,500m, whereupon Barrufaldi and Fossatti started to use oxygen. A few minutes later Fossatti called out 7,000m. Barrufaldi then noticed that the fuel was running low, but continued flying. At 7,400m the engine faltered, so he decided to descend. At 5,000m the engine quit, so he decided to land at San Isidro Aerodrome, where he was received by Maj Kingsley, who provided him with fuel to

Fronting this line-up are Nos.22 and 9, with three Avro 504s behind. *(Michael Magnusson)*

return to El Palomar. On 14 October 1921 Barrufaldi was killed while flying a SPAD.

The 1922 *Memoria anual* (annual report) of Grupo 1 de Bombardeo recorded the planned organisation of the Escuadrilla de Bombardeo (Bomber Squadron), which was to be commanded by a Capitán (captain). The unit was to have eight crews, each of them comprising a pilot and a bomber-gunner; four comprising Tenientes Primeros (1st Lts) and Tenientes (Lts), and the other

four 1st Sgts and Cabos Primeros (1st Cpls). They would also have one Cabo Armero (Corporal gunsmith) and a storekeeper.

From the outset the Escuadrilla was equipped with eight Bristol F.2B Mk III Fighters instead of the expected six, plus two Avro 504R Gosports and a Curtiss JN4 'Jenny'. The Commander, Capt Elisendo Pisano, (44hr 18min flying time), followed by Teniente (1st Lt) Primero Victoriano D. Martinez de Alegria (55hr 45min), Lt Abel

Left: **Rebuilt Hispano-engined Bristol Fighter 36 aloft.** (Ricardo Lezon)

April 1922 the Escuadrilla received conscripts from the disbanded civilian Compañía Aeronáutica, who were incorporated after undergoing brief military instruction.

Between 1922 and 1923 the Aviación de Ejercito set up a 'training cabinet' for their bomber crews, whose fleet comprised Caudron G.IIIs and the Bristol Fighters. This rudimentary simulator consisted of a tower provided with a sight and an extensive continuous series of aerial photographs arranged on a roll which was moved by an engine. The trainer simulated a bombing run over the ground. The final evaluation was carried out by establishing the concentration of the load dropped by the bomb aimer.

One of the most important operations performed by Grupo 1 de Aviación was military reconnaissance of the most important regions of the national territory, with the aim of establishing an efficient and adequate aeronautical infrastructure to aid the development of projected internal airlines.

In March 1922 Col Mosconi ordered to his staff to work on the Proyecto de Organización del Servicio Aéreo al Sud (Project for Organisation of the Southern Air Service). One of the missions of the recently formed Grupo 1 de Aviación, it entailed development of a programme that included exploratory flights over national territory that came within the compass of each unit.

The Director of the Servicio Aeronáutico del Ejercito (SAE) imparted the order to Mayor Bartolome Crespo, and five days later

Above: **One of ten Argentine F.2Bs reconstructed by the Fábrica Militar de Aviones at Cordoba during 1930-31, bearing the national insignia but still awaiting its individual number.** (Ricardo Lezon)

M. Gonzalez (48hr 45min) and Lt Alfredo Perez Aquino (37hr 40min.). There were the following Pilotos Militares: 1st Sgt Liborio Fernandez, 1st Cpl Ramón Calderón (55hr 5min), 1st Cpl Juan A. Farias (61hr 45min),

1st Cpl José A. Olmos (41hr 15min), 1st Cpl Ramón R. Gomez (70hr 12min), 1st Cpl Emilio Schaller, 1st Cpl Enrique Schneider, 1st Cpl José Fernandez and Cabo Secundino (2nd Cpl) Fuentes. Early, in

Below: **Bristol F.2B No.4 looking rather the worse for wear. This aircraft was C4823 in British service; in 1918 it was with 39 Home Defence Sqn at North Weald.** (Ricardo Lezon)

The nature of the terrain suggests that this photograph of No.12 depicts a forced landing. *(Ricardo Lezon)*

Rebuilt Bristol F.2B No.35 sits in the foreground as three Dewoitine D.21 fighters make a fly past in 1931. *(Philip Jarrett)*

a plan was made to fly over the following routes:

Escuadrilla de Bombardeo: El Palomar, Concordia, Posadas, Corrientes, Santa Fe and El Palomar.

Bristol No.7: 1st Lt Victoriano D. Martinez de Alegria (Jefe/Leader) and Capt Elisendo P. Pisano (observer).

Bristol No.8: Lt A. Perez Aquino (pilot) and Capt Rufino F. Tenreyro Bravo (observer).

Bristol No.11: 1st Sgt Pedro Mendez (pilot) and 1st Lt Pedro P. Pomo (observer).

Bristol No.9: Sgt Juan A. Farias (pilot) and Lt Mario Novazio (observer).

Bristol No.10: Sgt Ramon E. Gomez (pilot) and mechanic Pedro Radice.

The Escuadrilla set out to the north-east at 08:30hr on 22 November, and the flight schedule was as follows:

22 November: El Palomar-Gualeguaychu.
23 November: Gualeguaychu-Monte Caseros.
25 November: Monte Caseros-Santo Tome.
26 November: Santo Tome – Posadas.
29 November: Posadas-Paso de los Libres.
30 November: Paso de los Libres – Concordia
1 December: Concordia – Gualeguaychu
3 December: Gualeguaychu – El Palomar.

In total, the numbers of personnel involved were:
Three pilots, seven observers, eight sub-officials, 17 soldiers, nine mechanics and assistants.
The total distance covered: 1,792km, and seven landings were made en route.

Units involved:
Escuadrilla de Observación to the northeast.
1. El Palomar, Rosario, Santiago del Estero, Tucuman, Salta, Tucuman, La Rioja,

Argentine F.2B No.18 displays a jazzy colour scheme at an aviation meeting. *(Ricardo Lezon)*

Cordoba, Cañada de Gomez and El Palomar.
2. El Palomar, Rufino, Mendoza, San Rafael, Victorica, Carhue and El Palomar.
3. Carmen de Patagones, Trelew, Comodoro Rivadavia, Santa Cruz, Puerto Deseado, San Antonio Oeste, Olavarria, Bahia Blanca and El Palomar.

Primera Escuadrilla de Caza (Rio Gallegos)
Five Ansaldo SVA.5s
Four pilots, two observers, two sub-officials, two soldiers. 11 mechanics and assistants.
Distance covered: 2,313km; eight landings en route

Segunda Escuadrilla de Caza (Mendoza)
Five Ansaldo SVA.5s
Four pilots, two observers, three sub-officials, 20 soldiers, nine mechanics and assistants.
Distance covered: 4,085km: 12 landings en route

Escuadrilla de Bombardeo (Posadas)
Five Bristol Fighters (Nos.7, 8, 9, 10 and 11)
Three pilots, seven observers, eight sub-officials, 17 soldiers, nine mechanics and assistants.
Distance covered: 1,752km; seven landings en route

Escuadrilla de Observación (Jujuy):
Four Bristol Fighters (Nos.2, 4, 5 and 13)
Four pilots, six observers, one sub-official, eight soldiers, five mechanics and assistants.
Distance covered: 3,080km; 15 landings en route.

The operation started on 22 November 1922 and ended on 16 January 1923. Of fundamental importance were the performance of the telegraphic communications (both national and those of the railway companies), the involvement of the populations throughout the collaboration, and the hospitality received from different communities and municipalities at each stop. A final report, including 38 photographs taken during the flights, was submitted on 15 March. As a result of the flights, twelve fields were donated for transformation into landing grounds and aerodromes. Important information was also gathered on the terrain and the different regional climates of Argentina. A total of 11,230km had been surveyed, and the monopolistic market of the foreign suppliers of fuels and lubricants was appreciated, as well as their place in the framework of national defence.

By 21 April 1924 12 F.2Bs were still listed as being on hand and '10 more have been purchased from ADC in England,

although not yet delivered'. However, it seems these were not delivered. Instead, ten of the original 28 were rebuilt in 1930-31 (see later).

Grupo 1 de Observación 1925

Early in 1925 the organisation of military aviation in Argentina changed. It was decided to replace the Grupo 1 de Aviación, which was responsible for operational and training duties, so the Ministério de Guerra created the Grupo 1 de Observación. This unit comprised three squadrons (fighter, exploration and artillery co-operation, the last replacing the bomber squadron). The unit received five Bristol F.2Bs, and bombing training was carried out with these machines using 9kg Vickers bombs and training bombs built at the El Palomar facilities. In addition, 100 20lb bombs were supplied by ADC.

In the spring of 1925 the unit carried out training operations at Sierra de los Cóndores

in Córdoba. The Bristols were based at a camp at Rio Tercero.

Grupo 3 de Observación 1926

In 1926 the Grupo 3 de Observación was formed at Base Aérea Militar General Urquiza in Paraná, home of 3ª División de Ejército (Army Division). Upon completion of preparation of the unit's airfield and facilities on 22 December 1925, the unit was equipped with Bristol Fighter F.2B Mk IIIs Nos.4, 11, 13, 22 and 28.

On 12 May the Bristols departed El Palomar and set off for their new home at Paraná. En route, they landed to refuel at Rosario. While taxying, the propeller of one of the F.2Bs was broken, and a group of officers and mechanics were sent from Paraná to effect a repair.

The Bristols were employed solely on observation duties and did not participate in long-range flights, making only a few flights in squadron formation to Mesopotamia and

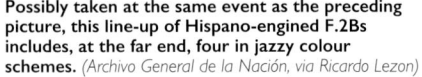

Jujuy. They operated until 1933. The F.2Bs and their crews were:

Bristol No.22: Capt Victoriano D. Martinez de Alegria and Lt Bernardo D. Menendez.
Bristol No.4: Lt Enrique R. Guntsche and 1st Lt Nabor W. Rocha.
Bristol No.11: Lt Hector F. Grisolia and 1st Lt Pedro Aviles.
Bristol No.13: Lt Guillermo Von Buren and mechanic Ortúzar.
Bristol No.28: Sargento Ayudante Piloto (Assistant Sgt Pilot) Ferrari and mechanic Dussi.

During 1926 five excercises were carried out with the army. The first took place at Sauce Viejo (Province of Buenos Aires) with Regimiento 12 de Infanteria, on observation duties. The others were at El Campo de El Paracao, in Paraná (Province of Entre Ríos). The last operations consisted of co-operation exercises with Grupo de Artilleria 3 de Diamante (Province of Entre Rios).

By 1928 the Army Aviation had 44 aircraft, organised as Grupo II de Observación (No.2 Observation Group) with 11 Bréguet XIXs and five Dewoitine D.21s at El Palomar (outside Buenos Aires and still an Air Force base today); the Escuela Militar de Aviación (Military Aviation School) with eight 504s and nine F.2Bs, also at El Palomar; Grupo III de Observación with two F.2Bs and six Bréguets at Paraná (moved from El Palomar in January 1926); and Grupo IV de Observación with three Bréguet XIXs at Mendoza. Thus by then they had 11 F.2Bs on strength, three presumably having been lost in accidents.

It is known that No.3 had crashed near Jujuy on 4 December 1923, losing its undercarriage, No.5 was possibly written-off at Tucuman on 30 November 1923, and No.16 was still current on 6 December 1928. Another, of Grupo III de Observación,

Six Argentine Bristol Fighters in vic formation. Their numbers, from nearest to furthest, appear to be 34, 30, 37, 36, 35 (all rebuilds) and 2. *(Philip Jarrett)*

The end of Argentine Bristol Fighter 28, in which Sargento Ayudante Farrari and Mechanic Dussi lost their lives. *(Ricardo Lezon)*

crashed on 14 January 1928 at Diamante, killing Lt Efrain Rivero Olazábal and Sgt Gil Valdez.

During 1930 and 1931 ten airframes were rebuilt at the Fábrica Militar de Aviones (FMA) in Córdoba (four in 1930 and six in 1931) and renumbered 29 to 38. (One source states that three were 'constructed' at Córdoba and six were 'rebuilt' at El Palomar, but this only accounts for nine aircraft, rather than ten, but the number could be made up by adding the long-serving No.2. It has also been stated that they were given Liberty engines and converted to single-seaters, but photographic evidence suggests that they retained the Hispano-Suiza engine and still had rear cockpits.) An Intelligence Report dated 1 July 1931 recorded the Army as having ten Bristol Fighters.

Records show that, at the start of 1931, four F.2Bs were in service, seven were undergoing maintenance and three needed maintenance. At the end of the year there were none in service, under maintenance or needing maintenance.

On 24 March 1931 F.2B No.33 suffered an accident in which its pilot, Lt Av Mil D. Miguel Castex Lainford, was killed, and Obs Mec de 3a Oscar Arregui was injured.

On 28 March 1931 three F.2Bs, No.34, piloted by Lt C.R. Ojeda and with Obs Mec J. Alesandretti aboard, No.30 crewed by Lt Uranga Imaz (pilot) and 1st Sgt A. Diaz, and No.35, carrying Lt J.P. Saadi and Cpl Zaporta, made a flight from El Palomar to Rosario, 260 miles distant. They returned the following day, with Saadi unaccompanied in 35, Imaz with Zaporta in 30, and Ojeda and Alesandretti again in 34.

On 22 July pilot 1st Sgt Ascencio Garraza and Obs 1st Sgt Claudio Vargas were both killed in the crash of F.2B No.35. It is also recorded that another F.2B, No.29, with pilot Aniceto Mendéz and Mec Victorio

Aircraft	No of flights	Total flying time
No.2	141	44hr 10min
No.29	Omitted from listing	
No.30:	219	76hr 40min
No.33:	35	6hr 15min (crashed)
No.34:	216	81hr 15min
No.35	109	36hr 50min (crashed)
No.36	97	30hr 35min
No.37	47	19hr 30min
No.38	66	23hr 15min

Meazzbotta aboard, was overturned and wrecked that same day. Whether the two accidents were connected is unknown.

As an accompanying photograph shows, No.28 had also crashed fatally at some point, killing Asst Sgt Farrari and Mechanic Dussi.

Total flights and flying times per aircraft during January-November 1931 are given in the adjacent table.

A record for 1932 lists 14 F.2Bs at El Palomar, all 'withdrawn'; 4 at Parana, also withdrawn; and 6 at 'D. Aerotecnica'.

By 1934 only FMA-rebuilt aircraft remained, this being the last year they are known to have been in service.

The following Anglo-Argentinians flew in F.2Bs during the First World War:

Capt Thomas Colvill-Jones (pilot)

Thomas Colville-Jones was born in Hurlingham, Provincia de Buenos Aires, Argentina, on 1 November 1897, the second son of British couple Abbie and Robert Colvill-Jones. In April 1910 the family arrived in England and Thomas and his elder brother went to Dulwich College, where they spent around nine months. Following this the they spent some time at Victoria College, then in the summer of 1912 the family returned to Argentina. Upon their return, Thomas took a position with the Central Argentine Railway, at first in the drawing office before being transferred to the position of assistant engineer in the San Martin section. In early 1917 he returned to England aboard the SS *Highland Rover*, upon arrival joining the Artists' Rifles, and subsequently being gazetted to a temporary position in the Royal Engineers. Thomas was fascinated by the idea of flight, however, and requested a transfer to the RFC, where he trained as a pilot. After going to the Western Front in late 1917, stationed near Ypres, he soon acquired a distinguished reputation for his prowess in aerial combat, and by the time the RFC was re-formed into the RAF he had already officially become an ace, having successfully downed nine German aircraft. During April 1918 he recorded another two

victories, for a total of eleven, making him the joint most successful South American-born pilot of the war. In late April 1918 he was reported as missing (he was shot down by Kurt Kressner). For a time his fate was uncertain, but it was later confirmed that he had been badly wounded and captured by the Germans on 25 April, and died at Limburg in the Netherlands, whilst still a German PoW, on 24 May.

Victories

1. 18 Oct 1917 16:10 20 Sqn Bristol F.2B (B1139) One Albatros D.V (DES) Gheluvelt, observer, 2nd Lt L.H. Phelps
2. 27 Nov 1917 15:25 20 Sqn Bristol F.2B (B1122) Two Albatros D.III (OOC) Westroosebeke, observer Capt L.R. Speakman
3. 13 [or 3] Jan 1918 14:25 20 Sqn Bristol F.2B (B1122) Three C (DES(F)) N of Moorslede, observer 2nd Lt Henry Crowe
4. 19 Jan 1918 20 Sqn Bristol F.2B One Albatros D.V (OOC) E of Moorslede, observer Capt John Hedley
5. 28 Jan 1918 13:50 20 Sqn Bristol F.2B (B1122) One Albatros D.V (OOC) NW of Westroosebeke, observer 2nd Lt J.A. Galbraith
6. 4 Feb 1918 10:55 20 Sqn Bristol F.2B Balloon (DES) 28K 5C, observer 2nd Lt D. Wishart-Orr
7. 4 Feb 1918 about 14:15 20 Sqn Bristol F.2B Four Albatros D.V (DES) Roulers-Menin Road, observer 2nd Lt W. Hart
8. 22 Mar 1918 16:20 48 Sqn Bristol F.2B (C4864) Five Albatros D.V (DES) SE of Monchy-Legache, observer 2nd Lt J.M.J. Moore
9. 24 Mar 1918 13:40 48 Sqn Bristol F.2B (C4864) Six LVG C (DES) E of Ham
10. 4 Apr 1918 13:30 48 Sqn Bristol F.2B (C4831) Seven Albatros D.V (DES) SE of Villers Brettoneux
11. 23 Apr 1918 15:50 48 Sqn Bristol F.2B (B1126) Eight Pfalz D.III (OOC) W of Bray

One Balloon, six destroyed, four out of control.

Argentine Bristol F.2Bs numbers 37 and 38 in pristine condition. *(Archivo General de la Nación Argentina)*

Shot down on 25 April 1918 in B1126 and PoW, along with his observer, AM1 F. Finney.

Norman George McNaughton

Born in May 1890, McNaughton went to Argentina, where he worked on a cattle ranch. When the war broke out, he joined the British Latin American Volunteers. Returned to the UK, he joined the RFC and was posted to 20 Sqn on 14 January 1916. He was wounded in a leg in an action on 21 April 1916. He joined 57 Sqn in 1917 as Captain and Flight Commander. He was shot down by Manfred von Richthofen on 24 June 1917 (von Richthofen's 55th victory). Both McNaughton and his observer, Lt A.H. Means, were killed.

2nd Lt Bertram Hutchinson Smyth (observer)

Bertram Hutchinson Smyth was born in Bernal, Provincia de Buenos Aires, Argentina, on 5 September 1894. He died in Buenos Aires on 6 February 1966.

Victories

1. 28 Jun 1918 20:00 88 Sqn Bristol F.2B (C787) One Halberstadt C (DES(F)) Houthulst Forest, pilot Lt K.B. Conn
2. 29 Jun 1918 20:10 88 Sqn Bristol F.2B (C787) One Fokker D.VII (DES(F)) Ghistelles, pilot Lt K.B. Conn
3. 29 Jun 1918 20:10 88 Sqn Bristol F.2B (C787) One Fokker D.VII (DES) Ghistelles, pilot Lt K.B. Conn
4. 14 Aug 1918 17:45 88 Sqn Bristol F.2B (E2153) Two Fokker D.VII (DES(F)) Dompierre, pilot?
5. 19 Aug 1918 10:25 88 Sqn Bristol F.2B (E2216) One Fokker D.VII (OOC) Oignies, pilot Lt K.B. Conn
6. 19 Aug 1918 10:30 88 Sqn Bristol F.2B (E2216) One Fokker DR.I (OOC) Oignies, pilot Lt K.B. Conn?

7. 4 Sep 1918 09:00 88 Sqn Bristol F.2B (E2153) Two Fokker D.VII (OOC) Seclin, pilot?
8. 4 Sep 1918 09:30 88 Sqn Bristol F.2B (E2153) Two Fokker DR.I (OOC) Provin

Four destroyed, four out of control.

Capt Thomas Caithcart Traill

Traill was born in Argentina on 6 August 1899 and was educated at Osbourne and Dartmouth. He joined the Royal Navy as a midshipman on 2 August 1914, was assigned to HMS *Nelson* and served in the Gallipoli campaign. Traill was transferred to the RFC to train as a pilot, and after completion of training was commissioned as a temporary Second Lieutenant on probation on 11 October 1917. He was posted to 20 Sqn, RFC. On 1 April 1918, as the RAF came into existence, Traill was promoted Lieutenant. He was promoted temporary Captain when he was appointed a Flight Commander on 20 September 1918.

Traill scored eight aerial victories. In the process, he had three other aces serve as his gunner/observer at various times. During a combat on 2 July 1918, Percy Griffith Jones called out a warning from the aeroplane's rear seat and Traill ducked. The German fighter behind them killed Jones and put a bullet through the cockpit and out through the windscreen, missing Traill. Traill's next observer took an incendiary bullet in his leg. Leslie William Burbidge then became Traill's observer.

On 23 October, while returning from the mission upon which he scored his eighth victory, Traill collided with another aeroplane in his flight while flying at 7,000ft. The accident knocked away part of the Bristol Fighter's wing, and as the aircraft began to spin out of control, Burbidge leaped out on to the opposite wing at Traill's command to counterbalance the spin while

Traill struggled for control. The resultant crash-landing hurled Burbidge on to his face but left Traill uninjured and saved the aeroplane. Both men were awarded the DFC for this incident.

Victories

1. 29 May 1918 18:40 20 Sqn Bristol F.2B (C856) One Fokker Dr.I (OOC) W of Armentieres, observer 2nd Lt P.G. Jones
2. 30 June 1918 07:30 20 Sqn Bristol F.2B (C938) One Albatros D.V (OOC) N of Comines, observer 2nd Lt P.G. Jones
3. 2 Jul 1918 08:40 20 Sqn Bristol F.2B (B1344) One Fokker D.VII (DES(F)) SE of Gheluvelt, observer 2nd Lt P.G. Jones
4. 29 Jul 1918 19:55 20 Sqn Bristol F.2B (E2452) One Fokker D.VII (OOC) Gheluwe, observer Lt R. Gordon-Bennett
5. 24 Sept 1918 16:00 20 Sqn Bristol F.2B (E2252) One Fokker D.VII (OOC) W of Busigny, observer Lt R. Gordon Bennett
6. 25 Sept 1918 18:20 20 Sqn Bristol F.2B (E2252) One Fokker D.VII (DES(F)) NE of St Quentin, observer Lt R. Gordon Bennett
7. 29 Sept 1918 10:25 20 Sqn Bristol F.2B (E2370) One Fokker D.VII (DES) N of St Quentin, observer Capt L.W. Burbidge
8. 23 Oct 1918 15:20 20 Sqn Bristol F.2B (E2403) One Fokker D.VII (DES) W Aulnoye, observer Capt L.W. Burbidge

Four destroyed, four out of control

George Henry Wythe

Wythe was born in Temperley, Provincia de Buenos Aires. He joined the Artists' Rifles OTC and then transferred to the RFC. He was posted to 49 Sqn and went to France with his unit on 7 November 1917. He was killed on 4 December 1917.

Five Argentine F.2Bs, with No.38 nearest and Nos.13 and 4 at the far end. *(Archivo General de la Nación, via Ricardo Lezon)*

Argentine Bristol Fighters: Individual Histories

1 ADC. Presented by Handley Page representative in Buenos Aires to Aviación de Ejercito 20/12/20. Possibly ex-H945 and originally Arab-powered. 300hp Hispano-Suiza 6Fb. Wfu before 1930.

2 ADC. Ordered late 1920. 300hp Hispano-Suiza Fb. Wfu during 1931/1932.

3 ADC. Ordered late 1920. 300hp Hispano-Suiza Fb. Aircraft hit post on take-off, undercarriage destroyed, 1/12/22. Pilot Teniente Primero Madariaga safe. Wfu 1923.

4 ADC. Ordered late 1920. 300hp Hispano-Suiza Fb. Wfu 1930.

5 ADC. Ordered late 1920. 300hp Hispano-Suiza Fb. Crash-landed after engine failure, 30/11/1922. Teniente Abel Gonzalez, pilot, and Jefe Interino Comando de la 5ta División de Ejército Teniente Coronel Villegas both safe. Aircraft remains sent by train to El Palomar.

6 ADC. Ordered late 1920. 300hp Hispano-Suiza Fb. Wfu before 1930.

7 ADC. Ordered late 1920. 300hpHispano-Suiza Fb. Wfu 1927 after accident on a long-distance flight to Provincia de Tucuman.

8 ADC. Ordered late 1920. 300hp Hispano-Suiza Fb. Wfu before 1930.

9 ADC. Ordered late 1920. 300hp Hispano-Suiza Fb. Wfu before 1930.

10 ADC. Ordered late 1920. 300hp Hispano-Suiza Fb. Wfu before 1930.

11 ADC. Ordered late 1920. 300hp Hispano-Suiza Fb. Wfu before 1930.

12 ADC. Ordered late 1920. 300hp Hispano-Suiza Fb. Wfu between 1931/1932.

13 ADC. Ordered late 1920. 300hp Hispano-Suiza Fb. Wfu before 1930.

14 ADC. Presented by Handley Page representative in Buenos Aires to Comisión Nacional Pro Aviación Civil y Militar and named *Ciudad de Avellaneda*. Wfu before 1930.

15 ADC. Ordered in 1923. 300hp Hispano-Suiza Fb. Wfu between 1931 and 1932.

16 ADC. Ordered in 1923. 300hp Hispano-Suiza Fb. Wfu before 1930.

17 ADC. Ordered in 1923. 300hp Hispano-Suiza Fb. Wfu between 1931 and 1932.

18 ADC. Ordered in 1923. 300hp Hispano-Suiza Fb. Wfu before 1930.

19 ADC. Ordered in 1923. 300hp Hispano-Suiza Fb. Wfu before 1930.

20 ADC. Ordered in 1923. 300hp Hispano-Suiza Fb. Wfu before 1930.

21 ADC. Ordered in 1923. 300hp Hispano-Suiza Fb. Wfu between 1931 and 1932.

22 ADC. Ordered in 1923. 300hp Hispano-Suiza Fb. Wfu before 1930.

23 ADC. Ordered in 1923. 300hp Hispano-Suiza Fb. Wfu before 1930.

24 ADC. Ordered in 1922. 300hp Hispano-Suiza Fb. Wfu before 1930.

25 ADC. Ordered in 1923. 300hp Hispano-Suiza Fb. Wfu before 1930.

26 ADC. Ordered in 1923. 300hp Hispano-Suiza Fb. Wfu before 1930.

27 ADC. Ordered in 1923. 300hp Hispano-Suiza Fb. Wfu before 1930.

28 ADC. Ordered in 1923. 300hp Hispano-Suiza Fb. Wfu after crash on 14/1/28 at Spazenkutter near Diamante, Provincia de Entre Rios. Teniente Efraín Rivero Olazabal and Sargento 1 Juan Gil Valdez killed.

29 Rebuild of earlier F.2B in 1930 at FMA. 300hp Hispano-Suiza Fb. Wfu 1931.

30 Rebuild of earlier F.2B in 1930 at FMA. 300hp Hispano-Suiza Fb. Wfu between 1931 and 1932.

31 Rebuild of earlier F.2B in 1930 at FMA. 300hp Hispano-Suiza Fb. Wfu 1931.

32 Rebuild of earlier F.2B in 1930 at FMA. 300hp Hispano-Suiza Fb. Wfu 1931.

33 Rebuild of earlier F.2B in 1931 at FMA. 300hp Hispano-Suiza Fb. Wfu after crash at Punta Indio, Veronica, Provincia de Buenos Aires, 26/3/31 Teniente Miguel Castex killed.

34 Rebuild of earlier F.2B in 1931 at FMA. 300hp Hispano-Suiza Fb. Wfu 1932.

35 Rebuild of earlier F.2B in 1931 at FMA. 300hp Hispano-Suiza Fb. Wfu after crash on 22/7/31 at Gonzalez Catán, Provincia de Buenos Aires, Sargento Primero Claudio Vargas and Sargento Primero Ascencio Garranza killed.

36 Rebuild of earlier F.2B in 1931 at FMA. 300hp Hispano-Suiza Fb. Wfu 1932.

37 Rebuild of earlier F.2B in 1931 at FMA. 300hp Hispano-Suiza Fb. Wfu 1932.

38 Rebuild of earlier F.2B in 1931 at FMA. 300hp Hispano-Suiza Fb. Wfu 1932.

Note:

In 1920 and 1921 civilian Anglo-Argentine pilot Eduardo Miguel Hearne made two long-distance staged flights in Hispano-engined F.2Bs. It is uncertain whether these were ex-Argentine military aircraft or were purchased from England. Further details will be found in Appendix 7.

Above and left: **The F.2B presented to King Albert of the Belgians by the Handley Page Company on 14 May 1920, with the regal insignia on its fuselage.** *(Philip Jarrett)*

Australia

On 29 January 1919 Gen W.R. Birdwood at Australian Imperial Force Headquarters in London cabled home recommendations for one squadron each of Bristol Fighters, Sopwith Snipes, Airco D.H.9As and Vickers Vimys. In the event only D.H.9s, D.H.9As, S.E.5as and Avro 504s were later delivered, and no military Bristol Fighters went to Australia.

Austro-Hungarian Air Force

Four captured F.2Bs were renumbered 00.58, 00.75 (ex-D8075), 00.80 (ex-D8069) and 00.83 (ex-D7966)

Belgium

The Bristol Fighter was first demonstrated to the Belgian authorities on 14 May 1920 at Evère, the meeting being organised by the Handley Page/ADC representative in Belgium, Jean Stampe, who was to become a well-known aircraft designer, later producing the famous Stampe S.V.4. Shortly afterwards the ADC, which had taken over all stocks of surplus wartime aircraft, offered His Majesty King Albert a Bristol F.2B Type 14 fighter fitted with a 275hp Rolls-Royce Falcon III. A deal was made by ADC's Mr Richards, and after being modified at Cricklewood the machine was ferried to Evère on 23 August 1920 by Maj E. Leslie Foot, probably with the temporary British civil registration G-EASU. On 10 March 1921 a second

F.2B reached Belgium, flown by a Mr A.F. Muir, this aircraft being presented to Her Majesty Queen Elisabeth. It probably bore the temporary British civil registration G-EASV.

In January 1923 the Aéronautique Militaire (Belgian Air Force) adopted the identification letter L for the Bristol F.2B. The King's aircraft was then serialled L-1 (green aircraft with letter A and a crown) and the Queen's aircraft became L-2 (white aircraft with letter E and a crown). Another 15 F.2Bs were supplied by the ADC and given the temporary British civil registrations G-EAYQ, G-EBAK, G-EBAL, G-EBAM, G-EBAT (believed crashed at Croydon on 28 January 1922 when taking off for delivery), G-EBAU, G-EBBD, G-EBBO, G-EBCU, G-EBCV, G-EBCW, G-EBDB, G-EBDN, G-EBEE, G-EBBO for their ferry flights to Belgium, where they were coded L-3 to L-17, though not necessarily in that order.

Further Bristol Fighters arrived in 1923, when the Bristol Aeroplane Co delivered six newly built Type 17As (s/nos 6223 to 6238) at a cost of £800 each. The first of these, delivered by air from Croydon to Evère (see below), had a 300hp Hispano-Suiza, the remainder being delivered engineless, according to Bristol records, to have the same engine fitted upon arrival. On 6 June 1923 they were given British C of A numbers from 623 to 637. On arrival in Belgium they received serial numbers L-18 to L-33 and were known in Aéronautique Militaire service as the Bristol 300.

The first of these aircraft, F.2B s/no 6223, registered G-EBCN, was sold to the Société Anonyme Belge de Constructions Aéronautiques (SABCA) as a pattern aircraft, its British registration being cancelled on 24 July 1923, and that same year licence-built production of the Bristol 300 version in Belgium began. SABCA had been created on 16 December 1920 in order to set up an independent aircraft industry. The Belgian Government made a commitment to SABCA to place orders worth six million Belgian francs. As the society was at that time unable to produce its own designs, the government signed the contracts and bought licences. The licences and all the production rights were then given free to SABCA, which was allowed to take a ten per cent profit margin. During 1922 and 1923 SABCA built 20 Morane-Saulnier 35s and 29 D.H.9s, then, between

The white F.2B which Handley Page, through ADC, presented to the Queen Elisabeth I of the Belgians, previously E2058, seen as G-EBCU before leaving the UK. *(Philip Jarrett)*

1923 and 1927, 45 Ansaldo A.300s, 88 Nieuport 29s, 15 D.H.4s and 40 Bristol 300s. The first Bristol (L-34) was taken on charge on 18 January 1923 and the last aircraft (L-73) on 7 March 1927.

Meanwhile, in June 1921, the Aéronautique Militaire was reorganised, there being seven Groupes (including the 1ᵉ Groupe at Wilrijk Berchem-Sainte Agathe (formerly at Groot-Bijgaarden), equipped with balloons). The first escadrille (squadron) to fly Bristol Fighters was the 6ᵉ escadrille at Haren, this being part of IIIᵉ Groupe based at Evère. This Groupe comprised four escadrilles (one more than in 1920) for army co-operation, each equipped with 12 aircraft, these being initially SPAD XIs, D.H.4s and D.H.9s, then later also Bristol Fighters. In 1922 the number of escadrilles was increased to 25, comprising 15 with operational aircraft and 4 with balloons, plus three escadrilles écoles (flying schools) at As and 3 escadrilles techniques (technical squadrons). A variety of aircraft types were flown, of which 125 were then serviceable, though the Aéronautique Militaire was attempting to standardise the types of aircraft in service. By 1923 there were eight Groupes.

From 1923 the Bristols were all operated by the squadrons based at Evère and the

Above and left: **One of the sixteen new-build Hispano-engined F.2Bs supplied to Belgium by the Bristol company, at Filton in 1921.** *(Bristol)*

d'Aéronautique, the Groupes being divided between them. There were now nine Groupes and 29 escadrilles, each Groupe also having an escadrille de dépôt et parc.

The 1ᵉʳ Groupement now comprised four Groupes, based at Zellik (Iᵉʳ Groupe with four balloon escadrilles), Gossoncourt (IIᵉ Groupe and IIIᵉ Groupe, each with three observation escadrilles flying D.H.9s and Ansaldos) and Evère (IVᵉ Groupe with the 1ᵉʳᵉ, 2ᵉ, 3ᵉ and 4ᵉ escadrilles all flying reconnaissance aircraft including Bristol Fighters).

The 2ᵉ Groupement controlled three Groupes based respectively at Schaffen (3 escadrilles de chasse), Nivelles (3 escadrilles de chasse) and Bierset-Awans (with 3 escadrilles de bombardement). None of these was equipped with Bristol Fighters.

Lastly, the 3ᵉ Groupement had two Groupes, one at Evère (three escadrilles techniques) and the other at Wevelgem (three escadrilles écoles), the latter having been based there since September 1924.

The 1ᵉʳᵉ, 2ᵉ, 3ᵉ and 4ᵉ Escadrilles, all equipped with Bristol Fighters, were now designated 1/IV/1Aé, 2/IV/1Aé, 3/IV/1Aé and 4/IV/1Aé (the escadrille numbers being in Arabic, the Groupe in Roman numerals and the Groupement in Arabic). In 1925 new purchases allowed an increase in the complement of each escadrille, there now being a total of 268 operational aircraft plus 144 for training. During this year it was decided to re-equip the first-line escadrilles with more modern and standardised types of aircraft. The Bréguet XIX was chosen to

Ecole de Pilotage at Wevelgem. At that time IIIᵉ Groupe at Evère had four reconnaissance Escadrilles (1ᵉʳᵉ, 2ᵉ, 3ᵉ and 4ᵉ). Then, during 1924 and 1925, IVᵉ Groupe at Evère had the same Escadrilles. Finally, between 1926 and 1929 IVᵉ Groupe of the 1ᵉʳ Régiment had 9ᵉ Escadrille ('Dragon') and 11ᵉ Escadrille (Marabout) – otherwise 9/IV/1Aé and 11/IV/1Aé. In 1929 the Bristols were replaced by Bréguet XIXs.

On 1 April 1924 the air arm was again reorganised to comprise three Groupements

Belgian F.2B (L)63, with an oleo-sprung undercarriage. *(Philip Jarrett)*

A line-up of Belgian F.2Bs, with the foremost machine about to have its propeller swung. *(Philip Jarrett)*

Belgian F.2B (L)56 carries its identity on the fuselage side and on the central rudder stripe. The Pingouin (Penguin) logo of the École d'Aviation Militaire Belge is also evident. *(Philip Jarrett)*

Right: **Belgian Air Force F.2Bs at Evere, circa 1920, with a German Zeppelin shed as a backdrop.** *(Philip Jarrett)*

An anonymous Belgian F.2B. *(Philip Jarrett)*

A Belgian pilot poses with an F.2B, possibly No.67, which has been fitted with an oleo-sprung undercarriage. *(Philip Jarrett)*

This pristine Hispano-engined F.2B in Belgium was probably photographed shortly after delivery, as it is devoid of national insignia apart from the stripes on its rudder, which also carries the constructor's number 'B No.9'. *(Philip Jarrett)*

Above: **A Belgian Falcon-engined Bristol Fighter, curiously carrying the numeral 1 above the letter B on its rudder, lined up with a de Havilland D.H.4. The large windshield and lack of a Scarff ring on the F.2B's rear cockpit suggest that it was being used to transport high-ranking officers or VIPs.**

Left: **This Belgian F.2B carries the later identity B4 on its rudder.** *(Philip Jarrett)*

replace all D.H.4s and D.H.9s in the six observation and reconnaissance escadrilles.

The Belgian Flying School (École d'Aviation Militaire Belge), which used a Pingouin (Penguin) logo and was based at Wevelgem from 25 September 1924, comprised 1ère, 2e and 3e Escadrille of II Groupe of 3e Groupements). The first course started there the following spring. Due to limited resources, *ab initio* training was given by civil schools at Deurne, Gosselies and later St Hubert. On return from there the pilots would undertake further training to gain a brevet moyen (intermediate licence) and then a brevet militaire (military pilot's licence). The school was organised into three escadrilles (1, 2 and 3/II/3Aé), initial training on arrival from the civilian schools being given by 3ème Escadrille on Caudron G.IIIs, RSV 32/90s and Avro 504Ks. They would next progress to 2ème Escadrille to fly Morane-Saulnier MS 35s and Fokker D.VIIs, then finally to 1ère Escadrille with D.H.9s and later Bristol 300s. In January 1926 the Aéronautique Militaire was reorganised to form Régiments d'Aéronautique, and the school now comprised 1ère and 3ème Escadrilles of IIème Groupe of 3ème Régiment d'Aéronautique, with 1ère flying D.H.9s, Fokker D.VIIs, Bréguet XIVs and Bristol 300s. The first Bristols (L-13, L-52, L-53, L-55, L-56 and L-57) were delivered to Wevelgem in March 1926, a second batch (L-62, L-67, L-69, L-70 and L-73) arriving in March 1927. The Bristols used in the Flying School, which were flown by student pilots of the 1ère Escadrille, had modified tail surfaces. In 1926 the squadrons of that unit were designated as 1/II/3Aé and 3/II/3Aé, but by the following year had become 1/III/3Aé and 3/III/3Aé. In 1929 the unit became Ecole de Pilotage or Ecole d'Aviation militaire.

Photographed at Croydon, probably during its delivery flight, Bristol Fighter Type 14 G-EBBO, ex-H1258, registered to the Aircraft Disposal Co Ltd, was ferried from Croydon to Brussels by E.D.C. Herne on 11 March 1922 and handed over to the Belgian Air Force. *(Philip Jarrett)*

King Albert of Belgium about to have a flight in an RAF Bristol Fighter at Peshawar in October 1925. *(Philip Jarrett)*

Queen Elisabeth of Belgium was also treated to a flight in an RAF Bristol Fighter at Peshawar in October 1925. *(Philip Jarrett)*

During the mid-1920s a Bristol Fighter made daily meteorological flights from Evère, as did another aircraft of unknown type from Goetsenhoven, the recording and measuring devices being contained in a tin box fitted between the wings. On completion of each flight the crews would land, put the recording tapes in a weighted tube and take off again towards the Royal Meteorological Observatory at Uccle, near Brussels, where on arrival they dropped the tube on to the grass around the observatory. On 20 May 1926 Sgt Félix Regel took off from Evère with Commandant Maurice Delva in the back seat of L-20. Over Uccle, Regel made a low run to allow Delva to drop the tube. Uncertain whether the manoeuvre had been successful, Regel made a low altitude turn but hit a tree and the

aircraft crashed near the observatory, killing both occupants.

On 1 January 1926 a further reorganisation saw the Groupements replaced by three Régiments d'Aéronautique, the escadrilles with paired numbers being disbanded as such. The new 1er Régiment comprised four Groupes with a total of eight escadrilles, the 2e Régiment had three Groupes with six escadrilles and the 3e Régiment had two Groupes with four escadrilles.

Early in 1929, owing to a worldwide recession and consequent budget limitations, the Aéronautique Militaire was reduced to two Régiments with 12 escadrilles. In addition to these were the Etablissements d'Aéronautique providing technical services at Evère and the Ecole de Pilotage (or Ecole d'Aviation Militaire) at Wevelgem. By the

following year, however, the Bristol Fighter was no longer in Belgian service.

A Bristol Fighter fitted with a Hispano-Suiza engine is on static display at the (Musée Royal de l'Armée et d'Histoire Militaire/Koninklijk Museum van het Leger en de Krijgsgeschiedenis in Brussels. With the Belgian fuselage marking '66' and constructor's number 'B4' vertically on the rudder nationality stripes, it also carries the Pingouin (Penguin) logo of the École d'Aviation Militaire Belge. A reconstruction based on one of several airframe components found at Weston-on-the-Green, Oxfordshire, it was built by Skysport Engineering at Hatch for Aero Vintage, then exchanged in 1989 for a Spitfire Mk.IX.

Belgian Bristol Fighters: Individual Histories

L-1 (Probably ex-G-EASU) Presented by Handley Page to King Albert of Belgium on 14.5.20; Ret'd to Cricklewood for special modification, then flown to Evère by Maj E. Leslie Foot 23.8.20, painted green overall with a letter 'A' and a crown.

L-2 (Probably ex-G-EBCU) Deld 10.3.21 from England to Evère by Mr A.F. Muir for Queen Elisabeth I, painted white overall with a letter 'E' and a crown.
[On 5.11.21 Lt Simonet and Lt Becquet, flying either L-1 or L-2, reached an altitude of 7,900m (25,920ft), recognised as a Belgian record by the Aéro Club de Belgique]

L-3 From VII Groupe to III Aé 23.8.22; WO IV/1 Aé 26.6.25

L-4 From VII Groupe to III Aé 23.8.22; From IV/1 Aé to I/3 Aé for repair 12.9.28

L-5 (later B-5) From IV Groupe to III Groupe 20.10.22; Crashed on to a train (no date); From IV/1 Aé to I/3 Aé for repair 16.7.25; WO at I/3 Aé 20.8.26

L-6 From VII Groupe to III Groupe 23.3.03; From I/3 Aé to IV/I Aé 16.7.27. At one time with Ecole de Perfectionnement (Penguin) fitted with night-flying hood.

L-7 From VII Groupe to III Groupe 11.9.22; From I/3 Aé to IV/I Aé 28.7.25

L-8 From VII Groupe to III Groupe 11.9.22; From III/3 EP to I/3 Aé rép 25.5.28

L-9 From VII Groupe to III Groupe 22.8.22; From IV/1Aé to I/3 Aé 17.3.26; WO at I/3 Aé 18.6.26

L-10 From VII Groupe to III Groupe 22.8.22; Crashed during International Concours Aviatique air display at Waalhaven, Rotterdam; three Bristols made a cross-over but the leader, in L-10, encountered turbulence, got into a spin and crashed, 10.9.22 (pilot 1st Lt Fernand N.A. Sauveur killed and observer 1st Lt Raymond Meuris injured); SOC 20.9.22

L-11 From VII Groupe to III Groupe 12.8.22; Crashed 19.8.22; VII Groupe for repairs 24.12.22; SOC 11.10.23

L-12 From VII Groupe to III Groupe 19.8.22; To VII Groupe for repair 20.9.22; Accident, from IV/1 Aé to I/3 Aé for repair 9.5.27; SOC 6.7.27

L-13 From VII Groupe to III Groupe 27.6.23; 1/II/3/Aé from 3.26; From IV/1Aé to II/3 EP 31.3.26

L-14 From VII Groupe to III Groupe 21.10.22; From IV/1 Aé to I/3 Aé for repair 25.6.28

L-15 From VII Groupe to III Groupe 20.9.22; Accident, from III Groupe to VII Groupe for repair 18.5.23; SOC 27.6.23

L-16 From VII Groupe to III Groupe 23.11.22; From IV/1 Aé to I/3 Aé for repair 6.7.27

L-17 From VII Groupe to III Groupe 19.1.23; Accident, to VII Groupe for repair 29.5.23; SOC 27.6.23

L-18 (later B-18) From VII Groupe to III Groupe 10.2.23; Accident, from IV/1 Aé to I/3 Aé for repair 9.5.27; SOC 6.7.27

L-19 (later B-19) TOC 1923; From VII Groupe to III Groupe 11.6.23; IV/1 Aé, overturned 31.5.28 (pilot Buchin); To I/3 Aé for repair 11.6.28

L-20 (later B-20) TOC 1923; From VII Groupe to III Groupe 11.6.23; Accident, from IV/1 Aé to I/3 Aé for repair 9.5.27; Crashed while dropping message to Uccle observatory, near Brussels 20.5.26 (Sgt Félix Regel and Observer Cdt Maurice Delva killed); SOC 2.7.26

L-21 TOC 1923; From VII Groupe to III Groupe 4.6.23; Accident, from III Groupe to VII Groupe for repair 24.12.23; SOC 30.1.24

L-22 TOC 1923; From VII Groupe to III Groupe 11.6.23; From IV/1 Aé to I/3 Aé for repair 25.6.28

L-23 TOC 1923; From VII Groupe to III Groupe 11.6.23; From I/3 Aé to IV/1 Aé 26.9.25

L-24 TOC 1923; From VII Groupe to III Groupe 11.6.23; Accident, from IV/1 Aé to I/3 Aé for repair 24.10.28

continued …

L-25   TOC 1923; From VII Groupe to III Groupe 19.6.23; Accident, from IV/1 Aé to I/3 Aé for repair 19.8.25; SOC at IV/1 Aé 4.6.26

L-26   TOC 1923; From VII Groupe to III Groupe 9.7.23; Accident, from IV/1 Aé to I/3 Aé for repair 19.8.24; SOC 29.10.24

L-27   TOC 1923; From VII Groupe to III Groupe 19.6.23; Accident, from IV/1 Aé to I/3 Aé for repair 2.8.24; SOC 29.10.24

L-28   TOC 1923; From VII Groupe to III Groupe 27.6.23; Crashed Evère 9.2.24 (Sgt Ernest L. Stiennon & S/Lt L. Englebin both killed); SOC 15.3.24

L-29   TOC 1923; From VII Groupe to III Groupe 27.6.23

L-30   TOC 1923; From VII Groupe to III Groupe 28.7.23; Accident, from IV/1 Aé to I/3 Aé for repair 24.6.27; SOC 8.8.27

L-31   TOC 1923; From VII Groupe to III Groupe 28.7.23; With IV/I Aé, caught by gust of wind while testing new equipment and crashed from 50ft, Woluwé-St-Etienne, near St-Lambert 9.2.25 (Lt Louis J. Debucuois & Lt Obs Droesbeke both injured); I/3 Aé for repair 16.2.25; SOC 10.6.25

L-32   TOC 1923; From VII Groupe to III Groupe 9.7.23; From I/3 Aé to IV/1 Aé 19.3.28

L-33   TOC 1923; From VII Groupe to III Groupe 7.8.23; Crashed Nivelles, 13.7.24 (Lt Edmiond R.H. Desclee killed and passenger Jean Verhaegen slightly injured)

L-34   From I/3 Aé to IV/1 Aé 18.1.26; I/3 Aé 6.7.27; III/3 EP 11.6.28; I/3 Aé for repair 20.7.28

L-35   From I/3 Aé to IV/1 Aé 18.1.26; I/3 Aé for repair 25.5.28

L-36   From I/3 Aé to IV/1 Aé 17.3.26

L-37   From I/3 Aé to IV/1 Aé 10.2.26; I/3 Aé for repair 24.8.28

L-38   From I/3 Aé to IV/1 Aé 27.1.26; I/3 Aé for repair 24.6.27

L-39   From I/3 Aé to IV/1 Aé 10.2.26; I/3 Aé for repair 16.8.26; IV/1 Aé 7.3.27

L-40   From I/3 Aé to IV/1 Aé 10.2.26; I/3 Aé 254.6.28

L-41   From I/3 Aé to IV/1 Aé 10.2.26; Major inspection 12.1.29 (cables & engine replaced); 9 Sqn/4 Groupe Ecole d'Aviation, stalled at 1,200m and crashed, Evère, 21.10.29 (Sgt Alfons E.J. de Rijck of 1 Escadrille killed)

L-42   From I/3 Aé to IV/1 Aé 17.3.26; Crashed at Evère 12.7.26 (Sgt Victor P.C. Van Caenegem killed); Wreckage to I/3 Aé; SOC 20.8.26

L-43   From I/3 Aé to IV/1 Aé 27.1.26

L-44   From I/3 Aé to IV/1 Aé 31.3.26; I/3 Aé to IV/1 Aé 23.5.27

L-45   (later B-45) From I/3 Aé to IV/1 Aé 26.2.26; I/3 Aé for repair 14.9.27; III/3 EP 20.7.28

L-46   From I/3 Aé to IV/1 Aé 10.2.26

L-47   From I/3 Aé to IV/1 Aé 19.5.26

L-48   From I/3 Aé to IV/1 Aé 10.2.26; Accident, to I/3 Aé for repair 10.12.26; SOC 2.2.27

L-49   From I/3 Aé to IV/1 Aé 10.2.26

L-50   From I/3 Aé to IV/1 Aé 10.2.26; Accident, to I/3 Aé for repair 24.8.28; SOC 24.12.28

L-51   From I/3 Aé to IV/1 Aé 10.2.26

L-52   (later B-52) From I/3 Aé to IV/1 Aé 10.2.26; II/3 EP 31.3.26; I/3 Aé for repair 25.2.27; III/3 EP 28.9.27; I/3 Aé for repair 25.5.28

L-53   (later B-53) From I/3 Aé to IV/1 Aé 26.2.26; II/3 EP 31.3.26; Pilot spun in while flying over parent's house at Wijtschate, Heuvelland, 21.4.28 (Kpl François Tyberghien killed); Wreckage to I/2 Aé; SOC 20.7.28

L-54   (later B-54) From I/3 Aé to IV/1 Aé 10.2.26

L-55   (later B-55) From I/3 Aé to IV/1 Aé 10.2.26; II/3 EP 31.3.26; Crashed at Tournai and badly damaged, 4.8.26 (1st Sgt E.P. Camille Spaens unhurt); I/3 Aé for repair 20.8.26; III/3 EP 25.4.28; I/3 for repair 25.5.28; Crashed on landing, Wevelghem, 5.28 (Kpl Franz Stienon unhurt); I/3 Aé for repair 25.5.28; SOC 13.8.28

L-56   From I/3 Aé to IV/1 Aé 26.2.26; II/3 EP 31.3.26; III/3 EP to I/3 Aé for repair 14.9.27 (also 28.9.27)

L-57   From I/3 Aé to II/3 EP 31.3.26

L-58   Deld I/3 Aé 16.8.26; IV/1 Aé 6.12.26

L-59   Deld I/3 Aé 6.12.26; IV/1 Aé 2.2.27

L-60   Deld I/3 Aé 6.12.26; IV/1 Aé 2.2.27 (also 25.2.27)

L-61   Deld I/3 Aé 6.12.26; IV/1 Aé 2.2.27; I/3 Aé for repair 19.3.28

L-62   (later B62) Deld I/3 Aé 6.12.26; II/3 EP 14.3.27

L-63   Deld I/3 Aé 6.12.26; WO23.3.27

L-64   Deld I/3 Aé 6.12.26; IV/1 Aé 25.2.27; Ground collision with another Bristol, to I/3 Aé for repair 23.3.27; SOC 20.4.27

L-65   Deld I/3 Aé 10.12.26; IV/1 Aé 25.2.27

L-66   Deld I/3 Aé 10.12.26; IV/1 Aé 7.3.27; Collided with L-71at Haren 14.10.27; Sgt Emile Dubuisson killed & Sgt Hilaire M.G. Mesdagh injured; crash-landed 500m from the other crashed a/c (not known which aircraft was which); Wreckage to I/3 Aé 24.10.27

L-67   Deld I/3 Aé 27.12.26; II/3 EP 14.3.27

L-68   Deld I/3 Aé 27.12.26; IV/1 Aé 2.2.27; I/3 Aé for repair 9.5.27; III/3 EP 25.4.28; Ran short of fuel, made emergency landing at Wevelgem, 12.6.28 (Kpl Joseph de Coninck killed); Wreckage to I/3 Aé 25.6.28; SOC 12.9.28

L-69   Deld I/3 Aé 27.12.26; II/3 EP 14.3.27

L-70   Deld I/3 Aé 27.12.26; II/3 EP 14.3.27; IV/1 Aé 14.5.28; I/3 Aé for repair 24.10.28

L-71   Deld I/3 Aé 2.2.27; IV/1 Aé 2.2.27; Mid-air collision with L-66 at Haren, 14.10.27; Sgt Emile Dubuisson killed and Sgt Hilaire M.G. Mesdagh injured but crash-landed 500m from the other crashed a/c. Not known which aircraft was which; Wreckage to I/3 Aé 24.10.27; SOC 23.11.27

L-72   Deld I/3 Aé 25.2.27; IV/1 Aé 25.2.27; I/3 Aé for repair 14.9.27

L-73   Deld I/3 Aé 7.3.27; II/3 EP 14.3.27

Unidentified

26.11.29 One aircraft crashed at Chée de Rodebeek a Schaarbeek (crew unhurt?).

Note

The dates given for delivery, accident or withdrawal of the aircraft are those of the relevant Ordres Matériel Aéronautique (OMA). The actual date could have been a short time before, after or on the same date as the OMA.

Canada's first F.2B in its original guise, as H4336, with the squadron number '1' inset in a maple leaf forward of the roundel. It became G-CYBC.

Canada

In 1919 the British government offered specific types of surplus military landplanes, including Bristol Fighters, to several Dominions, including Canada, as an Imperial Gift. The Canadian government was not happy with this, as much of the continent was unexplored and totally unsuited to landplane operations. However, there were many large lakes ideal for waterborne aircraft, and an additional allocation was made. During the war Canadian citizens had subscribed for 18 aeroplanes for use by the RFC and RAF in France, and with the ending of the war the same number of machines was to be returned to the Canadian government, the specific types to be selected by them. As these aircraft did not have to be surplus to

Canadian F.2B G-CYBC at Rockcliffe, Ontario, circa 1922. Previously it was a presentation aircraft, successively named *Zanzibar 17* and then *Huddersfield*. *(Library and Archives Canada / PA-062275)*

Bristol F.2B G-CYBC after a forced landing in Mountain Grove, Ontario, in May 1921. *(Tudhope Collection)*

RAF requirements they did not come under the Cabinet ruling regarding Imperial Gift aircraft, so the Canadians requested one Handley Page V/1500 and one O/400, nine Bristol Fighters and a single Fairey seaplane. After further negotiations, however, this was changed to eight Felixstowe F.3 flying boats and a single 'Fairey IIIC' seaplane (actually the Fairey IIIH originally intended for the transatlantic flight attempt), and all of the landplanes, including the nine F.2Bs, were cancelled.

However, two F.2Bs fitted with Falcon III engines were supplied from RAF stocks and given quasi-military registrations:

The other Canadian F.2B was G-CYDP, ex-D7869, seen here at its base, Camp Borden. *(Tudhope Collection)*

Canadian Bristol Fighters: Individual Histories

G-CYBC (ex-F4336 *Zanzibar No.17* and later *Huddersfield – Canada*) TOC 6.8.20; Based at Camp Borden. This aircraft was originally given to Maj A.E. McKeever, DSO, MC, in November 1918, when he was appointed to command the newly formed 1 Sqn, Canadian Air Force, for his personal use. It was then sent to Canada and taken on CAF strength (floats ordered); SOC 7.2.22

G-CYDP (ex-D7869) TOC 19.4.21. Based at Camp Borden; fate unknown.

Chile

Twelve Bristol Type 83B Lucifers were ordered in 1926 (s/nos 6924 to 6935) and numbered B.1 to B.12. Aluminium finish. Flight-tested at Filton from 26.2.26 and shipped from Liverpool 4.26. Four additional Type 83Bs were assembled in Chile in 1928, one being serialled B-13, but there is no trace of these in Bristol records.

China

A Bristol Fighter was reported to be on the strength of Sun Yat Sen's rebel air force in China. Its origin and identity are unknown.

Above right and right: **Bristol Type 83B Lucifer trainers serving in Chile, circa 1926.** *(via Bristol)*

area, and also to discourage the local ravenous wood-eating insects. During the three months' wait for the missing parts to arrive from the USA the aircraft was stored in an abandoned mill in San Pedro. It was then found that locally available petrol was below specification, and it took three weeks for higher-grade fuel to arrive. However, on 19 April Lamb flew solo to the Tegucigalpa through a driving northwest gale, arriving over the capital in 84min, a journey that normally took five days overland. The infant air force later acquired a motley collection of other aircraft, and the F.2B was later serialled H-9 and flown with an unmanned but uncovered Lewis machine-gun mounted on the Scarff ring in the rear cockpit.

Lamb later became too ambitious in his flights all over the Republic, and over-demanding for increases in his salary. An accident at 'Sitio de los Ninos' (Childrens' Place) during a 'goodwill' flight to Salvador on 15 September 1921 was perhaps the last straw, and he was invited to leave the country, on the excuse that he was wearing out the F.2B. The aircraft was trucked back to the Toncontin landing field at Tegucigalpa, where after lengthy repairs it was flown occasionally by various pilots engaged by the Government, among them the Italian Luigi Venditti (given in some documents as Luiz Vendetti) as late as 24 January 1923. It was finally burned by revolutionary forces at Toncontin in March 1924, together with other seized aircraft.

The Honduran F.2B protected by an armed guard who evidently means business. Note his reflection on the shiny fuselage side, coated with Valspar lacquer. *(Philip Jarrett)*

Greece

Six reconditioned F.2Bs (s/n's 6156 to 6161) were supplied to Greece. No gun mountings or gun gear was fitted. Later reserialled M-31 to M-36, they were still in use in 1928 for training purposes. One survivor was M-35, the type finally being withdrawn from use in 1934.

Honduras

Around 26 May 1920 a single F.2B appears to have been purchased for the Honduran Government, probably in either Canada or the USA, by a US citizen, Roy Gordon, who then seems to have dropped out of the picture. In January 1921 this aircraft arrived via freighter at the Caribbean port of Puerto Cortez, where it was met and removed from its crate by Dean Ivan Lamb and one Gaston de Prida. Lamb was an American mercenary, born in Pennsylvania in 1886, who had flown during the Mexican Revolution of 1913 and as a sergeant pilot with 4 Sqn in the RFC in France. He was hired by the

Honduran Government as Director General of Aviation, Commander of Artillery and Machine guns.

Despite the lack of some minor parts the F.2B was erected and treated as far as possible with Valspar lacquer to prevent deterioration of the fabric and wooden components in the hot, damp climate of the

Hungary

Five new-build Type 83 Lucifer School/PTMs (s/n 6922/G-EBNB, 6923/G-EBNC, 6960, 6961 & 6962) were supplied to the Hungarian Government. No details of use.

Irish Free State (Eire)

Individual histories of the F.2Bs operated by the Irish Army Air Corps are given in chapter 12.

Right: **A rear view at San Pedro Sula, with the nose and cockpits protected from the sun.** *(Philip Jarrett)*

Right: **Bristol Fighter B1124 of 48 Sqn under guard shortly after engine problems led to a forced landing at Zuidzande in Holland on 29 September 1917.** *(Philip Jarrett)*

Below right: **B1124 after purchase by the Dutch, adorned with the national orange roundel insignia and marked 'BR401 RR250'.** *(Philip Jarrett)*

Mexico

Around March 1928 a Mexican Air Service Commission headed by Brig Luis Amezcua returned from Europe after a six-month tour of France, Britain, Germany and Italy. Among the European aircraft they procured for the Mexican Air Force (Fuerza Aérea Mexicana; FAM) were ten new 200hp Hispano-Suiza-engined Bristol Type 17B Fighters (s/n 7222 to 7231) and two Bristol Boarhounds (s/n 7232 and 7233). Shipped in the SS *Novian*, they arrived at Veracruz in late March 1928. Described as being of Mk.III/IV standard, they had increased all-up weight, with strengthened longerons, an undercarriage incorporating oleo struts, Handley Page automatic slots and a redesigned fin and horn-balanced rudder, as well as a much better engine cowling. The Mexican national insignia had been incorrectly applied at the factory, facing the wrong way, but this was never corrected. They were numbered 1 to 10, and the Boarhounds were numbered 1 and 2, also having mis-painted national insignia.

The Fighters were erected early in April at Balbuena Field under the guidance of an English master mechanic. According to a contemporary official report, the F.2Bs were complete except for engines, and the FAM proposed to fit them with old overhauled 300hp Hispano-Suiza engines. An Intelligence Report dated 17 December 1929 stated that the engines were now to be replaced by 300hp Wright J-6s, though it is not clear whether this ever happened. Bandits were rife in Mexico at that time, so civilian passenger trains were escorted by armed air patrols, probably including F.2Bs, rebels being attacked both by machine-gun fire and light bombs. Aircraft were also much involved when a revolution broke out, attacking troop and supply concentrations in addition to rebel convoys and troop trains.

A report on 1 June 1933 said: 'the last Bristol Fighter, assigned to the 1/o Regiment, was lost 'several months ago'.' It went on to say, however, that 'the planes were dropped from the 1st Air Regiment during the latter part of last year and those which were fairly serviceable were used by pilots who were not members of the Regiment for practice flying. The MA had been informed, however, that the last serviceable Bristol was wrecked "several months ago" and none were then in use.' This conflicts with an AOB dated 26 March 1934 (the last report) which listed 12 Bristols, but since at least two are known to have been lost (one in 1929 and one in 1931) this is probably erroneous.

As seen here, BR401 later acquired a 'fighting cock' emblem on its fuselage flanks. *(Philip Jarrett)*

Netherlands

Only one interned wartime Bristol Fighter was ever flown by the Netherlands Air Force:

Netherlands Bristol Fighter: Individual History

BR401 (ex-B1124) 48 Sqn, interned 29.9.17 then purchased by the Netherlands government for £2,500 and taken over as BR401; served with the Luchtvaartafdeling until 1924.

New Zealand

Seven Bristol Fighters of various types were brought on charge by the New Zealand Permanent Air Force/Royal New Zealand Air Force (NZPAF/RNZAF) as follows:

Standard late-war F.2Bs: H1557 and H1558

Standard F.2B Mk IIs: 6856 and 6857

Mk III dual-control trainer: 7120

F.2B Mk IIIs: 7121 and 7122 with Mk IV fins and rudders but without Handley Page slats.

Left: **Although H1557 was one of the first F.2Bs to arrive in New Zealand, it was not assembled and flown until 1925. Its career ended shortly thereafter in a fatal accident on 17 March 1926.** *(Air Force Museum of New Zealand)*

Below left: **Photographer Charles Barton, in the rear cockpit of 6856, prepares to take air-to-air film of the visit of Fokker F.VIIB-3m** *Southern Cross* **following Kingsford Smith's successful trans-Tasman flight.** *(Warren P. Russell)*

The last five were in army co-operation configuration and were not regarded as fighters.

The first two, part of an Imperial Gift, arrived in August 1919. While H1557 remained in its packing case at Wigram, H1558 was assembled under the supervision of Capt John H. Don, who also made the type's first test flight in New Zealand, on 4 September.

In June 1923 the NZPAF was formed, and in late 1924 or early 1925 two more F.2Bs were ordered from Britain. They arrived aboard the *Suffolk* in late 1925. These aeroplanes' construction numbers initiated the practice in new Zealand of using c/ns as serial numbers; hence the serials 6856 and 6857.

Early in 1925 H1557 was finally assembled and flown, but its life was brief. On 17 March 1926, while being flown by Capt Frederick J. Horrell, with Lt Purcey A. Turner and Mr Lewis M. Reid as passengers, it was flown low over Papanui, Christchurch, and while performing aerobatics it crashed in the grounds of the Methodist Orphanage at Harewood Road and was destroyed.

Below: **A trio of F.2Bs, 6857, 6856 and another (7120?) prepare to take off from Wigram, possibly at the beginning of the 1928** *Southern Cross* **crew tour.** *(Air Force Museum of New Zealand)*

Right: **During the *Southern Cross* New Zealand tour the three escorting F.2Bs, 6856, 6857 and 7120, made an overnight stop at Westmere Racecourse on 23 or 24 September.** *(Alexander Turnbull Library Collection AT F21160)*

Below right: **Pilot 2nd Lt Ian C. Maclaine escaped unhurt when 6856 overturned at Wigram in January 1929 after encountering the slipstream of an Avro 504K.** *(RNZAF)*

Horrell was killed in the crash, and Reid died of his injuries en route to hospital, but Turner eventually recovered. An inquiry concluded that the aircraft was overloaded, and that Horrell should not have performed low-level aerobatics.

The three remaining F.2Bs were supplemented by 7120, 7121 and 7122, the latter two being fully equipped as army co-operation aircraft, upon arrival in the latter part of 1927.

Used extensively during 1927-1928, the Bristol Fighters also performed other than military duties. In July 1926 H1558 was specially equipped for an extensive photographic aerial survey of Christchurch City and its environs, and another, equipped with the necessary instrumentation, collected data for the New Zealand Meteorological Service.

In 1928, when Charles Kingsford Smith and his crew in the Fokker F.VIIB-3m *Southern Cross* arrived following their successful trans-Tasman flight, four F.2Bs took off from Wigram on 11 September to provide an escort to Wigram, one carrying a cine camera to record the event. The government then put 6856, 6857 and 7120 at the disposal of Kingsford Smith and his crew, and a tour of New Zealand was undertaken until the *Southern Cross* flew back to Australia on 13 October, escorted for part of the way by a brace of F.2Bs.

The five Fighters were still in service when the NZPAF became the RNZAF on 27 February 1934, and, to ensure that they remained serviceable until advanced trainers had been acquired, a quantity of Falcon engine spares was purchased from the RAF that year.

The annual refresher course of 1936 saw last use of the Bristol Fighter for intensive training. Unfortunately the course was marred by tragedy when Fg Off Graham M. Owen of the NZAF was killed. While carrying out ground-attack exercises in 7121 at the Lake Ellesmere range Owen circled the lake at 1,200ft and then dived on the target at an estimated angle of 80 degrees with the engine throttled back. He failed to pull out, and 7121 crashed 50 yards from the target and was destroyed. The accident was attributed to failure of the lower wing centre section. Shortly thereafter it was

Above right: **A nice study of 6856 at Wigram, probably before 1931, with its serial number also stencilled on the rudder.** *(Air Force Museum of New Zealand)*

Right: **Bristol F.2B 6856 aloft, with a camera gun on the rear-cockpit Scarff ring, probably in 1934.** *(RNZAF)*

Above: **A pristine 6857, probably photographed at Wigram about 1931.** *(RNZAF)*

Left: **A close-up of 6857, providing excellent detail of the forward fuselage and wing centre-section structure.** *(via Philip Jarrett)*

Below left: **The NZPAF's only dual-control F.2B, 7120, displays its distinctive cockpit shapes.** *(A.C. Elworthy via D.S. Wilson)*

Below right: **Dual-control 7120 in company with a pair of NZPAF Hawker Tomtits, 51 and 52. The Tomtits arrived in New Zealand in 1931.** *(via D.S. Wilson)*

Bottom left: **A pair of white cloth ground markers guide the crew of F.2B 7121, with its message hook lowered, over the two posts between which is stretched the wire attached to the message bag.** *(via D.P. Woodhall)*

Bottom right: **The rear-cockpit occupant of 7121 leans well over the side to ensure that the lowered message hook makes the necessary connection and collection. The later 'J'-type tail is well shown here.** *(RNZAF)*

Bristol F.2B 7122 in formation with a brace of Tomtits. *(D.S. Wilson)*

'Bombing up' an anonymous NZPAF F.2B with practice bombs; a view that shows often-obscured details of the type's cowling and undercarriage. Note the pump impeller on the starboard front undercarriage leg. *(D.P. Woodhall)*

Flanked by a Simmonds Spartan on the left and a de Havilland D.H.60G on the right, F.2B 7122 sits in a line-up at the Otago Aero Club Pageant at Taieri during the weekend of 21-22 February 1931. *(D.S. Wilson)*

The RNZAF's last surviving Bristol Fighter, probably 6857, stripped down and ready for burning on the rubbish tip, outside Wigram's No.4 hangar, 1938-39. *(Sqn Ldr Gerald S. Evatt)*

New Zealand Bristol Fighters: Individual Histories

Batch 1

Two Imperial Gift aircraft in 1919, retaining their RAF serial numbers:

H1557 To New Zealand 'on loan', for use by Lt Col A.V. Bettington, CMG, LofH(Fr), RAF, and party during his 1919 visit as 'Air Adviser' to New Zealand Government. Left UK on *Matatua* 28.6.19; arrived Auckland 8.8.19; By sea to Lyttelton c.18.8.19; received at Sockburn c.28.8.19; presented to NZ Govt/Defence Force as part of Imperial Gift by 22.9.19; New Zealand Permanent Air Force (NZPAF) 14.6.23 but not assembled until early 1925. Earliest known flight 28.2.25 (L.M. Isitt, 10min); NZPAF Wigram, spun in after two loops at 2,000ft over Papanui, crashed in rose garden of Methodist Orphanage, Harewood Rd, Wigram, 17.3.26; Capt F.J.

Horrell, New Zealand Air Force (NZAF) [Territorial] killed, Lt P.A. Turner, NZAF [Territorial] seriously injured; Mr L.M. Reid, passenger, died of injuries en route to hospital.

H1558 To New Zealand 'on loan', for use by Lt Col A.V. Bettington, CMG, LofH(Fr), RAF, and party during his 1919 visit as 'Air Adviser' to NZ Govt; Left UK on *Matatua* 28.6.19; Arrived Auckland 8.8.19. By sea to Lyttelton c.18.8.19; received at Sockburn c.28.8.19; first flight 4.9.19 (J.H. Don). Presented to NZ Govt/Defence Force as part of Imperial Gift by 22.9.19; NZPAF 14.6.23; Badly damaged in landing accident c.25.3.29; reduced to spares.

Batch 2

Two new army co-operation aircraft on order 'for some considerable time'. Supplied in 1925 and marked with the Bristol s/nos 6856 & 6857 on the fins:

6856 AW/CN 18.8.25; To Avonmouth for shipment 28.8.25; to New Zealand on *Suffolk* 9.25; NZPAF, earliest known flight 28.11.25 (L.M. Isitt, rigging and engine test, 30min). Badly damaged in landing accident 1.29; repaired. RNZAF 27.2.34; Last known flight 5.3.35 (I.E. Rawnsley). To ground instructional airframe 1936, scrapped at Wigram by burning post-1938.

6857 AW/CN 18.8.25; To Avonmouth for shipment 28.8.25; to New Zealand on *Suffolk* 9.25; NZPAF, earliest known flight 20.1.27 (M.W. Buckley, 'local passenger', 30min). RNZAF 27.2.34; Last known flight 24.10.36 (F.R. Dix). To ground instructional airframe 1936, scrapped at Wigram by burning post-1938.

Batch 3

Three further aircraft ordered c.9.26 and supplied in 1927, marked with Bristol s/nos 7120 to 7122 on the fins:

7120 (Mk III dual control) Arrived Wigram Jun-Jul 1927; NZPAF; Earliest known flight 2.11.27 (J.L. Findlay, to test dual controls, 15min). RNZAF 27.2.34. Last known flight 14.10.36 (I.E. Rawnsley); to ground instructional airframe 1936.

7121 ('J' type, Army Co-op); Air tested by makers at Filton 6.5.27; Arrived Wigram 3.8.27; NZPAF; first flight after erection 26.10.27 (M.W. Buckley, 10 min). RNZAF 27.2.34. Crashed during air-firing practice at Lake Ellesmere range, near

Christchurch 25.2.36 (Fg Off G.M. Owen, NZAF [Territorial] died of injuries) [TFH 669.15].

7122 ('J' type, Army Co-op) Arrived Wigram c.3.8.27; NZPAF; first flight after erection 8.9.27 (M.W. Buckley, 10min). RNZAF 27.2.34; Last known flight 29.9.36 (S. Wallingford); to ground instructional airframe 1936, scrapped at Wigram by burning post-1938.

Right: **An anonymous Puma-engined Bristol Fighter in Norway, one of five of obscure origin used by the Söndenfjeldske Flyavdeling (SFA) at Kjeller in the early 1920s.** *(Philip Jarrett)*

Below right: **Bristol F.2B No.253 of the SFA has the propeller of its Puma swung preparatory to a flight. Note the lack of wheel covers. This view emphasises the bulkiness of the Puma installation compared with those of earlier engines fitted in the Bristol Fighter. The numerals of the aircraft's serial number were yellow, outlined in black.** *(MiA – Museums in Akershus/Norway Lisens: CC: BY-NC-CA)*

decided to withdraw the remaining F.2Bs from active flying, and during November 1936 they were distributed for use as instructional airframes. The RNZAF's Bristol Fighters were the last of their kind in military service anywhere.

The fates of 6856, 6857, 7120 and 7122 are given below, but to which specific aircraft each account relates is uncertain. Around November 1936 one went to the Wellington Aero Club (for the Dominion School of Aeronautics?) for use as an instructional airframe after being struck off charge. Another, believed to be 7122, was also struck off charge and flown from Wigram to Palmerston North Technical College around late November or early December 1936 for a similar purpose. By May 1937 only one remained at Wigram, and although it was offered for sale in 1938 there were no takers, so either late that year or early in 1939, despite strenuous efforts by Wigram's CO, Sqn Ldr George Hodson, RAF, to have this aircraft sent to a museum, it was burnt in the rubbish pit on the eastern boundary of Wigram airfield.

Norway

On 10 August 1919 the Norwegian Defence Ministry decided to buy five new Puma-engined Bristol Fighters, an order being placed in May 1920. The aircraft eventually arrived in January 1921 at the main Army Air Force airfield at Kjeller, near Oslo. These were supposedly given sequence numbers 6140 to 6144, but Bristol records show these five as actually going to Spain, so the real origin of the Norwegian machines has not been established. Whatever their source, Norwegian serial numbers 104 to 108 were allotted, with individual numbers 251, 253,

An ambulance awaits while medics treat an injured occupant of SFA F.2B No.251 following a crash. *(Romsdalsmuseet photo archive)*

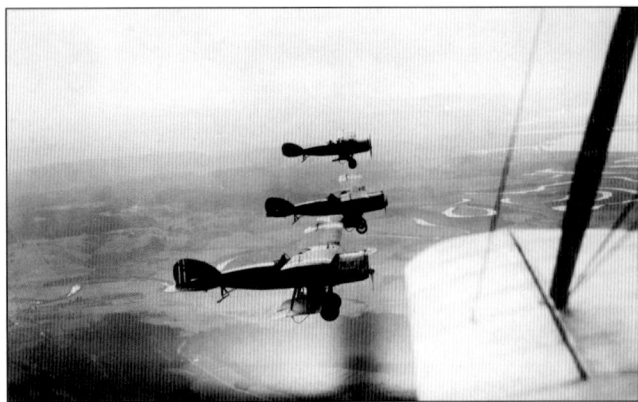

An air-to-air study of three SFA Puma-powered F.2Bs in echelon. The nearest aircraft has an indiscernible inscription over its rudder stripes. *(Photo by unknown/ Norwegian Aviation Museum. Distribution of images is not allowed)*

Another flying shot of the SFA F.2Bs aloft. The furthest machine again lacks wheel covers. *(Photo by unknown/Norwegian Aviation Museum. Distribution of images is not allowed)*

255, 257 and 259 painted in black on both sides of the fuselage in addition to national colours. These alternate odd numbers denote that they were army aircraft, even numbers being allocated to navy aircraft. All five were delivered on 6 June 1921 to the Söndenfjeldske Flyavdeling (SFA) at Kjeller, under the command of Premierlöytenant T.Vetlesen and were flown primarily as scouts with a range of 400km (250 miles) and a speed of 220km/h (140mph), until being struck off charge on 31 December 1933.

Persia (Iran)

In 1921 the Persian ambassador in Washington DC was asked to purchase aircraft in the USA, but his efforts were turned down under the terms of the First World War disarmament treaty. Iran therefore had to turn to European countries, and the UK appears to have been one of these. Bristol Fighter H1561 was intended to become No.4 with the Persian Air Force. It was flown from Farnborough to Gosport on 31 August 1920, but was badly damaged, returning to Farnborough on 5 October and then being retained for trial purposes. It was never replaced.

Peru

At least three Bristol Fighters were acquired for use by the Servicio de Aviación Militar del Ejercito del Peru (Peruvian Army Aviation Service) between 12 December 1920 and 11 January 1921. They were presentation aircraft, named after the towns or organisations which donated them via public subscription, namely *Apurimac*, *Camara de Diputados* (damaged on 11 January 1921) and *Pisco*.

By 1924 the Peruvian Army Flying Service had its main Air Station at Las Palmas, about nine miles for Lima, the capital city. *Jane's All the World's Aircraft* for that year listed the numbers and type of aircraft then in use by the service and these included three Bristol Fighters, presumably the above three. They remained in service until 1926.

Above: **On 13 October 1920 Bristol F.2B No.20.38 of 5 Eskadra Wywiadowcza, piloted by por. Boleslaw Lepszy, overturned on landing at Lwów Lewandówka Airfield.** *(T. Goworek)*

Poland

For Poland, the end of the First World War and the signing of the armistice meant that the nation was free after 123 years of occupation. Germany, Austria and Russia, the powers that had occupied Poland at the end of the 18th century, had been defeated or undergone revolution, but Poland now faced the task of defending its borders against the Czechoslovakians, Germans, Lithuanians, Russians and Ukrainians. Aviation units were among the first military forces established during November 1918. Based at the airfields taken from the previously occupying forces, these units' first operations started in November 1918, and by July 1919 the Polish Air Force comprised 15 *eskadras* (squadrons). By mid-1920 there were 20. Lack of aircraft was a major problem, and as there was no aviation industry in Poland it was necessary to purchase aircraft overseas. Among these was a quantity of Bristol Fighters bought from the Aircraft Disposal Company (ADC), a business run by Handley Page Ltd which held large stocks of surplus military aeroplanes.

Left and above: **Bristol F.2B 20.71 of 3 Pułk Lotniczy crashed at Poznan in 1925.** *(T. Goworek)*

Left: Photographed at Lwów on 10 June 1921, F.2B 20.24 was with 6 Eskadra Wywiadowcza, based at Luck. It had previously served with 10 Eskadra Wywiadowcza. (The late J.B. Cynk)

H5963) were allotted to the Polish Military Purchase Mission and despatched to Handley Page at Cricklewood ten days later. However, it transpired that the British would only let Poland buy Bristol Fighters powered by the 300hp Hispano-Suiza engine, because Falcon III production was totally taken up for British use. Consequently these aircraft were re-allotted to Inland Area for disposal on 19 April and were probably returned to storage at Henlow.

This meant that new flight tests were required, and these began in Paris on 26 April 1920, the aircraft being flown by Adam Haber-Wlynski. Although the machine's performance proved slightly inferior owing to the heavier engine, which increased its overall weight by nearly 175lb (80kg), this version was deemed acceptable. The problematic negotiations caused some delay, but an initial contract for 75 aircraft for £101,250 (£126,707 with spares) was signed on 10 June 1920. This was followed on 14 August 1920 by another for 30 more, and 60 engines were ordered on 22 September. This brought the total to 105 machines, the total value of the three contracts being £185,930. All of the aircraft had been delivered by the end of the year.

At one point Poland was informed that it would receive ten Puma-powered Bristol F.2Bs as part of an Imperial Gift, but as the negotiations with Handley Page were already at an advanced stage, these were replaced by de Havilland D.H.9s.

Above: Bristol F.2B 20.43 of 5 Eskadra Wywiadowcza at Przemyśl Airfield in May 1921. (The late J.B. Cynk)

On 1 December 1919 a team of Handley Page engineers arrived in Gdansk with two Falcon-powered Bristol Fighters powered by the 275hp Rolls-Royce Falcon III, one being F4409, and two Royal Aircraft Factory S.E.5as to serve as demonstration aircraft. These were shown and demonstrated to a Polish commission at Warsaw-Mokotów Airfield on 9 January 1920, and trial flights by Polish pilots proved that the aircraft was fast enough and very manoeuvrable. On the following day an intention to purchase 50 Bristol Fighters was announced, the number being increased to 125 on 18 January. The type's good performance was confirmed in further test flights on 14 January, when the virtues of its strong undercarriage and ease of landing were praised in view of Poland's poor terrain and under-trained pilots.

Initially, on 15 March 1920, ten aircraft in storage at No.5 (Eastern) ARD at Henlow (E2089, E2093, E2655, E2656, E5282, H1010, H1038, H5952, H5960 and

The two F.2Bs left behind at Mokotów by the ADC team in January 1920 were the first of their kind to enter Polish service. Initially they were still the property of Handley Page and could not be used by the Polish Air Force, so they were probably disassembled and stored at the Centralne Składy Lotnicze (CSL: Central Aircraft Depot). However, on 1 May 1920 Maj Aleksander Serednicki, Head of Field Aviation, asked the Minister of Military Affairs to arrange for them to be purchased by the Polish Government, and this was done early in July. Received from the British on 5 July 1920, F4409 was given the Polish military serial 20.1 at the Centralne Warsztaty Lotnicze (CWL: Central Aircraft Works). The other one (British serial unknown) was to be assembled between 10 and 25 July as 20.2. They were the only Polish Air Force F.2Bs to have Falcon IIIs.

F.2B 20.48 of 1 Eskadra Wywiadowcza, seen on the forward airfield at Dojlidy, near Bialystok, on 24 September 1920, is unusual in retaining its original British military serial number, H1279, on its rear fuselage. The crew are ppor. pil. Gustaw Gwizdalski and ppor. Obs. Ignacy Skorobohaty. (The late J.B. Cynk)

The first shipment of Hispano-Suiza-powered Bristol Fighters arrived by sea at Gdansk about 20 July and were shipped to Warsaw, where they were immediately erected, despite a lack of documentation. This was necessitated by the extremely difficult military situation, with Bolshevik armies approaching Warsaw and Lwów and threatening the newly formed Polish state. The 105 aircraft were to receive the serials 20.3 to 20.107 (the latter being the highest number recorded). They were used in the fighter, bomber and, primarily, ground-attack roles. Their observers' Lewis machine-guns were built under licence by Darne in France, and they were fitted with various items of equipment from Polish stocks, such as propellers manufactured by CWL, French radio sets and German Parabellum machine-guns.

The Polish Air Force suffered from a devastating shortage of equipment, having no more than 50 serviceable aircraft. The first two Fighters assembled at the CWL, 20.1 and 20.2, saw action even before they were allocated to any *eskadra*. On 5 and 6 August ppor. pil. Antoni Mroczkowski, with kpt. pil. Julian Słoniewski as observer, flew 20.1 on the first combat sorties, reconnoitring and strafing Bolshevik troops in the Wyszków and Ostrów Mazowiecka areas.

On 6 August Pilot Ppor. Stefan Żochowski of 16 Eskadra and 17 Eskadra observer ppor. Stefan Jeznach, flying in 20.2, were detailed to bomb Bolshevik troops at Ostrów, northwest of Warsaw. Żochowski had never previously flown the type and had not been instructed in the use of the variable-incidence tailplane to adjust the aircraft's longitudinal stability. The aircraft was overloaded with German bombs carried in observer's cockpit, and the aircraft, spun in and crashed on take-off. Both crew members were killed when the bombs exploded.

On the following day 20.1's engine malfunctioned and the pilot force-landed near the front line northwest of Warsaw, and crashed. Its crew, por. pil. Jan Matecki and plut. Franciszek Suchos, a 16 Eskadra observer, returned to safety uninjured.

Combat eskadra had now started to receive F.2Bs. First to receive the type was 10 Eskadra Wywiadowcza (11 aircraft), followed by 1 Eskadra Wywiadowcza (8) and 9 Eskadra Wywiadowcza (8). After brief conversion to their new mount the pilots started to go into action; 10 Eskadra on 7 August, followed by 1 and 9 Eskadra Wywiadowcza on 14 August.

In the fighting around Warsaw during August each Bristol-equipped eskadra flew thirty to forty sorties mainly comprising attacks on Bolshevik troops at Ostrów, Radzymin, Pułtusk, Ciechanów and, from 17 August, in the areas of Minsk Mazowiecki, Wegrów, Sokołów and Drohiczyn.

During September and October 1920 1 and 10 Eskadra participated in the victorious Battle of Niemen, 1 Eskadra being assigned to the 2nd Army, and 10 Eskadra to the 4th Army. Meanwhile, 9 Eskadra flew dozens of sorties in Wolyn in support of the3rd Army.

The Bolsheviks shot down only two Polish Bristol Fighters. The first, 20.12 of 9 Eskadra Lotnicza, was brought down on 17 August 1920 while attacking a Bolshevik column at Minsk Mazowiecki. After the ensuing forced landing the crew, pchor. pil.

At Deblin airfield on 24 April 1928 flying instructor sierz. Stanislaw Rybak and pupil sierz. Pchor. Jozef Szneider lost their lives when they crashed in F.2B 20.98 of Oficerska Szkoła Lotnictwa. It was the last fatal Bristol Fighter accident in Poland.

Jan Neumann and ppor. obs. Marian Sioda, were shooting at approaching enemy soldiers when the observer was wounded. He ordered his pilot to run, but was himself taken prisoner. Fortunately he spent only two days in captivity before he was released by Polish troops entering Otwock, near Warsaw.

On 18 August 1920 20.3, with a 10 Eskadra crew comprising kpr. pil. Eryk Szwencer and ppor. obs. Eugeniusz Tromszczynski, was shot down while attacking Bolshevik troops at Sokołów. The occupants escaped unharmed when the aircraft overturned on landing and hid in woods. They returned to their Eskadra on the following day. Although the retreating Bolsheviks failed to destroy the aircraft, they removed the observer's machine gun and three magazines and cut off the crews' harness.

During the war three F.2Bs were lost in crashes. The first, on 6 August in Warsaw, cost the lives of ppor. Żochowski and ppor. Jeznach. Then, on 16 September, sierz pil. Karol Biel and ppor. obs. Zygmunt Bem of 10 Eskadra, in 20.33, were killed at Brzesc nad Bugiem. On 25 September sierz. Jakub Kierojczyk, the pilot, and kpt. pil. Julian Słoniewski, the 9 Eskadra commander who was flying as observer, crashed in 20.18 while landing at Luck and lost their lives.

During the Polish-Bolshevik war 40 Bristols were used in combat by the Polish Air Force, 38 of these being assigned to 1, 9 and 10 Eskadras. When the war ended only 11 serviceable aircraft remained in these units, many having been damaged in forced landings owing to engine failures, usually a result of using incorrect petrol or water-polluted fuel. On 15 October 1920 20.49 of 9 Eskadra became the only F.2B to be captured by the Bolsheviks when it force-landed at Olesko, in enemy territory, owing to poor fuel. Its crew, kpt. pil. Bolesław Narkowicz, CO of 9 Eskadra, and ppor.

obs. Jan Latawiec, successfully evaded the enemy and returned to their unit. The aircraft, one of two Bristol Fighters used by the Soviets, was subsequently repaired and became the personal mount of I.U. Pavlov, commanding the 1st Soviet Combat Fighter Aviation Group. The fuselage bore his personal emblem, a skull with a bayonet in its teeth, beneath the motto *Gibel pobyezhdennym* (Death to the defeated). The fate of the other Soviet F.2B is unknown.

Before the war's end the Aviation HQ decided that two more Eskadra, 2 and 5, should convert to the Bristol Fighter. Stationed at Przemyśl, 5 Eskadra received its first two aircraft, 20.37 and 20.43, on 16 September 1920, and seven more (20.35, 20.36, 20.38, 20.39, 20.41, 20.42 and 20.44) on 27 September. The unit failed to reach combat capability before the war's end, partly because some of the aircraft lacked propellers owing to a delayed shipment from Britain. Based at Deblin in October 1920, 2 Eskadra, did not receive its F.2Bs (20.52, 20.56, 20.59, 20.60, 20.61, 20.64 and 20.68) until after the armistice with the Bolsheviks, on 12 October 1920.

Wartime experience only slightly modified the original opinions of the Bristol Fighter. Summarising the strengths and weaknesses of the aircraft types used by his unit, 1 Eskadra i Lotnicza, CO kpt. pil. Augustyn Domes wrote that while the Bristol Fighter had many of the advantages of the unit's other type, the Salmson 2A2, it was absolutely free of many of the French machine's shortcomings. He said it was a perfect example of a multi-role aircraft, incapable of long-range reconnaissance only because it lacked bigger tanks, or of bombardment because it lacked the weight-carrying capacity. Owing to the strong slipstream and the aircraft shuddering, it was not quite suited to aerial photography as the negatives were rarely sharp. It was best suited, he said, to short-range reconnaissance

and, because it was very fast and manoeuvrable and able to perform all manner of aerobatics and climb steeply, it was the perfect aircraft for attacks and even for dogfights. Its good armament ensured successful results in both instances, and the simple and direct communication between pilot and observer greatly facilitated any mission.

Domes added that the aircraft was very pleasant and easy to handle and did not require much space for take-off and landing. However, while the Hispano-Suiza engine was essentially very good, it often failed, which caused frequent forced landings.

Immediately after the Bolshevik War the F.2B equipped five eskadras, but by 18 January 1921 the total number of eskadras had been reduced in accordance with orders from the Supreme Command by combining units. Eskadra 1 and 2 formed the new 1 Eskadra, while 9 and 10 became the new 10 Eskadra. These two new units, together with 5 Eskadra, comprised the VII Dywizjon Wywiadowczy (a unit of 2-5 eskadras) of 3 Pułk Lotniczy (Air Regiment) at Poznan.

The Bristol Fighter gave lengthy service as the principal aircraft of the reconnaissance eskadras in 3 Pułk Lotniczy, its useful life being prolonged by general overhauls in the Pułk workshops from 1921. In September 1923 the design office of the Warsztaty Centralnych Zakładów Lotniczych (WCZL: Workshops of the Central Aircraft Works) in Warsaw developed a method of stiffening the fuselage structure in the region of the pilot's cockpit, its weakest area, by inserting 5mm plywood panels in the 3rd and 4th bays. this virtually eliminated the fuselage fractures which had hitherto occurred whenever an aircraft overturned on landing. As a result, the Bristol Fighter served as a front-line aircraft with 3 Pułk Lotniczy until its replacement by the Potez XV in mid-1925. In early February 1926 the Pułk still had 55 F.2Bs in storage, including four that were earmarked to be written off. After inspections in the spring of 1926 several machines were made serviceable again and went to the Eskadra Treningowa (advanced training squadron) of the Pułk.

The remaining aircraft were transferred to flying schools, where the type had been in use from late 1920. At Torun, the Oficerska Szkoła Obserwatorów Lotniczych (OSOL: Officers' School for Air Observers) used them to train observers, and the Wyższa Szkoła Pilotów (WSP: Advanced Pilots' School) at Grudziadz used them for flying training. In November 1925 the WSP was re-formed into the Oficerska Szkoła Lotnicza (OSL: Air Officers' School), and after this unit moved to Deblin in April 1927 the Lotnicza Szkoła Strzelania i Bombardowania (LSSiB: Air School of Gunnery and Bombardment) was established at Grudziadz. Thus, by the end of 1925, a number of Bristols reached

Deblin. The rest were kept by the LSSiB for bombing and air gunnery training, and for target towing, until early 1930s. Like those serving at Deblin, these aircraft were most usually equipped with twin Vickers Type F machine-guns in the observer's cockpit.

The Grudziadz school's Bristols were withdrawn around 1930 and transferred to the Szkoła Podchorazych Lotnictwa (SPL: Aviation Cadet Officers' School), established at Deblin in 1928 from the previous OSL. This school was Poland's last user of the type. In mid-1929 it had 29, only some of which were serviceable. On 1 April 1931 there were 47 Bristol Fighters in Poland, of which ten were serviceable (eight at Deblin).

Of the other 37, 20 were disassembled and in storage and 17 more were waiting to be written-off owing to damage or wear. Poland's last working Bristol Fighters were used for air gunnery training at Deblin until they were withdrawn from use in the autumn of 1932.

Polish Bristol Fighters: Individual Histories

20.1 (ex-F4409) (Falcon III) Arrived CWL from UK 5.7.20; delivered war front 1.8.20. Engine failure on operational sortie; forced-landed and crashed near front line northwest of Warsaw 7.8.20, por. Pil. Jan Matecki and plut. Franciszek Suchos of 16 Esk both unhurt.

20.2 (Falcon III) Assembled CWL 10-25.7.20; delivered war front 1.8.20. Took off from Warsaw Mokotów with heavy bomb load to bomb Bolshevik troops at Ostrów, northwest of Warsaw; spun and crashed, and bombs exploded, causing casualties among people nearby, Warsaw 6.8.20; ppor. pil. Stefan Żochowski of 16 Esk & ppor. obs. Stefan Jeznach of 17 Esk both killed.

20.3 (from here onwards all had 300hp Hispano-Suiza) Delivered 10 Esk 6.8.20. Shot down while attacking Bolshevik troops at Sokołów and overturned. 18.8.20 (kpr. pil. Eryk Szwencer & ppor. obs. Eugeniusz Tromszczyòski evaded capture). Abandoned by the Bolsheviks, taken for repair to CWL 26.8.20; 10 Esk 31.10.20; SL Bydgoszcz 1921.

20.4 Delivered 10 Esk 3.8.20; serviceable 18.10.20; 10 Esk, burnt in a Bessonneau hangar fire at Baranowicze, 25.11.20.

20.5 Delivered 10 Esk 3.8.20; crashed on test flight after repair, Warsaw Mokotów 1.8.22 (pilot kpt. Stefan Pawlikowski and fitter sierz. Ludwik Schultz). Delivered 10 Esk 8.8.20. Ret'd CWL 1.9.20; OSOL 10.12.28-30.1.29; CWL 10.10.29; OSL by 1930.

20.6 Delivered CSL to 10 Esk 3.8.20; Ret'd CWL 12.8.20; CWL 31.10.20-20.3.21; 10 Esk 20.6.21; 3 PL/1 EW 4.8.22; CWL as GI less skin 31.5.29.

20.7 Delivered 10 Esk 7.8.20; Ret'd CWL 7.8.20-31.10.20; OSL by 1928/9; CWL 10.10.29.

20.8 Delivered CSL to 10 Esk 4.8.20. Damaged before 17.9.20; 10 Esk 31.10.20.

20.9 Delivered CSL to 10 Esk 4.8.20. Damaged engine 26.9.20, sent back to IV Ruchomy park Lotniczy (RPL: Mobile aircraft park); 10 Esk to 10.1.21; WSP 31.7.22; OSL 1928/9; CWL 10.10.29.

20.10 Delivered 10 Esk 8.8.20; Damaged engine 26.9.20, sent back to IV RPL; CWL/CSL 31.1.21-20.4.21; WSP c.1922; 3 Pułk Lotniczy (PL: Air Regiment) Training Section 25.7.22-1924; OSL 1928/9; CWL 10.10.29.

20.11 (ex-E2713) Delivered 9 Esk 9.8.20. Damaged 5.9.20; still there 20.11.20; CWL 21.1.21; OSL by 30.1.29.

20.12 (ex-H1357) Delivered 9 Esk 14.8.20. Shot down attacking Bolshevik column at Minsk Mazowiecki, 17.8.20 (pchor pil. Jan Neumann evaded capture; ppor. obs. Marian Sioda shot and wounded on ground and taken PoW but released after two days by Polish troops entering Otwock). Aircraft recovered and repaired by CWL; 3 PL, crashed in ground test in Biedrusko, near Poznan, 29.8.23.

20.13 (ex-H913) Delivered 9 Esk 15.8.20. Propeller and radiator shot through by accident 30.8.20; damaged 5.9.20; 10 Esk 20.11.20.

20.14 (ex-H1353) CSL technical reception/acceptance 16.4.20; 5 Esk, crashed Poznan-Lawica 12.1.23 (kpt pil. Eugeniusz Pluszczewski killed and por. obs. Jan Szunejko seriously injured).

20.15 Delivered CWL; Cat. 1 repair 18.9.20. 1 Eskadra Wywiadowcza (EW: reconnaissance squadron), crashed 24.9.20; Cat. 2 repair 23.12.20.

20.16 (ex-E2734) Delivered 10 Esk 12.8.20-30.4.21; IV RPL 5.10.20; 1 Esk, accident 9.5.21; 3 PL/18 Esk 4.8.22. (The only identified radio-equipped Bristol Fighter.)

20.17 (ex-E2223) Delivered 9 Esk 10.8.20; serviceable 18.10.20. With 9 Esk until 20.6.21; 3 PL/1 Esk 18.7.22; Section IC RPL by 1924; OSL storage by 2.27-5.27.

20.18 (ex-E2695) Delivered 9 Esk 10.8.20. Crashed on landing 25.9.20 (sierz. pil. Jakub Kieroyczyk and kpt pil. Julian Sloniewski both killed).

20.19 Delivered 10 Esk 12.8.20; damaged before 10.9.20. Left 10 Esk 20.11.20; OSL 1928; SPL 13.6.30; CWOL 9.9.30, change of category, possibly to GI.

20.20 (ex-H975) Delivered 9 Esk 13.8.20; damaged 15.8.20. With 9 Esk until 20.11.20; CWL 23.12.20.

20.21 (ex-H1355) Delivered CWL to 1 Esk 12.8.20; damaged c. 25.9.20; Cat. 2 repair 18.12.20; Still 1 Esk 1923.

20.22 (ex-H1352) Delivered CWL to 1 Esk 13.8.20. Crashed 26.8.20 (ppor. Babinski); repaired; OSL by 1928/9; CWOL 10.10.29.

20.23 (ex-H1356) Delivered CWL 13.8.20; 1 Esk 18.8.20; damaged Mokotów 18.8.20 (ppor. Wiltsch). 10 Esk 10.10.20; OSL 10.12.28-30.1.29; CWOL 24.5.29-10.10.29.

20.24 (ex-H920) Delivered 10 Esk 12.8.20; damaged before 10.9.20. Left 10 Esk 31.10.20, III RPL 10.11.20-3.1.21; 10 Esk by 10.6.21; 1 PL/18 EW 17.8.22; crashed 6.23; repaired; OSL 1928; OSL 10.10.29.

20.25 (ex-H983) Delivered CSL to 1 Esk 15.8.20; damaged before 18.10.20. CWL 7.11.20; 3 PL, crashed, Poznan, 27.10.24 (kpr pil. Ignacy Zmuda and por. obs. Jan Wajda killed).

20.26 Delivered 1 Esk 13.8.20; nosed over on landing, autumn 1920. Serviceable 18.10.20. Left 1 Esk 10.1.21; OSL by 1928; CWL 10.10.29-1930.

20.27 (ex-H1354) Delivered 1 Esk 14.8.20; damaged c.1.10.20. CWL/CSL 8.11.20-20.4.21.

20.28 (ex-H1273) CSL 11.9.20; 10 Esk (32 Esk) 1924/5; OSL 1928/9; CWOL 18.6.29 (repair?); CWOL 30.9.29; still on strength 10.10.29.

20.29 (ex-H974) Delivered 1 Esk 15.8.20; crashed before 24.9.20. CWL 17.1.21; Esk Treningowa of 3 PL in 1926; 32 Esk, crashed Poznan 24.9.27 (por. pil. Ferdynand Pichler died of injuries 20.12.27).

20.30 (ex-H1358) Delivered 9 Esk 13.8.20. Serviceable 18.10.20. Left 9 Esk 20.6.21; 3 PL/1 EW 4.8.22; OSL 1928/9; CWOL – SOC 24.8.29.

20.31 (ex-H1351) Delivered CWL 14.8.20; 1 Esk, crashed 24.9.20. CWL 22.2.21; 10 Esk 20.6.21; 3 PL/18 EW 4.8.22.

20.32 (ex-H1360) Delivered 9 Esk 15.8.20; crashed Łuck 11.12.20 (ppor. pil. Seweryn Sacewicz killed and por.obs. Jan Latawiec seriously injured).

20.33 (ex-H1350) Delivered CSL 14.9.20; 10 Esk, crashed at Brzesc nad Bugiem on return from combat sortie 16.9.20 (sierz. pil. Karol Biel & ppor. obs. Zygmunt Bem killed); still with 10 Esk 31.10.20.

20.34 (ex-H972) Delivered CSL 1.9.20; 10 Esk 14.9.20; engine trouble, forced landing, crashed 30.9.20; 10 Esk, burnt in Bessonneau hangar fire at Baranowicze 25.11.20.

20.35 (ex-H915) Delivered CWL 11.9.20; 5 Esk 27.9.20?; 9 Esk 10.11.20-20.1.21; OSL 1928; CWOL 10.10.29-1930.

20.36 (ex-H1277) Delivered CWL 11.9.20; 5 Esk 27.9.20 [10.11.20?]-20.6.21; OSL 2.27-5.27.

20.37 (ex-E5217) Delivered 12.9.20; 5 Esk 16.9.20 [10.11.20?]-20.1.21; OSL 1928; CWOL 10.10.29.

20.38 (ex-H916) Delivered CSL 11.9.20; 5 Esk 27.9.20; nosed over on landing, Lwów Lewandówka, 13.10.20; repaired. OSL 1928/9; LSSiB 15.10.29.

20.39 (ex-H1278) Delivered CSL 11.9.20; 9 Esk 31.10.20; 5 Esk 10.11.20-28.8.21; 3 PL/5 Esk by 28.8.21.

20.40 (ex-H973) Delivered CSL 25.9.20; 5 Esk 1.11.20-20.6.20; 3 PL storage 20.7.21-28.8.21.

20.41 (ex-H1272) Delivered CSL 27.9.20; 5 Esk 10.11.20-31.7.21; 3 PL by 28.8.21; 3 PL from 30.11.26-1927.

20.42 (ex-H1270) Delivered CSL 16.9.20; 5 Esk [27.9.20?] 10.11.20-20.6.21; Park 3 PL 25.7.21; 3 PL/5 Esk by 28.8.21.

20.43 (ex-H979) Delivered CSL 14.9.20; 5 Esk 16.9.20 [10.11.20-20.1.21]; III RPL 20.6.21; 5 Esk 30.6.21; 3 PL by 8.21.

20.44 (ex-H1274) Delivered CSL 14.9.20; 5 Esk 27.9.20 [10.11.20-20.6.21]; 3 PL/5 Esk 4.8.22.

20.45 (ex-H911) Delivered CSL by 16.9.20; 9 Esk 18.11.20-10.11.21; 10 Esk 20.7.21; Park 3 PL 31.7.22.

20.46 (ex-H918) Delivered CWL 23.9.20; 9 Esk 18.11.20-10.11.21; 10 Esk 20.7.21; Park 3 PL 31.7.22; 3 PL 28.8.21.

20.47 (ex-H919) Delivered CSL 16.9.20; 1 Esk 16.9.20; serviceable 18.10.20. WSP, crashed Grudziadz 3.11.21 (por. pil. Aleksander Wojciechowski killed).

20.48 (ex-H1279) Delivered CSL 16.9.20; 1 Esk 16.9.20; hit by ground fire 24.9.20 (por. pil. Wacław Makowski and Lt Robert Vanderauvera (Belgian volunteer) both injured). Serviceable 18.10.20-10.1.21; 10 Esk 30.4.21; 1 Esk 30.4.21; 1 Esk 20.6.21; 3 PL/1 Esk 4.8.22; 3 PL 1923.

20.49 (ex-H971) Delivered CSL 20.9.20; 9 Esk 7.10.20; forced-landed in enemy territory owing to poor fuel and captured, 15.10.20 (kpt. pil. Bolesław Narkowicz and ppor. obs. Jan Latawiec evaded capture). Repaired and flown by the Soviet Russian Air Fleet up to at least 1924.

20.50 (ex-H912) Delivered CSL 20.9.20; 10 Esk 2.10.20; damaged between 10 and 18.10.20; CWL 17.1.21.

20.51 9 Esk by 20.11.20-10.1.21; 10 Esk 20.6.21; 3 PL/10 Esk 28.8.21; Park 3 PL 27.6.22. Reportedly ex-H1310, but this is doubtful, probably being based on a photograph with Polish marking on top of rudder stripes showing c/n 92222 and serial H...2. Possibly confused with 20.41 above.

20.52 (ex-H1367) Delivered CSL 28.9.20; 2 Esk 28.10.20-20.11.21; OSL by 1928; CWOL 10.10.29; LSSiB 1930.

20.53 (ex-H1366) Delivered CSL on or by 28.9.20; CWL 2-5.1.21; 1 Esk 20.6.21.

20.54 (ex-E5229) Delivered CSL 25.9.20; 1 Esk 18.10.20-10.1.21; 10 Esk 30.4.21; 3 PL/10 Esk 28.8.21-4.8.22.

20.55 (ex-H1331) Delivered CSL 20.9.20; CWL 16.11.20-10.3.21; 10 Esk 20.7.21; 3 PL Park 20.7.22 (to storage after repair); 3 PL Szkoła Obserwatorów Lotniczych (SOL: flying school) 1924.

20.56 (ex-H1379) Delivered CSL 28.9.20; 2 Esk 21.10.20-20.1.21; 10 Esk 30.4.21; 1 Esk 20.6.21; 3 PL/Park 20.7.22 (repair/overhaul).

20.57 (ex-H1301) Delivered CSL 2.10.20; CWL 15.1.21; 10 Esk 1924.

20.58 (ex-H1373) Delivered CSL 30.9.20; 10 Esk 2.10.20; serviceable 18.10.20. Burnt in the Bessonneau hangar fire at Baranowicze, 25.11.20.

20.59 (ex-H1368) Delivered CSL 28.9.20; 2 Esk 25.10.20-20.1.21; CWL/CSL 30.1.21-31.3.21; 20 Esk 30.4.21; 1 Esk 20.6.21; 3 PL/1 Esk 28.8.21-4.8.22; Training Section 3 PL 1924/7; 3 PL reserve storage 30.11.28; OSL by 1929; LSSiB 15.10.29; Deblin 1930.

20.60 (ex-H1308) Delivered CSL 28.9.20; 2 Esk 10.20-1921; 3 PL/1 Esk 4.8.22; 30.7.24 accident due to engine failure, kpr. pil. Lowak and por. obs. Wolski both seriously injured.

20.61 (ex-H1364) Delivered CSL 30.9.20; 2 Esk 19.10.20-20.1.21.

20.62 (ex-H1361) Delivered CSL 23.9.20; 10 Esk 2.10.20; serviceable 18.10.20. Burnt in Bessonneau hangar fire at Baranowicze 25.11.20; IV RPL 10.1.21; CWL SOC 13.4.21.

20.63 (ex-H1307) Delivered CSL 23.9.20; 1 Esk by 18.10.20-30.12.20.

20.64 (ex-H1388) Delivered CSL 23.9.20; 2 Esk 23.10.20-20.1.21; 10 Esk 30.4.21; 1 Esk 20.6.21; 3 PL Park 20.7.21 (repair/overhaul).

20.65 (ex-H1304) Deld CSL 28.9.20; 2 Esk 10.10.20-20.1.21; 10 Esk 30.4.21; 1 Esk by 3.21; 1 Esk 20.6.21; WSP 20.8.22.

20.66 No information.

20.67 OSL by 1928; CWOL 10.10.29.

20.68 2 Esk from or by 29.10.20-20.1.21; 10 Esk 30.4.21; 1 Esk 20.5.21; 3 PL/1 Esk 28.8.21.

20.69 WSP, collided with Albatros B.II 2577/17 on landing, Grudziadz 22.3.22 (st. szer. Wacek).

20.70 No information.

20.71 (ex-H1295) Delivered CSL 27.10.20; Crashed; 3 PL, crashed, Poznan aerodrome, 29 August 1923; also crashed there 1925.

20.72 OSOL – as GI 1928.

20.73 (ex-E9652) Delivered CSL 27.10.20; 3 PL 1923/4; 4 PL damage report 17.5.27.

20.74 3 PL/1 Esk 4.8.22; 10 Esk (32 Esk) 1926; OSL 10.12.28; CWOL 10.10.29.

20.75 3 PL/1 Esk 4.8.22; Training Section 3 PL 1924/5; 4 PL to Morski Dywizjon Lotniczy 1926; OSL 1928; CWOL, SOC 24.8.29.

20.76 (ex-H1305) Delivered CSL 29.10.20; 3 PL/1 Esk 1922; 10 Esk (32 Esk) 1926; OSL 1928; CWOL 10.10.29 ca. 1929; collided with 20.77.

20.77 (ex-H1296) Delivered CSL 27.10.20; 4 PL 23.5.24; OSL 1928; CWOL 10.10.29 ca. 1929; collided with 20.76.

20.78 (ex-H1275) Delivered CSL 29.10.20; 3 PL Park to 1 EW/3 PL 15.3.22 after repair/overhaul, with a cage for a message pigeon; range trials with the pigeon 4.8.22; 3 PL 1924; pigeon tests at Poznan, winter 1924.

20.79 OSL 1928; OWOL 10.10.29-1930.

20.80 3 PL/1 Esk 4.8.22; 3 PL 1923; OSL to 12.4.29.

20.81 (ex-H1288) Delivered CSL 11.11.209; 3PL/1 Esk 4.8.22.

20.82 (ex-H1284) Delivered CSL 11.11.20.

20.83 WSP 31.8.22.

20.84 WSP 20.8.22-1923.

20.85 (ex-H949) Delivered CSL 26.11.20; 3 PL/1 Esk 4.8.22.

20.86 (ex-H898) Delivered CSL 23.11.20; 3 PL Training Section 3.7.22; OSL 1928; CWOL 10.10.29.

20.87 Delivered CSL 15.3.21; CWL 20.3.21; 10 Esk 20.6.21.

20.88 (ex-H961) Delivered CSL 27.11.20; OSL Training Company as GI 20.6.28.

20.89 3 PL/1 Esk 4.8.22; 3 PL in reserve storage for Department of Aeronautics 30.11.27; LLSiB 15.10.29.

20.90 WSP 31.7.22.

20.91 3 PL storage park 15.4.26 (converted into a coffin carrier for ceremonial funerals of airmen).

20.92 3 PL in reserve storage for Department of Aeronautics 30.11.28; LSSiB 15.10.29; to be SOC 6.11.29.

20.93 (ex-H954) Delivered CSL 26.11.20.

20.94 3 PL 20.4.23-30.11.28 (reserve storage for Department of Aeronautics); LSSiB 15.10.29.

20.95 3 PL/1 Esk 4.8.22.

20.96 (ex-H1287) Delivered CSL 2.12.20; OSL 1928; CWOL 10.10.29; OSL by 1930.

20.97 (ex-H1297) Delivered CSL: 2.12.20; CWL storage 2.12.20; Training Section 3 PL 1924.

20.98 10 Esk 3.21 and 20.6.21; Park 3 PL 27.6.22; OSL, crashed, Deblin, 24.4.28 (sierz. pil. Stanisláv Rybak and sierz. pchor. student pilot Józef Szneider both killed).

20.99 Park 3 PL 21.6.22; 3 PL/1 Esk 4.8.22; OSL by 1928; CWOL 10.10.29-1930.

20.100 (ex-H1385) Delivered CSL 2.12.20; CWL storage 2.12.20; OSL 1928; CWOL, SOC 24.8.29.

20.101 (ex-H956) 9 Esk 11.11.20; CSL 21.12.20; Park 3 PL 20.7.22; OSL 1928/9 SPL 5.6.29; CWOL 10.10.29.

20.102 3 PL/Park 8.7.22; 3 PL/1 Esk 4.8.22.

20.103 10 Esk 3.21; LSSiB 1928-15.3.30.

20.104 10 Esk (32 Esk) 1924/5; CWOL 30.9.29.

20.105 (ex-H964) Delivered CSL 17.12.20; 1 Esk 20.6.21; 3 PL/1 Esk 28.8.21.

20.106 10 Esk 3.21/20.6.21; 3 PL/10 Esk 28.8.21; 3 PL 1922; 10 Esk, engine failed at 40m (130ft) on take-off; spun into ground, Poznan-Ławica, 25.9.23 (por. pil. Adam Swida of 10 Esk and fitter szer. Jozef Zachosc of 1 Esk both killed).

20.107 No information other than number mentioned in a document.

Unidentified

16.3.23 10 Esk, crashed Poznan (por. pil. Roman Marcinkiewicz killed).

10.8.23 1 Esk, crashed Poznan (por. pil. Stanisláv Korab-Kowalski & szer. mech. Antoni Wołoczko killed).

2.10.23 3 PL, crashed Poznan (por. Flaszynski and por. Bajan both safe)

6.5.24 WSP (por. Gawronski)

Units and Bases

Centrum Wyszkolenia Oficerów Lotnictwa, Deblin

1 Eskadra Wywiadowcza – Mokotów (Warsaw) c.8.20; Białystok c.9.20; Absorbed 2 Esk 1.21.

2 Eskadra Wywiadowcza – Deblin c.10.20; Absorbed by 1 Esk 1.21.

5 Eskadra Wywiadowcza – Przemyśl from 9.20–1921.

9 Eskadra Wywiadowcza – Mokotów (Warsaw) c.8.20; Chełm Lubelski c.9.20; Łuck c.12.20; Absorbed by 10 Esk 1.21.

10 Eskadra Wywiadowcza – Brzesc c.9.20; Lwów Lewandówka c.6.21; Absorbed 9 Esk 1.21 Kraków; Poznan-Ławica from c. 5.21; renumbered 32 Esk in 1925.

16 Eskadra Wywiadowcza – Kraków c.8.20; Wilno c. 1.21; Kraków c. 3.21.

32 Eskadra – formed 1925 at Poznan-Ławica by renumbering 10 Esk.

Lotnicza Szkoła Strzelania i Bombardowania – Formed 4.27 at Grudziadz [bombing and air gunnery training]; Bristol Fighters withdrawn c.1930

Morski Dywizjon Lotniczy (Naval Air Squadron) Puck (near Gdansk)

Oficerska Szkoła Lotnicza – Formed from WSP 11.25 at Grudziadz; to Deblin 4.27; Became SPL 1928

Oficerska Szkoła Obserwatorów Lotniczych – Toron [observer training]

3 Pułk Lotniczy – Ławica (Poznan) 1921–1923, replaced by Potez XV in 1925.

4 Pułk Lotniczy – Torun.

III RPL – Lwów.

IV RPL – Brzesc Litewski.

SOL – Warsaw – Mokotów (formed 1919).

II SOL – Poznan – Ławica (formed c. 5.20).

Szkoła Podchorazych Lotnictwa – Formed in 1928 from OSL at Deblin; became part of CWOL in 1929; Bristols withdrawn autumn 1932.

Wyższa Szkoła Pilotów – Grudziadz c.1922 [advanced flying training]; re-formed into OSL 11.25.

VII Dywizjon Wywiadowczy – Formed 1.21 of 3 Pułk Loniczy (comprised 'new' 1 and 10 Esk).

Abbreviations etc [military ranks (e. g. 'por.') and trades (e. g. 'pil.') in lower case]

CSL	Centralne Sklady Lotnicze (Central Aircraft Depot, Warsaw)	pchor.	Podchorazy (Cadet Officer)
CWL	Centralne Warsztaty Lotnicze (Central Aircraft Works, Warsaw)	pil.	pilot
		PL	Pułk Lotniczy (Air Regiment)
CWOL	Centrum Wyszkolenia Oficerów Lotnictwa (Air Force Officers' Training Centre, Deblin)	plut.	plutonowy (Platoon commander = Corporal)
		por	porucznik (Lieutenant = Flying Officer)
Esk.	Eskadra (roughly equivalent to a Flight)	ppor	podporucznik (Sub-lieutenant = Pilot Officer)
ET	Eskadra Treningowa (Training Flight)	RPL	Ruchomy Park Lotniczy (mobile aircraft storage park)
EW	Eskadra Wywiadowcza (Reconnaissance Flight)	sierz	sierzant (Sergeant)
kpr.	kapral (Aircraftman)	SL	Szkoła Lotnicza (Flying School)
kpt.	kapitan (Captain = Flight Lieutenant)	SOL	Szkoła Obserwatorów Lotniczych (School of Aircraft Maintenance)
LSSiB	Lotnicza Szkoła Strzelania i Bombardowania (School of Air Gunnery and Bombardment)	st.	starszy (Senior)
		st.sierz.	starszy sierzant (Senior Sergeant = Flight Sergeant)
mech.	mechanik (Mechanic)	szer.	szeregowy (Private = Aircraftsman)
obs.	obserwator (Observer)	WSP	Wyższa Szkola Pilotów (Advanced Pilots' School)
OSL	Oficerska Szkoła Lotnicza (Air Force Officers' School: became SPL, see above)		
OSOL	Oficerska Szkoła Obserwatorów Lotniczych (Officers' School of Air Observers)		

Romania

On 22 July 1921 a Mr S.A. Taylor, the Westinghouse Company's representative in Bucharest, signed a contact with the Romanian Government to supply 40 Puma-engined D.H.9s and 20 Rolls-Royce or Puma-engine Bristol F.2Bs at a price of £1,330 each, plus a quantity of spares valued at £40,904, a total of £120,750, the first instalment of £15,750 to be made by 15 September 1921. The aircraft were to be supplied from surplus RAF stocks, almost certainly those held by the ADC. It is questionable whether this contract was ever fully completed. [NTA file FO. 371/8932 refers.]

Russia

The only Polish Bristol Fighter to be captured by the Bolsheviks, No.20.49 of 9 Eskadra, forced-landed in enemy territory on 15 October 1920 owing to poor fuel. After being repaired it was flown by the Soviet Russian Air Fleet until at least 1924.

This aircraft has been mistakenly identified as ex-E2049.

Serbia

One F.2B was supplied to the Serbian Army in March 1923 with temporary British civil registration G-EBFD (ex-E2354). It was

flown there by Capt Norman Macmillan, as recounted in his book *Wings of Fate*.

Spain

Thirteen F.2Bs were supplied between August and December 1921 for military use but bearing civil-type registrations in the M-MR range. The F.2Bs were part of an order placed by the Spanish war office, which also included de Havilland D.H.4s and 9s, the aircraft being urgently required to counter the Riff rising in Spanish Morocco led by Ab-del-Krim. These aircraft, supplied by the Bristol Aeroplane Co Ltd, de Havilland Aircraft Co Ltd and the Aircraft Disposal Co Ltd, were flown from England to Madrid in Spain by a group of

ex-Service freelance pilots, as the suppliers found it quicker to erect the aircraft in England and deliver them by air than to crate, ship and rail them, and then erect and test them in Spain, where they were accepted. The aircraft left England with Spanish-language instrumentation and their Spanish registrations already applied.

The F.2Bs were flown from Bristol to Croydon or Lympne for Customs, then across the Channel by Folkestone-Gris Nez, where the pilots circled over a ground station to enable their aircraft to be recognised so that their safe arrival over France could be telephoned to Lympne. They then continued on via Le Bourget (Customs), the military aerodrome at Tours, Merignac-Bordeaux

Acquired from the Aircraft Disposal Co, M-MRAC went to Spain via Croydon on 7 September 1921. *(A.J. Jackson Collection at Brooklands Museum www.ajjcollection.co.uk)*

These four postcards pose something of a puzzle. They appear to be Spanish in origin, as 'Tarjeta Postal' is printed on their backs. The F.2B is probably F4466, which was tested at No.5 AAP at Bristol on 15 October 1918. Its Scarff ring has been removed and it has a union flag attached to its rudder, and it is apparently being used as a personal transport for the Flight Lieutenant in the rear cockpit, who has a leopard-skin flying helmet. The date, location, and reason for the visit are unknown. *(via Philip Jarrett)*

(Customs again), Lasarte-San Sebastian (Spanish Customs), across the Pyrenees to Burgos, and then across the Guadarrama mountains to Cuatro Vientos Aerodrome, Madrid. It has been recounted that the passage of the aircraft through France 'was not wholly popular', and that there was 'little alacrity in providing the essential petrol and oil at each stop'. Delays of several hours were the norm, more time being spent on the ground than in the air. However, the short stages were unavoidable, owing to the aircrafts' short endurance and relatively slow speed, the Hispano-engined F.2Bs cruising at about 110mph and having an endurance of about 2hr 40min at that speed, which meant they could cover somewhat less than 300 miles in still air.

At Lasarte, close to the foothills of the Pyrenees, the maximum possible ground run was only some 180 yards, and it is to the credit of the British pilots that not one of their machines was damaged there, even though their aircraft lacked the luxury of flaps and brakes. In fact, few machines crashed. It has been stated that one was written off in a clearing amid gum pines in the swamps of the Landes and two crashed near Bordeaux when their pilots were caught by nightfall, but others that were forced-landed were repaired by their pilots and flown on.

Above left: **Bristol F.2B M-MRAN is tanked up ready for its flight to Spain on 21 September 1921.** *(A.J. Jackson Collection at Brooklands Museum www.ajjcollection. co.uk)*

Left: **Hispano-engined F.2B M-MRAO taxying, probably at Croydon during its delivery flight to Spain on 22 September 1921.** *(Philip Jarrett)*

Photographed at Filton shortly after completion
and still awaiting its Spanish registration markings,
this is one of thirteen new F.2Bs built for Spain in
1921, powered by 300hp Hispano-Suiza engines.
(Bristol)

An excellent first-hand account by one of
the pilots, providing a vivid impression of
the vicissitudes encountered during these
flights, can be found in Capt Norman
Macmillan's book *Freelance Pilot*
(Heinemann, London, 1937). Macmillan
records that he ferried M-MRAK and
M-MRAG but does not provide dates. He
also states that 'less than a year later' H.B.
Richardson, another of the freelance pilots
who ferried Bristol Fighters to Spain, while
subsequently serving as an instructor with
the Army Flying Corps at Cuatro Vientos,
was killed in an F.2B crash along with two
other British pilots, Milne and Ortweiler,
who were flying with him as passengers.

For a brief period during 1922 Macmillan
served as a flying instructor at Quatro
Vientos, converting trainee pilots from the
ab initio Avro 504 to the more powerful
F.2B, using some F.2Bs which had been
converted to dual-control trainers by
Spanish engineers. Major Palanca, the
officer responsible for the technical side of
flying training at the base, had expressed
concern that accidents might occur owing to
a lack of rigidity in the aircraft's fuselages.
When Macmillan examined them he found
that, in the process of installing the dual
controls in the rear cockpits, an important

Right: **A Type 17A destined for Spain has its
propeller swung at Filton.** (Bristol)

Below: **One of the Type 17As of the later batch of
twelve for Spain approaches completion in a Filton
hangar in 1924.** (Bristol)

Left and below left: **This Type 17A in Spanish colours displays the stub exhausts of the 300hp Hispano-Suiza engine, the Frise balanced ailerons and the oleo-sprung undercarriage.** *(Bristol)*

cross-bracing had been removed to enable pupils to get their feet on the rudder bar, and that nothing had been substituted to take the loads. He designed an offset cross-bracing, fitted it to one F.2B and test-flew it himself. It proved satisfactory, and all the dual-control F.2Bs were similarly modified.

The Spanish Army in Morocco made extensive use of 15 Bristol Fighters in the early 1920s, and a further seven were used at Los Alcázares, near Cartagena, by the Escuela de Bombardo y Tiro (Bombing and Gunnery School). One is known to have been coded 50.

Twelve 300hp Hispano-Suiza engined Type 17As were supplied in 1924 (s/n's 6510 to 6521); Spanish serials unknown. (Possibly these too were registered in the M-MR series.)

Six F.2Bs with 300hp Hispano-Suiza 8Fb engines were still registered with the Compañía Española de Aviación at Albacete Aerodrome in 1936. These were identified as EC-AAJ (c/n 2301), EC-AJA (c/n 2601), EC-IAI (c/n 1916), EC-IIA (c/n 2300), EC-III (c/n 1982) and EC-JAA (c/n 2199).

A Bristol Fighter Type 17A for Spain undergoes a pre-delivery test flight in England. *(Bristol)*

This aircraft, M-MREF, was probably one of the 12 300hp Hispano-Suiza engined Type 17As supplied in 1924. *(Philip Jarrett)*

Spanish Bristol Fighters: Individual Histories

M-MRAC Delivered ex-ADC Croydon 7.9.21 (pilot Broome).

M-MRAE (s/n 3987) Delivered Filton to Croydon 30.8.21 and to Spain 31.8.21 (pilot Maj de Havilland).

M-MRAG (s/n 3981) (300hp Hispano-Suiza) Delivered Filton to Croydon 10.9.21 and to Spain 13.9.21 (pilot Norman Macmillan (or Tait-Cox?)). Crashed. Replaced by 4985 in 10/21.

M-MRAH (s/n 3977) Delivered Filton to Croydon 18.9.21 and to Spain via Paris and Beauvais 18.9.21 (pilot H.B. Richardson).

M-MRAI (s/n 3998) Delivered Filton to Croydon 12.9.21 and to Spain 13.9.21 (pilot Larry Carter).

M-MRAK Departed from Filton 'early in September' (pilot Norman Macmillan).

M-MRAL (s/n 4000) Delivered Filton to Croydon and to Spain same day 28.9.21 (pilot Frank Courtney). Damaged in France, returned to maker. Redelivered as s/n 4002 Filton to Croydon and to Spain same day 18.10.21 (pilot Carter).

M-MRAM (s/n 4001) Delivered Filton to Croydon and to Spain same day 17.9.21 (pilot Frank Courtney).

M-MRAN (s/n 3991) Delivered Filton to Croydon and to Spain same day 21.9.21 (pilot Milne).

M-MRAO (s/n 3997) Delivered Filton to Croydon and to Spain same day 22.9.21 (pilot Larry Carter).

M-MRAP Delivered ex-ADC Croydon via Paris 7.9.21 (pilot Wolley-Dod).

M-MRAQ Delivered ex-ADC Croydon via Paris 7.9.21 (pilot C.D. Barnard).

M-MRAR Ex-ADC. From Paris to Croydon 2.3.22 (pilot Piercey; test flown by Stocken 21.3.22; Croydon to St Inglevert (pilot Stocken) 30.3.22.

M-MRAU (s/n 4980) Delivered ex-ADC Croydon via Paris 13.10.21 (pilot Herne). Landed Le Crotoy 14.10.21 possibly damaged and returned to maker. Delivered Filton to Croydon 10.11.21 and to Spain 11.11.21 (pilot Herne). Returned Paris-Croydon 11.3.22 (pilot Piercey).

M-MRAV Delivered ex-ADC to Croydon then via St Inglevert and Paris to Spain same day 14.12.21 (pilot Herne).

[Curiously, surviving Bristol records show only five aircraft, s/n 6140 to 6144, registered M-MRAZ, M-MRAY, M-MRAX, M-MRAI and M-MRCO in that sequence, all with 300hp Hispano-Suiza engines]

This photograph, dated 27 July 1936, shows Bristol F.2B (Type 17A) M-MRAO or 'U at Cuatro Vientos near Madrid shortly after the outbreak of the Spanish Civil War. It was reportedly being used to carry bombs and leaflets. Keeping it company is an ancient de Havilland D.H.6, apparently devoid of markings but possibly B2938 and, in the background, a D.H.9. *(Philip Jarrett)*

Sweden

One Type 76A Fighter (ex-G-EBHG) was supplied to the Swedish Army as Fv.4300, later Fv.3667.

Swedish Bristol Fighter: Individual History

Fv.4300 (ex-G-EBHG) Taken over 6.5.24 by Flygkompaniet (Army Air Service); inspected and approved 23.7.24. To Flygvapnet 1.7.26; received designation Ö6 from 1.7.28; renumbered Fv.3667 3.32; SOC 3.34; became SE-AEE, registered 14.2.35

USA

Two UK-built F.2Bs, A7206 and C949, were sold to the US Government, the former being flown from April 1918 at McCook Field as P-30, fitted with a 300hp Hispano-Suiza engine to serve as prototype for the American version as originally envisaged, until being surveyed (struck off charge) on 19 February 1919. A second aircraft, almost certainly C949, was numbered P-37 and went to Wright Field, Ohio, on 9 June 1918 to be tested with the revised fitting of a 400hp Liberty engine. Two others, C4729 and D7879, were allotted to the British Aviation Mission in Washington. One of the latter may have been the Bristol Fighter stated to be of the British Air Mission RAF (USA), which on 22 September 1918 gave a flying display at Greenfield in support of the Fourth Liberty Loan War Bond Drive, but on returning to base it spun in from 600ft,

Right: **Bristol Aircraft-built F.2B D7879 is listed in British records as having been assigned from the factory to the British Aviation Mission in Washington D.C.**

Below: **A rather tired-looking British-built Falcon-engined F.2B in the USA.**

the port wing hit a tree and it crashed in a cornfield at Marion County Poor Farm, near the boundary with Indianapolis Speedway Field, Indiana, Capt J.J. Hammon RAF and Mr J.L. Kinder both being killed, and Lt R.W. Pickett USAS seriously injured.

In addition to these, several British-built F.2Bs were flown by the USAS at RAF Ford Junction, including E2147, E2156, E2207, E2216, E2221, E2222 and E2226. The American units based there between September and November 1918 were the 92nd, 140th and 326th Aero Squadrons, plus the US Night Bombardment Training School, whose proposed equipment was O/400s, the F.2Bs possibly being temporary equipment. One other American unit with a British-built F.2B on strength was the 148th US Aero Squadron in France, which had F5191. Another, unidentified, RAF aircraft crashed near Ithaca, New York State, on 8 October 1919.

American orders:
Engineering Division
    USB-1: 40046 to 40049 (cancelled)
    USB-2: 40050 to 40053 (cancelled)
    USB-1: 40096 to 40098 (cancelled)
    USXB-1: 40125 (P-90)
Dayton-Wright
    USXB-1A: 64155 to 64194
    (64158 = P-179; 64160 = P-181;
    64161 = P-182; 64177 = P-205)
    USXB-1A: 64300
    XB-1A: 94107 & 94108

See also Chapter 15 for details of US production and usage.

Yugoslavia

In February 1923 Capt Norman Macmillan flew a reconditioned F.2B with a 300hp Hispano-Suiza engine to Yugoslavia.

A line-up at Filton of Bristol Reserve Flying School Tourer/Trainers around 1923-25, including G-EBFU, G-EBFT, G-EBFZ and G-EBGC. *(Bristol)*

Chapter 19

CIVILIAN USE

Before the outbreak of the First World War Britain had a growing aircraft industry, partly based on French aircraft and engine designs. The remainder were the fruits of increasingly experienced all-British firms and designers. Among the latter was the British & Colonial Aeroplane Co Ltd of Filton, Bristol, whose aircraft flew under the Bristol marque. No organised standard method of external fuselage identification existed at that time, and such systems of constructor numbering that then existed were mostly somewhat rudimentary or non-existent.

By the time of the Armistice several British companies had taken advantage of large military aircraft and engine contracts to expand considerably. Among these was the Filton-based company, which by the end of 1919 had adopted the more logical and recognisable title of Bristol Aeroplane

Co Ltd. Exceptionally, all its individual aircraft were allocated 'sequence numbers' starting at 1, this nomenclature being exactly the same in purpose as the later more commonly-adopted term 'constructor's number'. The original company, The British & Colonial Aeroplane Co Ltd, was placed in (solvent) Members Voluntary Liquidation on 23 March 1920, ostensibly to avoid payment of excess profits tax. Its business and assets were formally transferred to The Bristol Aeroplane Co Ltd (albeit wef 31.12.19); this was a hitherto dormant company that had been formed on 19 February 1910.

Pre-war orders had been sparse, with sequence numbers barely exceeding 200 by the outbreak of war, and most orders were in single figures. With the advent of ever-growing military demands from both the War Office and the Admiralty, Bristol

sequence numbers had climbed to over 5700 by the time the war ended, including cancellations and orders in hand but not taking into account the many aircraft of Bristol design which had been built by other firms. Inevitably, 1919 was a rather traumatic year for industry in general, and for the aviation industry in particular. Large-scale cancellations became the order of the day as the RAF was run down and new aircraft were no longer required during this period of acute shrinkage. Companies were desperately trying to adapt to post-war civil needs, but orders were in short supply, as were materials to fulfil them. Many firms went out of business, and the aviation industry was no exception.

Unlike most other firms, Bristol still had a saleable product in the F.2B Fighter, especially as this type was one of the very few to be selected for the post-war RAF. It

Bristol F.2B G-ABYE, a Mk.IV civil conversion ex-F4721, was registered on 4 July 1932 to M. Emmett Voodley, and transferred two years later to Pt Off F.A. Ronald, who flew it to Baghdad and back the following month. Sadly, he was killed in a car accident on 18 November 1934. The aircraft was then taken over at Witney by Universal Aircraft Services Ltd until its registration was cancelled in April 1938. *(Philip Jarrett)*

Bristol Fighter Mk.III DC conversion G-ABXV was registered on 15 June 1932 to joint owners Philip H. Thomas and The Hon. John Grimston of Upper Heyford, Oxfordshire, and is seen here outside the Brooklands Aviation Hangar in 1932/33. It was written off on 18 September 1933 when Grimston crashed into a wall while landing at Capenoch, Dumfriesshire. *(Philip Jarrett)*

Sold in August 1932 to Anthony T. Wilson at Lympne, and jointly owned with Keith K. Brown, the CFI of the Cinque Ports Flying Club, Bristol Fighter G-ABYT took second place in the Folkestone Trophy Race in 1933. The following year it was sold to John P.W. Topham of Lympne, but following a collision with a barbed wire fence in 1936 it languished in a hangar at Lympne, as seen here, until it was scrapped. *(Philip Jarrett)*

was too early to expect new orders, and even when these were later forthcoming they were far smaller than those to which the company had become accustomed. The experienced design team turned their hands to a variety of civil aircraft types in the hope that one or more among them might prove saleable once a fresh pattern had emerged for non-military flying. The four-engined Pullman, for instance, was a commercial adaptation of the recently built prototype Braemar bomber, now no longer having any potential as such. It weighted was nearly 18,000lb fully loaded. At the other extreme was the lightweight and diminutive Babe tourer, with an engine of only 35-40hp and a quoted all-up weight of just 683lb. In between these extremes was the 2,300lb Bullet racer, which won the 1920 Aerial Derby when this popular pre-war flying sport was revived with more modern aircraft designs. Other new civil designs emerged, some of which were actually built, but none of the early attempts at meeting post-war civil needs, whatever these might prove to become, met with any great success.

However, the company's strength lay in the sturdy and reliable F.2B, with the added advantage that orders were on the horizon for both limited numbers of newer variants for the RAF and the reconditioning and rebuilding of some of the large surplus stocks of this type, then still in storage, starting in 1922. It might also prove possible to adapt the Fighter design to meet civil needs.

Many surplus wartime aircraft of different types were being sold off to the Croydon-based Aircraft Disposal Co Ltd, controlled by Handley Page Ltd and equally anxious to find both civil and military markets for wartime Bristol Fighters. In the event the first Fighters to grace the British civil register were four aircraft registered by ADC between April and November 1920,

G-EASH, G-EASU, G-EASV and G-EAWA. The first of these was flown as a demonstrator and the next two are believed to have gone to the Belgian Air Force, while G-EAWA never received a certificate of airworthiness and its registration lapsed. Bristol Fighters could be purchased for the then low price of £800, though running costs were to prove somewhat excessive. Between May 1921 and November 1923 the Aircraft Disposal Co Ltd and its new incarnation, ADC Aircraft Ltd, registered 17 more, the last being G-EBIO. As indicated in Chapter 18, most of these were

supplied to Belgium after only a brief spell on the British register for the purposes of test flying and subsequent delivery flights. In the event, none were the subject of orders from the home market.

In the meantime, however, the Bristol company had registered G-EBCN in April 1922, this being a variant powered by a 300hp Hispano-Suiza engine and given post-war sequence number 6223 and type number 17. (There seems to be confusion between that aircraft and G-EBFD. G-EBFD is shown on the original Air Ministry register sheets as c/n 6223, while

Above right and right: Photographed at Loughton Aerodrome (Abridge), G-ABZG was registered to Commercial Airways (Essex) Ltd, founded by Wilfred Lewington in the early 1930s. *(Philip Jarrett)*

Above: **Bristol Fighter G-ACAC, previously J8437, displays the extended slats in the outer leading edge of its starboard upper wing to advantage.** (Philip Jarrett)

Below: **Seen here at the far end of a line-up of machines outside the ADC sheds at Croydon, G-EBIO, the last F.2B to be registered to ADC, survived until 1935, at one time being the back-up aircraft for The Hon Mrs Victor Bruce's in-flight refuelling experiments.** (Philip Jarrett)

G-EBCN is shown as 3957.) Only three months later it went to Belgium as a pattern aircraft for proposed local production, materialising there within months as the Bristol 300, with the same engine. The Belgian Air Force eventually operated 73 machines, with military serial numbers L-1 to L-73 inclusive; their individual histories are given in Chapter 18.

The Spanish Air Force was another customer for the Fighter, being supplied between August 1921 and March 1922 with five of a modified design, now designated Type 17A. They had the 300hp Hispano-Suiza engine, an enlarged fin and Frise-type ailerons, and the old-style bungee-type undercarriage gave way to a new oleo design. With new sequence numbers 6140-6144, these were never given British civil registrations, but had the civil-type Spanish registrations M-MRAZ, M-MRAY, M-MRAX, M-MRAI and M-MRCO applied at the manufacturer. The first of these departed from Croydon on 13 September 1921 with Larry Carter at the controls. Several M-M Bristol Fighters were also delivered at the same time (see later notes); they included M-MRAC/MRAP and MRAQ on 7 September 1921, M-MRAU on 13 October 1921, and an unidentified one on 31 August 1921 (as reported in *The Aeroplane* magazine). They were supplemented by several similarly powered

Below: **Specially modified in 1932 to serve as an aerial refuelling tanker for The Hon Mrs Victor Bruce's Saunders-Roe Windhover, G-ABJP, F.2B G-ABXA had two 40gal tanks beneath its lower wings, and also served as a hoarding to advertise Regent Super petrol.** (Paul Smiddy)

Right: **Bristol F.2B Mk.III DC conversion G-ACCG had been converted to J-Type DC in 1925, while in RAF service as J6790. Early in 1933 it was sold to Universal Aircraft Services Ltd of Witney, and then went to Michel N. Mavrogordato, who based it at Hooton Park. Its registration was cancelled in July 1939. In 1944 National Studios at Elstree used it for taxying shots in the film *The World Owes Me a Living*. It ended up with a Guildford ATC squadron in 1948 and was scrapped three years later.** *(Philip Jarrett)*

ADC-modified machines, making 13 in all for the post-war Spanish Air Force. (See chapter 18)

By 1932 the Bristol Fighter was finally becoming obsolete in RAF service, and several were sold privately, the first being G-ABXA, formerly J8258, which was registered in June 1932 to The Honourable Mrs Mildred Bruce and based at Hanworth. Converted to serve as a tanker aircraft, with two large 40gal auxiliary fuel tanks attached beneath the inboard ends of the lower wings and a refuelling tube, it was named *Mercenary Mary* and was liberally painted with promotional advertising for Regent Super petrol. G-ABXA was used for in-flight refuelling of Mildred's Saro Windhover amphibian, *City of Portsmouth*, during her attempts to establish a new world endurance record by staying aloft for a month. The then current record was held by the brothers John and Kenneth Hunter of the USA, who had achieved a flight lasting 23 days in a Stinson Detroiter in June-July 1930. After tests at Cowes and Felixstowe, Mildred Bruce made three attempts to set a new record, the tanker F.2B transferring 80gal of fuel to the Windhover five times a day. After the first two attempts were aborted for various reasons, the third and final one, on 9 August 1932, was cut short after 54 hours by rising oil temperatures in the Windhover's engines. Although the British endurance record was 'unofficially' broken, the crew forfeited any mean of corroborating their flight, having thrown out the recording barograph with other equipment to save weight.

A further 20 Bristol Fighters graced the British civil register, the last being G-AFHJ,

Above: **Mark IV DC conversion G-ACPE was registered in 1934 to Arthur F. Cawthorn at Hanworth, then passed successively to Mrs Josephine J. Dudley, Charles S.W. Dudley and Richard G.J. Kingsmill, all at Hanworth. It was withdrawn from use in January 1939.** *(Philip Jarrett)*

registered in May 1938 to Sqn Ldr Nevile R. Buckle at RAF Hendon. In November 1932, in the process of obtaining a licence for an aerodrome at Abridge in Essex (this became Loughton Aerodrome (Abridge), and should not be confused with present-day Stapleford Aerodrome), Mr Wilfred Lewington of Waltham Cross requested and

was granted clearance for the Bristol Fighter to be operated from the airfield, as he proposed to purchase one or two of the type, and the Air Ministry agreed that the site was 'fit for instruction on Bristol Fighters'. Lewington then established the private company Commercial Airways (Essex) Ltd, to operate an air service from Abridge. On

This study of G-ACFP was probably taken after it had been re-registered to The Hon Mrs Victor Bruce at Hanworth. Although its C of A expired on 12 April 1934, its registration was not cancelled until January 1938. *(Philip Jarrett)*

Previously J8455, G-ADJR was registered on 18 June 1935 to Christopher Penrose Bartholomew Ogilvie of Willesden and based at Hanworth. C of A 4921 was issued on 22 June. The deployed upper wingtip slats are well shown. *(Philip Jarrett)*

22 March 1933 five ex-RAF Bristol Fighters were registered to the company: G-ABZG and G-ACFK, 'FL, 'FN and 'FO. These had been purchased from RAF Hornchurch, where large numbers of the type were being broken up. Although it was reported in January 1934 that the company had two 'Bristol Falcon IIIs' in its small fleet, in fact only one F.2B, G-ABZG, was converted. The other four were scrapped at Abridge in 1936. Despite announcements of imminent operations, Commercial Airways never managed to establish any scheduled services.

The most well-known of the civilianised F.2Bs, however, is G-AEPH, formerly D8096, which still survives. Rebuilt in the 1950s to near-Mk.II standard, then maintained for a time by the Bristol company bearing its old RAF serial number,

it is now part of the famous Shuttleworth Collection at Old Warden in Bedfordshire, where it can be seen flying regularly during the summer months.

Individual histories of the civil-registered Bristol Fighters and their derivatives will be found in Appendix 7.

Early in 1924, after being exhibited statically at the 1923 international aviation exhibition at Gothenburg, Type 76A Jupiter Fighter G-EBHG underwent cold-weather trials at Kiruna in Lapland, where it is seen on skis, which resulted in its sale to the Swedish Government. It became Fv 4300 until 1935, when it was sold off, being flown as SE-AEE until it crashed at Gothenburg in 1936. (See page 240.) *(Philip Jarrett)*

The two-seater, Puma-engined Bristol Seely G-EAUE, an enlarged Tourer derivative, was originally produced as an entry for the 1920 Air Ministry civil aeroplane competitions. Its later form is depicted on page 239. *(Bristol)*

Chapter 20

DERIVATIVES

At the end of the First World War there were large numbers of surplus airworthy Bristol Fighters in storage. Many of these went to ADC, but the Bristol company was very much still in business, with the type remaining in RAF service in smaller numbers and likely to be around for some years to come. This gave rise to the possibility of producing small numbers of both military and civil variants.

The first of these resulted from a request by Sir Frederick Sykes, the Controller of Civil Aviation, for three Bristol Fighters to be modified on the production line as unarmed dual-control two-seat communications aircraft with additional tankage to give a duration of five hours. The resulting aircraft, H1687-H1689, were delivered in July 1919. In addition to these, H1282 was converted on the line to a three-seater and delivered to the RAF, later becoming G-EAWZ.

In the early post-war years a major problem besetting civil aviation in general and commercial aviation in particular was finance. Having the advantage of an

established type continuing in RAF service, the obvious course was to try and develop the Fighter to meet likely civil requirements by adaptation, rather than starting to build and develop an entirely new design to meet future needs in a market not yet established.

On 1 May 1919, after a lapse of nearly five years, civil flying officially recommenced, and on that day Bristol test pilot C.F. Uwins flew Herbert Thomas in the unarmed H1460 from Filton to Hounslow for an official engagement. This aircraft, a one-off known as the Bristol Coupé and later given

the Bristol Type Number 27 when a numbering system was retrospectively introduced in 1923, had a hinged coupé cover over the rear passenger seat, resulting in an increased top speed of 128mph owing to the reduced drag. It never reached the new British civil register, being purchased 18 days later by the Air Board for use by the Air Council Inspection Squadron at Croydon, still with its RAF serial. This unit had a Director of Research Flight, and when the overall titling was changed on 1 February 1920 to become a re-established 24 Sqn,

The second of three F.2Bs built with dual controls and long-range fuel tanks, H1688 was delivered in July 1919. It eventually went to 24 Sqn at Kenley for the Directorate of Research. On 19 November 1921 H1688 suffered engine failure off Folkestone while returning from Le Bourget and was ditched by Flt Lt J.M. Robb, but it was salvaged.

Above: **The unique Coupé H1460, with the hood open. Other noteworthy features are the triangular transparencies in the sides of the rear cockpit and the short access ladder.**

Left: **The one-off Coupé H1460, subsequently designated Type 27, showing the hinged coupé cover over the rear passenger seat. On 1 May 1919 it was flown from Filton to Hounslow by C.F. Vivian with Herbert J. Thomas as passenger to enable Thomas to keep an appointment with Gen Seeley.** *(Bristol)*

The Bristol company had meanwhile been continuing with its efforts to develop a relatively affordable development of the Fighter, and the first fruit of this was the Tourer, later given type numbers 28 and 29 for the three-seater and two-seater versions respectively under the later numbering system, these being piloted from the front seat. The first of these to appear on the British civil register was s/n 5867, which became G-EAIZ on being given its Certificate of Registration (C of R) on 7 August 1919, followed by a Certificate of Airworthiness (C of A) on 10 September. Fitted out as a two-seater, it was powered by a 240hp Siddeley Puma salvaged from the wreckage of the sole experimental Bristol Badger X, which had been overturned at Filton on 22 May. It was used as a testbed and company hack. The following year it was demonstrated in Belgium and Norway before being withdrawn from use in September 1920.

On 23 September 1919 a second Type 29 two-seater, s/n 5868, also referred to as the P.T.2S, signifying Puma Tourer two-seat School, was registered as G-EANR. After being exhibited at the Paris Salon in December 1919 and January 1920 it was shipped to New York in May 1920, and is believed to have ended up in Nicaragua, transporting bullion from silver mines. This

and its base was changed to Kenley, H1460 continued with the Directorate of Research before being flown briefly in 1921 by No 1 FTS at Netheravon and No 2 FTS at Duxford.

Shortly after the Armistice the company had started work on a two- or three-seat biplane for peacetime operations. Never given a type number, it was known initially as the Rancher, and was to have been powered by a three-cylinder 100hp Cosmos Lucifer engine, one of several designs taken over by the Bristol Aeroplane Co Ltd when, in August 1920, it acquired the assets of the defunct Cosmos Engineering Co Ltd of Bristol. The name of the aircraft was changed from Rancher to Colonial, but it was overtaken by events when, in July 1919, an enquiry was received for a three-seat version known as the Tourer.

The first Bristol Type 29 Tourer, G-EAIZ, was registered to the Bristol Aeroplane Co Ltd in September 1919 and served as a demonstration aircraft until September 1920. *(Philip Jarrett)*

Right and below right: **Bristol Type 47 Tourer G-EART of Instone Air Line accommodated two passengers side-by-side in its rear cockpit.** *(Bristol)*

machine incorporated a high nose radiator with complementary pump and thermal syphon effects, having vertical shutters for temperature control. In this arrangement, a pump failure did not cause the system to fail, and in the event of a forced landing there was less likelihood of serious damage. Repair would therefore be easier; a factor to be taken into consideration for possible overseas operation over rough terrain.

The Tourer was by now proving so easy to produce that the planned Colonial design was abandoned, leaving Bristol free to produce two- and three-seat Tourer variants for an American market which the company's New York agent believed held promise. To accommodate a second passenger, Frank Barnwell designed a wide rear cockpit for side-by-side seating with either an open or coupé top.

Next were to have been two open-cockpit three-seaters, s/n 5873 and 5874, fitted with twin floats interchangeable with a wheeled chassis, but work on these was suspended. Work continued, however, on five open three-seaters (s/n 5876-5880) and a single two-seater (s/n 5881). However, the New York agent asked for a three-seater coupé, so s/n 5876 was retained to be replaced by an uncompleted s/n 5891, only 5877-5881 therefore being shipped in late May 1920. They were painted dark battleship grey with the cursive word 'Bristol' on the sides of the fuselage, the under surfaces being pale blue. Three-seater s/n 5891 followed in August, having been exhibited at Olympia in London the previous month. In the meantime, s/n 5876 had been registered as G-EART to S. Instone and Co Ltd of Croydon for its budding airline. Painted

blue and silver, it was used for about a year on charter work, including one engagement on 3 May 1920 when Capt F. L. Barnard flew it carrying Maj Gen Sir Frederick Sykes, the Controller General of Civil Aviation, and his bride on their honeymoon, the flight from Croydon to Cramlington, Newcastle, taking four hours.

Next off the line was open two-seater G-EAVU (s/n 5892), which was successfully demonstrated in both Belgium and Norway.

In anticipation of further orders from America, 16 more were laid down (s/n 6108-6123), but only initial deposits had been received when the New York agency ran into difficulties with import restrictions, so no more were shipped to the USA. These included s/n 5873 and 5874, the two seaplane variants. Aircraft from s/n 6108 onwards were fitted with the larger radiator designed for the firm's Seely, after Maj de Havilland reported overheating, at Cuatro

Alan Butler's Bristol Type 29 Tourer, G-EAWB, at Croydon Airport in April 1921. Butler had purchased the aircraft in November the previous year. After enclosing the gap between the fuselage and lower wing to reduce drag, he flew it the 1921 Aerial Derby at Hendon, taking third place in the handicap competition.
(Stuart McKay)

Left: **Bristol Tourer G-AUCA was supplied to Col Brinsmead, Australia's Controller of Civil Aviation, who used it for surveying new air routes, flying more than 9,000 miles in the process.** *(Philip Jarrett)*

Above: **Converted from 300hp Hispano-Suiza Fighter H1248, Tourer G-AUEB was flown by Qantas during 1922-23, and later became one of the first Flying Doctor ambulances in Australia's Northern Territories.** *(Philip Jarrett)*

Above: **Bristol Type 47 Tourer G-EAWR went to Spain as M-AEAA, being delivered to Madrid for Senõr Bayo by Hereward de Havilland on 24 April 1921.** *(Bristol)*

Left: **Bristol Type 29 Tourer G-EAXA first appeared in 1921. It was subsequently modified to a Type 81 Puma Trainer.** *(Bristol)*

Vientos in Mexico, on G-EAVU. This feature was to prove particularly invaluable later in Australia.

Work on the seaplanes was continued when an order came in from Siberia, and the first of these was flown on 15 October 1920 at Avonmouth with company test pilot C.F. Uwins at the controls. With two passengers and 40lb of ballast he was able to take off on calm water in 400 yards. The twin floats, designed by Maj Vernon, were of mahogany, with a single step and six watertight compartments in each. The Siberian order had, however, been cancelled, and instead efforts were made unsuccessfully to sell them in Canada. However, the last of the production batch, s/n 6123, was sold to the Newfoundland Air Survey Company, taking part in the gold rush to Stag Bay, Labrador, later that year, having been fitted with skis.

In late 1920 one of the unsold Tourers, s/n 6122, was purchased by Alan S. Butler, a private owner, and registered G-EAWB on 29 November 1920. He used it extensively for touring, based initially at Stag Lane and later Croydon, and it could often be seen flying in the London area. Butler left Croydon on 2 April 1921 for a tour of southern Europe starting on the French Riviera, returning safely two months later. On 16 July, after inserting a fairing to close the gap between the lower mainplane and the fuselage, he participated in the Aerial Derby at RAF Hendon, finishing fourth in the Handicap Race at an average speed of 106mph to win the £50 third prize. As a consequence Butler became enthusiastic about the value of private flying, joining Geoffrey de Havilland and later becoming chairman of the de Havilland Aircraft Company.

Meanwhile, Bristol was continuing with its efforts to find customers for the aircraft which it had hoped to be able to send to the USA. In April 1921 s/ns 6114 and 6112 were ordered through Spanish agents by a Senõr Bayo at Madrid, receiving the British registrations G-EAWQ and G-EAWR before becoming M-AAEA and M-AEAA respectively. The former was a three-seat Tourer Coupé (Type 28) and the latter a three-seat Open Tourer (later given the Type Number 47). The only authorised route from Le Bourget was via San Sebastian, where Lasarte Airfield was situated amidst mountains. The aircraft left towards the end of April, Andrew Forson departing first in M-AAEA, but on 23 April while en route to Madrid he ran into fog and was killed when, after landing safely at Lasarte to clear Customs, he took off again into a cloud

Above: **Bristol Type 81 Puma Trainer G-EBFS served with the Filton Reserve Flying School during 1923-24.** *(Bristol)*

Right: **Photographed at Filton in August 1920, the first Coupé Three-seater Tourer was sent for demonstration and sale in the USA.** *(Bristol)*

Above: **A comparative side view of the open-cockpit version of the Tourer.** *(Bristol)*

bank and crashed in the mountains close to the village of Anzuola. Forson had also been due to fly the second aircraft, but test pilot Cyril Uwins flew G-AEAA to Croydon on 25 April then on to Le Bourget the following week. From there it was flown safely to Madrid by Geoffrey de Havilland, who then discovered that he was required to give flying lessons to Senôr Bayo. Demonstrator G-EAVU (s/n 5892) was accordingly sent out to Madrid for this task, probably becoming M-AFAA, being returned to Bristol in September 1921 and then scrapped. It was then replaced by Type 29 M-AFFA (s/n 6121), one of three further Spanish purchases, the others being Type 47s M-AAAF (s/n 6109) and M-AFFF (s/n 6110).

This left eight unsold aircraft; s/ns 6108, 6111, 6113 and 6115 to 6119. Of these, 6113, a three-seat open Tourer, was recorded by the company as being unsold. A three-seat Tourer Coupé, 6117, became the first of several to go to Australia, being registered as G-AUCA on 28 June 1921 to the Department of Defence, Civil Aviation Branch, Melbourne. The Controller of Civil Aviation, Colonel Brinsmead, flew over 9,000 miles in it to survey proposed new air routes within Australia.

On 3 February, following a meeting with the Air Council, the Australian Minister for Defence had advised that plans were in hand to organise an aerial mail service, and that the Air Council would supply aircraft and personnel. Services were practical but would be costly to maintain, the route between Geraldton and Derby, Western Australia, being selected, initially only as an experiment. After putting the requirements out to tender, Western Australian Airways Ltd was formed at Perth and an order placed for six three-seat Tourer Coupés. The two pilots were to be C.E. Kingsford Smith and

L.T.E. Taplin, who arrived aboard the SS *Katoomba* on 16 November. They were followed on the next day by the arrival of six Tourers at Fremantle on board the SS *Surrey*. These were registered G-AUDF to G-AUDK inclusive by the end of the month, having the respective s/ns 6118, 6111, 6115, 6116, 6118 and 6119. Of these, G-AUDF had initially been registered in the UK as G-EAXK.

The service did not get off to an auspicious start. Demonstrations and joyrides were carried out on 3 December at The Esplanade, Perth, as well as the official opening of the service by Sir Francis Newdigate, the Governor of Western Australia. The following day G-AUDG, G-AUDI and G-AUDK left Perth for Geraldton carrying 2,500 letters. On 5 December G-AUDG suffered engine trouble but was successfully

Above: **Coupé Tourers G-AUDJ and G-AUDF, seen here, were two of six of their kind supplied to Maj Norman Brearley to serve on the Australian Federal Government's weekly air mail service between Geraldton and Perth.** *(Philip Jarrett)*

Right: **Initially registered G-EAWR, M-AEAA, seen here at Filton, was the ill-fated first Type 47 Open Tourer for Spain. On 23 April 1921, while en route to Madrid, ferry pilot Andrew Forson was killed in this aircraft when, after taking off from Lasarte, he flew into a cloud bank and crashed in the mountains near Anzuola.** *(Bristol)*

forced-landed near the Murchison River. However, G-AUDI crashed while circling them, killing pilot R. Fawcett and mechanic E.W. Broad. The service was then suspended pending surveying of the route for the provision of improved landing grounds. The Geraldton to Port Hedland (Western Australia) section of the service resumed on 21 February 1921, being extended to Derby on 6 April, followed in due course by further routes. The passenger rate was one shilling per mile, and the charter rate four shillings per mile.

On 16 March 1923 G-AUCA crashed at Bourke, New South Wales, while en route from Melbourne to Longreach. It was rebuilt, possibly with parts from unsold airframe s/n 6113, re-emerging as G-AUDX. The contract was renewed on 5 December 1923, being extended from Geraldton to Perth (250 miles) and also Derby to Wyndham (600 miles), all in Western Australia. G-AUDH crashed on 15 July 1924 when it dived vertically into Port Hedland Creek, Western Australia, but was rebuilt as G-AUDZ, surviving until February 1931. The Tourers of Western Australian Airways had flown over 200,000 miles by

September 1923 and nearly 485,000 miles by June 1926, having logged 6,400 flying hours and carried over 3,000 passengers and 400,000 letters and parcels, the latter including valuable consignments of pearls from the northwest coast fisheries. In June 1926 they were replaced by D.H.50s.

In January 1927 G-AUDJ and G-AUDK were bought by a syndicate of Western Australian Airways pilots operating as Interstate Flying Services Ltd and based at Longueville, New South Wales. After being flown 2,300 miles from Perth to Sydney,

G-AUDK was flown right round the Australian continent by Charles Kingsford Smith and Charles Ulm between 19 and 29 June 1927, some 7,500 miles being covered in 10 days and 5 hours, starting and finishing at Sydney. However, an attempt in September of the following year to fly it to England ended three days after leaving Camooweal on 9 September 1928, when Keith Anderson and passenger Hitchcock crashed at Pine Creek, Northern Territory. All the Australian Tourers eventually came to a similar end, none surviving.

Watched by pilot Charles Kingsford Smith, standing in his cockpit, passenger Mrs J.W. Marshall is helped out of G-AUDK at Sydney. This was another of the Coupé Tourers used for the Australian air mail service. *(Philip Jarrett)*

Right: **Charles Kingsford Smith (left) and Charles Ulm with Coupé Tourer G-AUDK, in which they made a 7,500-mile flight round the Australian continent between 19 and 29 June 1927. The flight, which started and finished at Sydney, took 10 days and 5hr.** *(Philip Jarrett)*

One other Australian tourer-type was G-AUEB, a conversion of F.2B H1248, fitted with a 300hp Hispano-Suiza and registered by Queensland and Northern Territories Aerial Services (QANTAS) and flown in 1922 and 1923. It was rebuilt in 1924 with a Puma engine and fitted with a stretcher, then marked with a red cross to become one of the first Flying Doctor ambulances in Northern Territories. However, it proved insufficiently robust for operations in the bush, eventually serving in the Bulolo goldfields until it crashed at Wau, New Guinea, on 17 April 1928.

Seely

In July 1919 the Air Ministry announced a Commercial Aeroplane Competition, to be held the following year, with separate categories of small and large civil aeroplanes incorporating specified standards of design, performance and economy of operation, having a minimum take-off run and able to land slowly. The competition began at Martlesham Heath on 3 August 1920, and Bristol submitted its new Seely design, later given Type Number 35, which had been specially designed to meet the requirements. A derivative of the Tourer, it incorporated many F.2B parts and carried a single passenger in an enclosed cabin behind the pilot. It had a deep fuselage, the bottom longerons being dropped to the level of the lower wings. In front of the pilot, the fuselage bays were constructed of steel tube instead of the Tourer's spruce, providing better protection in the event of a crash. It had multi-disc Ferodo brakes as well as a central forward steel skid to reduce the risk of turning over. The area of the three-bay wings was increased from that of the Tourer, a horn-balanced rudder and large fin were fitted, and the sprung tailwheel was linked to the rudder steering. The Puma engine had been tuned for increased economy, and efficient cooling was provided at low altitudes by a large-area radiator.

With sequence number 5870, it was first flown in December 1920 and was registered G-EAUE (see picture on page 233). During the competition it achieved a top speed of 108.3mph, and a week later achieved a slow-speed run of 49.07mph, but it failed to carry off any of the prize money, which was won by the Westland Limousine.

The Seely was afterwards retained at Filton, becoming a testbed in 1923 for the development of the Bristol Jupiter radial engine. On 22 December 1923 it was

The Seely subsequently served at Filton as a testbed for Jupiter engine development. After being fitted with a supercharged Jupiter III it was bought by the Air Ministry, serialled J7004, and underwent comprehensive testing in 1924. *(Bristol)*

Above: **The Bristol Type 34 Open Seaplane Tourer of 1920, fitted with mahogany single-step floats, first flew on 15 October 1920.** *(Bristol)*

purchased by the Air Ministry under contract No 408484/23 and fitted with an experimental exhaust-driven turbo-blown 435hp Jupiter III, in which form it first flew on 5 October 1923. It was then handed over to the RAE at Farnborough on 25 January 1924 with the military serial number J7004, sometimes being referred to as the Seely Mk.II, with the new type number 85. Fitted with a Leitner-Watts steel-bladed propeller, it was tested comprehensively in 1924, frequently climbing to 23,000ft, for which its low wing loading and enclosed observer's cabin made it particularly suitable.

Withdrawn from the RAE on 16 May 1924, it was returned to Bristol in July 1924 and dismantled there at the end of the year.

Jupiter-Fighter

By early 1923 Bristol was considering the possibility of fitting the company's 425hp Jupiter IV engine in a modified Bristol Fighter design. For cheapness, a spare F.2B airframe might be used, and W.T. Reid took on the task of assessing the feasibility. He reported on 22 January that the conversion was quite possible, though only two hours' flying time could be expected

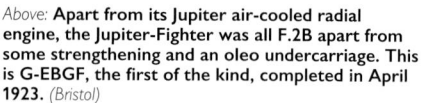

Above: **Apart from its Jupiter air-cooled radial engine, the Jupiter-Fighter was all F.2B apart from some strengthening and an oleo undercarriage. This is G-EBGF, the first of the kind, completed in April 1923.** (Bristol)

Above: **The first Bristol Tourer for Bulgaria was B-BECA, seen here before its markings were applied. It was a standard Fighter minus armament and with a Wolseley Viper engine and Tourer modifications to its fuselage and rear cockpit.** (Bristol)

the slipstream was too rough for the gunner when he was standing up. In addition, the low fuel capacity and the restricted view for the pilot led him to report that the design could not be recommended as a fighter. On the other hand, it was admirably suited to be a demonstrator for the Jupiter engine. The first machine, G-EBGF, was exhibited in the New Types Park at the annual RAF Display at Hendon on 30 June 1923. Two were selected to go to Sweden, where the exhibition was to be opened by King Gustav on 20 July. The third and last machine (s/n 6380), now registered G-EBHG, which was fitted with Frise ailerons but had no armament, would be shown on the Bristol stand at the exhibition, in which static displays from 36 countries participated, while the first machine was to be one of about 70 entrants taking part in various flying contests at the newly-opened Torslanda Airport. Given competition number 41, it was flown 755 miles from London to Gothenburg by Macmillan, accompanied by Raynham, for which they

with standard tankage. However, the aircraft would have an estimated top speed of 133mph, which was 3mph more than had been achieved by the recent Bloodhound fighter design, also powered by a Jupiter IV. Authority was therefore given for the construction of one Jupiter-Fighter (s/n 6379), to be available in time to be displayed at the International Aviation Exhibition (Internationella LuftUtställningen i Göteborg: ILUG) in Sweden, as a part of a celebration of the city's 300th Anniversary, this being the biggest aviation exhibition in the world up to that time. It was a simple conversion, as no exhaust manifold was fitted, the airframe being standard but with some local strengthening and an oleo undercarriage instead of the rubber-cord type. Completed in April 1923, at which time a second conversion was under way, it was registered G-EBGF on 3 May 1923. Two days later a third conversion was authorised, so while one was undergoing trials with A&AEE at Martlesham, two

would be available to go to Sweden. In June it was decided that one of the Sweden-bound machines would afterward be used for testing a Jupiter with alcohol fuel, for comparison tests with the supercharged 435hp Jupiter III fitted in the Bristol Seely II civil design (Type 85).

The first machine, G-EBGF, was flown early in June 1923 by Capt Norman Macmillan, who managed to reach a top speed of 134mph. However, at that speed

The second Tourer for Bulgaria was B-BEHA (s/n 6384). Both aircraft were sent to Bojourishte, near Sofia, to be proved in service. (Philip Jarrett)

Right: **The improved Bulgarian Tourers, represented here by B-BEKA, had an oleo undercarriage, Frise ailerons and the large fin and horn-balanced rudder designed for the Jupiter-Trainer.** *(Bristol)*

won the 'arrival prize' of 1,215 kroner. For the flying competition it was fitted with a special propeller to enhance its climbing abilities, and won the altitude prize by reaching 26,000ft. Although the aircraft was still climbing, Macmillan had no oxygen and had to break off. The aircraft greatly impressed the Swedish military pilots, especially as Macmillan also won an aerobatic contest for two-seater aircraft.

As a consequence, Sweden gave some consideration to purchasing the Jupiter-Fighter, provided it performed satisfactorily in Arctic conditions. Accordingly, a ski undercarriage and a carburettor heater muff were fitted to G-EBHG, which went north in November 1923 to Kiruna in Lapland. Unfortunately it proved impossible to operate aircraft at this latitude in winter, as the oil froze solid in a few hours even with an air-cooled engine. The Jupiter engine, however, behaved extremely well, repeatedly starting without trouble after spending long winter nights out in the open at temperatures down to -20°C, using standard petrol and arctic motor oil. It was the first water-cooled or rotary aircraft engine to be able to do this. The Swedish government decided to go ahead with the purchase, and G-EBHG was flown back by Lt Gardin of the Swedish Army, who covered the 800 miles from Kiruna to Malmslätt at an average speed of 124mph. Thereafter, G-EBHG was referred to as the Swedish Fighter. On return it was used for Jupiter engine demonstrations, undergoing repairs on 10 April. Then, on 14 March 1924, it was flown to Kiruna for cold-weather trials. It entered service with the Swedish Army in May 1924, being given the serial number Fv 4300, this being changed to Fv 1300 in 1926, then to Fv 3667 in 1932. Upon being declared surplus it was purchased by Hugo Fredrikson and registered SE-AEE on 14 February 1935. It crashed at Gothenburg the following year.

The design was given Bristol Type Number 76, the second machine, G-EBGF, being designated Type 76B. It did not survive long, however, as on 23 November 1923 its engine seized at 20,000ft while being flown from Filton by T.W. Campbell, and it crashed. The third machine, G-EBHH (s/n 6381), was fitted with a high-compression Jupiter engine and an experimental bi-fuel system with a special gravity tank for alcohol above the top centre-section, and designated Type 76A. On take-off it used alcohol, then on reaching an altitude at which detonation would not occur the pilot switched to petrol. It first flew in March 1924, but the Air Ministry abandoned the bi-fuel system in July owing to tank corrosion problems, preferring

Above: **Having flown Bristol Jupiter-Fighter G-EBGF from London to Göteborg in Sweden in a single day, freelance pilot Norman Macmillan poses with it at Torslanda, where it took part in the flying contest, on 20 July 1923. While being flown by T.W. Campbell on 23 November 1923 this aircraft suffered an engine seizure at 20,000ft and crashed.** *(Philip Jarrett)*

supercharging as a long-term development. In September 1924 G-EBHH was converted to Type 89 dual-control trainer standard for use by the Filton Reserve Flying School, but on 23 September 1925 it collided with Trainer G-EBJA over Filton and its pilot, Fg Off G.W. Thorpe, was killed. It was subsequently rebuilt but ended its days on 20 August 1929 when it was involved in another collision over Filton, this time with Trainer G-EBGB.

A dual-control advanced trainer version of the Jupiter-Fighter originated with demonstrator two-seat Tourer G-EAXA (s/n 6120), fitted with Frise ailerons to be evaluated in this role for possible use by the Filton Reserve Flying School and having Type Number 81. This proved satisfactory for the purpose; described as the Tourer/Trainer or Puma School 'B'; four (s/n 6239-6242) were built in March 1923, registered G-EBFR to G-EBFU. In June 1923 G-EBFS crashed and, as the rubber-cord suspension proved too weak to withstand repeated landings by trainees, the other three were fitted with an oleo undercarriage of the type first fitted to export Fighter Type 17A G-EBCN.

The success of the Jupiter-Fighter having by now been proved, a decision was reached

Jupiter-Fighter G-EBHG as 1300 in service with the Swedish Air Force at Malmslätt in 1926. *(Philip Jarrett)*

Left: **Type 76A Jupiter Fighter G-EBHH during trials of the high-compression bi-fuel Jupiter engine at Filton in June 1924. The gravity tank for alcohol above the top centre section is just visible.** *(Philip Jarrett)*

to fit a training version with a Jupiter engine, restricted to 290hp due to the higher insurance costs if it exceeded 300hp. The first of these, G-EBIH (s/n 6382), with a derated Jupiter III, had the new Type Number 89 and made its first flight on 14 April 1924. By that time four more were almost complete, G-EBJA to G-EBJC (s/n 6382-6385), of which G-EBJB was never completed; the last one was a spare airframe retained for stock purposes. To counteract the torque reaction of the Jupiter engine, the rating of which was later increased to 320hp despite the insurance penalty, Frise ailerons and an enlarged fin and horn-balanced rudder were fitted. Both G-EBJA and G-EBJB had been written off before the end of 1925. Two new machines were built as replacements, registered G-EBML (s/n 6918) and G-EBMN (s/n 6919), these having the Jupiter VI engine and being designated Type 89A Advanced Trainers. Four of this variant were ordered by Sir William Beardmore & Co Ltd of Dalmuir, near Glasgow, for use by the Beardmore Reserve School at Renfrew. The company had previously ordered two Type 89 Trainers, G-EBNZ (s/n 6963) and G-EBOA (s/n 6964), supplied in June 1926. The type remained in service with the school until it closed down in 1930.

Next came the first of further Type 89As, G-EBOC (s/n 6965), for the Filton school in October 1926. This was the first to have a fuselage strengthened by plywood covering instead of being braced with tie-rods. Its finish of black Cerric, with silver-doped wings and tail, earned it the nickname of 'Black Maria'. Ten more of the type were built for the Filton school, in addition to three for the Renfrew school, which also produced a final machine, G-EBWN (c/n R.58), using spares and salvaged components from the crashed G-EBOA and G-EBOD. Use of the type continued there until 1930. All of the Renfrew aircraft had the Jupiter VI, but Filton found it more economical to fit surplus Jupiter IVs which could be serviced at its own factory. The last Jupiter Trainers to be registered were G-ABPL (s/n 7711) and G-ABPM (s/n 7712) on 2 September 1931. The latter was retained at Filton for trials during 1932, undertaking taxying and landing tests with Dunlop 'doughnut' low-pressure wheels, with the aim of improving handling and serviceability when flown in tropical conditions. One of the Filton machines, G-EBYL, was equipped with Handley Page auto-slots, and another machine with steel wings, which proved trouble-free. The type remained in service at Filton until April 1933, when it was replaced by the Hawker Hart Trainer. None then went to civil owners, being regarded as unfit for this purpose.

Above: **A factory-fresh Puma-engined Bristol Type 81A for the Royal Hellenic Navy.** *(Bristol)*

Bristol Type 81 Puma Trainer G-EBFU was one of four of the type built in early 1923 and used at the Filton Reserve Flying School. *(Philip Jarrett)*

The prototype Bristol Type 89 Advanced Trainer, G-EBIH, powered by a Jupiter III radial, at Filton in April 1924. *(Bristol)*

Bristol Type 83A Primary Trainer Machine G-EBGA was the longest-lived of its kind, being registered to the Bristol Aeroplane Co Ltd in June 1923 and surviving until December 1933. *(Bristol)*

Bulgarian and Greek Tourers

In April 1923 the Department of Posts and Telegraphs of the Bulgarian Government at Sofia invited tenders for two different types of aircraft. One was to be a five- or six-seater and the other a two-seater for postal services. The latter was of interest to Bristol, which offered a Tourer variant with a 180hp Wolseley Viper. The engine power was limited because, at that time, Bulgaria was still regarded as an ex-enemy country, and therefore prohibited by the Treaty of Versailles, signed on 28 June 1919, from operating aircraft with engines exceeding 200hp. A contract was signed in August for four Tourers to be delivered by the end of 1923. The first two, completed on time in December, were given Bristol Type Number 88 and registered B-BECA (s/n 6383) and B-BEHA (s/n 6384). They were basically the same as the standard Fighters, but modifications included the absence of armament and the 15gal centre-section gravity tank of the Puma Tourer. Delivery did not take place for another four months, the two aircraft being sent in April 1924 to Bojourishte, near Sofia, where they were to be proved in service

before proceeding with the other two aircraft ordered.

In the event the Bulgarian Government seemed for a time as if they might accept an alternative offer of Lucifer-engined Primary Trainers, but in the end the next order, in April 1926, was for just one of these (which does not appear to have materialised) plus three improved Tourers. Like the first two they had Viper engines but were improved by the incorporation of an oleo undercarriage, Frise ailerons and the horn-balanced rudder, plus the large fin designed for the Jupiter-Trainer. They were also fitted with navigation lights and Holt flares for night operations. Given Type Number 88A and sequence numbers 6937 to 6939, they were registered B-BEBA, B-BETO and B-BEKA respectively. These Bulgarian Tourers were very neat machines, having a revised radiator to replace the earlier Hispano-Suiza type, and had their rudders painted in white, green and red vertical stripes.

Meanwhile, an order had come in from the Greek Government, whose aircraft were not restricted in engine power. They were already Bristol customers, having bought six standard Bristol Fighters in 1922. The order was for six unarmed Tourers for use by the Royal Hellenic Navy, and which had to be capable of conversion into fighters if required. These machines had oleo undercarriages,

strengthened tailskids, balanced ailerons and rudders, large-area fins and camera mountings. The first three were equipped with Marconi wireless apparatus. Given Type Number 81A and sequence numbers 6712 to 6717, they were test-flown at Filton between 24 April and 15 May 1925, each was fitted in turn with a single Puma engine supplied by the Greek government then shipped to Phaleron without engines, to have Pumas fitted on arrival. Initially serialled NAY131 to NAY136 and bearing Greek national blue-white-blue roundels and rudder stripes, they were later re-serialled M-31 to M-36 and were still in use for training in 1928. In March 1931 the company supplied Rolls-Royce Falcon conversion kits to be fitted locally by the Greek Navy to bring them up to a new standard, becoming in effect a modernised version of the original three Falcon-engined Tourers built for the Air Board in July 1919. They similarly had 15gal centre-section gravity tanks, although the rear fuselage decking remained flat, as in the fighter, and the rear cockpit incorporated a Scarff-ring base. Two of them, by then numbered M-51 and M-54, had under-nose auxiliary tropical radiators similar to those fitted on RAF Bristol Fighters in the Middle East and India. The last survivor was M-35, the type being finally withdrawn from use in 1934.

The sole Type 83E School G-EBYT, registered in June 1928, had a stronger airframe, initially to take the 250hp direct-drive Bristol Titan engine. In this form it competed in the 1928 two-day Round-Britain King's Cup Race, bearing racing number 20, and came in 14th overall. *(Bristol)*

Bristol Type 89A G-EBOC of late 1926 was the first of this version, which had the fuselage strengthened by being plywood covered. *(Bristol)*

A trio of Bristol Fighters belonging to the Cambridge University Air Squadron, 1930. In the lead is J8443, a Mk.III DC; nearest the camera is J8286, a Mk.IV; and the furthest aircraft is F4644, another Mk.IV. *(via Philip Jarrett)*

Chapter 21

FLYING THE BRISTOL FIGHTER

There is no shortage of accounts by pilots who have flown preserved F.2Bs or reproductions, but this chapter is based on official test reports and recollections taken from various autobiographies of pilots who flew the type in service.

Tests on an unidentified F.2A with a 190hp Rolls-Royce engine, dated October 1916, found lateral stability 'very good', and longitudinal and directional stability 'good'. The length of run to unstick was 100 yards, and the aircraft could be pulled up with the engine stopped in 30-40 yards. As regards controls, 'stick dual fittings' were supplied. The machine was '… comfortable and easy to fly. Lands extremely slowly but had a slight tendency to pancake. Is light on rudder and manoeuvres easily. Tail adjustment is good in use and is easily worked.' Approximately four minutes were required to prepare the engine for starting.

A CFS report resulting from tests of an F.2A with a 140hp Hispano-Suiza engine in December 1916 stated that, although lateral and directional stability were 'good', longitudinal stability was 'unsuitable at climbing speed' and 'neutral at high speed'. It continued: 'There is a strong tendency to put the nose down on sharp turns. The tail adjustment is insufficient and there is a tendency to stall when climbing, and to dive when the engine is shut off.' Dual stick fittings were again provided. As regards controllability the aircraft: 'Requires constant attention longitudinally. Very easy to land if tail is set for slow flying. Easy to manoeuvre. Length of run to unstick 75 yards. To pull up engine stopped 100 yards.' Regarding tactical features, the CFS noted that the aircraft had an armoured seat and a Scarff gun mounting for the observer. It comments: 'Pilot's view is bad for reconnaissance and bomb sighting. Both pilot and observer are too exposed to the rush of air at high speed, and in the case of the observer, the operation of his gun is prejudiced. Pilot cannot let go of controls in a fight. Observer's arc of fire 180 degrees, and facility for firing good upwards, downwards, and to the rear. Communication between pilot and observer difficult without telephone.'

Cecil Lewis sampled the Bristol Fighter after he was posted from the Western Front to the Testing Squadron at Upavon in November 1916, and the first aircraft type he flew there was an F.2B prototype. He writes: 'After the Morane [i.e. the Morane-Saulnier 'Bullets', Types N, I and V], the Bristol Fighter was comparatively heavy and slow on the controls; but it was well co-ordinated and gave the pilot confidence. This aeroplane would not let you down.' He then tried it with the upper wing centre-section removed in an attempt to improve the pilot's view upwards:

The sudden gap in the top plane made me feel naked, as if I was being spied on. But how would it behave?

Take-off, climb, flying level – all these seemed fairly normal. Perhaps the lack of that central hunk of lift made her a bit slow, but nothing much. However, on throttling back to glide, it was a very different matter. Here the difference in lift was at once noticeable. You had to put the nose right down to maintain speed.

Right: **The gunner looks over his pilot's shoulder as their F.2B, 'B' of an undetermined unit, passes by the photographer's aeroplane.** *(Philip Jarrett)*

She dropped like a brick. Approach and landing were hazardous owing to a wide variety in attitude with engine on or off. It wasn't, I suppose, really dangerous; but it was no aeroplane for general use. Better to accept a poor pilot view than upset the general excellent handling. So we put the centre-section back.

A preliminary performance report of F.2B A7183 with a 190-270hp Rolls-Royce Falcon II noted:

This is the standard machine with increased engine power. Controllability is good for a big machine, but heavy laterally and slow off steep bank. It is well balanced and will fly 'hands off'. The engine controls and tail adjustment lever are inconveniently placed and difficult to reach. Length of run to unstick, 85 yards; to pull up (engine stopped), 120 yards.

A similar performance report for B1201, powered by a 200hp Hispano-Suiza and tested in January 1918, states:

On this machine the view of the pilot and observer is good generally, though the pilot has some difficulty in seeing below him. The manoeuvrability is good, and controls conveniently placed and easily worked. The drift wires on either side pass directly across the ends of the exhaust pipes and are liable to get burnt. The internal diameter of the suction oil pipe from oil tank to pump has now been altered from ½in to ⅞in. Length of run to unstick, 75 yards; to pull up (engine stopped) 110 yards, (engine throttled) 150 yards.

Of the Falcon III engined F.2B, Maj Oliver Stewart writes:

Strictly speaking, the Bristol Fighter should be spoken of in terms of the heroes of classical mythology. It was, in the fullest sense, a hero after their pattern – a fighter by name, inclination and aptitude. … The aeroplane has the smallest possible quantity of wings, wires and wood and is so disposed about the men that it interferes as little as possible with their outlook and their gunnery. Add also the fullest powers of manoeuvre and enormous strength. …

The pilot, sitting behind the trailing edge of the top plane, with his observer in close touch with him and protecting his

Above: **An early F.2B, believed to have been photographed at Martlesham Heath during early trials.** *(Philip Jarrett)*

back, felt that he could see and manoeuvre. The machine seemed to be stripped for action, carrying nothing in the way of useless equipment. The way in which the fuselage was slung, half-way between the upper and lower planes, accentuated the stripped-for-action effect and set out the crew on a sort of all-way observation tower. A pilot so placed could go into action with confidence. His back was protected and he could concentrate

upon bringing his front fixed Vickers gun into action. …

The pilot could enter a dog-fight and turn almost as quickly and on almost as small a radius as the best single-seater. He could fling his machine about, go into vertical dives, pull it out quickly, turn it on its back, spin it, roll it and generally do every sort of manoeuvre if the need arose. And all the time there was the comfortable feeling that the observer was there with

A nice wartime study of a new-looking F.2B, apparently still awaiting application of a serial number and unit markings. There is a Sopwith Camel in the hangar on the left. *(Philip Jarrett)*

Above: **Take-off was a critical stage of flight, when an error often proved fatal, as in this example. The mangled remains of F.2B E2458 '9' of 88 Sqn at Nivelles, after 2nd Lt Kellough stalled during a climbing turn after take-off for a practice flight on 3 March 1919.** *(Eric Harlin)*

Above: **A new-looking F.2B has its Falcon engine run-up against the chocks at an undetermined location during the First World War. The number of personnel in civilian clothing suggests it might be a manufacturer's airfield.** *(Philip Jarrett)*

his pair of Lewis guns, watching and protecting. It is not to be wondered at … that the pilots who used the Bristol Fighter were ready to tackle tremendous odds. It is not to be wondered at that the machine came to be dreaded by enemy pilots.

… the thing which ought to be remembered about [Bristol Fighters] above all else was the heroism of the observers. Machines came back from patrol again and again with their observers dead in the rear cockpit, and the casualties among observers were exceptionally high.

The reason is to be found in the tactics used. … the pilots fought their machines as single-seaters and left the rear defence to the observer. Acts of prodigious courage were entailed in this defence work, for the observer, with no engine to protect him, had often to stand up in his narrow cockpit and face the fire of diving fighters and, at the same time, to attempt to bring offensive fire to bear upon them. At such moments the observer's twin Lewis guns must have seemed a poor counter to the fixed guns of the German machines. Yet, in spite of the difficulties and dangers of the observer's task, in spite of the heavy casualties, there was never a lack of volunteers for work with the Bristol Fighters.

The teething troubles encountered when units on the Western Front first received the F.2B are recounted by W.F.J. Harvey of 22 Sqn, previously equipped with the Royal Aircraft Factory F.E.2b (the 'Fee'), in his book *'Pi' in the Sky:*

… the change to Bristol Fighters created difficulties which required time for solution. Mechanics – good as they were – had to learn a new engine and airframe; the armourers a new gun, the Vickers, with its far from simple Constantinesco operating gear. As a result both engine trouble and gun stoppages were common on most flights – troubles which were apt

While the pilot runs up the F.2B's Falcon against the chocks, airmen take the opportunity to pose for a photograph, Cranwell, 1923. *(Philip Jarrett)*

Right: **This Cambridge UAS F.2B, C4740, photographed in 1930, is a 'J Type' DC.** *(via Philip Jarrett)*

to end fatally. Flight commanders joined the squadron from England, their previous fighting experience out of date; and new pilots arrived who had had no fighting instruction beyond the casual circling of another machine over their training aerodromes, and no experience of flying conditions at the heights which the Bristol could reach – heights which the enemy Albatros, Pfalz and Fokker triplane machines enforced. Ex-Fee pilots who had sat in the prow of a 'pusher' with nothing but the observer and his gun before them, now occupied a small cockpit with many strange controls whose adjustment controlled performance, the gunner now at the rear, and wings, a long engine cowling and the propeller in front. With the pilot's Vickers firing through the propeller [arc] in the line of flight, this aircraft was, by its tactical arrangement, a predominantly offensive one, and surviving Fee pilots had to re-think their attitude to war in the air. They realised that, although they had no instruction on how to use them in combat, their new machines were first rate aircraft. But they had to learn how to use them.

However, once pilots had become accustomed to their new mounts their attitudes soon changed, and Harvey states:

Much has been written about the Bristol, most of it by those never lucky enough to take one off the ground; some by those who flew them in peacetime conditions but never in their natural element of twelve to twenty thousand feet where their true qualities became apparent. This was a classic aeroplane, in looks, in performance for its period, and of a curiously perfect tactical design at a time when the future requirements of a fighting aircraft were not fully understood, nor the strategy and tactics of fighting in the air fully developed.

He continues:

As a fighter, the setting of the fuselage between the wings and its knife-edge taper at the tail ensured the minimum of blind spots, which could be uncovered by the slightest of tail switching. The back-to-back seating of pilot and rear gunner, classic position of those fighting against odds, made possible instant change from offence to defence, and back again. So close was the seating that an experienced Bristol war flying pilot could be recognised by the scar across the back of his flying coat, caused by friction from the

Right: **A pair of well-maintained F.2Bs on a Middle East airfield in the 1920s.** *(Philip Jarrett)*

Scarff gun mounting. And the point of an elbow into the rear gunner's kidney would spur him into action quicker than any inter-com.

Harvey also provides examples of the F.2B's capabilities and resilience:

A flight of five Bristols with full war load reached 20,350ft still climbing in formation in July 1918, a tribute to the quality of the Flight mechanics. Cold and lack of oxygen ended the climb.

A Falcon III Bristol without war load and with 1cwt ballast in place of the rear gunner was able to maintain level flight near ground with six of twelve cylinders out of action.

A Bristol left uncontrolled with tailplane set neutral and throttle slightly open, descended from 16,000ft in a series of letters 'J', of which the verticals were 4,000 to 5,000ft.

From the observed behaviour of the ASI which circled two and one third times before breaking, the speed of a

Above: **A moody study of an F.2B, possibly of 2 Sqn and with flight leader's pennants trailing from its rear outer interplane struts and rudder, over a cloudscape.** *(Philip Jarrett)*

Bristol dived with full engine was calculated by the wise men of Filton at between 234 and 245mph, possibly a world speed record for an aircraft which returned. This machine survived a sharp pull-up. The rigging was somewhat deranged and the steel main member of the tail distorted.

Another instance of the strength of the "stick and string" Bristol was the difficulty found in breaking one which had an undiscoverable jinx in both engine and frame, and which undoubtedly would have caused the death of a crew, sooner or later. It took three "landings" at 10 to 15ft up and with two unhappy "volunteers" in the back seat to break a longeron, and so make the machine a write-off.

A delightful quality of the Bristol was the perfection with which it could perform the rarely seen "falling leaf" acrobatic. After being put into the first sideslip with throttle nearly closed it would continue to slip to alternate sides almost without direction, and mixed with hovers and spins the series could be repeated with ease until landing out of a last turn.

An intimate first-hand account of a Bristol Fighter observer's experiences is found in Walter Noble's book, *With a Bristol Fighter Squadron*.

Vivian Voss, a South African who piloted F.2Bs in 48 and 88 Sqns, recalled his first solo in the type, at Netheravon:

So I climbed over into the pilot's seat, and opened the throttle. I felt at home at once in a Bristol even on this first solo. The engine, a 250hp Rolls-Royce, was infinitely more powerful than anything I had come cross so far. It gave a full-throated roar and shot away across the aerodrome and then up, soaring into the air like a great eagle. She was a massive machine but so beautifully designed that she did not feel heavy on the controls. She responded superbly to the least touch of the stick or rudder-bar. After flying around for half an hour, I brought her down and landed quite smoothly. I felt that up to the present I had only been playing at flying.

Later, Voss ditched an F.2B, and he describes his first flight following the mishap:

… when I found myself sitting once more in the pilot's seat of a Bristol Fighter, my knees were knocking together and it was all I could do to wave the mechanics away and open the throttle. But from watching three or four similar cases of nerves during the previous six months, I knew that if I gave way now I should inevitably crock up altogether. So that afternoon I stayed up for an hour, and forced myself to put the Bristol through all her paces. I looped her, side-slipped her, half-rolled, stalled, and finally, towards the end of the hour, I spun her. Unfortunately she was loosely rigged and I had some difficulty in pulling her out of the spin, and this, to some extent, destroyed the confidence which had been coming back to me.

Voss remarks that most of the F.2Bs in the squadron 'were fitted with long exhaust pipes, which terminated behind the observer's cockpit. They were thus not so noisy as those carrying short exhausts'.

In 1919 H.F.V Battle (later Air Cdre) had to ferry a Bristol Fighter from Filton; his first experience on the type:

This machine, with a Rolls Falcon, was very pleasant, but I did not like the position of the throttle, which, in the early models, was down alongside my right knee. As I was accustomed to land with my left hand on the throttle, holding the control column with my right, landing this machine was rather awkward. …

Immediately after taking off from Filton I headed east and looked around for my compass. Imagine my dismay when I could not find one in the cockpit! I searched everywhere, but that which should have been, by common standards, right in the centre of the instrument board was not to be found in the cockpit. I therefore started to follow the railway but getting cold feet decided to land at the next aerodrome, which proved to be Yate, where I asked for petrol. I also asked one of the pilots there "Where the heck is the compass kept on these 'blank' machines?". It was rather humiliating, therefore, to have it pointed out to me. There it was in the trailing edge of the top centre section, just above the windscreen! Just above my nose in fact.

Seen at Hendon during the 1921 RAF Display, H1484 served with No.2 FTS at Duxford and the CFS at Upavon. In the background is the dummy 'village occupied by enemy troops', built from parts of dismantled Handley Page bombers, that was subjected to a dramatic 'bombing and machine-gun attack' during the display and blown up by carefully synchronised explosives previously positioned in the structures. Bristol Fighters took part in this event, and 'passenger seats' in them could be booked by members of the public for five guineas each. *(Philip Jarrett)*

Right: **Three F.2Bs of 6 Sqn over hostile Middle Eastern terrain, with the Gara Dagh mountain behind. Another shot of this formation appears in chapter 13.** *(Philip Jarrett)*

Shortly thereafter, Battle was tasked to fly an F.2B with a Sunbeam Arab engine from Kenley to Marquise.:

> It was a rough engine, but kept going all the way, probably because I had been warned to treat it gently. My next had to be collected from Castle Bromwich for the same destination. However, after fifty minutes' flying this Arab had had enough and burst an oil pipe.

In the ensuing forced landing near Daventry he ended up across Watling Street. Two weeks later he again went to Castle Bromwich to collect another Arab engined F.2B. After reaching Hendon he discovered a water leak which had to be repaired before departure:

> There was very little wind ... and the take-off was quite hair-raising. The machine took the whole field from east to west before becoming airborne, and then it only just cleared the tops of the old pre-war hangars. But worse was to follow. When over Paddock Wood on the Redhill to Ashford railway, the engine burst a large water pipe, necessitating a hurried descent. Considering the millions of hop poles which covered the ground beneath me I was lucky to find one clear field to land in. After making a temporary repair I was able to continue to Lympne where I left the machine for a proper overhaul before the Channel hop.
>
> I took one more of these Arab Brisfits from Castle Bromwich on the same run, but this one only got me to Kenley before shedding a breather.
>
> It was explained to me later that the unreliability of the Sunbeam Arab engine was due to the hurry in which it had been put into production, the engine being never properly balanced. All I know is that one had only to put the machine into a couple of tight turns and get some work out of the engine and the resulting vibration would burst something.

Flying F.2Bs in the Middle East brought its own challenges. When C.H. Keith transferred from 70 Sqn to become CO of 6 Sqn in January 1928, while serving in Iraq, he went from flying Vickers Victoria transports to Bristol Fighters, flying regular patrols over the police posts dotted along the northern Turkish frontier in the Middle East. He remarks:

> Flying over these wild mountains and working from the various landing-

An anonymous and somewhat worn F.2B over Old Sarum in the 1920s. *(Philip Jarrett)*

Above: **A gunner's-eye-view in a formation of 6 Sqn F.2Bs over the Middle East in the late 1920s/early 1930s. The quartered wheel discs of the adjacent aircraft are noteworthy.** *(Philip Jarrett)*

grounds we have amongst them, calls for a high standard of flying, and it is a mercy that our Rolls-Royce Falcon engines are of exceptional reliability. It is rather funny to fly a small lively 'Brisfit' after the heavy stately Victorias.

On one occasion they had to drop a despatch on the village of 'an unruly shaikh', at the

bottom of a deep valley behind the great Ghai-Shirin range:

> ... into this Oddie dived to release the message – dived full engine on, his airspeed whistling up to nearly 200mph, in order that he might have enough speed to "zoom" up out of the valley. I stayed above, and watched him dive until his

and if you over-shoot, you go over a considerable "edge" into the rocky valley beyond. Also the altitude is 3,500[ft] above sea-level, so you have to come in faster than normal, and even so you seem to glide like a brick. You have just to clear the edge of a steep hillside, glide over a patch of broken country, just clear a waddi and touch your wheels down immediately you are over it. Otherwise – certain trouble.

And this is part of his description of a flight from Baghdad to Sheiba:

The wind was behind us and therefore a friend, for we were making nearly 90mph over the ground. My Brisfit was flying well, but occasionally coughed out a little lubricating oil on to the hot exhaust pipe, which made a foul stench, and I saw Mac [his passenger] swallowing down his breakfast several times when I looked behind. Sand-devils were staggering across the desert in such numbers that I couldn't dodge them all, and we got some pretty hefty bumps from them. Nearing Ur, I flew into some locusts, and they flattened themselves on my wind-screen, and splashed everything with their unpleasant-looking and evil-smelling green blood.

Above: **Bristol F.2B J6694 above the clouds. This aircraft served in various units, including a period with 2 Sqn in Shanghai in the late 1920s.** *(Philip Jarrett)*

The 305-mile trip took just under four hours. Likewise, a return flight from Billeh to Mosul in 1929 was not without its anxious moments:

Coming back it is essential to gain 6,000 feet before one can get out of the valley. That climb gave me grey hairs. To and fro I went, poking my nose skywards, and my engine roaring away at full throttle, yet I was often caught in a downward bump and lost height on the deal. Eventually I won and got enough height to set out across the Piris Dagh. When I got over the top I found that, with engine full on and my nose up for climbing, I was actually losing height. But I had height to spare and could laugh at those wicked peaks, and although I had a rough passage, I skimmed over them and reached the lowland country and eased down my engine. It is hard work flying in bumps such as those, and my arm ached through wrestling with my control column, which would otherwise have been wrenched out of my hand a dozen times.

aircraft was a mere speck. Down went the coloured streamer bearing the message, and up he shot and was soon by my side. And if his engine had failed, I suppose we should have been dropping a wreath there in a day or so!

On 23 April 1928 Keith led a flight formation of three F.2Bs to Babadi, their landing ground near Amadia:

It is a foul landing-ground, as the approach is bad, the slope considerable,

Keith also mentions using the Neil Robertson stretcher:

F.2B J7654 photographed from another of its kind. Evidently a dual-control machine at this time, it served with 4 Sqn at Farnborough in 1926. *(Philip Jarrett)*

Right: **Captioned as depicting a crash by Plt Off Lockyer at Heliopolis, this photograph reveals some underside detail of the F.2B.** *(Philip Jarrett)*

We have fearsome contraptions, called Roberston Stretchers, for strapping to the top of the fuselage of our aircraft, to evacuate sick cases from those mountain landing-grounds where a Victoria couldn't land. It is usual to give the victim a squirt of morphia before he is strapped in! We recently had to bring down a bad case from Billeh – an Assyrian levy with peritonitis – and he said he'd sooner die than go off that way, so George doubled him up and brought him back in the air gunner's seat. (The stretcher is illustrated in Appendix 2.)

Air-firing and bombing practice at Mosul is vividly described by Keith:

Flying for the practices of our air firing and bombing reminds me of riding on some fabulous scenic railway – with the difference that you go twice as fast and there aren't any rails to guide you. For my front gun firing, I approach the target at 1,000 feet, and then as I see the target disappearing under my lower plane, I shove my nose down and we start whistling earthwards, at two miles a minute. During the dive, one has to manoeuvre the aircraft so that the gun sights come "on" the target, and then let go a stream of bullets at it. It seems an age, as one's nerves are tee-ed up, but really it is all over in a few seconds. When you think you have gone low enough, you pull up out of the dive, and are pressed hard in your seat, and as you shoot up the earth seems to recede as

Above: **Mechanics restrain an F.2B as its Falcon undergoes a test run. The decorative wheel covers are noteworthy.** *(Philip Jarrett)*

Below: **A pristine F.2B at Henlow in the 1920s. The nearest two de Havilland D.H.9As in the hangar are E866 and J7010 (ex-H3496).** *(Philip Jarrett)*

Another message pick-up by an F.2B, probably in the Middle East. Other F.2Bs are lined up in the background on the right. *(Philip Jarrett)*

A good underside view of an H-serialled F.2B, probably in the Middle East. *(Philip Jarrett)*

though some giant hand had snatched it away from under you. Hard rudder, down goes one plane, and you are round and ready to begin again. In the cool grey dawn, on an empty "tummy" this is the king of liver tonics!

When I have had my little fun with my front gun, I fly level past the target, and my gunner. Atkins, attacks it with his moveable Lewis gun. As I skim the ground, to and fro, I can hear him firing, and I pray he won't continue long enough to hit my tailplane. Then we move over and play at bombing. Way below me I see the "Range Clear" signal, and I turn and do a steep dive at the target, releasing the bomb just when it seems we shall dive into the ground and be dashed to pieces. Again and again, until all my bombs are gone, and then we come out of the sky and let someone else have crack at the targets.

Allen Wheeler recalled his experiences with the F.2B in the UK during the interwar years.

… the Bristol Fighter was quite a revelation after the Avro [504K]. … One opened up the engine gently and it always seemed to give its full power. The water coolant temperature had to be watched, and controlled with the radiator shutters.

The pupil's chief worry … was the pressurisation system for the fuel tanks. There were two fuel tanks, one in front of the pilot and one under the seat. There were three air pressure pumps – one engine driven, one windmill and one hand pump. There were two pressure release valves, one automatic and one manually operated on the hand pressure pump. There was a pressure indicator gauge on the dashboard in front of the pilot. The pressure lines

from all these met on a sort of small brass control panel on the dashboard so that immediate action could be taken by the pilot in the case of any emergency arising from a variation of pressure.

In the unlikely event of the pressure going too high, it could be released either by tapping the release valve in case it had got stuck, by operating the manual release on the hand pump, or by turning off the pumps. In the much more likely event of a loss of pressure below the standard 2½lb the first action was to turn off the pressure line to the fuel tank not in use at the time and give a few supplementary strokes on the hand pump. If the pressure still dropped, one turned off the line to the pressure release valve since that clearly was not needed at that moment, and gave a few more hand pumps, but one had to remember to turn it on again when and if things returned to normal.

Thereafter, by a process of elimination, one could probably establish where the fault lay; at the worst one was left with all lines turned off except pressure to the tank in use and the hand pump, which was operated energetically until one could land at an aerodrome. We always took off on the front tank because it had a slight gravity feed effect when full, thus a sudden loss of air pressure would probably not cause a dead cut from the engine.

The pre-take-off check was fairly simple. After running up and checking oil pressure, water temperature, both magnetos, and take-off revs, one merely set the 'cheese-cutter' tail adjustment, wiggled all the controls to their full movement to check that they came to "meet the stick" in every case lest some mechanic had replaced one since the last flight and crossed the wires, and then one taxied out. Any repair or replacement in fact always involved a full test flight by one of the instructors.

Taxiing in light wind was fairly easy. There were no brakes, but the tail skid

F.2B F4320 'D' of 31 Sqn over Lahore in 1923. By 1927 it was with A Flight of 5 Sqn, still wearing the individual letter 'D'. *(Philip Jarrett)*

Right: **An aerial study of F.2B J6750 'L', the aircraft of C Flight commander, 5 Sqn, in India, 1924-25, complete with spare wheel beneath the gunner's cockpit.** *(Philip Jarrett)*

gave enough braking effect to need significant engine power before the aircraft moved, thus ensuring a fair slipstream over the rudder. Taxiing down wind was more tricky but use of the ailerons augmented the rudder control very effectively if they were operated as for a normal turn in the air. In this way the following wind acted on the "down" ailerons and helped the rudder. Taxiing into wind required aileron operation the other way.

Take-off was absolutely straightforward, with very little tendency to swing, and the Bristol Fighter flew itself off in a quietly graceful way which was a joy to watch and hear. ... It was very stable with rather heavy controls all round. We were told that the elevators were made specially heavy since the specification called for a maximum diving speed of 400mph, and light elevators at that speed could have been embarrassing. I doubt if the Bristol could have reached such a figure even in a vertical dive, but it certainly picked up speed very quickly in a shallow dive at full power – as for a loop, which one entered at speeds between 120 and 140mph.

Its spin characteristics were normal, but a lot of height was lost during recovery owing to the steep angle of spinning and the aircraft's relatively heavy weight. One of the most impressive aerobatic manoeuvres practised in the Bristol was the flick roll, induced by adjusting the speed to approximately 85mph in level flight and pulling the stick hard back with full rudder; it then did an impressive one turn of a spin horizontally, following which the pilot quickly normalised the controls to prevent it starting another. A "falling leaf" was also possible, and quite neat, but one had to use a little engine power during the change-over to keep the manoeuvre symmetrical. ... a slow roll was virtually impossible owing to the very heavy ailerons; furthermore, we only had lap straps in the Bristol Fighter.

Approach and landing was very straightforward. It stalled at 42mph and the approach correction was greatly assisted by the wonderful control one had in even the steepest side-slip. We looked upon the Bristol landing run as rather long – all of 100 yards on a calm day – but the grass aerodromes we operated from as pupils usually gave a landing or take-off run of at least 900 yards, often much more. In operational squadrons we

Above: **Five F.2Bs patrolling over featureless Middle Eastern terrain; not the best place for a forced landing.** *(Philip Jarrett)*

were expected to operate from 400-yard strips with reasonably clear approaches.

The use of the message hook is also described by Wheeler:

In this scheme two rifles with fixed bayonets (or just any poles) were stuck in the ground about 5 yards apart and a string was stretched between them with a message tied to it. The Bristol Fighter had a hook which could be let down below from the undercarriage; this hooked up the string as the Bristol flew close between the rifles and the hook was then drawn up until the observer in the rear seat could get hold if it through a hole in the floor. All very primitive but without any form of R/T which could pass such messages it was the only way we could devise.

NB Further information on the handling of the Bristol Fighter will be found in Appendix 3, in the extracts from *AP.129*, the *RAF Flying Training Manual*.

This sad picture of an unidentified crashed F.2B provides an excellent view of the camera gun installed on the upper wing centre section, the wing structure and covering, and the gunner's cockpit. Note also the propeller blade propped up against the nose. *(Philip Jarrett)*

This series of images depicts artwork incorporating images of the **Bristol F.2B.**

Left: This colour postcard by Geoffrey Watson was published during the First World War. Although it is a nice representation of the F.2B, the aircraft carries the spurious serial number B4824, allocated to a Maurice Farman S.11 Shorthorn. *(Philip Jarrett)*

Right: A product of the 1930s, this card of an anonymous Bristol Fighter, by Howard Leigh, was one of a large series published by the Air League of the British Empire, entitled *The Air Leaguers' Album of British Aircraft*, which junior members could buy in series of six every six months as part of their membership fee. The Bristol Fighter was included in Series Three. *(Philip Jarrett)*

Left: This study of Bristol Fighter J6694 is taken from a print believed to have been produced in the 1930s, which is a reproduction of a watercolour almost certainly by W.E. Johns. This F.2B initially served with 2 Sqn at Oranmore in 1921. Then went to 13 Sqn in 1924-25. It ended up with 2 Sqn again, this time in Shanghai. *(Philip Jarrett)*

Left: **This wash painting of A7131 by Leonard Bridgman was published in Oliver Stewart's classic book *The Clouds Remember*. The aircraft went to 11 Sqn in June 1917 but was short-lived, being wrecked in a landing accident only a month later.** *(Philip Jarrett)*

Below: **Leonard Bridgman's 1934 illustration for the dust wrapper of Vivian Voss's book *Flying Minnows*, first published by John Hamilton in 1935. The author used the pseudonym Roger Vee.**

Above: **A Bristol Fighter is disappearing off the bottom of this cover for piece of sheet music entitled *Out of the Blue*, a 'vocal march' by Hubert Bath 'specially written for and dedicated to the Royal Air Force Depot (Uxbridge)' and published in 1931.** *(Philip Jarrett)*

Right: **This post-Second World War Belgian playing card, depicting an Hispano-engined Bristol Fighter, was used to encourage recruiting for the Belgian Air Force. One of the slogans on the reverse states: 'The young pilot carries the world in his pocket!'.** *(Philip Jarrett)*

BRISTOL FIGHTER INDIVIDUAL LISTING

Abbreviations used in Individual Histories

@	at least
1st Lt	First Lieutenant (USAS)
2nd Lt	Second Lieutenant
AA	Anti-Aircraft
AAP	Aircraft Acceptance Park
A&AEE	Aircraft & Armament Experimental Establishment
a/c	aircraft
AC	Aircraftman
ACIS	Air Council Inspection Squadron
AD	Aircraft Depot
ADC	Aircraft Disposal Company
AEE	Aircraft Experimental Establishment (became A&AEE)
AEG	Allgemeine Elektricitäts-Gesellschaft (German aircraft manufacturer)
AEP	Aeroplane Erection Park
AES	Aeroplane Experimental Station
AFC	Australian Flying Corps
AG	Air Gunner
AGS	Armament & Gunnery School
AHQ	Air Headquarters
AIS	Air Issues Section
ALG	Advanced Landing Ground
AM	Air Mechanic
AMB	Aviation Militaire Belge
AMC	Aircraft Manufacturing Company
AP	Aircraft Park
APS	Air Pilotage School
ARS	Aeroplane Repair Section
ASC	Army Service Corps
ASD	Aeroplane Supply Depot
ARD	Aeroplane Repair Depot
Aux	Auxiliary
AZP	Anti Zeppelin Patrol
B&C	British & Colonial Aeroplane Co Ltd
Bde	Brigade
BEF	British Expeditionary Force
BF	British Forces
Bmdr	Bombardier (Artillery rank equivalent to a corporal)
c.	circa (around)
Capt	Captain
CAF	Canadian Air Force
CAS	Chief of the Air Staff
CC	Constantinescu synchronisation (interrupter) gear
CCS	Casualty Clearing Station
CDP	Central Delivery Pool London
CF	Communications Flight
CFS	Central Flying School
CO	Commanding Officer
Col	Colonel
Comms	Communications
Cpl	Corporal
CTD	Controller Technical Development
CUAS	Cambridge University Air Squadron
D	Depot
DAE	Director of Aeronautical Equipment
DC	Dual Control
DCM	Distinguished Conduct Medal
dd	delivered
Dept	Department
DFW	Deutsche Flugzeug-Werke (German aircraft manufacturer)
D of T	Director of Training
DSO	Distinguished Service Order
DTD	Directorate of Technical Development

E1	Department or section responsible for storage units
EA	Enemy Aircraft
EAD	Experimental Armament Department
(E)ARD	(Eastern) Aeroplane Repair Depot
ECD	Experimental Constructive Department
EF	Expeditionary Force
EKB	Enemy Kite Balloon
ES	Experimental Station
E&WS	Electrical & Wireless School
Fl.Abt(A)	Flieger Abteilung Artillerie (German artillery spotting unit)
Flik	Fliegerkompagnien (Austro-Hungarian flying company)
Flt	Flight
Flt Cdt	Flight Cadet
Flt Lt	Flight Lieutenant
Fg Off	Flying Officer
FPS	Fleet Practice Station
fr	freiherr (German Baron)
FS	Fighting School
FSL	Flight Sub-Lieutenant
FTL	Forced to Land
FTS	Flying Training School
GI	Ground Instructional (airframe)
Gnr	Gunner
HA	Hostile Aircraft
HAD	Home Aircraft Depot
HAP	Hostile Aircraft Patrol
HCF	Home Communications Flight
HD	Home Defence
Hon	Honourable
HQ	Headquarters
IAAD	Inland Area Aircraft Depot
IACF	Inland Area Communications Flight
IDE	Instrument Design Establishment
IIA	Injured in Action
IIFA	Injured in Flying Accident
IIGA	Injured in Ground Accident
IOAS	Injured on Active Service
IRA	Irish Republican Army
IRAS	Imperial Russian Air Service
Jasta	Jagdstaffel (German scout unit)
KIA	Killed in Action
KIFA	Killed in Flying Accident
KIGA	Killed in Ground Accident
KOAS	Killed on Active Service
LAC	Leading Aircraftman
LCpl	Lance Corporal
LFT	Luftfahrtruppe (Aviation Troops – Austro-Hungarian Air Service)
LG	Landing Ground
LH	Left Hand
LIA	Lost in Action
Lt	Lieutenant
Ltn	Leutnant (German 2nd Lieutenant)
LVG	Luft-Verkehrs Gesellschaft (German aircraft manufacturer)
MC	Military Cross
ME	Middle East
Mech	Mechanic
MFJa	Marine-Feldjagdstaffel (German Naval scout unit)
MM	Military Medal
MOS	Marine Operators School
NAF	National Aircraft Factory
NF	Night Flying
N/I	No Information
NLG	Night Landing Ground
NTS	Night Training School

NWF	North West Frontier
NZ	New Zealand
Obltn	Oberleutnant (German/Austrian [1st] Lieutenant)
Obs	Observers
O/C	Officer Commanding
Offstlvtr	Offizier Stellvertreter (German Warrant Officer)
OOC	Out of Control
OP	Offensive Patrol
OSPMR	Observers School of Photography and Maritime Reconnaissance?
o/t	over turned
OUAS	Oxford University Air Squadron
PD	Packing Depot
PO	Petty Officer
Plt Off	Pilot Officer
POW	Prisoner of War
Prob	Probationer
Pte	Private
RAE	Royal Aircraft Establishment
RAF	Royal Aircraft Factory
RAF	Royal Air Force
Regt	Regiment
RH	Right Hand
Rittm	Rittmeister (German Cavalry Captain)
RL	Royal Laboratory
RN	Royal Navy
RNAS	Royal Naval Air Service
RS	Reserve Squadron
SA	South Africa
SD	Special Duties
SAC	School of Army Co-operation
SAF	School of Aerial Fighting
SAFG	School of Aerial Fighting & Gunnery
(S)ARD	(Southern) Aeroplane Repair Depot
SEAFIS	South-Eastern Area Flying Instructors School
SF	Station Flight
Sgt	Sergeant
Sgt Maj	Sergeant Major
s/n	sequence number
snd	spinning nose dive
SoTT	School of Technical Training
Sqn	Squadron
Sqn Ldr	Squadron Leader
SS	Salvage Section
SSF	School of Special Flying
Stn	Station
Sub Lt	Sub-Lieutenant
T	Training
TS	Training Squadron
TDS	Training Depot Station
TO	Take Off
Uffz	Unteroffizier (German Corporal)
USA	United States of America
USAS	United States Air Service
VC	Victoria Cross
vict	combat victory
v	von (German nobility preposition 'of')
Vzfw	Vizefeldwebel (German Sergeant Major)
(W)ARD	(Western) Aeroplane Repair Depot
w/e	week ending
wef	with effect from
WEE	Wireless Experimental Establishment
Wg Cdr	Wing Commander
WIA	Wounded in Action
WT	Wireless Telegraphy/Telephony

2 BRISTOL R.2A ordered 28.8.16 under Contract 87/A/552 from The British & Colonial Aeroplane Co Ltd, Bristol and numbered A3303 & A3304. (Intended for 120hp Beardmore). [Consecutive works' sequence nos. 1379-1380].

A3303 Completed as F.2A (Falcon I) and first flown at Filton 9.9.16. **CFS** Upavon 21.9.16 (service trials); **2 AD** dd ex England 19.10.16 (Major Mills – engine 1/WD8168) and returned to England 22.10.16. **ES** Orfordness by 02:17, on HAP 7.7.17 (Lt F.D. Holder/Lt F.W. Musson both OK), on 08:20 HAP 22.7.17 (Lt F.D. Holder/Sgt S. Ashby both OK), on 17:45 HAP 12.8.17 (Lt F.D. Holder/Lt Wallace both OK), on 10:30 HAP 22.8.17 (Lt F.D. Holder/Capt B.M. Jones both OK) and still with unit until @ 14.5.18 (Lt J.A.W. Armstrong/AM2 Lowe on Visibility Test).

A3304 Completed as F.2A (150hp Hispano-Suiza) and first flown at Filton 25.10.16. **CFS** Upavon by 12.16.

50 BRISTOL FIGHTER F.2A ordered 28.8.16 under Contract 87/A/552 from The British & Colonial Aeroplane Co Ltd, Bristol and numbered A3305 to A3354. (190hp Falcon I). [Consecutive works' sequence nos. 1431 to 1480]. 10 delivered by 31.12.16 and contract fulfilled w/e 31.3.17.

A3305 **38 RS** Rendcomb by 20.12.16.

A3306 **38 RS** Rendcomb by 1.2.17 (Lt J.H.T. Letts/Lt Brockenhurst) until @ 5.5.17 (2nd Lt J.A.W. Armstrong).

A3307 **38 TS** Rendcomb by 1.2.17 (Lt J.H. Letts/Lt Dolbison) until @ 23.11.17. **62 Sqn** Rendcomb by 7.1.18. **38 TS** Rendcomb by 20.1.18 until @ 23.2.18.

A3308 **38 RS/TS** Rendcomb by 31.1.17 (Lt J.H. Letts/Lt Cooper) and wrecked 13.6.17 (Lt R. Dodds/passenger both OK, crashed into woodland).

A3309 On Delivery Flight to **38 RS**, crashed near Malmesbury 23.1.17 (2nd Lt B.F. Parsons fatally IIFA/2nd Lt C.B. Fenton IIFA, lost flying speed on downwind turn with failing engine – engine 1/190/213/WD10403). **38 TS** Rendcomb by 17.2.17 until @ 18.2.18.

A3310 **38 RS/TS** Rendcomb by 21.4.17 (2nd Lt J.A.W. Armstrong) and wrecked 11.7.17 (2nd Lt A.J. Cathie/2nd Lt H.W. Knowlson-Williams both KIFA, stalled in flat spin, dived in from 300ft – engine 215/WD10405).

A3311 **38 RS** Rendcomb and wrecked lost speed near ground, crashed 16.3.17 (2nd Lt J.H. Walker KIFA, lost flying speed near the ground after cutting off engine to achieve a slower landing – engine WD10420).

A3312 At maker's 20.3.17 allotted to BEF. En route to **(S)ARD** 13.4.17, BEF allotment cancelled and for O/C **DAE 2a Repair Section**. At (S)ARD 19.5.17 allotted to BEF. **1 AD** dd ex England 10.6.17 (engine 255/WD10458). **11 Sqn** dd ex 1 AD 11.6.17 (same engine) and wrecked on Practice Flight 28.6.17 (2nd Lt G.N. Hunstone KOAS/2nd Lt H.D. Duncan IOAS, attempted to turn back after engine failed at 250ft on take off, stalled and nosedived in – same engine). **2 AD** ex 11 Sqn 29.6.17 and deleted 30.6.17 (10hr 20min).

A3313 **48 Sqn** Rendcomb. **21st Wing ARS** Rendcomb ex 48 Sqn 15.2.17. **48 Sqn** ex 21st Wing ARS 24.2.17.

A3314 **35 RS** Northolt by 27.4.17 until @ 30.4.17. **39 (HD) Sqn** North Weald and wrecked 20.11.17 (2nd Lt T.B. Pritchard MC fatally IIFA/2nd Lt J.A. LLoyd IIFA, spun in from 1,200ft – engine 1/190/305/WD10448).

A3315 **1 AD** dd ex England 18.3.17 (engine 221/WD10410). **48 Sqn** dd ex 1 AD 6.4.17 (same engine) and damaged in successful combat on 18:00 OP, Arras, 9.4.17 (2nd Lt J.H.T. Letts OK/Lt H.G. Collins KIA, sent 2 Albatros D.III OOC – same engine). **2 AD** ex 48 Sqn 11.4.17. **11 Sqn** dd ex 2 AD 15.6.17 (engine 371/WD10481) and wrecked on Close Patrol 17.6.17 (Capt J.L. Williamson IOAS/Capt J.A. le Royer OK, o/t in long grass during forced landing after engine failure – same engine). **2 AD** ex 11 Sqn 19.6.17 and deleted 23.6.17 (not worth reconstruction, 29hr 25min).

A3316 **38 RS** Rendcomb and wrecked 7.2.17 (2nd Lt J.S. Brown IIFA, spun into the ground – engine 1/190/233/WD10414) and deleted by **48 Sqn** 10.2.17.

A3317 **48 Sqn** Rendcomb (Lt J.H. Letts), to BEF with unit and wrecked after combat NE of Arras 18:30, 7.4.17 (pilot Lt J.W. Warren OK/2nd Lt G.C. Burnand KIA, the machine was force landed near Saulty after engine failure – engine 225/WD10407). **2 AD** ex 48 Sqn 9.4.17, for reconstruction by 30.4.17 but deleted 23.6.17 (not worth reconstruction, 61hr 15min).

A3318 **48 Sqn** Rendcomb dd 13.2.17 (engine 239/WD10418), to BEF with unit 8.3.17, LIA after successful combat on 07:35 OP 11.4.17 (2nd Lt R.E. Adeney fatally WIA/2nd Lt L.G. Lovell KIA, shared in destroying 2 Albatros D.III with A3323 and A3338 near Fampoux then shot down c.09:05 – same engine) and deleted on unit that day (50hr 11min).

A3319 **38 TS** Rendcomb dd ex **21st Wing ARS** 27.7.17, marked as a/c *2* and wrecked returning from a forced landing 30.8.17 (Major E.J. Bannatyne fatally IIFA, machine caught fire in the air and crashed in a further forced landing – engine 205/WD10404).

A3320 **48 Sqn** Rendcomb dd 21.2.17 (engine 237/WD10417), to BEF with unit 8.3.17, LIA on OP, Douai, 5.4.17 (Lt L.H.A. Cooper/Lt A. Boldison both POW/WIA, probably brought down by Ltn Simon, Jasta 11 – same engine) and deleted on unit that day (18hr 44min).

A3321 **48 Sqn** Rendcomb (Lt J.H. Letts), to BEF with unit and wrecked after OP 22.4.17 (2nd Lt W.T. Price/2nd Lt M.A. Benjamin both OK, force landed on road near aerodrome after engine failure – engine 36/WD10425). **2 AD** ex 48 Sqn 23.4.17 and deleted 29.5.17 (not worth reconstruction, 56hr 27min).

A3322 **48 Sqn** as a/c *5*, LIA on 14:50 Line Patrol, Arras, 13.4.17 (2nd Lt H.D. Davies/2nd Lt R.S.L. Worsley both POW, brought down near Vitry by AA fire – engine 241/WD10419).

A3323 **48 Sqn** Rendcomb dd 13.2.17, to BEF with unit 8.3.17, vict 10.4.17 (2nd Lt G.N. Brockenhurst/2nd Lt C.B. Boughton shared a HA near Remy with A3338) then LIA after successful combats on OP, Arras, 11.4.17 (2nd Lt G.N. Brockenhurst/2nd Lt C.B. Boughton both POW/WIA, shared 2 Albatros D.III with A3318 & A3338 then brought down near Gavrelle, probably by Ltn L. v Richthofen, Jasta 11 – engine 229/WD10412) and deleted on unit that day (47hr 13min).

A3324 **48 Sqn** as a/c *2* and wrecked on OP 30.5.17 (2nd Lt J.F. Grose/2nd Lt H. Munro both OK, the machine caught fire in the air and burnt out on the aerodrome – engine 267/WD10453). **2 AD** ex 48 Sqn 1.6.17 and deleted 22.6.17 (not worth reconstruction, 159hr 35min).

A3325 **48 Sqn** Rendcomb, allotted 14.2.17 dd 14.2.17, marked as a/c *4*, to BEF with unit 8.3.17 and vict 2.5.17 (2nd Lt T.P. Middleton/2nd Lt C.G. Claye both OK, sent an Albatros C-type OOC near Adinfer Wood at c.10:00). **2 AD** ex 48 Sqn 26.5.17. **11 Sqn** dd ex 2 AD 8.6.17 (engine 26/WD10434). **1 AD** ex 11 Sqn 12.7.17 (same engine) and flown to England 13.7.17. **35 TS** Northolt and wrecked 22.9.17 (Cdt Novikov, IRAS, KIFA, stalled on turn and nosedived in – engine 447/WD15757).

A3326 **48 Sqn** Rendcomb allotted 13.2.17 and collected from Filton 23.2.17 but wrecked on Delivery Flight (2nd Lt A.D. Finney IIFA/Lt H.C. Fry KIFA, low flying in bad weather with insufficient height for safe landing after engine failed – engine 1/190/34/WD10428).

A3327 **48 Sqn** Rendcomb allotted 13.2.17, to BEF with unit 8.3.17, and wrecked after OP, Arras, 29.4.17 (2nd Lt W.T. Price/2nd Lt M.A. Benjamin both OK, crashed on landing – engine 257/WD10457). **2 AD** ex 48 Sqn and under repair by 1.6.17. **11 Sqn** dd ex 2 AD 29.6.17 (engine 337/WD10486) and wrecked on Delivery Flight to 2 AD 5.7.17 (2nd Lt R.H. Stacey IIFA, crashed after engine failure on take off – same engine). **2 AD** ex 11 Sqn 6.7.17 and deleted 24.7.17 (not worth reconstruction, 54hr 39min).

A3328 Allotted to **48 Sqn** Rendcomb 13.2.17. **38 TS** Rendcomb dd 23.2.17, damaged 17.6.17 (Lt R. Dodds OK, undercarriage collapsed on landing) and wrecked 10.11.17 (Sgt R. Lincoln fatally IIFA, nosedived in from 100ft after flat spin – engine 1/190/227/WD10415).

A3329 **48 Sqn** Rendcomb allotted 14.2.17, to BEF with unit 8.3.17 and wrecked before OP 8.4.17 (2nd Lt R.E. Adeney/2nd Lt H.L. Tomkins both OK, crashed on take off – engine 20/WD10422). **2 AD** ex 48 Sqn 9.4.17 and under reconstruction by 1.6.17. **11 Sqn** dd ex 2 AD 29.6.17 (engine 68/WD10465). **2 AD** ex 11 Sqn 4.5.17 (same engine). **1 AD** ex 2 AD 5.5.17 and flown to England 7.7.17. **38 TS** Rendcomb by 1.8.17 (2nd Lt T. Stephenson) until @ 23.1.18.

A3330 **48 Sqn** Rendcomb allotted 14.2.17, to BEF with unit 8.3.17, LIA on OP, Arras, 8.4.17 (2nd Lt O.W. Berry KIA/2nd Lt F.B. Goodison fatally IIA, brought down near Remyat c.14:00 after combat – engine 28/WD10427) and deleted on unit that day (25hr 58min).

A3331 **38 RS** Rendcomb allotted 21.2.17, dd ex **21st Wing ARS** 22.2.17 and wrecked 11.5.17 (Lt R.H. Spencer IIFA, forced landing after engine failure – engine 1/190/38/WD10431).

A3332 **35 RS** Northolt by 28.4.17 and wrecked 4.6.17 (Lt P.E. Welchman IIFA, pressure failed and stalled on a turn – engine 1/190/469/WD10520).

A3333 Allotted to **48 Sqn** 21.2.17. Presume reallotted to Training.

A3334 **48 Sqn** Rendcomb allotted 21.2.17, to BEF with unit 8.3.17 and damaged on OP 10.4.17 (Capt A.T. Cull/Cpl R. Edwards both OK, the machine was shot up and force landed near Queant – engine 48/WD10433). **2 AD** ex 48 Sqn 14.4.17. **48 Sqn** reissued ex 2 AD 26.5.17, marked as a/c *3* and wrecked after OP 4.6.17 (2nd Lt R.L. Curtiss OK/2nd Lt A.D. Light IOAS, the engine failed on landing approach and the machine hit a tree – engine 263/WD10450). **2 AD** ex 48 Sqn 5.6.17 and deleted 22.6.17 (not worth reconstruction, 51hr 20min).

A3335 Allotted to **48 Sqn** 21.2.17. Presume reallotted to Training. **(S)ARD** tested 16.5.17 (Sgt Cole/Lt E.H. Lawford, 'Test OK, 115mph, nice machine').

A3336 Allotted to **48 Sqn** 24.2.17. **1 AD** dd ex England 18.3.17 (engine 26/WD10434). **48 Sqn** dd ex 1 AD 27.3.17 (same engine), marked as a/c *1* and wrecked before OP 25.4.17; (2nd Lt E.G. Roberts/AM2 A. Trusson both OK, stalled on take off and crashed – engine 62/WD10446). **2 AD** ex 48 Sqn and deleted 2.5.17 (not worth reconstruction, 53hr 44min).

A3337 **48 Sqn** Rendcomb allotted 24.2.17, to BEF with unit 8.3.17, LIA on OP, Douai, 5.4.17 (Capt W.L. Robinson VC/2nd Lt E.D. Warburton both POW, brought down in combat with Jasta 11 – engine 54/WD10437) and deleted on unit that day (23hr 25min).

A3338 **48 Sqn** Rendcomb allotted 24.2.17, to BEF with unit 8.3.17, vict 10.4.17 (Capt D.M. Tidmarsh/2nd Lt C.B. Holland shared a HA OOC near Remy with A3323) then LIA after successful combats on 07:35 OP 11.4.17 (Capt D.M. Tidmarsh/2nd Lt C.B. Holland both POW, had shared destruction of 2 Albatros D.III near Fampoux with A3318 & A3323, then shot down near Gavrelle, possibly by Ltn K. Wolff, Jasta 11 – engine 50/WD10435) and deleted on unit that day (43hr 27min).

A3339 N/I

A3340 **48 Sqn**, LIA on OP, Douai 5.4.17 (2nd Lt A.N. Leckler POW wounded/2nd Lt H.D.K. George POW fatally wounded, brought down in combat c.10:50 by Obltn M. fr v Richthofen Jasta 11 – engine 30/WD10443) and deleted on unit that day (10hr 18min).

A3341 **48 Sqn**, LIA on 11:10 OP, Arras 20.5.17 (2nd Lt J.A.W. Armstrong/2nd Lt G. Baines both OK, brought down near Courcelette with radiator shot through in combat – engine 44/WD10429) and deleted on unit that day (97hr 14min).

A3342 **AEP** Lympne 20.3.17 reallotted from **48 Sqn** to BEF but allotment cancelled 11.4.17 and en route Lympne – **(S)ARD** for **DAE 2a Repair Section**. At (S)ARD 26.5.17, allotted to BEF. **1 AD** dd ex England 17.6.17 (engine 343/WD10501) and flown **8 AAP** Lympne 5.7.17 without issue to squadron (Lt H. Shaw, same engine). **82 Sqn** Waddington dd ex Lympne 4.8.17 (Lt Haig, via Chingford – same engine). **27th Wing ARS** engineless ex 82 Sqn 7.9.17. 82 Sqn reissued engineless ex **ARS** 27.9.17. **62 Sqn** Rendcomb by air ex 82 Sqn 6.10.17 (same engine).

A3343 **48 Sqn** LIA on OP, Douai, 5.4.17 (Lt A.T. Adams POW wounded/2nd Lt D.J. Stewart POW, brought down in combat at c.10:50, probably by Obltn M. fr v Richthofen, Jasta 11 – engine 22/WD10426) and deleted on unit that day (15hr 32min).

A3344 **35 RS** Northolt.

A3345 At Bristol 5.3.17 allotted to BEF. **1 AD** dd ex England 18.3.17 (engine 247/WD10440). **2 AD** dd ex 1 AD 23.3.17 (same engine). **48 Sqn** dd ex 2 AD 9.4.17 and damaged on OP 2.5.17, shot up in combat with Albatros D.IIIs (2nd Lt L.G. Harrison/2nd Lt H.L.E. Richards both WIA). **1 AD** ex 48 Sqn 12.6.17 and flown to England that day (same engine). **8 AAP** Lympne, on 11:10 HAP 13.6.17 (Lt R.S. Carroll) and tested 18.6.17 (2nd Lt H. Shaw). **35 TS** Northolt.

A3346 At Filton 8.3.17 allotted to BEF. In France by 19.3.17 reallotted to **48 Sqn**, wrecked on Practice Flight 23.3.17 (Capt A.T. Cull/Lt H.D.K. George both OK, crashed near Bellevue aerodrome after engine failure – engine 243/WD10424). **2 AD** ex 48 Sqn 26.3.17 and for overhaul 30.4.17. **48 Sqn** reissued ex 2 AD by 1.6.17. **1 AD** ex 48 Sqn 12.6.17 (engine 299/WD10460) and flown to England 13.6.17.

A3347 At Filton 8.3.17 allotted to BEF. **1 AD** dd ex England 24.3.17 (engine 251/WD10451). **2 AD** ex 1 AD 31.3.17 (same engine). **48 Sqn** dd ex 2 AD 8.4.17 (same engine), victs 2.5.17 (Lt O.J.F Scholte/AM2 F.W. Dame destroyed an Albatros D.III in flames and sent another OOC near Biache-Vitry at c.19:45, further vict 4.5.17 (2nd Lt H. Smither/AM2 V. Reed destroyed a HA C-type near Pelves at c.16:15, shared A3350) then damaged on 15:05 OP, Arras, 11.5.17 (2nd Lt J.A.W. Binnie OK/2nd Lt F.M. Magenais WIA, shot up in combat – same engine). **2 AD** ex 48 Sqn and for overhaul 1.6.17 but deleted 23.6.17 (not worth reconstruction, 76hr 52min).

A3348 At Filton 13.3.17 allotted to BEF. **1 AD** dd by air ex England 13.4.17 (engine 261/WD10449). **48 Sqn** dd ex 1 AD 28.4.17 (same engine), victs 2.5.17 (2nd Lt W.O.B. Winkler/2nd Lt E.S. Moore sent 2 Albatros D.III OOC and destroyed another, all near Brebieres-Biache 19.30-19.40). **1 AD** ex 48 Sqn 14.6.17 (engine 24/WD10423) and flown to England 15.6.17. **82 Sqn** Waddington dd ex **(S)ARD** 5.8.17 (engine 589/WD12566). **27th Wing ARS** ex 82 Sqn 23.8.17. **82 Sqn** reissued ex **ARS** 7.9.17. **27th Wing ARS** engineless ex 82 Sqn 19.10.17 and allotted to **35 TS** but allotment cancelled 24.10.17.

A3349 At Filton 13.3.17 allotted to BEF. **(S)ARD** by 29.3.17 with BEF allotment suspended and under repair. **1 AD** dd ex England by air 30.3.17 (engine 293/WD10459). **48 Sqn** dd ex 1 AD 6.4.17 (same engine), vict 2.5.17 (2nd Lt H.C. Farnes/2nd Lt Davis sent an Albatros C-type OOC, E of Adinfer Wood at c.10:00, shared A3325) then wrecked on 16:05 OP, Arras 10.5.17 (2nd Lt G.E. Hawksley/2nd Lt L. Speller both WIA, aircraft shot up and o/t in forced landing near Avesnes – same engine). **2 AD** ex 48 Sqn and deleted 29.5.17 (not worth reconstruction, 87hr 19min).

A3350 At Filton 13.3.17 allotted to BEF. **1 AD** dd ex England by air 28.3.17 (engine 299/WD10460) and tested 5.4.17. **48 Sqn** dd ex 1 AD 6.4.17 (same engine) and victs 4.5.17 (Capt J.H.T. Letts/2nd Lt L. Speller destroyed a HA C-type near Pelves at 16:15, shared A3347), 10.5.17 (2nd Lt T.P. Middleton/2nd Lt C.A. Malcolmson destroyed an Albatros D.III between Brebieres-Douai at 06:55), 11.5.17 (2nd Lt H. Smither & AM2 Rutherford sent an Albatros D.III OOC near Biache-Dury at 12:45, shared A7104) then damaged in successful combat 24.5.17 (Capt J.H.T. Letts OK/Lt L.W. Allen WIA, sent down a HA C-type near Vitry at c.15:40 but machine hit by enemy fire). **1 AD** ex 48 Sqn 14.6.17 (engine 289/WD10456) and flown to England that day. **8 AAP** Lympne and damaged on Patrol/Test 18.6.17 (2nd Lt H. Shaw OK, gun not timed and propeller shot away). **38 TS** Rendcomb by 27.6.17 until @ 26.12.17.

A3351 At Filton 13.3.17 allotted to BEF. En route to **(S)ARD** 11.4.17 with BEF allotment cancelled and for **DAE 2A Repair Section**. At (S)ARD 26.5.17 allotted to BEF but reallotted to Training 20.6.17. **35 TS** Northolt by 9.17.

A3352 At Filton 17.3.17 allotted to BEF. **1 AD** dd ex England by air 17.4.17 (engine 259/WD10448). **48 Sqn** dd ex 1 AD 9.4.17 (same engine), LIA on 18:20 OP, Arras, 25.5.17 (2nd Lt W.J. Clifford/2nd Lt H.L. Tomkies both KIA, probably brought down by Ltn K. Schafer, Jasta 11 – same engine) and deleted on unit that day (46hr 10min).

A3353 At Filton 21.3.17 allotted to BEF. **1 AD** dd ex England by air 5.4.17 (engine 253/WD10452). **48 Sqn** dd ex 1 AD 6.4.17 (same engine) and wrecked after Line Patrol 9.4.17 (2nd Lt A.B. Anstey IOAS/AM2 Rutherford OK, hit trees on aerodrome boundary when landing – same engine). **2 AD** ex 48 Sqn 11.4.17 and deleted 12.4.17 (6hr 15min).

A3354 At Filton 10.4.17 reallotted from Technical Controller to BEF. **1 AD** dd ex England 20.4.17 (engine 263/WD10450). **48 Sqn** dd ex 1 AD 21.4.17 and wrecked 24.4.17 (damaged in fire – same engine). **2 AD** ex 48 Sqn 25.4.17, intended for reconstruction 30.4.17 but deleted 20.7.18 (not worth reconstruction, 11hr 25min).

200 BRISTOL FIGHTER F.2B ordered 28.8.16 under Contract 87/A/552 (Additional) from The British & Colonial Aeroplane Co Ltd, Bristol and numbered A7101 to A7300. (190hp Falcon I or 220hp Falcon II, with some machines re-engined in service with 275hp Falcon III, or 210hp Arab). [Consecutive works' sequence nos. 2069 to 2268]. Deliveries from w/e 14.4.17.

A7101 (Falcon I) **AAP** Filton by 17.4.17, allotted to BEF. **1 AD** dd ex England 22.4.17 (engine 279/WD10466). **48 Sqn** dd ex 1 AD 22.4.17, LIA on 15:00 OP 11.5.17 (Capt A.T. Cull/AM1 A. Trusson both KIA, brought down in flames near Fresnes – same engine) and deleted on unit that day (57hr 58min).

A7102 (Falcon I) **AAP** Filton 21.4.17, allotted to BEF and despatched 21.4.17. **1 AD** dd ex England by air 24.4.17 (engine 273/WD10464). **48 Sqn** dd ex 1 AD 25.4.17 (same engine), vict 18.6.17 (Lt T.P. Middleton/2nd Lt A.W. Merchant destroyed an Albatros D.V, S of Rumaucourt 14:30) and on unit charge until @ 29.6.17. **22 Sqn** dd ex 1 AD 5.8.17 (engine 269/WD10454). **1 AD** ex 22 Sqn 10.8.17 and flown to England that day (same engine). **59 TS** Yatesbury by 3.9.17 and wrecked 11.9.17 (2nd Lt W.L. Woodman IIFA, mis-judged S-turns on approach, probably owing to mist; Woodman admitted to Chiseldon Military Hospital and discharged later in the month. – engine 190/269/WD10454).

A7103 (Falcon I) **AAP** Filton 21.4.17, allotted to BEF but reallotted to Training Bde 23.4.17; **35 TS** Northolt and wrecked on Practice Flight 27.7.17 (Lt I.B. Hart-Davies KIFA/2nd Lt A.D. Miller IIFA, bad landing after turning back with engine failure – engine 190/349/WD10518).

A7104 (Falcon I) **AAP** Filton 21.4.17, allotted to BEF. **1 AD** dd ex England by air 28.4.17 (engine 297/WD10468). **48 Sqn** dd ex 1 AD 28.4.17 (same engine) and wrecked on OP, Arras, 4.6.17 (2nd Lt W.A. Southey/Lt V.W.G. Nutkins both IOAS, on OP engine failed, hit telegraph wires in forced landing near Dainville and o/t – engine 58/WD10445). **2 AD** ex 48 Sqn 7.6.17 and deleted 8.6.17 (69hr 47min).

A7105 (Falcon I) **AAP** Filton 21.4.17, allotted to BEF. **1 AD** dd ex England 29.4.17 (engine 285/WD10472). **48 Sqn** dd ex 1 AD 29.4.17 (same engine) and wrecked on OP 30.4.17 (2nd Lt H.C. Patterson/Cpl R. Edwards both KOAS, collided with **66 Sqn** Sopwith Pup A7323 at over 2,000ft – same engine) and deleted on unit that day (5hr 10min).

A7106 (Falcon I) **AAP** Filton 25.4.17, allotted to BEF. **1 AD** dd ex England 29.4.17 (engine 291/WD10476). **48 Sqn** dd ex 1 AD 30.4.17 (same engine) and vict 13.7.17 (Lt R.D. Coath/2nd Lt A.W. Merchant sent an Albatros D.III OOC near Slype at 09:15). **1 AD** ex 48 Sqn 12.8.17 (engine 543/WD10549) and flown to England that day. **8 AAP** Lympne on 17:20 HAP 12.8.17 (Lt H. Slingsby OK) and on 11:00 HAP 22.8.17 (2nd Lt J.G. Dainty OK). **3 TDS** Lopscombe Corner.

A7107 (Falcon I) **AAP** Filton 25.4.17, allotted to BEF. **48 Sqn** by 1.6.17 and victs 16.6.17 (2nd Lt R.L. Curtiss/2nd Lt L.W. Allen destroyed an Albatros D.III at 07:30 near Fresnes les Montauban) and 21.7.17 (Capt B.E. Baker/Lt G.R. Spencer sent an Albatros D.V OOC near Slype at 18:00, shared with A7153, A7164). **1 AD** ex 48 Sqn 10.8.17 (2nd Lt H. Shaw – engine 321/WD10485) and flown to England, Lympne, that day. **WEE** Biggin Hill 1918, marked as a/c 6.

F.2B A7107 '6' of the Wireless Experimental Establishment at Biggin Hill in 1918. *(RAF Museum)*

A7108 (Falcon I) **AAP** Filton 26.4.17, allotted to BEF. **1 AD** dd ex England by air 29.4.17 (engine 323/WD10480). **48 Sqn** dd ex 1 AD 30.4.17 (same engine) victs 9.5.17 (Capt F.P. Holliday/Capt A.H.W. Wall destroyed a LVG C-type destroyed near Vitry-Noyelles at 08:20, shared A7110) and 20.5.17 (Lt H.J. Pratt/Lt H. Owen sent an Albatros D.III OOC near Brebières at 12:30, shared A7112), damaged in combat 27.5.17 (2nd Lt J.A.W. Armstrong OK/2nd Lt G. Baines fatally WIA) and further vict 27.7.17 (Capt F.P. Holliday DSO MC/Lt W. O'Toole sent a DFW C-type OOC near Lombartzyde-Westende at 16:30). **1 AD** ex 48 Sqn 10.8.17 (same engine). **20 Sqn** ex 1 AD and 48 Sqn 10.8.17, the unit's first F.2B, and wrecked on Instructional Flight 11.8.17 (Capt A.N. Solly/Lt D.Y. Hay both KOAS, the RH wings collapsed – same engine). **1 AD** ex 20 Sqn 12.8.17 and deleted 13.8.17 (125hr 12min).

A7109 (Falcon I) **AAP** Filton 28.4.17, allotted to BEF. **48 Sqn** by 1.6.17, LIA on 07:50 OP 6.7.17 Lt H.C. Farnes/Cpl J.T. Park both KIA, brought down in flames near Cambrai – engine 335/WD10479) and deleted on unit that day (115hr 50min).

A7110 (Falcon I) **AAP** Filton 30.4.17, allotted to BEF. **48 Sqn** and vict 9.5.17 (2nd Lt W.T. Price MC/Lt E.S. Moore destroyed a LVG C-type near Vitry-Noyelles at 08:20 shared A7108) then LIA after vict on further patrol that day (2nd Lt W.T. Price MC/Lt C.G. Claye both WIA, destroyed an Albatros D.III, E of Vitry-Fampoux then shot down within British lines NE of Fampoux, probably by Ltn L v Richthofen, Jasta11 – engine 387/WD10482) and deleted on unit that day (8hr 25min).

A7111 (Falcon I) **AAP** Filton 30.4.17, allotted to BEF. **48 Sqn** LIA on 15:00 OP 11.5.17 (Lt W.O.B. Winkler/2nd Lt E.S. Moore both POW, brought down near Gravelle – engine 301/WD10467).

A7112 (Initially Falcon I) at Filton 30.4.17, allotted to BEF. **48 Sqn** and victs 20.5.17 (Capt R. Raymond-Barker/Lt R.N.W. Jeff sent 2 Albatros D.III OOC near Brebieres at 12:30, one shared with A7108), 26.5.17 (Capt R. Raymond-Barker/Lt R.N.W. Jeff destroyed an Albatros D.III, E of Brebières at 19:59), 3.6.17 (Lt T.P. Middleton/Lt A.W. Merchant sent an Albatros D.III OOC, E of Douai at 10:50), 5.6.17 (Capt R. Raymond-Barker/Sgt Nicholson sent a HA C-type OOC, E of Bullecourt at 07:30) then damaged in successful combat 12.7.17 (2nd Lt G. Colledge/Sgt H. Lindfield ASC both OK, sent an Albatros D-type OOC near Ghistelles at 18:45 but machine was damaged by enemy fire – engine 261/WD10449). **1 AD** ex 48 Sqn 15.7.17. **22 Sqn** dd ex 1 AD 20.8.17 (engine Falcon II 45/WD22392) and wrecked on OP 12.9.17 (Lt H.S. Welby/Pte D.W. Clement both OK, force landed due to engine trouble and crashed on taking off – same engine). **1 AD** ex 22 Sqn 16.9.17. **2 AD** ex 1 AD 3.10.17. **1 AIS** ex 2 AD 18.11.17 (engine Falcon II 395/WD18474). **20 Sqn** dd ex 1 AIS 22.12.17 and wrecked on OP 2.1.18 (2nd Lt R.J. Gosse/Lt J.D. Boyd both OK crashed in forced landing after fuel pipe broke – same engine). **1 ASD** ex 20 Sqn 6.1.18 and deleted (111hr 10min).

A7113 (Falcon I) **AAP** Filton 4.5.17, allotted to BEF. **11 Sqn** dd ex **1 AD** 29.5.17 and wrecked on Target Practice 9.6.17 (2nd Lt C.W. Beatty/2nd Lt A. Jackson both OK, force landed with pressure trouble – engine 313/Wd10469). **2 AD** ex 11 Sqn 11.6.17 and deleted 12.6.17 (10hr 25min).

A7114 (Initially Falcon I) **AAP** Filton 4.5.17, allotted to BEF. **1 AD** by 1.6.17. **2 AD** ex 1 AD 6.6.17 (engine 315/WD10491). **11 Sqn** dd ex 2 AD 16.6.17 and wrecked on 18:55 OP 7.8.17 (2nd Lt M.S. West OK/2nd Lt F. Adams WIA, force landed near **20 CCS** – same engine). **2 AD** ex 11 Sqn 9.8.17. **1 AD** ex 2 AD 30.9.17 (engine Falcon II 191/WD22446). **22 Sqn** dd ex 1 AD 12.10.17 and wrecked after Practice Flight 16.10.17 (2nd Lt C.E. Ferguson/Gnr S. Beldire both OK, crashed on landing – same engine). **1 AD** ex 22 Sqn 16.10.17. **2 AD** ex 1 AD 28.10.17, unit re-named **2 ASD** 1.11.17. **2 AIS** ex 2 ASD 5.1.18 (engine Falcon III 67/WD18533). **2 ASD** ex 2 AIS 30.1.18. **2 AIS** ex 2 ASD 3.2.18. **48 Sqn** dd ex 2 AIS 5.2.18 (same engine), victs 8.3.18 (2nd Lt H.H. Harley/2nd Lt J.H. Robertson sent 2 Albatros D.V OOC near Busigny at 10:50 and destroyed an Albatros D.V, S of Bohain at 16:00) and 11.3.17 (2nd Lt H.H. Harley OK/2nd Lt J.H. Robertson fatally WIA, sent a Fokker Dr.I OOC near St Quentin at 12:55) then wrecked on Low OP 24.4.18 (2nd Lt T.G. Jackson/Lt A.E. Ansell both OK, shot up by enemy ground fire – engine Falcon III 257/WD18628). **2 ASD** ex 48 Sqn 27.4.18 and deleted 15.5.18 (not worth reconstruction).

A7115 (Falcon I) **AAP** Filton 4.5.17, allotted to BEF. **48 Sqn** by 1.6.17, vict 25.7.17 (2nd Lt J.A.W. Armstrong/2nd Lt P.N. Shone destroyed an Albatros D-type in flames, NE of Nieuport at 19:05) and reported as unfit for further operational service 13.10.17. **1 AD** ex 48 Sqn 14.10.17 (engine 383/WD10489) and flown to England 15.10.17.

A7116 (Falcon I) **AAP** Filton 4.5.17, allotted to BEF **AEP** Lympne dd ex Filton 14.5.17. **1 AD** by 18.5.17. **48 Sqn** by 1.6.17 and victs 15.6.17 (2nd Lt H.J. Pratt/2nd Lt H. Owen scnt an Albatros D.III OOC near Fampoux at 19:45, shared with A7117), 16.6.17 (2nd Lt H.J. Pratt/2nd Lt H. Owen sent an Albatros D.III OOC near Estree at 10:50) and 11.7.17 (2nd Lt H.J. Pratt/2nd Lt H. Owen drove down an Albatros D-type near Westende at 20:20). **1 AD** ex 48 Sqn 14.8.17 (engine 329/WD10471) and flown to England 15.8.17. **8 AAP** Lympne and on 11:20 HAP 22.8.17 (2nd Lt S.J. Riley OK).

A7117 (Falcon I) **AAP** Filton 7.5.17, allotted to BEF. **48 Sqn** by 1.6.17 and victs 15.6.17 (Lt H.M. Fraser/Lt M.A. Benjamin sent an Albatros D.III OOC near Fampoux at 19:45, shared with A7116) and 22.7.17 (2nd Lt H.P. Lale/2nd Lt G.R. Waters sent an Albatros D.III OOC, 2 miles E of Ostend at 13:30). **1 AD** ex 48 Sqn 12.8.17 and flown to England that day (engine 42/WD10462). **8 AAP** Lympne and on 17:30 HAP 12.8.17 (Lt R.S. Carroll OK).

A7118 (Initially Falcon I) **AAP** Filton 7.5.17, allotted to BEF. **48 Sqn** by 1.6.17 and victs 29.6.17 (Lt O.J.F. Scholte/2nd Lt A.W. Merchant sent an Albatros D.III OOC near Brebieres at 20:00) and 6.7.17 (Lt O.J.F. Scholte/2nd Lt A.W. Merchant destroyed an Albatros D.V, E of Cambrai at 09:30) then damaged on Low Patrol 19.7.17 (2nd Lt K.R. Park [NZ] OK/2nd Lt A.R. Noss IOAS, force landed in a cornfield after magneto trouble – engine 277/WD10475).

1 AD ex 48 Sqn 21.7.17. **22 Sqn** dd ex 1 AD 23.8.17 (engine Falcon II 111/WD22397), victs 22.9.17 (Capt R. Stuart-Wortley/2nd Lt P.V. Burton destroyed 2 Albatros D.V over Houthulst Wood at 09:00) then damaged on Escort 7.10.17 (Lt W.L. Wells/2nd Lt R.B.P. Wilson both OK, returned with 2 blades of 4-bladed propeller shot away and machine damaged by excessive vibration – same engine). **1 AD** ex 22 Sqn 8.10.17, deleted 11.10.17 (not worth reconstruction, 153hr 50min) but brought back on charge 21.10.17. **20 Sqn** dd ex 1 AD 7.11.17 (engine Falcon II 279/WD18416) and wrecked on 07:30 OP 9.11.17 (Lt J.C. Kirkpatrick OK/2nd Lt N. Couve IOAS, over the lines air pressure failed, engine lost revs and machine was force landed on ground that had been shelled – same engine). **1 ASD** ex 20 Sqn 12.11.17 and deleted 17.11.17 (not worth reconstruction, 155hr 40min).

A7119 (Falcon I) **AAP** Filton 10.5.17, allotted to BEF. **48 Sqn** by 1.6.17, victs 27.5.17 (Lt T.P. Middleton/2nd Lt A.W. Merchant destroyed an Albatros D.III and sent an EA C-type OOC, SW of Douai at 19:45) and 24.6.17 (Lt H.P. Lale/2nd Lt R.N.W. Jeff sent an Albatros D.III OOC near Douai at 20:15) then wrecked after Escort 4.8.17 (2nd Lt H.S. Gough/AM2 H. Lindfield both OK, caught telegraph wires on landing and crashed – engine 17/WD10524). **1 AD** ex 48 Sqn 16.8.17. **22 Sqn** dd ex 1 AD 28.9.17 (engine 503/WD12579) and wrecked after OP 30.9.17 (2nd Lt H.G. Robinson IOAS/2nd Lt F.J.B. Hammersley OK, crashed on landing – same engine). 1 AD ex 22 Sqn 1.10.17. **8 AAP** Lympne ex 1 AD 6.12.17 (Lt C.F. Uwins).

A7120 (Initially Falcon I) **AAP** Filton 10.5.17, allotted to BEF. **(S)ARD** 24.5.17, with BEF allotment cancelled and for **E1 Repair Section** then reallotted to BEF 14.6.17. **1 AD** dd ex England 2.7.17 (engine 555/WD12544). **22 Sqn** dd ex 1 AD 10.7.17 (same engine) and damaged on 08:20 OP 3.9.17 (Lt G.R. Carmichael OK/2nd Lt S. Cleobury WIA, force landed near Ypres due to the observer being badly wounded and machine damaged when being towed by lorry turning a sharp corner – same engine). **1 AD** ex 22 Sqn 6.9.17. **2 AD** ex 1 AD for reconstruction 16.10.17. **1 ASD** by 15.12.17. **22 Sqn** reissued ex 1 ASD 28.12.17 (engine Falcon II 343/WD18448) and wrecked on Practice Flight 25.1.18 (2nd Lt P.J.W. Reeves OK, bad landing – same engine). **1 ASD** ex 22 Sqn 27.1.18 and deleted 29.1.18 (57hr 36min).

A7121 (Falcon I) **AAP** Filton 10.5.17, allotted to BEF. **11 Sqn** dd ex **1 AD** 29.5.17 and wrecked on Observation Practice 30.11.17 (Sgt D.W. Beard/2nd Lt E.C. Gilroy both OK, hit telegraph pole when landing at Henin with engine trouble – engine 523/WD10546). **2 ASD** ex 11 Sqn and under repair by 31.12.17 but deleted 22.4.18 (not worth reconstruction, 169hr 30min).

A7122 (Falcon I) **35 TS** Northolt on 19:00 HAP 5.6.17 (Lt Child) and wrecked 14.6.17 (2nd Lt W. Coltman IIFA, rudder jammed, machine side-slipped and nosedived in – engine 190/367/WD10505).

A7123 (Initially Falcon I) **AAP** Filton 15.5.17, allotted to BEF. **48 Sqn** dd ex **1 AD** 31.5.17, victs 15.6.17 (2nd Lt J.A.W. Binnie/Cpl V. Reed sent an Albatros D.III OOC, SW of Douai at 19:40 and another down in flames N of Vitry at 20:20, the latter shared with A7149) and 28.7.17 (2nd Lt J.A.W. Binnie/Cpl V. Reed sent an Albatros D.V down in flames over Ghistelles-Zevecote at 08:15, shared A7170) then wrecked after OP 2.9.17 (Lt N.C. Millman/2nd Lt H.A. Cooper both OK, crashed landing in soft mud – engine 333/WD10512). **1 AD** ex 48 Sqn 4.9.17. **20 Sqn** dd ex 1 AD 23.9.17 (engine Falcon II 209/WD22453) and wrecked on OP 24.9.17 (Sgt F. Hopper/Lt Henry both OK, pilot lost bearings, force landed in mist and crashed – same engine). **1 AD** ex 20 Sqn 26.9.17 and deleted 29.9.17 (not worth reconstruction, 143hr 30min).

A7124 (Falcon I) **AAP** Filton 15.5.17, allotted to BEF. **AEP** Lympne ex Filton 22.5.17 (2nd Lt H. Shaw). **1 AD** dd ex England 21.5.17. **11 Sqn** dd ex 1 AD 29.5.17, LIA on OP 25.9.17 (Lt G.L. Miall-Smith MC/2nd Lt C.C. Dennis both KIA, shot down by EA over Le Catelet at 11:10, with machine seen to break up – engine 407/WD10498) and deleted on unit that day (152hr 35min).

A7125 (Initially Falcon I) **AAP** Filton 15.5.17, allotted to BEF. Despatched to Farnborough for BEF and force landed near Cheddington 22.5.17 (Lt H. Slingsby OK). **1 AD** dd ex England 1.6.17 (2nd Lt H. Shaw – engine 5/WD10521). **11 Sqn** dd ex 1 AD 2.6.17 (same engine) and wrecked on OP 20.6.17 (Lt A.E. McKeever [Can]/2nd Lt H.D. Duncan both OK, machine badly damaged by AA fire – same engine). **2 AD** ex 11 Sqn 22.6.17. **1 AD** ex 2 AD 17.8.17 (engine 337/WD10486). **48 Sqn** ex 1 AD 19.8.17; and wrecked on OP 22.8.17. Damaged in combat on 08:00 OP 22.8.17 (2nd Lt W.D. Bostock OK/2nd Lt H.R. Price

WIA, in aerial combat near Ostende – same engine). **1 AD** ex 48 Sqn 24.8.17. **22 Sqn** ex 1 AD 22.9.17 (engine 513/WD15776), LIA on 07:30 OP 18.10.17 (2nd Lt B.B. Berry/2nd Lt C.H. Bartlett both POW, brought down in combat over Ardoye – engine Falcon II 359/WD18456) and deleted on unit that day (65hr 32min).

A7126 (Falcon I) **AAP** Filton 15.5.17, allotted to BEF. **1 AD** dd ex England 23.6.17 (engine 373/WD10494). **2 AD** ex 1 AD 24.6.17 (same engine). **11 Sqn** dd ex 2 AD 9.7.17, LIA on OP 18.8.17 (2nd Lt T.W. Abbott/2nd Lt M. Nicholson both KIA, last seen over Douai at 06:15 – same engine) and deleted on unit that day (50hr 12min).

A7127 (Falcon I) **AAP** Filton 16.5.17, allotted to BEF. **11 Sqn** dd ex **1 AD** 29.5.17, marked as a/c *U*, LIA on Aerial Post 11.10.17 (2nd Lt A.E. Turvey POW/AM2 W. Hewitt POW WIA, brought down in combat near Ham at 15:50 – engine 311/WD10484) and deleted on unit that day (153hr 38min).

A7128 (Initially Falcon I) **AAP** Filton 16.5.17, allotted to BEF. **2 AD** by 1.6.17 (engine 15/WD10526). **11 Sqn** dd ex 2 AD 16.6.17 (same engine) and wrecked on OP 21.6.17 (2nd Lt T.W. Abbott/2nd Lt M. Nicholson both OK, force landed near Sombrin due to engine failure at 06:00 – same engine). **2 AD** ex 11 Sqn 22.6.17. **11 Sqn** reissued ex 2 AD 31.8.17 (engine Falcon II 333/WD18443), vict 27.10.17 (Lt R.D. Coath/2nd Lt K.F. Jones sent an Albatros D.V OOC over Ribecourt at 11:15) then damaged on OP 7.12.17 (2nd Lt R.H. Nixon/Lt P. Douglas both OK, force landed with failing engine – same engine). **2 ASD** ex 11 Sqn and for overhaul by 31.12.17. **48 Sqn** dd ex 2 AIS 29.3.18 (engine Falcon III 645/WD32722) and wrecked on Travelling Flight 15.6.18 (Lt Col T.A.E. Cairns DSO OK, landing crash – same engine). **2 ASD** ex 48 Sqn 16.6.18 and deleted 3.7.18 on reconstruction as F6121.

A7129 (Falcon I) **AAP** Filton 16.5.17, allotted to BEF. **2 AD** by 1.6.17. **48 Sqn** dd ex 2 AD 6.6.17 (engine 419/WD10503), victs 6.7.17 (Capt J.T. Milne/2nd Lt K.E. Tanner sent an Albatros D.III OOC, E of Cambrai at 09:00), 7.7.17 (Capt J.T. Milne/Lt A.D. Light destroyed an Albatros D.V, S of Vitry at 05:50) and 12.7.17 (Capt J.T. Milne/2nd Lt K.E. Tanner forced an Albatros D-type to land SW of Ghistelles at 09:45 and destroyed an Albatros D.V near Leffinghe at 18:15) then wrecked after Escort 27.7.17 (2nd Lt T.P. Middleton/2nd Lt G.R. Waters both OK, misjudged landing and crashed in ditch – same engine). **1 AD** ex 48 Sqn 29.7.17. **20 Sqn** 30.8.17 (same engine) and wrecked after Reconnaissance 9.9.17 (2nd Lt H.F. Tomlin/2nd Lt R.C. Purvis both OK, tyre burst on landing, machine swung and wrecked undercarriage – same engine). **1 AD** ex 20 Sqn 11.9.17. **2 ASD** ex **1 ASD** 11.11.17 (engine Falcon II 409/WD18481). **11 Sqn** dd ex 2 ASD 26.11.17 (same engine), attached to **15 Sqn** 2.2.18 (same engine) and passed on attachment to **59 Sqn** 6.4.18. **59 Sqn** ex 11 Sqn 23.4.18 (same engine) and wrecked on Engine Test 28.6.18 (Lt G.N. Prout/Sgt E. Nutter both OK, looped and on landing found to have suffered structural damage – same engine). **2 ASD** ex 59 Sqn 29.6.18 and deleted 8.7.18 on reconstruction as F6181 (220hr 10min).

A7130 (Falcon I) **AAP** Filton 19.5.17, allotted to BEF. While on unarmed delivery to France 25.5.17 attacked by EA over Ashford (Lt Baker OK, landed safely at Lympne). **1 AD** dd ex England 26.5.17 (engine 7/WD10528). **2 AD** ex 1 AD by 1.6.17. **11 Sqn** dd ex 2 AD 15.6.17 (same engine), marked as a/c *3* and named *Otazell*, LIA on 07:45 OP 19.9.17, last seen at 08:45, W of Bullecourt 19.9.17 (2nd Lt N.J. Taylor/Lt G.M. Mumford both POW WIA, probably brought down by Uffz F. Gille, Jasta 12 – engine 385/WD10506) and deleted on unit that day (130hr 11min).

A7131 (Initially Falcon I) **AAP** Filton 19.5.17, allotted to BEF. **1 AD** ex England. **2 AD** ex 1 AD 1.6.17 (engine 407/WD10498). **11 Sqn** dd ex 2 AD 18.6.17 and wrecked after OP 21.9.17 (Capt E.H.G. Sharples/2nd Lt S. Sutcliffe both OK, struck shell hole on landing and o/t – engine Falcon II 183/WD22444). **2 AD** ex 11 Sqn 24.9.17. **11 Sqn** reissued ex **2 ASD** 13.11.17 (engine Falcon II 269/WD18411), marked as a/c *5* and wrecked on Night Flying Practice 15.2.18 (2nd Lt J.S. Chick OK/Lt A. Reeve IOAS, crashed on landing – engine Falcon III 151/WD18575). **2 ASD** ex 11 Sqn 19.2.18 and deleted 20.2.18 (not worth reconstruction, 157hr).

A7132 (Falcon I) **AAP** Filton 19.5.17, allotted to BEF but reallotted to **62 Sqn (Mobilising)** 24.5.17. **62 Sqn** Filton 26.5.17, reallotted to BEF and **'X' Replacement Sqn**. To **1 AD** dd ex England 1.6.17 (engine 429/WD10500). **11 Sqn** ex 1 AD 1.6.17 (same engine) and wrecked on OP 13.6.17 (2nd Lt C. Pern/AM2 S.A. Mee both IOAS, dived through thick cloud and ground mist, side slipped to avoid trees and crashed – same engine). **2 AD** ex 11 Sqn 15.6.17 and deleted that day (23hr 5min).

A7133 (Falcon I) **AAP Filton** 21.5.17, allotted to BEF but reallotted to **62 Sqn (Mobilising)** 24.5.17. **62 Sqn** Filton 26.5.17, reallotted to BEF and **'X' Replacement Sqn**. To **1 AD** dd ex England 7.7.17 (engine 401/WD10513). **2 AD** ex 1 AD 20.7.17 (same engine). **22 Sqn** dd ex 2 AD 27.7.17 and wrecked after OP 6.9.17 (2nd Lt A.H. Gilbert/2nd Lt R.S. Gilbert both OK, crashed on landing – same engine). **1 AD** ex 22 Sqn 6.9.17. **22 Sqn** reissued ex 1 AD 10.10.17 (engine 577/WD12535). **1 ASD** ex 22 Sqn 5.12.17 (engine 481/WD12574), wrecked on Ferry Flight to **2 ASD** 8.12.17 (Lt C.H. Lick IOAS, stalled on turn at 100ft after take off and nosedived in – same engine) and deleted 12.12.18 (not worth reconstruction, 99hr 28min).

A7134 (Falcon I) **AAP Filton** 21.5.17, allotted to BEF. **1 AD** dd ex England 7.6.17 (engine 359/WD10492). **2 AD** ex 1 AD 8.6.17 (same engine). **11 Sqn** dd ex 2 AD 21.6.17, LIA on 18:30 OP 27.7.17 (2nd Lt J. Chapman/Lt W.R. Mackay both POW, last seen at 19:50 over Vis-en-Artois apparently under control, probably brought down by Ltn Wolff, Jasta 5 – same engine) and deleted on unit that day (38hr 40min).

A7135 (Falcon I) **35 TS** Northolt on 18:55 HAP 5.6.17 (Capt C.W.E. Cole-Hamilton), on 11:19 HAP 13.6.17 (Capt C.W.E. Cole-Hamilton OK/Capt C.H.C. Keevil KIA, in combat with Gotha – engine 395/WD10508) and on unit charge until @ 9.17.

A7136 (Falcon I) **35 TS** Northolt on 18:55 HAP 5.6.17 (Lt Walmsley OK, force landed near Barnet after engine failure), on 11:18 HAP 13.6.17 (2nd Lt J. Chapman/2nd Lt F.G.C. Weare both OK), on 08:02 HAP 4.7.17 (Capt A.C. Wright/Capt Bagnall both OK), on 09:40 HAP 7.7.17 (Capt G.D. Hill/Capt R. Stuart-Wortley both OK) and on unit charge until @ 9.17.

A7137 (Falcon I) **AAP Filton** 26.5.17, allotted from **62 Sqn** to BEF and **'X' Replacement Sqn**. To **1 AD** dd ex England 1.6.17 (engine 405/WD10497). **2 AD** ex 1 AD 2.6.17 (same engine). **48 Sqn** dd ex 2 AD 5.6.17 (same engine), LIA on 07:50 OP 6.7.17 (2nd Lt H. Smither/2nd Lt H.C. Clarke both KIA, brought down in flames E of Cambrai, probably by Ltn Wisseman, Jasta 3 – same engine) and deleted on unit that day (63hr).

A7138 (Falcon I) **AAP Filton** 26.5.17, allotted from **62 Sqn** to BEF and **'X' Replacement Sqn**. To **1 AD** dd ex England 5.6.17 (engine 427/WD10511). **2 AD** ex 1 AD 6.6.17 (same engine). **1 AD** ex 2 AD, wrecked, 7.6.17 (same engine). **2 AD** ex 1 AD 24.6.17 (same engine). **11 Sqn** dd ex 2 AD 11.7.17 (same engine), LIA on 16:45 OP 2.10.17 (Lt J.M. McKenna/2nd Lt S. Sutcliffe both KIA, last seen in combat between Douai and Cambrai at c.18:00 – engine 433/WD10504) and deleted on unit that day (104hr).

A7139 (Falcon I) **AAP Filton** 26.5.17, allotted from **62 Sqn** to BEF and **'X' Replacement Sqn**. To **1 AD** dd ex England 4.6.17 (engine 19/WD10541). **11 Sqn** dd ex 1 AD 5.6.17 (same engine), LIA on 05:00 OP 21.6.17 (2nd Lt D.C.H. MacBrayne KIA/Sgt W. Mollison POW, last seen at 06:45 between Bailleul and Oppy – same engine) and deleted on unit that day (32hr 1min).

A7140 (Falcon I) **AAP Filton** 29.5.17, allotted from **62 Sqn** to BEF and **'X' Replacement Sqn**. To **1 AD** dd ex England 4.6.17 (engine 425/WD10519). **11 Sqn** dd ex 1 AD 5.6.17 (same engine) and wrecked on OP 15.8.17 (2nd Lt F.H. Thorndike fatally IOAS/2nd Lt H.M. Drake IOAS, sideslipped and crashed onto Wagnonlieu ALG at 06:40). **2 AD** ex 11 Sqn and deleted 16.8.17 (84hr 3min).

A7141 (Initially Falcon I) **AAP Filton** 29.5.17, allotted from **62 Sqn** to BEF and **'X' Replacement Sqn**. To **1 AD** dd ex England 5.6.17 (engine 411/WD10510). **11 Sqn** dd ex 1 AD 5.6.17 (same engine), vict 17.6.17 (2nd Lt F.J. Foster/Lt D.G. Davidson sent an Albatros C-type OOC over Sailly-en-Ostrevert at 06:35) then wrecked on OP 10.7.17 (2nd Lt F.J. Foster/2nd Lt H.J. Day both IOAS, controls shot away and crashed on landing – same engine). **2 AD** ex 11 Sqn 12.7.17. **1 AD** ex 2 AD 14.9.17 (engine Falcon II 67/WD22390). **20 Sqn** dd ex 1 AD 20.9.17 (same engine), victs 21.9.17 (Lt R.K. Kirkman/2nd Lt J.P. Flynn sent an Albatros D.V in a vertical dive, smoking, over Becelaere at 11:10), 23.9.17 (Capt J.E. Johnston/Lt J.A. Hone crashed an Albatros D.V, N of Houthem at 18:30), and 17.10.17 (2nd Lt W. Durrand, 2nd Lt A.E. Woodbridge crashed a DFW C-type 2 miles N of Bousbecque at 09:25) then LIA on 11:25 OP 3.12.17 (2nd Lt W. Bevan/Lt F.B. Gloster both KIA, last seen N of Hollebeke – engine Falcon II 181/WD22442) and deleted on unit that day (83hr 41min).

A7142 (Falcon I) **AAP Filton** 29.5.17, allotted to **'X' Replacement Sqn** with BEF. **1 AD** dd ex England 6.6.17 (engine 399/WD10509). **11 Sqn** dd ex 1 AD 8.6.17 (same engine) and wrecked on Engine Test 5.7.17 (2nd Lt W.R. Exley/Capt J.A. LeRoyer both IOAS). **2 AD** ex 11 Sqn and deleted 8.7.17 (57hr 5min).

A7143 (Initially Falcon I) **AAP Filton** 4.6.17, allotted to BEF. **1 AD** dd ex England 10.6.17 (engine 235/WD10416). **11 Sqn** dd ex 1 AD 11.6.17 (same engine), LIA on 08:50 Reconnaissance 5.12.17 (Sgt M.H. Everix & Lt H. Whitworth both POW – engine Falcon II 73/WD22396) and deleted on unit that day (223hr 56min).

A7144 (Initially Falcon I) **AAP Filton** 4.6.17, allotted to BEF. **1 AD** dd ex England 7.6.17 (engine 351/WD12567). **11 Sqn** dd ex 1 AD 9.6.17 (same engine), victs 26.6.17 (Lt A.E. McKeever/2nd Lt E. Oake sent an Albatros D.III OOC over Etaing-Dury at 18:45), 26.6.17 (Lt A.E. McKeever/2nd Lt E. Oake claimed two Albatros D.V, one OOC, the other destroyed over Etaing-Dury at 18:45) and 7.7.17 (Lt A.E. McKeever/2nd Lt L.A. Powell sent three Albatros D.V OOC over Vitry at 20.30-20.40) then wrecked 10.7.17 (2nd Lt R.H. Stacey/2nd Lt L.A. Powell both OK, crashed on landing at **41 Sqn** – same engine). **2 AD** ex 11 Sqn 12.7.17. **1 AD** ex 2 AD 20.9.17 (same engine). **22 Sqn** dd ex 1 AD 21.9.17 (same engine). **1 AD** ex 22 Sqn 13.10.17 (same engine). **20 Sqn** dd ex **1 ASD** 15.11.17 (same engine), victs 5.12.17 (Sgt F. Johnson/Capt J.H. Hedley sent an Albatros D.V OOC near Dizeele at 09:25) and 10.12.17 (Sgt F. Johnson/Capt J.H. Hedley crashed an Albatros D.V, E of St Aden at 09:15) then wrecked before Defensive Patrol 29.12.17 (2nd Lt Pemberton/Cpl Mann both OK, pressure was lost after take off and the machine was force landed on rough ground – engine Falcon II 59/WD22404). **1 ASD** ex 20 Sqn 2.1.18 and deleted 16.1.18 (not worth reconstruction, 108hr 57min).

A7145 (Initially Falcon I) **AAP Filton** 4.6.17, allotted to BEF. **1 AD** dd ex England 7.6.17 (engine 11/WD12529). **2 AD** ex 1 AD 8.6.17 (same engine). **11 Sqn** dd ex 2 AD 23.6.17 (same engine) and wrecked on OP 7.7.17 (Lt R.F.S. Mauduit/Lt E.R. Dibbs both OK, force landed near aerodrome due to engine failure – same engine). **2 AD** ex 11 Sqn 10.7.17. **11 Sqn** reissued ex 2 AD 31.8.17 and wrecked after Patrol 16.2.18 (2nd Lt W.H. Park/2nd Lt H.J. Greenwood both OK, machine swung on landing and crashed – engine Falcon II 393/WD18473). **2 ASD** ex **11 Sqn** 19.2.18 and deleted 2.3.18 (not worth reconstruction, 175hr 25min).

A7146 (Falcon I) **AAP Filton** 4.6.17, allotted to BEF. **1 AD** dd ex England 11.6.17 (engine 190/281/WD10455). **48 Sqn** dd ex 1 AD 12.6.17 (same engine) and vict 22.7.17 (Capt B.E. Baker/Lt G.R. Spencer sent a Gotha into the sea a mile off Ostend at 10:40). **1 AD** ex 48 Sqn 14.8.17 and flown to England 15.8.17 (same engine). **Wireless Testing Park** Biggin Hill and wrecked 25.9.17 (2nd Lt C.W. Beatty OK/Lt C. Wormull fatally IIFA, stalled on take off from Stamford aerodrome and crashed near Wittering – same engine).

A7147 (Falcon I) **AAP Filton** 11.6.17, reallotted from Training Bde to BEF. **1 AD** dd ex England 20.6.17 (engine 307/WD10531). **2 AD** ex 1 AD 22.6.17 (same engine). **11 Sqn** dd ex 2 AD 5.7.17 (same engine), vict 7.7.17 (Lt H. Scandrett/Cpl S.A. Mee sent an Albatros D.V OOC, NW of Cambrai at 14:40) then LIA on 05:25 OP 18.8.17 (2nd Lt G.A. Rose/Cpl H.G. Bassenger both POW, last seen over Douai at 06:15 – same engine) and deleted on unit that day (39hr).

A7148 (Falcon I) **38 TS** Rendcomb by 13.6.17 and wrecked 4.11.17 (2nd Lt W.P. Lester-Jones IIFA, nosedived in after half spin – engine 275/WD19478).

A7149 (Initially Falcon I) **AAP Filton** by 7.6.17, allotted to BEF. **AEP** Lympne dd via Farnborough 11.6.17. **1 AD** dd ex England 13.6.17 (engine 389/WD10495). **48 Sqn** dd ex 1 AD 14.6.17 (same engine), victs 15.6.17 (Capt B.E. Baker/Lt H. Munro destroyed an Albatros D.III in flames N of Vitry at 20:20, shared A7123) and 3.7.17 (2nd Lt R.L. Curtiss/2nd Lt D.P. Fitzgerald-Uniacke sent a C-type OOC near Queant at 09:10) then wrecked on Ferry Flight 11.7.17 (Capt B.E. Baker MC/AM2 Newton both OK, tail broke on landing, longerons found to be cracked – same engine). **1 AD** ex 48 Sqn 14.7.17. **22 Sqn** dd ex 1 AD 20.8.17 (engine Falcon II 85/WD22398), LIA on 06:15 OP 21.9.17 (2nd Lt S.M. Spurway/AM1 H. Friend both KOAS, collided with A7233 at 10,000ft, pieces fell 2,000 yards E of Ypres – same engine) and deleted on unit that day (84hr 5min).

A7150 (Falcon I) **AAP Filton** 7.6.17, allotted to BEF. **1 AD** dd ex England 16.6.17 (engine 391/WD10507). **2 AD** ex 1 AD 18.6.17 (same engine). **48 Sqn** dd ex 2 AD 6.7.17 (same engine) and LIA on 18:40 OP Ostende-Dixmude, 27.9.17 (Sgt H. Clark KIA/Bmdr E.A. Nash fatally WIA, shot down in flames near Pervyse at 18:55 – engine 563/WD12577). **1 AD** ex 48 Sqn 1.10.17 and deleted 5.10.17 (135hr 30min).

A7151 (Initially Falcon I) **AAP Filton** 7.6.17, allotted to BEF. **1 AD** dd ex England 11.6.17 (engine 437/WD10533). **48 Sqn** dd ex 1AD

12.6.17 (same engine), victs 13.7.17 (Lt J.A.W. Binnie/Cpl V. Reed destroyed an Albatros D.V in flames over Slype at 09:40), 21.7.17 (2nd Lt H.W. Elliott/2nd Lt J.W. Ferguson sent an Albatros D.V OOC over Slype at 18:00) and 16.8.17 (2nd Lt R.L. Curtiss/2nd Lt D.P. Fitzgerald-Uniacke destroyed an Albatros D.V in flames at 19:55 and sent another OOC at 20:00) then wrecked on Collection Flight 18.8.17 (Capt B.E. Baker MC/Major A.V. Bettington both OK, engine failed just after take off, misjudged landing and crashed – same engine). **1 AD** ex 48 Sqn 21.8.17. **22 Sqn** dd ex 1 AD 18.9.17 (engine 463/WD10527) and wrecked after Patrol 27.9.17 (Lt W.M. Yool/AM1 Whitehouse both OK, crashed on landing – engine 533/WD12531). **1 AD** ex 22 Sqn 29.9.17. **2 AD** ex 1 AD for reconstruction 16.10.17. **1 AIS** dd ex 1 ASD 1.1.18 (engine Falcon II 191/WD22446). **20 Sqn** dd ex 1 AIS 19.1.18 (same engine) and wrecked 23.3.18 (caught fire on starting up, no crew). **1 ASD** ex 2 ASD by rail 1.4.18; and deleted 25.6.18 on reconstruction as F5814.

A7152 (Falcon I) **AAP** Filton 11.6.17, allotted to BEF. 1 AD dd ex England 14.6.17 (engine 345/WD10537). **2 AD** ex 1 AD 17.6.17 (same engine). **11 Sqn** dd ex 2 AD 23.6.17 (same engine) and wrecked before OP 30.9.17 (2nd Lt L.H. Clemetson/2nd Lt G.C. Leven both IOAS, crashed shortly after take off – same engine). **2 AD** ex 11 Sqn 2.10.17 and deleted 3.10.17 (not worth reconstruction, 151hr 59min).

A7153 (Initially Falcon I) **AAP** Filton 11.6.17, allotted to BEF. **1 AD** dd ex England 14.6.17 (engine 451/WD10516). **48 Sqn** dd ex 1 AD 15.6.17 (same engine), victs 3.7.17 (2nd Lt A. Riley/2nd Lt W. O'Toole sent an Albatros D.V OOC over Queant at 09:30), 2.7.17 (Lt R.B. Hay MC/Lt V.W.G. Nutkins sent an Albatros D.III OOC over Ghistelles at 18:40-19:00) and 21.7.17 (Lt R. Dodds/Lt T.C.S. Tuffield sent an Albatros D.III OOC near Slype at 18:00, shared A7107 & A7164) then wrecked after OP, Ostende, 14.9.17 (2nd Lt H.H. Hartley/AM2 H. Lindfield both OK, ran into a ditch on landing and crashed – engine 409/WD10499). **1 AD** ex 48 Sqn 17.9.17. **2 AD** ex 1 AD 27.9.17 for reconstruction. **11 Sqn** dd ex 2 AD 23.10.17 (engine Falcon II 267/WD18410) and damaged on Reconnaissance 20.11.17 (Capt J.C.L. Barnett/Cpl J. Mason both OK, machine shot through by gunfire and returned at 11:15 – same engine). **2 ASD** ex 11 Sqn 20.11.17. **2 AIS** ex 2 ASD 29.1.18 (engine Falcon III 209/WD18604). **11 Sqn** reissued ex 2 AIS 29.1.18 (same engine), vict 12.3.18 (2nd Lt J.P. Seabrook/2nd Lt C. Wrigglesworth destroyed an Albatros D.V, SE of Cambrai at 11:55) then wrecked 8.5.18 (when standing on aerodrome the machine was ran into by **70 Sqn** Sopwith Camel C8220 – same engine). **2 ASD** ex 11 Sqn 10.5.18; **2 AIS** by 20.6.18. **11 Sqn** reissued and LIA on Reconnaissance 3.10.18 (Lt J.W. Coons/Sgt Mech F.S. New, both KOAS, collided with C4753 at 07:00 – engine Falcon III 1753/WD51901) and deleted on unit that day.

A7154 (Falcon I) **AAP** Filton 11.6.17, allotted to BEF. **1 AD** dd ex England 15.6.17 (engine 435/WD10512). **11 Sqn** dd ex 1 AD 16.6.17 (same engine), damaged after vict 26.6.18 (2nd Lt P.C. Ross fatally WIA/2AM W. Woodward OK, sent an Albatros D.III OOC, E of Cambrai at 18:50, then force landed), LIA on 18:35 OP 12.7.17 (Capt C.E. Robertson/Sgt J.F. Carr both KIA, reported as shot down in flames by AA – same engine) and deleted on unit that day (53hr 40min).

A7155 (Initially Falcon I) **AAP** Filton 11.6.17, allotted to BEF. **1 AD** dd ex England 21.6.17 (engine 333/WD10512). **2 AD** ex 1 AD 23.6.17 (same engine). **48 Sqn** dd ex 2 AD 6.7.17 (same engine), victs 13.7.17 (Lt O.J.F. Scholte/Lt A.D. Light sent an Albatros D.V OOC over Slype at 09:40), 5.9.17 (2nd Lt R.L. Curtiss/2nd Lt H. Munro destroyed an Albatros D.V in flames 3 miles out to sea between Middelkerke and Westende Bains at 12:00) and damaged during vict 24.10.17 (2nd Lt H.F. Jenkins WIA/1AM E.J. Dunford OK, brought down an EA) then wrecked on OP 12.11.17 (2nd Lt J.W.D. Needham KOAS/Lt J.E.M. Evans IOAS, lost way and crashed landing after dark – engine Falcon II 29/WD22382). **1 ASD** ex 48 Sqn 15.11.17 and deleted 30.11.17 (162hr 32min).

A7156 (Falcon I) **AAP** Filton 11.6.17, allotted to BEF. **1 AD** dd ex England 17.6.17 (engine 483/WD10534). **2 AD** ex 1 AD 22.6.17 (same engine). **11 Sqn** dd ex 2 AD 6.7.17 (same engine), victs 17.7.17 (Lt H. Scandrett/Cpl J.W. Ross sent an Albatros D.V down OOC, E of Bullecourt at 19:15) and 5.8.17 (Lt H. Scandrett/Lt F.A. Herron sent an Albatros down OOC over Queant-Pronville at 19:15) then LIA on OP 4.9.17 (2nd Lt J.F. Wightman/AM2 J. Heedy both KIA, shot down in flames SE of Havrincourt at about 08:30, probably by Ltn Schobinger, Jasta 12 – same engine) and deleted on unit that day (90hr 14min).

A7157 (Falcon I) **AAP** Filton 11.6.17, allotted to BEF. **1 AD** dd ex England 21.6.17 (engine 477/WD10538). **2 AD** ex 1 AD 22.6.17 (same engine). **11 Sqn** dd ex 2 AD 4.7.17 (same engine), LIA on 09:30 OP 21.10.17 (Sgt C.J. Butler/AM1 W.T. Long both POW, last seen this side of the lines apparently with engine trouble – same engine) and deleted on unit that day (165hr 16min).

A7158 (Falcon I) **AAP** Filton 13.6.17, allotted to BEF. **1 AD** dd ex England 23.6.17 (engine 433/WD10504). **2 AD** ex 1 AD 26.6.17 (same engine). **11 Sqn** dd ex 2 AD 13.7.17 (same engine). **1 ASD** ex 11 Sqn 6.12.17 (engine 427/WD10511) and flown to England that day.

A7159 (Initially Falcon I) **AAP** Filton 13.6.17, allotted to BEF. **1 AD** dd ex Lympne 23.6.17 (engine 1/WD10532). **2 AD** ex 1 AD 26.6.17 (same engine). **11 Sqn** dd ex 2 AD 11.7.17 (same engine), victs 16.10.17 (Lt A.E. McKeever/2nd Lt L.A. Powell destroyed two Albatros D.V over Brebières-Douai at 10.20-10.25) then wrecked after Reconnaissance 30.10.17 (2nd Lt J.H. Wallace/Cpl F. Woodward both OK, landed downwind and struck a pile of timber – engine 235/WD10416). **2 ASD** ex 11 Sqn 2.11.17. **2 AIS** ex 2 ASD 15.2.18 (Lt Stiles – engine Falcon III 403/WD32601). **48 Sqn** dd ex 2 AIS 24.2.18 (same engine and reported 20.4.18 as unfit for further service in the field (218hr 50min – same engine). **2 ASD** ex 48 Sqn 22.4.18. **1 ASD** ex 2 ASD 25.4.18 and flown to England that day.

A7160 (Falcon I) **AAP** Filton 16.6.17, allotted to BEF. **(S)ARD** Farnborough 26.6.17. **AEP** Lympne 27.6.17. **1 AD** dd ex England 3.7.17 (engine 463/WD10527). **22 Sqn** dd ex 1 AD 10.7.17 (same engine) and wrecked on 06:15 OP 19.8.17 (Capt H. Patch/2nd Lt L.M. Quelch both OK, hit by AA fire and force landed at **5 Sqn** aerodrome – same engine). **1 AD** ex 22 Sqn 21.8.17 and deleted 28.8.17 (not worth reconstruction, 40hr 8min).

A7161 (Initially Falcon I) **AAP** Filton 16.6.17, allotted to BEF. **1 AD** dd ex England 23.6.17 (engine 403/WD10490). **2 AD** ex **1 AD** 26.6.17 (same engine). **22 Sqn** dd ex 2 AD 20.7.17 (same engine) and wrecked after OP 6.9.17 (Sgt J.M. Bainbridge/AM2 F. Scott both OK, crashed landing at **20 Sqn** aerodrome – engine 541/WD10543). **1 AD** ex 22 Sqn 8.9.17. **2 AD** ex 1 AD for reconstruction 6.10.17. **1 AIS** ex 1 ASD 1.1.18 (engine Falcon II 267/WD18410). **22 Sqn** reissued ex 1 AIS 26.1.18 (same engine) and vict 16.3.18 (2nd Lt W.F.J. Harvey/Sgt A. Burton destroyed a Pfalz D.III over Beaumont at 11:00). **2 AIS** ex 22 Sqn 10.4.18 as surplus to requirement (same engine). **2 ASD** 13.4.18 (same engine) and on unit charge until @ 24.10.18, apparently used as a communications machine.

A7162 (Falcon I) **AAP** Filton by 16.6.17, allotted to BEF. **1 AD** dd ex England 5.7.17 (engine 519/WD10542). **2 AD** ex 1 AD 22.7.17 (same engine). **22 Sqn** dd ex 2 AD 27.7.17 (same engine), LIA on Escort, Cortemarck, 17.8.17 (Lt R. Cornford/2nd Lt S.E. Raper both KIA, shot down in flames near Handzaeme at 09:10 – same engine) and deleted on unit that day (25hr 3min).

A7163 (Initially Falcon I) **AAP** Filton 16.6.17, allotted to BEF. **1 AD** dd ex England 25.6.17; **ARS 2 AD** 28.6.17 (engine 64/WD10438). **22 Sqn** dd ex 1 AD 15.7.17 (same engine) and wrecked after OP 11.9.17 (2nd Lt D.W.M. Miller/AM2 Loveland both OK, crashed in forced landing due to engine trouble – same engine). **1 AD** ex 22 Sqn 16.9.17. **2 AD** ex 1 AD 11.10.17. **1 AIS** ex 2 ASD 6.1.18 (engine Falcon II 159/WD22472). **1 ASD** ex 1 AIS 7.2.18 (same engine) and flown to England 17.3.18.

A7164 (Initially Falcon I) **AAP** Filton 20.6.17, allotted to BEF. **1 AD** dd ex England 2.7.17 (engine 505/WD10535). **22 Sqn** dd ex 1 AD 10.7.17 (same engine). **48 Sqn** and victs 21.7.17 (Lt R.D. Coath/2nd Lt K.E. Tanner sent an Albatros D.III down OOC over Slype at 18:00, shared A7107 & A7153), 22.7.17 (Lt R.D. Coath/2nd Lt A.D. Merchant attacked Gothas off Ostende at 10:40 and 1 EA ditched in shallows) and 12.8.17 (Lt R.D. Coath/AM2 Walker sent two Albatros D.III OOC over Slype at 10:45) then wrecked before OP 17.8.17 (2nd Lt H.E.T. Crocker/2nd Lt G.R. Waters both OK, ran into ditch on take off – engine 37/WD12538). **1 AD** ex 48 Sqn 17.8.17. **20 Sqn** dd ex 1 AD 30.9.17 (engine Falcon II 187/WD22441), victs 2.10.17 (Sgt F. Hopper/Capt L.W. Burbidge sent two Albatros OOC over Dadizeele at 11:55 but had to leave fight since elevator controls shot away and guns had jammed) and 29.11.17 (2nd Lt D. French/Lt A.D. Keith sent an EA down OOC at 10.54-12.54) then wrecked after OP 26.12.17 (Lt D.G. Campbell/2nd Lt W.H. Nash both OK, when about to land the machine was struck by a gust of wind and o/t when the undercarriage struck a ditch – engine Falcon II 431/WD18492). **1 ASD** ex 20 Sqn 1.1.18 and deleted 3.1.18 (not worth reconstruction, 79hr 15min).

A7165 (Falcon I) **AAP** Filton 20.6.17, allotted to BEF. **1 AD** dd ex England 1.7.17 (engine 495/WD10539). **22 Sqn** dd ex 1 AD 10.7.17 (same engine) and wrecked on Test Flight 14.8.17 Capt H. Patch/2nd Lt L.M. Quelch both OK, engine cut out at 1,000ft and machine crashed in forced landing – same engine). **2 AD** ex 22 Sqn 16.8.17 and deleted that day (not worth reconstruction, 29hr 10min).

A7166 (Falcon I) **AAP** Filton 20.6.17, allotted to BEF. **1 AD** dd ex England 28.6.17 (engine 501/WD10540). **48 Sqn** dd ex 1 AD 12.7.17 (same engine) LIA on 07:05 Photo Reconnaissance 17.7.17 (Lt R.B. Hay POW fatally WIA/Lt O.J. Partington POW WIA, believed to be the machine landed on the beach NE of Nieuport, probably brought down by Vzfw A. Werner, Jasta 17 – same engine) and deleted on unit that day (9hr 17min).

A7167 (Initially Falcon I) **AAP** Filton 22.6.17, allotted to BEF. **1 AD** dd ex England 2.7.17 (engine 497/WD10529). **22 Sqn** dd ex 1 AD 10.7.17 (same engine) and wrecked on Practice Flight 13.7.17 (Lt J.C. Bush OK, misjudged landing and o/t – same engine). **2 AD** ex 22 Sqn 16.7.17. **11 Sqn** dd ex 2 AD 30.8.17 (engine 529) and wrecked on Reconnaissance 2.12.17 (2nd Lt L.A. Rivers/Pte J.W. Scott both OK, engine hit by AA fire and crashed at 09:00 – engine Falcon II 197/WD22447). **2 ASD** ex 11 Sqn 2.12.17. **2 AIS** ex 2 ASD 28.2.18 (engine Falcon III 395/WD18697). **48 Sqn** dd ex 2 AIS 29.3.18 (same engine) and wrecked on OP 31.3.18 (2nd Lt B.G.A. Bell/2nd Lt W.H. Hanna both OK, damaged by ground fire – same engine). **22 Wing Salvage** 1.4.18. **2 ASD** ex Salvage 1.4.18 and deleted that day (154hr 31min).

A7168 (Initially Falcon I) **AAP** Filton 22.6.17, allotted to BEF. **1 AD** dd ex Filton, via Farnborough & Lympne, 5.7.17 (engine 499/WD10530). **11 Sqn** dd ex 1 AD 12.7.17 (same engine), damaged in combat 8.8.17 (Capt R. Raymond-Barker OK/2nd Lt H.J. Day fatally WIA) and wrecked on Practice Flight 23.8.17 (2nd Lt N.J. Taylor OK, stalled during landing and crashed – engine 517/WD10545). **2 AD** ex 11 Sqn 27.8.17. **11 Sqn** reissued ex 2 AD 22.10.17 (engine Falcon II 227/WD22452) and wrecked before Reconnaissance 11.3.18 (2nd Lt C.M. Smythe/Sgt R.D. Mason both OK, caught fire starting up on Bapaume ALG – same engine). **1 ASD** and deleted 8.4.18 (not worth reconstruction, 131hr 3min).

A7169 (Falcon I) **AAP** Filton 22.6.17, allotted to BEF. **AEP** Lympne dd ex Bristol 1.7.17 (2nd Lt H. Shaw). **1 AD** dd ex England 2.7.17 (engine 545/WD12527). **22 Sqn** dd ex 1 AD 10.7.17 (same engine), LIA on OP 11.8.17 (Capt P.W. Chambers POW fatally WIA/2AM W. Richman POW WIA, last seen in combat with 5 EA over Arleux at 07:45, probably brought down by Obltn A. Rittm v Tutschek, Jasta 12 – same engine) and deleted on unit that day (43hr 20min).

A7170 (Falcon II) **AAP** Filton 25.6.17, allotted to BEF. **1 AD** dd ex England 7.7.17 (engine 1/WD12543). **48 Sqn** dd ex 1 AD 21.7.17 (same engine), damaged on OP 24.7.17 (Capt B.E. Baker OK/Lt G.R. Spencer WIA by AA fire), victs 27.7.17 (Capt B.E. Baker/Lt G.R. Spencer sent an Albatros D-type down apparently OOC, but EA was then set on fire by a RNAS, **6N Sqn**, Sopwith Camel N6358 flown by FSL J.H. Forman and crashed in the sea NE of Nieuport at 17:10), 28.7.17 (Capt B.E. Baker/Lt G.R. Spencer destroyed an Albatros D.V in flames over Ghistelles-Zevecote at 08:15, shared A7123), 19.8.17 (Capt B.E. Baker & Lt H. Munro sent an Albatros D.III down OOC over Ostend at 06:50), 2.9.17 (Lt K.R. Park/2nd Lt A.D. Light sent an Albatros D.V down OOC, 5 miles E of Dixmude at 09:30 shared A7224 and another down OOC, SE of Dixmude at 09:35), 5.9.17 (2nd Lt R.L. Curtiss/2nd Lt D.P. Fitzgerald-Uniacke sent a DFW C-type down in vertical dive near Middelkerke at 08:40), 21.10.17 (Capt B.E. Baker/Lt E.F. Dixon sent an Albatros D.III down OOC over Ostend at 13:00), 31.10.17 (Capt B.E. Baker/Lt E.F. Dixon sent a Pfalz D.III down OOC NE of Dixmude at 16:15), 11.11.17 (Capt B.E. Baker/AM2 B. Jackman sent two Albatros D.III down OOC, NE of Dixmude at 17:10) and 29.11.17 (Capt B.E. Baker/AM2 B. Jackman sent an Albatros D.III down OOC over Houthulst Forest at 14:45 and captured another) then reported 24.12.17 as unfit for further service in the field (198hr 57min – engine 131/WD22470). **2 ASD** ex 48 Sqn 29.12.17 (time expired). **1 AIS** ex 2 ASD 1.1.18. **1 ASD** ex 1 AIS 3.1.18 and flown to England that day. **8 TS** Netheravon by 12.2.18. **33 TDS** Witney by 1.8.18 until @ 2.8.18 (2nd Lt G.A. Raybone).

A7171 (Falcon I) **AAP** Filton 25.6.17, allotted to BEF. **1 AD** dd ex England 6.7.17 (engine 575/WD12534). **48 Sqn** dd ex 1 AD 10.8.17 (same engine), LIA on 05:45 OP 19.8.17 (2nd Lt R. Dutton KIA/2nd Lt H.R. Hart-Davies POW WIA, shot down by

EA near Ostende – same engine) and deleted on unit that day (12hr 40min).

A7172 (Falcon I) **AAP** Filton 25.6.17, allotted to BEF. **1 AD** dd ex England 6.7.17 (engine 533/WD12531). **2 AD** ex 1 AD 13.7.17 (same engine). **22 Sqn** dd ex 2 AD 20.7.17 (same engine), victs 10.8.17 (Capt C.M. Clement/Pte D.W. Clement sent an Albatros D.V down OOC over Aubigny au Bac at 18:45) and 12.8.17 (Capt C.M. Clement/Lt R.B. Carter sent two Albatros D.V OOC over Biache St Vaast at 19:15 then sent two Albatros D.V OOC at 19:30 and 19:45 over Lens, both shared with A7174, the first also shared with Lt M.W. Turner/2nd Lt C.R. Edson) then LIA on 17:50 OP 19.8.17 (Capt C.M. Clement/Lt R.B. Carter both KIA, last seen in combat near Langemarck at 19:35 and shot down by AA – engine 535/WD10548) and deleted on unit that day (39hr 5min).

A7173 (Falcon I) **35 TS** Northolt on 10:32 HAP 22.8.17 (2nd Lt F.G.C. Weare OK) and wrecked 25.8.17 (2nd Lt C.S. Emery/2nd Lt D.H.H. Mayne both IIFA, stalled on a turn near the ground – engine 309/WD15745).

A7174 (Initially Falcon I) **AAP** Filton 28.6.17, allotted to BEF. **1 AD** dd ex England 10.7.17 (engine 547/WD12532). **2 AD** ex 1 AD 13.7.17 (same engine). **22 Sqn** dd ex 2 AD 20.7.17, marked as a/c F, victs 9.8.17 (Capt C.M. Clement/2nd Lt L.G. Davies destroyed an EA C-type in flames over Tortequesne at 06:50), 12.8.17 (Lt J.C. Bush/AM1 A.G. Whitehouse sent two Albatros D.V OOC at 19:30 and 19:45 over Lens, both shared with A7172 and the first also shared with Lt M.W. Turner/2nd Lt C.R. Edson, serial not known) and 17.8.17 (Lt J.C. Bush/Lt W.W. Chapman sent an Albatros D.V down OOC over Staden at 19:15) then wrecked after OP 20.9.17 (2nd Lt E.A. Bell/2nd Lt R.B.P. Wilson both OK, made bad landing in the dark – same engine). **1 AD** ex 22 Sqn 22.9.17. **2 AD** ex 1 AD for reconstruction 3.10.17. **11 Sqn** dd ex 2 ASD 3.12.17 (engine Falcon II 321/WD18437), marked as a/c F, LIA on 09:50 OP 13.1.18 (2nd Lt H.V. Biddington POW/2nd Lt J.H. Corbet KIA, hit by AA fire and last seen over Douai with smoke issuing from the engine – same engine) and deleted on unit that day (88hr 34min).

A7175 (Falcon I) presentation a/c *Malaya No.23, The Malacca*. **AAP** Filton 28.6.17, allotted to BEF. **1 AD** dd ex England 10.7.17 (engine 31/WD12547). **2 AD** ex 1 AD 28.7.17 (same engine). **11 Sqn** dd ex 2 AD 8.8.17 (same engine) and wrecked after Patrol 23.8.17 (2nd Lt F.J. Foster/Lt D.G. Davidson both KOAS, crashed near aerodrome on return at 18:30, machine completely burnt – same engine). **2 AD** ex 11 Sqn 28.8.17 and deleted that day (36hr 50min).

A7176 (Falcon I) presentation a/c *Montreal No.4*. **AAP** Filton 28.6.17, allotted to BEF. **1 AD** dd ex England 6.7.17 (engine 27/WD12546). **48 Sqn** dd ex 1 AD 19.7.17 (same engine), victs 24.7.17 (Lt K.R. Park/2nd Lt A.W. Merchant sent an Albatros D.III, grey and yellow with black tail, down OOC near Ravensyde at 17:40) and 12.8.17 (Lt K.R. Park/2nd Lt A.R. Noss sent an Albatros D.III down OOC, S of Slype at 10:45 12.8.17) then wrecked before OP 15.9.17 (2nd Lt L.A. Payne OK/AM2 H. Lindfield IOAS, engine cut out 10 minutes after take off and the machine crashed near the aerodrome – same engine). **1 AD** ex 48 Sqn 18.9.17 and deleted 20.9.17 (not worth reconstruction, 56hr 30min).

A7177 (Falcon I) presentation a/c *Auckland*. **AAP** Filton 2.7.17, allotted to BEF. Converted to F.2B Series 2 – prototype installation with Falcon III. **1 AD** dd ex England 9.7.17 (engine 21/WD12545). **48 Sqn** dd ex 1 AD 13.7.17 (same engine), LIA on 11:15 Photography 11.8.17 (2nd Lt G. Colledge/2nd Lt R.N.W. Jeff both POW, seen to land under control near Ostende – same engine) and deleted on unit that day (32hr 30min).

A7178 (Falcon I) presentation a/c *Australia No.1, The Sidney Kidman*. **AAP** Filton 2.7.17, allotted to BEF. **1 AD** dd ex England 15.7.17 (engine 283/WD12549). **2 AD** ex 1 AD 20.7.17 (same engine). **22 Sqn** dd ex 2 AD 27.7.17 and wrecked after OP 13.8.17 (2nd Lt S.M. Spurway/AM1 J. McRobert both OK, bad landing, overshot and ran into a hangar, crashing into A7120 – same engine). **2 AD** ex 22 Sqn 16.8.17. **1 AD** ex 2 AD 14.9.17 (same engine). **22 Sqn** reissued ex 1 AD 15.9.17 and wrecked on Practice Flight 18.10.17 (2nd Lt J. Kyle/Sub Lt H.K. Johnstone RN both IOAS, crashed on landing – same engine). **1 AD** ex 22 Sqn 18.10.17 and deleted 22.10.17 (not worth reconstruction, 84hr 4min).

A7179 (Falcon I) presentation a/c *Johore 6*. **AAP** Filton 2.7.17, allotted to BEF. **1 AD** dd ex Filton via Lympne 10.7.17 (engine 213/WD10403). **2 AD** ex 1 AD 13.7.17 (same engine). **22 Sqn** dd ex 2 AD 20.7.17 (same engine) LIA on 17:15 OP 11.8.17 Lt E.A.H

Ward/Lt K.W. Holmes AFC both KIA, last seen in combat NE of Douai at 18:00 and probably brought down by Oblt A. Rittm v Tutschek, Jasta 12 – same engine) and deleted on unit that day (28hr 3min).

A7180 (Falcon I) presentation a/c *Dominica*. **35 TS** Northolt by 16.7.17 (Lt J.H. Letts).

A7181 (Falcon I) presentation a/c *Newfoundland 4*. **AAP** Filton 4.7.17, allotted to BEF. **1 AD** dd ex Lympne 13.7.17 (2nd Lt H. Shaw – engine 23/WD12539). **22 Sqn** dd ex 1 AD 14.8.17 (same engine) LIA on 08:25 OP 11.10.17 (Lt R.I.V Hill/2nd Lt R.S. Gilbert both POW) and deleted on unit that day (57hr 30min).

A7182 (Falcon I) presentation a/c *Gold Coast II*. **AAP** Filton 4.7.17, allotted to BEF. **1 AD** dd ex England 13.7.17 (engine 355/WD12554). **48 Sqn** dd ex 1 AD 10.8.17 (same engine) and wrecked after Night Patrol 10.9.17 (Capt J.T. Milne MC/2nd Lt A.D. Light both IOAS (struck a car when landing at 22:15 and crashed – engine 451/WD10516). **1 AD** ex 48 Sqn 12.9.17 and deleted 16.9.17 (not worth reconstruction, 46hr 5min).

A7183 (Falcon III) **Testing Sqn** Martlesham Heath by 25.7.17 for performance tests with Falcon. **ES** Orfordness by 10.8.17 until @ 7.1.18 (Lt J.A.W. Armstrong/Capt Fairburn).

A7184 To Middle East. **X AP** and Palestine Bde dd ex **X AD** 26.8.17. **111 Sqn** dd ex X AP 22.9.17, damaged in combat 8.10.17 (Lt R.B. Sutherland OK, badly shot about in fight with Rumpler C-type & Albatros D.III) and damaged again during enemy bombing raid 29.11.17 (Cpl W. Richards WIA & AM2 P.L. Smith fatally WIA). **X AD** ex Palestine Bde 2.12.17. **X AP** ex X AD 31.8.18. **1 Sqn AFC** dd ex X AP 3.9.18 (engine WD12555). **X AP** ex 1 Sqn AFC 14.9.18 (same engine). **'X' Flt** dd ex X AP 17.9.18. **1 Sqn AFC** ex 'X' Flt 15.10.18 and deleted on unit 7.11.18 (probably the machine in which Lt W.E. Wright was WIA 26.10.18).

A7185 (Initially Falcon I) **AAP** Filton 6.7.17, allotted to BEF. **1 AD** dd ex England 16.7.17 (engine 363/WD12555). **2 AD** ex 1 AD 23.7.17 (same engine). **22 Sqn** dd ex 2 AD 27.7.17 (same engine), vict 5.9.17 (Lt J.C. Bush/Lt W.W. Chapman destroyed an Albatros D.V in flames E of Houthulst Wood at 19:00) then wrecked on 06:00 OP 17.9.17 (Lt W.M. Yool/Pte D.W. Clement both OK, shot up by EA, force landed near Coyecque due to dense mist and crashed – same engine). **1 AD** ex 22 Sqn 18.9.17. **22 Sqn** reissued ex 1 ASD 13.11.17 (engine Falcon II 415/WD18484) and wrecked on Practice Flight 7.1.18 (2nd Lt W.S. Smallwood/AM2 P. Hoolihan both OK, engine ran badly, force landed and crashed – same engine). **1 ASD** ex 22 Sqn 10.1.18 and deleted 11.1.18 (not worth reconstruction, 101hr 26min).

A7186 To Middle East. **X AP** and Palestine Bde dd ex **X AD** 26.8.18. **111 Sqn** dd ex X AP 12.9.17 and on unit charge until @ 15.10.17. **X AD** and deleted 29.7.18.

A7187 (Falcon I) **AAP** Filton 11.7.17, allotted to BEF. **1 AD** dd ex England 17.7.17 (engine 369/WD12556). **48 Sqn** dd ex 1 AD 27.7.17 (same engine), LIA on 09:35 D.H.4 Escort 11.9.17 (Sgt W.H. Roebuck/2nd Lt H.T. Batson both KIA, last seen at 16,000ft, S of Nieuport – same engine) and deleted on unit that day (67hr 50min).

A7188 To Middle East. **X AP** and Palestine Bde dd ex **X AD** 26.8.17 (engine 507/WD15785). **111 Sqn** dd ex X AP 15.9.17 and on unit charge until @ 10.17. **X AP** dd ex X AD 1.7.18 (engine WD15780). **'X' Flt** dd ex X AP 13.8.18 (same engine). **X AP** ex 'X' Flt 17.9.18. **1 Sqn AFC** dd ex X AP 13.10.18 (same engine) and deleted on unit 6.11.18.

A7189 (Falcon I) **AAP** Filton 12.7.17, allotted to BEF. **1 AD** dd ex England 17.7.17 (engine 587/WD12542). **2 AD** ex 1 AD 27.7.17 (same engine). **22 Sqn** dd ex 2 AD 27.7.17 (same engine) and wrecked on 14:25 OP 9.9.17 (2nd Lt E.O. Peel OK/AM1 S.W.T. Otley WIA, force landed after combat and o/t – same engine). **1 AD** ex 22 Sqn 11.9.17 and deleted 13.9.17 (54hr 45min).

A7190 Presentation a/c *New South Wales No.14. Women's Battleplane*. **X AP** and Palestine Bde dd ex **X AD** 26.8.17 (engine 579/WD15786). **111 Sqn** dd ex X AP 18.9.17. **X AP** dd ex X AD 1.6.18 (engine WD10470). **1 Sqn AFC** dd ex X AP 4.6.18. **X AD** ex 1 Sqn AFC 12.12.18 and deleted 19.12.18.

A7191 (Falcon I) **AAP** Filton 13.7.17, allotted to BEF. **1 AD** dd ex England 20.7.17 (engine 375/WD12557). **2 AD** ex 1 AD 27.7.17 (same engine). **11 Sqn** dd ex 2 AD 28.7.17 (same engine), LIA on 05:25 OP 18.8.17 (2nd Lt L.O. Harel/Capt W.H. Walker both KIA, last seen over Douai at 06:15 – same engine) and deleted on unit that day (11hr 25min).

A7192 To Middle East. **X AP** dd ex **X AD** 11.9.17. **111 Sqn** by 12:17 and victs 17.12.17 (Lt C.R. Davidson/2nd Lt L.A. Simmons destroyed an EA C-type N of Bireh at 11:15), 22.12.17 (Lt C.R. Davidson/

2nd Lt L.A. Simmons destroyed an EA C-type NE of Nablus at 14:30), 28.12.17 (Lt C.R. Davidson/AM2 F.J. Knowles destroyed an EA C-type near Nablus at 16:00) and 17.1.18 (Lt C.R. Davidson/AM2 F.J. Knowles destroyed an EA C-type near Kalkilieh at 09:20). **1 Sqn AFC** dd ex 111 Sqn 20.2.18. **X AP** ex 1 Sqn AFC 14.9.18 (engine WD15786). **5 FS** Helioopolis dd ex X AP 31.5.19 (engine WD 15747). **16 TDS** Abu Sueir. **111 Sqn** dd ex 16 TDS 5.10.19 (same engine). **Special Instruction Flt** Almaza by 7.20. A photograph shows this machine in Middle East, mispainted as B-7192 and named *Gubbins*.

A7193 (Initially Falcon I) **AAP** Filton 13.7.17, allotted to BEF. **1 AD** dd ex England 27.7.17 (engine 305/WD12549). **20 Sqn** dd ex 1 AD 13.8.17 (same engine), vict 11.9.17 (2nd Lt F. Babbage/2nd Lt R.C. Purvis destroyed an Albatros D.V in flames E of Menin at 14:00), damaged in combat 15.9.17 (Lt F. Babbage OK/2nd Lt J.E.L. Skelton WIA), further victs 2.10.17 (Lt J.P. Dalley/Lt O.A. Rowan sent an Albatros D.V down OOC over Moorslede at 12:00) and 15.10.17 (Lt J.C. Kirkpatrick/2nd Lt N. Couve sent an Albatros D.V down OOC over Wervicq at 14:10), damaged in combat 17.10.17 (Lt J.C. Kirkpatrick OK/Lt S.J. Veacock fatally WIA), vict 8.11.17 (Lt J.C. Kirkpatrick/Lt G.A. Brooke destroyed an EA in flames 12.10-14.15), LIA on 10:16 OP, Roulers, 19.1.18 (2nd Lt B. Starfield/Lt A. Hutchinson both KIA last seen near Wytschaete – engine Falcon II 435/WD18494) and deleted on unit 20.1.18 (165hr 25min).

A7194 (Falcon III) to Middle East. **X AD** dd ex England 11.9.17. **X AP** dd ex X AD 11.9.17. **111 Sqn** dd ex X AP 26.9.17 (engine 557/WD15783), vict 8.10.17 (2nd Lt R.C. Steele/Lt J.J. Lloyd-Williams captured an Albatros D.III) and on unit charge until @ 12.17. **1 Sqn AFC** by 17.1.18 and wrecked 27.3.18 (Lt Garson/Lt H.A. Letch both OK). **5 FS** Heliopolis and crashed 25.10.18 (2nd Lt F. Edmunds/2nd Lt W.F. Lane both OK, engine failed and forced landed – engine WD10454) and deleted on unit 21.3.19.

A7195 **AAP** Filton by 18.7.17, allotted to BEF but reallotted to Training 21.7.17. **82 Sqn** Waddington dd ex Filton by air 23.7.17 (engine 581/WD12561). **27th Wing ARS** engineless ex 82 Sqn 10.11.17. **1 SAF** Ayr by 14.2.18 until @ 26.4.18, marked with striped nose and interplane struts.

A7196 To Middle East. **X AP** and Palestine Bde dd ex **X AD** 11.9.17. **111 Sqn** dd ex X AP 26.9.17 (engine 571/WD12575), and vict 18.1.18 (Lt D. Baitken/Lt L.A.J. Barber destroyed an EA C-type over Jaffa-Arsuf at 11:30). **67 Sqn** by 1.18 on unit charge when redesignated as **1 Sqn AFC** 6.2.18 and LIA 1.5.18 (Lt F.W. Haig/Lt R.T. Challinor both POW, landed to rescue the crew of B1146 which had force landed due to ground fire, turned on nose after breaking a wheel on take off and machine burnt, near Amman).

A7197 **82 Sqn** Waddington dd ex from Filton by air 25.7.17 (engine 339/WD12552). **27th Wing ARS** ex 82 Sqn 3.9.17. **82 Sqn** ex ARS 20.9.17. **21st Wing** Rendcomb dd ex Waddington by air 28.9.17 **62 Sqn** Rendcomb and wrecked 5.12.17 (2nd Lt D.R. Eccles/Lt J.L. Sutherland both IIFA, stalled on climbing turn and nosedived in – engine 1/473/WD15765).

A7198 To Middle East. **X AD** dd ex England 11.9.17. **X AP** dd ex X AD 11.9.17. **111 Sqn** dd ex **X AP** 13.10.17, vict 18.1.18 (Capt A.L. Fleming/Cpl F.J. Knowles destroyed an EA C-type over Jaffa-Arsuf at 11:30, shared A7196). **67 Sqn** ex 111 Sqn 1.18, on unit charge when redesignated **1 Sqn AFC** 6.2.18 and vict 5.3.18 (Lt E.S. Headlam/Lt E.B.S. Beaton sent an Albatros D.III OOC, SE of Jiljulieh at 10:00).

A7199 **82 Sqn** Waddington dd ex Filton by air 29.7.17 (engine 331/WD12551). **27th Wing ARS** engineless ex 82 Sqn 11.9.17. Allotted to **35 TS** but allotment cancelled 24.10.17. **31 TS** Wyton 1917.

F.2B A7199 at Wyton around 1918, probably with No 31 Training Squadron.
(Philip Jarrett)

A7200 Presentation a/c *New South Wales No.12. The Macintyre Kayuga Estate*. To Middle East. **X AD** dd ex England 11.9.17. **X AP** ex X AD 11.9.17. **111 Sqn** dd ex X AP. **67 Sqn** dd ex 111 Sqn 27.1.18, on unit charge when redesignated **1 Sqn AFC** 6.2.18. **X AP** Kantara ex 1 Sqn AFC. Then reissued 1 Sqn AFC ex X AP 4.6.18 and vict 8.6.18 (Capt A.R. Brown/Lt G. Finlay destroyed an EA C-type SE of Amman aerodrome at 07:00). **X AD** ex 1 Sqn AFC 12.12.18 and deleted 19.12.18.

A7201 **AAP** Filton by 21.7.17, allotted to BEF. **1 AD** dd ex England 27.7.17 (engine 553/WD12540). **22 Sqn** dd ex 1 AD 5.8.17 (same engine), LIA on 18:00 OP 17.8.17 (2nd Lt R.S. Phelan POW WIA/Lt J.L. Macfarlane [SA] KIA, last seen side-slipping into cloud, Macfarlane's real name was E.E. White – same engine) and deleted on unit that day (13hr 57min).

A7202 To Middle East. **X AD** dd ex England 11.9.17. **X AP** ex X AD 11.9.17. **111 Sqn** by 25.11.17. **67 Sqn** and victs 12.12.17 (Capt R.M. Drummond/AM2 F.J. Knowles sent an Albatros D.V OOC over Tul Keram at 10:30, destroyed an Albatros D.V NW of Tul Keram at 10:35 and destroyed another over Wadi Auja at 10:45), 14.12.17 (Capt R.M. Drummond/AM2 F.J. Knowles destroyed an Albatros D.V, N of Beisan at 09:45) and on 29.12.17 (Lt C.R. Davidson/2nd Lt A. Simmons sent an Albatros D.III OOC at 08:30) then LIA on 08:30 Reconnaissance 20.1.18 (2nd Lt A.A. Poole/Lt F.W. Hancock both POW, engine hit by AA fire, force landed in enemy territoty and machine destroyed).

A7203 (Initially Falcon I) **AAP** Filton 23.7.17, allotted to BEF. **1 AD** dd ex England 9.8.17 (engine 577/WD12535). **20 Sqn** dd ex 1 AD 13.8.17 (same engine), vict 5.9.17 (2nd Lt R.M. Makepeace/Lt M.W. Waddington sent an Albatros D.V down OOC, W of Lille at 11:15), then damaged on OP 14.9.17 (2nd Lt H.F. Tomlin/2nd Lt R.M. Morris both OK, shot up in combat repairs could not be completed within the 36hr time limit and return to 1 AD recommended – same engine). **1 AD** ex 20 Sqn 19.9.17. **2 AD** ex 1 AD for reconstruction 7.10.17. **1 AIS** ex **2 ASD** 3.1.18 (engine Falcon II 177/WD15772). **1 ASD** ex 1 AIS 7.2.18 (same engine). **8 AAP** ex 1 ASD 9.3.18 (2nd Lt C.H. Drew/AM1 Lawson).

A7204 (Falcon I) **AAP** Filton 23.7.17, allotted to BEF. **1 AD** dd ex England 28.7.17 (engine 245/WD10420). **2 AD** ex 1 AD 30.7.17 (same engine). **22 Sqn** dd ex 2 AD 12.8.17 (same engine), LIA on OP 23.8.17 (2nd Lt H.G. Tambling/Sgt W. Organ both POW, part of a formation of six attacked by 5 EA and shot down – same engine) and deleted on unit that day (19hr).

A7205 (Falcon I) **AAP** Filton 24.7.17, allotted to BEF. **1 AD** dd ex England 5.8.17 (engine 32/WD10430). **22 Sqn** dd ex 1 AD 7.8.17 (same engine), LIA on 08:00 OP 22.9.17 (2nd Lt E.A. Bell/2nd Lt R.E. Nowell both KIA, attacked by EA and shot down in flames near Hollebeke, possibly by Oblt R. Berthold, Jasta 18 – same engine) and deleted on unit that day (53hr 10min).

A7206 Sold to US Government.

A7207 (Falcon I) **AAP** Filton 26.7.17, allotted to BEF. **1 AD** dd ex England 5.8.17 (engine 225/WD10407). **22 Sqn** dd ex 1 AD 17.8.17 (same engine), LIA on 14:25 Escort 9.9.17 (Sgt J.H. Hamer/Sgt G.E. Lambeth both KIA, shot down in flames near Wainbrechies – engine 511/WD15781) and deleted on unit that day (23hr 59min).

A7208 (Falcon I) **AAP** Filton 26.7.17, allotted to BEF. **1 AD** dd ex England 5.8.17 (engine 583/WD12565). **2 AD** ex 1 AD 9.8.17 (same engine). **22 Sqn** dd ex 2 AD 12.8.17 (same engine) and wrecked on Practice Flight 16.8.17 (2nd Lt D.K. Best KOAS/Lt J. Stevenson IOAS, spiralled in near aerodrome from 1,500ft – same engine). **1 AD** ex 22 Sqn 16.8.17 and deleted 19.8.17 (6hr 58min).

A7209 (Falcon I) **AAP** Filton 28.7.17, allotted to BEF. **1 AD** dd ex England 9.8.17 (engine 573/WD12562). **2 AD** ex 1 AD 12.8.17 (same engine). **11 Sqn** dd ex 2 AD 16.8.17 (same engine), vict 23.9.17 (Sgt T.F. Stephenson/AM1 S. Platel sent an Albatros D.V down OOC over Vitry at 16:25), LIA on Photography 17.10.17 (2nd Lt S.E. Stanley POW fatally WIA/2nd Lt E.L. Fosse POW, last seen in vertical dive during combat over La Sensée canal at c.10:00 – engine 1/WD10532) and deleted on unit that day (109hr 20min).

A7210 (Initially Falcon I) **AAP** Filton 28.7.17, allotted to BEF. **1 AD** dd ex England 9.8.17 (engine 377/WD12558). **48 Sqn** dd ex 1 AD 14.8.17 (same engine) and wrecked on 06:10 OP 17.8.17 (2nd Lt H.S. Gough WIA/Capt L.F. Reincke KIA, engine shot up in combat – same engine). **1 AD** ex 48 Sqn 18.8.17. **20 Sqn** dd ex 1 AD 20.9.17 (engine Falcon II 217/WD22450), LIA on 11:40 Photography 28.9.17 (Capt J.S. Campbell/Driver G. Tester both KIA, shot down in smoke and flames by EA at 12:30 – same engine) and deleted on unit that day (26hr 43min).

A7211 (Falcon I) **AAP** Filton 28.7.17, allotted to BEF. **1 AD** dd ex England 10.8.17 (engine 325/WD12550). **20 Sqn** dd ex 1 AD 13.8.17 (same engine) and wrecked on Practice Flight 11.9.17 (Sgt W.H. Roberts IOAS/2nd Lt A.E. West KOAS, stalled and spun in – same engine). **1 AD** ex 20 Sqn 14.9.17 and deleted 16.9.17 (30hr 56min).

A7212 (Falcon I) **82 Sqn** Waddington dd ex Filton by air 5.8.17 and damaged 4.9.17 (2nd Lt F.R. Hunt IIFA, flew into ground without flattening out and machine o/t – engine 1/48/WD10433). **27th Wing ARS** engineless ex 82 Sqn 6.9.17. **82 Sqn** reissued, engineless ex ARS 12.10.17. **35 TS** Northolt dd ex 82 Sqn by air 27.10.17 and wrecked 26.11.17 (2nd Lt S.A. Gomez IIFA, cause of accident not given – engine 1/379).

A7213 (Falcon I) **AAP** Filton 31.7.17, allotted to BEF. **1 AD** dd ex England 9.8.17 (engine 287/WD10473). **48 Sqn** dd ex 1 AD 15.8.17 (same engine), victs 21.8.17 (Lt R.D. Coath/Lt A.D. Light destroyed an Albatros D.V in flames E of Westende at 19:40) and 22.8.17 (Lt R.D. Coath/Lt A.D. Light sent an Albatros D.V down OOC, SW of Ostend at 09:00 and another OOC over Slype-Westende at 09:15), then wrecked after successful combat 15.9.17 (2nd Lt H.H. Hartley/2nd Lt E.C. Birch OK, destroyed an Albatros D.V, E of Dixmude at 18:50 but ran into a ditch on landing – same engine). **1 AD** ex 48 Sqn 18.9.17, **2 AD** ex 1 AD for reconstruction 27.9.17 but deleted for spares 25.10.17 (50hr 15min).

A7214 (Intitially Falcon I) **AAP** Filton 2.8.17, allotted to BEF. **1 AD** dd ex England 11.8.17 (engine 397/WD12560). **20 Sqn** dd ex 1 AD 13.8.17 (same engine), victs 3.9.17 (2nd Lt R.M. Makepeace/Lt M.W. Waddington destroyed an Albatros D.V in flames over Menin-Wervicq at 10:10), 5.9.17 (2nd Lt Campbell OK/AM W. Harrop WIA, shot off part of Albatros D-type tailplane W of Lille at 11:15) and 11.9.17 (2nd Lt R.M. Makepeace/Lt M.W. Waddington sent an Albatros D.V down OOC, E of Menin at 14:00) then wrecked on OP 1.10.17 (Capt D.D. Walrond-Skinner/Lt N.W. Sanders both OK, lost bearings due to mist and attempted to land at 1 AD but overshot and ran into rough ground – engine Falcon II 173/WD22429). Machine retained at 1 AD for repair and on charge when redesignated **1 ASD** 1.11.17. **1 AIS** ex 1 ASD 19.11.17 (engine Falcon II 435/WD18494). **20 Sqn** reissued ex 1 AIS 28.11.17 (same engine) and vict 3.12.17 (Sgt F. Johnson/2nd Lt S.H.P. Masding sent an Albatros D.V down OOC over Wervicq). **10 Sqn** dd ex 20 Sqn 2.2.18 (engine Falcon II 169/WD22440) and wrecked on Wireless Test 24.3.18 (Lt R.O. Williams/Lt S.S. Birbeck both OK, overran aerodrome on landing, hit road and smashed undercarriage – same engine). **1 ASD** ex 10 Sqn 28.3.18, repaired but crashed on Test Flight 30.4.18 (Lt Walls OK) and deleted 3.5.18 (not worth reconstruction, 112hr 18min).

A7215 (Initially Falcon I) **AAP** Filton 2.8.17, allotted to BEF. **1 AD** dd ex England 10.8.17 (engine 20/WD10422). **20 Sqn** dd ex 1 AD 11.8.17 (same engine), vict 9.9.17 (Lt H.E. Luchford/Lt R.F. Hill sent an Albatros D-type down OOC over Becelaere at 13:15) then wrecked after OP 20.9.17 (Capt J.S. Campbell/2nd Lt J.P.F. Adams both OK, stalled on landing and pancaked – same engine). **1 AD** ex 20 Sqn 22.9.17. **2 AD** ex 1 AD 27.9.17 for reconstruction and on unit charge when redesignated **2 ASD** 1.11.17. **2 AIS** ex 2 ASD 14.1.18 (engine Falcon II 103/WD18551). **11 Sqn** dd ex 2 AIS 2.2.18 (Lt J.P. Seabrook, same engine). **2 ASD** ex 11 Sqn 5.3.18, described as a bad climber. **1 ASD** by rail 2.4.18. **2 AIS** ex 2 ASD 25.5.18. **62 Sqn** dd ex 2 AIS 30.5.18 (engine Falcon III 501/WD32650), vict 24.6.18 (Lt L.W. Hudson/Lt H.E. Merritt destroyed a LVG C-type near Harnes at 08:00) then wrecked on Test Flight 16.7.17 (Lt J.K. Stewart OK – same engine). **2 ASD** ex 62 Sqn 18.7.18 and deleted 30.7.18 (not worth reconstruction, 110hr 40min).

A7216 (Initially Falcon II) **AAP** Filton 4.8.17, allotted to BEF. **1 AD** dd ex England 10.8.17 (engine 29/WD22382). **48 Sqn** dd ex 1 AD 12.8.17 (same engine), victs 20.8.17 (Capt J.T. Milne/2nd Lt W. O'Toole destroyed an Albatros D.V of MFJa1 and sent another OOC over Ghistelles at 19:15), 21.8.17 (Capt J.T. Milne/2nd Lt W. O'Toole destroyed an Albatros D.V, E of Westende at 19:45), 25.8.17 (Capt J.T. Milne/2nd Lt W. O'Toole sent an Albatros D.V down OOC over Westkerke at 12:10) and 9.9.17 (Capt J.T. Milne/Lt A.D. Light sent an Albatros D.V down OOC over Middelkerke at 16:15) then wrecked on Test Flight 18.2.18 (Sgt E.T. Hardeman OK, both top wings folded up in the air and machine crashed on Guizancourt aerodrome – engine 225/WD22451). **2 ASD** ex 48 Sqn 26.2.18. **48 Sqn** reissued ex 2 AIS 27.3.18 (engine Falcon III 613/WD32706) and wrecked on Travelling Flight 28.3.18 (2nd Lt C.D.B. Stiles/2nd Lt J.A.

Galbraith both OK, lost way and force landed near Bouval – same engine). **22 Wing Salvage** 1.4.18. **1 ASD** 7.4.18 and deleted 10.4.18 (not worth reconstruction, 175hr 52min).

A7217 (Initially Falcon II) **AAP** Filton 4.8.17, allotted to BEF. **1 AD** dd ex England 11.8.17 (engine 5/WD22375). **48 Sqn** dd ex 1 AD 12.8.17 (same engine), victs 25.8.17 (2nd Lt H.J. Pratt/Lt H. Owen sent an Albatros D.V down OOC over Westkerke at 12:10) and 31.8.17 (2nd Lt H.J. Pratt/Lt H. Owen sent an Albatros D.V down OOC over Zarren at 21:05) then wrecked after OP 15.9.17 (2nd Lt E.B. Corry IOAS/2nd Lt A.R. Noss fatally IOAS, nosedived in on landing and crashed near the aerodrome – same engine). **1 AD** ex 48 Sqn 17.9.17. **2 AD** ex 1 AD for reconstruction 7.10.17 and on unit charge when redesignated **2 ASD** 1.11.17. **2 AIS** ex 2 ASD 17.1.18 (engine Falcon III 59/WD18529). **2 ASD** ex 2 AIS 19.1.18. **2 AIS** ex 2 ASD 28.1.18. **48 Sqn** reissued ex 2 AIS 28.1.18 (same engine) and wrecked before OP 15.3.18 (2nd Lt E.R. Stock/Cpl J. Borwein both OK, crashed taking off in a gusty wind – same engine). **2 ASD** ex 48 Sqn 16.3.18. **1 ASD** ex 2 ASD by rail 2.4.18 and deleted 8.4.18 (not worth reconstruction, 98hr 50min).

A7218 **1 SAF** Ayr named *Panther* by 3.1.18. **59 TS** Lilbourne by 3.9.18 until @ 13.2.18. **35 TS** Port Meadow by 23.3.18.

A7219 (Falcon II) **AAP** Filton 7.8.17, allotted to BEF. **1 AD** dd ex England 11.8.17 (engine 21/WD22380). **48 Sqn** dd ex 1 AD 12.8.17, damaged on HAP 22.8.17 (Capt J.H.T. Letts IOAS/2nd Lt H.R. Power KIA, engaged a Gotha over sea, 30 miles off Nieuport at 11:30; observer shot, pilot hit by Lewis gun as observer slumped) then wrecked on OP 28.10.17 (2nd Lt H.S. McLaren/2nd Lt D.W. Hardie both OK, force landed on bad ground near Hondschoote at 10:25 after engine failure – engine 149/WD22415). **1 AD** ex 48 Sqn 30.10.17, unit redesignated **1 ASD** 1.11.17, and deleted 16.1.18 (not worth reconstruction, 129hr 46min).

A7220 (Initially Falcon II) **AAP** Filton 7.8.17, allotted to BEF. **1 AD** dd ex England 14.8.17 (Lt Dainty – engine 51/WD22384). **48 Sqn** dd ex 1 AD 14.8.17 (same engine), victs 19.8.17 (2nd Lt J.A.W. Binnie/Cpl V. Reed sent an Albatros D.V down OOC over Ostende at 06:50), 22.8.17 (2nd Lt J.A.W. Binnie/Cpl V. Reed destroyed an Albatros D.V in flames over Ghistellesat 09:00), 26.8.17 (2nd Lt J.A.W. Binnie/Cpl V. Reed destroyed an Albatros D.V and sent another OOC, W of Middelkerke at 08:30 and 11.9.17 (2nd Lt J.A.W. Binnie/2nd Lt T.C.S. Tuffield sent a DFW C-type down OOC over Dixmude at 10:15) then wrecked on 10:45 OP 21.2.18 (2nd Lt C.D.B. Stiles OK/Lt W.G.S. Gregson WIA, shot down by EA and crashed in forced landing 2,000yds E of Savy – same engine). **2 ASD** ex 48 Sqn 24.2.18. **2 AIS** ex 2 ASD 29.4.18 (engine Falcon III 615/WD32707). **11 Sqn** dd ex 2 AIS 10.5.18 (same engine) and wrecked on Reconnaissance 30.6.18 (Lt C.E. Lacoste OK/2nd Lt H.E. Power IOAS, o/t during forced landing in cornfield after engine failure – same engine). **2 ASD** ex 11 Sqn 1.7.18 and deleted 7.7.18 on reconstruction as F6179 (218hr 70min).

A7221 (Initially Falcon II) **AAP** Filton 10.8.17, allotted to BEF. **1 AD** dd ex England 15.8.17 (Lt Grosvenor – engine 23/WD22381). **48 Sqn** dd ex 1 AD 17.8.17 (same engine), vict 5.9.17 (Lt O.J.F. Scholte/2nd Lt G.R. Horsfall sent an Albatros D.V down OOC over Mariakerke at 12:00). **35 Sqn** ex 48 Sqn 4.2.18 (engine 247/WD13400), wrecked before Travelling Flight 24.3.18 (Capt G. McPherson/Lt C. Kniverton both OK, ran into a shell hole on take off and burnt out – engine Falcon III 471/WD32635) and deleted on unit that day (156hr 15min).

A7222 (Falcon II) **AAP** Filton 11.8.17, allotted to BEF. **1 AD** dd ex England 16.8.17 (engine 107/WD22407). **48 Sqn** dd ex 1 AD 18.8.17 (same engine), victs 3.9.17 (Lt R.E. Dodds/2nd Lt T.C.S. Tuffield sent an Albatros D.III down OOC and destroyed another in flames over Kayem, E of Dixmude, at 08:15) then wrecked in successful combat 17.9.17 (Sgt J. Oldham OK/AM2 W. Walker WIA, sent an EA C-type down OOC, shared A7224, then brought down in combat and crashed near Ferme de Moulin – same engine). **1 AD** ex 48 Sqn 19.9.17 and deleted 21.9.17 (not worth reconstruction, 55hr 54min).

A7223 (Falcon II) **AAP** Filton 11.8.17, allotted to BEF. **1 AD** dd ex England 16.8.17 (engine 113/WD22409). **22 Sqn** dd ex 1 AD 21.8.17 (same engine) and wrecked on 08:50 OP 11.10.17 (Lt W.G. Meggitt MC/Capt F.A. Durrad both OK, shot up in combat over 5th Army Front – engine 199/WD22436). **1 AD** ex 22 Sqn 11.10.17. **20 Sqn** dd ex 1 AD 7.11.17 (engine 271/WD18412) and wrecked on OP 14.11.17 (2nd Lt F. Babbage OK/AM2 J. McMechan IOAS, crashed in forced landing near Hondeghem due to thick fog – same engine). **1 ASD** ex 20 Sqn 15.11.17 and deleted 21.11.17 (not worth reconstruction, 91hr 44min).

A7224 (Falcon II) **AAP** Filton 13.8.17, allotted to BEF. **1 AD** dd ex Lympne 17.8.17 (Lt Slingsby – engine 129/WD22419). **48 Sqn** dd ex 1 AD 18.8.17 (same engine), victs 20.8.17 (2nd Lt R.L. Curtiss/2nd Lt D.P. Fitzgerald-Uniacke sent an Albatros D.V down OOC over Ghistelles at 20:05), 22.8.17 (2nd Lt R.L. Curtiss/2nd Lt D.P. Fitzgerald-Uniacke destroyed an Albatros D.V over Ostend and sent another down OOC at 09:08), 2.9.17 (2nd Lt R.L. Curtiss/2nd Lt D.P. Fitzgerald-Uniacke sent an Albatros D.V down OOC, E of Dixmude at 09:30, shared A7170), 14.9.17 (2nd Lt R.L. Curtiss/2nd Lt D.P. Fitzgerald-Uniacke destroyed an Albatros D.V over Ghistelles at 16:40) and 17.9.17 (2nd Lt R.L. Curtiss/2nd Lt D.P. Fitzgerald-Uniacke sent an EA C-type down OOC over Leke at 09:15) then LIA on OP 21.9.17 (2nd Lt R.L. Curtiss POW fatally WIA/2nd Lt D.P. Fitzgerald-Uniacke POW WIA, combat with 15 EA, chased down by 5 EA and last seen at 08:00 in a spin 10 miles NE of Roulers with observer trying to reach controls, probably brought down by Obltn H. Göring, Jasta 27 – same engine) and deleted on unit that day (51hr 25min).

A7225 Presentation a/c *Ajmeer*. **AAP** Filton by 18.8.17. **48 Sqn** as a/c *4*. **59 TS** Lilbourne by 31.8.18 until @ 4.9.17. Deleted by 2.12.17.

A7226 (Initially Falcon II) presentation a/c *Kotah No.2*. **AAP** Filton 16.8.17, allotted to BEF. **1 AD** dd ex England 21.8.17 (engine 147/WD22414). **22 Sqn** dd ex 1 AD 23.8.17 (same engine) and wrecked after OP 20.9.17 (Capt J.L. Williamson/Lt H.D. McGrath both OK, made bad landing in the dark – same engine). **1 AD** ex 22 Sqn 23.9.17. **2 AD** ex 1 AD 6.10.17 for reconstruction. **11 Sqn** dd ex 2 AD 28.10.17 (engine 213/WD22448), damaged in successful combat 6.1.18 (2nd Lt R.H. Nixon OK/2nd Lt E.H. Church WIA, sent an Albatros D.V down OOC over Estourmel at 14:15 but machine shot up) and wrecked after Reconnaissance 20.2.18 (2nd Lt R.K. Harrison/Lt D.S. Allison both OK, misjudged landing and crashed – same engine). **2 ASD** ex 11 Sqn 23.2.18. **2 AIS** ex 2 ASD 23.4.18 (engine Falcon III 627/WD32713). **11 Sqn** reissued ex 2 AIS 3.5.18 (same engine) and wrecked on OP 10.8.18 (Lt B.S.B. Thomas MC/2nd Lt C.E. Spinks both OK, centre-section hit by AA fire, force landed at Monchy au Bois and ran into barbed wire – engine Falcon III 1445/WD51747). **2 ASD** ex 11 Sqn 12.8.18 and deleted 23.8.18 (not worth reconstruction, 225hr 59min).

A7227 (Initially Falcon II) at maker's 11.8.17, allotted to BEF. **2 AD** dd ex England in packing case 31.8.17 (engine 15/WD22378). **1 AD** ex 2 AD 9.9.17 (same engine). **48 Sqn** dd ex 1 AD 11.9.17 (same engine) and wrecked on 11:40 OP, St. Quentin 11.3.18 (2nd Lt W.L. Thomas/Cpl J.H. Bowler both OK, machine shot up in combat at 12:00 – engine Falcon III 281/WD18640). **2 ASD** ex 48 Sqn 13.3.18. **1 ASD** ex 2 ASD by rail 1.4.18 and deleted 8.4.18 (not worth reconstruction).

A7228 (Falcon I) at maker's 11.8.17, allotted to BEF. **2 AD** dd ex England in packing case 7.9.17 (engine 431/WD15754). **1 AD** ex 2 AD 14.9.17 (same engine). **20 Sqn** dd ex 1 AD 19.9.17 (same engine) and wrecked after Photo Reconnaissance 21.9.17 (Sgt F. Johnson/2nd Lt J.P. Flynn both OK, engine stopped and machine stalled on landing – same engine). **1 AD** ex 20 Sqn 25.9.17 and deleted 26.9.17 (not worth reconstruction, 5hr 47min).

A7229 (Falcon II) at maker's 11.8.17, allotted to BEF. **2 AD** dd ex England in packing case 6.9.17 (engine 121/WD22413). **1 AD** ex 2 AD 15.9.17 (same engine). **48 Sqn** dd ex 1 AD 17.9.17, damaged in combat (Capt K.R. Park/Lt J.H. Robertson both, shot up by EA, E of St. Quentin and west of lines, both OK) then LIA on 11:00 Photography 16.2.18 (Sgt E.F. Hardeman/2nd Lt G.W. Croft both KIA, shot down in flames – engine 21/WD22380) and deleted on unit that day).

A7230 (Falcon II) at maker's 11.8.17, allotted to BEF. **2 AD** dd ex England in packing case 1.9.17 (engine 61/WD22394). **1 AD** ex 2 AD 9.9.17 (same engine). **22 Sqn** dd ex 1 AD 11.9.17 (same engine) and wrecked on 10:15 OP 3.12.17 (Lt L.R. Titchener/Sub Lt H.K. Johnstone RN both KOAS, collided with A7268 at 10:25 over Aire – same engine). **1 ASD** ex 22 Sqn 4.12.17 and deleted 7.12.17 (not worth reconstruction, 101hr 44min).

A7231 (Falcon I) at maker's 11.8.17, allotted to BEF. **2 AD** dd ex England in packing case 1.9.17 (engine 493/WD15759). **11 Sqn** dd ex 2 AD 7.9.17 (same engine) marked as a/c *1*, victs 30.9.17 (Lt H. Scandrett/Lt G. Watson sent two Albatros D.V down OOC over Etaing at 15:50-16:00), LIA on 08:50 Photo Reconnaissance, Douai-Denain-Caudry, 17.10.17 (2nd Lt E. Scholtz/2nd Lt H.C. Wookey both POW, last seen gliding down apparently under control over Cambrai at c.10:45 after combat with EA, probably brought down by Vzfw Bey, Jasta 5 – same engine) and deleted on unit that day (78hr 35min).

A7232 (Falcon I) at maker's 11.8.17, allotted to BEF. **2 AD** dd ex England in packing case 1.9.17 (engine 445/WD15775). **1 AD** ex 2 AD 9.9.17 (same engine). **22 Sqn** dd ex 1 AD 10.9.17 (same engine) and wrecked on OP 25.9.17 (Lt W.M. Yool/Pte D.W. Clement both OK, engine cut out, and crashed on landing at **21 Sqn** aerodrome – same engine). **1 AD** ex 22 Sqn 29.9.17 and deleted 30.9.17 (not worth reconstruction, 32hr 52min).

A7233 (Falcon I) **AAP** Filton 22.8.17, allotted to BEF. **1 AD** dd ex England 31.8.17 (Lt Rockey – engine 521/WD15784). **22 Sqn** dd ex 1 AD 6.9.17 (same engine), wrecked on 06:15 OP 21.9.17 (2nd Lt A.H. Gilbert/AM2 C. Loveland both KOAS, collided wth A7149 at 10,000ft and pieces fell 2,000 yards E of Ypres at 08:15 – same engine) and deleted on unit that day (29hr 30min).

A7234 (Falcon I) **AAP** Filton 23.8.17 allotted to BEF. **1 AD** dd ex England 31.8.17 (Lt Lichfield – engine 415/WD15750). **20 Sqn** dd ex 1 AD 4.9.17, vict 11.9.17 (Lt R.K. Kirkman/2nd Lt J.P. Flynn destroyed an Albatros D.V in flames, E of Menin at 14:00), LIA on 16:36 OP 21.9.17 (2nd Lt C.H. Woods/2nd Lt T.A. McLean both KIA, last seen between Menin and Wervicq, probably brought down by Ltn Kieckhafer, Jasta 29 – same engine) and deleted on unit that day (27hr 53min).

A7235 (Falcon I) **AAP** Filton 25.8.17, allotted to BEF. **1 AD** dd ex England 31.8.17 (Lt Carpenter – engine 441/WD15755). **11 Sqn** dd ex 1 AD 1.9.17 (same engine), wrecked after successful combats on 14:35 OP 31.10.17 (Sgt T.F. Stephenson OK/1AM S.H. Platel WIA, destroyed two Albatros D.V over Fresse at 15:30 then crashed landing on barbed wire during forced landing and machine unsalvageable – same engine) and deleted on unit that day (104hr 30min).

A7236 (Falcon I) presentation a/c *Australia No.1. The Sidney Kidman.* **X AP** dd ex England 26.10.17. **X AP** and Palestine Bde ex X AD 29.10.17. **111 Sqn**, tested new 6.11.17. **1 Sqn AFC** by 25.5.18, LIA 27.6.18 (Lt G.V. Oxenham KIA/Lt L.H. Smith POW, in combat with AEG C-types then hit by ground fire and crashed in the Hills of Lebanon, behind enemy lines – engine Falcon I WD12578) and deleted on unit 30.6.18.

A7237 (Falcon I) presentation a/c *New South Wales No.8. Australia No.9.* To Middle East. **X AD** dd ex England 26.10.17. **X AP** and Palestine Bde ex X AD 29.10.17. **111 Sqn** by 9.12.17. **1 Sqn AFC** by 5.5.18 until @ 16.6.18. **X AP** Kantara. **1 Sqn AFC** reissued ex X AP 30.10.18. **X AP** Kantara. **111 Sqn** reissued ex X AP 15.5.19 (engine Falcon I WD10501). **ASD ME** ex 111 Sqn and deleted 28.12.19.

A7238 **35 TS** Northolt by 15.11.17 until @ 18.11.17. **59 TS** Lilbourne/Rendcomb as a/c *6* by 6.1.18 until @ 24.6.18. **45 TDS** Rendcomb by 8.18.

A7239 (Initially Falcon I) **AAP** Filton by 27.8.17, allotted to BEF. **1 AD** dd ex England 2.9.17 (engine 91/WD22403). **22 Sqn** dd ex 1 AD 5.9.17 and wrecked on Test Flight 29.9.17 (Lt J.C. Bush/Lt W.W. Chapman both OK, crashed on landing – same engine). **1 AD** ex 22 Sqn 29.9.17. **2 AD** ex 1 AD for reconstruction 16.10.17. **22 Sqn** reissued ex **2 ASD** 11.12.17 (engine Falcon II 131/WD22444) and wrecked on Gunnery Practice 18.1.18 (2nd Lt G.G. Johnstone OK/2nd Lt G.J. Maynard IOAS, engine failed on take off, pilot tried to return to aerodrome but stalled and crashed – engine Falcon II 2111/WD22458). **1 ASD** ex 22 Sqn 21.1.18 and deleted 22.1.18 (not worth reconstruction, 48hr 33min).

A7240 (Initially Falcon II) **AAP** Bristol 27.8.17, allotted to BEF. **1 AD** dd ex England 3.9.17 (engine 115/WD22405). **20 Sqn** dd ex 1 AD 7.9.17 (same engine), victs 5.10.17 (Capt J.E. Johnston/Lt J.A. Hone sent an Albatros D-type OOC over Becelaere at 16:35, then around 16:45 attacked a C-type which went down into cloud, according to reports, the EA under the cloud fell into a formation of **1 Sqn** Nieuports and was shot down in flames) and 20.10.17 (2nd Lt J.L. Boles/Lt O.A. Rowan on 07:27 OP sent an Albatros D-type OOC over Adizeele) then wrecked on Test Flight 16.11.17 (2nd Lt D. French/Sgt T. Collins both OK, engine cut out at 50ft and machine crashed – engine 171/WD22428). **1 ASD** ex 20 Sqn 17.11.17. **1 AIS** ex 1 ASD 11.1.18 (engine Falcon III 237/WD18618). **20 Sqn** reissued ex 1 AIS 18.1.18 (same engine) and wrecked on 17:25 Patrol 1.4.18 (Major J.A. Dennistoun/2nd Lt H.G. Crowe both OK, machine hit by AA fire and crashed near Wulverghem – same engine). **1 ASD** ex 20 Sqn 5.4.18 and deleted 8.4.18 (146hr 7min).

A7241 (Falcon II) **AAP** Filton 28.8.17, allotted to BEF. **1 AD** dd ex England 4.9.17 (engine 143/WD22416). **20 Sqn** dd ex 1 AD 9.9.17, LIA on 11:40 Photo Reconnaissance, Wervicq-Hollebeke, 28.9.17 (2nd Lt H.F. Tomlin/2nd Lt H.T. Noble both KIA, shot down in flames by EA – same engine) and deleted on unit 29.9.17 (29hr 42min).

A7242 (Falcon II) **82 Sqn** Waddington dd ex Filton by air for **'B' Flt** 2.9.17 (engine 81/WD22401). Rendcomb dd ex Waddington by air 28.9.17 (same engine). **62 Sqn** Rendcomb by 14.11.17.

A7243 (Initially Falcon II) **AAP** Filton 29.8.17, allotted to BEF. **1 AD** dd ex England 6.9.17 (engine 25/WD12563). **22 Sqn** dd ex 1 AD 9.9.17 (same engine) and wrecked before Aerial Gunnery 23.12.17 (2nd Lt S.H. Wallace/AM2 P. Hoolihan both OK, damaged taxiing on frozen ground – engine 33/WD22467). **1 ASD** ex 22 Sqn 23.12.17. **1 AIS** ex 1 ASD 24.2.18 (engine Falcon III 27/WD18513). **22 Sqn** reissued ex 1 AIS 10.3.18 (same engine), victs 22.5.18 (2nd Lt E.C. Bromley/2nd Lt J.H. Umney sent an Albatros D-type down OOC SE of Arras at 10:30), 31.5.18 (Lt F.G. Gibbons/Sgt J.H. Jones sent a Pfalz D.III down OOC, SE of Armentieres at 19:15) and wrecked in successful combat 5.6.18 (Capt J.E. Gurdon OK/Sgt J.H. Hall WIA), sent an Albatros D.V down OOC, S of Laventie at 10:30 and destroyed a Pfalz D.III in flames NE of La Bassee at 19:15 but machine badly damaged by EA fire – engine 147/WD18573). **1 ASD** ex 22 Sqn 7.6.18 and deleted 26.6.18 (not worth reconstruction, 194hr 15min).

A7244 (Falcon II) **AAP** Filton by 30.8.17, allotted to BEF. **1 AD** dd ex England 5.9.17 (engine 31/WD22411). **22 Sqn** dd ex 1 AD 22.9.17 (same engine), LIA on OP 15.10.17 (Lt H.S. Wellby/2AM W. Nichol both POW, chased by several EA at 7,000ft over Maldeghem and going down under control but smoking at 13:15 – same engine) and deleted on unit that day.

A7245 (Falcon II) **AAP** Filton by 31.8.17, allotted to BEF. **1 AD** dd ex England 10.9.17 (engine 157/WD22424). **20 Sqn** dd ex 1 AD 11.9.17, vict 27.9.17 (2nd Lt F. Durrand/Sgt W.J. Benger destroyed an Albatros D.V in flames over Roulers at 13:00) then wrecked on 07:27 OP 20.10.17 (2nd Lt R.B. Slade/Lt G.B. Booth both IIA, engine and controls damaged by EA fire, over **6 Sqn**'s aerodrome the controls severed and the machine side-slipped in – same engine). **1 AD** ex 20 Sqn 21.10.17 and deleted 24.10.17 (not worth reconstruction, 68hr 8min).

A7246 (Falcon II) **AAP** Filton 1.9.17, allotted to BEF. **1 AD** dd ex England 6.9.17 (engine 155/WD22423). **20 Sqn** dd ex 1 AD 10.9.17 (same engine), and damaged in successful combats 19.9.17 (2nd Lt A.G.V. Taylor OK/2nd Lt H. Dandy WIA, destroyed an Albatros D.V in flames and sent more down OOC over Becelaere-Polygon Wood at 10:00 but machine damaged by EA fire and force landed at **4 Sqn** aerodrome – same engine). **1 AD** ex 20 Sqn 22.9.17. **2 AD** ex 1 AD for reconstruction 11.10.17. **1 AIS** dd ex 2 ASD 18.11.17. **22 Sqn** dd ex 1 AIS 23.12.17 (engine 407/WD18480) and wrecked on Gunnery Practice 25.1.18 (2nd Lt D.S. Smallwood/Sgt T. Kavanagh both KOAS, LH bottom plane collapsed and machine crashed – same engine). **1 ASD** ex 20 Sqn 27.1.18 and deleted 28.1.18 (36hr 40min).

A7247 (Falcon II) **AAP** Filton 4.9.17, allotted to BEF. **1 AD** dd ex England 9.9.17 (engine 165/WD22427). **22 Sqn** dd ex 1 AD 11.9.17 (same engine), victs 11.9.17 (Lt H.G.E. Luchford MC/Lt R.F. Hill MC sent an Albatros D.V down OOC, E of Menin at 14:00), 21.9.17 (Lt H.G.E. Luchford MC/Lt R.F. Hill MC sent an Albatros D.V down OOC over Becelaere at 17:00) and damaged in successful combat 27.9.17 (Lt J.P. Dalley/Lt O.A. Rowan both OK, destroyed an Albatros D.V in flames over Roulers but machine hit by EA fire) then LIA on 07:30 OP 18.10.17 (2nd Lt C.E. Ferguson/2nd Lt A.D. Lennox both KIA in combat over Ardoye at 08:45 – same engine) and deleted on unit that day (42hr 50min).

A7248 (Initially Falcon II) **AAP** Filton by 4.9.17, allotted to BEF. **1 AD** dd ex England 9.9.17 (engine 19/WD22387). **20 Sqn** dd ex 1 AD 9.9.17 (same engine) and wrecked on 12:33 Photo Reconnaissance 27.9.17 (Lt J.P. Dalley/Lt O.A. Rowan both OK, damaged by EA fire – engine Falcon I 305/WD12549). **1 AD** ex 20 Sqn 29.9.17. **2 AD** ex 1 AD for reconstruction 6.10.17. **11 Sqn** dd ex **2 ASD** 28.11.17 (engine Falcon II 273/WD18413) and wrecked on Reconnaissance 2.12.17 (2nd Lt J. Buckley/Cpl H.W. Scarnell both OK, engine cut out during change of tanks and failed to pick up, machine crashed at 08:40 – same engine). **2 ASD** ex 11 Sqn 2.12.17. **2 AIS** ex 2 ASD 3.2.18. **48 Sqn** dd ex 2 AIS 4.2.18 (engine Falcon III 323/WD18661). **62 Sqn** ex 48 Sqn 15.3.18 (same engine), LIA on Patrol 25.3.18 (2nd Lt V.K. Hilton/Cpl J. Borwein both OK, engine cut out over Albert and machine force landed and abandoned – same engine) and deleted on unit 27.3.18.

A7249 **35 TS** Northolt by 9.17. **39 Sqn** North Weald and on HAP 5.12.17 (2nd Lt C.P. Donnison/Lt W.N. Fraser) and on unit charge until @ 22.1.18.

A7250 (Falcon II) at maker's 1.9.17, allotted to BEF. **2 AD** dd ex England in packing case 21.9.17 (engine 175/WD22430). **1 AD** ex 2 AD 30.9.17 (same engine). **20 Sqn** dd ex 1 AD 6.10.17 (same engine), vict 27.10.17 (2nd Lt D.M. McGoun/2nd Lt N. Couve sent an Albatros D.III down OOC over Roulers at 13:10) then wrecked on 12:19 Photo Reconnaissance 5.12.17 (Sgt F. Hopper WIA/Capt R.H. Warden IIA, shot up by EA and force landed in shelled area – engine 125/WD15770). **1 ASD** ex 20 Sqn 7.12.17 and deleted 12.12.17 (not worth reconstruction, 70hr 15min).

A7251 (Falcon II) at maker's 1.9.17, allotted to BEF. **2 AD** dd ex England in packing case 20.9.17 (engine 145/WD22422). **1 AD** ex 2 AD 23.9.17 (same engine). **22 Sqn** dd ex **1 AD** 24.9.17 (same engine) and wrecked after OP 13.4.18 (2nd Lt O. StC. Harris/Lt H.F. Moore both OK, crashed landing on rough ground at St Andre – engine 151/WD15771). **1 ASD** ex 22 Sqn 14.4.18 and deleted 23.4.18 (not worth reconstruction, 184hr 56min).

A7252 (Falcon II) at maker's 1.9.17, allotted to BEF. **2 AD** dd ex England in packing case 21.9.17 (engine 55/WD22385). **11 Sqn** dd ex 2 AD 26.9.17 (same engine) and wrecked on Target Practice 11.11.17 (2nd Lt M.S. West/Capt J.A. Revill both KOAS, pulled up rather quickly from a dive and RH wings crumpled up – same engine). **2 ASD** ex 11 Sqn 13.11.17 and deleted 14.11.17 (41hr 55min).

A7253 (Falcon II) at maker's 1.9.17, allotted to BEF. **2 AD** dd ex England in packing case 19.9.17 (engine 75/WD22399). **1 AD** ex 2 AD 23.9.17 (same engine). **20 Sqn** dd ex 1 AD 30.9.17 (same engine), victs 12.11.17 (2nd Lt J.L. Boles/2nd Lt F.B. Wallis sent an Albatros D.V down OOC) and 13.11.17 (Lt R.K. Kirkman/Capt L.W. Burbidge sent an Albatros D.V down OOC over Becelaere at 15:00) then LIA on 10:54 OP 29.11.17 (2nd Lt E.V. Clark/2nd Lt G. Noon both KIA, in combat with EA over Moorslede and last seen near Westroosebeke 29.11.17 – same engine) and deleted on unit that day (74hr 54min).

A7254 (Initially Falcon II) at maker's 1.9.17, allotted to BEF. **2 AD** dd ex England in packing case 20.9.17 (engine 79/WD22391). **1 AD** ex 2 AD 23.9.17 (same engine). **48 Sqn** dd ex 1 AD 25.9.17 (same engine), vict 29.10.17 (2nd Lt H.H. Hartley/2nd Lt E.C. Birch destroyed an Albatros D.III in flames NE of Dixmude at 16:20, shared 2nd Lt L.A. Payne/2nd Lt V. Bourdillon) then wrecked after Camera Co-operation 4.1.18 (2nd Lt E.J. Smeetham-Jones/ 2nd Lt A.C. Cooper both OK, crashed landing on frozen ground – same engine). **2 ASD** ex 48 Sqn 9.1.18. **2 AIS** ex 2 ASD 28.2.18 (engine Falcon III 475/WD32637). **11 Sqn** dd ex 2 AIS 5.3.18 and wrecked on OP 21.3.18 (2nd Lt A.R. Knowles OK/Lt A.E. Matthews IOAS, crashed attempting to land near Gaudiempre in thick fog – same engine). **2 ASD** ex 11 Sqn 21.3.18 and deleted 25.3.18 (not worth reconstruction, 118hr 15min).

A7255 (Initially Falcon II) at maker's 1.9.17, allotted to BEF. **2 AD** dd ex England in packing case 20.9.17 (engine 59/WD22404). **1 AD** ex 2 AD 23.9.17 (same engine). **20 Sqn** dd ex 1 AD 24.9.17 (same engine), victs 25.9.17 (Lt J.P. Dalley/Sgt W.J. Benger sent an Albatros D.V down OOC over Becelaere at 18:30, shared), 27.9.17 (2nd Lt F. Babbage/2nd Lt R.C. Purvis sent an Albatros D.V down OOC over Moorslede at 13:00), 17.10.17 (Lt R.M. Makepeace/ Lt M.W. Waddington sent two Albatros D.V down OOC over Zonnebeke at 08:40 and 09:05) and 8.11.17 (2nd Lt B. Starfield/ Lt A. Hutchinson destroyed an EA, NE of Ypres at 06:53-08:47), damaged on Test Flight 13.11.17 (2nd Lt F.V. Tattersall/Capt J.H. Hedley both OK, crashed on landing) then wrecked on 10:42 OP 5.2.18 (Lt D.G. Campbell/2nd Lt W.H. Nash both OK, radiator shot through by machine gun fire and crashed near Crombeke at 11:20 – engine Falcon III 403/WD18478). **1 ASD** ex 20 Sqn 19.2.18 and deleted 22.2.18 (139hr 3min).

A7256 (Initially Falcon II) at maker's 1.9.17, allotted to BEF. **1 AD** dd ex England in packing case 22.9.17 (engine 171/WD22428). **20 Sqn** dd ex 1 AD 24.9.17 (same engine), vict 17.10.17 (2nd Lt Jooste/ Capt J.E. Johnston destroyed an EA in flames over Dadizeele at 10:00). **10 Sqn** dd ex 20 Sqn 2.2.18 (engine 365/WD18459). **1 AIS** ex 10 Sqn 11.4.18 (engine Falcon III 519/WD32659). **22 Sqn** dd ex 1 AIS 14.4.18 (same engine) and badly damaged on 08:30 OP 31.5.18 (2nd Lt O. StC. Harris/Sgt G. Shannon both OK, machine hit by fire from EA – same engine). **1 ASD** ex 22 Sqn 1.6.18 and deleted 8.10.18 on reconstruction as H7171.

A7257 (Falcon II) at maker's 1.9.17, allotted to BEF. **1 AD** dd ex England in packing case 25.9.17 (engine 105/WD22406). **48 Sqn** dd ex 1 AD 28.9.17 and wrecked after OP 9.10.17 (2nd Lt H.F. Jenkins/2nd Lt F. Cornish both OK, crashed on aerodrome after engine failed – same engine). **1 AD** ex 48 Sqn 12.10.17. **2 AD** ex 1 AD for reconstruction 30.10.17 with unit redesignated **2 ASD** 1.11.17. **2 AIS** ex 2 ASD 5.1.18 (engine 439/WD18496). **2 ASD** ex 2 AIS 1.2.18. **2 AIS** ex 2 ASD 15.2.18. **1 ASD** ex 2 ASD 7.3.18 (same engine) and flown to England 10.3.18.

A7258 At maker's 1.9.17, allotted to BEF but allotment cancelled 7.9.17.

A7259 (Initially Falcon II) at maker's 1.9.17, allotted to BEF. **1 AD** dd ex England 20.9.17 (engine 53/WD22993). **22 Sqn** dd ex 1 AD 21.9.17 (same engine). **16 Sqn** dd ex 22 Sqn 2.2.18 (same engine), marked as a/c *C* and wrecked before Artillery Patrol 21.5.18 (Lt Duffy/Lt North both OK, flew into a tree at Villers au Bois after take off – engine Falcon III 751/WD32775). **1 ASD** ex 16 Sqn 25.5.18 and deleted 26.5.18 (149hr 10min).

A7260 At maker's 1.9.17, allotted to BEF but allotment cancelled 7.9.17. Experimentally fitted with 200hp R.A.F. 4d. **RAF** Farnborough by 11.17, damaged 19.12.17 (broke tail skid landing at Farnbrough) and with unit when redesignated **RAE** 1.4.18. **ES** Orfordness ex RAE 15.6.18. **RAE** damaged 13.5.19 (force landed near Farnham, Surrey) and damaged 4.2.21 (crashed at Ascot, Berks).

A7261 (Initially Falcon II) at maker's 1.9.17, allotted to BEF, allotment cancelled 7.9.17. **AAP** Filton reallotted to BEF 14.9.17. **1 AD** dd ex England 20.9.17 (engine 35/WD22377). **22 Sqn** dd ex 1 AD 21.9.17 (same engine) and wrecked after OP 24.9.17 (Capt J.L. Williamson/Lt H.D McGrath both OK, collided with landing on the wreckage of B1104 – same engine). **1 AD** ex 22 Sqn 26.9.17 and awaiting reconstruction 30.9.17. **11 Sqn** dd ex 2 ASD 2.12.17 (engine Falcon I 491/WD10544). **1 ASD** ex 11 Sqn 5.12.17 (same engine) and flown to England 8.12.17. **1 (Aux) SAG Hythe** and wrecked 29.1.18 (Lt R.J. Macpherson/Lt C.B.O. Walker both IIFA, engine cut at 150ft after take off, glided down but undercarriage struck bank of drainage ditch – same engine).

A7262 (Falcon II) **AAP** Filton 15.9.17, allotted to BEF. **1 AD** dd ex England 19.9.17 (engine 89/WD22402). **48 Sqn** dd ex 1 AD 19.9.17 (same engine) and reported as unfit for further service in the field 4.3.18 (engine 1/WD12543). **2 ASD** ex 48 Sqn 8.3.17. **1 ASD** ex 2 ASD 9.3.18. **8 AAP** ex 1 ASD 11.3.18 (2nd Lt C.H. Drew/AM2 Jones). **1 (Obs) SAG** Hythe by 6.18 and wrecked 1.8.18; Mid-air collision with F.2B C4798 (Sgt F.T. Hoskins/ 2nd Lt J.S. Morbey both KIFA – engine 2/413/WD18483).

A7263 **35 TS** Northolt by 4.12.17.

A7264 (Falcon II) **AAP** Filton 17.9.17 allotted to BEF. **1 AD** dd ex England 20.9.17 (engine 119/WD22410). **22 Sqn** dd ex 1 AD 21.9.17, LIA on 07:30 OP 18.10.17 (Capt H. Patch fatally WIA/ Pte R. Spensley KIA, last seen in combat over Ardoye at 08:45 – engine 155/WD22423) and deleted on unit that day (30hr 47min).

A7265 **39 Sqn** North Weald and on HAPs 29/30.1.18 (2nd Lt W.B. Thomson/2nd Lt F.J.B. de S La Terrier, landed at Fyfield NLG), 16/17.2.18 (2nd Lt W.B. Thomson/Lt L.B. Hawkswell) and 7/8.3.18 (2nd Lt W.B. Thomson/2nd Lt F.J.B. de S La Terrier).

A7266 (Initially Falcon II) **AAP** Filton 18.9.17, allotted to BEF. **1 AD** dd ex England 22.9.17 (engine 69/WD22386). **48 Sqn** dd ex 1 AD 23.9.17 (same engine) and wrecked before OP 10.10.17 (2nd Lt I.R. Mees/2nd Lt L.N. Jones both OK, engine failed on take off and tailskid hit a ditch – engine 83/WD22421). **1 AD** ex 48 Sqn 13.10.17 with unit redesignated **1 ASD** 1.11.17. **2 ASD** ex 1 ASD 11.11.17 (engine 439/WD18496). **11 Sqn** dd ex 2 ASD 22.11.17 (same engine) and wrecked on Photo Reconnaissance, Cambrai, 5.12.17 (2nd Lt H.R. Child/Lt A. Reeve both OK, shot up in combat and returned at 10:50 – same engine). **2 ASD** ex 11 Sqn and for overhaul by 31.12.17. **2 AIS** ex 2 ASD 29.1.18 (engine Falcon III 345/WD18372). **11 Sqn** reissued ex 2 AIS 29.1.18 (same engine) and reported damaged 15.3.18. **1 ASD** and deleted 8.4.18 (78hr 27min) but reconstructed as F5815 and taken on charge 25.6.18.

A7267 Presentation a/c *Malaya No.23, The Malacca*. **AAP** Filton by 23.9.18. **35 TS** Northolt by 9.17. Deleted as presentation machine by 2.11.17. (Also noted at **39 Sqn** North Weald.)

A7268 (Falcon II) **AAP** Filton 21.9.17, allotted to BEF. **1 AD** dd ex England 23.9.17 (engine 179/WD22431). **22 Sqn** dd ex 1 AD 25.9.17 and wrecked on 10:10 OP 3.12.17 (2nd Lt F.A. Biner/ AM1 D.W. Clement both KOAS, collided with A7230 at 10:25 – same engine). **1 ASD** ex 22 Sqn 4.12.17 and deleted 7.12.17 (not worth reconstruction, 57hr 20min).

A7269 (Falcon II) **AAP** Filton 21.9.17, allotted to BEF. **1 AD** dd ex England 23.9.17 (engine 185/WD22432). **20 Sqn** dd ex 1 AD 24.9.17 (same engine) damaged on OP 9.10.17 (2nd Lt J.P. Dalley/Lt G.A. Brooke both OK, hit by a dud AA shell which wrecked the gun mounting and left through the side of the fuselage) then LIA on 13:12 OP 15.10.17 (2nd Lt J.P. Dalley/Lt L.H. Gould both KIA, in combat with EA and last seen over Wervicq at 15:10 – same engine) and deleted on unit 16.10.17.

A7270 (Initially Falcon II) **AAP** Filton 22.9.17, allotted to BEF. **1 AD** dd ex England 24.9.17 (engine 173/WD22429). **20 Sqn** dd ex 1 AD 26.9.17 (same engine) and wrecked after OP 28.9.17 (2nd Lt R.B. Slade/Capt J.E. Johnston both OK, collided on landing with a flare tin and wings caught fire – engine Falcon I, 397/WD12560). **1 AD** ex 20 Sqn 1.10.17 with unit redesignated **1 ASD** 1.11.17. **20 Sqn** reissued ex 1 ASD 13.11.17 (engine 377/WD18465), LIA on 09:45 OP 2.12.17 (Capt H.G.E. Luchford MC KIA/Capt J.E. Johnston POW IIA, last seen in combat with EA, SE of Passchendaele at 10:30 – same engine) and deleted on unit that day (24hr 30min).

A7271 (Falcon II) **AAP** Filton 22.9.17, allotted to BEF. **1 AD** dd ex England 24.9.17 (engine 17/WD22379). **20 Sqn** dd ex 1 AD 28.9.17 (same engine), vict 3.10.17 (Capt A.G.V. Taylor/Sgt W.J. Benger sent an Albatros D.V down OOC over Wervicq at 15:00) then LIA on 07:40 OP 17.10.17 (Capt A.G.V. Taylor/Sgt W.J. Benger both POW fatally WIA, last seen in combat with EA near Zonnebeke – same engine) and deleted on unit 18.10.17 (31hr 36min).

A7272 N/I

A7273 **35 TS** Northolt by 9.17 until @ 13.10.17.

A happy group pose with A7273 with cockpit unoccupied and engine running. This F.2B was with 35 TS at Northolt in September/October 1917. *(Philip Jarrett)*

A7274 **38 TS** Rendcomb.

A7275 (Falcon I) **5 AAP** Filton by 27.9.17, allotted to BEF. **1 AD** dd ex England 30.9.17 (engine 273/WD10464). **2 AD** ex 1 AD 3.10.17 (same engine). **11 Sqn** dd ex 2 AD 5.10.17 (same engine). **1 ASD** ex 11 Sqn 5.12.17 (same engine) and flown to England 8.12.17. **1 (Obs) SAG** Hythe as a/c *4* and photographed wrecked with undercarriage and port mainplanes smashed.

A7276 (Falcon I) **5 AAP** Filton by 27.9.17, allotted to BEF. **1 AD** dd ex England 5.10.17 (engine 40/WD10432). **2 AD** ex 1 AD 14.10.17 (same engine). **11 Sqn** dd ex 2 AD 18.10.17 (same engine). **1 ASD** ex 11 Sqn 5.12.17 (same engine) and flown to England 8.12.17.

A7277 (Falcon II) **AAP** Filton 29.9.17, allotted to BEF. **1 AD** dd ex England 5.10.17 (engine 47/WD22388). **48 Sqn** dd ex 1 AD 11.10.17 (same engine), damaged on OP 20.11.17 (Capt A.W. Field OK/2nd Lt G.R. Horsfall KIA in combat) then wrecked on 07:10 OP, Roye, 28.3.18 (Capt T. Colville-Jones/2nd Lt W. Hart both OK, machine badly damaged by ground fire – engine 339/WD18446). **22 Wing SS** ex 48 Sqn 1.4.18 (113hr 32min).

A7278 **62 Sqn** Rendcomb by 5.1.18. **59 TS** Rendcomb as a/c *11* by 26.6.18.

A7279 (Falcon II) **AAP** Filton by 29.9.17, allotted to BEF. **1 AD** dd ex England 8.10.17 (engine 207/WD22457). **22 Sqn** dd ex 1 AD 10.10.17 (same engine) and wrecked on Practice Flight 4.2.18 (2nd Lt A.H. Beamer KOAS, no passenger, wings collapsed in mid-air – same engine). **1 ASD** ex 22 Sqn 5.2.18 and deleted 7.2.18 (82hr 19min).

A7280 (Falcon II) **AAP** Filton 1.10.17, allotted to BEF. **1 AD** dd ex England 2.10.17 (engine 231/WD22455). **22 Sqn** dd ex 1 AD 5.10.17 (same engine), LIA on 06:28 Escort 7.10.17 (Lt J.C. Bush MC/Lt W.W. Chapman both KIA, last seen over Kruiseik at 07:30 – same engine) and deleted on unit that day (3hr).

A7281 (Initially Falcon II) **AAP** Filton 1.10.17, allotted to BEF. **1 AD** dd ex England 5.10.17 (engine 211/WD22458). **22 Sqn** dd ex 1 AD 11.10.17 (same engine), vict 27.10.17 (2nd Lt S.A. Oades/2nd Lt H.V.R. Hill sent a Rumpler C-type down OOC, N of Roulers at 10:15) then damaged on OP 2.12.17 (2nd Lt S.A. Oades/AM2 J.H. Jones both OK, fuselage strained in taking off and landing – engine 95/WD22469). **1 ASD** ex 22 Sqn 3.12.17. **2 AIS** ex 2 ASD 4.2.18 (engine Falcon III 369/WD18684). **2 ASD** ex 2 AIS 11.2.18 (same engine). **2 AIS** ex 2 ASD 19.2.18 (same engine). **11 Sqn** dd ex 2 AIS 23.2.18 (same engine) and wrecked on OP 21.3.18 (Lt E.A. Hay MC/Sgt P.A. Sherlock both OK,

force landed when ran out of fuel, machine dismantled and brought in by road – same engine). **2 ASD** ex 11 Sqn 21.3.18.

A7282 (Falcon II) **AAP** Filton 3.10.17, allotted to BEF. **1 AD** dd ex England 9.10.17 (engine 285/WD18419). **48 Sqn** dd ex 1 AD 10.10.17 (same engine) and wrecked on OP, Dixmude, 18.11.17 (2nd Lt W.S. McLaren fatally WIA/2nd Lt D.W. Hardie KIA, shot down in flames during combat at 12:40 – same engine). **1 ASD** ex 48 Sqn 19.11.17 and deleted 22.11.17 (44hr 46min).

A7283 (Falcon II) at maker's 3.10.17, allotted to BEF and to be delivered via Newhaven. **1 AD** dd ex England in packing case 14.10.17 (engine 251/WD18402). **2 AD** dd ex 1 AD 16.10.17 (same engine), LIA on 12:50 OP 8.11.17 (2nd Lt H.G. Robinson/Lt F.J.B. Hammersley both POW, shot down N of Moorslede – same engine) and deleted on unit that day (20hr 15min).

A7284 (Falcon II) at maker's 3.10.17, allotted to BEF. **2 AD** dd ex England in packing case 18.10.17 (engine 219/WD22456). **11 Sqn** dd ex 2 AD 20.10.17 (same engine) and reported in need of complete overhaul 2.4.18 (same engine). **2 AD** ex 11 Sqn 5.4.18. **1 ASD** ex **Advanced Salvage** 8.4.18 and deleted 10.4.18 (not worth reconstruction, 106hr 13min).

A7285 (Falcon II) at maker's 3.10.17, allotted to BEF. **1 AD** dd ex England in packing case 12.10.17 (engine 281/WD18417). **20 Sqn** dd ex 1 AD 16.10.17 (same engine), vict 12.11.17 (Capt Knight/Lt A.P. Wornum sent an Albatros D.V down OOC) and wrecked on Gunnery Practice 19.1.18 (2nd Lt B. Starfield/Sgt W. Ray both IOAS, caught some trees and sideslipped then crashed – same engine). **1 ASD** ex 20 Sqn 20.11.17 and deleted 3.1.18 (not worth reconstruction, 35hr 45min).

A7286 (Falcon II) at maker's 3.10.17, allotted to BEF. **2 AD** dd ex England in packing case 18.10.17 (engine 291/WD18422). **1 AD** ex 2 AD 20.10.17 (same engine). **22 Sqn** dd ex 1 AD 21.10.17 (same engine), LIA on 15:15 OP to Vauvillers, 2.4.18 (2nd Lt F. Williams/2nd Lt R. Critchley both KIA, shot down in flames, S of Albert in combat with Fokker Dr.I – engine 333/WD18443) and deleted on unit that day (110hr 5min).

A7287 (Falcon II) at maker's 3.10.17, allotted to BEF. **1 AD** dd ex England in packing case 12.10.17 (engine 281/WD18417). **20 Sqn** dd ex 1 AD 27.10.17 (engine 295/WD18424) and wrecked on OP 6.11.17 (2nd Lt R.M. Makepeace/Lt M.W. Waddington both OK, suffered magneto trouble and undercarriage gave way when landing on rough and muddy ground – same engine). **1 ASD** ex 20 Sqn 7.11.17 and deleted 11.11.17 (not worth reconstruction, 16hr 47min).

A7288 (Falcon II) at maker's 3.10.17, allotted to BEF. **2 AD** dd ex England in packing case 22.10.17 (engine 233/WD22463). **11 Sqn** dd ex 2 AD 28.10.17 (same engine), marked as a/c *7*, victs 11.11.17 (Capt A.E. McKeever [Can]/Lt L.V. Pogson destroyed a DFW C-type over Brebieres at 11:30) and 30.11.17 (Capt A.E. McKeever/2nd Lt L.A. Powell destroyed four Albatros D.V, S of Cambrai at 11:50-11:55) then LIA on 10:05 OP 28.1.18 (2nd Lt S. Reay/AM2 A. Patterson both KIA, shot down NW of Cambrai – engine 417/WD18485) and deleted on unit that day (56hr 30min).

A7289 At maker's 10.17, allotted to BEF. **1 AD** dd ex England in packing case 3.10.17 (engine 231/WD22455) and deleted without flying 16.1.18 (not worth reconstruction).

A7290 (Initially Falcon II) at maker's, allotted to BEF. **2 AD** dd ex England in packing case 21.10.17 (engine 289/WD18421). **11 Sqn** dd ex 2 AD 1.11.17 (same engine) and wrecked on Reconnaissance 20.11.17 (2nd Lt E.D. Perney/2nd Lt E.J. Blackledge both OK, lost way on return and machine damaged in forced landing – same engine). **2 ASD** ex 11 Sqn 20.11.17. **2 AIS** ex 2 ASD 2.2.18 (engine Falcon III 159/WD18579). **48 Sqn** dd ex 2 AIS 5.2.18 and wrecked after successful combats on 10:30 OP 12.3.18 (2nd Lt C.H. Hore MC OK/Cpl J. Cruikshank KIA, sent two Fokker Dr.I OOC over Catelat at 12:00 but machine damaged and force landed in a ploughed field – same engine). **1 ASD** ex 48 Sqn 14.3.18 and deleted 8.4.18 (not worth reconstruction).

A7291 (Falcon II) at maker's 3.10.17, allotted to BEF. **1 AD** dd ex England in packing case. **2 AD** ex 1 AD 28.10.17. **11 Sqn** dd ex **2 ASD** 13.11.17. **2 ASD** by 31.12.17. **2 AIS** ex 2 ASD 9.1.18 (engine 273/WD18413). **2 ASD** ex 2 AIS 1.2.18 (same engine). **1 ASD** ex 2 ASD 9.3.18 (same engine) and flown to England 10.3.18.

A7292 (Falcon II) at maker's 3.10.17, allotted to BEF. **2 AD** dd ex England in packing case 25.10.17 (engine 301/WD18427). **11 Sqn** dd ex **2 ASD** 7.11.17, LIA on 07:00 Reconnaissance 20.11.17 (Sgt T.F. Stephenson KIA/Lt T.W. Morse POW, shot down by ground fire – same engine) and deleted on unit that day (7hr 8min).

A7293 (Initially Falcon II) at maker's 3.10.17, allotted to BEF and despatched in packing case. **48 Sqn** dd ex **1 ASD** 6.11.17 (engine 283/WD18418) and wrecked after Photography 26.12.17 (Capt

K.R. Park MC/2nd Lt E.C. Birch both OK, crashed on landing – same engine). **2 ASD** ex 48 Sqn 31.12.17. **62 Sqn** dd ex **2 AIS** 15.3.18 (engine Falcon III 335/WD18667) and wrecked 24.3.18 (when standing on aerodrome, the machine was run into by C4692 – engine 179/WD18589). **1 ASD** ex 62 Sqn 1.4.18 and deleted 14.4.18 (not worth reconstruction, 40hr 50min).

A7294 (Falcon II) at maker's 3.10.17, allotted to BEF. **2 AD** dd ex England in packing case 25.10.17 (engine 313/WD18433). **1 AIS** ex 2 ASD 19.11.17 (same engine). **20 Sqn** dd ex 1 AIS 23.11.17 (same engine) and wrecked on Practice Flight 7.4.18 (Lt P.B. Holgate OK, machine swung on take off and struck a tree with the pilot unable to keep control of the rudder owing to the shortness of his legs – engine 235/WD22465). **1 ASD** ex 20 Sqn 10.4.18 and deleted 14.4.18 (not worth reconstruction, 109hr).

A7295 (Falcon II) at maker's 3.10.17, allotted to BEF and despatched in packing case. **48 Sqn** dd ex **1 ASD** 13.11.17 (engine 297/WD18425), wrecked on Photography Practice 1.3.18 (2nd Lt C.D.B. Stiles/2nd Lt H.J. Finnemore both OK, force landed in a snowstorm and machine caught fire and burnt out – same engine) and deleted on unit 2.3.18 (40hr 47min).

A7296 At maker's 3.10.17, allotted to BEF but reallotted to Training Division 19.10.17 and to be delivered to **4th Wing** Bulford Station. **8 TS** Netheravon by 11.1.18.

A7297 At maker's 3.10.17, allotted to BEF but reallotted to Training Division 19.10.17 and to be delivered to **4th Wing** Bulford Station. **8 TS** Netheravon by 6.1.18 and wrecked 16.2.18 (2nd Lt R.F. Overbury IIFA, dived on tarmac from too low an altitude and machine struck the ground – engine 291/WD10476).

A7298 (Initially Falcon II) presentation a/c *Presented by the Maharajah Bahadur Sir Rameswar Singh of Darbhangha No.1, The Lord Hardinge*. **AAP** Filton by 17.10.17, allotted to BEF. **2 AD** dd ex **1 AD** 21.10.17 (engine 277/WD18415), victs 27.10.17 (2nd Lt W. Durrand/2nd Lt A.E. Woodbridge destroyed an Albatros D.V, SW of Roulers at 13:10) and 5.12.17 (Lt R.K. Kirkman/Capt L.W. Burbidge sent an Albatros D.V down OOC over Ostnieuwkerke at 12:50) then wrecked on Instructional Flight 22.12.17 (Lt D. Leigh-Pemberton/Lt N.W. Taylor both OK, landed in the sea off Berck-sur-Mer and machine salvaged after being submerged for 12 hrs – same engine) and deleted on unit that day (57hr). **1 ASD** and returned to RFC charge. **2 ASD** ex 1 ASD 4.2.18 (engine Falcon III 135/WD18567). **2 AIS** ex 2 ASD 5.2.18 (same engine). **48 Sqn** dd ex 2 AIS 15.2.18 (same engine) and victs 8.3.18 (2nd Lt L.A. Payne/Lt G.H.H. Scutt sent two Albatros D.V down OOC over Mont d'Origny at 08:00). **62 Sqn** dd ex 48 Sqn 16.3.18 (same engine), LIA on 07:30 Trench Strafe 26.3.18 (2nd Lt J.M. Goller/2nd Lt E.C.W. Deacon both, force landed due to engine trouble and machine abandoned under shell fire – same engine) and deleted on unit that day.

A7299 (Falcon II) presentation a/c *Presented by the Maharajah Bahadur Sir Rameswar Singh of Darbhanga No.2, The Lord Chelmsford*. **AAP** Filton 18.10.17, allotted to BEF. **20 Sqn** dd ex **1 ASD** 15.11.17 (engine 317/WD18435), vict 5.12.17 (Lt J.C. Kirkpatrick/2nd Lt W.T.V. Harmer sent an Albatros D-type down O   O   C over Dadizeele at 09:25) then LIA on 08:26 OP 10.12.17 (Lt J.C. Kirkpatrick KIA/2nd Lt W.T.V. Harmer IIA, shot down by AA fire – same engine) and deleted on unit 11.12.17 (22hr 36min).

A7300 (Initially Falcon II) presentatiion a/c *Presented by the Maharajah Bahadur Sir Rameswar Singh of Darbhanga No.4*. **AAP** Filton 18.10.17, allotted to BEF and despatched by air. **22 Sqn** dd ex **1 AD** 21.10.17 (engine 329/WD18441) and wrecked on Practice Flight 12.3.18 (2nd Lt J.E. Gurdon OK, misjudged landing and crashed – same engine). **1 ASD** ex 22 Sqn 12.3.18 and deleted 13.3.18 (70hr 45min) but returned to RFC charge. **1 AIS** ex 1 ASD 16.4.18 (engine Falcon III 633/WD32716). **10 Sqn** dd ex 1 AIS 22.4.18 (same engine) and wrecked after Artillery Observation 26.5.18 (Lt S.C.P. Slattery/2nd Lt J.C. Anderson both OK, crashed on landing – same engine). **1 ASD** ex 10 Sqn 28.5.18 and deleted 25.6.18 on reconstruction as F5819.

2 BRISTOL FIGHTER F.2B, rebuilt by 1 (S)ARD Farnborough in range B701 to B900 reserved for reconstructions.

B817 (Falcon III) **20 Sqn** dd ex **1 ASD** 17.4.18 (engine 863/WD32831) and on unit charge 18.4.18.

B883 (Initially Falcon I) **1 (S)ARD** 24.9.17, allotted to BEF. **1 AD** dd ex England 11.10.17 (engine 467/WD15763). **20 Sqn** dd ex 1 AD 15.10.17 (same engine), victs 13.11.17 (2nd Lt W. Beaver/2nd Lt

C.J. Agelasto destroyed an Albatros D.V, SE of Houthoulst Forest at 15:00), 2.12.17 (2nd Lt W. Beaver/AM M. Mather destroyed an EA, SE of Passchendaele at 10:30) and 5.12.17 (2nd Lt W. Beaver/AM M. Mather sent an EA down OOC near Daizeele at 09:25) then LIA on 11:54 OP 25.1.18 (Sgt H.O. Smith/2nd Lt HS Clemons both POW WIA, hit by AA and force landed NE of Passchendaele near Houthulst Wood – engine Falcon II 175/WD22430) and deleted on unit 26.1.18 (84hr 51min).

250 BRISTOL FIGHTER F.2B ordered on running Contract 87/A/552 (Additional) dated 28.8.16 from The British & Colonial Aeroplane Co Ltd, Bristol and numbered B1101 to B1350. (190hp Falcon I/220hp Falcon II/275hp Falcon III or 210hp Arab). [Consecutive works' sequence nos. 2269 to 2518].

B1101 (Falcon I) **5 AAP** Bristol by 21.7.17. **1 AD** dd ex England 10.8.17 (engine 66/WD10439). **22 Sqn** dd ex 1 AD 16.8.17 (same engine), LIA on OP 23.8.17 (Sgt C.L. Randal/AM1 J.V. Hurley both KIA, last seen in combat with 5 EA at 07:30 – same engine) and deleted on unit that day (20hr 11min).

B1102 (Initially Falcon I) **5 AAP** Bristol by 24.7.17. **1 AD** dd ex England 9.8.17 (engine 525/WD12530). **20 Sqn** dd ex 1 AD 13.8.17 and wrecked on Practice Flight 17.8.17 (2nd Lt J.L. Boles OK, engine lost pressure and failed to pick up – same engine). **1 AD** ex 20 Sqn 21.8.17. **20 Sqn** reissued to 1 AD 29.9.17 (engine 531) and wrecked after OP 27.10.17 (2nd Lt F.H. Thompson/AM2 I. Townsend both OK, pilot became ill and crashed on landing – engine Falcon II 243/WD22464). **1 AD** ex 20 Sqn 28.10.17, unit redesignated **1 ASD** and deleted 16.1.18 (not worth reconstruction, 16hr 30min).

B1103 (Initially Falcon I) **5 AAP** Bristol by 24.7.17. **1 AD** dd ex Lympne 11.8.17 (engine 253/WD10452). **22 Sqn** dd ex 1 AD 15.8.17 (same engine) and wrecked on OP 9.9.17 (2nd Lt D.W.M. Miller/AM2 C. Loveland both OK, o/t in forced landing near St Venant after engine failure – same engine). **1 AD** ex 22 Sqn 11.9.17. **11 Sqn** dd ex 2 ASD 22.11.17 (engine Falcon II 191/WD22446) and wrecked after Reconnaissance 26.11.17 (Lt H.E.T. Crocker/2nd Lt J.E. Cross both OK, crashed on landing when trying to avoid a fence – same engine). **2 ASD** ex 11 Sqn 26.11.17 and to England 5.12.17. **38 TS** Rendcomb by 29.1.18.

B1104 (Initially Falcon I) **5 AAP** Filton by 4.8.17, allotted to BEF. **1 AD** dd ex England 11.8.17 (engine 209/WD10408). **22 Sqn** dd ex 1 AD 17.8.17 (same engine) and wrecked on Practice Flight 24.9.17 (2nd Lt R.I.V. Hill OK, crashed on landing – same engine). **1 AD** ex 22 Sqn 29.9.17. **20 Sqn** dd ex 1 AD 17.10.17 (engine Falcon II 223/WD22454), vict 27.10.17 (2nd Lt F. Babbage/Gnr J. McMechan sent an Albatros D.V OOC over Moorslede at 15:10) then wrecked on Practice Flight 5.11.17 (2nd Lt F.V. Tattersall/Pte B. Matthews both OK, pilot lost bearings, force landed and crashed – same engine). **1 ASD** ex 20 Sqn 30.11.17. **1 AIS** ex 1 ASD 25.1.18 (engine Falcon II 445/WD18499). **1 ASD** ex 1 AIS 9.3.18 (same engine) and flown to England 10.3.18. **1 (Obs) SAG** New Romney as a/c 11 by 6.18.

B1105 (Falcon I) **5 AAP** Filton by 4.8.17, allotted to BEF. **1 AD** dd ex Lympne 23.8.17 (engine 559/WD12541). **22 Sqn** dd ex 1 AD 1.9.17 (same engine), LIA on 08:00 OP 11.9.17 (2nd Lt R. de L. Stedman WIA/2nd Lt H.E. Jones fatally WIA, last seen at 2,000ft over Schapp Baillie engaged by EA and in a spin – same engine) and deleted on unit that day (19hr 48min).

B1106 (Falcon I) **5 AAP** Filton by 7.8.18, allotted to BEF but reallotted to Training 11.8.17. **59 TS** Yatesbury 30.8.17, Lt WM Yool, engine failure and crash, pilot uninjured.

B1107 (Falcon I) presentation a/c *Falkland*. **5 AAP** Bristol, despatched 16.8.17. Yatesbury 1917. **38 TS** Rendcomb by 23.11.17 until @ 29.1.18.

B1108 (Initially Falcon I) presentation a/c *Udaipur No.2* (also *Jaypores. Vizag*). **5 AAP** Filton by 15.8.17, allotted to BEF. **1 AD** dd ex England 21.8.17 (engine 149/WD22415). **48 Sqn** dd ex 1 AD 22.8.17 (same engine), vict 2.9.17 (Lt H.W. Elliott/2nd Lt J.W. Ferguson destroyed an Albatros D.V near Beerst at 09:15) then wrecked on OP 25.1.18 (Lt P. Burrows/AM1 B. Jackman both OK, force landed due to snow cloud – engine Falcon II 69/WD22386). **4 AP** ex 48 Sqn 18.2.18. **2 ASD** by 23.2.18. **1 ASD** ex 2 ASD for reconstruction 3.4.18. **1 AIS** ex 1 ASD 16.4.18 (engine Falcon III 663/WD32731). **20 Sqn** dd ex 1 AIS 17.4.18 (same engine) and wrecked after OP, 21.4.18 (Lt C.G. Lankin/Lt J.W. McHattie both OK, crashed on landing – same engine). **1 ASD** ex 20 Sqn 22.4.18 and deleted 25.4.18 (not worth reconstruction, 4hr 14min).

B1109 (Falcon II) presentation a/c *Udaipur No.1*. **5 AAP** Filton by 15.8.17, allotted to BEF. **1 AD** dd ex England 19.8.17 (engine 201/WD22434). **11 Sqn** dd ex 1 AD 20.8.17 (same engine), LIA on 14:34 OP 31.10.17 (2nd Lt S.W. Randall KIA/2nd Lt W. de C. Dodd POW fatally WIA, shot down by EA and last seen near Fressies (same engine) and deleted on unit that day (57hr 15min).

B1110 (Initially Falcon I) presentation a/c *Johore No.2*. **5 AAP** Filton by 20.8.17, allotted to BEF. **1 AD** dd ex England 31.8.17 (Major A.V. Bettington – engine 293/WD10459). **20 Sqn** dd ex 1 AD 6.9.17 (same engine), reported as nose heavy 11.9.17 and damaged on OP 21.9.17 (Sgt F. Hopper/2nd Lt R.S.V. Morris both OK, petrol tank shot through in combat – same engine). **1 AD** ex 20 Sqn 23.9.17. **2 ASD** after reconstruction. **11 Sqn** dd ex 2 ASD 23.11.17 (engine Falcon II 375/WD18464) and wrecked on OP 13.1.18 (2nd Lt J.H. Hartley/2nd Lt J.E. Cross both IOAS, crashed at Humber Camp – same engine). **1 ASD** ex 11 Sqn 22.1.18 and deleted 24.1.18 (not worth reconstruction, 52hr 13min).

B1111 (Initially Falcon I) presentation a/c *Punjab No.44, Lahore*. **5 AAP** Filton by 20.8.17, allotted to BEF. **1 AD** dd ex England 2.9.17 (engine 18/WD10421). **20 Sqn** dd ex 1 AD 4.9.17 (same engine), vict 25.9.17 (Sgt F. Hopper/Capt L.W. Burbidge sent an Albatros D.V OOC near Becelaere at 18:30, shared A7255) then wrecked on OP 30.9.17 (2nd Lt R.B. Slade/2nd Lt R.S.V. Morris both OK, pilot had to stall machine over telegraph wires, unable to regain flying speed and pancaked from 40ft – same engine). **1 AD** ex 20 Sqn 1.10.17, with unit redesignated **1 ASD** 1.11.17. **22 Sqn** dd ex 1 ASD 9.11.17 (engine Falcon II 421/WD18487) and wrecked after Gunnery Practice 10.12.17 (2nd Lt T. Ivison/2nd Lt A.P. Stoyle both OK, bad landing – same engine). **1 ASD** ex 22 Sqn 10.12.17. **2 AIS** ex 1 ASD 4.2.18 (engine Falcon III 407/WD32603). **48 Sqn** dd ex 2 AIS 6.2.18 (Lt Roberts – same engine) and wrecked after Reconnaissance 25.3.18 (Lt K.R. Little OK/Lt F.W. Irving IOAS, engine cut out and force landed on ploughed ground near aerodrome – same engine). **2 ASD** ex 48 Sqn 26.3.18. **1 ASD** ex 2 ASD by rail 1.4.18 and deleted 8.4.18 (not worth reconstruction, 127hr 20min).

B1112 (Initially Falcon I) **5 AAP** by 22.8.17, allotted to BEF. **1 AD** dd ex England 31.8.17 (engine 319/WD10474). **22 Sqn** dd ex 1 AD 6.9.17 (same engine) and marked as a/c *F*. **16 Sqn** ex 22 Sqn 2.2.18 (engine Falcon II 87/WD22468), still as a/c *F* and reported in need of overhaul 26.5.18 (167hr 50min – same engine). **1 ASD** ex 16 Sqn 31.5.18 and deleted 25.6.18 on reconstruction as F5821.

B1113 (Initially Falcon I) **5 AAP** Filton by 27.8.18, allotted to BEF. **1 AD** dd ex England 2.9.17 (engine 83/WD22421). **48 Sqn** dd ex 1 AD 3.9.17 (same engine) and reported as unfit for further service in the field 19.3.18 (185hr 55min – engine Falcon II 307/WD18430). **2 ASD** ex 48 Sqn 26.3.18. **2 AIS** ex 2 ASD 16.5.18 (engine Falcon III 771/WD32785). **48 Sqn** reissued ex 2 ASD 17.5.18 (same engine), LIA on 18:00 Reconnaissance 9.7.18 (1/Lt E.D. Shaw USAS/Sgt T.W. Smith both KIA, believed shot down in combat with 3 Pfalz a/c – engine Falcon III 829/WD32814) and deleted on unit that day (100hr – presume since re-issue).

B1114 (Initially Falcon II) presentation a/c *Auckland*. **5 AAP** Bristol 29.8.17, allotted to BEF. **1 AD** dd ex England 20.9.17 (engine 167/WD22425). **20 Sqn** dd ex 1 AD 21.9.17 (same engine), victs 5.10.17 (Lt R.B. Slade OK/Gnr E. Veale IIA, left at 10:35 and lost contact with the formation due to a storm, in combat with three Albatros D.V, one of which was sent down OOC Ledeghem at 11:30, but force landed near Armentieres with observer to hospital badly frost bitten about the face) and 17.10.17 (2nd Lt D. French/Gnr E. Veale destroyed an Albatros D.V near Zonnebeke at 08:40), damaged in combat 6.11.17 (2nd Lt E.S. Brander/AM A. Townsend both WIA) then wrecked on OP 14.11.17 (2nd Lt E.V. Clark OK/2nd Lt F.B. Wallis IOAS, o/t in force-landing near Morbecque due to thick fog – engine 67/WD22390). **1 ASD** ex 20 Sqn 16.11.17. **1 AIS** ex 1 ASD 24.2.18. **20 Sqn** reissued ex **1 AIS** 24.2.18 (engine Falcon III 245/WD18622), vict 27.5.18 (Lt A.T. Iaccaci [USA]/AM A. Newlands attacked by eight Pfalz D.IIIs and in a running fight one sent down in vertical dive smoking, crash confirmed by French AA, SW of Neuve Eglise at 12:15) then LIA on 16:25 OP 5.6.18 (Lt J.E.W. Sugden/Sgt W. O'Neill) both POW, last seen near Armentieres – engine Falcon III 589/WD32694) and deleted on unit 7.6.18 (186hr 25min).

B1115 (Falcon II) at maker's 7.9.17, allotted to BEF. **1 AD** dd ex England in packing case 22.9.17 (engine 237/WD22439). **22 Sqn** dd ex 1 AD 29.9.17 (same engine) and wrecked on OP 2.10.17 Lt R.I.V. Hill/2nd Lt C.H. Bartlett both OK, crashed in forced landing near Eisendamme – same engine). **1 AD** ex 22 Sqn 4.10.17. **48 Sqn** ex 1 AD 29.10.17 (engine 205/WD22466) and wrecked on Travelling Flight 22.12.17 (2nd Lt J.R. Mees/2nd Lt L.N. Jones both OK,

crashed in forced landing at Estree Blanche due to engine failure – same engine). **1 ASD** ex 48 Sqn 23.12.17 and deleted 16.1.18 (not worth reconstruction, 39hr 39min).

B1116 (Falcon II) at maker's 7.9.17, allotted to BEF. **1 AD** dd ex England in packing case 21.9.17 (engine 221/WD22437). **20 Sqn** dd ex 1 AD 22.9.17 (same engine) and wrecked on 09:30 OP 25.89.17 (Lt J.C. Kirkpatrick OK/Capt A.A. English WIA, shot up in combat and force landed on 29 Sqn aerodrome – same engine). **1 AD** ex 20 Sqn 29.9.17. **2 AD** ex 1 AD 7.10.17 for reconstruction. **11 Sqn** dd ex 2 AD 1.11.17 (engine 391/WD18472), LIA on 12:35 Reconnaissance 23.11.17 (2nd Lt E.D. Perney/2nd Lt E.J. Blackledge both KIA, last seen over Cambrai – same engine) and deleted on unit that day (4hr 35min).

B1117 (Falcon II) presentation a/c *Johore No.6*. **5 AAP** Filton by 4.9.17, allotted to BEF. **1 AD** dd ex England 11.9.17 (engine 141/WD22418). **48 Sqn** dd ex 1 AD 12.9.17 (Lt J.H. Letts – same engine), LIA on 15:45 OP 24.10.17 (Capt J.T. Milne MC/Lt J. Wright MC both KIA, probably the F.2B reported by the French to have been shot down at 16:25 near Merckem – same engine) and deleted on unit that day (68hr 20min).

B1118 (Falcon II) at maker's 7.9.17, allotted to BEF. **1 AD** dd ex England in packing case 24.9.17 (engine 229/WD22438). **20 Sqn** dd ex 1 AD 27.9.17 (same engine) and wrecked after OP 30.9.17 (Lt W.D. Chambers/Gnr E. Veale both OK, struck a ditch on landing – same engine). **1 AD** ex 20 Sqn 1.10.17 and deleted 5.10.17 (not worth reconstruction, 4hr 9min).

B1119 (200hp Hispano-Suiza) **5 AAP** Bristol 27.11.17, allotted to BEF. **1 ASD** dd ex England and test 3.12.17 and 6.12.17, then force landed near Ardres 16.12.17 (Lt Russell OK), re-tested 2.1.18 then flown to England 24.1.18 (engine 115316). **1 (S)ARD** ex **8 AAP** Lympne 4.2.18.

B1120 (Falcon II) at maker's 7.9.17, allotted to BEF. **1 AD** dd ex England in packing case 24.9.17 (engine 257/WD18405). **20 Sqn** dd ex 1 AD 25.9.17 (same engine) and wrecked on Practice Flight 26.9.17 (2nd Lt C.B. Stratton/Lt O.A. Rowan both OK, misjudged landing and crashed into a ditch – same engine). **1 AD** ex 20 Sqn 29.9.17. **22 Sqn** dd ex 1 AD 19.10.17 (engine 349/WD18451) and wrecked on 12:53 OP 8.11.17 (2nd Lt E.C. Bromley/2nd Lt A.H. Middleton both OK, force landed after combat with engine failure – same engine). **1 ASD** ex 22 Sqn 12.11.17. **1 AIS** ex 1 ASD 31.12.17 (engine 41/WD15773). **22 Sqn** reissued ex 1 AIS 9.1.18 (same engine) and wrecked on Practice Flight 18.1.18 (2nd Lt W.T.H. Shutt/AM2 J.H. Jones both IOAS, crashed on landing – same engine). **1 ASD** ex 22 Sqn 21.1.18 and deleted 22.1.18 (not worth reconstruction, 22hr 23min).

B1121 (Falcon II) **5 AAP** Filton by 19.7.17, allotted to BEF. **1 AD** dd ex England 23.9.17 (engine 259/WD18406). **22 Sqn** dd ex 1 AD 25.9.17 (same engine) and wrecked on Gunnery Practice 18.1.18 (2nd Lt G.A. Park/AM2 F.G. Kingsland both KOAS, crashed – same engine). **1 ASD** ex 22 Sqn 21.1.18 (98hr 21min), presume deleted.

B1122 (Initially Falcon II) presentation a/c *Dominica*. **5 AAP** Filton 19.9.17, allotted to BEF. **1 AD** dd ex; England 23.9.17 (engine 241/WD22462). **20 Sqn** dd ex 1 AD 24.9.17 (same engine), victs 25.9.17 (Lt H.G.E. Luchford MC/2nd Lt R.F. Hill MC destroyed an Albatros D.V, E of Gheluvelt at 18:30), 28.9.17 (Lt H.G.E. Luchford MC/2nd Lt R.F. Hill MC destroyed an Albatros D.V in flames and another crashed over Menin-Wervicq 12:30), 1.10.17 (Lt H.G.E. Luchford MC/2nd Lt R.F. Hill MC destroyed an Albatros D.V, SE of Roulers at 14:45), 11.10.17 (Lt H.G.E. Luchford MC/Sgt W.J. Benger destroyed an Albatros D.V in flames and sent another OOC Moorslede 07:15), 27.11.17 (2nd Lt T. Colville Jones/Capt L.R. Speakman sent an Albatros D.III down OOC over Westroosebeke at 15:25), 3.1.18 (Lt T. Colville-Jones/2/Lt H.G. Crowe destroyed an EA C-type in flames N of Moorslede at 14:25) and 28.1.18 (Capt T. Colville-Jones/Lt L.H. Phelps sent an Albatros D-type down OOC, NW of Westroosebeke at 13:50). **16 Sqn** ex 20 Sqn on loan 2.2.18. **20 Sqn** and wrecked on OP 24.3.18 (2nd Lt L. Campbell/Lt A. Mills both OK, damaged by enemy fire and force landed near Ypres – engine 379/WD18466). **1 ASD** ex 20 Sqn and deleted 29.3.18 (200hr 5min). Retaken on RAF charge at **1 ASD** and under reconstruction by 30.4.18. **1 AIS** ex 1 ASD 26.5.18 (engine Falcon III 965/WD32882). **20 Sqn** reissued ex 1 AIS 29.5.18 (same engine), victs 31.5.18 (Lt P.T. Iaccaci [USA]/AM1 A. Newlands destroyed a Pfalz D.III in flames E of Merville and destroyed an Albatros D-type which crashed on canal bank S of Merville, 07:45-08:00), 13.6.18 (Lt P.T. Iaccaci/Lt W. Noble sent an Albatros D.V down OOC, NW of Armentieres at 08:00) and 17.6.18 (Lt P.T. Iaccaci/Lt W. Noble destroyed a Pfalz D.III near Menin at 07:55) then wrecked on OP 23.6.18 (Lt H.C. McCreary/Sgt J.D.C. Summers both OK, fuel tank shot through and force landed near Tilques – same engine). **1 ASD** ex 20 Sqn 25.6.18 and deleted 27.6.18 (not worth reconstruction, 244hr 5min).

B1123   (Falcon II) **5 AAP** Filton 19.9.17, allotted to BEF. **1 AD** dd ex England 24.9.17 (engine 255/WD18404). **22 Sqn** dd ex 1 AD 29.9.17 (same engine), victs 2.10.17 (Lt J.C. Bush/AM1 A.G. destroyed an EA C-type N of Courtrai at 10:41) and 10.10.17 (Lt W.G. Meggitt/AM1 A. Whitehouse destroyed an Albatros D.V over Moorslede at 16:50) then LIA on 12:50 OP 8.11.17 (Lt W.G. Meggitt MC POW WIA/Capt F.A. Durrad KIA, separated in combat and went down in spin OOC – same engine) and deleted on unit that day (45hr 14min).

B1124   (Falcon II) **5 AAP** Filton 19.9.17, allotted to BEF. **1 AD** dd ex England 3.9.17 (engine 249/WD18401). **48 Sqn** dd ex 25.9.17 (same engine), LIA on 14:20 OP 29.9.17 (2nd Lt F.L. Smith/2nd Lt J. Frost both interned in Holland, engine hit by AA, last seen over Zeebrugge with engine failing and heading towards Holland, force landed near Zuidzorde – same engine) and deleted on unit that day (11hr 50min). Machine interned by Dutch, became *BR401* and served until 1924.

B1125   (Falcon II) **5 AAP** Filton 20.9.17, allotted to BEF. **1 AD** dd ex England 23.9.17 (engine 253/WD18403). **20 Sqn** dd ex 1 AD 24.9.17 (same engine), LIA on 15:19 Reconnaissance, Roulers-Menin, 9.10.17 (Lt W.D. Chambers/2nd Lt F.H. Berry both POW, engine failed and force landed on German aerodrome of Fl.Abt(A)217 – same engine) and deleted on unit that day (25hr 34min).

B1126   (Initially Falcon II) **5 AAP** Filton 20.9.17, allotted to BEF. **1 AD** dd ex England 23.9.17 (engine 139/WD22461). **20 Sqn** dd ex 1 AD 24.9.17 (same engine), vict 25.9.17 (2nd Lt N.V. Harrison/Lt V.R.S. White destroyed an Albatros D.V in flames over Becelaere at 18:30) then wrecked on OP 16.11.17 (2nd Lt D. French/2nd Lt G. Noon both OK crashed in forced landing after engine failure – 71hr 54min, same engine). **1 ASD** ex 20 Sqn 17.11.17. **2 AIS** ex 1 ASD 3.2.18 (engine Falcon III 255/WD18627). **48 Sqn** dd ex 2 AIS 11.2.18 (same engine), vict 23.4.18 (Capt T. Colville-Jones/2nd Lt J.M.J. Moore sent a Pfalz D.III down OOC, W of Bray at 15:50) then LIA on 16:05 OP 25.4.18 (Capt T. Colville-Jones POW fatally WIA/AM1 F. Finney POW, last seen in combat over Weincourt – same engine) and deleted on unit that day (134hr 50min).

B1127   To Middle East. **X AD** dd ex England 26.11.17. **X AP** and Palestine Bde ex X AD 30.11.17 and tested 12.12.17. **5 FS** Heliopolis dd ex X AD 27.4.19 (engine WD15780). **16 TDS** Abu Sueir and deleted on unit 8.8.19.

B1128   To Middle East. **111 Sqn** by 31.12.17. **67 Sqn** by 2.1.18, vict 3.1.18 (Lt R.A. Austin/Lt R.W. Sutherland destroyed an Albatros D.V between El Afule and Jenin at 09:20), on unit when redesignated **1 Sqn AFC** and LIA 19.3.18 (Capt R.A. Austin MC/Lt O.M. Lee both POW, landed at El Kutrani to help **142 Sqn**'s Martinsyde G.102 A3960 which had force landed with engine trouble but broke a wheel and both machines burnt).

B1129   To Middle East. **X AD** dd ex England 26.11.17. **X AP** and Palestine Bde ex X AD 30.11.17. **111 Sqn** by 13.12.17. **67 Sqn** by 2.1.18. Deleted 22.2.18.

B1130   (Falcon II) **5 AAP** Filton 22.9.17, reallotted from Training to BEF. **1 AD** dd ex England to **ARS** 25.9.17 (engine 245/WD22459). **20 Sqn** dd ex 1 AD 29.9.17 (same engine), vict 11.10.17 (Sgt F. Johnson/Lt N.M. Sanders sent an Albatros D.III down OOC over Moorslede at 07:15) then wrecked on OP 13.10.17 (2nd Lt T. Colville-Jones/Lt N.M. Sanders both OK, force landing with fuel problems near **23 Sqn** aerodrome – same engine). **1 AD** ex 20 Sqn 15.10.17 and deleted 17.10.17 (not worth reconstruction, 24hr 22min).

B1131   (Falcon II, short span tailplane) **5 AAP** Filton 22.9.17, allotted to BEF but allotment cancelled 25.9.17, machine en route to **(S)ARD** from Reading 25.9.17 for **E1 Repair Section**.

B1132   (Falcon II) **5 AAP** Filton 27.9.17, allotted to BEF. **1 AD** dd ex England 8.10.17 (engine 303/WD18428). **48 Sqn** dd ex 1 AD 14.10.17 (same engine) and reported as unfit for further service in the field 10.4.18 (125hr 10min – same engine). **2 ASD** ex 48 Sqn 12.4.18 **1 ASD** ex 2 ASD 17.4.18 and flown to England 20.4.18.

B1133   (Falcon II) **5 AAP** Filton 24.9.17, allotted to BEF. **1 AD** dd ex England 24.9.17 (engine 275/WD18414). **20 Sqn** dd ex 1 AD 29.9.17 (same engine), LIA on 07:39 OP 5.10.17 (Capt D.D. Walrond-Skinner/Pte F.F. Johns both POW, in combat with EA, N of Dadizeele and last seen going north over Roulers – same engine) and deleted on unit that day (12hr 44min).

B1134   (Falcon II) **5 AAP** Filton 24.9.17, allotted to BEF. **1 AD** dd ex England 24.9.17 (engine 307/WD18430). **48 Sqn** dd ex 1 AD 25.9.17 (same engine), vict 11.11.17 (Capt N.C. Millman/Lt T.C.S. Tuffield sent an Albatros D.V down OOC, E of St Georges at 15:10). **35 Sqn** dd ex 48 Sqn 4.2.18 (engine 215/WD22449) and wrecked on Travelling Flight to new aerodrome 24.3.18 (2nd Lt A.S. Hanna/2nd Lt R.A. Burnard both OK, ran into ridge on landing then o/t and machine caught fire – same engine). **2 ASD** ex 35 Sqn 24.3.18. **1 ASD** ex 2 ASD 7.4.18 and deleted 8.4.18 (not worth reconstruction).

B1135   (Initially Falcon II) **5 AAP** Filton 27.9.17, allotted to BEF. **1 AD** dd ex England 30.9.17 (engine 243/WD22464). **20 Sqn** dd ex 1 AD 3.10.17 (same engine) and wrecked on 15:35 OP 9.10.17 (Lt J.C. Kirkpatrick/AM J. McMechan both OK, longerons damaged by AA fire – engine Falcon I 491/WD10544). **1 AD** ex 20 Sqn 11.10.17. **2 AD** ex 1 AD for reconstruction 16.10.17. **2 AIS** ex 12.1.18 (engine Falcon III 93/WD18546). **2 ASD** ex 2 AIS 3.2.18 (Lt Plummer – same engine). **2 AIS** ex 2 ASD 15.2.18 (same engine). **2 ASD** ex 2 AIS. **2 AIS** ex 2 ASD 28.4.18 (engine Falcon III 513/WD32656). **48 Sqn** dd ex 2 AIS 4.5.18 (same engine) and wrecked on OP 7.7.18 (2nd Lt B.E. Sharwood-Smith/Sgt E. Collinson both OK, force landed near Amiens after radiator was shot through – same engine). **2 ASD** ex 48 Sqn 9.7.18 and deleted 29.7.17 (not worth reconstruction, 148hr 25min).

B1136   (Initially Falcon II) **5 AAP** Filton 5.10.17, allotted to BEF. **1 AD** dd ex England 8.10.17 (engine 311/WD18432). **22 Sqn** dd ex 1 AD 14.10.17 (same engine) and wrecked on OP 12.11.17 (2nd Lt G.C. Hughes/AM2 C. Hagan both OK, lost way and o/t landing at **1 ASD** – same engine). **1 ASD** ex 22 Sqn 14.11.17. **1 AIS** ex 1 ASD 25.1.18 (engine Falcon III 147/WD18573). **1 ASD** ex 1 AIS 7.2.18 (same engine). **1 AIS** ex 1 ASD 27.2.18 (same engine). **22 Sqn** dd ex 1 AIS 10.3.18 (same engine) and wrecked after OP 15.5.18 (Capt W.J. Mostyn & 2nd Lt A.E. Durling both OK, crashed on landing – engine Falcon III 191/WD18595). **1 ASD** ex 22 Sqn 18.5.18 and deleted 25.6.18 on reconstruction as F5817).

B1137   (Falcon II) **5 AAP** Filton 5.10.17, allotted to BEF. **1 AD** dd ex England 8.10.17 (engine 327/WD18440). **20 Sqn** dd ex 1 AD 9.10.17 (same engine) and wrecked on 10:15 Reconnaissance 14.10.17 Lt N.V. Harrison OK/2nd Lt J.P.F. Adams KIA, the formation was jumped by 8-10 Albatros D-types from the fringe of a cloud and the machine was chased back to the lines by three EA, badly shot up and crashed at **6 Sqn** aerodrome – same engine). **1 AD** ex 20 Sqn 15.10.17 and deleted 17.10.17 (not worth reconstruction, 8hr 31min).

B1138   (Falcon II) **5 AAP** Filton 6.10.17, allotted to BEF. **1 AD** dd ex England 8.10.17 (engine 261/WD18407). **20 Sqn** dd ex 1 AD 14.10.17, victs 18.10.17 (Capt H.G.E. Luchford/Lt V.R.S. White, saw three Albatros D.V diving on an R.E.8, attacked driving off two and shooting down the third which crashed between Houthem and Tenbrielen 08:45 then destroyed a DFW C-type near Dadizeele at 09:00) and 21.10.17 (Capt H.G.E. Luchford/Lt V.R.S. White destroyed a LVG C-type over Dadizeele-Menin at 15:20) then wrecked after OP 12.11.17 (Lt T. Colville-Jones/Lt L.H. Phelps both OK, overshot landing, tried again, lost flying speed banking and nosedived in – same engine). **1 ASD** ex 20 Sqn 15.11.17 and deleted 17.11.17 (not worth reconstruction, 45hr 3min).

B1139   (Falcon II) **5 AAP** Filton, allotted to BEF. **1 AD** dd ex England 8.10.17 (engine 335/WD18444). **20 Sqn** dd ex 1 AD 10.10.17 (same engine, vict 18.10.17 (Lt T. Colville-Jones/Lt L.H. Phelps destroyed an Albatros D.V over Gheluvelt at 16:10) then LIA on 07:22 OP 6.11.17 (2nd Lt C.B. Simpson/2nd Lt J.H.W. Duggan both KIA, believed hit by AA fire – same engine) and deleted on unit that day (34hr 5min).

B1140   **35 TS** Northolt by 5.12.17.

B1141   (Falcon II) **5 AAP** Filton 10.10.17, allotted to BEF. **1 AD** dd ex England 12.10.17 (engine 355/WD18454). **22 Sqn** dd ex 1 AD 17.10.17 (same engine) and wrecked on Practice Flight 20.10.17 (2nd Lt G.C. Hughes OK, crashed on landing – same engine). **1 AD** ex 22 Sqn 20.10.17, unit redesignated **1 ASD** 1.11.17, and deleted 16.1.18 (not worth reconstruction, 4hr 10min).

B1142   **5 AAP** Filton 19.10.17, reallotted to BEF from Training Division but reallotted that day to HD Bde.

B1143   (Initially Falcon II) presentation a/c *Kotah No.1*. **5 AAP** Filton 19.10.17, reallotted to BEF from Training Division. **11 Sqn** dd ex **1 AD** 27.10.17 (engine 389/WD18471) and wrecked on OP 24.11.17 (Capt G.H. Hooper MC/Lt H.G. Kent both OK, force landed with magneto trouble – same engine). **2 ASD** ex 11 Sqn 24.11.17. **2 AIS** ex 2 ASD 20.2.18 (engine Falcon III 357/

WD18678). **11 Sqn** reissued ex 2 AIS 8.3.18 (same engine) and wrecked after Reconnaissance 7.4.18 (2nd Lt R. Fitton/2nd Lt R.A. West both OK, crashed on landing when tail skid caught a ridge – same engine). **2 ASD** ex **2 Salvage Dump** 18.4.18 and deleted 22.4.18 (not worth reconstruction, 27hr 44min).

B1144 (Falcon II) **5 AAP** Filton 19.10.17, reallotted from HD Bde and **39 Sqn** to BEF. **22 Sqn** dd ex **1 AD** 21.10.17 (same engine) and wrecked before OP 4.1.18 (Sgt J.M. Bainbridge/AM2 J. Jones both OK, crashed on take off – same engine). **1 ASD** ex 22 Sqn 9.1.18 (46hr 30min) presume deleted.

B1145 Presentation a/c *Presented by Maharaja Bahadur Sir Rameswar Singh of Darbhanga No.3* wef 4.12.17.

B1146 Presentation a/c *New South Wales No.1. Bell Trees (Australia No.2).* To Middle East. **X AP** and Palestine Bde dd ex **X AD** 28.1.18. **67 Sqn** by 1.18, on unit charge when redesignated **1 Sqn AFC** and LIA 1.5.18 (Capt D.W. Rutherford/2nd Lt J. McElligott both POW, hit by ground fire near Amman, forced to land and machine burnt – A7196 crashed in an abortive rescue attempt).

B1147 Presentation a/c *South Australia No.2 (Australia 14), The Mrs Sidney Kidman.* **1 Sqn AFC** by 30.1.18. **19 TDS** El Rimal. **X AP** Kantara ex 19 TDS 16.8.18. **1 Sqn AFC** reissued ex X AP 16.8.18 (engine WD10545). **1 Sqn** ex 1 Sqn AFC 4.2.19. **ASD ME** Aboukir. **14 Sqn** dd ex ASD ME 12.2.20.

B1148 Presentation a/c *Australia No.3, New South Wales No.2. The White Edenglassie.* To Middle East. **X AD** Aboukir tested 26.1.18. **67 Sqn** by 1.18 and on unit charge when redesignated **1 Sqn AFC** in Palestine Bde. **X AP** ex 1 Sqn AFC 5.10.18 (engine WD10409) and deleted 16.10.18.

B1149 Presentation a/c *Australia No.11, New South Wales No.10. Government Duplicate The Tweed.* **67 Sqn** by 1.18, on unit charge when redesignated **1 Sqn AFC**, victs 3.5.18 (Capt A.R. Brown/Lt G. Finlay destroyed an EA C-type SW of Suweileh at 07:00, shared B1225) and 27.6.18 (Capt A.R. Brown/Lt G. Finlay destroyed an AEG C-type near Kutrani at 06:45) and deleted on unit 7.11.18.

B1150 To Middle East. **X AP** dd ex **X AD** 26.1.18. **1 Sqn AFC** dd ex X AP 27.1.18. **X AP** ex 1 Sqn AFC. **1 Sqn AFC** reissued ex X AP 18.7.18. **X AP** ex 1 Sqn AFC. **1 Sqn AFC** reissued ex X AP 28.10.18. **X AP** and deleted 9.9.19.

B1151 N/I

B1152 (Falcon II) **5 AAP** Filton 27.10.17, allotted to BEF. **1 AIS** dd ex **2 ASD** 18.11.18 (engine 361/WD18457). **22 Sqn** dd ex 1 AIS 3.12.17 (same engine), marked as a/c *C*, vict 18.3.18 (Capt F.G.C. Weare/Lt G.S.L. Hayward destroyed an Albatros D.V over Carvin at 11:15) then wrecked on Practice Flight 10.4.18 (2nd Lt C.E. Taylor OK, engine cut out and pilot misjudged landing on soft ground – same engine). **1 ASD** ex 22 Sqn 13.4.18 and deleted 23.4.18 (not worth reconstruction, 86hr 25min).

B1153 (Falcon II) **5 AAP** Filton 29.10.17, allotted to BEF. **22 Sqn** dd ex **1 ASD** 9.11.17 (engine 305/WD18429), LIA on 10:10 OP 3.12.17 (2nd Lt A.F. Goodchap/2nd Lt A.H. Middleton both POW, last seen going down over Poperinghe apparently with engine trouble – same engine) and deleted on unit 4.12.17 (10hr 26min).

B1154 (Falcon I) **5 AAP** Filton 27.10.17, allotted to BEF. **1 AIS** ex **2 ASD** 22.11.17, dismantled after forced landing near Coupelle Neuve (engine 44/WD10429). **1 ASD** ex 1 AIS 22.11.17. **8 AAP** Lympne ex 1 ASD 12.12.17 (2nd Lt C.H. Drew/AM1 Atkins).

B1155 (Falcon II) **5 AAP** Filton 29.10.17, allotted to BEF. **20 Sqn** dd ex **1 ASD** 7.11.17 (engine WD18478) and wrecked on OP 14.11.17 (2nd Lt R.M. Makepeace/2nd Lt W.T.V. Harmer both OK, force landed near Estaires in thick mist – engine 531/WD15779). **1 ASD** ex 20 Sqn 16.11.17. **1 AIS** ex 1 ASD 20.1.18 (engine 95/WD22469). **22 Sqn** dd ex 1 AIS 26.1.18 (same engine) and wrecked en route 1 ASD for wireless fitting 12.3.18 (2nd Lt W.S. Hill-Tout/Capt Stewart both OK, misjudged landing and crashed – same engine). **1 ASD** ex 22 Sqn 13.3.18 and deleted 14.3.18 (37hr 40min).

B1156 (Falcon II) **5 AAP** Filton 1.11.17, allotted to BEF. **20 Sqn** dd ex **1 ASD** 11.11.17 (engine 379/WD18466), LIA on Bombing 27.3.18 (Capt R.K. Kirkman/Capt J.H. Hedley both POW – engine 265/WD18409) and deleted on unit 29.3.18 (119hr 6min).

B1157 **39 Sqn** North Weald by 27.1.18, on HAP 28/29.1.18 (crew not named) and wrecked after HAP 30.1.18 (Lt E.S.C. Brooks OK/2nd Lt J.T. Baugh IIFA, crashed on landing – engine WD10445).

B1158 (Falcon II). **5 AAP** Bristol 9.11.17, allotted to BEF. En route to **3 (W)ARD** 27.11.17 with BEF allotment cancelled, and for **E1a Repair Section**.

B1159 **35 TS** Northolt by 16.11.17. (Also noted at **59 TS** by 10:17 until @ 4.18).

B1160 **1 SAF** Ayr by 3.1.18. **59 TS** Lilbourne/Rendcomb as a/c *8* by 11.1.18. **45 TDS** Rendcomb by 7.18 and wrecked 6.9.18 (Lt C.F.J. Thompson KIFA, the pilot apparently fainted and the machine side-slipped in – engine WD22403).

B1161 **1 SAFG** Turnberry by 5.6.18.

B1162 (Falcon II) **5 AAP** Bristol 9.11.17, allotted to BEF. **1 ASD** dd ex England 12.12.17. **1 AIS** ex 1 ASD 2.1.18 (engine 341/WD18447). **22 Sqn** dd ex 1 AIS 19.1.18 (same engine), LIA on 18:20 OP 12.5.18 (2nd Lt C.E. Taylor POW WIA/2nd Lt A.P. Bollins POW, last seen between Armentieres and Merville, believed shot down by AA – engine 325/WD18439) and deleted on unit that day (89hr 55min).

B1163 (Falcon II) **5 AAP** Bristol 9.11.17, allotted to BEF. **1 ASD** dd ex England 21.11.17 (engine 437/WD18495). **1 AIS** ex 1 ASD 3.12.17 (same engine). **22 Sqn** dd ex 1 AIS 4.12.17 (same engine) and wrecked on Practice Flight 7.12.17 (Lt M.W. Turner/AM1 D.E. Wareham both IOAS, crashed just after take off when engine failed – same engine). **1 ASD** ex 22 Sqn 8.12.17 and deleted 12.12.17 (not worth reconstruction, 6hr 30min).

B1164 (Falcon II) **5 AAP** Bristol 12.11.17, allotted to BEF. **1 ASD** dd ex England 22.11.17 (engine 433/WD18493). **22 Sqn** dd ex 1 AIS 2.12.17 (same engine), marked as a/c *D*, victs 7.5.18 (Capt A.C. Atkey/Lt C.G. Gass destroyed five Fokker D.VII, NE of Arras, two in flames, at 18:45-18:50) and damaged in successful combat 9.5.18 (Lt S.F.H. Thompson OK/Sgt L. Kendrick WIA, sent a Pfalz D.III down OOC, N of Douai at 18:45 – engine 291/WD18422). **1 ASD** ex 22 Sqn 13.5.18 and deleted 14.5.18 (not worth reconstruction, 129hr 50min). Also noted with **36 Sqn, 'A' Flt** by 20.9.18 until @ 22.9.18 (Lt E.T. Carpenter).

B1165 At maker's 6.11.17, allotted to BEF and to be delivered in packing case. **1 ASD** ex **2 ASD** 5.12.17 and flown to England that day.

B1166 (Falcon II) at maker's 6.11.17, allotted to BEF and to be delivered in packing case. **1 AIS** ex **1 ASD** 25.1.18 (engine 413/WD18483). **1 ASD** ex 1 AIS 10.3.18 (same engine) and flown to England 11.3.18.

B1167 (Falcon II) at maker's 6.11.17, allotted to BEF and to be delivered in packing case. **11 Sqn** dd ex **2 ASD** 6.12.17 (engine 429/WD18491) as **13 Wing** CO's machine, attached to **201 Sqn** 4.6.18, **11 Sqn** 20.7.18 and **218 Sqn** by 30.12.18 until @ 1.19. **8 Sqn** Sart. **1 ASD** Merheim ex 8 Sqn 16.7.19.

B1168 (Initially Falcon II) at maker's 6.11.17, allotted to BEF and to be delivered in packing case. **1 AIS** dd ex **1 ASD** 25.1.18 (engine 443/WD18498). **22 Sqn** dd ex 1 ASD 6.2.18 (same engine), damaged in successful combats 5.3.18 (2nd Lt S.A. Oades/2nd Lt S.W. Bunting both WIA, destroyed an EA C-type at 15:35 and sent an EA scout down OOC over Lens at 15:45 but Vickers continued firing after combat and shot away one blade of its propeller causing the machine to crash – same engine). **1 ASD** ex 22 Sqn 6.3.18. **1 AIS** ex 1 ASD 17.4.18 (engine Falcon III 477/WD32638). **20 Sqn** dd ex 1 AIS 22.4.18 (same engine) and wrecked on OP 2.8.18 (Lt J.J. Quinn/Prob K. Penrose both OK, crashed in forced landing after fuel tank holed – engine Falcon III 657/WD32728). **1 ASD** ex 20 Sqn 5.8.18 and deleted 7.8.18 (not worth reconstruction, 243hr 48min).

B1169 **8 TS** Netheravon/Witney by 23.1.18 until @ 15.6.18 (Sgt J. Gamble). **33 TDS** Witney and wrecked 18.7.18 (2nd Lt L.S. Ford IIFA, stalled at 20ft on downwind climbing turn – engine 15757).

B1170 (Falcon II) **5 AAP** Bristol 19.11.17, allotted to BEF. **1 ASD** dd ex England 23.11.17 (engine 357/WD18455). **1 ASD** ex **22 Sqn** 30.11.17. **20 Sqn** and wrecked on 09:44 OP 18.1.18 (Lt D. Leigh-Pemberton/AM1 M.B. Mather both OK, engine cut out whilst on the other side of the lines and force landed near Poperinghe striking a telegraph post – same engine). **1 ASD** ex 20 Sqn 23.1.18 (11hr 49min) presume deleted.

B1171 (Falcon II) **5 AAP** Bristol 19.11.17, allotted to BEF. **22 Sqn** dd ex **1 AIS** 5.1.18 (engine 381/WD18467), LIA on 09:05 OP 23.3.18 (Capt P. Thompson KIA/Lt D.W. Kent-Jones POW, last seen near Cambrai – same engine) and deleted on unit that day (60hr 10min).

B1172 (Falcon I) **5 AAP** Bristol 16.11.17, allotted to BEF but reallotted to Training 17.11.17. **35 TS** Port Meadow and wrecked 17.2.18 (Major V.O. Rees/2nd Lt S.J. Clinch both IIFA, lost flying speed in low turn and side-slipped in – engine 1/220/WD12547).

B1173 N/I

B1174 N/I

B1175 N/I

B1176 N/I

B1177 (Initially Falcon II) **5 AAP** Bristol 21.11.17, allotted to BEF. **20 Sqn** dd ex **1 ASD** 13.12.17 (engine 265/WD18409), victs

17.2.18 (Sgt F. Johnson/Capt J.H. Hedley destroyed a Pfalz D.III and sent another down OOC near Moorslede at 11:20-11:30). **1 ASD**, wrecked, ex 20 Sqn 15.4.18 (engine 347/WD18450) and under reconstruction by 30.5.18 (engine Falcon III 975/WD32887). **2 AIS** by 4.6.18. **1 AIS** by 21.6.18 (same engine). **22 Sqn** dd ex 1 AIS 26.6.18 (same engine) and reported 18.7.18 as unfit for further service in the field. **1 ASD** ex 22 Sqn 22.7.18 (13hr 50min) and deleted 14.9.18 on reconstruction as H7068.

B1178 (Falcon I, first flown 25.11.17) **1 SAFG** Turnberry/Ayr by 4.4.18 (Capt J.H. Letts). **1 SAFG** Turnberry/Ayr and wrecked 28.5.18 (Lt R.M. Makepeace/2nd Lt T.A. McClure both KIFA, RH wings folded in flight – engine 1/F/581/WD12561). Also noted with **1 Sqn AFC** by 7.18.

B1179 (Falcon I) **5 AAP** Bristol tested 26.11.17 (Lt C.F. Uwins – engine dud). **4 (Aux) SAG** Marske by 4.18, unit redesignated **2 FS** Marske 29.5.18, and wrecked 26.7.18 (Lt D.O. Driscoll fatally IIFA, stalled on overshoot, side-slipped in and burst into flames – engine 1/F/457/WD10517).

B1180 (Falcon I) **1 SAF** Ayr by 2.18, marked as a/c *3* and wrecked 26.4.18 (Sgt A. Woodfield IIFA, stalled to avoid collision with trees – engine 1/F/4189/WD10503).

B1181 (Falcon III) Presentation a/c *Baroda No.14*. **48 Sqn** and wrecked on Delivery Flight 4.1.18 (Lt B.H.M Jones/Major B.M. Jones both OK, crashed landing at Villers Bretonneaux – engine 17/WD18508). **2 ASD** ex 48 Sqn 8.1.18. **2 AIS** ex 2 ASD 12.2.18 (Lt Stock – same engine). **48 Sqn** reissued ex 2 AIS 24.2.18 and wrecked after OP 17.3.18 (2nd Lt A.C.G. Brown/Lt D. Wishart-Orr both OK, landed on soft ground and o/t – same engine). **2 ASD** ex 48 Sqn 20.3.18. **1 ASD** ex 2 ASD 3.4.18 and deleted 8.4.18 (not worth reconstruction, 62hr 15min).

B1182 (Falcon III) **5 AAP** Bristol 26.11.17, allotted to BEF. **48 Sqn** dd ex **2 AIS** 25.12.17 (engine 43/WD18521) and wrecked 5.2.18 (when stationary on aerodrome was run into by C4831 – same engine). **4 AP** ex 48 Sqn 18.2.18. **2 ASD** ex 4 AP 22.2.18. **2 AIS** ex 2 ASD 16.4.18 (engine 1/WD18500). **12 Sqn** dd ex 2 AIS 23.4.18 (same engine). **52 Sqn** ex 12 Sqn 13.7.18 and reported 29.7.18 as in need of complete overhaul (128hr 20min – engine 1319/WD51684). **2 ASD** ex 52 Sqn 31.7.18. **1 ASD** ex 2 ASD 3.8.18 and flown to England that day. **1 (S)ARD** Farnborough. **45 TDS** Rendcomb dd ex 1 (S)ARD 3.9.18 (Lt G.H. Richardson) and on unit charge until @ 12.18.

B1183 (Falcon III) **5 AAP** Bristol 26.11.17, allotted to BEF. **1 ASD** dd ex 5 AAP 3.12.17 (Lt C.F. Uwins). **11 Sqn** dd ex 1 ASD 6.12.17 (engine 21/WD18510) and wrecked en route to **2 ASD** for wireless fitting (Major R.F.S Morton/2nd Lt E.C. Gilroy both OK, crashed just after take off when engine failed – same engine). **2 ASD** ex 11 Sqn and deleted 16.3.18 (not worth reconstruction, 66hr 5min).

B1184 (Falcon III) **5 AAP** Bristol 28.11.17, allotted to BEF but reallotted to 6th Bde 5.12.17; **39 Sqn** North Weald on HAPs 18.12.17 (2nd Lt P.W.L. Jarvis/Lt Robbins) and 22.12.18 (Lt P.W. Deane/Lt A.L. Harrow-Bunn).

B1185 (Falcon III) **5 AAP** Bristol 29.11.17, allotted to BEF. **2 AIS** ex **1 ASD** 21.2.18 (engine 89/WD18544). **2 ASD** ex 2 AIS 26.2.18 to be packed in case for 7th Bde (same engine) and despatched by rail 2.3.18. **28 Sqn** dd ex **7 AP** 19.3.18 (same engine). **'Z' Flt, 34 Sqn** ex 28 Sqn 30.3.18 and damaged on 08:45 Reconnaissance 3.4.18 (2nd Lt W.L. Vorster/Lt C. leG. Amy both OK, Initially reported missing – same engine). **7 AP** ex 34 Sqn for repair 8.4.18. **'Z' Flt, 34 Sqn** reissued 5.5.18 (engine 83/WD18541), on charge when unit redesignated **139 Sqn** 3.7.18 and reported 14.7.18 as unfit for war flying. **7 AP** ex 139 Sqn 19.7.18. **139 Sqn** reissued ex 7 AP 4.11.18. **34 Sqn** ex 139 Sqn 28.12.18. **7 AP** ex 34 Sqn 10.2.18 (2nd Lt E.R. Williams).

B1186 (Falcon III) presentation a/c *Montreal No.4*. **5 AAP** Bristol by 28.11.17, allotted to BEF but reallotted to 6 Bde 5.12.17. **39 Sqn** North Weald on HAPs 18.12.17 (Lt C.R.W. Knight/Lt L. Speller), 29.1.18 (Lt C.R.W. Knight/2nd Lt E.J. Ralli) and 7/8.3.18 (Lt C.R.W. Knight/AM1 Easton). **33 Sqn 'C' Flt** Elshamand on AZP 5.8.18 (Capt A.B. Fanstone/AM Ridley). **36 Sqn, 'A' Flt** Hylton by 5.9.18 until @ 4.12.18 (Lt E.T. Carpenter).

B1187 (Falcon III) **5 AAP** Bristol 29.11.17, allotted to BEF. **48 Sqn** dd ex **2 AIS** 28.12.17 (engine 47/WD18523), victs 3.1.18 (Capt N.C. Millman/2nd Lt H.A. Cooper sent an Albatros C-type down OOC over Le Catelet at 11:30) and 15.3.18 (Lt H.W. Elliott/Lt R.S. Herring sent an Albatros D.III down OOC, NE of St Quentin at 14:25) then wrecked on OP 21.3.18 (2nd Lt C.D.G. Napier/2nd Lt J.M.J. Moore both OK, force landed after fuel tank shot through – engine 625/WD32712) and deleted on unit that day (96hr 5min). **1 ASD** ex Rouen 9.4.18, brought back onto RAF charge and ready by 29.5.18 (engine 977/WD32888). **1 AIS** ex 1 ASD

31.5.18 (same engine). **88 Sqn** dd ex 1 AIS 3.6.18 (same engine) and wrecked on OP 2.7.18 (Lt J.P. Findlay/2nd Lt G.E.D. Low both OK, engine cut out and pancaked in forced landing on Belgian aerodrome – same engine). **1 ASD** ex 88 Sqn 3.7.18 and deleted 6.7.18 (not worth reconstruction).

B1188 N/I

B1189 (Falcon III) **5 AAP** Bristol 29.11.17, allotted to BEF. **11 Sqn** dd ex **2 ASD** 14.12.17 (engine 125/WD18562), LIA on 10:05 OP, Cambrai, 28.1.18 (2nd Lt J.L. Milne-Henderson/2nd Lt E.A. Cunningham both KIA, engine trouble over Douai – engine 99/WD18459) and deleted on unit that day (17hr 25min).

B1190 (Falcon III) **5 AAP** Bristol 29.11.17, allotted to BEF and despatched 15.12.17. **2 ASD** ex **2 AIS** 24.1.18 (engine 145/WD18572). **2 AIS** ex 2 ASD 4.2.18 (same engine). **48 Sqn** dd ex 2 AIS 17.2.18 (same engine), victs 1.3.18 (Capt N.C. Millman/2nd Lt H.A. Cooper sent an EA C-type down OOC over Joncourt at 10:10 and an Albatros D.III down OOC, S of St Quentin at 10:30) and 8.3.18 (Capt N.C. Millman/2nd Lt H.A. Cooper sent an Albatros D.V down OOC over Bohain at 10:40 and another down OOC over Bohain at 15:55) then wrecked on OP 15.3.18 (Capt N.C. Millman/2nd Lt H.A. Cooper both OK, engine seized up and crashed on landing – same engine). **2 ASD** ex 48 Sqn 16.3.18. **1 ASD** ex 2 ASD by rail 2.4.18 and deleted 8.4.18 (not worth reconstruction, 33hr 25min).

B1191 (Falcon III) **5 AAP** Bristol 30.11.17, allotted to BEF and despatched by air. **20 Sqn** by 1.2.18, victs 13.3.18 (Lt E. Lindup/Cpl F. Archer sent a Pfalz D.III down OOC over Houthem at 12:20) and 28.3.18 (Lt E. Lindup/2nd Lt H.G. Crowe sent a Fokker Dr.I down OOC over Albert at 08:30) then wrecked after OP 25.4.18 (Lt C.G. Lankin/Lt J.W. McHattie both KOAS, overshot aerodrome when attempting to land, stalled and nosedived in – engine 123/WD18561). **1 ASD** ex 20 Sqn 27.4.18 and deleted 28.4.18 (114hr 59min).

B1192 (Falcon III) **5 AAP** Bristol 3.12.17, allotted to BEF and despatched 8.12.17. **48 Sqn** dd ex **2 ASD** 29.12.17 (engine 97/WD18548) and reported 6.5.18 as unfit for further service in the field (140hr 55min – engine 347/WD18673). **2 ASD** ex 48 Sqn 8.5.18. **1 ASD** ex 2 ASD 8.5.18 and flown to England 16.5.18.

B1193 (Falcon III) **5 AAP** Bristol 3.12.17, allotted to BEF and despatched by air. **48 Sqn** dd ex **2 AIS** 5.1.18 (engine 1/WD18500) and wrecked after OP 21.2.18 (Lt W.A. McMichael/2nd Lt W. Hart both OK, crashed on landing – same engine). **2 ASD** ex 48 Sqn 26.2.18. **1 ASD** ex 2 ASD 3.4.18. **1 AIS** ex 1 ASD 15.4.18 (engine 597/WD32698). **20 Sqn** dd ex 1 AIS 23.4.18 (same engine) and wrecked on 18:08 OP 27.5.18 (Sgt A. Stansfield OK/Prob J. Tulloch WIA, damaged by enemy fire and force landed at Clairmarais South – same engine). **1 ASD** ex 20 Sqn 29.5.18 and deleted 31.5.18 (not worth reconstruction, 64hr 26min).

B1194 (Falcon III) **5 AAP** Bristol 3.12.17, allotted to BEF and despatched 16.12.17. **2 AIS** ex **1 ASD** 5.2.18 (engine 5/WD18502). **11 Sqn** dd ex 2 AIS 10.3.18 (same engine), vict 22.3.18 (2nd Lt J.P. Seabrook/Lt A. Reeve destroyed an Albatros D.V in flames over Queant at 18:35) then wrecked after Reconnaissance 31.3.18 (2nd Lt J.P. Seabrook/2nd Lt C. Wrigglesworth both OK, crashed on landing after engine failed – same engine). **1 ASD** ex **Advanced Salvage** 4.4.18 and deleted 25.6.18 on reconstruction as F5812.

B1195 **SAF** Ayr. **4 (Aux) SAG** Marske by 4.18 until @ 3.5.18.

B1196 (Falcon III) **5 AAP** Bristol 3.12.17, allotted to BEF. **20 Sqn** dd ex **1 AIS** 22.1.18 (engine 155/WD18577) LIA on OP 26.3.18 (Lt D. Leigh-Pemberton WIA/Capt N.W. Taylor OK, crashed near Albert and abandoned owing to the advancing enemy – same engine) and deleted on unit 28.3.18 (22hr).

B1197 N/I

B1198 (Falcon I) to Middle East. **1 Sqn AFC** by 19.4.18 until @ 28.5.18. **111 Sqn**. **4 FTS** Abu Sueir dd ex **AD Aboukir** 29.11.21. **14 Sqn** by 23.2.22 until @ 4.22 (crashed into hangar at Ramleh and deleted).

B1199 (Falcon I) presentation a/c *Australia No.10. New South Wales No.9. The Tweed*. To Middle East. **1 Sqn AFC** dd ex **X AP** 12.4.18. **X AP** ex 1 Sqn AFC 3.10.18. **111 Sqn** dd ex **X AD** 27.9.19. **ASD ME** ex 111 Sqn 27.9.19 and deleted 13.11.19.

B1200 (200hp Hispano-Suiza) due to be dd to Testing Sqn Martlesham Heath w/e 22.12.17 (200hp Hispano-Suiza), but held up at Woodford, Essex with engine trouble 5.1.18. **ES** Martlesham Heath from 22.9.18 (200hp Wolseley Viper preformance tests). **1 (S)ARD** Farnborough by 10.10.18.

B1201 (200hp Hispano-Suiza) **ES** Martlesham Heath dd ex Bristol 26-31.12.17 (Lt J.H. Letts), performance trials with this engine, then top plane gravity tank tests, then engine transferred to Sopwith Dolphin C3778). **RAF** Farnborough 28.2.18 (became **RAE**

1.4.18), tested with 200hp Hispano-Suiza, and later with 200hp R.A.F. 4d then flown with both standard 2-bay wings & experimental 3-bay wings of 9.73 aspect ratio. **IDE** Biggin Hill by 17.1.22. **RAE** Farnborough by 9.3.22 until @ 12.23.

B1202 (Arab) **5 AAP** Bristol tested 24.1.18 (Lt C.F. Uwins & Cadet).

B1203 **5 AAP** Bristol tested 25.1.18 (Lt C.F. Uwins & Mechanic).

B1204 (Arab) **ES** Martlesham Heath dd ex **5 AAP** 8.2.18 for performance tests, producing Trials Report M224.

B1205 (Falcon III) to Middle East. **1 Sqn AFC** dd 27.4.18. **Z Sqn** by 10.2.19 (Sgt N. Madle). **16 TDS** Abu Sueir and deleted on unit 9.7.19.

B1206 **ES** Martlesham Heath dd 27.1.18 for performance with 230hp Puma. **2 AAP** Hendon by 3.4.18 until @ 9.6.18 (as station aircraft).

B1207 (Falcon III) **62 Sqn** Rendcomb, to BEF with unit 23.1.18, LIA on 09:00 OP 13.3.18 (2nd Lt C. Allen KIA/Lt N.T. Watson POW WIA, shot down in combat near Marcoing – engine 11/WD18505) and deleted on unit that day (67hr 20min).

B1208 **1 (Aux) SAG** Hythe dd ex **5 AAP** Filton 11.12.17 (Lt C.F. Uwins) and on unit charge until @ 24.4.18 (Lt E. Shamper).

B1209 (Falcon III) at maker's 4.12.17, allotted to BEF and to be despatched in packing case. **1 AIS** ex **1 ASD** 25.1.18 (engine 57/WD18528). **20 Sqn** dd ex 1 AIS 25.1.18 (same engine), wrecked on OP 17.2.18 (2nd Lt L.P. Roberts/2nd Lt W. Noble both OK, crashed near Woesten after combat with EA – same engine) and deleted on unit that day (13hr 22min). **1 ASD** and returned to RAF charge after reconstruction. **1 AIS** ex 1 ASD 15.4.18 (engine 277/WD18638). **22 Sqn** dd ex 1 AIS 17.4.18 (same engine), victs 20.5.18 (2nd Lt W.F.J. Harvey/Lt G. Thomson destroyed two EKBs in flames over Armentieres-Estaires at 16:45-17:45) and 26.5.18 (Lt H.H. Beddow/Sgt J. Goodman destroyed an Albatros D.V, SE of Armentieres at 19:45) then wrecked on Practice Flight 19.6.18 (2nd Lt J.J. Borrowman/AM Bates both OK, crashed on landing – same engine). **1 ASD** ex 22 Sqn 20.6.18 and deleted 17.9.18 on reconstruction as H7069.

B1210 (Falcon III) at maker's 4.12.17, allotted to BEF and to be delivered in a packing case. **2 ASD** by 31.12.17. **2 AIS** ex 2 ASD 11.1.18 (engine 91/WD18545). **48 Sqn** dd ex 2 AIS 4.2.18 (Sgt Hardiman – same engine) and wrecked on Photography, St Quentin, 9.2.18 (2nd Lt F.B. Hunt IOAS/Lt J.E.M. Evans fatally IOAS, force landed after engine failure – same engine). **3 AP** ex 48 Sqn 11.2.18. **2 ASD** ex 3 AP 17.2.18 and deleted 19.2.18 (58min).

Two views of an anonymous camera gun-equipped F.2B, possibly '30', at an RNAS airship station. *(Philip Jarrett)*

B1211 (Falcon III) at maker's 4.12.17, allotted to BEF and to be delivered in a packing case. **1 AIS** ex **1 ASD** 25.1.18 (engine 207/WD18602). **62 Sqn** dd ex 1 AIS 14.2.18 (same engine), LIA on 12:00 Trench Strafing 28.3.18 (2nd Lt M.H. Cleary KIA/2nd Lt V.G. Stanton fatally WIA, shot down E of Villers Bretonneux, probably by Ltn H. Weiss, Jasta 10 – same engine) and deleted on unit that day.

B1212 (Falcon III) presentation a/c *Ajmer*. At maker's 4.12.17, allotted to BEF and to be delivered in a packing case. **2 ASD** by 31.12.18. **2 AIS** dd ex 2 ASD 9.1.18 (engine 55/WD18527). **2 ASD** ex 2 AIS 6.2.18 (same engine). **2 ASD** ex 2 ASD 12.2.18 (same engine). To Italy and 7 Bde by rail 2.3.18 (same engine). **28 Sqn** dd ex **7 AP** 19.3.18 (same engine). **'Z' Flt, 34 Sqn** ex 28 Sqn 30.3.18, LIA on GHQ Reconnaissance 25.4.18 (2nd Lt P.G. Ratcliffe/ Lt H.N.V. Bankes both POW – same engine) and deleted on unit 25.4.18 (42hr 20min).

B1213 (Falcon III) at maker's 4.12.17, allotted to BEF and to be delivered in a packing case. **1 AIS** dd ex **1 ASD** 26.1.18 (engine 195/WD18957). **1 ASD** ex 1 AIS 7.2.18 (same engine). **1 AIS** ex 1 ASD 16.2.18 (same engine) and wrecked on Ferry Flight to **2 ASD** 22.3.18 (2nd Lt D.C. Townley IOAS, lost speed on take off – engine 675/WD32737). **1 ASD** ex 1 AIS 23.3.18. **1 AIS** ex 1 ASD 2.5.18 (engine 727/WD32763). **22 Sqn** dd ex 1 AIS 10.5.18 (same engine) and wrecked on Practice Flight 28.5.18 (Capt W.J. Mostyn/2nd Lt J.H. Umney both OK, crashed on landing – same engine). **1 ASD** ex 22 Sqn 31.5.18 and deleted 25.6.18 on reconstruction as F5820.

B1214 (Falcon III) at maker's 4.12.17, allotted to BEF and to be delivered in a packing case. **2 ASD** dd ex England in packing case 7.1.18 (engine 199/WD18599). **2 AIS** ex 2 ASD 20.1.18 (same engine). **2 ASD** ex 2 AIS 6.2.18 (same engine). **2 AIS** ex 2 ASD 14.2.18 (same engine). **2 ASD** ex 2 AIS 26.2.18 to be packed in case for Italy and 7th Bde. To 7 Bde by rail 2.3.18. **28 Sqn** dd ex **7 AP** 21.3.18 (same engine). **'Z' Flt, 34 Sqn** ex 28 Sqn 30.3.18, vict 4.4.18 (Lt T.C. Lowe/Lt H.N.V. Bankes both WIA, sent an Albatros D.V down OOC near Strigus) then wrecked 4.6.18 (engine 669/WD32734). **7 AP** for repair. **'Z' Flt, 34 Sqn** reissued ex 7 AP 28.6.18 (same engine), on charge when unit redesignated **139 Sqn** 3.7.18 and reported as unfit for war flying 24.7.18 (same engine). **34 Sqn** on attachment from 1.8.18, wrecked 26.9.18 and deleted on 139 Sqn.

B1215 (Falcon III) at maker's 4.12.17, allotted to BEF but allotment cancelled 6.12.17. **62 Sqn** Rendcomb by 26.12.17 to BEF with unit but wrecked en route 20.1.18 (2nd Lt D.A. Savage IOAS/ AM2 J. Ingham OK, left Lympne 16:25 and on arrival failed to find aerodrome and crashed at 17:15 – engine 25/WD18512). **1 ASD** ex 62 Sqn 31.1.18 and deleted 1.2.18 (not worth reconstruction, 20hr 25min).

B1216 (Falcon III) at maker's 4.12.17, allotted to BEF and to be delivered in a packing case. **2 ASD** dd ex England in packing case 6.1.18 (engine 133/WD18566). **2 AIS** ex 2 ASD 17.1.18 (same engine). **62 Sqn** dd ex 2 AIS 14.3.18 (same engine), victs 21.4.18 (Capt T.L. Purdom/2nd Lt P.V.G. Chambers destroyed an Albatros D.V, SE of Estaires at 09:45), 3.5.18 (Capt T.L. Purdom/2nd Lt P.V.G. Chambers sent an Albatros D-type OOC, S of Armentieres and destroyed an Albatros C-type N of Merville at 11:00), 15.5.18 (Capt T.L. Purdom/2nd Lt P.V.G. Chambers destroyed a DFW C-type near Pozieres at 17:45), 17.5.18 (Capt T.L. Purdom/2nd Lt P.V.G. Chambers sent a Fokker D.VII down OOC over Armentieres and sent a Rumpler C-type down in a vertical dive over Warneton at 10:45), and 19.5.18 (Capt T.L. Purdom/Sgt W.N. Holmes sent a Fokker D.VII down OOC, NW of Douai at 18:15) then wrecked on 06:05 Escort 22.8.18 (Lt C. Allday/2nd Lt L. Millar both OK, left aileron shot away over Pronville and followed by 4 EA back to the lines – engine 699/WD32749). **2 ASD** ex 62 Sqn and deleted 17.10.18 (not worth reconstruction).

B1217 (Falcon III) **5 AAP** Bristol 14.12.17, allotted to BEF and to be despatched by air. **1 AIS** ex **1 ASD** 24.1.18 (engine 191/WD18595). **22 Sqn** dd ex 1 AIS 24.1.18 (same engine), marked as a/c Z and wrecked on Compass Test 3.8.18 (Lt H.L. Christie/AM Fitter both OK, undercarriage smashed prior to take off due to the bad state of the ground – engine 1133/WD39459). **1 ASD** ex 22 Sqn 5.8.18.

B1218 **62 Sqn** Rendcomb by 27.12.17. **38 TS** Rendcomb by 17.2.18.

B1219 (Falcon III) **62 Sqn** Rendcomb, to BEF with the unit 23.1.18 and wrecked on Practice Flight 13.3.18 (Lt F.J. Batt/2nd Lt F.J. McNiff both KOAS, nosedived in on take off – engine 161/WD18580). **2 ASD** ex 62 Sqn 13.3.18 and deleted 20.3.18 (not worth reconstruction, 52hr).

B1220 WEE Biggin Hill 1918.

B1221 (Falcon III) **5 AAP** Bristol 14.12.17, allotted to BEF and to be despatched by air. **1 AIS** ex **1 ASD** 17.2.18 (engine 219/WD18609). **20 Sqn** dd ex 1 AIS 21.2.18 (same engine) and wrecked on Bombing 9.4.18 (Lt R.H. Harmer IOAS/Lt N. Peters OK, lost way in thick fog and crashed into sand hills near Wimereux – same engine). **1 ASD** ex 20 Sqn 11.4.18 and deleted 20.4.18 (65hr 30min).

B1222 (Falcon III) to Middle East. **1 Sqn AFC** by 6.2.18, vict 24.7.18 (Lt J.M. Walker/Lt H.A. Letch destroyed a Rumpler C-type over Tanturah at 05:30, shared B1278) then LIA 22.8.18 (Lt J.M. Walker/Lt H.A. Letch both KIA in combat with an EA C-type, fuel tank hit and went down in flames) and deleted on unit 26.8.18.

B1223 (Falcon III) presentation a/c *New South Wales No.16 The Upper Hunter Battleplane*. To Middle East. **1 Sqn AFC** dd 17.3.18 and vict 3.8.18 (Lt P.J. McGuiness/Lt H. Fysh destroyed an Albatros D.III, NE El Duba at 12:10, shared C4626). **111 Sqn** ex 1 Sqn AFC 4.2.19. **X AP** ex 111 Sqn 13.5.19 (engine WD51890). **ASD ME** ex X AP and Palestine Bde 20.8.19 and deleted 13.11.19.

B1224 Noted as accepted Brooklands 30.6.18.

B1225 To Middle East. **1 Sqn AFC** by 1.4.18, vict 3.5.18 (Lt G.V. Oxenham/Lt H.A. Letch destroyed an EA C-type 2-Str SW of Suweileh at 07:00, shared B1149), wrecked 19.9.18 (Lt D.R. Dowling/Lt E.A. Mulford both WIA) and deleted on unit 23.9.18.

B1226 **4 (Aux) SAG** Marske by 29.4.18 until @ 5.18.

B1227 (Falcon I) **4 (Aux) SAG** Marske by 4.18 as a/c *79*, unit redesignated **2 FS** 29.5.18, and wrecked 9.7.18 (pilot flew knowing the engine had faulty pressure – engine 1/F/14/WD10401).

B1228 N/I

B1229 (Falcon III) presentation a/c *Australia No.12. New South Wales No.11. The Macintyre Kayunga Estate*. To Middle East. **1 Sqn AFC** dd 17.3.18, victs 7.5.18 (Capt R.M. Smith/Lt E.A. Mustard destroyed an EA C-type in flames SE of Jenin aerodrome at 15:15, shared B1276), 22.5.18 (Capt R.M. Smith/Lt W.A. Kirk sent an Albatros D.III OOC, N of Nablus at 06:45), 11.6.18 (Capt R.M. Smith/Lt W.A. Kirk destroyed an EA C-type destroyed N of Tulkeram at 06:15, shared B1276), 19.6.18 (Capt R.M. Smith/Lt W.A. Kirk destroyed an EA C-type near Jericho at 06:05), 17.7.18 (Capt R.M. Smith/Lt W.A. Kirk destroyed two Albatros D.III, W of Huwarra at 06:40 the other near Wadi Auja at 06:45), 22.9.18 (Capt R.M. Smith/Lt E.A. Mustard destroyed an EA C-type near Mafrak at 10:00, and destroyed two Pfalz D.III near Mafrak at 10:45) and 19.10.18 (Capt R.M. Smith/Lt A.V. McCann destroyed a DFW C-type 25 miles SW of Aleppo at 10:30, shared B1295). **111 Sqn** ex 1 Sqn AFC 4.2.19. **X AP** ex 111 Sqn 15.5.19 (engine WD39412) and deleted 17.7.19 (earmarked for shipment to Australia, but F1284 possibly sent instead).

B1230 (Falcon III) presentation a/c *Montreal*. **5 AAP** Bristol 20.12.17, allotted to BEF and despatched by air. **2 AIS** ex **1 ASD** 23.2.18 (engine 83/WD18541). **2 ASD** ex 2 AIS 26.2.18, to be packed in case for 7th Bde. To Italy and 7 Bde by rail 2.3.18 (same engine). **28 Sqn** dd ex **7 AP** 12.3.18 and wrecked 26.3.18 (2nd Lt M.O. Ramsey/2nd Lt R.M. Ellis both IOAS, taxied into a ditch at Istrana). **7 AP** ex 28 Sqn 28.3.18 (same engine). **'Z' Flt, 34 Sqn** dd ex 7 AP 19.4.18 (engine 687/WD32743), marked as a/c *X* and wrecked on 08:55 Photography 31.5.18 (Lt H.O. Ramsey/Lt R. Walker both OK, force landed near Musestre after engine seized – engine 97/WD18539). **7 AP** ex 'Z' Flt 4.6.18 and deleted 9.6.18.

B1231 (Falcon III) presentation a/c *Winnipeg*. **5 AAP** Bristol 21.12.17, allotted to BEF and despatched by air. **2 AIS** ex **1 ASD** 21.2.18 (engine 113/WD18556). **48 Sqn** dd ex 2 AIS 6.3.18 (same engine) and wrecked on 17:15 OP 17.3.18 (2nd Lt N. Roberts/Cpl T. Ramsden both OK, badly damaged by AA fire nea St Quentin and force landed – same engine). **2 ASD** ex 48 Sqn 20.3.18. **1 ASD** ex 2 ASD by rail 1.4.18. **88 Sqn** dd ex 1 ASD 8.5.18 (engine 921/WD32860) and wrecked after OP 6.6.18 (Lt G.F. Anderson/AM A.J. Loton both OK, pancaked from 5ft on landing at Cappelle – same engine). **1 ASD** ex 88 Sqn 7.6.18 and deleted 12.7.18 on reconstruction as F5997.

B1232 (Falcon III) presentation a/c *Toronto*. **5 AAP** Bristol 20.12.17, allotted to BEF and tested 24.12.17 (Lt C.F. Uwins). **8 AAP** Lympne ex 5 AAP 26.12.17 (Lt C.F. Uwins). **1 AIS** ex **1 ASD** 17.2.18 (engine 187/WD18593). **20 Sqn** dd ex 1 AIS 24.2.18 (same engine), vict 21.4.18 (Lt D. Latimer/Lt T.C. Noel sent an Albatros D.V down OOC, N of Wervicq at 11:10) then LIA on 12:00 OP 16.5.18 (Lt F.E. Boulton/Prob H.G. Holman both POW WIA, last seen crossing the lines – engine 521/WD32660) snd, deleted on unit 17.5.18 (123hr 28min).

B1233 **5 AAP** Bristol 22.12.17, allotted to BEF but reallotted to **62 Sqn (Mobilising)** 28.12.17.

B1234 (Falcon III) presentation a/c *Edmonton*. **5 AAP** Bristol 21.12.17, allotted to BEF but reallotted to **62 Sqn (Mobilising)** 28.12.17. **62 Sqn** Rendcomb, to BEF with the unit 23.1.18, victs 12.4.18 (Lt D.A. Savage/2nd Lt L.M. Thompson sent a Pfalz D.III down OOC, E of Estaires at 14:20 and an Albatros D.V down OOC over Aubers 15:15) then wrecked after successful combats on 09:10 OP 21.4.18 (Lt D.A. Savage/2nd Lt L.M. Thompson destroyed an Albatros D.V at 09:45 and a Pfalz D.III at 09:50, both W of Lille, then force landed after hit by AA fire – engine 387/WD18693). **2 ASD** ex 62 Sqn 21.4.18 (104hr 10min). **10 Sqn** dd ex **1 AIS** 17.6.18 (engine 1131/WD39458) and wrecked after Artillery Observation 10.7.18 (Lt A.A. Webster/2nd Lt W.C. Stannard both OK, blown over landing in a storm – same engine). **1 ASD** ex 10 Sqn 10.7.17 and deleted 17.9.18 on reconstruction as H7070 (126hr 5min).

B1235 **5 AAP** Bristol 22.12.17, allotted to BEF but reallotted to **62 Sqn (Mobilising)** 28.12.17.

B1236 (Falcon III) **59 TS** Lilbourne by 21.1.18 and wrecked 22.1.18 (2nd Lt H.G. Nelson KIFA, fell out at 2,000ft – engine 3/F/175/WD18689).

B1237 N/I

B1238 (Falcon III) **62 Sqn** Rendcomb dd ex **5 AAP** 10.1.18 (Lt C.F. Uwins), to BEF with unit 23.1.18 and wrecked 23.3.18 (the engine was being run up by mechanics without chocks and the machine ran along ground and o/t – engine 221/WD18610). **2 ASD** ex 62 Sqn by 1.4.18. **1 ASD** ex 2 ASD by rail 2.4.18. **1 AIS** ex 1 ASD 19.5.18 (engine 971/WD32885). **2 AIS** ex 1 AIS 20.5.18 (same engine). **62 Sqn** reissued ex 2 AIS 1.6.18 (same engine) and reported 16.9.18 as unfit for further war service (112hr 30min – engine 191/WD18595). **2 ASD** ex 62 Sqn. **1 ASD** ex 2 ASD 18.9.18 and flown to England 20.9.18.

B1239 (Falcon III) **5 AAP** Bristol 22.12.17, allotted to BEF. **1 ASD** dd ex England 7.1.18 (engine 171/WD18585). **2 AIS** ex 1 ASD 26.2.18 (same engine). To Italy and 7 Bde by rail ex **2 ASD** 2.3.18 (same engine). **28 Sqn** dd ex **7 AP** 17.3.18 and wrecked 29.3.18 (Lt W.L. Worster OK/Lt Sharp IOAS, struck electric power stand [W/T mast] near aerodrome). **7 AP** ex 28 Sqn and deleted 8.4.18.

B1240 (Falcon III) **62 Sqn** Rencomb dd ex **5 AAP** Filton 19.1.18 (Lt C.F. Uwins), to BEF with unit 23.1.18 and reported 31.5.18 as in need of overhaul (96hr 50min – engine 117/WD18558). **2 ASD** ex 62 Sqn 2.6.18. **1 ASD** ex 2 ASD and flown to England 3.6.18.

B1241 N/I

B1242 Presentation aircraft *Ajmer*. **8 TS** Witney by 16.5.18 (Sgt J. Gamble). **33 TDS** Witney.

B1243 N/I

B1244 **5 AAP** Bristol 8.1.18, allotted to BEF. **8 AAP** Lympne 15.1.18, reallotted from BEF to Training. **8 TS** Netheravon by 12.12.18. **7 TS** Netheravon by 27.2.18 (2nd Lt H.A. Oaks).

B1245 **62 Sqn** Rendcomb and to BEF with unit 23.1.18. **2 ASD** ex 62 Sqn 10.4.18 (engine 293/WD18646). **62 Sqn** reissued ex 2 ASD 21.4.18 (same engine), vict 3.5.18 (Lt H.C.M. Nangle/2nd Lt T.C. Cooper sent a Fokker Dr.I down OOC over Armentieres at 10:45) then wrecked before OP 3.5.18 (Lt H.C.M. Nangle/2nd Lt T.C. Cooper both IOAS, collided on take off with a **58 Sqn** F.E.2b which had force landed – same engine). **2 ASD** ex 62 Sqn and deleted 5.5.18 (not worth reconstruction, 55hr 10min).

B1246 **5 AAP** Bristol 9.1.18, allotted to BEF but reallotted to **62 Sqn (Mobilising)** 15.1.18. **62 Sqn** Rendcomb, despatched to BEF with unit but ditched in English Channel en route France 29.1.18 (crew rescued).

B1247 **62 Sqn** dd ex **1 AIS** 18.2.18 (engine 299/WD18649), LIA on 09:30 OP 12.3.18 (Capt D.S. Kennedy/Lt H.G. Gill both KIA, seen to go down in flames E of Cambrai at about 11:10, probably brought down by Ltn L. v Richthofen, Jasta 11 – same engine) and deleted on unit that day (19hr 5min).

B1248 **5 AAP** Bristol 10.1.18, allotted to BEF but reallotted to 6th Bde 15.1.18. **39 Sqn** North Weald by 14.2.18 until @ 6.3.18.

B1249 **8 TS** Netheravon by 2.2.18. **24 TS** Witney and damaged 2.4.18 (2nd Lt H.C. Foley OK, undercarriage broken).

B1250 (Falcon III) **62 Sqn** Rendcomb, to BEF with the unit 23.1.18, LIA on OP 12.3.18 (2nd Lt C.B. Fenton/Lt H.B.P. Boyce both POW, in combat with EA at 11:10, shot down E of Cambrai – engine 241/WD18620) and deleted on unit that day (47hr 50min).

B1251 (Falcon III) at maker's 2.1.18, allotted to BEF and to be delivered in packing case. **1 ASD** dd ex England in packing case 18.1.18 (engine 275/WD18637). **1 AIS** ex 1 ASD 26.1.18 (same engine). **62 Sqn** dd ex 1 AIS 5.2.18 (same engine). LIA on 09:30 OP

12.3.18 (2nd Lt L.C.F. Clutterbuck/2nd Lt H.J. Sparks both POW WIA, shot down in flames E of Cambrai by Ritt M Fr v Richthofen at c.11:10 – same engine) and deleted on unit that day (27hr 20min).

B1252 (Falcon III) at maker's 2.1.18, allotted to BEF and to be delivered in packing case. **2 ASD** ex England in packing case 18.1.18 (engine 333/WD18666). **2 AIS** ex 2 ASD 4.2.18 (same engine). **11 Sqn** dd ex 2 AIS 19.2.18 (same engine) and wrecked 25.4.18 (when standing on the aerodrome, the machine was struck by a **70 Sqn** Camel – same engine). **2 ASD** ex 11 Sqn and deleted 30.4.18 (not worth reconstruction, 67hr 10min). Also noted at **39 Sqn** North Weald marked as a/c *8*.

B1253 (Falcon III) at maker's 2.1.18, allotted to BEF and to be delivered in packing case. **1 ASD** dd ex England 31.1.18 (engine 361/18680). **2 AIS** ex 1 ASD 22.3.18 (same engine). **22 Sqn** dd ex 2 AIS 25.3.18 (same engine), marked as a/c *E*, victs 7.5.18 (2nd Lt J.E. Gurdon/2nd Lt A.J.H. Thornton destroyed two Fokker D.VII in flames 10 miles NE of Arras at 18:45), 9.5.18 (2nd Lt A.C. Atkey/2nd Lt C.G. Gass destroyed an EA in flames and sent another down OOC over Hille at 09:40 then two Pfalz D-types down OOC and smoking 1 mile N of Douai at 18:40), 15.5.18 (2nd Lt A.C. Atkey/2nd Lt C.G. Gass sent two Pfalz D.III down OOC, 1 smoking, over Hille at 10:20), 22.5.18 (2nd Lt A.C. Atkey/2nd Lt C.G. Gass destroyed an EA scout which hit a tree 2 miles SE of Arras then sent an EA down OOC over Armentieres-Merville at 07:10-07:30), 27.5.18 (2nd Lt A.C. Atkey/2nd Lt C.G. Gass sent two Pfalz D.III down OOC, then destroyed another shared with a **40 Sqn** S.E.5a, NE of Dns [sic] at 20:00), 30.5.18 (2nd Lt A.C. Atkey/2nd Lt C.G. Gass destroyed a Pfalz D.III in flames and sent another down OOC at 19:40) and 31.5.18 (2nd Lt A.C. Atkey/2nd Lt C.G. Gass sent two Pfalz D-types OOC over Armentieres at 10:30) then LIA on 18:00 OP 5.6.18 (Lt C.H. Dunster POW WIA/Sgt L.A.F. Young KIA, last seen going down under control towards Lestrem at 19:15 – same engine) and deleted on unit that day (88hr 35min).

B1254 (Falcon III) at maker's 2.1.18, allotted to BEF and to be delivered in packing case. **2 ASD** dd ex England in packing case 23.1.18 (engine 337/WD18668). **2 AIS** ex 2 ASD 2.2.18 (same engine). **48 Sqn** dd ex 2 AIS 4.2.18, LIA on 10:05 Reconnaissance 14.2.18 (Capt S.J. Sibley/Lt O.G.S. Crawford both POW, hit by AA fire and last seen flying east over St Quentin – same engine) and deleted on unit that day (7hr 30min).

B1255 (Falcon III) at maker's 2.1.18, allotted to BEF and to be delivered in packing case. **1 ASD** dd ex England in packing case 22.1.18 (engine 251/WD18625). **2 AIS** ex 1 ASD 3.2.18 (same engine). **48 Sqn** dd ex 2 AIS 17.2.18 (Lt Jackson – same engine), wrecked on 16:05 OP 22.3.18 (2nd Lt N.H. Muirden/2nd Lt E.S. Herring both OK, badly shot up but returned to aerodrome – same engine) and deleted that day when burnt prior to evacuation of Flez (50hr 25min).

B1256 (Falcon III) at maker's 2.1.18, allotted to BEF and to be delivered in packing case. **2 ASD** dd ex England in packing case 21.1.18 (engine 253/WD18626). **2 AIS** ex 2 ASD 9.2.18 (same engine). **11 Sqn** dd ex 2 AIS 19.2.18 (Capt Haynes) and wrecked on OP 21.3.18 (2nd Lt A.D. Shannon/Sgt B.J. Maisey both OK, crashed in forced landing in mist – same engine). **2 ASD** ex 11 Sqn 21.3.18. **1 ASD** ex 2 ASD by rail 1.4.18 and deleted 14.4.18 (29hr 18min).

B1257 (Falcon III) at maker's 2.1.18, allotted to BEF and to be delivered in packing case. **1 ASD** dd ex England in packing case 30.1.18 (engine 359/WD18679). **1 AIS** ex 1 ASD 16.2.18 (same engine). **20 Sqn** dd ex 1 AIS 10.3.18 (same engine), LIA on 15:10 Bombing, Neuf Berquin, 12.4.18 (Lt A.L. Pemberton/Cpl F. Archer both POW then interned in Switzerland for repatriation – same engine). Machine salvaged and brought back on RAF charge by 12.11.18.

B1258 (Falcon III) **59 TS** Lilbourne by 28.1.18 and wrecked 9.3.18 (2nd Lt F.W.J. Tooley IIFA, stalled during forced landing – engine 3/F/375/WD18687).

B1259 **38 TS** Rendcomb by 5.2.18. **45 TDS** Rendcomb from 15.7.18 and wrecked 16.7.18 (Lt F.A. Hewens/Lt D.M. Mc Gregor both KIFA, mis-judgement by pilot – engine WD18418).

B1260 **39 Sqn** North Weald and on HAP 29/30.1.18 (2nd Lt H.P. Lale/Lt W.N. Fraser) and on unit charge until @ 17.2.18.

B1261 (Falcon III) **39 Sqn** North Weald on HAP 17.2.18 (Lt C. Evans/AM2 Parks) and wrecked 23.3.18 (2nd Lt P.W.L. Jarvis/Lt R.J. Robbins both IOAS, force landed after engine cut – engine 3/F/371/WD18685).

B1262 Presentation a/c *Presented by Maharaja Bahadur Sir Rameswar Singh of Darbhanga No.2. The Lord of Chelmsford.* **5 AAP** Bristol 12.1.18, allotted to BEF but reallotted to 6th Bde 15.1.18. **39 Sqn** North Weald by 12.2.18 until @ 8.8.18.

B1263 **39 Sqn** North Weald by 1.18, on HAP 19/20.5.18 (Capt W.T.F. Holland/AM1 Easton) and on unit charge until @ 9.18.

B1264 **5 AAP** Bristol 12.1.18, allotted to BEF but reallotted to 6th Bde 15.1.18. **39 Sqn** North Weald and on HAPs 29/30.1.18 (Lt P.W. Deane/AM1 W. Eatock), 16/17/2.18 (Lt P.W. Deane/AM1 W. Eatock), 17/18.2.18 (Lt P.W. Deane/AM1 L. Card) and 7/8.3.18 (Lt P.W. Deane/AM1 W. Eatock) then wrecked on HAP 20.5.18 (Lt P.W. Deane/Lt Robinson both OK, crashed after fire).

B1265 (Falcon III) at maker's 8.1.18, allotted to BEF and to be delivered in packing case. **2 ASD** dd ex England in packing case 28.1.18 (engine 173/WD18586). **2 AIS** ex 2 ASD 5.2.18 (same engine). **48 Sqn** dd ex 2 AIS 17.2.18 (same engine), victs 6.3.18 (Lt R.H. Little OK/Lt L.N. Jones WIA, destroyed a Pfalz D.III over La Fere at 09:50 but machine shot up) and 8.3.18 (Lt J.E. Drummond/2nd Lt N. Sillars sent an Albatros D.III down OOC, NE of Laon at 11:00) then wrecked on 06:55 OP 28.3.18 (Lt J.E. Drummond/2nd Lt J.J. Mackenzie both OK, machine badly damaged by machine gun fire near Roye – same engine). **22nd Wing SS** ex 48 Sqn 1.4.18 (70hr 30min) presume deleted.

B1266 (Falcon III) **5 AAP** Bristol 25.1.18, allotted to BEF, reallotted to **62 Sqn (Mobilising)** 30.1.18, still at Bristol. **39 Sqn** North Weald and wrecked 17.3.18 (Lt E.J. Stockman IOAS, crashed after engine failure – engine 3/F/193/WD15596).

B1267 (Falcon III) at maker's 8.1.18, allotted to BEF and to be delivered in packing case. **1 ASD** dd ex England in packing case 5.2.18 (engine 107/WD18553). **62 Sqn** dd ex 1 ASD 16.2.18 (same engine), vict 15.3.18 (Lt A.R. James/Lt J.M. Hay sent an Albatros D-type down OOC, 5 miles SE of Cambrai at 13:35) then LIA on 16:20 Trench Strafing 24.3.18 (Lt A.R. James/Lt J.M. Hay both KIRA near Peronne – same engine) and deleted on unit that day.

B1268 (Falcon III) **5 AAP** Bristol 25.1.18, allotted to BEF. **62 Sqn** Rendcomb, to BEF with the unit 23.1.18, LIA on 09:00 OP 13.3.18 (2nd Lt N.B. Wells/Lt G.R. Crammond both POW, in combat E of Cambrai and brought down near La Terrière – engine 71/WD18535) and deleted on unit that day (32hr 25min).

B1269 (Falcon III) at maker's 8.1.18, allotted to BEF and to be delivered in packing case. **2 ASD** dd ex England in packing case 31.1.18 (engine 295/WD18647). **2 AIS** ex 2 ASD 9.2.18 (same engine). **48 Sqn** dd ex 2 AIS 21.2.18 (same engine), vict 21.3.18 (2nd Lt E.R. Stock OK/Cpl J.H. Bowler WIA, sent a LVG C-type down OOC, E of Ephey but machine shot up and force landed) and wrecked on OP 2.4.18 (2nd Lt K.W. Pope/2nd Lt W.J. Battle both WIA in combat near Viller Bretonneaux – same engine). **2 ASD** ex 48 Sqn 8.4.18. **2 AIS** ex 2 ASD 18.6.18. **62 Sqn** dd ex 2 AIS 26.6.18 (engine 1215/WD51632) and reported 1.7.18 as unfit for further service in the field. **2 ASD** ex 62 Sqn and deleted 29.7.18 on reconstruction as H7069 (80hr 15min).

B1270 **1 FS** Turnberry by 1.7.18 (Capt J.H. Letts) until @ 24.7.18. **27 TDS** Crail by 21.10.17 until @ 27.10.18.

B1271 (Falcon III) at maker's 8.1.18, allotted to BEF and to be delivered in packing case. **1 ASD** dd ex England in packing case 31.1.18 (engine 265/WD18632). **2 AIS** ex **2 ASD** 22.3.18 (same engine). **48 Sqn** dd ex 2 AIS 22.3.18 (same engine), marked as a/c *22* and wrecked 16.5.18 (when standing on the aerodrome, was run into by C4745 – engine 739/WD32769). **2 ASD** ex 48 Sqn 18.5.18. **2 AIS** ex 2 ASD 29.6.18 (engine 955/WD32877). **62 Sqn** dd ex 2 AIS 1.7.18 (same engine) and wrecked after OP 11.7.17 (Lt J.S. Tarbolton IOAS/2nd Lt N.P. Adams OK, crashed at Auchy Au Bois – same engine). **2 ASD** ex 62 Sqn 14.7.18 and deleted 18.7.18 on reconstruction as F6206 (84hr 10min).

B1272 **1 SAF** Ayr by 4.3.18 until @ 12.4.18.

B1273 (Falcon III) at maker's 8.1.18, allotted to BEF and to be delivered in packing case. **2 ASD** dd ex England in packing case 9.2.18 (engine 153/WD18576). **2 AIS** ex 2 ASD (same engine). **48 Sqn** dd ex 2 AIS 24.3.18 (same engine) and wrecked on 09:55 OP 28.3.18 (2nd Lt E.R. Stock/2nd Lt W.D. Davidson both OK, radiator and fuel tank shot through and force landed near Allonville at 11:30). **22 Wing Salvage** ex 48 Sqn 1.4.18 (8hr 5min). **1 ASD** ex **Advanced Salvage** 5.4.18 and under reconstruction by 30.4.18. **2 AIS** ex 1 ASD 18.5.18 (engine 1003/WD39394). **62 Sqn** dd ex 2 AIS 20.5.18 (same engine), vict 24.6.18 (Lt T.H. Broadley OK/Sgt F.R. Bower WIA, sent a Pfalz D.III down OOC over Lille-Carvin at 07:10-07:30 but observer hit in the arm and machine crashed landing on the dummy aerodrome at Senlecques to obtain attention for observer – same engine). **2 ASD** ex 62 Sqn 26.6.18 and presume deleted.

B1274 N/I

B1275 (Falcon III) at maker's 8.1.18, allotted to BEF and to be delivered in packing case. **1 ASD** dd ex England in packing case 5.2.18

(engine 399/WD18699). **1 AIS** ex 1 ASD 24.2.18 (same engine). **20 Sqn** dd ex 1 AIS 31.3.18 (same engine) wrecked on 14:37 OP 11.4.18 (Major J.A. Dennistoun WIA/Lt J.J. Saramanga OK, force landed within range of enemy shell fire and machine unsalvageable – same engine) and deleted on unit 12.4.18 (50hr 49min).

B1276 (Falcon III) presentation a/c *Australia No.18, New South Wales No.17. The Upper Hunter Battleplane.* To Middle East. **1 Sqn AFC** dd 22.4.18, victs 7.5.18 (Lt A.V. Tonkin/Lt R.A. Camm destroyed an EA C-type in flames SE of Jenin aerodrome at 15:15, shared B1229), damaged on OP 4.6.18 (Lt A.V. Tonkin OK/Lt R.A. Camm WIA in combat with a Rumpler C-type), further vict 11.6.18 (Lt E.G.C. Stooke/Lt L.P. Krieg destroyed an EA C-type N of Tulkeram at 06:15, shared B1229) then wrecked and burnt out in forced landing 13.8.18 (engine WD18634) and deleted on unit 16.8.18.

B1277 (Falcon III) at maker's 8.1.18, allotted to BEF and to be delivered in packing case. **2 ASD** dd ex England in packing case 9.2.18 (engine 417/WD32608). **2 AIS** ex 2 ASD (same engine). **48 Sqn** dd ex 2 AIS 8.3.18 (same engine) and wrecked on Travelling Flight 28.3.18 (2nd Lt W.L. Thomas/2nd Lt C.S. Bissett both OK, crashed on landing – same engine). **1 ASD** ex **Advanced Salvage** 4.4.18 and deleted 8.4.18 (not worth reconstruction, 40hr 50min).

B1278 (Falcon III) to Middle East. **X AP** dd ex **X AD** 27.5.18 (engine WD18570). **1 Sqn AFC** dd ex X AP 27.6.18, victs 24.7.18 (Lt G.C. Peters/Lt J.H. Trail destroyed a Rumpler C-type over Tanturah at 05:30, shared B1222), 24.8.18 (Lt G.C. Peters/Lt J.H. Trail destroyed an LVG C-type and a Pfalz D.III E of Hanuteh at 08:15) and 22.9.18 (Lt G.C. Peters/Lt J.H. Trail destroyed a DFW C-type N of Deraa at 17:00) and deleted on unit 25.1.19.

B1279 (Falcon III) at maker's 8.1.18, allotted to BEF and to be delivered in packing case. **1 ASD** dd ex England in packing case 14.2.18 (engine 431/WD32615). **1 AIS** ex 1 ASD 9.3.18 (same engine). **20 Sqn** dd ex 1 AIS 11.3.18 (same engine) and wrecked on 06:15 OP 18.5.18 (Lt T.W. Williamson OK/Cpl W.A. Foster WIA, damaged by enemy fire and crashed near Vlamertinghe – same engine). **1 ASD** ex 20 Sqn 21.5.1 and deleted 23.5.18 (not worth reconstruction, 103hr 23min).

B1280 (Falcon III) to Middle East. **1 Sqn AFC** dd ex **X AP** 20.5.18, vict 29.5.18 (Lt E.C. Stooke/Lt W.J.A Weir destroyed a Rumpler C-type in flames NE of Nablus at 08:15, shared C4623) then wrecked 19.8.18 (Lt E.C. Stooke/Lt L.P. Krieg both KOAS) and deleted on unit 21.8.18.

B1281 (Falcon III) at maker's 8.1.18, allotted to BEF and to be delivered in packing case. **2 ASD** dd ex England in packing case 15.2.18 (engine 377/WD18688). **2 AIS** ex 2 ASD (same engine). **62 Sqn** dd ex 2 AIS 14.3.18 (same engine), vict 21.3.18 (2nd Lt H.N. Arthur/2nd Lt J. Bruce-Norton sent an Albatros D-type down OOC, NW of Cambrai at 15:30), wrecked on 07:15 OP 28.3.18 (2nd Lt H.N. Arthur/Cpl J. Borwein both WIA, port aileron and controls shot away and crashed on landing – same engine) and deleted on unit that day.

B1282 N/I

B1283 (Falcon III) at maker's 8.1.18, allotted to BEF and to be delivered in packing case. **1 ASD** dd ex England in packing case 14.2.18 (engine 473/WD32636). **2 AIS** ex 1 ASD 6.3.18 (same engine). **11 Sqn** dd ex 2 AIS 12.3.18 (same engine) and wrecked after Reconnaissance 28.3.18 (Capt W.H. Park/2nd Lt J.H. Greenwood both OK, crashed landing cross wind – same engine). **2 ASD** ex 11 Sqn for repair (33hr 45min). **11 Sqn** reissued ex 2 AIS 12.6.18 and wrecked before Target Practice 26.6.18 (Major H.B. Davey MC/Capt J.S. Chick both IOAS, propeller struck the ground in partially filled shell hole, one blade broke off, machine had sufficient speed to reach 200ft but on turning to get into aerodrome side slipped and crashed – engine 345/WD18672). **2 ASD** ex 11 Sqn and deleted 27.6.18 (not worth reconstruction, 12hr 55min – presume time since reissue).

B1284 (Falcon III) to Middle East. **X AP** ex **X AD** 29.6.18 (engine WD18691). **1 Sqn AFC** dd ex Kantara 29.6.18 and victs 28.7.18 (Capt A.R. Brown/Lt G. Finlay destroyed a Rumpler C-type near Wadi Fara at 12:00, shared C4627) and 22.8.18 (Capt A.R. Brown/Lt G. Finlay captured LVG C.V 3163/17 at Ramleh at 13:15). **111 Sqn** ex 1 Sqn AFC 4.2.19. **X AP** ex 111 Sqn 9.9.19. Possibly the F.2B shipped post-war to Australia in HMT *War Capital.*

B1285 (Falcon III) presentation a/c *Australia No.7, New South Wales No.6. The White Edenglassie.* To Middle East. **1 Sqn AFC** dd ex **X AP** 30.8.18 (engine WD18691). **X AD** ex 1 Sqn AFC 12.12.18 and deleted 19.12.18.

B1286 (Falcon III) to Middle East. **X AP** dd ex **X AD** 3.9.18. **1 Sqn AFC** dd ex X AP 5.9.18 (engine WD18540) and vict 22.9.18 (Lt E.S.

Headlam/Lt W.H. Lilly destroyed an EA C-type in flames near Mafrak at 10:00, shared B1229). **X AP** ex 1 Sqn AFC 3.10.18. **111 Sqn** dd ex X AP 14.5.19 (engine WD32790). **X AP** ex 111 Sqn 25.6.19 and deleted 9.9.19.

B1287 (Falcon III) to Middle East. **1 Sqn AFC** dd ex **X AP** 5.9.18 (engine WD39399). **111 Sqn** ex 1 Sqn AFC 4.2.19.

B1288 (Falcon I) **1(Obs)SAG** Hythe and wrecked 23.10.18 (2nd Lt G.H.E. Roxburgh IIFA/Sgt H.J. Wooley KIFA, probably jammed controls – engine 1/F/589/WD12566).

B1289 N/I

B1290 (Falcon) **EAD** Grain under erection by 25.5.18. Dover 18.6.18 (for temporary Special Duty). **ECD** Grain by 20.6.18 with visits to Hendon 6.7.18 and 10.7.18.

B1291 **WT School** Biggin Hill dd 20.5.18. **Wireless School** Chattis Hill as GI airframe by 5.18 until @ 29.11.18.

B1292 **Armament School** Uxbridge as GI airframe and deleted 10.18.

B1293 (Falcon III) to Middle East. **X AD** dd ex England 2.9.18. **5 FS** Heliopolis dd ex X AD 2.11.18 (engine WD10406). **X AD** ex 5 FS 20.2.19 (same engine). **111 Sqn** dd ex X AD 24.9.19 (engine WD32809).

B1294 (Falcon III) to Middle East. **X AD** dd ex England 2.9.18. **5 FS** Heliopolis dd ex X AD 22.11.18 (engine WD10549) and deleted on unit 15.2.19.

B1295 (Falcon III) to Middle East. **X AP** and Palestine Bde dd ex **X AD** 12.10.18. **1 Sqn AFC** dd ex X AP 14.10.18 (engine WD32612) and vict 19.10.18 (Lt E.S. Headlam/Lt W.H. Lilly destroyed a DFW C-type SW of Aleppo at 10:30, shared B1229). **111 Sqn** dd ex 1 Sqn AFC 4.2.19 (engine WD18677) and deleted on unit 30.4.19.

B1296 (Falcon III) to Middle East. **X AD** dd ex England 2.9.18. **X AP** and Palestine Bde ex X AD 30.10.18 (engine WD10502). **111 Sqn.**

B1297 N/I

B1298 (Facon III) to Middle East. **X AP** and Palestine Bde dd ex **X AD** 16.9.18. **1 Sqn AFC** dd ex X AP 28.9.18 (engine WD18623). **111 Sqn** ex 1 Sqn AFC 4.2.19 and deleted on unit 24.9.19.

B1299 **5 AAP** Bristol 31.1.18, allotted to BEF and despatched 5.2.18. **8 AAP** Lympne dd 9.2.18 via Newbury & Kenley after bad weather en route (Lt C.F. Uwins) and tested 19.2.18 (2nd Lt H. Shaw). **1 ASD** dd ex England 21.2.18 (engine 381/WD18690). **2 ASD** ex 1 ASD 5.3.18 (same engine). **48 Sqn** dd ex 2 ASD 24.3.18 (same engine), LIA on 14:30 OP 10.5.18 (Lt N.G. Stransom/Pte C.V. Taylor both KIA, last seen in a spin after combat – same engine) and deleted on unit that day (73hr 20min).

B1300 Presentation a/c *Presented by Maharaja Bahadur Sir Rameswar Singh of Darbhanga No.4.* **5 AAP** Bristol 31.1.18, allotted to BEF but reallotted to **62 Sqn** 5.2.18 then, still at Bristol, reallotted to BEF 6.2.18. **8 AAP** Lympne tested 23.2.18 (2nd Lt H. Shaw) and allotment to BEF cancelled 21.3.18.

B1301 (Falcon III) **5 AAP** Bristol 1.2.18, allotted to BEF. **1 ASD** dd air ex England 19.2.18 (engine 443/WD32621). **2 AIS** ex 1 ASD 5.3.18 (same engine). **48 Sqn** dd ex 2 AIS 13.3.18, LIA on 15:05 OP 22.3.18 (2nd Lt A.C. Hore MC/Lt S.R. Parker both WIA, shot down and crashed on British side of the lines SE of Flez and unsalvageable – same engine) and deleted on unit 23.3.18 (21hr 30min).

B1302 (Falcon III) **5 AAP** Bristol 1.2.18, allotted to BEF. **8 AAP** Lympne 6.2.18, reallotted to **62 Sqn**. **62 Sqn** dd ex 1 ASD 16.2.18 (engine 451/WD32625), vict 17.3.18 (Lt G.E. Gibbons/2nd Lt S.A.W. Knights sent an Albatros D-type down OOC, NE of Cambrai at 1130-12.00) then wrecked on Practice Flight 20.4.18 (2nd Lt A. Perren/2nd Lt C. Wealthal both OK, misjudged landing and crashed – same engine). **2 ASD** ex 62 Sqn (66hr). **2 AIS** by 17.6.18. **48 Sqn** dd ex 2 AIS 26.6.18 and wrecked before OP 18.8.18 (2nd Lt Weller/2nd Lt H.C. Wood both OK, crashed on take off when trying to avoid a collision – engine 157/WD18575). **2 ASD** ex 48 Sqn 20.8.18 and deleted 23.8.18 (not worth reconstruction).

B1303 N/I

B1304 **1 (Obs) SAG** Hythe and wrecked 6.6.18 (Lt S.J. Chapman/Flt Cdt T. Mathie both KIFA, broke up in air after mid-air collision with B8922 and caught fire on the ground – engine 3/F/397/WD18698).

B1305 (Falcon III) **5 AAP** Bristol 1.2.18, allotted to BEF. **1 ASD** dd ex England by air 10.3.18 (engine 467/WD32633). **2 AIS** ex 1 ASD 16.3.18 (same engine). **62 Sqn** dd ex 2 AIS 18.3.18 (same engine), victs 23.3.18 (Capt T.L. Purdom/2nd Lt P.V.G. Chambers sent an Albatros D-type down OOC, S of Havrincourt Wood at 14:45) and 24.3.18 (Capt T.L. Purdom/2nd Lt P.V.G. Chambers destroyed an Albatros D-type in flames near Peronne at 14:30, own fuel tank had been hit and engine stopped during ground attack and the Albatros was one of six attacking the BF) then LIA on

12:00 OP 26.3.18 (2nd Lt H.N. Arthur/2nd Lt J. Bruce-Norton both OK, engine damaged by AA fire, force landed near Mailly Maillet and machine abandoned owing to the proximity of the lines – same engine) and deleted on unit 28.3.18.

B1306 N/I

B1307 (Falcon III) **5 AAP** Bristol 4.2.18, allotted to BEF. **1 ASD** dd ex England by air 5.3.18 (engine 429/WD32614). **2 ASD** ex 1 ASD 9.3.18 (same engine). **11 Sqn** dd ex 2 ASD 16.3.18 and wrecked on OP 25.3.18 (Capt H.R. Child/Lt J.P.Y. Dickey both OK, engine cut out and force landed near St Leger – 16hr 45min, same engine). **2 ASD** ex 11 Sqn and under reconstruction 18.5.18. **2 AIS** ex 2 ASD 10.6.18. **20 Sqn** dd ex 1 ASD 17.6.18 (engine 437/WD32618), vict 30.6.18 (Lt D.J. Weston/Lt W. Noble destroyed a Pfalz D.III near Wervicq and then sent two Pfalz D-types down OOC at 07:30) then wrecked on Practice Flight 8.7.18 (Sgt Aldridge OK, tail skid caught in a hole on landing – same engine). **1 ASD** ex 20 Sqn 9.7.18 and deleted 8.10.18 on reconstruction as H7172.

B1308 (Falcon III) **ES** Orfordness and wrecked 14.4.18 (Lt B.H.M. Jones/ AM1 H.H. Palmert both KIFA, lost speed on a turn and spun in – engine 111/Fal/418).

B1309 (Falcon III) **5 AAP** Bristol 4.2.18, allotted to BEF. **1 ASD** dd ex England 27.2.18 (Lt C.F. Uwins – engine 261/WD18630). **11 Sqn** dd ex 1 ASD 29.3.18 (same engine) and wrecked 4.5.18 (Lt R.K. Harrison/Sgt R.D. Mason both OK, had force landed near Rouen due to heavy mist, engine failed on attempted take off and hit a tree – same engine). **2 ASD** ex 11 Sqn 8.5.18 and deleted 31.5.18 (not worth reconstruction).

B1310 **7 TS** Netheravon by 26.2.18.

B1311 N/I

B1312 **5 AAP** Bristol 6.2.18, reallotted from 7 Bde to BEF. **8 AAP** Lympne and wrecked on Ferry Flight 28.2.18 (Lt S. Chappell fatally IIFA, stalled and nosedived in – engine WD351). BEF allotment cancelled 5.3.18 (machine destroyed by fire).

B1313 **8 TS** Netheravon by 15.2.18 until @ 4.18. **24 TS** Witney by 8.5.18.

B1314 (Falcon III) **5 AAP** Bristol 6.2.18, reallotted from 7 Bde to BEF. **1 ASD** dd ex England 7.3.18 (engine 441/WD32620). **1 AIS** ex 1 ASD 11.3.18 (same engine). **22 Sqn** dd ex 1 AIS 13.3.18 (same engine) and wrecked 23.3.18 (2nd Lt F.M. Wood OK, lost way en route to 1 **AIS**, and force landed near Boisdinghem – same engine). **1 ASD** ex 22 Sqn 25.3.18. **2 AIS** ex 1 ASD 27.4.18 (engine 725/WD32762). **62 Sqn** dd ex 2 AIS 4.5.18 (same engine) and wrecked after OP 26.5.18 (Capt H. Rees-Jones/2nd Lt C. Wealthall both OK, collided with BF C4746 while landing – same engine). **1 ASD** ex 62 Sqn 29.5.18 and deleted 24.7.18 on reconstruction as F5998.

B1315 N/I

B1316 **39 Sqn.**

B1317 (Falcon I) to Middle East. **X AD** dd ex England 2.9.18. **X AP** and Palestine Bde ex X AD 1.11.18 (engine WD10476). **111 Sqn.**

B1318 N/I

B1319 N/I

B1320 (Falcon II) **1 (Obs)SAG** Hythe and wrecked 6.3.19 (Capt T.G. Jeffries/2nd Lt J.E. Brice both IIFA, stalled on turn after crosswind take off and spun in – engine 2/F/89/WD22402).

B1321 Coded a/c *36*

B1322 N/I

B1323 N/I

B1324 **8 AAP** Lympne, tested 30.6.18.

B1325 B&C for reconditioning to J Type (s/n 6673) and ready by 9.4.25. **2 Sqn** Manston. **16 Sqn/SAC** Old Sarum by 11.27.

B1326 B&C for reconditioning to J Type (s/n 6674) and ready by 9.4.25. **2 Sqn** Manston by 1925. B&C for reconditioning (s/n 7236) and ready by 29.6.28. **PD** Ascot.

B1327 (Falcon III) **5 FTS** Sealand and wrecked 3.12.23 (Plt Off R.E. Bath IIFA, hit telegraph wires and tree when landing at Sealand).

B1328 (Falcon III) **5 AAP** Bristol by 16.2.18, reallotted from Italian EF to BEF. Bristol to RNAS Eastbourne, and force landed with engine trouble 16.2.18. **8 AAP** Lympne by 11.3.18. **1 ASD** dd ex England 11.3.18 (engine 433/WD32616). **2 AIS** ex 1 ASD 15.3.18 (same engine). **48 Sqn** dd ex 2 AIS 16.3.18 (same engine) and wrecked after OP, Lamotte, 18.5.18 (Lt F.J. Cunningham/2nd Lt H. Knowles both OK, crashed on landing – engine 649/WD32724). **2 ASD** ex 48 Sqn 19.5.18 and deleted 3.7.18 on reconstruction as F6142 (85hr 55min).

B1329 **50 TS** Spittlegate by 30.2.18. **15 TS** Spittlegate by 12.5.18 until @ 30.7.18. **33 TDS** Witney by 29.10.18 (2nd Lt G.A. Raybone) until @ 11.18. **2 Sqn** post-war.

B1330 (Falcon III) presentation a/c *Presented by Maharaja Bahadur Sir Rameswar Singh of Darbhanga No.5*. **5 AAP** Bristol by 1.3.18. **1 AIS** dd ex **1 ASD** 7.7.18. **22 Sqn** dd ex 1 AIS 9.7.18 and wrecked 23.8.18; shot down by AA crashed nr Arras 07:30 23.8.18 (Lt J.S. Tarbolton WIA/Sgt T. Hooton OK, hit by AA fire and crashed near Arras – engine 516/WD32657). **1 ASD** and deleted 27.8.18 (120hr 20min).

B1331 (Falcon III) **5 AAP** Bristol by 1.3.18. **39 Sqn**, 'E' Flt by 3.5.18 (Capt O.V. Thomas/AM1 A.T.C. Stagg), on HAP 20.5.18 (Capt O.V. Thomas/Lt Fox) wrecked 29.7.18 (Capt O.V. Thomas/ 2nd Lt A.F. Cairns both fatally IIFA, a parachute flare stuck in the RL tube and exploded, the pilot descended but overshot the landing flares and hit a hedge, then the machine caught fire – engine 3/F/289/WD18644).

B1332 **5 AAP** Bristol by 28.2.18, allotted to BEF. **1 ASD** dd ex England 9.3.18 (engine 389/WD18694). **2 AIS** ex 1 ASD 17.3.18 (same engine). **11 Sqn** dd ex 2 AIS 22.3.18 (same engine), LIA on 11:15 Reconnaissance, Albert-Some, 27.3.18; (Capt H.R. Child/Lt A. Reeve both KIA) and deleted on unit that day (11hr 15min).

B1333 N/I

B1334 **5 AAP** Bristol by 26.2.18, allotted to BEF. **1 ASD** dd ex England 9.3.18 (engine 507/WD32653). **2 AIS** ex 1 ASD 17.3.18 (same engine). **11 Sqn** dd ex 2 AIS 22.3.18 (same engine) and wrecked 31.3.18 (when parked in front of a hangar the machine was crashed into by a **59 Sqn** R.E.8 – same engine). **1 ASD** ex 11 Sqn 31.3.18 and deleted 23.4.18 (not worth reconstruction, 8hr 45min).

B1335 Presentation a/c *Malaya No.23. The Malacca*. **5 AAP** Bristol by 1.3.18. **62 Sqn**. Deleted by 25.5.18.

B1336 (Falcon III) **5 AAP** Bristol 26.2.18, allotted to BEF. **1 ASD** dd ex **5 AAP** 18.3.18 (Lt C.F. Uwins – engine 527/WD32663). **2 AIS** ex 1 ASD 20.3.18 (same engine). **62 Sqn** dd ex 2 AIS 24.3.18 (same engine), victs 12.4.18 (Sgt F. Johnson DCM/Sgt W.M. Holmes MM destroyed two Albatros D.V, one near Allenes, the other near Chemy at 14:15-14:30) then wrecked in successful combat 19.5.18 (Lt D.A. Savage MC/Lt E.W. Collis both OK, sent an Albatros D.V down OOC over Bray at 10:30 but badly shot about and force landed near Corbie, 3,000yds behind the front line, with undercarriaige torn off by barbed wire – same engine) and deleted on unit that day (50hr 45min).

B1337 (Falcon III) **8 AAP** Lympne 27.4.18, reallotted from **88 Sqn (Mobilising)** to BEF and tested 1.5.18 (2nd Lt H. Shaw). **1 ASD** dd ex England by air 4.5.18 (engine 453/WD32626). **2 AIS** ex 1 ASD 8.5.18 (same engine). **48 Sqn** dd ex 2 AIS 10.5.18, LIA on 13:00 OP 15.5.18 (Capt C.D.G. Napier MC/Sgt P. Murphy both KIA, brought down in flames near La Motte – same engine) and deleted on unit that day (22hr).

B1338 **24 TS** Netheravon by 24.3.18 and wrecked 3.4.18 (Lt E.V.N. Grant IIFA, error of judgement, no further details given).

B1339 (Falcon III) **5 AAP** Bristol 28.2.18, allotted to BEF. **1 ASD** dd ex 5 AAP 16.3.18 (Lt C.F. Uwins). **2 AIS** ex 1 ASD 20.3.18 (same engine). **62 Sqn** dd ex 2 AIS 27.3.18 (same engine), victs 12.4.18 (2nd Lt L. Campbell/2nd Lt W. Hodgkinson sent an Albatros D.V down OOC near Lille at 15:00) and 8.7.18 (Lt L. Campbell/2nd Lt P. Pilkington destroyed a Fokker Dr.I NW of Carvin at 07:15) then wrecked on Escort 12.8.18 (2nd Lt J. Appleby OK/2nd Lt N.W. Jackson IOAS, crashed in forced landing between Doullens and Frevent – engine 1285/WD51667). **2 ASD** ex 62 Sqn and deleted 10.10.18 (not worth reconstruction).

B1340 **8 TS** Witney by 22.4.18 until @ 2.6.18 (Sgt J. Gamble).

B1341 (Falcon III) **88 Sqn** Harling Road, to BEF with the unit (via St Omer) 25.4.18, LIA on 18:15 OP 21.5.18 (Lt C.G. Scobie/2nd Lt F.J.D. Hudson both KIA, last seen in combat near the sea near Ostend – engine 697/WD32748) and deleted on unit 22.5.18.

B1342 **33 TDS** Witney by 27.10.18 until @ 14.11.18 (2nd Lt G.A. Raybone).

B1343 (Falcon III) at maker's 12.2.18, allotted to BEF and to be delivered in packing case. **1 ASD** dd ex England in packing case 12.3.18 (engine 517/WD32658). **62 Sqn** dd ex **1 AIS** 30.3.18 (same engine), victs 12.4.18 (2nd Lt G.M. Hemsworth/2nd Lt A.J. Todd sent an Albatros D-type down OOC over Bois de Biez at 15:00) and 8.5.18 (Lt G.K. Runciman/2nd Lt A.J. Todd sent a Fokker Dr.I down OOC over Wytschaete at 16:30) then wrecked after OP 17.6.18 (Lt G.K. Runciman/2nd Lt A.J. Todd both OK, crashed landing in long grass – engine 181/WD18590). **1 ASD** ex 62 Sqn 18.6.18 and deleted 20.6.18 (not worth reconstruction, 104hr 35min).

B1344 (Falcon III) at maker's 12.2.18, allotted to BEF and to be delivered in packing case. **62 Sqn** dd ex **1 AIS** 29.3.18 (engine 497/WD32648) and wrecked after OP 12.4.18 (2nd Lt H.K. Spoonley IOAS/Lt J. Bruce-Norton OK, returned with engine trouble and force landed in a ploughed field – same engine). **2 ASD** ex **2 Advanced Salvage** 20.4.18. **20 Sqn** dd ex 1 AIS 17.6.18 (engine 1139/WD39462), vict 22.7.18 (Lt T.C. Traill OK/Lt P.G. Jones KIA, destroyed a Fokker D.VII in flames SE of Gheluvelt at 08:40) then LIA on 16:26 OP 3.9.18 (Lt W.F. Washington/2nd Lt K. Penrose both KIA, last seen over Havrincourt Wood – engine 533/WD32676) and deleted on unit that day (182hr 48min).

B1345 (Falcon III) at maker's 12.2.18, allotted to BEF and to be delivered in packing case. **1 ASD** dd ex England in packing case 13.3.18 (engine 531/WD32665). **62 Sqn** dd ex 1 ASD 1.4.18 (same engine) and wrecked after OP 12.4.18 (2nd Lt C.F. Whistance/Sgt C. Brammer both OK, crashed on landing – same engine). **2 ASD** ex **2 Advanced Salvage** 18.4.18 and deleted 22.4.18 (not worth reconstruction, 1hr 40min).

B1346 (Falcon III) at maker's 12.2.18, allotted to BEF and to be delivered in packing case. **2 ASD** by 1.4.18. **2 AIS** ex 2 ASD 11.4.18 (engine 543/WD32671). **48 Sqn** dd ex 2 AIS 22.4.18 (same engine) and wrecked after Reconnaissance 25.4.18 (Capt H.C. Sootheran/Lt P.A. Cockeram both OK, crashed landing at Villers Bretonneux – same engine). **2 ASD** ex 48 Sqn 26.4.18 and deleted 12.5.18 (not worth reconstruction).

B1347 (Falcon III) at maker's 12.2.18, allotted to BEF and to be delivered in packing case. **1 ASD** dd ex England in packing case 16.3.18 (engine 365/WD18682). **2 AIS** ex 1 ASD 1.4.18 (same engine). **35 Sqn** dd ex 2 AIS 2.4.18 (same engine). **9 Sqn** ex 35 Sqn 7.7.18 (2nd Lt L.H. Button/2nd Lt T.J. Fazackerley) **2 ASD**, wrecked, ex 9 Sqn 2.9.18 (same engine) and deleted that day (not worth reconstruction, 93hr 45min).

B1348 (Falcon III) at maker's 12.2.18, allotted to BEF and to be delivered in packing case. **48 Sqn** dd ex 2 AIS 27.3.18 (engine 405/WD32602) and wrecked 11.4.18 (2nd Lt A.C. Campbell/ AM1 M. Lynch both OK, engine choked on take off, force landed in soft ground and o/t – same engine). **2 ASD** ex **2 Advanced Salvage** 18.4.18 and deleted 22.4.18 (not worth reconstruction, 21hr 5min).

B1349 (Falcon III) at maker's 12.2.18, allotted to BEF and to be delivered in packing case. **1 ASD** dd ex England in packing case 21.3.18 (engine 539/WD32669). **2 AIS** ex 1 ASD 1.4.18 (same engine). **48 Sqn** ex 2 AIS 1.4.18 (same engine) and wrecked before Travelling Flight 3.4.18 (Capt C.R. Steele/2nd Lt E.H. Stanes both OK, ran into a hole on take off – same engine). **2 ASD** ex 48 Sqn 4.4.18. **1 ASD** ex **Advanced Salvage** 9.4.18 and deleted 10.4.18 (not worth reconstruction, 1hr 55min).

B1350 At maker's 12.2.18, allotted to BEF and to be delivered in packing case. **2 ASD** by 24.3.18, destroyed by enemy fire 12.4.18 and deleted that day.

2 Bristol F.2B reconstructed from spares/salvage at 1 (S)ARD Farnborough in the serial block B7731-B8230 reserved for rebuilds under the Revised Aeroplane Repair Scheme. (Various engines).

B7763 (200hp Hispano-Suiza) **1 (S)ARD** by 3.12.17, allotted to BEF and still there 8.3.18 when allotment to BEF cancelled.

B7781 (230hp BHP) **1 (S)ARD** 27.11.17, allotted to BEF. **1 ASD** dd ex England 2.2.18 (engine 5107/WD2278), tested 10.1.18 and 13.1.18 and flown back to England 2.2.18.

34 Bristol F.2B reconstructed from spares/salvage at 3 (W)ARD Yate in the serial block B8831-B9030 reserved for rebuilds under the Revised Aeroplane Repair Scheme. (Various engines).

B8914 (Arab) **3 (W)ARD** by 16.1.18, allotted to BEF. **1 ASD** dd ex Lympne 25.1.18 (engine 16291). **11 Sqn** dd ex 1 ASD 28.1.18 (same engine). **12 Sqn** attached ex 11 Sqn 2.2.18 (same engine) and wrecked 3.4.18 (Casualty Report says machine fitted with a converted Rolls Royce radiator, various connections having been soldered on but this means of attachment not sufficiently strong, engine consistently overheated and was unfit for war flying). **2 ASD** ex 12 Sqn 3.4.18. **2 Salvage Dump** 6.4.18. **2 ASD** Repair Park by 15.4.18. **1 AIS** by 11.6.18. **22 Sqn** dd ex 1 AIS 19.6.18 (Falcon III – 1129/WD39457) and wrecked on OP 10.8.18 (Lt J.J. Borrowman IOAS/Lt T.J. Birmingham OK, o/t in corn during forced landing due to pressure trouble caused by leaking tank – same engine). **1 ASD** ex 22 Sqn 12.8.18 and deleted 14.8.18 (not worth reconstruction 99hr 35min).

B8915 (Arab) **3 (W)ARD** by 9.1.18, allotted to BEF but reallotted to Controller Technical Dept for Martlesham Heath 26.1.18. **ES** Martlesham Heath 8.2.18 (performance with Arab, later CC interrupter gear trials). **1 AAP** Coventry ex Martlesham for storage 27.6.18.

B8916 Issued for BEF w/e 18.2.18. **21st Wing WT Flt** Port Meadow by 30.9.18.

B8917 Issued for BEF w/e 18.2.18. **59 TS** Yatesbury by 10.17 until @ 4.18. **1 SSF** Gosport and wrecked 25.7.18 (Lt Col R.H. Austin-Sparks KIFA, stalled on turn and spun in).

B8918 (Falcon II) issued for BEF w/e 4.3.18. **8 TS** Witney and wrecked 3.5.18 (2nd Lt A.V. Flavell KIFA/Lt L.G. Harvey IIFA, rudder jammed after engine cut while over hangar, spun, crashed on aerodrome and burnt – engine 2/63/WD22389).

B8919 Issued for training w/e 18.3.18. **35 TS** Port Meadow by 3.18 until @ 3.4.18.

B8920 Issued for training w/e 25.3.18.

B8921 Issued for training w/e 25.3.18. **35 TS** Port Meadow by 29.3.18.

B8922 (Falcon II) issued for training w/e 1.4.18. **1 (Obs)SAG** Hythe and wrecked 6.6.18 (Lt N.R. Mitchell/Flt Cdt A.G. Harries both KIFA in mid-air collision with B1304 – engine 2/F/83/WD22421).

B8923 Issued for training w/e 1.4.18.

B8924 Issued for training w/e 25.3.18.

B8925 Issued for training w/e 1.4.18. **59 TS** Rendcomb as a/c *18* by 25.6.18.

B8926 Issued for training w/e 25.3.18; flown Rendcomb to Hendon 5.6.18. **59 TS** Rendcomb as a/c *13* by 7.6.18 until @ 25.6.18.

B8927 Issued for training w/e 15.4.18. **24 TS** Witney by 28.5.18. **33 TDS** Witney from 15.8.18 until @ 27.10.18 (2nd Lt G.A. Raybone).

B8928 Issued for training w/e 25.3.18 **8 TS** Netheravon by 6.18. **33 TDS** Witney by 31.8.18 until @ 24.10.18 (2nd Lt G.A. Raybone).

B8929 **AICS** Worthy Down by 5.18 until @ 8.18.

B8930 (Falcon II) issued for training w/e 6.5.18. **7 TS** Witney and wrecked 11.5.18 (2nd Lt B.F.L. Yeoman KIFA, overshot the aerodrome, engine failed and stalled on turn – engine 2/F/WD18415).

B8931 **24 TS** Witney by 24.3.18. **33 TDS** Witney by 1.9.18.

B8932 Issued for training w/e 6.5.18. **24 TS** Witney and wrecked (2nd Lt H.C. Foley OK, undercarriage smashed).

B8933 Issued for training w/e 20.5.18. **44 TS** Waddington by 28.6.18. **21st Wing, WT Flt** Port Meadow by 30.9.18.

B8934 (Falcon) issued for training w/e 10.6.18.

B8935 (Falcon) issued for training w/e 10.6.18.

B8936 (Falcon) issued for training w/e 10.6.18. **39 Sqn** North Weald by 6.8.18.

B8937 (Falcon III) issued for training w/e 17.6.18. **1 Torpedo Sqn** East Fortune and wrecked 13.7.18, spun in on TO 13.7.18 (Lt E.F. Kerruish KIFA, stalled at 400ft after take off, entered flat spin and caught fire on impact – engine WD22443).

B8938 (Falcon) issued for SW Area w/e 24.6.18. **2 FS** Marske marked as a/c *82*.

B8940 (Falcon) issued for SE Area w/e 24.6.18.

B8941 (Falcon III) **3 (W)ARD** by 20.6.18, allotted to BEF. **1 ASD** by 5.8.18 (engine 691/WD32745). **2 ASD** ex 1 ASD 23.8.18 (same engine). **11 Sqn** dd ex 2 AIS 31.8.18, victs 4.9.18 (Lt C.R. Smythe/2nd Lt W.T. Barnes destroyed a Fokker D.VII in flames S of St Hilaire at 10:45) and 3.10.18 (Lt C.R. Smythe/2nd Lt W.T. Barnes sent a Fokker D.VII down in vertical dive NE of Cambrai at 18:00) then LIA on 14:40 Reconnaissance 14.10.18 (Sgt Mech R. McCondach/2nd Lt C.E. Wainwright both KIA – engine 1749/ WD51899) and deleted on unit that day.

B8942 **201 TDS** East Fortune and wrecked 31.10.18 (Lt J.N. Bissell/Lt E.W. Bragg both KIFA, stalled in climbing turn, sideslipped to ground and smoke bombs exploded 31.10.18 – engine 22381).

B8943 **Fleet SAFG** Leuchars by 9.19 until @ 10.19.

B8945 (Falcon II) **201 TDS** East Fortune and wrecked 11.10.18 (2nd Lt P.L. Sant IIFA in collision with Avro 504 D7637 – engine 2/F/95/ WD22469).

B8946 **45 TDS** Rendcomb and wrecked 14.11.18 (2nd Lt A.R. Webster IIFA, misjudged landing and crashed – engine WD18425).

B8947 **1 (Obs) SAG** New Romney by 31.8.18 (Sgt J. Gamble).

B8948 N/I

B8950 **45 TDS** Rendcomb and wrecked 23.10.18 (2nd Lt O.M. Smith IIFA, misjudged landing in fog – engine 264/WD32897).

300 BRISTOL FIGHTER ordered 4.9.17 under Contract No A.S.17573/17 from The British & Colonial Aeroplane Co Ltd, Bristol and numbered C751 to C1050. (275hp Falcon III or 200hp Arab). [Consecutive works' sequence nos. 3151 to 3450].

C751 N/I

C752 **2 FS** Marske as a/c *75* by 17.7.18.

C753 N/I

C754 **2 FS** Marske by 19.7.18. Hendon 24.7.18. Manston by 25.7.18.

C755 **2 FS** Marske by 17.7.18

C756 4 (Aux)SAG Marske by 4.18, unit redesignated 2 FS 29.5.18 and on unit charge until @ 6.18.

C757 2 Sqn post-war.

C758 N/I

C759 44 TS Waddington by 1.7.18. 44 TDS Port Meadow dd 20.8.18 (Lt E.H. Westmoreland) and wrecked on Fighting Practice 20.8.18 (2nd Lt J. Packer KIFA, collided with C826 and crashed near Elsfield – engine 183/WD22444).

C760 N/I

C761 (Falcon III) 24 Sqn Kenley by 4.21. 6 FTS Manston and wrecked 15.8.21 (Fg Off S.L. Marcus KIFA, tried to turn too low after engine failure, stalled, crashed and burnt out).

C762 B&C for reconditioning to J Type (s/n 6449) and ready by 5.6.24. PD Ascot. To India. AD Drigh Road. To Egypt. 208 Sqn by 10.24 until @ 9.25. Heliopolis by 12.26 until @ 8.27. Also noted at 20 Sqn as a/c B in 1925.

C763 B&C for reconditioning to J Type (s/n 6391) and ready by 15.2.24. Staff College Flt 5.24 until @ 8.27. B&C for reconditioning to DC (s/n 7171) and ready by 4.5.28. 5 FTS Sealand by 11.28 and wrecked 11.1.29 (crashed in forced landing near Hinckley).

C764 B&C for reconditioning to J Type (s/n 6406) and ready by 6.3.24. PD Ascot. To Egypt. AD Aboukir. 14 Sqn by 30.1.25 until @ 11.25.

After being reconditioned to J Type, F.2B C764 served with 14 Sqn in 1925. *(Philip Jarrett)*

C765 B&C for reconditioning to J Type (s/n 6393) and ready by 18.2.24. 12 Sqn (Training Flt) Andover by 6.24. 11 Sqn Netheravon by 1.26 until @ 9.26.

C766 5 FTS Sealand by 1.24. B&C for reconditioning to J Type (s/n 6708) and ready by 15.5.25. PD Ascot. To Iraq. AD Hinaidi. To Egypt. 6 Sqn, damaged 17.10.28 (caught fire during refuelling), repaired and flying with unit by 12.29 but wrecked 1.4.30 (force landed due to fuel shortage near Roshpina, Lake Tiberius, Egypt and reduced to produce).

C767 5 FTS Sealand by 9.23 until @ 10.24. B&C for reconditioning to J Type (s/n 6672) and ready by 28.3.25. 2 Sqn Andover by 11.25 until @ 1.26. B&C for reconditioning to Mk.III (s/n 7152) and ready by 8.6.28. E&WS Worthy Down by 9.30 until @ 10.30. RAF College Cranwell by 2.31.

C768 RAF (Cadet) College Cranwell by 9.24.

C769 N/I

C770 2 SAF Eastburn. 18th Wing ARS Hounslow ex 2 SAF 23.5.18. 29 TS Hendon dd ex 18th Wing ARS 5.8.18.

C771 ACIS Worthy Down by 6.18 until @ 7.18.

C772 ACIS Worthy Down by 6.18 until @ 7.18.

C773 N/I

C774 (Falcon III) 88 Sqn Harling Road dd ex 5 AAP 23.3.18, to BEF with unit, vict 29.6.18 (Lt W.A. Wheeler/Lt T.S. Chilton destroyed a Fokker D.VII in flames NNW Dixmude at 20:10, shared C787, C983, D8022) and wrecked after OP 21.8.18 (Lt W.A. Wheeler/Sgt C. Hill both OK, crashed on landing and reported as time-expired with 207hr – engine 731/WD32765). 1 ASD ex 88 Sqn 24.8.18 and deleted 26.8.18 (not worth reconstruction, 209hr 40min).

C775 (Falcon III) 5 AAP Bristol 30.3.18, reallotted from 88 Sqn (Mobilising) to BEF. 1 ASD dd ex England by air to 1.4.18 (engine 745/WD32772). 2 AIS ex 1 ASD 2.4.18 (same engine). 11 Sqn dd ex 2 AIS 6.4.18 (same engine) and reported 21.10.18 as unfit for further war service, being unable to keep up with formation and in need of a complete overhaul, but fit to fly the Channel (226hr 30min – engine 1599/WD518240. 2 AIS ex 11 Sqn. 2 ASD ex 2 AIS 26.10.18 and on charge until @ 28.10.18. Also noted at 59 TS Rendcomb as a/c 20 by 23.6.18(?).

C776 (Falcon III) 5 AAP Bristol 30.3.18, reallotted from 88 Sqn (Mobilising) to BEF. 1 ASD dd ex England by air 1.4.18 (engine 635/WD32717). 2 AIS ex 1 ASD 1.4.18 (same engine). 22 Sqn dd ex 2 AIS 3.4.18, vict 22.5.18 (Capt W.F.J. Harvey & Lt G. Thomson sent a DFW C-type down OOC over Merville-Estaires at 19:25) then wrecked on 07:00 OP 18.6.18 (Capt W.F.J. Harvey DFC/Lt A.P. Stoyle both OK, damaged in combat and crashed – same engine). 1 ASD ex 22 Sqn 19.6.18 and deleted 1.8.18 on reconsruction as F6406, numbered in error and became H7065 (108hr 10min).

C777 (Falcon III) 88 Sqn Harling Road, to BEF with the unit 16.4.18 and wrecked after OP 4.6.18 (Lt J.P. Findlay/2nd Lt C.T. Gauntlett both OK, air pressure failed, pancaked in a small field). 1 ASD ex 88 Sqn 4.6.18 and deleted 12.7.18 on reconstruction as F5996.

C778 (Falcon III) 88 Sqn Harling Road, to BEF with the unit 16.4.18 and wrecked on Test Flight 1.8.18 (Lt R.H. Hammer/AM1 Racine both OK, crashed on take off when a tyre burst – engine 721/WD32760). 1 ASD ex 88 Sqn 3.8.18 and deleted 6.8.18 (not worth reconstruction, 141hr 55min).

C779 (Falcon III) 5 AAP Bristol 22.3.18, allotted to BEF. 1 ASD dd ex England by air 29.3.18 (engine 713/WD32756). 2 AIS ex 1 ASD 30.3.18 (same engine). 62 Sqn dd ex 2 AIS 31.3.18 (same engine), victs 3.5.18 (Capt S.E. Gibbons/Lt S.A.W. Knights destroyed an Albatros D-type in flames at 11:10, then destroyed an EA C-type N of Armentieres). Wrecked before OP 7.6.18 (Lt R.G. Taggart/2nd Lt I.P. Aitken both OK, collided on take off with C953 – engine 225/WD18612). 1 ASD ex 62 Sqn 9.6.18 and deleted 21.6.18 (not worth reconstruction, 68hr 5min).

C780 (Falcon III) 88 Sqn Harling Road, to BEF with the unit 16.4.18, vict 15.5.18 (Lt R.J. Cullen/2nd Lt E.H. Ward destroyed an Albatros D.V over Ghistelles at 06:35) then wrecked after successful combat 18.5.18 (Lt R.J. Cullen/2nd Lt E.H. Ward both OK, sent an Albatros D.III down OOC over Zandevoorde then engine cut out at 7,000ft, glided westward, force landed on a road at 08:00 and hit telegraph poles – engine 439/WD32619). 1 ASD ex 88 Sqn 18.5.18 and deleted 7.8.18 on reconstruction as F6402, numbered in error and renumbered H7062 (30hr 35min).

C781 (Falcon III) 5 AAP Bristol 30.3.18, reallotted from 88 Sqn (Mobilising) to BEF but again allotted to 88 Sqn 4.4.18. 88 Sqn Harling Road, to BEF with the unit 16.4.18 and wrecked on Travelling Flight to 1 ASD to have WT installed 8.5.18 (Lt T.E. Duffy/2nd Lt F.A. Lewis both OK, empty cartridge case jammed tail plane controls and crashed on landing – engine 705/WD32752). 1 ASD and under repair by 25.5.18. 1 AIS ex 1 ASD 26.5.18 (same engine). 88 Sqn reissued ex 1 AIS 5.6.18 and wrecked before Escort 21.6.18 (Lt C. Findlay/2nd Lt C.T. Gauntlett both OK, took off in strong wind, engine cut out and crashed – engine 741/WD32770). 1 ASD ex 88 Sqn 21.6.18 and deleted 25.7.18 on reconstruction as F6042 (40hr 5min).

C782 (Falcon III) 88 Sqn Harling Road, to BEF with the unit 16.4.18 and wrecked after OP 16.7.18 (Lt J.W. Addison/2nd Lt R.E. Hasell both OK, crashed from side-slip when landing at Cappelle – engine 811/WD32805). 1 ASD ex 88 Sqn 19.7.18 and deleted 21.7.18 (not worth reconstruction, 105hr 15min).

C783 (Falcon III) 5 AAP Bristol 30.3.18, reallottted from 88 Sqn (Mobilising) to BEF but again allotted to 88 Sqn 4.4.18. 88 Sqn Harling Road, to BEF with the unit 16.4.18, LIA on OP 18.5.18 (Lt L.G.S. Gadpaille/2nd Lt S. Griffin both KIA, last seen in spinning nose dive near Ypres – engine 793/WD32796) and deleted on unit 19.5.18.

C784 24 TS Witney by 2.5.18. 71 TS Port Meadow by 1.7.18. 44 TDS Port Meadow and wrecked 19.9.18 (Capt F.M. Hicks/Capt P. Newhouse both IIFA, spun in during practice forced landing – engine 1/F/7/WD10528).

C785 (Falcon III) 88 Sqn Harling Road, to BEF with the unit 25.4.18, marked as a/c JP, vict 31.5.18 (Lt J.P. Findlay/2nd Lt G.W. Lambert sent an Albatros D.V down OOC over Ostend at 19:50) and damaged in successful combat 2.6.18 (Lt J.P. Findlay OK/2nd Lt G.W. Lambert WIA, sent an Albatros D.V down OOC over Ostend at 19:45 but machine shot through the longerons – engine 703/WD32751). 1 ASD ex 88 Sqn 2.6.18 and deleted 25.6.18 on reconstruction as F5824.

C786 (Falcon III) 8 AAP Lympne 27.4.18, reallotted from 88 Sqn to BEF. 1 ASD dd ex England by air 2.5.18 (engine 503/WD32651). 2 AIS ex 1 ASD 7.5.18 (same engine). 48 Sqn dd ex 2 AIS 11.5.18 (same engine), LIA on 16:35 OP 8.8.18 (Lt J.C. Nuttall POW/2nd Lt B.C. Pearson POW WIA, missing near Lamotte – engine 1101/WD39443) and deleted on unit that day (148hr 5min).

C787 (Falcon III) **88 Sqn** Harling Road dd 22.3.18, to BEF with the unit 16.4.18, victs 5.6.18 (Lt K.B. Conn/2nd Lt B. Digby-Worsley destroyed two Albatros D.V over Messines at 20:15), 28.6.18 (Lt K.B. Conn/2nd Lt B.H. Smythe destroyed a Halberstadt C-type in flames over Houthulst Forest at 20:00), 29.6.18 (Lt K.B. Conn/ 2nd Lt B.H. Smythe destroyed two Fokker D.VII over Ghistelles at 20:10, one of them shared C774, C983 and D8022) and 1.7.18 (Lt K.B. Conn & 2nd Lt B. Digby-Worsley destroyed a Fokker D.VII in flames and sent another down OOC, W of Westroosebeke at 19:45) then reported 15.8.18 as unfit for further war service but fit as instructional machine (211hr – engine 723/WD32761). **8 AAP** Lympne ex 88 Sqn 26.8.18 (same engine).

C788 (Falcon III) **5 AAP** Bristol 30.3.18, reallotted from **88 Sqn (Mobilising)** to BEF. **1 ASD** dd ex England by air 1.4.18 (engine 661/WD32730). **2 AIS** ex 1 ASD 1.4.18 (same engine). **62 Sqn** dd ex 2 AIS 2.4.18 (same engine). **2 AIS** ex 62 Sqn 10.4.18 (same engine). **62 Sqn** reissued ex 2 AIS 21.4.18 (same engine), LIA on 06:15 OP 16.6.18 (Lt J.M. Godler/2nd Lt M. Ross-Jenkins both KIA, last seen in combat over Montdidier district, probably brought down by Ltn H. Viebig, Jasta 57 – engine 963/WD32881) and deleted on unit that day (84hr 5min).

C789 (Falcon III) **5 AAP** Bristol. At or en route to **8 AAP** Lympne ex 5 AAP 3.4.18, reallotted from **88 Sqn (Mobilising)** to BEF. **1 ASD** dd ex England by air 2.4.18 (engine 579/WD32779). **2 AIS** ex **1 ASD** 7.4.18 (same engine). **48 Sqn** dd ex 2 AIS 13.4.18 (same engine), LIA on 10:40 OP 25.6.18 (Lt F. Cabburn/Sgt W.E. Lawder both KIA, last seen in combat over Foucaucourt and went down OOC in flames – same engine) and deleted on unit that day (125hr 10min).

C790 (Falcon III) **5 AAP** Bristol. At or en route to **8 AAP** Lympne ex 5 AAP 3.4.18, reallotted from **88 Sqn (Mobilising)** to BEF. **1 ASD** dd ex England by air 1.4.18 (engine 683/WD32741). **2 AIS** ex 1 ASD 7.4.18 (same engine). **62 Sqn** dd ex 2 AIS 13.4.18 (same engine) and wrecked on Gunnery Practice 20.4.18 (2nd Lt G.K. Runciman/2nd Lt H.S. Hind both OK, misjudged landing and ran into C791 – same engine). **2 ASD** ex 62 Sqn 20.4.18 and deleted 3.7.18 on reconstruction as F6093 (2hr 10min).

C791 (Falcon III) **5 AAP** Bristol 22.3.18, allotted to BEF. **1 ASD** dd ex England by air 26.3.18 (engine 735/WD32767). **2 AIS** ex **1 ASD** 27.3.18 (same engine). **62 Sqn** dd ex 2 AIS 29.3.18 (same engine), vict 1.4.18 (2nd Lt H.C.M. Nangle/2nd Lt T.C. Cooper sent an Albatros D-type down OOC over Bouchoir at 17:00) then wrecked 20.4.18, run into by C790 which was landing – same engine). **48 Sqn** dd ex 2 AIS 26.6.18 (engine 621/WD32710), LIA on 07:15 Reconnaissance 5.7.18 (2nd Lt B.S. Hillis/Sgt S.J. Pratt both KIA, shot down Guillemont – same engine) and deleted on unit that day (48hr 40min).

C792 (Falcon III) **5 AAP** Bristol 23.3.18, allotted to BEF. **1 ASD** dd ex England by air 2.4.18 (engine 765/WD32782). **2 AIS** ex 1 ASD 3.4.18 (same engine). **11 Sqn** dd ex 2 AIS 8.4.18 (same engine) and wrecked on Reconnaissance, Bray, 8.7.18 (Lt H.C.M. Nangle/ Lt L.R. Reeves both OK, force landed due to pressure trouble into long crops and ran into barbed wire fence – engine 913/WD32856). **2 ASD** ex 11 Sqn 9.7.18 and deleted 25.7.18 on reconstruction as F6217 (97hr 55min).

C793 (Falcon III) **5 AAP** Bristol 23.3.18, allotted to BEF. **1 ASD** dd ex England by air 1.4.18 (engine 673/WD32736). **2 AIS** ex 1 ASD 2.4.18 (same engine). **48 Sqn** dd ex 2 AIS 7.4.18 (same engine) and wrecked on return from forced landing 4.6.18 (Lt E.A. Foord OK/Lt J.J. Mackenzie IOAS, o/t on landing – same engine). **2 ASD** and Salvage dump 5.6.18 and deleted that day (not worth reconstruction, 85 hr).

C794 (Falcon III) **5 AAP** Bristol 22.3.18, allotted to BEF. **1 ASD** dd ex England by air 29.3.18 (engine 775/WD32778). **2 AIS** ex 1 ASD 30.3.18 (same engine). Issue for **11 Sqn** but wrecked on Ferry Flight 3.4.18 (Sgt S.J. Mitchell fatally IOAS/Sgt J.E. O'Shea IOAS, hit a bank on landing and caught fire – same engine). **2 ASD** 3.4.18 and deleted that day.

C795 (Falcon III) **5 AAP** Bristol 22.3.18, allotted to BEF. **2 AAP** Hendon ex 5 AAP 29.3.18 (Lt C.F. Uwins/Major Stapleton-Cotton). **1 ASD** dd ex England by air 12.4.18 (engine 757/WD32778). **1 AIS** ex 1 ASD 15.4.18 (same engine). **22 Sqn** dd ex 2 AIS 17.4.18 (same engine), victs 8.5.18 (2nd Lt S.H. Wallage/Lt G. Thompson destroyed a Pfalz D.III, N of La Bassee at 19:00), 15.5.18 (2nd Lt S.H. Wallage/Lt G. Thompson sent two DFW C-type OOC over La Bassee at 10.40-10.45) and 22.5.18 (2nd Lt S.H. Wallage/ Lt A.P. Stoyle destroyed an Albatros D.V and sent another down OOC at 10:30) then LIA on 07:50 OP 10.7.18 Lt H.M. Dickinson

KIA/Lt M.H.K. Kane MC POW, last seen over Merville – engine 867/WD32833) and deleted on unit that day (129hr 15min).

C796 (Falcon III) **5 AAP** Bristol 22.3.18, allotted to BEF. **1 ASD** dd ex England 1.4.18 (engine 799/WD32799). **62 Sqn** ex 1 ASD 1.4.18 (same engine), vict 3.5.18 (Lt E.T. Morrow/Lt H.E. Merritt destroyed an Albatros D-type and another EA scout S of Armentieres at 11:20), LIA on 08:15 OP 19.5.18 (Lt H.C. Hunter POW WIA/Sgt J. Lake POW, last seen near Corbie at c.10:15, probably brought down by Obltn Greim, Jasta 34b [b for Bavarian] – same engine) and deleted on unit that day (26hr 25min).

C797 (Falcon III) **5 AAP** Bristol 23.3.18, allotted to BEF. **1 ASD** dd ex England by air 29.3.18 (engine 787/WD32793). **2 AIS** ex 1 ASD 1.4.18 (same engine). **22 Sqn** dd ex 2 AIS 1.4.18 (same engine). **11 Sqn** ex 22 Sqn 2.4.18 (same engine) and wrecked on OP 29.9.18 (2nd Lt C. Johnson/2nd Lt A. Nisbett both OK, o/t in forced landing at Selis after running into wires – engine 1413/WD51731). **2 ASD** ex 11 Sqn and deleted 6.10.18 (not worth reconstruction).

C798 B&C for reconditioning to J Type (s/n 6400) and ready by 29.2.24. **2 FTS** Digby by 6.24 until @ 2.25. **NF Flt** Biggin Hill by 12.25 until @ 9.27.

C799 B&C for reconditioning to J Type (s/n 6389) and ready by 20.2.24. **5 FTS** Sealand by 7.24, in starting accident 18.7.24 and wrecked 14.9.25 (caught fire, crashed near Sealand and burnt out).

C800 **24 Sqn** Kenley by 9.22 until @ 10.22.

C801 B&C for reconditioning to J Type (s/n 6416) and ready by 14.3.24. **PD** Ascot. To India. **AD** Drigh Road. **5 Sqn** as a/c A by 10.25 until @ 7.29.

C802 B&C for reconditioning to J Type (s/n 6445) and ready by 17.5.24. **PD** Ascot. To Egypt. **AD** Aboukir. **14 Sqn** by 11.24. **208 Sqn** and wrecked 18.10.26 (Fg Off V.B. Bingham-Hall/PO W. Higgins RN both KOAS, crashed and caught fire at Moascar).

C803 **PD** Ascot. To India. **AD** Drigh Road. **Stn Flt** Quetta by 5.29.

C804 B&C for reconditioning to J Type (s/n 6593) and ready by 20.1.25. **PD** Ascot. To India. **AD** Drigh Road. **5 Sqn** by 12.25 until @ 3.26.

C805 (Falcon III) **5 AAP** Bristol 28.3.18, allotted to BEF. **1 ASD** dd ex England by air 2.4.18 (engine 655/WD32727). **2 AIS** ex 1 ASD 3.4.18 (same engine). **48 Sqn** dd ex 2 AIS 8.4.18 (same engine), vict 21.5.18 (Lt J.E. Drummond/Lt C.C. Walmsley destroyed a Fokker Dr.I, S of Combles at 18:50) then wrecked on 04:00 Reconnaissance 2.6.18 (Lt J.E. Drummond/Lt C.C. Walmsley both OK, engine cut out and crashed in forced landing near aerodrome – same engine). **2 ASD** ex 48 Sqn 4.6.18 and deleted 3.7.18 on reconstruction as F6094 (87hr 10min).

C806 (Falcon III) **5 FTS** Sealand and wrecked 12.8.24 (Plt Off H.C.M. Shaw/Plt Off C.E. Hillier both KIFA, dived in after loop or roll at 2,000ft and crashed near Sealand).

C807 (Falcon III) **5 AAP** Bristol 28.3.18, allotted to BEF. **1 ASD** dd ex England by air 2.4.18 (engine 807/WD32803). **2 AIS** ex 1 ASD 3.4.18 (same engine). **11 Sqn** dd ex 2 AIS 6.4.18 (same engine) and wrecked on Rigging Test 18.6.18 (2nd Lt D.W. Beard/2nd Lt C. Littlejohn both OK, o/t trying to avoid personnel on aerodrome – same engine). **2 ASD** ex 11 Sqn 19.6.18. **2 AIS** ex 2 ASD 28.9.18. **5 AIS** ex 2 AIS 1.10.18. **11 Sqn** and wrecked before Reconnaissance 9.11.18 (crashed after engine failed on take off – engine 15671/WD51810).

C808 (Falcon III) **5 AAP** Bristol 28.3.18, allotted to BEF. **1 ASD** dd ex England by air 2.4.18 (engine 847/WD32823). **2 AIS** ex 1 ASD 3.4.18 (same engine). **48 Sqn** dd ex 2 AIS 6.4.18 (same engine) and damaged on 18:25 OP 2.7.18 (Lt E.D. Shaw USAS/Sgt T.W. Smith both OK, machine shot through in combat – engine 881/WD32840). **2 ASD** ex 48 Sqn 5.7.18. **2 AIS** ex 2 ASD 17.10.18. **20 Sqn** and damaged 27.1.19 (Chief Mech A.P. Welton OK, broke tailskid and damaged sternpost when taxiing to hangar – engine 1643/WD51846). **2 ASD** ex 20 Sqn 28.2.19.

C809 N/I

C810 B&C for reconditioning to J Type (s/n 6397) and ready by 29.2.24. **RAE** Farnborough by 4.1.26, for Davis landing light development, and wrecked 9.11.27 (Fg Off C. Mackenzie-Richards KIFA/ Mr H.N. Green OK, became lost when returning at night from Croydon, passenger parachuted safely but pilot killed jumping, machine crashed East Grinstead, Sussex).

C811 **20 Sqn**.

C812 B&C for reconditioning to J Type (s/n 6417) and ready by 14.3.24.

C813 (Falcon III) **5 AAP** Bristol 26.3.18, allotted to BEF. **1 ASD** dd ex England 3.4.18 (engine 815/WD32807). **2 AIS** ex 1 ASD 7.4.18 (same engine). **11 Sqn** dd ex **2 ASD** 12.4.18 (same engine) and reported 22.9.18 as in need of complete overhaul (201hr – engine

1195/WD51622). **2 ASD** ex 11 Sqn 25.9.18 and deleted 12.10.18 (not worth reconstruction).

C814 (Falcon III) **5 AAP** Bristol 27.3.18, allotted to BEF. **1 ASD** dd ex England 2.4.18 (engine 837/WD32818). **2 AIS** ex 1 ASD 8.4.18 (same engine). **48 Sqn** dd ex 2 ASD 17.4.18, marked as a/c *12*, LIA on 09:40 Reconnaissance, Villers Bretonneux, 3.5.18 (2nd Lt A.C.G. Brown POW fatally WIA/Cpl A.W. Sainsbury missing – same engine) and deleted on unit that day (33hr 30min).

C815 (Falcon III) **5 AAP** Bristol 28.3.18, allotted to BEF. **8 AAP** Lympne dd ex Bristol, via Eastbourne, 2.4.18. **1 ASD** ex England 7.4.18 (engine 499/WD32649), presumed wrecked/damaged in transit, and deleted 14.4.18 (not worth reconstruction, 2hr 25min).

C816 (Falcon III) **5 AAP** Bristol 28.3.18, allotted to BEF. **8 AAP** Lympne dd ex Bristol, via Eastbourne, 2.4.18. **1 ASD** dd ex England 2.4.18 (engine 825/WD32812). **2 AIS** ex 1 ASD 7.4.18 (same engine). **48 Sqn** collected ex 2 AIS 12.4.18 but wrecked on Delivery Flight (2nd Lt R.S. Wimpenny/AM1 E. North both OK, crashed on landing – same engine). **2 ASD** ex **Advanced Salavage** 18.4.18 and deleted 23.4.18 (not worth reconstruction, 4hr 45min).

C817 (Falcon III) **5 AAP** Bristol 28.3.18, allotted to BEF. **1 ASD** dd ex England 12.4.18 (engine 863/WD32831). **1 AIS** ex 1 ASD 12.4.18 (same engine). **20 Sqn** dd ex 1 AIS 17.4.18, victs 25.4.18 (2nd Lt W. Beaver/Cpl M. Mather destroyed an Albatros D.V in flames N of Ploegsteert Wood at 19:35), 3.5.18 (2nd Lt W. Beaver/Capt N.W. Taylor destroyed an Albatros D-type SE of Ypres at 11:05) and 9.5.18 (2nd Lt W. Beaver/Capt N.W. Taylor destroyed an Albatros D-type E of Warneton at 13:25) then LIA on 16:30 OP 5.6.18 (Lt E.A. Magee/Prob R.J. Gregory both POW, last seen near Armentieres – same engine) and deleted on unit that day (88hr 19min).

C818 (Falcon III) **5 AAP** Bristol 28.3.18, allotted to BEF. **1 ASD** dd ex England 2.4.18 (engine 845/WD32822). **2 AIS** ex 1 ASD 3.4.18 (same engine). **48 Sqn** dd ex 2 ASD 10.4.18 (same engine), LIA on 03:45 Reconnaissance 26.6.18 (Lt J.E. Doe/2nd Lt A.J. Elvin both POW – engine 1035/WD39410) and deleted on unit that day (132hr 25min).

C819 (Falcon III) **5 AAP** Bristol 29.3.18, allotted to BEF, but reallotted to 6 Bde 4.4.18. **141 Sqn** Biggin Hill. **1 AIS** ex 1 ASD 7.7.18. **20 Sqn** dd ex 1 AIS 11.7.18 (engine 779/WD32789) and wrecked on OP 15.7.18 (Lt L.H.T. Capel OK/Sgt E.A. Deighton IOAS, crashed avoiding mules in forced landing at Proven after engine failure – same engine). **1 ASD** ex 20 Sqn 16.7.18 and deleted 18.7.18 (not worth reconstruction, 87hr 1min).

C820 (Falcon III) **5 AAP** Bristol 29.3.18, allotted to BEF, but reallotted to 6 Bde 4.4.18. **141 Sqn** and on HAP 19/20.5.18 (Lt E.F. Haselden/Lt R.C. Cowl). **Development Sqn, 'B' Flt** Gosport by 6.19.

C821 (Falcon III) **5 AAP** Bristol tested 5.4.18 and allotted to BEF by 6.4.18. **88 Sqn** Harling Road, to BEF with unit 16.4.18, serving when officially reallotted 27.4.18, victs 17.5.18 (Capt A. Hepburn/2nd Lt G.W. Lambert sent an Albatros D.V down OOC, E of Middelkerke at 07:45), 31.5.18 (Capt A. Hepburn/AM2 T. Proctor sent an Albatros D.V down OOC over Ostend at 19:50), 2.6.18 (Capt A. Hepburn/AM2 T. Proctor destroyed an Albatros D.V in flames over Middelkerke-Ostend at 19:35), 31.7.18 (Capt A. Hepburn/Sgt E. Antcliffe destroyed a Fokker D.VII in flames over Bethune at 12:00), 11.8.18 (Lt G.R. Ramsden/Sgt E. Antcliffe destroyed a Fokker D.VII and sent another down OOC over Combles at 11:45) then reported time-expired 31.10.18 (308hr 40min – engine 1491/WD51770). **1 AIS** ex 88 Sqn 4.11.18 and flown to England 5.11.18.

C822 (Falcon III) **5 AAP** Bristol 29.3.18, allotted to BEF but reallotted to 6 Bde 4.4.18 and tested that day (Lt C.F. Uwins). **141 Sqn** Biggin Hill in striped fuselage scheme. **2 FS** Marske as a/c *84* by 6.3.19.

C823 (Falcon III) **5 AAP** Bristol 29.3.18, allotted to BEF but reallotted to 6 Bde 4.4.18 and tested 5.4.18 (Lt C.F. Uwins). **141 Sqn** on HAP 19/20.5.18 (Lt P.J. Kelsey) and wrecked on Searchlight Practice 18.8.18 (Lt P.J. Kelsey/2nd Lt M.R. Prodger both IOAS, crashed at night – engine 3/F/339/WD18669).

C824 N/I

C825 (Falcon III) **5 AAP** Bristol 29.3.18, allotted to BEF but reallotted to **88 Sqn (Mobilising)** 5.4.18 and tested that day (Lt C.F. Uwins). **88 Sqn** Harling Road, to BEF with the unit 16.4.18 and wrecked on OP 22.6.18 (Lt G.F. Anderson/AM T. Proctor both OK, engine failed and force landed on rough ground and o/t – engine 823/WD32811). **1 ASD** ex 88 Sqn 22.6.18 and deleted 1.8.18 on reconstruction as F6400 (88hr 45min), but new serial compromised and machine given new number H7060.

C826 (Falcon III) **44 TDS** Port Meadow and wrecked on Fighting Practice 20.8.18 (Lt E.H. Westmoreland KIFA in collision with C759, crashed near Elsfield – engine 3/F/585/WD32692).

C827 N/I

C828 **33 TDS** Witney by 18.8.18.

C829 **33 TDS** and wrecked 24.8.18 (2nd Lt H.H. Wilson IIFA, stalled on slack turn near the ground and spun in – engine WD22420).

C830 **44 TDS** Port Meadow in incident 26.7.18 (AM3 T. Fox IIGA, propeller accident – engine 283/WD12548). **35 TS** Port Meadow by 1.8.18. **71 TS** Port Meadow by 3.8.18. **154 Sqn, 'C' Flt** nucleus Port Meadow by 7.8.18.

C831 **35 TS** Port Meadow by 2.8.18. **71 TS** Port Meadow by 4.8.18. **154 Sqn, 'C' Flt** nucleus Port Meadow by 7.8.18.

C832 **154 Sqn, 'C' Flt** nucleus Port Meadow from 7.8.18 until @ 10.8.18.

C833 N/I

C834 **45 TDS** Rendcomb by 8.18 until @ 9.18.

C835 **71 TS** Port Meadow by 1.6.18.

C836 **8 TS** Witney by 5.18 until @ 8.6.18 (Sgt J. Gamble). **33 TDS** Witney by 16.8.18 until @ 29.10.18 (2nd Lt G.A. Raybone). **9 Sqn** from 9.5.19 until @ 6.19.

C837 **8 TS** Netheravon by 5.18 until @ 6.18. **33 TDS** Witney by 25.8.18.

C838 (Arab) **5 AAP** Bristol and tested 26.4.18 (Lt C.F. Uwins).

C839 (Falcon III) **5 AAP** Bristol and tested 12.4.18 (Lt C.F. Uwins). **88 Sqn** Harling Road, to BEF with the unit 25.4.18, LIA on 18:15 OP 21.5.18 (Lt K.O. Millar/2nd Lt S. Davidson both KIA, last seen in combat over the sea near Ostend – engine 729/WD32764) and deleted on unit 22.5.18.

C840 (Falcon III) **5 AAP** Bristol 10.4.18, allotted to BEF and tested 12.4.18 (Lt C.F. Uwins). **1 ASD** dd ex England by air 12.4.18 (engine 879/WD32839). **1 AIS** ex 1 ASD 17.4.18 (same engine). **22 Sqn** dd ex 1 AIS 22.4.18 (same engine), marked as a/c *M* and wrecked on Wireless Practice 30.8.18 (Lt M. Goldsmith/2nd Lt H.A. Felton both OK, collided with C4706 – engine 685/WD32742). **1 ASD** ex 22 Sqn 31.8.18 and presume deleted.

C841 (Falcon III) **5 AAP** Bristol 12.4.18, allotted to BEF and tested 15.4.18 (Lt C.F. Uwins). **1 ASD** dd ex England by air 20.4.18 (engine 875/WD32837). **48 Sqn** dd ex 1 ASD 27.4.18 (same engine), marked as a/c *11* and wrecked on Travelling Flight to 2 ASD 22.8.18 (2nd Lt H. Thomas OK, crashed on landing – engine 925/WD32862). **2 ASD** and deleted 19.9.18 (not worth reconstruction).

C842 (Falcon III) **5 AAP** Bristol 10.4.18, allotted to BEF. **1 ASD** dd ex England by air 18.4.18 (engine 867/WD32833). **1 AIS** ex 1 ASD 22.4.18 (same engine). **22 Sqn** dd ex 2 AIS 30.4.18 (same engine), marked as a/c *K*, vict 26.5.18 (2nd Lt W.F.J. Harvey/Lt G. Thomson sent a Pfalz D.III down OOC over Armentieres-Lille at 19:30-19:45) then wrecked in combat 4.7.18 (Lt I.O. Steed/2nd Lt W.A. Cowie both OK, radiator shot through and force landed near Barbure at 19:10 – engine 991/WD32895). **1 ASD** ex 22 Sqn 6.7.18 and deleted 8.10.18 on reconstruction as H7173.

C843 (Falcon III) **5 AAP** Bristol 10.4.18, allotted to BEF and tested 12.4.18 (Lt C.F. Uwins). **1 ASD** dd ex England by air 20.4.18 (engine 877/WD32838). **1 AIS** ex 1 ASD 22.4.18 (same engine). **20 Sqn** dd ex 1 AIS 15.5.18, victs 19.5.18 (Lt W.M. Thomson [Canadian]/Lt G.H. Kemp destroyed a Pfalz D.III which crashed on a house in Estaires at 10:30-10:45), 21.5.18 (Lt W.M. Thomson/Lt G.H. Kemp destroyed an Albatros D.V near Warneton at 08:35), 22.5.18 (Lt W.M. Thomson/Lt G.H. Kemp sent an Albatros D.V down OOC over Warneton at 18:40), 29.5.18 (Lt W.M. Thomson/Lt G.H. Kemp sent an Albatros D.V down OOC over Bac-St Maur at 18:30), 31.5.18 (Lt W.M. Thomson/Lt G.H. Kemp destroyed a Pfalz D.III near Bois Grenier at 18:50 and sent an Albatros D.V down OOC over Armentieres at 18:55), damaged in successful combat 1.6.18 (Lt W.M. Thomson OK/Lt G.H. Kemp KIA, destroyed two Pfalz D.III, NW of Comines at 06:30-06:35, then attacked from the rear by an Albatros), further victs 9.6.18 (Lt W.M. Thomson/Prob F.J. Ralphs destroyed Pfalz D.III over Comines-Houthem at 09:45), 17.6.18 (Lt W.M. Thomson/Prob F.J. Ralphs sent a Fokker D.VII down OOC over Boesinghe at 07:45, shared C987), 2.7.18 (Lt E.N. Sweeney/Prob C.G. Boothroyd destroyed a Fokker D.VII between Dadizeele and Gheluwe at 08:40), 19.7.18 (Lt W.M. Thomson/Sgt J.D.C. Summers destroyed a Fokker Dr.I, S of Gheluvelt at 08:45), 25.7.18 (Lt W.M. Thomson/Sgt J.D.C. Summers destroyed a Fokker D.VII over Gheluvelt at 08:55 and sent another down in flames NW of Comines, shared C4672, C4718) then wrecked on OP 1.9.18 (Lt F.E. Finch/Prob E.S. Harvey both OK, crashed near Villers Carbonel at 15:33 due to enemy action and abandoned under shell fire – engine 1587/WD51818) and deleted on unit that day (236hr 19min).

C844 **5 AAP** Bristol and tested 12.4.18, 14.4.18, 15.4.18, 18.4.18 and 19.4.18 (all Lt C.F. Uwins).

C845 (Falcon III) **5 AAP** Bristol 11.4.18, allotted to BEF and tested 12.4.18 (Lt C.F. Uwins). **1 ASD** dd ex England by air 20.4.18 (engine 831/WD32815). **2 AIS** ex 1 ASD 22.4.18 (same engine). **11 Sqn** dd ex 2 AIS 25.4.18, LIA after successful combat on 15:40 OP 15.5.18 (Lt H.W. Sellars MC KIA/Lt C.C. Robson MC POW, sent a Fokker Dr.I down OOC over Mametz at 17:20, shared C4882, then shot down over Bouchou – same engine) and deleted on unit that day (26hr 52min).

C846 (Falcon III) **5 AAP** Bristol 11.4.18, allotted to BEF. **1 ASD** dd ex England 20.4.18 (engine 881/WD32840). **2 AIS** ex 1 ASD 22.4.18 (same engine). **48 Sqn** dd ex 2 AIS 27.4.18 (same engine) and wrecked on 05:15 OP 8.8.18 (Lt J.C. Nuttall/2nd Lt B.C. Pearson both OK, force landed in low mist – engine 1001/WD39393). **2 ASD** ex 48 Sqn 11.8.18 and deleted 24.9.18 (213hr 10min).

C847 (Falcon III) **5 AAP** Bristol and tested 13.4.18 and 14.4.18 (both Lt C.F. Uwins). **141 Sqn** and wrecked on Searchlight Practice 8.5.18 (2nd Lt E.J. Ralli fatally IIFA, cause not apparent – engine 3/F/889/WD32844).

C848 **8 TS** Witney by 16.6.18 (Sgt J. Gamble).

C849 (Falcon III) **5 AAP** Bristol and tested 14.4.18 (Lt C.F. Uwins). **1 ASD** by 31.8.18 (engine 1071/WD39428). **1 AIS** ex 1 ASD 4.9.18. **48 Sqn** dd ex 1 AIS 9.9.18 and wrecked after OP 14.10.18 (2nd Lt W. Saunders/2nd Lt H.G. Lewis both OK, crashed on landing due to flat tyre – engine 1547/WD51798). **1 ASD** and deleted 18.10.18 (not worth reconstruction).

C850 (Falcon III) **5 AAP** Bristol 13.4.18, allotted to BEF and tested 19.4.18 (Lt C.F. Uwins). **1 ASD** dd ex England 22.4.18 (engine 777/WD32788). **1 AIS** ex 1 ASD 25.4.18 (same engine). **20 Sqn** dd ex 1 AIS 1.5.18 (same engine), vict 31.5.18 (Lt E. Lindup MC/Sgt E.A. Deighton destroyed a Pfalz D.III, S of Armentieres at 18:50) then LIA on 07:49 OP 2.7.18 (Lt B.T. Davidson/Sgt J. Helsby both KIA, last seen over Halluin, probably brought down by Jasta 56 pilot – engine 245/WD18622) and deleted on unit that day (128hr 9min).

C851 **5 AAP** Bristol and tested 15.4.18 (Lt C.F. Uwins). **141 Sqn** with vict on HAP 19/20.5.18 (Lt E.E. Turner/Lt H.B. Barwise both OK, brought down a Gotha near Frinsted).

C852 (Falcon III) **5 AAP** Bristol 13.4.18, allotted to BEF and tested 20.4.18. **1 ASD** dd ex England 22.4.18 (engine 641/WD32720). **1 AIS** ex 1 ASD 25.4.18 (same engine). **88 Sqn** dd ex 1 AIS 29.4.18 (same engine), victs 30.7.18 (Lt H.R. Little/Lt F.W. Addison sent one EA down OOC and destroyed another near Don at 10:30) then LIA on 16:55 OP 14.8.18 (Lt A.R. Stedman/2nd Lt G.R. Howard both POW, last seen in combat at 17:45 and to go down vertically near the Amiens-St Quentin road – engine 689/WD32744) and deleted on unit 15.8.18.

C853 **141 Sqn** Biggin Hill.

C854 N/I

The history of F.2B C854 is unknown, but here it is as '20' in an as yet undetermined unit, with an apparently enlarged fin and rudder. *(Philip Jarrett)*

C855 (Falcon III) **5 AAP** Bristol 15.4.18, allotted to BEF. **1 ASD** dd ex England 22.4.18 (engine 947/WD32873). **48 Sqn** dd ex 1 ASD 25.4.18 (same engine), LIA on 13:00 OP, Lamotte, 15.5.18 (2nd Lt C.E. Glover/2nd Lt J.C. Fitton both KIA, last seen in a spin with two EA on tail – same engine) and deleted on unit that day (29hr).

C856 (Falcon III) **5 AAP** Bristol 15.4.18, allotted to BEF and tested 15.4.18 (Lt C.F. Uwins). **1 ASD** dd ex England 20.4.18 (engine

753/WD32776). **1 AIS** ex 1 ASD 25.4.18 (same engine). **20 Sqn** dd ex 1 AIS 3.5.18 (same engine), victs 8.5.18 (Lt D. Latimer/Lt T.C. Noel MC destroyed an Albatros D.V on flames SE of Wervicq at 13:20 and then destroyed one Fokker Dr.I in flames and sent two more down OOC over Comines-Wervicq at 16:40), 14.5.18 (Lt D. Latimer/Lt T.C. Noel MC destroyed one Albatros D.V and captured another near Wervicq-Zillebeke at 18:50), 15.5.18 (Lt D. Latimer/Lt T.C. Noel MC sent a Pfalz D.III down OOC, NW of Lille at 10:45 and destroyed a Fokker Dr.I over Comines-Ypres at 11:15), 18.5.18 (Lt D. Latimer/Lt T.C. Noel MC destroyed a Pfalz D.III over Comines at 07:00 then destroyed a Pfalz D.III NE of Nieppe Forest at 11:40 and sent another down OOC over Merville at 11:45), 20.5.18 (Lt D. Latimer/Lt T.C. Noel MC were separated from the formation and attacked by three Albatros D.V, one was shot down in flames, another sent OOC, NE of Moorseele at 10:30 and upon linking up with two of the formation, they were joined by an Albatros which on realising its mistake dived down, followed by the formation to land and overturn), 22.5.18 (Capt T.P. Middleton/Lt A. Mills destroyed a LVG C-type between Wytschaete and St Eloi at 07:05) and wrecked after successful combat 29.5.18 (Lt T.C. Traill/2nd Lt P.G. Jones sent a Fokker Dr.I down OOC, W of Armentieres at 18:40, but machine damaged in the combat crashed near the aerodrome – same engine). **1 ASD** ex 20 Sqn 30.5.18 and deleted 1.6.18 (not worth reconstruction, 70hr 16min).

C857 **5 AAP** Bristol and tested 18.4.18 (Lt C.F. Uwins). **8 TS** Netheravon by 16.1.18 until @ 19.1.18. **7 TS** Netheravon and wrecked 15.2.18 (2nd Lt H.C. Little IIGA, crashed into by a landing machine whilst stationary – engine 417/WD15751). **ACIS** Worthy Down by 6.18.

C858 **5 AAP** Bristol and tested 24.4.18 (Lt C.F. Uwins). **141 Sqn** Biggin Hill by 9.18.

C859 (Falcon III) **5 AAP** Bristol 15.4.18, allotted to BEF. **1 ASD** dd ex England 22.4.18 (engine 887/WD32843). **1 AIS** ex 1 ASD 1.5.18 (same engine). **20 Sqn** dd ex 1 AIS 4.5.18 (same engine), vict 14.5.18 (Lt W.M. Thomson/2nd Lt G.H. Kemp destroyed an Albatros D.V over Wervicq-Zillebeke at 18:45), 17.5.18 (Lt W.M. Thomson/2nd Lt G.H. Kemp destroyed an Albatros D.V and sent another down OOC over Armentieres at 08:15), 18.5.18 (Lt W.M. Thomson/2nd Lt G.H. Kemp sent a Pfalz D.III down OOC, S of Merville at 11:40), 19.5.18 (Lt A.T. Iaccaci/AM1 A. Newlands destroyed a Fokker Dr.I, S of Vieux Berquin at 10:40) then LIA on 17:45 OP 31.7.18 (Lt W.H. Shell/Sgt J.D.C. Summers both POW, last seen SE of Merville and probably brought down by Obltn H. Auffort, Jasta 18 – engine 387/WD18693) and deleted on unit 2.8.18 (192hr 6min).

C860 **ACIS** Worthy Down by 6.18.

C861 **5 AAP** Bristol and tested 19.4.18 and 23.4.18 (Lt C.F. Uwins). **Artillery Co-operation Sqn** and wrecked 22.7.18 (Capt P.G.K. Bridgewood IIFA/Major R.J. Lowcock KIFA, crashed at Tilshead through error of judgement – engine 64).

C862 N/I

C863 **141 Sqn** and on HAP 19/20.5.18 (2nd Lt A.K. Bamber/2nd Lt R.G. Barker). **1 ASD** dd ex England 27.8.18. **1 AIS** ex 1 ASD 13.9.18 (engine 849/WD32824). **1 ASD** ex 1 AIS 22.9.18, destroyed in enemy bombing of Marquise 23.9.18 and deleted that day (143hr 25min).

C864 **5 AAP** Bristol and tested 18.4.18 and 19.4.18 (Lt C.F. Uwins).

C865 N/I

C866 (Falcon III) **5 AAP** Bristol 15.4.18, allotted to BEF, tested 18.4.18 (Lt C.F. Uwins) and despatched by air. **1 ASD** dd ex England 1.5.18 (engine 941/WD32870). **2 AIS** 7.5.18 (same engine). **62 Sqn** dd ex 2 AIS 7.5.18 (same engine) and wrecked before OP 4.9.18 (Lt J.W. Parsons/2nd Lt P. Pilkington both OK, crashed when engine failed on take off – engine 517/WD32658). **2 ASD** ex 62 Sqn, via **9 AP**, and deleted 15.9.18 (not worth reconstruction, 121hr 30min).

C867 (Falcon III) **5 AAP** Bristol 15.4.18, allotted to BEF. **1 ASD** dd ex England 25.4.18 (engine 917/WD32858). **11 Sqn** dd ex 1 ASD 27.4.18 (same engine), victs 15.5.18 (Capt J.P. Seabrook/2nd Lt C. Wrigglesworth sent a Pfalz D.III down OOC, SE of Albert at 17:22) and 16.5.18 (Capt J.P. Seabrook/2nd Lt C. Wrigglesworth destroyed an EA C-type E of Cambrai at 06:35) then reported 29.9.18 as in need of complete overhaul (214hr 20min – engine 1543/WD51796). **2 ASD** ex 11 Sqn, 1 ASD ex 2 ASD 3.10.18 and flown to England 7.10.18.

C868 Reconstructed as H7196 20.10.18.

C869 (Falcon III) **5 AAP** Bristol 15.4.18, allotted to BEF and tested 19.4.18 (Lt C.F. Uwins). **1 ASD** dd ex England 25.4.18 (engine 937/WD32868). **11 Sqn** dd ex 1 ASD 27.4.18 (same engine) and wrecked on Reconnaissance 2.5.18 (Lt R.F. Mullins/Lt H.M. Stewart both OK, hit ditch during forced landing in heavy mist near Beauvais – same engine). **2 ASD** ex 11 Sqn 2.5.18 and deleted 15.5.18 (not worth reconstruction).

C870 (Falcon III) **5 AAP** Bristol 20.4.18, allotted to BEF and tested 22.4.18 (Lt C.F. Uwins). **1 ASD** dd ex England 27.4.18 (engine 899/WD32849). **1 AIS** ex 1 ASD 2.5.18 (same engine). **88 Sqn** dd ex 1 AIS 8.5.18 (same engine) and wrecked on 17:00 OP 8.8.18 (Lt H.R. Little/Pte1 W.J. Spaulding both OK, damaged by AA fire – engine 795/WD32797). **1 ASD** ex 88 Sqn 11.8.18 and deleted 24.1.19 on reconstruction as H7169.

C871 (Falcon III) **5 AAP** Bristol 15.4.18, allotted to BEF. **1 ASD** dd ex England by air 28.4.18 (engine 951/WD32875). **2 AIS** ex 1 ASD 16.5.18 (same engine). **48 Sqn** dd ex 2 AIS 17.5.18 (same engine), LIA on 09:25 OP 30.5.18 (2nd Lt W.B. Yuille/2nd Lt W.D. Davidson both KIA brought down in flames near Bois de Senecat – engine 761/WD32780) and deleted on unit that day (26hr 10min).

C872 (Falcon III) **5 AAP** Bristol 20.4.18, allotted to BEF and tested 27.4.18 (Lt C.F. Uwins). **1 ASD** dd ex England by air 27.4.18 (engine 913/WD32856). **2 AIS** ex 1 ASD 29.4.18 (same engine). **11 Sqn** dd ex 2 AIS 6.5.18 (same engine) and wrecked before Reconnaissance 16.6.18 (Lt E.N. Underwood OK/2nd Lt E.F. Boyce IOAS, Engine, cut out just after take off, landed in long grass and o/t – engine 481/WD32640). **2 ASD** ex 11 Sqn 16.6.18 and deleted 3.7.18 on reconstruction as F6118 (69hr 5min).

C873 (Falcon III) **1 ASD** dd ex England by air 27.4.18 (engine 367/WD18663). **2 AIS** ex 1 ASD 1.5.18 (same engine). **20 Sqn** dd ex 2 AIS 4.5.18 (same engine) and wrecked after OP 6.7.18 (Lt G.H. Zellers/Cpl Hill both OK, damaged in bad landing – same engine). **1 ASD** ex 20 Sqn 7.7.18 and deleted 10.7.18 (not worth reconstruction, 119hr 45min).

C874 (Falcon III) **5 AAP** Bristol 18.4.18, allotted to BEF and tested 19.4.18 (Lt C.F. Uwins). **1 ASD** dd ex England by air 25.4.18 (engine 927/WD32863). **2 AIS** ex 1 ASD 27.4.18 (same engine). **62 Sqn** dd ex 2 AIS 4.5.18 (same engine), victs 22.5.18 (Capt W.E. Staton MC/Lt J.R. Gordon MC destroyed a LVG C-type N of L'Aventie at 08:00) and 29.5.18 (Capt W.E. Staton MC/Lt J.R. Gordon MC sent a LVG C-type down OOC over Aubigny at 19:15) then wrecked on Test Flight 1.7.18 (Capt W.E. Staton MC & 2nd Lt P. Pilkington both OK, turned on nose when landing – same engine). **2 ASD** ex 62 Sqn for repair. **2 AIS** ex 2 ASD 17.9.18 (engine 1163/WD51606). **20 Sqn** dd ex 2 AIS 25.9.18 (same engine) and wrecked on OP 20.9.18 (Lt P. Seagrave/2nd Lt A. Allen both OK, force landed near Equancourt after engine trouble – same engine). **2 ASD** and deleted 23.10.18 (not worth reconstruction).

C875 **5 AAP** Bristol and tested 22.4.18, 24.4.18 and 25.4.18 (Lt C.F. Uwins). **141 Sqn** and on HAP 19/20.5.18 (Lt H. Slingsby).

C876 (Falcon III) **48 Sqn** dd ex **2 ASD** 10.7.18 (engine 943/WD32871), LIA on 08:15 OP 8.8.18 (2nd Lt B.E. Sharwood-Smith/2nd Lt J.N. Kier both OK, machine caught alight due to bullet in rear tank, crashed near Bonnay and destroyed by fire – engine 1145/WD39465) and deleted on unit 9.8.18 (118hr 35min).

C877 (Falcon III) **5 AAP** Bristol 20.4.18, allotted to BEF and tested 23.4.18 and 24.4.18 (Lt C.F. Uwins). **8 AAP** Lympne dd via Eastbourne 29.4.18. **1 ASD** dd ex England by air 1.5.18 (engine 869/WD32834). **2 AIS** ex 1 ASD 12.5.18 (same engine). **48 Sqn** dd ex 2 AIS 15.5.18 (same engine), LIA on OP 27.6.18 (1st Lt J.M. Goad USAS/Sgt C. Norton both KIA, brought down in flames during combat over Villers Bretonneux – same engine) and deleted on unit that day (76hr 50min).

C878 (Falcon III) **5 AAP** Bristol 22.4.18, allotted to BEF and tested 23.4.18 (Lt C.F. Uwins). **1 ASD** dd ex England by air 27.4.18 (engine 939/WD32869). **2 AIS** ex 1 ASD 29.4.18 (same engine). **11 Sqn** dd ex 2 AIS 6.5.18 (same engine), LIA on 07:00 Reconnaissance, Cambrai-Le Cateau, 16.9.18 (2nd Lt L. Arnott/2nd Lt G.L. Bryars both KIA, shot down over Fontaine at 08:45 – same engine) and deleted on unit that day (157hr 14min).

C879 (Falcon III) **5 AAP** Bristol 22.4.18, allotted to BEF. **1 ASD** dd ex England by air 3.5.18 (engine 911/WD32855). **1 AIS** ex 1 ASD 9.5.18 (same engine). **88 Sqn** dd ex 1 AIS 19.5.18 (same engine) and wrecked on OP 2.6.18 (Lt J.L. Des Lauriers & 2nd Lt West both OK, crashed in forced landing on Petite Synthe aerodrome – same engine). **1 ASD** ex 88 Sqn 2.6.18 and deleted 8.6.18 (not worth reconstruction, 30hr 50min).

C880 **141 Sqn** Biggin Hill and wrecked 22.9.18 (Flt Cdt J.A. Jenkins/2nd Lt B.C. MacDougall both KIFA, stalled on climbing turn and spun in – engine WD22409).

C881 **20 Sqn.**

C882 (Falcon III) **5 AAP** Bristol 22.4.18, allotted to BEF and tested 24.4.18 (Lt C.F. Uwins). **1 ASD** dd ex England by air 1.5.18 (engine 969/WD32884). **1 AIS** ex 1 ASD 6.5.18 (same engine). **88 Sqn** dd ex 1 AIS 19.5.18 (same engine) and wrecked on OP 8.6.18 (Lt R.J. Cullen/2nd Lt F.A. Lewis both OK, longeron shot through by AA fire – same engine). **1 ASD** ex 88 Sqn 8.6.18 and deleted 24.7.18 on reconstruction as F6040 (44hr 55min).

C883 (Falcon III) **5 AAP** Bristol 24.4.18, allotted to BEF and tested 26.4.18 (Lt C.F. Uwins). **1 ASD** dd ex England by air 1.5.18 (engine 865/WD32832). **2 AIS** ex 1 ASD 7.5.18 (same engine). **48 Sqn** dd ex 2 AIS 8.5.18 (same engine), victs 21.5.18 (2nd Lt H.A. Oaks/2nd Lt C.S. Bissett sent a Fokker Dr.I down OOC over Carnoy-Mericourt and destroyed another 1 mile E of Mericourt), 25.6.18 (2nd Lt H.A. Oaks/2nd Lt G.J. Maynard sent a Fokker D.VII down OOC over Foucaucourt-Rosieres at 11:45) then wrecked after successful combats 2.7.18 (Capt H.A. Oaks/Lt G.J. Maynard both OK, destroyed two Pfalz D.III over Foucaucourt at 07:45 and Soyecourt at 08:40, the second one shared, but crashed on landing – engine 951/WD32875). **2 ASD** ex **48 Sqn** 4.7.18. **2 AIS** ex 2 ASD 29.10.18. Collected ex **2 AIS** by 11 Sqn 9.11.18 wrecked on Delivery Flight (2nd Lt D.A. Curtis OK, crashed in forced landing in rain at Lesdain – engine 529/WD32664).

C884 **5 AAP** Bristol and tested 26.4.18 (Lt C.F. Uwins).

C885 **5 AAP** Bristol and tested 29.4.18 (Lt C.F. Uwins).

C886 (Falcon III) **5 AAP** Bristol 24.4.18, allotted to BEF and tested 25.4.18 (Lt C.F. Uwins). **1 ASD** dd ex England by air 1.5.18 (engine 925/WD32862). **2 AIS** ex 1 ASD 8.5.18 (same engine). **62 Sqn** dd ex 2 AIS 9.5.18 (same engine) and wrecked on 12:25 Line Patrol 16.5.18 (Lt J.A. Chubb/2nd Lt E. Dumville both OK, force landed near Picquigny after hit by gunfire – same engine). **2 ASD** ex 62 Sqn 16.5.18. **48 Sqn** dd ex 2 ASD 24.7.18 (engine 311/WD18548), destroyed in enemy bombing attack on Bertangles aerodrome 24.8.18 (same engine) and deleted on unit 25.8.18.

C887 (Falcon III) **5 AAP** Bristol and tested 27.4.18 (Lt C.F. Uwins). **141 Sqn** Biggin Hill by 27.5.18. **1 ASD** by 31.8.18 (engine 851/WD32825). **1 AIS** ex 1 ASD 6.9.18 (same engine). **22 Sqn** dd ex **2 AIS** 17.9.18 and werecked on Travelling Flight to new aerodrome 22.11.18 (Lt L.N. Capel KOAS, crashed near Bettignies due to diving through thick fog – engine 1189/WD51619) and presume deleted on unit.

C888 **5 AAP** Bristol and tested 28.4.18 (Lt C.F. Uwins). **15 TS** Spittlegate by 16.5.18.

C889 (Falcon III) **5 AAP** Bristol 24.4.18, allotted to BEF and tested 28.4.18 (Lt C.F. Uwins). **1 ASD** dd ex England 2.5.18 (engine 981/WD32890). **1 AIS** ex 1 ASD 6.5.18 (same engine). **20 Sqn** dd ex 1 AIS 14.5.18 (same engine), victs 27.5.18 (Capt W. Beaver MC/Sgt E.A. Deighton DCM destroyed an Albatros D.V, NE of Armentieres then sent a Fokker Dr.I down OOC and destroyed another NE of Perenchies at 11.25-11.35), 29.5.18 (Capt W. Beaver MC/Sgt E.A. Deighton DCM destroyed a Fokker Dr.I near the river at Bac St Maur at 18:25) and 13.6.18 (Capt W. Beaver MC/Sgt E.A. Deighton DCM sent an Albatros D.V down OOC, NW of Armentieres at 08:00) then wrecked 29.6.18 (Casualty Report says machine caught fire, cause unknown, and a court of enquiry was to be held; it was thought that a falling tool had caused a spark and ignited spilt petrol – same engine). **1 ASD** ex 20 Sqn 2.7.18 and deleted 4.7.18 (not worth reconstruction, 51hr 23min).

C890 (Falcon II) **5 AAP** Bristol and tested 26.4.18 (Lt C.F. Uwins). **36 Sqn, 'A' Flt** and wrecked 24.10.18 (2nd Lt H. Croudace OK, Cpl E. Banks IIFA, engine choked at 70ft on take off, attempted to turn back, sideslipped, dived in – engine RR2/352/WD18453).

C891 **59 TS** Rendcomb as a/c 21 by 28.6.18.

C892 (Falcon III) **5 AAP** Bristol 1.5.18, allotted to BEF and tested 3.5.18 (Lt C.F. Uwins). **1 ASD** dd ex England 5.5.18 (engine 897/WD32848). **1 AIS** ex 1 ASD 7.5.18 (same engine). **20 Sqn** dd ex 1 AIS 19.5.18 (same engine) and wrecked on Practice Flight 4.8.18 (Lt F.S. Williams OK, hit a ridge on landing, bounced about 6ft, stalled and crashed – engine 1139/WD39426). **1 ASD** ex 20 Sqn 6.8.18 and deleted 8.8.18 (not worth reconstruction, 182hr 10min).

C893 N/I

C894 **AICS** Worthy Down by 6.18 and wrecked 31.8.18 (Lt A.J. Tremblay KIFA/2nd Lt S.R. Elworthy fatally IIFA, stalled at 30ft on downwind turn and dived in – engine WD22412).

C895 (Falcon III) **5 AAP** Bristol 30.4.18, allotted to BEF and tested 1.5.18 (Lt C.F. Uwins). **1 ASD** dd ex England by air 7.5.18 (engine 895/WD32847). **2 AIS** ex 1 ASD 12.5.18 (same engine). **62 Sqn** dd ex 2 AIS 20.5.18 (same engine), wrecked after successful combats on 06:05 OP 22.8.18 (Capt E.T. Morrow WIA/2nd Lt L.M. Thompson OK, sent a Fokker D.VII down OOC and destroyed another in flames over Pronville at 07:45 but petrol tank shot through, force landed near Ficheux and machine caught fire and burnt out – engine 1553/WD51801) and deleted on unit that day (114hr 45min).

C896   N/I

C897   (Falcon I) **5 AAP** Bristol and tested 3.5.18 (Lt C.F. Uwins). **44 TS** Waddington by 12.5.18 until @ 26.6.18, but also noted at **71 TS** Port Meadow by 13.6.18. **35 TS** Port Meadow by 27.7.18. **44 TDS** Port Meadow and wrecked 30.7.18 (Lt L.F. Gall/Lt R.S. Maclatchy both IIFA, stalled on turn and nosedived in from 50ft – engine 1/F/331/WD12551).

C898   (Falcon III) **5 AAP** Bristol 28.4.18, allotted to BEF and tested 2.5.18 (Lt C.F. Uwins) and despatched, via Eastbourne, 4.5.18. **1 ASD** dd ex England 7.5.18 (engine 985/WD32892). **2 AIS** ex 1 ASD 8.5.18. **11 Sqn** dd ex 2 AIS 11.5.18 and wrecked after Reconnaissance 30.7.18 (Lt E.F. Salter/2nd Lt H. Ellis both IOAS, crashed on landing due to thick mist – same engine). **2 ASD** ex 11 Sqn via **Advanced Salvage** 31.7.18 and deleted that day (not worth reconstruction, 91hr 15min).

C899   **1 (Obs) SAG** New Romney by 15.6.18 until @ 5.9.18 (Sgt J. Gamble).

C900   (Falcon III) **5 AAP** Bristol 30.4.18, allotted to BEF and tested 3.5.18 and 5.5.18 (Lt C.F. Uwins). **8 AAP** Lympne ex 5 AAP. **1 ASD** dd ex England by air 8.5.18 (engine 1009/WD39397). **2 ASD** ex 1 ASD 8.5.18 (same engine) and wrecked on Test Flight 11.5.18 (Sgt T.H.C. Davies/AM2 H. Higson both OK, engine cut out and hit railway embankment – same engine). **1 ASD** ex 2 ASD 15.5.18 and deleted 25.6.18 on reconstruction as F5816.

C901   (Falcon III) **5 AAP** Bristol 28.4.18, allotted to BEF and tested on flight to Yate 2.5.18 (Lt C.F. Uwins). **8 AAP** Lympne dd ex 5 AAP 4.5.18. **1 ASD** dd ex England by air 7.5.18 (engine 991/WD32895). **1 AIS** ex 1 ASD 9.5.18 (same engine). **22 Sqn** dd ex 1 AIS 16.5.18 (same engine), victs 20.5.18 (Capt W.J. Mostyn/Sgt J.H. Jones destroyed a Pfalz D.III, NW of Estaires at 18:50), 21.5.18 (Capt W.J. Mostyn/Sgt J.H. Jones sent two LVG C-types down OOC, SW of Vitry at 10:15), 22.5.18 (Capt W.J. Mostyn/Sgt J.H. Jones sent an Albatros D.V down OOC, SE of Arras), 26.5.18 (Capt W.J. Mostyn/Sgt J.H. Jones sent an Albatros D.V down OOC, SE of Armentieres at 19:45) and 2.6.18 (Lt F.G. Gibbons/2nd Lt J.H. Umney sent a Pfalz D.III down OOC, NE of Lens at 10:50) then wrecked on OP 2.7.18 (Capt W.J. Mostyn/Capt D.E. Waight both OK, o/t in forced landing on **13 Sqn** aerodrome – engine 885/WD32842). **1 ASD** ex 22 Sqn 4.7.18 and deleted 23.8.18 on reconstruction as H7064 (66hr).

C902   **3 SAFG** Eastburn. **Pool of Pilots** Manston dd ex Eastburn 28.6.18. **33 TDS** Witney by 4.11.18 (2nd Lt G.A. Raybone).

C903   **59 TS** Rendcomb by 3.18 until @ 5.5.18. **71 TS** Port Meadow by 11.6.18. **50 TDS** Eastbourne by 8.18. **45 TDS** Rendcomb by 11.18 until @ 12.18. **2 MOS** Eastchurch by 3.19 until @ 7.19. **RAF (Cadet) College** Cranwell by 1924. B&C for reconditioning to J Type (s/n 6583) and ready by 8.1.25. **PD** Ascot. To Iraq. **AD** Hinaidi. **6 Sqn**.

C904   **141 Sqn** Biggin Hill 28.6.18. **1 AIS** ex 1 ASD 7.7.18. **20 Sqn** dd ex 1 AIS 9.7.18 (engine 945/WD32872), LIA on 18:25 OP 30.7.18 (Lt G.H. Zellers USAS/Sgt J.D. Cormack both KIA, shot down in flames – same engine) and deleted on unit 2.8.18 (104hr 1min).

C905   **Pool of Pilots** Manston by 19.6.18 until @ 27.7.18.

C906   (Arab) **5 AAP** Bristol and tested 4.10.18 (Lt C.F. Uwins). **8 AAP** Lympne by 23.1.19, reallotted from BEF to SE Area for Store Weston-on-the-Green.

C907   (s/n 3307) **Pool of Pilots** Manston by 14.5.18 until @ 7.18.

C908   **5 AAP** Bristol and tested 4.5.18 and 6.5.18 (Lt C.F. Uwins). **24 TS** Witney by 6.5.18. **33 TDS** Witney by 19.8.18.

C909   **5 AAP** Bristol and tested 15.10.18 (Lt C.F. Uwins).

C910   (s/n 3310) **Pool of Pilots** Manston by 5.18 until @ 6.18.

C911   (Falcon III) **5 AAP** Bristol 2.5.18, allotted to BEF and tested 3.5.18 (Lt C.F. Uwins). **1 ASD** dd ex England by air 7.5.18 (engine 1047/WD39416). **2 AIS** ex 1 ASD 8.5.18 (same engine). **11 Sqn** dd ex 2 AIS 9.5.18 (same engine) and wrecked on Practice Flight 17.5.18 (Major R.F.S. Morton/Lt H.R. Kincaid both IOAS, hit a tree on landing – same engine). **2 ASD** ex 11 Sqn 17.5.18 and deleted 20.5.18 (16hr 15min).

C912   **5 AAP** Bristol and tested 24.5.18 (Lt C.F. Uwins).

C913   (Falcon III) **5 AAP** Bristol and tested 7.6.18 (Lt C.F. Uwins). Despatched to 7 Bde, Italy 6.5.18. **'Z' Flt** 34 Sqn dd ex 7 AP 28.5.18 (engine 907/WD32853) and wrecked after 04:45 Reconnaissance 9.6.18 (Capt T.C. Lowe MC/2nd Lt A.S. Withers

both IOAS, crashed on landing – same engine. **7 AP** ex 'Z' Flt 10.6.18.

C914   (Falcon III) **5 AAP** Bristol 2.5.18, allotted to BEF. **8 AAP** Lympne ex Bristol. **1 ASD** dd ex England by air 9.5.18 (engine 901/WD32850). **2 AIS** ex 1 ASD 14.5.18 (same engine). **48 Sqn** dd ex 2 AIS 16.5.18 (same engine) and wrecked on OP, Villers Bretonneux, 17.6.18 (Lt R.H. Davis/2nd Lt B. Rider both OK, radiator shot through by enemy fire and crashed in forced landing near Quirrieu – same engine). **2 ASD** ex 48 Sqn 18.6.18 and deleted 3.7.18 on reconstruction as F6131 (77hr 30min).

C915   **5 AAP** Bristol and tested 9.5.18, 10.5.18 and 7.6.18 (Lt C.F. Uwins).

C916   (Falcon III) despatched to 7 Bde, Italy 6.5.18. **'Z' Flt 34 Sqn** dd ex 7 AP 21.5.18 (engine 903/WD32851), damaged on OP 10.6.18 (Lt W.L. Voster OK/Lt R. Murdoch WIA, hit by AA fire), on charge when unit redesignated **139 Sqn** 3.7.18, vict 4.7.18 (Lt H.C.W. Walters/Lt C. Beagle destroyed an Albatros D.III near Asolo) then wrecked on 05:30 Reconnaissance 30.7.18 (Lt H.C.W. Walters WIA/2nd Lt W.F. Davies OK, crashed in forced landing near Sacca after pilot hit – engine 843/WD32821). **7 AP** ex 139 Sqn 3.8.18.

C917   (Falcon III) **2 AIS** dd ex **1 ASD** 7.7.18. **35 Sqn** dd ex 2 AIS 8.7.18 (engine 855/WD32827). **9 Sqn** ex 35 Sqn 8.7.18 (same engine) and safely force landed 7.9.18 (same engine). **'O' Flt** ex 9 Sqn 23.10.18 (same engine), in accident 7.1.19 and reported 8.1.19 as unfit for further service (139hr 20min – same engine).

C918   (Arab) **37 TDS** Yatesbury and wrecked 14.11.18 (2nd Lt L.E. Aldrich fatally IIFA/Lt E.J. McDougall IIFA, nosedived into the ground at New Leaze Farm, Showell – engine 2845/WD26970).

C919   (Falcon III) at maker's 1.5.18, allotted to BEF and to be despatched in packing case. **1 ASD** dd ex England 13.5.18 (engine 959/WD32879). **2 AIS** ex 1 ASD 16.5.18 (same engine). **62 Sqn** dd ex 2 AIS 18.5.18 (same engine), victs 22.5.18 (Capt G.E. Gibbons/Lt S.A.W. Knights destroyed a LVG C-type over W edge of Laventie at 08:05) and 28.5.18 (Capt G.E. Gibbons/Lt S.A.W. Knights destroyed a Fokker D.VII in flames W of Lille at 19:10 and sent a Rumpler C-type down OOC over La Creche at 19:45) then wrecked after OP 25.6.18 (Capt G.E. Gibbons/Lt H.E. Merritt both OK, landed in long grass on the aerodrome and the machine turned on nose – same engine). **1 ASD** and deleted 7.8.18 on reconstruction as F6401, but new serial compromised so renumbered H7061 (58hr 45min).

C920   (Falcon III) **5 AAP** Bristol 3.5.18, allotted to BEF. **1 ASD** dd ex England 30.5.18 (engine 987/WD32893). **1 AIS** ex 1 ASD 8.6.18 (same engine). **1 ASD** ex 1 AIS 13.6.18 (same engine). **4 Sqn** dd ex 1 AIS 14.6.18 (same engine) and wrecked on 18:35 Reconnaissance 15.6.18 (Lt H.N. Loch OK/Prob C.H. White WIA, attacked by three EA between Merville and Neuf Berquin and badly shot up – same engine). **1 ASD** ex 4 Sqn 15.6.18 and deleted 25.7.18 on reconstruction as F6041 (8hr 45min).

C921   (Arab) **5 AAP** Bristol and tested 10.5.18 (Lt C.F. Uwins).

C922   (Falcon III) **5 AAP** Bristol and tested 6.5.18 (Lt C.F. Uwins). **141 Sqn** Biggin Hill. **1 AIS** ex 1 ASD 7.7.18. **88 Sqn** dd ex 1 AIS 9.7.18, victs 20.9.18 (Lt G.R. Poole/Sgt C. Hill destroyed two Fokker D.VII over Quesnoy at 07:50-07:55, one shared E2216 and Capt E.C. Johnston/2nd Lt W.J.N. Grant) and 30.10.18 (Lt V. Voss/Sgt E. Antcliffe destroyed a Fokker D.VII near Caumont at 09:00) then reported 30.10.18 as having a general performance below standard (233hr 45min – engine 41/WD18520) and recommended for return to **ASD** and to England as an instructional machine). **8 AAP** ex 1 ASD.

C923   (Falcon III) **5 AAP** Bristol and tested 9.5.18 and 11.5.18 (Lt C.F. Uwins). **141 Sqn** Biggin Hill 1918. B&C for reconditioning to J Type (s/n 6611) and ready by 10.2.25. **PD** Ascot. To Mesoptamia. **AD** Hinaidi. **6 Sqn**.

C924   (Arab) **5 AAP** Bristol tested 10.5.18, allotted to BEF 10.5.18, and still a Bristol 1.10.18 (tested by Lt C.F. Uwins). **9 Sqn** by 25.2.19 and wrecked 19.4.19 (Capt J. McBain IOAS/2nd Lt J.A. Williams OK, force landed on aerodrome after engine failure – engine 53833). **8 SS** ex 9 Sqn 22.4.19.

C925   (Falcon III) **5 AAP** Bristol 3.5.18, allotted to BEF. **8 AAP** Lympne ex Bristol. **1 ASD** dd ex England 9.5.18 (engine 1037/WD39411). **2 AIS** ex 1 ASD 12.5.18 (same engine). **11 Sqn** dd ex 2 AIS 16.5.18 (same engine) and wrecked on Practice Flight 20.5.18 Lt A. Walker & Sgt W.A. Fraser both IOAS, ran into butts on landing – same engine). **2 ASD** ex 11 Sqn 21.5.18 and deleted that day (not worth reconstruction, 5hr 30min).

C926   (Falcon III) at maker's 29.4.18, allotted to BEF and to be delivered in packing case. **48 Sqn** dd ex 2 AIS 3.6.18 (engine 979/WD32889),

LIA on 05:10 OP 19.8.18 (2nd Lt E.S. Glasse/2nd Lt C.N. Woodend both KOAS, collided with D8027 at 10,000ft near Peronne, both machines fell locked together – same engine) and deleted on unit that day.

C927 (Arab) **5 AAP** Bristol 11.5.18, allotted to BEF. **1 ASD** by 30.9.18 (engine 19075). **'M' Flt** dd ex 1 ASD 7.10.18. **1 ASD** ex M Flight 18.11.18 (engine 19102). **'P' Flt** dd ex **1 ASD** 11.1.19. **8 Sqn** dd ex 'P' Flt 19.1.19 and wrecked on Aerial Mail 13.4.19 (Lt Baker/Lt Kelway both OK, crashed at Marquise). **1 ASD** ex 8 Sqn 12.7.18.

C928 (Falcon III) at maker's 29.4.18, allotted to BEF and to be delivered in packing case. **2 AIS** ex **2 ASD** 28.5.18. **48 Sqn** dd ex 2 AIS 3.6.18 (engine 1035/WD39410) and wrecked before Reconnaissance 7.6.18 (Lt E.A. Foord/2nd Lt A.J. Elvin both OK, engine cut out just after take off and crashed attempting to land – engine 845/WD32822). **2 ASD** ex 48 Sqn 9.6.18 and deleted 3.7.18 on reconstruction as F6118 (3hr 7min).

C929 (Falcon III) at maker's 29.4.18, allotted to BEF and to be delivered in packing case. **1 ASD** dd ex England 20.5.18 (engine 1043/WD39414). **1 AIS** ex 1 ASD 27.5.18 (same engine). **22 Sqn** dd ex 1 AIS 29.5.18 (same engine), vict 5.6.18 (Lt F.E. Gibbons/Sgt J.H. Jones sent a Pfalz D.III down OOC, NE of La Bassee at 19:15) then wrecked on OP 23.6.18 (Lt S.F.H. Thompson/Sgt R.M. Fletcher both OK, machine badly shot up in combat – same engine). **1 ASD** ex 22 Sqn 25.6.18 and deleted 30.7.18 on reconstruction as F6043 (39hr 40min).

C930 (Arab) **5 AAP** Bristol 11.5.18, allotted to BEF and despatched by air 3.19.

C931 (Falcon III) at maker's 29.4.18, allotted to BEF and to be delivered in packing case. **2 AIS** ex **2 ASD** 17.5.18. **11 Sqn** dd ex 2 AIS 18.5.18 and wrecked on Escort 8.9.18 (Sgt R.S. Hutt/Sgt R.A. Watson both OK, machine hit in tank by EA fire and crashed near St Just at 09:00 – engine 787/WD32793). **2 ASD** ex 11 Sqn and deleted 15.8.18 (78hr 45min).

C932 (Falcon III) at maker's 29.4.18, allotted to BEF and to be delivered in packing case. **48 Sqn** dd ex **2 AIS** 8.6.18 (engine 1067/WD39426) and wrecked on Reconnaissance, Villers Bretonneux, 14.6.18 (2nd Lt B.M. Battey USAS/Sgt H.F. Watson both OK, propeller shot away and o/t during forced landing in a wheatfield near Querrieu – same engine). **2 ASD** ex 48 Sqn 15.6.18 and deleted that day (not worth reconstruction, 13hr).

C933 (Arab) **5 AAP** Bristol by 13.5.18, allotted to BEF. **48 Sqn**.

C934 (Falcon III) at maker's 29.4.18, allotted to BEF and to be delivered in packing case. **1 ASD** dd ex England 13.5.18 (engine 235/WD18617). **1 AIS** ex 1 ASD 19.5.18 (same engine). **2 AIS** ex 1 AIS 20.5.18 (same engine). **11 Sqn** dd ex 2 AIS 2.6.18 (same engine) and wrecked after Reconnaissance, Cambrai, 13.6.18 (Lt N.G. Pring/AM1 H. Turner both IOAS, crashed on landing – same engine). **2 ASD** ex 11 Sqn 15.6.18. **2 AIS** ex 2 ASD 8.8.18. **62 Sqn** dd ex 2 AIS 16.8.18 and wrecked after OP 25.8.18 (Lt P.S. Manley/Sgt G.F. Hines both OK, caught in heavy thunder storm, unable to reach aerodrome and crashed in forced landing near Rocourt – engine 1259/WD51654). **2 ASD** ex 62 Sqn and deleted 6.10.18 (not worth reconstruction).

C935 (Falcon III) at maker's 29.4.18, allotted to BEF and to be delivered in packing case. **2 ASD** ex **1 ASD** 29.5.18. **2 AIS** ex 2 ASD 29.5.18. **48 Sqn** dd ex 2 AIS 15.6.18 (engine 1055/WD39420), LIA on 16:30 OP 27.6.18 (Lt E.A. Foord/Sgt L. James both KIA, shot down in flames near Villers Bretonneux – same engine) and deleted on unit that day (17hr 35min).

C936 (Arab) **5 AAP** Bristol by 13.5.18, allotted to BEF and tested 13.6.18, 5.9.18, 6.9.18 and 9.9.18 (Lt C.F. Uwins). **9 Sqn**.

C937 (Falcon III) at maker's 29.4.18, allotted to BEF and to be delivered in packing case. **2 AIS** ex **2 ASD** 28.5.18. **11Sqn** dd ex 2 AIS 12.6.18, vict 6.9.18 (Capt H.A. Hay/Lt A.H. Craig destroyed one Fokker D.VII and sent another down OOC, W of Cambrai at 10:30) then wrecked on Reconnaissance, Cambrai, 4.10.18 (2nd Lt D.R. Phillips/2nd Lt W. Connor both KOAS, collided in the air with D7978 near Bapaume at 08:45) and deleted on unit that day.

C938 (Falcon III) at maker's 29.4.18, allotted to BEF and to be delivered in packing case. **1 ASD** dd ex England 22.5.18 (engine 1081/WD39433). **1 AIS** ex 1 ASD 2.6.18 (same engine). **20 Sqn** dd ex 1 AIS 2.6.18 (same engine) and damaged in successful combat 30.6.18 (Lt T.C. Traill/2nd Lt P.G. Jones sent an Albatros D.V down OOC, N of Comines but force landed near St Momelin at 07:30 with petrol tank shot through – same engine). **1 ASD** ex 20 Sqn 2.7.18 and deleted 5.7.18 (not worth reconstruction, 53hr 46min).

C939 **5 AAP** by 13.5.18, allotted to BEF.

C940 (Falcon III) at maker's 29.4.18, allotted to BEF and to be despatched in packing case. **2 AIS** ex **2 ASD** 29.5.18. **48 Sqn** dd ex 2 AIS 7.6.18 (engine 1031/WD39408), victs 13.8.18 (Capt C.R. Steele/Lt J.B. Jameson destroyed one Fokker D.VII and sent two others down OOC, E of Roye at 17:00) then destroyed in enemy bombing attack on Bertangles aerodrome, night 24/25.8.18, and deleted on unit (same engine).

C941 (Falcon III) at maker's 29.4.18, allotted to BEF and to be delivered in packing case. **2 AIS** and damaged 30.5.18 (crashed into when stationary by R.E.8 E105 – engine 231/WD18615). **2 ASD** for repair. **2 AIS** ex 2 ASD 28.6.18. **48 Sqn** dd ex 2 AIS 29.6.18 (same engine) and wrecked on OP, Peronne, 24.8.18 (2nd Lt E. Allingham/2nd Lt R. Watson both OK, ran out of fuel, crashed and shelled – same engine). **1 ASD** ex 48 Sqn 31.8.18 and deleted 1.9.18.

C942 (Arab) **5 AAP** Bristol 13.5.18, allotted to BEF. **10 AAP** Brooklands dd ex Farnborough 7.11.18 (2nd Lt S.P.F. Rust).

C943 (Falcon III) at maker's 29.4.18, allotted to BEF and to be delivered in packing case. **1 ASD** dd ex England 21.5.18 (engine 1051/WD29418). **2 AIS** ex 1 ASD 6.6.18 (same engine). **48 Sqn** dd ex 2 AIS 15.6.18 (same engine) and damaged in successful combats 2.9.18 (2nd Lt J.B. Cowan/2nd Lt T.L. Jones both OK, destroyed a Fokker D.VII in flames W of Lille at 19:30 and sent another down OOC, E of Menin at 19:45 but machine hit by enemy fire – engine 1283/WD51666). **1 ASD** ex 48 Sqn 5.9.18.

C944 (Falcon III) at maker's 29.4.18, allotted to BEF and to be delivered in packing case. **2 AIS** ex **2 ASD** 29.5.18. **48 Sqn** dd ex 2 AIS 4.6.18 and wrecked on 16:25 OP 28.6.18 (2nd Lt B.M. Battey USAS/Sgt T.W. Smith both OK, propeller stopped due to prolonged glide, force landed and crashed near Croisy – engine 1097/WD39441). **2 ASD** ex 48 Sqn 29.6.18. **2 AIS** ex 2 ASD 15.8.18. **62 Sqn** dd ex 2 AIS 26.8.18, LIA on OP 27.9.18 (2nd Lt P.D. Mauby/Sgt G.F. Hines both POW, last seen in combat E of Douai – engine 1407/WD51728) and deleted on unit that day (88hr 20min).

C945 (Arab) **5 AAP** Bristol 13.5.18, allotted to BEF.

C946 (Falcon III) at maker's 29.4.18, allotted to BEF and despatched in packing case 8.5.18. **2 AIS** ex **2 ASD** 31.5.18. **11 Sqn** dd ex 2 AIS 16.6.18, LIA on 07:00 Reconnaissance, Cambrai-Le Cateau, 16.9.18 (Lt J.C. Stanley USAS POW WIA/2nd Lt E.J. Norris POW, shot down near Quievy at 08:50 – engine 1591/WD51820) and deleted on unit that day (120hr 5min).

C947 (Falcon III) **5 AAP** Bristol and tested 10.5.18 (Lt C.F. Uwins). **2 AIS** ex **2 ASD** 10.7.18. **48 Sqn** dd ex 2 AIS 15.7.18 (engine 1057/WD39421), LIA on 11:45 OP 8.8.18 (Lt C. Imeretinsky/Lt A. Urinowski both OK, engine hit by AA fire, force landed and crashed in shell hole near Lamotte – same engine) and deleted on unit that day (84hr 39min).

C948 (Arab) **5 AAP** Bristol by 5.6.18, allotted to BEF and tested 15.9.18 (Lt C.F. Uwins). **37 TDS** Yatesbury by 29.10.18 (Lt J.W. Baker).

C949 At maker's 29.4.18, allotted to BEF but allotment cancelled 1.5.18. Sold to US Government.

C950 (Falcon III) **5 AAP** Bristol 9.5.18, allotted to BEF and tested 10.5.18 and 11.5.18 (Lt C.F. Uwins). **1 ASD** dd ex England 15.5.18 (engine 1101/WD39443). **2 AIS** ex 1 ASD 17.5.18 (same engine). **48 Sqn** dd ex 2 AIS 19.5.18 (same engine), vict 2.7.18 (Capt F.J. Cunningham/2nd Lt H. Knowles sent a Pfalz D.III down OOC, SE of Foucaucourt at 19:50) then wrecked on OP 14.7.18 (2nd Lt G.W.D. Foggin KOAS/2nd Lt W.E. Harper IOAS, crashed in forced landing in fog near Villers-Bocage – engine 1327/WD51688). **2 ASD** ex 48 Sqn 16.7.18 and deleted that day (111hr 5min).

C951 (Falcon III) **5 AAP** Bristol 9.5.18, allotted to BEF and tested 10.5.18, 11.5.18 and 13.5.18 (Lt C.F. Uwins). **1 ASD** dd ex England 18.5.18 (engine 891/WD32845). **1 AIS** ex 1 ASD 21.5.18 (same engine). **20 Sqn** dd ex 1 AIS 25.5.18 (same engine), victs 29.5.18 (Capt T.P. Middleton/Lt A. Mills sent an Albatros D.V down OOC over Bac St Maur at 18:30), 30.5.18 (Capt T.P. Middleton/Lt A. Mills destroyed an Albatros D.V which crashed on the canal NW of Lille then destroyed a Pfalz D.III whose RH top plane fell off near Wez Macquart at 17:20), 31.5.18 (Capt T.P. Middleton/Lt A. Mills destroyed a Pfalz D.III over Armentieres-Est Aires at 07:40), 8.6.18 (Capt T.P. Middleton/Capt F. Godfrey destroyed two Pfalz D.III, SE of Comines at 17:20), 12.6.18 (Capt T.P. Middleton/Capt F. Godfrey destroyed an Albatros D.V, E of Zillebeke Lake at 19:10), 30.6.18 (Capt T.P. Middleton/Capt F. Godfrey destroyed a black Fokker Dr.I at 07:30 and a Pfalz D.III at 07:50, both E of Comines), 4.7.18 (Lt P.T. Iaccaci/2nd Lt R.W. Turner destroyed an Albatros D.V, sent another down OOC and destroyed a third N of Zillebeke Lake at 16:20-16:40), 29.7.18 (Capt T.P. Middleton DFC/Capt F. Godfrey DFC destroyed Fokker D.VII, S of Gheluwe at 19:50) and 16.9.18 (Lt A.R. Strachan/2nd Lt D.M. Calderwood destroyed a Fokker D.VII, NW of St Quentin at 08:20, shared E2514) then damaged in combat on OP 18.9.18 (Lt A.R. Strachan/Lt B.W. Wilson both OK – engine 1539/WD51794). **2 ASD** ex 20 Sqn 21.9.18 and deleted 28.9.18 (not worth reconstruction, 269hr 39min).

C952 (Falcon III) **5 AAP** Bristol 8.5.18, allotted to BEF and tested 9.5.18, 10.5.18, 13.5.18 and 14.5.18 (Lt C.F. Uwins). **1 ASD** dd ex England 17.5.18 (engine 1019/WD39402). **1 AIS** ex 1 ASD 20.5.18 (same engine). **88 Sqn** dd ex 1 AIS 22.5.18 (same engine) and wrecked after OP 2.7.18 (Lt C.J. Winstanley OK/2nd Lt T.S. Chilton IOAS, bounced on landing, stalled and fell on wing tip – same engine). **1 ASD** ex 88 Sqn 3.7.18 and deleted 6.7.18 (not worth reconstruction, 86hr 30min).

C953 (Falcon III) **5 AAP** Bristol 10.5.18, allotted to BEF and despatched by air 10.5.18. **1 ASD** dd ex England 12.5.18 (engine 1065/WD39425). **2 AIS** ex 1 ASD 18.5.18 (same engine). **62 Sqn** dd ex 2 AIS 20.5.18 (same engine) and wrecked on 06:05 OP 23.8.18 (Lt S.A.R. Solomon WIA/2nd Lt L. Egan OK, badly shot up in combat over Pronville and force landed at Dainville – same engine). Deleted 4.9.18 on reconstruction as F6283 (105hr 40min).

C954 **39 Sqn** North Weald by 10.18 until @ 11.18.

C955 (Falcon III) **5 AAP** Bristol 10.5.18, allotted to BEF and tested 11.5.18 (Lt C.F. Uwins). **1 ASD** dd ex England 15.5.18 (engine 1015/WD39400). **11 Sqn** dd ex 1 ASD 17.5.18 (same engine), damaged 26.5.18 (Lt E.M. De Zee OK, undercarriage collapsed in heavy landing) and wrecked on Formation Flight 8.4.19 (Lt A.K. Doull/Sgt L.K. Ward both OK, force landed near Brussels after engine failed – engine 1701/WD51875).

C956 (Arab) **5 AAP** Bristol 16.5.18, allotted to BEF.

C957 (Falcon III) **5 AAP** Bristol 10.5.18, allotted to BEF and tested 12.5.18 (Lt C.F. Uwins). **1 ASD** dd ex England 14.5.18 (engine 1073/WD39429). **2 AIS** ex 1 ASD 15.5.18 (same engine). **11 Sqn** dd ex 2 AIS 16.5.18 (same engine) and wrecked after Photography 11.6.18 (Lt B.S.B. Thomas/2nd Lt W.R.N. Cheetham both OK, crashed on landing – same engine). **2 ASD** ex 11 Sqn 11.6.18 and deleted 28.9.18.

C958 (Falcon III) **5 AAP** Bristol 11.5.18, allotted to BEF and tested that day (Lt C.F. Uwins). **1 ASD** dd ex England 16.5.18 (engine 43/WD18521). **2 AIS** ex 1 ASD 17.5.18 (same engine). **11 Sqn** dd ex 2 AIS 21.5.18 (same engine) and wrecked before Reconnaissance 17.6.18 (Lt L.C.H. Rutter IOAS/Sgt R. Allen OK, hit telegraph wires during forced landing after engine failed on take off – same engine). **2 ASD** ex 11 Sqn 17.6.18 and deleted 22.6.18 (not worth reconstruction, 37hr 10min).

C959 (Falcon III) **5 AAP** Bristol 11.5.18, allotted to BEF and tested 13.5.18, 14.5.18, 16.5.18 and 17.5.18 (Lt C.F. Uwins). **1 ASD** dd ex England 19.5.18 (engine 1059/WD39422). **2 AIS** ex 1 ASD 20.5.18 (same engine). **62 Sqn** dd ex 2 AIS 27.5.18 (same engine), vict 1.6.18 (Capt H. Rees-Jones/2nd Lt C. Wealthall destroyed a Fokker Dr.I, E of Montdidier at 10:50) and wrecked on Test Flight 8.1.19 (Lt R.C. McHenry OK, ran into a hole when taxiing in after landing – engine 1563/WD51806).

C960 (Falcon III) **5 AAP** Bristol 11.5.18, allotted to BEF and tested 13.5.18 and 14.5.18 (Lt C.F. Uwins). **1 ASD** dd ex England 18.5.18 (engine 91/WD18545). **2 AIS** ex 1 ASD 18.5.18 (same engine). **62 Sqn** dd ex 2 AIS 20.5.18 (same engine) and wrecked after OP 29.8.18 (2nd Lt J. Appleby/2nd Lt J.M. Holling both IOAS, had to land at **20 Sqn** to refuel, engine cut on take off and machine crashed – engine 264/WD1165). **2 ASD** ex 62 Sqn and deleted 9.10.18 (not worth reconstruction).

C961 (Falcon III) **5 AAP** Bristol 13.5.18, allotted to BEF and tested 15.5.18 (Lt C.F. Uwins). **1 ASD** dd ex England 18.5.18 (engine 1075/WD39430). **1 AIS** ex 1 ASD 19.5.18 (same engine). **22 Sqn** dd ex 1 AIS 22.5.18 (same engine), victs 30.5.18 (2nd Lt E.C. Bromley/2nd Lt J.H. Umney sent a Pfalz D.III down OOC, S of Armentieres at 19:40), 31.5.18 (2nd Lt E.C. Bromley/2nd Lt J.H. Umney destroyed a Pfalz D.III near Levantio, SW of Armentieres at 19:15), 1.6.18 (Lt F.G. Gibbons/2nd Lt J.H. Umney destroyed two Pfalz D.III over Erquinghem at 19:15), 2.6.18 (2nd Lt E.C. Bromley/2nd Lt J.H. Umney sent two EA C-type down OOC, E of Lens at 10:15) and 5.6.18 (2nd Lt E.C. Bromley/Lt C.G. Gass destroyed a Halberstadt C-type at 10:30 and sent an Albatros D.V down OOC at 10:36) then wrecked before OP 26.6.18 (Lt S.F.H Thompson/Sgt R.M. Fletcher both OK, crossed a rut on take off and smashed propeller, lost speed and crashed – same engine). **1 ASD** ex 22 Sqn 27.6.18 and deleted 29.6.18 (not worth reconstruction).

C962 (Falcon III) **5 AAP** Bristol 11.5.18, allotted to BEF and to be delivered by air. **1 ASD** dd ex England 20.5.18 (engine 821/WD32810). **2 AIS** ex 1 ASD 20.5.18 (same engine). **48 Sqn** dd ex 2 AIS 30.5.18 (same engine) and wrecked 5.7.18 (2nd Lt E. Allingham/2nd Lt J.W. London both OK, engine cut out on OP and crashed in forced landing near Bussy-les-Daours – same engine). **2 ASD** ex 48 Sqn 7.7.18 and deleted 30.7.18 (not worth reconstruction, 76hr 35min).

C963 (Arab) **5 AAP** Bristol 6.6.18, allotted to BEF.

C964 (Falcon III) **5 AAP** Bristol and tested 12.5.18 (Lt C.F. Uwins). **39 Sqn** and on HAP 20.5.18 (Capt C.L. Wauchope/AM1 L. Card) and on unit charge until @ 3.9.18 (Lt Cordes/AM1 A.T.C. Stagg).

C965 (Falcon III) **5 AAP** Bristol 13.5.18, allotted to BEF and tested that day (Lt C.F. Uwins). **1 ASD** dd ex England 14.5.18 (engine 1053/WD39419). **2 AIS** ex 1 ASD 16.5.18 (same engine). **62 Sqn** dd ex 2 AIS 18.5.18 (same engine) and wrecked after OP 6.6.18 (Lt F. Williams/2nd Lt W. Hodgkinson both OK, misjudged landing and ran into a hangar – same engine). **1 ASD** ex 62 Sqn 8.6.18 and deleted 11.6.18 (not worth reconstruction, 40hr 45min).

C966 (Arab) **5 AAP** Bristol 5.6.18, allotted to BEF and tested 13.8.18 (Lt C.F. Uwins). **1 ASD** by 15.9.18 (engine 16260) and on charge until @ 30.9.18. Flown to England 5.11.18.

C967 (Falcon III) **5 AAP** Bristol and tested 14.5.18 and 15.5.18 (Lt C.F. Uwins). **1 ASD** dd ex England 18.5.18 (engine 1079/WD39432). **1 AIS** ex 1 ASD 19.5.18 (same engine). **10 Sqn** dd ex 1 AIS 27.5.18 (same engine) and wrecked before Artillery Observation 16.6.18 (Capt E.H. Comber-Taylor KOAS/2nd Lt G.A. Cameron IOAS, engine failed on take off, stalled and crashed – same engine). **1 ASD** ex 10 Sqn 20.6.18 and deleted that day (not worth reconstruction, 41hr 5min).

C968 (Falcon III) **5 AAP** Bristol 13.5.18, allotted to BEF and tested 15.5.18 (Lt C.F. Uwins). **1 ASD** dd ex England 19.5.18 (engine 1087/WD39436). **1 AIS** ex 1 ASD 20.5.18 (same engine). **16 Sqn** dd ex 1 AIS 22.5.18 (same engine). **'L' Flt** ex 16 Sqn 1.7.18 (same engine) and wrecked after Artillery Observation 4.7.18 (Lt R.F. Buick/Lt J.E. Kendrick both OK, collided with small shed on landing – same engine). **1 ASD** ex 'L' Flt 9.7.18 and deleted 11.7.18 (not worth reconstruction, 41hr 55min).

C969 (Arab) **5 AAP** Bristol 5.6.18, allotted to BEF.

C970 (Falcon III) presentation a/c *Malaya XIX. The Singapore No.2.* **5 AAP** Bristol 13.5.18, allotted to BEF and tested 17.5.18 and 18.5.18 (Lt C.F. Uwins). **1 ASD** dd ex England 20.5.18 (engine 1027/WD39406). **2 AIS** ex 1 ASD 20.5.18 (same engine). **62 Sqn** dd ex 2 AIS 29.5.18 (same engine) and wrecked after OP 30.5.18 (Lt L.W. Hudson/AM1 F.R. Bower both OK, crashed on landing – same engine). **1 ASD** and deleted 25.6.18 on reconstruction as F5822.

C971 (Falcon III) **5 AAP** Bristol and tested 16.5.18 and 18.5.18 (Lt C.F. Uwins). **39 Sqn** North Weald and wrecked 11.6.18 (2nd Lt E.C. Slaght/2nd Lt F.T. West both IIFA, mis-judged landing, struck a ditch and hedge and o/t – engine 3/F/1091/WD39438).

C972 (Arab) **5 AAP** Bristol by 5.6.18, allotted to BEF.

C973 (Falcon III) **5 AAP** Bristol 13.5.18, allotted to BEF and tested 16.5.18 (Lt C.F. Uwins). **1 ASD** dd ex England 19.5.18 (engine 1041/WD39413). **2 AIS** ex 1 ASD 20.5.18 (same engine). **62 Sqn** dd ex 2 AIS 27.5.18 (same engine) and wrecked after OP 22.7.18 (Lt J.W. Parsons/2nd Lt P. Pilkington both OK, ran into a plough on landing – same engine). **2 ASD** ex 62 Sqn 23.7.18 and deleted 30.7.18 (not worth reconstruction, 66hr 50min).

C974 (Falcon III) **5 AAP** Bristol and tested 14.5.18 (Lt C.F. Uwins). **2 AIS** dd ex 1 ASD 10.7.18. **48 Sqn** dd ex 2 AIS 11.7.18 (engine 1069/WD39427), LIA on 19:25 OP, Lamotte, 21.7.18 (2nd Lt B.M. Battey USAS/2nd Lt J. Gondre both POW, last seen over the lines – same engine) and deleted on unit that day (52hr 29min).

C975 (Arab) **5 AAP** Bristol by 5.6.18, allotted to BEF.

C976 (Falcon III) **5 AAP** Bristol 13.5.18, allotted to BEF and tested 16.5.18, 18.5.18 and 24.5.18 (Lt C.F. Uwins). **1 ASD** dd ex England 25.5.18 (engine 1007/WD39396). **1 AIS** ex 1 ASD 27.5.18 (same engine). **20 Sqn** dd ex 1 AIS 30.5.18 (same engine), damaged on OP 24.6.18 (Lt A.B.D. Campbell OK, controls damaged by AA fire and force landed near Boisdinghem Hospital) then LIA on 07:51 OP 25.7.18 (Lt F.J. Shearer/Sgt D. Malpas both KIA, last seen in combat over Menin – engine 1111/WD39448) and deleted on unit that day (145hr 46min).

C977 (Falcon III) **5 AAP** Bristol and tested 16.5.18 (Lt C.F. Uwins). **141 Sqn** Biggin Hill 1918.

C978 (Falcon III) **5 AAP** Bristol 15.5.18, allotted to BEF and tested 20.5.18 and 21.5.18 (Lt C.F. Uwins). **1 ASD** dd ex England 23.5.18 (engine 1033/WD39409). **1 AIS** ex 1 ASD 27.5.18 (same engine). **22 Sqn** dd ex 1 AIS 31.5.18 (same engine), marked as a/c *O* and wrecked on 08:05 OP 16.9.18 (Lt L.N. Caple/Lt G.S. Routhier both OK, fuselage shot through by fire from EA – engine 1415/WD51732). **1 ASD** ex 22 Sqn 18.9.18 and presume deleted.

C979 (Falcon III) **5 AAP** Bristol 15.5.18, allotted to BEF and tested 16.5.18 and 18.5.18 (Lt C.F. Uwins). **1 ASD** dd ex England 20.5.18 (engine 905/WD32852). **1 AIS** ex 1 ASD 26.5.18 (same engine). **20 Sqn** dd ex 1 AIS 27.5.18 (same engine), vict 30.5.18 (Lt D.J. Weston/Lt W. Noble destroyed a Pfalz D.III near Lille at 17:20) then wrecked after OP 17.6.18 (Lt G.H. Zellers/Sgt J.D. Cormack both OK, tail skid caught in a hole on landing, causing cracked longerons – same engine). **1 ASD** ex 20 Sqn 18.6.18 and deleted 8.8.18 (not worth reconstruction, 46hr 35min).

C980 (Falcon III) **5 AAP** Bristol 15.5.18, allotted to BEF. **1 ASD** dd ex England 20.5.18 (engine 1093/WD39439). **1 AIS** ex 1 ASD 25.5.18 (same engine). **20 Sqn** dd ex 1 AIS 3.6.18 (same engine) and wrecked on Practice Flight 4.7.18 (Lt A.J. McAllister/Prob T.V. Robinson both KOAS, stalled on climbing turn and nosedived in – same engine). **1 ASD** ex 20 Sqn 5.7.18 and deleted 7.7.18 (not worth reconstruction, 94hr 22min).

C981 (Falcon III) **5 AAP** Bristol and tested 25.5.18 (Lt C.F. Uwins). **141 Sqn** by Biggin Hill 29.5.18 until @ 28.6.18.

C982 (Arab) **5 AAP** Bristol 31.5.18, allotted to BEF and tested 1.6.18 (Lt C.F. Uwins). **1 (S)ARD** Farnborough by 25.1.19 with BEF allotment cancelled and for deletion.

C983 (Falcon III) **5 AAP** Bristol 16.5.18, allotted to BEF and tested 17.5.18 and 19.5.18 (Lt C.F. Uwins). **8 AAP** Lympne by 20.5.18. **1 ASD** dd ex England 21.5.18 (engine 1103/WD39444). **1 AIS** ex 1 ASD 21.5.18 (same engine). **88 Sqn** dd ex 1 AIS 22.5.18 (same engine) and wrecked after successful combat 29.6.18 (Capt K.R. Simpson/Sgt C. Hill both OK, destroyed a Fokker D.VII over Ghistelles at 20:10, shared C774, C787, D8022, but o/t in forced landing near Beveren after the combat – same engine). **1 ASD** ex 88 Sqn 30.6.18 and deleted 20.10.18 on reconstruction as H7197.

C984 (Falcon III) **39 Sqn** North Weald by 26.6.18 (Lt Arkell/AM1 A.T.C. Stagg) until @ 29.6.18. **1 AIS** dd ex 1 ASD 9.7.18 **10 Sqn** dd ex 1 ASD 13.7.18 (engine 1045/WD39415) and wrecked after Artillery Observation 23.8.18 (Lt R. Johnstone/2nd Lt M.G. Ryan both OK, broke longeron on landing – same engine). **1 ASD** ex 10 Sqn 23.8.18 and deleted 27.8.18 (not worth reconstruction, 73hr 15min).

C985 (Arab) **5 AAP** Bristol 3.6.18, allotted to BEF. **1 ASD** and flown to England 4.9.18.

C986 (Falcon III) **5 AAP** Bristol 16.5.18, allotted to BEF and tested 19.5.18 and 20.5.18 (Lt C.F. Uwins). **1 ASD** dd ex England 20.5.18 (engine 1049/WD39417). **1 AIS** ex 1 ASD 25.5.18 (same engine). **16 Sqn** dd ex 1 AIS 28.5.18 (same engine). **'L' Flt** dd ex 16 Sqn 11.7.18 (same engine) and wrecked before Photography 9.8.18 (Lt G.L. Barnett/Lt R.L. Rice both OK, crashed on take off due to rough ground – same engine). **1 ASD** ex 'L' Flt 11.8.18 and deleted 14.8.18 (not worth reconstruction, 65hr 21min).

C987 (Falcon III) **5 AAP** Bristol 24.5.18, allotted to BEF and tested 26.5.18 (Lt C.F. Uwins). **1 ASD** dd ex England 29.5.18 (engine 1061/WD39423). **1 AIS** ex 1 ASD 30.5.18 (same engine). **20 Sqn** dd ex 1 AIS 7.6.18 (same engine), victs 17.6.18 (Capt D. Latimer/Lt T.C. Noel sent a Fokker D.VII down OOC over Boesinghe at 07:45, shared C843) and 11.8.18 (Lt E.W. Sweeney/2nd Lt C.G. Boothroyd burnt an EKB on the ground S of Heule at 13:40) then LIA on 17:00 OP 14.8.18 (Lt D.E. Smith KIA/2nd Lt J. Hills POW – engine 1263/WD51656) and deleted on unit that day (123hr).

C988 (Arab) **5 AAP** Bristol 3.6.18, allotted to BEF and first flown 21.8.18. **5 TDS** Easton on Hill; Flying from Farnborough to Stamford, engine failed near Dunstable, tried to force land, commenced to side slip, could not straighten out, crashed 24.9.18 (2nd Lt H. Marsden/2nd Lt R.A. McAvity both IIFA).

C989 (Falcon III) presentation a/c *Bhopal, presented by Her Highness the Begum of Bhopal.* **5 AAP** Bristol by 24.5.18, allotted to BEF. **1 ASD** dd ex England 29.5.18 (engine 1115/WD39450). **1 AIS** ex 1 ASD 2.6.18. **22 Sqn** dd ex 1 AIS 6.6.18 (same engine), victs 28.6.18 (Lt F.G. Gibbons & Lt V. StB. Collins destroyed a Fokker Dr.I, N of Estaires at 10:15) and 10.7.18 (Lt F.G. Gibbons/Lt V. StB. Collins sent a Fokker Dr.I OOC over Lille at 09:45) on OP 9.8.18 (Lt F.C. Stanton/Lt C.J. Tolman both OK, force landed at Lilliers on return from patrol, due to engine cutting out from pressure failure – engine 1331/WD51690). **1 ASD** ex 22 Sqn 10.8.18.

C990 (Falcon III) to 7 Bde Italy. **'Z' Flt, 34 Sqn** dd ex 7 AP 22.6.18 (engine 1089/WD39437), on unit charge when redesignated **139 Sqn** 3.7.18 and wrecked on 06:25 Photo-Reconnaissance 29.7.18 (Lt A.E. Ryan WIA/Lt C. LeG. Amy, shot up in combat and crashed in forced landing – same engine). **7 AP** ex 139 Sqn 3.8.18.

C991 (Falcon III) to 7 Bde Italy. **'Z' Flt, 34 Sqn** dd ex 7 AP 28.6.18, on unit charge when redesignated **139 Sqn** 3.7.18 and wrecked on 09:25 Escort 1.7.18 (Lt R.R. Evans/Lt M.I. Hough both OK, crashed in forced landing near Crocetta at 11:45 after engine cut out – engine 1121/WD39453). **7 AP** ex 139 Sqn 15.7.18.

C992 (Falcon III) to 7 Bde Italy. **'Z' Flt, 34 Sqn** dd ex 7 AP 24.6.18 (engine 1117/WD39451), on unit charge when redesignated **139 Sqn** 3.7.18 and wrecked on 07:30 Reconnaissance 1.9.18 (Lt A.N. Martyn/2nd Lt G.L. Kaye both OK, badly shot up and forced to land, with estimated 3 weeks for repair – same engine). **7 AP** ex 139 Sqn 5.9.18.

C993 (Falcon III) to 7 Bde Italy. **'Z' Flt, 34 Sqn** dd ex 7 AP 21.6.18 (engine 1029/WD39407), LIA on 18:00 Escort 28.6.18 (Lt F.S. Williams/Lt D. Thomas both KIA, received a direct hit from AA fire and down in flames – same engine) and deleted on unit (9hr 5min).

C994 (Falcon III) to 7 Bde Italy. **139 Sqn** dd ex 7 AP 12.7.18 (engine 1141/WD39463), damaged in forced landing on Reconnaissance 24.10.18 (Lt H.V. Jellicoe/Sgt F.H. Shanks both OK, engine cut out and forced landed near the Piave – engine 551/WD32675) and wrecked on Reconnaissance, Piave, 31.10.18 (Capt Holland/Lt Fullager both OK, force landed near Pordenone after engine failure – same engine). **7 AP** ex 139 Sqn 7.11.18.

C995 (Arab) **5 AAP** Bristol by 3.6.18, allotted to BEF. **(3 Sqn AFC). O Flight** dd 1.11.18 and deleted, burnt, on unit 6.11.18.

C996 (Falcon III) to 7 Bde Italy. **139 Sqn** dd ex 7 AP 5.7.18 (engine 1099/WD39442) and in need of overhaul by 28.7.18 (3hr 5min). **7 AP**, wrecked, ex 139 Sqn 3.8.18. **139 Sqn** reissued ex 7 AP 12.11.18 and marked as a/c *K.* **34 Sqn** ex 139 Sqn 28.1.19 and on unit charge until @ 12.2.19. To India. **20 Sqn** by 4.21 and wrecked 10.6.21 (undercarriage collapsed during forced landing after engine failure).

C997 (Falcon III) to 7 Bde Italy. **'Z' Flt, 34 Sqn** dd ex 7 AP 29.6.18, on unit charge when redesignated **139 Sqn** 3.7.18, and wrecked 28.10.18 (2nd Lt J.R. Dean OK, taxied into a hangar – engine 957/WD32878). **7 AP** ex 139 Sqn 31.10.18.

C998 (Arab) **5 AAP** Bristol 3.6.18, allotted to BEF. **37 TDS** Yatesbury. **7th TS AFC** dd ex 37 TDS 2.11.18 and tested 4.11.18.

C999 (Falcon III) to 7 Bde Italy. **'Z' Flt, 34 Sqn** dd ex 7 AP 2.7.18, on unit charge when redesignated **139 Sqn** 3.7.18 and vict 4.7.18 (Lt W.C. Simon/Lt W. Smith sent an Albatros OOC over Levico) and damaged in successful combats 30.7.18 (Lt W.C. Simon OK/Lt W.W. Smith WIA, destroyed an Albatros D-type and sent an Albatros D-type and an EA C-type OOC over Motta). **7 AP** ex 139 Sqn 3.8.18. **34 Sqn** by 3.9.18. **139 Sqn** ex 34 Sqn 29.9.18 and wrecked on Test Flight 12.11.18 (2nd Lt G.A. Hadley IOAS, crashed on landing). **7 AP** ex 139 Sqn 12.11.18.

C1000 (Falcon III) **5 AAP** Bristol 24.5.18, allotted to BEF. **1 AIS** by 6.6.18. **88 Sqn** dd ex 1 AIS 9.6.18 and wrecked on Wireless Instruction 15.7.18 (Lt H. Allbut/2nd Lt A.N. Ealand both KOAS, machine entered a spinning nose dive and crashed – engine 215/WD18607). **1 ASD** ex 88 Sqn 16.7.18 and deleted 18.7.18 (not worth reconstruction, 47hr 5min).

C1001 (Arab) **5 AAP** Bristol by 3.6.18, allotted to BEF and tested 13.8.18 (Lt C.F. Uwins). **37 TDS** Yatesbury by 31.10.18 (Lt J.W. Baker).

C1002 (Falcon III) **5 AAP** Bristol by 24.5.18, allotted to BEF. **2 AIS** ex **1 ASD** 6.6.18. **62 Sqn** dd ex 2 AIS 17.6.18 (engine 767/WD32783), LIA on 06:10 OP 8.7.18 (Lt J.A. Chubb/Sgt J. Borwein both POW, last seen in a dive near Carvin, under control with three EA on its tail – same engine) and deleted on unit that day (27hr 10min).

C1003 (Falcon III) **5 AAP** Bristol by 24.5.18, allotted to BEF and tested 25.5.18 and 26.5.18 (Lt C.F. Uwins). **1 ASD** dd ex England 27.5.18 (engine 1149/WD39467). **1 AIS** ex 1 ASD 29.5.18 (same engine). **22 Sqn** dd ex 1 AIS 6.6.18, damaged in successful combats 10.7.18 (Lt J.E. Gurdon DFC WIA/Lt J.J. Scaramanga fatally WIA, destroyed a Pfalz D.III in flames and sent two others OOC over Armentieres-Lille at 09:30, but machine damaged in the combat – same engine). **1 ASD** ex 22 Sqn 11.7.18 and deleted 19.9.18 on reconstruction as H7066 (36hr).

C1004 (Arab) **5 AAP** Bristol by 3.6.18, allotted to BEF and tested 17.6.18 (Lt C.F. Uwins). **2 AIS** ex 1 ASD 21.6.18. **HQ Communications Sqn** by 11.10.18 and still on unit charge 3.4.19.

C1005 N/I

C1006 N/I

C1007 (Arab) **5 AAP** Bristol by 3.6.18, allotted to BEF and tested 22.8.18 (Lt C.F. Uwins).

C1008 N/I
C1009 **2 FS** Marske as a/c *85*, photographed o/t.
C1010 (Arab) **5 AAP** Bristol by 3.6.18, allotted to BEF. **1 ASD** by 15.9.18 (engine 2886). **2 ASD** ex 1 ASD 24.10.18 but force landed en route (Lt Dolby OK, same engine). **8 Sqn** Bellevue dd ex **2 AIS** 8.11.18. **1 ASD** ex 8 Sqn 3.5.19.
C1011 **PD** Ascot. To India. **AD** Drigh Road by 4.23. **20 Sqn** by 8.23 until @ 6.24. **AP** Lahore by 10.24.
C1012 N/I
C1013 (Arab) **5 AAP** Bristol by 3.6.18, allotted to BEF and tested 12.7.18 (Lt C.F. Uwins). **1 ASD** by 26.7.18 (engine 19039). **'P' Flt** dd ex **1 AIS** 3.9.18 (same engine) and destroyed on Patrol 6.11.18 (Capt L.H. Jones/Lt V. Lockey both OK, force landed and burnt out after fuel tank hit by enemy machine gun fire – engine E2916).
C1014 B&C for reconditioning to J Type (s/n 6425) and ready by 3.4.24. **4 Sqn** Farnborough by 11.25. **SAC** Old Sarum by 9.25 until @ 4.29. **2 Sqn** Manston by 5.29 until @ 7.29.
C1015 **24 Sqn** Kenley 1921. B&C for reconditioning to J Type (s/n 6568) and ready by 19.12.24. **PD** Ascot. To Egypt. **AD** Aboukir. **208 Sqn** by 5.2.25. **8 Sqn** by 3.27 until @ 5.27 (listed as J1015).
C1016 (Arab) **5 AAP** Bristol by 3.6.18, allotted to BEF and tested 13.7.18 and 14.8.18 (Lt C.F. Uwins).
C1017 **2 FTS** Duxford by 1.24 until @ 4.24.
C1018 **2 FTS** Duxford by 10.21 until @ 2.22. **SAC** Old Sarum.
C1019 (Arab) **5 AAP** Bristol by 3.6.18, allotted to BEF.
C1020 (Falcon III) **IAAD** Henlow in incident 23.6.22 (Fg Off B.K.D. Robertson OK/LAC H. Biggs IIGA, propeller accident at Hendon) **1 FTS** Netheravon by 8.22.
C1021 N/I
C1022 (Arab) **5 AAP** Bristol by 3.6.18, allotted to BEF.
C1023 N/I
C1024 N/I
C1025 (Arab) **5 AAP** Bristol by 3.6.18, allotted to BEF, still at Bristol 9.1.19, reallotted from BEF to SW Area for **CTD**, to be railed to RAE Farnborough, and tested 4.9.18 and 8.10.18 (Lt C.F. Uwins).
C1026 N/I
C1027 B&C for reconditioning to J Type (s/n 6557) and ready by 8.12.24. **PD** Ascot. To Iraq. **AD** Hinaidi. **AHQ Iraq Command Training Flt** by 5.27 until @ 9.28.
C1028 (Arab) **5 AAP** Bristol by 3.6.18, allotted to BEF and tested 12.10.18 (Lt C.F. Uwins).
C1029 N/I
C1030 **45 TDS** Rendcomb 1918.
C1031 (Arab) **5 AAP** Bristol by 3.6.18, allotted to BEF and tested 8.10.18 and 10.10.18 (Lt C.F. Uwins). **12 Sqn** as a/c *A2* by 3.19 until @ 5.19.

Showing the early style of unit marking on its fin, F.2B C1039 'B' of 5 Sqn climbs gently. This aircraft served in this unit during 1926-28. *(Philip Jarrett)*

C1032 **CFS** Upavon by 2.22 until @ 3.22. B&C for reconditioning to J Type (s/n 6591) and ready by 19.1.25.
C1033 **4 TS** North Shotwick and wrecked 4.7.19 (2nd Lt G.C. Kemp/2nd Lt R.M. Tate both IIFA, engine failure and telegraph wires prevented a safe landing).
C1034 (Falcon III) presentation a/c *Zanzibar No.7*. **5 AAP** Bristol by 30.5.18, allotted to BEF and tested 3.6.18., 4.6.18 and 5.6.18 (Lt C.F. Uwins, 6 flights). **1 AIS** dd ex **1 ASD** 11.6.18. **1 ASD** 13.6.18. **1 AIS** 14.6.18 (engine 665/WD32732). **2 Sqn** dd ex 1 ASD 19.6.18 (same engine). **'L' Flt** dd ex 2 Sqn 1.7.18 and wrecked after Artillery Observation 21.8.18 (Capt B.E. Catchpole/Lt J.E.

Kendrick both OK, force landed on edge of the aerodrome due to shortage of petrol – engine 543/WD32671). **1 ASD** ex 'L' Flt and deleted 28.8.18 (not worth reconstruction, 56hr 55min).
C1035 (Falcon III) **5 AAP** Bristol by 30.5.18, allotted to BEF and tested 3.6.18 and 4.6.18 (Lt C.F. Uwins). **1 AIS** ex 1 ASD 7.6.18. **22 Sqn** dd ex 1 ASD 9.6.18 (engine 1155/WD51602), victs 25.8.18 (Lt C.E. Hurst/Sgt H.C. Hunt destroyed a Pfalz D.III, W of Peronne at 18:30 then destroyed a Fokker Dr.I and sent a Pfalz D.III down OOC near Maricourt at 18:35) then wrecked 22.11.18 (Capt A.J.F. Bawden/Lt D.C. Davies both OK, crashed landing on uneven section of aerodrome – engine 1127/WD39456). **2 ASD** ex 22 Sqn.
C1036 (Falcon III) **5 AAP** Bristol by 30.5.18, allotted to BEF. **2 AIS** ex **1 ASD** 4.6.18. **4 Sqn** dd ex 1 ASD 18.6.18 (engine 1157/WD51603) and wrecked 20.9.18 (Lt R.H. Schroeder OK/2nd Lt B.R. Jones KIA, in combat with EA near Passchendaele – same engine). **1 ASD** ex 4 Sqn 28.9.18 and deleted 3.10.18 (not worth reconstruction, 56hr 10min).
C1037 (Falcon III) **5 AAP** Bristol by 30.5.18, allotted to BEF. **2 AIS** ex **1 ASD** 4.6.18. **11 Sqn** dd ex **2 ASD** 17.6.18 and wrecked after Reconnaissance, Cambrai, 27.6.18 (Lt J.W. Coons/Lt R.A. West both OK, crashed landing in strong wind when wing tip hit the ground – engine 151/WD18575). **2 ASD** ex 11 Sqn. **2 AIS** ex 2 ASD 5.9.18. **11 Sqn** reissued ex 2 AIS 6.9.18 and on unit charge until @ 18.7.19. **12 Sqn** Bickendorf by 6.22. **SAC** Old Sarum by 1922 until @ 1923.
C1038 (Arab) **5 AAP** Bristol by 5.6.18, allotted to BEF.
C1039 B&C for reconditioning to J Type (s/n 6609) and ready by 11.2.25. **PD Ascot**. To India. **AD** Drigh Road. **5 Sqn** as a/c *B* by 8.26 until @ 10.28.
C1040 (Falcon III) **5 AAP** Bristol 31.5.18, allotted to BEF and tested 6.6.18 (Lt C.F. Uwins). **22 Sqn** attached ex **2 ASD** 21.6.18 for experimental purposes, taken on unit charge 14.8.18, vict 21.8.18 (Lt T.W. Martin/Sgt G. Shannon sent a Fokker D.VII OOC, N of Cambrai at 19:45) then wrecked after OP 5.9.18 (Lt Ramsden/ Lt Felton both OK, on landing ran into a French civilian who was bending down and obscured by a small hillock – engine 1609/WD51829). **1 ASD** ex 22 Sqn 6.9.18.
C1041 (Arab) **5 AAP** Bristol by 5.6.18, allotted to BEF.
C1042 B&C for reconditioning to J Type (s/n 6248) and ready by 19.6.23. **13 Sqn** Andover by 1924 until @ 1926.
C1043 N/I
C1044 (Arab) **5 AAP** Bristol by 5.6.18, allotted to BEF. **36 TDS** Yatesbury by 1.19 until @ 2.19 (Lt W.R. Parkhouse).
C1045 **22 Sqn.**
C1046 N/I
C1047 (Arab) **5 AAP** Bristol by 7.6.18, allotted to BEF. **5 FTS** Sealand as a/c *7*.
C1048 **PD** Ascot. To Iraq. **AD** Hinaidi by 5.23. **6 Sqn** by 28.6.23 and wrecked 31.3.24 (collided with H1048).
C1049 **AD** Aboukir. **14 Sqn** by 3.5.23 until @ 12.23. To India. **AP** Lahore. Returned to UK. B&C for reconditioning to J Type (s/n 6864) and ready by 21.11.25. **RAF (Cadet) College** Cranwell by 1.28 until @ 12.30.
C1050 (Arab) at maker's 13.6.18, allotted to BEF. **8 AAP** Lympne by 23.1.19, reallotted from BEF to SE Area for Store Weston-on-the-Green.

200 BRISTOL FIGHTER F.2B ordered 23.7.17 under Contract AS.20379 from Harris & Sheldon and to be numbered C1951 to C2150. Contract cancelled and serials re-allocated.

1 BRISTOL FIGHTER F.2B built from spares by 18th Wing ARS under reference 87/Allot/86, serial number issued 17.12.17.

C4548 Allotment to Southern Training Brigade cancelled 26.12.17. **1 (Obs) SAG** New Romney dd ex 18th Wing ARS 16.2.18 and on unit charge until @ 3.18.

200 BRISTOL FIGHTER F.2B ordered 4.9.17 under Contracts AS.8871/1 & AS.17573 from British & Colonial Aeroplane Co Ltd, Bristol and numbered C4601 to C4800. (275hp Falcon III or 200hp Arab). [Consecutive works' sequence nos. 2951 to 3150]. Deliveries from w/e 20.11.17.

C4601 (Falcon III) **5 AAP** Bristol by 29.11.17, allotted to BEF. **11 Sqn** dd ex **2 AIS** 7.12.17 (engine 157/WD18578), marked as a/c *V* and wrecked on Test Flight 24.4.18 (Capt W.H. Park/Sgt C. Wilson both OK, ran into butts on landing – engine 39/WD18519). **2 ASD** ex 11 Sqn. **2 AIS** by 13.6.18. **1 AIS** by 21.6.18 (engine 643/WD32721). **88 Sqn** dd ex 1 AIS 22.6.18 and wrecked on

Delivery Flight to new aerodrome 21.10.18 (2nd Lt J. Thibadeau/ Cpl J. Hughes both OK, crashed on landing – engine 1249/WD51649). **1 ASD** ex 88 Sqn 23.10.18 and deleted 26.10.18 (not worth reconstruction).

C4602 (Falcon III) **5 AAP** Bristol by 30.11.17, allotted to BEF. **1 ASD** by 24.2.18. **2 AIS** dd ex 1 ASD 15.3.18. **62 Sqn** dd ex 2 AIS 18.3.18 (engine 115/WD18557). **2 AIS** ex 62 Sqn 10.4.18 (same engine). **62 Sqn** reissued ex 2 AIS 20.4.18 (same engine) and wrecked on Practice Flight 6.5.18 (Lt G. Palardy fatally IOAS, stalled and nosedived in – same engine). **1 ASD** ex 62 Sqn 9.5.18 and deleted 11.5.18 (not worth reconstruction, 25hr 25min).

C4603 (Falcon III) **5 AAP** Bristol 30.11.17, allotted to BEF and despatched by air by 15.12.17. **2 AIS** ex **2 ASD** 1.2.18 (engine 111/WD18555). **48 Sqn** dd ex 2 AIS 4.2.18 (2nd Lt N. Roberts, same engine), vict 12.3.18 (2nd Lt N. Roberts/Cpl W. Lawder destroyed a Fokker Dr.I and sent another down OOC, NE of St Quentin at 12:00) then wrecked after OP, Roye, 28.3.18 (2nd Lt N. Roberts/2nd Lt W.F. Hanna both OK, crashed on landing – engine 47/WD18523). **22 Wing SS** ex 48 Sqn 1.4.18. **1 ASD** ex Advanced Salvage 12.4.18 and deleted 23.4.18 (not worth reconstruction, 100hr 50min).

C4604 (Falcon III) **5 AAP** Bristol by 1.12.17, allotted to BEF. **1 AIS** ex **1 ASD** 18.12.17. **20 Sqn** dd ex 1 AIS 21.1.18 (engine 61/WD18530), victs 19.5.18 (Lt P.T. Iaccaci/Sgt W. Sansome destroyed a Fokker Dr.I near Merville at 10:55), 31.5.18 (Lt L.H.T. Capel/Prob F.J. Ralph destroyed an Albatros D.V, N of Laventie at 07:30), 17.6.18 (Lt L.H.T. Capel/Sgt E.A. Deighton DCM sent a Pfalz D.III down OOC and destroyed another NE of Gheluvelt at 07:40) and 23.6.18 (Lt L.H.T. Capel/Sgt E.A. Deighton DCM destroyed a Pfalz D.III over Laventie at 07:30) then LIA on 19:00 OP 24.7.18 (Sgt H.D. Aldridge POW/Sgt M.S. Samson POW, last seen N of Armentieres – engine 1023/WD39404) and deleted on unit 25.7.18 (288hr 11min).

C4605 (Falcon III) **5 AAP** Bristol by 1.12.17, allotted to BEF. **1 ASD** dd ex 5 AAP 6.12.17 (Lt C.F. Uwins). **1 AIS** dd ex 1 ASD 19.12.17. **20 Sqn** dd ex 1 AIS 28.1.18 (engine 123/WD18561), victs 5.2.18 (Lt D.G. Cooke/2nd Lt C.J. Agelasto sent two Albatros D.V down OOC, N of Staden at 11:20) and 9.3.18 (Lt D.G. Cooke/2nd Lt J.J. Scaramanga sent an Albatros D.V down OOC, S of Comines at 08:00) then wrecked on 15:14 OP 12.4.18 (Lt D.G. Cooke/ Lt H.G. Crowe both OK, machine badly shot up by enemy fire – engine 319/WD18659). **1 ASD** ex 20 Sqn 15.4.18 and deleted 23.4.18 (not worth reconstruction, 99hr 40min).

C4606 (Falcon III) **5 AAP** Bristol by 3.12.17, allotted to BEF. **2 AIS** ex **1 ASD** 10.12.17. **48 Sqn** dd ex 2 AIS 10.1.18 (engine 127/WD18563) and wrecked on Reconnaissance 15.4.18 (2nd Lt A.C.G. Brown/2nd Lt W. Hart both OK, machine shot up by ground machine gun fire – same engine). **2 Salvage Section** ex 48 Sqn 17.4.18. **2 ASD** ex 2 SS 22.4.18 and deleted 30.4.18 (not worth reconstruction).

C4607 **5 AAP** Filton tested 10.12.17 (Lt C.F. Uwins).

C4608 N/I

C4609 (Falcon III) **62 Sqn** Rendcomb by 24.12.17, to BEF with unit 23.1.18, vict 24.3.18 (2nd Lt S.W. Symons/Sgt W.N. Holmes destroyed an Albatros D-type 10 miles NE of Peronne at 15:55) then wrecked on OP 31.3.18 (2nd Lt L. Campbell/2nd Lt W. Hodgkinson both OK, crashed near Planques aerodrome – engine 49/WD18524) and deleted on unit that day (94hr 15min).

C4610 (Falcon III) **62 Sqn** Rendcomb by 22.12.17 and wrecked 11.1.18 (2nd Lt G.L.R. Parrish/fatally IIFA/Lt A.V. Collins IIFA, side-slipped to 50ft, stalled, dived in and caught fire – engine 3/F/119/WD18559).

Bristol F.2B C4611 in the snow, with its radiator covered against the cold, at the Wireless Experimental Establishment at Biggin Hill. *(RAF Museum)*

C4611 **WEE** Biggin Hill dd ex **5 AAP** 15.12.17 (Lt C.F. Uwins), marked as a/c *1* and on unit charge until @ 7.19.

C4612 **59 TS** Lilbourne by 23.2.18.

C4613 (Falcon III) **62 Sqn** Rendcomb by 29.12.17, to BEF with the unit 23.1.18 and wrecked on 12:00 Trench Straffing 28.3.18 (2nd Lt E.T. Morrow/Lt H.E. Merritt both OK, badly hit, force landed close to the lines and came under shell fire – engine 243/WD18621). **2 ASD** ex **2 Advanced Salvage** 19.4.18 and deleted 22.4.18.

C4614 **62 Sqn** Rendcomb by 19.12.17 but not to BEF with the unit. To India post-war and wrecked 13.12.19 (Lt Davies IOAS, crashed at Ambala).

C4615 (Falcon III) **5 AAP** Bristol 11.12.17, allotted to BEF and dd 18.12.17. **1 AIS** ex **1 ASD** 28.12.17 (engine 105/WD18552). **20 Sqn** dd ex 1 AIS 24.1.18 (same engine), vict 13.3.18 (Lt D. Latimer/2nd Lt J.J. Scaramanga sent an Albatros D.V down OOC over Comines-Wervicq at 12:55) then wrecked on 09:58 Patrol 1.4.18 (Lt R.B.T. Hedges/Lt A.C. Horlock both WIA, machine hit by AA fire, caught alight and came down near Pypegaale – engine 545/WD32672). **1 ASD** ex 20 Sqn 5.4.18 and deleted 7.4.18 (70hr 29min).

C4616 (Falcon III) **5 AAP** Bristol 12.12.17, allotted to BEF. **1 AIS** ex **1 ASD** 6.1.18 (engine 77/WD18538). **20 Sqn** dd ex 1 AIS 21.1.18 (same engine) and wrecked on 19:35 OP 13.4.18 (Lt H. Wesley-Segui/2nd Lt W.L. Pinder both IOAS, crashed landing in darkness at Clairmarais – same engine). **1 ASD** ex 20 Sqn 16.4.18 and deleted 23.4.18 (81hr 41min).

C4617 (Falcon III) **5 AAP** Bristol 12.12.17, allotted to BEF. **1 ASD** dd ex Bristol 18.12.17 (Lt C.F. Uwins). **1 AIS** ex 1 ASD 28.12.17 (engine 239/WD18619). **20 Sqn** dd ex 1 AIS 6.1.18 (same engine) and wrecked on Test Flight 23.2.18 (2nd Lt L.P. Roberts/LCpl G. Oxtoby ASC both KOAS, failed to pullout of a vertical dive – same engine). **1 ASD** ex 20 Sqn 26.2.18 and deleted 1.3.18 (52hr 3min).

C4618 (Falcon III) **5 AAP** Bristol 18.12.17, allotted to BEF. **1 ASD** by 24.2.18. **2 ASD** ex 1 ASD 26.2.18 (engine 109/WD18554). **7 Bde** Italy, ex 2 ASD by rail 2.3.18 (same engine). **28 Sqn** dd ex **7 AP** 16.3.18 (same engine) and wrecked 28.3.18 (Lt G. Ward IOAS/Lt Shorn OK, crashed on landing at **34 Sqn** aerodrome. **7 AP** and deleted 8.4.18.

C4619 (Falcon III) **62 Sqn** Rendcomb, marked as a/c *R* and later *C*, to BEF with the unit 23.1.18, victs 13.3.18 (2nd Lt W.E. Staton/Lt H.E. Merritt sent a Fokker Dr.I and an Albatros D.V down OOC over Cambrai), 21.3.18 (Lt W.E. Staton MC/Lt J.R. Gordon MC destroyed a Fokker Dr.I in flames near Cambrai at 15:20), 1.4.18 (Lt W.E. Staton MC/Lt J.R. Gordon MC sent an Albatros D.V down OOC over Bouchoir at 17:00) and 3.5.18 (Lt W.E. Staton MC/Lt J.R. Gordon MC destroyed a Pfalz D.III in flames E of Armentieres at 11:30, then destroyed an EA C-type 1 mile SE of Ploegsteert Wood). **2 ASD** ex 62 Sqn 20.7.18 (time expired, 198hr 55min – engine 605/WD32702) and flown to England 28.7.18.

C4620 **5 AAP** Filton tested 24.12.17 (Lt C.F. Uwins).

C4621 (Falcon III) **62 Sqn** Rendcomb dd ex **5 AAP** 23.12.17 (Lt C.F. Uwins), to BEF with the unit 23.1.18 and wrecked on Practice Flight 25.3.18 (2nd Lt J.M. Goller OK, engine failed, pilot attempted to land down wind and crashed – engine 409/WD32604). **1 ASD** ex **2 ASD** 3.4.18 for repair but deleted 25.6.18 on reconstruction as F5813 (60hr 50min).

C4622 (Falcon III) **5 AAP** Bristol 20.12.17, reallotted from ME Bde for service in Egypt to BEF and tested 23.12.17 and 24.12.17 (Lt C.F. Uwins). **1 ASD** dd ex England 6.1.18 (engine 79/WD18539). **2 AIS** ex 1 ASD 24.2.18 (same engine). **2 ASD** 26.2.18 to be packed in case for 7 Bde Italy. **7 Bde** dd ex 2 ASD by rail 2.3.18 (same engine). **28 Sqn** dd ex **7 AP** 16.3.18 and wrecked 19.3.18 (2nd Lt D.W. Pratt OK/AM2 W.T. Jackson IOAS, controls broke away from control lever and machine crashed (same engine). **7 AP** ex 28 Sqn 21.3.18.

C4623 (Falcon III) presentation a/c *Australia No.8, New South Wales No.7. The Mrs P. Kirby & Son.* To Middle East. **X AP** and Palestine Bde dd ex **X AD** 18.3.18. **1 Sqn AFC** dd ex X AP 19.3.18, damaged in combat on 11:45 Patrol 26.6.18 (Lt A.W. Murphy OK/Lt A.W.K Farquhar KIA in combat with an Albatros C-type over Ramleh). **X AP** ex 1 Sqn AFC. **1 Sqn AFC**, reissued ex X AP 10.8.18, victs 24.8.18 (Lt P.J. McGuiness/Lt H.B. Fletcher destroyed Pfalz D.III in flames and destroyed another on the ground after forcing it to land near Kalkilieh at 08:30), 31.8.18 (Lt P.J. McGuiness/Lt H. Fysh captured a LVG C-type near Rantieh and destroyed another E of Kalkilieh at 14:30), 14.9.18 (Lt P.J. McGuiness/Lt H. Fysh destroyed a Rumpler C-type E of Jenin at 11:30, shared B1223). **111 Sqn** ex 1 Sqn AFC 4.2.19. **X AP** ex 111 Sqn 13.5.19 (engine WD30399). **ASD ME** ex X AP 24.7.19 (same engine).

C4624 Presentation a/c *Australia No.13, Australia No.12, The Macintyre Abayuga Estate*. To Middle East. **1 Sqn AFC** dd ex **X AP** 25.3.18 and on unit charge until @ 16.6.18.

C4625 To Middle East. **1 Sqn AFC** by 21.3.18

C4626 (Falcon III) presentation a/c *Australia No.16, New South Wales No.7. The Women's Battleplane*. To Middle East. **X AD** and tested 23.3.18. **X AP** ex **X AD** 24.3.18 **1 Sqn AFC** dd ex **X AP** 30.3.18, victs 28.4.18 (Lt E.P. Kenny/Lt F.C. Hawley sent an Albatros D.III down OOC, S of Nablus at 17:45), 30.7.18 (Lt E.P. Kenny/Lt L.W. Sutherland destroyed a DFW C-type near Wadi Aujah at 07:10), 3.8.18 (Lt E.P. Kenny/Lt L.W. Sutherland destroyed an Albatros C-type FTL NW of Afuleh at 11:30, sent an Albatros C-type down OOC over Leijun at 11:45 and destroyed another Albatros C-type 2 miles NE of Ez Buba at 12:10 the last shared with B1223), 23.9.18 (Lt E.P. Kenny/Lt L.W. Sutherland destroyed a DFW C-type FTL NW of Deraa at 07:15), 28.9.18 (Lt E.P. Kenny/Lt L.W. Sutherland destroyed a DFW C-type over Damascus aerodrome at 08:15) and 23.10.18 (Lt S.H. Harper/Lt W.H. Lilly forced a DFW C-type down onto Babannit aerodrome near Aleppo at 06:00). **111 Sqn** ex 1 Sqn AFC 4.2.19. **X AP** ex 111 Sqn 31.5.19 (engine WD18691).

C4627 (Falcon III) presentation a/c *City of Adelaide. Presented by Mrs Harry Bickford*. To Middle East. **X AP** dd ex **X AD** 21.3.18. **1 Sqn AFC** dd ex **X AP** 22.3.18, victs 23.5.18 (Lt C.S. Paul/Lt W.J.A. Weir sent an Albatros D.V down OOC and destroyed another near Nablus at 07.00-07.15), 13.6.18 (Lt C.S. Paul/Lt W.J.A. Weir destroyed a Rumpler C-type 8 miles N of Nablus at 04:30), 28.7.18 (Lt C.S. Paul/Lt W.J.A. Weir destroyed a Rumpler C-type NW of Wadi Farah at 12:00, shared B1284) and 16.8.18 (Lt C.S. Paul/Lt W.J.A. Weir destroyed a Rumpler C-type over Kefr Kaddum at 08:30). **111 Sqn** ex 1 Sqn AFC 4.2.19. **X AP** ex 111 Sqn 15.5.19 (engine 32725). **ASD ME** ex X AP 23.7.19 (same engine).

C4628 (Falcon III) **5 AAP** Bristol 22.12.17, allotted to BEF. **2 AIS** ex **1 ASD** 10.1.18 (engine 205/WD18602). **48 Sqn** dd ex 2 AIS 4.2.18 (same engine), vict 9.2.18 (2nd Lt H.H. Hartley/2nd Lt R.S. Herring sent an Albatros D.III down OOC, S of Guise at 12:00) then wrecked after OP 4.4.18 (2nd Lt F.C. Ransley/2nd Lt C.W. Dacies both OK, crashed on landing and o/t – same engine). **2 ASD** ex 48 Sqn 6.4.18. **1 ASD** ex **2 ASD** 10.4.18 and deleted that day (not worth reconstruction, 93hr 50min).

C4629 (Falcon III) **5 AAP** Bristol 22.12.17, allotted to BEF. **1 ASD** by 24.2.18. **2 AIS** ex 1 ASD 6.3.18 (engine137/WD18568). **62 Sqn** dd ex 2 AIS 13.3.18 (same engine), vict 21.3.18 (Capt T.L. Purdom/2nd Lt P.V.G. Chambers destroyed an Albatros D.V, N of Cambrai at 15:30) and damaged on Trench Strafing 28.3.18 (2nd Lt H.C.M. Nangle OK/AM1 A. Boxall WIA, machine shot up and landed at **12 Sqn** aerodrome – same engine). **2 ASD** ex 62 sqn 11.4.18 (same engine). **48 Sqn** dd ex 2 AIS 22.4.18 (same engine), destroyed in enemy bombing of aerodrome 24.8.18 (engine 943/WD32871) and deleted on unit that day.

C4630 (Falcon III) **5 AAP** Bristol 27.12.17 allotted to BEF but re-allotted to **62 Sqn** 28.12.18. **62 Sqn** Rendcomb, as a/c *J*, to BEF with the unit 23.1.18, victs 23.2.18 (Capt G.F. Hughes MC/Capt H. Claye destroyed a large two-seat EA at 7,000ft over Armentières), 13.3.18 (Capt G.F. Hughes MC/Capt H. Claye sent down a Fokker Dr.I flown by Ltn L. v Richthofen, shared with **73 Sqn** Camel B7282 of Capt A.H. Orlebar, and destroyed another E of Cambrai at 10:30), 12.4.18 (Capt G.F. Hughes MC/Capt H. Claye sent an Albatros D.V down OOC over Bois de Biez at 14:15 and destroyed an LVG C-type near Seclin at 15:15), 10.5.18 (Capt G.F. Hughes MC/Capt H. Claye sent an EA C-type down OOC over Albert at 18:30) then LIA on 08:15 on OP 19.5.18 (Lt H.A. Clarke/Capt H. Claye both POW, last seen under control near Corbie at c.10:15, probably brought down by Ltn Delling, Jasta 34b – engine 249/WD18624) and deleted on unit that day (106hr 5min).

C4631 (Falcon III) **5 AAP** Bristol 27.12.17, allotted to BEF. **1 ASD** dd ex England 7.1.18 (engine 285/WD18642). **1 AIS** ex 1 ASD 24.1.18 (same engine). **1 ASD** ex 1 AIS 2.2.18 (same engine). **1 AIS** ex 1 ASD 27.2.18 (same engine). **22 Sqn** dd ex 1 AIS 7.3.18 (same engine), marked as a/c *T*, victs 28.5.18 (2nd Lt W.F.J. Harvey/Lt G. Thomson destroyed an EA C-type and another EA over La Bassee-Rickebourg at 11:09). **1 ASD** ex 22 Sqn 23.6.18 (unfit for further war service, 118 hr – same engine) and flown to England 25.6.18. **141 Sqn** Biggin Hill 1918. **APS** Andover by 7.19 until @ 2.20. **SAC** Old Sarum by 12.22 until @ 7.23. B&C for reconditioning to J Type (s/n 6658) and ready by 17.3.25. **SAC** Old Sarum by 9.25 until @ 2.28. B&C for reconditioning (s/n 7242) and ready by 12.7.28. **PD** Ascot.

C4632 (Falcon III) **5 AAP** Bristol 31.12.17, allotted to BEF. **1 ASD** dd ex England 10.1.18 (engine 139/WD18569). **2 AIS** ex 1 ASD 6.3.18 (same engine). **62 Sqn** dd ex 2 AIS 13.3.18 (same engine) and wrecked on OP 17.3.18 (2nd Lt S.W. Symons/Sgt W.N. Holmes both OK, radiator hit by AA fire and hit shell hole during forced landing near Les Boeufs – same engine). **2 ASD** ex 62 Sqn 17.3.18. **1 ASD** ex 2 ASD 3.4.18 and deleted 8.4.18 (not worth reconstruction, 3hr 25min).

C4633 (Falcon III) **5 AAP** Bristol 31.12.17, allotted to BEF. **1 ASD** dd ex England 10.1.18 (engine 197/WD18598). **2 AIS** ex 1 ASD 6.3.18 (same engine). **62 Sqn** dd ex 2 AIS 13.3.18 (same engine), victs 21.4.18 (2nd Lt G.M. Yuille/Lt E.W. Collis sent a Pfalz D.III down OOC over Bois de Ploegsteert at 11:30) and 22.5.18 (Lt W.K. Swayze/Lt W.E. Hall destroyed an LVG C-type at 08:00) then reported 29.5.18 as in need of thorough overhaul and re-rigging (same engine). **2 ASD** ex 62 Sqn 29.5.18 (Lt Hudson) and flown to England via **1 ASD** 30.5.18.

C4634 **8 TS** Netheravon by 21.1.18. **7 TS** Netheravon by 24.2.18 (2nd Lt H.A. Oaks). **8 TS** Netheravon by 8.3.18 (Sgt J. Gamble).

C4635 **39 Sqn** North Weald by 31.1.18 (Lt C.P. Donnison/AM1 A.T.C. Stagg) and on HAPs 16/17.2.18 (Lt C.P. Donnison/AM1 A.T.C. Stagg) and 17/18.2.18 (Lt C.P. Donnison/AM1 A.T.C. Stagg) and on unit charge until @ 3.6.18 (Lt C.P. Donnison/AM1 A.T.C. Stagg).

C4636 **39 Sqn** North Weald as a/c *A-6* named *Devil in the Dusk*, on HAPs 28/29.1.18 (crew not named), 16/17.2.18 (2nd Lt A.J. Arkell/AM1 E. Gedgeon), 17/18.2.18 (2nd Lt A.J. Arkell/Sgt Major Wyatt), 7/8.3.18 (2nd Lt A.J. Arkell/AM1 E. Gudgeon), vict on HAP 19/20.5.18 (2nd Lt A.J. Arkell/AM1 A.T.C. Stagg brought down a Gotha near East Ham at 00:20) and on unit charge until @ 9.18.

C4637 (Falcon III) **62 Sqn** Rencomb, to BEF with the unit 23.1.18 and wrecked on Test Flight 14.2.18 (2nd Lt J. Reid Miller/Lt E.W. Collis both IOAS, in bad visibility flew into a wooded hillside – engine 331/WD18665). **1 ASD** ex 62 Sqn 16.2.18 and deleted 17.2.18 (10hr 20min).

C4638 **39 Sqn** North Weald damaged on HAPs 28.1.18 (2nd Lt J.G. Goodyear OK/AM1 W.T. Merchant WIA, landed safely – engine 18658) and 7/8.3.18 (Lt J.G. Goodyear/Lt Forrest) and on unit charge until @ 14.5.18 (Lt C.P. Donnison/AM1 A.T.C. Stagg).

C4639 **39 Sqn** North Weald and on HAPs 29.1.18 (Lt A.E. Simmons/AM1 Coombs returned early with engine trouble) and 17.2.18 (Lt C.R.W. Knight/2nd Lt E.J. Ralli).

C4640 (Falcon III) **5 AAP** Bristol by 7.1.18, allotted to BEF. **1 ASD** dd ex England 13.1.18 (engine 165/WD18582). **2 AIS** ex 1 ASD 23.2.18 (same engine). **48 Sqn** dd ex 2 AIS 12.3.18 and wrecked on 12:45 Ground Patrol 14.3.18 (2nd Lt H.H. Hartley KIA/2nd Lt G. Dixon WIA, hit by ground fire at 100ft over the trenches near Estrees and crashed – same engine). **2 ASD** ex 48 Sqn 16.3.18. **1 ASD** ex 2 ASD by rail 2.4.18 and deleted 14.4.18 (not worth reconstruction).

C4641 (Falcon III) **5 AAP** Bristol by 7.1.18, allotted to BEF. **1 ASD** dd ex 5 AAP 13.1.18 (Lt C.F. Uwins, departed 12.1.18 – engine 319/WD18569). **1 AIS** ex 1 ASD 28.1.18 (same engine). **20 Sqn** dd ex 1 AIS 15.2.18 (same engine), vict 17.2.18 (Lt E. Lindup/Cpl M. Mather destroyed a Pfalz D.III in flames over Westroosebeke at 11:30) then wrecked on OP 22.5.18 (Lt R.G. Bennett/Lt G.T.C. Salter both OK, fuselage badly strained in a nose dive – engine 187/WD18593). **1 ASD** ex 20 Sqn 24.5.18 and deleted 12.7.18 on reconstruction as F5995.

C4642 (Falcon III) **7 TS** Netheravon and wrecked 15.2.18 (2nd Lt R.B. Tapp IIFA, dived out of cloud with empty main tank and flew into the ground while trying to change tanks – engine 311/WD18655).

C4643 **PD** Ascot. To Egypt. **AD** Aboukir. Force landed near Balir, Transjordan after engine failure 5.30.

C4644 **8 TS** Netheravon dd ex **5 AAP** by 23.1.18 and on unit charge until @ 2.18. **SAC** Old Sarum by 9.25 until @ 9.26.

C4645 Presentation a/c *Presented by Maharaja Bahadur Sir Rameswar Singh of Darbhanga No.3*. **39 Sqn** North Weald by 2.18 until @ 24.8.18.

C4646 **39 Sqn** North Weald and on HAP 29.1.18 (2nd Lt A.S. Dickens/Lt N.C. Crombie). **33 TDS** Witney by 8.18.

C4647 (Falcon III) **5 AAP** tested 20.1.18 (Lt C.F. Uwins). **35 TS** Port Meadow and wrecked 15.3.18 (Capt E.F. Norris/AM2 R.R. Humphries both KIFA, machine collapsed when looping at 3,000ft and crashed near Wolvercote – engine 3/F/201/WD18600).

C4648 (Falcon III) **1 (Obs) SAG** Hythe by 24.4.18 (Lt E. Shamper) and wrecked 3.9.18 (Lt G.W. Armstrong/2nd Lt K.C.W. Garden both KIFA in mid-air collision with C4781 – engine 203/WD18601).

C4649 **5 AAP** tested 20.1.18 (Lt C.F. Uwins). Arrived Eastbourne with C4822 and to New Romney 28.4.18. **1 (Obs) SAG** New Romney by 16.6.18 until @ 20.8.18 (Sgt J. Gamble).

C4650 **39 Sqn** North Weald marked as a/c *1* and on HAPs 16/17.2.18 (Capt J.M. Clarke/Lt L. Speller), 17/18.2.18 (Capt J.M. Clarke/Lt L. Speller) and 7/8.3.18 (Capt J.M. Clarke/Lt L. Speller) and on unit charge until @ 10.8.18.

C4651 (Falcon III) to Middle East. **X AD** dd ex England 25.7.18. **5 FS** Heliopolis dd ex X AD 16.9.18 and wrecked on Camera Gun Practice 25.10.18 (2nd Lt J. Edmonds/2nd Lt W.F. Lane both OK, engine cut out on take off – engine WD10468). **16 TDS** Abu Sueir. **ASD ME** ex 16 TDS 16.5.19 (same engine). **208 Sqn** by 12.21 until @ 1.22. **4 FTS** Abu Sueir by 8.23 until @ 9.23. **AD** Aboukir and rebuilt as CR4651. **14 Sqn** by 22.4.24, wrecked 5.5.24 (crashed on landing Ramleh) and deleted.

C4652 (Falcon III) to Middle East. **X AD** dd ex England 25.7.18. **X AP** and Palestine Bde ex X AD 29.10.18. **111 Sqn** dd ex X AP 31.3.19 (engine WD18592). **X AP** ex 111 Sqn 25.6.19. **ASD ME** ex Palestine Bde 20.8.19 and deleted 13.11.19.

C4653 To Middle East. **X AD** dd ex England 1.7.18. **5 FS** Heliopolis dd ex X AD 28.11.18 (engine WD10499). **16 TDS** Abu Sueir and deleted on unit 2.6.19.

C4654 (Arab) **ES** Martlesham Heath dd 14.8.18. **2 AAP** Hendon 19.9.18 (and fitted with 290hp high compression Puma). **ES** Martlesham Heath reissued 22.9.18, producing test report M230a 12.10.18. **RAE** Farnborough by 7.7.22 fitted with Falcon III and damaged 11.9.22 (Fg Off J.S. Chick MC OK, engine fire at 200ft after take off but landed safely). **AEE** (later A&AEE) Martlesham Heath. **RAE** Farnborough by 4.4.23 for cooling tests and, later, meteorological research. **HAD** Henlow by 7.9.27.

C4655 (BHP) in France 19.6.18 reallotted from SE Area to BEF. **1 ASD** by 19.6.18. **1 AIS** by 21.6.18 (engine 5812/WD23486). **42 Sqn** dd ex 2 ASD 23.6.18 (same engine). **'L' Flt** ex 42 Sqn 5.7.18 (engine 6613). **42 Sqn** ex 'L' Flt 31.7.18 (same engine). **1 ASD** ex 42 Sqn 1.8.18 (same engine) and flown to England 7.8.18. **RAE** Farnborough by 10.9.18, fitted with Puma engine by 1.20 and given enlarged fin and rudder by 8.26. **HAD** Henlow 13.9.27. B&C for reconditioning to J Type (s/n 7242) and ready by 12.7.28. **PD** Ascot.

C4656 N/I

C4657 (Arab) **3 (W)ARD** by 14.2.18, allotted to BEF.

C4658 (Arab) **3 (W)ARD** by 14.2.18, allotted to BEF. **1 ASD** dd ex England 11.3.18 (engine 19035). **2 ASD** ex 1 ASD 18.4.18 (same engine) and on unit charge until @ 30.4.18. **1 ASD** and flown to England 12.5.18 (same engine). **2 TDS** Gullane by 2.19 until @ 4.19.

C4659 (Initially Arab) **3 (W)ARD** 14.2.18, allotted to BEF. **1 ASD** dd ex England 15.3.18 (engine 16288). **2 ASD** ex 1 ASD 21.4.18 (same engine). Converted to Falcon III. **62 Sqn** dd ex 2 ASD 8.6.18 (engine 93/WD18546) and wrecked on Practice Flight 26.7.18 (Lt N.N. Coope/2nd Lt J. Hall both OK, engine failed, force landed in cornfield and o/t – same engine). **2 ASD** ex 62 Sqn 28.7.18 and deleted 11.8.18 (not worth reconstruction, 36hr).

C4660 **35 TS** Port Meadow 23.3.18.

C4661 N/I

C4662 (Arab) **3 (W)ARD** 14.2.18, allotted to BEF. **1 ASD** dd ex England 23.3.18 (engine 16271) and flown back to England 18.5.18, apparently without squadron service (same engine).

C4663 (Arab) **3 (W)ARD** 14.2.18, allotted to BEF and despatched 10.3.18. **11 Sqn** dd ex **1 ASD** 3.4.18 (engine 19041). **12 Sqn** attached ex **11 Sqn** 23.4.18 (same engine). **2 ASD** ex 12 Sqn 23.4.18 and flown to England 15.5.18.

C4664 (Arab) **3 (W)ARD** 14.2.18, allotted to BEF but allotment cancelled 26.3.18 with machine deleted.

C4665 (Arab) **(S)ARD** Farnborough, photographed with re-applied serial.

C4666 **33 TDS** Witney by 15.8.18 (2nd Lt G.A. Raybone). **IACF** Northolt by 6.21.

C4667 N/I

C4668 Rendcomb to Eastbourne 9.8.18.

C4669 **45 TDS** Rendcomb by 7.18 until @ 28.8.18.

C4670 **39 Sqn** North Weald by 26.2.18 and on HAP 7/8/3/1918 (Lt J.L.N. Bennett-Baggs/Lt A.J.F. Bawden).

C4671 **39 Sqn** North Weald and wrecked on HAP 20.5.18 (Lt S.H. Love/AM1 W.T. Merchent both OK, crashed on landing).

C4672 (Falcon III) **5 AAP** Bristol 14.2.18, reallotted from 7 Bde Italy to BEF. **1 ASD** dd ex England 5.3.18 (engine 469/WD32634). **1 AIS** ex 1 ASD 11.3.18 (same engine). **20 Sqn** dd ex 1 AIS 27.3.18 (same engine), victs 31.5.18 (Lt A.T. Iaccaci/Sgt D. Malpas sent an Albatros D.V down OOC, SW of Armentieres at 08:00), 24.7.18 (Lt L.M. Price/Lt A. Mills DFC destroyed a Fokker D.VII, N of Comines at 20:00) and 25.7.18 (Lt D.E. Smith/Prob J. Hills destroyed a Fokker D.VII and sent another down OOC over Comines at 08:50) then damaged on Formation Practice 21.8.18 (2nd Lt S. Rendle/2nd Lt D.M. Calderwood both OK, bad landing and reported as unfit for further service in the field and not fit to fly the Channel – engine 1325/WD51657). **1 ASD** ex 20 Sqn 23.8.18 and deleted 26.8.18 (not worth reconstruction, 288hr 8min).

C4673 (Falcon III) **5 AAP** Bristol 14.2.18, reallotted from 7 Bde Italy BEF. **1 ASD** dd ex England 24.2.18 (engine 379/WD18689). **2 AIS** ex 1 ASD 28.2.18 (same engine). **11 Sqn** dd ex 2 AIS 5.3.18 (same engine), marked as a/c *11*, victs 12.3.18 (Lt H.W. Sellars/Lt C.C. Robson captured an LVG near Dorignies at 14:40), 13.3.18

Dual-control Bristol F.2B C4666, seen in the snow at Port Meadow, Oxfordshire, in May 1919, was the personal mount of Fg Off Walter Longton. *(Philip Jarrett)*

(Lt H.W. Sellars/Lt C.C. Robson sent an Albatros D.V down OOC near Oisy at 14:00), 15.3.18 (Lt H.W. Sellars/Lt C.C. Robson sent an Albatros D.V down OOC near Rumilly at 11:15), 18.3.18 (Lt H.W. Sellars/Lt C.C. Robson sent an Albatros D.V down OOC, N of St Quentin at 11:00), 21.3.18 (Lt H.W. Sellars/Lt C.C. Robson destroyed and Albatros C-type and sent an Albatros D.V down in flames near Morchies at 16:15) and 2.4.18 (Lt H.W. Sellars/Lt C.C. Robson sent a Fokker Dr.I down OOC, SE of Albert at 18:20) then wrecked on Reconnaissances 24.4.18 (2nd Lt E.W.P. Lamb/Sgt B.J. Maisey both KOAS, hit trees in thick fog – same engine) and deleted on unit that day (73hr 40min).

C4674 **35 TS** Port Meadow by 27.7.18. **71 TS** Port Meadow by 5.8.18.

C4675 **44 TDS** Port Meadow and wrecked 19.8.18 (2nd Lt C.J. Buckland KIFA, spun in from 100ft after take off – engine 353/WD15746).

C4676 **45 TDS** Rendcomb 1918. B&C for reconditioning to J Type (s/n 6569) and ready by 19.12.24. **16 Sqn** Old Sarum. B&C for reconditioning (s/n 6968) and ready by 8.7.26 as the first machine to be fitted with new type Holt Flare brackets. **16 Sqn/SAC** Old Sarum by 7.27 until @ 1.28.

C4677 **45 TDS** Rendcomb by 11.18 until @ 1.19. **Staff College Flt** Andover by 5.25.

C4678 **45 TDS** Rendcomb by 8.18.

C4679 N/I

C4680 B&C for reconditioning to J Type DC (s/n 6441) and ready by 6.5.24. B&C for reconditioning to Mk.III DC (s/n 7130) and ready by 31.3.27. **CFS** Upavon named *The Old Biff 1928* by 12.28 until @ 4.29. B&C for repair and ready by 23.12.29.

C4681 **1 SAFG** Ayr by 15.4.18 (Capt J.H. Letts). B&C for reconditioning to J Type (s/n 6436) and ready by 10.5.24. **16 Sqn/SAC** Old Sarum by 12.25.

C4682 B&C for reconditioning to J Type (s/n 6446) and ready by 6.6.24. To Iraq. Rebuilt as CR4682. **6 Sqn** by 4.29 until @ 6.30 and also on unit charge by 1.32 until @ 6.32.

C4683 B&C for reconditioning to J Type (s/n 6424) and ready by 22.3.24. **CFS** Upavon by 6.24 until @ 10.25. B&C for reconditioning (s/n 7238) and ready by 30.6.28. **PD** Ascot. To Egypt. **AD** Aboukir. **6 Sqn** by 4.19 and wrecked 23.2.32 (crash landed at Ismailia and deleted).

C4684 **1 SAF** Ayr by 4.18. **1 FS** Turnberry by 20.8.18. **27 TDS** Crail by 6.11.18. **2 FTS** Digby and wrecked 21.11.24 (crashed near Warboys, Hunts).

C4685 **1 SAFG** Ayr by 26.6.18 (Capt J.H. Letts) and transferred to Turnberry with unit becoming **1 FS** and on charge until @ 28.7.18 (Capt J.H. Letts).

C4686 N/I

C4687 **8 TS** Netheravon by 14.3.18. **SSF** Gosport. **1 SAFG** Ayr by 12.4.18 until @ 26.5.16 (Capt J.H. Letts).

C4688 (Falcon III) **1 SAF** Ayr, given as C7688, and wrecked 2.4.18 (2nd Lt J.E. Doe/Cpl H.R. Young USAS both IIFA, failed to exit a spin – engine 3/F/723/WD32611).

C4689 (Falcon II) **1 SAFG** Ayr by 18.4.18 and wrecked 23.4.18 (Lt L.W. Wheelock/Lt N. Berry USAS both IIFA, flat turn after take off, dived in and caught fire on impact – engine 2/F/111/WD22397).

C4690 **1 SAFG** Turnberry by 26.4.18, unit retitled **1 FS** and on unit charge until @ 6.9.18 (Capt J.H. Letts).

C4691 **1 SAF** Ayr by 27.3.18.

C4692 (Falcon III) **2 FS** Marske as a/c *43* and wrecked 28.10.18 (2nd Lt D.D. McAlpin/Flt Cdt A.E. Johnson both KIFA in mid-air collision over North Sea with E2550 – engine WD22414).

C4693 N/I

C4694 **2 SAFG** Marske as a/c *16* by 4.18 and photographed completely wrecked.

C4695 **2 FS** Marske as a/c *76* by 19.7.18. **1 FS** Turnberry.

C4696 **1 (S)ARD** Farnborough dd ex Catterick as salvage 2.7.18 and deleted 24.3.19.

C4697 **SAC** Old Sarum by 3.20.

C4698 (Falcon III) **33 Sqn, 'A' Flt** Scampton and wrecked on AZP 5.8.18 (Lt F.A. Benitz KOAS/Lt H. Lloyd-Williams IAOS, crashed landing at Atwick in adverse weather – engine WD18506).

C4699 (Falcon III) **5 AAP** Bristol 21.2.18, reallotted from 7 Bde Italy to BEF. **8 AAP** Lympne by 25.2.18. **1 ASD** dd ex England 5.3.18 (engine 521/WD32660). **1 AIS** ex 1 ASD 11.3.18 (same engine). **20 Sqn** dd ex 1 AIS 27.3.18 (same engine), victs 31.5.18 (Lt D.J. Weston/Lt W. Noble sent an Albatros D.V down OOC over Estaires at 07:40 and Lt P.T. Iaccaci/AM1 S.W. Melbourne sent an Albatros D.V down OOC, NW of Armentieres at 18:55) then wrecked after OP 13.6.18 (Lt Davidson/Sgt J.D. Cormack both OK, crashed on landing – engine 343/WD18171). **1 ASD** ex 20 Sqn 15.6.18 and deleted 22.7.18 on reconstruction as F5999 (141hr 13min).

C4700 (Falcon III) **5 AAP** Bristol 22.2.18, allotted to BEF. **8 AAP** dd ex 5 AAP 25.2.18 (Lt C.F. Uwins). **1 ASD** dd ex England 26.2.18 (engine 559/WD32679). **2 ASD** ex 1 ASD 27.2.18 (same engine) and to 7th Bde, Italy by rail 2.3.18 (same engine). **28 Sqn** dd ex 7 AP 27.3.18 (same engine) and wrecked 29.3.18 (Lt D.W. Pratt OK/Lt Wilton IOAS, crashed on landing). **7 AP** for repair. **Z Flight, 34 Sqn** dd ex 7 AP 10.5.18, in combat 2.6.18 (2nd Lt E.M. Brown/2nd Lt H. Milburn claimed an Albatros D.III shot down), LIA on Reconnaissance 9.6.18 (Lt E.M. Brown/2nd Lt C.A. Gordon both POW, brought down over Trento at 09:00 – same engine) and deleted on unit 10.8.18 (48hr 50min).

C4701 (Falcon III) **5 AAP** Bristol 22.2.18, allotted to BEF. **1 ASD** dd ex England 26.2.18 (engine 533/WD32666). **2 AIS** ex 1 ASD 27.2.18 (same engine). **48 Sqn** dd ex 2 AIS 16.3.18, damaged in combat 28.3.18 (Capt W.L. Wells fatally WIA/Cpl W. Beales WIA) and wrecked on 17:05 OP 2.4.18 (2nd Lt C.E. Glover/Cpl W. Beales both OK, machine shot up in combat – same engine). **2 ASD** ex 48 Sqn 7.4.18 and deleted 12.4.18 (not worth reconstruction).

C4702 **8 TS** Netheravon by 23.2.18. **24 TS** Netheravon and wrecked 13.3.18 (2nd Lt C.W. Hurst IIFA, failed to flatten out on landing – engine 435/WD32617).

C4703 **1 (Obs) SAG** Hythe and wrecked 31.3.18 (Lt Bain OK, crashed on landing after engine failure).

C4704 (Falcon III) **1 (Obs) SAG** Hythe and wrecked 8.4.18 (Lt A.H. Phillips/Lt A.G. Rees both IIFA, engine cut on take off and crashed attempting to land – engine 3/F/393/WD18696).

C4705 N/I

C4706 (Falcon III) **5 AAP** Bristol 25.2.18, allotted to BEF. **1 ASD** dd ex 5 AAP 5.3.18 (Lt C.F. Uwins – engine 541/WD32670). **1 AIS** ex 1 ASD 11.3.18 (same engine). **22 Sqn** dd ex 1 AIS 13.3.18, marked as a/c *Q* and wrecked on Wireless Practice 30.8.18 (Lt E.R. Zealley/Lt C. Partington both KOAS, collided with another machine, elevator damaged and crashed – engine 1389/WD51719). **1 ASD** ex 22 Sqn 30.8.18 and deleted 2.9.18 (245hr 51min).

C4707 (Falcon III) **5 AAP** Bristol 25.2.18, allotted to BEF. **1 ASD** dd ex England 7.3.18 (engine 587/WD32693). **2 AIS** ex 1 ASD 8.3.18 (same engine). **48 Sqn** dd ex 2 AIS 15.3.18 (same engine), LIA on 17:05 OP 2.4.18 (2nd Lt C.D.B. Stiles WIA/2nd Lt F.F. Walker fatally WIA, shot down in combat close to the front-line trenches with machine unsalvageable – same engine) and deleted on unit that day (38hr 35min).

C4708 **37 TS** Spittlegate by 4.18. **15 TS** Spittlegate by 4.18 until @ 11.8.18.

C4709 (Falcon III) **5 AAP** Bristol 27.2.18, allotted to BEF. **1 ASD** dd ex England 10.3.18 (engine 565/WD32685). **2 AIS** ex 1 ASD 15.3.18 (same engine). **62 Sqn** dd ex 2 AIS 16.3.18, marked as a/c *8* and vict 24.3.18 (2nd Lt M.H. Cleary/2nd Lt V.G. Stanton sent an Albatros D.V down OOC, E of Peronne at 13:10). **2 AIS** ex 62 Sqn 10.4.18. **62 Sqn** ex 2 AIS 22.4.18 (same engine) and wrecked after successful combat on 09:55 Patrol 3.5.18 (Capt H. Rees Jones/2nd Lt J. Bruce-Norton both OK, destroyed an Albatros D-type in flames S of Armentieres and sent another down OOC at 11:00 but controls damaged in combat, and crashed in forced landing – same engine). **1 ASD** ex 62 Sqn 7.5.18 and deleted 25.6.18 on reconstruction as F5811 (37hr).

C4710 (Falcon III) **5 AAP** Bristol 28.2.18 allotted to BEF. **1 ASD** dd ex England 9.3.18 (engine 647/WD32723). **2 AIS** ex 1 ASD 15.3.18 (same engine). **48 Sqn** dd ex 2 AIS 16.3.18 (same engine), LIA on 17:05 OP 24.3.18 (Capt C.R. Steele/2nd Lt E.H. Stanes both OK, brought down by ground fire near Foucaucourt, machine destroyed and impossible to salvage due to the proximity of the enemy – same engine) and deleted on unit that day (13hr 45min).

C4711 **39 Sqn** North Weald and on HAP 19/20.5.18 (Lt A.F. Barker/AM1 Hill). At Rendcomb (**45 TDS**?) 3.12.18

C4712 **50 TS** Spittlegate by 2.4.18. **15 TS** Spittlegate by 14.5.18 until @ 12.8.18.

C4713 **88 Sqn** and wrecked on Practice Flight 6.5.18 (Lt Foster/Lt Chilton both OK, crashed on landing – engine 213/WD18606). **1 ASD** ex 88 Sqn and deleted 11.5.18 (not worth reconstruction, 32hr 20min).

C4714 **ES** Orfordness by 9.8.18 until @ 29.8.18. **ECD** Grain dd ex Orfordness 4.7.19.

C4715 (Falcon III) **141 Sqn**, on HAP 19/20.5.18 (Lt F.R.S. Southen) and wrecked 26.7.18 (Lt E.H. Rowlands IIFA, landed outside flares and searchlights – engine 3/F/1071/WD39428).

C4716 **45 TDS** Rendcomb by 8.18.

C4717 (Falcon III) **8 TS** Witney by 24.4.18 (Sgt J. Gamble) and wrecked 8.6.18 (2nd Lt N.R. Scully IIFA, stalled on low LH turn and nosedived in – engine 3/F/509/WD32654).

C4718 (Falcon III) **88 Sqn** Harling Road, to BEF with unit 25.4.18 and wrecked on Practice Flight 27.4.18 (Sgt Lile/2nd Lt Hinchliffe both OK, crashed landing at Capelle – engine 691/WD32745). **1 ASD** ex 88 Sqn 1.5.18. **1 AIS** ex 1 ASD 25.6.18 (engine 553/WD32676). **20 Sqn** dd ex 1 AIS 29.6.18, victs 25.7.18 (Capt H.P. Lale/2nd Lt F.J. Ralph destroyed a Fokker D.VII crashed just N of Comines and sent another down in flames, shared with the patrol at 08:55) and 13.8.18 (Lt F.G. Harlock/2nd Lt A.S. de Aisey destroyed a Fokker D.VII near Quesnoy at 19:05) then wrecked on 07:27 OP 16.9.18 (Lt H.E. Johnston/2nd Lt E.S. Harvey, both OK, force landed near Vignacourt with combat damage – engine 777/WD32788). **2 ASD** ex 20 Sqn 19.9.18. **1 FTS** Netheravon. **PD** Ascot. To India. **AD** Drigh Road. **AP** Lahore 20 Sqn NW Frontier.

C4719 (Falcon III) **5 AAP** Bristol 7.3.18, reallotted from storage at 1 SD to BEF. **1 ASD** dd ex England 18.3.18 (engine 629/WD32714). **2 ASD** ex 1 ASD 24.3.18 (same engine). **2 AIS** ex 2 ASD 20.4.18 (same engine). **48 Sqn** dd ex 2 AIS 25.4.18 (same engine), LIA on 10:40 OP 25.6.18 (2nd Lt N.H. Muirden POW fatally WIA/2nd Lt E. Roberts POW, last seen falling OOC over Foucaucourt – same engine) and deleted on unit that day (130hr 10min).

C4720 (Falcon III) **88 Sqn** Harling Road dd 21.2.18, to BEF with unit 25.4.18 and reported 7.8.18 with performance below the proper standard, and recommended for return to UK as an instructional machine (198hr – engine 1085/WD39435). **8 AAP** ex 88 Sqn, via **1 ASD**, 11.8.18.

C4721 (Falcon III) Eastbourne by 5.18. At Grain 27.5.18 and at Hendon 30.5.18 (communications machine?). **MAEE** Grain by 11.22 and wrecked 15.11.24 (Flt Lt W.R. Curtis/Sqn Ldr S.M. Cleverly both KIFA, made a sharp turn at 150ft after take off and dived in).

C4722 N/I

C4723 **PD** Ascot. To Egypt. **AD** Aboukir and later re-built as CR4723. **208 Sqn** 1926.

C4724 **44 TS** Waddington by 15.7.18.

C4725 To Middle East. **X AD** Aboukir dd ex England 17.8.18. Palestine Bde ex **XD** 2.11.18 (engine WD32600). **111 Sqn**.

C4726 To Middle East. **X AD** Aboukir dd ex England 17.8.18. Palestine Bde ex **XD** 1.11.18 (engine WD10503). **111 Sqn** dd ex X AP 14.5.19 (same engine) and deleted on unit 18.9.19.

C4727 To Middle East. **X AD** Aboukir dd ex England 17.8.18. Palestine Bde ex **XD** 1.11.18 (engine WD32680). **111 Sqn**.

C4728 To Middle East. **X AD** Aboukir dd ex England 2.9.18. Palestine Bde ex **XD** 3.11.18 (engine WD15759). **111 Sqn** Palestine. **X AP** ex 111 Sqn 25.6.19 and deleted 9.9.19.

C4729 To British Aviation Mission, Washington.

C4730 To Middle East. **X AD** Aboukir dd ex England 10.6.18. **X AP** and Palestine Bde ex X AD 26.10.18 (engine WD18508). **1 Sqn AFC** dd ex X AP 28.10.18. **111 Sqn** ex 1 Sqn AFC 4.2.19 and deleted on unit 22.2.19 (engine WD18608).

C4731 To Middle East. **X AD** Aboukir dd ex England 10.6.18. **X AP** and Palestine Bde ex X AD 30.10.18 (engine WD10508). **111 Sqn** Palestine. **ASD ME** ex 111 Sqn 29.12.19.

C4732 To Middle East. **X AD** Aboukir dd ex England 10.6.18. **X AP** and Palestine Bde ex X AD 30.10.18 (engine WD10483). **111 Sqn** dd ex X AP 30.10.18 (same engine).

C4733 Ex RFC, engineless to RNAS Tregantle & Withnoe store w/e 30.3.18.

C4734 B&C for reconditioning to J Type (s/n 6423) and ready by 22.3.24. **CFS** Upavon by 8.25 until @ 2.26.

C4735 (Falcon III) **5 FTS** Sealand and wrecked 31.8.22 (Plt Off M.V. Ward OK, became lost on cross-country, force landed in field and struck hedge near Minshull Vernon, Cheshire).

C4736 N/I

C4737 **SAC** Old Sarum by 6.24 until @ 9.26. B&C for reconditioning to J Type (s/n 7169) and ready by 23.3.28. **SAC** Old Sarum by 10.28.

C4738 B&C for reconditioning to J Type (s/n 6392) and ready by 16.2.24.

C4739 N/I

C4740 **RAF (Cadet) College** dd ex **ARS** 6.7.23 and on unit charge until @ 3.25. B&C for reconditioning to J Type DC (s/n 6867) and ready by 26.11.25. **RAF (Cadet) College** by 9.27 until @ 3.29. B&C for reconditioning and ready by 1.5.30. **Cambridge UAS** dd 6.6.30. **RAF College** by 11.30 until @ 1.31.

C4741 B&C for reconditioning to J Type (s/n 6426) and ready by 7.4.24. **2 Sqn** Manston by 5.24 until @ 5.25.

C4742 To Egypt. **4 FTS** Abu Sueir by 8.23, crashed 15.8.23 (control column broke on landing) and on unit charge until @ 10.23.

C4743 **PD** Ascot. To Egypt. **AD** Aboukir and rebuilt as CR4743. **208 Sqn** (heart badge on fin) 1925.

Rebuilt F.2B CR4743 of 208 Sqn over RAF Ismailia in 1925 displays a heart Flight motif on its fin. *(Philip Jarrett)*

C4744 (Falcon III) **5 AAP** 25.3.18 allotted to BEF. **1 ASD** dd ex England 29.3.18 (engine 711/WD32755). **2 AIS** ex 1 ASD 30.3.18 (same engine). **62 Sqn** dd ex 2 AIS 31.3.18 (same engine), LIA on 09:55 OP 3.5.18 (Lt P.R. Hampton/Lt L.C. Lane both POW WIA, probably brought down by Jasta 10 pilot) and deleted on unit that day (15hr).

C4745 (Falcon III) **5 AAP** Bristol 26.3.18, allotted to BEF. **1 ASD** dd ex England 1.4.18 (engine 797/WD32798). **2 AIS** ex 1 ASD 1.4.18 (same engine). **48 Sqn** dd ex 2 AIS 3.4.18 (same engine) and wrecked 16.5.18 (2nd Lt E.R. Stock OK/2nd Lt W.D. Davidson WIA, machine badly shot up and ran into B1271 on landing – same engine). **2 ASD** ex 48 Sqn 18.5.18. **2 AIS** ex 2 ASD 27.6.18. **11 Sqn** dd ex 2 AIS 3.7.18, LIA on 08:45 Reconnaissance, Le Cateau, 6.9.18 (Lt C.B. Seymour/2nd Lt E.G. Bugg both POW WIA, last seen over Cambrai being chased by EA – engine 1229/WD51639) and deleted on unit that day (139hr 5min).

C4746 (Falcon III) **5 AAP** Bristol by 25.3.18, allotted to BEF. **1 ASD** dd ex England 29.3.18 (engine 789/WD32794). **2 AIS** ex 1 ASD 30.3.18 (same engine). **62 Sqn** dd ex 2 AIS 31.3.18 (same engine) and wrecked 26.5.18 (when stationary, was run into by B1314 which was landing – same engine). **1 ASD** ex 62 Sqn 29.5.18 and deleted 8.10.18 on reconstruction as H7174.

C4747 (Falcon III) **5 AAP** Bristol by 22.1.18 (Lt C.F. Uwins/Cadet, 'joyride') and allotted to BEF by 25.3.18. **1 ASD** dd ex England 1.4.18 (engine 591/WD32695). **1 AIS** ex 1 ASD 3.4.18 (same engine). **22 Sqn** dd ex 1 AIS 11.4.18 (same engine, victs 6.5.18 (2nd Lt E.C. Bromley/2nd Lt J.H. Umney sent an Albatros D-type down OOC, believed crashed, E of Arras, 8.5.18 (2nd Lt E.C. Bromley/2nd Lt J.H. Umney destroyed two EA C-type SE of Arras at 10:05), 9.5.18 (2nd Lt E.C. Bromley/2nd Lt J.H. Umney sent a Pfalz D.III down OOC over Douai at 18:40), 16.5.18 (2nd Lt E.C. Bromley/2nd Lt J.H. Umney destroyed two Pfalz D.III at 10:05-10:30), 19.5.18 (2nd Lt A.C. Atkey/2nd Lt C.G. Gass destroyed an Albatros C-type S of Douai at 10:50 and sent two LVG C-type OOC, W of Hille at 18:45) then wrecked on OP 20.5.18 (2nd Lt C.H. Dunster/2nd Lt J.H. Umney both OK, engine damaged by EA fire and crashed on landing – same engine). **1 ASD** ex 22 Sqn 22.5.18 and deleted 24.5.18 (not worth reconstruction, 60hr 10min).

C4748 (Falcon III) **5 AAP** Bristol 28.3.18, allotted to BEF. **1 ASD** dd ex England 3.4.18 (engine 737/WD32768). **1 AIS** ex 1 ASD 3.4.18 (same engine). **20 Sqn** dd ex 1 AIS 12.4.18 (same engine) and wrecked on Reconnaissance 17.4.18 (Lt J.H. Colbert IOAS/2nd Lt R.W. Turner OK, crashed near Tardeghem due to engine failure – same engine). **1 ASD** ex 20 Sqn 22.4.18 and deleted 25.4.18 (7hr 30min).

C4749 (Falcon III) **5 AAP** Bristol 28.3.18, allotted to BEF. **1 ASD** dd ex England 2.4.18 (engine 781/WD32790). **1 AIS** ex 1 ASD 2.4.18 (same engine). **20 Sqn** dd ex 1 AIS 17.4.18 (same engine), victs 19.5.18 (Capt D.G. Cooke/Lt S.H.P Masding destroyed two Fokker D.VII, one in flames, near Laventie at 10:25) then wrecked on 05:24 OP 1.6.18 (Lt T.C. Traill/2nd Lt P.G. Jones both OK, front petrol tank shot up and force landed near Poperinghe – same engine). **1 ASD** ex 20 Sqn 3.6.18 and deleted 25.6.18 on reconstruction as F5823.

C4750 (Falcon III) **5 AAP** Bristol 28.3.18, allotted to BEF. **1 ASD** dd ex England 2.4.18 (engine 829/WD32814). **2 AIS** ex 1 ASD 7.4.18 (same engine). **48 Sqn** dd ex 2 AIS 13.4.18 (same engine) and damaged in successful combat 9.5.18 (Capt C.D.G Napier MC/ Sgt W. Beales DCM sent three Fokker Dr.I down OOC over

Wiencourt-Mericourt at 15:40 but machine badly shot up in combat – engine 607/WD32703). **2 ASD** ex 48 Sqn 11.5.18. **2AIS** ex 2 ASD 15.6.18 (engine 1147/WD39466). **62 Sqn** dd ex 2 AIS 25.6.18 (same engine) and wrecked on Test Flight 5.7.18 (Lt C.F. Whitstance OK, crashed on landing – same engine). **2 ASD**, repaired by 25.10.18. **2AIS** ex 2 ASD 26.10.18. B&C for reconditioning to J Type (s/n 6541) and ready by 22.11.24. **5 FTS** Sealand by 12.26. B&C for reconditioning to Mk.III (s/n 7137) and ready by 8.5.28. **2 Sqn** Manston by 9.29 until @ 5.30. Crashed and repaired. To Civilian Register as *G-ACFO*, registered to Commercial Airways 22.3.33. Sold for scrap 5.36.

C4751 (Falcon III) **5 AAP** Bristol 28.3.18, allotted to BEF. **1 ASD** dd ex England 3.4.18 (engine 809/WD32804). **2 AIS** ex 1 ASD 7.4.18 (same engine). **62 Sqn** dd ex 2 AIS 11.4.18 (same engine), LIA on 08:15 OP 19.5.18 (2nd Lt F. Atkinson POW fatally WIA/Sgt C.C. Brammer POW, last seen under control near Corbie at c.10:15 and probably brought down by Vzfw Kahlow, Jasta 34b – same engine) and deleted on unit that day (28hr).

C4752 **5 AAP** Bristol 29.3.18, allotted to BEF but allotment cancelled 4.4.18, machine had crashed near Hook en route to (S)ARD Farnborough.

C4753 (Falcon III) **5 AAP** Bristol 29.3.18, allotted to BEF. **1 ASD** dd ex England 2.4.18 (engine 817/WD32808). **2 AIS** ex 1 ASD 2.4.18 (same engine). **48 Sqn** dd ex 2 AIS 3.4.18 (same engine) and wrecked on 12:25 Reconnaissance 6.4.18 (2nd Lt C.D.G Napier/ 2nd Lt J.M.J. Moore both OK). **1 ASD** ex **2 ASD** 8.4.18 and under repair by 30.4.18. **11 Sqn** dd ex 2 AIS 15.6.18 and wrecked on Engine Test 1.7.18 (Lt R.N. Underwood/2nd Lt G.S. Turner both OK, a wheel had dropped off on take off and machine crashed landing at **20 Sqn** aerodrome – engine 717/WD32758). **2 ASD** for repair 1.7.18. **2 AIS** ex 2 ASD 25.9.18. **11 Sqn** and LIA on 07:00 Reconnaissance 3.10.18 (2nd Lt T. Peacock/2nd Lt G.W.A. Kelty both KOAS, collided with A7153 at 9,000ft and crashed near Duollens – engine 1657/WD51853) and deleted on unit that day.

C4754 (Falcon III) at maker's 6.4.18, allotted to 7 Bde, Italy. **'Z' Flt, 34 Sqn** dd ex **7 AP** 4.5.18 (engine 785/WD32792) and wrecked 7.5.18 (crashed in storm). **7 AP** ex 'Z' Flt 7.5.18. **139 Sqn** dd ex 7 AP 3.9.18, marked as a/c *M* and wrecked on Travelling Flight, 34 Sqn to 139 Sqn, 24.10.18 (Lt R.F.S. Johnson IOAS/AM2 R.S. Hudson OK, crashed due to mist at Lendenara – same engine). **7 AP** ex 139 Sqn 31.10.18.

C4755 At maker's 6.4.18, allotted to 7 Bde, Italy. **'Z' Flt, 34 Sqn** dd ex 7 **AP** 2.5.18, LIA on 06:40 Reconnaissance 11.5.18 (Lt J.B. Guthrie/ Lt H.B. Thornton both KIA, last seen at 08:15 at 16,000ft over Levico in combat with four EA and brought down by Obltn F. Linke-Crawford, Flik 51 – engine 801/WD32800) and deleted on unit 12.5.18 (7hr 40min).

C4756 (Falcon III) at maker's 6.4.18, allotted to 7 Bde, Italy. **'Z' Flt, 34 Sqn** dd ex **7 AP** 30.4.18 (engine 839/WD32819) and damaged on Reconnaissance 3.5.18 (Lt T.C. Lowe/2nd Lt T. Newey both OK, machine hit by AA fire – same engine). **7 AP** ex 'Z' Flight 5.5.18. **'Z' Flt** reissued ex 7 AP 27.6.18, on charge when unit redesignated **139 Sqn** 3.7.18 and wrecked on 08:45 OP 11.7.18 (2nd Lt J.B. Isaacs OK/2nd Lt F.F. Crump IOAS, became lost in clouds, ran out of petrol and crashed in forced landing – same engine). **7 AP** ex 139 Sqn 14.7.18.

C4757 (Falcon III) at maker's 6.4.18, allotted to 7 Bde, Italy. **'Z' Flt, 34 Sqn** dd ex **7 AP** 1.5.18 (engine 199/WD18599), vict 9.6.18 (Lt G. Robertson/2nd Lt H. Milburn sent an Albatros D.III down OOC), damaged on Bombing 16.6.18 (Lt C.E.G. Gill/Lt T. Newey both OK, machine hit by enemy gunfire), on charge when unit redesignated **139 Sqn** 3.7.18 and wrecked by 16.7.18. **7 AP** ex 139 Sqn 16.7.18 (same engine).

C4758 At maker's 6.4.18, allotted to 7 Bde, Italy. **'Z' Flt, 34 Sqn** dd ex 7 **AP** 1.5.18 (engine 803/WD32801) and damaged 21.5.18 (fuel tank burst). **7 AP** ex 'Z' Flight 21.5.18. **'Z' Flt** reissued ex 7 AP 1.6.18, vict 9.6.18 (2nd Lt A.E. Ryan/2nd Lt T. Newey destroyed an Albatros D.III over Trento) then wrecked on 09:10 Bombing, Piave, 16.6.18 (Lt G.H. Wood/Lt C. leG. Amy both OK, brought down over the Italian lines and machine came under shellfire – engine 841/WD32820). **7 AP** ex 'Z' Flight 27.6.18.

C4759 (Falcon III) at maker's 6.4.18, allotted to 7 Bde, Italy. **'Z' Flt, 34 Sqn** dd ex **7 AP** 17.6.18 (engine 873/WD32836), on charge when unit redesignated **139 Sqn** 3.7.18, LIA on 07:30 Reconnaissance 23.7.18 (Lt W.L. Vorster/Sgt H.G. Frow both KIA, shot down over Trento, probably by Obltn R. Schmidt, Flik 30 – same engine) and deleted on unit 24.7.18 (68hr 20min).

C4760 (Falcon III) at maker's 6.4.18, allotted to 7 Bde, Italy. **'Z' Flt, 34 Sqn** dd ex **7 AP** 4.6.18 (engine 861/WD32830), on charge when unit redesignated **139 Sqn** 3.7.18, LIA on 12:20 Bombing 30.10.18 (2nd Lt J.B. Isaacs/Capt M.G. Cahill-Byrne both POW, shot down and machine burnt – engine 1099/WD39442) and deleted on unit 31.10.18 (223hr 35min).

C4761 (Falcon III) at maker's 6.4.18, allotted to 7 Bde, Italy. **'Z' Flt, 34 Sqn** dd ex **7 AP** 2.6.18 (engine 857/WD32828) and wrecked on Escort 21.6.18 (2nd Lt A.E. Ryan OK/2nd Lt Davies IOAS, engine cut out and crashed near aerodrome – same engine). **7 AP** ex 'Z' Flt 24.6.18.

C4762 (Falcon III) at maker's 6.4.18, allotted to 7 Bde, Italy. **'Z' Flt, 34 Sqn** dd ex **7 AP** 17.6.18 (engine 805/WD32802), on charge when unit redesignated **139 Sqn** 3.7.18, LIA on 07:30 Reconnaissance 23.7.18 (Lt V.D. Fernald/2nd Lt W. Watkins both KIA, last seen over Belluno – engine 89/WD18544) and deleted on unit 24.7.18 (48hr 18min).

C4763 (Falcon III) **5 AAP** Bristol 12.4.18, allotted to BEF and tested 14.4.18 (Lt C.F. Uwins). **1 ASD** dd ex England 22.4.18 (engine 859/WD32829). **20 Sqn** dd ex 1 ASD 25.4.18 (same engine), victs 16.5.18 (Lt D.J. Weston/Sgt E.A. Deighton destroyed an Albatros D.V over Wervicq at 18:30) and 19.5.18 (Lt D.J. Weston/Sgt E.A. Deighton sent a Pfalz D.III down OOC smoking near Armentieres, destroyed another in flames over Merville and crashed a third N of Frelinghem, all during a general engagement 10:35-10:40) then LIA on 09:17 OP 28.5.18 (Lt R.G. Bennett/Lt G.T.C. Salter both KIA, last seen near Neuf Berquin at 10:30 – same engine) and deleted on unit 29.5.18 (71hr 23min).

C4764 (Falcon III) **5 AAP** Bristol 12.4.18, allotted to BEF and tested 14.4.18 (Lt C.F. Uwins). **1 ASD** dd ex 5 AAP, via Eastbourne, 22.4.18 (engine 871/WD32835). **20 Sqn** dd ex 1 ASD 25.4.18 (same engine), vict 1.6.18 (Lt V.E. Groom/2nd Lt E. Hardcastle destroyed a Pfalz D.III, N of Comines and sent another down OOC to crash NW of Comines at 06:30) then wrecked on OP 8.7.18 (Lt V.E. Groom/2nd Lt E. Hardcastle both OK, returned with pressure trouble, landed downwind and o/t (engine 891/WD32845). **1 ASD** ex 20 Sqn 10.7.18 and deleted 11.7.18 (not worth reconstruction, 163hr 15min).

C4765 (Falcon II) **5 AAP** Bristol 13.4.18, allotted to BEF and tested 15.4.18 and 19.4.18 (Lt C.F. Uwins). **1 ASD** dd ex England 22.4.18 (engine 209/WD22453). **8 AAP** ex 1 ASD 27.4.18 (2nd Lt C.H. Drew/Sgt observer).

C4766 **5 AAP** Bristol and tested 18.4.18 (Lt C.F. Uwins). **1 (Obs) SAG** New Romney by 6.18. **APS** Andover by 7.19 until @ 2.20. B&C for reconditioning to J Type (s/n 6619) and ready by 12.2.25. To Egypt. **208 Sqn** 1926. To India. **20 Sqn** by 10.26.

C4767 **5 AAP** Bristol and tested 19.4.18 (Lt C.F. Uwins).

C4768 **5 AAP** Bristol and tested 19.4.18 (Lt C.F. Uwins).

C4769 **5 AAP** Bristol and tested 20.4.18 (Lt C.F. Uwins). Cranwell 24.4.18 (transit). **15 TS** Spittlegate by 25.4.18 until @ 18.5.18.

C4770 (Falcon I) **5 AAP** Bristol and tested 27.4.18 (Lt C.F. Uwins). **15 TS** Spittlegate and wrecked 28.4.18 (Lt P.W.D. Thurley IIFA, hit shed roof landing – engine WD10459).

C4771 **24 TS** Witney by 16.6.18.

C4772 **33 TDS** Witney by 29.10.18 (2nd Lt G.A. Raybone).

C4773 **5 AAP** Bristol and tested 23.4.18 (Lt C.F. Uwins). **33 TDS** Witney by 11.9.18.

C4774 (Falcon II) **5 AAP** Bristol and tested 22.4.18 (Lt C.F. Uwins). **45 TDS** Rendcomb by 8.18 until @ 9.18 **21st Wing WT Flt** Port Meadow and wrecked 1.11.18 (Capt L.S. Arbuthnot/ 2nd Lt A.V. Scholes both KIFA, undercarriage struck ground when stunting low, zoomed, stalled and nosedived in – engine 2/F/77/WD22400).

C4775 **59 TS** Rendcomb as a/c *19* by 28.6.18.

C4776 **5 AAP** Bristol 20.4.18, allotted to BEF and tested 23.4.18 (Lt C.F. Uwins). **1 ASD** dd ex England 27.4.18 (engine 289/WD18421). England ex 1 ASD 4.5.18. **2 AAP** Hendon dd ex **14 AAP** Hawkinge 6.7.18 (2nd Lt C.H. Drew). Brooklands by 8.20. **RAE** Farnborough for trials with modified fin and rudder 21.4.21, force landed near Wanborough, Surrey, 28.4.21 (crew OK) and still at Farnborough 8.6.33.

C4777 **39 Sqn** North Weald by 31.8.18 (Lt Kendall/AM1 A.T.C. Stagg) until @ 6.9.18. (Also noted at **189 NTS** Suttons Farm.)

C4778 **141 Sqn** and on HAP 19/20.5.18 (Capt B.E. Baker). **WEE** Biggin Hill by 7.18.

C4779 **5 AAP** Bristol and tested 24.4.18 (Lt C.F. Uwins). **39 Sqn** North Weald by 15.8.18 (Capt Deane/AM1 A.T.C. Stagg). **44 TDS** Bicester dd ex 39 Sqn 16.12.18.

C4780 (Falcon III) **5 AAP** Bristol and tested 25.4.18 (Lt C.F. Uwins). **36 Sqn, 'A' Flt** Hylton by 18.8.18 and wrecked 22.9.18 (2nd Lt H. Croudace OK/AM3 J.E. Barlow IIFA, overshot landing at

Hylton and crashed into a fence – engine 220/WD10535). Remains at Hornchurch, Essex 1930.

C4781 5 AAP Bristol and tested 27.4.18 (Lt C.F. Uwins). **1 (Obs) SAG** New Romney dd 29.4.18 and wrecked 3.9.18 (Lt L.J. Boswood KIFA/2nd Lt F.A. Parfait fatally IIFA in mid-air collision with C4648 – engine 2/F/389/WD18471).

C4782 5 AAP Bristol and tested 25.4.18 (Lt C.F. Uwins).

C4783 2 AIS dd ex **1 ASD** 27.8.18. **62 Sqn** and reported as unfit for service in the field 29.9.18 (150hr 35min, engine 285/WD18642). **1 ASD** ex **2 ASD** 1.10.18 and flown to England that day. Farnborough dd ex **8 AAP** Lympne 3.10.18 (Lt G.H. Richardson).

C4784 5 AAP Bristol and tested 27.4.18 (Lt C.F. Uwins). **76 Sqn, 'A' Flt**. To **36 Sqn, 'C' Flt** dd ex Copmanthorpe 21.6.18 (Lt E.W. Watt, 76 Sqn) and with **'A' Flt** by 12.9.18 until @ 1.19.

C4785 5 AAP Bristol and tested 30.4.18 (Lt C.F. Uwins). **36 Sqn, 'A' Flt** by 29.9.18 until @ 1.19.

C4786 15 TS Spittlegate, crashed 6.5.18. **ARS** Harlaxton 5.18.

C4787 5 AAP Bristol and tested 29.4.18 (Lt C.F. Uwins).

C4788 5 AAP Bristol first flown 30.4.18 and tested 1.5.18 (Lt C.F. Uwins). **44 TDS** Port Meadow and wrecked 21.7.18 (Capt E.E. Froneman/Lt W.F. Beachcroft both KIFA, spun in from 500ft – engine WD15749).

C4789 (Falcon I) **5 AAP** Bristol and tested 1.5.18 (Lt C.F. Uwins). **33 TDS** Witney and wrecked on Fighting Practice 8.10.18 (2nd Lt C.M. Doolittle KIFA, port top plane failed owing to the excessive stress induced when machine suddenly pulled out of a high-speed dive – engine 10450).

C4790 5 AAP Bristol and tested 1.5.18 (Lt C.F. Uwins).

C4791 5 AAP Bristol and tested 2.5.18 (Lt C.F. Uwins). **1 (Obs) SAG** New Romney dd 5.18.

C4792 5 AAP Bristol and tested 3.5.18 (Lt C.F. Uwins).

C4793 5 AAP Bristol and tested 5.5.18 (Lt C.F. Uwins). **62 Sqn** dd ex **2 AIS** 2.9.18.

C4794 5 AAP Bristol and tested 6.5.18 (Lt C.F. Uwins). B&C for reconditioning to J Type (s/n 6547) and ready by 29.11.24. **16 Sqn** by 3.25. B&C for reconditioning (s/n 6950) and ready by 23.6.26.

C4795 5 AAP Bristol and tested 9.5.18 (Lt C.F. Uwins).

C4796 N/I

C4797 5 AAP Bristol and tested 18.6.18 (Lt C.F. Uwins). **1 (Obs) SAG** Hythe by 7.18.

C4798 (Falcon I) **1 (Obs) SAG** Hythe and wrecked 1.8.18 (2nd Lt H.S. Richards NZ/Flt Cdt G. Finney both KIFA in mid-air collision with A7262 – engine 1/F/39/WD12566).

C4799 1 (Obs) SAG Hythe and damaged 30.10.18 (Lt G. Norton IIFA, hit a bank on the edge of the aerodrome when landing).

C4800 5 AAP Bristol and tested 9.5.18 and 10.5.18 (Lt C.F. Uwins). **18th Wing ARS** Hounslow dd ex 5 AAP 10.5.18. Hendon dd ex Hounslow 21.6.18 until @ 24.7.18. **29 TS** Hendon dd ex 18th Wing ARS 5.8.18 (engine 31/WD12547). At Cologne for BEF 30.4.19, reallotted from SE Area.

100 BRISTOL FIGHTER F.2B ordered 14.9.17 under Contracts A.S.22909/1/17 & A.S.17573 from British & Colonial Aeroplane Co Ltd, Bristol and numbered C4801 to C4900. (275hp Falcon III or 200hp Arab). [Consecutive works' sequence nos. 2851 to 2950].

C4801 (Falcon II) presentation a/c *Presented by the Maharaja Bahadur Sir Rameswar Singh of Darbhanga No.5* wef 19.10.17. **5 AAP** Bristol 19.10.17, allotted to BEF. **22 Sqn** dd ex **1 AD** 21.10.17 (engine 293/WD18423), missing on 10:35 Escort 28.12.17 (Lt D.G. Barnett/AM2 G.L. Sims both WIA, seen going down over Nieppe Forest at 11:00 – same engine) and deleted on unit that day (46hr). Salvaged by **2 ASD** and returned to RFC charge but deleted 16.1.18.

C4802 (Falcon II). **5 AAP** Bristol 9.11.17, reallotted from Training to BEF. **1 ASD** dd ex England 18.11.17 (235/WD22465). **1 AIS** ex 1 ASD 19.11.17 (same engine). **20 Sqn** dd ex 1 AIS 4.12.17 and wrecked on Practice Flight 22.4.18 (Sgt Stansfield OK, crashed on landing – engine 313/WD18433). **1 ASD** ex 20 Sqn 24.4.18 and deleted 25.4.18 (not worth reconstruction, 69hr 20min).

C4803 5 AAP Bristol by 9.11.17, reallotted from Training to BEF. En route from **2 Wireless School** Penhurst to **3 (W)ARD** 15.11.17, allotment to BEF cancelled, and for **E1a Repair Section**.

C4804 35 TS Northolt/Port Meadow by 10.17.

C4805 (Falcon II) **2 TS** Northolt and wrecked 6.11.17 (Lt Morris OK/2nd Lt E. Henriques IIFA, machine ran over ruts after landing and o/t – engine 2/190/309).

C4806 8 TS Netheravon and wrecked 18.12.17 (2nd Lt J.V. Audas SA IIFA, stalled at 100ft on climbing turn with insufficient speed and dived in – engine 263/WD18408).

C4807 N/I

C4808 (Falcon II) **5 AAP** Bristol 26.10.17, took part in armament trials at Orfordness, allotted to BEF. **22 Sqn** dd ex **1 ASD** 8.12.17 (engine 315/WD18434), victs 18.2.18 (2nd Lt S.H. Wallage/Sgt J.H. Jones sent and EA C-type OOC over Seclin) and 16.3.18 (Lt W.L. Wells/Lt G.S.L. Hayward sent a Pfalz D.III OOC at Oignes and destroyed an Albatros D.V over Beaumont) then 18.3.18 (2nd Lt W.F.J. Harvey/2nd Lt J.L. Morgan destroyed an Albatros D.V, Carvin) and 2.4.18 (2nd Lt G.N. Traunweiser/Sgt S. Belding destroyed a Fokker Dr.I at Vauvilliers) then LIA on 13:50 Reconnaissance 15.4.18 (2nd Lt G.N. Traunweiser/Sgt S. Belding both KIA, fired on and brought down by British infantry at 14:30 in a shelled area at Haverskerque – same engine) and deleted on unit that day (132hr).

C4809 8 TS Netheravon by 1.1.18 and wrecked 24.2.18 (Lt T.E. Bulteel KIFA, collided at 50ft with DH6 C2003 – engine 231/WD10413).

C4810 (Falcon II) presentation a/c *Gold Coast No.11*. **5 AAP** Bristol 27.10.17, allotted to BEF. **1 ASD** by 7.11.17. **1 AIS** by 31.12.17. **22 Sqn** dd ex 1 AIS 19.1.18 (engine 325/WD18439), marked as a/c *N*, vict 6.3.18 (2nd Lt G.W. Bulmer USA/2nd Lt S.J. Hunter sent a Pfalz D.III OOC, E of La Bassée at 11:15) then wrecked before OP 22.4.18 (2nd Lt F.M. Ward/Sgt A. Burton both KOAS, stalled on take off and crashed – engine 357/WD18455). **1 ASD** ex **Advanced Salvage** 23.4.18 and deleted 25.4.18 (85hr 26min).

C4811 62 Sqn Rendcomb by 7.12.17. **35 TS** Port Meadow and wrecked 8.3.18 (Cap C.J. Campbell IIFA, no further details given).

C4812 (Falcon I) **35 TS** Port Meadow and wrecked 30.1.18 (2nd Lt H.F. Robinson IIFA, hit ridge on the aerodrome and machine stood on nose – engine 1/F/205/WD10404). Also noted as having collided with Avro 504J B4276 at the **CFS** 2.18.

C4813 (Falcon I) **35 TS** Northolt dd ex **5 AAP** 1.11.17 and wrecked 6.11.17 (pilot OK/AM2 A.J. Gardner IIFA, pilot mis-judged landing distance and struck a tree – engine 1/F/13/WD10523).

C4814 (Falcon I) **5 AAP** Bristol 31.10.17, allotted to BEF. **11 Sqn** dd ex **2 ASD** 24.11.17 (engine 455/WD15759). **1 ASD** ex 11 Sqn 5.12.17 (same engine) and flown to England 12.12.17 (2nd Lt H. Shaw). **8 AAP** Lympne 12.12.17.

C4815 39 Sqn North Weald by 11.17, on HAPs 18.12.17 (Capt O.V. Thomas/Cpl Gee), 29/30.1.18 (Capt O.V. Thomas/Sgt Riches) and 16/17.2.18 (Capt O.V. Thomas/Sgt Riches) and wrecked on Formation Flight 13.6.18 (Lt J.L. Boles/Flt Cdt J.W. Mackay both KIFA, engine failed at 150ft, tried to turn back but crashed and caught fire).

C4816 (Falcon II) **5 AAP** Bristol 1.11.17, allotted to BEF. **48 Sqn** dd ex **1 ASD** 6.11.17 (engine 363/WD18454), LIA on Counter Battery Photography 9.1.18 (Capt A.W. Field/2nd Lt W.S. Smith both KIA, last seen going down OOC near Estrees with LH wings shot off – same engine) and deleted on unit that day (45hr).

C4817 (Initially Falcon I) **5 AAP** Bristol 3.11.17, allotted to BEF. **1 AIS** ex **1 ASD** 15.11.17 (engine 15/WD10528). **20 Sqn** dd ex 1 AIS 18.11.17 (same engine) and damaged on 09:32 OP 29.11.17 (2nd Lt W. Beaver/AM1 G. Thomas both OK, force landed near Steenworde after engine seized when hit by fire from EA – engine Falcon II 187/WD22441). **1 ASD** ex 20 Sqn and under reconstruction by 24.2.18. **1 AIS** ex 1 ASD 9.3.18 (engine Falcon III 411/WD32605). **2 AIS** ex 1 AIS 23.3.18 (same engine). **22 Sqn** dd ex 2 AIS 25.3.18, marked as a/c *D* and wrecked on OP 15.4.18 (2nd Lt W.S. Hill-Tout/2nd Lt P.S. Williams both OK, machine shot through in combat – same engine). **1 ASD** ex 22 Sqn 19.4.18. **1 AIS** ex 1 ASD 8.5.18 (same engine). **22 Sqn** reissued ex 1 AIS 14.5.18 (same engine) and wrecked on Practice Flight 25.6.18 (Lt T.W. Martin/AM Dowell both, crashed on landing – same engine). **1 ASD** ex 22 Sqn 26.6.18 and deleted 8.10.18 on reconstruction as H7175.

C4818 (Initially Falcon II) presentation a/c *Newfoundland No 4*. **5 AAP** Bristol 2.11.17, allotted to BEF. **22 Sqn** dd ex **1 ASD** 10.11.17 (engine 325/WD18439) and wrecked after OP 3.12.17 (2nd Lt E.C. Bromley/2nd Lt S.J. Hunter both OK, crashed on landing – same engine). **1 ASD** ex 22 Sqn 4.12.17. **1 AIS** ex 1 ASD 29.1.18 (engine Falcon III 363/WD18681). **62 Sqn** dd ex 1 AIS 17.2.18 (same engine). **1 ASD** ex 62 Sqn 18.2.18 as surplus to establishment (same engine). **1 AIS** ex 1 ASD 24.2.18 (same engine). **10 Sqn** dd ex 1 AIS 27.3.18 (same engine). **1 AIS** ex 10 Sqn 12.4.18 (same engine). **20 Sqn** dd ex 1 AIS 20.4.18 (same engine) and wrecked on OP 3.5.18 (Lt F.E. Boulton/AM W.H. Foster both OK, fuel tank shot through in combat and crashed in forced landing near Wormhoudt – same engine). **1 ASD** ex 20 Sqn 7.5.18 and deleted 25.6.18 on reconstruction as F5818.

C4819 (Falcon I) **5 AAP** Bristol 3.11.17, allotted to BEF. **2 AIS** ex **1 ASD** 11.11.17 (engine 38/WD10431). **11 Sqn** dd ex 2 AIS 3.12.17

(same engine). **1 ASD** ex 11 Sqn 5.12.17 (same engine). **8 AAP** Lympne ex 1 ASD 6.12.17. **3 (Aux) SAG** New Romney dd ex Lympne 13.12.17 (2nd Lt H. Shaw). Photographed alongside Handley Page V/1500, marked as a/c *56*.

C4820 (Initially Falcon II) at maker's 6.11.17, allotted to BEF and to be delivered in packing case. **1 ASD** dd ex England in packing case 16.11.17 (engine 399/WD18476). **20 Sqn** dd ex 1 ASD 4.12.17 (same engine), wrecked on OP 14.1.18 (Lt D.G. Campbell/Lt J.H. Stream both OK, crashed near Westoutre due to engine trouble – engine Falcon III 327/WD18663 and deleted on unit that day (16hr 58min). Wreckage at 1 ASD 22.1.18.

C4821 (Falcon II) **5 AAP** Bristol 8.11.17, allotted to BEF. **1 AIS** ex **1 ASD** 15.11.17 (engine 365/WD18459). **20 Sqn** dd ex 1 AIS 18.11.17 (same engine) and wrecked after OP 19.12.17 (2nd Lt D.J. Weston/Pte B. Matthews both OK, tail skid caught a ditch when landing – same engine). **1 ASD** ex 20 Sqn 22.12.17 and deleted 16.1.18 (not worth reconstruction, 27hr 27min).

C4822 At maker's 6.11.17, allotted to BEF. **1 ASD** and flown to England 15.12.18. **8 AAP** Lympne tested 18.12.17 (2nd Lt H. Shaw). **3 (Aux) SAG** New Romney dd ex Lympne 24.12.17 (2nd Lt H. Shaw). **141 Sqn** Biggin Hill 1918. **1 (Obs) SAG** New Romney dd via Eastbourne 28.4.18.

C4823 **39 Sqn** North Weald on HAP 5.12.18 (Lt C.J. Chabot/Lt V.A. Lanos).

C4824 (Initially Falcon II) at maker's 6.11.17, allotted to BEF and to be delivered in packing case. **1 ASD** dd ex England in packing case 19.11.17 (engine 397/WD18475). **62 Sqn** dd ex 1 ASD 15.2.18 (engine Falcon III 373/WD18686), LIA on 09:30 OP 12.3.18 (Lt J.A.A. Ferguson/Sgt L.S. Long both POW, shot down in flames E of Cambrai at c.11:10, probably by Ltn W. Steinhauser, Jasta 1 – same engine) and deleted on unit that day (26hr 35min).

C4825 (Falcon II) **5 AAP** Bristol 9.11.17, allotted to BEF. **1 ASD** dd ex England 19.11.17 (engine 419/WD18486). **1 AIS** ex 1 ASD 23.11.17 (same engine). **20 Sqn** dd ex 1 AIS 5.12.17 (same engine, LIA on 10:30 OP, St Julien, 22.1.18 (2nd Lt A.R. Paul/ AM2 A. Mann both POW fatally WIA, last seen at 10:30 – same engine) and deleted on unit 23.1.18 (32hr 21min).

C4826 (Falcon II) at maker's 6.11.17, allotted to BEF and to be despatched in packing case. **1 ASD** ex **2 ASD** 5.12.17. **20 Sqn** dd ex 1 ASD 9.12.17 (engine 347/WD18450) and wrecked on Practice Flight 2.5.18 (Lt P.B. Holgate OK, crashed after hitting a bank on landing – engine 441/WD18497). **1 ASD** ex 20 Sqn 3.5.18 and deleted 4.5.18 (not worth reconstruction, 120hr 35min).

C4827 (Falcon II) **5 AAP** Bristol 12.11.17, allotted to BEF. **1 ASD** dd ex England 22.11.17 (engine 345/WD18449). **22 Sqn** dd ex 1 ASD 5.12.17 (same engine), LIA on 09:25 OP 23.3.18 (2nd Lt H.L. Christie/2nd Lt N.T. Berrington both OK, engine damaged in combat with EA at 11:30, force landed in shelled area near Ham and abandoned – engine 99/WD22473) and deleted on unit that day (46hr 45min).

C4828 (Initially Falcon II) at maker's 6.11.17, allotted to BEF and to be despatched in packing case. **1 ASD** dd ex England in packing case 22.11.17 (engine 411/WD18482). **2 AIS** ex 1 ASD 3.2.18 (same engine). **22 Sqn** dd ex 2 AIS 6.2.18 (same engine) and wrecked on OP 20.4.18 (2nd Lt O. St C. Harris/Lt W.B. Ives both OK force landed on rough ground near Hazebrouck due to ignition trouble – same engine). **1 ASD** ex 22 Sqn 23.4.1. **22 Sqn** reissued ex 1 ASD 22.6.18 (engine Falcon III 1137/WD39461) and wrecked on Test Flight 18.7.18 (Capt W.F.J. Harvey/AM Elliott both OK, slewed on landing after wing hit the ground – same engine). **1 ASD** ex 22 Sqn 19.7.18 and deleted 21.7.18 (not worth reconstruction, 131hr).

C4829 (Falcon I) at maker's 6.11.17, allotted to BEF but allotment cancelled 26.11.17 with machine en route from Bristol to **3 (W)ARD** for O/C **E1a Repair Section**.

C4830 (Falcon I) at maker's 6.11.17 allotted to BEF but allotment cancelled 9.11.17. **5 AAP** Bristol by 12.11.17, reallotted to BEF then reallotted to Training 17.11.17. **35 TS** Port Meadow and wrecked 2.1.18 dived in 2.1.18 (2nd Lt J.R. Nickson/1st Lt W.S. Ely USAS both KIFA, nosedived in – engine 255/WD10458).

C4831 (Initially Falcon II) presentation a/c *Presented by the Government of Johore No.6*. **5 AAP** Bristol 14.11.17, allotted to BEF. **1 ASD** dd ex England 23.11.17 (engine 371/WD18462). **48 Sqn** dd ex 1 ASD 26.11.17 (same engine) and wrecked on OP 20.4.18 (2nd Lt A.C.G. Brown/AM1 M.E. Lynch both OK, o/t during forced landing near Neufchatel owing to lack of fuel – same engine). **2 ASD** ex 48 Sqn 23.4.18. **2 AIS** ex 2 ASD 21.6.18 **48 Sqn** reissued ex 2 AIS 27.6.18 (engine Falcon III 1187/WD51618) and wrecked on Practice Flight 10.7.18 (2nd Lt B.E. Sharwood Smith/Sgt T.R.

Turner both OK, crashed on landing – same engine). **2 ASD** ex 48 Sqn 12.7.18 and deleted 6.8.18 (not worth reconstruction, 129hr 30min).

C4832 (Falcon II) presentation a/c *Udaipur No.1*. At maker's 6.11.17, allotted to BEF but allotment cancelled 9.11.17. **5 AAP** Bristol 14.11.17, reallotted to BEF. **1 ASD** dd ex England 22.11.17 (engine 385/WD18469). **22 Sqn** dd ex 1 ASD 5.12.17 (same engine), LIA on 10:35 OP 30.1.18 (2nd Lt G.G. Johnstone KIA/ AM3 R.A. Duff fatally WIA, shot down in flames by EA – same engine) and deleted on unit that day (30hr 25min).

C4833 (Falcon I) **5 AAP** Bristol by 15.11.17, allotted to BEF but reallotted to Training 17.11.17. **35 TS** Port Meadow by 14.3.18.

C4834 (Falcon I) at maker's 6.11.17, allotted to BEF but allotment cancelled 9.11.17. **5 AAP** Bristol by 16.11.17, reallotted to BEF but reallotted to Training 17.11.17.

C4835 (Initially Falcon II) **5 AAP** Bristol 16.11.17, allotted to BEF. **1 ASD** dd ex England 22.11.17 (engine 383/WD18468). **22 Sqn** dd ex 1 ASD 30.12.17 (same engine), marked as a/c *R* and wrecked on OP 13.7.18 (Lt C.E. Hurst/Lt S.G. Birch both OK, o/t in forced landing near Lilliers after rear fuel tank shot through by EA fire – engine Falcon III 1257/WD51653). **1 ASD** ex 22 Sqn 16.7.18 and deleted 14.9.18 on reconstruction as H7067 (202hr 5min).

C4836 (Falcon II) at maker's 6.11.17, allotted to BEF but allotment cancelled 9.11.17. **5 AAP** Bristol 17.11.17, reallotted to BEF. **8 AAP** Lympne tested 11.12.17, 2nd Lt H. Shaw). **1 AIS** ex **1 ASD** 15.12.17. **20 Sqn** dd ex 1 AIS 30.12.17 (engine 387/WD18470) and wrecked on OP 26.1.18 (2nd Lt D. Latimer/Cpl F. Asher both OK, crashed near Crombeke due to stoppage in petrol pipe – same engine). **1 ASD** ex 20 Sqn 27.1.18 and deleted 29.1.18 (16hr 54min).

C4837 (Falcon II) **5 AAP** Bristol 17.11.17, allotted to BEF. **1 ASD** dd ex 5 AAP 22.11.17 (Lt C.F. Uwins – engine 423/WD18488). **20 Sqn** dd ex 1 ASD 4.12.17 (same engine) and LIA on OP 19.2.18 (Lt D.G. Campbell/Lt J.H. Stream both KIA, brought down in flames – same engine). **1 ASD** ex 20 Sqn 26.2.18 and deleted 1.3.18 (68hr 50min).

C4838 (Falcon II) at maker's 6.11.17, allotted to BEF but allotment cancelled 9.11.17. **5 AAP** Bristol 19.11.17, reallotted to BEF. **1 ASD** dd ex England 23.11.17 (engine 405/WD18479). **22 Sqn** dd ex 1 ASD 4.12.17 (same engine) and wrecked on Gunnery Practice 29.12.17 (2nd Lt W.W.M. Dulin/2nd Lt N.P. Barrington both IOAS, crashed on aerodrome – same engine). **1 ASD** ex 22 Sqn 1.1.18 and presume deleted (18hr).

C4839 (Falcon III) **5 AAP** Bristol 19.11.17, allotted to BEF and despatched 30.11.17. **2 AIS** ex **1 ASD** 15.12.17. **11 Sqn** dd ex 2 AIS 17.1.18 (engine 7/WD18503), damaged on OP 4.5.18 (Lt L.R. Fitton WIA) and wrecked on Practice Flight 15.5.18 (Lt J.W. Coons/Lt R.A. West both OK, crashed on landing – same engine). **2 ASD** ex **2 SS** 16.5.18 and deleted 18.5.18 (not worth reconstruction, 70hr 40min).

C4840 (Falcon III) presentation a/c *New South Wales No.3. The Mrs P. Kirby & Son*. **1 Sqn AFC** dd ex **X AP** 17.3.18. **111 Sqn** ex 1 Sqn AFC 4.2.19. **ASD ME** ex Palestine Bde 20.8.19 and deleted 13.11.19.

C4841 **2 (Aux)SAG** Turnberry and wrecked 13.2.18 (2nd Lt F.G. Sutton/ AM1 W.G. Hoyes both IIFA, stalled on low turn and spun in – engine 1/F/389/WD10495).

C4842 (Falcon III) **5 AAP** Bristol 22.11.17, allotted to BEF. **1 AIS** ex **1 ASD** 5.12.17. **11 Sqn** dd ex **2 ASD** 12.12.17 (engine 29/WD18514) and wrecked on Engine Test 25.1.18 (Sgt G. Pickard/Sgt H. Mills both KOAS, crashed 1 mile from aerodrome – same engine). **2 ASD** ex 11 Sqn 28.1.18 and deleted 29.1.18 (25hr 34min).

C4843 (Falcon III) **5 AAP** Bristol 23.11.17, allotted to BEF. **11 Sqn** dd ex **1 ASD** 6.12.17 (engine 31/WD18515), damaged on Reconnaissance 27.3.18 (2nd Lt R. Fitton/2nd Lt R.A. West both OK, machine shot through by enemy fire with longeron hit – same engine). **2 ASD** and under repair by 30.4.18. **2 AIS** ex 2 ASD 10.6.18 (engine 1123/WD39454). **1 AIS** by 21.6.18 (same engine). **22 Sqn** dd ex 1 AIS 22.6.18 and wrecked after OP 2.7.18 (2nd Lt J.J. Borrowman/2nd Lt T.J. Birmingham both OK, crashed when returning with engine trouble – same engine). **1 ASD** ex 22 Sqn 3.7.18 and presume deleted.

C4844 (Falcon III) **5 AAP** Bristol 23.11.17, allotted to BEF. **1 ASD** dd ex 5 AAP 29.11.17 (Lt C.F. Uwins – engine 33/WD18516). **11 Sqn** dd ex 1 ASD 6.12.17 (same engine), LIA on 09:30 OP 18.3.18 (Capt A.P. Malean POW fatally WIA/Lt F.H. Canton MC KIA, brought down in combat over Fresnoy Le Grand-Bohain – engine 309/WD18654) and deleted on unit that day (87hr 15min).

C4845 (Falcon III) **5 AAP** Bristol 24.11.17, allotted to BEF. **8 AAP** Lympne dd ex 5 AAP 2.12.17 (Lt C.F. Uwins, via Croydon 1.12.17). **2 AIS** ex **1 ASD** 15.12.17. **11 Sqn** dd ex 2 AIS 14.1.18 (engine 65/WD18532), victs 9.5.18 (Lt J.S. Chick/Lt E.C. Gilroy sent two Albatros D.V down OOC, S of Albert at 12:20) and wrecked 10.5.18 (crashed into by C4852 – same engine). **2 ASD** ex 11 Sqn 11.5.18. **2 AIS** ex 2 ASD 15.6.18. **62 Sqn** dd ex 2 AIS 26.6.18 (engine 265/WD18632) and reported 10.8.18 as in need of complete overhaul (133hr 30min – engine 995/WD32897). **2 ASD** ex 62 Sqn 11.8.18 and flown to England via 1 ASD 12.8.18. B&C for reconditioning to J Type (s/n 6696) and ready by 4.5.25.

C4846 (Falcon III) **5 AAP** Bristol 24.11.17, allotted to BEF. **11 Sqn** dd ex **1 ASD** 6.12.17, marked as a/c *16* and named *Amy*, victs 1.1.18 (2nd Lt J.S. Chick/Lt H.R. Kinkead sent an Albatros D.V down OOC over Crevecoeur at 13:30), 9.3.18 (2nd Lt D.W. Beard/Sgt H.W. Scarnell sent a Pfalz D.III down OOC over Douai at 11:30), 15.3.18 (2nd Lt D.W. Beard/Sgt H.W. Scarnell destroyed an Albatros D.V and sent two more down OOC over Rumilly at 11:15) and 22.3.18 (2nd Lt D.W. Beard/2nd Lt H.M. Stewart destroyed an Albatros D.V in flames over Queant at 18:35), mistakenly reported as missing on 19:05 Reconnaissance 1.6.18 (Lt R.F. Mullins/2nd Lt F.C.B. Phillips both OK, returned safely) then reported 10.6.18 as in need of general overhaul (192hr 4min – same engine). **2 ASD** ex 11 Sqn 12.6.18. **1 ASD** ex 2 ASD 14.6.18 and flown to England 15.6.18 (194hr 54min).

C4847 (Falcon III) **5 AAP** Bristol 26.11.17, allotted to BEF. **11 Sqn** dd ex **1 ASD** 6.12.17 (engine 63/WD18531), victs 12.3.18 (2nd Lt J.S. Chick/2nd Lt P. Douglas sent an EA C-type down OOC at 11:15 and then sent four Fokker Dr.I down OOC over Caudray at 11:45-11:55) then wrecked on Reconnaissance 11.4.18 (2nd Lt E.A. Magee/2nd Lt A.H. Craig both OK, collided on landing with another machine after pilot became ill in the air – engine 35/WD18517). **2 ASD** ex **2 SS** 18.4.18. **11 Sqn** reissued ex **2 AIS** 19.6.18 (engine 667/WD32733) and wrecked on Height Test 29.6.18 (2nd Lt D.W. Beard/AM1 R.G. Clegg both OK, engine failed and crashed during forced landing in a wheat field same engine). **2 ASD** ex 11 Sqn 1.7.18 and deleted 17.7.18 on reconstruction as F6195 (130hr 50min).

C4848 (Falcon III) **5 AAP** Bristol 26.11.17, allotted to BEF. **1 ASD** and deleted 16.1.18 (presume wrecked on delivery, 45min).

C4849 (Falcon III) **5 AAP** Bristol 28.11.17, allotted to BEF. **11 Sqn** dd ex **1ASD** 6.12.17 (engine 51/WD18525) and wrecked on Reconnaissance, Arras-Cambrai, 10.12.17 (2nd Lt R.H. Nixon/Lt P. Douglas both OK, crashed in forced landing near Doullens at 13:00 after engine trouble – same engine). **2 ASD** and under repair by 31.12.17. **2 AIS** ex 2 ASD 28.1.18 (engine 235/WD18617). **11 Sqn** dd ex 2 AIS 28.1.18 (same engine). **2 ASD** ex 11 Sqn 5.3.18 (poor performance). **35 Sqn** dd ex 2 AIS 1.4.18 (Lt Smith – engine 391/WD18695) and wrecked on 18:05 Shoot 1.7.18 (Lt A. McGregor WIA/Lt R.J. Fitzgerald MC KIA, force landed near Coisy at 19:30 after attacked and shot up by EA – same engine). **2 ASD** ex 35 Sqn 2.7.18 and deleted 9.7.18 (not worth reconstruction, 64hr).

C4850 (Falcon III) **5 AAP** Bristol 28.11.17, allotted to BEF but reallotted to 6th Bde 5.12.17. **39 Sqn** North Weald and on HAPs 16/17.2.18 (Lt P. Thomson/Lt G.T. Stoneham), 17/18.2.18 (Lt P. Thomson/ Lt G.T. Stoneham) and 7/8.3.18 (Lt P. Thomson/Lt G.T. Stoneham). **36 Sqn** spring 1919.

C4851 (Falcon III) at maker's 12.2.18, allotted to BEF and to be delivered in packing case. **1 ASD** dd ex England in packing case 12.3.18 (engine 561/WD32680). **1 AIS** ex 1 ASD 2.4.18 (same engine). **20 Sqn** dd ex 2 AIS 6.4.18 (same engine), vict 9.5.18 (Lt W.M. Thomson/2nd Lt G.H. Kemp destroyed an Albatros D.V, W of Comines at 13:30) then wrecked on 15:58 OP 10.5.18 (Lt D.E. Smith OK/Prob F.J. Ralph WIA, machine damaged by enemy fire and force landed near Hazebrouck – same engine). **1 ASD** ex 20 Sqn 13.5.18 and deleted 25.6.18 on reconstruction as F5810.

C4852 (Falcon III) at maker's 12.2.18, allotted to BEF and to be delivered in packing case. **11 Sqn** dd ex **2 AIS** 28.3.18 and wrecked before Reconnaissance 10.5.18 (Lt B.S.B. Thomas/AM1 H. Turner both OK, crashed into C4845 on take off – engine 33/WD18516). **2 ASD** ex 11 Sqn 10.5.18 and deleted 3.7.18 on reconstruction as F6158 (22hr 5min).

C4853 Photographed at Gosport.

C4854 **8 TS** Netheravon by 9.3.18.

C4855 (Falcon III) **5 AAP** Bristol 25.2.18, allotted to BEF. **1 ASD** dd ex England 6.3.18 (engine 609/WD32704), wrecked on Test Flight 7.3.18 (2nd Lt H.F.D. Lay/2nd Lt G.W.A. Watson both KIFA, cut out at 150ft on take off, machine side-slipped and nosedived in) and deleted 9.3.18 (not worth reconstruction, 4hr 25min).

C4856 (Falcon III) **5 AAP** Bristol 25.2.18, allotted to BEF. **1 ASD** dd ex England 8.3.18 (engine 603/WD32701). **1 AIS** ex 1 ASD 11.3.18 (same engine). **20 Sqn** dd ex 1 AIS 2.4.18 (same engine) and wrecked on OP 3.5.18 On OP lost way, force landed and crashed 3.5.18 (Lt T.W. Williamson/AM1 S.W. Melbourne both OK, pilot lost his way and crashed in a forced landing near Henneveux – same engine). **1 ASD** ex 20 Sqn 7.5.18 and deleted 8.5.18 (not worth reconstruction, 30hr 6min).

C4856 N/I

C4857 **5 AAP** Bristol 25.2.18, allotted to BEF. **3 (W)ARD** 19.3.18 with BEF allotment cancelled and for deletion.

C4858 **44 TS** Waddington by 14.5.18. **71 TS** Port Meadow by 25.6.18. **45 TDS** Rendcomb 1918.

C4859 (Falcon III) **5 AAP** Bristol 28.2.18, allotted to BEF. **1 ASD** dd ex England 11.3.18 (engine 523/WD32661). **2 ASD** ex 1 ASD 23.3.18 (same engine). **62 Sqn** dd ex **2 AIS** 26.3.18, victs 12.4.18 (2nd Lt C.H. Arnison/Lt S. Parry sent an all white Albatros D.V OOC near La Bassee at 14:15) and 21.4.18 (2nd Lt C.H. Arnison/ Lt S. Parry sent two Pfalz D.III OOC, one by the pilot, the other by the observer, Estaires-Lille at 10:00), damaged in successful combat 3.5.18 (2nd Lt C.H. Arnison OK/Lt S. Parry KIA when sending two Albatros D.V OOC and destroying another in flames E of Armentieres, 11.15-11.17), further victs 9.5.18 (2nd Lt C.H. Arnison/Lt H.E. Merritt destroyed a Pfalz D.III and sent another OOC) and 15.5.18 (2nd Lt C.H. Arnison/Lt C.D. Wells destroyed an EA C-type, Albert-Ayette at 17:45) then wrecked on 12:15 OP 16.5.18 (2nd Lt C.H. Arnison WIA/Lt C.D. Wells MC KIA, brought down in combat, crash landed within the allied lines and abandoned under shell fire), deleted on unit 17.5.18 (60hr).

C4860 (Falcon III) **5 AAP** Bristol 27.2.18, allotted to BEF. **1 ASD** dd ex England 10.3.18 (engine 551/WD32675). **2 ASD** ex 1 ASD 16.3.18 (same engine) and despatched by rail to 7 Bde Italy 28.3.18. **'Z' Flt, 34 Sqn** dd ex **7 AP** 27.4.18 (same engine) and wrecked in crash near Padua. **7 AP** ex 'Z' Flt 1.5.18 (same engine).

C4861 (Falcon III) **5 AAP** Bristol 28.2.18, allotted to BEF. **1 ASD** dd ex England 15.3.18 (engine 583/WD32691). **2 ASD** ex 1 ASD 17.3.18 (same engine). **11 Sqn** dd ex 2 ASD 22.3.18, vict 7.4.18 (Lt H.A. Hay/Sgt P.A. Sherlock sent an Albatros C-type OOC near Grevillers at 12:05) and 4.5.18 (Lt H.A. Hay/Sgt P.A. Sherlock destroyed a Pfalz D.III in flames near Marquion at 18:40) then wrecked after Reconnaissance 7.6.18 (Lt R.J. Pring/AM1 H. Turner both OK, longeron broken in bad landing – engine 63/WD18531). **2 ASD** ex 11 Sqn 7.6.18 and deleted 3.7.18 on reconstruction as F6101.

C4862 (Falcon III) **5 AAP** Bristol 28.2.18, allotted to BEF. **1 ASD** dd ex 5 AAP 11.3.18 (Lt C.F. Uwins engine 549/WD32674). **2 ASD** ex 1 ASD 16.3.18 (same engine). **11 Sqn** dd ex 2 ASD 22.3.18 (same engine), LIA on 17:00 OP 2.4.18 (2nd Lt A.R. Knowles/Lt A.E. Matthews both KIA, last seen diving on EA – same engine) and deleted on unit that day (26hr 45min).

C4863 N/I

C4864 (Falcon III) **5 AAP** Bristol 27.2.18, allotted to BEF. **1 ASD** dd ex England 10.3.18 (engine 567/WD32683). **2 ASD** ex 1 ASD 15.3.18 (same engine). **48 Sqn** dd ex **2 AIS** 18.3.18 (same engine), LIA on 14:35 OP 6.4.18 (2nd Lt B.G.A. Bell/2nd Lt C.G. Bartlett both KIA near Villers Bretonneaux – same engine) and deleted on unit that day (21hr 45min).

C4865 **8 TS** Netheravon dd ex **5 AAP** 10.3.18 (Lt C.F. Uwins/Lt Elshaw).

C4866 **8 TS** Netheravon by 9.3.18. **24 TS** Netheravon by 13.3.18.

C4867 (Falcon III) **88 Sqn** Harling Road dd ex **5 AAP** 14.3.18, to BEF with unit 25.4.18, in BEF 18.5.18 (Capt E.C. Johnston/2nd Lt J. Rudkin destroyed an Albatros D.V in flames and sent another OOC, N of Langemarck at 07:35), 1.7.18 (Capt E.C. Johnston/2nd Lt J. Rudkin destroyed a Fokker D.VII in flames near Westroosebeke) and 19.8.18 (Capt E.C. Johnston/2nd Lt J. Rudkin sent a Fokker D.VII OOC near Oignies at 10:30, shared E2216) then wrecked in further successful combat 4.9.18 (Capt E.C. Johnston/2nd Lt W.J.N. Grant destroyed a Fokker D.VII in flames over Seclin at 09:00, sent another OOC over Phalempin at 09:15 and sent a Fokker Dr.I OOC over Provin at 09:30 but own machine badly shot up by EA fire – engine 1255/WD51652). **1 ASD** ex* 88 Sqn 7.9.18 and deleted 11.9.18 (not worth reconstruction, 220hr 35min).

C4868 (Falcon III) presentation a/c *Presented by the Government of Johore No.2*. **5 AAP** Bristol 8.3.18, allotted to BEF. **1 ASD** dd ex England 27.3.18 (engine 459/WD32629). **2 ASD** ex 1 ASD 27.3.18 (same engine). **11 Sqn** dd ex 2 ASD 28.3.18. **2 ASD** ex 11 Sqn 22.8.18 and deleted 8.9.18 on reconstruction as F6288 (183hr 15min).

C4869 N/I

C4870 (Falcon III) **1 FTS** Netheravon by 4.20 and wrecked 5.8.20 (Fg Off D. Ankers IIFA/Flt Lt M.A.J. Orde KIFA, took off steeply, stalled, then dived in, off a turn at Netheravon – control had been wrongly adjusted).

C4871 N/I

C4872 N/I

C4873 N/I

C4874 (Falcon II) **45 TDS** Rendcomb and wrecked 27.11.18 (2nd Lt H.C. Craddock KIFA, engine cut, stalled and nosedived in – engine 2/F/149/WD22415).

C4875 **36 Sqn, 'C' Flt** Seaton Carew by 24.12.18. **IDE** Biggin Hill by 2.20.

C4876 Cranwell by 5.19.

C4877 N/I

C4878 **39 TDS** Spittlegate by 24.8.18.

C4879 (Falcon III) **33 TDS** Witney named *The Crocodile*. **Netheravon Flying School** and wrecked 14.8.19 (Flt Cdt H.S. Morris KIFA, stalled on gliding turn and spun in – engine 51978).

C4880 (Falcon III) **88 Sqn** Harling Road, to BEF with unit 25.4.18, LIA on 18:30 OP 28.6.18 (Lt J.P. West/Pte A.J. Loton both KIA, probably brought down in flames near Clerkem) and deleted on unit 29.6.18 (77hr 53min).

C4881 **24 TS** Witney by 29.4.18.

C4882 (Falcon III) **5 AAP** Bristol 7.3.18, allotted to BEF. **1 ASD** dd ex England 20.3.18 (engine 571/WD32685). **2 ASD** ex 1 ASD 26.3.18. **11 Sqn** dd ex 2 ASD 28.3.18, LIA after vict on 15:40 OP 15.5.18 (Capt J.V. Aspinall/Lt P.V. de la Cour both KIA, sent a Fokker Dr.I OOC near Mametz, shared C845, then shot down over Bouchou) and deleted on unit that day (50hr 13min).

C4883 N/I

C4884 N/I

C4885 (Falcon III) Hendon by 5.18. **1 Comms Sqn** Hendon 23.7.18 and wrecked on Communications Flight, Martlesham-Hendon, 26.8.18 (Col B. Hopkinson KIFA, sideslipped and dived in near Paston, Essex – engine 3/F/659/WD32729).

C4886 (Falcon III) **5 AAP** Bristol 8.3.18, allotted to BEF. **1 ASD** dd ex England 17.3.18 (engine 679/WD32739). **2 ASD** ex 1 ASD 23.3.18 (same engine). **48 Sqn** dd ex **2 AIS** 25.3.18 and wrecked on Low OP 24.4.18 (Lt F.C. Ransley/2nd Lt C.W. Davies both OK, machine shot up by enemy machine-gun fire – same engine). **2 ASD** ex 48 Sqn 27.4.18 and deleted 12.5.18 (not worth reconstruction).

C4887 (Falcon III) **5 AAP** Bristol 8.3.18, allotted to BEF. **1 ASD** dd ex England 20.3.18 (engine 681/WD32740). **2 ASD** ex 1 ASD 23.3.18 (same engine). **2 AIS** ex 2 ASD 27.4.18 (same engine). **62 Sqn** dd ex 2 AIS 4.5.18 (same engine) and wrecked after OP 8.5.18 (Lt A.W. Blowes/2nd Lt H.S. Hind both OK, misjudged landing – same engine). **1 ASD** ex 62 Sqn 12.5.18 and deleted 25.6.18 on reconstruction as F5809 (5hr 8min).

C4888 (Falcon III) **5 AAP** Bristol 7.3.18, allotted to BEF. **1 ASD** dd ex England 18.3.18 (engine 685/WD32742). **2 ASD** ex 1 ASD 20.3.18 (same engine). **22 Sqn** marked as a/c *P* by 8.4.18, victs 6.5.18 (2nd Lt G.W. Bulmer/2nd Lt H.E. Elsworth sent a Pfalz D.III OOC near Fresnay at 18:25), 17.5.18 (2nd Lt G.W. Bulmer/2nd Lt P.S. Williams destroyed a Pfalz D.III near Brebières at 10:15) and 27.6.18 (Capt G.W. Bulmer/Observer sent a Fokker D.VII completely OOC near Ognies Courriers at 09:45) then wrecked on Practice Flight 22.10.18 (Capt K.C. Gill fatally IOAS/2nd Lt J.V. Scorton IOAS, crashed at **102 Sqn** aerodrome – engine 1561/WD51805) and deleted on unit that day.

C4889 **Medical Flt** Hendon dd ex **2 AAP** 4.4.18. Brooklands by 21.7.18. **29 TS** Hendon dd ex 2 AAP 26.7.18.

C4890 N/I

C4891 **36 Sqn, 'A' Flt** Hylton by 4.8.18. To Iraq. **8 Sqn** by 6.27 until @ 7.27.

C4892 **2 FS** Marske as a/c *48*.

C4893 (Falcon III) **36 Sqn** and wrecked 27.7.18 (Lt A.H. Carmen OK/Flt Cdt A.V. Kidd IIFA, overshot landing and engine failed when trying to take off again – engine 3/677/WD32738).

C4894 (Falcon III) **5 AAP** Bristol 8.3.18 allotted to BEF. **1 ASD** dd ex England 18.3.18 (engine 701/WD32861). **2 ASD** ex 1 ASD 20.3.18 (same engine). **22 Sqn** dd ex 2 ASD 20.3.18, marked as a/c *L*, vict 30.3.18 (Lt W.F.J. Harvey/2nd Lt H.F. Moore destroyed an EKB, NE of Albert at 18:45) and wrecked on 19:40 Wireless Test 8.6.18 (Lt C.W.M. Thompson/AM Rich both OK, landed badly – same engine) **1 ASD** ex 22 Sqn 10.6.18 and deleted 8.8.18 (not worth reconstruction, 100hr 25min).

C4895 (Falcon III) **1 ASD** by 31.8.18 (engine 923/WD32861) and flown to England 23.9.18, apparently without issue to squadron. **39 Sqn**.

C4896 (Falcon I) **36 Sqn, 'A' Flt** Hylton by 1.5.18 and wrecked 3.7.18 (Lt A. Wald MC OK, Flt Cdt Horsington IIFA, propeller struck the gound on landing and machine o/t – engine 1/Fal/577/WD52688).

C4897 **36 Sqn** by 9.18. **APS** Andover by 7.19 until @ 2.20. B&C for reconditioning to J Type (s/n 6435) and ready by 26.4.24. **13 Sqn** by 9.27. **E&WS** by 1.28 until @ 7.28. B&C for reconditioning to Mk.III (s/n 7570), ready by 1.12.30 and delivered 15.12.30. Sold and to civilian register as G-ACFL 22.3.33 for Commercial Airways (Essex) Ltd. Sold for scrap 5.36.

C4898 **36 Sqn, 'A' Flt** by 7.5.18 until @ 28.8.18 and with **'C' Flt** by 8.1.19 until @ 16.1.19.

C4899 To Middle East. **X AD** dd ex England 2.9.18. Palestine Bde. **X AD** ex Palestine Bde 1.11.18.

C4900 **ES Grain** 9.20 until @ 1.23.

150 BRISTOL FIGHTER F.2B ordered 30.10.17 under Contract A.S.32796 from The Gloucestershire Aircraft Co Ltd, Cheltenham and numbered C9836 to C9985. (200hp Arab).

C9836 **5 AAP** Bristol and tested 10.5.18 (Lt C.F. Uwins).

C9837 **5 AAP** Bristol 17.5.18, allotted to BEF. **8 Sqn** marked as a/c *B4* and *C4* and reported wrecked at **12 Sqn** aerodrome 18.7.19.

C9838 **5 AAP** Bristol 27.5.18, allotted to BEF.

C9839 **5 AAP** Bristol 27.5.18, allotted to BEF and tested 1.9.18 (Lt C.F. Uwins). **1 ASD** by 4.9.18 until @ 15.9.18 (engine 53789).

C9840 (Arab) **5 AAP** Bristol 3.6.18, allotted to BEF but reallotted to SW Area for D of T and ACIS Winchester 6.6.18 and tested 4.9.18 (Lt C.F. Uwins). Photographed o/t.

C9841 (Arab) **5 AAP** Bristol 27.5.18, allotted to BEF. **1 Comm Sqn** Hendon by 12.11.18 (2nd Lt C.H. Drew).

C9842 (Arab) **5 AAP** Bristol 3.6.18, allotted to BEF but reallotted to SW Area for D of T and AICS Winchester 6.6.18 and tested 5.7.18, 6.7.18, 7.7.18 and 17.7.18 (Lt C.F. Uwins, 7 flights). **AES** Martlesham Heath dd 31.7.18 and allotted to **(S)ARD** 31.8.18. **1 (S)ARD** Farnborough by w/e 14.9.18.

C9843 (Arab) **5 AAP** Bristol 3.6.18, allotted to BEF but reallotted to SW Area for D of T and the Artillery and Infantry Co-operation School Winchester 6.6.18.

C9844 (Arab) **5 AAP** Bristol 3.6.18, allotted to BEF but reallotted to SW Area for D of T and AICS Winchester 6.6.18. **7th TS AFC** Minchinhampton.

C9845 **5 AAP** Bristol tested 14.8.18 (Lt C.F. Uwins).

C9846 N/I

C9847 (Arab) **5 AAP** Bristol 3.6.18, allotted to BEF but reallotted to SW Area for D of T and the Artillery and Infantry Co-operation School Winchester 6.6.18.

C9848 N/I

C9849 **5 AAP** Bristol tested 9.7.18 (Lt C.F. Uwins).

C9850 **7th TS AFC** Minchinhampton dd ex **5 AAP** 5.11.18.

C9851 **5 AAP** Bristol tested 16.8.18 (Lt C.F. Uwins).

C9852 N/I

C9853 **7th TS AFC** Minchinhampton dd 27.9.18 and on unit charge until @ 17.11.18. (Also noted **59 Sqn** 1919).

C9854 **1 (Obs) SAG** New Romney and wrecked 16.7.18 (2nd Lt A.F. Rogers/Flt Cdt W.K. Smith both KIFA, stalled in steeply banked turn near the ground, nosedived in and caught fire – engine 19112/WD19162).

C9855 **5 AAP** Bristol tested 8.7.18 (Lt C.F. Uwins).

C9856 (Arab) at maker's 5.6.18, allotted to BEF but reallotted to SW Area for D of T for the Artillery and Infantry Co-operation School Winchester 6.6.18.

C9857 (Arab) at maker's 5.6.18, allotted to BEF. En route to **5 AAP** Bristol 6.6.18, reallotted to SW Area for D of T for the Artillery and Infantry Co-operation School Winchester.

C9858 (Arab) at maker's 5.6.18, allotted to BEF. En route to **5 AAP** Bristol 6.6.18, reallotted to SW Area for D of T for AICS Winchester. **7th TS AFC** Leighterton dd ex 5 AAP 27.9.18 and on unit charge until @ 26.1.19.

C9859 (Arab) at maker's 5.6.18, allotted to BEF. En route to **5 AAP** Bristol 6.6.18, reallotted to SW Area for D of T for the Artillery and Infantry Co-operation School Winchester. **7th TS AFC** Leighterton dd ex 5 AAP 5.11.18.

C9860 (Arab) at maker's 5.6.18, allotted to BEF. En route to **5 AAP** Bristol 6.6.18, reallotted to SW Area for D of T for the Artillery and Infantry Co-operation School Winchester. **AICS** Worthy Down by 8.18.

C9861 (Arab) at maker's 5.6.18, allotted to BEF. **5 AAP** Bristol tested 12.8.18 (Lt C.F. Uwins). En route to 5 AAP Bristol 6.6.18, reallotted to SW Area for D of T for the Artillery and Infantry Co-operation School Winchester. **AICS** Worthy Down by 8.18. **Artillery Co-operation Sqn** Tilshead by 11.18.

C9862 (Arab) at maker's 5.6.18, allotted to BEF. En route to **5 AAP** Bristol 6.6.18, reallotted to SW Area for D of T for the Artillery and Infantry Co-operation School Winchester. **AICS** Worthy Down by 7.18 until @ 8.18.

C9863 (Arab) at maker's 5.6.18, allotted to BEF but reallotted 7.6.18 to SW Area for D of T and the Wireless Telephony School, Chattis Hill.

C9864 (Arab) at maker's 5.6.18, allotted to BEF but reallotted 7.6.18 to SW Area for D of T and the Wireless Telephony School, Chattis Hill. **5 AAP** Bristol tested 21.7.18 (Lt C.F. Uwins).

C9865 (Arab) at maker's 5.6.18, allotted to BEF but reallotted 7.6.18 to SW Area for D of T and the Wireless Telephony School, Chattis Hill. **5 AAP** Bristol tested 21.7.18, 26.7.18 and 29.7.18 (Lt C.F. Uwins).

C9866 Presentation a/c *No.1 Bircham Newton, 1918*. **5 AAP** Bristol tested 25.7.18 (Lt C.F. Uwins).

C9867 Photographed marked as a/c 6.

C9868 N/I

C9869 **7th TS AFC** Leighterton dd 30.10.18 and on unit charge until @ 26.1.19.

C9870 N/I

C9871 (Arab) at maker's 12.6.18, allotted to BEF. **5 AAP** Bristol tested 29.7.18 (Lt C.F. Uwins). **1 ASD** Repair Park by 31.8.18 (engine 2858) and deleted 23.9.18 (destroyed by enemy action, 2hr 20min).

C9872 (Arab) at maker's 12.6.18, allotted to BEF. **5 AAP** Bristol tested 21.8.18 (Lt C.F. Uwins).

C9873 (Arab) at maker's 12.6.18, allotted to BEF. **'L' Flt** 1918. **8 Sqn** dd ex 'L' Flt 20.1.19 (Lt Buick) and wrecked on Aerial Post, St Omer, 11.4.19 (Lt W.J. Tarring/2nd Lt H.E. Sheffield both OK), crashed in forced landing (engine 53858).

C9874 (Arab) at maker's 12.6.18, allotted to BEF.

C9875 (Arab) at maker's 12.6.18, allotted to BEF. **5 AAP** Bristol tested 23.8.18 (Lt C.F. Uwins). **37 TDS** Yatesbury by 17.10.18 until @ 28.10.18 (Lt J.W. Baker).

C9876 (Arab) at maker's 22.6.18, allotted to BEF. **5 AAP** Bristol tested 19.7.18 and 8.9.18 (Lt C.F. Uwins). **9 Sqn** dd ex **6 AIS** 18.4.19 (engine 19116).

C9877 (Arab) at maker's 22.6.18, allotted to BEF. **5 AAP** Bristol tested 17.7.18 (Lt C.F. Uwins). **1 ASD** by 30.9.18 (engine 19069). **8 Sqn** by 26.12.18. **59 Sqn** dd ex 8 Sqn 28.1.19 and wrecked 15.2.19 (Lt F.A. Markham/AM3 G.G. Stewart both OK, machine o/t after a wheel came off on landing – same engine).

C9878 (Arab) at maker's 22.6.18, allotted to BEF. **5 AAP** Bristol tested 25.7.18 and 26.7.18 (Lt C.F. Uwins). **1 ASD** Repair Park by 31.8.18 (engine 19151) and deleted 23.9.18 (destroyed by enemy action, 2hr 15min).

C9879 (Arab) at maker's 22.6.18, allotted to BEF. **5 AAP** Bristol tested 25.7.18 (Lt C.F. Uwins). **1 ASD** by 15.9.18 (engine 19116). **6 Sqn** dd ex 1 ASD 14.10.18. **9 Sqn** by 26.4.19 and wrecked on Patrol 29.5.19 (2nd Lt Foster/Lt Miller both OK, the machine crashed in a forced landing – same engine). **8 SS** ex 9 Sqn 31.5.19.

C9880 (Arab) at maker's 22.6.18, allotted to BEF. **5 AAP** Bristol tested 24.7.18 (Lt C.F. Uwins). **ES Martlesham Heath** dd w/e 3.8.18 until @ 9.8.18 (Capt G.W. Gathergood). **1 (S)ARD** Farnborough 15.8.18. In France by 3.19, allotted 1 (S)ARD Farnborough, but reallotted to BEF 17.3.19.

C9881 (Arab) at maker's 22.6.18, allotted to BEF.

C9882 (Arab) at maker's 22.6.18, allotted to BEF. **1 ASD** by 15.9.18 (engine 19199). **13 Sqn** dd ex **2 ASD** 30.10.18 and on unit charge until @ 15.1.19.

C9883 (Arab) at maker's 22.6.18, allotted to BEF. **ES Martlesham Heath** dd w/e 3.8.18 (engine 53793) used to produce Report M.224 and left w/e 15.2.19.

C9884 (Arab) at maker's 22.6.18, allotted to BEF.

C9885 (Arab) at maker's 22.6.18, allotted to BEF. **28th Wing** Yatesbury as Wing Examining Officer's machine.

C9886 (Arab) at maker's 27.6.18, allotted to BEF. **36 TDS** Yatesbury by 12.18 (Lt W.R. Parkhouse).

C9887 (Arab) presentation a/c *No.7 Bircham Newton*. At maker's 27.6.18, allotted to BEF. **5 AAP** Bristol tested 18.8.18 and 19.8.18 (Lt C.F. Uwins).

C9888 (Arab) at maker's 27.6.18, allotted to BEF. **5 AAP** Bristol tested 2.9.18 (Lt C.F. Uwins). **1 ASD** Repair Park by 15.9.18 (engine 19240) and deleted 23.9.18 (destroyed by enemy action, 3hr 20min).

C9889 (Arab) at maker's 27.6.18, allotted to BEF. **5 AAP** Bristol tested 8.8.18 (Lt C.F. Uwins). **37 TDS** Yatesbury.

C9890 (Arab) at maker's 27.6.18, allotted to BEF. **36 TDS** Yatesbury by 1.19 (Lt W.R. Parkhouse).

C9891 (Arab) at maker's 27.6.18, allotted to BEF. **1 ASD** by 31.8.18 (engine 19225). **'P' Flt** dd ex **1 AIS** 3.9.18 (same engine), wrecked

after Test Flight 19.1.19 (Lt Vaile OK, overshot landing and ran into a ditch – engine 53861) and deleted on unit 1.2.19.

C9892 (Arab) at maker's 27.6.18, allotted to BEF.

C9893 (Arab) at maker's 27.6.18, allotted to BEF. **5 AAP** Bristol tested 14.8.18, 15.8.18 and 15.10.18 (Lt C.F. Uwins).

C9894 (Arab) at maker's 27.6.18, allotted to BEF. **1 ASD** by 31.8.18 (engine 19235). **'L' Flt** dd ex 1 ASD 21.9.18, accident 1.19 and for deletion on unit 24.1.19 (awaiting radiator bracket, to be dismantled and destroyed – engine 2983/WD27108).

C9895 (Arab) at maker's 27.6.18, allotted to BEF. **5 AAP** Bristol tested 19.7.18 (Lt C.F. Uwins) and wrecked on ground engine tuning 29.7.18 (Lt L. Wood/AM3 A.W. Churchyard both IIGA, engine started without the tail being secured – engine 19177). **3 (W)ARD** 25.1.19 with BEF allotment cancelled and machine for deletion.

C9896 (Arab) at maker's 27.6.18, allotted to BEF. **5 AAP** Bristol tested 6.8.18 (Lt C.F. Uwins). **1 ASD** by 31.8.18 (engine 19202). **N Flight** dd ex 1 ASD 28.9.18 and wrecked on Weather Test 22.10.18 (Lt Bowker OK/Lt Grant IOAS, pancaked on landing and turned over – engine 53770). **2 ASD** and deleted 9.11.18 on reconstruction as H6893.

C9897 (Arab) at maker's 27.6.18, allotted to BEF. **1 ASD** by 4.9.18. **3 Sqn AFC** dd 27.11.18 (engine 19180/WD10180). **59 Sqn** by 2.19. **1 ASD** ex 59 Sqn 19.7.19.

C9898 (Arab) at maker's 27.6.18, allotted to BEF.

C9899 (Arab) at maker's 27.6.18, allotted to BEF. **1 ASD** by 15.9.18 (engine 19246). **9 Sqn** dd ex 1 ASD 29.5.19 (same engine). **1 ASD** ex 9 Sqn 19.7.19.

C9900 to **C9940** } N/I

C9941 **'P' Flt**, wrecked on Delivery Flight ex **1 ASD** 11.1.19 (Lt Vaile/Lt Muir both OK, force landed near Longuenese).

C9942 N/I

C9943 In France 28.4.19, reallotted from **5 (E)ARD** to BEF. **9 Sqn** dd ex **6 AIS** 16.6.19 (engine 2977/WD27102).

C9944 N/I

C9945 N/I

C9946 N/I

C9947 (Arab) **1 (S)ARD** 23.1.19, allotment to BEF cancelled, after crash but reallotted to BEF 27.1.19. **12 Sqn** named *Charlestown* and wrecked on Formation Flight 5.4.19 (Lt Frost/Lt Jenkins both OK, landed on soft ground and o/t – engine E3204/WD27329).

C9948 **'N' Flt** and wrecked on Travelling Flight, Bovillers-Bertangles 21.12.18 (Lt Peterson/Lt Pratt both OK, force landed near Auxi-le-Chateau – engine 53738).

C9949 N/I

C9950 **5 AAP** Bristol and tested 12.9.18 (Lt C.F. Uwins). **9 Sqn** dd ex **1 ASD** 9.4.19 (engine 53709). **1 ASD** ex 9 Sqn 21.7.19.

C9951 to **C9971** } N/I

C9972 Photographed wrecked at **1 ASD**.

C9973 **59 Sqn** Duren. **1 ASD** ex 59 Sqn 17.7.19.

C9974 **8 Sqn** Sart. **1 ASD** Merheim ex 8 Sqn 12.7.19 (Lt J.W. Baker).

C9975 Reallotted from **5 (E)ARD** to BEF 6.3.19.

C9976 **9 Sqn** dd ex **6 AIS** 2.6.19 (engine 2971/WD27096).

C9977 N/I

C9978 N/I

C9979 **5 AAP** Bristol and tested 16.10.18 (Lt C.F. Uwins).

C9980 **5 AAP** Bristol and tested 11.10.18 (Lt C.F. Uwins).

C9981 N/I

C9982 **8 Sqn** Bellevue. **2 ASD** ex 8 Sqn 28.1.19. **12 Sqn** marked as a/c *A1* by 3.19 until @ 5.19.

C9983 **8 Sqn** Bellevue. **2 ASD** ex 8 Sqn 28.1.19.

C9984 N/I

C9985 (Arab) **8 AAP** Lympne by 23.1.19, reallotted from BEF to SE Area for Storage at Weston-on-the-Green

500 BRISTOL FIGHTER F.2B ordered 22.11.17 under Contract A.S.34276 from National Aircraft Factory No.3 (Cunard Steamship Co Ltd), Aintree and numbered D2126 to D2625. (200hp Hispano-Suiza 8B).

D2126 (Arab) **5 AAP** Bristol 13.6.18, allotted to BEF. **1 ASD** by 30.9.18 (engine 19130). **'L' Flt** Bruay dd ex 1 ASD 5.10.18 and wrecked on Travelling Flight 14.1.19 (Capt Brettell/AC2 Edwards both OK, longeron broken and machine to be dismantled and deleted – same engine).

D2127 (Arab).

D2128 (Arab) first flown 12.7.18. **37 TDS** Yatesbury and crashed on take-off from Yatesbury 5.10.18 (Lt G.H. Turner OK, fuselage fractured caused by the violent impact of the tail skid with the ground – engine 2845, 13hr).

D2129 (Arab) at maker's 21.6.18, allotted to BEF and to be delivered to **5 AAP**. **8 Sqn** and damaged on Travelling Flight 28.11.18 (Lt Filmer/Lt Oates both OK, force landed near Boyeffelles due to darkness – engine E2860).

D2130 (Arab) at maker's 21.6.18, allotted to BEF and to be delivered to **5 AAP**. **1 ASD** Marquise and flown to England 4.9.18.

D2131 (Arab) **36 TDS** Yatesbury by 1.19 until @ 2.19 (Lt W.R. Parkhouse).

D2132 N/I

D2133 (Arab) NAF Aintree 25.6.18, allotted to BEF and to be delivered to **5 AAP**.

D2134 (Arab) NAF Aintree 25.6.18, allotted to BEF and to be delivered to **5 AAP**. **1 ASD** Reception Park by 30.9.18 (engine 19229). **2 AIS** dd ex 1 ASD 24.10.18. **8 Sqn** and wrecked on Aerial Post 14.12.18 (Lt Jaconsen/Lt Ptynne both OK, force landed near Bousignies and ran into a ditch – engine WD53863).

D2135 (Arab) NAF Aintree 25.6.18, allotted to BEF and to be delivered to **5 AAP**.

D2136 (Arab) NAF Aintree 25.6.18, allotted to BEF and to be delivered to **5 AAP**. **'P' Flt** and wrecked on Travelling Flight 24.12.18 (Lt Vaile/AM Battley both OK, ran into a shell hole when landing at Saultain – engine 53761).

D2137
to   } N/I
D2145

D2146 **12 Sqn** 1919.

D2147 N/I

D2148 (Arab) in France 27.12.18 reallotted from **5 (E)ARD** to BEF.

D2149 N/I

D2150 (Arab) **9 Sqn** dd ex 6 AIS 23.4.19 (engine 53810). **1 ASD** ex 9 Sqn 15.7.19.

D2151 (Arab) **8 Sqn** 7.19. **1 ASD** ex 8 Sqn 12.7.19.

D2152 (Arab) **8 AAP** Lympne 23.1.19, reallotted from BEF to SE Area for Storage at Weston-on-the-Green.

D2153 N/I

D2154 N/I

D2155 N/I

D2156 N/I

D2157 **141 Sqn** Biggin Hill 1918.

D2158 N/I

D2159 **141 Sqn** Biggin Hill 1918.

D2160 N/I

D2161 **8 Sqn** dd ex 1 ASD 20.4.19.

D2162 **'P' Flt** dd ex 1 ASD 11.1.19. **8 Sqn** dd ex 'P' Flt 19.1.19 (Lt Wilkinson). **2 ASD** ex 8 Sqn 28.1.19.

D2163 N/I

D2164 N/I

D2165 (Arab) **37 TDS** Yatesbury by 29.10.18 (Lt J.W. Baker).

D2166 N/I

D2167 (Arab) **48 Sqn** named *Shifnal*. **12 Sqn** and wrecked on Air Test 29.3.19 (Lt P.F. Bovingdon/Lt Turpin both OK, crashed landing in bad weather – engine E3038).

D2168 N/I

D2169 **39 TDS** Spittlegate by 1.19.

D2170
to   } N/I
D2182

D2183 **'L' Flt** Bruay by 28.9.18.

D2185
to   } N/I
D2190

D2191 **5 TDS** Easton-on-the-Hill by 31.8.18 until @ 6.9.18 (Capt B.C. Rice).

D2192 **5 TDS** Easton-on-the-Hill by 2.9.18 (Capt B.C. Rice).

D2193
to   } N/I
D2198

D2199 **15 AAP** Manchester by 28.3.19 allotted to BEF.

D2200 N/I

D2201 N/I

D2202 N/I

D2203 **15 AAP** Manchester by 10.1.19.

D2204 **15 AAP** Manchester by 28.3.19 allotted to BEF, but allotment cancelled and for deletion 30.4.19.

D2205 N/I

D2206 N/I

D2207 N/I

D2208 Cranwell, o/t late 1918 or early 1919.

D2209 N/I

D2210 **15 AAP** Manchester by 21.3.19 allotted to BEF, but reallotted to Ministry of Munitions Salvage Depot, Waddon, 29.3.19.

D2211 **141 Sqn** 1918.

D2212 **20 Sqn** by 9.10.18.

D2213 N/I

D2214 **20 Sqn** by 9.10.18.

D2215 N/I

D2216 N/I

D2217 N/I

D2218 (Arab) **15 AAP** Manchester and wrecked 15.1.19 (Capt C.A. Brown/Pte C.J.T. Cafferty both KIFA, turned without bank and entered flat spin at 1,500ft then caught fire on impact – engine 53877).

D2219 N/I

D2220 N/I

D2221 N/I

D2222 (Arab) **37 TDS** Yatesbury by 10.18 (Lt W.R. Parkhouse), stalled from 10ft and crashed 17.10.18 (Lt F.E.W. Perry IIFA and admitted to Chiseldon Military Hospital).

D2223 N/I

D2224 **20 Sqn**.

A product of National Aircraft Factory No.3 (the Cunard Steamship Co Ltd) at Aintree, Hispano-engined D2222 undergoes a trial run of its 200hp Hispano-Suiza 8B engine at 37 TDS, Yatesbury. *(C&C/Trevor Henshaw)*

D2225 ⎫
to ⎬ N/I
D2231 ⎭
D2232 **8 Sqn** to **2 ASD** 28.1.19 (possibly E2232).
D2233 ⎫
to ⎬ N/I
D2239 ⎭
D2240 HD Bde.
D2241 N/I
D2242 N/I
D2243 N/I
D2244 **141 Sqn** 1918.
D2245 **20 Sqn** by 24.9.18.
D2246 N/I
D2247 **141 Sqn** 1918.
D2248 N/I
D2249 N/I
D2250 dd 4.1.19.
D2251 ⎫
to ⎬ cancelled by 1.1.19.
D2625 ⎭

150 BRISTOL FIGHTER F.2B ordered under Contract A.S.35822 (B.R.270) dated 22.11.17 from Marshall, Sons & Co Ltd, Gainsborough and numbered D2626 to D2775. (200hp Arab). [H1746 to H1895 also allotted in error, then cancelled].

D2626 (Arab) at maker's 5.6.18, allotted to BEF and to be delivered to **5 AAP**.
D2627 (Arab) at maker's 15.6.18, allotted to BEF and to be delivered to **5 AAP**. To **37 TDS** Yatesbury by 10.18 (Lt W.R. Parkhouse).
D2628 (Arab) at maker's 26.6.18, allotted to BEF and to be delivered to **5 AAP**. To **3 (W)ARD** by 25.1.19 with BEF allotment cancelled and machine for deletion.
D2629 (Arab) at maker's 18.6.18, allotted to BEF and to be delivered to **5 AAP**. To **36 TDS** Yatesbury by 11.18. **7 TS AFC** Leighterton, engineless, by 18.11.18.
D2630 (Arab) at maker's 28.6.18, allotted to BEF and to be delivered to **4 AAP** Lincoln.
D2631 (Arab) at maker's 28.6.18, allotted to BEF and to be delivered to **4 AAP** Lincoln.
D2632 ⎫
to ⎬ N/I
D2642 ⎭
D2643 **20 Sqn** by 11.18.
D2644 **20 Sqn** by 24.12.18.
D2645 N/I
D2646 **33 TDS** Witney by 5.11.18 until @ 9.11.18 (2nd Lt G.A. Raybone).
D2647 N/I
D2648 N/I
D2649 Presentation a/c *Gold Coast No.14* wef 10.18. **4 AAP** Lincoln by 3.10.18. **1 ASD** dd ex **4 ASD** 9.10.18. **2 AIS** ex 1 ASD 24.10.18. **8 Sqn** by 22.1.19. **6 SS** ex 8 Sqn 12.5.19.
D2650 **20 Sqn** by 5.12.18.
D2651 N/I
D2652 (Arab) presentation a/c *Armenia Malaya No.7*. **4 AAP** Lincoln by 3.10.18. **1 ASD** by 17.10.18. **1 AIS** ex 1 ASD 18.10.18. **'P' Flt** dd 22.10.18, force landed on Artillery Patrol 25.10.18 (Lt Brown/Lt Gutheridge both OK, hit in fuel and oil tanks and came down in no man's land, machine for repair on unit – engine E2196/WD27041) and wrecked on Test Flight 30.12.18 (Lt C. Goldsworthy IIFA, crashed near aerodrome – engine E3063). **1 ASD** ex 'P' Flt 5.1.19.
D2653 ⎫
to ⎬ N/I
D2658 ⎭
D2659 (Arab) **8 Sqn** dd ex **1 ASD** 12.5.18. **1 ASD** ex 8 Sqn 15.7.19.
D2660 Presentation a/c *Zanzibar No.5* by 10.18. **4 AAP** Lincoln by 3.10.18. **8 Sqn** dd 27.11.18 with forced landing at Treizennes. **3 Sqn AFC** ex 8 Sqn 28.1.19. **59 Sqn** by 2.19 until @ 17.7.19.
D2661 ⎫
to ⎬ N/I
D2675 ⎭
D2676 **22 Sqn** marked as a/c *B* and photographed crashed on nose.
D2677 ⎫
to ⎬ N/I
D2686 ⎭
D2687 (Arab) **7 TS AFC** Leighterton, photographed crashed on nose.
D2688 N/I
D2689 N/I

D2690 N/I
D2691 **7 TS AFC** Leighterton by 18.11.18.
D2692 N/I
D2693 N/I
D2694 N/I
D2695 N/I
D2696 ADC Waddon and to Spanish civilian register as M-CAJA.
D2697 **7 TS AFC** Leighterton dd ex **4 AAP** 1.11.18.
D2698 ⎫
to ⎬ N/I
D2702 ⎭
D2703 **RAF (Cadet) College** by 7.19.
D2704 N/I
D2705 (Arab) **4 AAP** Lincoln 4.4.19, allotted to BEF.
D2706 (Arab) **4 AAP** Lincoln 3.4.19, allotted to BEF.
D2707 (Arab) **4 AAP** Lincoln 31.1.19, allotted to BEF. **9 Sqn** dd ex **1 ASD** 7.5.19 (engine 19038). **1 ASD** ex 9 Sqn 15.7.19.
D2708 (Arab) **4 AAP** Lincoln 16.1.19, allotted to BEF and still at Lincoln 24.4.19. **59 Sqn** by 13.6.19 and wrecked on Test Flight 12.7.19 (Lt R. Jones/AM2 R. Harvey both OK, mis-judged landing and crashed into cornfield – engine 16287). **1 ASD** ex 59 Sqn 17.7.19.
D2709 N/I
D2710 Despatched to BEF 2.19.
D2711 ⎫
to ⎬ N/I
D2716 ⎭
D2717 (Arab) **4 AAP** Lincoln 25.1.19, reallotted from SW Area for D of T and RAF and Army Co-operation School Winchester to BEF.
D2718 N/I
D2719 N/I
D2720 (Arab) **4 AAP** Lincoln 27.1.19, reallotted from Midland Area to BEF.
D2721 (Arab) **4 AAP** Lincoln 27.1.19, reallotted from Midland Area to BEF. **8 Sqn** dd ex **1 ASD** 3.5.19. **1 ASD** ex 8 Sqn 7.5.19 (engine E3258).
D2722 ⎫
to ⎬ N/I
D2728 ⎭
D2729 (Arab) **4 AAP** Lincoln 14.4.19, allotted to BEF. **9 Sqn** dd ex **1 ASD** 7.5.19 (engine 3263/WD27338) and on unit charge until @ 14.6.19.
D2730 (Arab) **4 AAP** Lincoln 14.1.19, allotted to BEF. **9 Sqn** dd ex **1 ASD** 7.5.19 (engine 3291/WD27416). **1 ASD** ex 9 Sqn 15.7.19.
D2731 (Arab) **4 AAP** Lincoln 19.4.19, allotted to BEF.
D2732 ⎫
to ⎬ N/I
D2739 ⎭
D2740 (Arab) **59 Sqn** and wrecked on Delivery Flight 14.6.19 (Lt A.G. Peasland OK, o/t on landing when undercarriage caught in corn – engine WD27597).
D2741 N/I
D2742 (Arab) **4 AAP** 14.4.19 reallotted from Weston-on-the-Green for Storage to BEF. **9 Sqn** dd ex **6 AIS** 17.5.19 (engine 3316/WD27441) and on unit charge until @ 14.6.19.
D2743 ⎫
to ⎬ N/I
D2752 ⎭
D2753 **4 AAP** 28.4.19 allotted to BEF. **9 Sqn** dd ex **1 ASD** 7.5.19 (engine 3455/WD27680). **8 SS** ex 9 Sqn 20.5.19 (same engine).
D2754 N/I
D2755 **59 Sqn** Duren. **1 ASD** ex 59 Sqn 17.7.19.
D2756 ⎫
to ⎬ N/I
D2764 ⎭
D2765 dd by about 3.19.
D2766 ⎫
to ⎬ cancelled 12.18.
D2775 ⎭

300 BRISTOL FIGHTER F.2B Mk.I ordered 11.1.18 to Contract AS.17573 (B.R.120 & B.R.162) from British & Colonial Aeroplane Co. Ltd and numbered D7801 to D8100 (275hp Falcon III or Sunbeam Arab). [Consecutive works' sequence nos. 3451 to 3750].

D7801 B&C for reconditioning to J Type (s/n 6399) and ready by 27.2.24. **2 FTS** Digby by 6.24 and wrecked 19.5.25 (hit stationary Sopwith Snipe E6476 in ground accident at Digby). B&C for repair and reconditioning (s/n 6955) and ready by 29.6.26. **13 Sqn** Andover 1927. **16 Sqn/SAC** Old Sarum by 12.27.

D7802 **PD** Ascot. To Egypt. **AD** Aboukir. **208 Sqn** as a/c *11* by 8.24 until @ 12.24. **AD** Aboukir and reconstructed as DR7802 2.26 until @ 2.27.

This reconstructed F.2B, DR7802, has been modified as a two-seat communications hack, with the Scarff ring removed and the rear fuselage top-decking raised. The insignia forward of the fuselage roundel comprises a winged 'B' (B Flight?) with the numeral '1' inside it. *(Philip Jarrett)*

D7803 **1 FTS** Netheravon by 8.21 until @ 3.22.

D7804 **5 FTS** Sealand and wrecked 2.5.22 (Plt Off I.P. Anderson IIFA/ AC2 S. Thompson KIFA, turned at 100ft after take off and spun in near Shotwick).

D7805 (Arab) at maker's 7.6.18, allotted to BEF. **5 AAP** Bristol tested 9.8.18 (Lt C.F. Uwins). **1 ASD** by 31.8.18 (engine 19063). **L Flight** dd ex **1 AIS** 3.9.18 and wrecked after Touring Lines 15.9.18 (Lt I.C.R. Mackenzie/2nd Lt C.C.G. Ravine both OK, crashed due to heavy landing on rough ground – engine 2997). **1 ASD** ex 'L' Flt 18.9.18 and deleted 20.9.18 (not worth reconstruction, 13hr 55min).

D7806 N/I

D7807 **PD** Ascot. To India. **AD** Drigh Road. **AP** Lahore by 8.24. **31 Sqn** by 7.25 until @ 10.25. **AD** Drigh Road by 1926. **5 Sqn** by 9.26 until @ 3.27. **AD** Drigh Road 1927. **31 Sqn** as a/c *A* by 3.10.27. **5 Sqn** by 10.28. **20 Sqn** as a/c *N* by 6.30 until @ 1.31.

D7808 (Arab) at maker's 7.6.18, allotted to BEF. **1 ASD** by 31.8.18 (engine 19120), wrecked in enemy bombing and deleted 23.9.18.

D7809 **PD** Ascot. To India. **AD** Drigh Road. **AP** Lahore. **5 Sqn** by 16.7.24. **20 Sqn** by 2.26 until @ 9.26. **28 Sqn** as a/c *J*. **Quetta SF** by 8.29.

D7810 **CFS** Upavon. **1 FTS** Netheravon by 3.22.

D7811 (Arab) at maker's 7.6.18, allotted to BEF and to be delivered to **5 AAP**.

D7812 B&C for reconditioning to J Type (s/n 6434) and ready by 3.5.24. **AGS** Eastchurch by 11.24. B&C for reconditioning (s/n 6952) and ready by 25.6.26. **13 Sqn** Andover.

D7813 **PD** Ascot. To India. **AD** Drigh Road by 4.23 until @ 5.23. **31 Sqn** NW Frontier. **AD** Drigh Road by 8.23 until @ 11.23. **20 Sqn** by 3.24 until @ 7.24. **5 Sqn** NW Frontier. **Quetta SF** by 5.29.

D7814 (Arab) at maker's 7.6.18, allotted to BEF and to be delivered to **5 AAP**. At **1 ASD** by 31.8.18 (engine 19083). **'L' Flt** dd ex **1 AIS** 3.9.18. **8 Sqn** dd ex 'L' Flight 25.1.19 (Lt Mackenzie/AC Simpson). **2 ASD** ex 8 Sqn 28.1.19 and reported as salvage 5.19. **PD** Ascot. To Iraq. **AD** Hinaidi. **6 Sqn** and force landed on Hillah LG after engine failure 22.10.20. **HQ Iraq** and wrecked 31.5.22 (crashed in forced landing 90 miles from Kyri Railhead and 180 miles NNE Baghdad).

D7815 **PD** Ascot. To Egypt. AD Aboukir. **14 Sqn** Palestine. **AD** Aboukir for overhaul 29.4.25. B&C for reconditioning to J Type (s/n 6945) and ready 17.6.26. **PD** Ascot. To Iraq. **AD** Hinaidi by 8.29.

D7816 **1 FTS** Netheravon by 3.24; and wrecked 4.4.24 (Plt Off J.H. Pledger KIFA, caught fire at 1,000ft and crashed out of control in flames at West Kennett, Wilts).

D7817 (Arab) at maker's 7.6.18, allotted to BEF and to be delivered to **5 AAP**.

D7818 B&C for reconditioning to J Type (s/n 69944) and ready 16.6.26. **PD** Ascot. To Iraq. **AD** Hinaidi by 8.29.

D7819 **PD** Ascot. To Egypt. **AD** Aboukir. **208 Sqn** by 12.23 until @ 2.25.

D7820 (Arab) at maker's 7.6.18, allotted to BEF and to be delivered to **5 AAP**. At **PD** Ascot. To India. **AD** Drigh Road. **AP** Lahore by 12.22.

D7821 To India. **20 Sqn** and wrecked 16.5.24 (climbed steeply on take off, turned and fell to ground).

D7822 (Falcon I) **33 TDS** Witney and wrecked 15.10.18 (Flt Cdt S.V. Little IIFA, collided on take off with another machine – engine 1/F/10539).

D7823 (Arab) at maker's 7.6.18 allotted to BEF. **8 Sqn** by 1.19. **1 ASD** Merheim ex 8 Sqn 12.7.19.

D7824 **33 TDS** Witney and wrecked 10.10.18 (Capt N.A. Doggart KIFA, spun in and crashed near Witney – engine 333/WD10512).

D7825 N/I

D7826 (Arab) at maker's 7.6.18, allotted to BEF and to be delivered to **5 AAP** Bristol. Tested at 5 AAP 2.9.18 and 9.9.18 (Lt C.F. Uwins).

D7827 **8 Sqn** by 1.19.

D7828 N/I

D7829 (Arab) at maker's 7.6.18, allotted to BEF and to be delivered to **5 AAP** Bristol. Tested at 5 AAP 10.9.18 (Lt C.F. Uwins).

D7830 **PD** Ascot. Despatched ex UK for Egypt and **AD** Aboukir 12.3.20. To India. **AD** Drigh Road. **5 Sqn** by 10.22 and wrecked 26.1.24 (stalled on landing at Kutwa LG).

D7831 **PD** Ascot. Despatched ex UK for Egypt and **AD** Aboukir 12.3.20. **208 Sqn** by 8.20 and wrecked 14.4.21 (collided with E2298 and crashed at Bilbeis).

D7832 **PD** Ascot. To Iraq. **AD** Hinaidi. **6 Sqn** and wrecked 26.8.20 (undercarriage collapsed on landing at Hillah and machine o/t). **AP** Baghdad for repair. **6 Sqn** reissued by 11.22 and totally wrecked 8.3.23 (Fg Off H.J. Bradley IOAS/Sgt R.A. Long OK, crashed on landing at Kirkuk).

D7833 Despatched ex UK for Egypt and **ASD** Aboukir 26.2.20. **6 Sqn** by 9.20 and totally wrecked 8.2.21 (engine failed on take off and machine crashed).

D7834 At maker's 4.6.18, allotted to BEF and to be erected at **5 AAP** Bristol. Tested at 5 AAP 11.8.18, 12.8.18, 14.8.18, 16.8.18 and 30.9.18 (Lt C.F. Uwins). To Iraq. **6 Sqn** and damaged 22.10.20 (force landed on Hillah aerodrome after engine failure). **HQ Iraq** and wrecked 31.5.22 (crashed in forced landing 90 miles from Kyri raihead & 180 miles NNE of Baghdad).

D7835 Handley Page Ltd for fitting slots 1.28. **SAC** Old Sarum by 3.28 until @ 3.29. B&C for reconditioning, ready by 19.12.29 and issued 17.1.30. **4 Sqn** Farnborough. **RAE** Farnborough by 18.3.31. **Practice Camp** Sutton Bridge by 4.4.31.

D7836 N/I

D7837 At maker's 7.6.18, allotted to BEF and to be erected at **5 AAP**. At **PD** Ascot. To Egypt. **AD** Aboukir. **4 FTS** Abu Sueir by 3.27 until @ 4.27.

D7838 To Middle East. **208 Sqn** 1921. **6 Sqn** and totally wrecked 8.8.22 (Fg Off V.C. Cordingly OK, stalled on night landing and crashed).

D7839 **5 AAP** Bristol tested 7.7.18 (Lt C.F. Uwins). To Middle East. **208 Sqn** by 5.21 until @ 1.22. **14 Sqn** 1922. **4 FTS** Abu Sueir by 6.23. To UK. B&C for reconditioning to J Type DC (s/n 6816) and ready by 24.9.25. **PD** Ascot. To Egypt. **AD** Aboukir. **4 FTS** Abu Sueir by 8.27 until @ 7.28. **AD** Aboukir and reconstructed as DR7839. **4 FTS** Abu Sueir by 20.3.29 until @ 1.30.

D7840 (Arab) at maker's 4.6.18, allotted to BEF.

D7841 N/I

D7842 To Civilian Register as *G-EBBD* registered to Aircraft Disposal Co Ltd (s/n 3492).

D7843 (Arab) at maker's 7.6.18, allotted to BEF. **8 AAP** Lympne dd ex **1 ASD** 4.9.18 (2nd Lt C.H. Drew/AM Ransom).

D7844 To Iraq. **6 Sqn** and wrecked 22.10.20, crashed at Hillah after engine failure. **AP** Baghdad by 6.21 (after reconstruction?).

D7845 **PD** Ascot. To Iraq. **AD** Hinaidi. **6 Sqn** and wrecked 16.5.22 (Fg Off L.C. Hooton MC/AC2 G.W. Butler both KOAS, crashed at Baghdad West and burnt out).

D7846 (Arab) at maker's 4.6.18, allotted to BEF and to be erected at **5 AAP** Bristol. Tested at 5 AAP 25.7.18 (Lt C.F. Uwins).

D7847 B&C for reconditioning to J Type (s/n 6681) and ready by 8.4.25. **SAC** Old Sarum by 11.25 until @ 10.28.

D7848 **AGS** Eastchurch by 2.24. B&C for reconditioning to J Type (s/n 6690) and ready by 30.4.25. **PD** Ascot. **AD** Aboukir. **AHQ Iraq Command** by 17.6.27 until @ 28.6.27 (tested fully tropical radio, not recommended). **6 Sqn** by 6.29 and wrecked 2.1.30, undercarriage collapsed when taxiing.

D7849 (Arab) at maker's 7.6.18, allotted to BEF. **5 AAP** Bristol tested 18.8.18 (Lt C.F. Uwins).

D7850 B&C for reconditioning to J Type (s/n 6691) and ready 24.4.25.

D7851 B&C for reconditioning to J Type (s/n 6401) and ready by 11.3.25. **PD** Ascot. To India. **AD** Drigh Road. **20 Sqn** by 21.3.25 until @ 11.25. **AD** Drigh Road 1926. **28 Sqn** marked as a/c *E*. **AD** Drigh Road 1928. **AP** Lahore by 1.29. **20 Sqn** marked as a/c *D* 1929 until 1930.

D7852 (Arab) at maker's 4.6.18, allotted to BEF and to be erected at **5 AAP**. At **36 TDS** Yatesbury by 12.18 until @ 1.19 (Lt W.R. Parkhouse). **PD** Ascot. **AD** Hinaidi. **8 Sqn** Iraq.

D7853 **AGS** Eastchurch by 5.22.

D7854 B&C for reconditioning to J Type (s/n 6455) and ready by 24.5.24. **16 Sqn** Old Sarum by 9.24 until @ 11.24.

D7855 (Arab) at maker's 7.6.18, allotted to BEF and to be erected at **5 AAP**.

D7856 **100 Sqn** and wrecked 10.2.22 (Flt Lt P.J. Parry/AC J. Harris both KOAS, crashed in forced landing at Baldonnel after engine failure).

D7857 **5 FTS** Sealand and wrecked 20.11.22 (Plt Off J.S. Phillips IIFA, hit a tree and crashed near Chester).

D7858 (Arab) at maker's 4.6.18, allotted to BEF but allotment cancelled 15.6.18, still at maker's. **PD** Ascot. To Egypt. **AD** Aboukir. **6 Sqn** by 5.22 until @ 7.22.

D7859 **Test Dept Grain** from 9.19 for meteorological tests.

D7860 (200hp R.A.F. 4d) **RAE** Farnborough, fitted with single bay wings of 4.69 aspect ratio, by 1.20, force landed near Swallowfield, Berks, 31.3.20, repaired and on charge until @ 25.6.20.

D7861 N/I

D7862 N/I

D7863 (Arab) at maker's 7.6.18, allotted to BEF. **5 AAP** Bristol and tested 28.6.18 (Lt C.F. Uwins). **1 ASD** by 26.7.18 until @ 31.8.18 (engine 19127). **'N' Flt** dd ex **1 AIS** 3.9.18 and wrecked on Travelling Flight 5.9.18 (2nd Lt S.C. Sutcliffe/AM Devonshire both OK, force landed near Conteville after engine failed en route to 1 ASD for wireless fitting – same engine). **1 ASD** and deleted 11.9.18 on reconstruction as H7146 (7hr 20min).

D7864 (First with HP slots). B&C for reconditioning to J Type (s/n 6641) and ready by 7.3.25. **24 Sqn** Kenley. **2 Sqn** Manston by 9.26 until @ 3.27. **AGS** Eastchurch by 4.28 until @ 6.28.

D7865 To Irish Air Corps as BF5 and crashed 8.24.

D7866 (Arab) at maker's 7.6.18, allotted to BEF. **5 AAP** Bristol and tested 22.6.18, 24.6.18, 26.6.18 and 27.6.18 (Lt C.F. Uwins).

D7867 To Egypt. Shipped UK to **ASD ME** Aboukir 26.2.20. To Iraq. **6 Sqn** by 6.20 and wrecked 14.12.20 (crashed in desert landing at Tank, Mespotamia).

D7868 N/I

D7869 (Arab) at maker's 7.6.18, allotted to BEF. **5 AAP** Bristol and tested 7.10.18 (Lt C.F. Uwins). To Canada; Became *G-CYDP* and taken on CAF charge 19.4.21. Used at Camp Borden.

D7870 N/I

D7871 N/I

D7872 (Arab) at maker's 7.6.18, allotted to BEF. **5 AAP** Bristol tested 1.7.18, 2.7.18, 4.7.18 and 10.7.18 (Lt C.F. Uwins). **1 ASD** by 26.7.18 until @ 5.8.18 (engine 53711). **59 Sqn** by 14.8.18. **'N' Flight** ex 59 sqn 2.9.18 and wrecked on Shoot 14.9.18 (2nd Lt J.F. Robb/2nd Lt N.B. Eames both OK, force landed near Boisleux au Mont due to engine trouble – same engine). **2 ASD** ex 'N' Flt 14.9.18 and deleted 12.10.18 (not worth reconstruction).

D7873 B&C for reconditioning to J Type (s/n 6437) and ready by 10.5.24. **AGS** Eastchurch by 11.24.

D7874 B&C for reconditioning to J Type (s/n 6433) and ready by 15.4.24. **PD** Ascot. To Egypt. **AD** Aboukir. **6 Sqn**. Returned to UK. **HAD** Henlow by 9.27. **13 Sqn** Andover by 9.27. **SAC** Old Sarum by 4.28 until @ 4.29. B&C for reconditioning and ready by 5.2.30. Retaken on RAF charge 27.2.30. **Andover SF** by 1.31 until @ 1.32.

D7875 (Arab) at maker's 7.6.18, allotted to BEF. **5 AAP** Bristol and tested 11.9.18 (Lt C.F. Uwins). **8 Sqn** with Army of Occupation. **1 ASD** ex 8 Sqn 12.7.19.

D7876 B&C for reconditioning to J Type (s/n 6438) and ready by 10.5.24. **PD** Ascot. To Iraq. **AD** Hinaidi. **6 Sqn** and damaged 27.5.25 (caught fire when Very light fired in cockpit), repaired and on unit charge until @ 11.26.

D7877 **5 FTS** Shotwick and wrecked 21.9.22 (Plt Off A.L. Harris OK, banked steeply on landing, and sideslipped in).

D7878 (Arab) at maker's 7.6.18, allotted to BEF and to be delivered to **5 AAP**. To 'M' Flt dd ex **1 ASD** 8.10.18. **1ASD** ex 'M' Flt 17.11.18 (engine 19256).

D7879 To British Aviation Mission, Washington.

D7880 N/I

D7881 (Arab) at maker's 7.6.18, allotted to BEF and to be delivered to **5 AAP**. At **1 ASD** by 15.9.18 (engine 19148). **8 Sqn** dd ex 1 ASD 13.10.18. **2 ASD** ex 8 Sqn 28.1.19.

D7882 To Irish Air Corps as BF7. Deleted for spares 1924.

D7883 N/I

D7884 (Arab) at maker's 7.6.18, allotted to BEF and to be delivered to **5 AAP**. At **1 ASD** by 31.8.18 (engine E2838). **'P' Flt** dd ex 1 ASD 7.9.18 (same engine) and wrecked on Artillery Patrol 5.10.18 (2nd Lt J.T. Brown/2nd Lt H.V. Irving both OK, hit at 1,200ft by AA fire and force landed (engine 53782). **1 ASD** ex 'P' Flt.

D7885 To Irish Air Corps as BF8 and crashed 8.23.

D7886 To Irish Air Corps as BF6 and crashed 9.25.

D7887 (Arab) at maker's 7.6.18, allotted to BEF. **5 AAP** Bristol tested 21.8.18 (Lt C.F. Uwins). **8 Sqn** dd 20.12.18. **1 ASD** ex 8 Sqn 15.7.19.

The crew of Bristol-built Arab-engined F.2B Mk.I D7887 of 8 Sqn in the early post-war period. After re-equipping with Arab Bristol Fighters late in 1918 the unit moved to Sart in Belgium on 11 May 1919 but was short-lived, being reduced to a cadre in July. Its aircraft were withdrawn before it returned home to Duxford. *(Philip Jarrett)*

D7888 N/I

D7889 N/I

D7890 B&C for reconditioning to J Type (s/n 6635) and ready by 4.3.25. To Egypt. **AD** Aboukir and reconstructed as DR7890. **208 Sqn** by 10.28 until @ 7.29.

D7891 N/I

D7892 (Arab) at maker's 17.6.18, allotted to BEF and to be delivered to **5 AAP**. To **8 Sqn**.

D7893 (Falcon III) **5 AAP** Bristol and tested 23.6.18 and 24.6.18 (Lt C.F. Uwins). **2 AIS** ex **1 ASD** 7.7.18. **48 Sqn** dd ex 2 AIS 8.7.18 (engine 1163/WD51606) and wrecked on OP 18.7.18 (2nd Lt S.N. Waddy/Sgt W.J. Shuker both OK, force landed near Villers-Bocage due to failing light – same engine). **2 ASD** ex 48 Sqn 20.7.18 and deleted 7.8.18 on reconstruction as F6235 (23hr 40min).

D7894 (Falcon III) presentaton a/c *Kotah No.1*. At maker's 17.6.18, allotted to BEF. **5 AAP** Bristol and tested 28.6.18, 29.6.18, 8.7.18 and 9.7.18 (Lt C.F. Uwins). **1 AIS** dd ex **1 ASD** 15.7.18. **22 Sqn** dd ex 1 AIS 16.7.18, victs 28.9.18 (Lt F.G. George/Sgt G. Shannon destroyed two Fokker D.VII over Haynecourt at 11:15) and wrecked on OP 28.9.18 (2nd Lt T.D. Smith/Lt B. Caillard both OK, machine shot up in combat – engine 1597/WD51823). **1 ASD** ex 22 Sqn 30.9.18 and deleted 2.10.18 (not worth reconstruction).

D7895 (Arab) at maker's 17.6.18, allotted to BEF. **5 AAP** in incident 21.7.18 (Pte F. Rowland IIGA, struck by propeller – engine Arab 53729).

D7896 (Falcon III) at maker's 17.6.18, allotted to BEF. **5 AAP** Bristol and tested 23.6.18 (Lt C.F. Uwins). **1 AIS** ex **1 ASD** 25.6.18 (engine 1245/WD51647). **22 Sqn** dd ex 1 AIS 25.6.18 (same engine), victs 9.7.18 (Lt T.W. Martin/Sgt J.H. Hall destroyed two Albatros D.V, N of La Bassee at 11:00 and W of Steenwerck at 11:30), 10.7.18 (Lt T.W. Martin, Capt D.E. Waight sent a Pfalz D.III down OOC over Lille at 10:00) and 26.7.18 (Lt S.F.H. Thompson/Lt C.G. Gass sent a Fokker Dr.I down OOC over Laventie at 09:00) then wrecked after OP 31.7.18 (Lt S.F.H. Thompson MC/Lt J.H. Umney both OK, crashed on landing – same engine). **1 ASD** ex 22 Sqn 1.8.18 and still on unit charge 5.8.18.

D7897 (Falcon III) at maker's 17.6.18, allotted to BEF. **5 AAP** Bristol tested 29.6.18 (Lt C.F. Uwins). **1 AIS** ex **1 ASD** 30.6.18 (engine 1235/WD51642). **20 Sqn** dd ex 1 AIS 30.6.18 (same engine) and wrecked before OP 23.8.18 (2nd Lt W.F. Carson OK/2nd Lt G.L. Shaw IOAS, crashed after engine cut out on take off – engine 149/WD18574). **1 ASD** ex 20 Sqn 24.8.18 and deleted 26.8.18 (not worth reconstruction, 115hr 43min).

D7898 (Falcon III) at maker's 17.6.18, allotted to BEF and to be delivered to **5 AAP**. At **8 Sqn** by 6.5.19 (Lt J.W. Baker). **6 SS** ex 8 Sqn 12.5.18 (dismantled at Fosse).

D7899 (Falcon III) **5 AAP** Bristol and tested 28.6.18 (Lt C.F. Uwins). **62 Sqn** dd ex **2 AIS** 2.7.18, victs 8.7.18 (Capt W.E. Staton/Sgt W.N. Holmes destroyed a Fokker Dr.I, NW of Carvin at 07:10), 22.8.18 (Capt W.E. Staton/Lt L.E. Mitchell destroyed a Fokker D.VII in flames over Pronville at 09:45), 3.9.18 (Capt W.E.

Staton/Lt L.E. Mitchell destroyed a Fokker D.VII, SE of Marquion at 18:30) and 4.9.18 (Capt W.E. Staton/Lt L.E. Mitchell sent a Fokker D.VII down OOC, N of Cambrai 09:30) then wrecked on Escort 14.10.18 (2nd Lt A.J.P. Evans/2nd Lt A.A. Simpson both OK, engine cut out and force landed near Armentieres – engine 1371/WD51710) and deleted on unit that day.

D7900 (Falcon III) at maker's 17.6.18, allotted to BEF. **5 AAP** Bristol and tested 28.6.18 (Lt C.F. Uwins). **2 AIS** ex **1 ASD** 2.7.18. **48 Sqn** dd ex **2 AIS** 25.7.18 (engine 97/WD18548) then wrecked on Practice Flight 5.9.18 (2nd Lt N. Davies KOAS, entered a spin and crashed – engine 39/WD18519) and deleted on unit 6.9.18 (71hr 15min). Wreckage to 1 ASD 8.9.18.

D7901 **5 AAP** Bristol tested 9.7.18 (Lt C.F. Uwins). **8 Sqn** Bellevue. **53 Sqn** dd ex 8 Sqn 28.1.19.

D7902 (Falcon III) presentation a/c *Presented by Maharaja Bahadur Sir Rameswar Singh of Darbhanga No.4*. At maker's 21.6.18, allotted to BEF. **5 AAP** Bristol and tested 28.6.18, 29.6.18 and 8.7.18 (Lt C.F. Uwins). **2 AIS** ex **1 ASD** 13.7.18. **48 Sqn** dd ex 2 AIS 14.7.18 (engine 1223/WD51636), LIA on 06:00 OP 24.7.18 (2nd Lt S.N. Waddy/Sgt W.J. Shuker both KIA, brought down in flames over Faucoucourt after combat over Lamotte – same engine) and deleted on unit that day (11hr 25min).

D7903 (Falcon III) at maker's 21.6.18, allotted to BEF. **5 AAP** Bristol tested 29.6.18 (Lt C.F. Uwins). **2 AIS** ex **1 ASD** 2.7.18. **35 Sqn** dd ex 2 AIS 2.7.18 (engine 1277/WD51663) and wrecked on Delivery Flight to **9 Sqn** 7.7.18 (Lt C.N. Hardwick/2nd Lt L.M. Moffat both OK, the propeller hit the ground on take off, the machine rose but was forced to land – same engine). **2 ASD** ex 35 Sqn 8.7.18 and deleted 29.7.18 (not worth reconstruction, 4hr 5min).

D7904 (Arab) **5 AAP** Bristol tested 7.7.18 (Lt C.F. Uwins). **39 TDS** Spittlegate and wrecked 15.8.18 (Lt J. Thompson OK, oil pipe burst and crashed during forced landing in rough field). Photographed marked as a/c *B*.

D7905 (Falcon III) at maker's 21.6.18, allotted to BEF. **5 AAP** Bristol and tested 27.6.18 (Lt C.F. Uwins). **2 AIS** ex **1 ASD** 29.6.18. **88 Sqn** dd ex 2 AIS 30.6.18 and wrecked on Patrol 16.7.18 (Lt V. Voss OK/2nd Lt G.E.D. Low IOAS, o/t in forced landing after fuel supply not turned on – engine 1329/WD51689). **1 ASD** ex 88 Sqn 17.7.18 and deleted 19.7.18 (not worth reconstruction, 19hr 25min).

D7906 (Falcon III) at maker's 21.6.18, allotted to BEF and to be delivered to **5 AAP**. **2 AIS** ex **1 ASD** 1.7.18. **11 Sqn** dd ex 2 AIS 3.7.18, LIA on 08:40 Reconnaissance, Le Cateau, 6.9.18 (Lt E.N. Underwood/2nd Lt C.M. Coleman both KIA, last seen W of Cambrai and being chased by EA – engine 1495/WD51772) and deleted on unit that day (86hr).

D7907 **ES** Martlesham Heath dd w/e 13.7.18 for engine performance tests and wrecked 3.9.18.

D7908 (Falcon III) at maker's 21.6.18, allotted to BEF. **5 AAP** Bristol tested 29.6.18 (Lt C.F. Uwins). **8 AAP** dd ex 5 AAP 1.7.18 (2nd Lt C.H. Drew). **1 ASD** dd ex 8 AAP 2.7.18. **1 AIS** ex 1 ASD 2.7.18. **22 Sqn** dd ex 1 AIS 3.7.18, damaged 5.4.18 (Capt Heap/Lt Pople both OK, swung on take off after propeller hit the ground – engine 187/WD18593) and wrecked on Wireless Practice 16.7.18 (Lt Beddow/AM Peters both OK, collided with a cow when landing – engine 1301/WD51675).

D7909 (Falcon III) at maker's 21.6.18, allotted to BEF and to be delivered to **5 AAP**. At **48 Sqn** dd ex **1 ASD** 3.7.18 (engine 1239/WD51644), vict 7.7.18 (Capt C.R. Steele/Lt A.E. Ansell destroyed a Pfalz D.III which crashed onto the Amiens-St Quentin road at 11:30) then destroyed in German bombing raid on Bertangles aerodrome on the night of 24/25.8.18 and deleted on unit.

D7910 (Arab) **5 AAP** Bristol tested 25.7.18 (Lt C.F. Uwins). **ES** Martlesham Heath by 7.8.18 and allotted to **(S)ARD** 31.8.18. **ECD** Grain 1.9.18 for flotation gear and hydrovane tests, being floated off slipway 18.9.18 and to be tested again off HMS *Slinger*.

D7911 **5 AAP** Bristol and tested 28.6.18 (Lt C.F. Uwins). **2 AIS** ex **1 ASD** 29.6.18. **11 Sqn** dd ex 2 AIS 30.6.18 and wrecked after Reconnaissance 7.7.18 (Lt H.C.M. Nangle/2nd Lt L.R. Reeves both OK, crashed on crosswind landing – engine 1275/WD51662). **1 ASD** ex 11 Sqn 8.7.18 and deleted 22.7.18 on reconstruction as F6208 (14hr 45min).

D7912 (Falcon III) **5 AAP** Bristol tested 30.6.18 (Lt C.F. Uwins). **2 AIS** ex **1 ASD** 7.7.18. **11 Sqn** dd ex 2 AIS 8.7.18, victs 13.8.18 (Lt E.S. Coler/2nd Lt C.W. Gladman destroyed three Fokker D.VII in flames and sent two more down OOC over Peronne at c.08:40) then wrecked on 07:10 Escort 14.8.18 (Lt E.S. Coler/2nd Lt C.W. Gladman both WIA, crashed in forced landing after machine damaged by EA fire – engine 1305/WD51677). **2 ASD** ex 11 Sqn and deleted 6.10.18 (not worth reconstruction).

D7913 (Arab) presentation a/c *Malaya XXIII The Malacca*. **1 ASD** by 31.8.18 (engine 2823). **'N' Flt** dd ex **1 AIS** 3.9.18. **8 Sqn** by 21.3.19 (Lt J.W. Baker) and reported as being dismantled on unit 29.4.19 (split propeller – engine 53817).

D7914 (Falcon III) **5 AAP** Bristol and tested 28.6.18 and 29.6.18 (Lt C.F. Uwins). **88 Sqn** dd ex **1 AIS** 27.6.18 and on charge until @ 30.9.18. **2 ASD** and deleted 6.10.18 (not worth reconstruction).

D7915 (Falcon III) at maker's 22.6.18, allotted to BEF. **5 AAP** Bristol tested 29.6.18 (Lt C.F. Uwins). **1 AIS** ex **1 ASD** 2.7.18. **20 Sqn** dd ex 1 AIS 3.7.18 (engine 1267/WD51658) and wrecked after OP 10.10.18 (Lt F.R. Goodearle/2nd Lt P.B. de Moyse-Bucknell both OK, struck a filled shell hole and thrown into another shell hole – engine 1457/WD51753). **2 ASD** ex 20 Sqn and deleted 21.10.18 (not worth reconstruction).

D7916 (Arab) at maker's 22.6.18, allotted to BEF. **5 AAP** Bristol tested 10.7.18 (Lt C.F. Uwins). **1 ASD** by 22.7.18 (engine E2859). **21 Sqn** dd ex **1 AIS** 28.7.18 (same engine). **'P' Flt** ex 21 Sqn 1.9.18 and wrecked before Artillery Patrol 25.10.18 (2nd Lt N.A. Talbot/2nd Lt V. Lockey both OK, engine failed on take off and crashed onto aerodrome – engine 53845). **1 ASD** ex 'P' Flt.

D7917 (Arab) at maker's 22.6.18, allotted to BEF and to be delivered to **5 AAP**. At 5 AAP Bristol tested 4.9.18 and 6.9.18 (Lt C.F. Uwins). Also noted at **21 Sqn**.

D7918 To Middle East. **X AD** dd ex England 19.10.18, with unit redesignated **ASD ME**. To **111 Sqn** dd ex ASD ME 7.11.19 (engine WD18596) and deleted on unit 3.1.20.

D7919 (Arab) at maker's 22.6.18, allotted to BEF. **5 AAP** Bristol tested 17.7.18 (Lt C.F. Uwins). **1 ASD** by 31.8.18 (engine 19244). **N Flight** dd ex **1 AIS** 3.9.1, LIA on 10:40 Artillery Patrol 28.10.18 (Lt J. Thomson/2nd Lt A.F. Perry both KIA – engine 53865) and deleted on unit that day.

D7920 (Arab) at maker's 22.6.18, allotted to BEF and to be delivered to **5 AAP**.

D7921 To Middle East. **X AD** dd ex England 19.10.18. **AD** Aboukir postwar. **4 FTS** Abu Sueir by 12.21 until @ 10.22.

D7922 (Arab) at maker's 22.6.18, allotted to BEF and to be delivered to **5 AAP**. At 5 AAP Bristol tested 18.7.18 (Lt C.F. Uwins).

D7923 (Arab) at maker's 22.6.18, allotted to BEF and to be delivered to **5 AAP**. At **1 ASD** by 15.9.18 (engine E2848) and still on unit charge 30.9.18. **8 Sqn** Bellevue. **12 Sqn** dd ex 8 Sqn 28.1.19.

D7924 To Middle East. **ASD ME** Aboukir post war. **14 Sqn** dd ex Aboukir 4.2.20.

D7925 (Arab) at maker's 22.6.18, allotted to BEF and to be delivered to **5 AAP**. To **1 ASD** dd ex **8 AAP** 15.7.18 (2nd Lt C.H. Drew). **42 Sqn** dd ex **1 AIS** 22.7.18 (engine 2870). **'L' Flt** ex 42 Sqn. **42 Sqn** ex 'L' Flt 31.7.18. **'P' Flt** ex 42 Sqn 3.9.18 (engine 53802) and wrecked after Patrol 14.10.18 (Lt D. King OK/2nd Lt Currington IOAS, crashed on landing – same engine). **1 ASD** ex P Flight and deleted 18.10.18 (not worth reconstruction).

D7926 (Arab) at maker's 22.6.18, allotted to BEF and to be delivered to **5 AAP**. At 5 AAP Bristol tested 4.9.18 (Lt C.F. Uwins). **5 TDS** Easton-on-the-Hill by 20.9.18 until @ 22.9.18 (Capt B.C. Rice).

D7927 To Middle East. **X AD** dd ex England 19.10.18. **16 TDS** dd ex **ASD ME** 11.11.19 (engine WD39398). **Special Instruction Flt** Almaza by 2.20. **70 Sqn** wrecked 27.5.20 (spun in at Almaza due to fuel shortage) and deleted.

D7928 (Arab) at maker's 22.6.18, allotted to BEF and to be delivered to **5 AAP**.

D7929 (Arab) at maker's 22.6.18, allotted to BEF and to be delivered to **5 AAP**. At 5 AAP Bristol tested 19.7.18 (Lt C.F. Uwins). **1 ASD** by 30.9.18 (engine E2905).

D7930 **X AD** dd ex England 18.10.18. **5 FS** Heliopolis dd ex X AD 14.3.19 (engine WD10537). **208 Sqn** by 10.22 until @ 5.23.

D7931 (Arab) at maker's 22.6.18, allotted to BEF and to be delivered to **5 AAP**. At 5 AAP Bristol tested 12.7.18 (Lt C.F. Uwins). **1 ASD** by 26.7.18 (engine 2834) and on unit charge until @ 29.8.18. **P Flight** dd ex **1 AIS** 3.9.18 (same engine), force landed on Artillery Patrol 8.9.18 (Capt L.H. Jones/2nd Lt V. Lockey both OK) and on unit charge @ 30.9.18. **1 ASD** and deleted 14.10.18 (not worth reconstruction).

D7932 (Arab) at maker's 22.6.18, allotted to BEF and to be delivered to **5 AAP**.

D7933 To Middle East. **X AD** dd ex England 18.10.18. **17 TDS** El Firdan dd ex X AD 30.11.18 (engine WD10440). **16 TDS** Abu Sueir. **X AP** and Palestine Bde ex 16 TDS 17.6.19 (engine WD10409). **16 TDS** Abu Sueir. **ASD ME** ex 16 TDS 2.10.19. **4 FTS** Abu Sueir by 8.22 until @ 10.22.

D7934 (Arab) at maker's 29.6.18, allotted to BEF and to be delivered to **5 AAP**. At **1 ASD** by 31.8.18 (engine 2880). **'L' Flt** dd ex **1 AIS**

3.9.18, marked as a/c *D* and wrecked on Engine Test 1.10.18 (Lt H.O. Thornton/3AM P.H. Bates both IOAS, engine cut out and o/t landing on rough ground – same engine). **1 ASD** and deleted 11.10.18 (not worth reconstruction).

D7935 (Arab) at maker's 29.6.18, allotted to BEF and to be delivered to **5 AAP**.

D7936 (Arab) at maker's 29.6.18, allotted to BEF and to be delivered to **5 AAP**. At 5 AAP Bristol tested 5.7.18 (Lt C.F. Uwins). **2 AIS** ex **1 ASD** 7.7.18. **48 Sqn** dd ex 2 AIS 8.7.18 (engine 51673), destroyed in enemy bombing 24.8.18 (same engine) and delted on unit that day.

D7937 At maker's 29.6.18, allotted to BEF and to be delivered to **5 AAP**. To **12 Sqn** marked as a/c *A5* and photographed crashed.

D7938 (Arab) at maker's 29.6.18, allotted to BEF and to be delivered to **5 AAP**. At **1 ASD** by 30.9.18 (engine 53717). **'L' Flt** dd ex 1 ASD 1.10.18. **8 Sqn** dd ex 'L' Flt 20.1.19 (2nd Lt Cowan). **1 ASD** Merheim ex 8 Sqn 16.7.19.

D7939 (Arab) presentation a/c *Toronto*. At maker's 29.6.18, allotted to BEF and to be delivered to **5 AAP**. At **1 AIS** ex **1 ASD** 9.7.18. **20 Sqn** dd ex 1 AIS 11.7.18 (engine 1303/WD51676), marked as a/c *P*, LIA on 16:30 OP 15.9.18 (2nd Lt A.B.D. Campbell/Sgt T.A. Stack both POW, brought down by AA near Epehy – same engine) and deleted on unit that day (138hr 40min).

D7940 (Arab) at maker's 29.6.18, allotted to BEF and to be delivered to **5 AAP**. At **2 AIS** and presumed crashed near Faucquenhem. **1 ASD** ex 2 AIS as salvage 22.1.19.

D7941 (Arab) at maker's 29.6.18, allotted to BEF and to be delivered to **5 AAP**. At **1 ASD** by 31.8.18 (engine 2817) and on unit charge until @ 30.9.18.

D7942 (Falcon III) presentation a/c *Falkland*. At maker's 29.6.18, allotted to BEF and to be delivered to **5 AAP**. At **1 AIS** ex **1 ASD** 8.7.18. **88 Sqn** dd ex 1 AIS 9.7.18, victs 29.7.18 (Capt W.G. Westwood/2nd Lt W. Tinsley sent a Fokker D.VII OOC over Bois Grenier at 18:20) and 4.11.18 (Lt J.B. Aird/Lt A.B. Radford destroyed a Fokker D.VII near Renaix at 09:15) then wrecked on Cross Country 6.4.19 (2nd Lt N.L. Head OK, force landed near Antwerp after engine failed on take off – engine 1537/WD51793).

D7943 (Arab) at maker's 29.6.18, allotted to BEF and to be delivered to **5 AAP**.

D7944 (Arab) at maker's 29.6.18, allotted to BEF and to be delivered to **5 AAP**.

D7945 (Falcon III) presentation a/c *Gold Coast No.11*. At maker's 29.6.18, allotted to BEF and to be delivered to **5 AAP**. At **2 AIS** dd ex **1 ASD** 15.7.18. **62 Sqn** dd ex 2 AIS 16.7.18 (engine 1217/WD51633), LIA on 08:15 OP 4.9.18 (Lt W.K. Swayze/Lt W.E. Hall both POW, in a general combat N of Cambrai suffered engine failure and attacked and forced to land by Ltn M. Demisch, Jasta 58 – same engine) and deleted on unit that day (71hr 25min).

D7946 (Arab) at maker's 29.6.18, allotted to BEF and to be delivered to **5 AAP**. At **1 ASD** by 31.8.18 (engine 19207). **'N' Flt** dd ex **1 AIS** 3.9.18, damaged 3.10.18 (2nd Lt T.C. Sutcliffe WIA/2nd Lt N.J. Dalgleish fatally WIA in 14:20 combat near Estomel) then wrecked on Practice Flight 31.10.18 (Lt Hawkins OK, longerons strained – same engine).

D7947 (Arab) at maker's 29.6.18, allotted to BEF and to be delivered to **5 AAP**. At **1 ASD** by 31.8.18 (engine 53705). **'P' Flt** dd ex **1 AIS** 6.9.18 (same engine). **1 ASD** ex 'P' Flt 7.9.18 (no wireless had been fitted), destroyed in enemy bombing 23.9.18 and deleted that day (3hr 40min).

D7948 (Falcon III) at maker's 29.6.18, allotted to BEF and to be delivered to **5 AAP**. At 5 AAP Bristol tested 10.7.18 (Lt C.F. Uwins). **62 Sqn** dd ex **2 AIS** 21.7.18 (engine 1349/WD51699), LIA on OP 4.11.18 (Lt F.C.D. Scott/2nd Lt C. Rigby both KIA, brought down by Vzfw Paul Keusla, Jasta 2 – engine 1683/WD51866) and deleted on unit.

D7949 (Arab) at maker's 29.6.18, allotted to BEF and to be delivered to **5 AAP**. At 5 AAP Bristol tested 10.8.18 (Lt C.F. Uwins). **9 Sqn** Duren. **1 ASD** ex 9 Sqn 19.7.19.

D7950 (Arab) at maker's 29.6.18, allotted to BEF and to be delivered to **5 AAP**.

D7951 (Falcon III) at maker's 29.6.18, allotted to BEF and to be delivered to **5 AAP**. At 5 AAP Bristol tested 9.7.18 (Lt C.F. Uwins). **20 Sqn** dd ex **1 ASD** 17.7.18 (engine 1273/WD51661), victs 24.7.18 (Lt J.H. Colbert/Lt R.W. Turner destroyed a Fokker D.VII 3 miles N of Comines at 20:00) and 29.7.18 (Lt J.H. Colbert/Lt R.W. Turner destroyed a Fokker D.VII, NW of Wervicq at 20:10) then wrecked on OP 25.9.18 (Lt F.E. Turner OK/Sgt Mech E.G. Mitchell IOAS, force landed at **23 Sqn** with engine trouble – engine 105/WD18552). **2 ASD** ex 20 Sqn 27.9.18 and deleted 17.10.18 (not worth reconstruction).

D7952 (Arab) **5 AAP** Bristol tested 3.9.18 (Lt C.F. Uwins). **8 Sqn** dd ex **2 ASD** 12.11.18. **2 ASD** ex 8 Sqn 28.1.19. **12 Sqn** and wrecked 21.3.19 (Lt Blackford OK, crashed landed at Duren – engine 53739).

D7953 5 AAP Bristol tested 6.9.18 (Lt C.F. Uwins).

D7954 (Falcon III) to 7 Bde Italy. **139 Sqn** dd ex **7 AP** 28.12.18 and wrecked 11.1.19 (Lt T.B. Service/Lt J.G. Acheson both OK, left Ferrara at 10:15, ran into low clouds over mountains and force landed at Borgo, S of Lorenza, when petrol ran out – engine 1281). **7 AP** ex 139 Sqn 23.1.19.

D7955 7th TS AFC Leighterton by 23.11.18 until @ 26.1.19.

D7956 N/I

D7957 (Falcon III) to 7 Bde Italy. **34 Sqn** dd ex **7 AP** 26.9.18. **139 Sqn** dd ex 34 Sqn 1.10.18 (engine 1315/WD51682) and wrecked on 08:25 Reconnaissance/Bombing 8.10.18 (Capt S.H. Holland OK/2nd Lt R.G. Fullager WIA, damaged in combat over Borgo – same engine). **7 AP** ex 139 Sqn 13.10.18.

D7958 5 AAP Bristol and tested 18.10.18 (Lt C.F. Uwins).

D7959 37 TDS Yatesbury by 10.18 (Lt W.R. Parkhouse).

D7960 To 7 Bde Italy. **139 Sqn** dd ex **7 AP** 14.9.18, unconfirmed vict 26.9.18 (Lt H.V. Jellicoe/Lt W. Mackay destroyed an Albatros D.III, crashed just S of Lavis, Pergine-Lavis 10:10) then wrecked on 07:45 Reconnaissance, Citteldella, 28.10.18 (2nd Lt A.A. Bartram/2nd Lt C.A. Sander both OK, crashed in forced landing near Borghetto – engine 1289/WD51669). **7 AP** ex 139 Sqn 3.11.18.

D7961 N/I

D7962 N/I

D7963 (Falcon III) to 7 Bde Italy. **139 Sqn** dd ex **7 AP** 10.11.18 and wrecked on Photography Practice 21.12.18 (Lt T.B. Service/Lt J.G. Acheson both OK, crashed landing at Grossa – engine 1279/WD51664). **7 AP** ex 139 Sqn 21.12.18.

D7964 N/I

D7965 (Arab) **ES** Martlesham Heath dd 20.7.18 for engine performance tests, generating Report M.224. **RAE** Farnborough 6.9.18. **ES** Martlesham Heath 5.10.18 for engine performance tests, generating Report M.224A and flown until @ 15.10.18 (Capt G.W. Gathergood). **ES** Orfordness. **ECD** Grain dd ex Orfordness 8.8.19. For release 8.20.

D7966 To 7 Bde Italy. **139 Sqn** marked as a/c *A*, dd ex **7 AP** 16.8.18, LIA on 07:00 Reconnaissance 23.8.18 (Lt C.E.G. Gill/Lt T. Newey both POW, machine captured and flown by Austro-Hungarian LFT as 00.83 – engine 1295/WD51672) and deleted on unit that day (10hr 50min).

D7967 N/I

D7968 (Arab) **ES** Martlesham Heath dd 20.7.18 for engine performance tests.

D7969 (Falcon III) to 7 Bde Italy. **139 Sqn** dd ex **7 AP** 23.8.18, vict 27.10.18 (Lt A.A. Bartram/2nd Lt C.A. Sander sent an EA scout down OOC over Cimaldormo) then wrecked on 11:25 Bombing 30.10.18 (Capt L.F. Hursthouse WIA/2nd Lt W.W. Smith OK, hit by ground fire and crashed in forced landing on **28 Sqn** aerodrome – engine 1141/WD39462). **7 AP** ex 139 Sqn 3.11.18.

D7970 5 AAP Bristol and tested 11.9.18 and 13.9.18 (Lt C.F. Uwins). **7th TS AFC** Leighterton dd ex Yatesbury 30.10.18.

D7971 (Arab) **5 AAP** Bristol tested 7.8.18 (Lt C.F. Uwins). **ES Martlesham Heath** dd 19.7.18 for engine performance tests and wrecked 13.9.18 (pilot OK/AM1 H. Chadwick IIFA, the engine cut at 100ft and the pilot landed downwind into a sandpit – engine 53749).

D7972 (Falcon III) to 7 Bde Italy. **139 Sqn** dd ex **7 AP** 23.8.18 and wrecked on Test Flight 20.9.18 (Lt E. Exton OK/AM3 R.W. Hare IOAS, crashed – engine 1307/WD51678). **7 AP** ex 139 Sqn 24.9.18.

D7973 N/I

D7974 N/I

D7975 (Falcon III) to 7 Bde Italy. **139 Sqn** dd ex **7 AP** 1.9.18 and wrecked on Reconnaissance 14.9.18 (Lt H.V. Jellicoe/Sgt F.H. Shanks both OK, machine shot through by enemy fire and crashed – engine 1353/WD51701). **7 AP** ex 139 Sqn 16.9.18.

D7976 5 AAP Bristol and tested 17.10.18 (Lt C.F. Uwins).

D7977 N/I

D7978 (Falcon III) **1 ASD** by 26.7.18 (engine 1387/WD51718). **2 AIS** ex 1 ASD 31.7.18. **11 Sqn** dd 12.8.18, wrecked on Reconnaissance, Cambrai, 4.10.18 (Lt B.S.B. Thomas MC/2nd Lt C.E. Spinks both KOAS, collided in the air with C937 near Bapaume at 08:45 – same engine) and deleted on unit that day.

D7979 N/I

D7980 N/I

D7981 (Falcon III) **2 AIS** ex **2 ASD** 29.7.18. **11 Sqn** dd ex 2 AIS 30.7.18, victs 22.8.18 (Lt C.R. Smythe/Lt W.T. Barnes destroyed a Fokker D.VII in flames near Bapaume at 07:40) and 29.8.18 (Lt C.R. Smythe/Lt W.T. Barnes sent a Fokker D.VII down OOC over Bourlon Wood at 18:30) then damaged on 17:20 Escort 30.8.18 (Lt C.R. Smythe/Lt W.T. Barnes both OK, machine hit by enemy fire – engine 1321/WD51685). **2 ASD** ex 11 Sqn 31.8.18 and flown to England 2.9.18 **SEAFIS** Shoreham by 12.18 until @ 1.19.

D7982 **12 Sqn** and wrecked 2.19 (Lt Evans OK, nosed up in ploughed field).

D7983 N/I

D7984 (Falcon III) presentation a/c *Kotah No.1*. **5 AAP** Bristol tested 20.7.18 (Lt C.F. Uwins). **1 ASD** by 26.7.18 (engine 1287/WD51668). **2 AIS** ex 1 ASD 30.7.18. **48 Sqn** dd ex 2 AIS 11.8.18, victs 5.9.18 (Capt H.A. Oaks/Lt T. Beck destroyed a Fokker D.VII in flames and sent another OOC at 12:40) and on unit charge until @ 30.9.18.

D7985 N/I

D7986 **22 Sqn**. **139 Sqn** by 8.18.

D7987 (Falcon III) **5 AAP** Bristol tested 18.7.18 (Lt C.F. Uwins). **141 Sqn** Biggin Hill dd 26.6.18. **44 TDS** Bicester by 3.12.18.

D7988 (Arab) **ES** Martlesham Heath by 30.11.18.

D7989 **8 Sqn**.

D7990 (Falcon III) **1 ASD** by 26.7.18 (engine 1291/WD51670). **1 AIS** ex 1 ASD 1.8.18. **22 Sqn** dd ex 1 AIS 4.8.18, LIA on 08:25 OP 2.9.18 (Capt B.L. Dowling/Lt V. St B. Collins both KIA, last seen E of Cambrai) and deleted on unit that day 65hr 10min).

D7991 N/I

D7992 N/I

D7993 (Falcon III) **1 ASD** by 26.7.18 (engine 1385/WD51717). **1 AIS** ex 1 ASD 28.7.18 (same engine). **20 Sqn** dd ex 1 AIS 5.8.18 (same engine), victs 14.8.18 (Capt D. Latimer/Sgt A. Newland DFM destroyed two Pfalz D.III near Dadizeele at 18:00-18:30) and 21.8.18 (Capt D. Latimer/Sgt A. Newland DFM destroyed three Pfalz D.III, crashed at Menin, Dadizeele and Gheluwe 19:10-19:15, one shared with E2158 and E2467), LIA on 07:30 OP 22.8.18 (Capt D. Latimer DFC MC POW/Lt T.C. Noel MC & Bar KIA, shot down near Westroosebeke, probably by Ltn Nebgen Jasta 7 – same engine) and deleted on unit 23.8.18 (36hr 46min).

D7994 N/I

D7995 N/I

D7996 N/I

D7997 **9 Sqn** Ludendorf. **1 ASD** ex 9 Sqn 21.7.19.

D7998 **Development Sqn** Gosport.

D7999 N/I

D8000 N/I

D8001 (Falcon III) **39 Sqn** North Weald on HAP 20.5.18 (Capt J.M. Clarke/Lt L. Speller) and on unit charge until @ 16.8.18.

D8002 **5 AAP** Bristol and tested 10.5.18 (Lt C.F. Uwins).

D8003 (Falcon III) **5 AAP** Bristol and tested 10.5.18 (Lt C.F. Uwins). **33 Sqn**, 'C' **Flt** Elsham and on AZP 5.8.18 (Lt G.A. Cameron/Cpl Booth). **36 Sqn**, 'A' **Flt** Hylton by 9.9.18 until @ 18.11.18.

D8004 (Falcon III) **36 Sqn**, 'C' **Flt** Seaton Carew by 14.12.18 until @ 3.2.19.

D8005 **5 AAP** Bristol and tested 11.5.18 (Lt C.F. Uwins).

D8006 N/I

D8007 **5 AAP** Bristol and tested 16.5.18 (Lt C.F. Uwins).

D8008 N/I

D8009 **5 AAP** Bristol and tested 16.5.18 (Lt C.F. Uwins). **1 (Obs) SAG** New Romney by 6.18. B&C for reconditioning to J Type (s/n 6616) and ready by 14.2.25.

D8010 **5 AAP** Bristol and tested 15.5.18 (Lt C.F. Uwins). **1 (Obs) SAG** New Romney by 5.18.

D8011 N/I

D8012 (Falcon I) **5 AAP** Bristol and tested 17.5.18 and 19.5.18 (Lt C.F. Uwins). **44 TDS** Bicester and wrecked 9.10.18 (2nd Lt J.H. Lamb KIFA, returning from Fowlmere, stalled and crashed near Islip whilst making a forced landing due to engine failure, weather conditions were described as unfavourable for flying – engine I/Fal/389/WD10495).

D8013 **WT School** Chattis Hill 1918.

D8014 N/I

D8015 N/I

D8016 **5 AAP** Bristol and tested 25.5.18 (Lt C.F. Uwins). **1 (Obs) SAG** New Romney by 6.18. **WT School** Chattis Hill 1918.

D8017 **15 TS** Spittlegate and wrecked 6.6.18 (2nd Lt H.J. Gye IIFA, stalled near the ground avoiding collision – engine 403/WD18478).

D8018 N/I

D8019 N/I

D8020 (Falcon II) **1 (Obs) SAG** New Romney and wrecked 18.5.19 (Lt T.H. Jackson IIFA, landed on rough ground – engine 2/Fal/313/WD18433).

D8021 (Falcon III) **5 AAP** Bristol 28.5.18, allotted to BEF. **Central Despatch Pool**, in incident 1.6.18 (Lt J.A. Roth USAS, no further details on Casualty Card – engine 3/F/1107/WD39446).

D8022 (Falcon III) **5 AAP** Bristol by 28.5.18, allotted to BEF and tested 2.6.18 (Lt C.F. Uwins). **1 AIS** dd ex **1 ASD** 6.6.18. **88 Sqn** dd ex 1 AIS 8.6.18, victs but wrecked 29.6.18 (Lt R.J. Cullen WIA/2nd Lt H.H. Ward OK, sent a Fokker D.VII down OOC and destroyed two more, one of which was shared with C774, C787 and C983, over Ghistelles at 20:10 but machine combat damaged and force landed 300yds this side of the lines and then unsalvageable owing to enemy shell fire – engine 933/WD32866). **1 ASD** by 22.7.18 and deleted 25.7.18 (not worth reconstruction, 42hr).

D8023 (Falcon III) **5 AAP** Bristol by 28.5.18, allotted to BEF. **1 ASD** dd ex England 30.5.18 (engine 1083/WD39434). **1 AIS** ex 1 ASD 3.6.18. **20 Sqn** dd ex 1 AIS 14.6.18 (same engine) and wrecked 17.6.18 (when stationary, was run into by a taxiing machine – engine 877/WD32838). **1 ASD** ex 20 Sqn 18.6.18 and deleted 7.8.18 on reconstruction as F6403 – serial in error and later re-numbered H7063.

D8024 (Falcon III) **5 AAP** Bristol by 28.5.18, allotted to BEF. **2 AIS** dd ex **1 ASD** 4.6.18 (engine 75/WD18537). **62 Sqn** dd ex 2 AIS 17.6.18 (same engine and wrecked after OP 25.8.18 (Lt L.W. Hudson/2nd Lt J. Hall both OK, force landed and collided with two cows after caught in a heavy thunder storm and unable to reach own aerodrome – engine 1335/WD51692). **2 ASD** ex 62 Sqn and deleted 9.10.18 (not worth reconstruction).

D8025 (Falcon III) **5 AAP** Bristol by 28.5.18, allotted to BEF. **1 ASD** dd ex England 30.5.18 (engine 1125/WD39455). **1 AIS** ex 1 ASD 3.6.18 (same engine). **2 Sqn** dd ex 1 AIS 19.6.18 (same engine). **L Flight** dd ex 2 Sqn 1.7.18 and wrecked after Artillery Observation 31.7.18 (Lt H.O. Thornton/Lt A.G. Fletcher both IIFA, crashed on landing – same engine). **1 ASD** ex 'L' Flt 4.8.18 and deleted 7.8.18 (not worth reconstruction, 38hr 15min).

D8026 (Falcon III) **5 AAP** Bristol by 28.5.18, allotted to BEF. **1 ASD** dd ex England 29.5.18 (engine 983/WD32891). **1 AIS** ex 1 ASD 31.5.18 (same engine). **88 Sqn** dd ex 1 AIS 3.6.18 and wrecked after OP 1.7.18 (Lt J.L. Des Lauriers/AG A.M. Spaulding both OK, crashed onto nose after tyre burst on landing – same engine). **1 ASD** ex 88 Sqn 2.7.18 and deleted 5.7.18 (not worth reconstruction, 44hr 20min).

D8027 (Falcon III) **5 AAP** Bristol by 28.5.18, allotted to BEF. **2 AIS** ex **1 ASD** 6.6.18. **48 Sqn** dd ex 2 AIS 17.6.18 (engine 1145/WD39465), LIA on 05:10 OP 19.8.18 Lt R.H. Davis/2nd Lt E.G. Locke both KOAS, collided with C926 at 10,000ft W of Peronne and fell locked together – engine 1405/WD51727) and deleted on unit that day.

D8028 (Falcon III) **5 AAP** Bristol by 28.5.18, allotted to BEF. **1 ASD** dd ex England 30.5.18 (engine 163/WD18581). **2 AIS** dd ex 1 ASD 6.6.18. **62 Sqn** dd ex 2 AIS 6.6.18 (same engine), LIA on 06:15 OP 24.6.18 (Lt F. Williams/2nd Lt E. Dumville both KIA, in combat with EA near Lille and probably brought down by Ltn P. Billik, Jasta 52 – same engine) and deleted on unit that day (28hr 5min).

D8029 **WEE** Biggin Hill as a/c *5*. **ES** Martlesham Heath by 11.9.18 (Lt J.A.W. Armstrong/Lt Spencer on Sextant Tests).

D8030 (Falcon III) **Acoustic ES** Butley and in incident 10.11.18 (Capt H.J.O. Windsor OK/Lt O.B.W. Wills KIFA, passenger fell out of machine – engine 409/WD32604). **ES Orfordness** and wrecked 28.2.19 (Capt G. Gibbons/AC2 G. Milligan both IIFA, engine failed at low height on landing approach).

D8031 B&C for reconditioning to J Type (s/n 6448) and ready by 6.6.24. **PD** Ascot. To Egypt. Reconstructed as DR8031. **Aden Flt**, wrecked 19.2.26 (Flt Lt E.B. Mason OK) and deleted.

D8032 **ES** Orfordness and wrecked 28.2.19 (Capt C. Gibbons/AC2 G. Milligan both IIFA, undershot while landing, engine failed to pick up and hit a tree – listed as A8032). **5 FTS** Sealand and wrecked 8.11.22 (Fg Off D.L. Evans MC DFC/Plt Off J.S. Phillips both OK, engine failed at 50ft on take off, turned back and crashed near Shotwick).

D8033 Photographed wrecked and marked as a/c *15*. **24 Sqn** Kenley by 5.22. **RAF Staff College Flt** Andover by 7.24. B&C for reconditioning to J Type DC (s/n 6826) and ready by 6.10.25. **2 FTS** Digby by 4.26 until @ 9.26. B&C for reconditioning to Mk.III DC (s/n 7131) and ready by 1.9.27. **Andover SF** by 1.29 until @ 7.31.

D8034 **PD** Ascot. To India. **AD** Drigh Road. **28 Sqn** by 22.1.22. **31 Sqn** as a/c *A* by 3.23 and crashed at Tank. **AP** Lahore by 12.24.

D8035 PD Ascot. To India. **AD** Drigh Road. **AP** Lahore by 7.24. **5 Sqn** as a/c *H* by 11.24 until @ 5.25. **AP** Lahore by 9.25. **5 Sqn** as a/c *M* by 4.26 until @ 10.26. **AD** Drigh Rd 1927. **5 Sqn** as a/c *A* 1927. **20 Sqn** as a/c *M* and collided in formation with F4396 at Peshawar 20.3.28. **Quetta SF** by 5.29.

D8036 PD Ascot. To India. **AP** Lahore by 11.22 until @ 2.23. **5 Sqn** as a/c *H*. **28 Sqn** by 3.23. **AD** Drigh Road. **20 Sqn** by 25.4.24 and damaged 7.5.24 (blown on to starboard wing tip by gust and swung on nose). **AD** Drigh Road and wrecked on Ferry Flight 14.11.24 (engine failed en route Lahore and crashed at Karoudi). **AP** Lahore by 12.24. **5 Sqn** by 12.25 until @ 7.26. **Quetta SF** by 8.28 until @ 11.29. **1** (Indian) Group. **30 Sqn** 1930. **20 Sqn** by 7.30 until @ 9.30.

D8037 To Egypt, despatched 26.2.20. **ASD ME** Aboukir by 26.2.20. To Iraq. **6 Sqn** and wrecked 1.5.22 (collided with H1453 and crashed at Baghdad West).

D8038 PD Ascot. To Iraq. **AD** Hinaidi. **6 Sqn** dd ex AD 22.5.23, wrecked 31.3.24 (collided with C1048) and deleted.

D8039 PD Ascot. To India. **AD** Drigh Road. **20 Sqn** by 8.23 and wrecked 25.1.24 (hit telephone wires at Quetta in forced landing after engine failure).

D8040 To Middle East. **6 Sqn** by 6.20. **AD** Hinaidi by 1.23. **6 Sqn** by 26.2.23 until @ 5.23.

D8041 In use by 2 Group Uxbridge and wrecked 15.12.19 (Fg Off G.R. St.C Gwynne-Timothy IIFA, engine failed en route Halton, attempted forced landing in bad weather but stalled and crashed nr Swansbottom – engine WD18479).

D8042 N/I

D8043 N/I

D8044 B&C for reconditioning to J Type (s/n 6580) and ready by 7.1.25.

D8045 B&C for reconditioning to J Type DC (s/n 6898) and ready by 26.1.26. **5 FTS** Sealand by 5.27 until @ 8.27.

D8046 N/I

D8047 N/I

D8048 (Falcon III) to 7 Bde Italy. **139 Sqn** dd ex **7 AP** 14.10.18, wrecked on OP 29.10.18 (Major H.H. Kitchener OK/Lt H.H. Dowse WIA, shot up and engine seized, crashed in forced landing near Conegliano – engine 1315/WD51682) and deleted 30.10.18.

D8049 To India. **31 Sqn** and wrecked 6.3.20 (engine failed, stalled and crashed while turning on ground to avoid uneven surface at Risalpur).

D8050 29 TS Stag Lane dd ex Ascot 8.9.18.

D8051 To Iraq. **6 Sqn** wrecked 19.10.20 (crashed in sandstorm at Kufrah LG) and deleted on unit.

D8052 PD Ascot. To Iraq. **AD** Hinaidi by 7.22. **6 Sqn** by 8.22. **AD** Hinaidi by 3.23. **6 Sqn** 1923 until @ 5.25.

D8053 N/I

D8054 N/I

D8055 B&C for reconditioning to J Type (s/n 6419) and ready by 15.3.24. **AGS** Eastchurch by 11.24 until @ 11.26. **207 Sqn** Eastchurch by 5.27.

D8056 PD Ascot. To Iraq. **AD** Hinaidi and reconstructed as DR8056. **6 Sqn** by 2.5.23. **70 Sqn** by 12.24. Returned to UK. B&C for reconditioning to J Type (s/n 6942) and ready by 12.6.26. **PD** Ascot. To Egypt. **AD** Aboukir. **208 Sqn** by 9.29. **6 Sqn** by 12.29 until @ 11.31.

D8057 PD Ascot. To India. **AD** Drigh Road. **AP** Lahore by 7.24. **28 Sqn**, crashed at 4.8.24 and deleted.

D8058 PD Ascot. To Egypt. **AD** Aboukir. **14 Sqn** by 10.24. **AD** Aboukir for overhaul 15.6.25. **14 Sqn** by 12.26 until @ 1.28.

D8059 12 Sqn as a/c *B5* by 3.19, collided with H1566 at Cologne/Lindenthal 17.5.20 and deleted.

D8060 To 7 Bde Italy. **139 Sqn** dd ex **7 AP** 20.7.18. Presumed crashed. **7 AP** ex 139 Sqn for repair 27.7.18.

D8061 (Falcon III) presentation a/c *Zanzibar No.18*. At maker's 7.6.18, allotted to BEF and to be delivered to **5 AAP**. At 5 AAP Bristol and tested 19.6.18 (Lt C.F. Uwins). **1 ASD** by 22.6.18 (engine 51/WD18525). **2 AIS** dd ex 1 ASD 27.6.18. **48 Sqn** dd ex **2 ASD** 28.6.18 (same engine), LIA on 09:05 OP 8.8.18 (2nd Lt B.J. McCutcheon/2nd Lt V.S. Gray both KIA, last seen near Faucoucourt, probably brought down by Offstlvtr J. Mai, Jasta 5 – same engine) and deleted on unit that day (19hr 55min).

D8062 (Falcon III) presentation a/c *Zanzibar No.19*. At maker's 7.6.18, allotted to BEF and to be delivered to **5 AAP**. At 5 AAP Bristol and tested 21.6.18 (Lt C.F. Uwins). **1 AIS** dd ex **1 ASD** 23.6.18. **88 Sqn** dd ex 1 AIS 23.6.18 and wrecked after successful combats on 08:10 OP 17.9.18 (Lt F. Jeffreys/Lt F.W. Addison both OK, destroyed a Fokker D.VII in flames and another which broke up at 10:10 over Lomelet, then crashed with fuel shortage – engine 899/WD32849). **1 ASD** ex 88 Sqn 21.9.18 (and presume deleted).

D8063 To 7 Bde Italy. **139 Sqn** dd ex **7 AP** 26.7.18 and marked as a/c *D*. **34 Sqn** ex 139 Sqn 26.12.18 and on unit charge until @ 5.2.19. To UK. **PD** Ascot. To India. **AD** Drigh Road. **28 Sqn** by 12.22 until @ 2.23.

D8064 (Falcon III) presentation a/c *Zanzibar No.20*. At maker's 7.6.18, allotted to BEF and to be delivered to **5 AAP**. At 5 AAP Bristol and tested 21.6.18 (Lt C.F. Uwins). **1 AIS** ex **1 ASD** 23.6.18. **1 ASD** ex 1 AIS 25.6.18. **1 AIS** ex 1 ASD 29.6.18 (engine 271/WD18635). **88 Sqn** dd ex 1 AIS 30.6.18, vict 31.7.18 (Lt G.R. Poole/Sgt C. Hill sent a Fokker D.VII down OOC over Estaires-Merville at 09:45) then wrecked on OP 20.9.18 (Capt K.R. Simpson/2nd Lt F.A. Lewis both OK, force landed with engine trouble and crashed into a shell hole – same engine). **1 ASD** ex 88 Sqn 22.9.18 and deleted 25.9.18 (not worth reconstruction, 134hr 5min).

D8065 (Falcon III) presentation a/c *Australia No.24, South Australia No.2, Mrs Sydney Kidman,* presented 7.5.17 by Mrs Kidman, Eringa, Kapunda, South Australia. At maker's 7.6.18, allotted to BEF and to be delivered to **5 AAP**. At 5 AAP Bristol and tested 22.6.18 (Lt C.F. Uwins). **1 ASD** by 28.6.18 (engine 233/WD18611). **1 AIS** dd ex 1 ASD 23.6.18. **1 ASD** ex 1 AIS 25.6.18. **1 AIS** ex 1 ASD 29.6.18. **88 Sqn** dd ex 1 AIS 1.7.18 and wrecked 5.7.18 (Lt FW Addison OK, crashed landing at 1 ASD when taking machine for fitting of wireless – same engine). **1 ASD** and deleted 6.11.18 on reconstruction as H7198.

D8066 To 7 Bde Italy. **139 Sqn** dd ex **7 AP** 24.7.18. **34 Sqn** ex 139 Sqn 26.12.18 and on unit charge until @ 20.2.19.

D8067 (Falcon III) at maker's 7.6.18, allotted to BEF. **5 AAP** Bristol tested 21.6.18 and 22.6.18 and reallotted from BEF to SE Area for D of T for **3 SAFG** Bircham Newton 24.6.18. **1 (Obs) SAG** New Romney by 6.18 until @ 7.18. Maidstone by 4.8.18.

D8068 N/I

D8069 (Falcon III) to 7 Bde Italy. **139 Sqn** dd ex **7 AP** 1.8.18 and LIA on 07:05 Bombing 16.8.18 (Lt C.R.H. Jackson/Lt W.F. Keepin both KIA, in combat with 4 EA over Trento and seen to fall in flames – engine 1161/WD51605). Machine captured and flown by Austro-Hungarian LFT as *00.80*.

D8070 N/I

D8071 N/I

D8072 (Falcon III) to 7 Bde Italy. **139 Sqn** dd ex **7 AP** 1.8.18 and wrecked on Special Duty 22.11.18 (Lt Jones OK/Lt Mortimer IOAS, machine crashed – engine 109/WD22781). **7 AP** ex 139 Sqn 22.11.18.

D8073 (Falcon III) at maker's 7.6.18, allotted to BEF. **5 AAP** Bristol by 24.6.18, reallotted from BEF to SE Area for D of T and **3 SAFG** Bircham Newton.

D8074 (Falcon III) at maker's 7.6.18, allotted to BEF. **5 AAP** Bristol tested 22.6.18 and reallotted from BEF to SE Area for D of T and **3 SAFG** Bircham Newton 24.6.18.

D8075 (Falcon III) to 7 Bde Italy. **139 Sqn** as a/c *L*, dd ex **7 AP** 15.7.18 and LIA on 07:00 Reconnaissance 22.8.18 (Lt N.E. Gwyer/2nd Lt T.R. Hilton both POW – 14hr 55min, engine 1173/WD51611). Machine captured and flown by Austro-Hungarian LFT as *00.75*.

D8076 4 Sqn Farnborough.

D8077 N/I

D8078 (Falcon III) to 7 Bde Italy. **139 Sqn** dd ex **7 AP** 4.8.18 and damaged 15.9.18 (Lt G.R.B. Playfair WIA/AM J.C. Ings OK, hit by AA fire). **34 Sqn** ex 139 Sqn 26.12.18. **7 AP** ex 34 Sqn 10.2.19 (2nd Lt H. Shone/Lt Lilbourne).

D8079 N/I

D8080 Deleted 24.1.19 on reconstruction as H7170.

D8081 (Falcon III) to 7 Bde Italy. **139 Sqn** dd ex 7 AP 30.7.18 and wrecked on 14:40 Patrol 1.8.18 (Lt M.O. Ramsey/2nd Lt F.F. Crump both IOAS, crashed nr Italian aerodrome at S Pietro in Gu after combat – engine 1159/WD51604). **7 AP** ex 139 Sqn 2.8.18 and deleted 3.8.18 (2hr 25min).

D8082 N/I

D8083 RAF (Cadet) College Cranwell as a/c *5* by 9.23 until @ @11.23. **2 FTS** Duxford by 5.24. **RAF (Cadet) College** by 7.24. **Staff College Flt** Andover 7.24 until @ 1925. B&C for reconditioning to J Type DC (s/n 6905) and ready by 12.2.26. **RAF (Cadet) College** Cranwell.

D8084 (Falcon III) to 7 Bde Italy. **139 Sqn** dd ex **7 AP** 29.7.18, marked as a/c *S*, and wrecked on Test Flight 25.9.18 (Lt W.C. Simon/AM Gay both OK, shot through propeller when testing gun – engine 903/WD32851). **7 AP** ex 139 Sqn 2.10.18.

D8085 PD Ascot. To Iraq. **AD** Hinaidi. **6 Sqn** by 11.22. **AD** Hinaidi. **6 Sqn** reissued ex AD 31.5.23 and on unit charge until 1924. To UK. B&C for reconditioning to J Type DC (s/n 6846); and ready by 28.10.25. **Home Communications Flt** Henlow by 1.28 until

@ 3.28. **4 Sqn** Farnborough by 5.28 until @ 8.29. B&C for reconditioning (s/n 7557). Retaken onto RAF charge 12.8.30.

D8086 (Falcon III) at maker's 7.6.18, allotted to BEF. **5 AAP** Bristol tested 29.6.18 (Lt C.F. Uwins). **1 AIS** ex **1 ASD** 2.7.18. **20 Sqn** dd ex **1 AIS** 3.7.18 (engine 149/WD18574), victs 24.7.18 (Lt G.E. Randall/Lt G.V. Learmond destroyed a Fokker D.VII, N of Wervicq at 20:15) and 14.8.18 (Lt G.E. Randall/Lt G.V. Learmond sent a Pfalz D.III down OOC over Dadizeele at 18:00-18:30) then wrecked on Engine test 24.8.18 (Lt G.E. Randall/Lt G.V. Learmond both OK, crashed on landing after hitting a mound – engine 1441/WD51745). **1 ASD** ex 20 Sqn 25.8.18 and deleted 21.9.18 on reconstruction as H7170.

D8087 (Falcon III) at maker's 7.6.18, allotted to BEF. **5 AAP** Bristol and tested 23.6.18 (Lt C.F. Uwins). **1 ASD** by 28.6.18 (engine 1193/WD51621). **2 AIS** ex **1 ASD** 29.6.18 (same engine). **59 Sqn** dd ex **2 AIS** 1.7.18 (same engine). **52 Sqn** ex 59 Sqn 13.7.18 (same engine) and wrecked on Artillery Observation/Photography 22.7.18 (Lt L.A. Brereton/2nd Lt G.R. la Cecilia both WIA, hit by AA fire over Bapaume at c.18:30 and force landed near Monchy with propeller shot away – same engine). **2 ASD** ex 52 Sqn 22.7.18 and deleted 26.7.18 (not worth reconstruction, 16hr 30min).

D8088 (Falcon III) at maker's 7.6.18, allotted to BEF and to be delivered to **5 AAP**. At **2 AIS** ex **1 ASD** 28.6.18. **11 Sqn** dd ex **2 AIS** and wrecked on 09:10 Reconnaissance, Cambrai-Le Cateau, 16.9.18 (Capt A. Morrison/Sgt R. Allan both OK, machine hit by enemy AA fire – engine 1461/WD51755). **2 ASD** ex 11 Sqn 18.9.18 and deleted 24.10.18 (not worth reconstruction).

D8089 (Falcon III) at maker's 22.6.18, allotted to BEF. **5 AAP** Bristol and tested 23.6.18, 24.6.18 and 25.6.18 (Lt C.F. Uwins). **1 AIS** ex **1 ASD** 25.6.18. **22 Sqn** dd ex 1 AIS 26.6.18 (engine 1227/WD51638), vict 16.9.18 (Lt T.W. Martin/Sgt M. Jones destroyed a Fokker D.VII over Quesnoy Wood at 15:30) then LIA on OP 27.9.18 (Lt I.F. Smith POW/2nd Lt B.G. Shum KIA, last seen over Cambrai – same engine) and deleted on unit that day (110hr 43min).

D8090 (Falcon III) at maker's 22.6.18, allotted to BEF. **5 AAP** Bristol and tested 23.6.18 (Lt C.F. Uwins). **1 AIS** ex **1 ASD** 25.6.18. **20 Sqn** dd ex 1 AIS 26.6.18 (engine 1207/WD51628), vict 22.6.18 (Lt P.T. Iaccaci/2nd Lt F.J. Ralphs sent a Pfalz D.III down OOC over Armentieres at 19:00, one of 5 attacking EA) then LIA on 07:48 OP 2.7.18 (Lt H.C. McCreary/Sgt W.H. Barter both KIA, last seen over Halluin and probably brought down by Jasta 56 pilots – same engine) and deleted on unit that day (14hr 13min).

D8091 N/I

D8092 **SAC** Old Sarum by 12.22 until @ 7.23. B&C for reconditioning to J Type (s/n 6647) and ready by 11.3.25. **PD** Ascot. To India. **AD** Drigh Road. **20 Sqn** by 10.26 until @ 5.27. Presume to depot. **20 Sqn** by 9.31 until @ 11.31.

D8093 N/I

D8094 (Falcon III) with 4 Group 16.12.18, reallotted from SE Area to BEF but reallotted to SE Area 17.2.19. **Pool of Pilots** Joyce Green, tested 31.3.19 then wrecked 2.4.19 (Lt V.S.E. Lindop IIFA/Lt P.L. Stephens OK, force landed after ignition failure and o/t when wheels hit water furrows – engine 105/WD22406).

D8095 **PD** Ascot. To Iraq. **AD** Hinaidi by 11.23. **70 Sqn** by 11.23 until @ 12.23.

D8096 **PD** Ascot. To Egypt. **AD** Aboukir. **208 Sqn** by 14.10.22 until @ 8.23. **AD** Aboukir. **208 Sqn** reissued by 9.10.23 until @ 3.24. Returned to UK. B&C for reconditioning to J Type DC (s/n 6848) and ready by 30.10.25. **E&WS** Worthy Down by 8.27. B&C 1928. **E&WS** Worthy Down reissued 2.8.28. B&C for reconditioning to Mk.III DC (s/n 7575). Retaken onto RAF charge 21.3.31. At Andover for storage. Sold by B&C, rebuilt for Warden Aviation Ltd. To civilian register as *G-AEPH* but not taken up. First flown at Old Warden 14.2.51 and currently with the Shuttleworth Trust.

D8097 **PD** Ascot. To India. **AD** Drigh Road. **AP** Lahore by 11.24. **31 Sqn** and wrecked 2.12.24 (crashed on landing at Ambala). Repaired. **31 Sqn** by 1.25 until @ 4.25.

D8098 **PD** Ascot. To Egypt. **AD** Aboukir. **208 Sqn** by 12.22 until @ 11.24. Rebuilt as DR8098. **Aden Flt** and wrecked on Co-operation 1.26 (Flt Lt E.B. Mason OK).

D8099 **PD** Ascot. To Iraq. **AD** Hinaidi. **45 Sqn** by 7.23. **AD** Hinaidi by 8.23. To Egypt. **AD** Aboukir. **208 Sqn** by 10.24.

D8100 B&C for reconditioning to J Type DC (s/n 6889) and ready by 12.1.26. **4 Sqn** Farnborough. **5 FTS** Sealand by 5.27 until @ 10.27.

500 BRISTOL FIGHTER F.2B ordered 15.2.18 under Contract A.S.3117 from British & Colonial Aeroplane Co Ltd, Filton and to be numbered E1101 to E1600 but order cancelled and serials re-allocated.

250 BRISTOL FIGHTER F.2B ordered 22.2.18 under Contract No 35A/46/C.20 (B.R.360) from Sir W.G. Armstrong Whitworth & Co Ltd, Gosforth and numbered E1901 to E2150. (200hp Arab unless noted otherwise). [Work stopped 20.9.19].

E1901 Flying by 30.8.18 at **9 AAP** Newcastle (Capt F. Crawford, 180min – 'Special Test on 1st machine') and tested again 4.9.18 (Capt F. Crawford, 60min – 'Special Test').

E1902 **Fleet SAFG** Leuchars and wrecked 10.7.19 (Lt E.J. Campbell Kirby fatally IIFA/2nd Lt K.C. McKenzie IIFA, forced to land downwind after engine failure – engine E2874/WD2699)

E1903 N/I

E1904 N/I

E1905 N/I

E1906 **8 Sqn** dd 27.11.18 and wrecked on Tank Reconnaissance 14.12.18 (Lt Jacobson/Lt Wood both OK, hit shell hole in forced landing near Plateau after fuel failure).

E1907 N/I

E1908 **9 Sqn** dd ex Reception Park 1.6.19 (engine 16253) and wrecked on Travelling Flight, Ludendorf-Sart, 14.6.19 (same engine). **8 SS** ex 9 Sqn 16.6.19.

E1909 N/I

E1910 N/I

E1911 **39 TDS** Spittlegate and wrecked 30.9.18 (2nd Lt H.L. Martin KIFA, stalled at 100ft and nosedived in – engine 16258).

E1912 N/I

From the last of a batch of 300 F.2Bs built by the parent company, Falcon-engined D8100 was reconditioned to J Type in 1925/26, then going to 4 Sqn at Farnborough and No.5 FTS at Sealand in 1927. *(C&C)*

E1913 N/I
E1914 N/I
E1915 N/I
E1916 **ADC** Waddon. Converted to Tourer and to Spanish civilian register as *M-CIAI* 25.9.28.
E1917 to **E1924** } N/I
E1925 **2 Sqn** Manston post-war.
E1926 N/I
E1927 N/I
E1928 N/I
E1929 N/I
E1930 **PD** Ascot. To Middle East. **Egypt AD** Aboukir. **208 Sqn** by 11.22.
E1931 to **E1957** } N/I
E1958 To Irish Army Air Corps as *B.F.IV*, but crashed on delivery to Baldonnel mid-9.22 and deleted.
E1959 N/I
E1960 N/I
E1961 N/I
E1962 **ADC** Waddon. To Spanish civilian register as *M-CIII* 25.9.28.
E1963 N/I
E1964 **Fleet SAFG** Leuchars. Turnhouse ex Leuchars 25.3.19.
E1965 N/I
E1966 N/I
E1967 N/I
E1968 N/I
E1969 Cranwell and wrecked on Delivery Flight to Liverpool 31.7.19 (Lt W.A. Roberts/Lt E. Ireland both KIFA, lost speed on climbing turn after take off, stalled, nosedived in and caught fire – engine WD23883).
E1970 Harlaxton (a/c *B*).

An Arab-engined F.2B built by Armstrong Whitworth, E1970 'B' was taken on charge in November 1918 and served at Harlaxton. (*Eric Harlin*)

E1971 Cranwell by 6.19. **RAF (Cadet) College**.
E1972 N/I
E1973 N/I
E1974 N/I
E1975 N/I
E1976 First post-war delivery.
E1977 N/I
E1978 **9 AAP** Newcastle 13.1.19, allotted to BEF. **59 Sqn** by 12.6.19 and wrecked on Engine Test 16.7.19 (2nd Lt J. Owen/Lt H.C. MacEwan both OK, ran onto road when landing and turned on nose – engine E3045). **1 ASD** ex 59 Sqn 17.7.19.
E1978 **9 AAP** Newcastle 13.1.19, allotted to BEF.
E1979 to **E1984** } N/I
E1984 At maker's 6.2.19, reallotted from Storage to BEF.
E1985 N/I
E1986 N/I
E1987 N/I
E1988 N/I
E1989 At maker's 6.2.19, reallotted from Storage to BEF.
E1990 **9 AAP** Newcastle by 21.3.19, allotted to BEF.
E1991 N/I
E1992 At maker's 6.2.19, reallotted from Storage to BEF. **59 Sqn** and wrecked on Delivery Flight from Merheim 30.6.19 (2nd Lt L.S. Mersh OK/2nd Lt C.W.C. Peene IOAS, crashed in forced landing at Duren after oil tank burst – engine 16220).
E1993 **9 AAP** Newcastle by 28.1.19, allotted to BEF.

E1994 to **E2013** } N/I
E2014 At maker's 6.2.19, reallotted from Storage to BEF. **59 Sqn** and wrecked after Reconnaissance 7.6.19 (2nd Lt W.L. Alston/2nd Lt H. Ball both OK, machine o/t on landing when undercarriage caught in corn – engine 19289).
E2015 At maker's 6.2.19, reallotted from Storage to BEF. **59 Sqn** by 15.5.19. **1 ASD** ex 59 Sqn 17.7.19.
E2016 At maker's 6.2.19, reallotted from Storage to BEF. **59 Sqn** by 20.5.19. **1 ASD** ex 59 Sqn 17.7.19. Yatesbury (named *Rita*).
E2017 At maker's 6.2.19, reallotted from Storage to BEF.
E2018 to **E2027** } N/I
E2028 At maker's 6.2.19, reallotted from Storage to BEF. **59 Sqn** by 19.5.19. **1 ASD** ex 59 Sqn 17.7.19.
E2029 At maker's 6.2.19, reallotted from Storage to BEF. **59 Sqn** Duren. **1 ASD** ex 59 Sqn 17.7.19.
E2030 At maker's 6.2.19, reallotted from Storage to BEF. **59 Sqn** dd ex Merheim 30.6.19. **1 ASD** ex 59 Sqn 17.7.19.
E2031 At maker's 6.2.19, reallotted from Storage to BEF.
E2032 to **E2041** } N/I
E2042 At maker's 6.2.19, reallotted from Storage to BEF.
E2043 At maker's 6.2.19, reallotted from Storage to BEF.
E2044 At maker's 6.2.19, reallotted from Storage to BEF.
E2045 At maker's 6.2.19, reallotted from Storage to BEF.
E2046 At maker's 6.2.19, reallotted from Storage to BEF.
E2047 At maker's 6.2.19, reallotted from Storage to BEF.
E2048 At maker's 6.2.19, reallotted from Storage to BEF.
E2049 At maker's 6.2.19, reallotted from Storage to BEF. Soviet Russian Air Fleet.
E2050 At maker's 6.2.19, reallotted from Storage to BEF. **59 Sqn** dd ex Merheim 30.6.19 and wrecked on Test Flight 12.7.19 (2nd Lt W.L. Alston/2nd Lt A.H. Winham both OK, crashed on landing due to engine not throttling down – engine 3418). **1 ASD** ex 59 Sqn 16.7.19.
E2051 to **E2057** } N/I
E2058 To civilian register as *G-EBCU* 25.4.22. To AMB 5.22.
E2059 to **E2068** } N/I
E2069 **RAE** Farnborough with experimental 230hp Puma.
E2070 to **E2088** } N/I
E2089 (230hp Puma) **5 (E)ARD** Henlow, allotted to Polish Military Purchase Mission 15.3.20, despatched to Handley Page, Cricklewood 25.3.20 for delivery but reallotted to Inland Area for disposal 19.4.20.
E2090 N/I
E2091 N/I
E2092 N/I
E2093 (230hp Puma) **5 (E)ARD** Henlow, allotted to Polish Military Purchase Mission 15.3.20, despatched to Handley Page, Cricklewood 25.3.20 for delivery but reallotted to Inland Area for disposal 19.4.20.
E2094 to **E2125** } N/I
E2126 **37 TDS** Yatesbury by 1.19 until @ 2.19.
E2127 **5 AAP** Bristol tested 10.7.18 (Lt C.F. Uwins).
E2128 **5 AAP** Bristol tested 12.7.18 (Lt C.F. Uwins). **62 Sqn** by 4.9.18.
E2129 **8 AAP** Lympne dd ex **1 (S)ARD** Farnborough 13.10.18 (Lt G.H. Richardson).
E2130 **5 AAP** Bristol tested 17.7.18 (Lt C.F. Uwins).
E2131 to **E2135** } N/I
E2136 **5 AAP** Bristol tested 10.8.18 (Lt C.F. Uwins).
E2137 N/I
E2138 N/I
E2139 **8 Sqn** by 17.5.19.
E2140 N/I
E2141 N/I

E2142   **204 TDS** Eastchurch by 25.9.18.
E2143   N/I
E2144   N/I
E2145   N/I
E2146   N/I
E2147   To USAS at Ford Junction.
E2148   N/I
E2149   **5 AAP** Bristol and tested 10.10.18 (Lt C.F. Uwins).
E2150   **9 Sqn** dd 28.4.19. **1 ASD** 15.7.19.

500 BRISTOL FIGHTER F.2B ordered 5.2.18 under Contract No A.S.3117/1/18 (B.R.335) from The Bristol Aeroplane Co Ltd, Filton and numbered E2151 to E2650. (200hp Arab or 275hp Falcon III). [Consecutive works' sequence nos. 3754 to 4253].

E2151   (Falcon III) **1 ASD** by 26.7.18 (engine 1409/WD51729). **48 Sqn** dd ex **2 AIS** 10.8.18 (same engine) but crashed on arrival (Lt N. Hunt OK). **2 ASD** ex 48 Sqn 12.8.18 and deleted 23.8.18 (not worth reconstruction, 3hr).
E2152   (Falcon III) **5 AAP** Bristol tested 22.7.18 (Lt C.F. Uwins). **39 Sqn** by 14.8.18 (Lt Taylor/AM1 A.T.C. Stagg) until @ 22.8.18. **1 ASD** by 31.8.18 (engine 1365/WD51707). **2 AIS** ex 1 ASD 31.8.18. **62 Sqn** dd ex 2 AIS 5.9.18 and on unit charge until @ 12.18.
E2153   (Falcon III) **5 AAP** Bristol tested 24.7.18 (Lt C.F. Uwins). **1 ASD** by 5.8.18 (engine 1323/WD51686). **1 AIS** ex 1 ASD 10.8.18. **88 Sqn** dd ex 1 AIS 11.8.18 (same engine), LIA on 12:55 Patrol 27.9.18 (Lt C. Foster/Sgt T. Proctor both KIA in combat near Abancourt – same engine) and deleted on unit that day (106hr 10min).
E2154   (Falcon III) **1 ASD** by 26.7.18 (engine 1343/WD51696). **1 AIS** ex 1 ASD 28.7.18 (same engine). **20 Sqn** dd ex 1 AIS 1.8.18 (same engine), vict 15.8.18 (Lt W.M. Thomson MC/Lt M.A. Mckenzie MC destroyed a Fokker D.VII near Becelaere at 07:10) then wrecked 17.9.18 (Lt J. Nicholson/Cpl Heartfield both IOAS, crashed landing after fuel problems – engine 1579/WD51814). **2 ASD** ex 20 Sqn 19.9.18.
E2155   (Falcon III) **5 AAP** Bristol tested 21.7.18 and 24.7.18 (Lt C.F. Uwins). **1 ASD** by 26.7.18 (engine 1313/WD51681). **1 AIS** ex 1 ASD 28.7.18 (same engine). **20 Sqn** dd ex 1 AIS 31.7.18 (same engine), vict 15.8.18 (Lt W.H. Markham WIA/2nd Lt E.S. Harvey OK, sent down an EKB in flames W of Comines at 07:35) then LIA on 12:33 OP 26.9.18 (2nd Lt L.G. Smith/2nd Lt E.S. Harvey both POW fatally WIA, brought down in flames after combat NW of St Quentin – engine 1225/WD51637) and deleted on unit that day (108hr 48min).
E2156   **5 AAP** Bristol tested 23.7.18 (Lt C.F. Uwins). **39 Sqn** North Weald as a/c *3* by 28.8.18 (Lt Goodyear/AM1 A.T.C. Stagg) until @ 12.18. To USAS at Ford Junction.
E2157   **5 AAP** Bristol tested 24.7.18 (Lt C.F. Uwins).
E2158   (Falcon III) **5 AAP** Bristol tested 23.7.18 (Lt C.F. Uwins). **1 ASD** by 26.7.18 (engine 1253/WD51651). **1 AIS** ex 1 ASD 29.7.18. **20 Sqn** dd ex 1 AIS 31.7.18 (same engine), victs 21.8.18 (Lt J.H. Colber/2nd Lt H.L. Edwards destroyed a Fokker D.VII, N of Menin and sent another down in flames, shared by the patrol) and 22.8.18 (Lt G.E. Randall/Sgt A. Newland DFM shot down one of four Fokker D.VII, E of Comines at 08:40) then LIA on 09:30 OP 20.9.18 (Lt A.R. Strachan/2nd Lt D.M. Calderwood both KIA, brought down in flames) and deleted on unit that day (82hr 54min).
E2159   N/I
E2160   (Falcon III) **5 AAP** Bristol tested 26.7.18 and 27.7.18 (Lt C.F. Uwins). **39 Sqn** North Weald by 16.8.18 and wrecked 25.9.18 (2nd Lt R.H. Kemp/Lt R.G. Underwood both KIFA, crashed due to engine failure – engine 3/F/485).
E2161   (Arab) **1 ASD** by 31.8.18 (engine 53754). **'L' Flt** dd ex **1 AIS** 17.9.18 (same engine). **8 Sqn** ex 'L' Flt 20.1.19 (Lt Mckenzie) and wrecked after Ferry Flight 29.4.19 (Lt Weaver/passenger both OK, hit a sunken track when landing – same engine).
E2162   (Arab) **5 AAP** Bristol tested 26.7.18 (Lt C.F. Uwins). **1 ASD** by 31.8.18 (engine 19178). **'M' Flt** dd ex 1 ASD 3.10.18. **1 ASD** ex 'M' Flt 17.11.18 (engine 3132). **8 Sqn** ex 1 ASD. **2 ASD** ex 8 Sqn 28.1.19 and still on unit charge 14.2.19.
E2163   (Arab) **1 ASD** by 31.8.18 (engine 53722). **'L' Flt** dd ex 1 ASD 21.9.18, LIA on 11:55 Practice Photography (2nd Lt C.A. Harrison/Lt J.A. Parkinson both POW – same engine) and deleted on unit that day (9hr 5min).
E2164   **5 AAP** Bristol tested 30.7.18 (Lt C.F. Uwins).
E2165   N/I
E2166   (Arab) **5 AAP** Bristol tested 30.7.18 (Lt C.F. Uwins). **5 TDS** Easton-on-the-Hill and wrecked 6.3.19 (Lt I.H. Grabowsky/2nd Lt

J.W. Hammond both IIFA, engine failed on downwind take off, attempted to turn back, stalled and crashed – engine 53470).

E2167
to   } N/I
E2180

E2181   (Falcon III) **5 AAP** Bristol 25.7.18, allotted to BEF and tested 28.7.18 (Lt C.F. Uwins). **1 ASD** by 5.8.18 (engine 1379/WD51714). **1 AIS** ex 1 ASD 17.8.18. **20 Sqn** dd ex 1 AIS 23.8.18 (same engine), victs 3.9.18 (Capt H.P. Lale OK/2nd Lt F.J. Ralph DFC KIA, sent a Fokker D.VII OOC, S of Havrincourt Wood at 17:45) and 6.9.18 (Capt H.P. Lale/Lt H.L. Edwards sent down two Fokker D.VII in flames near St Quentin at 08:45) then wrecked on OP 24.9.18 (2nd Lt H.E. Johnston/2nd Lt E.C. Harvey both OK, forced to land by enemy action – same engine). **2 ASD** ex 20 Sqn 27.9.18 and deleted 28.9.18 (not worth reconstruction, 55hr 12min).
E2182   (Falcon III) **5 AAP** Bristol tested 29.7.18 (Lt C.F. Uwins). **1 ASD** by 5.8.18 (engine 1483/WD51766). **2 AIS** ex 1 ASD 10.8.18. **62 Sqn** dd ex 2 AIS 12.8.18 and wrecked 24.9.18 (Lt R. Shallane/2nd Lt R. Lowe both IOAS, force landed near Ovillers due to fuel shortage – engine 209/WD18604). **2 ASD** and deleted 8.10.18 (not worth reconstruction).
E2183   (Falcon III) **1 ASD** by 5.8.18 (engine 1435/WD51742). **1 AIS** ex 1 ASD 6.8.18 (same engine). **88 Sqn** dd ex 1 AIS 9.8.18 and wrecked on 06:05 OP, Armentieres, 20.9.18 (Lt A. Williamson/2nd Lt A.C. Craig both OK, a bullet from EA pierced the water jacket, engine seized and machine was force landed near Strazeele – same engine). **1 ASD** ex 88 Sqn 22.9.18 and deleted 25.9.18 (not worth reconstruction, 48hr).
E2184   (Falcon III) **5 AAP** Bristol tested 31.7.18 (Lt C.F. Uwins). **1 ASD** by 5.8.18 (engine 1471/WD51760). **1 AIS** ex 1 ASD 11.8.18. **L Flight** dd ex 1 AIS 15.8.18 and wrecked on Escort 28.10.18 (Lt A.H. Read/Lt H. Jardine MC both OK, ran into a rut during forced landing – engine 1465/WD51757). **1 ASD** ex 'L' Flt.
E2185   (Falcon III) to 7 Bde Italy. **139 Sqn** dd ex **7 AP** 21.9.18, marked as a/c *S* and on unit charge until @ 31.12.18.
E2186   (Falcon III) to 7 Bde Italy. **139 Sqn** dd ex **7 AP** 26.10.18 and wrecked 22.11.18 (Lt A. Bell/Lt Homer both OK, the machine crashed at Garda). **7 AP** ex 139 Sqn 22.11.18.
E2187   (Falcon III) to 7 Bde Italy. **139 Sqn** dd ex **7 AP** 29.9.18, marked as a/c *P* and damaged in combat 1.11.18 (2nd Lt H. Baldwin WIA). **34 Sqn** ex 139 Sqn 28.1.19 and wrecked after Practice Flight 5.2.19 (2nd Lt A. Newark/2nd Lt W.F. Watson both OK, crashed on landing).
E2188   (Falcon III) to 7 Bde Italy. **139 Sqn** dd ex **7 AP** 1.10.18, marked as a/c *V* and wrecked on Practice Flight 7.12.18 (Lt J.A. Carr/AM Brown both OK, crashed after engine failure).
E2189   (Falcon III) to 7 Bde Italy. **139 Sqn** dd ex **7 AP** 26.10.18 and marked as a/c *C*. **34 Sqn** ex 139 Sqn 28.1.19. **7 AP** ex 34 Sqn 10.2.19 (2nd Lt L.B. Ramsey).
E2190   (Falcon III) to 7 Bde Italy. **139 Sqn** dd ex **7 AP** 31.10.18. **34 Sqn** ex 139 Sqn 28.12.18.
E2191   (Falcon III) **5 AAP** Bristol tested 10.8.18 and 12.8.18 (Lt C.F. Uwins). To 7 Bde Italy. **139 Sqn** dd ex **7 AP** 3.11.18.
E2192   To 7 Bde Italy. **139 Sqn** dd ex **7 AP** 11.18.
E2193   (Arab) **5 AAP** Bristol tested 6.8.18 (Lt C.F. Uwins). **1 ASD** by 31.8.18 (engine 2887/WD27012). **'M' Flt** dd ex 1 ASD 4.10.18 and on unit charge until @ 27.11.18 (same engine). Flown to England 16.12.18.
E2194
to   } N/I
E2198
E2199   To Spanish civilian register as *M-CJAA*.
E2200   N/I
E2201   N/I
E2202   N/I
E2203   **22 Sqn** by 12.18.
E2204   N/I
E2205   N/I
E2206   N/I
E2207   To USAS at Ford Junction.
E2208   N/I
E2209   N/I
E2210   N/I
E2211   **1 ASD** and deleted 14.9.18 (ex England destroyed by fire, 2hr 45min).
E2212   **141 Sqn** Biggin Hill 1918.
E2213   (Falcon III) **1 AIS** ex **1 ASD** 11.8.18. **20 Sqn** dd ex 1 AIS 15.8.18 (engine 1377/WD51713), victs 23.9.18 (Lt N.S. Boulton/2nd Lt

H.L. Edwards destroyed two Fokker D.VII and sent another down OOC, NE of St Quentin at 18:15-18:20) then wrecked on Firing Practice 14.10.18 (Lt D. Seagrave/2nd Lt J.E. Kidd both OK, two propellor blades shot off and force landed in a shellhole – engine 823/WD32811) but still on unit charge 23.10.18.

E2214 (Falcon III) **2 AIS** ex **1 ASD** 13.8.18. **48 Sqn** dd ex 2 AIS 22.8.18 (engine 1363/WD51706), LIA on 18:10 OP 2.9.18 (2nd Lt O. O'Connor/2nd Lt J.J. Ambler both POW, last seen in combat near Lille at 19:15 – same engine) and deleted on unit that day (23hr 50min).

E2215 (Falcon III) **2 AIS** ex **1 ASD** 10.8.18. **11 Sqn** dd ex 2 AIS 13.8.18, victs 30.8.18 (Capt E.S. Coler/2nd Lt B.E.J.D. Tuke destroyed a Pfalz D.XII and a Fokker D.VII, NW of Havrincourt at 18:40), 6.9.18 (Capt E.S. Coler/Lt D.F. Conyngham destroyed a Fokker D.VII and sent another down OOC, W of Cambrai at 10:30) and 15.9.18 (Capt E.S. Coler/Lt E.J. Corbett destroyed two Fokker D.VII, W of Esnes at 12:00) then wrecked after successful combat on Reconnaissance 16.9.18 (Capt E.S. Coler/Lt E.J. Corbett both IIA, destroyed a Pfalz D.XII and a Fokker D.VII, E of Cambrai but radiator hit and force landed near Beugny – engine 1425/WD51737) and deleted on unit that day (44hr 55min).

E2216 (Falcon III) **1 ASD** by 14.8.18 (engine 751/WD32775). **88 Sqn** dd ex 1 ASD 15.8.18 (same engine), victs 19.8.18 Lt K.B. Conn/Lt B.H. Smyth sent a Fokker D.VII down OOC over Oignies at 10:30, shared C4867), 4.9.18 (Lt K.B. Conn/Sgt C.M. Maxwell sent a Fokker Dr.I down OOC over Provin at 09:30), 5.9.18 (Lt K.B. Conn/2nd Lt B. Digby-Worsley sent a Fokker D.VII down OOC over Armentieres at 18:40) and 16.9.18 (Lt K.B. Conn/2nd Lt B. Digby-Worsley destroyed two Fokker D.VII over Habourdin at 17:55) then wrecked 26.10.18 (Lt K.B. Conn/2nd Lt K.C.W. Craig both OK, force landed just after take off and tail hit the ground heavily – engine 1655/WD51852). **1 ASD** ex 88 Sqn.

E2217 **5 AAP** Bristol tested 8.8.18 (Lt C.F. Uwins). **2 AIS** ex 1 ASD 14.8.18. **62 Sqn** dd ex 2 AIS 23.8.18 and presumed crashed 2.9.18 (reported as missing, 18hr). **2 ASD** ex 2 AIS 4.9.18 and deleted 18.11.18 (not worth reconstruction).

E2218 **5 AAP** Bristol tested 7.8.18 (Lt C.F. Uwins). **2 AIS** ex 1 ASD 13.8.18. **62 Sqn** dd ex 2 AIS 23.8.18 and wrecked on OP 17.9.18 (2nd Lt R.A. Boxall/2nd Lt L. Millar both OK, crashed into a shellhole during forced landing near Remy after fuel tank hit in combat – engine 1479/WD51764).

E2219 (Falcon III) **5 AAP** Bristol tested 7.8.18 (Lt C.F. Uwins). **1 ASD** by 14.8.18 (engine 1447/WD51748) and deleted there 30.8.18 on reconstruction as F6408 (2hr 10min). Serial compromised and machine given new serial H7293.

E2220 (Falcon III) **1 ASD** by 14.8.18 (engine 1467/WD51758). **1 AIS** ex 1 ASD 16.8.18. **88 Sqn** dd ex 1 AIS 17.8.18 (same engine, marked as a/c *22* and on unit charge until @ 10.18. **12 Sqn** as a/c *C1* by 9.19 and wrecked 23.12.19 (Capt P.F. Fullard DSO MC DFC OK).

E2221 (Arab) **36 TDS** Yatesbury as a/c *C*. **37 TDS** Yatesbury by 10.18. To USAS at Ford Junction.

E2222 (Arab) **37 TDS** and wrecked 17.10.18 (Lt F.E.W. Perry IIFA, stalled at 10ft – engine WD19184).

E2223 **5 AAP** Bristol tested 18.8.18 (Lt C.F. Uwins). (Photographed marked as a/c *G*, unit unknown).

E2224 (Arab) **36 TDS** Yatesbury by 9.18 and photographed o/t at Yatesbury winter 1918/1919 (Sgt L. Fowler OK).

E2225 **20 Sqn**.

E2226 **5 AAP** Bristol tested 20.8.18 (Lt C.F. Uwins). To USAS at Ford Junction.

E2227 to **E2232** N/I

E2233 Presentation a/c *Alresford District Council*. **8 Sqn** dd 21.12.18. **2 ASD** ex 8 Sqn 28.1.19. **12 Sqn** marked as a/c *B4* and wrecked on Test Flight 21.4.19 (Lt Purefoy/Lt Taylor both OK, port wing hit tree in landing at Duren after engine failure – engine 53819).

E2234 N/I

E2235 N/I

E2236 N/I

E2237 **5 AAP** Bristol tested 7.9.18 (Lt C.F. Uwins). To Middle East. **ASD ME** ex **111 Sqn** 31.12.19.

E2238 **5 AAP** Bristol tested 7.9.18 (Lt C.F. Uwins). **20 Sqn** by 10.18.

E2239 N/I

E2240 **5 AAP** Bristol tested 8.9.18 (Lt C.F. Uwins).

E2241 **5 AAP** Bristol tested 9.8.18 (Lt C.F. Uwins).

E2242 (Falcon III) **5 AAP** Bristol tested 13.8.18 (Lt C.F. Uwins). **1 AIS** ex **1 ASD** 18.8.18. '**L**' **Flt** 22.8.18. '**L**' **Flt** dd ex 1 ASD 22.8.18 and wrecked before Reconnaissance/Photography 26.8.18 (Lt G.

Russell IOAS/2nd Lt J.W.R. Anderson OK, bottom plane struck the ground on take off – engine 649/WD32724). **1 ASD** ex L Flight.

E2243 (Falcon III) **5 AAP** Bristol tested 14.8.18 (Lt C.F. Uwins). **1 AIS** ex **1 ASD** 23.8.18. **22 Sqn** dd ex 1 AIS 31.8.18 (engine 15/WD18507), LIA on OP 27.9.18 (Lt J.R. Drummond KIA/2nd Lt C.H Wilcox POW, last seen over Cambrai – same engine) and deleted on unit that day (44hr 45min).

E2244 (Falcon III) **5 AAP** Bristol tested 15.8.18 (Lt C.F. Uwins). **2 AIS** ex **1 ASD** 21.8.18. **62 Sqn** dd ex 2 AIS 30.8.18 and LIA on 07:45 Escort 16.9.18 (2nd Lt R.H. Stone/2nd Lt N.F. Adams both POW last seen going down NE of Douai – engine 607/WD32703) and deleted on unit that day (21hr).

E2245 **5 AAP** Bristol tested 15.8.18 (Lt C.F. Uwins). **141 Sqn** Biggin Hill 1918.

E2246 (Falcon III) **5 AAP** Bristol tested 15.8.18 (Lt C.F. Uwins). **2 AIS** ex **1 ASD** 23.8.18. **20 Sqn** dd ex 2 AIS 1.9.18 (engine 1429/WD51749) and wrecked on OP 9.11.18 (Lt N.P.B. Giddens/Sgt W.R. Greenfield both OK, force landed after controls jammed – same engine).

E2247 (Falcon III) **5 AAP** Bristol tested 16.8.18 (Lt C.F. Uwins). **1 AIS** ex **1 ASD** 23.8.18. **22 Sqn** dd ex 1 AIS 31.8.18 (engine 1531/WD51790) and wrecked 1.9.18 (Capt W.F.J. Harvey/Capt D.E. Waight both OK, a wheel came off and machine crashed on landing – same engine). **1 ASD** ex 22 Sqn 2.9.18 and deleted 10.10.18 (not worth reconstruction).

E2248 **5 AAP** Bristol tested 18.8.18 (Lt C.F. Uwins). **39 Sqn** North Weald. **141 Sqn** Biggin Hill ex North Weald 30.11.18. To India. **114 Sqn** 1919 and on charge when unit redesignated **28 Sqn** 1.2.20. AP Lahore by 9.5.21.

E2249 (Falcon III) **5 AAP** Bristol tested 20.8.18 (Lt C.F. Uwins). **1 AIS** ex **1 ASD** 24.8.18. **20 Sqn** dd ex 1 AIS 25.8.18 (engine 1463/WD51756) and wrecked after OP 17.9.18 (2nd Lt Kiernanden/2nd Lt D.M. Calderwood both OK, crashed landing in the dark – same engine). **2 ASD** ex 20 Sqn 21.9.18 and deleted 6.10.18 (not worth reconstruction).

E2250 (Falcon III) **1 AIS** ex **1 ASD** 23.8.18. **10 Sqn** dd ex 1 AIS 24.8.18 (engine 7/WD18503) and wrecked on 09:00 Photography 1.10.18 (Lt A.W. Bennett/2nd Lt G.H.E. Kime MM bothWIA, machine damaged in combat with Fokker D.VIIs over Courtrai – same engine). **1 ASD** ex 10 Sqn and deleted 4.10.18 (not worth reconstruction).

E2251 N/I

E2252 (Falcon III) **1 AIS** ex **1 ASD** 18.8.18. **20 Sqn** dd ex 1 AIS 23.8.18 (engine 1505/WD51777), vict 24.9.18 (Capt T.C. Traill/Lt. R Gordon-Bennett sent a Fokker D.VII down OOC, W of Busigny at 16:00), damaged in successful combat 25.9.18 (Capt T.C. Traill OK/Lt R Gordon-Bennett WIA, destroyed a Fokker D.VII in flames NE of St Quentin at 18:20) then wrecked on Practice Flight 21.11.18 (2nd Lt J.L. Boyd/2nd Lt W.A. Rogers both OK, force landed near Cambrai in mist – engine 1213/WD51631).

E2253 **20 Sqn** by 11.18.

E2254 **5 AAP** Bristol tested 18.8.18 (Lt C.F. Uwins). **1 ASD** and deleted 27.8.18 on reconstruction as F6407. Serial compromised and so machine given new serial H7292.

E2255 (Falcon III) **5 AAP** Bristol tested 20.8.18 (Lt C.F. Uwins). **2 AIS** ex **1 ASD** 28.8.18. **20 Sqn** dd ex 2 AIS 17.9.18 (engine 1529/WD51789) and wrecked 13.10.18 (hit when stationary on the ground by **205 Sqn** D.H. 9A F1044 – engine 1715/WD51882).

E2256 (Falcon III) **5 AAP** Bristol 20.8.18 allotted to **154 Sqn (Mobilising)** as a training machine but reallotted to BEF 26.8.18. **1 ASD** by 31.8.18 (engine 1311/WD51680). **2 AIS** ex 1 ASD 2.9.18. **62 Sqn** dd ex 2 AIS 16.9.18, LIA after successful combat on 06:45 OP 9.10.18 (Capt L. Campbell/2nd Lt W. Hodgkinson both KIA, destroyed a Fokker D.VII over Preseau then last seen going down over the Forêt de Mormal with two EA on its tail – same engine) and deleted on unit that day.

E2257 **5 AAP** Bristol tested 21.8.18 (Lt C.F. Uwins). B&C for reconditioning to J Type (s/n 6585) and ready by 9.1.25. To India. **31 Sqn** as a/c *E* by 3.26. **5 Sqn** by 6.28 until @ 7.28.

E2258 (Falcon III) **5 AAP** Bristol 20.8.18 allotted to **154 Sqn (Mobilising)** as a training machine but reallotted to BEF 26.8.18. **1 ASD** by 31.8.18 (engine 797/WD32798). **2 AIS** ex 1 ASD 31.8.18. **20 Sqn** dd ex 2 AIS 5.9.18 (same engine), victs 20.9.18 (Lt F.G. Harlock/2nd Lt A.S. Draisey destroyed two Fokker D.VII over Mesnil at 10.00-10.15) then wrecked 23.9.18 (Lt F.G. Harlock/AM1 S. Roberts both OK, force landed due to pressure trouble – same engine). **2 ASD** ex 20 Sqn and deleted 28.9.18 (23hr 36min).

E2259 **5 AAP** Bristol tested 23.8.18 (Lt C.F. Uwins), allotted to **154 Sqn (Mobilising)** 25.8.18 but allotment cancelled 30.8.18. **ACIS** Kenley by 8.19 (for General Groves). B&C for reconditioning to J Type (s/n 6553) and ready by 5.12.24.

E2260 (Falcon III) **1 ASD** by 31.8.18 (engine 135/WD18567). **1 AIS** ex 1 ASD 1.9.18. **48 Sqn** dd ex 1 AIS 5.9.18, LIA on 09:20 OP 20.9.18 (Lt M.F.J.R. Mahony/2nd Lt C.N. Kier both POW, last seen in combat over Roubaix at 11:00 – same engine) and deleted on unit that day (26hr 20min).

E2261 **5 AAP** Bristol tested 20.8.18 (Lt C.F. Uwins). **141 Sqn** and wrecked 8.8.19 (Lt G.R. Barker IIFA, engine cut at 50ft after take off and the machine struck a haystack attempting a forced landing near Tallaght – engine 1503/WD51776).

E2262 **39 Sqn** North Weald by 8.18 until @ 10.18. **141 Sqn** Biggin Hill 1918.

E2263 (Falcon III) **1 AIS** ex 1 ASD 23.8.18 (engine 1533/WD51791). **22 Sqn** dd ex 1 AIS 31.8.18 and wrecked on Travelling Flight to new aerodrome 15.12.18 (Lt J. Sewell OK crashed due to engine pressure trouble – same engine).

E2264 (Falcon III) **5 AAP** Filton by 26.8.18. **8 AAP** dd ex Bristol 26.8.18. **1 ASD** dd ex Lympne 27.8.18 (Lt G.H. Richardson – engine 1489/WD51769). **2 ASD** ex 1 ASD 31.8.18. B&C for reconditioning to J Type (s/n 6582) and ready by 7.1.25.

Running up E2264's Falcon engine against the chocks. This F.2B was with 1 ASD and then 2 ASD, and then went back to Bristol's for reconditioning to 'J' Type. *(Eric Harlin)*

E2265 (Falcon III) **48 Sqn** dd ex 1 ASD 27.8.18 (engine 431/WD32615), LIA on 16:15 OP 1.10.18 (Capt W. Buckingham MC POW/Lt T. Beck MC POW fatally WIA, brought down in combat near Thielt, engine 1287/WD51668) and deleted on unit that day.

E2266 (Falcon III) **1 ASD** by 31.8.18 (engine 393/WD18696). **1 AIS** ex 1 ASD 1.9.18. **22 Sqn** dd ex 1 AIS 2.9.1, LIA on OP 29.9.18 (Lt E. Adams USAS/Sgt G. Bissell both KIA, last seen in combat over Cambrai – same engine) and deleted on unit that day (33hr 40min).

E2267 (Falcon III) **5 AAP** Bristol tested 24.8.18 (Lt C.F. Uwins). **48 Sqn** dd ex 1 ASD 27.8.18 (engine 65/WD18532) and wrecked after OP 5.9.18 (Capt E.N. Griffiths IOAS/Sgt H.F. Monday OK collided when landing with E2482 – same engine). **1 ASD** ex 48 Sqn 6.9.18 and deleted 9.9.18 (not worth reconstruction, 25hr 40min).

E2268 (Falcon III) **1 ASD** by 31.8.18 (engine 153/WD51781). **1 AIS** ex 1 ASD 31.8.18. **48 Sqn** dd ex 1 AIS 4.9.18 (same engine) and wrecked on OP 22.10.18 (Sgt W. Eade/2nd Lt Knowles-Brown both OK, crashed in forced landing after engine trouble on rough ground on the aerodrome – same engine).

E2269 (Falcon III) **1 ASD** by 31.8.18 (engine 1555/WD51802). **1 AIS** ex 1 ASD 1.9.18. **22 Sqn** dd ex 1 AIS 3.9.18, marked as a/c *Z* and wrecked before Practice Flight 4.4.19 (Lt Lavery IOAS, turned on nose during take off – same engine).

E2270 (Falcon III) to 7 Bde Italy. **139 Sqn** dd ex 7 AP 16.11.18 and wrecked on Travelling Flight, Grossa-Florence, 25.1.19 (Sgt Bromley/Lt Griffiths both OK, crashed near Sienna and machine destroyed by fire – engine WD18630). **7 AP** ex 139 Sqn 29.1.19 and deleted.

E2271 (Arab) **1 ASD** by 30.9.18 (engine 53791). **2 AIS** ex 1 ASD 24.10.18. **8 Sqn** Bellevue. **9 Sqn** ex 8 Sqn 28.1.19 (same engine). And wrecked 19.7.18 (Capt Skeate OK). **1 ASD** ex 9 Sqn 19.7.18.

E2272 (Arab) **9 Sqn** dd ex 1 ASD 9.5.19 (engine 53794). **1 ASD** ex 9 Sqn 19.7.19.

E2273 N/I

E2274 (Arab) **8 AAP** dd ex **1 ASD** 4.9.18 (2nd Lt C.H. Drew/AM2 Hoeden).

E2275 (Falcon III) **1 ASD** ex **1 (S)ARD** Farnborough 3.9.18 (Lt G.H. Richardson) and flown back to England 4.9.18.

E2276 to E2280 } N/I

E2281 (Falcon III) **1 AIS** ex **1 ASD** 7.9.18 (engine 315/WD18657). **48 Sqn** dd ex 1 AIS 22.9.18 (same engine), vict 9.10.18 (Lt T.G. Rae/Sgt C.F. Perkin destroyed a Fokker D.VII, N of Courtrai at 10:45) and wrecked on Test Flight 15.3.19 (Major F.W. Stent/2nd Lt Lang both IOAS, landed in the River Rhine near Schiffbrucke Bridge – engine 531/WD32665).

E2282 (Falcon III) **5 AAP** Bristol tested 25.8.18 (Lt C.F. Uwins). **1 ASD** by 31.8.18 (engine 115/WD18557). **1 AIS** ex 1 ASD 31.8.18. **48 Sqn** dd ex 1 AIS 3.9.18 (same engine) on OP 26.9.18 (2nd Lt J.B. Cowan/Lt L.N. Jones both OK, crashed in forced landing near Hazebroucke after engine shot through in combat – same engine). **1 ASD** ex 48 Sqn 30.9.18 and deleted 5.10.18 (not worth reconstruction).

E2283 To USAS at Ford Junction. To India. **48 Sqn** by 2.20. **5 Sqn** by 6.20. **28 Sqn** by 1920 until @ 1923.

E2284 (Falcon III) to 7 Bde Italy. **139 Sqn** 1918. **28 Sqn** by 18.12.18 and tested 22.12.18. **7 AP** by 8.2.19.

E2285 (Falcon III) to 7 Bde Italy. **139 Sqn** dd ex 7 AP 6.11.18, marked as a/c *A* and damaged in forced landing 30.1.19. **7 AP** ex 139 Sqn 30.1.19.

E2286 (Falcon III) to Middle East. **X AD** dd ex England 24.11.18. **X AP** ex X AD 17.4.19. **111 Sqn** and deleted on unit 24.9.19.

E2287 (Falcon III) to Middle East. **X AD** dd ex England 24.11.18. **X AP** ex X AD 21.4.19. **111 Sqn** dd ex X AP 23.6.18 (engine WD32614). **208 Sqn** by 9.20 until @ 1.21. To India. **31 Sqn.**

E2288 (Falcon III) to Middle East. **X AD** dd ex England 24.11.18. **X AP** ex X AD 21.4.19. **111 Sqn** dd ex X AP 1.6.19 (engine WD32614), on charge 1.2.20 when unit redesignated **14 Sqn** and wrecked 18.4.21 (crashed in forced landing at Ramleh after petrol tube broke and throttle jammed).

E2289 (Falcon III) to Middle East. **X AD** dd ex England 24.11.18. **X AP** ex X AD 21.4.19. **111 Sqn** dd ex X AP 10.7.19 (engine WD51886) and deleted on unit 8.9.18.

E2290 (Falcon III) to Middle East. **X AD** dd ex England 24.11.18. **X AP** ex X AD 17.4.19. **111 Sqn** dd ex X AP 6.7.19 (engine WD51890), on unit charge 1.2.20 when redesignated **14 Sqn** and wrecked 22.2.20 (undercarriage torn off in forced landing at Kilo 99). **AD** Aboukir and repaired. **Special Instruction Flt** Almaza by 7.20. **4 FTS** Abu Sueir by 6.21 until @ 9.21.

E2291 (Falcon III) to 7 Bde Italy. **139 Sqn** dd ex 7 AP 3.11.18, wrecked on Test Flight 7.11.18 (Capt G.W. Curtiss/2nd Lt T.W. Smith both OK, crashed in forced landing near Nova after oil pressure gave out – engine 1567/WD51808) but still on unit charge 10.11.18.

E2292 (Falcon III) to 7 Bde Italy. **139 Sqn** dd ex 7 AP 26.10.18 and wrecked after Reconnaissance 30.1.18 (Lt G.W. Curtiss/2nd Lt R.G. Fullager both OK, perfect landing then taxied into a concealed ditch – engine 165/WD18582). **7 AP** ex 139 Sqn 31.10.18.

E2293 (Falcon III) to Middle East. **X AD** dd ex England 18.11.18. **17 TDS** El Firdan dd ex X AD 2.12.18. **X AP** ex 17 TDS 28.3.19 (engine WD15753). **111 Sqn** by 1.20, on charge when unit redesignated **14 Sqn** 1.2.20 and wrecked on Travelling Flight, Ramleh-Ismailia, 14.6.20 (Fg Off N. Fitzgerald-Eager fatally IOAS/AC1 P.W.J. Thacker KOAS, flew off course and force landed Sinai Desert, 30 miles W of Nekhl, Palestine).

E2294 To Middle East. **X AD** dd ex England 18.11.18. **17 TDS** El Firdan dd ex X AD 22.11.18. **16 TDS** Heliopolis. **ASD ME** ex 16 TDS 2.10.19. **208 Sqn** 9.20. Returned to UK. **CFS Upavon** by 7.26.

E2295 To Middle East. **X AD** dd ex England 18.11.18. **17 TDS** El Firdan dd ex X AD 22.11.18. **16 TDS** Heliopolis. **ASD ME** ex 16 TDS 17.6.19. **208 Sqn** by 9.20 until @ 1.21.

E2296 N/I

E2297 B&C for reconditioning to J Type (s/n 6662) and ready by 21.3.25. To India. **AD** Drigh Road. **31 Sqn** by 23.10.27. **20 Sqn** by 7.31 until @ 10.31.

E2298 To Middle East. **208 Sqn** and wrecked 14.4.21 (collided with D7831 and crashed near Bilbeis).

E2299 To Middle East. **208 Sqn** Ismailia 1920; Tested after reconstruction but force landed near El Arish 24.9.20. **208 Sqn** by 9.20 until @ 5.22. **4 FTS** Abu Sueir by 5.23.

E2300 **PD** Ascot. To India. **AD** Drigh Road. **70 Sqn** by 12.22 until @ 8.23. (Also noted at **20 Sqn**, crashed 29.5.23.) Returned to UK.

B&C for reconditioning to J Type (s/n 6831) and ready by 10.10.25. **CFS** Upavon by 7.26 until @ 8.26.

E2301 To Spanish Civilian Register as *M-CAAJ* (s/n E2301) 25.9.28 registered to ADC Aircraft.

E2302 N/I

E2303 N/I

E2304 N/I

E2305 N/I

E2306 (Arab) **5 AAP** Bristol by 28.9.18 and tested 3.10.18 (Lt C.F. Uwins). **ES** Martlesham Heath from 4.10.18 until 31.12.18 for strengthening of engine mounting and engine & carburettor trials.

E2307 N/I

E2308 N/I

E2309 N/I

E2310 N/I

E2311 **CFS** Upavon by 4.26.

E2312 to **E2318** } N/I

E2319 (Arab) **8 Sqn** Bellevue dd 27.11.18. **2 ASD** ex 8 Sqn 28.1.19. **8 Sqn** reissued ex **1 ASD** 12.5.19. **1 ASD** ex 8 Sqn 26.6.19.

E2320 (Arab) **5 AAP** Bristol and in incident 9.9.18 (AM3 H. Burrows KIGA, walked into running propeller – engine 2829) and tested 12.9.18 (Lt C.F. Uwins).

E2321 to **E2325** } N/I

E2326 **3 Sqn AFC** by 11.18.

E2327 N/I

E2328 N/I

E2329 **5 AAP** Bristol and tested 11.9.18 (Lt C.F. Uwins). **3 Sqn AFC** 1918. **'O' Flt**.

E2330 **5 AAP** Bristol and tested 16.9.18 and 16.10.18 (Lt C.F. Uwins).

E2331 To India. **20 Sqn** by 9.19 and wrecked 1.2.20 (shot down by rebel fire).

E2332 N/I

E2333 N/I

E2334 To India. **31 Sqn** and wrecked on Travelling Flight, Cawnpore-Peshawar, 15.10.21 (crashed near Agra after engine failure).

E2335 N/I

E2336 N/I

E2337 (Falcon III) **1 ASD** by 15.9.18 (engine 59/WD18529). **2 AIS** ex 1 ASD 16.9.18. **20 Sqn** dd ex 2 AIS 17.9.18 (same engine) and on unit charge until @ 30.9.18.

E2338 (Falcon III) **1 ASD** dd ex **2 AAP** 16.9.18 (Major Ainslie – engine 1635/WD51842). **2 AIS** ex 1 ASD 20.9.18. **20 Sqn** dd ex 2 AIS 25.9.18 (same engine), victs 27.9.18 (Lt F.G. Harlock/2nd Lt A.S. Draisey destroyed a Fokker D.VII, NE of Marcy at 10:30) and 3.10.18 (Lt F.G. Harlock/Lt J.F. Kidd destroyed a Fokker D.VII over Mericourt at 10:05) then reported 21.3.19 as unsafe to fly after being left outside in wet weather – same engine (101hr 41min).

E2339 (Falcon III) **1 ASD** by 15.9.18 (engine 213/WD18606). **1 AIS** ex 1 ASD 18.9.18. **88 Sqn** dd ex 1 AIS 20.9.18 (same engine) and wrecked on Test Flight 26.10.18 (Lt G.F. Anderson/2nd Lt C.M.W. Elliott both OK, ran into shell hole on landing – engine 1631/WD51840). **1 ASD** ex 88 Sqn. **20 Sqn** by 12.18.

E2340 (Falcon III) **5 AAP** Bristol tested 9.9.18 and 10.9.18 (Lt C.F. Uwins). **1 ASD** by 15.9.18 (engine 1605/WD51827). **2 AIS** ex 1 ASD 16.9.18. **20 Sqn** dd ex 2 AIS 17.9.18 (same engine), victs 25.9.18 (Lt F.G. Harlock/2nd Lt A.S. Draisey destroyed two Fokker D.VII over Magny at 18:20) then wrecked 6.10.18 (Lt A.D. Keirnander/2nd Lt L. Allden both OK, struck a covered shell hole when landing at Proyart – same engine).

E2341 N/I

E2342 (Arab) **2 AIS** ex **1 ASD** 24.10.18. **8 Sqn** and wrecked on Practice Flight 30.10.18 (Lt Putwaine/Lt Smith both OK, force landed Estrees after engine trouble – engine 53834). Noted at **39 Sqn** Biggin Hill by 25.10.19.

E2343 (Arab) **2 AIS** ex **1 ASD** 24.10.18. **8 Sqn** and wrecked on Contact Patrol 5.11.18 (Lt A. Glenn/2nd Lt H. Roberts both IOAS, crashed in Forêt de Mormal after engine trouble – engine 53846).

E2344 (Arab) **2 ASD** dd ex **1 ASD** 24.10.18. **8 Sqn** dd ex 2 ASD 26.10.18 and wrecked 4.11.18 (Lt Grundy/Lt Mitchell both OK, force landed near Ruemont after throttle control worked loose – engine 53819).

E2345 (Arab) **8 Sqn** dd 23.10.18.

E2346 to **E2350** } N/I

E2351 (Arab) **5 AAP** Bristol and tested 16.9.18 (Lt C.F. Uwins). **'O' Flt** dd ex **2 AIS** 29.10.18. Photographed wrecked at **1 ASD**.

E2352 (Arab) **8 Sqn** dd 22.1.19, force landed near Valenciennes and for **6 Salvage Section** 7.5.19 (engine 53856).

E2353 (Arab) **8 Sqn** dd 20.12.18. **2 ASD** and **8 SS** ex 8 Sqn 20.5.19.

E2354 **5 AAP** Bristol and tested 12.9.18 (Lt C.F. Uwins). To Civilian Register as G-EBFD.

E2355 to **E2359** } N/I

E2360 To Spanish Civilian register as *M-CIIA* (s/n E2360) 25.9.28, registered to ADC Aircraft Ltd.

E2361 (Falcon III) **5 AAP** Bristol tested 9.9.18, 10.9.18 and 11.9.18 (Lt C.F. Uwins). **39 Sqn** North Weald by 17.9.18 until @ 27.10.18. **37 Sqn** dd ex Biggin Hill 3.12.18 (engine 347/WD18673) but transfer cancelled 18.12.18.

E2362 **'M' Flt** by 10.18. **141 Sqn** Biggin Hill 1918.

E2363 (Falcon III) **1 ASD** by 15.9.18 (engine 1663/WD51856). **11 Sqn** dd ex **2 ASD** 17.9.18 and damaged on Photography 24.9.18 (2nd Lt C. Johnson/Sgt C.H. Hampson both WIA, machine hit by enemy AA fire and force landed at Bellevue – same engine). **2 ASD** ex 11 Sqn 25.9.18 and deleted 8.10.18 (not worth reconstruction).

E2364 (Falcon III) **2 AIS** ex **1 ASD** 28.9.18. **5 AIS** ex 2 AIS 3.10.18. **11 Sqn** and wrecked on Travelling Flight 24.11.18 (Lt H.S. Malik/AM2 J. Watt both OK, force landed near Lay/Remy after oil pipe broke in the air – engine 1631/WD51835). **6 AP** ex 11 Sqn 28.11.18. **3 AD** ex 6 AP 28.11.18.

E2365 (Falcon III) **1 ASD** by 15.9.18 (engine 1661/51855). **2 AIS** ex 1 ASD 16.9.18. **11 Sqn** by 11.18 and wrecked on Travelling Flight, Aulnoye-Bonneville, 14.12.18 (Sgt Mech A.W. Wallace/2nd Lt J.F. Rowbotham both OK, ran into a plough during forced landing near Charleroi and o/t – same engine).

E2366 (Falcon III) **5 AAP** Bristol and tested 13.9.18 (Lt C.F. Uwins). **2 AIS** ex **1 ASD** 23.9.18. **11 Sqn** dd ex 2 AIS 26.9.18 and wrecked on 07:00 Reconnaissance, Le Cateau-Cambrai, 1.10.18 (Sgt Mech A.L. Cridlan/2nd Lt W. Connor both OK, machine damaged by enemy AA fire – engine 739/WD32769). **2 ASD** ex 11 Sqn and deleted 8.10.18 (not worth reconstruction).

E2367 (Falcon III) **1 AIS** ex **1 ASD** 21.9.18 and on unit charge 30.9.18 (engine 175/WD18587). **48 Sqn** and wrecked on Line Patrol, Escauaissles, 29.10.18 (Lt I.O. Gaze/2nd Lt C.W. Newstead both OK, force landed near Deerlyke after hit by enemy AA at 15:00 – same engine).

E2368 **5 AAP** Bristol and tested 13.9.18 (Lt C.F. Uwins). **141 Sqn** Biggin Hill by 23.11.18.

E2369 (Falcon III) **1 AIS** ex **1 ASD** 29.9.18 (engine 439/WD32619) and tested 3.10.18.

E2370 (Falcon III) **5 AAP** Bristol and tested 15.9.18 (Lt C.F. Uwins). **2 AIS** ex **1 ASD** 19.9.18. **20 Sqn** dd ex 2 AIS 21.9.18 (engine 153/WD18576) and wrecked after OP 9.11.18 (2nd Lt G. Thompson/2nd Lt F. Bland both OK, crashed after hit soft ground on landing – engine 1645/WD51847).

E2371 to **E2381** } N/I

E2382 **48 Sqn** by 9.18.

E2383 to **E2389** } N/I

E2390 **39 Sqn** by 25.10.19.

E2391 to **E2399** } N/I

E2400 (300hp Hispano-Suiza) at maker's 28.9.18 for Martlesham Heath. **ES** Martlesham Heath dd 27.11.18 (new type Bristol mounting), producing Test Report M249A 2.19 and on unit charge until 6.19.

E2401 N/I

E2402 N/I

E2403 (Falcon III) **2 AIS** ex **1 ASD** 26.9.18. **HQ Communications Sqn** dd ex 2 AIS 29.9.18 (engine 547/WD32673). **2 ASD** and tested 3.10.18. **5 AIS** ex 2 ASD 7.10.18. **20 Sqn** dd ex 2 AIS 13.10.18 and wrecked after successful combat on OP 23.10.18 (Capt R.C. Traill OK/Capt L.W. Burbidge IOAS, destroyed a Fokker D.VII, W of Aulnoye at 15:20 but collided mid-air with E2590 and crashed S of Cambrai – engine 1009/WD39397).

E2404 (Falcon III) **2 AIS** ex **1 ASD** 26.9.18. **20 Sqn** dd ex 2 AIS 1.10.18 and wrecked 10.10.18 (Lt A.W. McHardy/AM2 Doyle both OK, force landed near La Houssoye after losing their way and running short of fuel during return from a forced landing at Soissons –

engine 379/WD18689). **2 ASD** ex 20 Sqn and deleted 17.10.18 (not worth reconstruction).

E2405 **2 AIS** ex **1 ASD** 2.10.18. **5 AIS** ex 2 AIS 8.10.18.

E2406 (Falcon III) **2 AIS** ex **1 ASD** 28.9.18. **20 Sqn** dd 1.10.18 and wrecked after OP 8.10.18 (Lt F.R. Goodearle/2nd Lt P.B. de Moyse-Bucknell both OK, crashed when struck a shell hole on landing – engine 705/WD32752). **2 ASD** ex 20 Sqn.

E2407 (Falcon III) **5 AAP** Bristol and tested 3.10.18 (Lt C.F. Uwins). **2 AIS** ex **1 ASD** 8.10.18. **20 Sqn** by 23.10.18 and wrecked on Practice Flight 12.1.19 (Lt J.O. Boyd/Lt P.B. de Moyes-Bucknell both OK, tail skid broke in forced landing at Ghent Arsenal – engine 1667/WD51858).

E2408 (Falcon III) **2 AIS** ex **1 ASD** 28.9.18. **22 Sqn** 1918. **62 Sqn** and wrecked on Test Flight 8.4.19 (2nd Lt N.P.B. Giddens/2nd Lt F.D.R. McLaren both OK, crashed near Nivelles – engine WD51874).

E2409 (Falcon III) **2 AIS** ex **1 ASD** 2.10.18. **5 AIS** ex 2 AIS 3.10.18. **62 Sqn** and wrecked on Delivery Flight to new aerodrome 14.12.18 (Lt Edwards/Cpl Brownridge both OK, crashed landing on bad ground at Bouge – engine 1823/WD51936).

E2410 (Falcon III) **1 ASD** by 30.9.18 (engine 519/WD32659) and tested 8.10.18. **22 Sqn** marked as a/c *F*, damaged 7.1.19 (Lt W. Martin OK, forced landed near Waterloo) and wrecked on Practice Flight 8.4.19 (Lt Laver OK, crashed on landing at Nivelles – same engine).

E2411 (Falcon III) **141 Sqn, 'C' Flt** Tallaght and wrecked 5.6.19 (force landed near Lucan). Repaired at Tallaght. **100 Sqn** Castlebar and wrecked 6.8.20 (crashed on landing). To Fermoy for repair. **2 Sqn** Fermoy, and wrecked 15.10.20 (engine failed on take off and force landed 1 mile NW of aerodrome). Repaired at Fermoy. **Irish Flt** Collinstown. Transferred to Irish Air Corps at Baldonnel 12.7.22 as *BFI* and crashed 2.24.

E2412 (Falcon III) **1 AIS** ex **1 ASD** 22.9.18. **88 Sqn** dd ex 1 AIS 28.9.18 (engine 1409/WD51729), victs 30.10.18 (Lt A.H. Berg/2nd Lt W.J.N. Grant destroyed a Fokker D.VII in flames over Caumont at 09:00) and 4.11.18 (Lt C.E. Lacoste/Lt I.W.F. Agabeg destroyed a Fokker D.VII over Foucaumont at 13:05).

E2413 (Falcon III) **1 AIS** ex **1 ASD** 22.9.18. **48 Sqn**, victs 26.10.18 (Lt T.G. Rae/2nd Lt F.G. Smith destroyed a Fokker D.VII near Flobecq at 13:30, shared E2608) and 30.10.18 (Sgt N. Hunt/Sgt C.F. Levett sent a Fokker D.VII down OOC, SW of Audenarde at 13:30) then wrecked on OP, Brussels-Charleroi, 22.11.18 (Lt W. Grant/Sgt R.L.G. Waite both OK, force landed after running out of fuel – engine 1027/WD39411).

E2414 (Falcon III) **1 ASD** and destroyed by enemy action 23.9.18 (2hr 30min).

E2415 (Falcon III) **1 AIS** ex **1 ASD** 24.9.18. **48 Sqn** dd ex 1 AIS 29.9.18 (engine 1047/WD39416) and on unit charge until @ 30.9.18.

E2416 (Falcon III) **2 AIS** ex **1 ASD** 22.9.18. **62 Sqn** dd ex 2 AIS 25.9.18 and wrecked on Cross Country 16.2.19 (Lt E.R. Danks IOAS, force landed in mist near Yersekle, Holland – engine 1659/WD51854).

E2417 (Falcon III) **2 AIS** ex **1 ASD** 22.9.18. **62 Sqn** dd ex 2 AIS 25.9.18 and on unit charge until @ 30.9.18.

E2418 N/I

E2419 (Falcon III) **2 AIS** ex **1 ASD** 24.9.18. **20 Sqn** dd ex 2 AIS 26.9.18 (engine 417/WD32608) and wrecked on Practice Flight 11.4.19 (Lt Talbot/Lt Ford both OK, landed on rough ground on Ossogne aerodrome – engine 295/WD18647).

E2420 (Falcon III) **2 AIS** ex **1 ASD** 25.9.18. **20 Sqn** dd ex 2 AIS 1.10.18, LIA on 15:40 OP 8.10.18 (Lt F.W. Ely/2nd Lt J.G. McBride both KIA – engine 565/WD32682).

E2421 (Falcon III) **2 AIS** ex **1 ASD** 25.9.18. **11 Sqn** dd ex 2 AIS 28.9.18 and on unit charge until @ 2.8.19. **PD** Ascot. To India. **AD** Drigh Road. **5 Sqn**, marked as a/c *C* and named *Palace* by 10.24 until @ 1927.

E2422 (Falcon III) **2 AIS** ex **1 ASD** 26.9.18. **62 Sqn** dd ex 2 AIS 25.9.18 and on unit charge until @ 30.9.18.

E2423 (Falcon III) **1 ASD** by 30.9.18 (engine 257/WD18628). **5 AIS** ex 1 ASD 8.10.18. **20 Sqn** and vict 21.10.18 (Lt T.G. Rae/2nd Lt H.G. Lewis sent a Fokker D.VII down OOC over Petegem at 10:20) and on unit charge until @ 12.18. **24 Sqn** Kenley by 4.21.

E2424 (Falcon III) **2 AIS** ex **1 ASD** 28.9.18. **5 AIS** ex 2 AIS 1.10.18. **11 Sqn** by 1.11.18 until @ 1.8.19. **200 NTS** South Carlton by 11.9.19. **PD** Ascot. To Iraq. **AD** Hinaidi. **6 Sqn** by 11.22 until @ 5.25.

E2425 (Falcon III) **1 ASD** by 30.9.18 (engine 1073/WD39429). **1 AIS** ex 1 ASD 1.10.18. **22 Sqn** dd ex 1 AIS 9.10.18 and wrecked on Travelling Flight 19.3.19 (Lt Dixon Davis OK, crashed in snowstorm near Castle Bromwich when on special leave to England – same engine).

E2426 (Falcon III) **1 AIS** ex **1 ASD** 29.9.18 (engine 1689/WD51869) and on unit charge until @ 30.9.18. **'M' Flt** by 10.18 until @ 16.7.18.

E2427 (Falcon III) **1 ASD** by 30.9.18 (engine 1747/WD51898). **1 AIS** ex **1 ASD** 1.10.18 and tested 2.10.18.

E2428 (Falcon III) **1 ASD** dd ex Bristol 27.9.18 (Lt G.H. Richardson – engine 901/WD32850). **5 AIS** ex **1 ASD** 8.10.18. **11 Sqn** by 31.10.18 and wrecked 4.7.19 (Lt Shreeve/Lt W. Cougle both OK).

E2429 (Falcon III) **1 ASD** by dd ex **5 AAP** 27.9.18 (engine 1091/WD39438). **5 AIS** ex 1 ASD 4.10.18. **1 AIS** and tested 8.10.18. **20 Sqn** dd ex 2 AIS 13.10.18 and on unit charge until @ 12.18. **PD** Ascot. To India. **AD** Drigh Road. **20 Sqn**.

E2430 (Falcon III) **1 AIS** dd ex **1 ASD** 13.10.18 and tested that day. **48 Sqn** and wrecked after Travelling Flight from Sart 9.4.18 (2nd Lt L.C. Taylor OK, bad landing in gale conditions – engine 611/WD32703).

E2431 **RAF (Cadet) College** Cranwell by 5.23 and wrecked 31.7.23 (Flt Cdt F.W.L. Beaumont IIFA, stalled on landing).

E2432 **RAF (Cadet) College** Cranwell by 6.23 until @ 5.24. B&C for reconditioning to J Type (s/n 6909) and ready by 25.2.26. **CFS** Upavon by 5.26 until @ 6.26.

E2433 **PD** Ascot. To India. **AD** Drigh Road by 8.23 until @ 12.23. **20 Sqn** by 2.24. **AD** Drigh Road and caught fire in the air 4.3.24.

E2434 **RAF (Cadet) College** Cranwell as a/c *8* by 8.23 until @ 7.25. B&C for reconditioning to J Type (s/n 6911) and ready by 3.3.26. **1 FTS** Netheravon. **2 FTS** Duxford. **RAF (Cadet) College** Cranwell by 1.27 until @ 3.27.

F.2B E2450 of 31 Sqn at Lahore, India, in 1922. *(C&C)*

E2435 At Rouen ex SS *Hunsgate* for **2 ASD** 11.11.18. **1 ASD** dd ex Rouen 15.11.18. Old Sarum by 9.19 until @ 10.19. B&C for reconditioning to J Type (s/n 6530) and ready by 7.11.24. **2 FTS** Digby by 12.24 until @ 2.25. B&C for reconditioning. **2 FTS** Digby by 8.3.27.

E2436 **PD** Ascot. To India. **AD** Drigh Road. **AP** Lahore by 12.22 until @ 1.23. **5 FTS** by 12.23 until @ 6.24.

E2437 To India. **20 Sqn** by 12.20.

E2438 To Middle East **ASD ME** Aboukir dd ex England 13.10.19. **208 Sqn** and wrecked 2.9.20 (landed on rough ground at Helmiah).

E2439 At Rouen ex SS *Hunsgate* for **2 ASD** 11.11.18. **2 ASD** by 17.1.19.

E2440 (Falcon III) at Rouen ex SS *Hunsgate* for **2 ASD** 11.11.18. **1 ASD** by 15.11.18. **7 Sqn** and wrecked 14.4.19 (2nd Lt Edwards/2nd Lt boyd both OK, o/t on landing at Spich in gusty conditions – engine 63/WD18531).

E2441 N/I

E2442 To India. **28 Sqn** by 8.20 and wrecked 3.3.22 (collided with H1548 20 miles from Lahore).

E2443 N/I

E2444 **2 AIS** ex **1 ASD** 24.10.18.

E2445 N/I

E2446 To India. **20 Sqn** by 9.19.

E2447 To India. **20 Sqn** 6.21 until @ 7.21.

E2448 **PD** Ascot. To India. **AD** Drigh Road. **28 Sqn** and wrecked 7.5.21 (struck goalpost during practice bomb dropping on Ambala aerodrome). Repaired. **20 Sqn** as a/c *M* 1922.

E2449 N/I

E2450 **PD** Ascot. To India. **AD** Drigh Road. **31 Sqn** 1922.

E2451 (Falcon III) at maker's 21.6.18, allotted to BEF and to be delivered to **5 AAP**. At 5 AAP Bristol and tested 6.7.18 (Lt C.F. Uwins). **1 AIS** ex **1 ASD** 9.7.18. **88 Sqn** dd ex 1 AIS 9.7.18, victs 15.9.18 (Lt G.F. Anderson/Lt T.S. Chilton sent a Fokker D.VII down OOC, E of Seclin at 17:30) then wrecked after successful combat 30.10.18 (Lt G.F. Anderson/2nd Lt C.M.W. Elliott both WIA, destroyed a Fokker D.VII in flames and sent another OOC over Caumont at 09:00 then force landed within 400yds of an enemy outpost and abandoned under shell fire – engine 1221/WD51635) and deleted on unit. Salvaged and brought back onto RAF charge 16.11.18.

E2452 (Falcon III) presentation a/c *Montreal*. At maker's 21.6.18, allotted to BEF and to be delivered to **5 AAP**. At 5 AAP Bristol and tested 6.7.18 (Lt C.F. Uwins). **1 AIS** ex **1 ASD** 9.7.18. **20 Sqn** dd ex 1 AIS 9.7.18 (engine 1213/WD51631), vict 29.7.18 (Capt T.C. Traill/Lt R. Gordon-Bennett sent a Fokker D.VII down OOC, W of Gheluwe at 19:55) and wrecked after OP 22.8.18 (2nd Lt F.E. Finch/2nd Lt E.S. Harvey both OK, made bad landing in the dusk 20:30 – engine 1235/WD51642). **1 ASD** ex 20 Sqn 25.8.18 and deleted 26.8.18 (not worth reconstruction, 121hr 44min).

E2453 (Falcon III) presentation a/c *Dominica*. At maker's 21.6.18, allotted to BEF and to be delivered to **5 AAP**. At 5 AAP Bristol and tested 8.7.18 (Lt C.F. Uwins). **22 Sqn** dd ex **1 ASD** 12.7.18, LIA on 05:40 OP 27.8.18 (Lt J.J. Borrowman/2nd Lt J. Amos both KIA, last seen going S over the Arras-Cambrai road, apparently under control – engine 1205/WD51627) and deleted on unit that day (296hr 45min).

E2454 (Falcon III) at maker's 21.6.18, allotted to BEF and to be delivered to **5 AAP**. At **22 Sqn** dd ex **1 ASD** 12.7.18, victs 8.8.18 (Capt J.E. Gurdon/Lt C.G. Gass sent an Albatros D.V down OOC over Douai at 10:30 and destroyed a Pfalz D.III in flames NE of Vitry at 10:40, the Pfalz shared with E2466), 10.8.18 (Capt J.E. Gurdon/Lt C.G. Gass destroyed two Fokker D.VII, SW of Peronne at 18:10), 13.8.18 (Capt J.E. Gurdon/Lt C.G. Gass sent a Fokker D.VII down OOC over Auberchicourt at 11:20), 27.8.18 (Lt F.G. Gibbons/Lt J. McDonald sent a Fokker D.VII down OOC over Douai at 13:45), 5.9.18 (Lt F.G. Gibbons/Sgt G. Shannon sent a Fokker D.VII down OOC over Douai at 17:00) and 16.9.18 (Lt F.G. Gibbons/Sgt G. Shannon sent a Fokker D.VII down OOC over Quesnoy Wood at 15:30) then wrecked on Travelling Flight, Nivelles-Spich, 17.5.19 (Capt E.D. Atkinson/AC2 Edwards both OK, crashed in forced landing at Nivelles after engine failure – engine 1189/WD51619).

E2455 (Falcon III) presentation a/c *Udaipur No.2*. At maker's 21.6.18, allotted to BEF and to be delivered to **5 AAP**. At 5 AAP Bristol and tested 8.7.18 (Lt C.F. Uwins). **48 Sqn** dd ex **1 ASD** 13.7.18 (engine 1201/WD51625), LIA on 18:10 OP, Menin, 2.9.18 (2nd Lt I.M.B. McCulloch POW/2nd Lt L.P. Perry KIA, last seen E of Lille at 19:15 – same engine) and deleted on unit that day (124hr 5min).

E2456 (Falcon III) at maker's 21.6.18, allotted to BEF and to be delivered to **5 AAP**. At 1 AIS by 26.7.18 (engine 189/WD18594). **62 Sqn** dd ex 1 AIS 28.7.18 (same engine) and wrecked after OP 17.10.18 (2nd Lt L.A. Williamson/2nd Lt R. Davison both OK, smashed undercarriage in misjudged landing – engine 1509/WD51779). **2 ASD**.

E2457 (Falcon III) presentation a/c *Punjab No.44 Lahore No.4*. At maker's 21.6.18, allotted to BEF and to be delivered to **5 AAP**. At 5 AAP Bristol and tested 8.7.18 (Lt C.F. Uwins). **2 AIS** ex **1 ASD** 15.7.18. **62 Sqn** dd ex 2 AIS 18.7.18 (engine 1237/WD51643), marked as a/c *9*, victs 13.8.18 (Capt G.E. Gibbons/2nd Lt T. Elliott destroyed an EA C-type over Bullecourt at 10:25), 22.8.18 (Capt G.E. Gibbons/2nd Lt T. Elliott destroyed two Fokker D.VII, W of Pronville at 07:40), 3.9.18 (Capt G.E. Gibbons/2nd Lt T. Elliott sent two Fokker D.VII down OOC, N of Cambrai at 18:45) and 4.9.18 (Capt G.E. Gibbons/2nd Lt T. Elliott destroyed a Fokker D.VII and sent another down OOC over Abancourt at 09:30) then wrecked on Escort 24.9.18 (2nd Lt L. Hudson/2nd Lt A. Palmer both OK, machine damaged in combat near Cambrai and force landed on **107 Sqn** aerodrome – same engine). **2 ASD** ex 62 Sqn and deleted 6.10.18 (not worth reconstruction).

E2458 (Falcon III) at maker's 21.6.18, allotted to BEF and to be delivered to **5 AAP**. At 5 AAP Bristol and tested 12.7.18 (Lt C.F. Uwins). **1 AIS** ex **1 ASD** 19.7.18. **88 Sqn** dd ex 1 AIS 21.7.18, marked as a/c *8*, vict 30.10.18 (Lt W.A. Wheeler/2nd Lt W.B. Clarke sent a Fokker D.VII down OOC over Caumont at 09:00) and wrecked on Practice Flight 3.3.19 (2nd Lt W.R. Kellough KOAS, crashed from stall on climbing turn after take off – engine 213/WD18606).

E2459 (Falcon III) at maker's 21.6.18, allotted to BEF and to be delivered to **5 AAP**. At **1 AIS** ex **1 ASD** 16.7.18. **88 Sqn** dd ex 1 AIS 17.7.18, marked as a/c *12* and vict 18.18.18 (Lt Jeffrey/2nd Lt Woods sent a Fokker D.VII down OOC over Tournai at 12:45). 18.10.18 (Lt Jeffrey/2nd Lt Woods).

E2460 (Falcon III) at maker's 21.6.18, allotted to BEF and to be delivered to **5 AAP**. At **1 AIS** ex **1 ASD** 17.7.18. **88 Sqn** dd ex 1 AIS 18.7.18 and wrecked on Reconnaissance, Lille, 20.7.18 (2nd Lt V. Voss/2nd Lt C. Whinstanley both OK, crashed into wire fence during forced landing in the dark near Furnes – engine 1211/WD51630). **1 ASD** ex 88 Sqn 26.7.18 and deleted 29.7.18 (not worth reconstruction, 9hr 20min).

E2461 **5 AAP** Bristol tested 13.7.18 (Lt C.F. Uwins). **2 AIS** to **11 Sqn** 28.9.18.

E2462 **5 AAP** Bristol tested 13.7.18 (Lt C.F. Uwins). **39 Sqn** North Weald by 1.8.18 (Lt Manning/AM1 A.T.C. Stagg) until @ 9.8.18. Wrecked 6.1.19 (Lt C. McLaughlin IIFA, failed to accomplish crosswind take off and drifted into another machine – Casualty Card gives no further details).

E2463 **5 AAP** Bristol tested 13.7.18 (Lt C.F. Uwins). **141 Sqn** Tallaght and wrecked 6.5.19 (hit trees during forced landing in fog). **PD** Ascot. To India. **AD** Drigh Road. **5 Sqn** by 7.24.

E2464 **1 FS** Turnberry by 25.7.18.

E2465 **1 FS** by 1.8.18 until @ 1.10.18 (Capt J.H. Letts). **27 TDS** Crail by 14.10.18 until @ 4.11.18.

E2466 (Falcon III) **5 AAP** Bristol tested 14.7.18 (Lt C.F. Uwins). **2 AIS** ex **2 ASD** 21.7.18. **22 Sqn** dd ex 2 AIS 22.7.18, marked as a/c *I* (possibly also *T*), victs 8.8.18 (Capt W.F.J. Harvey/Capt D.E. Waight destroyed two Pfalz D.III NE of Vitry at 10:40, one shared with E2454) and reported on unit 19.8.19 as unsafe to fly (engine 2409/WD52049).

E2467 (Falcon III) **2 AIS** ex **2 ASD** 25.7.18. **20 Sqn** dd ex 2 AIS 28.7.18 (engine 1181/WD51615), vict 16.9.18 (Lt N.S. Boulton/Sgt J. Dodds sent a Fokker D.VII down OOC, W of Lesdin at 08:25) then wrecked 8.10.18 (Lt H.B. Hartland/2nd Lt B.M. La Praike both OK, struck hangar on landing – engine 1313/WD51681). **2 ASD** ex 20 Sqn and deleted 22.10.18 (not worth reconstruction).

E2468 (Falcon III) **5 AAP** Bristol tested 18.7.18 (Lt C.F. Uwins). **1 AIS** ex **1 ASD** 22.7.1018. **62 Sqn** dd ex 1 AIS 24.7.18 (engine 1203/WD51626), LIA on Escort (Lt A.B. Cort/2nd Lt J.N. Mitchell both KIA, shot down in flames at 10,000ft N of Peronne, crew fell out when machine turned on back – same engine) and deleted on unit that day (28hr 40min).

E2469 (Falcon III) **5 AAP** Bristol tested 16.7.18 (Lt C.F. Uwins). **2 AIS** ex **1 ASD** 28.7.18. **48 Sqn** dd ex 2 AIS 9.8.18 (engine 1179/WD51614), LIA on 18:10 OP, Menin, 31.8.18 (2nd Lt J.B. Cowan/Sgt R.L.G. White both OK, machine hit by AA fire and forced to land in bad country near Elverdinghe at 20:00 (same engine). **1 ASD** ex 48 Sqn 4.9.18 and deleted 7.9.18 (not worth reconstruction, 51hr 10min).

E2470 (Falcon III) **5 AAP** Bristol tested 17.7.18 (Lt C.F. Uwins). **1 AIS** ex **1 ASD** 1.8.18 (engine 1225/WD51637). **20 Sqn** dd ex 1 AIS 4.8.18 (same engine), LIA on 14:33 OP 23.10.18 (Lt H.L. Pennal/ Sgt G. Aitken both KIA, last seen in combat low over Aulnoye – engine 1593/WD51821) and deleted on unit that day.

E2471 (Falcon III) **5 AAP** Bristol tested 21.7.18 (Lt C.F. Uwins). **1 ASD** by 26.7.18 (engine 1183/WD51616). **20 Sqn** dd ex 1 ASD 28.7.18 (same engine), vict 29.7.18 (Sgt Mech J.J. Cowell MM/ Cpl C.W. Hill sent a Fokker D.VII down OOC, NW of Wervicq), LIA on 18:25 OP 30.7.18 (Sgt J.J. Cowell DCM MM & Bar/Cpl C. Hill both KIA, shot down in flames near Ypres – same engine) and deleted on unit that day (12hr 9min).

E2472 (Falcon III) **5 AAP** Bristol tested 20.7.18 (Lt C.F. Uwins). **1 ASD** by 26.7.18 (engine 1395/WD51722). **2 AIS** ex 1 ASD 28.7.18. **48 Sqn** dd ex 2 AIS 8.8.18 (same engine), destroyed in enemy bombing raid on Bertangles aerodrome on the night of 24/25.8.18 (engine 539/WD32669) and deleted on unit.

E2473 (Falcon III) **1 ASD** by 26.7.18 (engine 1361/WD51705). **1 AIS** ex 1 ASD 8.8.18. **'L' Flt** dd ex 1 AIS 9.8.18 and wrecked after Artillery Observation 14.8.18 (Lt A.H. Read/2nd Lt L.A. Hooper both OK, overshot landing and collided with roller – same engine). **1 ASD** ex 'L' Flt and presume deleted.

E2474 (Falcon III) **5 AAP** Bristol tested 20.7.18 (Lt C.F. Uwins). **2 AIS** ex **1 ASD** 25.7.18. **88 Sqn** dd ex 2 AIS 28.7.18 (engine 1375/WD51712), victs 29.7.18 (Lt J.P. Findlay/2nd Lt R.E. Hasell destroyed a Fokker D.VII in flames over Bois Grenier at 18:20), 6.9.18 (Lt J.P. Findlay/2nd Lt W. Tinsley sent a Fokker D.VII down OOC, E of Douai at 18:45) and 30.10.18 (Lt J.G. Fleming/Sgt W.J. Spaulding sent two Fokker D.VII down OOC over Caumont at 09:00) then wrecked on Firing Practice 2.4.19 (2nd Lt T. Blythe/2nd Lt H. Bradbury both OK, force landed after propeller shot through – engine 1437/WD51743). To England. **PD** Ascot. To India. **AD** Drigh Road. Risalpur 8.23.

E2475 (Falcon III) **5 AAP** Bristol tested 19.7.18 (Lt C.F. Uwins). **62 Sqn** dd ex **2 AIS** 27.7.18 (engine 1355/WD51702) and wrecked before Practice Patrol 16.8.18 (2nd Lt L.B. Raymond/2nd Lt D.S. Hamilton both OK, swerved on take off and ran into long corn – same engine).

E2476 (Falcon III) **5 AAP** Bristol tested 20.7.18 (Lt C.F. Uwins). **1 ASD** by 26.7.18 (engine 1399/WD51724). **2 AIS** ex 1 ASD 28.7.18. **11 Sqn** dd ex 2 AIS 9.8.18, vict 11.8.18 (Lt H.A. Hay/2nd Lt E.J. Norris destroyed an Albatros near Peronne at 19:10) and still on unit charge 29.7.19. **12 Sqn** Heumar. To UK 12.20. **PD** Ascot. To Iraq. **AD** Hinaidi. **AHQ Iraq Command Training Flt** by 9.28 until @ 10.28.

E2477 (Falcon III) **5 AAP** Bristol tested 19.7.18 (Lt C.F. Uwins). **1 ASD** by 26.7.18 (engine 1431/WD51740). **1 AIS** ex 1 ASD 28.7.18. **22 Sqn** dd ex 1 AIS 1.8.18, vict 25.9.18 (Lt F.G. Gibbons/2nd Lt J.A. Oliver destroyed Fokker D.VII over Bourlon Wood at 18:10), LIA on OP 27.9.18 (Capt S.F.H. Thompson/2nd Lt C.J. Tolman both KIA, last seen over Cambrai – engine 1627/WD51838) and deleted on unit that day (100hr 45min).

E2478 (Falcon III) **5 AAP** Bristol tested 21.7.18 (Lt C.F. Uwins). Farnborough dd ex 5 AAP 16.10.18 (Lt G.H. Richardson). **141 Sqn** Biggin Hill 1918.

E2479 (Falcon III) **1 ASD** by 26.7.18 (engine 681/WD32740). **1 AIS** ex 1 ASD 4.8.18 (same engine). **2 AIS** ex 1 AIS 4.8.18. **62 Sqn** dd ex 2 AIS 11.8.18, LIA on OP 1.9.18 (2nd Lt L.B. Raymond/2nd Lt D.S. Hamilton both POW, last seen going down under control near Cambrai at 13:40 – same engine) and deleted on unit that day (30hr 40min).

E2480 (Falcon III) **2 AIS** ex **1 ASD** 30.7.18. **48 Sqn** dd ex 2 AIS 9.8.18 (engine 1341/WD51695), destroyed in enemy bombing raid on Bertangles aerodrome on the night of 24/25.8.18 (same engine) and deleted on unit.

E2481 (Falcon III) **5 AAP** Bristol tested 24.7.18 and 25.7.18 (Lt C.F. Uwins). **1 AIS** ex **1 ASD** 1.8.18. **88 Sqn** dd ex 1 AIS 2.8.18. (engine 1437/WD51743) and victs 18.10.18 (Lt Hanmer/2nd Lt A. Trantor sent a Fokker D.VII down OOC over Tournai at 12:45) and 30.10.18 (Lt J.L. Des Lauriers/2nd Lt F.A. Lewis sent a Fokker D.VII down OOC over Caumont at 09:00).

E2482 (Falcon III) **48 Sqn** dd ex **1 ASD** 27.8.18 (engine 1403/WD51726) and wrecked after OP 5.9.18 (2nd Lt W. Sanders/2nd Lt C.R. Pickering both OK, collided on landing with E2267 – same engine). **1 ASD** ex 48 Sqn 6.9.18 and deleted 9.9.18 (not worth reconstruction, 53hr 27min).

E2483 (Falcon III) **5 AAP** Bristol 25.7.18, allotted to BEF and tested 27.7.18. **1 ASD** and deleted 8.8.18 on reconstruction as F6404 (2hr 55min) but serial compromised and given new serial H7291.

E2484 (Falcon I) **5 AAP** Bristol tested 29.7.18 (Lt C.F. Uwins). **1 (Obs) SAG** New Romney and wrecked 18.11.18 (2nd Lt R.F. Allen/Lt G.C. Scarr both KIFA, crashed in forced landing – engine 1/F/205/WD10404).

E2485 N/I

E2486 **5 AAP** Bristol tested 29.7.18 (Lt C.F. Uwins). **AGS** Eastchurch by 1.21.

E2487 **5 AAP** Bristol tested 27.7.18 (Lt C.F. Uwins). **1 (Obs) SAG** New Romney marked as a/c *24* and crashed at Manston.

E2488 N/I

E2489 N/I

E2490 N/I

E2491 (Falcon III) **5 AAP** Bristol tested 31.7.18 (Lt C.F. Uwins). **1 ASD** by 14.8.18 (engine 1347/WD51698). **1 AIS** ex 1 ASD 23.8.18. **22 Sqn** dd ex 1 AIS 29.8.18 and wrecked on Wireless Practice 30.8.18 (2nd Lt J.G. Walker/2nd Lt D.B. Halley both KOAS, stalled near the ground, bounced and crashed – same engine). **1 ASD** ex 22 Sqn 30.8.18 and deleted 2.9.18 (5hr 30min).

E2492 (Falcon III) **5 AAP** Bristol tested 30.7.18 and 31.7.18 (Lt C.F. Uwins). **1 ASD** by 5.8.18 (engine 1393/WD51721). **2 AIS** ex 1 ASD 10.8.18. **48 Sqn** dd ex 2 AIS 20.8.18 (same engine), vict 2.9.18 (2nd Lt W.S. Rycroft/2nd Lt H.C. Wood sent a Fokker D.VII down OOC, N of Menin at 19:30) then wrecked on OP, Commines, 6.9.18 (2nd Lt W.S. Rycroft WIA/2nd Lt H.C. Wood OK, force landed near Poperinghe after fuel pressure system damaged by AA fire – same engine). **1 ASD** ex 48 Sqn 9.9.18 and deleted 13.9.18 (not worth reconstruction, 43hr 25min).

E2493 (Falcon III) **5 AAP** Bristol tested 31.7.18 and 6.8.18 (Lt C.F. Uwins). **1 ASD** by 14.8.18 (engine 1457/WD51753). **1 AIS** ex 1 ASD 15.8.18. **20 Sqn** dd ex 1 AIS 22.8.18 (same engine), victs 15.9.18 (Lt N.S. Boulton/Lt G.W. Pearce sent a Fokker D.VII down OOC, NE of St Quentin at 11:10) and 20.9.18 (Lt N.S. Boulton/Sgt E.G. Mitchell destroyed a Fokker D.VII, NE of St Quentin at 10:15) then wrecked on OP 10.11.18 (2nd Lt H. Foster/Sgt W.R. Greenfield both OK, force landed near Esqueheries after engine pressure trouble – engine 1821/WD51935).

E2494 (Falcon III) **5 AAP** Bristol tested 11.8.18 (Lt C.F. Uwins). **2 AIS** ex **1 ASD** 18.8.18. **62 Sqn** dd ex 2 AIS 27.8.18 and wrecked on 12:15 OP 1.9.18 (Lt L.W. Hudson OK/2nd Lt J. Hall WIA, controls shot through in combat near Cambrai and crashed in forced landing near Monchy aux Bois – engine 1359/WD51704). **2 ASD** ex 48 Sqn via **9 AP** and deleted 24.9.18 (not worth reconstruction, 14hr 30min).

E2495 (Falcon III) **1 ASD** by 14.8.18 (engine 1459/WD51754). **1 AIS** ex 1 ASD 24.8.18 (same engine). **48 Sqn** dd ex 1 AIS 3.9.18 (same engine), LIA on 11:10 OP, Menin, 5.9.18 (2nd Lt R. Beesley/2nd Lt A.M. Miller both POW, brought down in combat – same engine) and deleted on unit that day (5hr 50min).

E2496 **39 Sqn** North Weald by 6.8.18 until @ 10.8.18 (Lt Kirkes/ AM1 A.T.C. Stagg). **48 Sqn** dd ex **1 ASD** 27.8.18 (engine 535/WD32667) and wrecked on OP 3.9.18 (Lt G. Thornton-Norris/2nd Lt A.M. Miller both OK, had to leave the formation due to the engine overheating and crashed on landing – same engine). **1 ASD** ex 48 Sqn 5.9.18.

E2497 (Falcon III) **2 AIS** ex **1 ASD** 10.8.18. **62 Sqn** dd ex 2 AIS 12.8.18 and on unit charge until @ 30.9.18.

E2498 (Falcon III) **2 AIS** ex **1 ASD** 13.8.18. **48 Sqn** dd ex 2 AIS 22.8.18 (engine 1401/WD51725), LIA on 17:00 OP 3.10.18 (Lt J.A. Sykes KIA/Sgt S. Kitchin POW, brought down in combat over Ingelmunster – engine 1685/WD39409) and deleted on unit that day.

E2499 (Falcon III) **1 ASD** by 5.8.18 (engine 1127/WD39456). **1 AIS** ex 1 ASD 9.8.18. **22 Sqn** dd ex 1 AIS 11.8.18, victs 13.8.18 (Lt H.H. Beddow/2nd Lt T.J. Birmingham sent two Pfalz D.III down OOC over Auberchicourt at 11:00) and wrecked after OP 14.8.18 (Lt H.H. Beddow/2nd Lt T.J. Birmingham both OK, over-estimated distance in landing and collided with the armoury – engine 1033/WD39409). **1 ASD** ex 22 Sqn 15.8.18 and presume deleted.

E2500 (Falcon III) **1 ASD** by 5.8.18 (engine 1527/WD51788). **1 AIS** ex 1 ASD 9.8.18. **22 Sqn** dd ex 1 AIS 9.8.18, victs 21.8.18 (Lt F.C. Stanton/2nd Lt C.J. Tolman sent an EA C-type down OOC over Albert at 19:45) and 27.8.18 (Lt F.C. Stanton/2nd Lt C.J. Tolman sent a Fokker D.VII down OOC, SE of Seulemont at 14:00) then wrecked after OP 2.9.18 (Lt F.C. Stanton/2nd Lt C.J. Tolman both OK, landed at 20:10 in semi darkness in a ploughed field near the aerodrome and o/t – same engine). **1 ASD** ex 22 Sqn 4.9.18.

E2501 **5 AAP** Bristol tested 6.8.18 (Lt C.F. Uwins). B&C for reconditioning to J Type (s/n 6614) and ready by 9.2.25. To India.

Reconditioned J-Type F.2B E2501 'R' of 5 Sqn aloft over India, complete with spare wheel beneath the gunner's cockpit. *(RAF Museum)*

31 Sqn by 1.26 until @ 2.26. **5 Sqn** as a/c *R* by 6.27 until @ 2.28. Photographed in India marked as a/c *5*.

E2502 N/I

E2503 N/I

E2504 B&C for reconditioning to J Type (s/n 6610) and ready by 9.2.25.

E2505 **5 AAP** Bristol tested 7.8.18 (Lt C.F. Uwins). **24 Sqn** Kenley by 6.22. **Irish Flt** Collinstwown by 8.22. **24 Sqn** Kenley by 2.23. **1 FTS** Netheravon.

E2506 (Falcon III) **1 ASD** by 14.8.18 (engine 1357/WD51793). **1 AIS** ex 1 ASD 15.8.18 (same engine). **88 Sqn** dd ex 1 AIS 20.8.18 (same engine) and vict 30.10.18 (Lt J. Baird/Sgt C. Hill destroyed a Fokker D.VII over Caumont at 09:00). **12 Sqn** marked as a/c *A2* 12.18 until @ 8.19.

E2507 (Falcon III) **5 AAP** Bristol tested 11.8.18 (Lt C.F. Uwins). **1 ASD** dd ex 5 AAP 12.8.18 (Lt G.H. Richardson – engine 1525/WD51787). **2 AIS** ex 1 ASD 18.8.18. **48 Sqn** dd ex 2 AIS 27.8.18 (same engine), victs 3.10.18 (Capt F.J. Cunninghame/Lt R.A. Brunton MC destroyed two Fokker D.VII, one in flames and another crashed N of Lendelede at 17:50) then wrecked after successful combat on OP, Courtrai, 14.10.18 (Capt F.J. Cunninghame/Lt T.C. Jones sent a Fokker D.VII down OOC, W of Thielt at 08:55 but crashed on landing when trying to avoid a crashed machine in the centre of the aerodrome – same engine). **1 ASD** ex 48 Sqn and deleted 18.10.18 (not worth reconstruction).

E2508 (Falcon III) **1 ASD** by 14.8.18 (engine 1411/WD51730). **2 AIS** ex 1 ASD 16.8.18. **62 Sqn** dd ex 2 AIS 23.8.18, wrecked on Test Flight 18.9.18 (Lt J.V. Lind/Pte W.J. Gale both KOAS, engine cut out at 100ft, pilot tried to turn but machine dived in and burst into flames – same engine) and deleted on unit that day (45hr 5min).

E2509 (Falcon III) **5 AAP** Bristol tested 17.8.18 (Lt C.F. Uwins). **2 AIS** dd ex 1 ASD 18.8.18. **62 Sqn** dd ex 2 AIS 23.8.18, wrecked on Line Patrol 29.9.18; Shot down by AA 29.9.18 (Lt R.R. O'Reilly/2nd Lt L.E. Mitchell both KIA, machine broke up in the air at 6,000ft over Dury, possibly hit by artillery shell – same engine) and deleted on unit that day (48hr 45min).

E2510 (Falcon III) **5 AAP** Bristol tested 15.8.18 (Lt C.F. Uwins). **2 AIS** ex 1 ASD 21.8.18. **48 Sqn** dd ex 2 AIS 27.8.18 (engine 1501/WD51775), and wrecked on 15:45 OP (2nd Lt H. Thomas/2nd Lt F.H.V. Coomer both OK, shot up in combat – same engine). 1 ASD and deleted 14.10.18 (not worth reconstruction).

E2511 (Falcon III) **2 AIS** ex **1 ASD** 21.8.18. **48 Sqn** dd ex 2 AIS 27.8.18 (engine 889/WD32844), victs 5.10.18 (Sgt J. Moffat/AM S. Julian destroyed a Fokker D.VII, E of Armentieres, pilot seen to jump), 22.10.18 (Sgt N. Hunt/Sgt C.F. Levett destroyed a Fokker near Peldenhoek at 10:20) and 4.11.18 (Sgt N. Hunt/Sgt Maj C.J. O'Toole destroyed a Fokker D.VII in flames NW of Lessines at 15:15) then wrecked on Practice Flight 2.1.19 (Sgt N. Hunt/Sgt C.F. Perkin both OK, bad landing in gale – engine 1401/WD51725).

E2512 (Falcon III) **5 AAP** Bristol tested 17.8.18 (Lt C.F. Uwins). **1 AIS** ex 1 ASD 23.8.18. **20 Sqn** dd ex 1 AIS 25.8.18 (engine 827/WD32813), LIA on 10:20 OP 15.9.18 (Lt F.E. Finch POW WIA/2nd Lt C.G. Russell POW, last seen near St Quentin – same engine) and deleted on unit that day (43hr 30min).

E2513 (Falcon III) **5 AAP** Bristol tested 17.8.18 (Lt C.F. Uwins). **2 AIS** ex **1 ASD** 23.8.18. **62 Sqn** dd ex 2 AIS 2.9.18, LIA on OP 4.11.18 (Lt F. Sumsion/Capt W.G. Walford both KIA, brought down in combat SW of Mons, probably by Ltn H. Lange, Jasta 36 – engine 1565/WD51807) and deleted on unit that day.

E2514 (Falcon III) **1 AIS** ex 1 ASD 23.8.18. **22 Sqn** dd ex 1 AIS 24.8.18, marked as a/c *K*, LIA on 05:40 OP 27.8.18 (Lt F.M. Sellars POW/2nd Lt T.B. Collis KIA, last seen going SE of Arras under control and probably brought down by Obltn Frommherz, Jasta 27 – engine 1497/WD51773) and deleted on unit that day (10hr 50min).

E2515 (Falcon III) **2 AIS** ex 1 ASD 24.8.18. **62 Sqn** dd ex 2 AIS 2.9.18, LIA on Escort 24.9.18 (Lt N.N. Coope/2nd Lt H.S. Mantle both POW WIA, last seen near Cambrai at 08:00 and machine captured – engine 1477/WD51763) and deleted on unit that day (30hr 50min).

E2516 (Falcon III) **5 AAP** Bristol tested 19.8.18 (Lt C.F. Uwins). **1 AIS** ex 1 ASD 24.9.18 (engine 575/WD32687). **22 Sqn** dd ex 1 AIS 31.8.18 and wrecked after successful combat on 08:25 OP 2.9.18 (Lt I.O. Stead OK/2nd Lt W.A. Cowie WIA, sent a Fokker D.VII down OOC over Arras-Cambrai road at 09:15 but shot through tank in combat and force landed in shelled area at 09:30 – same engine). **1 ASD** ex 22 Sqn 5.9.18 and presume deleted.

E2517 (Falcon III) **5 AAP** Bristol tested 19.8.18 (Lt C.F. Uwins). **1 AIS** ex 1 ASD 1.9.18 (engine 1545/WD51797). **22 Sqn** dd ex 1 AIS 17.9.18, LIA on OP 29.9.18 (Lt C.W. Thompson/Lt L. James both POW, last seen in combat E of Cambrai – same engine) and deleted on unit that day (50hr).

E2518 (Falcon III) **5 AAP** Bristol 20.8.18 for **154 Sqn (Mobilising)** as a training machine and tested that day (Lt C.F. Uwins). **154 Sqn** Chingford dd ex Bristol 21.8.18 (engine 1557/WD31803) but reallotted to BEF 26.8.18. **1 ASD** by 31.8.18 (same engine). **1 AIS** ex 1 ASD 12.9.18 (same engine). **62 Sqn** dd ex 1 AIS 17.9.18 and on unit charge until @ 12.18.

E2519 (Falcon III) **5 AAP** Bristol 20.8.18 allotted to **154 Sqn (Mobilising)** as a training machine. **154 Sqn** Chingford dd 22.8.18 but reallotted to BEF 26.8.18. **1 ASD** by 31.8.18 (engine 323/WD18661). **1 AIS** ex 1 ASD 31.8.18. **22 Sqn** dd ex 1 AIS 3.9.18, LIA on 14:30 OP 16.9.18 (2nd Lt W. Kellow/2nd Lt H.A. Felton both KIA, last seen going down OOC, E of Cambrai – same engine) and deleted on unit that day (20hr 15min).

E2520 (Falcon III) **5 AAP** Bristol tested 22.8.18 (Lt C.F. Uwins). **1 ASD** by 31.8.18 (engine 297/WD18648). **1 AIS** ex 1 ASD 3.9.18. **48 Sqn** dd ex 1 AIS 6.9.18 and wrecked on OP 29.9.18 (2nd Lt J. Cowan/2nd Lt L.N. Jones both OK, collided in mid-air with E2530, escorted back to aerodrome by S.E.5a but crashed on landing – engine 1585/WD51817). **1 ASD** ex 48 Sqn 30.9.18 and deleted 4.10.18 (not worth reconstruction).

E2521 (Falcon III) **5 AAP** Bristol tested 20.8.18, 21.8.18 and 22.8.18 (Lt C.F. Uwins). **1 AIS** ex **1 ASD** 23.8.18. **'L' Flt** dd ex 1 AIS 27.8.18, LIA on 11:00 Photography 1.9.18 (Lt G.L. Barritt/2nd Lt R.H.G. Boys both POW, brought down OOC by EA over canal de la Sensee – engine 603/WD32701) and deleted on unit that day (13hr 20min).

E2522 (Falcon III) **5 AAP** Bristol tested 20.8.18 (Lt C.F. Uwins). **48 Sqn** dd ex **1 ASD** 27.8.18 (engine 282/WD18640) and wrecked after vict 4.10.18 (2nd Lt T.G. Rae/2nd Lt R. Pickering both OK, destroyed a Fokker D.VII near Wambrechies at 12:50 then force landed in mist near Mont des Cats – engine 1573/WD51811). **1 ASD** ex 48 Sqn and deleted 9.10.18 (not worth reconstruction).

E2523 (Falcon III) **48 Sqn** dd ex **1 ASD** 27.8.18 (engine 675/WD32737), LIA on 17:00 OP, Courtrai 3.10.18 (2nd Lt J.B. Cowan/Lt L.N. Jones both KIA, brought down in flames in combat over Ingelmunster at 18:30 – engine 1705/WD51877) and deleted on unit that day.

E2524 (Falcon III) **48 Sqn** dd ex **1 ASD** 27.8.18 (engine 1549/WD51799, vict on Bombing, Coutrai 9.10.18 (Lt G.F. Manning/Sgt H.F. Monday sent a Fokker D.VII down OOC and on fire at 10:50) and wrecked on OP, Tournai-Renaix 1.11.18 (Lt G.F. Manning/Lt W.E. Harper both OK, became lost in fog and force landed near Le Frein – engine 675/WD32737).

E2525 (Falcon III) presentation a/c *Auckland*. **5 AAP** Bristol tested 24.8.18 (Lt C.F. Uwins). **2 AIS** ex **1 ASD** 29.8.18. **62 Sqn** dd ex 2 AIS 4.9.18, LIA on Escort 15.9.18 (Lt T.H. Broadley/2nd Lt R.H. Dillaway both KIA, last seen going down under control after combat with 20 EA near Cambrai at 16:30 – engine 433/WD32616) and deleted on unit that day (11hr 30min).

E2526 (Falcon III) **5 AAP** Bristol tested 23.8.18 and 24.8.18 (Lt C.F. Uwins). **1 ASD** by 31.8.18 (engine 531/WD32665). **1 AIS** ex 1 ASD 31.8.18. **48 Sqn** dd ex 1 AIS 4.9.18 (same engine) and on unit charge until @ 30.9.18. **2 FTS** by 4.25.

E2527 (Falcon III) **5 AAP** Bristol 23.8.18 allotted to **154 Sqn (Mobilising)** but reallotted to BEF 26.8.18. **48 Sqn** dd ex **1 ASD** 27.8.18 (engine 1585/WD51817), vict 2.9.18 (Lt H.A. Cole/2nd Lt J.W. London sent a Fokker D.VII down OOC over Menin at 17:00-17:30), LIA on OP, Menin, 12.9.18 (Lt H.A. Cole/2nd Lt C.R. Gage both POW, became lost in thunderstorm – engine 1197/WD51623) and deleted on unit that day (31hr 25min).

E2528 (Falcon III) **1 ASD** by 15.9.18 (engine 237/WD18618). **2 AIS** ex 1 ASD 17.9.18. **62 Sqn** dd ex 2 AIS 19.9.18, LIA on 06:45 Escort 9.10.18 (Lt J.E. Sitch/2nd Lt D.S. Fox both POW, last seen going down SE of Cambrai at about 08:00 after combat – same engine) and deleted on unit that day.

E2529 (Falcon III) **5 AAP** Bristol 23.8.18 allotted to **154 Sqn (Mobilising)** but reallotted to BEF 26.8.18. **1 ASD** by 31.8.18 (engine 1577/WD51813). **2 AIS** ex 1 ASD 4.9.18. **9 Sqn** dd ex 2 AIS 5.9.18 (same engine). **3 Sqn AFC** on loan by 30.9.18. **O Flight** ex 9 Sqn 23.10.18 (same engine) and wrecked before Travelling Flight 9.11.18 (2nd Lt Paistra/2nd Lt Sturgeon both OK, ran into a sunken road on take off – same engine). **PD** Ascot. To Iraq. **AD** Hinaidi. **6 Sqn**.

E2530 (Falcon III) **1 ASD** by 31.8.18 (engine 789/WD32794). **1 AIS** ex 1 ASD 4.9.18. **48 Sqn** dd ex 1 AIS 6.9.18, wrecked on OP 29.9.18 (2nd Lt W.S. Rycroft/2nd Lt H.C. Wood both IOAS, collided in mid-air and crashed in forced landing in no man's land – same engine) and deleted on unit that day.

E2531 (Falcon III) **1 ASD** by 31.8.18 (engine 1575/WD51812). **1 AIS** ex 1 ASD 7.9.18. **48 Sqn** dd ex 1 AIS 9.9.18 (same engine) and wrecked on 11:00 OP 1.10.18 (Lt E.C. Shirley/Sgt R.L.G White both OK, machine badly shot up in aerial combat – same engine). **1 ASD** ex 48 Sqn and deleted 9.10.18 (not worth reconstruction).

E2532 (Falcon III) **1 AIS** ex **1 ASD** 7.9.18. **48 Sqn** dd ex 1 AIS 13.9.18 (engine 21/WD18510), vict 28.9.18 (Capt F.J. Cunninghame/2nd Lt R.A. Brunton destroyed one of 6 Fokker D.VII, SE of Roulers at 14:45), LIA on 12:15 OP 26.10.18 (2nd Lt H. Thomas POW/2nd Lt F.H.V. Coomer POW WIA, last seen over Tournai – same engine) and deleted on unit that day.

E2533 (Falcon III) **1 AIS** ex **1 ASD** 5.9.18. **88 Sqn** dd ex 1 AIS 7.9.18 (engine 1433/WD51741) and victs 2.10.18 (Capt E.C. Johnston/Sgt C.M. Maxwell destroyed two Fokker D.VII in flames and drove down another over Neuve Chapelle at 08:10-08:25). **12 Sqn** as a/c C6 by 10.19 until @ 18.5.20. **SAC** Old Sarum by 12.22, in propeller accident 26.3.23 (Plt Off E.B. Forester OK/AC2 F. Willock IIGA) and on unit charge until @ 6.23; B&C for reconditioning to J Type (s/n 6550) and ready by 29.11.24. **PD** Ascot. To Egypt. **AD** Aboukir. **208 Sqn** by 10.28 until @ 11.28. **6 Sqn** by 4.31. **AD** Aboukir by 30.6.32.

E2534 (Falcon III) **1 ASD** by 31.8.18 (engine 613/WD32706). **1 AIS** ex 1 ASD 3.9.18. **48 Sqn** dd ex 1 AIS 4.9.18 (same engine), vict 3.10.18 (2nd Lt G. Thornton-Norris/Sgt R.L.G. White destroyed a Fokker D.VII in flames NW of Iseghem at 17:50) then wrecked on OP 25.10.18 (2nd Lt G. Thornton-Norris/Sgt R.L.G. White both OK, force landed near Deerlyck after hit by enemy AA fire – same engine). **1 ASD** ex 48 Sqn and deleted 31.10.18 (not worth reconstruction).

E2535 **141 Sqn** Biggin Hill 1918.

E2536 (Falcon III) **1 ASD** dd ex **5 AAP** Filton 1.9.18 (Lt G.H. Richardson). **2 AIS** ex 1 ASD 7.9.18. **20 Sqn** dd ex 2 AIS 17.9.18 (engine 1629/WD51839) and on unit charge until @ 30.9.18.

E2537 (Falcon III) **2 AIS** ex **1 ASD** 4.9.18. **11 Sqn** dd ex 2 AIS 6.9.18 and wrecked on Travelling Flight, Aulnoye-Bonneville, 14.12.18 (Sgt Mech R. McGlasson OK, o/t by wind when axle bent on landing and smashed wheel – engine 1261/WD51655).

E2538 N/I
E2539 At Rouen ex SS *Hunsgate* 11.11.18 for **2 ASD**.
E2540 N/I
E2541 N/I
E2542 N/I
E2543 To India. **20 Sqn** by 9.19 until @ 4.10.19. **114 Sqn**. Returned to UK. **5 FTS** Sealand by 3.30.
E2544 N/I
E2545 **AGS** Eastchurch by by 5.22.
E2546 (Falcon III) **2 Sqn** Manston and wrecked 29.4.21 (Fg Off R.G. Mullette/AC2 L.H. Hall both IOAS, stalled and sideslipped into trees on take off from Fermoy).
E2547 N/I
E2548 N/I
E2549 N/I
E2550 **5 AAP** Bristol tested 3.9.18 (Lt C.F. Uwins). **2 FS** Marske and wrecked 28.10.18 (2nd Lt E. Taviner/Flt Cdt E. Lloyd both KIFA, in mid-air collision and crashed into sea – engine WD18400).
E2551 **100 Sqn** Baldonnel by 5.21 until @ 6.21.
E2552 B&C for reconditioning to J Type (s/n 6628) and ready by 25.2.25. **PD** Ascot. To India. **AD** Drigh Road by 11.30 until @ 6.31.

E2553 **106 Sqn** Fermoy.
E2554 (Falcon III). **1 ASD** by 15.9.18 (engine 1603/WD51826). **11 Sqn** dd ex **2 ASD** 17.9.18 and wrecked on Practice Flight 8.4.19 (Lt C. Simar/2nd Lt Jackson both OK, misjudged landing and crashed – engine 1721/WD51885).
E2555 (Falcon III) **20 Sqn** by 7.9.18. **11 Sqn** dd ex **1 ASD** 8.12.18 and wrecked 20.5.19 (Lt C.H.N. Ashlin/AC Wright both OK, crashed near Lontzen).
E2556 (Falcon III) **5 AAP** Bristol 21.8.18 allotted to **154 Sqn** but allotment cancelled 21.8.18. **1 AIS** ex **1 ASD** 13.9.18 (engine 1257/WD51653). **22 Sqn** dd ex 1 AIS 20.9.18 and wrecked on Cross Country 1.7.19 (Lt G.J. Hole/Lt W.A. Hall both OK, crashed near Liege – engine 1107/WD39446). **10 SS** ex 22 Sqn.
E2557 (Falcon III) **5 AAP** Bristol 21.8.18 allotted to **154 Sqn** but allotment cancelled 21.8.18. **1 ASD** by 15.9.18 (engine 1613/WD51831). **2 AIS** ex 1 ASD 17.9.18. **11 Sqn** dd ex 2 AIS 17.9.18 and wrecked on Passenger Flight 26.4.19 (Lt H.Y. Lewis/Major General Watson both OK, crashed landing at Penhurst).
E2558 **5 AAP** Bristol 21.8.18 allotted to to **154 Sqn** Chingford.
E2559 (Falcon III) **5 AAP** Bristol allotted to **154 Sqn** but allotment cancelled 21.8.18 and tested 9.9.18 (Lt C.F. Uwins). **1 ASD** by 15.9.18 (engine 1607/WD51828). **2 AIS** ex 1 ASD 16.9.18. **62 Sqn** dd ex 2 AIS 16.9.18 and wrecked on Test Flight 29.3.19 (Lt H.V. Edwards/Lt Davidson both OK, force landed near Marcq – same engine).
E2560 (Falcon III) **1 AIS** ex **1 ASD** 13.9.18. (engine 1611/WD51830). **22 Sqn** dd ex 1 AIS 17.9.18 and wrecked on Practice Flight 12.6.19 (Lt Huxley OK, struck standing corn and o/t when undershot landing – same engine).
E2561 (Falcon III) **1 ASD** by 15.9.18 (engine 1533/WD51792). **2 AIS** ex 1 ASD 17.9.18. **20 Sqn** dd ex 2 AIS 18.9.18 (same engine), LIA on OP 29.9.18 (Lt N.S. Boulton/Lt C.H. Case both KIA, last seen over the lines – same engine) and deleted on unit that day (16hr 35min).
E2562 (Falcon III) **5 AAP** Bristol and tested 11.9.18 (Lt C.F. Uwins). **1 ASD** by 15.9.18 (engine 725/WD32762). **2 AIS** ex 1 ASD 17.9.18. **20 Sqn** dd ex 2 AIS 20.9.18 (same engine), LIA on OP 23.9.18 (Lt J. Nicholson/2nd Lt B.W. Wilson both KIA, brought down in flames near Villers Outreux at 17:25, brobably by Vzfw Ungewitter, Jasta 24 – same engine) and deleted on unit that day (6hr 25min).
E2563 **5 AAP** Bristol and tested 12.9.18 and 8.10.18 (Lt C.F. Uwins). **1 AIS** ex **1 ASD** 18.10.18. **88 Sqn** dd ex 1 AIS 4.11.18.
E2564 **5 AAP** Bristol tested 10.9.18 (Lt C.F. Uwins). **Development Sqn** Gosport by 6.19.
E2565 (Falcon III) **1 ASD** by 15.9.18 (engine 1639/WD51844). **11 Sqn** dd ex **2 AIS** 17.9.18 and wrecked before Travelling Flight 22.4.19 (Lt J.P. Cox/Lt P.C. Bayley both OK, ran into a hole on take off – same engine).
E2566 (Falcon III) **1 AIS** ex **1 ASD** 21.9.18. **22 Sqn** dd ex 1 AIS 29.9.18 and wrecked after Travelling Flight 27.9.18 (Lt F.E. Turner/Lt C.E. Clarke both OK, ran into a ditch on landing – engine 1653/WD51851). **1 ASD** ex 22 Sqn 28.10.18 and deleted 31.10.18 (not worth reconstruction).
E2567 N/I
E2568 (Falcon III) **5 AAP** Bristol and tested 13.9.18 (Lt C.F. Uwins). **2 AIS** ex **1 ASD** 19.9.18. **20 Sqn** dd ex 2 AIS 20.9.18 (engine 1615/WD51832), LIA on 09:30 OP 27.9.18 (2nd Lt F. Turner/2nd Lt C. Clarke both KIA, last seen near St Quentin – same engine) and deleted on unit that day (16hr 58min).
E2569 (Falcon III) **5 AAP** Bristol and tested 15.9.18 (Lt C.F. Uwins). **2 AIS** ex **1 ASD** 19.9.18. **11 Sqn** dd ex 2 AIS 24.9.18 and wrecked on Reconnaissance 27.9.18 (2nd Lt E.T. Clacey IOAS/2nd Lt A. Nisbett OK, crashed in dark in ploughed field near Duoullens during second forced landing due to petrol trouble – engine 775/WD32787). **2 ASD** ex 11 Sqn 27.9.18 and deleted 29.9.18 (9hr 25min).
E2570 (Falcon III) **1 AIS** ex **1 ASD** 21.9.18. **4 Sqn** dd ex 1 AIS 29.9.18 (engine 1671/WD51860) and on unit charge until @ 30.9.18. **M Flight** and wrecked on Weather Test 23.10.18 (Lt McLeod IOAS/Lt Watson OK, landed on rough ground short of the aerodrome and crashed – same engine). **1 ASD** ex 'M' Flt and deleted 26.10.18 (not worth reconstruction).
E2571 **5 AAP** Bristol and tested 14.9.18 (Lt C.F. Uwins).
E2572 N/I
E2573 (Falcon III) **5 AAP** Bristol and tested 15.9.18 and 16.9.18 (Lt C.F. Uwins). **11 Sqn** and victs 1.10.18 (Lt C.R. Smythe/2nd Lt W.T. Barnes destroyed a Fokker D.VII at 08:20 and sent another down OOC at 08:25 both S of Le Cateau).

E2574 **5 AAP** Bristol and tested 16.9.18 (Lt C.F. Uwins). **141 Sqn** Biggin Hill, to Ireland with unit 14.3.19 and on unit charge until @ 29.7.19.

E2575 (Falcon III) **1 ASD** dd ex **8 AAP** 19.9.18. **1 AIS** ex 1 ASD 23.9.18. **22 Sqn** dd ex 1 AIS 29.9.18. **8 AAP** Lympne ex 22 Sqn 19.8.19 (Lt Gregson). **APS** Andover until @ 3.20.

E2576 (Falcon III) **1 AIS** ex **1 ASD** 21.9.18. **22 Sqn** dd ex 2 AIS 29.9.18. **8 AAP** Lympne ex 22 Sqn 19.8.19 (Lt Wrathall).

E2577 **39 Sqn** North Weald by 19.9.18 until @ 10.18.

E2578 (Falcon III) **1 AIS** ex **1 ASD** 24.9.18 (engine 377/WD18688). **22 Sqn** dd ex 1 AIS 1.10.18 and wrecked on OP 21.10.18 (2nd Lt F.C. Stanton OK/2nd Lt J.A. Oliver IOAS, force landed near Arras after engine seized – same engine). **1 ASD** ex 22 Sqn 23.10.18 and deleted 26.10.18 (not worth reconstruction).

E2579 (Falcon III) **1 AIS** ex **1 ASD** 21.9.18. **88 Sqn** dd ex 1 AIS 22.9.18 (engine 533/WD18688) and wrecked on Special Mission 18.10.18 (Capt A. Hepburn/2nd Lt D.A. Vavasour both OK, longerons shot through by enemy ground fire – same engine). **1 ASD** ex 88 Sqn 19.10.18 and deleted 21.10.18 (not worth reconstruction).

E2580 (Falcon III) **2 AIS** ex **1 ASD** 25.9.18. **62 Sqn** dd ex 2 AIS 28.9.18 and on unit charge until @ 30.9.18. **PD** Ascot. To Mesoptamia. **AD** Hinaidi. **6 Sqn** by 1930.

E2581 **1 Communications Sqn** Hendon. **39 Sqn**. Preserved with IWM.

E2582 N/I

E2583 (Falcon III) **1 ASD** by 30.9.18 (engine 407/WD32603). **1 AIS** ex 1 ASD 18.10.18 and tested 19.10.18. **48 Sqn** and LIA on OP, Tournai-Ath, 4.11.18 (Lt I. Glaze/2nd Lt C.W. Newstead both POW, last seen in combat over Lessines – same engine).

E2584 (Falcon III) **2 AIS** ex **1 ASD** 23.9.18. **20 Sqn** dd ex 2 AIS 26.9.18 (engine 401/WD32603) and on unit charge until @ 30.9.18.

E2585 **141 Sqn** Biggin Hill 1918.

E2586 **2 AIS** ex **1 ASD** 26.9.18. **5 AIS** ex 2 AIS 3.10.18. **11 Sqn** by 1.11.18 until @ 1.19.

E2587 (Falcon III) **2 AIS** ex **1 ASD** 28.9.18. **11 Sqn** and wrecked on Travelling Flight 1.11.18 (Sgt Mech R. McGlasson/2nd Lt F. Brown OK, crashed in a misjudged landing at Beauvois – engine 1703/WD51876).)

E2588 (Falcon III) **2 AIS** ex **1 ASD** 24.9.18. **20 Sqn** dd ex 2 AIS 27.9.18 (engine 1741/WD51895) and wrecked after OP 28.10.18 (Lt R.B. Tapp/2nd Lt W.H. Welch both OK, tail skid struck hole on landing and broke longerons – same engine).

E2589 (Falcon III) **1 AIS** ex **1 ASD** 5.10.18 and tested 8.10.18. **48 Sqn** and wrecked before OP, Courtrai-Renaix, 28.10.18 (Sgt J. Moffatt/ AM1 E. Norris both OK, crashed shortly after take off due to engine failure – engine 673/WD32736). **1 ASD** ex 48 Sqn.

E2590 (Falcon III) **1 ASD** by 30.9.18 (engine 717/WD32758). **5 AIS** ex 1 ASD 4.10.18. **20 Sqn**, wrecked on OP 23.10.18 (Lt F.R. Goodearle KOAS/Lt A. McBride IOAS, collided in the air with E2403 – same engine) and deleted on unit that day.

E2591 (Falcon III) **2 AIS** ex **1 ASD** 28.9.18. **5 AIS** ex **2 ASD** 1.10.18. **11 Sqn**, LIA on 09:50 Reconnaissance, Cambrai area, 7.10.18 (Sgt Mech A.L. Cridlan/Sgt Mech G.E. Fuller both KIA) and deleted on unit that day.

E2592 (Falcon III) **1 AIS** ex **1 ASD** 29.9.18 (engine 1733/WD51891) and on unit charge until @ 30.9.18. **48 Sqn** LIA on OP, Tournai-Ath, 4.11.18 (2nd Lt J. McNamara/2nd Lt J. Pugh both POW, last seen in combat over Lessines – same engine). Presume deleted on unit.

E2593 (Falcon III) **1 ASD** by 30.9.18 (engine 1719/WD51884). **2 AIS** ex 1 ASD 2.10.18. **20 Sqn** dd ex 2 AIS 7.10.18, wrecked after OP 27.10.18 (Lt S.L. Walters OK/Lt P.B. de Moyse-Bucknell IOAS, landed in rough ground on the aerodrome – engine 1377/WD51713) and deleted on unit that day.

E2594 (Falcon III) **'M' Flt** by 11.18 and wrecked before Travelling Flight to Elsenborn 22.12.18 (Lt Mcleod/Sgt Hassall both OK, engine cut out at 50ft on take off and in landing the machine was caught by a gust of wind and the wing hit the ground – engine 1751/WD51900).

E2595 (Falcon III) **1 ASD** by 30.9.18 (engine 609/WD32704). **1 AIS** ex 1 ASD 8.10.18. **62 Sqn** and wrecked on Test Flight 7.1.19 (Capt F.G.C. Weare/Lt S.B. Perry both OK, stalled over trees after engine failure and crashed onto aerodrome – same engine).

E2596 (Falcon III) **1 ASD** by 30.9.18 (engine 1759/WD51904). **1 AIS** ex 1 ASD 1.10.18 and tested 3.10.18. **48 Sqn** and victs 30.10.18 (Lt T.G. Rae/Lt E. Watson destroyed a Fokker D.VII in flames near Meldon at 15:45) and 4.11.18 (Lt T.G. Rae/2nd Lt R. Evans destroyed a Fokker D.VII in flames over Enerbeck at 15:15).

E2597 (Falcon III) **1 ASD** by 30.9.18 (engine 1777/WD51913). **2 AIS** ex 1 ASD 1.10.18. **20 Sqn** dd ex 2 AIS 14.10.18 and wrecked after OP 17.10.18 (Lt R.B. Tapp/2nd Lt W.H. Welsh both OK, collided with hangar on landing – same engine). **2 ASD** ex 20 Sqn. **Andover SF** by 9.29.

E2598 (Falcon III) **1 ASD** by 30.9.18 (engine 1743/WD51896). **5 AIS** ex 1 ASD 4.10.18.

E2599 (Falcon III) **1 ASD** by 5.10.18. **'M' Flt** dd ex 1 ASD 19.11.18 and wrecked on Patrol 22.11.18 (Lt R.H. Schroeder/Lt F.A. Franklin both OK, ran short of fuel due to leaking tank, landed

Above: **On 23 November 1918 the D.H.9s of 211 Sqn at Clary were inspected by the CO of the 22nd Wing. Two of the three seen here are E8880 'S' and D551. Also at Clary on that day, Lt W. Knight of 20 Sqn misjudged his landing in Bristol F.2B E2603 following a practice patrol. Although Knight and his observer, Lt D.M. Lapraik, both escaped unharmed, the Bristol was wrecked. Its sad remains are seen on the extreme right of the main picture, and in the inset enlargement.**
(Philip Jarrett)

on rough ground just clear of the aerodrome and o/t – engine 1745/WD51897).

E2600 (Falcon III) **1 ASD** by 30.9.18 (engine 1633/WD51841). **2 AIS** ex 1 ASD 1.10.18. **11 Sqn** by 1.11.18 until @ 10.19. **PD** Ascot. To India. **AD** Drigh Road. **AP** Lahore by 7.24. Transferred to Afghan Air Force 8.24.

E2601 (Falcon III) **1 AIS** ex **1 ASD** 5.10.18. **22 Sqn** dd ex **2 AIS** 9.10.18. **8 AAP** Lympne ex 22 Sqn 20.8.19 (Lt Feathers).

E2602 **5 AAP** Bristol and tested 30.9.18 (Lt C.F. Uwins). **2 AIS** ex **1 ASD** 8.10.18. **11 Sqn** by 1.11.18 and wrecked 7.6.19 (Sgt J. Gamble/ Sgt A. Bell both OK).

E2603 **5 AAP** Bristol and tested 30.9.18 (Lt C.F. Uwins). **5 AIS** ex **1 ASD** 5.10.18. **20 Sqn** and wrecked on Practice Patrol 23.11.18 (Lt W. Knight/2nd Lt D.M. Lapraik both OK, misjudged landing – engine 1505/WD51777).

E2604 **5 AAP** Bristol and tested 30.9.18 (Lt C.F. Uwins). **141 Sqn** Biggin Hill 1918.

E2605 (Falcon III) **5 AAP** Bristol and tested 1.10.18 (Lt C.F. Uwins). **2 ASD** ex **1 ASD** 17.10.18. **20 Sqn** 10.18. **11 Sqn** by 8.4.19 (Capt M.leB. Smith) and still on unit charge 30.7.19. **PD** Ascot. To India. **AD** Drigh Road. **AP** Lahore by 29.1.24. **28 Sqn** as a/c *C* by 7.24 and wrecked 7.7.25 (wheel collapsed in rough ground at Akora, NWF). Repaired. **20 Sqn** as a/c *L* by 8.24 until @ 11.25.

E2606 **5 AIS** ex **1 ASD** 4.10.18. **2 ASD** and deleted 23.10.18 (not worth reconstruction).

E2607 **5 AAP** Bristol and tested 2.10.18 (Lt C.F. Uwins). **Experimental Flt** Gosport for RN Signal School, Portsmouth by 10.18 until @ 4.19. **Development Sqn, 'D' Flt** Gosport by 6.19 until 1920.

E2608 (Falcon III) **1 AIS** dd ex **1 ASD** 5.10.18. **48 Sqn** and victs 26.10.18 (Capt F.J. Phillips/2nd Lt J.W. London destroyed a Fokker D.VII near Flobecq at 13:30, shared with E2413) and 28.10.18 (Capt F.J. Phillips/2nd Lt J.W. London forced an LVG C-type to land near Cellas at 10:00, shared E2281). **11 Sqn** by 26.6.19.

E2609 (Falcon III) **1 AIS** dd ex **1 ASD** 5.10.18 and tested 7.10.18. **48 Sqn** LIA on Line Patrol, R. Scheldt, 27.10.18 (2nd Lt W. Saunders/ 2nd Lt H. Lewis both POW – engine 464/WD32632) and deleted on unit that day.

E2610 (Falcon III) **5 AAP** Bristol and tested 2.10.18 (Lt C.F. Uwins). **1 AIS** dd ex **1 ASD** 13.10.18 and tested 16.10.18. **88 Sqn** dd ex 1 AIS 18.10.18, marked as a/c *3* and wrecked on Travelling Flight to new aerodrome 21.11.18 (2nd Lt Dair IOAS, crashed on Mons Road, near Bavay, due to bad weather – engine 85/WD18542).

E2611 **5 AAP** Bristol and tested 6.10.18 (Lt C.F. Uwins). **27 TDS** Crail by 26.10.18 until @ 9.11.18 (Lt F.A. Beardmore) and photographed there unarmed.

E2612 **1 AIS** dd ex **1 ASD** 13.10.18. **88 Sqn** and victs 30.10.18 (Lt K.B. Conn/2nd Lt K.C.W. Craig destroyed a Fokker D.VII and sent another down in flames near Caumont at 09:00) and 4.11.18 (Lt K.B. Conn/2nd Lt K.C.W. Craig destroyed a Fokker D.VII near Foucaumont at 13:05).

E2613 **5 AAP** Bristol and tested 7.10.18 and 10.10.18 (Lt C.F. Uwins). **5 FTS** Sealand by 3.30.

E2614 (Falcon III) **5 AAP** Bristol and tested 7.10.18 (Lt C.F. Uwins). **27 TDS** Crail by 13.10.18 until @ 23.10.18 (Lt F.A. Beardmore).

E2615 (Falcon III) **5 AAP** Bristol and tested 7.10.18 (Lt C.F. Uwins). **1 AIS** dd ex **1 ASD** 18.10.18. **22 Sqn** dd ex 1 AIS 22.10.18 and wrecked on Travelling Flight 24.4.19 (Lt-Col L.A. Strange OK, turned on nose during forced landing at Cognelee in bad weather – engine WD32837).

E2616 **27 TDS** Crail 11.18 photographed unarmed.

E2617 (Falcon III) **22 Sqn** and wrecked on Passenger Flight 24.1.19 (Lt D.C. Davis/Capt Phillips both OK, hit a tree during forced landing after becoming lost in mist – engine 1815/WD51932).

E2618 (Falcon III) **5 AAP** Bristol and tested 10.10.18 and 12.10.18 (Lt C.F. Uwins). **1 ASD** and wrecked on Ferry Flight to **70 Sqn** 8.11.18 (Lt W.J. Rivett-Carnac OK, machine turned on nose when landing, due to wind and soft ground – engine 1819/WD51934).

E2619 N/I

E2620 **5 AAP** Bristol and tested 10.10.18 (Lt C.F. Uwins).

E2621 N/I

E2622 N/I

E2623 **ES** Orfordness. **ECD** Grain dd ex Orfordness 28.6.19.

E2624 **5 AAP** Bristol and tested 12.10.18 (Lt C.F. Uwins). **33 TDS** Witney by 12.18. **4 Sqn** Farnborough as a/c *4A* 1921. B&C for reconditioning to J Type (s/n 6575) and ready by 22.12.24. B&C for reconditioning to J Type (s/n 6866) and ready by 25.11.25. **RAF College** Cranwell by 5.28 until @ 1.31.

E2625 (Falcon III) **48 Sqn** and LIA on OP, Tournai-Ath, 4.11.18 (Capt A. Harcourt-Vernon/2nd Lt D. Lee both POW, last seen in combat over Lessines – engine 615/WD32707).

E2626 **5 AAP** Bristol and tested 11.10.18 (Lt C.F. Uwins).

E2627 **5 AAP** Bristol tested 13.8.18 (Lt C.F. Uwins). Yatesbury.

Evidently undergoing an engine test, E2627 has its cowlings off, and it seems that an unfortunate air mechanic is sitting on the tailskid in the snow. *(Ken Smy/ SAAF Museum)*

E2628 (Falcon III) **22 Sqn** and wrecked on Travelling Flight, Nivelles-Spich, 17.5.19 (Lt D.E. Davies/AC Jones both OK, crashed in forced landing at Liege after engine failure – engine 701/WD32750).

E2629 **5 AAP** Bristol tested 18.7.18 (Lt C.F. Uwins). **12 Sqn** by 20.8.19 (Lt J.W. Baker). B&C for reconditioning to J Type (s/n 6552) and ready by 4.12.24. **PD** Ascot. To Egypt. **AD** Abouokir. **6 Sqn** marked as a/c *4*.

E2630 **5 AAP** Bristol and tested 13.10.18 (Lt C.F. Uwins). **12 Sqn** as a/c *A3* by 27.6.19 until @ 15.11.20 (Lt J.W. Baker). Force landed 27.11.19. B&C for reconditioning to Mk.III DC (s/n 7119) and ready by 18.7.27. **HAD** Henlow. **Home Communications Flt** dd ex HAD by road 27.4.28.

E2631 **2 FS** Marske marked as a/c *77* early 1919.

E2632 N/I

E2633 **5 AAP** Bristol and tested 15.10.18, 16.10.18 and 18.10.18 (Lt C.F. Uwins).

E2634 **5 AAP** Bristol and tested 13.10.18 (Lt C.F. Uwins). **27 TDS** Crail 11.18, photographed with leader's streamer.

E2635 (Falcon III) **5 AAP** Bristol and tested 15.10.18 (Lt C.F. Uwins). **48 Sqn** and wrecked on Test Flight 9.11.18 (Major K.R. Park/Sgt E. Curson both OK, hit telephone wires when landing with missing engine – engine 219/WD18609).

E2636 (Falcon) **1 ASD** dd ex **8 AAP** Lympne 24.2.19.

E2637 (Falcon) **88 Sqn** dd ex **1 AIS** 4.11.18.

E2638 N/I

E2639 **5 AAP** Bristol and tested 13.10.18 (Lt C.F. Uwins).

E2640 **33 TDS** Witney by 12.18.

E2641 (Falcon III) **5 AAP** Bristol and tested 17.10.18 (Lt C.F. Uwins). **M Flight** dd ex **1 ASD** 18.11.18 (engine 1829/WD51939) and on unit charge until @ 3.3.19.

E2642 **33 TDS** Witney and wrecked 29.10.18 (Flt Cdt J.H.L. Cowin IIFA, hit trees and crashed – engine 51883).

E2643 **12 Sqn** dd ex **1 ASD** 25.8.19 and marked as a/c *A5*. **IAAD** Henlow tested 24.1.24-29.1.24. **AGS** Eastchurch by 3.24. B&C for reconditioning to J Type (s/n 6838) and ready by 27.10.25. **2 FTS** Digby by 4.26 until @ 1.27. B&C for reconditioning to DC (s/n 7175) and ready by 20.6.28.

E2644 (Falcon III) **20 Sqn** and wrecked on Practice Flight 31.12.18 (Lt S.L. Walters/Lt E.W. Kirkpatrick both OK, landed on soft ground – engine 667/WD32733).

E2645 (Falcon III) **6 AIS** and wrecked on Delivery Flight 11.2.19 (Lt Fowler OK, broke tail skid and longerons on landing – engine 1974/WD51998).

E2646 N/I

E2647 **5 AAP** Bristol and tested 19.10.18 (Lt C.F. Uwins). **PD** Ascot. To Egypt. **AD** Aboukir. **4 FTS** Abu Sueir by 5.30.

E2648 (Falcon III) **1 ASD** and wrecked on Ferry Flight 28.10.18 (Lt Lyon OK, overshot landing at Reception Park and flew into a hangar – engine 1941/WD51995).

E2649 (Falcon III) delivered 11.18. **88 Sqn** and wrecked 25.4.19 (Lt R.J. Twilton/Sgt P. Gaillard both OK, misjudged landing and crashed on aerodrome – engine 1895/WD51972). **8 Sqn** by 8.19.

E2650 Delivered 28.12.18. **20 Sqn** 1919.

250 BRISTOL FIGHTER F.2B ordered 22.2.18 under Contract 35A/62/C.33 (B.R.360) from Angus Sanderson & Co, Newcastle-upon-Tyne and numbered E2651 to E2900. (200hp Arab). Deliveries from w/e 3.5.19. 100 cancelled and 126 delivered by 23.8.19.

E2651 dd w/e 3.5.19.
E2652 N/I
E2653 N/I
E2654 N/I
E2655 **5 (E)ARD** Henlow reallotted from Southern Area to Polish Military Purchase Mission 15.3.20 and despatched to Handley Page, Cricklewood 29.3.20. Replaced by D.H.9 for Poland and reallotted Inland Area for disposal 19.4.20.
E2656 **5 (E)ARD** Henlow reallotted from Southern Area to Polish Military Purchase Mission 15.3.20 and despatched to Handley Page, Cricklewood 29.3.20. Replaced by D.H.9 for Poland and reallotted Inland Area for disposal 19.4.20.
E2657 to E2661 } N/I
E2662 **PD** Ascot. To Egypt. **AD** Aboukir. **6 Sqn** and wrecked 24.9.24 (Shot down by machine gun fire, Shiram Irlag, Iraq).
E2663 to E2755 } N/I
E2756 **SAC** Worthy Down by 18.4.19.
E2757 to E2762 } N/I
E2763 **141 Sqn** wrecked 7.5.19 (2nd Lt W.F. King KIFA/Pte M. Fyfe IIFA, crashed in misjudged landing at Tallaght – engine 3325/WD88987).
E2764 to E2771 } N/I
E2772 **27 Sqn.**
E2773 to E2799 } N/I
E2800 Delivered 9.9.19.
E2801 to **E2900** cancelled 1.19.

250 BRISTOL FIGHTER F2B ordered 20.3.18 under Contract 35a/47/C.27 from the Standard Motor Co Ltd, Coventry and numbered E5179 to E5428. (200hp Arab). [E5253 to E5428 transferred to parent company as sequence nos. 5659 to 5714, mostly to store?]. E5309-E5428 cancelled. Only the following identified:

E5179 (Arab) **1 AAP** Coventry by 21.3.19, allotted to BEF but reallotted to Ministry of Munitions Aircraft Salvage Depot Waddon 29.3.19, with machine and engine surplus to RAF requirements.
E5219 Became *G-EBDB*. To AMC 7.22.
E5282 **5 (E)ARD** Henlow allotted to Polish Military Purchase Mission 15.3.20 but reallotted to Inland Area for disposal 19.4.20.

[E5253/87 Puma engine, 1919, s/n 5659 to 5664 & E5259/5308 1919, s/n 5665 to 5714].

150 BRISTOL FIGHTER F.2B ordered 20.3.18 on B.R.392 under Contract 35a/428/C.307 (B.R.392) from The Gloucestershire Aircraft Co Ltd, Cheltenham and numbered E9507 to E9656. Work stopped 20.9.19. (200hp Arab).

E9507 to E9523 } N/I
E9524 **5 AAP** Bristol and tested 20.10.18 (Lt C.F. Uwins).
E9525 N/I
E9526 N/I
E9527 N/I
E9528 N/I
E9529 **AICS** Worthy Down and wrecked 12.11.18 (Capt J. Bussey/Sgt Millar both OK, crashed into hedge near aerodrome during forced landing after engine failure).
E9530 to E9541 } N/I
E9542 Delivered 5.4.19.
E9543 N/I
E9544 **20 Sqn.**

E9545 to E9571 } N/I
E9572 (Arab) in France 16.12.18, allotted to BEF.
E9573 (Arab) **8 Sqn** dd ex **2 ASD** 7.12.18 and wrecked on Aerial Post 15.12.18 (Lt Trites/Lt Hicklin both OK, landed on soft ground near Bousignies after engine failure – engine E2013).
E9574 N/I
E9575 (Arab) **8 Sqn** dd 16.12.18. **1 ASD** Merheim ex 8 Sqn 12.7.19.
E9576 (Arab) in France 4.1.19, allotted to BEF. **8 Sqn.**
E9577 (Arab) in France 23.12.18, allotted to BEF.
E9578 (Arab) in France 23.12.18, allotted to BEF. **8 Sqn** dd ex **1 ASD** 26.12.18. **2 ASD** ex 8 Sqn 28.1.19. **12 Sqn** marked as a/c *B3* and photographed crashed (Lt Curry).
E9579 (Arab) in France 21.12.18, allotted to BEF.
E9580 (Arab) in France 22.1.19, allotted to BEF.
E9581 N/I
E9582 (Arab) **5 (E)ARD** Henlow 15.2.19, allotted to BEF. **9 Sqn** by 5.7.19. **1 ASD** ex 9 Sqn 19.7.19.
E9583 (Arab) in France 9.1.19, allotted to BEF. **59 Sqn** Duren. **1 ASD** ex 59 Sqn 17.7.19.
E9584 (Arab) in France 2.1.19, allotted to BEF.
E9585 N/I
E9586 N/I
E9587 (Arab) in France 4.1.19, allotted to BEF.
E9588 (Arab) in France 4.1.19, allotted to BEF. **9 Sqn** dd ex **1 ASD** 14.5.19 (engine 3075/WD27240). **1 ASD** ex 9 Sqn 15.7.19.
E9589 (Arab) in France 2.1.19, allotted to BEF.
E9590 (Arab) **5 (E)ARD** Henlow 15.2.19, allotted to BEF and despatched 2.19.
E9591 N/I
E9592 (Arab) **5 (E)ARD** Henlow 15.2.19, allotted to BEF and despatched 3.19.
E9593 **3 (W)ARD** Yate 8.2.19, allotted to BEF.
E9594 (Arab) **5 (E)ARD** Henlow 6.3.19, allotted to BEF.
E9595 (Arab) in France 22.1.19, allotted to BEF. **9 Sqn** dd ex **6 AIS** 27.4.19 (engine 3053/WD27178). **1 ASD** ex 9 Sqn 15.7.19.
E9596 **3 (W)ARD** Yate 8.2.19, allotted to BEF and despatched 3.19.
E9597 (Arab) en route to BEF 14.2.19, reallotted from **5 (E)ARD** to BEF. **12 Sqn** as a/c *C3* and photographed nosed up on landing 1919.
E9598 **8 Sqn** dd ex **6 AIS** 6.6.19. **1 ASD** ex 8 Sqn 15.7.19.
E9599 N/I
E9600 N/I
E9601 N/I
E9602 (Arab) **5 (E)ARD** Henlow 15.2.19, allotted to BEF and despatched 3.19. **9 Sqn** dd ex **6 AIS** 27.4.19 (engine 3089/WD27214) and on unit charge until @ 14.6.19.
E9603 (Arab) en route from **5 (E)ARD** to BEF 11.2.19, allotted to BEF.
E9604 (Arab) en route from **5 (E)ARD** to BEF 11.2.19, allotted to BEF.
E9605 N/I
E9606 **59 Sqn** by 30.6.19. **1 ASD** ex 59 Sqn 17.7.19.
E9607 With BEF by 21.3.19. **1 ASD** and wrecked on Ferry Flight to **6 AIS** 2.4.19 (Sgt N.V. Morgan OK, o/t during forced landing in ploughed field – engine 53882).
E9608 N/I
E9609 With BEF by 21.3.19. **12 Sqn** marked as a/c *A6*.
E9610 **8 Sqn** dd ex **6 AIS** 20.5.19. **8 SS** ex 8 Sqn 29.5.19.
E9611 **33 TDS** Witney by 5.11.18 until @ 16.11.18 (2nd Lt G.A. Raybone). With BEF ex **5 (E)ARD** 10.4.19. **8 Sqn** dd ex **6 AIS** 21.5.19. **1 ASD** ex 8 Sqn 17.7.19.
E9612 **33 TDS** Witney by 27.10.18 until @ 19.11.18 (2nd Lt G.A. Raybone) 11.18.
E9613 (Arab) **3 (W)ARD** Yate 1.3.19, allotted to BEF. **8 Sqn** dd ex **6 AIS** 21.5.19. **8 SS** ex 8 Sqn 30.5.19.
E9614 (Arab) **3 (W)ARD** Yate 1.3.19, allotted to BEF.
E9615 N/I
E9616 To India. **5 Sqn** by c.24 until @ 1927. **20 Sqn** NW Frontier. **AP** Drigh Road by 11.5.29.
E9617 (Arab) France 26.2.19, allotted to BEF. **9 Sqn** dd ex **6 AIS** 28.4.19. **1 ASD** ex 9 sqn 20.6.19.
E9618 To India. **20 Sqn.**
E9619 (Arab) **5 AAP** Bristol by 24.12.18, allotted to BEF. To India. **20 Sqn.**
E9620 to E9650 } N/I
E9651 **5 (E)ARD** by 14.3.19 with BEF allotment cancelled and for deletion.

E9652
to   } N/I
E9656

200 BRISTOL FIGHTER F.2B ordered 9.4.18 from Standard Motor Co Ltd under Contract 35a/47/C.27 to be numbered F301 to F550. Cancelled.

200 BRISTOL FIGHTER F.2B ordered from British & Colonial Aeroplane Co Ltd, Bristol and numbered F1231 to F1430. Order cancelled and serials reallocated.

700 BRISTOL FIGHTER F.2B ordered 12.4.18 (and 5.6.18) under Contracts 35a/779/C658 & AS.3117/1/18 (B.R.448) from The British & Colonial Aeroplane Co Ltd, Filton and numbered F4271 to F4970. (175hp Falcon III). [Consecutive works' sequence nos. 4257 to 4956].

F4271   **5 AAP** Bristol and tested 23.10.18 (Lt C.F. Uwins).
F4272   N/I
F4273   N/I
F4274   Presentation a/c *Barnstaple (Devon)*. **'M' Flt** by 11.18 until @ 5.3.19.
F4275   (Falcon III) **20 Sqn** and wrecked 25.1.19 (2nd Lt W. Knight OK, tailskid broke on landing at Thuilles and sternpost hit the ground – engine 59/WD18529).
F4276   **5 AAP** Bristol 24.10.18 for **138 Sqn (Mobilising)** Chingford as a training machine, despatched to squadron 2.11.18 but crashed en route.
F4277   Presentation a/c *Carlton Colville*.
F4278   **CFS** Upavon by 11.20 until @ 3.21. B&C for reconditioning to J Type (s/n 6687) and ready by 18.4.25.
F4279   N/I
F4280   To 7 Bde Italy. **34 Sqn** dd ex **7 AP** 21.1.19. **7 AP** ex 34 Sqn 24.2.19.
F4281   **5 AAP** Bristol 25.10.18 allotted to **138 Sqn (Mobilising)**. **138 Sqn** by 10.18 until @ 11.18. Northolt dd ex B&C 13.10.27.
F4282   **1 FTS** Netheravon by 6.24.
F4283   **5 AAP** Bristol 30.10.18 for **138 Sqn (Mobilising)** Chingford. **138 Sqn** dd 2.11.18. Reallotted to D of T Worthy Down 9.12.18.
F4284   **CFS** Upavon by 7.21 until 10.21. **School of Photography** Farnborough by 1.24.
F4285   (Falcon III) At **1 (S)ARD** 17.4.19, reallotted from 7 Bde to 1 (S)ARD. **CFS** Upavon by 2.21. B&C for reconditioning to J Type (s/n 6551) and ready by 29.11.24. **PD** Ascot. To Egypt. **AD** Aboukir. **14 Sqn** by 11.25. **AD** Aboukir and rebuilt as FR4285. Swung on nose landing, Ramleh, 17.5.30 and deleted.
F4286   **5 AAP** 29.10.18 for **138 Sqn (Mobilising)**. To **138 Sqn** Chingford. **2 FS** Marske as a/c *79* early 1919. **PD** Ascot. To India. **AD** Drigh Road. **AP** Lahore by 11.23 until @ 12.23. **28 Sqn** and wrecked 28.7.24, flew into hillside near Ramzak, NWF, in heavy cloud and bombs exploded. Deleted.

Photographed in a hangar at Marske early in 1919, while serving with No.2 Fighting School, F.2B F4286 '79' was later shipped to India. it was with 28 Sqn by 28 July 1924, when it was flown into a hillside in heavy cloud while returning from a bombing operation. Both Fg Off T.C. Anderson and AC K. Taylor were killed when its bombs exploded. *(C&C)*

F4287   **Observers School** Eastchurch by 3.19 until @ 7.19. **2 FTS** Duxford by 5.24 until @ 6.24.
F4288   **PD** Ascot. To India. **AD** Drigh Road. **27 Sqn** and damaged 26.4.21, force landed at Nowshera after engine failure. **28 Sqn** by 12.22.
F4289   (Falcon) **5 AAP** 29.10.18 for **138 Sqn (Mobilising)** and despatched 2.11.18. **138 Sqn** Chingford 11.18.
F4290   (Falcon III) **5 AAP** 29.10.18 for **138 Sqn (Mobilising)**. To **138 Sqn** and wrecked 15.11.18 (Lt J.W. Williamson IIFA/2nd Lt W.L. Folkard KIFA, hit a tree on take off – engine 3/F/264/WD1999).

F4291   **5 AAP** 29.10.18 for **138 Sqn (Mobilising)**. To **138 Sqn** by 4.11.18. **AICS** Worthy Down by 12.18.
F4292   **5 AAP** 30.10.18 for **138 Sqn (Mobilising)**. To **138 Sqn** Chingford. **RAF & Army Co-operation School** Worthy Down and wrecked 21.5.19 (Lt W.C. Taylor/Lt J.E. Robbins both IIFA, o/t in forced landing after engine failure – engine WD52002).
F4293   **5 AAP** 30.10.18 for **138 Sqn (Mobilising)**. To **138 Sqn** Chingford by 4.11.18.
F4294   **5 AAP** 31.10.18 for **138 Sqn (Mobilising)**. To **138 Sqn** Chingford by 4.11.18. Same unit as F4527, 8.19.
F4295   **5 AAP** 31.10.18 for **138 Sqn (Mobilising)** and despatched to squadron 7.11.18. **138 Sqn** 11.18. **RAF & Army Co-operation School** Worthy Down by 31.5.19 until @ 16.6.19.
F4296   N/I
F4297   **'M' Flt** by 1.19 until @ 6.19.
F4298   N/I
F4299   (Falcon III) **62 Sqn** and wrecked 18.3.19 (Capt F.G.C. Weare/ 2nd Lt E.G. Holloway both OK, crashed on aerodrome – engine 1951/WD52000).
F4300   **5 AAP** 4.11.18 for **138 Sqn (Mobilising)** at Chingford, despatched to unit 7.11.18 but crashed en route.
F4301   **5 AAP** Bristol 4.11.18 for **138 Sqn (Mobilising)**. To **138 Sqn** Chingford dd 7.11.18. Reallotted to D of T for Worthy Down 9.12.18. B&C for reconditioning to J Type (s/n 6578) and ready by 3.1.25.
F4302   N/I
F4303   N/I
F4304   **PD** Ascot. To India. **AD** Drigh Road. **20 Sqn** by 4.23 until @ 2.24.
F4305   **'M' Flt** by 6.19 until @ 18.7.19.
F4306   Presentation a/c *Burgate*. **'L' Flt** 1918. **141 Sqn** Biggin Hill.
F4307   **'O' Flt** and wrecked on Practice Flight 8.2.19 (Lt Mcmann/Lt Simpson both IOAS, crashed on landing – engine 2009/WD52029).
F4308   (Falcon III) **8 AAP** Lympne 24.12.18, reallotted from BEF to SE Area for D of T for Pilots' Pool. **Pool of Pilots** Joyce Green by 5.19.
F4309   (Falcon III) **88 Sqn** and wrecked 25.2.19 (Capt Simpson OK, turned on nose by wind when taxiing in from landing at Marquise – engine 1857/WD51953).
F4310   (Falcon III) **2 AAP** Hendon 16.1.19, reallotted from BEF to Storage.
F4311   **48 Sqn** marked as a/c *19*.
F4312   N/I
F4313   **44 TDS** Bicester and wrecked 10.1.19 (Lt F.J. Frape OK/Lt H.H. Kernick IIFA, crashed on landing – engine 2/F/153/WD22471).
F4314   N/I
F4315   **2 FS** Marske by 23.1.19 until @ 11.3.19. **PD** Ascot. To India. **AD** Drigh Road by 3.23. **31 Sqn** by 6.23. **AP** Lahore and crashed near Amarsaded, NWF, 8.12.31.
F4316   **5 AAP** Bristol by 12.11.18 for **138 Sqn (Mobilising)**.
F4317   N/I
F4318   **5 AAP** Bristol by 12.11.18 for **138 Sqn (Mobilising)**.
F4319   **2 FS** Marske as a/c *80*, photographed o/t.
F4320   To India. **31 Sqn** as a/c *D*, 1923. Returned to UK. B&C for reconditioning to J Type (s/n 6262) and ready by 31.7.23. **PD** Ascot. To India. **AD** Drigh Road. **AP** Lahore by 4.24. **5 Sqn** as a/c *D*. **AP** Lahore and wrecked 8.12.31 force landed after engine failure at Amarsidedhu, hit telegraph wires and ran into small mullah and o/t).
F4321   **2 FS** Marske as a/c *76*, crashed on nose 2.3.19 (2nd Lt F.A. Beardmore). **2 Sqn** Fermoy by 9.20 until @ 11.20. **PD** Ascot. To India. **AD** Drigh Road by 4.23. **20 Sqn** by 5.23 until @ 10.24.
F4322   **5 AAP** Filton dd w/e 21.11.18. **Fleet Practice Station** Turnhouse dd w/e 12.12.18 and on unit charge until @ 5.19. **Fleet SAFG** Leuchars by 6.19.
F4323   **33 TDS** Witney by 12.18.
F4324   N/I
F4325   N/I
F4326   **2 FS** Marske by 23.1.19. B&C for reconditioning to J Type (s/n 6285) and ready by 6.9.23. **PD** Ascot. To Egypt. **AD** Aboukir. **6 Sqn** by 9.24 until @ 5.25.
F4327   N/I
F4328   **Pool of Pilot**s Joyce Green, tested 12.12.18.
F4329   **RAE** Farnborough by 1.20 as standard machine for comparison tests and stalling tests, damaged 16.10.22 (force landed near Basingstoke after engine failure), repaired and fitted with RAF.30 section wings by 1925. **HAD** Henlow by 12.9.27. B&C for reconditioning to J Type. At makers (s/n 7244) and ready by 19.7.28. **PD** Ascot. To Egypt. **AD** Aboukir. **208 Sqn** by 1.5.29 until @ 4.30. **6 Sqn** by 1.32.

F4330 (Falcon III) presentation a/c *Wingate (Co. Durham)*. **8 AAP** Lympne 24.12.18, realloted from BEF to 11 Group for **105 Sqn**, then reallotted to BEF 22.1.19. **105 Sqn** to 2.20. **SAC** Old Sarum by 11.23 until @ 3.24. To B&C, reconditioned to J Type (s/n 6661) and ready by 19.3.25. **PD** Ascot. To India. **AD** Drigh Road. **20 Sqn** as a/c *B* by 1930.

F4331 N/I

F4332 (Falcon III) presentation a/c *Forehoe Union (Durham)*. **8 AAP** Lympne 24.12.18, reallotted from BEF to 11 Group for **105 Sqn**, Ireland. In France 21.1.19, reallotted to BEF. **105 Sqn** until 2.20.

F4333 (Falcon III) presentation a/c *Dominica*. **8 AAP** Lympne 31.12.18, reallotted from BEF to 5 (Operations) Group but reallotted at Lympne 21.1.19 to BEF. Despatched to BEF 3.19. **62 Sqn** and wrecked 7.4.19 (Capt F.G.C. Weare/Lt Holloway both OK, force landed near Aix-le-Chappelle – engine 2111/WD52080).

F4334 (Falcon III) presentation a/c *Montreal*. **8 AAP** Lympne by 24.12.18, reallotted from BEF to 11 Group for **105 Sqn**. In France by 21.1.19, allotted to BEF. **105 Sqn** until 2.20.

F4335 (Falcon III) **8 AAP** Lympne by 24.12.18, reallotted from BEF to D of T for **29 TS** Croydon.

F4336 (Falcon III) presentation a/c *Zanzibar No.17*. **8 AAP** Lympne 17.1.19, reallotted from BEF to SE Area for the use of the Imperial Air Fleet and presentation at Hendon on 21.1.19. **1 Sqn CAF** Shoreham. Imperial Gift to Canada; Became *G-CYBC*, taken on charge 6.8.20 and used at Camp Borden (floats ordered). Deleted 7.2.22.

F4337 Presentation a/c *Zanzibar 18*. **5 AAP** Bristol by 17.1.19. To BEF and recorded with **25 Sqn** 5.19.

F4338 B&C for reconditioning to J Type. At makers (s/n 6394) and ready by 21.2.24.

F4339 B&C for reconditioning to J Type. At makers (s/n 6404) and ready by 4.3.24. **2 FTS** Duxford and wrecked 22.5.24 (Fg Off G.G. Walker/Cpl K.V. Raylor both OK, went to help force landed Sopwith Snipe, but burst into flames after landing at Castor, near Peterborough, and burnt out).

F4340 AGS Eastchurch and wrecked 29.11.22 (Fg Off W.J. Gayes KIFA, collided with Sopwith Snipe E6479 during aerial gunnery practice and crashed near Eastchurch).

F4341 **24 Sqn** Kenley by 12.19 until @ 2.22. **2 FTS** Duxford by 3.24 until @ 5.24. B&C for reconditioning to J Type (s/n 6686) and ready by 23.4.25. To Iraq. **AHQ Iraq Command Communications Flt** by 11.26, wrecked 4.4.27 (Flt Lt F.E.C. Benstead OK, ran into D.H.9A E8658 when pilot left it unattended with the engine running) and deleted.

F4342 **24 Sqn** Kenley by 4.21. B&C for reconditioning to J Type DC (s/n 6430) and ready by 29.4.24. **5 FTS** Sealand by 10.24 until @ 10.26. B&C for reconditioning to Mk.III DC (s/n 7127) and ready by 30.8.27. **2 FTS** Digby by 1.30. B&C for reconditioning (s/n 7578) and ready by 15.5.31. **2 FTS** Digby by 8.31. **HAD** Henlow. Sold and to civilian register 24.7.33 as G-ACHR, registered to R.C. Simpson and crashed at Guigmes, Seine-et-Marne, France 19.9.33.

F4343 N/I

F4344 B&C for reconditioning to J Type. At makers (s/n 6640) and ready by 5.3.25. **PD** Ascot. To Iraq. **AD** Hinaidi **AHQ Iraq Command Training Flt** by 6.28. **AD** Aboukir. **6 Sqn** by 11.29 and wrecked 5.30 (undercarriage collapsed on take off from Balir).

F4345 **6 FTS** Manston by 20.5.21.

F4346 AGS Eastchurch by 5.22 and wrecked 13.7.23 (Sgt F.W. Bone IIFA, engine failed on turn, crashed and went on nose at Eastchurch).

F4347 N/I

F4348 N/I

F4349 B&C for reconditioning to J Type (s/n 6447) and ready by 30.5.24. **PD** Ascot. To Egypt. **AD** Aboukir. **8 Sqn** as a/c *B*. **14 Sqn** by 10.25 until @ 11.25. **AD** Aboukir by 11.26 until @ 4.27. **208 Sqn** by 1.29 until @ 4.29. **6 Sqn** and wrecked 1.9.30 (crashed in night landing at Ismailia) and deleted.

F4350 N/I

F4351 N/I

F4352 **106 Sqn** Fermoy and wrecked 9.3.19 (crew OK, force landed in a bog near Skibereen, Co Cork).

F4353 SoTT Halton and wrecked 10.6.19 (Cpl D. Davies IIFA, o/t in forced landing on Halton aerodrome – engine 32839).

F4354 **2 Sqn** and wrecked 1.11.20 (hit a cow on take off from Fermoy).

F4355 (Falcon III) presentation a/c *Presented by Maharaja Bahadur Sir Rameswar Singh of Darbhanga No.4*. **5 AAP** Bristol by 7.12.18, allotted to BEF. **8 AAP** Lympne 24.12.18, reallotted to 11 Group for **105 Sqn**. In France 22.1.19 reallotted to BEF. **88 Sqn**.

F4356 AGS Eastchurch by 3.24.

F4357 **2 FS** Marske, photographed early 1919.

F4358 Allocated Croydon 8.19. **IACF** Northolt by 6.20 until @ 7.20.

F4359 N/I

F4360 APS Andover by 23.12.19. **RAE** Farnborough by 16.4.20, fitted with single bay wings of 4.69 aspect ratio 1923, in stalled flight experiments 1925, fitted with RAF.30 section wings 4.26, damaged landing at Farnborough 17.7.26, repaired, fitted with M2 section wings 1927 and on charge until @ 11.1.28.

F4361 (Falcon III) **9 AAP** Newcastle for RAF Aircraft Exhibition and wrecked 24.3.19 (Lt F. Fenwick/AM2 J.H. Underwood both KIFA, flew into kite balloon cable during wireless demonstration – engine 3/F/2001/WD52025).

F4362 To Iraq. **6 Sqn** by 1920. Returned to UK. **IAAD** Henlow by 15.11.23 until @ 23.11.23. **2 FTS** Duxford/Digby by 1.24 until @ 9.24. B&C for reconditioning to J Type (s/n 6695) and ready by 1.5.25. **PD** Ascot. To Iraq. **AD** Hinaidi. **AHQ Iraq Command Training Flt** by 9.27 untill @ 9.28. **AD** Aboukir. **6 Sqn** by 2.30, wrecked 4.6.30 (a tyre burst and undercarriage collapsed after wheel sank in hole landing at Ramleh) and deleted.

F4363 Photographed at Sedgeford (**3 FS**?).

F4364 N/I

F4365 Cowes. **RAE** Farnborough by 11.6.19.

F4366 **Pool of Pilots** Joyce Green by 5.19. B&C for reconditioning to J Type (s/n 6564) and ready by 15.12.24. **2 Sqn** Manston. **16 Sqn/SAC** Old Sarum by 8.25 until @ 8.26. B&C for reconditioning to Mk.III (s/n 7091) and ready by 27.5.27 as first machine with factory painted serials under lower wings. **Duxford SF** by 8.27. B&C for reconditioning to Mk.IV (s/n 7258) and ready by 29.9.28. **2 Sqn** Manston by 9.28. **4 Sqn**. Farnborough. **School of Photography Flt** Kenley by 3.30 until @ 10.30.

Just how RAF F.2B F4379, complete with Scarff ring, came to be sharing the beach at Rhyl with a pair of joyriding civilian Avro 504Ks, G-EAMP (ex-J745) and G-EAMQ (ex-J748), on Whit Monday in 1920, is no known. According to the contemporary caption, a ride in a 504 cost 'a guinea a flip'. Both 504s were withdrawn from use by Avro in October 1920. *(Philip Jarrett)*

F4367 N/I

F4368 N/I

F4369 B&C for reconditioning to J Type (s/n 6597) and ready by 22.1.25. **13 Sqn** Andover. **2 Sqn** Manston by 7.25. B&C for reconditioning to DC (s/n 6873) and ready by 7.12.25. **13 Sqn** Andover by 12.26 until @ 9.27. **2 Sqn** Manston by 3.28 until @ 4.29.

F4370 IAAD Henlow tested 18.1.24. **5 FTS** Sealand and wrecked 31.3.24 (crashed when throttle switch failed).

F4371 N/I

F4372 N/I

F4373 **106 Sqn** Fermoy 1920.

F4374 N/I

F4375 ACIS Kenley by 8.19 (for General Groves). PD Ascot. To Egypt. AD Aboukir. To India. **31 Sqn** by 10.24. Returned to UK B&C for reconditioning to J Type (s/n 6563) and ready by 13.12.24. **2 FTS** Digby by 5.25. B&C for reconditioning to DC (s/n 6903) and ready by 10.2.26. **IACF** Northolt by 6.26.

F4376 APS Andover by 23.12.19 until @ 2.20. B&C for reconditioning to J Type (s/n 6566) and ready by 17.12.24. **SAC** Old Sarum by 2.28 until @ 11.28.

F4377 (Falcon III) **5 AAP** Bristol 25.1.19, reallotted from 11 Group to BEF. To India. **48 Sqn** 1919 and on charge when unit redesignated **5 Sqn** 1.4.20.

F4378 (Falcon III) **5 AAP** Bristol 25.1.19, reallotted from 11 Group to BEF. At or en route to **3 (W)ARD** 21.2.19, crashed and with BEF allotment cancelled.

F4379 B&C for reconditioning to J Type (s/n 6581) and ready by 3.1.25.

F4380 **105 Sqn** Omagh by 11.18 until @ 2.19. 11 Group Collinstown/ Tallaght by 1.7.19 until @ 23.6.20. **106 Sqn** Fermoy 1921.

F4381 (Falcon III) **5 AAP** Bristol 25.1.19, reallotted from 11 Group to BEF. B&C for reconditioning to J Type (s/n 6546) and ready by 28.11.24. **16 Sqn/SAC** Old Sarum by 3.25 until @ 9.26. B&C for reconditioning Mk.III (s/n 7148) and ready by 19.5.28. **16 Sqn/SAC** Old Sarum by 9.29 until @ 7.30.

F4382 N/I

F4383 (Falcon III) **5 AAP** Bristol 25.1.19, reallotted from NW Area to BEF.

F4384 (Falcon III) **5 AAP** Bristol 14.4.19, allotted to BEF.

F4385 (Falcon III) **5 AAP** Bristol 25.1.19, reallotted from NW Area to BEF. **3 (W)ARD** Yate by 2.19. **24 Sqn** Kenley by 11.20 until @ 6.22. B&C for reconditioning to J Type (s/n 6555) and ready by 6.12.24. **SoTT** Halton by 5.25. B&C for reconditioning to DC (s/n 6871) and ready by 3.12.25. **RAF (Cadet) College** Cranwell by 12.26 until @ 7.27.

F4386 (Falcon III) **5 AAP** Bristol 25.1.19, reallotted from NW Area to BEF and despatched 3.19.

F4387 (Falcon III) **5 AAP** Bristol 28.3.19, allotted to BEF and despatched 3.19. **AGS** Eastchurch by 3.24. **Northolt SF** by 1925 until @ 1926 for **Dept of CAS**.

F4388 (Falcon III) **5 AAP** Bristol 25.1.19, reallotted from NW Area to BEF. **2 Sqn** Oranmore/Fermoy by 2.20 until 1921. **RAF Staff College Flt** Andover by 5.24 until @ 6.24. **AGS** Eastchurch by 11.24. **2 Sqn** Manston by 9.28 until @ 12.28.

F4389 **2 FTS** Duxford and destroyed by fire 22.5.24.

F4390 Northolt 1.24. **PD** Ascot. To India. **AD** Drigh Road. **31 Sqn** marked as a/c *R*.

F4391 **School of Photography** Farnborough by 4.21. **4 Sqn** Farnborough by 5.22.

F4392 **5 AAP** Bristol by 18.4.19 allotted to BEF. B&C for reconditioning to J Type (s/n 6636) and ready by 10.3.25. **PD** Ascot. To Egypt. **AD** Aboukir marked as a/c *B* by 3.26 until @ 8.26.

F4393 (Falcon III) **5 AAP** Bristol by 25.1.19, reallotted from SW Area for RAF and Army Co-operation School to BEF and still at Bristol 7.4.19.

F4394 (Falcon III) **5 AAP** Bristol by 19.4.19, allotted to BEF. **PD** Ascot. To India. **AD** Drigh Road. **5 Sqn** marked as a/c *W* by 1.21 until @ 5.21.

F4395 (Falcon III) **5 AAP** Bristol 25.1.19, reallotted from Midland Area for **OSPMR** Shrewsbury to BEF. **RAF (Cadet) College** Cranwell by 11.25.

F4396 (Falcon III) **5 AAP** Bristol by 19.4.19, allotted to BEF. B&C for reconditioning to J Type (s/n 6621) and ready by 20.2.25. **PD** Ascot. To India. **AD** Drigh Road by 1926. **20 Sqn** as a/c *B* and collided in formation with D8035 near Peshawar, 20.3.28 but still flying 1932 (20 Sqn?).

F4397 **5 AAP** Bristol by 7.4.19, allotted to BEF. **11 Sqn** Spich by 31.7.19. **RAF (Cadet) College** Cranwell by 2.25 until @ @7.26.

F4398 (Falcon III) **5 AAP** Bristol by 19.4.19, allotted to BEF. **11 Sqn** Spich dd 29.5.19 and on unit charge until @ 1.8.19.

F4399 **11 Sqn** Spich by 26.6.19. **IACF** Henlow by 1.24 until @ 3.24. **PD** Ascot. To India. **AD** Drigh Road. **AP** Lahore by 11.24.

F4400 **5 AAP** Bristol by 3.4.19, allotted to BEF.

F4401 B&C for reconditioning to J Type (s/n 6660) and ready by 18.3.25. To India. **AD** Drigh Road 1926. **20 Sqn** by 12.26.

F4402 **12 Sqn** Heumar as a/c *B3* by 3.7.19 and wrecked in crash 13.5.20.

F4403 (Falcon III) **5 AAP** Bristol by 24.1.19, allotted to BEF. To India. **48 Sqn** as a/c *C* on charge when unit redesignated **5 Sqn** 1.4.20, still as a/c *C* and wrecked 16.8.22 (crashed landing, at Pislim, NWF). **AP** Lahore repaired by 10.24.

F4404 (Falcon III) **5 AAP** Bristol by 24.1.19, allotted to BEF.

F4405 (Falcon III) **5 AAP** Bristol by 25.1.19, allotted to BEF and still at Bristol 11.4.19.

F4406 (Falcon III) **5 AAP** Bristol by 24.1.19, allotted to BEF and still at Bristol 5.4.19. **APS** Andover by 23.12.19 until @ 2.20.

F4407 (Falcon III) **5 AAP** Bristol by 25.1.19, allotted to BEF. **22 Sqn** Spich and wrecked 17.6.19 (Lt J.M. Huxley/2nd Lt T.J. Leighs both IIFA, o/t on landing after bouncing on overshot landing – engine 2265/WD88957). To India. **48 Sqn** by 10.19 and on unit charge when redesignated **5 Sqn** 1.4.20. Also noted at Kenley 10.26.

F4409 (Falcon III) **5 AAP** Bristol by 29.1.19, allotted to BEF. **22 Sqn** Spich, tested 11.6.19. **8 AAP** Lympne ex 22 Sqn 19.8.19 (Lt Head).

F4410 (Falcon III) **5 AAP** Bristol by 29.1.19, allotted to BEF. **208 Sqn** by 8.8.19. To UK 1.21. Yeovil. **RAE** Farnborough by 24.6.26 and last flown 25.1.27.

F4411 (Falcon III) **5 AAP** Bristol 29.1.19, allotted to BEF.

F4412 (Falcon III) **5 AAP** Bristol 30.1.19, allotted to BEF. **12 Sqn** Heumar/Bickendorf 1919. To UK 12.20. B&C for reconditioning to Mk.III (s/n 7104) and ready by 1.7.27. **2 Sqn** Manston. B&C for reconditioning to Mk.IV (s/n 7263) and ready by 10.10.28. **2 Sqn** Manston by 10.28. **RAF (Cadet) College** Cranwell. **4 Sqn** Farnborough.

F4413 (Falcon III) **5 AAP** Bristol by 30.1.19, allotted to BEF. **12 Sqn** Bickendorf as a/c *A2*, later *A1*, by 12.19. **HQ Flt** by 15.12.20. **RAF College** Cranwell by 5.29.

F4414 (Falcon III) **5 AAP** Bristol 31.1.19, allotted to BEF. **12 Sqn** Heumar by 7.19 as a/c *B* until @ 15.11.20 (Lt J.W. Baker). To UK 15.12.20. **5 FTS** Sealand by 5.22 until @ 9.24 and in incident 27.5.22 (Plt Off A.D. Drysdale OK/AC2 Day IIGA, propeller accident at High Leigh). B&C for reconditioning to J Type (s/n 6699) and ready by 11.5.25. **PD** Ascot. To India. **AD** Drigh Road. **AP** Lahore by 2.29. **20 Sqn** as a/c *N*, wrecked on Ferry Flight to Lahore 5.5.30 (port wing hit telephone wire when circling to land and and aircraft hit ground at Jhelum) and deleted.

F4415 **PD** Ascot. To India. **AD** Drigh Road. **20 Sqn** as a/c *N*. **31 Sqn**.

F4416 **APS** Andover by 7.19 until @ 2.20. **2 FTS** Duxford by 10.23 until @ 4.24. **HAD** Henlow by 5.24. **2 FTS** Digby by 6.24. B&C for reconditioning to J Type (s/n 6698) and ready by 4.5.25.

F4417 **5 AAP** Bristol by 5.2.19, allotted to BEF.

F4418 **5 AAP** Bristol by 5.2.19, allotted to BEF. **6 FTS** Manston by 23.5.21. B&C for reconditioning to J Type (s/n 6532) and ready by 8.11.24. B&C for reconditioning to DC (s/n 6875) and ready by 18.12.25. **CFS** Upavon by 7.26, damaged 15.7.26 (swung while taxying for take off and collided with stationary Sopwith Snipe E6656 at Upavon), repaired and on unit charge until @ 1.29.

F4419 **5 AAP** Bristol by 6.2.19 allotted to BEF.

F4420 **4 Sqn** Farnborough by 4.20 until @ 6.20. **24 Sqn** Kenley by 4.21. **2 FTS Duxford** and wrecked 8.4.22 (crashed at Chettisham, Cambs).

F4421 (Falcon III) **2 AIS** ex **1 ASD** 17.10.18. **20 Sqn** and LIA on OP 10.11.18 (Lt E.A.C. Britton POW/Sgt R.S. Dodds KIA, last seen in combat over Charleroi – engine 357/WD18678).

F4422 **2 FTS** Duxford and wrecked 7.4.22 (Plt Off G. Hopkins KIFA, fell to ground on sharp turn when low flying over Chettisham, near Ely).

F4423 **88 Sqn** dd ex **1 ASD** 22.10.18 (engine 1767/WD51908). **CFS** Upavon by 2.21. **24 Sqn** Kenley by 1.23 until @ 3.23. B&C for reconditioning to J Type (s/n 65998) and ready by 27.1.25. B&C for reconditioning to DC (s/n 6868) and ready by 28.11.25. **13 Sqn** Andover by 1925 until @ 1926. **RAF (Cadet) College** Cranwell by 9.27 until @ 5.29.

F4424 To India. **31 Sqn** and wrecked on Radiator Test to 10,000ft 22.9.29 (crashed near Mhow).

F4425 **1 AIS** dd ex **1 ASD** 13.10.18. **48 Sqn** by 11.18 until 1919. **22 Sqn** by 12.6.19. **12 Sqn** Bickendorf as a/c *B1* by 6.20 **HQ Flt** from 1.21. **RAF (Cadet) College** Cranwell by 6.28 until @ 5.29.

F4426 **5 AAP** Bristol and tested 3.10.18 and 4.10.18 (Lt C.F. Uwins). **1 AIS** dd ex **1 ASD** 18.10.18. **88 Sqn** by 10.18. **12 Sqn** Bickendorf as a/c *A3* and wrecked 8.19 (Fg Off P.F. Bovingdon OK).

F4427 **5 AAP** Bristol and tested 4.10.18 (Lt C.F. Uwins). **2 AIS** dd ex **1 ASD** 17.10.18. **20 Sqn** by 25.10.18, wrecked on Practice Flight 27.10.18 (Lt H. Packard/Sgt W. Gibson both OK, spun in) and deleted on unit that day.

F4428 **2 Sqn** Manston. **CFS** Upavon by 8.24. **School of Photography Flt Kenley** by 3.28 until @ 4.28.

F4429 **88 Sqn** dd ex **1 AIS** 4.11.18. **12 Sqn** Bickendorf as a/c *A4*.

F4430 **5 AAP** Bristol and tested 4.10.18 (Lt C.F. Uwins). **22 Sqn** by 18.5.19 and wrecked 2.7.19 (Lt West/Lt Hermon both OK, crashed on aerodrome).

F4431 **5 FTS** Sealand and wrecked 2.10.22 (Plt Off K.R. Boulton OK, force landed near Childs Ercall, Shropshire after engine failure and ran into a hedge).

F4432 **13 Sqn** Andover. **RAF (Cadet) College** Cranwell by 3.25.

F4433 N/I

F4434 'M' Flt and wrecked on Test Flight 31.12.18 (Lt Dunlop/AM Connolly both OK, crashed on aerodrome after engine failure). B&C for reconditioning to J Type DC (s/n 6865) and ready by 25.11.25. **RAF (Cadet) College** Cranwell by 1.28 until @ 5.29. B&C for reconditioning to Mk.III DC (s/n 7581) and ready by 2.6.31. Andover for storage. Sold and to civilian register as *G-ACFP* 13.4.33, registered to Empire Air Services Ltd Feltham. To Hon Mrs Victor Bruce 11.33. Sold for scrap 1.38.

F4435 'M' Flt dd ex **1 ASD** 19.11.18 and on unit charge until @ 6.19. **12 Sqn** Bickendorf as a/c *C2* by 9.19. To UK 10.1.21. **RAF (Cadet) College** Cranwell. **PD** Ascot. To Egypt. **AD** Aboukir by 12.24. **4 FTS** Abu Sueir by 4.26. **208 Sqn** by 8.25 until @ 10.29.

F4436 **2 AIS** dd ex **1 ASD** 24.10.18 **20 Sqn** by 25.10.18 and wrecked on Practice Flight 8.4.19 (Lt Hawkins/Lt Edwards both OK, tail skid caught in rough ground and ran into a hollow – engine 1763/WD51909). **PD** Ascot. To India. **AD** Drigh Road. **5 Sqn** by 5.23.

F4437 **5 AAP** Bristol and tested 10.10.18 (Lt C.F. Uwins). **11 Sqn** dd ex **1 ASD** 9.1.19.

F4438 **5 AAP** Bristol and tested 10.10.18 (Lt C.F. Uwins). 'P' Flt by 11.11.18. **8 Sqn** dd ex 'P' Flt 19.1.19 (Lt de Boer). **2 ASD** ex 8 Sqn 22.1.19.

F4439 **20 Sqn** and wrecked on Practice Flight 3.4.19 (2nd Lt Knight OK/ AC2 Creed IIFA, engine failed on take off and force landed into ploughed field – engine 1773/WD51911).

F4440 Presentation a/c *Presented by Maharaja Bahadur Sir Rameswar Singh of Darbhanga No.1*. **5 AAP** Bristol by 16.10.18, allotted to BEF. **1 ASD** dd ex England by 18.10.18 and tested 24.10.18. **18 Sqn** 1919. **RAF Staff College Flt** Andover by 6.24.

F4441 Presentation a/c *Maharajah of Darbaughar No.1*. **5 AAP** Bristol and tested 10.10.18 (Lt C.F. Uwins).

F4442 **88 Sqn** as a/c *1*. **Meteorological Flt** by 20.8.19. **12 Sqn** by 11.19. To UK 12.20.

F4443 'O' Flt and wrecked on Practice Flight 19.11.18 (Capt F.H. Hodgson/2nd Lt J.H. Taylor both KOAS, nosedived in on take off – engine 1691/WD51890).

F4444 'P' Flt dd ex **1 ASD** 13.11.18 and on unit charge until @ 19.1.19.

F4445 **22 Sqn** dd ex **1 ASD** 10.11.18 and on unit charge until @ 18.5.19. **12 Sqn** Bickendorf as a/c *B* by 12.19 until @ 1.20.

F4446 **208 Sqn** by 23.5.19 until @ 7.8.19 (presume replaced by F4410).

F4447 **PD** Ascot. To India. **AD** Drigh Road. **20 Sqn** and wrecked 20.3.20 (crashed on bombing raid, Sherrani, NWF).

F4448 **13 Sqn** Andover by 1924 until @ 1926.

F4449 N/I

F4450 B&C for reconditioning to J Type (s/n 6576) and ready by 1.1.25. **4 Sqn** Farnborough by 8.26.

F4451 N/I

F4452 N/I

F4453 HMS *Eagle* **Trials Flt** Gosport by 6.20 for deck landing trials.

F4454 B&C for reconditioning to J Type (s/n 6326) and ready by 26.10.23. **E&WS** Worthy Down by 7.24 until @ 6.26.

F4455 **PD** Ascot. To Egypt. **AD** Aboukir. **4 FTS** Abu Sueir by 5.22. Returned to UK. **SAC** Old Sarum by 6.23 and wrecked 27.8.23 (Plt Off R.N. Waite/Major Wingfield-Stratford MC, Royal West Kent Regt both OK, engine failed taking off after forced landing and side-slipped in l mile N of Totton, Hants).

F4456 **SAC** Old Sarum and wrecked 15.7.21 (Fg Off B.H. Cook/Sgt J.F. Hall both IIFA, force landed downwind into cornfield near Moreton-in-the-Marsh after fuel shortage, struck a furrow and o/t).

F4457 N/I

F4458 N/I

F4459 **PD** Ascot. To Egypt. **AD** Aboukir. **14 Sqn** by 8.23 and wrecked 3.9.23 (crashed from a turn near Abu Sueir).

F4460 N/I

F4461 **PD** Ascot. To India. **AD** Drigh Road. **AP** Lahore by 8.1.24. **5 Sqn** dd ex Lahore by 12.24 and on unit charge until @ 5.25.

F4462 **PD** Ascot. To India. **AD** Drigh Road by 7.23 until @ 8.23. Risalpur by 9.23.

F4463 B&C for reconditioning to J Type (s/n 6291) and ready by 14.9.23. **PD** Ascot. To India. **AD** Drigh Road. **AP** Lahore by 10.24 until @ 11.24. **5 Sqn** by 12.24 until @ 10.25. **AD** Drigh Road 1926. **31 Sqn** as a/c *L*. **AP** Lahore by 1.29. **20 Sqn** as a/c *L* by 2.30 and wrecked 18.3.30 (after landing at Peshawar, taxied into stationary Westland Wapiti J9396).

F4464 B&C for reconditioning to J Type (s/n 6306) and ready by 27.9.23. **PD** Ascot. To India. **AD** Drigh Road. **31 Sqn** by 12.24.

F4465 **12 Sqn** by 12.19 until 1920. To UK 11.20. B&C for reconditioning to J Type (s/n 6323) and ready by 19.10.23. **1 SoTT (Boys)** Halton by 4.24 until @ 9.24. B&C for reconditioning (s/n 6959) and ready by 3.7.26.

F4466 **5 AAP** Bristol and tested 15.10.18 (Lt C.F. Uwins).

F4467 N/I

F4468 (Falcon III) wrecked on Collection Flight for **48 Sqn** 27.10.18 (Lt Taylor OK, had to return due to bad weather and whilst taxiing collided with a **52 Sqn** R.E.8 – engine 243/WD18621).

F4469 (Falcon III) **1 ASD** deleted 23.10.18 (not worth reconstruction).

F4470 (Falcon III) presentation a/c *Newfoundland No.4*. **5 AAP** Bristol and tested 17.10.18 (Lt C.F. Uwins). **6 Sqn** and wrecked 23.4.19 (Capt H.J. Hunter OK, crashed landing at Sart after engine trouble – engine 645/WD32722). To India. **48 Sqn** and on unit charge when redesignated **5 Sqn** 1.2.20.

F4471 N/I

F4472 (Falcon III) **6 Sqn** and wrecked on Special Mission 14.4.19 (Lt Owen/Major Ford both OK, crashed at St Andre – engine 1833/WD51941).

F4473 B&C for reconditioning to J Type (s/n 6567) and ready by 17.12.24. **SAC** Old Sarum by 9.25 until @ 4.28.

F4474 (Falcon III) **88 Sqn** by 10.18 and wrecked 26.11.18 (hit on the ground by **42 Sqn** R.E.8 C3467 (engine 1175/WD51612).

F4475 (Falcon III) **48 Sqn** and wrecked on Practice Flight 18.2.19 (Capt L.A. Payne KOAS/Lt R.L. Ford OK, struck water and o/t into the river Rhine near Merheim – engine 205/WD18602).

F4476 **5 AAP** Bristol and tested 16.10.18 (Lt C.F. Uwins).

F4477 **11 Sqn** dd ex **2 ASD** 10.11.18 and still on unit charge 21.7.19. **5 FTS** Sealand and wrecked 12.11.23 (Fg Off G.H. Stainforth OK, crashed in forced landing near Great Saughall, Chester). B&C for reconditioning to J Type (s/n 6602) and ready by 29.1.25. **PD** Ascot. To Iraq. **AD** Hinaidi. **6 Sqn** by 1.26.

F4478 **5 AAP** Bristol and tested 15.10.18 (Lt C.F. Uwins). **24 Sqn** Kenley by 2.20 until @ 3.21. **6 FTS** Manston by 26.5.21.

F4479 **33 TDS** Witney by 12.11.18 (2nd Lt G.A. Raybone) until @ 12.18. **106 Sqn** Fermoy 1920.

F4480 N/I

F4481 B&C for reconditioning to J Type (s/n 6321) and ready by 17.10.23. **13 Sqn** Andover by 1924, damaged 13.7.25 (Plt Off J. Warburton/Sgt Tilbury both OK, lost power after take off and o/t in forced landing into cornfield near Odiham) and on unit charge until @ 1926. **PD** Ascot. To India. **AD** Drigh Road by 1927.

F4482 **1 FTS** Netheravon and wrecked 11.1.23 (Cpl A.J. Amess KIFA, engine failure at 500ft after take off and spun in near Netheravon).

F4483 **1 FTS** Netheravon and wrecked 3.3.23 (hit air pocket and crashed near Netheravon).

F4484 **2 Sqn** Ireland by 1920 until 1921. B&C for reconditioning to J Type (s/n 6281) and ready by 31.8.23. **1 SoTT (Boys)** Halton and wrecked 9.10.23 (Flt Lt F.H. Sims IIFA/AC2 Hawes OK, pilot misjudged height on landing and landed in a copse near Halton). B&C for reconditioning to J Type (s/n 6457) and ready by 15.5.24. **2 Sqn** Manston as a/c *A* and wrecked 6.8.24 (stalled on a turn and crashed near Manston).

F4485 **1 FTS** Netheravon. B&C for reconditioning to J Type (s/n 6284) and ready by 8.9.23. **2 FTS** Duxford by 3.24 and wrecked 2.5.24 (Plt Off E. Martin KIFA, collided with Avro 504K F8945 1 mile from aerodrome).

F4486 B&C for reconditioning to J Type (s/n 6347) and ready by 17.11.23. **School of Photography**, Farnborough by 8.25 until @ 9.25. B&C for reconditioning (s/n 6985) and ready by 30.7.26. **HAD** Henlow by 8.27.

F4487 B&C for reconditioning to J Type (s/n 6304) and ready by 26.9.23.

F4488 To Middle East. **14 Sqn** 1919. To India. **48 Sqn** 1919 and on unit charge when redesignated **5 Sqn** 1.2.20. **E&WS** Worthy Down by 10.22. B&C for reconditioning to J Type (s/n 6544) and ready by 22.11.24. **13 Sqn** Andover by 11.24 until @ 1.26.

F4489 B&C for reconditioning to J Type (s/n 6316) and ready by 12.10.23. **2 Sqn** Manston as a/c *A* by 25.8.25. B&C for reconditioning to Mk.III (s/n 7097) and ready by 15.6.27. Converted to Mk.III DC and delivered 31.8.29. **2 FTS** Digby by 8.31 until @ 9.31.

F4490 B&C for reconditioning to J Type (s/n 6313) and ready by 8.10.23. **2 Sqn** Manston by 5.24 until @ 11.24. B&C for reconditioning to DC (s/n 6836) and ready by 22.10.25. **2 Sqn** Manston reissued 1925 and on unit charge until 1926 marked with diamond on fin. **5 FTS** Sealand by 10.26 until @ 4.27.

F4491 B&C for reconditioning to J Type (s/n 6298) and ready by 24.9.23. **24 Sqn** Kenley 1924. **Dept of CAS Comms Flt** Kenley by 1925 until 1926. At Kenley 10.26. **RAE** Farnborough 1926 until @ 1928.

F4492 **B&C** for reconditioning to J Type (s/n 6335) and ready by 1.11.23. **1 SoTT (Boys)** Halton by 2.24 until @ 2.25. Also noted at Hal Far 1925. B&C for reconditioning to DC (s/n 6842) and ready by 26.10.25. **RAF (Cadet) College** Cranwell and wrecked 12.7.26 (ran into stationary Avro 504K on take off at Cranwell and o/t). B&C for reconditioning to Mk.III DC (s/n 7118) and ready by 15.7.27. **School of Photography Flt** Farnborough by 3.30. **16 Sqn/SAC** Old Sarum by 2.30 until @ 6.30. **School of Photography Flt Kenley** by 8.30 until @ 9.30.

F4493 **1 FTS** Netheravon by 7.21. **AGS** Eastchurch.

F4494 **1 FTS** Netheravon by 4.21 until @ 7.22. B&C for reconditioning to J Type (s/n 6617) and ready by 12.2.25. **PD** Ascot. To India. **AD** Drigh Road. **31 Sqn** as a/c *F*. **20 Sqn** by 6.30 until @ 2.31.

F4495 B&C for reconditioning to J Type (s/n 6303) and ready by 26.9.23. **PD** Ascot. To India. **AD** Drigh Road. **AP** Lahore by 10.24 until @ 11.24. **31 Sqn** NW Frontier. **AP** Lahore by 8.25 (at Ambala).

F4496 B&C for reconditioning to J Type (s/n 6296) and ready by 14.9.23. **24 Sqn** Kenley by 4.24 and in ground collision with Avro 504K after overshooting, 20.7.25. **Dept of CAS Comms Flt** Northolt 1925 until @ 1926. B&C for reconditioning to Mk.III DC and retaken on charge 23.8.29. **2 FTS** Manston by 7.31 until @ 9.31.

F4497 B&C for reconditioning to J Type (s/n 6299) and ready by 24.9.23. **RAF (Cadet) College** Cranwell by 6.24 until @ 6.25. B&C for reconditioning to DC (s/n 6908) and ready by 22.2.26. **RAF (Cadet) College** reissued by 3.27. **CFS** by 5.28 until @ 1929.

F4498 B&C for reconditioning to J Type (s/n 6594) and ready by 28.1.25. **PD** Ascot. To India. **AD** Drigh Road. **5 Sqn** by 12.25 until @ 4.28.

F4499 **RAF (Cadet) College** Cranwell as a/c *6* by 9.23 until @ 7.25.

F4500 B&C for reconditioning to J Type (s/n 6287) and ready by 11.9.23. **5 Sqn** by 7.24. B&C for reconditioning (s/n 6598) and 2.7.26. **2 Sqn** Manston by 1928 until 1929. **16 Sqn** Old Sarum by 4.30.

F4501 **1 FTS** Netheravon by 7.22; B&C for reconditioning to J Type (s/n 6533) and ready by 8.11.24. **23 Group HQ** Spittlegate 4.26. O/t landing 16.2.28 and deleted.

F4502 **RAF (Cadet) College** as a/c *7*, later *B7*, by 10.23 until @ 1.24. **2 FTS** Digby by 1.26 until @ 12.27.

F4503 **1 FTS** Netheravon by 4.21 until @ 7.22. B&C for reconditioning to J Type (s/n 6537) and ready by 14.11.24. **13 Sqn** Andover by 1924 until @ 1926.

F4504 B&C for reconditioning to J Type (s/n 6330) and ready by 27.10.23. **CFS** Upavon by 3.24 until @ 6.24. **HAD Stn Flt** Henlow by 7.26 until @ 2.28.

F4505 B&C for reconditioning to J Type (s/n 6322) and ready by 19.10.23. **PD** Ascot. To Egypt. **AD** Aboukir by 9.24.

F4506 B&C for reconditioning to J Type (s/n 6314) and ready by 10.10.23. **16 Sqn/SAC** Old Sarum by 6.24 until @ 7.27.

F4507 B&C for reconditioning to J Type (s/n 6277) and ready by 27.8.23. **2 FTS** Duxford/Digby by 2.24, wrecked 6.8.24 (Plt Off G.S. Hall KIFA, engine failed at 200-300ft on take off and dived in vertically), presumed repaired and damaged 20.4.25 (Plt Off C.H. Noble IIFA, hit a tree on landing and o/t). B&C for reconditioning to DC (s/n 6845) and ready by 2.11.25. **RAF (Cadet) College** Cranwell by 9.26, in mid-air collision with F4940 13.9.26, repaired and on unit charge until @ 3.29.

F4508 B&C for reconditioning to J Type (s/n 6320) and ready by 18.10.23. **5 FTS** Sealand by 10.24 until @ 12.24. **HAD** Henlow by 11.26.

F4509 B&C for reconditioning to J Type (s/n 6561) and ready by 12.12.24.

F4510 B&C for reconditioning to J Type (s/n 6310) and ready by 4.10.23. **1 FTS** Netheravon by 12.23 until @ 1.24. B&C for reconditioning to DC (s/n 6878) and ready by 19.12.25. **2 FTS** Digby by 9.26.

F4511 B&C for reconditioning to J Type (s/n 6700) and ready by 7.5.25. **RAF (Cadet) College** Cranwell as a/c *3*, later *B3*. **23 Group HQ** Spittlegate by 4.27. To Egypt. **6 Sqn** by 5.30 until @ 11.30.

F4512 **PD** Ascot. To Egypt. **AD** Aboukir. **14 Sqn** by 1.24 until @ 10.25.

F4513 **16 Sqn** by 11.18. B&C for reconditioning to J Type (s/n 6317) and ready by 12.10.23. **16 Sqn/SAC** Old Sarum by 2.25 until @ 7.25.

F4514 B&C for reconditioning to J Type (s/n 6309) and ready by 4.10.23. **1 FTS** Netheravon by 12.23 and wrecked 24.11.24 (became lost in cloud and crashed on hill top).

F4515 B&C for reconditioning to J Type (s/n 6339) and ready by 2.11.23. **RAF (Cadet) College** Cranwell by 12.24 until @ 7.25. B&C for reconditioning DC (s/n 6907) and ready by 20.2.26. **CFS** Upavon by 5.26.

F4516 B&C for reconditioning to J Type (s/n 6351) and ready by 3.12.23. **13 Sqn** Andover by 9.24. B&C for reconditioning to Mk.III (s/n 7110) and ready by 13.7.27. B&C for reconditioning to DC (s/n 7434) and retaken on RAF charge 27.6.29. **RAF College** Cranwell by 7.29 until @ 10.29. To Civilian Register as *G-ACAA*, registered to C.R.A. Oakley 20.1.33, H.A. Carson 5.34 and A.E. Green & A.P. Fraser 2.36. Registration cancelled 12.46.

F4517 B&C for reconditioning to J Type (s/n 6333) and ready by 29.10.23. **School of Photography** Farnborough by 4.25 until @ 9.25. B&C for reconditioning to Mk.III (s/n 7136) and ready by 16.6.28. **HCF** Northolt by 23.6.28. **AGS** Eastchurch by 1.3.29 until @ 7.30.

F4518 **SAC** Old Sarum by 12.22. B&C for reconditioning to J Type (s/n 6345) and ready by 16.11.23. **SAC** Old Sarum by 12.23 and wrecked 3.10.24 (Plt Off G.D. Gibson/Plt Off G.J. Southam both IIFA, spun in near Old Sarum).

F4519 B&C for reconditioning to J Type (s/n 6343) and ready by 8.11.23. **16 Sqn/SAC** Old Sarum by 3.24 until @ 7.25. B&C for reconditioning to Mk.III DC (s/n 7129) and ready by 31.8.27. **5 FTS** Sealand as a/c *5* by 10.28 until @ 10.29.

F4520 N/I

F4521 N/I

F4522 **2 FS** Marske and photographed wrecked.

F4523 **5 AAP** Bristol 24.10.18 for **138 Sqn (Mobilising)**. To **138 Sqn** Chingford by 29.10.18. Reallotted to D of T for Worthy Down 9.12.18. **1 FTS** Netheravon by 4.21 until @ 7.22. B&C for reconditioning to J Type (s/n 6595) and ready by 22.1.25.

F4524 **33 TDS** Witney by 6.11.18 (2nd Lt G.A. Raybone).

F4525 **5 AAP** Bristol by 24.10.18 for **138 Sqn (Mobilising)**. To **138 Sqn** Chingford by 31.10.18. Reallotted to D of T for Worthy Down 9.12.18.

F4526 **5 AAP** Bristol by 24.10.18 for **138 Sqn (Mobilising)**. To **138 Sqn** Chingford by 31.10.18. Reallotted to D of T for Worthy Down 9.12.18. **RAF (Cadet) College** Cranwell by 5.28.

F4527 **5 AAP** Bristol by 24.10.18 for **138 Sqn (Mobilising)**. To **138 Sqn** Chingford 2.11.18. Reallotted to D of T for Worthy Down 9.12.18. Same unit as F4294, 9.19.

F4528 **5 AAP** Bristol by 24.10.18 for **138 Sqn (Mobilising)** and still at Bristol 2.11.18 when reallotted to 6 Bde.

F4529 **12 Sqn**.

F4530 **5 AAP** Bristol by 24.10.18 for **138 Sqn (Mobilising)**. To **138 Sqn** Chingford dd 1.11.18. Reallotted to D of T for Worthy Down 9.12.18.

F4531 **5 AAP** Bristol and tested 24.10.18 (Lt C.F. Uwins).

F4532 N/I

F4533 N/I

F4534 **HAD SF** Henlow by 2.28.

F4535 N/I

F4536 **39 Sqn** North Weald dd ex **8 AAP** 26.8.19.

F4537 Presentation a/c *Bingley, Yorkshire*. **2 Sqn** as a/c *V* by 1920 until @ 1921. B&C for reconditioning to J Type (s/n 6604) and ready by 29.1.25. **2 Sqn** Manston.

F4538 **138 Sqn**, collected from Bristol but crashed en route to Chingford 4.11.18. **5 AAP** by 7.11.18 under repair. **20 Sqn** by 30.11.18. **P Flight** and in accident 21.12.18.

F4539 N/I

F4540 **138 Sqn**, collected from Bristol but crashed en route to Chingford 4.11.18.

F4541 B&C for reconditioning to J Type (s/n 6289) and ready by 13.9.23. To India. **Quetta SF** by 5.28 until @ 11.29.

F4542 **SAC** Old Sarum by 1922 until 1923. B&C for reconditioning to J Type (s/n 6282) and ready by 5.9.23. **SAC** Old Sarum, reissued by 2.24 until @ 10.25. **31 Sqn** as a/c *H*. B&C for reconditioning to Mk.III (s/n 7144) and ready by 15.5.28. **2 Sqn** Manston by 4.29 until @ 12.29. **CUAS** Duxford 1931. To Civilian Register as *G-ACFN*, registered 22.3.33 to Commercial Airways. Sold for scrap 5.36.

F4543 B&C for reconditioning to J Type (s/n 6354) and ready by 4.12.23. **PD** Ascot. To India. **AD** Drigh Road. **AP** Lahore by 11.23. **28 Sqn** NW Frontier.

F4544 **4 Sqn** Farnborough. B&C for reconditioning to J Type (s/n 6360) and ready by 30.11.23. **PD** Ascot. To India. **AD** Drigh Road. **AP** Lahore by 11.24 until @ 2.25. **5 Sqn** as a/c Y 1925. **AP** Lahore by 1.26. **5 Sqn** by 4.28 and wrecked 5.12.29 (hit a stationary aircraft). **20 Sqn** by 1.31 until @ 8.31.

F4545 B&C for reconditioning to J Type (s/n 6471) and ready by 14.7.24. **4 Sqn** Farnborough by 7.24. **13 Sqn** Andover 1924 until @ 1926 and known to have crashed. B&C for reconditioning to Mk.III (s/n 7133) and possibly not fully converted. **A&AEE** Martlesham Heath by 6.28 until @ 8.28. B&C for reconditioning to Mk.IV (s/n 7248) and possibly not converted. ready by 4.10.23. **2 Sqn** Manston by 7.29. **16 Sqn** Old Sarum by 2.30.

F4546 **FPS** Turnhouse by 1.10.19. B&C for reconditioning to J Type (s/n 6332) and ready by 3.11.23. **2 Sqn** Manston by 1.25 and wrecked 9.25 (Flt Lt Culley/Fg Off Reedman both OK, crashed and o/t at Worthy Down). **Home Comms Flt** Henlow by 7.26. **RAF (Cadet) College** Cranwell by 2.28.

F4547 B&C for reconditioning to J Type (s/n 6300) and ready by 21.9.23. **RAF (Cadet) College** Cranwell by 12.23 until @ 12.24.

F4548 B&C for reconditioning to J Type (s/n 6325) and ready by 22.10.23. **24 Sqn** Kenley by 2.25 and wrecked 30.6.25 (Fg Off R.E. Rose/passenger both OK, Engine temperature rose whilst over Epping Forest, force landed in a field on Nazing Common, struck a mound, went over on nose and broke undercarriage). B&C for reconditioning to DC (s/n 6869) and ready by 1.12.25. **RAF (Cadet) College** Cranwell by 5.27. B&C for reconditioning 7.12.28. **RAF (Cadet) College** Cranwell by 2.29 until @ 3.30. B&C for reconditioning to J Type (s/n 6325) and ready by 22.10.23. B&C for reconditioning to Mk.III DC (s/n 7569), ready by 25.11.30 and retaken on RAF charge 11.12.30. **CUAS** Duxford until @ 1931.

F4549 B&C for reconditioning to J Type (s/n 6328) and ready by 26.10.23. **13 Sqn** Andover by 3.25 and crashed. **RAF (Cadet) College** Cranwell by 9.27.

F4550 B&C for reconditioning to J Type (s/n 6344) and ready by 9.11.23. **SAC** Old Sarum by 1.24. **16 Sqn/SAC** Old Sarum by 1.4.24 until @ 11.24.

F4551 B&C for reconditioning to J Type (s/n 6297) and ready by 21.9.23. **24 Sqn** Kenley.

F4552 **RAF (Cadet) College** Cranwell by 3.24 and wrecked 29.7.24 (Flt Cdt H.H. Aspinall KIFA, spun in from 500ft on approach to Spittlegate).

F4553 B&C for reconditioning to J Type (s/n 6350) and ready by 16.11.23. B&C for reconditioning to Mk.III (s/n 7134) and ready by 13.6.28. **Andover SF** by 10.28 until @ 4.30.

F4554 B&C for reconditioning to J Type (s/n 6349) and ready by 29.11.23.

F4555 B&C for reconditioning to J Type (s/n 6366) and ready by 14.12.23. **PD** Ascot. To India. **AD** Drigh Road. **31 Sqn** by 3.25. **AP** Lahore by 6.25 until 7.25. **31 Sqn** 7.9125 until @ 10.25. **5 Sqn** by 10.26 until @ 3.27. **31 Sqn** marked as a/c E. **20 Sqn** as a/c E by 7.30 until @ 10.30.

F4556 B&C for reconditioning to J Type (s/n 6639) and ready by 7.3.25. **24 Sqn** Kenley.

F4557 **2 FS** Marske, photographed early 1919.

F4558 **16 Sqn** Old Sarum by 5.24. B&C for reconditioning to J Type (s/n 6642) and ready by 4.3.25. **PD** Ascot. To Iraq. **AD** Hinaidi. **HQ Iraq Command Comms Flt** by 8.27.

F4559 B&C for reconditioning to J Type (s/n 6637) and ready by 4.3.25.

F4560 **AGS** Eastchurch and wrecked 7.2.24 (crashed avoiding another aircraft on take off at Eastchurch).

F4561 **115 Sqn** by 11.18 until @ 1.2.20. **24 Sqn** Kenley by 3.24. B&C for reconditioning to J Type (s/n 6302) and ready by 21.9.23. B&C for reconditioning to DC (s/n 6912) and ready by 4.3.26. **23 Group HQ** Spittlegate by 6.26 until @ 7.26. **School of Photography Flt** Kenley by 3.28. **AGS** Eastchurch by 10.28.

F4562 B&C for reconditioning to J Type (s/n 6693) and ready by 1.5.25. **PD** Ascot. To India. **AD** Drigh Road. **20 Sqn** as a/c C by 1927 and wrecked 14.5.30 (crashed at Ali Masjid, near Peshawar).

F4563 B&C for reconditioning to J Type (s/n 6370) and ready by 21.12.23. **13 Sqn** Andover 1924. **1 FTS** Netheravon by 5.25. Handley Page for test 3.2.28. **2 Sqn** Manston by 4.28 until @ 9.28.

F4564 **RAF (Cadet) College** Cranwell as DC machine by 18.7.23 until @ 9.4.25. B&C for reconditioning to J Type DC (s/n 6906) and ready by 15.2.26. **IACF** Northolt by 6.26 until @ 10.26.

F4565 B&C for reconditioning to J Type (s/n 6327) and ready by 25.10.23. **SAC** Old Sarum by 6.24 until @ 9.26. B&C for

reconditioning to J Type (s/n 6344) and ready by 9.11.23. B&C for reconditioning to Mk.III (s/n 7154) and ready by 9.6.28. **13 Sqn** Andover by 7.28. **PD** Ascot. To India. **AD** Drigh Road. **AP** Lahore by 10.28.

F4566 B&C for reconditioning to J Type (s/n 6290) and ready by 12.9.23. **PD** Ascot. To India. **AD** Drigh Road. **AP** Lahore. **5 Sqn** by 10.24 and wrecked 1.11.24 (spun in on turn at Dardoni).

F4567 **RAE** Farnborough 1919. B&C for reconditioning to J Type (s/n 6276) and ready by 24.8.23. **CFS** Upavon by 11.23. **2 Sqn** Manston and wrecked 8.5.24 (crashed at Manston). B&C for reconditioning (s/n 6941) and ready by 12.6.26. **16 Sqn/SAC** Old Sarum by 10.27 until @ 4.29.

F4568 B&C for reconditioning to J Type (s/n 6280) and ready by 30.8.23. **PD** Ascot. To India. **AD** Drigh Road. **AP** Lahore by 5.3.24 until @ 5.24. **5 Sqn** and wrecked 3.7.24 (crashed from 500ft whilst photographing).

F4569 B&C for reconditioning to J Type (s/n 6278) and ready by 28.8.23. **CFS** Upavon by 3.24 until @ 6.26. **16 Sqn** Old Sarum. B&C for reconditioning to Mk.III (s/n 7153) and ready by 5.6.28.

F4570 B&C for reconditioning to J Type (s/n 6288) and ready by 8.9.23. **PD** Ascot. To Iraq. **AD** Hinaidi. **6 Sqn** by 12.24 until @ 5.25.

F4571 **RAF (Cadet) College** Cranwell as a/c 4 by 1.23. B&C for reconditioning to J Type (s/n 6340) and ready by 8.11.23. **208 Sqn** by 1.25. **RAF Cadet College** Cranwell 1925. B&C for reconditioning to (s/n 6957) and ready by 2.7.26. **24 Sqn** Kenley by 4.28 until @ 4.30.

F4572 B&C for reconditioning to J Type (s/n 6352) and ready by 21.11.23. **13 Sqn** Andover and wrecked 2.10.24 (Fg Off A.H. Stirling/AC1 W.J.A. Turton both KIFA, spun in from 2,000-3,000ft, at Penton Mewsey, Wilts).

F4573 B&C for reconditioning to J Type (s/n 6460) and ready by 4.7.24. **4 Sqn** Farnborough by 5.25 until @ 5.26. **PD** Ascot. To Iraq. **AD** Hinaidi. **HQ Iraq Command Comms Flt** by 5.28.

F4574 B&C for reconditioning to J Type (s/n 6329) and ready by 24.10.23. **PD** Ascot. To Egypt. **AD** Aboukir. **208 Sqn** by 6.25 until @ 8.25.

F4575 Presentation a/c *1st Reserve Battalion Honourable Artillery Company No.1*. **PD** Ascot. To Egypt. **AD** Aboukir. **208 Sqn** by 3.25 until @ 4.25.

F4576 (Falcon III) **5 AAP** Bristol 29.10.18 for **138 Sqn (Mobilising)**. **138 Sqn** Chingford and wrecked 6.11.18 (Lt J.S. Bower-Binns/Sgt W.H. Martin both KIFA, forced landing into trees – engine 3/F/264/WD51965).

F4577 **5 AAP** Bristol 29.10.18 for **138 Sqn (Mobilising)**. To **138 Sqn** Chingford dd 2.11.18.

F4578 **5 AAP** Bristol 29.10.18 for **138 Sqn (Mobilising)**. To **138 Sqn** Chingford dd 2.11.18.

F4579 **5 AAP** Bristol 29.10.18 for **138 Sqn (Mobilising)**. To **138 Sqn** Chingford by 11.18. **SAC** Worthy Down by 17.5.19. **Netheravon Flying School** and wrecked on Practice Flight 14.8.19 (side-slipped and spun in near Harley 14.8.19).

F4580 **5 AAP** Bristol 29.10.18 for **138 Sqn (Mobilising)**. To **138 Sqn** Chingford by 11.18. **16 Sqn** by 5.24. **6 Sqn**.

This F.2B, F4580 'M', was one of those supplied to 138 Sqn at Chingford in 1918, but the unit did not become operational before the Armistice and was disbanded on 1 February 1919. By May 1924 F4580 was with 16 Sqn. *(Eric Harlin)*

F4581 B&C for reconditioning to J Type (s/n 6336) and ready by 31.10.23. **1 SoTT (Boys)** Halton by 2.24 until @ 1.25.

F4582 **PD** Ascot. To Egypt. **AD** Aboukir reconditioned as FR4582. **208 Sqn** by 9.22 and wrecked 24.11.22 (force landed near Shile on Ismid Peninsula after engine failure and burnt by salvage party).

F4583 B&C for reconditioning to J Type (s/n 6359) and ready by 4.12.23. **PD** Ascot. To Egypt. **AD** Aboukir and reconditioned as FR4583.

14 Sqn by 1.25 until @ 10.25. **208 Sqn** by 12.25 until @ 11.28. **AD** Aboukir. **6 Sqn** by 24.7.30. **AD** Aboukir by 2.12.31. **6 Sqn** by 2.32.

F4584 B&C for reconditioning to J Type (s/n 6293) and ready by 19.9.23. **24 Sqn** Kenley by 1.25. B&C for reconditioning to DC (s/n 6877) and ready 19.12.25. **2 FTS** Digby by 3.27. **RAF (Cadet) College Cranwell** by 5.27.

F4585 **2 FTS** Duxford by 6.24. **2 Sqn** Manston by 10.24. B&C for reconditioning to J Type DC (s/n 6822) and ready by 2.10.25. **2 Sqn** Manston by 1.26 until @ 6.26. **2 FTS** Digby by 11.27 until @ 1.28.

F4586 B&C for reconditioning to J Type (s/n 6334) and ready by 9.11.23. B&C for reconditioning to DC (s/n 6904) and ready by 11.2.26. **6 Sqn** by 6.30. **24 Sqn** dd ex RAE Farnborough 19.1.37.

F4587 B&C for reconditioning to J Type (s/n 6331) and ready by 27.10.23. **16 Sqn** Old Sarum. **School of Photography Flt Kenley** by 4.25 until @ 10.25. B&C for reconditioning to Mk.III (s/n 7146) and ready 23.5.28. **A&AEE** Martlesham Heath by 9.28 until @ 2.29. **Handley Page Ltd. RAE** Farnborough by 15.1.30. Handley Page Ltd by 9.12.31 (rudder and spinning trials). **24 Sqn** Hendon by 19.1.37 (stored for display purposes) and exhibited at Hendon Air Pageant 26.6.37. To Civilian Register as *G-AFHJ* 1.9.38, registered to Sqn Ldr N.R. Buckle. Destroyed by enemy action during WWII.

F4588 B&C for reconditioning to J Type (s/n 6338) and ready by 3.11.23. **RAF (Cadet) College** Cranwell by 10.24 until @ 12.24. B&C for reconditioning to DC (s/n 6901) and ready by 28.1.26. B&C for reconditioning (s/n 7172) and ready 4.5.28. **PD** Ascot. **AD** Aboukir and reconditioned as FR4588. **208 Sqn** Ismailia.

F4589 B&C for reconditioning to J Type (s/n 6273) and ready by 23.8.23. **2 FTS** Duxford and wrecked on cross-country 24.10.23 (Plt Off C.F. Roupell OK, forced landed near Market Harborough after fuel failure). **PD** Ascot. To Egypt. **AD** Aboukir. **208 Sqn** 1926. **AD** Aboukir and reconstructed as FR4589. **208 Sqn** Ismailia.

F4590 B&C for reconditioning to J Type (s/n 6353) and ready by 20.11.23. **SAC** Old Sarum. **2 Sqn** Manston by 11.25 until @ 1.26. **IAAD, ARS** Henlow by 2.26. B&C for reconditioning to Mk.III (s/n 7094) and ready by 28.5.27. B&C for reconditioning to Mk.IV (s/n 7255) and ready by 21.9.28. **PD** Ascot. To Iraq. **AD** Hinaidi. **6 Sqn**.

F4591 **138 Sqn** Chingford by 22.10.18. B&C for reconditioning to J Type (s/n 6283) and ready by 3.9.23. **PD** Ascot. To Egypt. **AD** Aboukir. **6 Sqn** by 11.23 until @ 5.25. Noted at B&C for reconditioning (s/n 6947) and ready by 18.6.26. **PD** Ascot. To Egypt. **AD** Aboukir. **6 Sqn** by 4.30 until @ 11.30.

F4592 B&C for reconditioning to J Type (s/n 6292) and ready by 13.9.23. **PD** Ascot. To India. **AD** Drigh Road. **20 Sqn** by 7.24. **5 Sqn** as a/c *D* by 8.24 until 1927 (named *White City*). (Noted as having been taxied into at Henlow by Avro 504K D7535 2.6.25 – damaged Cat R).

F4593 **PD** Ascot. To India. **AD** Drigh Road. **5 Sqn** by 12.23. **31 Sqn** and wrecked 6.10.24 (controls jammed and struck ground while landing).

F4594 B&C for reconditioning to J Type (s/n 6412) and ready by 15.3.24. **PD** Ascot. To India. **AD** Drigh Road. **31 Sqn** by 8.25 until @ 8.26.

F4595 B&C for reconditioning to J Type (s/n 6398) and ready by 28.2.24. **2 FTS** Digby by 8.24 until @ 1.25.

F4596 B&C for reconditioning to J Type (s/n 6337) and ready by 2.11.10.23.

F4597 **PD** Ascot. To India. **AD** Drigh Road. **5 Sqn** as a/c *U* by 11.20 and wrecked 16.6.22 (stalled on take off at Quetta). Repaired. **20 Sqn** by 11.22 until @ 5.23.

F4598 B&C for reconditioning to J Type (s/n 6356) and ready by 1.12.23. **PD** Ascot. To India. **AD** Drigh Road. **5 Sqn** by 12.24 until @ 6.25. **AD** Drigh Road 1927. **20 Sqn** by 23.4.27.

F4599 B&C for reconditioning to J Type (s/n 6307) and ready by 3.10.23. **PD** Ascot. To India. **AD** Drigh Road. **AP** Lahore by 10.24 until @ 12.24. **6 Sqn** as a/c *H*. **AD** Drigh Road 1926. **20 Sqn** by 11.31 until @ 2.32.

F4600 B&C for reconditioning to J Type (s/n 6358) and ready by 28.11.23. **SAC** Old Sarum and wrecked 8.4.24 (crashed on camera gun practice at Old Sarum). **PD** Ascot. To Iraq. **AD** Hinaidi and reconstructed as FR4600. **6 Sqn** Mosul. **14 Sqn** by 11.25. Heliopolis by 5.27 until @ 7.27. **208 Sqn** by 9.29. **6 Sqn** by 5.30 until @ 5.32.

F4601 B&C for reconditioning to J Type (s/n 6371) and ready by 21.12.23. **PD** Ascot. To Egypt. **AD** Aboukir by 8.24. **208 Sqn** by 10.24 until @ 10.25, **6 Sqn**.

F4602 B&C for reconditioning to J Type (s/n 6365) and ready by 19.12.23. **PD** Ascot. To India. **AD** Drigh Road. **AP** Lahore by 11.24 until @ 12.24. **20 Sqn** by 3.25 until @ 4.25. **HQ India** and in starting accident, 5.4.29.

F4603 B&C for reconditioning to J Type (s/n 6466) and ready by 8.7.24. **SAC** Old Sarum by 9.25. B&C for reconditioning (s/n 6981) and ready by 24.7.26. **4 Sqn** Farnborough by 3.26 until @ 9.26. **HAD** Henlow by 4.27. Shipped China (for **2 Sqn** Shanghai?). **HQ India** by 4.29. **20 Sqn**.

F4604 B&C for reconditioning to J Type (s/n 6362) and ready by 5.12.23. **PD** Ascot. To India. **AD** Drigh Road. **31 Sqn** by 3.25 until @ 5.26. **AD** Drigh Road 1927 (converted to DC). **20 Sqn** by 1930.

F4605 B&C for reconditioning to J Type (s/n 6685) and ready by 21.4.25. **PD** Ascot. To Mesopotamia. **AD** Hinaidi. **AHQ Iraq Command Comms Flt** by 25.6.5.27.

F4606 B&C for reconditioning to J Type (s/n 6346) and ready by 14.11.23. **SAC** Old Sarum and wrecked 8.4.24 (Plt Off F.F.R Goldsmith/LAC H.S. Nicholls both KIFA, stalled on turn and crashed at Old Sarum).

F4607 B&C for reconditioning to J Type (s/n 6301) and ready by 27.9.23. **RAF (Cadet) College** Cranwell by 12.24 and wrecked 30.6.25 (Flt Cdt F. Priestman OK, engine failed at 200ft after take off and hit a hedge in forced landing near Bircham Newton). B&C for reconditioning to DC (s/n 6891) and ready by 14.1.26. **PD** Ascot. To India. **AD** Drigh Road. **5 Sqn** by 6.26.

F4608 N/I

F4609 B&C for reconditioning to J Type (s/n 6465) and ready by 7.7.24. **E&WS** Worthy Down by 11.25 until @ 10.26. **PD** Ascot. To India. **AD** Drigh Road. In India 10.28.

F4610 B&C for reconditioning to J Type (s/n 6342) and ready by 9.11.23. B&C for reconditioning to DC (s/n 6913) and ready by 10.3.26. B&C for reconditioning (s/n 7245) and ready by 6.9.28. **HAD** Henlow. **RAF (Cadet) College** Cranwell by 10.28 until @ 8.29. B&C for reconditioning and ready by 5.5.30. Returned to RAF charge 16.6.30. **5 FTS** Sealand by 8.30 until @ 8.31.

F4611 To India. **48 Sqn** as a/c *D* by 12.19, on unit charge when redesignated **5 Sqn** 1.2.20 and wrecked 16.8.22 (crashed on take off at Pislim).

F4612 To Middle East. **ASD ME** dd ex England 13.10.19. **14 Sqn** by 12.22 until @ 5.23. Crashed (Colonel Lawrence).

F4613 N/I

F4614 **PD** Ascot. To India. **AD** Drigh Road. **28 Sqn** by 6.21 until @ 9.21. **20 Sqn** by 9.22. **5 Sqn** by 10.22 until @ 1.23.

F4615 N/I

F4616 (Falcon III) **8 AAP** Lympne 24.12.18, reallotted from BEF to 11 Group Ireland for **105 Sqn** then again allotted to BEF 22.1.19. **105 Sqn** Omagh by 11.19 until @ 2.20. To India. **5 Sqn** marked as a/c *M*. To Egypt. **208 Sqn** by 7.25.

F4617 N/I

F4618 (Falcon III) **2 AAP** Hendon 16.1.19, reallotted from BEF to storage. **2 FTS** Duxford by 9.21. B&C for reconditioning to J Type (s/n 6570) and ready by 19.12.24. **16 Sqn/SAC** Old Sarum by 5.25. **2 FTS** Digby. B&C for reconditioning to Mk.III (s/n 7101) and ready by 29.6.27. B&C for reconditioning to Mk.IV (new type undercarriage fitted) and ready by 29.9.27. B&C dd 19.1.28 (demonstration). **A&AEE** Martlesham Heath by 5.28.

F4619 (Falcon III) **2 AAP** Hendon 16.1.19, reallotted from BEF to storage. B&C for reconditioning to J Type (s/n 6482) and ready by 10.9.24. **RAF (Cadet) College** Cranwell.

F4620 **5 FTS** Sealand by 10.26.

F4621 B&C for reconditioning to J Type (s/n 6305) and ready by 28.9.23. **PD** Ascot. To India. **AD** Drigh Road. **AP** Lahore by 10.24. **5 Sqn** by 10.26 until @ 3.27. **20 Sqn** as a/c *K* by 8.30 until @ 3.31.

F4622 **SAC** Old Sarum by 12.22 until @ 6.23. B&C for reconditioning to J Type DC (s/n 6840) and ready by 22.10.25. **RAF (Cadet) College** Cranwell by 2.26 until @ 3.28.

F4623 **208 Sqn** by 1.21. B&C for reconditioning to J Type (s/n 6315) and ready by 11.10.23. **16 Sqn/SAC** Old Sarum by 12.24 until @ 8.26.

F4624 B&C for reconditioning to J Type (s/n 6312) and ready by 10.10.23. B&C for reconditioning (s/n 6977) and ready by 17.7.26. **HAD** Henlow by 4.27. Shipped China (for **2 Sqn** Shanghai?). **2 Sqn** Manston by 1.30.

F4625 To India. **48 Sqn** by 12.19 and on unit charge when redesignated **5 Sqn** 1.2.20.

F4626 To India. **20 Sqn** and damaged on Patrol 30.7.19, fired at Simla (Capt G. Eastwood WIA/2nd Lt D.M. Lapraik OK, hit by ground fire at Simla).

F4627 To India. **48 Sqn** by 12.19 and on unit charge when redesignated **5 Sqn** 1.2.20 and wrecked 16.4.20 (crashed at Loralei LG).

F4628 To India. **20 Sqn** by 9.19.

F4629 To India. **20 Sqn** by 11.20.

F4630 To India. **114 Sqn** by 12.19; and on unit charge when redesignated **28 Sqn** 1.2.20. **RAF School (India)** by 11.21. **5 Sqn** and wrecked 29.1.24 (crashed on turn when approaching Sangor Maia LG).

F4631 (Arab) with B&C by 10.11.18 until @ 20.11.18 (Lt C.F. Uwins). **ES** Martlesham Heath dd 27.11.18 (new type mounting) and with unit when redesignated **A&AEE**, still at Martlesham. **SAC** Old Sarum by 4.28.

F4632 N/I

F4633 To India. **20 Sqn** by 6.20.

F4634 To India. **114 Sqn** by 12.19, unit redesignated **28 Sqn** 1.2.20 and wrecked 16.4.20. Repaired. **28 Sqn** by 6.21 until @ 9.21. **5 Sqn** by 11.22 until @ 1.24.

F4635 To India. **5 Sqn** and wrecked 10.4.20 (force landed in river bed after engine failure).

F4636 To India. **114 Sqn** by 11.19, unit redesignated **28 Sqn** 1.2.20 and on charge until @ 6.20. **RAF School (India)** by 11.21. **5 Sqn** by 10.11.21 until @ 10.23.

F4637 To India. **48 Sqn** as a/c *A* by 11.19 and on charge when unit redesignated **5 Sqn** 1.2.20.

F4638 N/I

F4639 **PD** Ascot. To India. **AD** Drigh Road. **60 Sqn** as DC by 2.23 until @ 7.23.

F4640 (Arab) to India. **114 Sqn** by 12.19 and on unit charge when redesignated **28 Sqn** 1.2.20. **AD** Drigh Road and reconstructed as FR4640. **AP** Lahore. **28 Sqn** reissued ex AP 9.5.21 (replaced E2248).

F4641 **PD** Ascot. To India. **AD** Drigh Road. **AP** Lahore by 2.23.

F4642 B&C for reconditioning to J Type DC (s/n 6443) and ready by 7.5.24. Photographed as a/c *3*, crashed into a hedge.

F4643 B&C for reconditioning to J Type (s/n 6590) and ready by 20.1.25. To India. **31 Sqn** as a/c *L*, later *J*, by 6.28. **Quetta SF** by 6.28. **20 Sqn** by 1.29 until @ 1.30.

F4644 B&C for reconditioning to J Type (s/n 6454) and ready by 31.5.24. To India. **5 Sqn** as a/c *F*. B&C for reconditioning (to Mk.IV?) and ready by 30.1.30. **CUAS** Duxford by 6.30 until @ 7.30.

F4645 B&C for reconditioning to J Type (s/n 6427) and ready by 22.3.24. **24 Sqn** Kenley marked as a/c *Q*. B&C for reconditioning (s/n 7160) and ready by 28.2.28. **CUAS** Duxford by 10.28 until @ 7.29. **School of Photography** Farnborough by 4.30 until @ 8.30.

F4646 B&C for reconditioning to J Type (s/n 6458) and ready by 6.6.24. **24 Sqn** Kenley by 9.24 until @ 7.25. **HAD** Henlow by 11.26. **SAC** Old Sarum by 10.28 until @ 4.29. **2 Sqn** Manston by 5.29.

F4647 B&C for reconditioning to J Type DC (s/n 6429) and ready by 2.4.24. **5 FTS** Sealand by 10.24 until @ 12.24.

F4648 B&C for reconditioning to J Type DC (s/n 6439) and ready by 26.4.24. **2 FTS** Duxford by 9.24 until @ 11.24. **4 Sqn** Farnborough by 4.27.

F4649 B&C for reconditioning to J Type (s/n 6459) and ready by 30.6.24. **24 Sqn** Kenley.

F4650 B&C for reconditioning to J Type DC (s/n 6442) and ready by 3.5.24. **2 FTS** Duxford by 11.24 until @ 2.19.27.

F4651 (Falcon III) **8 AAP** Lympne by 24.12.18, reallotted from BEF to 11 Group for **105 Sqn**. In France 22.1.19, allotted to BEF. **105 Sqn** Omagh until 1.2.20. To Egypt. **208 Sqn** Maoscar. **14 Sqn** by 1922. **4 FTS** Abu Sueir by 10.19.23. To UK. B&C for reconditioning to J Type DC (s/n 6855) and ready by 9.11.25. **1 FTS** Netheravon.

F4652 **PD** Ascot. To India. **AD** Drigh Road; **1 (Indian) Group**.

F4653 N/I

F4654 N/I

F4655 **PD** Ascot. To Egypt. **AD** Aboukir. **208 Sqn** by 7.29 until @ 5.30.

F4656 **5 AAP** Filton dd w/e 21.11.18. **FPS** Turnhouse dd w/e 12.12.18 until @ 30.1.19. **27 TDS** Crail. **FPS** Turnhouse ex Crail 5.3.19 until @ 4.10.19.

F4657 **4 Sqn** Farnborough and wrecked 20.1.22 (Fg Off E.A.C. Bilton DFC IIFA, ran into thick fog at 300ft en route Henlow-Farnborough, attempted to turn back but flew into the ground at Monks Wood, near Stevenage, Herts, and machine burnt out).

F4658 B&C for reconditioning to J Type (s/n 6294) and ready by 13.9.23. **PD** Ascot. To India. **AD** Drigh Road. **5 Sqn** by 11.24 until @ 6.25. **20 Sqn** as a/c *H*. **AD** Drigh Road 1927. **31 Sqn**.

F4659 **ACIS** by 8.19 (for Directorate of Research). **WEE** Biggin Hill by 9.19.

F4660 **5 FTS** Sealand and wrecked 9.11.22 (Plt Off G.A.F. Bucknall OK, ran into hedge during forced landing after engine failure near Shotwick). B&C for reconditioning to J Type (s/n 6626) and ready by 25.2.25. To India. **AD** Drigh Road. **5 Sqn** by 7.26 until @ 9.26.

F4661 **12 Sqn** as a/c *B6* by 23.10.19 (Lt J.W. Baker) and wrecked 9.8.21 (side-slipped and crashed at Bickendorf).

F4662 N/I

F4663 N/I

F4664 Presentation a/c *Tyldesley*. **PD** Ascot. To India. **AD** Drigh Road. **31 Sqn**.

F4665 Eastchurch (AGS?). B&C for reconditioning to J Type (s/n 6618) and ready by 14.2.25. **PD** Ascot. To India. **AD** Drigh Road. **31 Sqn** by 3.26. **AD** Drigh Road 1927. **AP** Lahore by 3.29. **20 Sqn** as a/c *K* by 5.30 – until @ 10.31.

F4666 **APS** Andover and wrecked 20.7.21 (Fg Off A.J. Warwick/AC2 Heaton both OK; ran into boundary hedge at Andover after engine failed on take off).

F4667 B&C for reconditioning to J Type (s/n 6600) and ready by 26.1.25. **Staff College Flt** Andover by 5.25.

F4668 To India. **20 Sqn** marked as a/c *H*.

F4669 **105 Sqn** Oranmore and wrecked 5.6.19 (2nd Lt D.W. Beard IIFA/2nd Lt F. Clarke fatally IIFA, machine was rigged nose-heavy and was unable to exit spin – engine 18659).

F4670 **ACIS** Worthy Down by 8.19 (for use by General Longmore). B&C for reconditioning to J Type (s/n 6615) and ready by 11.2.25. **PD** Ascot. To India. **AD** Drigh Road. **5 Sqn** by 12.25 until @ 3.26. **AD** Drigh Road 1927.

F4671 (Falcon III) **5 AAP** Bristol by 25.1.19, reallotted from NW Area to BEF. **2 FTS** Digby by 7.24.

F4672 N/I

F4673 **22 Sqn** by 18.5.19 and wrecked 27.6.19 (Lt Kent OK, force landed in cornfield near Marquise – engine WD52062).

F4674 N/I

F4675 **RAE** Farnborough dd 2.1.19 (Handley Page slotted wings and used for rudder surface trials). **A&AEE** Martlesham Heath by 20.11.28. **SD Flt** Netheravon by 12.10.29 until @ 4.30.

F4676 **1 SoTT (Boys)** Halton by 2.25.

F4677 Presentation a/c *Kotah No.3.* **5 AAP** Bristol by 17.1.19. **Staff College Flt** Andover by 7.25.

F4678 (Falcon III) presentation a/c *Winnipeg*. **8 AAP** Lympne 24.12.18, reallotted from BEF to 11 Group for **105 Sqn**. In France 21.1.19, allotted to BEF.

F4679 (Falcon III) presentation a/c *Presented by Maharaja Bahadur Sir Rameswar Singh of Darbhanga No.5.* **8 AAP** Lympne by 24.12.18, reallotted from BEF to 11 Group for **105 Sqn**. In France 11.2.19, reallotted from 11 Group to BEF. **12 Sqn** by 3.8.19 until @ 27.8.19 (Lt J.W. Baker). Old Sarum by 3.20. **SAC** Old Sarum by 6.23 and wrecked 7.6.23 (Plt Off A. King-Lewis OK/Plt Off F.W.M. Downer IIFA, engine cut out over aerodrome and machine crashed).

F4680 (Falcon III) presentation a/c *Johore No.6.* **8 AAP** Lympne 24.12.18, reallotted from BEF to 11 Group for **105 Sqn**. In France 21.1.19, allotted to BEF. B&C for reconditioning to J Type (s/n 6558) and ready by 9.12.24. **6 Sqn**. To **CFS** Upavon by 10.28 until @ 5.29. **5 FTS** Sealand by 11.26 until @ 12.26.

F4681 **PD** Ascot. To Iraq. **AD** Hinaidi. **6 Sqn** by 11.22 until @ 5.23. B&C for reconditioning to J Type (s/n 6476) and ready by 29.8.24. B&C for reconditioning to Mk.III (s/n 7143) and ready by 15.6.28. **4 Sqn** Farnborough by 7.28. **23 Group HQ** Spittlegate by 2.29 until @ 11.29. **3 FTS** Spittlegate and wrecked on Ferry Flight, Grantham-Eastchurch, 23.12.30 (hit a tree during forced landing near High Ongar, Essex).

This picture captures F.2B Mk.III F4681 at an interesting stage in its life. It has evidently been modified to serve as a communications aircraft, and a greatly enlarged rear fuselage top-decking has been fitted. This might well have been done when it was on charge with 23 Group HQ at Spittlegate in 1929. The following year F4681 was allocated to No.3 FTS, but was wrecked while being ferried from Grantham to Eastchurch on 23 December 1930 when it hit a tree during a forced landing near High Ongar in Essex. *(Philip Jarrett)*

F4682 B&C for reconditioning to J Type (s/n 6479) and ready by 3.9.24. **PD** Ascot. To Egypt. **AD** Aboukir. **208 Sqn** by 5.25 until @ 9.25. **AD** Aboukir. **208 Sqn** by 28.5.29 and in starting accident, 3.7.29. **6 Sqn** by 1.32 until @ 6.32.

F4683 **CFS** Upavon by 6.24. B&C for reconditioning to J Type (s/n 6480) and ready by 5.9.24. **16 Sqn/SAC** Old Sarum by 2.28 until @ 2.30. **31 Sqn**. **PD** Ascot. To Egypt. **AD** Aboukir by 2.12.31. **6 Sqn** by 2.32.

F4684 B&C for reconditioning to J Type (s/n 6478) and ready by 3.9.24. B&C for reconditioning (s/n 6987) and ready by 19.8.26. **24 Sqn** Kenley by 5.29.

F4685 B&C for reconditioning to J Type (s/n 6440) and ready by 3.5.24. **2 FTS** Digby by 9.24, damaged 21.11.24 (Flt Lt D.P. Hadow MC/ Plt Off A.B. Smith MC both OK, bracing wire fractured at 1,000ft, went on nose when landing) and on unit charge until @ 5.28.

F4686 **IAAD** Henlow tested 12.6.23. **SAC** Old Sarum by 3.24 until @ 9.24. B&C for reconditioning to J Type (s/n 6701) and ready by 8.5.25. **PD** Ascot. To Iraq. **AD** Hinaidi. **6 Sqn** by 6.29, damaged 2.30 (force landed near Jericho after engine failure) and on unit charge until @ 9.30.

F4687 B&C for reconditioning to J Type (s/n 6477) and ready by 30.8.24. To Iraq. **AHQ Iraq Command Comms Flt** by 11.25 until @ 1.26.

F4688 B&C for reconditioning to J Type (s/n 6428) and ready by 22.3.24. **24 Sqn** Kenley by 1926.

Aviation author, editor and artist Leonard Bridgman photographed F.2B F4688 when it was serving as a communications aircraft with 24 Sqn at Kenley. Another 24 Sqn F.2B, H1456, is in the background. *(Philip Jarrett)*

F4689 B&C for reconditioning to J Type (s/n 6481) and ready by 9.9.24. **PD** Ascot. To India. **AD** Drigh Road. **31 Sqn** as a/c *B* by 7.25 until @ 10.25. **20 Sqn** and crashed on nose. **AD** Drigh Road 1927. **AP** Lahore by 13.8.27. **5 Sqn** by 3.28 until @ 6.28.

F4690 **2 FTS** Duxford by 3.24 until @ 4.24.

F4691 B&C for reconditioning to J Type DC (s/n 6431) and ready by 29.4.24. **2 FTS** Digby by 7.24 until @ 4.25. B&C for reconditioning to Mk.III DC (s/n 7126) and ready by 26.8.27. **School of Photography Flt Kenley** by 8.27. **AGS** Eastchurch by 9.28 until @ 9.29. **School of Photography Flt Kenley** by 3.30. **16 Sqn/SAC** Old Sarum by 3.30 until @ 6.30. **5 FTS** Sealand by 7.31 until @ 8.31.

F4692 B&C for reconditioning to J Type (s/n 6432) and ready by 1.5.24. **2 FTS** Digby by 10.24 and wrecked 30.3.25 (collided on take off at Cranwell with Avro 504K D4432).

F4693 B&C for reconditioning to J Type (s/n 6418) and ready by 15.3.24. To India. **AD** Drigh Road. **31 Sqn** by 7.25 until @ 9.25. **AD** Drigh Rd 1927. **20 Sqn** by 6.27. **5 Sqn** by 4.28 until @ 7.28.

F4694 B&C for reconditioning to J Type (s/n 6475) and ready by 19.7.24.

F4695 **4 FTS** Abu Sueir by 9.23. Returned to UK. B&C for reconditioning to J Type (s/n 6492) and ready by 29.9.24.

F4696 **AGS** Eastchurch and wrecked 22.12.20 (crashed on landing at Eastchurch after engine failed at low altitude). **PD** Ascot. To Egypt. **AD** Aboukir by 8.26 until @ 10.26.

F4697 B&C for reconditioning to J Type (s/n 6451) and ready by 17.5.24. **SAC** Old Sarum by 3.28 until @ 4.28. B&C for reconditioning (to Mk.IV?) and ready by 20.12.29. Retaken onto RAF charge 31.1.30. **School of Photography Flt Kenley** by 9.30 until @ 10.30. **4 Sqn** Farnborough by 11.30.

F4698 B&C for reconditioning to J Type (s/n 6474) and ready by 17.7.24. **24 Sqn** Kenley. B&C for reconditioning (s/n 6983) and ready by 30.7.26. **24 Sqn** Kenley by 10.27 until @ 5.30.

F4699 B&C for reconditioning to J Type (s/n 6472) and ready by 15.7.24. **2 Sqn** Manston by 11.24.

F4700 **1 FTS** Netheravon by 2.24 until @ 7.24. B&C for reconditioning to J Type (s/n 6683) and ready by 17.4.25. **PD** Ascot. To India. **AD** Drigh Road. **20 Sqn** as a/c *N* 1927-1928.

F4701 B&C for reconditioning to J Type (s/n 6497) and ready by 6.10.24. **School of Photography Flt Kenley** by 4.25 until @ 11.25. B&C for reconditioning to Mk. III DC (s/n 7117) and ready by 18.7.27.

F4702 B&C for reconditioning to J Type (s/n 6367) and ready by 19.12.23.

F4703 B&C for reconditioning to J Type (s/n 6368) and ready by 20.12.23. Heliopolis by 11.26 until @ 8.27. **13 Sqn** Andover by 10.27.

F4704 B&C for reconditioning to J Type (s/n 6311) and ready by 5.10.23.

F4705 B&C for reconditioning to J Type C (s/n 6502) and ready by 17.10.24. **RAF (Cadet) College** Cranwell as a/c *B5* by 12.24 until @ 7.25. B&C for reconditioning to DC (s/n 6881) and ready by 31.12.25. **16 Sqn/SAC** Old Sarum by 4.27 until @ 10.29. Repaired (by B&C?) and retaken onto RAF charge 14.3.30. Returned for cockpit packing. **16 Sqn** Old Sarum.

F4706 B&C for reconditioning to J Type (s/n 6341) and ready by 14.11.23. B&C for reconditioning (s/n 6632) and ready by 26.2.25. To India. **5 Sqn** by 7.26 until @ 3.28. **20 Sqn** as a/c *H* by 8.30 until @ 3.31.

F4707 **PD** Ascot. To India. **AD** Drigh Road. **5 Sqn** by 4.22. **31 Sqn** as a/c *A* and crashed by Sqn Ldr Maltby.

F4708 B&C for reconditioning to J Type DC (s/n 6500) and ready by 11.10.24. **13 Sqn** Andover 1924. **5 FTS** Sealand by 9.25 until @ 5.28.

F4709 **PD** Ascot. To Egypt. **AD** Aboukir. **14 Sqn** by 2.22. **AD** Aboukir by 2.5.23.

F4710 **1 FTS** Netheravon by 1.24. B&C for reconditioning to J Type (s/n 6679) and ready by 9.4.25. **16 Sqn/SAC** Old Sarum by 9.25 until @ 6.27.

F4711 B&C for reconditioning to J Type (s/n 6464) and ready by 7.7.24. **E&WS** Worthy Down by 10.25 until @ 10.26. To Civilian Register as *G-ABXV* 2.11.32 registered to P.H. Thomas/Hon J. Grimston and crashed near Capenoch, Dumfrieshire, 18.9.33.

F4712 B&C for reconditioning to J Type (s/n 6319) and ready by 15.10.23. **PD** Ascot. To Egypt. **AD** Aboukir. **14 Sqn** by 8.24 until @ 10.25.

F4713 B&C for reconditioning to J Type (s/n 6363) and ready by 18.12.23. **PD** Ascot. To India. **AD** Drigh Road. **31 Sqn** by 3.25.

F4714 B&C for reconditioning to J Type (s/n 6357) and ready by 27.11.23. **2 Sqn** Manston. **PD** Ascot. To Egypt. **AD** Aboukir. **208 Sqn** by 4.25 until @ 10.25.

F4715 B&C for reconditioning to J Type (s/n 6468) and ready by 9.7.24. **SAC** Old Sarum by 8.24 until @ 5.25. B&C for reconditioning to DC (s/n 6311) and ready by 4.1.26. **1 SoTT** Halton by 12.26 until @ 7.28.

F4716 B&C for reconditioning to J Type (s/n 6295) and ready by 19.9.23. **24 Sqn** Kenley by 3.24, damaged 31.7.24 (o/t in forced landing near Sandridge, Kent), repaired and on unit charge until @ 12.24.

F4717 B&C for reconditioning to J Type (s/n 6473) and ready by 16.7.24. Northolt by 12.24. **2 Sqn** Manston by 4.26 until @ 9.28 (Mk.IV).

F4718 **1 FTS** Netheravon by 2.24 and wrecked 28.3.24 (force landed near Netheravon after engine failure).

F4719 B&C for reconditioning to J Type (s/n 6369) and ready by 20.12.23. **PD** Ascot. To Egypt. **AD** Aboukir by 4.29 until @ 6.29.

F4720 B&C for reconditioning to J Type (s/n 6361) and ready by 6.12.23. **PD** Ascot. To India. **AD** Drigh Road. **20 Sqn** by 4.25.

F4721 **1 FTS** Netheravon by 10.23 until @ 4.24. B&C for reconditioning to J Type (s/n 6680) and ready by 9.4.25. **16 Sqn/SAC** Old Sarum by 7.25. B&C for reconditioning to DC (s/n 6874) and ready by 17.12.25. B&C for reconditioning to Mk.III DC (s/n 7116) and ready by 16.7.27. **5 FTS** Sealand by 6.28 until @ 11.29. B&C for reconditioning to (s/n 7559). Retaken onto RAF charge 25.8.30. To Civilian Register as *G-ABYE* 14.12.32 registered to M. Emmett. Universal Aircraft Services Ltd 3.35. Registration cancelled 4.38.

F4722 **5 FTS** Sealand and wrecked 1.12.23 (crashed landing at Sealand). B&C for reconditioning to J Type DC (s/n 6495) and ready by 4.10.24. **2 Sqn** Manston by 9.25 until @ 3.27.

F4723 B&C for reconditioning to J Type (s/n 6308) and ready by 2.10.23. **PD** Ascot. To India. **AP** Lahore by 11.24 until @ 12.24.

F4724 **IDE** Biggin Hill by 3.21 until @ 4.22 **A&AEE (15 Sqn)** Martlesham Heath by 5.25 until @ 11.26.

F4725 Marske by 2.20. **A&AEE (15 Sqn)** Martlesham Heath.

F4726 B&C for reconditioning to J Type (s/n 6266) and ready by 2.8.23. **PD** Ascot. To India. **AD** Drigh Road. **AP** Lahore by 4.24 until @ 5.24.

F4727 B&C for reconditioning to J Type (s/n 6251) and ready by 13.7.23. **PD** Ascot. To Iraq. **AD** Hinaidi and reconstructed as FR4727.

6 Sqn by 11.23. **AD** Hinaidi by 12.23. To UK 1.25. B&C for reconditioning to DC as F4727 (s/n 6847) and ready by 29.10.25. **HCF Northolt** by 9.27 until deletion authorised 11.4.28.

F4728 Scopwick. **RAE** Farnborough by 21.4.20 with three bay wings of 9.73 aspect ratio and RAF.32, used for stalling experiments 1925 and wrecked 12.9.25 (crashed after take off from Farnborough).

F4729 B&C for reconditioning to J Type (s/n 6252) and ready by 13.7.23. **PD** Ascot. To Iraq. **AD** Hinaidi. **6 Sqn** by 1924 until @ 1925.

F4730 (DC) **PD** Ascot. To India. **AD** Drigh Road. **5 Sqn** by 1.10.24 until @ 3.25. **20 Sqn** by 2.26 until @ 5.27. **5 Sqn** by 7.28.

F4731 To Egypt. **208 Sqn** by 8.20. **AD** Aboukir by 22.2.22. **208 Sqn** by 4.22. To UK. B&C for reconditioning to J Type (s/n 6253) and ready by 18.7.23. **PD** Ascot. To Iraq. **AD** Hinaidi. **6 Sqn** and wrecked 9.12.24 (caught fire at 100ft).

F4732 B&C for reconditioning to J Type (s/n 6257) and ready by 24.7.23. **PD** Ascot. To Iraq. **AD** Hinaidi. **6 Sqn** by 1924 until @ 1925. To UK. B&C for reconditioning (s/n 6946) and ready by 17.6.26.

F4733 B&C for reconditioning to J Type (s/n 6268) and ready by 10.8.23. **PD** Ascot. To India. **AD** Drigh Road. **AP** Lahore by 8.24. Transferred to Afghan Air Force 8.24.

F4734 B&C for reconditioning to J Type (s/n 6264) and ready by 3.8.23. **PD** Ascot. To India. **AD** Drigh Road. **AP** Lahore by 2.24 until @ 4.24. **5 Sqn** by 5.24.

F4735 B&C for reconditioning to J Type (s/n 6255) and ready by 17.7.23. **PD** Ascot. To India. **AD** Drigh Road. **AP** Lahore. **5 Sqn** by 1.25.

F4736 (Falcon III) **5 AAP** Bristol 25.1.19, reallotted from NW Area to BEF. **Fleet SAFG** Leuchars 2.4.19 with BEF allotment cancelled and for deletion.

F4737 B&C for reconditioning to J Type (s/n 6355) and ready by 26.11.23. B&C for reconditioning (s/n 6456) and ready by 5.6.24. **24 Sqn** Kenley 1924. **13 Sqn** Andover by 1925 until @ 6.26. **SAC** Old Sarum by 2.29 until @ 4.29. **2 Sqn** Manston by 6.29 until @ 7.29.

F4738 **4 Sqn** Farnborough and wrecked 24.1.22 (Fg Off A.A. Ward OK, force landed in bad weather and after engine trouble en route Henlow to Farnborough). Repaired. **Duxford SF** by 10.26 until @ 3.27.

F4739 **24 Sqn** Kenley and wrecked 4.2.20 (crashed at Eastchurch).

F4740 (DC) **RAF (Cadet) College** Cranwell by 6.7.23 until @ 3.29.

F4741 B&C for reconditioning to J Type (s/n 6259) and ready by 25.7.23. **16 Sqn/SAC** Old Sarum by 8.24 until @ 5.25. B&C for reconditioning to Mk.III (s/n 7106) and ready by 7.7.27. B&C for reconditioning to Mk.IV (s/n 7427). Retaken onto RAF charge 2.5.29. B&C for repair ready by 2.6.30. **16 Sqn** Old Sarum by 9.30. **RAE** Farnborough. **Practice Camp** Sutton Bridge by 31.3.31.

F4742 B&C for reconditioning to J Type (s/n 6247) and ready by 18.6.23. To Egypt. **216 Sqn** and wrecked 5.11.23 (control column broke and undercarriage collapsed on landing at Heliopolis). **AGS** Eastchurch by 2.24 until @ 3.24.

F4743 B&C for reconditioning to J Type (s/n 6258) and ready by 24.7.23. To Egypt. **208 Sqn** by 3.25. **Staff College Flt** Andover by 10.26 and on charge when unit renamed **Andover Comms Flt** 14.4.27 until @ 9.27. **A&AEE/22 Sqn** Martlesham Heath by 5.27 until @ 10.27.

F4744 B&C for reconditioning to J Type (s/n 6256) and ready by 21.7.23. **24 Sqn** Kenley by 10.23. **2 FTS** Duxford by 9.24 until @ 3.25. B&C for reconditioning (s/n 6940) and ready by 11.6.26. **PD** Ascot. To Iraq. **AD** Hinaidi. **AHQ Iraq Command Comms Flt** by 23.5.27 until @ 25.5.27. To Egypt. **AD** Aboukir and reconstructed as FR4744. **6 Sqn** by 11.29 damaged 2.30 (nosed up landing at Roshpina) and 27.2.30 (wheel collapsed on take off from Balir) but on unit charge until @ 4.32.

F4745 B&C for reconditioning to J Type (s/n 6246) and ready by 18.6.23. **NF Flt** Biggin Hill by 10.25. **Signal Co-operation Flt** Old Sarum and wrecked 10.11.23 (Flt Lt J.A.G. Haslam MC DFC/AC1 J.G. Ranson both OK, hit ridge landing at Kenley). B&C for reconditioning (s/n 6949) and ready by 21.6.26. **A&AEE/15 Sqn** Martlesham Heath by 5.27 until @ 2.28. **RAE** Farnborough by 10.4.28. Manston by 3.8.28 (2 Sqn?). **SD Flt** Netheravon by 10.28 until @ 9.29.

F4746 B&C for reconditioning to J Type (s/n 6265) and ready by 2.8.23. **PD** Ascot. To India. **AD** Drigh Road. **AP** Lahore by 14.4.24. **5 Sqn** as a/c *B* and named *Wembley* by 16.5.24 until @ 1.26, later marked as a/c *L* and o/t in crash at Quetta. **AD** Drigh Road.

F4747 B&C for reconditioning to J Type (s/n 6271) and ready by 20.8.23. **RAF (Cadet) College** Cranwell by 7.25. **Inland Area Comms Flt** Henlow by 8.25. **Inland Area Comms Flt Northolt** by 2.26. **APC** North Coates Fitties by 25.5.27. **HCF Northolt** by 10.27.

F4748 B&C for reconditioning to J Type (s/n 6260) and ready by 25.7.23. **24 Sqn** Kenley by 9.23 and wrecked 18.12.24 (crashed on landing at Kenley).

F4749 B&C for reconditioning to J Type (s/n 6245) and ready by 16.6.23.

F4750 N/I

F4751 B&C for reconditioning to J Type (s/n 6261) and ready by 30.7.23. **RAF (Cadet) College** Cranwell as a/c *B4* 1924. B&C for reconditioning to DC (s/n 6834) and ready by 16.10.25. **5 FTS** Sealand by 1.26 until @ 5.27. **24 Sqn** Kenley by 12.27.

F4752 **PD** Ascot. To India. **AD** Drigh Road. **AP** Lahore by 11.23 until @ 12.23. **28 Sqn** by 1.24. **6 Sqn** by 1929.

F4753 B&C for reconditioning to J Type (s/n 6263) and ready by 31.7.23. B&C for reconditioning (s/n 6707) and ready by 13.5.25. **PD** Ascot. To Iraq. **AD** Hinaidi. **AHQ Iraq Command Comms Flt** by 27.5.27. To Egypt. **AD** Aboukir. **6 Sqn** by 4.32 until @ 5.32.

F4754 B&C for reconditioning to J Type (s/n 6452) and ready by 24.5.24. **16 Sqn/SAC** Old Sarum by 9.24 until @ 3.26. B&C for reconditioning to Mk.III (s/n 7151) and ready by 4.6.28. **E&WS** Worthy Down by 9.30 until @ 12.30.

F4755 B&C for reconditioning to J Type (s/n 6243) and ready by 15.6.23.

F4756 B&C for reconditioning to J Type (s/n 6250) and ready by 11.7.23. **PD** Ascot. To Iraq. **AD** Hinaidi. **6 Sqn** by 12.24 until @ 5.25. Returned to UK. B&C for reconditioning to DC (s/n 6835) and ready 21.10.25. **5 FTS** Sealand by 1.26 until @ 12.26. **CFS** Upavon. B&C for reconditioning to Mk.III DC (s/n 7132) and ready by 6.9.27. B&C for reconditioning and ready by 30.4.30. **5 FTS** Sealand by 10.31.

F4757 **1 FTS** Netheravon by 3.23. **IAAD** Henlow by 10.12.23 until @ 24.1.24. **Henlow SF** named *Lady Cherry* by 7.24 until @ 11.24. **24 Sqn** Kenley by 10.24. B&C for reconditioning to J Type DC (s/n 6916) and ready by 15.3.26. **5 FTS** Sealand by 7.27 until @ 8.28.

F4758 B&C for reconditioning to J Type (s/n 6269) and ready by 3.8.23. **PD** Ascot. To India. **AD** Drigh Road. **AP** Lahore by 24.4.24 until @ 5.24. **31 Sqn** by 11.24 until @ 2.25.

F4759 N/I

F4760 To Middle East. **6 Sqn** by 5.20. Returned to UK. B&C for reconditioning to J Type (s/n 6272) and ready by 21.8.23. **5 FTS** Sealand by 10.24. **1 FTS** Netheravon and wrecked 15.12.24 (turned on nose when avoiding another aircraft at Netheravon).

F4761 **5 FTS** Sealand and wrecked 20.3.23 (Plt Off L.B.W.B. Wride KIFA, stalled when turning to land at Sealand).

F4762 **RAF (Cadet) College** Cranwell 9.19.

F4763 N/I

F4764 (Falcon III) **5 AAP** Bristol 16.12.18, allotted to BEF but reallotted to NW Area 21.12.18.

F4765 N/I

F4766 **2 FTS** Duxford by 1.24 until @ 2.24. **PD** Ascot. To India. **AD** Drigh Road. **5 Sqn** as a/c *H* by 11.27 until @ 7.28. **Quetta SF** by 7.29. **20 Sqn** by 11.30 until @ 3.31.

F4767 **2 Sqn** Fermoy by 9.20 until @ 12.20.

F4768 **2 Sqn** Fermoy by 12.20.

F4769 Cowes. **RAE** Farnborough by 11.6.19. **2 Sqn** Fermoy by 18.10.20 until @ 1.21. **SAC** Old Sarum by 5.24.

F4770 N/I

F4771 **1 FTS** Netheravon by 4.21 until @ 7.22. B&C for reconditioning to J Type (s/n 6554) and ready by 5.12.24. **PD** Ascot. To Iraq. **AD** Hinaidi. **6 Sqn** by 6.25 until @ 5.27.

F4772 **APS** Andover by 7.19 until @ 2.20 (prefix unconfirmed). **5 FTS** Sealand and wrecked 29.11.23 (Flt Lt D. Colyer OK, turned to avoid airmen on the aerodrome when landing and ran into gun butts).

F4773 N/I

F4774 (Falcon III) presentation a/c *Presented by Maharaja Bahadur Sir Rameswar Singh of Darbhanga No.3.* **5 AAP** Bristol 16.12.18, allotted to BEF but reallotted to NW Area 21.12.18. **PD** Ascot. To Egypt. **AD** Aboukir. **208 Sqn** by 4.25.

F4775 **IAAD** Henlow by 1.25.

F4776 **RAE** Farnborough by 21.4.20 until @ 8.4.21.

F4777 N/I

F4778 N/I

F4779 **2 Sqn** Fermoy by 5.20 and on unit charge until 1921.

F4780 N/I

F4781 Left UK for **AD** Aboukir 19.3.20 (for Iraq).

F4782 Left UK for **AD** Aboukir 26.2.20. **AP** Baghdad. **6 Sqn** and wrecked 15.9.20 (force landed after engine failure 3 miles W of Khan Nuqtah, Iraq, and burnt by Arabs).

F4783 Left UK for **AD** Aboukir 26.2.20. **AP** Baghdad. **6 Sqn** by 5.20 and destroyed 20.8.20 (engine cut after take off, force landed on bad ground at Qilat-Sikar, Iraq, 13.8.20, abandoned on evacuation and burnt by Arabs).

F4784 N/I

F4785 **PD** Ascot. To Iraq. **AD** Hinaidi by 1.23. **6 Sqn** by 22.3.23 until @ 1924. **AD** Aboukir. **6 Sqn** by 12.31.

F4786 B&C for reconditioning to J Type (s/n 6499) and ready by 11.10.24.

F4787 Left UK for **AD** Aboukir 26.2.20. **6 Sqn** as a/c *C* by 7.19 until @ 2.20.

F4788 **PD** Ascot. To Iraq. **AD** Hinaidi by 1.23. **6 Sqn** by 17.2.23 until @ 1.24.

F4789 B&C for reconditioning to J Type (s/n 6494) and ready by 2.10.24. **PD** Ascot. To India. **AD** Drigh Road. **20 Sqn** by 11.26 until @ 2.27.

F4790 To Iraq. **6 Sqn** by 4.21. **AD** Hinaidi by 3.23.

F4791 **PD** Ascot. To Egypt. **AD** Aboukir. **208 Sqn** Ismailia.

F4792 N/I

F4793 N/I

F4794 N/I

F4795 **1 AAP** Coventry by 24.4.19, reallotted from 11 Group Ireland to BEF. **11 Sqn** 11.6.18 until @ 26.6.19. **2 Sqn** Fermoy by 4.20 until @ 1.21.

F4796 **105 Sqn** Oranmore and wrecked 2.8.19 (2nd Lt W.E. Lowrie IIFA, crashed due to engine failure – engine 2145). **106 Sqn** Collinstown by 12.19.

F4797 **2 Sqn** Fermoy and wrecked 1.4.21 (Fg Off J. McBain/AC2 Jarrett both OK, force landed between Banteer and Kanturk after engine failed, ran into hedge and o/t). Returned to Fermoy by rail 2.4.21.

F4798 **2 Sqn** Fermoy 1920-1921.

F4799 N/I

F4800 (Falcon III) **5 AAP** Bristol 25.1.19, reallotted from 11 Group to BEF. **12 AAP** Hawkinge by 15.4.19 reallotted from BEF to SE Area. At Cologne 30.4.19 with allotment to SE Area cancelled, again allotted to BEF.

F4801 **105 Sqn** Omagh as a/c *15* by 28.2.19 until @ 5.5.20.

F4802 **23 Group HQ** Spittlegate by 8.27.

F4803 N/I

F4804 B&C for reconditioning to J Type (s/n 6555) and ready by 6.12.24.

F4805 (Falcon III) **5 AAP** Bristol 25.1.19, reallotted from NW Area to BEF and still with unit 3.2.19, reallotted to Midland Area for 27 Group Bircham Newton. **274 Sqn** Bircham Newton by 6.20 (sic – 1919?) and on unit charge when disbanded into **207 Sqn** 1.2.20.

F4806 (Falcon III) **5 AAP** Bristol 25.1.19, reallotted from NW Area to BEF and still with unit 3.2.19, reallotted to Midland Area for 27 Group Bircham Newton. **274 Sqn** Bircham Newton and on unit charge when disbanded into **207 Sqn** 1.2.20.

F4807 **2 FTS** Duxford and wrecked 25.2.22 (Plt Off B.A.C. South KIFA, spun in off turn after take off from Duxford).

F4808 (Falcon III) **5 AAP** Bristol 25.1.19, reallotted from NW Area to BEF and wrecked on Delivery Flight 13.2.19 (Lt J.L. Pugh CDP IIFA, spun in from 100ft after fast turns around aerodrome – engine 2171/WD88910). At Upavon 21.2.19 with allotment to BEF cancelled.

F4809 **PD** Ascot. To India. **AD** Drigh Road. **20 Sqn** by 1930.

F4810 B&C for reconditioning to J Type (s/n 6562) and ready by 13.12.24. **2 FTS** Digby by 4.25 until @ 5.26. B&C for reconditioning to Mk.III DC (s/n 7115) and ready by 20.7.27.

F4811 B&C for reconditioning to J Type DC (s/n 6498) and ready by 10.10.24. **RAF (Cadet) College** Cranwell by 12.24 until @ 7.25. B&C for reconditioning to Mk.III DC (s/n 7113) and ready by 14.7.27. **2 FTS** Digby by 6.29 and wrecked 17.2.30 (swung on landing at Digby and struck stationary Avro 504N J9691). B&C for reconditioning (s/n 7556). Retaken onto RAF charge 20.8.30. **2 FTS** Digby by 7.31.

F4812 B&C for reconditioning to J Type (s/n 6463) and ready by 6.7.24. **16 Sqn/SAC** Old Sarum by 9.24 until @ 3.26. B&C for reconditioning (s/n 6982) and ready by 30.7.26. **HAD** Henlow by 4.27. Shipped to China (for **2 Sqn** Shanghai?). **2 Sqn** Manston by 10.29.

F4813 **SAC** Old Sarum by 12.22 until @ 3.24. B&C for reconditioning to J Type (s/n 6671) and ready by 30.3.25.

F4814 **PD** Ascot. To India. **AD** Drigh Road. **31 Sqn** as a/c *F*. B&C for reconditioning to J Type DC (s/n 6820) and ready by 29.9.25. **RAF (Cadet) College** Cranwell as a/c *D1* by 9.25 until @ 3.28. Photographed crashed on nose.

F4815 B&C for reconditioning to J Type (s/n 6692) and ready by 24.4.25.

F4816 N/I

F4817 Fell in Irish Sea 19.10.20.

F4818 N/I

F4819 **ES** Martlesham Heath by 7.20. **RAE** Farnborough by 10.20 (Mk.V Gyro). **ES** Martlesham Heath by 4.21 until @ 6.21 (metal propeller tests). B&C for reconditioning to J Type (s/n 6612) and ready by 16.2.25.

F4820 **APS** Andover by 2.20 and wrecked 6.9.20 (stalled onto hangar roof on take off from Andover).

F4821 (Falcon III) **5 AAP** Bristol 25.1.19, reallotted from NW Area to BEF.

F4822 **RAF (Cadet) College** Cranwell by 1925 until @ 1.26.

F4823 **24 Sqn** Kenley by 3.21. **RAF (Cadet) College** Cranwell by 11.23.

F4824 **30 TS** Northolt and wrecked 28.9.19 (force landed at Rochford after engine failure and burnt).

F4825 **100 Sqn** and wrecked 28.8.20 (Fg Off N.H. Dimmock IIFA, elevator controls jammed. **PD** Ascot. To India. **AD** Drigh Road. **5 Sqn** as a/c *X* 1925.

F4826 B&C for reconditioning to J Type DC (s/n 6841) and ready by 22.10.25. **RAF (Cadet) College** Cranwell by 9.26 until @ 10.28.

F.2B F4826 '11', with quartered wheel discs, was photographed at Hendon during the 1924 RAF Display there. Shortly thereafter it was reconditioned to a J-Type DC. *(Philip Jarrett)*

F4827 (300hp Hispano-Suiza) **ACIS** Worthy Down ex France by 8.19. **RAE** Farnborough. B&C for reconditioning to J Type DC (s/n 6444) and ready by 9.5.24. **5 FTS** Sealand by 5.26 until @ 12.26.

F4828 N/I

F4829 (Falcon III) **5 AAP** Bristol 25.1.19, reallotted from Midland Area for **Observers School** Shrewsbury to BEF and still with unit under same allotment 5.4.19. **24 Sqn** Kenley by 6.20. To India. **5 Sqn** as a/c *X*.

F4830 **CFS** Upavon by 10.21 until @ 3.22. B&C for reconditioning to J Type (s/n 6572) and ready by 22.12.24. **16 Sqn/SAC** Old Sarum by 3.25 until @ 9.27.

F4831 **24 Sqn** Kenley by 11.20 and wrecked 24.10.22 (Plt Off M.C. Hayer KIFA, spun in off turn landing Kenley).

F4832 **1 SoTT** Halton and wrecked 4.5.21 (Fg Off A. Knox OK/Fg Off H.W. Whale IIFA, struck tree tops on landing at Halton).

F4833 **CFS** Upavon by 2.26 until @ 4.26.

F4834 N/I

F4835 **Development Sqn, 'B' Flt** Gosport by 6.19.

F4836 **SAC** Old Sarum 1922-1923. B&C for reconditioning to J Type (s/n 6529) and ready by 7.11.24. **2 FTS** Digby by 3.25 until @ 6.26. B&C for reconditioning (s/n 6980) and ready by 24.7.26. **HAD** Henlow by 4.27. Shipped China (for **2 Sqn** Shanghai?). **2 Sqn** Manston by 2.28 and wrecked 27.3.28 (crashed near Stamford, Lincs).

F4837 (Falcon III) **5 AAP** Bristol 25.1.19, reallotted from Midland Area for **Observers School** Shrewsbury to BEF.

F4838 (Falcon III) **5 AAP** Bristol 11.4.19, allotted to BEF. **1 ASD** Repair Park Marquise and lost in Channel 9.5.19 (Lt L.L. Evans CDP/ Lt H.J.E. Stokes 8 AAP/Sgt R.F. Fillmore all KIFA – engine 2137/WD52093).

F4839 (Falcon III) **5 AAP** Bristol 24.3.19, allotted to BEF. B&C for reconditioning to J Type (s/n 6620) and ready by 14.2.25. **PD** Ascot. To India. **AD** Drigh Road. **31 Sqn** as a/c *F*. **20 Sqn** as a/c *E* by 12.30 until @ 1.32.

F4840 B&C for reconditioning to J Type (s/n 6453) and ready by 24.5.24. **16 Sqn/SAC** Old Sarum by 8.24 until @ 1.26. **RAF Staff College** Andover by 11.25.

F4841 **School of Administration** Halton by 6.19. **1 SoTT (Boys)** Halton and wrecked 29.8.23 (Flt Lt M. Ballard IIFA/AC1 J. Rudd OK, crashed after engine failed on take off from Halton).

F4842 **16 Sqn/SAC** Old Sarum by 7.24 until @ 9.26.

F4843 N/I

F4844 **Development Sqn, 'F' Flt** Gosport by 6.19. **1 SoTT** Halton as a/c 6 by 1924.

F4845 (Falcon III) **5 AAP** Bristol 7.4.19, allotted to BEF. **12 Sqn** 1919. **1 SoTT** as a/c 6 by 1923. **1 FTS** Netheravon by 3.24 until @ 4.24. B&C for reconditioning to J Type (s/n 6531) and ready by 8.11.24. **2 FTS** Digby by 2.25 until @ 3.25. B&C for reconditioning (s/n 6956, first machine fitted with Uniflex cable for wireless) and ready by 2.7.26. **School of Photography Flt** Kenley by 5.28 until @ 8.28. **RAF College** Cranwell by 6.29. B&C for reconditioning (to Mk.IV?) and ready by 16.1.30. **16 Sqn/SAC** Old Sarum by 9.30. **RAE** Farnborough. **Practice Camp** Sutton Bridge by 31.3.31.

F4846 N/I

F4847 (Falcon III) **5 AAP** Bristol 25.1.19, reallotted from Midland Area for **Observers School** Shrewsbury to BEF and still with unit under same allotment 11.4.19. **22 Sqn** dd ex **207 Sqn** aerodrome 24.7.19 (Capt Day/Capt Caillard). **12 Sqn** by 22.6.20, marked as a/c B5 and wrecked 23.11.20 (Fg Off Young OK, struck roller and o/t avoiding horse and cart while landing, at Bickendorf).

While serving as 'B5' with 12 Sqn, F4847 was wrecked on 23 November 1920 when it was overturned by Fg Off Young, who was trying to avoid a horse and cart while landing at Bickendorf and struck a roller instead. Young escaped 'OK'. *(Philip Jarrett)*

F4848 (Falcon III) **5 AAP** Bristol 25.1.19, reallotted from Midland Area for **Observers School** Shrewsbury to BEF and still with unit under same allotment 5.4.19. **22 Sqn** by 18.5.19 (Lt Young). **8 AAP** Lympne ex 22 Sqn 19.8.19 (Lt Walkington).

F4849 **5 AAP** Bristol by 14.4.19 allotted to BEF. **Meteor Flt** by 14.8.19.

F4850 (Falcon III) **5 AAP** Bristol 25.1.19, reallotted from 6 Bde to BEF and still with unit under same allotment 21.3.19. At Farnborough 9.4.19, with BEF allotment cancelled and to be deleted.

F4851 **5 AAP** Bristol by 28.3.19, allotted to BEF. **SAC** Old Sarum by 1.24.

F4852 (Falcon III) **5 AAP** Bristol by 28.3.19, allotted to BEF. **22 Sqn** by 18.5.19 until @ 2.7.19. **24 Sqn** Kenley and wrecked 4.11.20 (Fg Off H. Prouyt/Fg Off H. Fenwick both KIFA, struck a tree in fog, 1 mile from Kenley).

F4853 (Falcon III) **5 AAP** Bristol 25.1.19, reallotted from 6 Bde to BEF and still with unit under same allotment 11.4.19. B&C for reconditioning to J Type (s/n 6538) and ready by 15.11.24. **School of Photography Flt** Kenley by 4.25 until @ 10.25. **CFS** Upavon by 5.29.

F4854 (Falcon III) **5 AAP** Bristol 25.1.19, reallotted from 6 Bde to BEF and still with unit under same allotment 11.4.19. **2 Sqn** Fermoy by 1920 until @ 1921. B&C for reconditioning to J Type (s/n 6573) and ready by 22.12.24. **4 Sqn** Farnborough.

F4855 (Falcon III) **5 AAP** Bristol 24.1.19, allotted to BEF and still with unit under same allotment 14.4.19. **12 Sqn** as a/c B4 by 8.19 and wrecked 22.9.21 (Plt Off Brookham OK, force landed at Lehman, near Coblenz, after engine failure).

F4856 (Falcon III) **5 AAP** Bristol 24.1.19, allotted to BEF. **'M' Flt** by 16.7.19. **12 Sqn** as a/c C5 by 9.19. To UK 13.1.21. **PD** Ascot. To Iraq. **AD** Hinaidi. **AHQ Iraq Command Comms Flt** Hinaidi. **6 Sqn** and wrecked 5.30 (struck a wadi near Zerka LG).

F4857 (Falcon III) **5 AAP** Bristol 24.1.19, allotted to BEF and still with unit under same allotment 24.4.19. B&C for reconditioning to J Type (s/n 6623) and ready by 21.3.25. **PD** Ascot. To India. **AD** Drigh Road. **20 Sqn** by 10.26.

F4858 (Falcon III) **5 AAP** Bristol 24.1.19, allotted to BEF and still with unit under same allotment 24.4.19.

F4859 (Falcon III) **5 AAP** Bristol 24.1.19, allotted to BEF and still with unit under same allotment 24.4.19.

F4860 (Falcon III) presentation a/c *Government of Johore No.6*. **5 AAP** Bristol 25.1.19, allotted to BEF. **PD** Ascot. To Iraq. **AD** Hinaidi. **6 Sqn**.

F4861 (Falcon III) **5 AAP** Bristol 24.1.19, allotted to BEF and still with unit under same allotment 24.4.19. To India. **48 Sqn** by 12.19 and on unit charge when redesignated **5 Sqn** 1.2.20.

F4862 (Falcon III) **5 AAP** Bristol 25.1.19, allotted to BEF. To India. **20 Sqn** by 2.20.

F4863 (Falcon III) **5 AAP** Bristol 25.1.19, allotted to BEF and still with unit under same allotment 27.3.19.

F4864 (Falcon III) **5 AAP** Bristol 24.1.19, allotted to BEF. **AES** Martlesham Heath. **A&AEE** Martlesham Heath. **25 Sqn** Hawkinge by 5.29.

F4865 (Falcon III) **5 AAP** Bristol 25.1.19, allotted to BEF and still with unit under same allotment 24.4.19. **88 Sqn** as a/c 13 by 6.19. **Meteor Flt** by 28.8.19. **12 Sqn** as a/c B3 from 17.6.20. **PD** Ascot. To Egypt. **AD** Aboukir by 5.25. **Aden Flt** and wrecked 25.10.25 (crashed and burnt out).

F4866 (Falcon III) **5 AAP** Bristol 25.1.19, allotted to BEF. To India. **48 Sqn** by 1.20 and wrecked 29.2.20 (became lost in mist and flew into the ground during forced landing 23 miles NW of Barkham, India).

F4867 (Falcon III) **5 AAP** Bristol 25.1.19, allotted to BEF; **20 Sqn** by 2.20.

F4868 (Falcon III) **5 AAP** Bristol 25.1.19, allotted to BEF and wrecked 6.3.19 (Lt A.W. Parr **CDP** IIFA, no further details given – engine 3/F/2179/WD88914). **PD** Ascot. To Iraq. **AD** Hinaidi. **6 Sqn** by 1923 until @ 1924.

F4869 (Falcon III) **5 AAP** Bristol 29.1.19, allotted to BEF.

F4870 (Falcon III) **5 AAP** Bristol 29.1.19, allotted to BEF. **11 Sqn** by 29.5.19 (Capt M. leB. Smith) until @ 30.5.19. **APS** Andover by 7.19 until @ 2.20. B&C for reconditioning to J Type (s/n 6267) and ready by 13.8.23. **PD** Ascot. To India. **AD** Drigh Road. **28 Sqn** by 7.24. **5 Sqn** by 4.26. Returned to UK. **RAF (Cadet) College** Cranwell by 9.28.

F4871 (Falcon III) **5 AAP** Bristol 24.1.19, allotted to BEF and still with unit under same allotment 19.4.19.

F4872 (Falcon III) **5 AAP** Bristol 24.1.19, allotted to BEF.

F4873 (Falcon III) **5 AAP** Bristol 29.1.19, allotted to BEF and still with unit under same allotment 24.4.19. **11 Sqn** by 29.5.19 (Capt M. leB. Smith) until @ 30.7.19.

F4874 (Falcon III) **5 AAP** Bristol 25.1.19, allotted to BEF and still with unit under same allotment 24.4.19.

F4875 (Falcon III) **5 AAP** Bristol 25.1.19, allotted to BEF. **IDE** Biggin Hill by 1.20 until @ 3.20. To BEF. **88 Sqn** as a/c 11 by 6.19. **12 Sqn** by 12.20. To UK 1.21.

F4876 (Falcon III) **5 AAP** Bristol 29.1.19, allotted to BEF.

F4877 (Falcon III) **5 AAP** Bristol 29.1.19, allotted to BEF. **12 Sqn** by 11.20. To UK 12.20. In storage at Kenley 12.20. B&C for reconditioning to J Type. **PD** Ascot. To Iraq. **AD** Hinaidi by 8.24. **6 Sqn** by 8.24 and wrecked 16.9.24 (crashed on Zakho LG).

F4878 (Falcon III) **5 AAP** Bristol 29.1.19, allotted to BEF. To India, **48 Sqn** by 5.19 and on unit charge when redesignated **5 Sqn** 1.2.20. **24 Sqn**.

F4879 (Falcon III) **5 AAP** Bristol 30.1.19, allotted to BEF. **24 Sqn** Kenley by 2.20. **12 Sqn** 1920.

F4880 (Falcon III) **5 AAP** Bristol 31.1.19, allotted to BEF. **PD** Ascot. To Iraq. **AD** Hinaidi. **6 Sqn** by 12.123 until @ 1.24.

F4881 B&C for reconditioning to J Type (s/n 6364) and ready by 19.12.23. **PD** Ascot. To India. **AD** Drigh Road. **5 Sqn** by 3.25 until @ 6.26. **AD** Drigh Road 1927. **20 Sqn** by 12.28.

F4882 B&C for reconditioning to J Type (s/n 6348) and ready by 21.11.23. **Staff College Flt** Andover by 6.25 until @ 7.25. B&C for reconditioning to DC (s/n 6899) and ready by 27.1.26. **1 FTS** Netheravon by 8.27.

F4883 B&C for reconditioning to J Type (s/n 6372) and ready by 10.12.23. **PD** Ascot. To Egypt. **AD** Aboukir. **4 FTS** Abu Sueir by 4.26. **208 Sqn** by 5.11.28 and wrecked 26.4.29 (static electricity caused front cockpit to catch fire after landing).

F4884 B&C for reconditioning to J Type (s/n 6318) and ready by 13.10.23. **Staff College Flt** Andover by 7.24 until @ 11.25. **School of Photography Flt** Kenley. **RAF College** Cranwell by 3.29.

F4885 B&C for reconditioning to J Type DC (s/n 6830) and ready by 13.10.25. **2 FTS** Digby by 1.26 until @ 1.27.

F4886 B&C for reconditioning to J Type (s/n 6668) and ready by 19.3.25. **RAE** Farnborough with RAF.30-section wings by 19.10.26 and last flown 26.8.27.

F4887 B&C for reconditioning to J Type (s/n 6493) and ready by 2.10.24. **PD** Ascot. To Egypt. **AD** Aboukir by 5.25. **208 Sqn** by 9.25 until @ 10.25. **4 FTS** Abu Sueir by 11.25.

F4888 **PD** Ascot. To Iraq. **AD** Hinaidi by 5.22 until @ 6.22. **6 Sqn** by 8.22 until @ 9.22.

F4889 **PD** Ascot. To Egypt. **AD** Aboukir. **4 FTS** Abu Sueir by 3.22 and wrecked 14.6.22 (crashed while low flying at El Birka, 2 miles N of Heliopolis).

F4890 **PD** Ascot. To Iraq. **AD** Hinaidi. **6 Sqn** by 1923 until @ 1924.

F4891 (Falcon III) **5 AAP** Bristol 29.1.19, allotted to BEF. **12 Sqn** as a/c *N* by 9.19. **22 Sqn** and flown to UK 19.8.19 (Lt Allen). **24 Sqn** Kenley by 2.24. B&C for reconditioning to J Type (s/n 6702) and ready by 8.5.25.

F4892 (Falcon III) **5 AAP** Bristol 29.1.19, allotted to BEF. **22 Sqn** and flown to UK 19.8.19 (Lt E.R. Danks). **2 FTS** Digby by 1.24 until @ 5.25. B&C for reconditioning to J Type (s/n 6682) and ready by 9.4.25. **Duxford SF** by 10.26 until @ 11.26.

F4893 (Falcon III) **5 AAP** Bristol 31.1.19, allotted to BEF. **22 Sqn** by 24.7.19. **12 Sqn** as a/c *C1* by 2.1.20 until @ 5.12.20 (Lt J.W. Baker). To UK 15.10.20. Reconstructed. **6 Sqn** by 10.26. **RAF (Cadet) College** Cranwell by 5.28.

F4894 (Falcon III) **5 AAP** Bristol 31.1.19, allotted to BEF. **11 Sqn** 11.6.19 until @ 1.8.19. **24 Sqn** Kenley by 9.23 and wrecked 12.7.24 (crashed near Wealdstone, Middlesex).

F4895 (Falcon III) **5 AAP** Bristol 7.2.19, allotted to BEF. **22 Sqn** by 2.7.19 (Lt Davies/Sgt May). **12 Sqn** as a/c *C3* by 9.19 and wrecked 4.5.21 (Fg Off Perhouse OK, hit telephone wires at Cologne Lindenthal). Repaired. **2 Sqn** Manston and damaged 6.5.24 (caught by gust of wind and hit a bump while landing, at Martlesham). **2 FTS** Digby by 1.27.

F4896 (Falcon III) **5 AAP** Bristol 7.2.19, allotted to BEF. **11 Sqn** by 30.6.19 until @ 29.7.19. B&C for reconditioning to J Type (s/n 6274) and ready by 22.8.23. B&C for reconditioning (s/n 6663) and ready by 20.3.25. **PD** Ascot. To India. **AD** Drigh Road. **5 Sqn** by 10.28.

F4897 (Falcon III) **5 AAP** Bristol 7.2.19, allotted to BEF. **PD** Ascot. To Iraq. **AD** Hinaidi. **6 Sqn** by 12.23 until @ 1.24.

F4898 (Falcon III) **5 AAP** Bristol 6.2.19, allotted to BEF. **22 Sqn** by 20.8.19 (Lt Moloney/Capt Day). **12 Sqn** as a/c *C2* by 3.20 until @ 5.12.20 (Lt J.W. Baker). **24 Sqn** Kenley by 11.22 until @ 12.22. **RAF (Cadet) College** Cranwell by 10.24. B&C for reconditioning to J Type (s/n 6584) and ready by 9.1.25. **RAF (Cadet) College** Cranwell by 6.25 until @ 3.29.

F4899 (Falcon III) **5 AAP** Bristol 7.2.19, allotted to BEF.

F4900 (Falcon III) **5 AAP** Bristol 7.2.19, allotted to BEF. **12 Sqn** by 9.20. To UK 5.22.

F4901 B&C for reconditioning to J Type (s/n 6469) and ready by 9.7.24. **SAC** Old Sarum by 9.25 until @ 4.28.

F4902 **2 FTS** Duxford/Digby by 3.24 until @ 7.24. B&C for reconditioning to J Type (s/n 6275) and ready by 24.8.23. **PD** Ascot. To Egypt. **AD** Aboukir. **208 Sqn** by 6.25. Returned to UK. B&C for reconditioning (s/n 6972) and ready by 13.7.26.

F4903 B&C for reconditioning to J Type (s/n 6286) and ready by 7.9.23. **PD** Ascot. To Iraq. **AD** Hinaidi by 9.24. **6 Sqn** by 9.24 until @ 1.25. Returned to UK. B&C for reconditioning (s/n 6953) and ready by 25.6.26. **13 Sqn** Andover by 10.27. **E&WS** Worthy Down by 25.11.27 until @ 9.30.

F4904 B&C for reconditioning to J Type (s/n 6279) and ready by 30.8.23. **2 FTS** Duxford by 12.23 until @ 2.24. **4 Sqn** Farnborough by 9.26.

F4905 B&C for reconditioning to J Type (s/n 6324) and ready by 20.10.23. **16 Sqn/SAC** Old Sarum by 8.24 until @ 1.26. **PD** Ascot. To India. **AD** Drigh Road. **20 Sqn**.

F4906 B&C for reconditioning to J Type (s/n 6694) and ready by 25.4.25.

F4907 B&C for reconditioning to J Type (s/n 6489) and ready by 19.9.24. **PD** Ascot. To India. **AD** Drigh Road. **AP** Lahore. **31 Sqn** by 27.8.25 until @ 5.26.

F4908 **2 Sqn** Manston by 11.22. B&C for reconditioning to J Type (s/n 6587) and ready by 16.1.25. **16 Sqn** Old Sarum by 3.25. **PD** Ascot. To India. **AD** Drigh Road 1926. **20 Sqn** NW Frontier. **Quetta SF** by 8.28.

F4909 N/I

F4910 **PD** Ascot. To Egypt. **AD** Aboukir. **208 Sqn** by 8.20 until @ 4.22. **14 Sqn** by 7.22, damaged 9.2.23 (undercarriage collapsed) and on unit charge until @ 3.23. **208 Sqn** by 12.23.

F4911 **PD** Ascot. To Iraq. **AD** Hinaidi by 5.22. **6 Sqn** by 1923 until @ 1924. Returned to UK. B&C for reconditioning to J Type DC (s/n 6469) and ready by 13.10.25. **5 FTS** Sealand by 3.26 until @ 4.27.

F4912 To Egypt. **14 Sqn** 1922. Returned to UK. B&C for reconditioning to J Type DC (s/n 6833) and ready by 22.10.25. **5 FTS** Sealand by

3.26 until @ 7.26. B&C for reconditioning to Mk.III DC (s/n 7128) and ready by 31.8.27. **RAF (Cadet) College** Cranwell by 9.28 until @ 4.29. B&C for repair and ready by 31.12.29. **CFS** Upavon by 5.30.

F4913 B&C for reconditioning to J Type DC (s/n 6496) and ready by 6.10.24. **24 Sqn** Kenley by 1.25 and for use by CAS until @ 1926. B&C for reconditioning (s/n 7177) and ready by 22.6.28.

F4914 B&C for reconditioning to J Type (s/n 6487) and ready by 18.9.24. **PD** Ascot. To India. **AD** Drigh Road. **20 Sqn** by 1927 until @ 1928; and again on unit charge by 4.30.

F4915 B&C for reconditioning to J Type (s/n 6488) and ready by 19.9.24. **PD** Ascot. To India. **AD** Drigh Road. **31 Sqn** as a/c *H* and damaged 9.27. **20 Sqn** by 8.29 until @ 10.31.

F4916 B&C for reconditioning to J Type (s/n 6485) and ready by 15.9.24. **PD** Ascot. To India. **AD** Drigh Road 1926. **20 Sqn** by 3.27 until @ 1.28.

F4917 **SAC** Old Sarum and damaged 7.9.21 (heavy landing at Old Sarum). **RAF (Cadet) College** as a/c *C9* and wrecked 13.10.24.

F4918 N/I

F4919 **PD** Ascot. To Egypt. **AD** Aboukir. **14 Sqn** by 5.22 until @ 10.22.

F4920 **PD** Ascot. To Egypt. **AD** Aboukir. **4 FTS** Abu Sueir by 8.21 until @ 3.22. **AD** Aboukir and reconstructed as as FR4920. **14 Sqn** c.24.

F4921 B&C for reconditioning to J Type (s/n 6624) and ready by 19.2.25. **PD** Ascot. To India. **AD** Drigh Road 1926. **20 Sqn** by 1.27, in propeller accident at Peshawar 4.12.30, and on unit charge until @ 4.31.

F4922 **PD** Ascot. To Egypt. **AD** Aboukir. **Aden Flt** 1922. **4 FTS** Abu Sueir and wrecked 15.6.23 (stalled and spun in when landing at Khormaksar).

F4923 Despatched to Egypt 26.2.20. **AD** Aboukir. To Iraq. **6 Sqn** by 5.20 until @ 6.20. **AD** Hinaidi by 6.23.

F4924 Despatched UK to **AD** Aboukir 19.3.20 (for Iraq). To India. **AD** Drigh Road. **5 Sqn** as a/c *V* by 12.20 and wrecked 1922 (crashed at Sheik Manda).

F4925 **PD** Ascot. To Iraq. **AD** Hinaidi. **70 Sqn** by 3.23. **AD** Hinaidi by 5.23 until @ 10.24. **6 Sqn** 1924 until @ 5.25. Returned to UK. B&C for reconditioning to J Type DC (s/n 6817) and ready by 25.9.25. **PD** Ascot. To Egypt. **AD** Aboukir. Heliopolis by 11.26 until @ 6.27. **AD** Aboukir and reconstructed as FR4925. **6 Sqn** by 2.30, force landed near Deir el Bela after engine failure 12.4.30 and wreaked during salvage 14.4.30.

F4926 To Egypt. **208 Sqn** by 3.21, damaged 1.6.21 (stalled on landing at Suez) and wrecked 15.8.21 (stalled in on a turn at Heliopolis).

F4927 **PD** Ascot. To Egypt. **AD** Aboukir. **4 FTS** Abu Sueir by 5.21 and tested 17.10.21 for issue to Ramleh. **14 Sqn** by 11.21 until @ 5.22. To India. **20 Sqn** as a/c *G*.

F4928 **PD** Ascot. To Iraq. **AD** Hinaidi. **6 Sqn** by 5.22. **AD** Hinaidi. **6 Sqn** reissued ex AD 29.3.23. **AD** Hinaidi ex 6 Sqn 11.24, reconstructed as FR4928 by 8.25 and on unit charge until @ 13.8.26. **AHQ Iraq Training Flt** by 7.27 until @ 8.28. **AD** Hinaidi by 12.29 until @ 7.30. **6 Sqn** by 12.29. To Egypt. **AD** Aboukir by 24.7.30.

F4929 B&C for reconditioning to J Type (s/n 6484) and ready by 12.9.24. **PD** Ascot. To India. **AD** Drigh Road. **AP** Lahore. **5 Sqn** by 21.9.25 until @ 1.26. **20 Sqn** by 11.28 until @ 12.28.

F4930 **PD** Ascot. To Egypt. **AD** Aboukir. **208 Sqn** by 10.22 until @ 7.23.

F4931 **PD** Ascot. To India. **AD** Drigh Road. **AP** Lahore by 5.12.23. **28 Sqn** by 2.24.

F4932 B&C for reconditioning to J Type (s/n 6470) and ready by 12.7.24. **4 Sqn** Farnborough by 7.24. **13 Sqn** Andover by 9.25 until @ 5.26.

F4933 **SAC** Old Sarum and wrecked 15.4.21 (Fg Off B.F. Deane/AC2 P.F. Elliot both KIFA (dived in off turn after take off from Andover).

F4934 **Irish Flt** Baldonnel by 8.22. B&C for reconditioning to J Type (s/n 6545) and ready by 28.11.24. B&C for reconditioning to DC (s/n 6902) and ready by 6.2.26. **HAD** Henlow by 7.26 until @ 5.27.

F4935 B&C for reconditioning to J Type (s/n 6461) and ready by 4.7.24. **4 Sqn** Farnborough and wrecked 22.12.24 (engine failed on landing at Farnborough).

F4936 To Iraq. **6 Sqn** by 7.19 until @ 2.20. To India. **AD** Drigh Road by 1927.

F4937 **PD** Ascot. To Iraq. **AD** Hinaidi. **6 Sqn** by 11.21 and wrecked 8.4.22 (Fg Off A.E. Beibby DSC OK, struck a ridge on landing).

F4938 **PD** Ascot. To Egypt. **AD** Aboukir. **6 Sqn** by 6.21 and wrecked 8.4.22 (Fg Off A.G. Smart OK, struck a bank on landing at Kumait LG). **AD** Aboukir. Returned to UK. **RAF (Cadet) College** Cranwell by 3.28.

F4939 PD Ascot. To Egypt. **AD** Aboukir. **208 Sqn** by 9.22. **14 Sqn** by 11.22. **AD** Aboukir by 7.2.23. Returned to UK. B&C for reconditioning to J Type DC (s/n 6818) and ready by 26.9.25. **RAF (Cadet) College** Cranwell as a/c *B6* by 10.26 and wrecked 4.2.29 (crashed on landing at Cranwell).

F4940 B&C for reconditioning to J Type DC (s/n 6819) and ready by 26.9.25. **RAF (Cadet) College** Cranwell by 9.26, in mid-air collision with F4507 13.9.26, repaired and on unit charge until @ 3.27.

F4941 At maker's 6.2.19, allotted to BEF. **24 Sqn** Kenley and wrecked 2.11.23 (Plt Off M.W. Keey OK, ran out of fuel and o/t on rough ground during forced landing at Andover).

F4942 At maker's 6.2.19, allotted to BEF. **12 Sqn** as a/c *A6*, later *A*, and wrecked 27.5.22 (Plt Off Brookham OK). B&C for reconditioning to J Type (s/n 6556) and ready by 6.12.24. **PD** Ascot. To India. **AD** Drigh Road. **31 Sqn** as a/c *H*.

F4943 At maker's 6.2.19, allotted to BEF. **24 Sqn** Kenley by 2.24.

F4944 At maker's 6.2.19, allotted to BEF. **4 Sqn** Farnborough 1921. B&C for reconditioning to J Type (s/n 6540) and ready by 21.11.24. B&C for reconditioning to Mk.III (s/n 7135) and ready by 14.6.28. **4 Sqn** Farnborough and in starting accident, at Farnborough, 11.9.29. **16 Sqn/SAC** Old Sarum by 1.30 until @ 2.30.

F4945 (DC) **PD** Ascot. **AD** Hinaidi by 7.24.

F4946 B&C for reconditioning to J Type (s/n 6388) and ready by 16.2.24. **5 FTS** Sealand by 10.24. B&C for reconditioning to DC (s/n 6821) and ready by 30.9.25. **2 FTS** Digby by 3.26 until @ 9.26. B&C for reconditioning (s/n 7174) and ready by 4.6.28. **HQ 23 Group** Spittlegate by 6.29. **CFS** Upavon by 9.29 until @ 11.30.

F4947 B&C for reconditioning to J Type (s/n 6411) and ready by 12.3.24. **13 Sqn** Andover as a/c *G* 1924. **PD** Ascot. To India. **AD** Drigh Road. **5 Sqn** as a/c *C* by 3.25 until @ 4.25. **20 Sqn** by 7.25 until @ 8.25. **5 Sqn** as a/c *G* by 9.26 until @ 5.27. **AD** Drigh Road 1927. **AP** Lahore by 13.8.27.

F4948 B&C for reconditioning to J Type (s/n 6405) and ready by 8.3.24. **13 Sqn** Andover by 1924 until @ 6.26.

F4949 X **AD** Aboukir dd ex Taranto **AP** 11.4.19. B&C for reconditioning to J Type (s/n 6403) and ready by 29.2.24. **A&AEE** Martlesham Heath by 5.24 and wrecked 28.1.25 (crashed near King's Lynn, Norfolk).

F4950 B&C for reconditioning to J Type (s/n 6407) and ready by 11.3.24. **SAC** Old Sarum by 4.25. To Egypt. **208 Sqn** by 8.25 until @ 1.28.

Judging by the partly obscured fuselage roundel and the empty circle for the Flight emblem on its fin, this F.2B of 208 Sqn, F4950, has had a recent respray. Immediately behind it is FR4583. *(Via Philip Jarrett)*

F4951 B&C for reconditioning to J Type (s/n 6408) and ready by 11.3.24. **PD** Ascot. To India. **AD** Drigh Road. **31 Sqn** as a/c *J* and wrecked 6.25 (hit a church spire at Delhi).

F4952 B&C for reconditioning to J Type (s/n 6244) and ready by 15.6.23. **IAAD** Henlow and in ground collision with Avro 504K D7535 2.6.25. **ARS IAAD** Henlow by 4.26, on charge when unit retitled **HAD** and on unit charge until @ 6.26. B&C for reconditioning to Mk.III (s/n 7093) and ready by 28.5.27. B&C for reconditioning to Mk.IV (s/n 7259) and ready by 30.9.28. **SAC** Old Sarum by 9.28 until @ 1.30.

F4953 B&C for reconditioning to J Type (s/n 6249) and ready by 12.7.23. **PD** Ascot. To India. **AD** Drigh Road. **AP** Lahore by 7.24 until @ 8.24. **Quetta SF** by 5.28. **20 Sqn** by 5.30 until @ 11.30.

F4954 B&C for reconditioning to J Type (s/n 6395) and ready by 16.2.24. **5 FTS** Sealand and wrecked 29.4.24 (Fg Off T.P.T. Jones/AC2 C.S. Richards both KIFA, spun in and burnt out near Shotwick).

F4955 B&C for reconditioning to J Type (s/n 6413) and ready by 19.3.24. **13 Sqn** Andover by 7.24 and wrecked on Photo Reconnaissance 26.8.24 (Fg Off J.W.C. Harcourt-Vernon/AC1 Carpenter both KIFA, crashed near Lavant, Sussex).

F4956 B&C for reconditioning to J Type (s/n 6387) and ready by 19.2.24. **2 Sqn** Manston by 5.24 until @ 7.25. B&C for reconditioning to DC (s/n 6880) and ready by 22.12.25. **RAF (Cadet) College** Cranwell by 5.28. **16 Sqn/SAC** Old Sarum by 8.28 until @ 1.30.

F4957 **AGS** Eastchurch by 9.20 until @ 10.20. B&C for reconditioning to J Type (s/n 6414) and ready by 21.4.24. **13 Sqn** Andover by 1925 until @ 1926. **16 Sqn** Old Sarum. B&C for reconditioning to Mk.III (s/n 7147) and ready by 4.6.28. **AGS** Eastchurch by 10.29 until @ 7.30.

F4958 To Iraq and wrecked 16.9.22 (struck a bank on landing at Kumait LG – **6 Sqn**?). Returned to UK. B&C for reconditioning to J Type (s/n 6410) and ready by 14.3.24. **PD** Ascot. To India. **AD** Drigh Road. **31 Sqn** as a/c *L* by 11.25 until @ 12.25. **5 Sqn** as a/c *F* by 6.27 until @ 3.28. **20 Sqn** as a/c *A* by 12.29 until @ 3.30.

F4959 N/I

F4960 B&C for reconditioning to J Type (s/n 6386) and ready by 18.2.24. **16 Sqn/SAC** Old Sarum by 6.24 until @ 4.25. B&C for reconditioning to DC (s/n 6882) and ready by 1.1.26. **1 SoTT** Halton by 7.26 until @ 10.27.

F4961 B&C for reconditioning to J Type (s/n 6409) and ready by 12.3.24. **PD** Ascot. To Egypt. **AD** Aboukir. **6 Sqn** by 1.25 and wrecked 18.4.25 (crashed in flames while bombing).

F4962 B&C for reconditioning to J Type (s/n 6402) and ready by 3.24. **PD** Ascot. To Egypt. **AD** Aboukir. **208 Sqn** by 7.25. Heliopolis by 7.27 until @ 9.27.

F4963 B&C for reconditioning to J Type (s/n 6415) and ready by 6.3.24. B&C for reconditioning to DC (s/n 6894) and ready by 15.1.26.

F4964 B&C for reconditioning to J Type (s/n 6390) and ready by 25.2.24. **5 FTS** Sealand by 12.24 until @ 2.25. **HAD SF** Henlow by 8.26 until @ 1.29.

F4965 B&C for reconditioning to J Type (s/n 6422) and ready by 22.3.24. **2 Sqn** Manston by 5.24 until @ 8.25. B&C for reconditioning (s/n 6976) and ready by 17.7.26. **HAD** Henlow by 4.27. Shipped China. **2 Sqn** Shanghai/Manston by 6.27 and wrecked 30.5.28 (crashed on landing at Sutton Bridge).

F4966 Fermoy 1921. **24 Sqn** Kenley by 11.21. **1 SoTT** Halton by 2.27.

F4967 B&C for reconditioning to J Type (s/n 6421) and ready by 21.3.24. **2 Sqn** Manston by 4.26 until 5.26. At B&C for reconditioning to Mk.III (s/n 7102) and ready by 20.6.27; **RAE** by 22.7.27. Handley Page Cricklewood and fitted with Handley Page slots 11.10.27. **A&AEE** Martlesham Heath 10.27. To B&C. **RAE** Farnborough by 31.5.28. Worthy Down by 18.9.30. **RAE** Farnborough by 20.12.30 and last flown 3.3.31.

F4968 B&C for reconditioning to J Type (s/n 6254) and ready by 19.7.23. **PD** Ascot. To Iraq. **AD** Hinaidi. **6 Sqn** 1924 until 1925. Returned to UK. B&C for reconditioning to DC (s/n 6839) and ready by 30.10.25.

The circumstances of this accident to F4968 are not known, but it was one of a batch of 700 Falcon-powered F.2Bs ordered from Bristol in 1918. *(Philip Jarrett)*

F4969 B&C for reconditioning to J Type (s/n 6396) and ready by 26.2.24. **5 FTS** Sealand by 12.24 until @ 1.25.

F4970 B&C for reconditioning to J Type (s/n 6385) and ready by 15.2.24. B&C for reconditioning to DC (s/n 6886) and ready by 7.1.26. **4 Sqn** Farnborough by 31.5.26. **1 SoTT** Halton by 9.26 until @ 1.28. B&C for reconditioning (s/n 7246) and ready by 7.9.28. **HAD** Henlow. **RAF College** Cranwell by 3.29 until @ 2.31.

100 BRISTOL F.2B (200hp Arab) ordered 21.5.18 under Contract 351/1218/C.1158 (BR.488) from Harris & Sheldon, Birmingham and numbered F5074 to F5173. Final 20 machines cancelled.

F5074 N/I

F5075 N/I

F5076 **14 AAP** Castle Bromwich and tested 9.11.18 (Lt G.H. Richardson).

F5077
to   } N/I
F5086

F5087 Photographed at Elsham (in transit?).

F5088 N/I

F5089 N/I

F5090 **14 AAP** Castle Bromwich and tested 2.12.18 (Lt G.H. Richardson).

F5091 (Arab) **14 AAP** Castle Bromwich by 27.1.19, reallotted from SW Area to BEF and still on unit charge 19.3.19.

F5092 (Arab) **14 AAP** Castle Bromwich by 25.1.19, allotted to BEF and still on unit charge 26.3.19. **8 Sqn** dd ex **1 ASD** 20.4.19. **1 ASD** ex 8 Sqn 12.7.19.

F5093 N/I

F5094 **7 TS AFC** dd ex Castle Bromwich 8.2.19 (engine 16272). **1 (T) Wing AFC ARS** Leighterton ex 7 TS AFC 8.2.19.

F5095 (Arab) **14 AAP** Castle Bromwich by 27.1.19, reallotted from SW Area to BEF and still on unit charge 19.3.19.

F5096 **37 TDS** Yatesbury by 22.1.19 (Lt J.W. Baker) until @ 2.19.

F5097 (Arab) **14 AAP** Castle Bromwich by 27.1.19, reallotted from SW Area to BEF and still on unit charge 19.3.19. **8 Sqn** dd ex **1 ASD** 3.5.19. **1 ASD** ex 8 Sqn 12.7.19.

F5098 (Arab) **14 AAP** Castle Bromwich 19.4.19, allotted to BEF and wrecked 28.4.19 (Capt E.T. Hayen KIFA/Major M.N. Perrin fatally IIFA, engine failed on take off, stalled trying to turn back and nosedived in – engine E3271/WD27396).

F5099
to   } N/I
F5108

F5109 (Arab) **14 AAP** Castle Bromwich by 27.12.18, allotted to BEF; at London Colney 7.4.19, reallotted to Ministry of Munitions ASD, surplus to RAF requirements, and to go to Hendon by road.

F5110 (Arab) **14 AAP** Castle Bromwich by 19.4.19, reallotted from SW Area to BEF and still on unit charge 19.4.19. **8 Sqn** dd ex **6 AIS** 31.5.19. **1 ASD** ex 8 Sqn 12.7.19.

F5111 (Arab) **14 AAP** Castle Bromwich by 27.1.19, reallotted from Midland Area to BEF and still on unit charge 27.3.19. At London Colney 7.4.19, reallotted to Ministry of Munitions ASD, surplus to RAF requirements, and to go to Hendon by road.

F5112 (Arab) **14 AAP** Castle Bromwich by 25.4.19, reallotted from SE Area to BEF.

F5113 (Arab) **14 AAP** Castle Bromwich by 25.4.19, reallotted from SE Area to BEF.

F5114 N/I

F5115 N/I

F5116 N/I

F5117 (Arab) **59 Sqn** Duren. **1 ASD** ex 59 Sqn 17.7.19.

F5118 (Arab) **59 Sqn** by 30.6.19. **1 ASD** ex 59 Sqn 17.7.19.

F5119
to   } N/I
F5129

F5130 (Arab) **14 AAP** Castle Bromwich by 28.4.19, allotted to BEF. **59 Sqn** Duren dd 2.6.19. **1 ASD** ex 59 Sqn 17.7.19.

F5131 (Arab) **14 AAP** Castle Bromwich 28.4.19, allotted to BEF.

F5132 (Arab) **14 AAP** Castle Bromwich by 28.4.19, allotted to BEF. **59 Sqn** by 30.6.19. **1 ASD** ex 59 Sqn 17.7.19.

F5133 (Arab) **14 AAP** Castle Bromwich by 28.4.19, allotted to BEF.

F5135 (Arab) **14 AAP** Castle Bromwich 28.4.19, allotted to BEF. **8 Sqn** by dd ex **6 AIS** 25.5.19. **8 SS** ex 8 Sqn 20.6.19.

F5136 (Arab) **14 AAP** Castle Bromwich by 28.4.19, allotted to BEF. **8 Sqn** dd ex **1 ASD** 5.5.19. **1 ASD** ex 8 Sqn 7.7.19.

F5137 (Arab) **14 AAP** Castle Bromwich by 30.4.19, allotted to BEF. **9 Sqn** dd ex **1 ASD** by 31.5.19 (engine 3333/WD27458). **2 SS** ex 9 Sqn 7.6.19.

F5138 (Arab) **14 AAP** Castle Bromwich by 28.4.19, allotted to BEF. **9 Sqn** dd ex **1 ASD** 9.5.18 (engine 3375/WD27500). **1 ASD** 22.7.19.

F5139 **9 Sqn** 14.5.19.

F5140 (Arab) **14 AAP** Castle Bromwich by 28.4.19, allotted to BEF. **12 Sqn** as a/c *A5* 1919.

F5141 N/I

F5142 (Arab) **12 Sqn** and wrecked 1919 (Lt V. Fowler OK, nosed up on landing at Lille).

F5143 N/I

F5144 N/I

F5145 (Arab) **14 AAP** Castle Bromwich by 28.4.19, allotted to BEF.

F5146
to   } N/I
F5152

F5153 **8 Sqn** by 11.6.19.

At least 51 Bristol F2B reconstructed by Aircraft Depots in France

F5809 (Falcon III) taken on charge 25.6.18 on reconstruction from C4887. **2 AIS** ex **1 ASD** 28.6.18. **48 Sqn** dd ex 2 AIS 29.6.18 (engine 1177/WD51613) and wrecked on Test Flight 8.7.18 (Lt B.M. Battey USAS/Cpl R. Lund both OK, force landed at **2 ASD** after air lock in fuel supply – same engine). **2 ASD** ex 48 Sqn 9.7.18. **2 AIS** ex 2 ASD 23.8.18. **9 Sqn** dd ex 2 AIS 2.9.18 (engine 955/WD32877) and wrecked on return from ALG 3.9.18 (Lt G.W. Miller/Lt H.C.G. Newton both OK, over-ran on landing and collided with R.E.8 D4935 – same engine). **2 ASD** ex 9 Sqn 6.9.18 and deleted 22.9.18 (not worth reconstruction, 21hr 55min).

F5810 (Falcon III) taken on charge 25.6.18 on reconstruction from C4851. **1 ASD** by 26.8.18 (engine 1309/WD51679). **2 AIS** ex 1 ASD 4.7.18. **62 Sqn** dd ex 2 AIS 6.7.18, LIA on 07:00 OP 22.7.18 (Lt W.E. Coulson/2nd Lt W.H.E. Labett both POW, last seen diving on three enemy triplanes over Laventie – same engine) and deleted on unit that day (9hr 40min).

F5811 (Falcon III) taken on charge 25.6.18 on reconstruction from C4709. **1 ASD** by 28.6.18 (engine 1251/WD51650). **48 Sqn** dd ex 1 ASD 3.7.18, marked as a/c *3*, vict 8.8.18 (Capt C.R. Steele/2nd Lt E. Vickers destroyed a DFW C-type over Rosieres-Chaulnes at 09:50) then wrecked in enemy bombing raid on Bertangles aerodrome 24/25.8.18 and deleted on unit (burnt out).

F5812 (Falcon III) taken on charge 25.6.18 on reconstruction from B1194. **1 ASD** by 7.7.18. **'L' Flt** dd ex **1 AIS** 9.7.18, marked as a/c *A* and wrecked on Travelling Flight 24.10.18 (Capt B.E. Catchpole MC DFC/2nd Lt C. Edwards both OK, engine cut out and crashed in forced landing on rough ground near Monchy le Preax – engine 1373/WD51711). **1 ASD** ex 'L' Flt and deleted 30.10.18 (not worth reconstruction).

F5813 (Falcon III) taken on charge 25.6.18 on reconstruction from C4621. **1 ASD** by 26.7.18 (engine 1137/WD39461). **1 AIS** ex 1 ASD 31.7.18 and wrecked on Ferry Flight to **2 AIS** 9.8.18 (Lt E.W. Walls OK, overshot on arrival to avoid other landing machine and landed in a cornfield – same engine). **2 ASD** ex 2 AIS and deleted 19.9.18 (not worth reconstruction, 2hr 50min).

F5814 (Falcon III) taken on charge 25.6.18 on reconstruction from A7151. **1 ASD** by 9.7.18. **2 AIS** ex 1 ASD 9.7.18. **11 Sqn** dd ex 2 AIS 10.7.17, LIA on OP 29.9.18 (2nd Lt T.T. Smith/Lt J.L. Bromley both KIA – engine 1269/WD51659) and deleted on unit that day (114hr 40min).

F5815 (Falcon III) taken on charge 25.6.18 on reconstruction from A7266. **1 ASD** by 24.7.18. **52 Sqn** dd ex **2 ASD** 25.7.18. **59 Sqn** on attachment ex 52 Sqn from 3.8.18 until 2.9.18. **'N' Flt** by 30.9.18 and wrecked after Artillery Observation 1.11.18 (2nd Lt Illsley/2nd Lt Crowther both OK – returned with full load and broke longerons on landing – engine 1757/WD51903).

F5816 (Falcon III) taken on charge 25.6.18 on reconstruction from C900. **1 ASD** by 28.8.18. **2 AIS** ex 1 ASD 29.8.18. **20 Sqn** dd ex 2 AIS 3.9.18 (engine 1579/WD51814), and wrecked on 10:20 OP 15.9.18 (Lt A.B.D. Campbell OK/Sgt A.J. Winch WIA, machine force landed after shot up by enemy fire – engine 1343/WD51696). **2 ASD** ex 20 Sqn 19.9.18.

F5817 (Falcon III) taken on charge 25.6.18 on reconstruction from B1136. **48 Sqn** and wrecked on Formation Flight 12.3.19 (2nd Lt C.A. Allen/2nd Lt W. Kennedy both KOAS, dived in vertically near Lohmar – engine 435/WD32617).

F5818 (Falcon III) taken on charge 25.6.18 on reconstruction from C4818. **1 ASD** by 14.9.18 (engine 575/WD32687) and wrecked by enemy bombing of Marquise 23.9.18 (burnt out) and deleted 26.9.18 (50min).

F5819 (Falcon III) taken on charge 25.6.18 on reconstruction from A7300. **1 ASD** by 26.7.18 (engine 975/WD32887). **1 AIS** ex 1 ASD 3.8.18. **'L' Flt** dd ex 1 AIS 4.8.18 and wrecked after Artillery Observation/Photography 21.8.18 (Lt R.F. Buick/Lt B. Donald both OK, struck a rut when landing on rough ground – same engine). **1 ASD** ex 'L' Flt and deleted 29.8.18 (not worth reconstruction, 41hr).

F5820 (Falcon III) taken on charge 25.6.18 on reconstruction from B1213. **1 ASD** by 5.8.18 (engine 1485/WD51767). **1 AIS** ex 1 ASD 8.8.18. **22 Sqn** dd ex 1 AIS 15.8.18 and wrecked on 07:00

OP 6.9.18 (Lt L.C. Rowney OK/Sgt J. Goodman WIA, brought down by enemy AA fire – same engine). **1 ASD** ex 22 Sqn 8.9.18 and deleted 11.9.18 (not worth reconstruction, 51hr 5min).

F5821 (Falcon III) taken on charge 25.6.18 on reconstruction from B1112.

F5822 (Falcon III) taken on charge 25.6.18 on reconstruction from C970. **1 ASD** by 22.7.18. **1 AIS** by 26.7.18 (engine 223/WD18611). **L Flight** dd ex 1 AIS 22.8.18 and wrecked on Travelling Flight 16.9.18 (Lt G.A.J. Ashwin/2nd Lt C.C.G. Ravine both KOAS, crashed at **16 Sqn** aerodrome, being seen to hang at the top of a loop, then go into a steep dive with engine full on before the RH wing crumpled up at 50ft – same engine). **1 ASD** ex 'L' Flt and deleted 20.9.18 (39hr 40min).

F5823 (Falcon III) taken on charge 25.6.18 on reconstruction from C4749. **1 ASD** by 30.8.18 (engine 441/WD32620). **1 AIS** ex 1 ASD 3.9.18. **22 Sqn** dd ex 1 AIS 7.9.18, reported as unfit for war flying 13.10.18 (same engine) and wrecked after OP 4.11.18 (2nd Lt E. Bannister/2nd Lt C. Spooner both OK, engine failed on landing due to fuel shortage and machine crashed – engine 1431/WD51740). **1 ASD** ex 22 Sqn 7.11.18.

F5824 (Falcon III) taken on charge 25.6.18 on reconstruction from C785. **1 ASD** by 22.7.18. **2 AIS** ex 1 ASD 24.7.18. **22 Sqn** dd ex 2 AIS 28.7.18, victs 16.8.18 (Lt C.E. Hurst/Sgt H.C. Hunt destroyed an EA C-type near Fresnoy at 11:00) and 31.8.18 (Lt C.E. Hurst/Sgt H.C. Hunt sent a Fokker D.VII down OOC, SE of Vitry at 17:10) then wrecked on 08:05 OP 16.9.18 (Lt T.D. Smith/2nd Lt S.C. Barrow both OK, machine damaged in combat and force landed at **16 Sqn** aerodrome – engine 893/WD32846). **1 ASD** ex 22 Sqn 17.9.18 and deleted 19.9.18 (not worth reconstruction, 77hr 34min).

F5995 (Falcon III) taken on charge 12.7.18 on reconstruction from C4641. **48 Sqn** and wrecked on Travelling Flight to Nivelles 14.2.19 (Lt G. Thornton-Norris/Capt C. Campbell both OK, became lost in fog and force landed near Albeneyck – engine 543/WD32671).

F5996 (Falcon III) taken on charge 12.7.18 on reconstruction from C777. **1 ASD** by 14.9.18 (engine 683/WD32741). **1 AIS** by 4.10.18. **22 Sqn** dd ex 2 AIS 25.10.18 and on unit charge until @ 24.7.19. **24 Sqn** as a/c **P** 1919. B&C for reconditioning to J Type (s/n 6596) and ready by 24.1.25. B&C for reconditioning to Mk.III (s/n 7141) and ready by 7.5.28. **2 Sqn** Manston by 1.29 until @ 2.29.

F5997 (Falcon III) taken on charge 12.7.18 on reconstruction from B1231. **1 ASD** and tested 26.10.18. **88 Sqn**. **80 Sqn**. **6 Sqn** and wrecked before Practice Flight 19.3.19 (Lt D. McD. Northcombe IOAS, collided with a R.E.8 taken off at Sart – engine 413/WD32606).

F5998 (Falcon III) taken on charge 24.7.18 on reconstruction from B1314. **1 ASD** by 14.9.18 (engine 975/WD32887), reported in need of reconstruction 23.9.18 and still on unit charge 30.9.18.

F5999 (Falcon III) taken on charge 24.7.18 on reconstruction from C4699. **1 ASD** by 13.9.18. **1 AIS** ex 1 ASD 15.9.18 (engine 451/WD32625). **88 Sqn** dd ex 1 AIS 21.9.18 (same engine) and wrecked on Engine Test 9.4.19 (Lt L.S. Delapena/2nd Lt D.A. Vavasour both OK, hit a ridge on landing).

F6040 (Falcon III) taken on charge 24.7.18 on reconstruction from C882. **1 ASD** by 31.8.18 (engine 1559/WD51804). **1 AIS** ex 1 ASD 4.9.18. **22 Sqn** dd ex 1 AIS 7.9.18, vict 27.9.18 (Lt F.G. Gibbons/Sgt G. Shannon sent a Fokker D.VII down OOC over Sensee Canal-Cambrai at 07:30) then wrecked on 06:00 OP 30.10.18 (Lt O.H. Williamson/Capt G.B. Crawford both OK, machine damaged by EA fire with longeron shot through – same engine). **1 ASD** ex 22 Sqn by 15.11.18.

F6041 (Falcon III) taken on charge 25.7.18 on reconstruction from C920. **1 ASD** by 14.9.18 (engine 231/WD18615). **1 AIS** ex 1 ASD 1.10.18 and tested 10.10.18. **48 Sqn**, vict 4.11.18 (Capt L.A. Payne MC/2nd Lt R.L. Ford sent a Fokker D.VII down OOC smoking over Lessines-Gramont at 15:15) then wrecked on OP, Audenarde-Tournai, 12.11.18 (Capt L.A. Payne MC/2nd Lt T.L. Jones both OK, force landed near Elsegem after engine failure – same engine). **8 SS** ex 48 Sqn.

F6042 (Falcon III) taken on charge 25.7.18 on reconstruction from C781. **5 Sqn** and wrecked on Travelling Flight 24.3.19 (Lt R. Blake/2nd Lt R. Franklin both OK, forced to make a second landing approach at Coblenz and force landed in rough ground after engine failed – engine 111/18555).

F6043 (Falcon III) taken on charge 30.7.18 on reconstruction from C929. **1 ASD** by 26.10.18.

F6093 (Falcon III) taken on charge 30.7.18 on reconstruction from C790. **2 AIS** ex **2 ASD** 29.7.18. **48 Sqn** dd ex 2 AIS 9.8.18 (engine 1215/WD51632) and wrecked after OP, Peronne, 21.8.18 (2nd Lt G.C.S. Browning/Sgt W.B. Dodd both OK, crashed on landing

– same engine). **2 ASD** ex 48 sqn and deleted 10.10.18 (not worth reconstruction).

F6094 (Falcon III) taken on charge 3.7.18 on reconstruction from C805. **48 Sqn** dd ex **2 ASD** 20.8.18 (engine 961/WD32880), destroyed during enemy bombing of Bertangles 24/25.8.18 (same engine) and deleted on unit.

F6101 (Falcon III) taken on charge 3.7.18 on reconstruction from C4861. **52 Sqn** dd ex **2 ASD** 31.7.18. **59 Sqn** on attachment ex 52 Sqn from 9.8.18 until 2.9.18. **'N' Flt** by 30.9.18 and reported 26.12.18 as having cracked engine bearer, probably caused in a forced landing on 9.12.18 – engine 1051/WD39418). **2 ASD** ex 'N' Flt.

F6116 (Falcon III) taken on charge 3.7.18 on reconstruction from C872. **2 ASD** and tested 21.10.18. **2 AIS** ex 2 ASD 22.10.18. **20 Sqn** by 29.10.18, LIA on OP 1.11.18 (2nd Lt P. Segrave/Lt J.F. Kidd both KIA, last seen over Forêt de Mormal – engine 1651/WD51850).

F6118 (Falcon III) taken on charge 3.7.18 on reconstruction from C928. **48 Sqn** dd ex **2 AIS** 8.8.18 (engine 1277/WD51663) and wrecked in enemy bombing of Bertangles 24/25.8.18 (same engine). **2 ASD** ex 48 Sqn 29.8.18 and deleted 8.9.18 (not worth reconstruction).

F6121 (Falcon III) taken on charge 3.7.18 on reconstruction from A7128. **2 ASD** and tested 8.10.18. **2 AIS** ex 2 ASD 22.10.18. **20 Sqn** marked as a/c **S**.

F6131 (Falcon III) taken on charge 3.7.18 on reconstruction from C914. **2 AIS** ex **2 ASD** 13.8.18. **11 Sqn** dd ex 2 AIS 20.8.18, wrecked on Reconnaissance, Le Cateau, 17.10.18 (Sgt Mech J. Gamble/Sgt Mech E.C. Taylor both OK, force landed near Inchy after engine failure, hit a trench and fuselage broke in two – engine 1391/WD51720) and deleted on unit that day.

F6142 (Falcon III) taken on charge 3.7.18 on reconstruction from B1328. **2 AIS** ex **2 ASD** 21.9.18. **62 Sqn** dd ex 2 AIS 25.9.18 and on unit charge until @ 12.18.

F6158 (Falcon III) taken on charge 3.7.18 on reconstruction from C4852. **62 Sqn** dd ex 2 AIS 16.7.18 (engine 1247/WD51648) and wrecked on Bombing 23.8.18 (2nd Lt T.K. Stewart/2nd Lt E.M. Buckley both OK, machine shot up in combat near Douai – same engine). **2 ASD** ex 62 Sqn and deleted 6.10.18 (not worth reconstruction).

F6179 (Falcon III) taken on charge 7.7.18 on reconstruction from A7220.

F6181 (Falcon III) taken on charge 8.7.18 on reconstruction from A7129. **2 ASD** and tested 21.10.18. **2 AIS** ex 2 ASD 22.10.18. **20 Sqn** and wrecked 3.12.18 (Lt S.E. Booth/Cpl Mech R. Moors both KOAS, spun into the ground – engine 1617/WD51833).

F6195 (Falcon III) taken on charge 17.7.18 on reconstruction from C4847. **2 AIS** ex **2 ASD** 29.9.18. **5 AIS** ex 2 AIS 3.10.18. **20 Sqn** LIA on OP 10.11.18 (Lt A.W. McHardy/Lt W.A. Rodgers both KIA, last seen in combat over Charleroi – engine 403/WD32601) and deleted on unit that day.

F6206 (Falcon III) taken on charge 18.7.18 on reconstruction from B1271. **2 ASD** and tested 29.10.18. **2 AIS** ex 2 ASD 30.10.18. **11 Sqn** by 15.12.18 until @ 17.7.19.

F6208 (Falcon III) taken on charge 22.7.18 on reconstruction from D7911. **2 AIS** ex **2 ASD** 26.10.18. **20 Sqn** as a/c **X** by 1.12.18.

F6217 (Falcon III) taken on charge 25.7.18 on reconstruction from C792. **2 AIS** dd ex **2 ASD** 29.10.18. **11 Sqn** dd ex 2 AIS 11.11.18 and wrecked on Travelling Flight 14.12.18 (2nd Lt E.E.W.C. Sharpe/Capt A. Morrison both OK, hit road after overshoot on landing – engine 597/WD32698).

F6235 Taken on charge 7.8.18 on reconstruction from D7893. **ACIS** Kenley by 8.19 (for General Brooke-Popham). Also noted at **RAE** ex Kenley 5.2.19. Last flown 19.8.27.

F6283 Taken on charge 4.9.18 on reconstruction from C953.

F6400 (Falcon III) taken on charge 1.8.18 on reconstruction from C825 and at **1 ASD** 14.9.18 (engine 1623/WD51836) but serial applied in error and given new one, H7060, 9.18.

F6401 (Falcon III) taken on charge 7.8.18 on reconstruction from C919, at **1 ASD** by 14.9.18 (engine 543/WD32671) and damaged on Test Flight 20.9.18 (Lt Stewart OK, force landed after engine failure) but serial applied in error and given new one, H7061, 9.18.

F6402 Taken on charge 7.8.18 on reconstruction from C780 but serial applied in error and given new one, H7062, by 9.18.

F6403 (Falcon III) taken on charge 7.8.18 on reconstruction from D8023, at **1 ASD** by 14.9.18 (engine 633/WD32716) but serial applied in error and given new one, H7063, 9.18.

F6404 (Falcon III) taken on charge 8.8.18 on reconstruction from E2483. **2 ASD** ex **1 ASD** 12.8.18. **48 Sqn** dd ex **2 AIS** 20.8.18 (engine 1481/WD51765) and damaged 24.8.18. **2 ASD** ex 48 Sqn 28.8.18. Serial applied in error and given new one, H7291, 9.18.

F6405 Taken on charge 23.8.18 on reconstruction from C901 but serial applied in error and given new one, H7064, 9.18.

F6406 Taken on charge 23.8.18 on reconstruction from C776 but serial applied in error and given new one, H7065, 9.18.

F6407 (Falcon III) taken on charge 27.8.18 on reconstruction from E2254, at **1 ASD** by 31.8.18 (engine 1517/WD51783) and to **1 AIS** 15.9.18 but serial applied in error and given new one, H7292, by 9.18.

F6408 (Falcon III) taken on charge 30.8.18 on reconstruction from E2219, at **1 ASD** 31.8.18 (engine 1447/WD51748) and to **1 AIS** 12.9.18 but serial applied in error and given new one, H7293, 9.18.

BRISTOL FIGHTER F2B airframes reconstructed from salvage/spares.

F9396 The first of a batch of rebuilds of various aircraft types by the **45th Wing**, as a/c *8* may have been with **28 TDS** at Crail.

F9403 (Falcon II) rebuilt by **4th Wing ARS** Netheravon. **33 TDS** Witney and wrecked 17.10.18 (Flt Cdt A.E. Kaye KIFA, spun into the ground – engine 2/F/18449).

F9502 Reconstructed by **5 (E)ARD** Henlow.

F9504 (Falcon III) reconstructed by **5 (E)ARD** Henlow. **IAAD** Henlow and totally wrecked 4.2.21 (Flt Lt G.C. Rhodes OK, heavy landing).

F9516 Reconstructed by **5 (E)ARD** Henlow (ex E2560) and taken on charge 28.8.18.

F9549 (Arab) erected by Marshall & Sons additional to contract dated 19.7.18.

F9598 Reconstructed by **3 (W)ARD** Yate.

F9606 Reconstructed by **3 (W)ARD** Yate.

F9616 Reconstructed by **3 (W)ARD** Yate.

F9638 Reconstructed by **RAF & Army Co-operation School**, Worthy Down.

250 BRISTOL FIGHTER F.2B ordered 19.7.18 under Contract No.35a/2114/C2448 (B.R.575) from The Gloucestershire Aircraft Co Ltd, Cheltenham and numbered H834 to H1083. Mostly stored. (Engines?). Deliveries from w/e 9.11.18 and 222 delivered by w/e 23.8.19.

H834 N/I

H835 N/I

H836 (Arab) in France 19.3.19, allotted to BEF. **9 Sqn** dd ex **1 ASD** 7.5.19 (engine 53812) and on unit charge until @ 14.6.19.

H837 (Arab) **3 (W)ARD** Yate by 8.2.19, allotted to BEF.

H838 to **H901** } N/I

H902 (Arab) **5 AAP** Bristol by 14.1.19, allotted to BEF.

H903 N/I

H904 N/I

H905 (Arab) **5 AAP** Bristol by 15.1.19, allotted to BEF.

H906 to **H925** } N/I

H926 To Civilian Register 13.7.22 as *G-EBEE*, registered to the Aircraft Disposal Co Ltd. To AMB 7.22.

H927 To Civilian Register 21.6.22 as *G-EBDN*, registered to the Aircraft Disposal Co Ltd. To AMB 7.22.

H928 to **H950** } N/I

H951 To Civilian Register 22.11.20 as *G-EAWA*, registered to Handley Page Ltd.

H952 to **H1008** } N/I

H1009 **2 FS** Marske by 6.2.19 until @ 17.2.19.

H1010 **5 (E)ARD** Henlow 15.3.20, allotted Polish Military Purchase Mission and to be despatched to Handley Page, Cricklewood 4.20 but reallotted to Inland Area for disposal 19.4.20.

H1011 N/I

H1012 N/I

H1013 N/I

H1014 **4 Sqn** Farnborough.

H1015 **24 Sqn** Kenley by 4.21. **SAC** Old Sarum by 9.25 until @ 9.26.

H1016 N/I

H1017 (Puma) first flown 16.10.19. Storage Station Brockworth and wrecked on Ferry Flight to Waddon 12.2.20 (Fg Off G.V. Howard/ RAF passenger both OK, force landed on cliff near Maidenhead after port aileron cable failed).

H1018 N/I

H1019 First flown 13.8.19. Loaned to Handley Page and wrecked 17.2.20 (Mr E.F. Jones OK, crashed after take off en route Waddon-Cricklewood).

H1020 to **H1037** } N/I

H1038 **5 (E)ARD** Henlow 15.3.20, allotted Polish Military Purchase Mission but reallotted to Inland Area 19.4.20.

H1039 to **H1045** } N/I

H1046 **5 FTS** Sealand by 9.23.

H1047 to **H1083** } N/I

500 BRISTOL FIGHTER F.2B ordered 18.7.18 under Contract 35a/2100/C2393 (B.R.574) from The British & Colonial Aeroplane Co Ltd, Filton and numbered H1240 to H1739. (Falcon III). [Consecutive works sequence nos. 4957 to 5424]. Deliveries from w/e 22.2.19 and 447 delivered by w/e 5.7.19 with no others recorded before Ministry of Munitions ledger closed w/e 23.8.19. H1708 – H1739 cancelled 20.9.19.

H1240 To Civilian Register 21.12.21 as *G-EBAM*, registered to the Aircraft Disposal Co Ltd. To AMB 7.22.

H1241 N/I

H1242 To Civilian Register 31.12.21 as *G-EBAT*, registered to the Aircraft Disposal Co Ltd. To AMB 7.22.

H1243 N/I

H1244 To Civilian Register 31.12.21 as *G-EBAU*, registered to the Aircraft Disposal Co Ltd. To AMB 7.22.

H1245 To Civilian Register 25.4.22 as *G-EBCW*, registered to the Aircraft Disposal Co Ltd. To AMB 7.22.

H1246 N/I

H1247 N/I

H1248 (Hispano-Suiza) to Civilian Register 12.4.23 as *G-AUEB*, registered to H. Miller.

H1249 N/I

H1250 N/I

H1251 To Irish Air Corps at Baldonnel 5.7.22 as *BF.II*.

H1252 N/I

H1253 N/I

H1254 To Civilian Register 24.12.24 as *G-EBIO*, registered to the Aircraft Disposal Co Ltd. Scrapped 1935.

H1255 N/I

H1256 N/I

H1257 N/I

H1258 To Civilian Register 27.2.22 as *G-EBBO*, registered to the Aircraft Disposal Co Ltd. To AMB.

H1259 to **H1269** } N/I

H1270 To Polish Air Force as *20.42*.

H1271 N/I

H1272 To Polish Air Force as *20.41*.

H1273 To Polish Air Force as *20.28*.

H1274 To Polish Air Force as *20.44*.

H1275 To Polish Air Force as *20.78*.

H1276 N/I

H1277 To Polish Air Force as *20.36*.

H1278 To Polish Air Force as *20.39*.

H1279 To Polish Air Force as *20.48* (300hp Hispano-Suiza).

H1280 N/I

H1281 To Civilian Register 25.4.22 as *G-EBCV*, registered to the Aircraft Disposal Co Ltd. To AMB.

H1282 To Civilian Register 23.5.21. As *G-EAWZ* 13.7.22, registered to the Aircraft Disposal Co Ltd. To AMB and crashed 1921.

H1283 N/I

H1284 **44 TDS** Bicester and wrecked 7.7.19 (2nd Lt J.B. Stockbridge IIFA, engine failed on take off, stalled and side-slipped in – engine 2487/WD89068).

H1285 N/I

H1286 N/I

H1287 To Polish Air Force as *20.71*.

H1288 To Polish Air Force as *20.96*.

H1289 N/I

H1290 N/I

H1291 To Civilian Register 21.12.21 as *G-EBAK*, registered to the Aircraft Disposal Co Ltd. To AMB 1922.

H1292 To Civilian Register 21.12.21 as *G-EBAL*, registered to the Aircraft Disposal Co Ltd. To AMB 3.22.

H1293 N/I

H1294 N/I

H1295 To Polish Air Force as *20.71*.

H1296 To Polish Air Force as *20.77*.

H1297 To Polish Air Force as *20.97*.

H1298 N/I

H1299 N/I

H1300 N/I

H1301 To Polish Air Force as *20.57*.

H1302 N/I

H1303 N/I

H1304 To Polish Air Force as *20.65*.

H1305 To Polish Air Force as *20.76*.

H1306 N/I

H1307 To Polish Air Force as *20.63*.

H1308 To Polish Air Force as *20.60*.

H1309 N/I

H1310 To Polish Air Force as *20.51*.

H1311
to } N/I
H1324

H1325 5 FTS Sealand by 9.24.

H1326 5 FTS Sealand by 9.23 until @ 1.24.

H1327 N/I

H1328 N/I

H1329 N/I

H1330 N/I

H1331 To storage at Waddon. To Polish Air Force as *20.55*.

H1332
to } N/I
H1349

H1350 To Polish Air Force as *20.33*.

H1351 To Polish Air Force as *20.31*.

H1352 To Polish Air Force as *20.22*.

H1353 To Polish Air Force as *20.14*.

H1354 To Polish Air Force as *20.27*.

H1355 To Polish Air Force as *20.21*.

H1356 To Polish Air Force as *20.23*.

H1357 To Polish Air Force as *20.12*.

H1358 To Polish Air Force as *20.30*.

H1359 N/I

H1360 To Polish Air Force as *20.32*.

H1361 To Polish Air Force as *20.62*.

H1362 N/I

H1363 N/I

H1364 To Polish Air Force as *20.61*.

H1365 N/I

H1366 To Polish Air Force as *20.53*.

H1367 To Polish Air Force as *20.52*.

H1368 To Polish Air Force as *20.59*.

H1369 N/I

H1370 N/I

H1371 N/I

H1372 To storage at Waddon.

H1373 To storage at Waddon. To Polish Air Force as *20.58*.

H1374 N/I

H1375 N/I

H1376 To Civilian Register 27.11.20 as *G-EASH*, registered to Handley Page Ltd.

H1377 N/I

H1378 N/I

H1379 To Polish Air Force as *20.56*.

H1380
to } N/I
H1384

H1385 To Polish Air Force as *20.100*.

H1386 N/I

H1387 N/I

H1388 To Polish Air Force as *20.64*.

H1389 To Civilian Register 21.12.21 as *G-EAYQ*, registered to the Aircraft Disposal Co Ltd. To AMB.

H1390 B&C for reconditioning to J Type DC (s/n 6505) and ready by 23.10.24. **16 Sqn/SAC** Old Sarum by 5.25. **1 SoTT** Halton 1925. B&C for reconditioning to Mk.III and ready by 2.9.26. **E&WS** Worthy Down by 3.28 until @ 5.28. **RAF College** Cranwell by 1.31 until @ 5.31. **2 FTS** Digby by 7.31.

H1391 B&C for reconditioning to J Type (s/n 6703) and ready by 5.5.25. **2 Sqn** Manston.

H1392 B&C for reconditioning to J Type DC (s/n 6501) and ready by 15.10.24. **RAF (Cadet) College** Cranwell by 11.26 until @ 6.27.

H1393 B&C for reconditioning to J Type (s/n 6534) and ready by 14.11.24.

H1394 24 Sqn Kenley by 3.23. **IACF** Northolt by 6.23 until @ 4.24. B&C for reconditioning to J Type (s/n 6704) and ready by 13.5.25. **PD** Ascot. To Egypt. **AD** Aboukir. **6 Sqn** and wrecked 2.30 (force landed in hills during bad weather and burnt on site).

H1395 SAC Old Sarum by 12.22 until @ 6.23. B&C for reconditioning to J Type (s/n 6649) and ready by 15.3.25. **SAC** Old Sarum by 5.25 until @ 6.26.

H1396 B&C for reconditioning to J Type DC (s/n 6504) and ready by 18.10.24. **2 FTS** Digby. **16 Sqn/SAC** Old Sarum by 7.25 until @ 7.26. B&C for reconditioning to Mk.III DC (s/n 7111) and ready by 11.7.27. **HCF Northolt. 5 FTS** Sealand by 8.2.29 and wrecked 6.12.29 (hit a hedge to avoid cables during forced landing near Mollington, Cheshire). **HAD** Henlow. B&C for reconditioning (s/n 7558). Retaken on RAF charge 15.8.30. **Practice Camp** North Coates Fitties by 4.31. **2 FTS** Digby by 6.31.

H1397 2 FTS by Digby by 5.23. B&C for reconditioning to J Type (s/n 6598) and ready by 24.1.25.

H1398 B&C for reconditioning to J Type DC (s/n 6506) and ready by 23.10.24. **RAF Display** 27.6.25. **HAD** Henlow. **5 FTS** by 5.26. **IACF** Northolt by 5.26 until @ 9.26. B&C for reconditioning to (s/n 7247) and ready by 22.9.28. **PD** Ascot. To India. **AD** Aboukir. **4 FTS** Abu Sueir by 6.29 until @ 2.31.

H1399 N/I

H1400 N/I

H1401 N/I

H1402 N/I

H1403 2 FTS Digby by 10.24 until @ 11.24. **16 Sqn** Old Sarum.

H1404 6 FTS Manston by 23.5.21.

H1405 16 Sqn Old Sarum.

H1406 N/I

H1407 24 Sqn Kenley by 5.21. **PD** Ascot. To India. **AD** Drigh Road. **AP** Lahore by 3.23.

H1408 24 Sqn Kenley by 9.21 and wrecked on Forced Landing Practice 21.11.22 (Flt Lt the Hon H.J.B. Rodney/Plt Off D. Macfadyn both OK, stalled low down and crashed near Addington, Surrey).

H1409 N/I

H1410 To Egypt. **208 Sqn** dd 1.12.21. To UK. **2 FTS** Duxford by 1.24. B&C for reconditioning to J Type (s/n 6652) and ready by 16.3.25.

H1411 1 FTS Netheravon by 9.21 until @ 1.22. **IAAD** Henlow tested 6.12.23 until 18.12.23. **1 FTS** Netheravon by 1.24.

H1412 N/I

H1413 India 1920 (**28 Sqn?**). Returned to UK. B&C for reconditioning to J Type (s/n 6486) and ready by 16.9.24.

H1414 N/I

H1415 4 Sqn Farnborough as a/c *A2* by 1921. **IDE** Biggin Hill by 5.22. **24 Sqn** Kenley 1924. **19 Sqn** Duxford 6.24. B&C for reconditioning to J Type (s/n 6676) and ready by 1.4.25. **School of Photography Flt** Kenley by 9.25. **4 Sqn** Farnborough by 11.25 until @ 2.26. B&C for reconditioning (s/n 6970) and ready by 9.7.26. **SAC** Old Sarum by 9.26.

H1416 B&C for reconditioning to J Type (s/n 6462) and ready by 5.7.24. **16 Sqn/SAC** Old Sarum by 8.24 until @ 6.25.

H1417 2 FTS Duxford by 8.21 until @ 1.22. B&C for reconditioning to J Type (s/n 6536) and ready by 15.11.24. **24 Sqn** Kenley by 1.25. B&C for reconditioning to Mk.III (s/n 7090) and ready by 22.3.27. **RAE** Farnborough dd 23.3.27 and on charge until @ 3.5.27.

H1418 N/I

H1419 2 FTS Duxford and wrecked 19.8.21 (Plt Off E.R. Lush/Plt Off E.A. Rush both KIFA, became lost, ran short of fuel, stalled on turn and crashed at Croxted, near Thetford).

H1420 B&C and reconditioned to Mk.III prototype (s/n 6669). **SAC** Old Sarum dd 21.8.25. B&C 9.1.26 for further modifications. **SAC** Old Sarum by 4.3.26. B&C from 23.7.26 until 9.26. B&C for reconditioning to Mk.IV with large rudder and cambered fin (s/n 7249) and ready by 8.9.28. **4 Sqn** by 9.28.

H1421 2 FTS Duxford by 2.21 until @ 1.22.

H1422 RAF (Cadet) College Cranwell by 3.20 until @ 5.20.

H1423 B&C for reconditioning to J Type (s/n 6565) and ready by 15.12.24. Caught fire on ground by accidental firing of Very pistol, 29.7.26. Repaired. **2 FTS** Digby by 3.30.

H1424 B&C for reconditioning to J Type (s/n 6483) and ready by 11.9.24. **PD** Ascot. To Iraq. **AD** Hinaidi. **6 Sqn** until 1.26. Returned to

Reconditioned F.2B H1420, which served as the mock-up for the Mk.III, was completed in August 1925. It subsequently underwent further modification to meet RAF requirements, and in 1928 was converted to a MK.IV. *(Philip Jarrett)*

UK. **B&C** for reconditioning (s/n 6984) and ready by 14.8.26. **24 Sqn** Kenley by 5.28 until @ 3.30.

H1425 2 FTS Duxford and wrecked 8.3.21 (Flt Lt H.A. Whistler DSO/ Fg Off C.W.S. Chalmers both OK, crashed at Duxford after engine failed at 150ft on take off).

H1426 24 Sqn Kenley by 12.22 and wrecked 20.1.23 (Plt Off C.H.A. Stevens IIFA, hit trees during forced landing on Ladywell Recreation Ground, Lewisham, after engine failure).

H1427 2 FTS Duxford and wrecked 17.8.21 (Fg Off H.D. Wardle/Plt Off F.V. Gauntlett both IIFA, while landing at Duxford, was landed on by H1429).

H1428 2 FTS Duxford by 12.21. **B&C** for reconditioning to J Type (s/n 6588) and ready by 16.1.25. **PD** Ascot. To India. **AD** Drigh Road. **31 Sqn** as a/c *L*. **20 Sqn** by 10.26 until @ 6.27. **5 Sqn** by 7.28 and wrecked 21.9.28 (undershot in night landing at Risalpur and hit a mound).

H1429 2 FTS Duxford and wrecked 17.8.21 (Plt Off R.E. Baugh IIFA, landed on top of H1427 which was landing at Duxford).

H1430 2 FTS Duxford by 2.21 until @ 11.21. **B&C** for reconditioning to J Type (s/n 6607) and ready by 30.1.25.

H1431 N/I

H1432 SAC Old Sarum by 12.22 until @ 6.23. **B&C** for reconditioning to J Type (s/n 6535) and ready by 14.11.24. Kenley by 9.25. **B&C** for reconditioning to Mk.III (s/n 7138) and ready by 8.5.28. **B&C** for repair ready by 16.12.29. **16 Sqn** Old Sarum by 5.30 until @ 6.30.

H1433 IDE Biggin Hill by 11.20. **2 FTS** Duxford and wrecked 5.11.23 (Plt Off E.R. Newbigging IIFA, force landed near Hitchin, Herts, after engine failure).

H1434 IACF Northolt by 6.22. **RAF (Cadet) College** Cranwell by 3.27.

H1435 1 FTS Netheravon by 8.21 until @ 9.21. **PD** Ascot. To Egypt. **AD** Aboukir and reconstructed as HR1435. **208 Sqn** Ismailia.

H1436 AEE/A&AEE/22 Sqn by 6.21 until @ 3.27, used in parachute development trials.

H1437 SAC Old Sarum and wrecked 30.5.22 (Plt Off G.W. Gay/Flt Lt J. Everidge both OK, swung on landing and hit a hangar at Old Sarum). **Irish Flt** Baldonnel by 8.22. **SAC** Old Sarum by 9.25 until @ 9.26.

H1438 RAF (Cadet) College Cranwell by 7.22. **B&C** for reconditioning to J Type DC (s/n 6705) and ready by 14.5.25. **SAC** Old Sarum by 9.25 until @ 9.26. **PD** Ascot. To Iraq. **AD** Hinaidi. **AHQ Iraq Command** by 24.5.27. **6 Sqn** by 1.30 and wrecked 11.8.30 (o/t after struck ridge on landing at Imshash, Egypt).

H1439 RAF (Cadet) College Cranwell by 11.22 until @ 4.24. **B&C** for reconditioning to J Type DC (s/n 6828) and ready by 8.10.25. **2 FTS** Digby by 5.26 until @ 8.27.

H1440 1 FTS Netheravon by 8.20 until @ 7.22. **B&C** for reconditioning to J Type (s/n 6577) and ready by 1.1.25. **13 Sqn** Andover 1925 until @ 1926. **B&C** for reconditioning to (s/n 7167) and ready by 16.3.28. **SAC** Old Sarum by 3.29 until @ 10.30.

H1441 106 Sqn Fermoy 1920. **105 Sqn** Omagh 1920. **2 Sqn** Oranmore by 4.20 until @ 1921.

H1442 106 Sqn Fermoy by 1920. **AGS** Eastchurch by 5.22.

H1443 N/I

H1444 B&C for reconditioning to J Type DC (s/n 6503) and ready by 18.10.24. **SAC** Old Sarum by 9.25 until @ 2.28.

H1445 2 Sqn Oranmore by 1920 until @1921.

H1446 N/I

H1447 CFS Upavon by 11.20 until @ 9.22.

H1448 2 Sqn Oranmore and wrecked on Mail Flight 16.8.20 (spun in from 80ft during forced landing at Fermoy after engine failure).

H1449 1 FTS Netheravon by 8.21. **AGS** Eastchurch and wrecked 31.8.23 (Sqn Ldr P.C. Sherren/AC1 F. Mangleshat both OK, hit a ridge on landing). To India. **AD** Drigh Road 1923. **HAD** Henlow by 8.25.

H1450 IDE Biggin Hill by 2.20 until @ 5.22. **PD** Ascot. To Iraq. **AD** Hinaidi. **6 Sqn** by 1924 until @ 1925. Gosport by 3.26 (flown by officers of Directorate of Scientific Research & Technical Development). **RAE** Farnborough by 31.12.26. Yeovil by 4.27. **RAE** Farnborough by 12.4.27. Yeovil by 29.4.27. **RAE** from 30.4.27 until @ 1932.

H1451 School of Photography Farnborough by 2.21. To Egypt. **14 Sqn** Palestine. **208 Sqn** dd ex 14 Sqn 14.2.22. Returned to UK. **B&C** for reconditioning to J Type (s/n 6579) and ready by 3.1.25. **RAF (Cadet) College** Cranwell by 1.25 until @ 9.25. **B&C** for reconditioning (s/n 6971) and ready by 9.7.26. **16 Sqn/SAC** Old Sarum by 4.27 until @ 12.27.

H1452 4 Sqn Farnborough and wrecked 8.6.20 (downwind force landing at Frensham, near Farnham, Surrey).

H1453 24 Sqn Kenley by 9.21; **PD** Ascot. To Iraq. **AD** Hinaidi. **6 Sqn** by 11.21 and wrecked 1.5.22 (Fg Off J.G. Argles OK, collided with D8037 and crashed at Baghdad West).

H1454 PD Ascot. To Iraq. **AD** Hinaidi by 1.23. **6 Sqn** by 18.2.23. **208 Sqn** by 5.23. **6 Sqn** by 1924 until 1925. Returned to UK. **B&C** for reconditioning to J Type (s/n 6806) and ready by 4.9.25. 1.1.25. Kenley (**24 Sqn**?) by 10.25 and wrecked while night flying 11.25.

H1455 2 Sqn Manston by 4.20. **PD** Ascot. To Egypt. **AD** Aboukir. **208 Sqn** by 8.21 until @ 8.23. **B&C** for reconditioning to J Type (s/n 6807) and ready by 4.9.25. **2 Sqn** Manston by 2.27, crashed 22.2.27, repaired and on unit charge until @ 4.27. **SAC** Old Sarum by 4.29 until @ 9.29.

H1456 PD Ascot. To Egypt. **AD** Aboukir. **208 Sqn** by 10.22 until @ 8.23. Returned to UK. **B&C** for reconditioning to J Type (s/n 6853) and ready by 5.11.25. **24 Sqn** Kenley 1926. **1 FTS** Netheravon by 8.26. **5 FTS** Sealand by 6.27 until @ 1.28.

H1457 B&C for reconditioning to J Type (s/n 6613) and ready by 11.2.25. To India. **31 Sqn** as a/c *E* and in propeller accident at Quetta 11.12.30.

H1458 B&C for reconditioning to J Type (s/n 6491) and ready by 25.9.24. To India. **31 Sqn** by 9.25. **5 Sqn** by 2.28 until @ 10.28. **31 Sqn** as a/c *E* 1930. Marked as a/c *A* in India at one time. (Also noted at **B Base Training Flt** Leuchars by 1.31).

H1459 RAF Staff College Flt Andover by 5.24 until @ 6.24. **24 Sqn** Kenley by 10.26 until @ 3.29.

H1460 Modified to coupe and purchased by Air Board 19.5.19. **ACIS** Kenley. **AGS** Eastchurch ex AICS 17.11.19. **24 Sqn** Kenley by 1.1.20 until @ 5.21 (for Directorate of Research use). **1 FTS** Netheravon by 8.21. **2 FTS** Duxford by 10.21.

H1461 B&C for reconditioning to J Type (s/n 6490) and ready by 24.9.24. **PD** Ascot. To India. **AD** Drigh Road. **5 Sqn** by 12.25 until @ 2.26. **AP** Lahore. **5 Sqn** by 28.4.28 until @ 7.28. **31 Sqn** as a/c *F* 1930. In Delhi air display 2.31.

H1462 Despatched from UK for AD Aboukir 25.3.20, for **6 Sqn**. To **AP** Baghdad. **8 Sqn** and wrecked on Reconnaissance 1.8.20 (spun in from 3,000ft).

H1463 **PD** Ascot. To Egypt. **AD** Aboukir. **4 FTS** Abu Sueir by 7.21 until @ 9.21. **AD** Aboukir and reconstructed as HR1463. **208 Sqn** by 2.23 and wrecked 10.7.23. Returned to B&C for reconditioning to J Type DC (s/n 6825) and ready by 3.10.25. **5 FTS** Sealand by 4.27 until @ 7.27.

H1464 **PD** Ascot. To Iraq. **AD** Hinaidi by 7.22 until @ 1.23 AD Hinaidi by 10.23 for reconstruction. **6 Sqn** 1924 until @ 1925.

H1465 **PD** Ascot. To Egypt. **AD** Aboukir. **14 Sqn** by 7.22. **ARS** Aboukir for overhaul. **14 Sqn** by 27.4.23. Returned to UK. B&C for reconditioning to J Type DC (s/n 6854) and ready by 7.11.25. **5 FTS** Sealand by 3.30.

H1466 **E&WS** Worthy Down by 1.22.

H1467 To Egypt. **14 Sqn** and wrecked 25.5.22.

H1468 **PD** Ascot. To Egypt. **AD** Aboukir. **208 Sqn** 1924. Returned to UK. B&C for reconditioning to J Type DC (s/n 6876) and ready by 18.12.25. **4 Sqn** Farnborough by 6.26 until @ 2.28.

H1469 B&C for reconditioning to J Type DC (s/n 6827) and ready by 7.10.25. **PD** Ascot. To Egypt. **AD** Aboukir. **208 Sqn**.

H1470 To Egypt. **Special Instruction Flt**, Almaza by 12.20. **4 FTS** Abu Sueir by 4.21 until @ 5.21.

H1471 N/I

H1472 N/I

H1473 **RAF (Cadet) College** Cranwell by 2.21; B&C for reconditioning to J Type (s/n 6706) and ready by 16.5.25.

H1474 to **H1482** } N/I

H1483 B&C for reconditioning to J Type (s/n 6571) and ready by 20.12.24. **16 Sqn/SAC** Old Sarum by 5.27.

H1484 **IAAD** Henlow tested 28/29.11.23. **2 FTS** Duxford. **CFS** Upavon by 4.24.

H1485 **2 Sqn** Oranmore by 1920 until 1922. **4 Sqn** Aldergrove by 5.22. To Irish Army Air Service at Baldonnel 12.7.22 as *BF.III* and wrecked 17.2.22 (crashed at Naas). Scrapped 1925.

H1486 **2 Sqn** Oranmore 1921. **4 Sqn** Aldergrove by 4.22. B&C for reconditioning to J Type (s/n 6543) and ready by 22.11.24. **4 Sqn** Farnborough. **SAG** Eastchurch and wrecked 8.4.25 (Plt Off A.A.C. Mason KIFA, hit sea while diving on floating target off Leysdown).

H1487 **141 Sqn** Tallaght. **2 Sqn** Oranmore 1920 and wrecked 10.2.21 (Fg Off N.V. Moreton/Fg Off E.F. MacKay both OK, force landed 3 miles NW of Kilfinane after engine failure and set on fire by IRA).

H1488 **106 Sqn** and crashed at Fermoy 1921. **4 Sqn** Aldergrove 1921. B&C for reconditioning to J Type (s/n 6646) and ready by 12.3.25. **1 SoTT** Halton 1925.

H1489 **24 Sqn** Kenley by 6.22. **Irish Flt** Collinstown by 7.22 and wrecked 1.8.22 (Flt Lt Wigglesworth OK/Pte McCafferty IIFA, engine failed on take off from Collinstown and port wheel collapsed on landing).

H1490 **4 Sqn** Aldergrove and wrecked 17.11.20 (struck wireless mast while dropping mail on barracks). **PD** Ascot. To Egypt. **AD** Aboukir. **208 Sqn** by 2.21. Returned to UK. **A&AEE** Martlesham Heath by 3.27.

H1491 **PD** Ascot. To Egypt. **AD** Aboukir. **208 Sqn** by 8.20. **14 Sqn** by 3.21 until @ 6.22.

H1492 **PD** Ascot. To Egypt. **AD** Aboukir. **208 Sqn** by 10.22 until @ 6.24. Returned to UK. B&C for reconditioning to J Type DC (s/n 6849) and ready by 2.11.25. **5 FTS** Sealand by 9.27 until @ 10.27.

H1493 **PD** Ascot. To Egypt. **AD** Aboukir. **4 FTS** Abu Sueir by 29.11.21 until @ 4.22. Returned to UK. B&C for reconditioning to J Type DC (s/n 6823) and ready by 1.10.25. **2 FTS** Digby by 3.26 until @ 3.27. B&C for reconditioning (s/n 7176) and ready by 21.6.28. To Iraq. **6 Sqn** by 11.29, in starting accident 21.11.29, in fatal starting accident 26.3.31 and on unit charge until @ 5.32.

H1494 **PD** Ascot. To Egypt. **AD** Aboukir. **208 Sqn** by 8.22 until @ 8.23. Returned to UK. B&C for reconditioning to J Type DC (s/n 6852) and ready by 5.11.25. B&C for reconditioning to Mk.III DC (s/n 7125) and ready by 24.8.27. **Andover CF** by 7.29 until @ 10.30.

H1495 **PD** Ascot. To Egypt. **AD** Aboukir. **Aden Flt** and wrecked on Ferry Flight, Berbera-Aden, 28.4.22 (crashed on landing at Perim Island and fell into 14ft of water).

H1496 **PD** Ascot. To Egypt. **AD** Aboukir. **4 FTS** Abu Sueir by 12.22 until @ 12.23. **208 Sqn** by 6.24. Returned to UK. B&C for reconditioning to J Type DC (s/n 6824) and ready by 2.10.25. **5 FTS** Sealand by 3.26 until @11.26.

H1497 To India. **AD** Drigh Road. **5 Sqn** by 2.20 until @ 4.21. **AD** Drigh Road 1923. **AP** Lahore by 2.23. **31 Sqn** by 8.23 until @ 9.23.

H1498 To India. **AD** Drigh Road. **5 Sqn** as a/c *T* by 5.20 and crashed at Chaman 1922.

H1499 To India. **114 Sqn** 1919, on unit charge when redesignated **28 Sqn** 1.2.20 and crashed 19.4.21.

H1500 **PD** Ascot. To Iraq. **AD** Hinaidi by 7.22. **6 Sqn** by 9.22 until 1.23. **AD** Hinaidi by 1.23.

H1501 **PD** Ascot. To Egypt. **AD** Aboukir. **4 FTS** Abu Sueir by 9.22. **AD** Aboukir. **208 Sqn** by 29.12.22 until @ 7.23. Returned to UK. B&C for reconditioning to J Type (s/n 6808) and ready by 7.9.25.

H1502 **PD** Ascot. To Egypt. **AD** Aboukir. **14 Sqn** by 10.22 until @ 3.23. Returned to UK. B&C for reconditioning to J Type DC (s/n 6844) and ready by 31.10.25. **RAF (Cadet) College** Cranwell by 1.27 until @ 7.28.

H1503 N/I

H1504 **PD** Ascot. To Egypt. **AD** Aboukir. **14 Sqn** and wrecked 30.9.21 (engine failed on take off from LG1, Jerusalem).

H1505 **1 FTS** Netheravon and wrecked 1.12.23 (Plt Off F. Boston IIFA, undershot landing and hit a ridge). **2 FTS** Digby by 8.24. **PD** Ascot. To Egypt. **AD** Aboukir. **4 FTS** Abu Sueir. **AD** Aboukir by 26.5.25.

H1506 **SAC** Old Sarum and wrecked 28.4.24 (Fg Off A.F. Ingram IIFA/AC2 J. Renton OK, engine failed on take off from Old Sarum, stalled and side-slipped in).

H1507 To India. **20 Sqn** by 2.20.

H1508 **PD** Ascot. To India. **AD** Drigh Road. **28 Sqn** by 6.21 until @ 9.21. **20 Sqn** as a/c *P* by 8.22. **5 Sqn** by 9.23.

H1509 To India. **114 Sqn** 1919, on charge when unit redesignated **28 Sqn** 1.2.20. **RAF School (India)** by 11.21.

H1510 **PD** Ascot. To India. **AD** Drigh Road. **31 Sqn** as a/c *H* by 1921.

H1511 N/I

H1512 To India. **114 Sqn** 1919, on charge when unit redesignated **28 Sqn** 1.2.20 and wrecked 28.2.20 (crashed E of Ambala after engine failure).

H1513 To India. **5 Sqn** by 2.20 until @ 4.20.

H1514 **12 Sqn**.

H1514 To India. **114 Sqn** 1919, on charge when unit redesignated **28 Sqn** 1.2.20.

H1515 To India. **AP** Lahore by 11.22. **5 Sqn** and wrecked 3.9.23 (force landed at Rajpur Rd, Ambala, after engine failure).

H1516 **PD** Ascot. To India. **AD** Drigh Road. **5 Sqn** by 5.22.

H1517 N/I

H1518 **PD** Ascot. To India. **AD** Drigh Road. **5 Sqn** as a/c *P* and wrecked 1922 (undercarriage collapsed on landing at Quetta). **20 Sqn** by 11.22.

H1519 N/I

H1520 To India. **114 Sqn** 1919 and on charge when unit redesignated **28 Sqn** 1.2.20. **20 Sqn** by 11.20. **5 Sqn** by 4.21.

H1521 To India. **20 Sqn** by 11.20. **28 Sqn**.

H1522 **PD** Ascot. To India. **AD** Drigh Road. Wrecked on Ferry Flight from Tank 13.4.22 (**27 Sqn** pilot OK, crashed in forced landing at Parachinar).

H1523 To India. **5 Sqn** by 5.20 and wrecked on height test to 16,000ft, 11.9.22.

H1524 **PD** Ascot. To India. **AD** Drigh Road. **20 Sqn**, damaged 13.4.20 (force landed near Datta Khal, NWF), repaired and on unit charge until @ 11.20.

H1525 N/I

H1526 **2 Sqn** Oranmore as a/c *A2* by 1920 until @ 1921. **4 Sqn** Farnborough as a/c *A2* 1921. **PD** Ascot. To Egypt. **ASD** Aboukir. **14 Sqn** by 4.21 until @ 6.21. Returned to UK. B&C for reconditioning to J Type (s/n 6809) and ready by 8.9.25. **4 Sqn** Farnborough by 1.26 and wrecked 1.2.27 (collided with stationary aircraft after landing at Farnborough). B&C for reconditioning (s/n 7162) and ready by 2.3.28. **4 Sqn** Farnborough by 8.28. B&C for modification. Retaken onto RAF charge 14.2.30.

H1527 **ASD ME** Aboukir dd ex UK 6.1.20.

H1528 **PD** Ascot. To India. **AD** Drigh Road. **5 Sqn** by 3.20 until @ 8.21.

H1529 **PD** Ascot. To India. **AD** Drigh Road. **20 Sqn** by 8.20. **28 Sqn** by 16.10.21.

H1530 PD Ascot. To India. **AD** Drigh Road. **48 Sqn** as a/c *A* by 1.20, on charge when unit redesignated **5 Sqn** 1.2.20, marked as a/c *A* and wrecked 10.3.22 (crashed in high altitude landing at Quetta). **AP** Lahore by 6.24.

H1531 N/I

H1532 N/I

H1533 IDE Biggin Hill by 4.21. To Egypt. **14 Sqn** and wrecked 14.4.21 (pilot Collingwood OK, crashed from stall after engine failure at Ramleh).

H1534 PD Ascot. To Egypt. **AD** Aboukir from 2.20. **14 Sqn** damaged 26.2.21 (stalled on landing at Ramleh), repaired and on unit charge by 1.22 until @ 4.22.

H1535 PD Ascot. **AD** Aboukir dd ex England 2.20. To India. **AD** Drigh Road by 12.21, crashed on Delivery Flight 2.2.22 and repaired by 4.22. **5 Sqn** by 8.22. **20 Sqn** by 8.23 until @ 11.24.

H1536 PD Ascot. To India. **AD** Drigh Road and tested 17.4.22. **28 Sqn** by 12.22 and wrecked 22.12.24 (engine cut during forced landing in bad weatherat Rawalpindi).

H1537 PD Ascot. To India. **AD** Drigh Road. **28 Sqn** by 6.21 until wrecked 9.21 (crashed at Parachinar NWF in sandstorm).

H1538 PD Ascot. To India. **AD** Drigh Road and tested 16.4.22. **AP** Lahore by 2.23. **28 Sqn** by 2.23 and wrecked 1.8.23 (overshot landing at Peshawar). **AP** Lahore by 5.24. **AD** Drigh Road 1927.

H1539 PD Ascot. To India. **AD** Drigh Road. **AP** Lahore by 2.23. **28 Sqn** by 2.23. **5 Sqn** marked as a/c *A*.

H1540 At maker's 6.2.19, allotted to BEF.

H1541 At maker's 6.2.19, allotted to BEF. To India. **114 Sqn** 1919, on charge when redesignated **28 Sqn** 1.1.20 and on unit charge until @ 9.21.

H1542 At maker's 6.2.19, allotted to BEF.

H1543 At maker's 6.2.19, allotted to BEF.

H1544 At maker's 6.2.19, allotted to BEF. To India. **48 Sqn** by 10.19 and on unit charge when redesignated **5 Sqn** 1.2.20.

H1545 At maker's 6.2.19, allotted to BEF.

H1546 At maker's 6.2.19, allotted to BEF. **PD** Ascot. To India. **AD** Drigh Road. **5 Sqn** as a/c *O* by 4.20 until @ 1.22.

H1547 At maker's 6.2.19, allotted to BEF.

H1548 At maker's 6.2.19, allotted to BEF. **PD** Ascot. To India. **AD** Drigh Road. **28 Sqn** by 6.21 until @ 3.22. **20 Sqn** and wrecked 3.3.22 (collided with E2442 20 miles from Lahore and deleted).

H1549 At maker's 6.2.19, allotted to BEF. To India. **20 Sqn** by 9.19 until @ 7.21. **28 Sqn** by 1921 until @ 1923.

H1550 N/I

H1551 At maker's 6.2.19, allotted to BEF.

H1552 At maker's 6.2.19, allotted to BEF. To India. **48 Sqn** by 12.19 and on charge when unit redesignated **5 Sqn** 1.2.20.

H1553 At maker's 6.2.19, allotted to BEF. To India. **20 Sqn** by 9.20 until @ 6.21.

H1554 At maker's 6.2.19, allotted to BEF. **PD** Ascot. To India. **AD** Drigh Road. **31 Sqn** and wrecked 3.3.22 (struck rough ground landing at Peshawar and o/t). **28 Sqn** by 1924 and still in India 1927.

H1555 At maker's 6.2.19, allotted to BEF. **2 FTS** Digby by 9.23 until @ 9.24. **B&C** for reconditioning to J Type (s/n 6697) and ready by 29.4.25. **PD** Sealand. To India. **AD** Drigh Road. **AP** Lahore by 12.28 until @ 4.29.

H1556 At maker's 6.2.19, allotted to BEF. **AGS** Eastchurch by 10.24 until @ 11.24. **HAD** Henlow by 7.26 until @ 8.26.

H1557 Imperial Gift to New Zealand.

H1558 Imperial Gift to New Zealand.

H1559 RAE Farnborough by 1.20 and wrecked 11.2.20 (crashed on take off for Martlesham). Repaired. **A&AEE** Martlesham Heath as DC machine dd ex Halton 16.3.21 for parachute work and wrecked 16.3.21 (rudder jammed and crashed on landing).

H1560 RAE Farnborough by 22.2.26. **HAD** Henlow by 8.9.27. **B&C** for reconditioning (s/n 7243) and ready by 13.7.28. **PD** Ascot. To Iraq. **AD** Hinaidi. **6 Sqn** by 12.29 until @ 6.32.

H1561 RAE Farnborough by 6.1.20, to Gosport 31.8.20 as *Persia No.4* but badly damaged, returned RAE 5.10.20 and wrecked 12.10.20 (crashed in forced landing at Bagshot, Surrey). **AEE** Martlesham Heath by 8.7.21. **RAE** Farnborough by 6.3.22 (modified to test Calthorp Al parachute) and last flown 5.9.28.

H1562 B&C for reconditioning to J Type (s/n 6420) and ready by 15.3.24. **SAC** Old Sarum; **AGS** Eastchurch by 4.26. **B&C** for reconditioning to Mk.III (s/n 7095) and ready by 2.6.27. **B&C** for reconditioning to Mk.IV (s/n 7257) and ready by 29.9.28. **16 Sqn/SAC** Old Sarum by 9.28. **2 Sqn** Manston by 5.29 until @ 7.29.

H1563 N/I

H1564 N/I

H1565 B&C for reconditioning to J Type (s/n 6270) and ready by 15.5.23. **PD** Ascot. To India. **AD** Drigh Road. **AP** Lahore by 7.24. **5 Sqn** as a/c *H* named *Silver Star* by 20.8.24 until @ 7.26.

H1566 12 Sqn as a/c *B1* by 19.3.20 (Lt J.W. Baker) and wrecked 17.5.20 (Fg Off Toomer OK, collided in formation with D8059 over Cologne Lindenthal).

H1567 2 Sqn Oranmore. Missing over Irish Sea while ferrying from (or to?) **100 Sqn**, 21.2.20.

H1568 (DC) 12 Sqn as a/c *C6* by 24.4.20 (Lt J.W. Baker), wrecked 12.12.21 and deleted.

Although it is recorded as being a dual-control machine, this photograph of H1568 'C6' with 12 Sqn in India shows it with a Scarff ring on its rear cockpit. It was written off in a crash on 12 December 1921. *(RAF Museum)*

H1569 12 Sqn as a/c *8* by 8.20 until @ 20.1.21 (Lt J.W. Baker). To UK 5.22.

H1570 24 Sqn Kenley by 1.1.20 until @ 11.20 (for Directorate of Research use). **2 Sqn** Fermoy 1920. **24 Sqn** Kenley by 2.21 until @ 3.31.

H1571 12 Sqn. To UK. **2 Sqn** Fermoy and wrecked 21.8.20 (force landed at Garrybritas, near Lismore, after engine failure and set on fire by IRA).

H1572 SAGB Eastchurch by 1.21. **SoTT** Manston by 3.21.

H1573 N/I

H1574 12 Sqn as a/c *C4* by 9.19 until @ 12.10.20 (Lt J.W. Baker). To UK 31.5.22 **AGS** Eastchurch and wrecked 18.6.9123 (Flt Lt R.S. Capon OK, o/t in forced landing on rough ground near Sudbury, Essex, after engine failure).

H1575 N/I

H1576 N/I

H1577 APS Andover by 12.19 until 2.20.

H1578 N/I

H1579 11 Sqn by 7.19.

H1580 N/I

H1581 12 Sqn as a/c *Al* by 10.20 until @ 8.2.21 (Lt J.W. Baker). To UK 5.22. **24 Sqn** Kenley by 11.22. **B&C** for reconditioning to J Type (s/n 6622) and ready by 20.2.25. **PD** Ascot. To Iraq. **AD** Hinaidi. Still in Iraq 1928.

H1582 N/I

H1583 APS Andover by 23.12.19 until @ 2.20. **B&C** for reconditioning to J Type (s/n 6601) and ready by 27.1.25. **PD** Ascot. To Egypt. **AD** Aboukir. **208 Sqn** Ismaila. **84 Sqn.**

H1584 N/I

H1585 N/I

H1586 PD Ascot. To India. **AD** Drigh Road. **31 Sqn.**

H1587 12 Sqn as a/c *A5* by 8.19.

H1588 APS Andover by 7.19 until @ 2.20. **B&C** for reconditioning to J Type (s/n 6542) and ready by 22.11.24. **AGS** Eastchurch by 11.26.

H1589 12 Sqn as a/c *A5* by 8.19. **B&C** for reconditioning to J Type DC (s/n 6507) and ready by 25.10.24. **24 Sqn** Kenley by 11.27 until @ 3.29.

H1590 106 Sqn Fermoy. **2 Sqn** Fermoy by 1920 and wrecked 1921 (crashed at Fermoy).

H1591 N/I

H1592 N/I

H1593 N/I

H1594 12 Sqn and wrecked 5.7.20 (Fg Off McQueen OK, crashed at Heumar after engine failure on take off from Cologne Lindenthal, though also noted as coded *18* in 1922).

H1595 2 Sqn Oranmore 1920 until 1921. **2 FTS** Digby by 9.25.

H1596 12 Sqn by 11.20. To UK 12.20 and strorage at Kenley. **B&C** for reconditioning to Mk.III (s/n 7145) and ready by 25.5.28. **AGS** Eastchurch by 9.29 until @ 3.31.

H1597 AGS Eastchurch by 9.21 until @ 9.22.

H1598 RAE Farnborough by 8.8.19 being fitted with enlarged fuel tank for use on No.1 Aerial Route to Egypt. Ferried to France 9.19. B&C for reconditioning to J Type (s/n 6539) and ready by 20.11.24. **RAF (Cadet) College** Cranwell by 4.25 until @ 5.25. **IACF** Northolt by 1.26. B&C for reconditioning to Mk.III (s/n 7140) and ready by 17.5.28. **16 Sqn/SAC** Old Sarum by 2.30 until @ 1.31.

When the late Peter Capon photographed F.2B H1598 during its visit to de Havilland's airfield at Stag Lane in May 1925, it was on the strength of the RAF (Cadet) College at Cranwell, having recently been reconditioned to J Type. Its next user was to be the Inland Area Communication Flight at Northolt. *(Philip Jarrett)*

H1599 12 Sqn by 9.20, damaged 10.3.21 (force landed near Aachen after engine failure), repaired and wrecked 6.21 (Fg Off Sinclair OK). **SAC** Old Sarum by 12.22 until @ 7.24. B&C for reconditioning to J Type (s/n 6643) and ready by 13.3.25.

H1600 B&C for reconditioning to J Type (s/n 6684) and ready by 21.4.25. **16 Sqn/SAC** Old Sarum by 4.26 until @ 4.27.

H1601 APS Andover by 1.20. B&C for reconditioning to J Type (s/n 6586) and ready by 12.1.25. **PD** Ascot. To India. **AD** Drigh Road 1927. **20 Sqn** by 6.27.

H1602 APS Andover by 23.12.19 until @ 4.20. **2 FTS** Duxford by 2.24 until @ 3.24.

H1603 APS Andover by 23.12.19 until @ 2.20. **SAC** Old Sarum by 12.22 until 7.23. **2 Sqn** Manston and wrecked 27.7.23 (Fg Off H.P.L. Gardner/Lt J.C. Holmes, Royal Sussex Regt, both IIFA, crashed after stall during landing at Old Sarum.

H1604 B&C for reconditioning to J Type (s/n 6605) and ready by 29.1.25. **24 Sqn** Kenley and wrecked 21.6.26.

H1605 *Eagle* Trials Flt, Gosport by 6.20 until @ 8.20.

H1606 APS Andover by 23.12.19. **4 Sqn** Farnborough by 4.12.20. B&C for reconditioning to J Type (s/n 6606) and ready by 7.2.25.

H1607 N/I

H1608 SAC Old Sarum by 3.20 until @ 1.24.

H1609 APS Andover by 23.12.19 until @ 2.20. B&C for reconditioning to J Type (s/n 6450) and ready by 14.5.24.

H1610 2 Sqn Fermoy by 1920 until @ 1921.

H1611 1 FTS Netheravon by 4.21 until @ 7.22.

H1612 100 Sqn and missing on Ferry Flight 21.2.20 (Fg Off H.L. Holland missing, presumed lost in Irish Sea and drowned).

H1613 N/I

H1614 APS Andover by 23.12.19 until @ 2.20. **1 FTS** Netheravon. **AEE** Martlesham Heath by 6.24. B&C for reconditioning to J Type DC (s/n 6885) and ready by 7.1.26. **1 SoTT** Halton by 11.27 until @ 10.28.

H1615 2 Sqn Oranmore 1920 until @ 1921.

H1616 APS Andover by 23.12.19 until @ 2.20. B&C for reconditioning to J Type (s/n 6638) and ready by 27.2.25. **PD** Ascot. To Egypt. **AD** Aboukir. **47 Sqn** by 16.8.26.

H1617 1 FTS Netheravon by 4.21 until @ 7.22. B&C for reconditioning to J Type (s/n 6608) and ready by 10.2.25. **24 Sqn** Kenley by 9.26. **HCF** Northolt by 2.27.

H1618 N/I

H1619 N/I

H1620 2 Sqn Fermoy by 1920 until @ 1921.

H1621 2 Sqn and lost on Ferry Flight from Fermoy 21.2.20 (Fg Off H. de Waller missing, presumed lost in Irish Sea and drowned).

H1622 N/I

H1623 PD Ascot. To Egypt. **AD** Aboukir. **208 Sqn** by 12.21 until @ 9.23. Returned to UK. B&C for reconditioning to J Type (s/n 6810) and ready by 9.9.25. **13 Sqn** Andover 1925 until 1926. **RAF Staff College Flt** Andover by 3.26.

H1624 IAAD Henlow tested 6.12.23. **24 Sqn** Kenley 1924. B&C for reconditioning to J Type (s/n 6689) and ready by 22.4.25. B&C for reconditioning to Mk.III (s/n 7139) and ready by 8.5.28. B&C for reconditioning to Mk.IV and ready by 31.1.30. Retaken onto RAF charge 22.2.30. **E&WS** Worthy Down by 9.30 until @ 10.30. Hawkinge. **RAE** Farnborough by 20.5.31. North Coates Fitties by 17.6.31.

H1625 IAAD Henlow. Duxford (**2 FTS**?) by 8.4.24. **RAE** Farnborough by 1926 until @ 1928.

H1626 PD Ascot. To Egypt. **AD** Aboukir. **4 FTS** Abu Sueir and wrecked 22.6.22. Force landed in rough country near Helmiah (after engine failure).

H1627 PD Ascot. To Iraq. **AD** Hinaidi. **6 Sqn** by 1923 until @ 1924. Returned to UK. B&C for reconditioning to J Type (s/n 6811) and ready by 12.9.25. **13 Sqn** Andover from 1925 until @ 1926.

H1628 PD Ascot. To Egypt. **AD** Aboukir. **208 Sqn** by 8.21 until @ 9.21. **14 Sqn** by 9.22 until @ 12.23.

H1629 N/I

H1630 To Iraq. **6 Sqn** and wrecked 14.7.20 (force landed N of Diwaniyah after engine failure and burnt).

H1631 PD Ascot. To Iraq. **AD** Hinaidi. **6 Sqn** by 2.20 and wrecked 13.3.22 (Fg Off Shipwright OK, hit barbed wire fence landing at night). **AD** Hinaidi for repair 3.22.

H1632 B&C for reconditioning to J Type (s/n 6559) and ready by 11.12.24. **PD** Ascot. To Egypt. **AD** Aboukir. **6 Sqn** by 6.25. **AHQ Iraq Command Training Flt** by 8.27 until @ 9.27.

H1633 PD Ascot. To Egypt. **AD** Aboukir. Aden 10.23. **14 Sqn** and wrecked 14.4.21 (crashed after engine failure). **Aden Flt** by 11.22, wrecked and deleted 14.11.23.

H1634 B&C for reconditioning to J Type (s/n 6467) and ready by 8.7.24. B&C for reconditioning to DC (s/n 6910) and ready by 26.2.26. **CFS** Upavon by 8.26. **2 FTS** Digby by 1.27. Practice Camp Sutton Bridge 7.28. **5 FTS** Sealand as a/c 6 by 4.29 and wrecked 16.5.30 (collided with DH.60G Gipsy Moth J9927 over Sealand).

H1635 PD Ascot. To Egypt. **AD** Aboukir. **4 FTS** Abu Sueir by 8.21 until @ 1.22. **AD** Aboukir and reconstructed as HR1635. **208 Sqn** and wrecked 1924 (crashed at Ismailia).

H1636 B&C for reconditioning to J Type (s/n 6812) and ready by 12.9.25. **PD** Ascot. To Egypt. **AD** Aboukir. **208 Sqn** by 8.24 until @ 1.25.

H1637 E&WS Worthy Down by 1.22. B&C for reconditioning to J Type (s/n 6667) and ready by 26.3.25.

H1638 To Civilian Register 29.4.20 as *G-EASV*, registered to Handley Page Ltd (s/n 5355).

H1639 To Civilian Register 29.4.20 as *G-EASU*, registered to Handley Page Ltd (s/n 5356).

H1640 To Iraq. **6 Sqn** by 8.22. Returned to UK. **1 FTS** Netheravon by 4.23. B&C for reconditioning to J Type (s/n 6548) and ready by 27.11.24. **SAC** Old Sarum. B&C for reconditioning (s/n 7166) and ready by 8.3.28. **SAC** Old Sarum by 1.29 until @ 4.29. **2 Sqn** Manston by 6.29 until @ 7.29. B&C for reconditioning (to Mk. IV?) and ready by 13.7.30. Retaken onto RAF charge 19.7.30.

H1641 To Egypt. **208 Sqn** by 9.21 until @11.21.

H1642 **PD** Ascot. To Egypt. **AD** Aboukir. Aden Flight 1922. **208 Sqn** and wrecked 31.1.24 (crashed on Moascar aerodrome). Returned to UK. B&C for reconditioning to J Type DC (s/n 6843) and ready by 29.10.25. **RAF (Cadet) College** Cranwell by 11.25 until @ 12.26. B&C for reconditioning (s/n 7173) and ready by 4.6.28. **4 FTS** Abu Sueir by 9.30 until @ 10.30.

H1643 N/I

H1644 **PD** Ascot. To Egypt. **AD** Aboukir. **4 FTS** Abu Sueir by 3.22 until @ 6.23. **208 Sqn** by 8.24 until @ 10.24. Returned to UK. B&C for reconditioning to J Type DC (s/n 6829) and ready by 10.10.25. **CFS** Upavon by 4.26 until @ 6.26. **2 FTS** Digby. B&C for reconditioning to Mk.III DC (s/n 7112) and ready by 14.7.27. **2 FTS** Digby and wrecked 19.9.29 (dived in at Halton le Moor, Cambs, after engine failure).

H1645 **PD** Ascot. To Iraq. **AD** Hinaidi by 6.22. **6 Sqn** 1923 until @ 1924.

H1646 **PD** Ascot. To Egypt. **AD** Aboukir. **208 Sqn** by 8.20 until @ 6.22. **14 Sqn** by 7.22 until @ 9.22.

H1647 **PD** Sealand. To Egypt. **AD** Aboukir. **4 FTS** Abu Sueir by 3.22 and wrecked 29.4.22 (overshot on landing at Heliopolis).

H1648 To Egypt. **208 Sqn** by 8.20 until @ 1.22.

H1649 **PD** Ascot. To Egypt. **AD** Aboukir. **208 Sqn** by 2.21 until @ 6.22. **14 Sqn** 1922.

H1650 **PD** Ascot. To Egypt. **AD** Aboukir. **208 Sqn** by 4.30.

H1651 **PD** Ascot. To Egypt. **14 Sqn** by 2.11.22. **AD** Aboukir and reconstructed as HR1651. **14 Sqn** by 7.22 until @ 8.23.

H1652 (DC) **PD** Ascot. To Egypt. **AD** Aboukir. **4 FTS** Abu Sueir by 19.9.21 until @ 3.22. **208 Sqn** by 10.22 until @ 11.22. **4 FTS** Abu Sueir by 9.23.

H1653 **PD** Ascot. To Egypt. **AD** Aboukir. **208 Sqn** dd ex AD 8.9.21. **14 Sqn** and wrecked 3.2.22 (o/t landing at Jerusalem).

H1654 N/I

H1655 N/I

H1656 To India. **AD** Drigh Road and wrecked 21.11.20 (landed on bad ground after engine failure).

H1657 To India. **AD** Drigh Road. **RAF School (India)** by 11.21. **5 Sqn** by 1.23 until @ 2.24. **AP** Lahore by 2.26. **AD** Drigh Road 2.26 until @ 1927. **20 Sqn** by 8.30 until @ 12.30.

H1658 **20 Sqn** by 12.20 and wrecked 19.1.21 (force landed in Afghanistan, crew repatriated).

H1659 **PD** Ascot. To India. **AD** Drigh Road. **31 Sqn** and wrecked 12.4.22 (side-slipped on landing).

H1660 **ASD** Aboukir dd 12.11.19 and on unit charge until @ 24.2.20. Returned to UK. B&C for reconditioning to J Type DC (s/n 6851) and ready by 4.11.25. B&C for reconditioning (s/n 7170) and ready by 4.5.28. **5 FTS** Sealand by 10.28 until @ 1.30. B&C for reconditioning to Mk.IV DC (s/n 7572) and ready by 13.2.31. Retaken onto RAF charge 5.3.31. **5 FTS** Sealand 1931.

H1661 **ASD** Aboukir dd ex UK 26.2.20. **14 Sqn** and wrecked 30.9.21 (flew into bank on edge of LG1 Jerusalem).

H1662 N/I

H1663 Despatched from UK to Iraq 23.2.20. **6 Sqn** by 9.20. Returned to UK. **5 FTS** Sealand by 2.27.

H1664 **PD** Ascot. **ASD** Aboukir dd UK 2.20. **14 Sqn** by 5.22 until @ 11.22.

H1665 Despatched from UK to Iraq 23.2.20. **6 Sqn** and wrecked 4.12.22 (Fg Off C.E. Gibbs OK, port wheel detached in the air and machine o/t on landing). **AD** Hinaidi for repair by 1.23. **6 Sqn** 1923 until @ 1924.

H1666 To Egypt. **4 FTS** Abu Sueir by 5.21.

H1667 N/I

H1668 **PD** Ascot. To Iraq. **AD** Hinaidi. **6 Sqn** by 11.21 until @ 1.24. **AD** Hinaidi by 1.23. **6 Sqn** by 16.2.23. Returned to UK. B&C for reconditioning to J Type (s/n 6813) and ready by 14.9.25. **SAC** Old Sarum by 2.28 until @ 11.28.

H1669 **12 Sqn** with Army of Occupation. To Egypt. **208 Sqn** by 9.20 until @ 12.21. **4 FTS** Abu Sueir by 2.23 until @ 8.23. Returned to UK. B&C for reconditioning to J Type DC (s/n 6837) and ready by 23.10.25. **5 FTS** Sealand by 2.27 until @ 6.28.

H1670 To Egypt. **208 Sqn** by 2.21.

H1671 To Iraq. **6 Sqn** by 11.20. **AD** Hinaidi by 5.22. **6 Sqn**, damaged 12.12.22 (Fg Off T.J. Desmond OK, undercarriage collapsed on landing), repaired and on unit charge until @ 1924.

H1672 To Egypt. **14 Sqn** by 11.21. **AD** Hinaidi.

H1673 To Egypt. **208 Sqn** by 2.21.

H1674 **PD** Ascot. To Iraq. **AD** Hinaidi by 10.23 for reconstruction. **6 Sqn** by 1923 until @ 1924.

H1675 **PD** Ascot. To Iraq. **AD** Hinaidi. **6 Sqn** by 1923 until @ 1924.

H1676 **PD** Ascot. To Egypt. **AD** Aboukir. **14 Sqn** and wrecked 26.8.21 (force landed at LGl Jerusalem after engine failure).

H1677 **PD** Ascot. To Egypt. **AD** Aboukir. **14 Sqn** by 6.22 until @ 3.23. **4 FTS** Abu Sueir by 8.23 until @ 10.23. **AD** Aboukir and reconstructed as HR1677. **208 Sqn** by 1.24 until @ 8.24. **4 FTS** Abu Sueir. Returned to UK. B&C for reconditioning to J Type (s/n 6814) and ready by 15.9.25.

H1678 **PD** Ascot. To Egypt. **AD** Aboukir. **208 Sqn** by 9.10.22 and wrecked 10.7.23 (o/t when undercarriage collapsed on landing at San Stefano). Repaired.

H1679 To Egypt. **208 Sqn** by 12.21 until @ 3.22.

H1680 N/I

H1681 To Egypt. **14 Sqn** by 10.21 until @ 12.22. Returned to UK. B&C for reconditioning to J Type DC (s/n 6850) and ready by 3.11.25. **1 FTS** Netheravon.

H1682 **PD** Ascot. To Egypt. **AD** Aboukir. **208 Sqn** by 2.21 until @ 1923.

H1683 N/I

H1684 **PD** Ascot. To Egypt. **AD** Aboukir. **14 Sqn** by 29.1.23 until @ 12.23.

H1685 **PD** Ascot. To Egypt. **AD** Aboukir. **208 Sqn** by 10.22 until @ 6.24. Returned to UK. B&C for reconditioning to J Type (s/n 6815) and ready by 16.9.25. **IACF** Northolt by 11.25 until @ 1.26.

H1686 B&C for reconditioning to J Type (s/n 6592) and ready by 23.1.25. **PD** Ascot. To India. **AD** Drigh Road. **20 Sqn** by 5.27 until @ 10.28. **31 Sqn** by 11.25 until @ 1.26.

H1687 Converted to 'Tourer' and with B&C at Bristol by 29.7.19.

H1688 Converted to 'Tourer' and with B&C at Bristol by 9.8.19 until @ 10.9.19 (Lt C.F. Uwins). **24 Sqn** Kenley by 12.19 (for Directorate of Research and fitted with 5hr tank) and damaged 19.11.21 (Flt Lt J.M. Robb OK, ditched 5 miles off Folkestone, engine failed on return from Le Bourget). Salvaged.

H1689 Converted to 'Tourer' and with B&C at Bristol by 29.8.19. Croydon. **RAE** Farnborough by 21.11.19 until @ 27.12.19. **24 Sqn** Kenley by 1.1.20 until @ 12.22 (for Directorate of Research – long range). **CFS** Upavon by 23.6.21. **APS** Andover by 7.22 until @ 7.23. **Staff College Flt** Andover by 2.24 until @ 3.26.

H1690 (Puma) reported as not entering RAF service.

H1691 Reported as not entering RAF service.

H1692 Reported as not entering RAF service.

H1693 Reported as not entering RAF service.

H1694 Reported as not entering RAF service. (Though also noted as at **PD** Ascot. To Egypt. **AD** Aboukir. **208 Sqn** by 1922 until @ 1923.)

H1695 Reported as not entering RAF service.

H1696 Reported as not entering RAF service.

H1697 Reported as not entering RAF service.

H1698 Reported as not entering RAF service.

H1699 Reported as not entering RAF service.

H1700 Reported as not entering RAF service.

H1701 Reported as not entering RAF service.

H1702 Reported as not entering RAF service.

H1703 Reported as not entering RAF service.

H1704 Reported as not entering RAF service.

H1705 Reported as not entering RAF service.

H1706 Reported as not entering RAF service.

H1707 Reported as not entering RAF service.

150 BRISTOL FIGHTER F.2B ordered 15.8.18 under Cont No A.S.35822/18 from Marshall & Sons & Co Ltd, but serials cancelled as batch previously allotted serials D2626 to D2775.

200 BRISTOL FIGHTER F.2B ordered under Contract 35a/2113/C.2447 from Sir W.G. Armstrong, Whitworth & Co Ltd, Gosforth, Newcastle-upon-Tyne and numbered H3796 to H3995. Order cancelled.

600 BRISTOL FIGHTER F.2B (Puma) ordered 14.8.18 under Contract 35a/2532/C.2768 (B.R.635) from The Austin Motor Co (1914) Ltd, Birmingham and numbered H5940 to H6539. Mainly to storage. (Puma). Order reduced to 125 on 20.12.18. Deliveries from w/e 5.7.19 and 45 delivered by w/e 23.8.19.

H5940
to   } N/I
H5951

H5952 **5 (E)ARD** Henlow, allotted Polish Military Purchase Mission 15.3.20. Despatched Handley Page, Cricklewood 25.3.20; reallotted Inland Area for disposal 19.4.20.

H5953
to   } N/I
H5959

H5960 **5 (E)ARD** Henlow, allotted Polish Military Purchase Mission 15.3.20. Despatched Handley Page, Cricklewood 25.3.20; reallotted Inland Area for disposal 19.4.20.

H5961 N/I

H5962 N/I

H5963 **5 (E)ARD** Henlow, allotted Polish Military Purchase Mission 15.3.20. Despatched Handley Page, Cricklewood 25.3.20; reallotted Inland Area for disposal 19.4.20.

H5964 to H6042 } N/I

H6043 **1 ASD** 26.10.18.

H6044 to H6054 } N/I

H6054 N/I

H6055 **RAE** Farnborough dd 15.3.20 on on charge until @ 17.7.20.

H6056 to H6063 } N/I

H6064 dd 10.19.

26 Bristol F2B reconstructed by Aircraft Depots in France from salvage and spares, including 8 machines which had been previously given incorrect serials.

H6893 Taken on charge 9.11.18 on reconstruction from C9896.

H7060 Taken on charge 1.8.18 on reconstruction from C825. **1 ASD** destroyed by German bombing 23.9.18 and deleted 26.9.18 (22min).

H7061 Taken on charge 7.8.18 on renumbering from incorrectly marked F6401 (formerly C919). **1 ASD** damaged by German bombing 23.9.18 and re-built by 30.9.18 (engine 543/WD32671). **11 Sqn** by 31.7.19. **22 Sqn** 1919. **12 Sqn** by 13.11.20 until @ 21.1.21 (Lt J.W. Baker). To UK 5.22.

H7062 Taken on charge 7.8.18 on renumbering from incorrectly marked F6402 (formerly C780). **1 ASD** by 30.9.18 (engine 1609/WD51829). **22 Sqn** dd ex **1 AIS** 9.11.18 and wrecked on Travelling Flight 21.11.18 (Lt L.C. Rowney OK, crashed landing on soft ground at new aerodrome – same engine). **2 ASD** ex 22 Sqn.

H7063 Taken on charge 7.8.18 on renumbering from incorrectly marked F6403 (formerly D8023). **1 ASD** destroyed by German bombing 23.9.18 and deleted 26.9.18 (30min).

H7064 Taken on charge 23.8.18 on renumbering from incorrectly marked F6405 (formerly C901). **'M' Flt** dd ex **1 ASD** 27.11.18 (engine 745/WD32772). **24 Sqn** Kenley by 12.22 until @ 3.23. B&C for reconditioning to J Type (s/n 6603) and ready by 27.1.25.

H7065 Taken on charge 23.8.18 on re-numbering from incorrectly marked F6406 (formerly C776). **62 Sqn** by 12.18 and wrecked 17.3.19 (2nd Lt E.G. Schafer IOAS, crashed at Foedekenskerke, Holland – engine 1809/WD51929). Deleted 21.3.19.

H7066 Taken on charge 14.9.18 on reconstruction from C1003. **11 Sqn** dd ex **6 AIS** 8.1.19.

H7067 Taken on charge 14.9.18 on reconstruction from C4835.

H7068 Taken on charge 14.9.18 on reconstruction from B1177.

H7069 Taken on charge 17.9.18 on reconstruction from B1209.

H7070 Taken on charge 17.9.18 on reconstruction from B1234.

H7146 (Arab) taken on charge 11.9.18 on reconstruction from D7863. **1 ASD** by 30.9.18 (engine 53796). **1 AIS** dd ex **1 ASD** 5.10.18. **1 ASD** by 22.10.18. **1 AIS** ex **1 ASD** 24.10.18. **'M' Flt** dd ex **1 ASD** 17.11.18 (same engine).

H7169 Taken on charge 24.1.19 on reconstruction from C870.

H7170 Taken on charge 24.1.19 on reconstruction from D8080.

H7171 Taken on charge 8.10.18 on reconstruction from A7256.

H7172 Taken on charge 8.10.18 on reconstruction from B1307.

H7173 Taken on charge 8.10.18 on reconstruction from C842.

H7174 Taken on charge 8.10.18 on reconstruction from C4746. B&C for reconditioning to J Type DC (s/n 6892) and reissued 14.1.26.

H7175 Taken on charge 8.10.18 on reconstruction from C4817.

H7196 Taken on charge 20.10.18 on reconstruction from C868.

H7197 Taken on charge 8.10.18 on reconstruction from C983.

H7198 Taken on charge 6.11.18 on reconstruction from D8065.

H7291 Taken on charge 8.8.18 on renumbering from incorrectly marked F6404 (formerly E2483). **48 Sqn** and wrecked by enemy bombing 24.8.18. **2 ASD** and deleted 8.9.18 (not worth reconstruction).

H7292 Taken on charge 27.8.18 on renumbering from incorrectly marked F6407 (formerly E2254).

H7293 Taken on charge 30.8.18 on renumbering from incorrectly marked F6408 (formerly E2219). **62 Sqn** dd ex **1 AIS** 19.9.18.

435 BRISTOL FIGHTER F.2B (Arab) ordered from H.H. Martyn & Co, Sunningend, Cheltenham (renamed Gloucester Aircraft Co 5.6.17). Presume cancelled. Serials allocated, if any, unknown.

500 BRISTOL FIGHTER F.2B ordered on Contracts AS.33803 & 35a/3244/C3754 (B.R.682) dated 26.10.18 from British & Colonial Aeroplane Co Ltd and numbered J1231 to J1730. J1231-J1430 cancelled 21.12.18 and J1431-J1730 cancelled 1.19.

200 BRISTOL FIGHTER F.2B ordered on Contracts 35a/3293/C3839 & AS.33803/2 dated 26.10.18 from Standard Motor Co Ltd and numbered J1731 to J1930 but contracts cancelled 4.11.18.

100 BRISTOL FIGHTER F.2B ordered on Contracts 35a13379/C3965 and AS.34500 (B.R.691) dated 12.10.18 from Marshall & Sons & Co Ltd and numbered J2292 to J2391. 7 delivered by w/e 21.12.18 and J2299-J2391 cancelled 21.12.18.

J2292 to J2298 } Delivered to storage by 28.12.18.

215 BRISTOL FIGHTER F.2B (275hp Falcon III) ordered from Bristol Aeroplane Co Ltd to Contract 211474/20, dated 24.6.20, to Mk.II standard. Survivors later reconditioned to J Type, Mk.III, Mk.IV or Dual Control Trainer. [Consecutive works sequence nos.5893-6107].

J6586 First flown 12.20. **AEE** Martlesham Heath by 15.1.21 until @ 7.23 for performance tests, then tests with tropical radiator (5.21), Leitner-Watts metal airscrew (7.21) and navigation lights (12.21). B&C for reconditioning to J Type DC (s/n 6509) and ready by 25.10.24. **E&WS** Worthy Down by 9.25 until @ 9.26.

J6587 **PD** Ascot. To India. **AD** Drigh Road by 5.23 until @ 8.23, crashed at Drigh Road and deleted.

J6588 **PD** Ascot. To India. **AD** Drigh Road by 5.23. **20 Sqn** by 3.25 until @ 7.25. **28 Sqn** NW Frontier. **20 Sqn** by 6.27.

J6589 **PD** Ascot. To Egypt. **AD** Aboukir. **14 Sqn** by 19.12.22 until @ 1.23. Returned to UK. B&C for reconditioning to J Type DC (s/n 6887) and ready by 9.1.26. **1 SoTT** Halton by 7.26 until @ 2.28.

J6590 **PD** Ascot. To Egypt. **AD** Aboukir. **4 FTS** Abu Sueir by 3.23.

J6591 **PD** Ascot. To India. **AD** Drigh Road. **28 Sqn** NW Frontier. **5 Sqn** by 8.23 until @ 3.24. **AP** Lahore by 18.3.24. **5 Sqn** reissued by 4.24 until @ 7.24.

J6592 **2 Sqn** Manston. **PD** Ascot. To Egypt. **AD** Aboukir. **14 Sqn** by 7.23. **AD** Aboukir by 11.24 and reconditioned as JR6592. **208 Sqn** 1925.

J6593 **PD** Ascot. To Egypt. **AD** Aboukir. **14 Sqn** by 7.23, crashed landing at Beersheba 9.9.23, returned by road and on unit charge until @ 5.24. **AD** Aboukir by 5.25. **14 Sqn** reissued by 8.25 and on unit charge until @ 1.26.

J6594 **PD** Ascot. To India. **AD** Drigh Road. **20 Sqn** and damaged 21.11.22 (crashed near Kach, NWF). **AD** Drigh Road by 1.23, repaired. **20 Sqn** and damaged 7.3.23 (crashed on take off). **AD** Drigh Road 3.23. **20 Sqn** and damaged. **AD** Drigh Road by 2.4.23 and repaired. **20 Sqn**, wrecked 7.4.23 (crashed, 13 miles from Quetta) and deleted.

J6595 **2 Sqn** Manston and wrecked 26.3.23 (Plt Off E. Reid IIFA, made a sharp turn at 500ft after take off from Farnborough and spun in). **PD** Ascot. To Egypt. **AD** Aboukir. **208 Sqn** by 3.25.

J6596 (s/n 5903) **PD** Ascot. To Egypt. **AD** Aboukir. **208 Sqn** and wrecked 22.5.29 (caught fire during refuelling). Deleted.

J6597 **IACF** Northolt by 6.23.

J6598 **PD** Ascot. To India. **AD** Drigh Road. **5 Sqn** by 1.24.

J6599 **PD** Ascot. To India. **AD** Drigh Road. **28 Sqn** by 9.23. **AP** Lahore by 4.3.24. **5 Sqn** by 4.24 and wrecked 26.6.24 (crashed in bumpy conditions at Razmak).

J6600 **PD** Ascot. To Egypt. **AD** Aboukir. **4 FTS** Abu Sueir by 4.23 until @ 11.23, o/t on landing. **AD** Aboukir and reconstructed as JR6600. **208 Sqn** by 20.2.25. Returned to UK. B&C for reconditioning to J Type DC (s/n 6892) and ready by 14.1.26. **12 Sqn** Northolt by 6.26 until @ 8.27. **HQ Wessex Area** by 8.27. **NF Flt** Biggin Hill by 20.9.27.

J6601 **PD** Ascot. To India. **AD** Drigh Road. **20 Sqn** by 2.25, damaged 13.3.25 (force landed at Gharwalla, NWF), repaired and on unit charge until @ 6.25. **5 Sqn** by 5.27. **20 Sqn** by 6.27. **5 Sqn** as a/c C by 1.28 until @ 3.28. **28 Sqn** and damaged 28.4.29 (crashed landing after Reconnaissance). **20 Sqn** by 11.31 until @ 2.32.

J6602 **PD** Ascot. To Egypt. **AD** Aboukir. **14 Sqn** by 8.24. **AD** Aboukir for overhaul 29.4.25. **14 Sqn** by 10.25. Returned to UK. B&C for reconditioning to J Type DC (s/n 6897) and ready by 19.1.26. **HQ 23 Group** Spittlegate by 9.27 until @ 12.28. B&C for reconditioning to Mk.III and ready by 13.5.30. Retaken onto RAF charge 30.5.30. **CUAS** Duxford by 6.30 until @ 7.30. **5 FTS** Sealand by 12.30 until @ 8.31.

J6603 N/I

J6604 **PD** Ascot. To Egypt. **AD** Aboukir and reconditioned as JR6604. **208 Sqn** by 10.25 and damaged 1925 (o/t in crash, Lake Timsah). **4 FTS** Abu Sueir by 8.27 until @ 7.28 and photographed nosed over on landing.

J6605 **PD** Ascot. To Egypt. **AD** Aboukir by 7.3.25. **4 FTS** Abu Sueir by 26.5.25. **AD** Aboukir by 6.25 until @ 1.26. **4 FTS** Abu Sueir by 8.27 and damaged 1928 (crashed on nose).

J6606 **PD** Ascot. To Egypt. **AD** Aboukir. **4 FTS** Abu Sueir by 12.22 and wrecked 9.4.23 (spun in from 300ft at Heliopolis).

J6607 N/I

J6608 **4 Sqn** Farnborough and wrecked 26.7.21 (Fg Off G.V. Wheatley/ AC1 R.P. Thompson both OK (undercarriage collapsed in heavy landing at Farnborough).

J6609 **24 Sqn** Kenley by 7.23.

J6610 N/I

J6611 **2 FTS** Duxford by 1.23. **RAE** Farnborough by 2.10.23. **2 FTS** Digby by 10.25.

J6612 **IDE** Biggin Hill by 6.21 and in starting accident at Farnborough 6.7.21 (AC2 F.C. Ashcroft Died of Injuries 7.7.21). **Signal Co-operation Flt** Biggin Hill and wrecked 11.9.22 (Fg Off E. Wormell/Mr J. Balfour both IIFA stalled from 20ft and undercarriage collapsed on landing at Biggin Hill).

J6613 **PD** Ascot. To India. **AD** Drigh Road. **AP** Lahore as DC by 16.1.24. **5 Sqn** as a/c *D* by 2.24 until @ 7.24. **20 Sqn** NWF. **AD** Drigh Road. **5 Sqn** as a/c *O* by 15.10.26 until @ 11.28 and in landing accident at Fort Sandeman, 1928.

J6614 **PD** Ascot. To Egypt. **AD** Aboukir. **6 Sqn** by 6.30 until @ 3.31.

J6615 **PD** Ascot. To Egypt. **AD** Aboukir. **4 FTS** Abu Sueir by 2.23 and crashed there.

J6616 **PD** Ascot. To India. **AD** Drigh Road by 1.23. **20 Sqn** by 4.23 until @ 3.24. **31 Sqn** as a/c *C* and wrecked 27.4.30 (struck telegraph wires on take off from Fort Sandeman and o/t). **AP** Lahore.

J6617 **PD** Ascot. To Egypt. **AD** Aboukir. **4 FTS** Abu Sueir by 10.23 and damaged (crashed and o/t). **208 Sqn** by 3.25. **AD** Hinaidi. **6 Sqn** by 12.30, damaged 23.12.31 (force landed and salvaged the next day) and on unit charge until @ 4.32.

J6618 **PD** Ascot. To Egypt. **AD** Aboukir. **14 Sqn** by 11.24.

J6619 **PD** Ascot. To Egypt. **AD** Aboukir. **14 Sqn** by 5.23 and damaged 3.10.23 (force landed between Ludd & Ramleh after engine failure).

J6620 **PD** Ascot. To India. **AD** Drigh Road. **AP** Lahore by 8.3.24.

J6621 **PD** Ascot. To India. **AD** Drigh Road. **AP** Lahore by 2.1.24. **31 Sqn** 1.24 until @ 4.24. **20 Sqn** by 11.24 until @ 4.25. **20 Sqn** by 1.27 until @ 6.27. **28 Sqn** as a/c *E* 1928. **20 Sqn** as a/c *H* by 3.29.

J6622 **PD** Ascot. To Iraq. **AD** Hinaidi by 9.23 until @ 10.23. **6 Sqn** 1923. **AD** Hinaidi by 4.24. Returned to UK. B&C for reconditioning to J Type (s/n 6943) and ready by 14.6.26. **PD** Ascot. To India. **AD** Drigh Road. **20 Sqn** 1928. To Iraq. **6 Sqn** by 3.30 and wrecked 14.4.30 (undercarriage collapsed on landing at Ramleh).

J6623 **25 Sqn** Hawkinge 1921 until 1922. **2 Sqn** Oranmore 1922. **Irish Flt** Collistown by 7.22. **PD** Ascot. To India. **AD** Drigh Road by 2.23. **31 Sqn** by 6.23 and damaged 29.10.23 (crashed, at Sararogba, NWF). **20 Sqn** by 3.24 and wrecked 27.9.24 (crashed, on Khanai LG and deleted).

J6624 **PD** Ascot. To India. **AD** Drigh Road by 2.23. **AP** Lahore by 21.2.24. **5 Sqn** by 5.24 until @ 9.24. **28 Sqn**.

J6625 **PD** Ascot. To India. **AD** Drigh Road by 7.23. **31 Sqn** by 9.24 until @ 10.24.

J6626 **PD** Ascot. To India. **AD** Drigh Road by 2.23. **28 Sqn** by 7.23. **31 Sqn** and wrecked 10.8.23 (force landed after engine failure).

J6627 **PD** Ascot. To India. **AD** Drigh Road by 2.23. To Iraq. **AD** Hinaidi by 5.23. **6 Sqn** by 7.23 until @ 1925.

J6628 **PD** Ascot. To India. **AD** Drigh Road. **5 Sqn** as a/c *D* by 1.24 and wrecked 17.3.24 (crashed near Razani, NWF, after engine failure).

J6629 N/I

J6630 **PD** Ascot. To India. **AD** Drigh Road. **AP** Lahore by 5.24 until @ 6.24. **28 Sqn** by 8.24.

J6631 **PD** Ascot. To India. **AD** Drigh Road. **AP** Lahore by 7.24. **5 Sqn** as a/c *P* by 8.24 until @ 3.25. **20 Sqn** by 3.26 and wrecked 1.10.26 (Fg Off P.H. Nicholls fatally IOAS/LAC G. Cairns IOAS (hit obstruction on take off at Peshawar, crashed, caught fire and burnt out).

J6632 B&C for reconditioning to J Type (s/n 6630) and ready by 26.2.25. **PD** Ascot. To India. **AD** Drigh Road. **AP** Lahore. **5 Sqn** by 9.26. **AD** Drigh Road 1927.

J6633 **PD** Ascot. To Egypt. **AD** Aboukir. **14 Sqn** and damaged 12.29 (broke undercarriage V-strut when landing at Ramleh).

J6634 **PD** Ascot. To India. **AD** Drigh Road by 2.23. **31 Sqn** by 9.24 until @ 12.24. **5 Sqn** as a/c *V* 1925. **AD** Drigh Road 1927. **20 Sqn** as a/c *L* by 10.31 until @ 3.32.

J6635 **PD** Ascot. To Egypt. **AD** Aboukir and reconditioned as JR6635. **14 Sqn** by 20.6.25. **6 Sqn** by 7.30, successfully force landed at Gaza LG 8.30 and wrecked 28.8.30 (struck a hill and overturned on landing at Kolundia LG, near Jerusalem).

J6636 **PD** Ascot. To Iraq. **AD** Hinaidi by 3.23.

J6637 **PD** Ascot. To India. **AD** Drigh Road. **AP** Lahore by 2.2.24. **5 Sqn** by 3.24 and wrecked 5.5.25 (starboard wheel went into a ditch during forced landing at Dardoni after engine failure).

J6638 **PD** Ascot. To India. **AD** Drigh Road by 2.23. **AP** Lahore by 4.23. **AD** Drigh Road by 7.23. **5 Sqn** by 11.23 until @ 4.24. **28 Sqn** NWF. **20 Sqn** by 3.25 until @ 8.25 and also on unit charge 6.27.

J6639 **PD** Ascot. To India. **AD** Drigh Road. **28 Sqn** and wrecked 28.5.24 (crashed into a field in the Splitor area). **31 Sqn** by 1925.

J6640 **PD** Ascot. To India. **AD** Drigh Road. **AP** Lahore by 8.12.23. **HQ RAF India** by 11.24. **31 Sqn** as a/c *K* by 11.24 and wrecked 1.8.26 (Fg Off J.C. Marcy IOAS/LAC P.W.E. Crunden fatally IOAS, crashed on take off at Multan).

J6641 **PD** Ascot. To India. **AD** Drigh Road by 2.23. **AP** Lahore by 4.23. **5 Sqn** by 10.23 until @ 6.24. **20 Sqn** by 3.25 until @ 4.25. **31 Sqn** as a/c *E* by 2.27. **28 Sqn** as a/c *T*. **AD** Drigh Road by 12.32.

J6642 **PD** Ascot. To India. **AD** Drigh Road. **AP** Lahore by 19.12.23. **31 Sqn** and wrecked 16.6.24 (crashed on Night Flying Practice at Ambala).

J6643 **PD** Ascot. To India. **AD** Drigh Road by 1.24. **AP** Lahore as DC by 1.24. **5 Sqn** by 4.24 until @ 10.26. **20 Sqn** as a/c *G* 1927. **31 Sqn** by 4.29 and damaged 22.5.30 (engine started when the cockpit was unmanned and the a/c ran into a ditch). **AP** Lahore and repaired. **20 Sqn** by 9.31 until @ 2.32.

J6644 **PD** Ascot. To India. **AD** Drigh Road 1923. **20 Sqn** by 1.24, damaged 8.2.24 (stalled and crashed at Quetta) and wrecked 31.3.24 (stalled on low turn at Quetta).

J6645 **PD** Ascot. To India. **AD** Drigh Road by 8.23 until @ 9.23. **20 Sqn** by 1.24 until @ 10.24 and also on unit charge as a/c *K* by 11.31.

J6646 **PD** Ascot. To India. **AD** Drigh Road by 3.23. **AP** Lahore by 4.23. **28 Sqn** by 7.24.

J6647 **PD** Ascot. To India. **AD** Drigh Road by 2.23. **AP** Lahore by 3.23 until @ 4.23. **31 Sqn** as a/c *K* by 7.23 and damaged 11.1.24 (engine failed and starboard wheel went into a ditch at Dardoni). **20 Sqn** as a/c *F* by 6.24 until @ 12.25 and also marked as a/c *D*. **31 Sqn** and wrecked 26.11.28 (crashed at Hyderabad).

J6648 **PD** Ascot. To Egypt. **AD** Aboukir. **14 Sqn** by 5.24. **AD** Aboukir by 2.26. **208 Sqn** by 5.30 until @ 6.30.

J6649 **PD** Ascot. To India. **AD** Drigh Road. **31 Sqn** by 4.26 until @ 5.26.

J6650 **PD** Ascot. To India. **AD** Drigh Road. **31 Sqn** by 10.23 until @ 11.24. **28 Sqn** NWF. **AD** Drigh Road. **20 Sqn** by 6.27. **1 (Indian) Group** by 7.29 until 1930. **20 Sqn** by 4.30 and damaged 17.6.30 (force landed at Basawal, Afghanistan). **20 Sqn** by 18.6.30 until @ 8.30.

J6651 **PD** Ascot. To India. **AD** Drigh Road. **31 Sqn** as a/c *B* and crashed. **AP** Lahore by 18.12.23. **5 Sqn** as a/c *C* by 31.12.23 until @ 6.24. **20 Sqn** by 3.25. **28 Sqn**.

J6652 **PD** Ascot. To India. **AD** Drigh Road by 3.23. **AP** Lahore by 4.23. **31 Sqn** as a/c *A* and wrecked 12.12.23 (hit telegraph wires and crashed at Dardoni).

J6653 **PD** Ascot. To India. **AD** Drigh Road. **AP** Lahore by 7.6.24. **5 Sqn** by 3.25 until @ 6.25.

J6654 **PD** Ascot. To India. **AD** Drigh Road. **AP** Lahore by 9.1.24. **31 Sqn** as a/c *O* by 3.24 until @ 2.25. **5 Sqn** as a/c *B* by 11.27 until @ 3.28. **20 Sqn** 1928 and on unit charge 1930. **AD** Drigh Road by 7.31.

J6655 **PD** Ascot. To India. **AD** Drigh Road. **20 Sqn** by 8.23 until @ 4.24.

J6656 **PD** Ascot. To India. **AD** Drigh Road by 2.23. **AP** Lahore by 2.23. **AD** Drigh Road by 11.23 until @ 12.23. **20 Sqn** by 3.25. **AD** Drigh Road 1927. **20 Sqn** by 6.27 until @ 11.28. **28 Sqn** as a/c *C* by 1930 until @ 1932.

J6657 **PD** Ascot. To India. **AD** Drigh Road **31 Sqn** as a/c *P* and wrecked 11.8.24 (hit tree on landing at Ambala).

J6658 **PD** Ascot. To Egypt. **AD** Aboukir. To Iraq. **6 Sqn** 1923. **AD** Hinaidi, reconstructed 1.24 and on unit charge until @ 6.24. **6 Sqn** by 9.24 until 1.25. Returned to UK 1.25. B&C for reconditioning to J Type DC (s/n 7103) and ready by 16.1.26. **1 FTS** Netheravon by 8.26.

J6659 **PD** Ascot. To Iraq. **AD** Hinaidi by 5.23. **6 Sqn** by 28.6.23. **AD** Hinaidi by 6.26 and converted to DC. **AHQ Iraq Command Training Flt** by 12.26 until @ 6.29. **AD Hinaidi Training Flt** by 6.12.29 until @ 11.30. **30 Sqn**.

J6660 **PD** Ascot. To India. **AD** Drigh Road by 1.23. **AP** Lahore by 11.24. **20 Sqn** by 8.23 and damaged 30.4.24 (hit a water channel and o/t at Chaman LG). **5 Sqn** by 11.24.

J6661 **IACF** Henlow by 3.21 until @ 10.22. **24 Sqn** Kenley by 4.24 until @ 6.24. **B&C** for reconditioning to J Type DC (s/n 6883) and ready by 6.1.26. **1 SoTT** Halton by 5.26. **4 Sqn** Farnborough by 23.8.26. **1 SoTT** Halton by 10.26 until @ 11.27. **B&C** for reconditioning to Mk.III DC and ready by 16.5.30. Retaken onto RAF charge 23.6.30. **5 FTS** Sealand by 8.30 until @ 8.31.

J6662 **B&C** for reconditioning to J Type (s/n 6574) and ready by 22.12.24. **2 Sqn** Manston by 3.26 until @ 6.26. **B&C** for reconditioning to Mk.III (s/n 7103) and ready by 6.7.27. **B&C** for reconditioning to Mk.IV (s/n 2623) and ready by 6.10.28. **2 Sqn** Manston by 6.29. **AGS** Eastchurch by 9.29 until @ 4.30.

J6663 **2 Sqn** Manston. **B&C** for reconditioning to J Type (s/n 6631) and ready by 2.3.25. **PD** Ascot. To India. **AD** Drigh Road. **31 Sqn** as a/c *C*. **20 Sqn** as a/c *B* 1927 and as a/c *M* by 5.30 until @ 11.31.

J6664 **B&C** for reconditioning to J Type (s/n 6549) and ready by 29.11.24.

J6665 **CFS** Upavon and wrecked 15.10.23 (stalled from flat turn on on approach to Farnborough).

J6666 **100 Sqn** Baldonnel by 12.21 until @ 4.22. **4 Sqn** Farnborough and wrecked 20.6.22 (Fg Off A.A. Ward/Capt D.F. Ward, Bombay University Cadet Corps, both OK, force landed at Chobham Ridges, near Pirbright Camp, Surrey, after engine failure).

J6667 **PD** Ascot. To India. **AD** Drigh Road. **AP** Lahore by 4.23.

J6668 **2 Sqn** Manston by 2.22 until @ 6.22. **NF Flt** Biggin Hill by 1.27. **B&C** for reconditioning to J Type (s/n 7158) and ready by 28.2.28. **PD** Ascot. To India. **AD** Drigh Road. **20 Sqn** by 1930.

J6669 **2 Sqn** Manston 1927.

J6670 **24 Sqn** Kenley by 4.24. **B&C** for reconditioning to J Type (s/n 6629) and ready by 27.2.25. **PD** Ascot. To India. **AD** Drigh Road 1925. **AP** Lahore. **5 Sqn** by 10.26 until @ 6.27. **AD** Drigh Road 1927.

J6671 **2 Sqn** Oranmore 1920. **100 Sqn** Baldonnel 1921. **AGS** Eastchurch and wrecked 16.1.23 (Fg Off J.H. Vickers/AC2 A.E. Bayliss IIFA, engine failed on turn while landing at Eastchurch and sideslipped in).

J6672 **AGS** Eastchurch and wrecked 4.10.22 (Fg Off F.V. Gauntlett OK, force landed on the sea 80yds off Leysdown after engine failed on take off).

J6673 **1 FTS** Netheravon. Shotwick (**5 FTS**?) by 1.4.21. **2 Sqn** Manston and wrecked 24.5.22 (Fg Off E.G. Green/Sgt W.J. Skivey both KIFA, stalled on turn near ground in beat up of Digby).

J6674 **2 Sqn** Oranmore and wrecked 29.6.21 (Fg Off S.L.H. Potter OK/ Fg Off S.E. Sutcliffe IOAS, hit a fence when force landed due to fuel shortage at Mallow, Co Cork, while low flying as escort to troop train). **PD** Ascot. To India. **AD** Drigh Road. **31 Sqn** as a/c *K* by 7.23. **AD** Drigh Road 1926.

J6675 **100 Sqn** Baldonnel by 5.21. **PD** Ascot. To India. **AD** Drigh Road. **31 Sqn**.

J6676 **IAAD** Henlow by 12.23. **RAE** Farnborough by 15.1.24. **B&C** for reconditioning to J Type DC (s/n 6508) and ready by 30.10.24. **AGS** Eastchurch by 1.28 until @ 7.28. **PD** Ascot. To Egypt. **AD** Aboukir. **208 Sqn** by 5.29.

J6677 **APS** Andover by 10.22 until @ 11.22. **Staff College Flt** Andover by 6.23 until @ 5.24. **B&C** for reconditioning to J Type (s/n 6645) and ready by 9.3.25. **B&C** for reconditioning to DC (s/n 6895) and ready by 18.1.26. **1 FTS** Netheravon by 8.26. **1 SoTT** Halton.

J6678 **100 Sqn** Baldonnel by 5.21. **2 Sqn** Oranmore by 1.22. **IACF** Henlow by 6.23. **B&C** for reconditioning to J Type (s/n 6589) and ready by 16.1.25. **RAF (Cadet) College** Cranwell by 3.25 until @ 7.26.

J6679 **2 Sqn** Oranmore by 2.22. **5 FTS** Sealand and wrecked 6.7.23 (Plt Off G.G. Hopkins IIFA, landing overshoot at Shotwick).

J6680 **1 SoTT** (Boys) Halton as a/c *7*, later as a/c *6* by 9.23 until @ 1.25. **B&C** for reconditioning to J Type (s/n 6973) and ready by 15.7.26.

J6681 **B&C** for reconditioning to J Type (s/n 6654) and ready by 14.3.25. **NF Flt** Biggin Hill by 1.27. **24 Sqn** Kenley by 1.27 until @ 8.28.

J6682 **16 Sqn/SAC** Old Sarum by 7.24 until @ 10.26. **23 Group HQ** Spittlegate by 10.27.

J6683 **16 Sqn/SAC** Old Sarum by 2.24 until @ 3.25.

J6684 To Iraq. **6 Sqn** 1922. **AD** Hinaidi by 10.23. **6 Sqn** 1925.

J6685 **PD** Ascot. To Egypt. **AD** Aboukir. **Khartoum Flt**. Returned to UK. **B&C** for reconditioning to J Type DC (s/n 6888). **5 FTS** Sealand by 4.27 until @ 4.29. **B&C** for reconditioning to Mk.III DC and ready by 9.5.30. Retaken onto RAF charge 28.5.30. **E&WS** Worthy Down by 9.30 until @ 11.30. **OUAS** Upper Heyford by 7.31. **2 FTS** Digby by 9.31 until @ 10.31.

J6686 **PD** Ascot. To Egypt. **AD** Aboukir. **208 Sqn** by 5.24 until @ 8.24.

J6687 N/I

J6688 **24 Sqn** Kenley by 5.22. **2 Sqn** Collinstown by 7.22 until 8.22. **Irish Flt** Collinstown 8.22 and wrecked 3.9.22 (crashed in forced landing after engine failure at Dundalk, Co Louth). Repaired. **2 Sqn** Manston by 13.10.22, damaged 1.5.23 (force landed on soft ground near Bracknell, Herts), repaired and on unit charge until @ 9.23.

J6689 **IDE** Biggin Hill by 7.21. **RAE** Farnborough by 8.5.22, damaged 12.7.22 (crashed at Aston Tirrold, Berks) and wrecked 16.10.23 (Fg Off H.R. Junor/Flt Lt R. deH Haig both IIFA, crashed when testing landing lights at night at Farnborough). **A&AEE** Martlesham Heath for night flying trials 2.10.24. **RAE** Farnborough by 9.10.24 and damaged 16.9.27 (crashed on landing at Martlesham). Repaired. **A&AEE** Martlesham Heath by 24.10.30.

J6690 **100 Sqn** Baldonnel and wrecked on Travelling Flight, Oranmore-Baldonnel, 16.6.21 (Fg Off H.C. Black OK/Cpl J.E. Brown IIFA, force landed, hit a bank and o/t in at Ballinasloe, Galway, after engine failure). **1 SoTT** Halton by 6.23.

J6691 **2 Sqn** Oranmore 1921. **B&C** for reconditioning to J Type (s/n 6677) and ready by 28.3.25. **2 Sqn** Manston by 12.25.

J6692 **2 Sqn** Oranmore and wrecked 18.7.22 (crashed on landing at Collinstown). Repaired. **Irish Flt** Collinstown by 8.22 until @ 11.22. **24 Sqn** Kenley and wrecked 12.22 (Plt Off L.K. Barnes OK, force landed on golf links near Walsall, Staffs, due to fuel shortage and hit a hedge on take off).

J6693 **100 Sqn** Baldonnel by 8.21. **2 Sqn** Manston and wrecked 6.7.23 (Flt Lt D. Gilley/Fg Off F.L. Hudson both IIFA, hit trees during forced landing near Crowthorne, Berks).

J6694 **2 Sqn** Oranmore 1921. **IAAD** Henlow by 6.24. **13 Sqn** Andover 1924 until 1925. **E&WS** Worthy Down by 10.25 until @ 3.26. **B&C** for reconditioning to J Type (s/n 6979) and ready by 23.7.26. **HAD** Henlow by 4.27. Shipped to China. **2 Sqn** Shanghai by 7.27, returned to UK with unit and on charge until @ 7.29.

J6695 **IACF** Henlow by 3.23 until @ 5.23. **5 FTS** Sealand by 9.24 until @ 10.24. **B&C** for reconditioning to J Type (s/n 6975) and ready by 16.7.26. **HAD** Henlow by 4.27. Shipped China. **2 Sqn** Shanghai.

J6696 **2 Sqn** Oranmore as a/c *2* by 1920 until @ 1921. **1 FTS** Netheravon by 7.22 until @ 8.22. **5 FTS** Sealand and wrecked 31.3.25 (collided with D.H.9A J7347 while landing and caught fire). **B&C** for reconditioning to J Type (s/n 6917) and ready by 5.2.26. **SAC** Old Sarum by 9.28 until @ 1.29.

J6697 **Staff College Flt** Andover by 7.22 until @ 10.22. **IACF** Henlow by 10.22 and wrecked 11.12.22 (Flt Lt D. Craik IIFA, force landed near Lichford en route Shotwick-Northolt and hit a plough). **2 FTS** Digby by 6.25 and damaged 19.8.25 (caught fire in mid-air). **B&C** for reconditioning to J Type (s/n 6914) and ready by 9.3.26.

J6698 **4 Sqn** detachment Baldonnell and wrecked on Delivery Flight to **5 FTS** 20.1.22 (Fg Off G.E. Pratt/AC2 L. Brooks both OK, force landed near Rhos-on-Sea, N. Wales, after engine failure).

J6699 **100 Sqn** Baldonnel by 5.21. **PD** Ascot. To Egypt. **AD** Aboukir. **6 Sqn** 1928.

J6700 **2 Sqn** Aldergrove by 5.22 until @ 1922. **B&C** for reconditioning to J Type (s/n 6625) and ready by 19.2.25. **PD** Ascot. To India. **AD** Drigh Road. **5 Sqn** by 1.26 until @ 7.26. **AD** Drigh Road 1927. **20 Sqn** by 6.27 and damaged 19.7.28 (a/c ran away while unattended with engine running). 19.7.28; repaired. **Quetta SF** 1929. **20 Sqn** by 11.29.

J6701 **2 Sqn** Aldergrove by 5.22 until @ 9.22. **B&C** for reconditioning to J Type (s/n 6655) and ready by 12.3.25. **B&C** for reconditioning (s/n 6969) and ready by 8.7.26. **16 Sqn** Old Sarum by 8.27 until @ 5.30.

J6702 Farnborough by 5.22 until @ 6.24. **13 Sqn** Andover 1924. **B&C** for reconditioning to J Type DC (s/n 6890) and ready by 14.1.26. **5 FTS** Sealand by 7.26 until @ 4.28.

J6703 **2 Sqn** Oranmore by 12.21 until @ 8.22. **4 Sqn** Farnborough by 10.22. **2 Sqn** Manston and wrecked 3.2.24 (force landed near Boodle Station, Sussex, after engine failure).

J6704 **1 FTS** Netheravon by 5.22. **24 Sqn** Kenley by 7.22. **Irish Flt** Collinstown by 8.22. **4 Sqn** Farnborough by 1.23 until @ 3.23.

J6705 **2 Sqn** Aldergrove by 6.22 and wrecked 9.10.22 (Fg Off D. Craik/ Wing Cdr A.V. Bettington both IIFA, flew into water in mist, 3 miles from eastern shore of Lough Neagh, and 6 miles from Aldergrove).

J6706 **100 Sqn** Baldonnel and wrecked on Delivery Flight to **5 FTS** Sealand 29.1.22 (Fg Off A. Knox/AC2 C.G. Scott both OK, force landed at Dyserth, near Rhyl, due to lack of fuel).

J6707 **100 Sqn** Oranmore and wrecked 27.6.21 (Flt Lt B.M. Fleming/ Cpl R.F. Bond both IIFA, force landed on water in Galway Bay after engine failure, crew rescued by destroyer HMS *Urchin*).

J6708 **APS** Andover by 10.22. **2 Sqn** Manston by 6.23. B&C for reconditioning to J Type (s/n 6678) and ready by 9.4.25. B&C for reconditioning to J Type DC (s/n 6872) and ready by 4.12.25. **HQ Wessex Bombing Area** Andover by 8.26 until @ 9.27. **5 FTS** Sealand by 11.27 until @ 12.27. **Andover CF** by 7.28. **School of Photography Flt** Kenley by 3.28.

J6709 **100 Sqn** Baldonnel and wrecked 1.7.21 (Fg Off V. Croome IOAS/ LAC C. Grant OK, hit a tree during forced landing near Mullingar, Ireland).

J6710 **100 Sqn** Baldonnel by 12.21. **4 Sqn** Farnborough by 10.22 until @ 3.23. **13 Sqn** Andover 1925.

J6711 **2 Sqn** Aldergrove by 7.22 until @ 9.22. **4 Sqn** Farnborough by 4.23. B&C for reconditioning to J Type (s/n 6670) and ready by 21.3.25. **PD** Ascot. To India. **AD** Drigh Road. **5 Sqn** 1925. **AD** Drigh Road. **5 Sqn** by 4.27 until @ 2.28. **20 Sqn** as a/c *F* by 9.31 until @ 10.31.

J6712 **2 Sqn** Oranmore 1920. **100 Sqn** Baldonnel by 8.21 until @ 1.22. **School of Photography** Farnborough by 5.22. **4 Sqn** Farnbrough and wrecked 17.6.24 (force landed near Guildford, Surrey after becoming lost in bad weather).

J6713 **4 Sqn** Farnborough as a/c *A4* by 1923. **IAAD** Henlow by 12.23. **2 FTS** Duxford by 12.23 until @ 5.24. **19 Sqn** Duxford and damaged 14.5.24 (dived in when avoiding Sopwith Snipe after take off). Repaired. **4 Sqn** Farnborough. **2 FTS** Duxford and wrecked 24.7.24 (crashed avoiding a Sopwith Snipe on landing at Duxford).

J6714 **2 Sqn** Aldergrove by 3.22. **NF Flt** Biggin Hill by 10.25 until @ 3.26. **21 Group HQ** Northolt. **Northolt CF** by 7.26 until @ 11.27. **2 FTS** Digby.

J6715 **4 Sqn** Farnborough as a/c *A1* by 1.22 until @ 8.23. B&C for reconditioning to J Type (s/n 6634) and ready by 28.2.25. To India. **AD** Drigh Road. **AP** Lahore. **5 Sqn** as a/c *R* by 30.8.26 until @ 3.27. **5 Sqn** by 10.28.

J6716 **2 Sqn** Digby by 4.22 until @ 7.22. **SAC** Old Sarum by 5.24. B&C for reconditioning to J Type (s/n 6651) and ready by 17.3.25.

J6717 **2 Sqn** Digby/Manston by 4.22 and wrecked 13.8.23 (Fg Off A. Maybaum OK/AC2 F.G. Richardson IIFA, force landed near Elsted, Sussex, due to fuel shortage).

J6718 **24 Sqn** Kenley by 2.23 until @ 3.24. B&C for reconditioning to J Type (s/n 6650) and ready by 14.3.25. B&C for reconditioning to Mk.III DC and ready by 20.7.27. **22 Group** Farnborough as ferry aircraft by 1.29 until @ 9.29.

J6719 **16 Sqn/SAC** Old Sarum by 11.24 until @ 6.26. **4 Sqn** Farnborough. B&C for reconditioning to Mk.III (s/n 7105) and ready by 6.7.27. B&C for reconditioning to Mk.III DC (s/n 7430) and ready by 16.6.29. **RAF College** Cranwell by 12.30 until @ 1.31.

J6720 **4 Sqn** Farnborough by 5.22, to Turkey with the unit 9.22 and wrecked 14.12.22 (missing in cloud and found crashed at Chan-Bazar Kevi, 34 miles E of Chanak).

J6721 **4 Sqn** Kilya Bay by 10.22. B&C for reconditioning to J Type (s/n 6665) and ready by 21.3.25. Stag Lane. **RAE** Farnborough by 16.11.26 for tests with steel bi-convex wings, later evaporation cowling and adjustable pitch propeller, force landed at Worthy Down 7.3.32 and on delivery @ 1934.

J6722 **24 Sqn** Kenley by 24.6.22, participated in Hendon Air Pageant. **RAE** Farnborough by 28.11.22. **2 Sqn** Manston by 10.4.23. **RAE** Farnborough by 2.10.23 until @ 2.24. **16 Sqn/SAC** Old Sarum by 8.24 until @ 10.2. B&C for reconditioning to J Type (s/n 7168) and ready by 17.3.28. **SAC** Old Sarum by 8.28. **16 Sqn** Old Sarum by 2.30 until @ 4.30.

J6723 **2 FTS** Duxford and wrecked 19.3.23 (force landed upside down at Long Melford Ridge Railway Station, Suffolk).

J6724 **SAC** Old Sarum by 1922 and wrecked 1.6.23 (Plt Off M.C.W. Flint/Flt Lt J.W. Brenna both IIFA, became lost and struck chimney and fell into pond during forced landing near Westbury Station, Wilts).

J6725 **100 Sqn** Baldonnel and wrecked 2.9.21 (Fg Off F.F. Tattam IIFA/ Cpl S.H. Roadnight KIFA, dived into ground after spnning from 1,500ft to 150ft over Baldonnel).

J6726 **SAC** Old Sarum. **PD** Ascot. To Egypt. **AD** Aboukir and reconditioned as JR6726. **14 Sqn** by 17.7.25.

J6727 **1 FTS** Netheravon by 5.22. **E&WS** Worthy Down and damaged 15.1.24 (force landed after engine failure). **IAAD ARS** Henlow by 1.26 until @ 4.26. **Henlow SF** by 4.26 until @ 8.27. **4 Sqn** Farnborough by 3.9.27 until @ 3.28.

J6728 **2 Sqn** Manston by 6.22 until @ 8.22. **SAC** Old Sarum.

J6729 **1 FTS** Netheravon by 5.22 until @ 1.24. B&C for reconditioning to J Type (s/n 6653) and ready by 13.3.25. **Dept of CAS CF** Northolt 1925 until @ 1926.

J6730 **1 FTS** Netheravon by 5.22. **24 Sqn** Kenley by 9.22 until @ 11.22. **2 Sqn** Manston by 5.23 until @ 6.23. B&C for reconditioning to J Type (s/n 6689) and ready by 28.4.25. **PD** Ascot. To India. **AD** Drigh Road. **AP** Lahore. **20 Sqn** as a/c *M*.

J6731 **PD** Ascot. To India. **AD** Drigh Road 1923. **20 Sqn** and wrecked 9.4.24 (starboard wheel came off after landing).

J6732 **1 FTS** Netheravon by 4.21. **2 Sqn** Oranmore. **Irish Flt** Collinstown by 14.8.22. Shotwick (**5 FTS**?) by 12.11.22. **CFS** Upavon by 10.24 and wrecked 29.6.26 (overshot on landing at Upavon and collided with Sopwith Snipe E6342). Repaired.

J6733 **1 FTS** Netheravon. **PD** Ascot. To India. **AD** Drigh Road by 4.23 until @ 6.23.

J6734 **APS** Andover by 8.22 until @ 10.22. **1 FTS** Netheravon. **16 Sqn/ SAC** Old Sarum by 1.24 until @ 4.25. B&C for reconditioning to J Type DC (s/n 6896) and ready by 20.1.26.

J6735 **APS** Andover by 8.22 until @ 11.22. B&C for reconditioning to J Type (s/n 6644) and ready by 10.3.25. **2 Sqn** Manston by 12.26 until @ 1.27. Shipped to China. **2 Sqn** Shanghai by 2.6.27 until @ 8.27. To India. **AP** Lahore by 2.29.

J6736 **24 Sqn** Kenley by 1.22 until @ 9.22. **2 Sqn** Manston by 12.22 until @ 5.23. B&C for reconditioning to J Type (s/n 6666) and ready by 20.3.25. **PD** Ascot. To India. **AD** Drigh Road by 5.31. **20 Sqn** by 2.32.

J6737 **CFS** Upavon and wrecked 7.9.23 (hit a steep ridge on landing at Upavon, bounced and o/t).

J6738 **IAAD** Henlow by 4.12.24. **24 Sqn** Kenley by 12.2.25. **IAAD** Henlow by 20.2.25 until @ 8.25. B&C for reconditioning to J Type DC (s/n 6915) and ready by 13.3.26.

J6739 **1 FTS** Netheravon by 5.22 and wrecked 9.2.23 (Cpl E.A. Grose IIFA, stalled and crashed on take off from Netheravon).

J6740 **APS** Andover by 10.22. **Staff College Flt** Andover by 4.23 until @ 7.23. B&C for reconditioning to J Type (s/n 6659) and ready by 19.3.25. **PD** Ascot. To India. **AD** Drigh Road. **28 Sqn** as a/c *L* by 1929 until @ 1930.

J6741 **PD** Ascot. To India. **AD** Drigh Road by 3.23. **31 Sqn** by 9.23. **5 Sqn** as a/c *C* by 1924 until 1. 1925. **20 Sqn** 1.25 until @ 11.25. **AD** Drigh Road by 7.31.

J6742 **5 FTS** Sealand and wrecked 16.3.22 (crashed near Brentwood, Essex). **Staff College Flt** Andover by 1925 until @ 2.26. **AGS** Eastchurch by 11.26 until @ 1.27. B&C for reconditioning to J Type (s/n 7239) and ready by 2.7.28. **PD** Ascot. To Egypt. **AD** Aboukir and wrecked at Zangai 4.2.29 on Delivery Flight to **6 Sqn**.

J6743 **24 Sqn** Kenley by 9.22 until @ 10.22. **2 Sqn** Manston by 1.23 until @ 7.23. **Staff College Flt** Andover by 6.24 until @ 3.26 and damaged (Sqn Ldr E.A. Bealah OK, in ground collision with Avro 504K J6743). **HAD** Henlow for repair. **2 FTS** Digby by 28.7.25. **HQ Wessex Area** Andover by 3.8.26. **13 Sqn** Andover 1926. B&C for reconditioning to J Type (s/n 7163) and ready by 2.3.28.

J6744 **24 Sqn** Kenley, participating in Hendon Air Pageant 24.6.22. **Irish Flt** Collinstown by 8.22. **24 Sqn** Kenley by 6.23.

J6745 **24 Sqn** Kenley by 12.22. **2 Sqn** Manston by 6.23. **2 FTS** Digby by 1.26.

J6746 **1 FTS** Netheravon by 5.22 until @ 11.22. B&C for reconditioning to J Type (s/n 6633) and ready by 28.2.25. **PD** Ascot. To India. **AD** Drigh Road. **5 Sqn** by 9.26.

J6747 **IACF** Henlow by 9.24. B&C for reconditioning to J Type (s/n 6954) and ready by 26.6.26. **13 Sqn** Andover by 9.27.

J6748 **2 Sqn** Aldergrove by 8.22. **12th Wing** by 14.8.22. **Irish Flt** Collinstown by 10.22. **RAF (Cadet) College** Cranwell by 7.24.

J6749 **2 Sqn** Oranmore and damaged 29.6.21 (crashed in forced landing due to fuel shortage at Mallow, Co Cork). **24 Sqn** Kenley, participating in Hendon Air Pageant 24.6.22. **2 Sqn** Manston by 12.22 and damaged 10.7.23 (undercarriage collapsed on landing at Farnborough). Repaired. **RAE** Farnborough by 2.10.23. **PD** Ascot. To Egypt. **AD** Aboukir by 10.25. Returned to UK. B&C for reconditioning to Mk.III (s/n 7092) and ready by 28.5.27. B&C for reconditioning to Mk.IV (s/n 7261) and ready by 6.10.28. **AGS** Eastchurch by 9.29 until @ 7.30.

J6750 **PD** Ascot. To India. **AD** Drigh Road. **AP** Lahore by 11.4.24. **5 Sqn** as a/c *L* by 12.24 until @ 10.25. **31 Sqn**.

J6751 **2 FTS** Duxford by 3.24.

J6752 **4 Sqn** Farnborough by 7.23 and damaged 13.3.24 (o/t when undercarriage collapsed on landing at Andover). Repaired. **1 FTS** Netheravon by 3.24. **PD** Ascot. To India. **AP** Lahore by 6.24. Returned to UK. B&C for reconditioning to J Type (s/n 6648) and ready by 6.3.25. **PD** Ascot. To India. **AD** Drigh Road. **20 Sqn** as a/c *K* by 27.4.27. **20 Sqn** by 10.31.

J6753 **AEE** Martlesham Heath by 7.21 for radiator and parachute trials and wrecked 11.8.22 (o/t after Parachute Test when starboard wheel came off during landing at Martlesham Heath).

J6754 **SAC** Old Sarum by 12.22 until @ 6.23. **School of Photography Flt** Kenley by 5.25 until @ 9.25. To India. **31 Sqn**.

J6755 N/I

J6756 **Irish Flt** Collinstown by 8.22. **2 Sqn** Oranmore 9.22. **Irish Flt** Collinstown 9.22 and damaged 9.10.22, force landed on seashore at Betaghstown, 5 miles N of Gormanston). Shotwick (**5 FTS**?) by 12.11.22. **2 FTS** Duxford and damaged 26.1.23 (pilot injured by debris on take off from Duxford). **2 Sqn** Manston by 5.23. B&C for reconditioning to J Type (s/n 6657) and ready by 16.3.25. **16 Sqn/SAC** Old Sarum by 4.25 until @ 10.26.

J6757 **APS** by 10.22. Damaged on Delivery Flight to **RAE** Farnborough 16.10.22 (force landed near Maidenhead, Berks). **PD** Ascot. To India. **AD** Drigh Road. **AP** Lahore by 7.3.24 until @ 5.24. **31 Sqn** by 12.24.

J6758 **PD** Ascot. To Egypt. **AD** Aboukir. **4 FTS** Abu Sueir by 7.23 until @ 9.23. **208 Sqn** by 3.24. **AD** Aboukir. **208 Sqn** 1928. To India. **AD** Drigh Road. **31 Sqn** and wrecked (crashed on landing).

J6759 **PD** Ascot. To India. **AD** Drigh Road. **AP** Lahore by 5.24. **5 Sqn** as a/c *L*.

J6760 **APS** Andover by 11.22. **Staff College Flt** Andover by 7.23 until @ 8.24. B&C for reconditioning to J Type (s/n 7159) and ready by 28.2.28. **4 Sqn** Farnborough by 8.29.

J6761 **4 Sqn** Farnborough as a/c *C1* by 10.22. B&C for reconditioning to J Type (s/n 6664) and ready by 21.3.25. **PD** Ascot. To India. **AD** Drigh Road. **31 Sqn** as a/c *A* by 10.27. **5 Sqn** 10.27 until @ 7.28. **28 Sqn** 1930.

J6762 **1 FTS** Netheravon by 4.21 until 7.22. **Irish Flt** Collinstown by 8.22. **5 FTS** Sealand by 9.22. **PD** Ascot. To India. **AD** Drigh Road 1924. **AP** Lahore by 2.5.24. **28 Sqn** by 8.24. **5 Sqn** by 1925 until @ 4.27. **AD** Drigh Road 1927.

J6763 **2 Sqn** Oranmore by 9.21. **Irish Flt** Collinstown and damaged 21.10.22 (crashed at Phoenix Park, Dublin). Repaired. **2 Sqn** Aldergrove by 1.11.22 and damaged 22.11.19 (Fg Off Gemmel/ wireless operator both OK, force landed 4 miles from Aldergrove). Repaired. Force landed at Camberley, Surrey, 22.11.23.

J6764 **PD** Ascot. **4 Sqn** by 12.22 and wrecked 5.1.23 (o/t taxiing on soft ground at Kilid el Bahr, Turkey).

J6765 **1 FTS** Netheravon by 2.24 until @ 3.24. B&C for reconditioning to J Type (s/n 6675) and ready by 7.4.25. **HAD** Henlow by 3.29 until @ 4.29.

J6766 **13 Sqn** Andover 1924. B&C for reconditioning to Mk.III (s/n 7142) and ready by 14.5.28.

J6767 **PD** Ascot. To Egypt. **AD** Aboukir and reconditioned as JR6767. **14 Sqn** Palestine. **AD** Aboukir for overhaul 15.6.25. Heliopolis by 12.26 until @ 1.27. **208 Sqn** 1927 until @ 1928.

J6768 N/I

J6769 **PD** Ascot. To India. **AD** Drigh Road by 12.22. **AP** Lahore by 1.23. **28 Sqn** by 28.1.23 and wrecked 21.8.23 (spun in at Peshawar).

J6770 **PD** Ascot. To India. **AD** Drigh Road. **AP** Lahore. **28 Sqn** by 23.12.22. **AD** Drigh Road. 1923. **AP** Lahore by 14.1.24 and damaged 19.4.23 (force landed near Gunjan Wallah). **5 Sqn** as a/c *L* by 6.24 and wrecked 15.11.24 (o/t on landing, at Dardoni).

J6771 **PD** Ascot. To India. **AD** Drigh Road by 12.22. **AP** Lahore by 2.23 until @ 4.23. **5 Sqn** as a/c *T* 1924. **20 Sqn** damaged 11.3.25 (force landed at Idak, NWF). **AP** Lahore by 3.25. **20 Sqn** by 6.27. **31 Sqn**.

J6772 **PD** Ascot. To India. **AD** Drigh Road. **AP** Lahore by 27.2.24. **5 Sqn** by 11.3.24 until @ 8.24.

J6773 **Aden Flt**, crashed and deleted.

J6774 **PD** Ascot. To India. **AD** Drigh Road 1923. **20 Sqn** by 8.23 until @ 6.24. **31 Sqn** by 3.25. **5 Sqn** as a/c *W* 1925. **AD** Drigh Road 1926. **5 Sqn** as a/c *C* by 1927 until @ 1928. **20 Sqn** as a/c *C* by 1930 until 1931. **20 Sqn** by 8.31 until @ 9.31.

J6775 **RAF Staff College Flt** Andover by 5.24. **IAAD** Henlow by 2.25 until @ 7.25. B&C for reconditioning to J Type (s/n 6974) and ready by 16.7.26. **HAD** Henlow by 4.27. Shipped China (For **2 Sqn** Shanghai?). **2 Sqn** Manston by 2.28 and wrecked 27.3.28 (dived in near Woldingham, Surrey, from 1,000ft in bad weather).

J6776 **RAE** Farnborough by 3.22 until @ 5.24. Cricklewood 9.25. B&C for reconditioning to J Type (s/n 7241) and ready by 7.7.28. **PD** Ascot. To Egypt. **AD** Aboukir. **208 Sqn** by 6.29. To India. **31 Sqn**.

J6777 **PD** Ascot. To India. **AD** Drigh Road. **AP** Lahore by 2.23. **5 Sqn** by 9.24 until @ 6.25.

J6778 **PD** Ascot. To India. **AD** Drigh Road. **AP** Lahore. **28 Sqn** 23.12.22.

J6779 **PD** Ascot. To India. **AD** Drigh Road. **28 Sqn** as a/c *D* by 12.22 and wrecked 16.3.23 (crashed near Dardoni after strut hit by vulture).

J6780 **PD** Ascot. To India. **AD** Drigh Road. **AP** Lahore by 11.22. **28 Sqn** as a/c *F* by 5.12.22 until @ 1.23. **AP** Lahore by 2.24.

J6781 **PD** Ascot. To India. **AD** Drigh Road. **28 Sqn** as a/c *C* by 12.22 until @ 3.23. **AD** Drigh Road by 5.23. New **Wing HQ Quetta** as a/c *B* by 6.24. **6 Sqn** by 9.24 until @ 10.24. **20 Sqn** as a/c *B* by 11.24 until @ 2.25. **31 Sqn** NW Frontier. **Quetta SF** by 5.28.

J6782 **PD** Ascot. To India. **AD** Drigh Road. **28 Sqn** as a/c *H* by 11.22 until @ 2.23. **AD** Drigh Road 1923. **31 Sqn** as a/c *C* by 7.23. **20 Sqn** by 18.3.24 until @ 7.24. To new **Wing HQ Quetta** as a/c *C* by 6.24. **5 Sqn** as a/c *O* by 12.24. **AP** Lahore by 11.1.26. **28 Sqn** as a/c *O* by 5.26. **20 Sqn** as a/c *M* by 6.30 until @ 12.30. **SF Quetta**.

J6783 **PD** Ascot. To India. **AD** Drigh Road. **28 Sqn** by 12.22. **20 Sqn** by 6.24 until @ 10.24. **31 Sqn** as a/c *L*.

J6784 **4 Sqn** Farnborough by 11.23 and wrecked 9.4.24 (Plt Off C.W. Moss KIFA, spun in from 400ft after take off from Farnborough).

J6785 **PD** Ascot. To Egypt. **AD** Aboukir. **208 Sqn** by 12.24 until @ 3.25. **AD** Aboukir and reconditioned as JR6785. **208 Sqn** by 4.29 until @ 9.29. **6 Sqn** by 10.30 and wrecked 24.9.31 (crashed while landing at Heliopolis).

J6786 N/I

J6787 **School of Photography Flt** Kenley by 6.25 until @ 10.25. **4 Sqn** Farnborough by 9.26.

J6788 **4 Sqn** by 2.23 and wrecked 20.2.24 (collided with goal posts during forced landing at Farnborough after engine failure). Repaired. **PD** Ascot. To Egypt. **AD** Aboukir and reconditioned as JR6788. **208 Sqn** as single seater.

J6789 **PD** Ascot. To Egypt. **AD** Aboukir. **208 Sqn** by 11.23 until @ 9.24. **AD** Aboukir by 12.24 and there 1.26, reconditioned as JR6789. **208 Sqn** Ismailia.

J6790 **AEE** Martlesham Heath by 3.22 and wrecked 26.6.22 (drifted and stalled on landing at Martlesham). B&C (for repair?). **AEE** Martlesham Heath by 3.23. **RAE** Farnborough by 28.1.24. **A&AEE** Martlesham Heath by 5.2.24 until @ 16.3.25. B&C for reconditioning to J Type DC (s/n 6879) and ready by 21.12.25. **5 FTS** Sealand by 1.30. B&C for reconditioning to Mk.III (s/n 7576) and ready by 27.3.31, at Andover for storage. To Civilian Register as *G-ACCG* by 24.3.33, registered to Universal Aircraft Services Ltd, sold to M.N. Mavrogordato 10.33 and survived until 1937.

J6791 B&C for reconditioning to J Type DC (s/n 6870) and ready by 2.12.25. **RAF (Cadet) College** Cranwell by 4.28 until @ 5.28.

J6792 **PD** Ascot. To India. **AD** Drigh Road. **28 Sqn** by 12.22 until @ 6.23. **20 Sqn** as a/c *A* by 11.24 and wrecked 15.4.25 (crashed and o/t). **AD** Drigh Road. **20 Sqn** as a/c *E* by 6.27.

J6793 **4 Sqn** Farnborough by 1.23. **3 Group HQ** Spittlegate by 7.25. B&C for reconditioning to J Type DC (s/n 6900) and ready by 4.2.26. **1 FTS** Netheravon by 10.26.

J6794 To Egypt. **208 Sqn** Ismailia. To India. **AD** Drigh Road. **28 Sqn** by 12.22. **20 Sqn** by 7.24. Returned to UK. **2 Sqn** Manston as a/c *G* by 1928 and wrecked 19.7.29 (crashed at Tilshead, Wilts).

J6795 **PD** Ascot. To India. **AD** Drigh Road. **AP** Lahore by 1.23 until @ 4.23. **31 Sqn** by 10.24 until @ 1.25. **28 Sqn** as a/c *B*.

J6796 To India. **AP** Lahore by 11.22. **28 Sqn** by 8.12.22. **AP** Lahore by 1.23. **AD** Drigh Road 1923. **31 Sqn** by 6.23 until @ 1.24. **20 Sqn** by 9.24 and wrecked 5.12.24 (tyre burst on take off and undercarriage collapsed on landing at Pad Idan).

J6797 Grain. **RAE** Farnborough by 19.4.23. **A&AEE** Martlesham Heath by 2.25.

J6798 **PD** Ascot. To Egypt. **AD** Aboukir. **14 Sqn** by 21.1.24 until @ 1.25. Returned to UK. B&C for reconditioning to J Type (s/n 6948) and ready by 18.6.26. **PD** Ascot. To Egypt. **AD** Aboukir. **208 Sqn** 1928. **AD** Aboukir and reconditioned as JR6798. **6 Sqn** and wrecked 5.12.30 (crashed after striking incinerator chimney on take off from Ramleh).

J6799 **PD** Ascot. To India. **AD** Drigh Road. **28 Sqn** by 2.23 and wrecked 31.3.24 (side-slipped in at Nowshera).

J6800 **AEE** Martlesham Heath by 2.1.22 (for long range trials). **24 Sqn** Kenley by 20.2.22 until @ 3.24. B&C for reconditioning to J Type (s/n 6656) and ready by 14.3.25. **13 Sqn** Andover.

84 BRISTOL FIGHTER Mk II from Bristol Aeroplane Co Ltd and numbered J7616 to J7699. To Specification 3/25 (275hp Falcon III). [Consecutive works' sequence nos. 6721 to 6804]. Reconditioned and converted 1925.

J7616 Taken on RAF charge 20.5.25. **B&C** for reconditioning to Mk.III (s/n 7100). Retaken onto RAF charge 22.6.27. **SAC** Old Sarum by 5.28. **B&C** for reconditioning to Mk.IV (s/n 7420). Retaken onto RAF charge 8.4.29. **16 Sqn** Old Sarum damaged 13.2.30 (force landed in fog and ran into a ditch) repaired and on unit charge until @ 9.30.

J7617 Taken on RAF charge 22.5.25. **E&WS** Worthy Down by 9.25. **RAF (Cadet) College** Cranwell by 6.28.

J7618 Taken on RAF charge 23.5.25. **SAC** Old Sarum by 9.25 until @ 9.26. **4 Sqn** Farnborough until @ 1.27. **B&C** for reconditioning to J Type DC. Retaken onto RAF charge 7.27.

J7619 Taken on RAF charge 21.5.25; **16 Sqn/SAC** Old Sarum by 9.25 until @ 3.26. **4 Sqn** Farnborough as a/c *A3* by 4.26 until @ 7.27.

J7620 Taken on RAF charge 25.5.25. **B&C** for reconditioning to J Type (s/n 6986). Retaken onto RAF charge 16.8.26. **HAD** Henlow by 7.27.

F.2B J7620 'B' at an unknown location. Taken on RAF charge on 25 May 1925, it was subsequently reconditioned to J Type and then re-taken on to RAF charge on 16 August 1926. It was at Home Aircraft Depot, Henlow by July 1927. *(Philip Jarrett)*

J7621 Taken on RAF charge 29.5.25. **B&C** for reconditioning to Mk.III (s/n 7096). Retaken onto RAF charge 2.6.27. **B&C** for reconditioning to Mk.IV (s/n 7256). Retaken onto RAF charge 22.9.28. **AGS** Eastchurch and wrecked 4.4.29 (the machine ran away while unattended with engine running).

Bristol F.2B J7621 'C4'. After being reconditioned to Mk.IV standard in 1928 it went to the Armament and Gunnery School at Eastchurch, but was wrecked on 4 April 1929 when it was left unattended with the engine running, and ran away. *(Philip Jarrett)*

J7622 Taken on RAF charge 27.5.25. **PD** Ascot. To Iraq. **AD** Hinaidi. **30 Sqn** and wrecked 19.12.27 (struck by D.H.9A E8513 on take off).

J7623 Taken on RAF charge 26.5.25. **PD** Ascot. To Egypt. **AD** Aboukir. **6 Sqn** by 3.30, damaged 1.10.31 (force landed SW of Shaikh Zowaid after engine failure), repaired and returned to Ramleh 4.10.31.

J7624 Taken on RAF charge 29.5.25.

J7625 Taken on RAF charge 26.5.25. **AGS** Eastchurch by 9.27 until 3.28.

J7626 Taken on RAF charge 29.5.25. **AGS** Eastchurch by 12.27 until 6.28.

F.2B J7626 of the Armament and Gunnery School at Eastchurch in 1927, with a camera gun on the upper wing centre-section. *(RAF Museum)*

J7627 Taken on RAF charge 29.5.25. **AGS** Eastchurch by 12.27 until 5.28. **HAD** Henlow by 4.29 until @ 5.29. **AGS** Eastchurch by 9.29 until 12.29.

J7628 Taken on RAF charge 29.5.25. **AGS** Eastchurch by 12.26 until 6.28.

J7629 Taken on RAF charge 9.6.25. **E&WS** Worthy Down by 8.27 until @ 7.28.

J7630 Taken on RAF charge 8.6.25. **E&WS** Worthy Down by 10.27 until @ 6.28.

J7631 Taken on RAF charge 5.6.25.

J7632 Taken on RAF charge 3.6.25.

J7633 Taken on RAF charge 8.6.25. **E&WS** Worthy Down by 9.27 until @ 10.27.

J7634 Taken on RAF charge 4.6.25. **SAC** Old Sarum 1925. **4 Sqn** Farnborough by 8.26.

J7635 Taken on RAF charge 8.6.25. **RAE** Farnborough by 4.6.26 until @ 1.28.

J7636 Taken on RAF charge 9.6.25. **4 Sqn** Farnborough by 8.26. **B&C** for reconditioning to Mk.III (s/n 7109). Retaken onto RAF charge 11.7.27. **B&C** and converted to Mk.III DC. Retaken onto RAF charge 13.8.29. **OUAS** Upper Heyford as a/c *Y* by 4.30. Hawkinge, in storage, 23.2.32 (obsolete). Remains at Abridge, Essex 23.4.35.

J7637 Taken on RAF charge 10.6.25. **13 Sqn** Andover by 12.26 until @ 9.27.

J7638 Taken on RAF charge 11.6.25. **B&C** for reconditioning to J Type (s/n 7237). Retaken onto RAF charge 29.6.28. **PD** Ascot. To Iraq. **AD** Hinaidi. **6 Sqn** and wrecked 7.6.29 (Fg Off F. Townsend/Sgt Gunn both OK, engine failed on take off and stalled turning back).

J7639 Taken on RAF charge 11.6.25.

J7640 Taken on RAF charge 12.6.25. **4 Sqn** Farnborough by 3.27. **B&C** for reconditioning to J Type (s/n 7240). Retaken onto RAF charge 6.7.28. **PD** Ascot. To Egypt. **AD** Aboukir. **208 Sqn** by 12.28 until @ 2.29.

J7641 Taken on RAF charge 12.6.25.

J7642 Taken on RAF charge 29.8.25. **RAE** Farnborough by 2.2.26 until @ 12.26. **B&C** 27.4.27. **HAD** Henlow by 6.27. **2 Sqn** Manston by 12.27. **HAD** Henlow by 7.28. **2 Sqn** Manston by 12.28 until @ 10.29.

J7643 Taken on RAF charge 13.6.25. **A&AEE** Martlesham Heath 1926. **RAE** Farnborough by 15.11.26. **A&AEE/15 Sqn** Martlesham Heath by 21.3.27 until @ 10.28 (armament trials and detached to Eastchurch 2.9.27).

J7644 Taken on RAF charge 13.6.25. **PD** Ascot. To India. **AD** Drigh Road. **AP** Lahore by 2.29 until @ 3.29. **20 Sqn** by 11.30 until @ 3.4.31.

J7645 Taken on RAF charge 16.6.25. **PD** Ascot. To India. **AD** Drigh Road. **AP** Lahore by 3.29.

J7646 Taken on RAF charge 22.6.25.

J7647 Taken on RAF charge 16.6.25. **13 Sqn** Andover. **PD** Ascot. To Iraq. **AD** Hinaidi. **6 Sqn** and wrecked 25.4.28 (swung and crashed when taxiing to take off). Deleted 11.5.28.

J7648 Taken on RAF charge 17.6.25. **PD** Ascot. To India. **AD** Drigh Road. **AP** Lahore 1930 and in propellor accident 21.11.30. **CF Delhi** by 11.30 until @ 2.31.

J7649 Taken on RAF charge 20.6.25. **HAD** Henlow by 9.27. **16 Sqn/SAC** Old Sarum by 12.27 until @ 2.28. Crashed deleted (2.29?).

J7650 Taken on RAF charge 22.6.25. **13 Sqn** Andover by 9.27 until @ 11.27. **E&WS** Worthy Down by 12.27 until @ 2.28.

J7651 Taken on RAF charge 22.6.25. **2 Sqn** Manston by 7.6.27 until @ 7.27. Wrecked and deleted 2.4.28 (hit a tree in low strafing exercise and crashed, near Colchester, Essex).

J7652 Taken on RAF charge 22.6.25. Shipped to China. **2 Sqn** Shanghai by 7.6.27, force landed on racecourse at Shanghai 15.8.27, returned to UK and on unit charge until @ 3.29. B&C for reconditioning to Mk.III DC and ready by 21.1.30. Retaken onto RAF charge 10.2.30.

J7653 Taken on RAF charge 23.6.25. **HAD** Henlow by 5.29 until @ 11.29. **16 Sqn/SAC** Old Sarum by 1.30 until @ 4.30.

J7654 Taken on RAF charge 23.6.25. **4 Sqn** Farnborough 1926.

J7655 Taken on RAF charge 24.6.25.

J7656 Taken on RAF charge 25.6.25. **2 Sqn** Manston by 2.26. B&C for reconditioning to Mk.III (s/n 7164). Retaken onto RAF charge 5.3.28. **School of Photography Flt** Kenley by 6.28 until @ 7.28.

J7657 Taken on RAF charge 25.6.25. **2 Sqn** Manston by 1.26. B&C for reconditioning to J Type (s/n 7108). Retaken onto RAF charge 8.7.27. B&C for reconditioning to Mk.III (s/n 7422). Retaken onto RAF charge 16.4.29. B&C for repair. Retaken onto RAF charge 6.6.30.

J7658 Taken on RAF charge 25.6.25. **4 Sqn** Farnborough and damaged 27.10.25 (caught fire in the air and crash landed). B&C for reconditioning to J Type (s/n 6951). Retaken onto RAF charge 25.6.26. **4 Sqn** Farnborough by 3.27 until @ 7.27.

J7659 Taken on RAF charge 2.7.25. **2 Sqn** Manston by 12.25. **4 Sqn** Farnborough by 8.26. B&C for reconditioning to Mk.III DC (s/n 7150). **SAC** Old Sarum dd 14.6.28 and wrecked 23.5.29 (engine failed after take off and force landed in a field near Old Sarum).

J7660 Taken on RAF charge 27.6.25. **13 Sqn** Andover. B&C for reconditioning to J Type (s/n 7161). Retaken onto RAF charge 2.3.28. **4 Sqn** Farnborough by 6.28 until @ 6.29.

Having initially served with 13 Sqn at Andover, after being reconditoned to J Type J7660 went to 4 Sqn at Farnborough as 'C2' in the late 1920s.
(RAF Gutersloh)

J7661 Taken on RAF charge 30.6.25. **4 Sqn** Farnborough and damaged 17.12.25 (mid-air collision with Avro 504K H2150 during aerobatics). Repaired. **4 Sqn** Farnborough and in starting accident 5.6.29.

J7662 Taken on RAF charge 1.7.25. **16 Sqn/SAC** Old Sarum by 12.25 and wrecked 21.4.26 (crashed on landing at Old Sarum).

J7663 Taken on RAF charge 1.7.25. **16 Sqn/SAC** Old Sarum and wrecked 4.6.26 (hit hillock and o/t on take off from Tilshead LG, Wilts).

J7664 Taken on RAF charge 3.7.25. Shipped China. **2 Sqn** by 6.27 and wrecked 22.7.27, crashed on landing at Shanghai).

J7665 Taken on RAF charge 3.7.25. Shipped to China. **2 Sqn** Shanghai by 7.6.27 until @ 8.27. Returned to UK. **HAD** Henlow by 5.29.

J7666 Taken on RAF charge 10.7.25. **2 Sqn** Manston and wrecked 13.4.28 (Fg Off H.J.J. Mumford-Mathews/Lt D.F.C. Scott, 1st Essex Regt, both KIFA, mid-air collision with Vickers Virginia J8239 of **9 Sqn**).

J7667 Taken on RAF charge 6.7.25. **2 Sqn** Manston 1925.

J7668 Taken on RAF charge 14.7.25. **13 Sqn** Andover by 9.28 until @ 1.29. **SAC** Old Sarum by 3.29 until @ 6.29.

J7669 Taken on RAF charge 7.7.25. **13 Sqn** Andover.

J7670 Taken on RAF charge 7.7.25. B&C for reconditioning to Mk.III (s/n 7149). Retaken onto RAF charge 19.5.28. **School of Photography Flt** Kenley by 6.28 until @ 12.30.

J7671 Taken on RAF charge 9.7.25. **SAC** Old Sarum, **13 Sqn** Andover and wrecked 18.7.27 (Plt Off W.H. Shorter/AC1 L. Rogers both KIFA, engine caught fire and a/c dived into road at Camberley, Surrey).

J7672 Taken on RAF charge 9.7.25. **School of Photography Flt** Kenley by 3.28 until @ 6.28. **HAD** Henlow by 10.28.

J7673 Taken on RAF charge 9.7.25. **HAD** Henlow by 9.28 until @ 3.29. **2 Sqn** Manston by 9.29.

J7674 Taken on RAF charge 15.7.25.

J7675 Taken on RAF charge 17.7.25. **16 Sqn/SAC** Old Sarum by 3.27.

J7676 Taken on RAF charge 22.7.25. **PD** Ascot. To Iraq. **AD** Hinaidi. **6 Sqn** 1925.

J7677 Taken on RAF charge 13.8.25. **PD** Ascot. To India. **AD** Drigh Road. **5 Sqn** by 4.26 until @ 1.27. **28 Sqn** 1927. **1 (India) Wing HQ** by 1.28. **20 Sqn** by 4.30 until @ 7.30. **60 Sqn** and wrecked at Bangalore.

J7678 Taken on RAF charge 16.7.25.

J7679 Taken on RAF charge 18.7.25.

J7680 Taken on RAF charge 15.8.25. **PD** Ascot. To India. **AD** Drigh Road. **20 Sqn** NWF. **31 Sqn** and wrecked 9.6.28 (while stationary, hit at night by J7681). Repaired. **Staff College** Quetta by 5.31.

J7681 Taken on RAF charge 22.7.25. **PD** Ascot. To India. **AD** Drigh Road. **20 Sqn** by 8.26 until @ 4.27. **31 Sqn** and wrecked 9.6.28 (overshot flare path and collided with stationary J7680). **28 Sqn** and in starting accident 18.9.29.

J7682 Taken on RAF charge 24.7.25. **PD** Ascot. To India. **AD** Drigh Road. **20 Sqn** as a/c *C* and wrecked 31.5.26.

J7683 Taken on RAF charge 28.7.25. **PD** Ascot. To India. **AD** Drigh Road. **31 Sqn** as a/c *L* by 12.25 until @ 4.26.

J7684 Taken on RAF charge 28.7.25. **PD** Ascot. To India. **AD** Drigh Road. **20 Sqn** by 2.26 until 2.27. **20 Sqn** (as DC?) in starting accident 17.7.29 and on unit charge until @ 12.31.

J7685 Taken on RAF charge 31.7.25. B&C for reconditioning to J Type (s/n 6978). Retaken onto RAF charge 23.7.26. **HAD** Henlow by 4.27. Shipped China (for **2 Sqn** Shanghai?). **2 Sqn** Manston by 3.28 until @ 6.28. **4 Sqn** Farnborough.

J7686 Taken on RAF charge 31.7.25. **2 Sqn** Manston by 8.25 until @ 11.25. B&C for reconditioning to Mk.III (s/n 7098). Retaken onto RAF charge 22.6.27. Shipped China. **2 Sqn** Shanghai. **4 Sqn**. Returned to UK. B&C for reconditioning to Mk.IV DC (s/n 7419). Retaken onto RAF charge 6.4.29. **16 Sqn/SAC** Old Sarum as a/c *11* by 30.4.29 until @ 9.30.

J7687 Taken on RAF charge 13.8.25. **SAC** Old Sarum by 9.25. **4 Sqn** Farnborough by 4.26 until @ 8.26. **16 Sqn/SAC** Old Sarum by 8.28 unti @ 4.30.

J7688 Taken on RAF charge 17.8.25. **4 Sqn** Farnborough by 11.25 until @ 3.27.

J7689 Taken on RAF charge 18.8.25. **13 Sqn** Andover 1925 until @ 1926. B&C for reconditioning to Mk.III (s/n 7107). Retaken onto RAF charge 7.7.27. **SAC** Old Sarum by 8.28. B&C for reconditioning to Mk.III DC (s/n 7429). Retaken onto RAF charge 8.6.29. **CUAS** Duxford by 7.29. **RAF College** Cranwell by 9.29 until @ 3.30.

J7690 Taken on RAF charge 20.8.25. **13 Sqn** Andover 1925 until @ 1926. B&C for reconditioning to J Type (s/n 7165). Retaken onto RAF charge 7.3.28. **13 Sqn** Andover by 9.28. **SAC** Old Sarum by 2.29 until @ 5.30.

J7691 Taken on RAF charge 20.8.25. **16 Sqn**, Old Sarum.

J7692 Taken on RAF charge 21.8.25. **16 Sqn/SAC** Old Sarum by 7.27 until @ 9.27. B&C for reconditioning to Mk.III DC and ready by 8.1.30. **Andover CF** dd 31.3.30 and on unit charge until @ 3.31.

J7693 Taken on RAF charge 22.8.25. **AGS** Eastchurch by 12.29.

J7694 Taken on RAF charge 27.8.25. **AGS** Eastchurch by 12.25 and wrecked 4.27 (crashed on night flying from Eastchurch).

J7695 Taken on RAF charge 31.8.25.

J7696 Taken on RAF charge 29.8.25. B&C for reconditioning to Mk.III DC and ready by 24.1.30. **E&WS** Worthy Down by 9.30 until @ 10.30.

J7697 Taken on RAF charge 31.8.25. **16 Sqn/SAC** Old Sarum by 9.26 until @ 9.27.

J7698 Taken on RAF charge 31.8.25.

J7699 Taken on RAF charge 2.9.25. **2 Sqn** Manston by 4.26 until @ 6.28.

50 BRISTOL FIGHTER Mk.III ordered 9.26 from Bristol Aeroplane Co Ltd to Contract No 709172/26 and numbered J8242 to J8291. [Consecutive works' sequence nos.7040 to 7089]. Constructed to Specification 8126 (275hp Falcon III).

J8242 Delivered engineless to storage 16.10.26. **A&AEE (15 Sqn)** Martlesham Heath by 3.28 until @ 12.30.

J8243 Delivered engineless to storage 16.10.26. B&C for conversion to DC and tested 20.8.29. **RAF College** Cranwell by 10.29 until @ 2.31.

J8244   Delivered engineless and to storage 16.10.26. B&C for reconditioning to Mk.IV (s/n 7419). Retaken onto RAF charge 22.11.28. Andover for storage. **PD** Sealand. To Egypt. **AD** Aboukir **6 Sqn** by 4.31. **AD** Aboukir by 6.31 until 7.31. **6 Sqn** 7.31.

J8245   Delivered engineless and to storage 16.10.26. Worthy Down by 10.27. **2 Sqn** Manston. B&C for reconditioning to DC (s/n 7435), ready by 21.6.29 and tested 19.7.29. **Andover CF** by 1.8.30 until @ 2.32. To Civilian Register as *G-ABZG* 9.8.33, registered to Commercial Airways (Essex) Ltd. Scrapped 5.38.

J8246   Delivered engineless and to storage 26.10.26. B&C for reconditioning to Mk.IV (s/n 7313). **4 Sqn** Farnborough dd 10.12.28. B&C for reconditioning to Mk.III. Retaken onto RAF charge 5.12.29.

J8247   Delivered engineless and to storage 27.10.26. B&C for reconditioning to Mk.IV (s/n 7321). Retaken onto RAF charge 22.12.28 for storage at Andover. **PD** Sealand. To Egypt. **AD** Aboukir. **208 Sqn** by 7.29. **6 Sqn** by 12.30 until @ 7.31.

J8248   Delivered engineless and to storage 29.10.26. **SAC** Old Sarum by 8.28. B&C for reconditioning to Mk.IV (s/n 7320). Retaken onto RAF charge 3.12.28 for storage at Andover. B&C for reconditioning to Mk.III. Retaken onto RAF charge 16.12.29. **16 Sqn** Old Sarum by 6.30.

J8249   Delivered engineless and to storage 29.10.26. B&C for reconditioning to Mk.IV (s/n 7302). **24 Sqn** Kenley dd 23.10.28. **OUAS** Upper Heyford by 7.31 until @ 8.31.

J8250   Delivered engineless and to storage 29.10.26. **1 FTS** Netheravon. B&C for reconditioning to Mk.IV DC. **OUAS** as a/c *X* dd 28.8.29 and on unit charge until @ 7.31.

J8251   Ready by 7.10.26. **A&AEE** Martlesham Heath dd 25.10.26. **RAE** Farnborough by 27.4.28 until @ 1.33.

J8252   Delivered engineless and to storage 5.11.26. **A&AEE** Martlesham Heath by 7.27. **2 Sqn** Manston by 12.27. B&C for reconditioning to Mk.IV (s/n 7305). Retaken onto RAF charge 24.10.28 for storage at Andover. **2 Sqn** Manston by 10.29 until @ 12.29. **16 Sqn** Old Sarum by 5.30 and wrecked 20.1.31 (undercarriage collapsed on landing at Old Sarum and crashed on nose).

J8253   Delivered engineless and to storage 6.11.26. **2 Sqn** Manston by 12.27. B&C for reconditioning to Mk.IV (s/n 7421). **RAF College** Cranwell dd 10.4.29 and on charge until @ 7.29. **2 Sqn** Manston by 8.29 until @ 12.30.

After being reconditioned to Mk.IV standard, J8253 went to the RAF College at Cranwell on 10 April 1929, but in August it was transferred to 2 Sqn. *(Philip Jarrett)*

J8254   Delivered engineless and to storage 8.11.26. B&C for reconditioning to DC. Retaken onto RAF charge 27.8.29. **2 FTS** Digby by 12.30 until @ 9.31.

J8255   Delivered engineless and to storage 9.11.26. **2 Sqn** Manston by 12.27. B&C for reconditioning to Mk.IV (s/n 7424). Retaken onto RAF charge 18.4.29. **2 Sqn** Manston by 12.29 until @ 1.30. **North Coates Fitties SF** by 6.30.

J8256   Delivered engineless and to storage 11.11.26. B&C for reconditioning to DC. **12 Sqn** Andover dd 31.8.29 and on charge until 1.30. **Andover CF** 1.30 until @ 3.31.

J8257   Delivered engineless and to storage 13.11.26. B&C for reconditioning to DC. Retaken onto RAF charge 12.8.29. **SAC** Old Sarum by 3.9.29. **Andover CF** by 9.29 until @ 1.30. Reconditioned to Mk.IV DC. **OUAS** Upper Heyford as a/c *Z* by 9.31 until @ 1932.

J8258   Delivered engineless and to storage 17.11.26. B&C for reconditioning to Mk.IV (s/n 7303). **24 Sqn** Kenley dd 23.10.28. To Civilian Register 1.7.32 as *G-ABXA* registered to Mrs V. Bruce, to Inca Aviation Ltd 11.33 and withdrawn from use 11.34.

F.2B Mk.IV DC J8257 of the Oxford University Air Squadron at Upper Heyford flying over the Thames Estuary, probably during a Summer Camp at Manston in August 1930. *(via Philip Jarrett)*

J8259   Delivered engineless and to storage 18.11.26. B&C for reconditioning to DC (s/n 7433). **RAF College** Cranwell dd 22.6.29 and on charge until @ 3.31.

J8260   Delivered engineless and to storage 22.11.26. B&C for reconditioning to Mk.IV (s/n 7425). Retaken onto RAF charge 23.4.29. **SAC** Old Sarum by 28.5.29. **RAE** Farnborough by 16.6.31. Catfoss by 17.6.31.

J8261   Delivered engineless and to storage 24.11.26. B&C for reconditioning to DC. Retaken onto RAF charge 23.8.29. **RAF College** Cranwell by 4.30 until @ 11.30.

J8262   Taken on RAF charge 6.11.26. B&C for reconditioning to Mk.IV (s/n 7264). **24 Sqn** dd 10.10.28. **Andover CF** by 2.29 until @ 6.29.

J8263   Taken on RAF charge 6.11.26. **RAE** Farnborough with modified rudder. B&C 8.3.27 with wings set back 3 in for spinning tests. Handley Page Ltd 3.10.27 for leading edge slot tests. B&C. **RAE** Farnborough by 8.2.28. **A&AEE** Martlesham Heath by 24.4.28 until @ 10.31.

J8264   Taken on RAF charge 10.11.26. **4 Sqn** Farnborough. **RAE** Farnborough by 5.9.27 until @ 12.28.

J8265   Taken on RAF charge 12.11.26. **2 Sqn** Manston. B&C for reconditioning to Mk.IV (s/n 7250). **24 Sqn** dd 10.9.28 and on unit charge until @ 10.30.

J8266   Taken on RAF charge 12.11.26. **4 Sqn** Farnborough.

J8267   Taken on RAF charge 18.11.26. **4 Sqn** Farnborough by 11.1.28. B&C for reconditioning to Mk.IV (s/n 7253). **2 Sqn** Manston dd 15.9.28. **Andover CF** by 12.29.

J8268   Taken on RAF charge 19.11.26.

J8269   Taken on RAF charge 22.11.26. **2 Sqn** Manston by 12.27. B&C for reconditioning to Mk.IV (s/n 7251). **2 Sqn** reissued 14.9.28 and on unit charge until @ 8.29.

J8270   Taken on RAF charge 22.11.26. B&C for reconditioning to Mk.IV (s/n 7254). **2 Sqn** Manston dd 19.9.28. **School of Photography Flt** Kenley by 3.30 until @ 5.30.

J8271   Retaken onto RAF charge 25.11.26. **16 Sqn/SAC** Old Sarum by 3.27 until @ 1.28. B&C for reconditioning to Mk.IV (s/n 7260). **4 Sqn** Farnborough dd 6.10.28 and on unit charge until @ 4.29. **SAC** Old Sarum by 12.29 until @ 2.30.

J8272   Retaken onto RAF charge 25.11.26. **16 Sqn/SAC** Old Sarum by 1.28. **4 Sqn** Farnborough. B&C for reconditioning to Mk.IV (s/n 7252). **AGS** Eastchurch dd 15.9.28 and on unit charge until @ 10.30.

J8273   Delivered engineless and to storage 2.12.26. B&C for reconditioning to Mk.IV (s/n 7304). **24 Sqn** Kenley dd 23.10.28 and on unit charge until @ 8.30. **4 Sqn** Farnborough by 18.3.31. **North Coates Fitties CF** by 1.4.31.

J8274   Delivered engineless and to storage 2.12.26. **4 Sqn** Farnborough. B&C for reconditioning to Mk.IV (s/n 7315). Retaken onto RAF charge 14.12.28. Andover for storage. **PD** Ascot. To Egypt. **AD** Aboukir. **208 Sqn** Ismailia. **6 Sqn** and wrecked 24.2.31 (force landed at Abu Zabul, Egypt, and burnt).

J8275   Delivered engineless and to storage 6.12.26. **4 Sqn** Farnborough. B&C for reconditioning to Mk.IV (s/n 7312). **4 Sqn** Farnborough dd 10.12.28 and on unit charge until @ 8.29. **School of Photography Flt** Kenley by 3.30 until @ 5.30. **RAF College** Cranwell 1931.

J8276   Delivered engineless and to storage 6.12.26. B&C for reconditioning to Mk.IV (s/n 7318). Retaken onto RAF charge

3.12.28. Andover for storage. **4 Sqn** Farnborough and in starting accident 23.8.29. **16 Sqn** Old Sarum by 7.30.

J8277 Delivered engineless and to storage 8.12.26. B&C for reconditioning to Mk.IV (s/n 7426). Retaken onto RAF charge 30.4.29. Andover for storage. **PD** Ascot. To Egypt. **AD** Aboukir. **6 Sqn** by 8.30 until @ 7.31.

J8278 Delivered engineless and to storage 10.12.26. B&C for reconditioning to DC. **2 FTS** Digby dd 22.8.29 and on unit charge until @ 8.31.

J8279 Delivered engineless and to storage 13.12.26. B&C for reconditioning to Mk.IV (s/n 7310). Retaken onto RAF charge 25.10.28. Andover for storage. **AGS** Eastchurch by 7.29 and wrecked 9.9.30 (dived in when recovering from spin, near Leysdown, Isle of Sheppey).

J8280 Delivered engineless and to storage 13.12.26. B&C for reconditioning to Mk.IV (s/n 7309). Retaken onto RAF charge 24.10.28. Andover for storage. To Iraq. **6 Sqn** by 1.31.

J8281 Delivered engineless and to storage 15.12.26. B&C for reconditioning to Mk.IV (s/n 7307). Retaken onto RAF charge 24.10.28. Andover for storage. **PD** Ascot. To Egypt. **AD** Aboukir. **6 Sqn** by 12.30 until @ 7.31.

J8282 Delivered engineless and to storage 15.12.26. B&C for reconditioning to DC (s/n 7432). Retaken onto RAF charge 27.6.29. **5 FTS** Sealand as a/c **4** by 10.29 until @ 7.31.

J8283 Delivered engineless and to storage 15.12.26. B&C for reconditioning to Mk.IV (s/n 7314). Retaken onto RAF charge 10.12.28. Andover for storage.

J8284 Delivered engineless and to storage 20.12.26. B&C for reconditioning to Mk.IV (s/n 7316). Retaken onto RAF charge 14.12.28. Andover for storage. **PD** Ascot. To Egypt. **AD** Aboukir. **6 Sqn** by 23.3.30 and wrecked 11.2.31 (crashed after hitting bush on take off at Ain Hosb LG and burnt in situ).

J8285 Delivered engineless and to storage 20.12.26. B&C for reconditioning to DC. Retaken onto RAF charge 17.6.29. B&C and tested 1.7.29. To Iraq. **6 Sqn**. To Civilian Register as *G-ACFK*, registered to Commercial Airways (Essex). Sold for scrap 5.36.

J8286 Delivered engineless and to storage 20.12.26. B&C for reconditioning to Mk.IV (s/n 7301). Retaken onto RAF charge 18.10.28. **DTD** Bristol. B&C and tested 7.11.28. **CUAS** Duxford by 5.29 until @ 3.30.

J8287 Delivered engineless and to storage 22.12.26. B&C for reconditioning to Mk.IV (s/n 7308). Retaken onto RAF charge 24.10.28. Andover for storage. **AGS** Eastchurch by 12.28 until @ 7.31.

J8288 Delivered engineless and to storage 22.12.26. B&C for reconditioning to Mk.IV (s/n 7423) and ready by 17.4.29. **RAF College** Cranwell dd 16.5.29. **16 Sqn/SAC** Old Sarum by 1.30 until @ 2.30.

J8289 Delivered engineless and to storage 23.12.26. **Andover CF** by 7.29. B&C for reconditioning to Mk.IV (s/n 7306). Retaken onto RAF charge 24.10.28. Andover for storage. **Andover CF**. Handley Page, Radlett 14.6.30 until 6.31. **AGS** Eastchurch by 7.31. **RAE** Farnborough by 11.12.31.

J8290 Delivered engineless and to storage 23.12.26. B&C for reconditioning to Mk.IV (s/n 7428). Retaken onto RAF charge 7.5.29. **SAC** Old Sarum by 17.6.29. **4 Sqn** Farnborough by 8.29. **13 Sqn** Andover by 9.29.

J8291 Delivered engineless and to storage 23.12.26. B&C for reconditioning to Mk.IV (s/n 7317). Retaken onto RAF charge 14.12.28. Andover for storage. **16 Sqn** Old Sarum by 11.29 until @ 5.30.

30 BRISTOL FIGHTER Mk.III DC ordered from Bristol Aeroplane Co Ltd under Contract No 733811/26 to Specification 30/26 and numbered J8429 to J8458 [consecutive s/n 6988 to 7017]. (275hp Falcon III), [Type 96 per BR].

J8429 Taken on RAF charge 17.1.27. **5 FTS** Sealand by 10.28 until @ 1.30. B&C for reconditioning to Mk.IV DC (s/n 7573) and ready by 17.2.31. Andover dd for storage 13.3.31. To Civilian Register 17.12.32 as *G-ABYF*, registered to D.V. Ivins, Jersey, and to Airmedia Ltd 4.35. Scrapped at Redhill 1939.

J8430 Taken on RAF charge 24.1.27. **24 Sqn** Kenley by 6.27 until @ 10.29 (flown by HRH Prince of Wales 27.4.28-19.7.28.) **Andover CF** by 4.30. **HQ Fighting Area** Northolt 1930. **5 FTS** Sealand by 4.31.

J8431 Taken on RAF charge 26.1.27. **2 FTS** Digby by 10.28 until @ 1.29. B&C for reconditioning to Mk.IV and ready by 5.6.30. Retaken onto RAF charge 8.7.30. Scrapped at Wingletyne Yard, Hornchurch 4.33.

J8432 Taken on RAF charge 17.1.27. **HAD** Henlow by 2.29.

J8433 Taken on RAF charge 24.1.27. **5 FTS** Sealand by 5.28 until @ 5.29.

J8434 Taken on RAF charge 29.1.27. **CUAS** Duxford by 9.27, damaged at Farnborough 8.9.27 but returned to Duxford that day and on unit charge until @ 3.30. B&C for reconditioning to Mk.IV DC (s/n 7568) and ready by 18.11.30. Retaken onto RAF charge 5.12.30. **HAD** Henlow and in propellor accident there 26.3.31. **5 FTS** Sealand 1931 until 1932. To Civilian Register 27.8.33 as *G-ABYT*, registered to A.T. Wilson, to J.P.W. Topham 4.34 and scrapped 1935 after collision with barbed wire fence at Lympne.

J8435 Taken on RAF charge 17.1.27.

J8436 Taken on RAF charge 20.1.27.

J8437 Taken on RAF charge 20.1.27. **HAD** Henlow by 11.27 until @ 5.28. Woodford. **HAD** Henlow by 9.7.28 until @ 11.28. **2 FTS** Digby 1929. **HAD** Henlow by 31.5.29. B&C for reconditioning to Mk.IV DC (s/n 7571) and ready by 8.12.30. Retaken onto RAF charge 19.12.30. **2 FTS** Digby by 10.31 until @ 11.31. To Civilian Register 12.4.32 as *G-ACAC*, registered to W.L. Handley. Scrapped at Hooton 1.36.

J8438 Taken on RAF charge 26.1.27. **HAD** Henlow by 5.27 until @ 7.27. **CUAS** Duxford. **RAE** Farnborough by 29.8.27. **CUAS** Duxford by 14.9.27 until @ 11.27. B&C and tested 21.12.27. **CUAS** Duxford 1928. **RAE** Farnborough 26.3.28. **CUAS** Duxford by 10.4.28. **RAE** Farnbrough by 13.6.29. **CUAS** Duxford by 19.7.29 until @ 10.29.

J8439 Taken on RAF charge 28.1.27. **41 Sqn** Northolt by 9.28 until @ 6.30.

J8440 Taken on RAF charge 4.2.27. **Andover CF** by 23.9.27 until @ 7.29. B&C for reconditioning and ready by 26.5.30. Retaken onto RAF charge 28.6.30.

J8441 Taken on RAF charge 7.2.27. **2 FTS** Digby by 10.28 until @ 6.29.

J8442 Taken on RAF charge 10.2.27. **2 FTS** Digby by 4.29 until 1930. **5 FTS** Sealand and wrecked 4.5.31 (while landing at Sealand, the wheels struck upper plane of Armstrong Whitworth Siskin J9223).

J8443 Taken on RAF charge 11.2.27. **HCF** Henlow. **24 Sqn** Kenley by 12.4.28. **CUAS** Duxford by 6.30 until @ 7.30.

J8444 Taken on RAF charge 16.2.27. **HAD** Henlow by 6.28 until @ 5.30. B&C for reconditioning to Mk.IV DC (s/n 7579) and ready by 21.5.31. Andover dd for storage. To Civilian Register 14.10.32 as *G-ABYL*, registered to E.B.H. Wright. Scrapped 1933.

J8445 Taken on RAF charge 22.2.27. **5 FTS** Sealand by 4.29 until @ 7.31. Scrapped at Wingletyne Yard, Hornchurch 4.33.

J8446 Taken on RAF charge 22.2.27. **5 FTS** Sealand as a/c **4** by 12.28 until @ 2.30. B&C for reconditioning to Mk.IV DC (s/n 7574) and ready by 12.12.30. Andover dd for storage 22.12.30. **2 FTS** Digby by 7.31 until @ 10.31. To Civilian Register 14.10.32 as *G-ABYD*, registered to M. Cresswell. Scrapped 3.33.

J8447 Taken on RAF charge 22.2.27. **5 FTS** Sealand by 10.29 until @ 11.29.

J8448 Taken on RAF charge 26.2.27. **RAE** Farnborough 1927. **Andover CF** by 8.27 until @ 9.27. In starting accident at Netheravon 11.9.28 (**1 FTS**?). **2 FTS** Digby by 1.30 until @ 2.30. B&C for reconditioning to Mk.IV DC (s/n 7577) and tested 10.4.31. Retaken onto RAF charge 15.4.31. Andover for storage. To Civilian Register 9.10.34 as *G-ACPE* registered to A.F. Cawthorn, then to Mrs J. Dudley 7.35 and R.C. Kingshill 8.36. Scrapped 1.39.

J8449 Taken on RAF charge 1.3.27. **2 FTS** Digby by 1.29. **5 FTS** Sealand by 8.30 until @ 6.31.

After spending time at HAD Henlow, J8457, a Mk.III DC and the penultimate Bristol Fighter to be built, went to No.5 FTS at Sealand. It is seen here with a Handley Page Hinaidi bomber for company. *(Philip Jarrett)*

J8450 Taken on RAF charge 4.3.27. **2 FTS** 1929. B&C for repair. Retaken onto RAF charge 17.12.29. **2 FTS** by 5.30 until @ 5.32.

J8451 Taken on RAF charge 4.3.27. **HAD** Henlow by 2.29. **5 FTS** Sealand by 7.29.

J8452 Taken on RAF charge 5.3.27. **2 FTS** Digby by 6.29 until @ 9.31. Hamble by 31.7.34.

J8453 Taken on RAF charge 8.3.27. **24 Sqn** Kenley by 11.27. **CFS** Upavon by 10.28 until @ 2.29. **HAD** Henlow by 4.29. **CFS** Upavon by 10.29 until @ 11.29. **5 FTS** Sealand by 12.30.

J8454 Taken on RAF charge 9.3.27. **HAD** Henlow by 11.28 and wrecked 3.12.29, dived in inverted at Clifton, near Henlow (after becoming lost).

J8455 Taken on RAF charge 9.3.27. **HAD** Henlow by 11.28 until @ 11.29. B&C for reconditioning to Mk.IV DC (s/n 7580), ready by 29.5.31 and tested 25.6.31. Andover for storage. To Civilian Register 22.6.35 as *G-ADJR*, registered C.P.B. Ogilvie and to London Film Productions Ltd 8.35. Scrapped 1.38.

J8456 Taken on RAF charge 11.3.27. **HAD** Henlow by 11.28 until @ 3.29.

J8457 Taken on RAF charge 13.6.27. **HAD** Henlow by 11.28 until @ 5.29. **HAD** Henlow by 12.29. **5 FTS** Sealand 1930.

J8458 Delivered 27.6.27. **2 FTS** Digby wrecked 22.9.30 (stalled due to engine failure on take off near Rotherham, Yorks) and deleted as damaged beyond repair.

Unidentified

5.4.17   **48 Sqn**, Albatros D.III sent down OOC at 10:15 (Capt A. Wilkinson/Lt L.G. Allen).

8.4.17   **48 Sqn**, Albatros D.III sent down OOC over Remy, shared with 2nd Lt G.N. Brockhurst/2nd Lt C.B. Boughton (2nd Lt A.G. Riley/2nd Lt L.G. Hall).

11.5.17   **48 Sqn**, two Albatros D.III destroyed, shared with A3318, A3323 & A3338 (2nd Lt A.G. Riley/2nd Lt L.G. Hall).

2.6.17   **48 Sqn**, OP, shot up (pilot OK/2nd Lt G. Rogers WIA).

27.6.17   **11 Sqn**, hit by AA on OP (Lt T.E. Wylde fatally WIA/observer OK).

1.1.17   **11 Sqn**, Shot up in combat on OP (pilot OK/Cpl S. Brett KIA).

29.7.17   **22 Sqn**, EA C-type sent down OOC over Tortequesne at 06:50 (2nd Lt E.A.H. Ward/Lt G.G. Bell).

9.8.17   **11 Sqn**, on OP (pilot OK/Capt J.A. Revill WIA).

11.8.17   **22 Sqn**, shot up (Lt R.N. Treadwell fatally WIA/observer OK).

17.8.17   **22 Sqn**, OP (Lt M.W. Turner WIA/2nd Lt C.R. Edson AFC fatally WIA).

21.8.17   **22 Sqn**, shot up (pilot OK/AM1 G. Brown fatally WIA).

22.8.17   **22 Sqn**, OP (pilot OK/AM2 S.C. Boxall WIA).

6.9.17   **22 Sqn**, in action (pilot OK/AM2 F. Scott WIA).

30.9.17   **11 Sqn**, shot up on OP (2nd Lt A.R. Browne WIA/observer OK).

3.10.17   **48 Sqn**, OP (pilot OK/2nd Lt G.R. Horsfall WIA).

18.11.17   **20 Sqn**, in action (pilot OK/2nd Lt F.B. Wallis WIA).

18.11.17   **20 Sqn**, in action (pilot OK/2nd Lt L.H. Phelps WIA).

20.11.17   **11 Sqn**, combat on patrol (pilot OK/2nd Lt P.J. Cayley WIA).

23.11.17   **11 Sqn**, reconnaissance (Lt R.D Coath WIA/observer OK).

22.12.17   **20 Sqn**, in combat on OP (pilot OK/Lt N.M. Sanders WIA).

6.1.18   **11 Sqn**, in combat on OP (2nd Lt N.E. Gwyer wounded)

4.2.18   **20 Sqn**, in action (pilot OK/2nd Lt F.D. Miller KIA).

26.2.18   **22 Sqn**, in combat (pilot OK/Sgt C. Hagan WIA).

9.3.18   **22 Sqn**, HAP, attacked spotter EA, shot up and force landed (Major L.W. Learmount DSO MC WIA/observer OK).

13.3.18   **20 Sqn**, in action (pilot OK/2nd Lt D.E. Stevens KIA).

13.3.18   **48 Sqn**, in action (Sgt E.J. Elton OK/2nd Lt E.G. Humphrey WIA).

14.3.18   **62 Sqn**, in action (pilot OK/Sgt J. Lake WIA).

24.3.18   **62 Sqn**, in action (pilot OK/2nd Lt F. Keith WIA).

25.3.18   **48 Sqn**, in action (pilot OK/Lt D.W. Orr WIA).

26.3.18   **48 Sqn**, in action (pilot OK/2nd Lt R.S. Herring WIA).

27.3.18   **48 Sqn**, in action (pilot OK/2nd Lt H.J. Finnimore fatally WIA).

27.3.18   **62 Sqn**, in action (pilot OK/2nd Lt V.K. Hilton WIA).

28.3.18   **48 Sqn**, in action (pilot OK/2nd Lt E.G. Humphrey fatally WIA).

28.3.18   **62 Sqn**, in action (pilot OK/2nd Lt S.W. Symons WIA).

6.4.18   **22 Sqn**, in action (pilot OK/2nd Lt B.C.M. Ward WIA).

13.4.18   **22 Sqn**, hit by machine gun fire (2nd Lt H.F. Davison WIA, pilot or observer?).

3.5.18   **62 Sqn**, hit by ground machine gun fire (Lt H.K. Spoonley/Lt E.G. Grant both WIA?).

4.5.18   **11 Sqn**, in action (2nd Lt R. Fiton WIA).

15.5.18   **48 Sqn**, in action (Lt W.A. McMichael WIA).

15.5.18   **48 Sqn**, in action (pilot OK/2nd Lt H.F. Lumb WIA).

19.5.18   **48 Sqn**, in action (2nd Lt E.R. Stock WIA).

19.5.18   **48 Sqn**, hit by ground machine gun fire (Capt R.C. StJ Dix WIA).

26.5.18   **20 Sqn**, hit by AA fire (pilot OK/2nd Lt W. Jacklin WIA).

27.5.18   **48 Sqn**, in action (pilot OK/Lt C.J.R. Gibson WIA).

25.6.18   **48 Sqn**, in action (pilot OK/2nd Lt J.W. Whitmarsh WIA).

30.6.18   'A8716', **20 Sqn** combat report has Fokker D.VII crashed near Menin 07:30 (Capt H.P. Lale/2nd Lt E. Hardcastle).

1.1.18   **88 Sqn**, hit by AA fire (pilot OK/Lt C.B. Marshall WIA).

11.8.18   **48 Sqn**, in combat (pilot OK/2nd Lt H. Knowles fatally WIA).

13.8.18   **48 Sqn**, in combat (pilot OK/Capt M.S. Anthony WIA).

1.9.18   **48 Sqn**, hit by AA fire (pilot OK/2nd Lt J.N. Kier WIA).

1.9.18   **62 Sqn**, in combat (pilot OK/2nd Lt J.K. Stewart WIA).

1.9.18   **'L' Flt**, in combat (pilot OK/2nd Lt M. Wallace WIA).

2.9.18   **20 Sqn**, in action (pilot OK/Sgt L. Bradshaw WIA).

16.9.18   **22 Sqn**, in combat (pilot OK/Sgt Mech M. Jones WIA).

16.9.18   **62 Sqn**, Fokker D.VII destroyed, own machine shot up (2nd Lt C.H. Moss WIA/2nd Lt R. Lowe OK).

23.9.18   **20 Sqn**, in combat (pilot OK/Sgt N.C. Dodds WIA).

24.9.18   **22 Sqn**, in combat (pilot OK/Capt G. McCormack WIA).

24.9.18   **62 Sqn**, bomber escort, general combat with 30 EA, one sent down OOC E of Cambrai, shot up on return (Capt W.E. Station WIA/2nd Lt L.E. Mitchell OK).

27.9.18   **62 Sqn**, in action (pilot OK/2nd Lt R.F. Hunter WIA or IOAS).

6.10.18   **20 Sqn**, in combat (pilot OK/Capt H. Dinwoodie MC WIA).

9.10.18   **62 Sqn**, in combat (pilot OK/2nd Lt R.A. Clarke WIA).

18.10.18   **88 Sqn**, in combat (pilot OK/Capt J.P. Findlay WIA).

5.11.18   **20 Sqn**, hit by mg fire (pilot OK/Sgt Mech W. Gibson WIA).

20.11.18   **27 TDS** Crail (Flt Cdt AJ Kettlewood KIFA, turned into aerodrome with engine off, stalled and dived in – engine 10441).

23.11.18   **27 TDS** Crail (Lt C.R. Mundy/AM1 F. Creen both KIFA, came out of spin too low and crashed – engine 1793/WD51221).

15.12.18   **RAF & Army Co-operation School**, Worthy Down, crashed (2nd Lt J.R. Kirby KIFA – listed as 'D267').

2.8.19   **105 Sqn** Omagh (Lt A.B. Jones/Lt E. Lowne both IIFA, engine failure – engine 2145).

6.1.23   **4 Sqn** (engine failed on take off from San Stefano). Deleted.

14.9.24   **6 Sqn** LIA (shot down by ground fire, near Zakho – listed as F1731).

7.1.25   **14 Sqn**, crashed Ramleh (Flt Lt R.R.H. Bruce fatally IOAS/LAC A. Sutton IOAS).

17.1.25   **208 Sqn**, crashed at Ismailia (Fg Off J.A. McLaren MC KOAS).

30.3.25   **28 Sqn**, crashed at Quetta (Fg Off T.D. Berridge KOAS/AC2 A. Bidmead IOAS).

4.5.25   **6 Sqn**, crashed at Khaniutman, Iraq (Flt Lt W.A.B. Savile IOAS/Lt J.E. Griffiths, Iraq Levies, KOAS).

9.5.25   **31 Sqn**, crashed at Ambala (Fg Off R.R.S. Waller fatally IOAS).

15.5.25   **28 Sqn**, on Close Reconnaissance, struck telephone wires across mullah near Fort Sandeman and crashed (crew OK).

20.5.25   **31 Sqn**, crashed at Sialkot (Fg Off A. Findlay/Capt G. Rich, Indian Army, both KOAS).

14.9.25   **5 FTS**, crashed in flames near Sealand (Plt Off W.L. Spurway fatally IIFA).

16.9.25   **2 FTS**, spun in from 1,800ft near Digby (Plt Off F.M. Kellaway KIFA/Fg Off W. Cave Williams fatally IIFA).

16.9.25   (Or earlier?) **2 FTS**, caught fire at 800ft and landed safely near Duxford (Plt Off N.K. Howard).

This is what happens when the apparently firm surface on which you attempt to make a forced landing turns out to be softer than expected. The recovery crew have taken the opportunity to pose for a snapshot, at the same time providing a good view of the F.2B's underwing ordnance carriers. *(Philip Jarrett)*

2.10.25 **20 Sqn**, crashed at Kohat (Fg Off E.T. O'N Hogben fatally IOAS).

16.10.25 **SAC**, crashed at Wilton, near Salisbury (Plt Off J.S. Branch/Plt Off J.A. Ballantyne both KIFA).

6.2.26 Crashed at Heliopolis (Fg Off A.C. Tremellon KIFA/Flt Lt G.P. Simpson IIFA – unit?).

5.3.26 **AD** Karachi, crashed at Karachi (Fg Off C.P.M.B. Caillard KIFA/LAC A. Barron fatally IIFA).

7.4.26 **28 Sqn**, crashed at Quetta (Fg Off R.E.J. Willson/LAC A.J. Burgess both fatally IOAS).

6.7.26 **5 Sqn**, crashed at Razmak, India (Fg Off C.C. Harris KOAS/LAC C.C. Avery fatally IOAS).

15.8.26 **20 Sqn**, crashed at Dalbandin, Baluchistan (Wg Cdr J.O. Archer CBE IOAS/LAC W.S. Bolam fatally IOAS).

31.8.26 **16 Sqn**, crashed at Marchwood, Hants (Plt Off A.L.R. Page KIFA/LAC E.A.L Lowe IIFA).

10.9.26 **2 Sqn**, crashed at Tilshead (Fg Off R.R. Reedman KIFA/Major O. Birkbeck Royal Artillery IIFA).

14.9.26 **31 Sqn**, crashed near Lahore (Plt Off D.C. Sherman KOAS).

21.9.26 **5 Sqn**, crashed at Attock, India, sank in River Indus (Fg Off D. Robinson IOAS/AC1 P. Jones KOAS).

9.11.26 **4 Sqn**, crashed at Farnborough (Plt Off C.V. Mossman/AC2 C.H. Hayward both KIFA).

29.12.26 **28 Sqn**, crashed at Ambala (Flt Lt A.N. Macneal/LAC C.A. Overy both fatally IOAS).

13.5.27 **RAF College**, whilst en route Cranwell-Henlow-Cranwell, landed downwind and crashed at Henlow (Flt Cdt Cpl A.C. Bentley KIFA).

24.6.27 **31 Sqn**, crashed at Old Chaman, India (Fg Off R.E. Slacke/LAC A.C. Hart both KOAS).

1.8.27 **13 Sqn**, en route Andover to Manston met rain and bad visibility, landed Farnborough but crashed (Fg Off A.G. Boon/LAC S.M. Vincent both KIFA).

13.9.27 **30 Sqn**, crashed at Hinadi (Wg Cdr A.B. Gaskell DSC KOAS/LAC W.R. Kittow-Roberts fatally IOAS).

9.1.28 **6 Sqn**, crashed near Mosul (Plt Off L.E.R. Fisher MC KOAS/Lt S.G. Haserick, King's Own Yorkshire Light Infantry, fatally IOAS).

9.3.28 **6 Sqn**, damaged in heavy landing in wadi near Mosul and burnt out (pilot Evans).

11.5.28 **16 Sqn**, struck ground after dive from 150ft at Old Sarum (Fg Off G.A. Underdown/LAC M. Thomas both KIFA).

8.6.28 **6 Sqn**, spun in near Mosul (Sgt A.J. Garner/Sgt W.F. Futcher both KOAS).

7.28 **6 Sqn**, heavy landing at Diana LG, Iraq (Flt Lt F.C. Farrington).

3.7.28 **31 Sqn**, crashed at Quetta (Fg Off C.R. McEvoy/LAC J.L. Mason both KOAS).

4.7.28 **6 Sqn**, hit telegraph wires across Mosul Bridge and crashed in River Tigris (Fg Off A.B. Kay fatally IOAS/LAC A.H. Bolton IOAS).

19.4.29 **6 Sqn**, force landed near Hinaidi due to air lock in radiator and undercarriage (Sqn Ldr C.H. Keith).

21.4.29 **6 Sqn**, crashed at Billeh, Iraq (pilot Plt Off Hodder).

15.2.30 **6 Sqn**, crashed 5 miles E of Kolundia, Palestine (pilot McCallum – H1394?).

1.3.30 **6 Sqn**, crashed at Balir, Transjordan (pilot Fairhead).

1.5.30 **2 FTS**, pilot abandoned on solo flight.

H167x **PD** Ascot. To Egypt. **AD** Aboukir. **208 Sqn** as a/c *IV* crashed on nose 13.11.24 (last digit of serial unknown).

Tailpiece: Abused Biffs

Above: **This 'main line F.2B' was created by airmen for the RAF Display at Andover on 20 June 1930, when it was seen taxying about during the show.** *(Philip Jarrett)*

Above: **'The Spirit of Salts' was designed, built and 'piloted' by Mr Kirby, the engineer of the Mousehold Brigade Flying Club of Norwich, and was paraded at Mousehold Aerodrome on 26 July 1930 during a Norwich and Norfolk Aero Club flying meeting. It had a 90hp RAF engine, but mercifully never left terra firma.** *(via Philip Jarrett)*

Right: **Precisely when and where this formidable 'Bristol battleship' made its appearance during the interwar years is unknown.** *(Philip Jarrett)*

BRISTOL FIGHTER INDIVIDUAL LISTING
NAME INDEX

Brown, 2nd Lt J.T., D7884
Brown, Lt, D2652
Brown, AM, E2188
Browne, 2nd Lt A.R., 30.9.17
Browning, 2nd Lt G.C.S., F6093
Brownridge, Cpl, E2409
Bruce, Flt Lt R.R.H., 7.1.25
Bruce-Norton, 2nd Lt, Lt J., B1281,
    B1305, B1344, C4709
Brunton, 2nd Lt, Lt R.A., E2507,
    E2532
Bryars, 2nd Lt G.L., C878
Buckingham, Capt W., E2265
Buckland, 2nd Lt C.J., C4675
Buckley, 2nd Lt E.M., F6158
Buckley, 2nd Lt J., A7248
Bucknall, Plt Off G.A.F., F4660
Bugg, 2nd Lt E.G., C4745
Buick, Lt R.F., C968, F5819
Buick, Lt, C9873
Bulmer, 2nd Lt, Capt G.W., C4810,
    C4888
Bulteel, Lt T.E., C4809
Bunting, 2nd Lt S.W., B1168
Burbidge, Capt L.W., A7164,
    A7253, A7298, B1111, E2403
Burgess, LAC A.J., 7.4.26
Burnand, 2nd Lt G.C., A3317
Burnard, 2nd Lt R.A., B1134
Burrows, Lt P., B1108
Burton, Sgt A., A7161, C4810
Burton, 2nd Lt P.V., A7118
Bush, Lt J.C., A7167, A7174,
    A7185, A7239, A7280, B1123
Bussey, Capt J., E9529
Butler, Sgt C.J., A7157
Butler, AC2 G.W., D7845
Button, 2nd Lt L.H., B1347

Cabburn, Lt F., C789
Cafferty, Pte C.J.T., D2218
Cahill-Byrne, Capt M.G., C4760
Caillard, Lt B., D7894
Caillard, Fg Off C.P.M.B., 5.3.26
Caillard, Capt, F4847
Cairns, 2nd Lt A.F., B1331
Cairns, LAC George, J6631
Cairns, Lt Col T.A.E., A7128
Calderwood, 2nd Lt D.M., C951,
    C4672, E2158, E2249
Cameron, 2nd Lt, Lt G.A., C967,
    D8003
Camm, Lt R.A., B1276
Campbell, 2nd Lt A.C., B1348
Campbell, 2nd Lt, Lt A.D.B., C976,
    D7939, F5816
Campbell, Capt C.J., C4811
Campbell, Lt D.G., A7164, C4820,
    C4837
Campbell, Capt J.S., A7210, A7215
Campbell, 2nd Lt, Lt, Capt L.,
    B1122, B1339, C4609, E2256
Campbell, 2nd Lt, A7214
Campbell, Capt, F5995
Campbell-Kirby, Lt E.J., E1902
Canton, Lt F.H., C4844
Capel, Lt L.H.T., C819, C4604
Capel, Lt L.N., C887, C978
Capon, Flt Lt R.S., H1574
Card, AM1 L., B1264, C964
Carmen, Lt A.H., C4893
Carmichael, Lt G.R., A7120
Carpenter, Lt E.T., B1164
Carpenter, Lt, A7235
Carpenter, AC1, F4955
Carr, Lt J.A., E2188
Carr, Sgt J.F., A7154
Carroll, Lt R.S., A3345, A7117
Carson, 2nd Lt W.F., D7897

Carter, Lt R.B., A7172
Carthew, 2nd Lt J.H., C855
Case, Lt C.H., E2561
Catchpole, Capt B.E., C1034,
    F5812
Cathie, 2nd Lt A.J., A3310
Cave-Williams, Fg Off W., 16.9.25
Cayley, 2nd Lt P.J., 20.11.17
Chabot, Lt C.J., C4823
Chadwick, AM1 H., D7971
Challinor, Lt R.T., A7196
Chalmers, Fg Off C.W.S., H1425
Chambers, 2nd Lt P.V.G., B1216,
    B1305, C4629
Chambers, Capt P.W., A7169
Chambers, Lt W.D., B1118, B1125
Chapman, 2nd Lt J., A7134, A7136
Chapman, Lt S.J., B1304
Chapman, Lt W.W., A7174, A7185,
    A7239, A7280
Chappell, Lt S., B1312
Cheetham, 2nd Lt W.R.N., C957
Chick, 2nd Lt, Capt, Fg Off J.S.,
    A7131, B1283, C4654, C4845,
    C4846, C4847
Child, 2nd Lt, Capt H.R., A7266,
    B1307, B1332
Child, Lt, A7122
Chilton, 2nd Lt, Lt T.S., C774,
    C952, E2451
Chilton, Lt, C4713
Christie, 2nd Lt D., C4604
Christie, 2nd Lt, Lt H.L., B1217,
    C4827
Chubb, Lt J.A., C886, C1002
Church, 2nd Lt E.H., A7226
Churchyard, AM3 A.W., C9895
Clacey, 2nd Lt E.T., E2569
Clark, 2nd Lt E.V., A7253, B1114
Clark, Sgt H., A7150
Clarke, 2nd Lt C., E2568
Clarke, Lt C.E., E2566
Clarke, 2nd Lt F., F4669
Clarke, 2nd Lt H.C., A7137
Clarke, Capt J.M., C4650, D8001
Clarke, 2nd Lt R.A., 9.10.18
Clarke, 2nd Lt W.B., E2458
Claye, 2nd Lt, Lt C.G., A3325,
    A7110
Claye, Capt H., C4630
Clayson, 2nd Lt P.A., E2611
Cleary, 2nd Lt M.H., B1211, C4709
Clegg, AM1 R.G., C4847
Clement, Capt C.M., A7172, A7174
Clement, Pte D.W., A7112, A7172,
    A7185, A7232, A7268
Clemetson, 2nd Lt L.H., A7152
Clemons, 2nd Lt H.S., B883
Cleobury, 2nd Lt S., A7120
Cleverly, Sqn Ldr S.M., C4721
Clifford, 2nd Lt W.J., A3352
Clinch, 2nd Lt S.J., B1172
Clutterbuck, 2nd Lt L.C.F., B1251
Coath, Lt R.D., 23.11.17, A7106,
    A7128, A7164, A7213
Cockeram, Lt P.A., B1346
Colber, Lt J.H., E2158, C4748,
    D7951
Cole, Lt H.A., E2527
Cole, Sgt, A3335
Cole-Hamilton, Capt C.W.E., A7135
Coleman, 2nd Lt C.M., D7906
Coler, Lt, Capt E.S., D7912, E2215
Colledge, 2nd Lt G., A7112, A7177
Collins, Lt A.V., C4610
Collins, Lt H.G., A3315
Collins, Sgt T., A7240
Collins, Lt V.StB., C989, D7990
Collinson, Sgt E., B1135

Collis, Lt E.W., B1336, C4633,
    C4637
Collis, 2nd Lt T.B., E2514
Coltman, 2nd Lt W., A7122
Colville-Jones, 2nd Lt, Lt, Capt T.,
    A7277, B1130, B1138, B1139,
    B1122, B1126
Colyer, Flt Lt D., F4772
Comber-Taylor, Capt E.H., C967
Conn, Lt K.B., C787, E2216,
    E2612
Connolly, AM., F4434
Connor, 2nd Lt W., C937, E2366
Conyngham, Lt D.F., E2215
Cook, Fg Off B.H., F4456
Cooke, Lt, Capt D.G., C4605,
    C4749
Coombs, AM1 C4639, F4485
Coomer, 2nd Lt F.H.V., E2510,
    E2532
Coons, Lt J.W., A7153, C1037,
    C4839
Coope, Lt N.N., C4659, E2515
Cooper, 2nd Lt A.C., A7254
Cooper, 2nd Lt H.A., A7123,
    B1187, B1190
Cooper, Lt L.H.A., A3320
Cooper, 2nd Lt T.C., B1245, C791
Cooper, Lt, A3308
Corbet, 2nd Lt J.H., A7174
Corbett, Lt E.J., E2215
Cordes, Lt, C964
Cordingly, Fg Off V.C., D7838
Cormack, Sgt J.D., C904, C979,
    C4699
Cornford, Lt R., A7162
Cornish, 2nd Lt F., A7257
Corry, 2nd Lt E.B., A7217
Cort, Lt A.B., E2468
Cougle, Lt W., E2428
Coulson, Lt W.E., F4330, F5810
Couve, 2nd Lt N., A7118, A7193,
    A7250
Cowan, 2nd Lt J., E2520
Cowan, 2nd Lt J.B., C943, E2282,
    E2469, E2523
Cowan, 2nd Lt, D7938
Cowell, Sgt J.J., E2471
Cowie, 2nd Lt W.A., C842, E2516
Cowin, Flt Cdt J.H.L., E2642
Cox, Lt J.P., E2565
Craddock, 2nd Lt H.C., C4874
Craig, 2nd Lt A.C., E2183
Craig, 2nd Lt, Lt A.H., C937,
    C4847
Craig, 2nd Lt K.C.W., E2612
Craik, Fg Off D., J6705
Crammond, Lt G.R., B1268
Crawford, Capt F., E1901
Crawford, Capt G.B., F6040
Crawford, Lt O.G.S., B1254
Creed, AC2 F4439
Creen, AM1 F., 23.11.18
Cridlan, Sgt Mech A.L., E2366,
    E2591
Critchley, 2nd Lt R., A7286
Crocker, 2nd Lt, Lt H.E.T., A7164,
    B1103
Croft, 2nd Lt G.W., A7229
Crombie, Lt N.C., C4646
Croome, Fg Off V., J6709
Cross, 2nd Lt J.E., B1103, B1110
Croudace, 2nd Lt H., C890, C4780
Crowe, 2nd Lt, Lt H.G., A7240,
    B1122, B1191, C4605
Crowther, 2nd Lt, F5815
Cruikshank, Cpl J., A7290
Crump, 2nd Lt F.F., C4756, D8081
Crunden, LAC P.W.E., J6640

Cull, Capt A.T., A3334, A3346,
    A7101
Cullen, Lt R.J., C780, C882, D8022
Culley, Flt Lt, F4546
Cunningham, 2nd Lt E.A., B1189
Cunninghame, Lt, Capt F.J., B1328,
    C950, E2507, E2532
Currington, 2nd Lt, D7925, E9578
Curson, Sgt E., E2635
Curtis, 2nd Lt D.A., C883
Curtis, Flt Lt W.R., C4721
Curtiss, Capt G.W., E2291, E2292
Curtiss, 2nd Lt R.L., A3334, A7107,
    A7149, A7151, A7155, A7170,
    A7224

Dacies, 2nd Lt C.W., C4628
Dainty, 2nd Lt J.G., A7106
Dainty, 2nd Lt, Lt, A7220, E2610
Dalgleish, 2nd Lt N.J., D7946
Dalley, 2nd Lt, Lt J.P., A7193,
    A7247, A7248, A7255,
    A7269
Dame, AM2 F.W., A3347
Dandy, 2nd Lt H., A7246
Danks, Lt E.R., E2416, F4892
Davey, Major H.B., B1283
Davidson, Lt B.T., C850
Davidson, Lt C.R., A7192, A7202
Davidson, Lt D.G., A7141, A7175
Davidson, 2nd Lt S., C839
Davidson, 2nd Lt W.D., B1273,
    C871, C4745
Davidson, Lt, C4699, E2559
Davies, 2nd Lt C.W., C4886
Davies, Cpl D., F4353
Davies, Lt D.C., C1035
Davies, 2nd Lt D.E., E2628
Davies, 2nd Lt H.D., A3322
Davies, 2nd Lt L.G., A7174
Davies, 2nd Lt N., D7900
Davies, Sgt T.H.C., C900
Davies, 2nd Lt W.F., C916
Davies, 2nd Lt, Lt, C4614, C4761,
    F4895
Davis, Lt D.C., E2617
Davis, Lt R.H., C914, D8027
Davis, 2nd Lt, A3349
Davison, 2nd Lt H.F., 13.4.18
Davison, 2nd Lt R., E2456
Day, 2nd Lt H.J., A7141, A7168
Day, AC2, F4414
Day, Capt, F4847, F4898
De Zee, Lt E.M., C955
Deacon, 2nd Lt E.C.W., A7298
de AIsey, 2nd Lt A.S., C4718
Dean, 2nd Lt J.R., C997
Deane, Fg Off B.F., F4933
Deane, Lt P.W., B1184, B1264
Deane, Capt, C4779
de Boer, Lt, F4438
Deighton, Sgt E.A., C819, C850,
    C889, C4604, C4763
de la Cour, Lt P.V., C4882
Delapena, Lt L.S., F5999
de Moyes-Bucknall, 2nd Lt, Lt P.B.,
    D7915, E2406, E2407, E2593
Dennis, 2nd Lt C.C., A7124
Dennistoun, Major J.A., A7240,
    B1275
deS La Terrier, 2nd Lt F.J.B., A7265
des Lauriers, Lt J.L., C879, D8026,
    E2481
Desmond, Fg Off T.J., H1671
Devonshire, AM, D7863
de Waller, Fg Off H., H1621
Dibbs, Lt E.R., A7145
Dickens, 2nd Lt A.S., C4646
Dickey, Lt J.P.Y., B1307

McHenry, Lt R.C., C959
McKeecer, Lt, Capt A.E., A7144, A7125, A7144, A7159, A7288
McKenna, Lt J.M., A7138
McKenzie, 2nd Lt K.C., E1902
Mckenzie, Lt M.A., E2154
Mckenzie, Lt, E2161
McLaren, 2nd Lt F.D.R., E2408
McLaren, 2nd Lt H.S., A7219
McLaren, Fg Off J.A., 17.1.25
McLaren, 2nd Lt W.S., A7282
McLaughlin, Lt C., E2462
McLean, 2nd Lt T.A., A7234
McLeod, Lt, E2570, E2594
McMann, Lt, F4307
McMechan, AM2, Gnr J., A7223, B1104, B1135
McMichael, Lt W.A., 15.5.18, B1193
McNamara, 2nd Lt J., E2592
McNiff, 2nd Lt F.J., B1219
McPherson, Capt G., A7221
McQueen, FG Off, H1594
McRobert, AM1 J., A7178
Mee, AM2, Cpl S.A., A7132, A7147
Mees, 2nd Lt I.R., A7266
Mees, 2nd Lt J.R., B1115
Meggitt, Lt W.G., A7223, B1123
Melbourne, AM1 S.W., C4699, C4856
Merchant, 2nd Lt A.D., A7164
Merchant, 2nd Lt, Lt A.W., A7102, A7106, A7112, A7118, A7119, A7176
Merchant, AM1 W.T., C4638, C4671
Merritt, Lt H.E., A7215, C796, C919, C4613, C4619, C4859
Mersh, 2nd Lt L.S., E1992
Miall-Smith, Lt G.L., A7124
Middleton, 2nd Lt A.H., B1120, B1153
Middleton, 2nd Lt, Lt, Capt T.P., A3325, A3350, A7102, A7112, A7119, A7129, C856, C951
Milburn, 2nd Lt H., C4700, C4757
Millar, Lt K.O., C839
Millar, 2nd Lt L., B1216, E2218
Millar, Sgt, E9529
Miller, 2nd Lt A.D., A7103
Miller, 2nd Lt A.M., E2495, E2496
Miller, 2nd Lt D.W.M., A7163, B1103
Miller, 2nd Lt F.D., 4.2.18
Miller, Lt G.W., F5809
Miller, Lt, C9879
Milligan, AC2 G., D8030, D803.
Millman, Lt, Capt N.C., A7123, B1134, B1187, B1190
Mills, Lt A., B1122, C856, C951, C4672
Mills, Sgt H., C4842
Mills, Major, A3303
Milne, Capt J.T., A7129, A7182, A7216, B1117
Milne-Henderson, 2nd Lt J.L., B1189
Mitchell, Sgt Mech E.G., D7951, E2493
Mitchell, 2nd Lt J.N., E2468
Mitchell, 2nd Lt, Lt L.E., 24.9.18, D7899, E2509
Mitchell, Lt N.R., B8922
Mitchell, Sgt S.J., C794
Mitchell, Lt, E2344
Moffat, Sgt J., E2511
Moffat, 2nd Lt L.M., D7903
Moffatt, Sgt J., E2589
Mollison, Sgt W., A7139

Moloney, Lt, F4898
Monday, Sgt H.F., E2267, E2524
Moore, 2nd Lt, Lt E.S., A3348, A7110, A7111
Moore, 2nd Lt, Lt H.F., A7251, C4894
Moore, 2nd Lt J.M.J., B1126, B1187, C4753
Moors, Cpl Mech R., F6181
Morbey, 2nd Lt J.S., A7262
Moreton, Sgt, Fg Off N.V., H1487, E9607
Morgan, 2nd Lt J.L., C4808
Morris, Flt Cdt H.S., C4879
Morris, 2nd Lt R.M., A7203
Morris, 2nd Lt R.S.V., B1110, B1111
Morris, Lt, C4805
Morrison, Capt A., D8088, F6217
Morrow, 2nd Lt, Lt, Capt E.T., C796, C895, C4613
Morse, Lt T.W., A7292
Mortimer, Lt, D8072
Morton, Major R.F.S., B1183, C911
Moss, 2nd Lt C.H., 16.9.18
Moss, Plt Off C.W., J6784
Mossman, Plt Off C.V., 9.11.26
Mostyn, Capt W.J., B1136, B1213, C901
Muir, Lt, C9941
Muirden, 2nd Lt N.H., B1255, C4719
Mulford, Lt E.A., B1225
Mullette, Fg Off R.G., E2546
Mullins, Lt R.F., C869
Mumford, Lt G.M., A7130
Mumford-Mathews, Fg Off H.J.J., J7666
Mundy, Lt C.R., 23.11.18
Munro, 2nd Lt, Lt H., A3324, A7149, A7155, A7170
Murdoch, Lt R., C916
Murphy, Lt A.W., C4623
Murphy, Sgt P., B1337
Musson, Lt F.W., A3303
Mustard, Lt E.A., B1229

Nangle, 2nd Lt, Lt H.C.M., B1245, C791, C792, C4629, D7911
Napier, 2nd Lt, Capt C.D.G., B1187, B1337, C4750, C4753
Nash, Bmdr E.A., A7150
Nash, 2nd Lt W.H., A7164, A7255
Needham, 2nd Lt J.W.D., A7155
Nelson, 2nd Lt H.G., B1236
New, Sgt.Mech F.S., A7153
Newark, 2nd Lt A., E2187
Newbigging, Plt Off E.R., H1433
Newey, 2nd Lt, Lt T., C4756, C4757, C4758, D7966
Newhouse, Capt P., C784
Newland, Sgt A., D7993, E2158
Newlands, AM1 A., B1114, B1122, C859
Newstead, 2nd Lt C.W., E2367, E2583
Newton, Lt H.C.G., F5809
Newton, AM2, A7149
Nichol, 2AM W., A7244
Nicholls, LAC H.S., F4606
Nicholls, Fg Off P.H., J6631
Nicholson, Lt J., E2154, E2562
Nicholson, 2nd Lt M., A7126, A7128
Nicholson, Sgt, A7112
Nickson, 2nd Lt J.R., C4830
Nisbett, 2nd Lt A., C797, E2569
Nixon, 2nd Lt R.H., A7128, A7226, C4849

Noble, Plt Off C.H., F4507
Noble, 2nd Lt H.T., A7241
Noble, 2nd Lt, Lt W., B1122, B1209, B1307, C979, C4699
Noel, Lt T.C., B1232, C856, C987, D7993
Noon, 2nd Lt G., A7253, B1126
Norris, AM1 E., C816
Norris, Capt E.F., C4647
Norris, 2nd Lt E.J., C946, E2476
North, AM1 E., C816
North, Lt, A7259
Norton, Sgt C., C877
Norton, Lt G., C4799
Noss, 2nd Lt A.R., A7118, A7176, A7217
Novikov, Cdt, A3325
Nowell, 2nd Lt R.E., A7205
Nutkins, Lt V.W.G., A7104, A7153
Nuttall, Lt J.C., C786, C846
Nutter, Sgt E., A7129

Oades, 2nd Lt S.A., A7281, B1168
Oake, 2nd Lt E., A7144
Oaks, 2nd Lt, Capt H.A., C883, B1244, C4634, D7984
Oates, Lt, D2129
O'Connor, 2nd Lt O., E2214
Oldham, Sgt J., A7222
Oliver, 2nd Lt J.A., E2477, E2578
O'Neill, Sgt W., B1114
Orde, Flt Lt M.A.J., C4870
O'Reilly, Lt R.R., E2509
Organ, Sgt W., A7204
Orr, Lt D.W., 25.3.18
O'Shea, Sgt J.E., C794
Otley, AM1 S.W.T., A7189
O'Toole, Sgt Maj C.J., E2511
O'Toole, 2nd Lt W., A7153, A7216
Overbury, 2nd Lt R.F., A7297
Overy, LAC C.A., 29.12.26
Owen, 2nd Lt, Lt H., A7108, A7116, A7217
Owen, 2nd Lt J., E1978
Owen, Lt, F4472
Oxenham, Lt G.V., A7236, B1225
Oxtoby, LCpl G., C4617

Packard, Lt H., F4427
Packer, 2nd Lt J., C759
Page, Plt Off A.L.R., 31.8.26
Paistra, 2nd Lt, E2529
Palardy, Lt G., C4602
Palmer, 2nd Lt A., E2457
Palmert, AM1 H.H., B1308
Parfait, 2nd Lt F.A., C4781
Park, 2nd Lt G.A., B1121
Park, Cpl J.T., A7109
Park, 2nd Lt, Lt, Capt K.R., A7118, A7170, A7176, A7229, A7293, E2635
Park, 2nd Lt, Capt W.H., A7145, B1283, C4601
Parker, Lt S.R., B1301
Parkhouse, Lt W.R., C1044, C9886, C9890, D2131, D2222, D2627, D7852, D7959
Parkinson, Lt J.A., E2163
Parks, AM2, B1261
Parr, Lt A.W., F4868
Parrish, 2nd Lt G.L.R., C4610
Parry, Flt Lt P.J., D7856
Parry, Lt S., C4859
Parsons, 2nd Lt B.F., A3309
Parsons, Lt J.W., C866, C973
Partington, Lt C., C4706
Partington, Lt O.J., A7166
Patch, Capt H., A7160, A7264

Patterson, AM2 A., A7288
Patterson, 2nd Lt H.C., A7105
Paul, 2nd Lt A.R., C4825
Paul, Lt C.S., C4627
Payne, 2nd Lt, Capt L.A., A7176, A7298, F4475, F6041
Peacock, 2nd Lt T., C4753
Pearce, Lt G.W., E2493
Pearson, 2nd Lt B.C., C786, C846
Peel, 2nd Lt E.O., A7189
Peene, 2nd Lt C.W.C., E1992
Pemberton, Lt A.L., B1257
Pemberton, 2nd Lt, A7144
Pennal, Lt H.L., E2470
Penrose, Prob, 2nd Lt K., B1168, B1344
Perhouse, Fg Off, F4895
Perkin, Sgt C.F., E2281, E2511
Pern, 2nd Lt C., A7132
Perney, 2nd Lt E.D., A7290, B1116
Perren, 2nd Lt A., B1302
Perrin, Major M.N., F5098
Perry, 2nd Lt A.F., D7919
Perry, Lt F.E.W., E2222
Perry, 2nd Lt L.P., E2455
Perry, Lt S.B., E2595
Peters, Lt G.C., B1278
Peters, Lt N., B1221
Peters, AM, D7908
Peterson, Lt, C9948
Phelan, 2nd Lt R.S., A7201
Phelps, 2nd Lt, Lt L.H., 18.11.17, B1122, B1138, B1139
Phillips, Lt A.H., C4704
Phillips, 2nd Lt D.R., C937
Phillips, 2nd Lt F.C.B., C4846
Phillips, Capt F.J., E2608
Phillips, Plt Off J.S., D7857, D8032
Phillips, Capt, E2617
Pickard, Sgt G., C4842
Pickering, 2nd Lt C.R., E2482
Pickering, 2nd Lt R., E2522
Pilkington, 2nd Lt P., B1339, C866, C874, C973
Pinder, 2nd Lt W.L., C4616
Platel, AM1 S.H., A7209, A7235
Playfair, Lt G.R.B., D8078
Pledger, Plt Off J.H., D7816
Plummer, Lt, B1135
Pogson, Lt L.V., A7288
Poole, 2nd Lt A.A., A7202
Poole, Lt G.R., C922, D8064
Pope, 2nd Lt K.W., B1269
Pople, Lt, D7908
Potter, Fg Off S.L.H., J6674
Powell, 2nd Lt L.A., A7144, A7159, A7288
Power, 2nd Lt H.E., A7220
Power, 2nd Lt H.R., A7219
Pratt, 2nd Lt, Lt D.W., C4622, C4700
Pratt, Fg Off G.E., J6698
Pratt, 2nd Lt, Lt H.J., A7108, A7116, A7217
Pratt, Sgt S.J., C791
Pratt, Lt, C9948
Price, 2nd Lt H.R., A7125
Price, Lt L.M., C4672
Price, Lt W.T., A3321, A3327, A7110
Priestman, Flt Cdt F., F4607
Pring, Lt N.G., C934
Pring, Lt R.J., C4861
Pritchard, 2nd Lt T.B., A3314
Proctor, AM2, AM1, Sgt T., C821, C825, E2153
Prodger, 2nd Lt M.R., C823
Prout, Lt G.N., A7129
Prouyt, Fg Off H., F4852

Spaulding, Pte1, Sgt W.J., C870, E2474
Speakman, Capt L.R., B1122
Speller, 2nd Lt, Lt L., A3349, A3350, B1186, C4650, D8001
Spencer, Lt G.R., A7107, A7146, A7170
Spencer, Lt R.H., A3331
Spencer, Lt, D8029
Spensley, Pte R., A7264
Spinks, 2nd Lt C.E., A7226, D7978
Spooner, 2nd Lt C., F5823
Spoonley, Lt H.K., 3.5.18, B1344
Spurway, 2nd Lt S.M., A7149, A7178
Spurway, Plt Off W.L., 14.9.25
Stacey, 2nd Lt R.H., A3327, A7144
Stack, Sgt T.A., D7939
Stagg, AM1 A.T.C., B1331, C964, C984, C4635, C4638, C4777, C4779, E2152, E2156, E2462
Stainforth, Fg Off G.H., F4477
Stanes, 2nd Lt E.H., B1349, C4710
Stanley, Lt J.C., C946
Stanley, 2nd Lt S.E., A7209
Stannard, 2nd Lt W.C., B1234
Stansfield, Sgt A., B1193
Stansfield, Sgt, C4802
Stanton, 2nd Lt, Lt F.C., C989, E2500, E2578
Stanton, 2nd Lt V.G., B1211, C4709
Stapleton-Cotton, Major, C795
Starfield, 2nd Lt B., A7193, A7255, A7285
Station, 2nd Lt, Lt, Capt W.E., 24.9.18, C874, C4619, D7899
Stead, Lt I.O., E2516
Stedman, Lt A.R., C852
Stedman, 2nd Lt R.deL., B1105
Steed, Lt I.O., C842
Steele, Capt C.R., B1349, C940, C4710, D7909, F5811
Steele, 2nd Lt R.C., A7194
Stent, Major F.W., E2281
Stephens, Lt P.L., D8094
Stephenson, 2nd Lt T., A3329
Stephenson, Sgt T.F., A7209, A7235, A7292
Stevens, Plt Off C.H.A., H1426
Stevens, 2nd Lt D.E., 13.3.18
Stevenson, Lt J., A7208
Stewart, 2nd Lt D.J., A3343
Stewart, AM3 G.G., C9877
Stewart, 2nd Lt H.M., C869, C4846
Stewart, 2nd Lt, Lt J.K., 1.9.18, A7215
Stewart, 2nd Lt T.K., F6158
Stewart, Capt, B1155
Stewart, Lt, F6401
Stiles, 2nd Lt C.D.B., A7216, A7220, A7295, C4707
Stiles, Lt, A7159
Stirling, Fg Off A.H., F4572
Stock, 2nd Lt E.R., 19.5.18, A7217, B1269, B1273, C4745
Stock, Lt, B1181
Stockbridge, 2nd Lt J.B., H1284
Stockman, Lt E.J., B1266
Stokes, Lt H.J.E., F4838
Stone, 2nd Lt R.H., E2244
Stoneham, Lt G.T., C4850
Stooke, Lt E.C., B1280
Stooke, Lt E.G.C., B1276
Stoyle, 2nd Lt, Lt A.P., B1111, C776, C795
Strachan, Lt A.R., C951, E2158
Strange, Lt-Col L.A., E2615
Stransom, Lt N.G., B1299
Stratton, 2nd Lt C.B., B1120

Stream, Lt J.H., C4820, C4837
Stuart-Wortley, Capt R., A7118, A7136
Sturgeon, 2nd Lt, E2529
Summers, Sgt J.D.C., B1122, C843, C859
Sumsion, Lt F., E2513
Sutcliffe, 2nd Lt S., A7131, A7138
Sutcliffe, 2nd Lt S.C., D7863
Sutcliffe, Fg Off S.E., J6674
Sutcliffe, 2nd Lt T.C., D7946
Sutherland, Lt J.L., A7197
Sutherland, Lt L.W., C4626
Sutherland, Lt R.B., A7184
Sutherland, Lt R.W., B1128
Sutton, LAC A., 7.1.25
Sutton, 2nd Lt F.G., C4841
Swayze, Lt W.K., C4633, D7945
Sweeney, Lt E.N., C843
Sweeney, Lt E.W., C987
Sykes, Lt J.A., E2498
Symons, 2nd Lt S.W., 28.3.18, C4609, C4632

Taggart, Lt R.G., C779
Talbot, 2nd Lt N.A., D7916
Talbot, Lt, E2419, F4838
Tambling, 2nd Lt H.G., A7204
Tanner, 2nd Lt K.E., A7129, A7164
Tapp, 2nd Lt, Lt R.B., C4642, E2588, E2597
Tarbolton, Lt J.S., B1271, B1330
Tarring, Lt W.J., C9873
Tate, 2nd Lt R.M., C1033
Tattam, Fg Off F.F., J6725
Tattersall, 2nd Lt F.V., A7255, B1104
Taviner, 2nd Lt E., E2550
Taylor, 2nd Lt, Capt A.G.V., A7246, A7271
Taylor, 2nd Lt C.E., B1162
Taylor, Pte C.V., B1299
Taylor, Sgt Mech E.C., F6131
Taylor, 2nd Lt J.H., F4443
Taylor, 2nd Lt L.C., E2430
Taylor, 2nd Lt N.J., A7130, A7168
Taylor, Lt, Capt N.W., A7298, B1196, C817
Taylor, Lt W.C., F4292
Taylor, Lt, E2152
Taylor, Lt, F4468
Tester, Dvr G., A7210
Thacker, AC1 P.W.J., E2293
Thibadeau, 2nd Lt J., C4601
Thomas, Lt B.S.B., A7226, C957, C4852, D7978
Thomas, Lt D., C993
Thomas, AM1 G., C4817
Thomas, 2nd Lt H., C841, E2510, E2532
Thomas, LAC M., 11.5.28
Thomas, Capt O.V., B1331, C4815
Thomas, 2nd Lt W.L., A7227, B1277
Thompson, Lt C.F.J., B1160
Thompson, Lt C.W., E2517
Thompson, Lt C.W.M., C4894
Thompson, 2nd Lt F.H., B1102
Thompson, 2nd Lt, Lt G., C795, E2370
Thompson, Lt J., D7904
Thompson, 2nd Lt L.M., B1234, C895
Thompson, Capt P., B1171
Thompson, AC1 R.P., J6608
Thompson, AC2 S., D7804
Thompson, Lt, Capt S.F.H., B1164, C929, C961, D7896, E2477

Thomson, Lt G., B1209, C776, C842, C4631
Thomson, Lt J., D7919
Thomson, Lt P., C4850
Thomson, 2nd Lt W.B., A7265
Thomson, Lt W.M., C843, C859, C4851, E2154
Thorndike, 2nd Lt F.H., A7140
Thornton, 2nd Lt A.J.H., B1253
Thornton, Lt H.B., C4755
Thornton, Lt H.O., D7934, D8025
Thornton-Norris, 2nd Lt, Lt G., E2496, E2534, F5995
Thurley, Lt P.W.D., C4770
Tidmarsh, Capt D.M., A3338
Tilbury, Sgt, F4481
Tinsley, 2nd Lt W., D7942, E2474
Titchener, Lt L.R., A7230
Todd, 2nd Lt A.J., B1343
Tolman, 2nd Lt, Lt C.J., C989, E2477, E2500
Tomkies, 2nd Lt H.L., A3352, A3329
Tomlin, 2nd Lt H.F., A7203, A7241
Tonkin, Lt A.V., B1276
Tooley, 2nd Lt F.W.J., B1258
Toomer, Fg Off, H1566
Townley, 2nd Lt D.C., B1213
Townsend, AM A., B1114
Townsend, Fg Off F., J7638
Townsend, AM2 I., B1102
Trail, Lt J.H., B1278
Traill, Capt R.C., E2403
Traill, Lt, Capt T.C., B1344, C856, C938, C4749, E2252, E2452
Trantor, 2nd Lt A., E2481
Traunweiser, 2nd Lt G.N., C4808
Treadwell, Lt R.N., 11.8.17
Tremblay, Lt A.J., C894
Tremellon, Fg Off A.C., 6.2.26
Trites, Lt, E9573
Trusson, AM2 A., A3336, A7101
Tuffield, 2nd Lt, Lt T.C.S., A7153, A7222, B1134
Tuke, 2nd Lt B.E.J.D., E2215
Tulloch, Prob J., B1193
Turner, Lt E.E., C851
Turner, 2nd Lt F., E2568
Turner, Lt F.E., D7951, E2566
Turner, Lt G.H., D2128
Turner, 2nd Lt G.S., C4753
Turner, AM1 H., C934, C4852, C4861
Turner, Lt M.W., 17.8.17, B1163
Turner, 2nd Lt, Lt R.W., C951, C4748, D7951
Turner, Sgt T.R., C4831
Turpin, Lt, D2167
Turton, AC1 W.J.A., F4572
Turvey, 2nd Lt A.E., A7127
Twilton, Lt R.J., E2649

Umney, 2nd Lt, Lt J.H., A7243, B1213, C901, C961, C4747, D7896
Underdown, Fg Off G.A., 11.5.28
Underwood, Lt E.N., C872, D7906
Underwood, AM2 J.H., F4361
Underwood, Lt R.G., E2160
Underwood, Lt R.N., C4753
Urinowski, Lt A., C947
Uwins, Lt C.F., B1179, B1183, B1202, B1203, B1208, B1232, B1238, B1240, B1299, B1309, B1336, B1339, C795, C822, C823, C825, C838, C839, C840, C841, C843, C845, C849, C850, C851, C856, C857, C858, C861, C864, C866, C869, C870, C872,

C874, C875, C877, C878, C882, C883, C884, C885, C886, C887, C888, C889, C890, C892, C895, C897, C898, C900, C901, C906, C908, C909, C911, C912, C913, C915, C921, C922, C923, C924, C936, C947, C948, C950, C951, C952, C955, C957, C958, C959, C960, C961, C964, C965, C966, C967, C968, C970, C971, C973, C974, C976, C977, C978, C979, C981, C982, C983, C986, C987, C1001, C1003, C1004, C1007, C1013, C1016, C1025, C1028, C1031, C1034, C1035, C1040, C4605, C4607, C4611, C4617, C4620, C4621, C4622, C4641, C4647, C4649, C4700, C4706, C4747, C4763, C4764, C4765, C4766, C4767, C4768, C4769, C4770, C4773, C4774, C4776, C4779, C4780, C4781, C4782, C4784, C4785, C4787, C4788, C4789, C4790, C4791, C4792, C4793, C4794, C4795, C4797, C4800, C4837, C4844, C4845, C4862, C4865, C9836, C9839, C9840, C9842, C9845, C9849, C9851, C9855, C9861, C9864, C9865, C9866, C9871, C9872, C9875, C9876, C9877, C9878, C9879, C9880, C9887, C9888, C9889, C9893, C9895, C9896, C9950, C9979, C9980, D7805, D7826, D7829, D7834, D7839, D7846, D7849, D7863, D7866, D7869, D7872, D7875, D7887, D7893, D7894, D7896, D7897, D7899, D7900, D7901, D7902, D7903, D7904, D7905, D7908, D7910, D7911, D7912, D7914, D7915, D7916, D7917, D7919, D7922, D7926, D7929, D7931, D7936, D7948, D7949, D7951, D7952, D7953, D7958, D7970, D7971, D7976, D7984, D7987, D8002, D8003, D8005, D8007, D8009, D8010, D8012, D8016, D8022, D8061, D8062, D8064, D8065, D8086, D8087, D8089, D8090, E2127, E2128, E2130, E2136, E2149, E2152, E2153, E2155, E2156, E2157, E2158, E2160, E2162, E2164, E2166, E2181, E2182, E2184, E2191, E2193, E2217, E2218, E2219, E2223, E2226, E2237, E2238, E2240, E2241, E2242, E2243, E2244, E2245, E2246, E2247, E2248, E2249, E2254, E2255, E2257, E2259, E2261, E2267, E2282, E2306, E2320, E2329, E2330, E2340, E2351, E2354, E2361, E2366, E2368, E2370, E2407, E2451, E2452, E2453, E2455, E2457, E2458, E2461, E2462, E2463, E2466, E2468, E2469, E2470, E2471, E2472, E2474, E2475, E2476, E2477, E2478, E2481, E2484, E2486, E2487, E2491, E2492, E2493, E2494, E2501, E2505, E2507, E2509, E2510, E2512, E2513, E2516, E2517, E2518, E2520, E2521, E2522, E2525, E2526, E2550, E2559, E2562, E2563, E2564, E2568, E2569, E2571, E2573, E2574, E2602, E2603, E2604, E2605, E2607, E2610,

E2611, E2613, E2614, E2615,
E2618, E2619, E2624, E2626,
E2627, E2629, E2630, E2633,
E2634, E2635, E2639, E2641,
E2647, E9524, F4271, F4426,
F4427, F4430, F4437, F4438,
F4441, F4466, F4470, F4476,
F4478, F4531, F4631, H1688

Vaile, Lt, C9891, C9941, D2136
Vavasour, 2nd Lt D.A., E2579,
F5999
Veacock, Lt S.J., A7193
Veale, Gnr E., B1114, B1118
Vickers, 2nd Lt E., F5811
Vickers, Fg Off J.H., J6671
Vincent, LAC S.M., 1.8.27
Vorster, 2nd Lt, Lt W.L., B1185,
C4759
Voss, 2nd Lt, Lt V., C922, D7905,
E2460
Voster, Lt W.L., C916

Waddington, Lt M.W., A7203,
A7214, A7255, A7287
Waddy, 2nd Lt S.N., D7893, D7902
Waight, Capt D.E., C901, D7896,
E2247, E2466
Wainwright, 2nd Lt C.E., B8941
Waite, Sgt R.L.G., E2413
Waite, Plt Off R.N., F4455
Wald, Lt A., C4896
Walford, Capt W.G., E2513
Walker, Lt A., C925
Walker, Lt C.B.O., A7261
Walker, 2nd Lt F.F., C4707
Walker, Fg Off G.G., F4339
Walker, 2nd Lt J.G., E2491
Walker, 2nd Lt J.H., A3311
Walker, Lt J.M., B1222
Walker, Lt R., B1230
Walker, AM2 W., A7222
Walker, Capt W.H., A7191
Walker, AM2, A7164
Walkington, Lt, F4848
Wall, Capt A.H.W., A7108
Wallace, Sgt Mech A.W., E2365
Wallace, 2nd Lt J.H., A7159
Wallace, 2nd Lt M., 1.9.18
Wallace, 2nd Lt S.H., A7243
Wallace, Lt, A3303
Wallage, 2nd Lt S.H., C795, C4808
Waller, Fg Off R.R.S., 9.5.25
Wallis, 2nd Lt F.B., 18.11.17, A7253
Wallis, 2nd Lt F.C., B1114
Walls, Lt E.W., F5813
Walls, Lt, A7214

Walmsley, Lt C.C., C805
Walmsley, Lt, A7136
Walrond-Skinner, Capt D.D.,
A7214, B1133
Walters, Lt H.C.W., C916
Walters, Lt S.L., E2593, E2644
Warburton, 2nd Lt E.D., A3337
Warburton, Plt Off J., F4481
Ward, Fg Off A.A., F4738, J6666
Ward, 2nd Lt B.C.M., 6.4.18
Ward, Capt D.F., J6666
Ward, 2nd Lt, Lt E.A.H., 29.7.17,
A7179
Ward, 2nd Lt E.H., C780
Ward, 2nd Lt F.M., C4810
Ward, Lt G., C4618
Ward, 2nd Lt H.H., D8022
Ward, Sgt L.K., C955
Ward, Plt Off M.V., C4735
Warden, Capt R.H., A7250
Wardle, Fg Off H.D., H1427
Wareham, AM1 D.E., B1163
Warren, Lt J.W., A3317
Warwick, Fg Off A.J., F4666
Washington, Lt W.F., B1344
Waters, 2nd Lt G.R., A7117, A7129,
A7164
Watkins, 2nd Lt W., C4762
Watson, Lt E., E2596
Watson, Lt G., A7231
Watson, 2nd Lt G.W.A., C4855
Watson, Sgt H.F., C932
Watson, Lt N.T., B1207
Watson, 2nd Lt R., C941
Watson, Sgt R.A., C931
Watson, 2nd Lt W.F., E2187
Watson, Major General, E2557
Watson, Lt, E2570
Watt, Lt E.W., C4784
Watt, AM2 J., E2364
Wauchope, Capt C.L., C964
Wealthall, 2nd Lt C., B1302, B1314,
C959
Weare, 2nd Lt, Capt F.G.C., A7136,
A7173, B1152, E2595, F4299
Weaver, Lt, E2161
Webster, Lt A.A., B1234
Webster, 2nd Lt A.R., B8946
Weir, Lt W.J.A., B1280, C4627
Welch, 2nd Lt W.H., E2588
Welchman, Lt P.E., A3332
Wellby, Lt H.S., A7244
Weller, 2nd Lt, B1302
Wells, Lt C.D., C4859
Wells, 2nd Lt N.B., B1268
Wells, Lt, Capt W.L., C4701, C4808
Welsh, 2nd Lt W.H., E2597

Welton, Chief Mech A.P., C808
Wesley-Segui, Lt H., C4616
West, 2nd Lt A.E., A7211
West, 2nd Lt F.T., C971
West, Lt J.P., C4880
West, 2nd Lt M.S., A7114, A7252
West, 2nd Lt, Lt R.A., B1143,
C1037, C4839, C4843
West, 2nd Lt, Lt C879, F4430
Westmoreland, Lt E.H., C759,
C826
Weston, Lt D.J., B1307, C979,
C4699, C4763, C4821
Westwood, Capt W.G., D7942
Whale, Fg Off H.W., F4832
Wheatley, Fg Off G.V., J6608
Wheeler, Lt W.A., C774, E2458
Wheelock, Lt L.W., C4689
Whinstanley, 2nd Lt C., E2460
Whistance, 2nd Lt C.F., B1345
Whistler, Flt Lt H.A., H1425
White, Prob C.H., C920
White, Sgt R.L.G., E2469, E2531,
E2534
White, Lt V.R.S., B1126, B1138
Whitehouse, AM1 A.G., A7174,
B1123
Whitmarsh, 2nd Lt J.W., 25.6.18
Whitstance, Lt C.F., C4750
Whitworth, Lt H., A7143
Wigglesworth, Flt Lt, H1489
Wightman, 2nd Lt J.F., A7156
Wilcox, 2nd Lt C.H., E2243
Wilkinson, Capt A., 5.4.17
Wilkinson, Lt, D2162
Williams, 2nd Lt E.R., B1185
Williams, 2nd Lt F., A7286, C965,
D8028
Williams, Lt F.S., C892, C993
Williams, 2nd Lt J.A., C924
Williams, 2nd Lt P.S., C4817,
C4888
Williams, Lt R.O., A7214
Williamson, Lt A., E2183
Williamson, Capt J.L., A3315,
A7226, A7261
Williamson, Lt J.W., F4290
Williamson, 2nd Lt L.A., E2456
Williamson, Lt O.H., F6040
Williamson, Lt T.W., B1279, C4856
Willock, AC2 F., E2533
Wills, Lt O.B.W., D8030
Willson, Fg Off R.E.J., 7.4.26
Wilson, 2nd Lt, Lt B.W., C951,
E2562
Wilson, Sgt C., C4601
Wilson, 2nd Lt H.H., C829

Wilson, 2nd Lt R.B.P., A7118,
A7174
Wilton, Lt, C4700
Wimpenny, 2nd Lt R.S., C816
Winch, Sgt A.J., F5816
Windsor, Capt H.J.O., D8030
Wingfield-Stratford, Major, F4455
Winham, 2nd Lt A.H., E2050
Winkler, 2nd Lt, Lt W.O.B., A3348,
A7111
Winstanley, Lt C.J., C952
Wishart-Orr, Lt D., B1181
Withers, 2nd Lt A.S., C913
Wood, 2nd Lt F.M., B1314
Wood, Lt G.H., C4758
Wood, 2nd Lt H.C., B1302, E2492,
E2530
Wood, Lt L., C9895
Wood, Lt, E1906
Woodbridge, 2nd Lt A.E., A7298
Woodend, 2nd Lt C.N., C926
Woodfield, Sgt A., B1180
Woodman, 2nd Lt W.L., A7102
Woods, 2nd Lt C.H., A7234
Woods, 2nd Lt, E2459
Woodward, Cpl F., A7159
Woodward, 2AM W., A7154
Wookey, 2nd Lt H.C., A7231
Wooley, Sgt H.J., B1288
Wormell, Fg Off E., J6612
Wormull, Lt C., A7146
Wornum, Lt A.P., A7285
Worsley, 2nd Lt R.S.L., A3322
Worster, Lt W.L., B1239
Wrathall, Lt, E2576
Wride, Plt Off L.B.W.B., F4761
Wrigglesworth, 2nd Lt C., A7153,
B1194, C867
Wright, Capt A.C., A7136
Wright, Lt J., B1117
Wright, Lt W.E., A7184
Wright, AC, E2555
Wyatt, Sgt Major., C4636
Wylde, Lt T.E., 27.6.17

Yeoman, 2nd Lt B.F.L., B8930
Yool, Lt W.M., A7151, A7185,
A7232, B1106
Young, Cpl H.R., C4688
Young, Sgt L.A.F., B1253
Young, Fg Off, F4847
Young, Lt, F4848
Yuille, 2nd Lt G.M., C4633
Yuille, 2nd Lt W.B., C871

Zealley, Lt E.R., C4706
Zellers, Lt G.H., C873, C904, C979

Appendix I

BRISTOL FIGHTER SPECIFICATION

Manufacturers

The British & Colonial Aeroplane Co Ltd, Filton and Brislington, Bristol.
The Bristol Aeroplane Co Ltd, Filton, Bristol.
Angus Sanderson & Co Ltd, Newcastle-upon-Tyne.
Sir W.G. Armstrong Whitworth & Co Ltd, Gosforth and Elswick, Newcastle-upon-Tyne.
Austin Motors Ltd, Longbridge, Birmingham.
Cunard Shipping Co Ltd, National Aircraft Factory No.3, Aintree, Lancashire.
Gloucestershire Aircraft Co Ltd, Sunningend, Cheltenham, Gloucestershire.
Harris & Sheldon Ltd, Stafford Street, Birmingham.
Standard Motor Co Ltd, Coventry, Warwickshire.
Curtiss Aeroplane & Motor Corporation, Buffalo, New York, USA.
Dayton-Wright Airplane Co, Dayton, Ohio, USA.
Engineering Division, Bureau of Aircraft Production, McCook Field, Dayton, Ohio, USA.

Engines

190hp Rolls-Royce Falcon I
150hp Hispano-Suiza (second prototype F.2A only)
220hp Rolls-Royce Falcon II
275hp Rolls-Royce Falcon III
200hp Sunbeam Arab
200hp Hispano-Suiza
230hp Siddeley Puma
290hp Siddeley Puma (high compression)
300hp Hispano-Suiza
200hp R.A.F. 4d.
200hp Wolseley W.4a Viper
290hp Liberty 8 (USA O-1)
400hp Liberty 12 (USA O-1)

Armament

One fixed Vickers 0.303in machine-gun centrally mounted beneath the engine cowling, synchronised by means of Constantinesco gear so as to fire forward through the arc of the revolving propeller, and one moveable Lewis 0.303in machine-gun or double-yoked pair mounted on a Scarff ring on the rear cockpit. Two 112lb bombs, or up to 12 20lb Cooper bombs, carried on racks beneath the lower wings.

Costs

Airframe:	
Without engine, instruments and guns	£1,350.10
Engines:	
Rolls-Royce Falcon I, II and III	£1,210.00
Sunbeam Arab	£1,017.10
200hp Hispano-Suiza	£1,004.00
Siddeley Puma	£1,089.00
Wolseley Viper	£814.00

Performance

Falcon

Maximum speed:	110mph at sea level; 108mph at 13,000ft
Climb:	838 ft/min; 11min 15sec to 10,000ft
Endurance:	3hrs
Service ceiling	20,000ft

Arab

Maximum speed:	104mph at 10,000ft, 94 mph at 15,000 ft
Climb:	14min 25sec to 10,000ft; 29min 45sec to 15,000ft
Service ceiling:	17,000ft

Dimensions

Wingspan	F.2A prototypes 39ft 2½ in
	F.2A production and standard F.2B 39ft 3in
Wing chord	5ft 6in
Wing gap	5ft 4½in
Wing stagger	Production F.2A 17.1in; F.2B (Falcon I) 16.9in; (Falcon II) 18.1in; (200hp Hispano-Suiza) 19.7in
Wing dihedral	3° 30'
Wing incidence	(Falcon) 1° 45'; (200hp Hispano) 1°42' at centre-section, 1° 24' at inner struts, 1° at outer struts
Length	F.2A (A3303) 25ft 9in. F.2A (A3304) 24ft 10in F.2B (Falcon) 25ft 10in; (200hp Hispano-Suiza) 24ft 8½in; (Arab) 24ft 10in; (230hp Puma) 26ft; (Viper) 24ft 9in; (Liberty 12) 27ft 1in; (Liberty 8 and Wright H) 25ft 5in
Height	F.2A (A3303) 9ft 4in. (A3304) 9 ft 6in F.2B: (with Falcon I) 9ft 4in; (Falcon II and III) 9ft 9in; (200hp Hispano-Suiza and Viper) 9ft 6in; (Arab and 230hp Puma) 9ft 5in

Tailplane span	F.2A 12ft; F.2B 12ft 10in
Wheel track	5ft 5½in
Tyres	750 × 125mm.

Propeller diameters:
A3303, four-blade propeller, 9ft 2½in, two-blade 9ft 9in
A3304 8ft 10.3in
With Falcon II and III, four-blade, 9ft 4in; two-blade, 9ft 8in;
With 200hp Hispano-Suiza, 9ft 4in;
With 230hp Puma, 9ft 6in;
With Viper, 8ft 4½in;
With 300hp Hispano-Suiza, 9ft

Areas

Wings:	F.2A 389sq ft; F.2B 405.6sq ft
Ailerons:	each 13sq ft, total 52sq ft
Tailplane:	22.25sq ft
Elevators:	23.25sq ft.
Fin:	upper 6.9sq ft, lower 3.8sq ft, total 10.7sq ft
Rudder:	7.2sq ft

Tankage (Gallons)	Petrol				Oil	Water
	Main tank	Gravity tank	Rear tank	Total		
F.2A A3303	31	—	19	50	4	9
F.2A A3304	40	—	14	54	3¼	6
F.2B Falcon III	—	—	—	45	4	6½
F.2B 200hp Hispano-Suiza	27	—	18	45	3½	9½
F.2B Arab	26½	4½	14	45	4½	—
F.2B 230hp Puma	26	—	18	44	2¾	—
F.2B 230hp Puma	—	—	38	—	—	7
F.2B Viper	—	—	—	48¼	4½	8½
F.2B 300hp Hispano-Suiza	—	—	—	51	4½	—

	Tourer	Tourer Seaplane	Seely	Jupiter-Fighter and Advanced Trainers	Greek and Belgian Tourers
Engine	230 hp Siddeley Puma	230 hp Siddeley Puma	230 hp Siddeley Puma	Fighter: 425hp Bristol Jupiter IV Trainer: 320hp Bristol Jupiter IV or VI (both de-rated)	Greek: 230hp Siddeley Puma, later 275hp Rolls-Royce Falcon Bulgarian: 180hp Wolseley Viper
Wingspan	39ft 5in	39ft 5in	47ft 1in	39ft 3in	39ft 5in
Length	26ft 10in	29ft 6in	29ft 6in	25ft 0in	Puma 26ft 0in Falcon 26ft 0in Viper 24ft 11in
Height	10ft 0in	11ft 5in	12ft 0in	9ft 6in	10ft 0in
Wing Area	407sq ft	407sq ft	560sq ft	405sq ft	407sq ft
Weight empty	Two-seater 1,700lb Three-seater 1,900lb	2,100lb		Fighter 2,190lb Trainer 2,326lb	Puma 1,750lb; Falcon 1,800lb; Viper 1,650lb
Weight loaded/ all-up	Two-seater 2,800lb Three-seater 3,000lb	3,000lb	3,000lb	Fighter 3,079lb Trainer 3,250lb	Puma 2,800lb; Falcon 3,000lb; Viper 2,700lb
Cruising speed				Trainer 94mph	
Maximum speed	Two-seater and three-seater coupé: 120mph Three-seater open: 117mph	110mph	128mph at sea level	Fighter 134mph at sea level Trainer 110 mph	Puma 120mph Falcon 125mph Viper 120mph
Initial climb at sea level			10,000ft in 11½min	Fighter 1,250ft/min	
Service ceiling	Two-seater: 22,000ft; three-seater: 20,000ft	17,000ft		Fighter 22,150ft	
Range				Fighter 400 miles Trainer 340 miles	
Endurance					Puma 5hrs; Falcon 4hrs; Viper 5½ hrs

An annotated photograph of J Type F.2B JR7623 laden with an assortment of armament and equipment. The spare wheel between the undercarriage legs and the canister on the upper surface of the lower wing root have not been included in the annotations, and the 'bomb sight' arrow is actually pointing to the wireless generator, the bombsight being immediately in front of it. It was rare to see an F.2B carrying all of this. *(Philip Jarrett)*

Appendix 2

ARMAMENT AND EQUIPMENT

Initially one fixed 0.303in Lewis machine-gun mounted to starboard and synchronised by CC Fire Control Timing Gear to fire forward through the disc of the revolving airscrew. One moveable 0.303in Lewis machine-gun mounted on a pillar-type mounting to the rear; on later multi-seat aircraft it could be stowed in the fuselage decking.

Then one fixed 0.303in Vickers machine-gun mounted centrally under the cowling, synchronised by Constantinesco gear to fire forward through the disc of the revolving airscrew. One or twin moveable double-yoked 0.303in Lewis machine-guns on Scarff ring-mounting on the rear cockpit, this being attached to the upper longerons immediately behind the pilot. Six or more double ammunition drums were provided, there being firing steps and a folding seat.

Production aircraft were fitted with both ring-and-bead and Aldis optical sights, the former being bracketed to the top centre-section. The latter was offset to starboard and fixed to a special fore-and aft tubular mounting, similarly attached to the centre-section and carrying two circular clamps. The Constantinesco gear was of Type B, with a Hyland Type B loading handle.

Up to 12 20lb Cooper fragmentation bombs could be carried on racks under the inner lower wings and the centre section. A negative lens bombsight could be fitted.

For Home Defence night fighting, a Neame illuminated sight was fitted on the centre-section, pointing upwards at 45 degrees from the pilot's eye. The procedure was for the pilot to take aim, then the gunner aligned his gun accordingly, being ready to fire on receiving a signal from the pilot. A device that enabled the pilot to rotate the gun mounting was also tested, but did not go into production.

During 1918 trials were undertaken with an early 0.30in Browning Model 1918, B1 aircraft machine-gun, somewhat similar to those fitted two decades later to the Hurricane and Spitfire.

After the war, the guns were removed for army co-operation trials to offset the heavy weight of contemporary wireless gear. From 1921 Type C Constantinesco CC Fire Control Timing Gear was standardised on all Falcon-engined aircraft. This was in conjunction with a new type of nose piece for the engine, incorporating the generator brackets in the castings.

For later operations on the North West Frontier region of India, an operational load of eight 20lb Cooper fragmentation bombs and one 112lb HE bomb, the final Mk.IV variant being capable of carrying two 112lb HE bombs. As an alternative to 112lb bomb, a canister containing 200 BIB incendiary bombs could be carried. In India all of this was in addition to an extra tropical radiator and an additional fuel tank under the rear seat. For squadron transport purposes, the wing bomb racks could carry two bundles of bedding, complete with mosquito nets and poles, and a nosepiece comprising galvanised iron washbowls, in place of bombs.

The later M.R.1 carried much the same armament as the Bristol Fighter, the fuselage being built in sections, the second of which incorporated the pilot's cockpit with Vickers machine-gun and ammunition box, and the third the observer's seat and Scarff ring mounting. CC Fire Control Timing Gear was fitted.

A beast of burden
During the interwar years, the F.2B relinquished its fighter role and became an army co-operation aircraft, and therefore it was burdened with all manner of equipment, most of which was carried externally. It included a telescopic wireless mast, petrol cans, screw pickets, a hand generator and an air-driven generator, a message hook, a canister containing kit, etc, wingtip flares and a spare tyre. In addition, a Neil Robertson stretcher carrying a patient could be carried on the rear fuselage top-decking.

A 'stripped' Lewis machine gun (i.e. with its cooling jacket removed) lacking sights and with a 47-round magazine, on the gunner's Scarff No.2 ring of an F.2B.

Lieutenant Fred Haigh of 1 Sqn AFC in Palestine poses with a selection of F.2B weaponry, including a Vickers machine gun (mounted for airfield defence), a stripped Lewis gun, and the 112lb RL, 20lb Hale, 16lb HE, and 100lb Hale bombs. *(Philip Jarrett)*

An observer demonstrates the technique of oblique aerial photography. *(Philip Jarrett)*

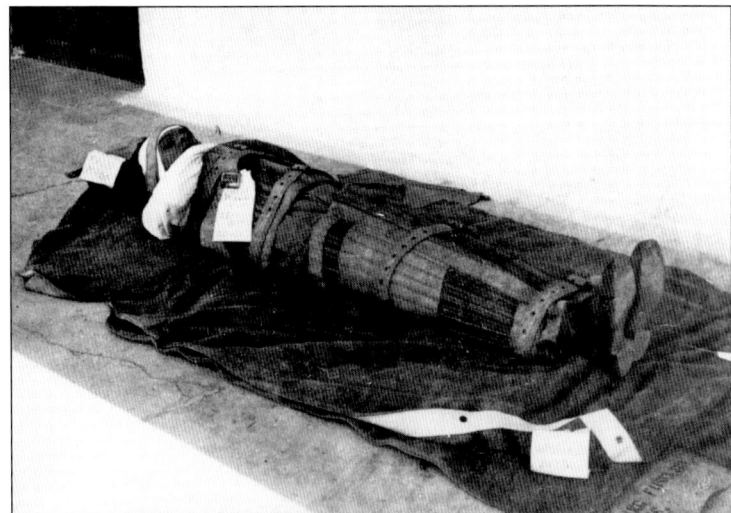

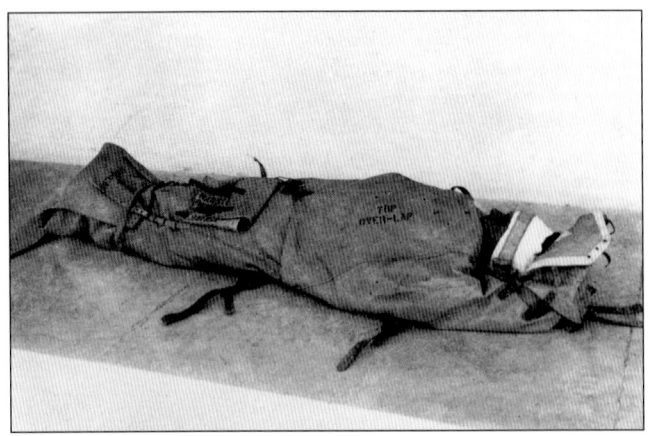

Above: **Four pictures showing the Neil Robertson stretcher: laid out; with patient strapped in; with the covering wrapped around it; with the stretcher and patient fastened on the top-decking of F4599 of 20 Sqn in India.** *(Philip Jarrett)*

Right: **The Neil Robertson stretcher: F4942 of 31 Sqn aloft with a stretcher patient** *in situ.* (Philip Jarrett)

Below left: **A nice view of J6765 with its message hook deployed. This F.2B served with No.1 FTS at Netheravon in 1924.** (Philip Jarrett)

Below right: **A Cranwell F.2B with a movie camera mounted on the rear cockpit rim.** (Philip Jarrett)

An F.2B with a free-flying aerial glider target mounted on its upper centre section, to be air-launched to enable gunners to practice their marksmanship. (Philip Jarrett)

This J-serialled F.2B has a Hythe camera gun mounted on the upper wing centre section, and Aldis and ring sights for the pilot. Camera guns might also be mounted on the lower wing or could be carried on the gunner's Scarff ring mounting. (Philip Jarrett)

This Arab-engined F.2B has a camera gun mounted on the forward fuselage, offset to starboard. Also noteworthy is the camera shaft between the fuselage underside and the lower wing centre-section for a downward-pointing camera installed in the floor of the pilot's cockpit. (Philip Jarrett)

Auxiliary servicing equipment could include such luxuries as this mobile crane to facilitate an engine change. (Philip Jarrett)

Left: **A pair of Duxford-based Cambridge University Air Squadron F.2Bs during gunnery practice, circa 1931. The gunner in F4542 (which is equipped with a message hook) is using a camera gun on his Scarff ring while the pilot of F4548 presents his machine as a target. Both aircraft were modified to J-Type standard. In 1933 F4542 became G-ACFN, registered to Commercial Airways. In 1930 F4548 was again modified, this time as a Mk.III DC.** *(Charles E. Brown)*

Below left: **An engine change in the field was another matter, and it was often simply a case of sheer legs and manpower, as with this F.2B of 5 Sqn at Fort Dardoni in India in 1922-23.** *(Philip Jarrett)*

Below: **Another form of mobile hoist, possibly made on site, is being used to remove the engine from this F.2B Mk.III at Ismailia, Egypt, in the late 1920s/early 1930s. The auto slot-equipped aircraft has the supplementary under-nose radiator, underwing baggage panniers and wingtip flare brackets, and its tail is supported on a tailskid dolly incorporating a pair of aircraft wheels.** *(Philip Jarrett)*

At establishments such as the RAE there was often a Hucks starter available to swing the propeller, as seen here with F.2B J6611. *(RAE)*

Right: **Generally, however, the propeller was swung by a two- or three-man chain, as seen here with H1403 at Cranwell, which also displays a rather appealing devil emblem on its fin.** *(Philip Jarrett)*

A three-man chain heaves on the propeller of a Falcon-engined F.2B, probably of 12 Sqn. *(Philip Jarrett)*

This F.2B of 20 Sqn in India carries 25lb Cooper bombs beneath its wings and a larger bomb beneath the lower centre-section. The auxiliary under-nose radiator is also well depicted. *(Philip Jarrett)*

This F.2B, 'R' of a B Flight detachment of 5 Sqn at Sakhakot in India (now in Pakistan), was the Flight Commander's aircraft, and a rigger is seated in its cockpit. The aircraft displays a number of interesting features: a spare wheel beneath the gunner's cockpit; twin tricolour streamers on the lower wing trailing edges; a large generator mounted on the inboard end of the lower starboard wing; a first-aid red cross on the fuselage just aft of the Scarff ring; and, retracted against the fuselage side, a very unconventional message hook with a stabilising fin. *(Philip Jarrett)*

Appendix 3

DATA, WEIGHTS AND PERFORMANCE

Introduction

In addition to the weight and performance data listed below, this appendix also includes relevant pages from three period documents, as follows: data on the Bristol F.2A from Volume 1 of the Aeronautical Inspection Department loose–leaf *Data Book of 1917*; data and interchangeability drawings from Volume 3 of the Aeronautical Inspection Directorate loose–leaf *Confidential Aeroplane Data Book of 1918*; and relevant pages from Air Ministry Air Publication AP129, *Royal Air Force Flying Training Manual, Part 1 Flying Instruction*, 1923.

Aircraft Type	F.2A Prototypes		F.2A Prodn	F.2B										
Engine	Falcon	Hispano-Suiza	Falcon Hispano	Falcon I Puma	Falcon II Puma	Falcon III Hispano	Falcon III	200hp	Arab	230hp	290hp	Viper	300hp
Trial Report No	M.69	M.78	–		A.7	M.128A	M.163	M.168	M.186	M.178	M.230A	M.237	M.249a
Date of Report	16.10.16	6.12.16	–		12.11.17	7.17–8.17	13.12.17	16.1.18	17.3.18	26.2.18	20.9.18	11.10.18	18.2.19
Aircraft serial	A3303	A3304	–		C4808	A7l83	B1181	B1201	B1204	B1206	C4654	B1200	E2400
Airscrew type	D2800	P3026	–		P3045	–	P3040	P3046	AB8210	DGB2627	AB7931	AB6625	AB8831
Weight empty	1,727	1,474	1,727	1,700	–	1,934	–	1,733	1,886	1,918	1,944	1,867	2,067
Military load	180	160	180	150	–	185	–	192	185	185	185	185	185
Crew	360	360	360	360	–	360	–	360	360	360	360	360	360
Fuel and oil	486	479	400	440	–	300	–	345	347	347	344	394	408
Weight loaded	2,753	2,473	2,667	2,650	2,860	2,779	2,848	2,630	2,804	2,810	2,833	2,806	3,020
Max speed mph													
Ground level	110	–	–	–	–	–	–	–	–	–	–	–	–
1,000ft	109	–	–	–	–	–	–	–	–	–	–	–	–
4,000ft	–	99.5	–	–	–	123	–	–	–	–	–	–	–
5,000ft	106	–	–	–	–	121.5	–	–	–	–	–	–	–
6,500ft	–	99	–	–	–	119	–	–	–	–	–	100.5	–
7,000ft	104	–	–	–	–	118	–	–	–	–	–	–	–
7,300ft	–	98	–	–	–	–	–	–	–	–	–	–	–
8,400ft	–	97	–	–	–	–	–	–	–	–	–	–	–
9,000ft	102	–	–	–	–	115	–	–	–	–	–	–	–
10,000ft	–	95	–	–	111.5	113	–	105	104	104	110	95	107
11,000ft	100	–	–	–	110.5	111.5	–	–	–	–	–	–	–
12,000ft	–	94	–	–	109.5	110	–	–	–	–	–	–	–
13,000ft	96	–	–	–	108	108	–	100.5	98	101.5	106.5	89	104
14,000ft	–	–	–	–	106	106.5	–	–	–	–	–	–	–
14,500ft	–	87	–	–	–	–	–	–	–	–	–	–	–
15,000ft	96	–	–	–	103.5	105	105	97.5	94	99	103.5	–	101
16,000ft	–	–	–	–	100	–	–	–	–	–	–	–	–
16,500ft	–	–	–	–	–	102	–	–	–	–	–	–	–
Climb to (in minutes and seconds)													
1,000ft	1 50	1 20	–	–	–	0 50	0 50	1 10	1 00	1 00	–	–	–
2,000ft	1 55	2 35	–	–	2 00	1 45	1 54	2 20	2 10	2 05	1 55	3 10	1 50
3,000ft	3 00	4 10	–	–	–	2 45	2 45	3 35	3 20	3 10	–	–	–
4,000ft	4 10	5 50	–	–	4 15	3 45	3 50	5 00	4 45	4 25	–	–	–
5,000ft	5 25	7 30	–	–	5 30	4 50	4 55	6 25	5 55	5 40	5 05	8 45	5 10
6,000ft	6 50	9 25	–	–	6 50	5 55	6 05	7 50	7 20	7 00	–	–	–
7,000ft	8 15	11 30	–	–	–	7 05	7 20	9 30	8 55	8 25	–	–	–
8,000ft	10 00	13 55	–	–	9 50	8 25	8 45	11 10	10 30	9 55	–	–	–
9,000ft	12 00	16 10	–	–	–	9 45	10 15	13 05	12 25	11 35	–	–	–
10,000ft	14 30	19 00	–	–	13 15	11 15	11 50	15 05	14 25	13 30	11 55	22 20	12 20
11,000ft	17 00	22 00	–	–	–	12 55	13 40	17 15	16 40	15 15	–	–	–
12,000ft	19 25	25 30	–	–	17 35	14 40	15 40	19 40	19 10	17 20	–	–	–
13,000ft	22 05	29 25	–	–	–	16 40	18 00	22 20	22 05	19 35	–	36 20	18 40
14,000ft	27 00	34 00	–	–	23 15	18 50	20 40	25 20	25 35	22 15	–	–	–
15,000ft	31 00	–	–	–	–	21 20	23 45	28 50	29 45	25 10	22 10	–	24 50
16,000ft	–	–	–	–	31 25	24 10	–	32 50	35 05	28 35	–	–	–
17,000ft	–	–	–	–	–	–	–	37 30	42 25	32 35	–	–	–
18,000ft	–	–	–	–	–	–	–	43 25	54 20	37 30	32 25	–	–
19,000ft	–	–	–	–	–	–	–	–	–	43 50	–	–	–
20,000ft	–	–	–	–	–	–	–	–	–	52 40	–	–	–

Performance data for the F.2A from Volume 1 of the Aeronautical Inspection Department loose-leaf *Data Book of 1917*.

Instructions for Erecting — BRISTOL FIGHTER F.2A

1. Set up Machine with propeller shaft horizontal by placing a spirit level on top of either top longitudinal of fuselage inside cockpit. Check transverse level and any vertical lines.
2. Dihedral 3½°
3. Angle of incidence of main planes 1½°
4. Stagger 1'7·1"
5. Angle of incidence of tail plane 1°
6. Flaps should be wired so that the trailing edges are ¾" below the trailing edges of the planes.

Bristol Fighter F.2.A. 190 Rolls Royce CLIMBING TRIAL.

Barometer on ground 29·6". Temperature on ground 47°F. Gross Total Weight 2753.

Height	Time Min.	Time Secs.	Rate of Climb feet per min.	Engine revolutions	Airspeed by Indicator m.p.h.	Temperature
1000		50	1208	1790	64	45°F
2000	1	55	923	1770	61	42
3000	3	0	923	1790	62	37
4000	4	10	857	1770	57	34
5000	5	25	860	1750	56	30
6000	6	50	766	1740	55	26
7000	8	15	706	1730	55	22
8000	10	0	571	1730	55	21
9000	12	0	500	1710	52	20
10000	14	30	400	1680	50	15·5
11000	17	0	400	1710	55	15
12000	19	25	414	1700	56	14
13000	22	5	375	1690	52	11
14000	27	0	263	1670	51	10
15000	31	0	250	1670	51	7

BRISTOL FIGHTER F.2.A. 190 ROLLS ROYCE

LEADING FEATURES	Biplane	2 seats	Tractor	Aspect Ratio 7·14 Dihedral 3½° Stagger 1'-5·1"
ENGINE	Rolls Royce	190 HP	Water cooled	Incidence 1½°
AIRSCREW	9'·2"[4] diam 9'·8"[2]	9'-3 6"pitch	4/2 blades	Chord 5'-8" Gap C to C 5·45

WEIGHTS in lbs.	Power unit dry 874	Aeroplane 853	Fuel, Oil & Water 486
	Military load 180	Human load 360	Total 2753 W/S = 14·5

AREAS in sq.ft.	Wings including Flaps 389	Tail Plane 26
	Elevators 22·5	Fin Top 6·6 Bottom 2·8 Rudder 7·1
	Wings & flaps, tail planes & elevators 430	Load 2753/430 = 6·4 lbs sq ft

DIMENSIONS	Wing Span 39'3"	Tail Span 12' 0"	Overall length 26' 3"
	Height from ground to highest point of machine 11' 2"		

CAPACITY OF TANKS	Petrol 50 galls	Oil 4 galls	Water 9 galls

BRISTOL FIGHTER F.2.A. 190 ROLLS ROYCE CONSUMPTION TRIALS 18.10.16

Barometer on Ground 29·4"   Temperature on Ground 52°F
Total Weight in lbs 2753   Height of Test 8000 feet.

	Engine r.p.m.	Air Speed	Consumption
Climbing at full throttle	1780	66 m.p.h.	13·5 Galls per hour
Flying level at full throttle	1920	102 "	14·6 " " "
" " throttled down	1750	90·5 "	12·8 " " "
" " "	1600	79 "	9·8 " " "
" " "	1450	68 "	7·5 " " "

Air endurance at full speed   3 hours   25 min. including 10 min to climb 8000 ft

Tractor biplane, 2 seats. 140 Hispano Suiza BRISTOL FIGHTER. F.2.A.

TANKS	Main Pressure tank 40 galls. Auxiliary pressure divided tank 7 galls each compartment Total Petrol capacity 54 galls Oil 3·25 galls. Water 6 galls. Petrol Consumption at 10,000 ft at 92·5 m.p.h. at 1450 r.p.m. = 9 galls. Oil Consumption Endurance 6 hours.
AIRSCREW	2 blades 8"-10·5"diam 6-6·8" pitch Type Drawing No. P.3026
DIMENSIONS	Wing span upper 39'-3" lower 39'- 3" Chord 5'- 6" Gap 5'- 4·5" Tail span 12'-0" Overall length 24'-10" Overall height 9'-6"
AREAS sq ft	Wings and flaps 389 Tail plane 26 Elevators 22·5 Fin Top 6·8 Bottom 2·8 Rudder 7·1

USEFUL LOAD.	Human 360	Military equipment 160	
	Fuel oil and water 479		Total 999

POWER PLANT.	Engine bare 417	Radiator, say 60	
	Exhaust manifold say 22	Petrol tank say 87	
WEIGHTS lbs.	Oil tank say 7	Piping say 25 Airscrew 28	Total 646
AEROPLANE say 828			828
		Total Flying Weight	2473

Weight per HP 17·7. Loading per □' of main planes and flaps

Tractor biplane, two seats, 140 Hispano Suiza BRISTOL F.2.A.

STABILITY and CONTROL. C.F.S Report

STABILITY — Lateral and directional good. Longitudinal unstable at climbing speed neutral at high speed. There is a strong tendency to put the nose down on sharp turns. The tail adjustment is insufficient and there is a tendency to stall when climbing, and to dive when engine is shut off.

CONTROLABILITY — Stick dual. Requires constant attention longitudinally. Very easy to land if tail is set for slow flying. Easy to manoeuvre.

Length of run to unstick 78 yards. To pull up engine stopped 100 yards.

TACTICAL FEATURES. C.F.S. Report

Armoured seat. Scarff gun mounting for observer. Pilot's view is bad for reconnaissance and bomb sighting. Both pilot and observer are too exposed to the rush of air at high speed, and in the case of the observer the operation of his gun is prejudiced. Pilot cannot let go of controls in a fight. Observers arc of fire 150° and facility for firing good upwards, downwards, and to the rear. Communication between Pilot and observer difficult without telephone.

CHASSIS

Wheel track   Tyres   shock absorbers.

BRISTOL FIGHTER F.2A 190 ROLLS ROYCE SPEED TRIAL 16-10-16

Total Weight in lbs 2753   Barometer on Ground 29·65   Temperature on Ground 47°F

Height in feet	1000	3000	5000	7000	9000	11000	13000	15000
Temperature	45°F	36°F	29°F	22°F	17°F	15°F	11°F	6°F
Engine r.p.m.		2040	1980	1950	1910	1890	1810	1790
SPEED m.p.h.	109	109	106	104	102	100	96	96

Stalling Speed mph With engine on   With Engine off

STABILITY AND CONTROL.

Stability | Lateral Very Good | Longitudinal Good | Directional Good
Length of run to unstick 100 yds to pull up (engine stopped) 30-40 yds.
Control | Stick Dual fittings supplied. Machine is comfortable & easy to fly. Lands extremely slowly but has a slight tendency to pancake. Is light on rudder & manoeuvres easily. Tail adjustment is good in use & is easily worked.

Length of time to prepare engine for starting   4 mins. approx.

BRISTOL FIGHTER F.2A

SPEED TRIAL CFS 6.12.16

Height feet	Temperature	Engine r.p.m.	SPEED m.p.h	Average speed for type
Ground 4600	42°F	1590	99·5	
6500	42°	1560	99·0	
7500	40°	1550	99·0	
8400	39°	1525	97·0	
10200	39°	1500	95·0	
12000	36°	1450	92·0	
14500	26°	1410	87·0	

Total Weight 2473 lbs
Best starting
" cruising
Maximum
Stalling speed engine on
" " off
Best landing speed
Trimming speed

CLIMBING TRIAL C.F.S 6.12.16

Height feet	Time mins. secs.	Rate of climb ft p.min.	Engine r.p.m.	Airspeed m.p.h	Temperature	Average climb for type
Ground 1000	1 20	760	1350	57	40°F	
1000	2 55	800	"	57	39°	
3000	4 10	632	"	64	35°	
4000	5 50	600	"	54	39°	
5000	7 30	600	"	60	40°	
6000	9 25	622	"	60	39°	
7000	11 30	480	"	56	35°	
8000	13 55	414	"	56	31°	
9000	16 10	444	"	59	31°	
10000	19 0	353	"	62	29°	
11000	22 0	333	"	56	28°	
12000	25 30	296	"	55	26°	
12000	29 25	255	"	54	26°	
14000	34 0	219	"	57	26°	
14885	38 30	222				

Total Weight including military load 2473 lbs
Best climbing speed at start for type

The following pages, from Volume 3 of the loose-leaf *Aeronautical Inspection Directorate Confidential Aeroplane Data Book,* include drawings prepared in December 1917 to provide dimensions and gauges affecting the interchangeability of spare parts for the **F.2B.**

AERONAUTICAL INSPECTION DIRECTORATE.

. BRISTOL F. 2.B.
190–270 H.P. (Falcon)
ROLLS ROYCE, MARK II.

SHEET 2.

PRELIMINARY **CONSTRUCTION** REPORT.

o (33) AS 4525—I Wt 277/3 300 1/18 E & S

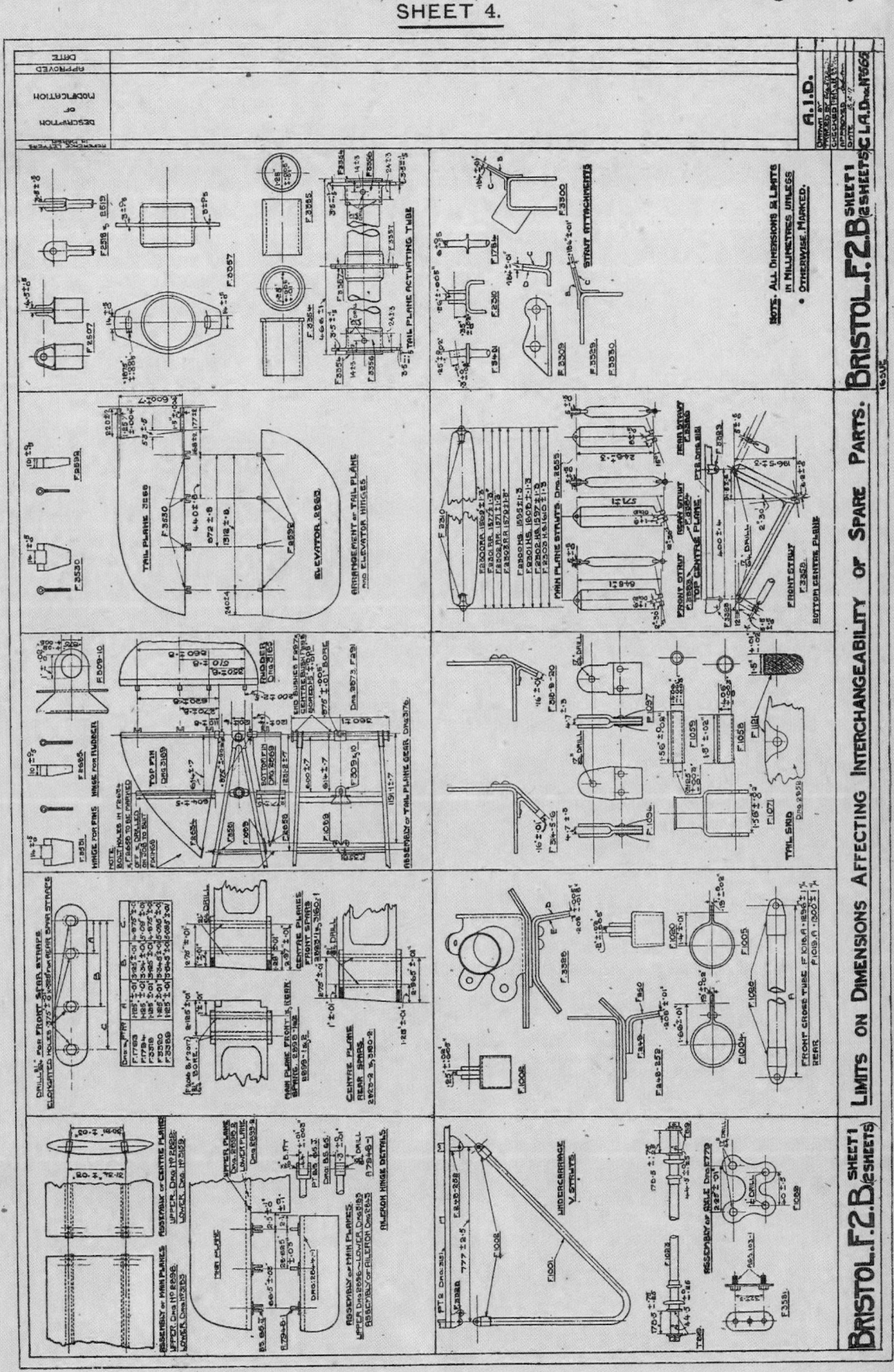

AERONAUTICAL INSPECTION DIRECTORATE.

BRISTOL F.2.B.

Interchangeability.

SHEET 4 a.

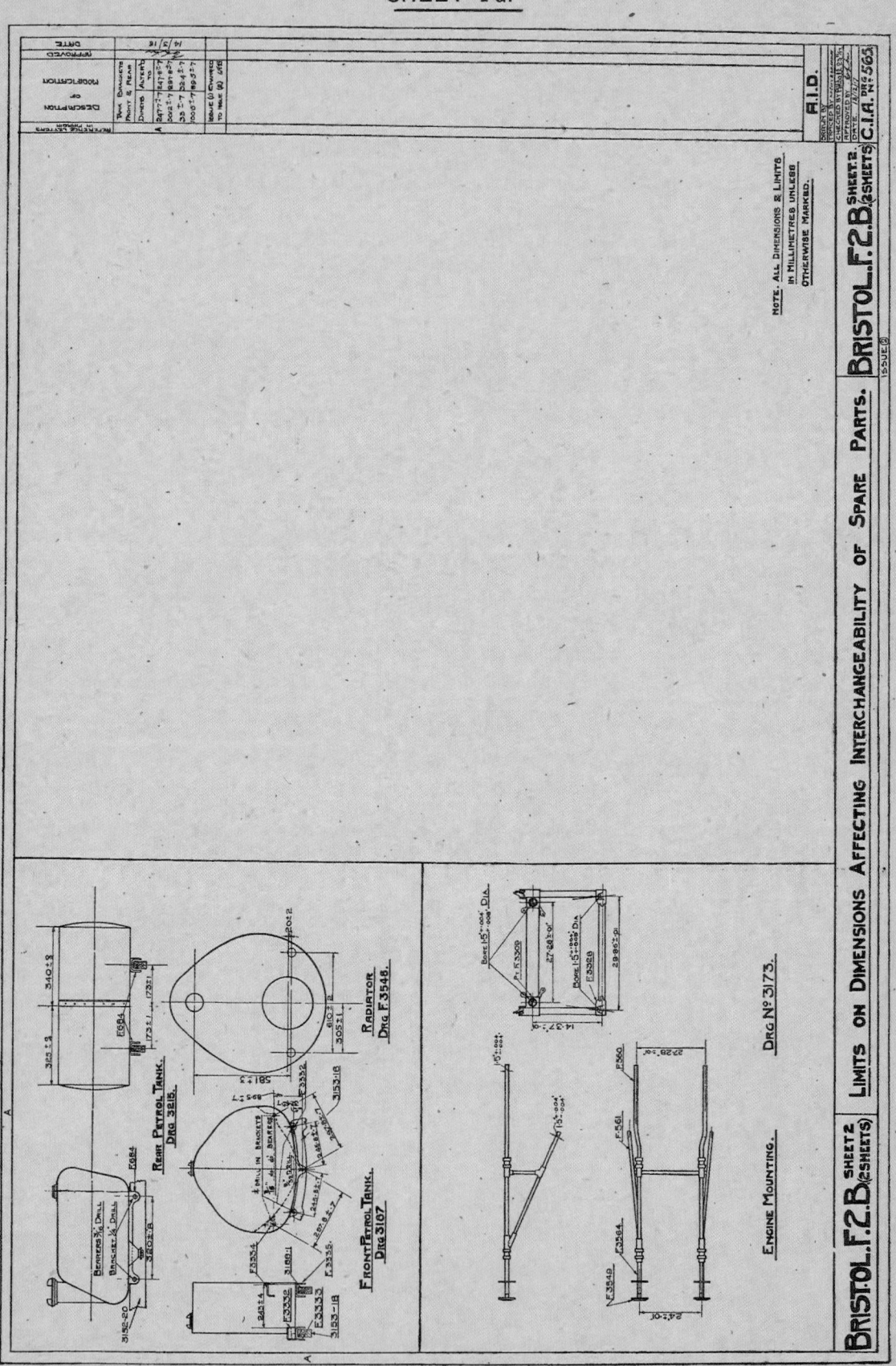

BRISTOL.F.2.B. SHEET 2 (2SHEETS) LIMITS ON DIMENSIONS AFFECTING INTERCHANGEABILITY OF SPARE PARTS. BRISTOL.F.2.B. SHEET 2 (2SHEETS) C.I.A. Nº565.

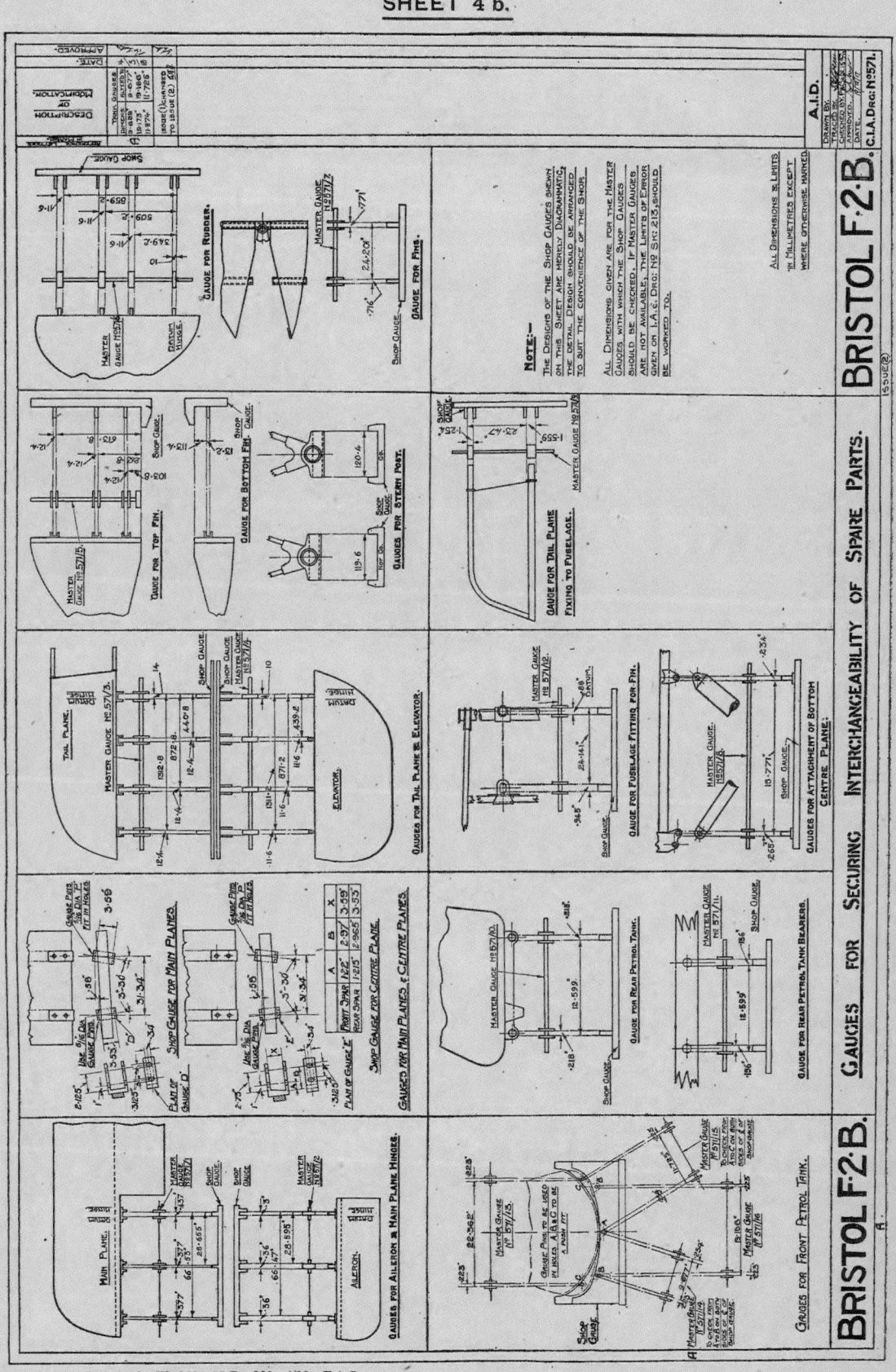

<u>AERONAUTICAL INSPECTION DIRECTORATE.</u>

BRISTOL F. 2. B.

SHEET 5.

PRELIMINARY **CONSTRUCTION** REPORT.

ARMAMENT, INSTRUMENTS AND FITTINGS.

ARMAMENT.

GUNS.—VICKERS, 1. LEWIS, 1.	SIGHTS.—Aldis, Ring & Bead, Norman (and Hutton*).
GUN MOUNTING.—Scarff Ring.	WIND SCREEN.—Avro Type.
INTERRUPTER GEAR.—Constantinesco (C.C.).	BOMB RIBS.—Under Wings.
LOADING HANDLES.—Hyland Type " B."	BOMB SIGHTS.—Negative Lens.
BRACKETS for Aldis Sight.	STANDARD R.L. TUBE.*

INSTRUMENTS AND FITTINGS.

Aneroid	Radiator Thermometer, Mk 1.	Navigation Lights.*
Rev. Indicator, Mk. 5.	Holt Flare Brackets.*	Accumulator.
Flex Drive, Mk. 4A.	Cross Level, Mk. 5A.	Starting Magneto.
Gear Box.	Telephone.	Dashboard Lighting Set, Mk. 3.
A.S. Indicator, Mk. 4A.	Pitôt Head, Mk. 4A.	Oil and Air Pressure Gauges.
Clinometer.	Pressure Gauge.	Petrol Level Gauge.
Altimeter, Mk. 5B.	Safety Belts, 2.	Generator for Clothing and Gun Heaters.*
Compass.	Engine Starter.	
Watch and Holder.		

* Fitted by Squadrons to Home Defence and Night Flying Machines only.

NOTE.—The above is a complete list of the Armament, Instruments, and Fittings usually apportioned to this type of machine.

o . (33) AS 4325—37 Wt 277/3 300 5/18 E & S

AERONAUTICAL INSPECTION DIRECTORATE.

BRISTOL F. 2.B.
190—270-H.P. (Falcon)
ROLLS ROYCE, MARK II.

SHEET 6.

PRELIMINARY **PERFORMANCE** REPORT.

TWO-SEAT TRACTOR BIPLANE.

Machine No., A. 7183. Contract No., 87/A/552. Engine No., 27.
Military Duty:—Fighter. W.D. No., 22376.

DIMENSIONS.

Wings.—Span, top........39′ 3″; bottom.......39′ 3″. Chord, top ....5′ 6″; bottom..........5′ 6″.
Dihedral, top ....3° 30′; bottom.......3° 30′. Incidence, top.......1° 42′; bottom.........1° 42′.
Gap ......5′ 0″. Stagger ......16·9″. Wing and flap area......372 sq. ft. Flap area..54·6 sq. ft.
Centre plane area, top...17 sq. ft.; bottom...17 sq. ft. Top planes only

Empennage.—Tail, span.............13′ 10″. Area.............22 sq. ft. Incidence...........Controlled.
Elevator area ....23 sq. ft. Rudder area.....7·2 sq. ft. Fin area....{Top.....6·9 sq. ft. Bottom..3·8 sq. ft.}

Overall.—Span.......................39′ 3″. Length ....26′ 2″. Height (Tail skid on ground) 8′ 9″.
Chassis.—Type..........Vee. Track..........5′ 5¼″. Tyres..........750 × 125. Brakes ....None.

WEIGHTS CARRIED ON TRIAL.	LBS.	LOADING.	TANK CAPACITY.	GALLS.	AIRSCREW USED ON TRIAL.
Military Load.—Lewis gun (Scarff ring mounting), 16 lbs.; Ammunition, 32 lbs.; Vickers gun, fixed over engine, 35 lbs.; Ammunition, 28 lbs.; Extra deadweight, 74 lbs.; Pilot and Gunner at 180 lbs. = 360 lbs.	545	Per square foot of Wings and Flaps—6 lbs.	Petrol.—Front tank, top of fore end of fuselage (pressure)	26	Drawing No., P. 3045.
Fuel and Oil.—(Petrol, 38 galls.; Oil, 3 galls.)	300	Per H.P., 9·6 lbs.	Rear tank, below Pilot's seat (pressure)	19	Maker—British & Colonial.
Machine, empty.—(With water, 6½ galls.)	1,745		Total	45	Series No., 6470.
Gross Weight	2,590		Oil tank (on R.H. engine bearer tube)	4	No. of Blades, 4.
			Water	6½	Diameter, 9′ 4″.
					Pitch, 8′ 11·5″.

CONSUMPTION TRIAL AT 11,000 FEET.

Engine R.P.M.	Air Speed.	Galls. per hour.	Endurance, including Climb at Full Throttle.	
			R.P.M.	Hours.
1,970	112	12	1,970	About 3 hrs.
1,700	91½	9	1,810	„ 3¾ „
1,600	84	8¼	1,680	„ 4¼ „
1,500	76	7¾	1,550	„ 4½ „
1,400	68½	7¼	1,420	„ 5 „

SPEED TRIAL.

Variation in load. Nil.

Height, Feet.	% of Standard Density.	Galls. per Hour.	R.P.M.	True Speed. M.P.H.
3,000	93·2	17	2,100	125
6,500	83·2	14½	2,050	119
10,000	74	12½	1,995	113
13,000	67·3	11	1,945	108
16,500	60	9½	1,890	102

CLIMBING TRIAL.

Variation in load. Nil.

Height, Feet.	Time, Minutes. M. S.	Rate of Climb, Feet per Minute.	R.P.M.	Air Speed.	% of Standard Density.	Consumption, Galls. per Hour.
1,000	0 50	1,200	—	—	99·4	—
6,000	5 55	923	1,785	63	84·5	14½
10,000	11 15	666	1,770	61	74	12¾
12,000	14 40	571	1,770	61	69·5	11¾
14,000	18 50	461	1,745	61	65·2	11¾
16,000	24 10	353	1,730	57	61	10¼

NOTES.

This is the standard machine with increased engine power. Controllability is good for a big machine, but heavy laterally and slow off steep bank. It is well balanced and will fly "hands off." The engine controls and tail adjustment lever are inconveniently placed and difficult to reach.

Length of run to unstick, 85 yards; to pull up (engine stopped), 120 yards.

o (33) AS 4076—88 Wt 277/8 300 1/18 E & S

AERONAUTICAL INSPECTION DIRECTORATE.

BRISTOL F. 2.B.
200 H.P. HISPANO SUIZA.
FALCON ROLLS ROYCE No. 2.

SHEET 6.

SUPPLEMENTARY PERFORMANCE REPORT.

TWO-SEAT TRACTOR BIPLANE.

Machine No., B 1201.   Contract No., 87/A/552.   Engine No., 16456. W.D. 11334.
Military Duty :—Fighter and Reconnaissance.   Date of trials :—January 1918.

STANDARD DIMENSIONS.

WEIGHTS.		LOADING.	TANK CAPACITY.		AIRSCREW USED ON TRIAL.
	LBS.			GALLS.	
Military Load.—Vickers gun, 35 lbs.; Lewis gun and Scarff ring, 23 lbs.; Ammunition, 60 lbs., deadweight, 74 lbs.; Pilot and observer, 360 lbs.	552	Per square foot of Wings and Flaps, 6·5 lbs.	Petrol.—Tank immediately behind engine (pressure) Under Pilot's seat (pressure)	27 18	Drawing No., P. 3046. Maker—British and Colonial. Series No. G 126 1/7647.
Fuel and Oil - - - - -	345	Per H.P., 13·2 lbs.	Total -	45	No. of Blades, 2.
Machine, empty (with water) -	1,733		Oil.—Under engine (pressure) - - -	3½	Diameter, 9′ 4″.
Gross Weight - - - -	2,630		Water - - -	9½	Pitch, 6′ 11″.

SPEED TRIAL.

Height, Feet.	% of Standard Density.	Galls. per Hour.	R.P.M.	True Speed.
10,000	74·0	—	1,995	105 m.p.h.
13,000	67·3	—	1,945	100½ ,,
15,000	63·0	—	1,915	97½ ,,

CLIMBING TRIAL.

Height, Feet.	Time, Minutes.		Rate of Climb, Feet per Minute.	R.P.M.	Air Speed.	% of Standard Density.	Consumption, Gallons per Hour
	M.	S.					
1,000	1	10	857	—	—	99·4	—
2,000	2	20	857	1,880	76	96·3	—
5,000	6	25	706	1,850	72	87·4	—
8,000	11	10	600	1,825	68	79·2	—
10,000	15	05	500	1,810	66	74·0	—
12,000	19	40	414	1,790	—	69·5	—
15,000	28	50	286	1,765	64	63·0	—
18,000	43	25	169	1,740	60	57·1	—
	Approximate ceiling, 21,000 feet.						

NOTES.—On this machine the view of the pilot and observer is good generally, though the pilot has some difficulty in seeing below him. The manœuvreability is good, and controls conveniently placed and easily worked. The drift wires on either side pass directly across the ends of the exhaust pipes and are liable to get burnt. The internal diameter of the suction oil pipe from oil tank to pump has now been altered from ½ in. to ⅞ in. Length of run to unstick, 75 yds.; to pull up—(engine stopped) 110 yds., (engine throttled) 150 yds.

Machine No., C 4808.   Gross Weight, 2,860 lbs.

Fitted with "Falcon" Rolls Royce, No. 2. Two-bladed Tractor Propeller (Drawing No., P. 3033).

SPEED TRIAL.

Height, Feet.	% of Standard Density.	Galls. per Hour.	R.P.M.	True Speed.
10,000	74·0	—	2,030	109¾ m.p.h.
13,000	67·3	—	1,975	106 ,,
15,000	63·0	—	1,925	101 ,,

CLIMBING TRIAL.

Height, Feet.	Time, Minutes.		Rate of Climb, Feet per Minute.	R.P.M.	Air Speed.	% of Standard Density.	Consumption, Gallons per Hour.
	M.	S.					
2,000	2	00	945	1,905	—	96·3	—
5,000	5	30	785	1,900	—	87·4	—
10,000	13	15	520	1,880	—	74·0	—
15,000	26	55	250	1,825	—	63·0	—

NOTE.—The photographs on Sheet 2 show this machine fitted with a four-bladed propeller.

o (33) AS 4525—15 Wt 277/3 300 3/18 E & S

SHEET 7.

INTERIM CONSTRUCTION REPORT.

INSTRUCTIONS FOR ERECTING.

FLYING POSITION.—Machine is in flying position when top longerons at Gunner's cockpit are horizontal laterally and longitudinally. Stretch a line from point "A" on fuselage (*see diagram*) to tail, bisecting fuselage from strut 4 to rear. This line should be perfectly horizontal.

TRUING UP FUSELAGE.—Commence at forward end of machine, and working towards the rear adjust top, bottom, and internal bracing wires, making each pair equal, checking with trammels. Adjust side bracing wires, making diagonals equal, from strut 8 to rear, and top and bottom longerons equal distance from the line on side of fuselage.

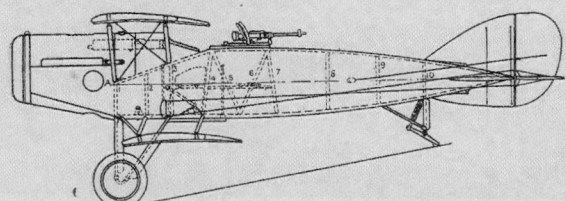

TAIL PLANE.—Adjust tail plane to allow full movement (2 inches). When tail plane control lever is in neutral position, leading edge of tail plane should be $\frac{7}{8}$ inch below the horizontal line. When the handle of the lever is raised the leading edge of tail plane is depressed, and vice versa.

ELEVATORS.—With control column in normal position (vertical) adjust elevator controls until elevators continue in the horizontal line of machine.

DIHEDRAL.—Adjust bracings to give main planes an angle of Dihedral of $3\frac{1}{2}$ degrees. Check by use of dihedral board and spirit level, or straightedge and Abney level, and test for correct by stretching a line from points on the upper surface of planes directly above outer struts. Vertical measurements from the line to top of centre section plane should show $9\frac{1}{4}$ inches. It is important that dihedral be perfectly balanced about the vertical centre-line of machine. Check by measurement from point at centre of leading edge of top centre plane to bottom of front outer struts—corresponding measurements should be equal.

STAGGER.—Adjust stagger wires at centre section to give a stagger of 16·9 inches. Drop plumb lines from leading edges of top plane in front of each wing strut. Horizontal measurements from line to leading edge of lower planes should show 16·9 inches. The horizontal distance from the leading edge of top centre plane to foremost surface of first fuselage strut = 13 inches.

INCIDENCE.—Adjust incidence bracings to give 1° 42′ incidence. Check by means of straightedge and Abney level.

AILERONS.—With control column fixed central ailerons should droop $\frac{5}{8}''$ below the trailing edge of main planes.

MAIN DIMENSIONS.

Wings.—Span, top and bottom .... 39′ 3″ ; Chord, top and bottom .... 5′ 6″.

Dihedral, top and bottom .... 3° 30′ ; Incidence, top and bottom .... 1° 42″.

Stagger .... 16·9″ ; Gap .... 5′ 0″.

Overall.—Length .... 26′ 2″ ; Height (tail skid on ground) .... 8′ 9″.

o (33) AS 4076—113 Wt 277/3 300 1/18 E & S

Issued

BRISTOL F.2.B.
CONTRACTS.

SHEET 9.

INTERIM CONSTRUCTION REPORT.

	Bristol Fighter F.2b. Falcon Rolls-Royce or Arab Sunbeam.				Bristol Fighter F.2b. Arab Sunbeam.	
Machine ...						
Contractor ...	British and Colonial Aero Co., Brislington and Filton, Bristol.				Gloucester Aircraft Co., Cheltenham.	
Contract No.	87/A/552	A.S.17573	A.S.3117	35A/779/C.658	A.S.32796	35A/428/C.307
Date ...	28/8/16	4/9/17	5/2/18	5/6/18	30/10/17	20/3/18
Number off...	602	800	500	700	150	150
Increase and authority						
Required delivery per week ...	8					
Date completed						
Machine numbers allotted ...	A.3303-3354 A.7101-7300 B.1101-1350 C.4801-4900	C.751-1050 C.4601-4800 D.7801-8100	E.2151-2650	F.4271-4970	C.9836-9985	E.9507-9656
Notes ...	Cancelled 28/9/17					

	Bristol Fighter F.2b. Arab Sunbeam.	Bristol Fighter F.2b. 200 H.P. Hispano.	Bristol Fighter F.2b. Arab Sunbeam.	Bristol Fighter F.2b. Arab Sunbeam.	Bristol Fighter F.2b.	Bristol Fighter F.2b.
Machine ...						
Contractor ...	Marshall & Sons, Gainsborough.	National Aircraft Factory, No. 3.	Standard Motor Co., Coventry.	Armstrong Whitworth & Co., Newcastle.	Angus Sanderson & Co., Newcastle.	Harris & Sheldon, Birmingham.
Contract No.	A.S.35822	A.S.34276	35A/47/C.27	35A/46/C.20	35A/62/C.33	35A/1218/C1158.
Date ...	22/11/17	22/11/17	22/2/18	22/2/18	22/2/18	21.5.18
Number off...	150	500	250	250	250	100
Increase and authority						
Required delivery per week ...						
Date completed						
Machine numbers allotted ...	D.2626-2775	D.2126-2625	E.5179-5428	E.1901-2150	E.2651-2900	F.5074-5173
Notes ...					Arab Sunbeam will probably be fitted.	Arab Sunbeam will probably be fitted.

The section relating to the F.2B from Air Ministry Air Publication *AP129, Royal Air Force Flying Training Manual, Part 1 Flying Instruction,* 1923.

THE BRISTOL FIGHTER (FALCON).

210. The engine controls. (i) The engine controls are :—

(*a*) Petrol tap (centre of dashboard).

(*b*) Petrol pressure exchange (on port side of cock-pit).

(*c*) Throttle lever (on starboard side of cock-pit).

(*d*) Altitude control (on port side of cock-pit).

(*e*) Magneto advance (on port side of cock-pit).

(*f*) Main switch (outside fuselage on port side).

(*g*) Hand starting magneto switch (in passenger's seat).

(*h*) Radiator shutter adjustment (on starboard side of pilot's seat).

(*i*) Hand pump (on port side of cock-pit).

(ii) *The Altitude Control.*—The operation of this control varies with individual engines and should be adjusted by the pilot until smooth running is obtained. The altitude control must usually not be opened under 4,000 ft., but this will depend on the engine and on atmospheric conditions. The best position for the control is not that at which the highest number of revolutions is obtained, but slightly further open at a point at which the revolutions have dropped a little below the original figure. The control should be gradually closed during the descent, and should usually be closed completely at 4,000 ft.

---

160   **Secs. 210—212.**

(iii) *The Radiator Shutter Adjustment.*—In operating this lever, care must be taken that it has engaged one of the ratchets before the butterfly nut is screwed up, otherwise the shutters are liable to close with vibration.

(iv) *Ignition.*—Ignition should be retarded when the engine is running very slowly, and fully advanced when the throttle is opened out.

211. The petrol system.—The Bristol Fighter is fitted with two petrol tanks ; the front tank contains about 24 galls. and the rear tank under the pilot's seat 17 galls. Both these tanks are pressure fed, the initial pressure being supplied by hand pump, and during flight by engine driven pump on camshaft and a wind driven pump attached to forward strut of under-carriage.

The main petrol tap is simple to use and is clearly marked, but care must be taken to see that the pointer on petrol cock handle registers exactly with that on ivorine plate indicating front and rear tanks, and that when the pointer is pointing at front or rear the tap to that tank is fully open. A ratchet inside the tap engages when the tap is open, even though the pointer may not be pointing exactly to front or rear, and the tap cannot then be easily moved either way. Quite a small error in turning on the petrol may result in a restricted supply, which will starve the engine on full throttle.

212. The pressure exchange (*see* fig. 90).—This includes five small taps which are marked as follows :—" Front tank," " rear tank," " release valve," " engine pump," " mechanical (windmill) pump."

At the bottom of the hand pump is another " 3-way " tap. If turned one way, this tap shuts off the hand pump from the pressure system ; if turned along the pressure pipe, it connects the hand pump to the pressure system ; if turned the other way it releases pressure from the tanks. All these taps should be opened before starting the engine, and the hand pump should be connected to the pressure system.

The range of pressure is $\frac{1}{2}$ lb. to 4 lb. per sq. in., but a constant pressure of $2\frac{1}{2}$ lb. should be maintained. The pressure can be regulated by adjustment of air release valve in pilot's cock-pit. Pressure failure in the air can be overcome almost always by correct use of these taps, as they enable that section of the system which is at fault to be isolated.

If the pressure begins to fail, the best procedure is to work on the following system :—

(i) Release valve tap should be turned off ; if this does not eliminate the trouble—

(ii) Pressure from the tank not in use should be turned off ; if this fails—

(iii) The pressure tap of this tank should be opened, the petrol turned on from it, and the other tank shut off ; if this fails—

(iv) Mechanical and engine pumps should be shut off in turn.

Whatever may be the cause of pressure failure, the section of the system in which it has occurred can thus be isolated.

Sec. 212.   161

If the pressure becomes too great :—

(i) Release valve must be adjusted ; if this fails—

(ii) Either mechanical or engine pump should be turned off ; if this fails—

(iii) Pressure must be released at intervals by tap on hand pump.

If a change be made from one tank to another in the air, the pressure tap of the new tank should always be turned on before making the change.

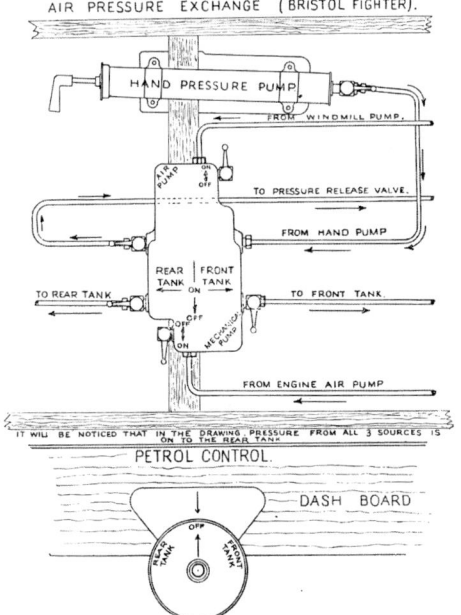

FIG. 90.—**Air Pressure Exchange.**

The oil tank holds 3 galls., but space for one gall. (3 in. from top of tank) should be left, when filling, so as to allow for the oil left in the engine sump when at rest. On starting up the scavenging pump delivers this oil to the tank, and if this is already full, surplus oil is forced out through air vent in filler cap and blown back on to pilot and observer.

(6802)   H

162   Secs. 212—215.

All petrol pipes in the Bristol Fighter between tanks and engine are made of rubber metal tubing known as " rub-metal " (rubber with lining of coiled brass wire), and care should be exercised when connecting this tubing between tanks, petrol cock and filter box, to see that the coiled wire does not restrict the flow of petrol by entering filter box connections. The petrol pipe system should be watched with care, especially if a mixture of petrol and benzole be used, as this mixture is more injurious to rubber tubing than petrol.

213. Starting and running up the engine.—The ease with which the engine can be started depends largely on the temperature of the atmosphere. In cold weather the radiator should be filled with hot water. To suck in, the throttle should be about a quarter open and ignition retarded. With about four revolutions of the airscrew and eight charges of the doper, the engine should start up, when it is switched on and the hand starting magneto is operated.

The radiator shutters should be closed and the engine run slowly until the thermometer shows 60°C. and the oil gauge 40-60 lb. pressure per sq. in. The engine may then be run up gradually, until the necessary revolutions are obtained.

214. Rigging characteristics.—The aileron controls should not be too tight, as they are exposed to air pressure and " take up " a little in flight.

The cross bracings of the two fuselage bays above the tail skid should be frequently examined, as they become loose and sometimes break. Neglect of this precaution may result in broken longerons.

The fastenings of the engine cowling should always be screwed right home in the circular slots, as a really steep dive will pull open the cowling if it is carelessly fastened.

Care should be taken not to allow the skids on the lower planes to get bent or they may foul the aileron king posts.

The drag wires from the front of the engine bearers to the top of the inner forward interplane struts should not be kept too taut, or an undue strain may be brought to bear on the compression ribs concerned.

A combined use of the adjustable tail plane and elevator is necessary to fly the Bristol Fighter well. When flying level or climbing, the pilot should adjust the tail plane till the aeroplane will fly hands off at required speed and engine revolutions.

215. Flying characteristics.

(i) *Taking off.*—Before taking off, the pilot should ascertain that :—

(a) All pressure taps are on, and pressure is at 2½ lb.

(b) Altitude control is closed.

(c) Tail plane adjusting lever is in the half-way position.

(d) Ignition is fully advanced.

A little forward pressure on the control lever is necessary to get the tail off the ground at once, followed by a slight backward movement to take the aeroplane off the ground.

The pilot should always run his engine on the front tank when taking off.

Secs. 215—216.   163

(ii) *Gliding.*—The tail plane should be so adjusted that the aeroplane glides at the required speed " hands off."

For sharp turns and aerobatics, the tail should be so adjusted that the aeroplane is slightly tail-heavy.

(iii) *Turning.*—Rather more rudder is required than on the Avro and it is not necessary to hold off so much bank.

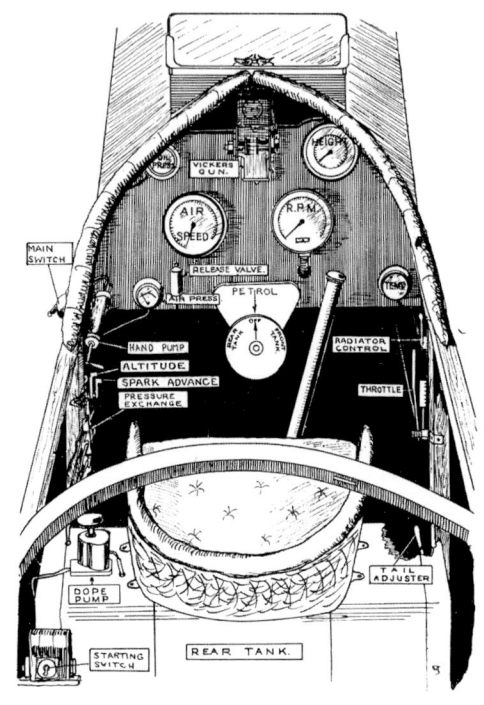

FIG. 91.—**Bristol Fighter. Pilot's Cockpit.**

216. Landing.—The method of approach is the same as that explained in chapter IV. The final turn should not be made too near the ground, as the Bristol Fighter is heavy and is not handled as easily as the Avro.

164   Secs. 216—219.

The tail plane adjustment lever should be right up when near the ground, as this facilitates a slow landing; but the Bristol Fighter stalls rather easily if the glide is too flat.

The radiator shutters should be closed while gliding in to land, in order to prevent the engine from getting cold.

217. Aerobatics.

(i) *Diving.*—The Bristol Fighter has a very steady dive, and the angle of the dive can be regulated by the position of the tail plane adjustment lever

The further forward the lever is set, the steeper the dive. The lever should be eased back while coming out of a dive.

(ii) *Spinning.*—The Bristol Fighter spins rather quickly and loses height rapidly in a spin. She spins more readily against airscrew torque, but full rudder is required to keep her in a spin.

(iii) *Looping.*—The loop should be commenced with a speed of about 90 m.p.h. by pulling back the control column gently but steadily. Rudder to port must be applied to keep her straight on top of the loop, and when over the top the throttle should be closed.

(iv) *Rolling.*—This type rolls best against the airscrew torque, and at a speed of from 60 to 70 m.p.h., otherwise the manoeuvre is carried out as explained in chapter IV.

(v) *Side-slipping.*—The Bristol Fighter is heavier than an Avro, necessitating more care when side-slipping near the ground.

Bristol F.2B H1451 at Farnborough around 1921, probably with the School of Photography Flight, has a container or fairing beneath the lower wing centre section. The observer has a camera gun, and, protruding beneath the fuselage immediately behind the end of the exhaust pipe, there is a Klaxon signal horn. *(C&C)*

Appendix 4

CONTRACTS

Production and Allocation

A total of 3,101 Bristol Fighters was produced up to the end of 1918. Of these, 1,349 were built by the British & Colonial Aeroplane Co. at Filton and 853 at Brislington, a total of 2,202. Production under wartime contracts continued at Bristol until July 1919, by which time a total of 3,126 were completed, 2,081 at Filton and 1,045 at Brislington. By 1926 3,571 Bristol Fighters had been built at Bristol.

Of the 1,754 which were delivered to the RAF up to 31 October 1918, 934 went to the Expeditionary Force in France; 68 went to Italy; 68 to the Middle East; 115 to Home Defence squadrons; 569 to training units.

On 31 October 1918 the RAF had 1,583 Bristol Fighters on charge. Of these, 721 had Sunbeam Arab engines. On that date 249 Falcon and 79 Arab machines were with the squadrons in France; 58 (Falcon)

were with Home Defence units; 48 (Falcon) were in Italy; 26 (Falcon) were in transit to the Middle East; and 42 (Falcon) were in Egypt and Palestine. At training aerodromes at home were 62 (Falcon) and 20 (Arab); at Aeroplane Repair Depots 21 (Falcon) and 62 (Arab); in store 172 (Falcon) and 345 (Arab); at Aircraft Acceptance Parks 46 (Falcon) and 101 (Arab); at various other home stations 138 (Falcon) and 114 (Arab).

Serials	Version	Total	Engines	Contract No	Contract Date	British Requisition	Contractor
A3303	F.2A (ex R.2A)	1	Falcon I	87/A/552	28.8.16	?	British & Colonial
A3304	Falcon or Arab	1	Hispano-Suiza	87/A/552	28.8.16	?	British & Colonial
A3305–A3354	F.2A	50	Falcon II	87/A/552	28.8.16	?	British & Colonial
A7101	F.2B prototype	1	Falcon I	87/A/552 (Addl)	28.8.16	?	British & Colonial
A7102–A7176	F.2B Srs.I		Falcon I	87/A/552 (Addl)	28.8.16	?	British & Colonial
A7177	F.2B Srs.II proto		Falcon I	87/A/552 (Addl)	28.8.16	?	British & Colonial
A7178–A7250	F.2B Srs.I		Falcon I	87/A/552 (Addl)	28.8.16	?	British & Colonial
A7251–A7300	F.2B Srs.2B		Falcon II	87/A/552 (Addl)	28.8.16	?	British & Colonial
B1101–B1350	F.2B	250	Falcon III or Arab	87/A/552 (Addl)	28.8.16	?	British & Colonial
C751–C1050	F.2B	300	Falcon III or Arab	A.S.17573/17	4.9.17	?	British & Colonial
C1951–C2150	F.2B	(200)	–	A.S.20379	23.7.17	?	Harris & Sheldon
C4601–C4800	F.2B	200	Falcon III or Arab	A.S.8871/17 & A.S.17573	4.9.17	?	British & Colonial
C4801–C4900	F.2B	100	Falcon III or Arab	A.S.22909/1/17 & 87/A/552 (Addl)	14.9.17	?	British & Colonial

Serials	Version	Total	Engines	Contract No	Contract Date	British Requisition	Contractor
C9836–C9985	F.2B	150	Arab	A.S.32796	30.10.17	?	Gloucester
D2126–D2625	F.2B	500	Hispano-Suiza	A.S.34276	22.11.17	–	NAF No.3/Cunard
D2626–D2775	F.2B	150	Arab	A.S.35822	22.11.17	270	Marshall & Sons
D7801–D8100	F.2B Mk.I	300	Falcon III	A.S.17573	11.1.18	120, 162	British & Colonial
E1101–E1600	F.2B	(500)	–	A.S.3117	15.2.18	?	British & Colonial
E1901–E2150	F.2B	250	Arab	35a/46/C20	22.2.18	360	Armstrong-Whitworth
E2151–E2650	F.2B	500	Falcon III or Arab	A.S.3117/1/18	5.2.18	335	British & Colonial
E2651–E2900	F.2B	250	Arab	35a/62/C33	22.2.18	360	Angus, Sanderson
E5179–E5428	F.2B	250	Arab	35a/47/C27	20.3.18	360	Standard Motor Co
E9507–E9656	F.2B	150	Arab	35a/428/C307	20.3.18	392	Gloucester
F301–F550	F.2B	(250)	–	35a/47/C27	9.4.18	?	Standard Motor Co
F1231–F1430	F.2B	(200)	–	?	?	?	British & Colonial
F427 –F4970	F.2B	700	Falcon III	35a/779/C658 & A.S.3117/18	12.4.18 & 5.6.18	448	British & Colonial
F5074–F5173	F.2B	100	Arab?	35a/1218/C1158	21.5.18	488	Harris & Sheldon
H834–H1083	F.2B	250		35a/2114/C2448	19.7.18	575	Gloucester
H1240–H1707	F.2B	468	Falcon III	35a/2100/C2393	18.7.18	574	British & Colonial
H1708–H1739	F.2B	(32)	–	35a/2100/C2393	18.7.18	?	British & Colonial
H1746–H1895	F.2B	(150)	–	A.S.35822/18	15.8.18	?	Marshall Sons & Co
H3796–H3995	F.2B	(200)	–	35a/2113/C2447	19.7.18	576	Armstrong Whitworth
H5940–H6539	F.2B	600		35a/2532/C2788	14.8.18	635	Austin Motor Co
J1231 –J1730	F.2B	(500)	–	A.S.33803 & 35a/3244/C3754	26.10.18	682	British & Colonial
J1731–J1930	F.2B	(200)	–	A.S.33803/2 & 35a/3293/C3839	26.10.18	?	Standard Motor Co
J2292–J2391	F.2B	100	?	35a/3379/C3965 & A.S.34500	12.10.18	691	Marshall Sons & Co
J6586–J6800	F.2B Mk.II	215	Falcon III	211474/20	24.6.20	–	Bristol
J7616–J7699	F.2B Mk.II	84	Falcon III	?	?	–	Bristol
J8242–J8291	F.2B Mk.III	50	Falcon III	709172/26	9.26	–	Bristol
J8429–J8458	F.2B Mk.III(DC)	30	Falcon III	733811/26	?	–	Bristol
–	F.2B	(435)	Arab				H.H. Martyn & Co
–	F.2B	(200)	?			577	Angus, Sanderson

UK Contractors

Angus, Sanderson & Co, Newcastle-upon-Tyne.

Sir W.G. Armstrong Whitworth & Co Ltd, Gosforth and Elswick, Newcastle-upon-Tyne.

The Austin Motor Co (1914) Ltd, Northfield, Birmingham (and/or Longbridge).

The British & Colonial Aeroplane Co Ltd, Filton and Brislington, Bristol (Became Bristol Aeroplane Co Ltd 31.12.19).

Harris & Sheldon, Stafford Street, Birmingham.

Marshall Sons & Co Ltd, Gainsborough.

H.H. Martyn & Co, Sunningend, Cheltenham, Glos (Became The Gloucester Aircraft Co Ltd 5.6.17, then Gloster Aircraft Co Ltd in 1926).

National Aircraft Factory No.3 (Cunard Shipping Co Ltd), Aintree, Liverpool.

Standard Motor Co Ltd, Coventry.

American production

Curtiss Aeroplane & Motor Corporation, Buffalo, New York, USA

Dayton-Wright Airplane Co., Dayton, Ohio, USA

Engineering Division, Bureau of Aircraft Production, McCook Field, Dayton, Ohio, USA

The fuselage of this F.2B at the RAF and Army Co-operation School at Worthy Down around 1919 has been given what appears to be a lozenge-pattern colour scheme reminiscent of that applied to German aeroplanes during the First World War. (Philip Jarrett)

Pilot Capt B.I. Catchpole and observer Lt A.J. Findlay seated in F.2B F5812 'A' of 'L' Flight at Bruay around August 1918. This aircraft was a rebuild of B1194. *(C&C)*

Appendix 5

F.2Bs REBUILT BY THE RFC/RAF AND INTERWAR RECONSTRUCTIONS BY BRISTOL AT FILTON

Wartime rebuilds

By No.1 (Southern) Aircraft Repair Depot, Farnborough: B808, B857, B883

By No.1 (Southern) Aircraft Repair Depot, Farnborough: B7763, B7781, B7947

Believed all by No.3 (Western) Aircraft Repair Depot, Yate: B8914 to B8938, B8940 to B8943, B8945 to B8953

By 18th Wing ARS Hounslow; C4548

By Repair Park, No.1 Aeroplane Supply Depot, in France: F5809 to F5824, F5995 to F5999, F6040 to F6043

By Repair Park, No.2 Aeroplane Supply Depot, in France: F6093, F6094, F6101, F6116, F6118, F6121, F6131, F6142, F6158, F6195, F6206, F6208, F6217, F6235, F6283, F6400, F6401, F6402 to F6408

By unknown units: F9395, F9396, F9397, F9404

By 5th Wing ARS: F9403

By No.33 Training Depot Station, Witney: F9404

By No.5 (Eastern) Aircraft Repair Depot, Henlow: F9502, F9504, F9516

By No.3 (Western) Aircraft Repair Depot, Yate: F9598, F9606, F9616

By RAF & Army Co-operation School, Worthy Down: F9638

By Repair Park, No.2 Aeroplane Supply Depot, in France: H6893

By Repair Park, No.1 Aeroplane Supply Depot, in France: H7060 to H7070, H7146, H7169 to H7175, H7196 to H7198, H7291 to H7293

Post-war rebuilds

By Aircraft Depot, Aboukir: CR4651, CR4723, CR4743, DR7802, DR7839, DR8031, DR8098, FR4285, FR4582, FR4583, FR4588, FR4589, FR4600, FR4744, FR4920, FR4925, HR1435, HR1463, HR1635, HR1651, HR1677, JR6592, JR6600, JR6604, JR6635, JR6726, JR6767, JR6785, JR6788, JR6789, JR6798

By Aircraft Depot, Hinaidi: CR4682, DR8056, FR4727, FR4928

By Aircraft Depot, Drigh Road: FR4640

A rebuild by No.3 (Western) Aircraft Repair Depot at Yate, F.2B B8916 appears to have been a dual-control trainer. By late September 1918 it was with the 21st Wing Wireless Telegraphy Flight at Port Meadow. *(Eric Harlin)*

Rebuild F5817 '11' of 48 Sqn, formerly B1136, was lost on 13 March 1919 when it dived in vertically while leading a formation and crashed at Lohmar, south-east of Cologne, Germany. Both occupants, 2nd Lt C.V.A. Allen and 2nd Lt W. Kennedy, were killed. *(C&C)*

Bristol Fighter B8946 was one of a batch rebuilt by No.3 (Western) Aircraft Repair Depot at Yate, and is believed to have been serving with No.45 TDS at Rendcomb when this photograph was taken. It was wrecked on 14 November 1918 in a misjudged landing by 2nd Lt A.R. Webster, who was injured. *(SAAF Museum via Ken Smy)*

F.2Bs Reconditioned by Bristol Interwar, by batches

The information on Bristol Aeroplane Company production contracts listed below was copied from the company's handwritten ledger, and the order in which the aircraft are listed is as it appears in that document. The date of the final stamp of approval by the Aeronautical Inspection Directorate (AID) representative at the Filton factory is also given.

Despite extensive research, the authors were unable to ascertain the exact meaning of the abbreviation 'O/o', but it is thought it might denote the 'Office order' number.

O/o 6135

150 aircraft converted to J type. Electrically bonded throughout and fitted for wireless. Engine fitted to each machine but taken out before despatch. Petrol pipes fitted with metal couplings. Doping scheme ADP & V84. Scarff gun ring moved back.

Dope: Cellon Scheme 'B' pigmented dope. B.E.S A Specification 2 D101. Four coats of dope, one coat of V84; put into operation 10 December 1923. Fuselages of F4702, F4703, F4719, F4563 and F4601 given Scheme 'B' dope.

Serial	Final AID stamp	Remarks	Serial	Final AID stamp	Remarks	Serial	Final AID stamp	Remarks
F4755	15/6/23		F4902	24/8/23		F4599	3/10/23	
F4952	15/6/23		F4567	24/8/23		F4723	2/10/23	
F4749	16/6/23		F4507	27/8/23		F4514	4/10/23	
F4745	18/6/23		F4569	28/8/23		F4510	4/10/23	
F4742	18/6/23		F4904	30/8/23		F4704	5/10/23	
C1042	19/6/23		F4568	30/8/23		F4624	10/10/23	
F4953	12/7/23		F4484	31/8/23		F4490	8/10/23	
F4756	11/7/23		F4542	5/9/23		F4506	10/10/23	
F4727	13/7/23		F4591	3/9/23		F4623	11/10/23	
F4729	13/7/23		F4485	8/9/23		F4489	12/10/23	
F4731	18/7/23		F4326	6/9/23		F4513	12/10/23	
F4698	19/7/23		F4903	7/9/23		F4884	13/10/23	
F4735	17/7/23		F4500	11/9/23		F4712	15/10/23	
F4744	21/7/23		F4570	8/9/23		F4508	18/10/23	
F4732	24/7/23		F4541	13/9/23		F4481	17/10/23	
F4743	24/7/23		F4566	12/9/23		F4505	19/10/23	
F4741	25/7/23		F4463	14/9/23		F4465	19/10/23	
F4748	25/7/23		F4592	13/9/23		F4905	20/10/23	
F4751	30/7/23		F4584	19/9/23		F4548	22/10/23	
F4320	31/7/23		F4658	13/9/23		F4454	26/10/23	
F4753	31/7/23		F4716	19/9/23		F4565	25/10/23	
F4734	3/8/23		F4496	14/9/23		F4549	26/10/23	
F4746	2/8/23		F4551	21/9/23		F4574	24/10/23	
F4726	3/8/23		F4491	24/9/23		F4504	27/10/23	
F4870	13/8/23		F4497	24/9/23		F4587	27/10/23	
F4733	10/8/23		F4547	21/9/23		F4546	3/11/23	
F4758	14/8/23		F4607	27/9/23		F4517	29/10/23	
H1565	15/8/23		F4561	25/9/23		F4586	9/11/23	
F4747	20/8/23		F4495	26/9/23		F4492	1/11/23	
F4760	21/8/23		F4487	26/9/23		F4581	31/10/23	
F4589	23/8/23		F4621	28/9/23		F4596	2/11/23	
F4896	22/8/23		F4464	27/9/23		F4588	3/11/23	

Previously A7128, rebuild F6121 'S' of 20 Sqn, seen here at Boisdinghem, spun into the ground on 3 December 1918, killing Lt S.E. Booth and Cpl Mech R. Morse. *(C&C)*

The first of a batch of rebuilds of various aircraft types by the 45th Wing, F9396 '8' may have been with No.28 TDS at Crail. *(via Phil Cooksey)*

Serial	Final AID stamp	Remarks	Serial	Final AID stamp	Remarks	Serial	Final AID stamp	Remarks
F4515	2/11/23		F4516	3/12/23		F4604	5/12/23	
F4571	8/11/23		F4572	21/11/23		F4713	18/12/23	
F4706	14/11/23		F4590	20/11/23		F4881	19/12/23	
F4610	9/11/23		F4543	4/12/23		F4602	19/12/23	
F4519	8/11/23		F4737	26/11/23		F4555	14/12/23	
F4550	9/11/23		F4598	10/12/23		F4702	19/12/23	
F4518	16/11/23		F4714	27/11/23		F4703	20/12/23	
F4606	14/11/23		F4600	28/11/23		F4719	20/12/23	
F4486	17/11/23		F4583	4/12/23		F4563	21/12/23	
F4882	21/11/23		F4544	30/11/23		F4601	21/12/23	
F4554	29/11/23		F4720	6/12/23		F4883	10/12/23	
F4553	16/11/23							

O/o 6525

75 aircraft converted to J type. 25 to be fitted with dual control. (Ten machines only fitted with dual control on this o/o, indicated by *; 15 machines fitted on o/o 6764, below.)

Serial	Final AID stamp	Remarks	Serial	Final AID stamp	Remarks	Serial	Final AID stamp	Remarks
F4970	15/2/24		F4958	14/3/24		C4897	26/4/24	
F4960	18/2/24		F4947	12/3/24		C4681	10/5/24	
F4956	19/2/24		F4594	15/3/24		D7873	10/5/24	
F4946	16/2/24		F4955	19/3/24		D7876	10/5/24	
C799	20/2/24		F4957	21/3/24		F4648*	26/4/24	
F4964	25/2/24		F4963	6/3/24		F4685*	3/5/24	
C763	15/2/24		C801	14/3/24		C4680*	6/5/24	
C4738	16/2/24		C812	14/3/24		F4650*	3/5/24	
C765	18/2/24		F4693	15/3/24		F4642*	7/5/24	
F4338	21/2/24		D8055	15/3/24		F4827*	9/5/24	
F4954	16/2/24		H1562	15/3/24		C802	17/5/24	
F4969	26/2/24		F4967	21/3/24		C4682	6/6/24	
C810	29/2/24		F4965	22/3/24		F4349	30/5/24	
F4595	28/2/24		C4734	22/3/24		D8031	6/6/24	
D7801	27/2/24		C4683	22/3/24		C762	5/6/24	
C798	29/2/24		E1014	3/4/24		H1609	14/5/24	
D7851	11/3/24		C4741	7/4/24		F4697	17/5/24	
F4962	6/3/24		F4645	22/3/24		F4754	24/5/24	
F4949	29/2/24		F4688	22/3/24		F4840	24/5/24	
F4339	4/3/24		F4647*	26/4/24		F4644	31/5/24	
F4948	8/3/24		F4342*	29/4/24		D7854	24/5/24	
C764	6/3/24		F4691*	29/4/24		F4737	5/6/24	
F4950	11/3/24		F4692*	1/5/24		F4484	15/5/24	
F4951	11/3/24		D7874	15/4/24		F4646	6/6/24	
F4961	12/3/24		D7812	3/5/24		F4649	30/6/24	

O/o 6764
75 aircraft converted to J type, sequence numbers 6460 to 6509.

First 16 machines fitted with engines and screened and bonded for short-wave radio transmission (SWRT).

Next 19 machines less engines but screened and bonded for SWRT. Ballast weights, new type pistol case, R/L bomb cases for 8x4 bombs.

Last 15 machines fitted with dual control (*), not screened and bonded for SWRT. Ballast weights not fitted to these machines; CC firing gear not fitted; no lighting cables in fuselage; wings fitted with lighting and Holt flare cables.

Serial	Final AID stamp	Remarks	Serial	Final AID stamp	Remarks	Serial	Final AID stamp	Remarks
F4573	4/7/24		F4682	3/9/24		F4695	29/9/24	
F4935	4/7/24		F4683	5/9/24		F4887	2/10/24	
H1416	5/7/24		F4689	9/9/24	1st machine with new type rudder lamp bracket	F4789	2/10/24	
F4812	5/7/24					F4722*	4/10/24	
F4711	7/7/24					F4913*	6/10/24	
F4609	7/7/24		F4619	10/9/24		F4701*	6/10/24	
F4603	8/7/24		H1424	11/9/24		F4811*	10/10/24	
H1634	8/7/24		F4929	12/9/24		F4786*	11/10/24	
F4715	9/7/24		F4916	15/9/24	1st machine with batten for 2 terminal block in rear fuselage	F4708*	11/10/24	
F4901	9/7/24					H1392*	15/10/24	
F4932	12/7/24					F4705*	17/10/24	
F4545	14/7/24					H1444*	18/10/24	
F4699	15/7/24		H1413	16/9/24		H1396*	18/10/24	
F4717	16/7/24		F4914	18/9/24		H1390*	23/10/24	
F4698	17/7/24		F4915	19/9/24		H1398*	23/20/24	
F4694	19/7/24		F4907	19/9/24		H1589*	25/10/24	
F4681	29/8/24		H1461	24/9/24		J6676*	30/10/24	
F4687	30/8/24		H1458	25/9/24		J6586*	25/10/24	
F4684	3/9/24							

O/o 6827
100 aircraft converted to J type, sequence numbers 6529 to 6628. Delay caused on this contract by old and new type tailplane and elevator hinges.

Serial	Final AID stamp	Remarks	Serial	Final AID stamp	Remarks	Serial	Final AID stamp	Remarks
F4386	7/11/24	1st machine with ⅜in copper bonding strip & silencer type exhaust pipes	H1640	27/11/24		F4473	17/12/24	
			J6664	29/11/24		C1015	19/12/24	
			E2533	29/11/24		C4676	19/12/24	
			F4285	29/11/24		F4618	19/12/24	
			E2629	14/12/24		H1483	20/12/24	
E2435	7/11/24		E2259	5/12/24		F4830	22/12/24	
F4645	8/11/24		F4771	5/12/24		F4854	22/12/24	
F4418	8/11/24		F4804	6/12/24		J6662	22/12/24	
F4501	8/11/24		F4942	6/12/24		E2624	22/12/24	
H1393	14/11/24	1st machine with hole in radiator fairing	C1027	8/12/24		F4450	1/1/25	
			F4680	9/12/24		H1440	1/1/25	
			H1632	11/12/24	1st machine with new type fire bulkhead & tie rods for CPX bracing	F4301	3/1/25	
H1432	14/11/24					H1451	3/1/25	
H1417	15/11/24					D8044	7/1/25	
F4503	14/11/14					F4379	3/1/25	
F4853	15/11/24					E2264	7/1/25	
H1598	20/11/24	1st machine with new type swivelling arm	F4385	12/12/24	1st machine with fibre between incidence wires & ash stripe on gunner's seat rail	C903	8/1/25	
						F4898	9/1/25	
						E2257	9/1/25	
F4944	21/11/24					H1601	12/1/25	
C4750	22/11/24					F4908	16/1/25	
H1588	22/11/24		F4509	12/12/24		H1428	16/1/25	
H1486	22/11/24		F4810	13/12/24		J6678	16/1/25	
F4488	22/11/24		F4375	13/12/24		F4643	20/1/25	
F4934	28/11/24		F4366	15/12/24		C1032	19/1/25	
F4381	28/11/24		H1423	15/12/24		H1686	23/1/25	
C4794	29/11/24		F4376	17/12/24		C804	20/1/25	

Serial	Final AID stamp	Remarks	Serial	Final AID stamp	Remarks	Serial	Final AID stamp	Remarks
F4498	28/1/25		H1606	7/2/25		F4665	14/2/25	
F4523	22/1/25		H1430	30/1/25		C4766	12/2/25	
F5996	24/1/25		H1617	10/2/25		F4839	14/2/25	
F4369	22/1/25		C1039	11/2/25		F4396	20/2/25	
H1397	24/1/25		E2504	9/2/25		H1581	20/2/25	
F4423	27/1/25		C923	10/2/25		F4857	21/2/25	
F4667	26/1/25		F4819	16/2/25		F4921	19/2/25	
H1583	27/1/25		H1457	11/2/25		J6700	19/2/25	
F4477	29/1/25		E2501	9/2/25		F4660	25/2/25	
H7064	27/1/25		F4670	11/2/25		F9616	25/2/25	
F4537	29/1/25		D8009	14/2/25		E2552	25/2/25	
H1604	29/1/25		F4494	12/2/25				

O/o 7120

80 aircraft converted to J type, sequence numbers 6629 to 6708.

Serial	Final AID stamp	Remarks	Serial	Final AID stamp	Remarks	Serial	Final AID stamp	Remarks
6670	27/2/25		J6740	19/3/25		D7847	8/4/25	
J6632	26/2/25		F4401	18/3/25		F4892	9/4/25	
J6663	2/3/25		F4430	19/3/25		F4700	17/4/25	
F4706	26/2/25		E2297	21/3/25		H1600	21/4/25	
J6746	28/2/25		F4896	20/3/25		F4605	21/4/25	
J6715	28/2/25		J6761	21/3/25		F4341	23/4/25	
D7890	4/3/25		JJ6721	21/3/25		F4278	18/4/25	
F4392	10/3/25		J6736	20/3/25		H1624	22/4/25	
F4559	4/3/25		H1637	26/3/25		J6730	28/4/25	
H1616	27/2/25		F4886	19/3/25		D7848	30/4/25	
F4556	7/3/25		H1420	This machine used as a mock-up for new layout. Mock-up completed & machine sent aerodrome 21/8/25. Returned from Old Sarum 19/1/26 for further modifications. Flown to Old Sarum 4/3/26. Returned to works 23/7/26.		D7850	24/4/25	
F4344	5/3/25					F4815	24/4/25	
D7864	7/3/25					F4562	1/5/25	
F4558	4/3/25					F4906	28/4/25	
H1599	13/3/25					F4362	1/5/25	
J6735	10/3/25					C4845	4/5/25	
J6677	9/3/25					H1555	29/4/25	
H1488	12/3/25					F4416	4/5/25	
D8092	11/3/25					F4414	11/5/25	
J6752	6/3/25		J6711	21/3/25		F4511	7/5/25	
H1395	17/3/25		F4813	30/3/25		F4686	8/5/25	
J6718	14/3/25		C767	28/3/25		F4891	8/5/25	
J6716	17/3/25		B1325	9/4/25		H1391	5/5/25	
H1410	16/3/25		B1326	9/4/25		H1394	13/5/25	
J6729	13/3/25		J6765	7/4/25		H1438	14/5/25	
J6681	14/3/25		H1415	1/4/25		H1473	16/5/25	
J6701	12/3/25		J6691	28/3/25		F4753	13/5/25	
J6800	14/3/25		J6708	9/4/25		C766	15/5/25	
J6756	16/3/25		F4710	9/4/25				
C4631	17/3/25		F4721	9/4/25				

O/o 8005

84 aircraft converted to J type.

Serial	Final AID stamp	Remarks	Serial	Final AID stamp	Remarks	Serial	Final AID stamp	Remarks
J7616	20/5/25		J7622	27/5/25		J7628	29/5/25	
J7617	22/5/25		J7623	26/5/25		J7629	9/6/25	
J7618	23/5/25		J7624	29/5/25		J7630	8/6/25	
J7619	21/5/25		J7625	26/5/25		J7631	5/6/25	
J7620	25/5/25		J7626	29/5/25		J7632	3/6/25	
J7621	29/5/25		J7627	29/5/25		J7633	8/6/25	

Serial	Final AID stamp	Remarks	Serial	Final AID stamp	Remarks	Serial	Final AID stamp	Remarks
J7634	4/6/25		J7652	22/6/25		J7676	22/7/25	
J7635	8/6/25		J7653	23/6/25		J7677	13/8/25	
J7636	9/6/25		J7654	23/6/25		J7678	16/7/25	
J7637	10/6/25		J7655	24/6/25		J7679	18/7/25	
J7638	11/6/25		J7656	25/6/25		J7680	15/8/25	
J7639	11/6/25		J7657	25/6/25		J7681	22/7/25	
J7640	12/6/25		J7658	26/6/25		J7682	24/7/25	
J7641	12/6/25		J7659	2/7/25		J7683	28/7/25	
J7642	29/8/25	Fitted with new type engine bearer. Modified F3328. i.e. – Socket at bottom of diagonal tube. (1st design)	J7660	27/6/25		J7684	31/7/25	
			J7661	30/6/25		J7685	31/7/25	
			J7662	1/7/25		J7686	31/7/25	
			J7663	1/7/25		J7687	13/8/25	
			J7664	3/7/25		J7688	17/8/25	
			J7665	3/7/25		J7689	18/8/25	
			J7666	10/7/25		J7690	20/8/25	
J7643	13/6/25		J7667	6/7/25		J7691	20/8/25	
J7644	13/6/25		J7668	14/7/25		J7692	21/8/25	
J7645	16/6/25		J7669	7/7/25		J7693	22/8/25	
J7646	22/6/25		J7670	7/7/25		J7694	27/8/25	
J7647	16/6/25		J7671	9/7/25		J7695	31/8/25	
J7648	17/6/25		J7672	9/7/25		J7696	29/8/25	
J7649	20/6/25		J7673	9/7/25		J7697	31/8/25	
J7650	22/6/25		J7674	15/7/25		J7698	31/8/25	
J7651	22/6/25		J7675	17/7/25		J7699	2/9/25	

O/o 8092

50 aircraft converted to J type, sequence numbers 6806 to 6855. Dual control (*).

Serial	Final AID stamp	Remarks	Serial	Final AID stamp	Remarks	Serial	Final AID stamp	Remarks
H1454	4/9/25		H1493*	1/10/25		F4622*	22/10/25†	
H1455	4/9/25		H1496*	2/10/25		F4826*	22/10/25†	
H1501	7/9/25		H1463*	3/10/25		F4492*	26/10/25†	
H1526	8/9/25		D8033*	6/10/25		H1642*	29/10/25†	
H1623	9/9/25		H1469*	7/10/25		H1502*	31/10/25†	
H1627	12/9/25		H1439*	8/10/25		F4507*	2/11/25†	
H1636	12/9/25		H1644*	10/10/25		D8085*	28/10/25	
H1668	14/9/25		F4885*	13/10/25		F4727*	29/10/25	
H1677	15/9/25		E2300*	10/10/25		D8096*	30/10/25	
H1685	16/9/25		F4911*	13/10/25		H1492*	2/11/25	
D7839*	24/9/25		F4912*	22/10/25		H1681*	3/11/25	
F4925*	25/9/25		F4751*	16/10/25		H1660*	4/11/25	
F4939*	26/9/25		F4756*	21/10/25		H1494*	5/11/25	
F4940*	26/9/25		F4490*	22/10/25		H1456*	5/11/25	
F4814*	29/9/25		H1669*	23/10/25		H1465*	7/11/25	
F4946*	30/9/25		E2643*	27/10/25		F4651*	9/11/25	
F4585*	2/10/25		F4968*	30/10/25				

† Fitted with engine & sent to the aerodrome re-rigged for flight test.

O/o 8302

54 aircraft converted to J type, sequence numbers 6864 to 6917. All dual control (*) apart from last machine (J6696).

Serial	Final AID stamp	Remarks	Serial	Final AID stamp	Remarks	Serial	Final AID stamp	Remarks
C1049*	21/11/25		F4548*	1/12/25		F4721*	17/12/25	1st machine with Mod. F.2B 598, & all subsequent machines.
F4434*	25/11/25		J6791*	2/12/25				
E2624*	25/11/25		F4385*	3/12/25				
C4740*	26/11/25		J6708*	4/12/25				
F4423*	28/11/25		F4369*	7/12/25		F4418*	18/12/25	

Serial	Final AID stamp	Remarks	Serial	Final AID stamp	Remarks	Serial	Final AID stamp	Remarks
H1468*	18/12/25		J6702*	14/1/26		F4586*	11/2/26	
F4584*	19/12/25		F4607*	14/1/26		D8083*	12/2/26	
F4510*	?		J6600*	14/1/26		F4564*	15/2/26	
J6790*	21/12/25		J6658*	16/1/26		F4515*	20/2/26	
F4956*	22/12/25		F4963*	15/1/26		F4497*	22/2/26	
F4705*	31/12/25		J6677*	18/1/26		E2432*	25/2/26	
F4960*	1/1/26		J6734*	20/1/26		H1634*	26/2/26	
J6661*	6/1/26		J6602*	19/1/26		E2434*	3/3/26	
F4715*	4/1/26		D8045*	26/1/26		F4561*	4/3/26	
H1614*	7/1/26		F4882*	27/1/26		F4610*	10/3/26	
F4970*	7/1/26		J6793*	4/2/26		J6697*	9/3/26	
J6589*	9/1/26		F4588*	28/1/26		J6738*	13/3/26	
J6685*	12/1/26		F4934*	6/2/26		F4757*	15/3/26	
D8100*	12/1/26		F4375*	10/2/26		J6696	5/2/26	

O/o 8673

40 aircraft converted to J type. Built to Spec 425 Appendix A Serial No 140. Lewis gun stowage as H1420 (see O/o 7120). Divided doors on Vickers gun mtg. Adjustable mounting for Vickers gun. HA drift sight mounting fitted and bottom plane modified to suit. New exhaust pipe on starboard side, also new brackets. Voltage control box fitted. Stick and clips for R/L bomb tube. Oil thermometer fitted, also map and photo boards, writing pad, message picking up gear, cockpit and engine covers. Wireless as H1420 as far as possible. Fixed aerial omitted. Hand starter mag to Mod 570 not as H1420.

Serial	Final AID stamp	Remarks	Serial	Final AID stamp	Remarks	Serial	Final AID stamp	Remarks
F4744†	11/6/26		D7801	29/6/26		J6775	16/7/26	
F4567†	12/6/26		F4845	2/7/26	1st machine fitted with Uniflex cable for wireless	J6695	16/7/26	
D8056†	12/6/26					F4965	17/7/26	
J6622†	14/6/26					F4624	17/7/26	
D7818†	16/6/26		F4571	2/7/26		J7685	23/7/26	
D7815†	17/6/26		F4500	2/7/26		J6694	23/7/26	
F4732†	17/6/26		F4465	3/7/26		F4836	24/7/26	
F4591†	18/6/26		C4676	8/7/26	1st machine fitted with new type Holt flare points	F4603	24/7/26	
J6798†	18/6/26					F4812‡	30/7/26	
F4745†	21/6/26					F4698‡	30/7/26	
C4794†‡	23/6/26		J6701	8/7/26		H1424‡	14/8/26	
J7658†‡	25/6/26		H1415	9/7/26		F4486‡	30/7/26	
D7812	25/6/26		H1451	9/7/26		J7620‡	16/8/26	
F4903	25/6/26		F4902	13/7/26		F4684‡	19/8/26	
J6747	26/6/26		J6680	15/7/26				

† Hand starter switches not fitted. ‡ Aerial reel not fitted

O/o 9789

30 aircraft; nine to be dual control, 21 to be standard type, sequence numbers 7090 to 7119. Last 9 dual control (*).

Serial	Final AID stamp	Remarks	Serial	Final AID stamp	Remarks	Serial	Final AID stamp	Remarks
H1417	22/3/27		J7686	22/6/27	Wings set back 4in	J7636	11/7/27	
F4366	27/5/27	1st machine with serial numbers under lower wings	F4496	24/6/27		F4516	13/7/27	
			J7616	22/6/27		H1396*	11/7/27	
			F4618	29/6/27		H1644*	14/7/27	
J6749	28/5/27		F4967	20/6/27		F4811*	14/7/27	
F4952	28/5/27		J6662	6/7/27		J6718*	20/7/27	
F4590	28/5/27		F4412	1/7/27		F4810*	20/7/27	
H1562	2/6/27		J6719	6/7/27		F4721*	16/7/27	
J7621	2/6/27	Longerons strengthened	F4741	7/7/27		F4701*	18/7/27	
			J7689	7/7/27		F4492*	15/7/27	
F4489	15/6/27	New top & bottom fins & rudders (balanced)	J7657	8/7/27		E2630*	18/7/27	

O/o 42 (Contract 742470/27)

30 aircraft; eight to be dual control (*), 22 to be Mk.III, sequence numbers 7125 to 7154.

Serial	Final AID stamp	Remarks	Serial	Final AID stamp	Remarks	Serial	Final AID stamp	Remarks
H1494*	24/8/27		F4944	14/6/28		H1596	25/5/28	
F4691*	26/8/27		F4517	16/6/28		F4587	23/5/28	Became G-AFHJ
F4342*	30/8/27		C4750	8/5/28	Became G-ACFO	F4957	4/6/28	
F4912*	31/8/27		H1432	8/5/28		F4381	19/5/28	
F4519*	31/8/27		H1624	8/5/28		J7670	19/5/28	
C4680*	31/8/27		H1598	17/5/28		J7659	14/6/28	
D8033*	1/9/27		F5996	7/5/28		F4754	4/6/28	
F4756*	6/9/27		J6766	14/5/28		C767	8/6/28	
F4545	?		F4681	15/6/28		F4569	5/6/28	
F4553	13/6/28		F4542	12/5/28	Became G-ACFN	F4565	9/6/28	

O/o 161

20 aircraft; first 12 J Type, final 8 dual control (*).

The wings on the J Type machines were fixed in the original position and not set back. Fuselage longerons were not stiffened up. They had old basket-type pilot's seat and sliding gunner's seats. Map case and writing pad fitted. Auster windscreens. Latest type wireless installation. HA drift sight not fitted. Old type rudders (unbalanced) and fins fitted. Wooden tailskids. Old type undercarriage and shock absorbers. No message picking-up gear. No swivelling arm. DP generator fitted to bottom port wing. Straight tube gun steady fitted. External ballast weights without modification to flange collars and bearer tube. Old type IAG lever fitted. Starting magneto as Mk.III. Latest type Vickers gun mounting. Canvas bulkhead fitted. Last modified bonding. One Pyrene (extinguisher) only fitted in camera bay.

The first three dual-control machines were sent away less autoslots. Other five machines fitted with autoslots. Longerons were reinforced, but old type rudders and fins fitted. Also wooden tailskid. Mk.III windscreen on front cockpit fairing and Auster windscreen on rear cockpit fairing. Old type undercarriage and shock absorbers fitted.

Serial	Final AID stamp	Remarks	Serial	Final AID stamp	Remarks	Serial	Final AID stamp	Remarks
J6668	28/2/28		J7690	7/3/28		F4588*	4/5/28	
J6760	28/2/28		H1640	8/3/28		H1642*	4/6/28	
F4645	28/2/28		H1440	16/3/28		F4946*	4/6/28	
J7660	2/3/28		J6722	17/3/28		F2643*	20/6/28	
H1526	2/3/28		C4737	23/3/28		H1493*	21/6/28	
J6743	2/3/28		H1660*	4/5/28		F4913*	22/6/28	
J7656	5/3/28		C763*	4/5/28				

O/o 315 (Contract 793687//27)

12 aircraft: first nine J Type, all sent to Packing Depot, RAF Ascot; final three dual control (*), all sent to Home Aircraft Depot, Henlow.

Serial	Final AID stamp	Remarks	Serial	Final AID stamp	Remarks	Serial	Final AID stamp	Remarks
B1326	29/6/28		J7640	6/7/28		F4329	19/7/28	
J7638	29/6/28		J6676	7/7/28		F4610*	6/9/28	
C4683	30/6/28		C4655	12/7/28		F4970*	7/9/28	
J6742	2/7/28		H1560	13/7/28		H1398*	22/9/28	

O/o 468 (Contract 79687//27)

17 aircraft: recondition where necessary and convert to Mk.IV. All less engines. Essex Fire Extinguishers fitted to all except F4545.

Serial	Final AID stamp	Remarks	Serial	Final AID stamp	Remarks
F4545?	?		J8269	14/9/28	Inland Area for 2 (AC) Sqn Manston
H1420	8/9/28	Fitted with large-type rudder & cambered fin. Extra bay of top longerons stiffened up to 40mm sq. (see o/o 7120). Inland Area for 4 (AC) Sqn Farnborough	J8272	15/9/28	Inland Area for Armament & Gunnery School Eastchurch
			J8267	15/9/28	Inland Area for 2 (AC) Sqn Manston
			J8270	19/9/28	Inland Area for 2 (AC) Sqn Manston
J8265	10/9/28	Fighting area for 24 Sqn Northolt	F4590	21/9/28	Inland Area for SoAC Old Sarum

Serial	Final AID stamp	Remarks	Serial	Final AID stamp	Remarks
J7621	22/9/28	Inland Area for Armament & Gunnery School Eastchurch	J6749	6/10/28	Inland Area for Armament & Gunnery School Eastchurch
H1562	29/9/28	Inland Area for SoAC Old Sarum	J6662	6/10/28	Inland Area for Armament & Gunnery School Eastchurch
F4366	29/9/28	Inland Area for 4 (AC) Sqn Farnborough	F4412	10/10/28	Inland Area for 4 (AC) Sqn Farnborough
F4952	30/9/28	Inland Area for SoAC Old Sarum	J8262	?	Fighting Area for 24 Sqn Northolt
J8271	6/10/28	Inland Area for 4 (AC) Sqn Farnborough			

O/o 1143

10 aircraft reconditioned to Mk.IV and Mk.III dual. (22 aircraft listed, dual machines not identified)

Serial	Final AID stamp	Despatched	Remarks	Serial	Final AID stamp	Despatched	Remarks
F4697	20/12/29	31/1/30		J6661	16/5/30	23/6/30	
J7692	8/1/30	31/1/30		C4740	1/5/30	6/6/30	
F4644	2/1/30	30/1/30		J6602	13/5/30	30/5/30	
D7835	19/12/29	17/1/30		F4610	5/5/30	16/6/30	
J7696	24/1/30	18/2/30		J6685	9/5/30	28/5/30	
D7874	5/2/30	27/2/30		J8440	26/5/30	28/6/30	
J7652	21/1/30	10/2/30		J8431	5/6/30	8/7/30	
F4845	16/1/30	4/2/30		F4811	?	20/8/30	s/n 7556
H1624	31/1/30	22/2/30		D8085	?	12/8/30	s/n 7557
H1640	13/7/30	19/7/30		H1396	?	15/8/30	s/n 7558
F4756	30/4/30	27/5/30		F4721	?	25/8/30	s/n 7559. Became G-ABYE

O/o 1167

10 aircraft for repair; two dual control (*).

Serial	Final AID stamp	Remarks	Serial	Final AID stamp	Remarks	Serial	Final AID stamp	Remarks
J8246	5/12/29	Mk.III	C4680*	23/12/29	Mk.III dual	J8450	17/12/29	
F4912*	3/12/29	Mk.III dual	J8248	16/12/29	Mk.III	J7657	6/6/30	
H1432	16/12/29	Mk.III	F4741	2/6/30				

O/o 1589 (Contract 27633/30)

14 aircraft reconditioned to Mk.IV and Mk.III, all dual control (*). First 10 machines only fitted with new-type Sorbo rubber front and rear cockpit padding. Modification cancelled, not to apply to subsequent machines. Raking instrument board in rear cockpit, also new anchorage for passenger's harness. Sequence numbers 7568 to 7581.

Serial	Sent to aerodrome	Despatched	Remarks
J8434*	18/11/30	5/12/30	Became G-ABYT
F4548*	25/11/30	11/12/30	
C4897*	1/12/30	15/12/30	Became G-ACFL
J8437*	8/12/30	19/12/30	Became G-ACAC
H1660*	13/2/31	5/3/31	
J8429*	17/2/31	13/3/31	Wessex Area for Andover. Became G-ABYF
J8446*	12/12/30	22/12/30	Wessex Area for Andover. Became G-ABYD
D8096*	?	21/3/31	Wessex Area for Andover. Became G-AEPH
J6790*	?	27/3/31	Wessex Area for Andover. Became G-ACCG
J8448*	?	15/4/31	Wessex Area for Andover. Became G-ACPE
F4342*	15/5/31		Became G-ACHR
J8444*	21/5/31		Wessex Bombing Area for Andover Store. Became G-ABYL
J8455*	29/5/31		Wessex Bombing Area for Andover Store. Became G-ADJR
F4434*	2/6/31		Wessex Bombing Area for Andover Store. Became G-ACFP

This F.2B, with stereoscopic cameras mounted on the rear cockpit, has the name *Murielle* inscribed below the exhaust pipe. *(Philip Jarrett)*

Appendix 6

NAMED AIRCRAFT

Presentation aircraft

Serial	Presentation name
A7175	Malaya No.23 'The Malacca'
A7176	Montreal No.4
A7177	Auckland
A7178	Australia No.1, South Australia No.1 'The Sidney Kidman'
A7179	Presented by the Government of Johore No.6
A7180	Dominica
A7181	Newfoundland No.4
A7182	Gold Coast No.11
A7190	Australia No.15, New South Wales No.14 'Womens Battleplane'

(subscribed and collected by women of New South Wales)

A7200	Australia No.13, New South Wales No.12 'The Macintyre Kayuga Estate
A7225	Ajmeer
A7226	Kotah No.2
A7236	Australia No.1, South Australia No.1 'The Sidney Kidman'
A7237	Australia No.9, New South Wales No.8 'The White Saumarez & Baldblair'
A7267	Malaya No.23 'The Malacca'
A7299	Presented by the Maharaja Bahadur Sir Rameswar Singh of Darbhanga No.2

A7300	Presented by the Maharaja Bahadur Sir Rameswar Singh of Darbhanga No.4
B1105	Kotah No.1
B1107	Falkland
B1108	Udaipur No.2, also Jaypores Vizag
B1109	Udaipur No.1
B1110	Johore No.2
B1111	Punjab No.44 Lahore No.4
B1114	Auckland
B1117	Presented by the Government of Johore No.6
B1122	Dominica
B1143	Kotah No.1
B1145	Presented by Maharaja Bahadur Sir Rameswar Singh of Darbhanga No.3
B1146	Australia No.2, New South Wales No.1. 'The White Bell Trees'
B1147	'South Australia No.2' Presented by the People of South Australia
B1148	Australia No.3, New South Wales No.2 'The White Edenglassie'
B1149	Australia No.11, New South Wales No.10 'Duplicate Tweed No.9'
B1181	Baroda No.14
B1186	Montreal No.4
B1199	Australia No.10, New South Wales No.9 'The Tweed'

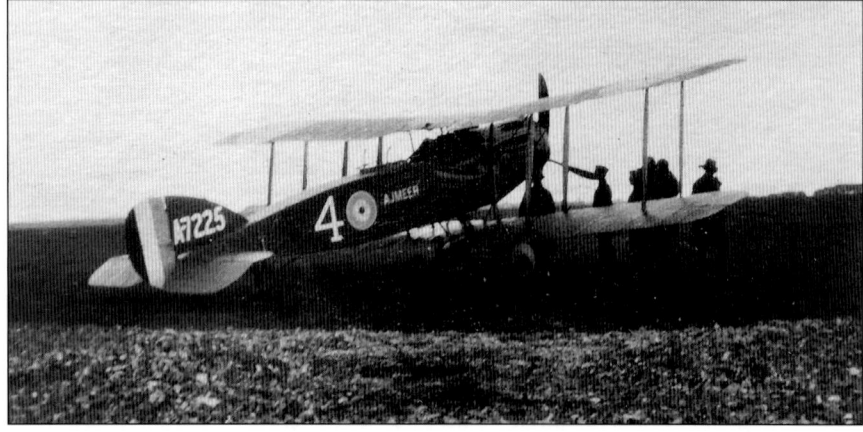

Probably photographed while serving with No 59 TS, F.2B A7225, carrying number '4' was named *Ajmeer*. *(SAAF Museum via Ken Smy)*

B1223	Australia No.17, New South Wales No.16 'The Upper Hunter Battleplane' (presented by the Residents of the Upper Hunter District, NSW)
B1229	Australia No.12, New South Wales No.11 'The Macintyre Kayuga Estate'
B1230	Montreal
B1231	Winnipeg
B1232	Toronto
B1234	Edmonton
B1242	Ajmeer (from India)
B1262	Presented by the Maharaja Bahadur Sir Rameswar Singh of Darbhanga No.2 'The Lord of Chelmsford'
B1276	Australia No.18, New South Wales No.17 'The Upper Hunter Battleplane'
B1285	Australia No.7, New South Wales No.6 'The White Edenglassie'
B1330	Presented by Maharaja Bahadur Sir Rameswar Singh of Darbhanga No.5
B1331	Presented by Maharaja Bahadur Sir Rameswar Singh of Darbhanga No.1 'The Lord Hardinge'
B1335	Malaya No.23 'The Malacca'
C773	Brigham Young
C797	Udaipur No.1
C970	Malaya No.19 'The Singapore No.2'
C989	'Bhopal' Presented by His Highness the Begum of Bhopal
C1034	Zanzibar No.17 (presented by the Government of Zanzibar)
C4623	Australia No.20, New South Wales No.18 'The McClaughey Battleplane', also Australia No.8, New South Wales No.7 'The Mrs P.Kirby & Son'
C4624	Australia No.13, New South Wales No.12 'The Macintyre Kayuga Estate'
C4626	Australia No.16, New South Wales No.7 'The Upper Hunter'
C4627	City of Adelaide, Presented by Mrs Harry Bickford
C4635	Presented by the Maharaja Bahadur Sir Rameswar Singh of Darbhanga No.3
C4805	Montreal No.4
C4810	Gold Coast No.11
C4818	Newfoundland No.4
C4831	Presented by the Government of Johore No.6
C4832	Udaipur No.1
C4840	Australia No.4, New South Wales No.3 'The Mrs P.Kirby & Son'
C4868	Presented by the Government of Johore No.2
C9866	No.1 Bircham Newton, 1918
C9887	No.7 Bircham Newton
D2167	Shifnal
D2649	Gold Coast No.14
D2652	Malaya No.7 'The Armenia'
D2660	Zanzibar No.5
D7894	Kotah No.1
D7902	Presented by the Maharaja Bahadur Sir Rameswar Singh of Darbhanga No.4
D7913	Malaya No.23 'The Malacca'
D7939	Toronto
D7942	Falkland
D7945	Gold Coast No.11
D8061	Zanzibar No.18
D8062	Zanzibar No.19
D8064	Zanzibar No.20

Above: **Two studies of F4274, named** *Barnstaple* **after the Devon town, with a civilian-looking gentleman in the pilot's cockpit and standing at the wingtip, wearing his flat cap reversed in the style of pre-First World War aviators. The pictures are captioned as being taken at Ruislip Aerodrome, Middlesex, in 1919.**
(Philip Jarrett)

D8065	Australia No.24, South Australia No.2 'The Mrs Sidney Kidman' (presented by Mrs Sidney Kidman, Eringa, Kapunda, South Australia)		F4306	Burgate
			F4330	Wingate (County Durham)
E2233	Alresford Rural District Council		F4332	Forehoe Union (County Durham)
E2404	No.1 Company RAMC Cambridge Hospital		F4333	Dominica
			F4334	Montreal
E2452	Montreal		F4336	Zanzibar No.17 later Huddersfield – Canada
E2453	Dominica			
E2455	Udaipur No.2		F4337	Zanzibar No.18
E2457	Punjab No.44, Lahore No.4		F4355	Presented by the Maharaja Bahadur Sir Rameswar Singh of Darbhanga No.4
E2525	Auckland			
F4274	Barnstaple (Devon)			
F4277	Carlton Colville. (named after a village near Lowestoft)		F4440	Presented by the Maharaja Bahadur Sir Rameswar Singh of Darbhanga No.l 'The Lord Hardinge'
			F4470	Newfoundland No.4

F.2B F4440 bore the lengthy inscription *Presented by the Maharaja Bahadur Sir Rameswar Singh of Darbhanga No.l. 'The Lord Hardinge'.* **It was with to 18 Sqn in 1919 and was on the RAF Staff College Flight at Andover in 1924.** *(C&C)*

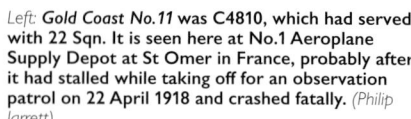

Left: *Gold Coast No.11* was C4810, which had served with 22 Sqn. It is seen here at No.1 Aeroplane Supply Depot at St Omer in France, probably after it had stalled while taking off for an observation patrol on 22 April 1918 and crashed fatally. *(Philip Jarrett)*

F4537	Bingley, Yorkshire
F4664	Tyldesley
F4677	Kotah No.2
F4678	Winnipeg
F4679	Presented by the Maharaja Bahadur Sir Rameswar Singh of Darbhanga No.5
F4680	Presented by the Government of Johore No.6
F4774	Presented by the Maharaja Bahadur Sir Rameswar Singh of Darbhanga No.3
F????	Royal Marines Chatham No.IV

Other known names:

Serial	Name	Unit
A7192	Gubbins	Middle East
A7218	Panther	59 TS
A7238	Tiger	59 TS
C852	Gladys?	88 Sqn
C4680	The Old Biff 1928	CFS
C4846	Amy	11 Sqn
C4879	The Crocodile 33	TDS
C9947	Charlestown	12 Sqn
E2016	Rita	Yatesbury
E2421	Palace	5 Sqn
F4592	White City	5 Sqn
F4746	Wembley	5 Sqn
F4757	Lady Cherry	Station Flight IAAD
H1565	Silver Star	5 Sqn

Unidentified

Blokes
Murielle
The Fair Maid

Above: This F.2B sharing a wintry Upper Heyford with a Sopwith Dolphin in February 1919 is F4336, originally named *Zanzibar No.17* and later *Huddersfield – Canada.* Both aircraft are captioned as belonging to 81 (Canadian) Sqn, previously No.1 Sqn CAF. Subsequently gifted to Canada, F4336 later became G-CYBC (see chapter 18). *(Philip Jarrett)*

Bristol F.2B F4277 carries the name of *Carlton Colville*, a village near Lowestoft. *(Ken Smy/SAAF Museum)*

Above: Appropriately, *Zanzibar No.18* was F4337, seen in wintry conditions in these two views. The three-quarter rear view reveals that it has for some reason acquired the rudder from C9894, an Arab-engined machine. *(Ken Smy/ SAAF Museum)*

Named *Tyldesley* after the town in the Metropolitan Borough of Wigan, in Greater Manchester, Bristol F.2B F4664, seen here inverted at Bickendorf in 1919, subsequently went to 31 Sqn in India. *(Philip Jarrett)*

Panther was F.2B A7218 '1' of No.59 TS. *(Eric Harlin)*

The serial number of this Arab-engined F.2B of 8 Sqn, named *Blokes*, is undetermined. *(Philip Jarrett)*

Above: **Another F.2B of unknown identity was 'K',** *The Fair Maid*, **of an undetermined unit. It was photographed at Old Sarum in 1918, and might be a visiting machine from 22 Sqn.** *(Philip Jarrett)*

Right: **Having served with 59 Sqn, Arab-engined F.2B E2016, named** *Rita*, **was detached to 5 Sqn and flown by Lt H.S.R. Burt early in 1919.** *(via Philip Jarrett)*

Registered to the Bristol Aeroplane Co Ltd on 10 April 1922, G-EBCN, powered by a 300hp Hispano-Suiza, went to SABCA of Belgium to serve as a pattern for local production. *(Philip Jarrett)*

Appendix 7

CIVILIAN REGISTERED BRISTOL FIGHTERS AND DERIVATIVES

NOTE: Bristol referred to its individual aircraft production by sequence number, rather than the more generally accepted 'constructor's number'. To avoid confusion for civil aircraft researchers we have used 'c/n' in this listing, rather than the correct 's/n'.

British Civil Register

G-EASH c/n 5093 ex-**H1376**. Regd [CofR 490] 7.4.20 to Handley Page Ltd; used by Aircraft Disposal Co Ltd, Croydon, as demonstrator, with Hispano-Suiza engine, later flown as hack. Flown Cricklewood to Brussels 15.8.20 for HP Transport. CofA 445 issued 27.11.20. Regn cld 4.21 but still in use for demos 2.22.

G-EASU c/n 5356 ex-**H1639**. Regd [CofR 505] 29.4.20 to Handley Page Ltd for Aircraft Disposal Co Ltd, Croydon. No CofA issued. Flown to Paris 5.20 for King of the Belgians. Regn cld 9.20. Probably to Belgian Air Force as L-1.

G-EASV c/n 5355 ex-**H1638**. Regd [CofR 506] 29.4.20 to Handley Page Ltd for Aircraft Disposal Co Ltd, Croydon. No CofA issued. Operated by Handley Page Transport 8.6.20-5.7.20. Regn cld 11.20. Possibly to Belgian AF as L-2.

G-EAWA ex-**H951**. Regd [CofR 618] 22.11.20 to Handley Page Ltd for Aircraft Disposal Co Ltd, Croydon. No CofA issued & regn lapsed.

G-EAWZ F.2B ex-**H1282** (c/n 4999). Bought ex-ADC by Philip John Pinckney c.5.20 and shipped to Buenos Aires and operated without regn as 3-seater with a passenger cabin and made c.150 local flights. Returned to England, rebuilt by ADC Ltd who renewed everything but the original fuselage owing to transport damage. Regd [CofR 659] 23.5.21 to Aircraft Disposal Co Ltd (but as nominee for Pinckney). Test flown on 23.5.21, then flown Croydon to Lymington on the 24th. Returning from Lymington to AV Roe's aerodrome at Hamble, the port aileron cable jammed while the aircraft was banked to the right at 300ft on approach. The aircraft spun and crashed c.15.30 on 25.5.21; owner Pinckney and pilot T.L. Tebbitt killed, passenger Miss F. Pinckney seriously injured. Regn cld 6.21.

G-EAYQ c/n 5106 ex-**H1389**. Regd [CofR 713] 4.10.21 to Aircraft Disposal Co Ltd. No CofA issued. Departed Croydon 6.10.21 on delivery to Belgian Air Force but hit trees during forced landing in France. Regn cld 13.10.21.

G-EBAK c/n 5008 ex-**H1291**. Regd [CofR 767] 21.12.21 to Aircraft Disposal Co Ltd. No CofA issued. Delivered ex Croydon 29.12.21 to Belgian Air Force. Regn cld 2.3.22.

G-EBAL c/n 5009 ex-**H1292**. Regd [CofR 768] 21.12.21 to Aircraft Disposal Co Ltd. No CofA issued. To Belgian Air Force 1.22. Regn cld 2.3.22.

G-EBAM c/n 4957 ex-**H1240**. Regd [CofR 769] 21.12.21 to Aircraft Disposal Co Ltd. No CofA issued. Crashed Croydon 28.1.22 on delivery to Belgian Air Force; repaired and re-flown 24.2.22 and delivered ex Croydon 25.2.22. Regn cld 2.3.22.

G-EBAT c/n 4959 ex-**H1242**. Regd [CofR 776] 31.12.21 to Aircraft Disposal Co Ltd. No CofA issued. Delivered ex Croydon to Belgian Air Force 28.1.22. Regn cld 2.3.22.

G-EBAU c/n 4961 ex-**H1244**. Regd [CofR 777] 31.12.21 to Aircraft Disposal Co Ltd. No CofA issued. Delivered ex Croydon to Belgian Air Force 15.2.22. Regn cld 2.3.22.

G-EBBD c/n 3492 ex-**D7842**. Regd [CofR 788] 12.1.22 to Aircraft Disposal Co Ltd. No CofA issued. Delivered ex Croydon to Belgian Air Force 28.1.22 by A.F. Muir & formally presented to the Queen of the Belgians; painted in all-white c/s. Regn cld 4.4.22.

G-EBBO c/n 4975 ex-**H1258**. Regd [CofR 800] 27.2.22 to Aircraft Disposal Co Ltd. No CofA issued. Delivered ex Croydon to Belgian Air Force 11.3.22. Regn cld 4.4.22.

G-EBCN c/n 3957 (although Bristol records show c/n 6223, fitted with a 300hp Hispano-Suiza engine; but see **G-EBFD**). Regd [CofR 828] 10.4.22 to Bristol Aeroplane Co Ltd. CofA 604 issued 31.1.23. To SABCA, Belgium, as pattern aircraft for local production. Regn cld 24.7.23.

G-EBCU ex-**E2058**. Regd [CofR 840] 25.4.22 to Aircraft Disposal Co Ltd. No CofA issued. Official gift to the Queen of the Belgians and delivered ex Croydon 6.5.22. Regn cld 12.7.22.

Acquired at a postcard fair in May 2019, this intriguing faded, unevenly exposed and uncaptioned photograph shows a Hispano-Suiza-engined Bristol F.2B with a claustrophobic coupé top over the rear cockpit and a fixed access ladder on the starboard side. There are no visible markings. It might well be G-EAWZ, ex-H1282, which went to Buenos Aires and was operated as a three-seater with cabin by Philip John Pinckney in 1920. *(Philip Jarrett)*

G-EBCV c/n 4998 ex-**H1281**. Regd [CofR 841] 25.4.22 to Aircraft Disposal Co Ltd. No CofA issued. To Belgian Air Force 7.22. Regn cld 12.7.22.

G-EBCW c/n 4962 ex-**H1245**. Regd [CofR 842] 25.4.22 to Aircraft Disposal Co Ltd. No CofA issued. To Belgian Air Force 7.22. Regn cld 18.9.22.

G-EBDB ex-**E5219**. Regd [CofR 847] 1.5.22 to Aircraft Disposal Co Ltd. No CofA issued; test-flown 2.5.22. To Belgian Air Force 7.22. Regn cld 12.7.22.

G-EBDN ex-**H927**. Regd [CofR 866] 21.6.22 to Aircraft Disposal Co Ltd. No CofA issued. To Belgian Air Force 7.22. Regn cld 12.7.22.

G-EBEE ex-**H926**. Regd [CofR 885] 13.7.22 to Aircraft Disposal Co Ltd. No CofA issued. To Belgian Air Force 7.22. Regn cld 18.9.22.

G-EBFD c/n 6223 (per Air Ministry register – see **G-EBCN**) ex-**E2354**. Regd [CofR 932] 25.1.23 to Bristol Aeroplane Co Ltd. CofA 605 issued 10.2.23. To Serbian Army. Regn cld 27.3.23.

G-EBIO c/n 4971 ex-**H1254** (though originally regd as **D2258**). Regd [CofR 1051] 11.23 to Aircraft Disposal Co Ltd; (renamed ADC

Aircraft Ltd 30.7.25), Croydon. CofA 845 issued 24.12.24. Operated by The Marconi Wireless Telegraph Co Ltd, Croydon 2.28-9.30 on radio trials. CofA lapsed 8.11.30. Regd [CofR 3411] 9.31 to Flt Lt Donald Vernon Ivins, RAF Henlow; CofA renewed 5.9.31. To The Hon Mrs Victor Bruce 5.32 as back-up aircraft on flight-refuelling trials at Cowes; painted in Regent Super c/s from sponsor Regent Petrol Co; trials moved to Felixstowe/Ipswich 8.32. CofA lapsed 4.9.32. For sale by Ivins [5.34]. Regd [CofR 5475] 30.11.34 to Robert Clive Parker, London W9 (based Redhill); CofA not renewed. Regn cld 12.35.

G-ABXA Type 96 F.2B Mk.IV ex-**J8258** (c/n 7303) [regd with original c/n 7056]. Regd [CofR 3768] 5.32 to The Hon Mrs Mary Mildred Bruce, Esher (based Hanworth). CofA 3522 issued 1.7.32. Loaned/provided to Mrs Bruce by Regent Petrol Co for flight-refuelling experiments 6.32-8.32 at Cowes/Felixstowe; named *Mercenary Mary* and painted in Regent Super titles. Used as a tanker aircraft to refuel owner's Saro Windhover during

The Bristol Fighter adapted as an aerial tanker for The Hon Mrs Victor Bruce's attempts to set a new world endurance record, G-ABXA, has its underwing tanks refuelled. *(Paul Smiddy)*

abortive attempt on world endurance record in 1932. Briefly used by Bruce's company, Air Dispatch Ltd, for newspaper/freight operations. For sale 11.32 by Luxury Air Tours Ltd [Mrs Bruce]. CofA lapsed 30.6.33. Regd [CofR 4697] 31.10.33 to Inca Aviation Co Ltd, Hanworth; but CofA not renewed. Regn cld 11.34.

G-ABXV Type 96 F.2B Fighter Mk.IIIDC ex-**F4811** (c/n 7556). [Also identified as ex-**F4711** c/n 6464]. Regd [CofR 3804] 15.6.32 to Philip Heriot Thomas, Dumfries and The Hon John Grimston, London NW11 (based Upper Heyford). CofA 3636 issued 2.11.32. While flown by its second joint owner it crashed into wall on landing at Capenoch, Dumfriesshire, on 18.9.33 and broke its back. Regn cld 12.34.

G-ABYD Type 96A F.2B Fighter Mk.IV ex-**J8446** (c/n 7574) [regd as ex-**J8440**]. Regd [CofR 3834] 4.7.32 to Michael Justin Creswell, Ewhurst, Surrey (based Abingdon). CofA 3620 issued 14.10.32. Crashed in Spain 2.33 during European tour with owner. Regn cld 3.33.

Seen here during its time with No.5 FTS and fitted with a Leitner-Watts adjustable-pitch metal propeller, F.2B J8446 became G-ABYD in 1932, but was scrapped following an accident in 1933. *(Philip Jarrett)*

G-ABYE Type 96A F.2B Fighter Mk.IV ex-**F4721** (c/n 7559). Regd [CofR 3835] 4.7.32 to Arthur Maitland Emmet, Oxford (based Woodley). CofA 3687 issued 14.12.32. Emmet was a teacher at St Edwards School, Oxford, and bought the aircraft to give pupils rides (including Guy Gibson). Regd [CofR 5282] 1.8.34 to Plt Off Ronald Franklin Arthur Edelsten, London SW16 (based with Oxford UAS, Witney). Flown by owner and Peter Hogg on trip Witney-Baghdad-Witney 10.8.34-17.9.34. CofA lapsed 17.12.34 after owner was killed in motor accident on 18.11.34. Regd [CofR 5696] 12.3.35 to Universal Aircraft Services Ltd, Witney, but CofA not renewed and believed used for ground instruction. Regn cld 4.38.

G-ABYF Type 96A F.2B Fighter Mk.IV ex-**J8429** (c/n 7573). Regd [CofR 3837] 4.7.32 to Flt Lt Donald Vernon Ivins, RAF Henlow. CofA 3692 issued 17.12.32. Regd [CofR 5820] 15.4.35) to Airmedia Ltd; used for banner towing, initially at Hanworth and then Redhill. CofA lapsed 12.8.35; still stored Redhill 8.39 when allocated Directorate of Training. Regn cld 15.8.45.

This snapshot of G-ABYF was probably taken on a Jersey beach during the aircraft's ownership by D.V. Ivins. *(Philip Jarrett)*

G-ABYL Type 96 F.2B Fighter ex-**J8444** (c/n 7579). Assembled at Croydon by Rollason Aircraft Services and regd [CofR 3864] 21.7.32 to Edmund Basil Higham Wright, Beckenham (based Croydon; later to Gravesend). CofA 3619 issued 14.10.32. CofA lapsed 13.10.33. Regn cld 12.33.

The previous identity of G-ABYL was J8444. It was owned by Edmund B.H. Wright of Croydon, and held a CofA for only a year, during 1932-33. *(Philip Jarrett)*

G-ABYT Type 96A F.2B Fighter Mk.IV ex-**J8434** (c/n 7568). Regd [CofR 3893] 3.8.32 to Anthony Thomas Wilson, London SW (based Lympne and owned jointly with Keith Kendle Brown, CFI of Cinque Ports Flying Club). Assembled at Lympne and CofA 3992 issued 28.7.33. Raced and came second in 1933 Folkestone Trophy. Regd [CofR 4944] 29.3.34 to John Patrick Wakelyn Topham, Folkestone (based Lympne). Overshot at Lympne and damaged in contact with wire fence some time before CofA expiry 12.12.35. Still in store in damaged state at Lympne 8.37. Regn cld 16.11.45.

G-ABZG Type 96 F.2B Fighter Mk.III ex-**J8245** (c/n 7435) [regd with original c/n 7043]. Regd [CofR 3906] 9.32 to unknown party. Regd [CofR 4287] 22.3.33 to Commercial Airways (Essex) Ltd, Abridge. CofA 4006 issued 9.8.33 for operation by East Anglian Aero Club as a flying school trainer. CofA lapsed 8.8.34; sold for scrap 5.36. Regn cld 5.38.

G-ACAA (1) Type 96 F.2B Fighter Mk.IV ex-**F4516** (c/n 7434). Regd [CofR 3976] 10.32 to Charles Richard Andrew Oakley, London EC3 (based Woodley). CofA 3732 issued 20.1.33. Reportedly used in 1933 film *I was a Spy*. Owned [34/35] by Ralph Dundas, Edinburgh. Regd [CofR 5776] 8.4.35 to Herbert Arthur Carson, Bonnybridge (based Renfrew). Regd [CofR 6722] 12.2.36 to Alfred Ernest Green, London W1 and Alistair Pringle Fraser, Pontypool (based Aldenham). CofA lapsed 30.10.36. In March 1937 Fraser was prosecuted for flying an unlicensed aircraft. Regn cld 1.12.46.

Seeing the state of F4516 in this shot of it under scrutiny by Cranwell cadets in 1929, it is hard to believe that in 1933 it joined the British civil register as **G-ACAA**. *(Philip Jarrett)*

G-ACAA (2) Rebuild based on fuselage frame found at Weston-on-the-Green, Oxfordshire, and transferred to the RAF Museum, which then exchanged it for a Lockheed Hudson turret. Regd 25.10.91 to Patina Limited (The Fighter Collection) [using original identity of **G-ACAA** but no known connection]. Rebuilt by Skysport Engineering at Hatch and fitted with a Rolls-Royce Falcon III from the National Technical Museum in Prague. Completed minus engine, moved to Duxford 1993 and first flown there 30.6.98. Returned to Skysport Engineering at Hatch and packed for delivery to New Zealand. Regn cld 8.1.07 as sold New Zealand.

Two pleasing studies of the evidently well-maintained G-ACCG, which passed through several owners before it was donated to a Guildford Air Training Corps unit in 1948 as an instructional airframe. *(Philip Jarrett)*

G-ACAC Type 96 F.2B Fighter Mk.IV ex-**J8437** (c/n 7571). Built up by Phillips & Powis at Woodley 9.32-11.32 and regd (CofR 3986) 1.11.32 to Walter Leslie Handley, Sheldon, Birmingham (based Castle Bromwich). CofA 3862 issued 12.4.33. CofA lapsed 11.4.34. Regn cld 1.36 as sold and reportedly to Hooton Park but not overhauled.

G-ACCG Type 96 F.2B Fighter ex-**J6790** (c/n 7576). Regd [CofR 4075] 2.33 to Universal Aircraft Services Ltd, Witney. CofA 3842 issued 24.3.33. Operated an air taxi service from The Rock Hotel, Llandrindod Wells, wef 3.8.33. Sold 16.9.33 and regd [CofR 4675] 10.10.33 to Michel Noel Mavrogordato, Westerham, Kent (based Witney). Advertised for sale in *The Aeroplane* magazine 29.9.37 at £130; then at £80 9.2.38. CofA lapsed 10.6.38. Regn cld 4.7.39. Used by National Studios Ltd, Elstree, 1944, for taxying shots in the film *The World Owes Me a Living*. For sale 1.45 by WS Shackleton Ltd. Sold .45 to Cecil James Packer, Burton Garage, Acton Turville, nr Chippenham. Sold [by 12.45] to Vokes Ltd and donated to Guildford Air Training Corps unit in 1948 as an instructional airframe. Believed scrapped .51.

G-ACFK Type 96 F.2B Fighter ex-**J8285** (c/n 7431). Regd [CofR 4275] 22.3.33 to Commercial Airways (Essex) Ltd, Abridge. Civil conversion completed 7.33 but no C of A issued. Sold for scrap 5.36. Regn cld 5.38.

G-ACFL Type 96 F.2B Fighter ex-**C4897** (c/n 7570). Regd [CofR 4276] 22.3.33 to Commercial Airways (Essex) Ltd, Abridge, but civil conversion not completed. Sold for scrap 5.36. Regn cld 5.38.

G-ACFN Type 96 F.2B Fighter ex-**F4542** (c/n 7144). Regd [CofR 4277] 22.3.33 to Commercial Airways (Essex) Ltd, Abridge, but civil conversion not completed. Sold for scrap 5.36. Regn cld 5.38.

G-ACFO Type 96 F.2B Fighter ex-**C4750** (c/n 7137). Regd [CofR 4278] 22.3.33 to Commercial Airways (Essex) Ltd, Abridge, but civil conversion not completed. Sold for scrap 5.36. Regn cld 5.38.

G-ACFP Type 96 F.2B Fighter ex-**F4434** (c/n 7581). Regd [CofR 4283] 22.3.33 to Empire Air Services Ltd, Wembley (based Hanworth; later Heston). CofA 3861 issued 13.4.33. Regd [CofR 4709] 9.11.33 to The Hon Mrs Victor Bruce, Cobham, Surrey (based Hanworth). CofA lapsed 12.4.34. Regn cld 1.38.

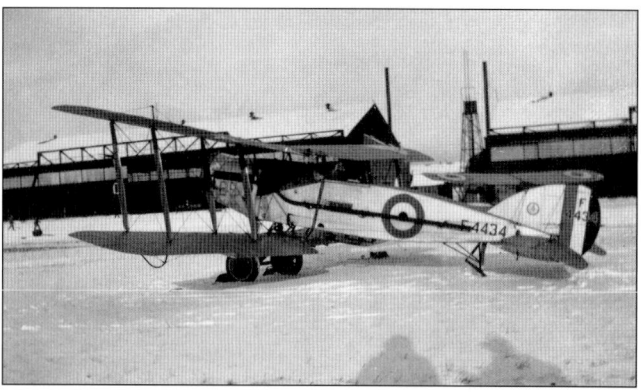

Seen here in the snow at RAF Cranwell in 1928-29, F4434 was destined to become G-ACFP in 1933. *(Philip Jarrett)*

Above: Previously F4434, G-ACFP is seen while being operated by Hanworth-based Empire Air Services, its first civilian owner, in 1933. *(Philip Jarrett)*

Right: **Bristol F.2B G-ACPE at Hanworth in the 1930s, with a Cierva C.30 Autogiro keeping it company on the left. This F.2B, ex-J8448, was based at Hanworth for its entire civilian life, from March 1934 until its registration was cancelled in January 1939.** *(Richard Riding collection)*

G-ACHR Type 96 F.2B Fighter ex-**F4342** (c/n 7578). Regd [CofR 4390] 6.6.33 to Major Reginald Calvert Empson, London NW (based Brooklands). CofA 4000 issued 24.7.33. Crashed 19.9.33 (or 20.9.33) at Guignes, Seine-et-Marne, France, on *Bienvenue Aerienne European* tour when suitcase fouled rudder bar. Regn cld 11.33.

G-ACPE Type 96 F.2B Fighter ex-**J8448** (c/n 7577). Regd [CofR 493x] 3.34 to unknown party. Regd [CofR 5391] 9.10.34 to Arthur Fleetwood Cawthorn, Surbiton, Surrey (based Hanworth). CofA 4529 issued 9.10.34. Regd [CofR 6032] 2.7.35 to Josephine Jessie Dudley, Brixton (based Hanworth). CofA lapsed 8.10.35. Regd [CofR 6502] 16.11.35 to Charles Samuel William Dudley, Brixton (based Hanworth). Regd [CofR 7232] 1.8.36 to Richard George John Kingsmill of RASC Aldershot (based Hanworth). CofA not renewed. Regn cld 13.1.39.

G-ADJR Type 96 F.2B Fighter ex-**J8455** (c/n 7530). Regd [CofR 5978] 18.6.35 to Christopher Penrose Bartholomew Ogilvie, Willesden (based Hanworth). CofA 4921 issued 22.6.35. Regd [CofR 6098] 20.7.35 to London Film Productions Ltd, London SW1 (based Hanworth, later Heston and Denham); operated by their technical adviser and author, Nigel Trevithick Tangye. CofA expired 8.6.37. Regn cld 1.38.

Disguised in pseudo-military markings, this is actually G-ADJR, ex-J8455, as it appeared in Event No.10, 'Special Aircraft – Past and Present', at the 1936 RAF Pageant at Hendon. It had joined the civil register the previous year. *(Philip Jarrett)*

Here is G-ADJR in its true civil markings, as a 'camera ship' for Alexander Korda's London Film Productions in the second half of the 1930s, with a camera mounting on its rear cockpit. *(Philip Jarrett)*

This crashed British civil-registered Bristol Fighter could be G-ABXV, the Type 96 Mk.III DC which crashed into wall on landing at Capenoch, Dumfriesshire, on 18 September 1933, but further information as to location and date are lacking. *(Philip Jarrett)*

For the 1937 RAF Pageant the Bristol Fighter was represented by another masquerading civil-registered example. This time it was G-AFHJ, previously F4587, the identity it still carries on its rudder. Apparently it was not flown at this event. *(Philip Jarrett)*

G-AEPH Type 96 F.2B Fighter Mk.III ex-**D8096** (c/n 7575). Sold 33/34 to Christopher Ogilvie and stored at Primrose Garage, Watford. Regd [CofR 7451] 13.11.36 to Christopher Penrose Bartholomew Ogilvie, Willesden; remained in store. No CofA issued. Regn cld 1.12.46 by Secretary of State. Still in store Watford 1946 but reported to Elstree [47/48]. Regd 25.8.48 (back) to Ogilvie (but entry in register then deleted) Sold 1948 to The Shuttleworth Trust, Old Warden; to Filton for overhaul 12.50 and 'conversion' back to stock F2B; re-flown 14.2.51 by Bill Pegg. Subsequently operated unregistered under special Shuttleworth permit until formally regd 29.10.81 to The Shuttleworth Collection. Extant and flown marked as 'D8096', then as 'B1162' from 2020.

G-AFHJ Type 96 F.2B Fighter Mk.III ex-**F4587** (c/n 7146). Regd [CofR 8514] 23.5.38 to Sqn Ldr Neville Raby Buckle of HQ Fighter Command, Bentley Priory (based RAF Hendon). CofA 6388 issued 1.9.38. CofA lapsed 31.8.39. Destroyed by enemy action during WWII. Regn cld 1.1.46 at census.

The following were granted a CofA to ADC Aircraft Ltd:

E1916   C of A 1619 issued 25.9.28
E1962   C of A 1620 issued 25.9.28
E2199   C of A 1621 issued 25.9.28
E2301   C of A 1622 issued 25.9.28
E2360   C of A 1623 issued 25.9.28
D2696   C of A 1624 issued 25.9.28

A batch of new-build Bristol Fighters for delivery to Belgium were given a UK CofA prior to delivery:
C/ns 6224 to 6238 were issued CsofA 623 to 637 on 6.6.23.

Bristol Fighter Derivatives (registered in UK)

5867 Type 29 Open Tourer/PTS Two-seater. Regd **G-EAIZ** (CofR 234) 7.8.19 to British & Colonial Aeroplane Co Ltd. CofA 214 issued 10.9.19. Fitted with 230hp Siddeley Puma, used as testbed and company hack. Used for demonstrations in Belgium and Norway in February 1920. CofA lapsed 9.9.20. Regn cld 10.20.

5868 Type 29 Open Tourer/PTS Two-seater. Regd **G-EANR** (CofR 358) 23.9.19 to British & Colonial Aeroplane Co Ltd. Exhibited at Paris Salon in 12.19-1.20. No CofA issued. Regn cld 9.20. Shipped to New York 5.20 and sold by local Bristol agent and believed to have been the Tourer used by Joseph F. Thorne for bullion transport from his silver mines in Nicaragua.

5870 Type 36 Seely [Puma]. Regd **G-EAUE** (CofR 553) 3.7.20 to Bristol Aeroplane Co Ltd. Built for the August 1920 Air Ministry Commercial Aeroplane competition at Martlesham Heath. CofA 447 issued 11.12.20. Failed to win and used as a company hack until CofA lapsed 10.12.21. Regn cld 30.6.23. Sold to Air Ministry as **J7004** under Contract No.408484/23 dated 24.3.23; original 240hp Siddeley Puma replaced by a 435hp Bristol Jupiter III and f/f 5.10.23 as Type 85 (sometimes referred to as the Seely Mark II). Continued as a testbed on RAE charge from 25.1.24 to 16.5.24. Returned to Bristol 7.24 and dismantled 12.24.

5876 Type 47 Open Tourer Three-seater [Puma]. Regd **G-EART** [CofR 471] 17.3.20 to S. Instone & Co Ltd, Croydon. CofA 345 issued 21.4.20. Damaged when overturned in forced landing in field nr Abbeville, France, 15.6.20 following engine failure (pilot H.W. Chataway). Regn cld 2.21.

5892 Type 47 Coupé Tourer Two-seater. Regd **G-EAVU** [CofR 609] 21.10.20 to Bristol Aeroplane Co Ltd. CofA 430 issued 26.10.20. Replaced **G-EAIZ** as dual-control demonstrator initially in Norway. Regn cld 4.21 and flown to Madrid to give dual-control instruction to Snr Bayo with Hereward de Havilland. Reported as returned to Bristol 9.21 when replaced by **M-AFFA** (c/n 6121) and scrapped when replaced by **G-EAXA**.

6108 Type 28 Coupé Tourer Three-seater [Puma] Regd **G-EAXK** [CofR 674] 18.6.21 to Bristol Aeroplane Co Ltd. CofA 492 issued 21.6.21. Regn cld 5.7.22 as sold. Regd in Australia as **G-AUDF** [CofR 52] 28.11.21 to W.A. Airways Ltd (Western Australian Airways), Perth. Dbf Onslow, WA 27.1.25.

6109 Type 28 Open Tourer Three-seater C of A 508 issued 16.7.21. To Spain as **M-AAAF**, regd 9.21.

6110 Type 28 Open Tourer Three-seater CofA 512 issued 23.8.21. Ferried to Spain 27.8.21 and regd as **M-AFFF** 10.21.

6112 Type 47 Open Tourer Three-seater. Regd **G-EAWR** [CofR 647] 16.4.21 to Bristol Aeroplane Co Ltd. CofA 467 issued 19.4.21. Delivered to Croydon 24.2.21 and onward to Le Bourget as **M-AEAA** (pilot C. Uwins). Regn cld 5.21. Regd **M-AEAA** 21.5.21 to Sociedad del Monte Archanda, Bilbao. Current .30.

6114 Type 28 Tourer Coupé Three-seater (Puma). Regd **G-EAWQ** [CofR 646] 16.4.21 to Bristol Aeroplane Co Ltd. CofA 453 issued 6.1.21 [prior to regn and probably for frustrated export]. Delivered (as **M-AAEA**) to Croydon 22.4.21 and departed for Madrid via Le Bourget 23.4.21. Collected by ADC pilot Andrew Forson from Le Bourget en route to new owner Snr Bayo, Madrid (who Forson was going to teach to fly) but crashed into mountain nr Anzuola 19.5.21 in fog shortly after taking off from Lasarte Airfield, San Sebastian; Forson killed. Regn cld 5.21.

6120 Type 29 Tourer/PT2S 2-seater [Puma]. Regd **G-EAXA** [CofR 660] 23.5.21 to Bristol Aeroplane Co Ltd. CofA 491 issued 17.6.21. Used by makers as a demonstrator. Fitted with Frise ailerons and evaluated as a Type 81 Trainer .23. Abandoned and crashed Purton, nr Swindon, 9.5.24; pilot Flt Lt A.A. Downs baled out successfully. Regn cld 10.5.24.

6122 Type 29 Tourer/PT2S Two-seater. Regd **G-EAWB** [CofR 620] 29.11.20 to Alan Samuel Butler, London W1 (based Stag Lane, later Croydon). CofA 452 issued 1.1.21. Flown by Butler on Southern European tour 2.4.21-6.21. Flown in Aerial Derby, Hendon, 16.7.21. Reportedly sold 11.21 to US millionaire William Bateman Leeds but sale probably fell through. CofA lapsed 31.12.21 and regn lapsed 11.22. Regn renewed 1.23 but again lapsed 11.23.

6153 Type 73 L3S Three-seater/Taxiplane [Lucifer]. Regd **G-EBEW** [CofR 919] 23.10.22 to Bristol Aeroplane Co Ltd. To AEE Martlesham Heath 9.4.23 until 17.5.23. CofA 641 issued 19.5.23. Converted to Type 83A and CofA renewed 15.7.24. CofA lapsed 14.7.25. Regn cld 6.1.26.

6154 Type 73 L3S Three-seater/Taxiplane [Lucifer]. Regd **G-EBEY** [CofR 923] 10.11.22 to Bristol Aeroplane Co Ltd. Regd **G-EBFX** [CofR 963] 3.5.23 [as Bristol Taxiplane] in error; regn cld 12.6.23. CofA 642 issued 19.5.23. To Martlesham Heath for tests 1.24. CofA lapsed 18.5.25 and dismantled at Filton. Regn cld 6.1.26.

6155 Type 73 L3S Taxiplane [Lucifer]. Regd **G-EBFY** [CofR 964] 3.5.23 to Bristol Aeroplane Co Ltd. CofA 643 issued 19.5.23. CofA lapsed 18.5.24 and dismantled at Filton for spares. Regn cld 6.1.26.

6239 Type 81 Tourer/Trainer [Puma School 'B']. Regd **G-EBFR** [CofR 956] 19.4.23 to Bristol Aeroplane Co Ltd; for operation by Bristol Reserve Flying School. Crashed into hedge on landing Yeovil (or Filton?) 31.5.23 on tests before issue of CofA; pilot Arthur Keep. Regn cld 25.7.23.

6240 Type 81 Tourer/Trainer [Puma School 'B']. Regd **G-EBFS** [CofR 957] 19.4.23 to Bristol Aeroplane Co Ltd; operated by Bristol Reserve Flying School. CofA 648 issued 8.6.23. Became lost in mist and crashed, location unknown 7.7.23 (Fg Off R.A. Seaton unhurt). Regn cld 7.5.24.

6241 Type 81 Tourer/Trainer [Puma School 'B']. Regd **G-EBFT** [CofR 958] 19.4.23 to Bristol Aeroplane Co Ltd; operated by Bristol Reserve Flying School. CofA 649 issued 8.6.23. Crashed on take-off 5.6.24 (Plt Off L.D.P. Joseph unhurt); repaired. Stalled and crashed Filton 10.3.25; pilot P.H. Davies. Regn cld 6.1.26.

6242 Type 81 Tourer/Trainer [Puma School 'B']. Regd **G-EBFU** [CofR 959] 19.4.23 to Bristol Aeroplane Co Ltd; operated by Bristol Reserve Flying School. CofA 650 issued 8.6.23. Crashed on landing 20.6.24 (Fg Off J.T. Rymer); repaired. Crashed at Filton [no details] sometime prior to CofA expiry 8.7.28. Regn cld 1.29.

6373 Type 83A Trainer/PTM [Lucifer]. Regd **G-EBFZ** [CofR 965] 3.5.23 to Bristol Aeroplane Co Ltd; operated by Bristol Reserve Flying School. CofA 644 issued 31.5.23. Later converted to Type 83B. Grazed hedge landing, took off again, crashed on landing 27.8.29 (Plt Off P. Johnson injured); repaired. Wfu 6.31. Regn cld 12.31.

6374 Type 83A Trainer/PTM [Lucifer]. Regd **G-EBGA** [CofR 966] 3.5.23 to Bristol Aeroplane Co Ltd. CofA 645 issued 19.6.23. Converted to Type 83B 3.26; then later 83C .28. Crashed in field Liberty Lane, Long Ashton, 17.2.30 (pilot Lt A. Djernal of Turkish Army); repaired. Regn cld 12.31 before CofA expiry on 14.4.32. Regd [CofR 4183] 11.2.33 to Leslie George Anderson, Kensington (based Hanworth); converted to Taxiplane standard and CofA renewed 6.4.33. Operated by British Hospitals Air Pageant 4.33-10.33. Regn cld 12.33.

6375 Type 83A Trainer/PTM [Lucifer]. Regd **G-EBGB** [CofR 967] 3.5.23 to Bristol Aeroplane Co Ltd; operated by Bristol Reserve Flying School. CofA 646 issued 19.6.23. Converted to Type 83B 1926. While stationary, struck by Puma Trainer **G-EBIH** taking off from Filton 20.8.29 (Plt Off B. Brahr unhurt). Regn cld 1.30.

6376 Type 83A Trainer/PTM [Lucifer]. Regd **G-EBGC** [CofR 968] 3.5.23 to Bristol Aeroplane Co Ltd; operated by Bristol Reserve Flying School. CofA 704 issued 16.7.23. Converted to Type 83B 1926. Wfu 6.31 with current CofA. Regn cld 12.31.

6377 Type 83A Trainer/PTM [Lucifer]. Regd **G-EBGD** [CofR 969] 3.5.23 to Bristol Aeroplane Co Ltd; operated by Bristol Reserve Flying School. CofA 696 issued 2.10.23. Converted to Type 83B 1925. Forced-landed owing to fuel shortage, minor damage 3.8.28 (Plt Off R.C.C. Gale unhurt); repaired. Crashed nr farmhouse at Southmead Road, nr Filton, 20.1.30; repaired. Wfu 6.31 with current CofA. Regn cld 12.31.

6378 Type 83A Trainer/PTM [Lucifer]. Regd **G-EBGE** [CofR 970] 3.5.23 to Bristol Aeroplane Co Ltd; operated by Bristol Reserve Flying School. CofA 697 issued 2.10.23. Converted to Type 83B 1926. Badly damaged when crashed on landing Upavon 26.8.30; repaired. Wfu 6.31 with current CofA. Regn cld 12.31.

6379 Type 76 Fighter [Jupiter]. Regd **G-EBGF** [CofR 971] 3.5.23 to Bristol Aeroplane Co Ltd. First flown 6.23; CofA 654 issued 2.8.23. To Sweden 8.23 to participate in the ILUG international aviation exhibition at Gothenburg, flown with competition number '41' by Capt Norman Macmillan and Raynham. Crashed Filton 23.11.23 after engine failure at 20,000ft on test flight. Regn cld 7.4.25.

6380 Type 76A Fighter [Jupiter]. Regd **G-EBHG** [CofR 1009] 25.7.23 to Bristol Aeroplane Co Ltd. Used for Jupiter engine demonstrations and tests from 11.23, arrived Kiruna, Northern Sweden, 14.3.24 for Arctic cold-weather trials; flown by Lt Gardin of Swedish Army. Regn cld 6.5.24 but CofA 755 issued 10.5.24 for sale to Swedish Army as **Fv.4300**; later **Fv.1300** .26; to **Fv.3667** .32. Regd **SE-AEE** (CofR 121) 14.2.35 to EH Fredrikzon, Malmsätt. Crashed Sannegårdshamnen, Göteborg, 30.10.36 after engine failure. Regd 29.12.36 to Svensk Flygtjanst AB, Stockholm. Regn cld 19.9.37 as destroyed.

6381 Type 76B Fighter [Jupiter]. Regd **G-EBHH** [CofR 1010] 25.7.23 to Bristol Aeroplane Co Ltd; operated by Bristol Reserve Flying School. Mod 2.25 to Type 89; CofA 847 issued 27.2.25. Collided with **G-EBJA** and crashed on landing, Filton 23.9.25 (Fg Off G.W. Thorpe killed). Regn cld. Tipped on nose while running-up engine 29.12.26. Regn cld.

6382 Type 89 Trainer. Regd **G-EBIH** (CofR 1041) 15.10.23 to Bristol Aeroplane Co Ltd; operated by Bristol Reserve Flying School. First flight 4.24; CofA 775 issued 5.7.24. Crashed on landing 31.10.25 (Fg Off W.M. Hirons unhurt). Dived into the ground from 50ft, Filton 8.8.27; repaired. Pilot stopped engine in the air in error, crashed 25.4.29 (LAC W.C. Hayden injured); repaired. Struck **G-EBGB** on take-off Filton 20.8.29 (Plt Off L.H.A. Fry unhurt). Regn cld 9.29.

6522 Type 89 Advanced Trainer [Jupiter School]. Regd **G-EBJA** [CofR 1070] 8.5.24 to Bristol Aeroplane Co Ltd; operated by Bristol Reserve Flying School. CofA 788 issued 23.7.24. While landing at Filton collided with stationary **G-EBHH** 23.9.25 (Fg Off P.A. Cox killed). Regn cld 23.9.25.

6523 Type 89 Advanced Trainer [Jupiter School]. Regd **G-EBJB** [CofR 1071] 8.5.24 to Bristol Aeroplane Co Ltd; operated by Bristol Reserve Flying School. CofA 851 issued 9.4.25. Crashed into garage on landing and dbf nr Filton 15.12.25 (Fg Off D.C. Anderson killed). Regn cld 18.12.25.

6524 Type 89 Advanced Trainer [Jupiter School]. Regd **G-EBJC** [CofR 1072] 8.5.24 to Bristol Aeroplane Co Ltd. No CofA issued – aircraft not completed. Regn cld 11.5.25.

6525 Type 89 Advanced Trainer [Jupiter School] Spare airframe for stock [see **R.58** later].

6918 Type 89A Advanced Trainer [Jupiter]. Regd **G-EBML** [CofR 1206] 19.11.25 to Bristol Aeroplane Co Ltd; operated by Bristol Reserve Flying School. CofA 928 issued 17.12.25. Tyre burst on landing, overturned 12.7.26 (Plt Off C.W. Carter unhurt); repaired. Lost revs in circuit, forced-landed and crashed outside Filton Aerodrome 14.5.27 (Plt Off C.S. Dawson injured). Regn cld 3.2.28.

6919 Type 89A Advanced Trainer [Jupiter]. Regd **G-EBMN** [CofR 1208] 19.11.25 to Bristol Aeroplane Co Ltd; operated by Bristol Reserve Flying School. CofA 929 issued 17.12.25. Undershot landing, hit hedge, overturned 28.7.26 (Plt Off J.H.A. Wells unhurt); repaired. Partial engine failure when low over sea and ditched 17.3.27 (Fg Off H.I. Townsend injured). Regn cld 2.4.27.

6922 Type 83 Trainer [Lucifer School/PTM]. Regd **G-EBNB** [CofR 1222] 14.12.25 to Bristol Aeroplane Co Ltd. Regn cld 25.2.26 as sold. CofA 967 issued 28.4.26 and delivered to Hungarian Govt.

6923 Type 83 Trainer [Lucifer School/PTM]. Regd **G-EBNC** [CofR 1223] 14.12.25 to Bristol Aeroplane Co Ltd. Regn cld 25.2.26 as sold. CofA 968 issued 28.4.26 and delivered to Hungarian Govt.

6963 Type 89 Advanced Trainer [Jupiter]. Regd **G-EBNZ** [CofR 1256] 26.4.26 to William Beardmore & Co Ltd; operated by Beardmore Reserve School, Renfrew. CofA 991 issued 9.6.26. Crashed on landing 29.6.27 (Fg Off J. James injured). Wfu 10.28 (and for sale 12.28) with CofA current to 21.10.29. Regn cld 14.1.30.

6964 Type 89 Trainer [Jupiter]. Regd **G-EBOA** [CofR 1257] 26.4.26 to William Beardmore & Co Ltd; operated by Beardmore Reserve School, Renfrew. CofA 992 issued 5.6.26. Spun in and crashed/dbf Moor Park Aerodrome, Renfrew, 10.3.27 (Fg Off John Walker killed). Regn cld 15.3.27. Parts used in rebuild as **G-EBWN**.

6965 Type 89A Trainer [Jupiter]. Regd **G-EBOC** [CofR 1263] 14.5.26 to Bristol Aeroplane Co Ltd; operated by Bristol Reserve School. CofA 1057 issued 28.10.26. Pilot became lost, landed to enquire whereabouts, hit ridge, overturned 18.2.27 (Plt Off N.M. Browning unhurt); repaired. Undershot landing Upavon, crashed and overturned 4.9.30 (Fg Off E.T. Scott injured); repaired. Collided with Type 89A Trainer **G-AAWJ** at 200ft while landing at Filton 7.7.31 (Flt Lt E.H. Bryant injured). Regn cld 8.31 as crashed.

6966 Type 89A Trainer [Jupiter]. Regd **G-EBOD** [CofR 1264] 14.5.26 to Bristol Aeroplane Co Ltd. CofA 1096 issued 4.4.27. Regd [CofR 1368] 13.4.27 to William Beardmore & Co Ltd; operated by Beardmore Reserve School, Renfrew. Crashed on railway embankment nr Pollockshaws Station, Glasgow, 26.5.27; rebuilt as **G-EBWN** [c/n R.58 – see below]. Regn cld 14.1.30.

6967 Type 89A Trainer [Jupiter]. Regd **G-EBQS** [CofR 1358] 4.27 to Bristol Aeroplane Co Ltd. Regd [CofR 1412] 24.6.27 to William Beardmore & Co Ltd; operated by Beardmore Reserve School, Renfrew. CofA 1147 issued 27.6.27. Wfu 10.28 and for sale 12.28 prior to CofA lapse 17.6.29. Regn cld 14.1.30.

7124 Type 89A Trainer [Jupiter School]. Regd **G-EBQT** [CofR 1359] 4.27 to unknown. CofA 1146 issued 11.6.27. Regd [CofR 1413] 24.6.27 to Bristol Aeroplane Co Ltd; operated by Bristol Reserve Flying School. Became lost, came down, engine cut at 400-500ft, forced-landed on hilly ground, overturned 28.6.27 (Fg Off G. Vereers Carlew injured); repaired. Stalled and crashed Tewkesbury, Glos, 23.8.28 (Plt Off R.C.C. Gale injured). Regn cld 1.29.

7156 Type 89A Advanced Trainer [Jupiter School]. Regd **G-EBSB** [CofR 1408] 13.6.27 to William Beardmore & Co Ltd; operated by Beardmore Reserve School, Renfrew. CofA 1151 issued 5.7.27. Wfu 10.28 & for sale 12.28 prior to CofA lapse 30.7.29. Regn cld 14.1.30.

7157 Type 89A Advanced Trainer [Jupiter School]. Regd **G-EBSH** [CofR 1419] 8.7.27 to Bristol Aeroplane Co Ltd; operated by Bristol Reserve Flying School. CofA 1200 issued 1.9.27. Undershot landing, hit hedge, overturned 27.8.28 (Plt Off R.G. Shaw unhurt); repaired. Hit hedge landing in field 17.5.29 (Fg Off A.J. Plummer unhurt); repaired. Badly damaged when struck stationary aircraft on ground while taxying at Filton 23.7.30 (Fg Off A.L. Muir unhurt); repaired. CofA lapsed 28.11.33. Regn cld 8.35. [Note: Also quoted incorrectly as c/n **7159**]

7221 Type 89A Advanced Trainer [Jupiter School]. Spare airframe for stock 1928.

7234 Type 89A Advanced Trainer [Jupiter School]. Regd **G-EBVR** [CofR 1547] 11.1.28 to William Beardmore & Co Ltd; operated

by Beardmore Reserve School, Renfrew. CofA 1327 issued 10.3.28. Wfu 10.28 & for sale 12.28 prior to CofA lapse 9.3.29. Regn cld 14.1.30.

R.58 Type 89A Advanced Trainer [Jupiter] [rebuild by Beardmore of G-EBOA/EBOD plus various spares]. Regd **G-EBWN** [CofR 1580] 1.3.28 to William Beardmore & Co Ltd; operated by Beardmore Reserve School, Renfrew. CofA 1348 issued 31.7.28. Wfu 10.28 & for sale 12.28, prior to CofA lapse 30.7.29. Regn cld 14.1.30. [Bristol c/n 6525 has been quoted for this and may have used this spare airframe.]

7265 Type 89A Advanced Trainer [Jupiter School]. Regd **G-EBYL** [CofR 1654] 4.6.28 to Bristol Aeroplane Co Ltd; operated by Bristol Reserve Flying School. CofA 1598 issued 14.9.28. Swung after landing Upavon, minor damage to propeller and undercarriage 20.8.30 (Fg Off R.D. Wayman unhurt); repaired. CofA lapsed 3.10.33. Regn cld 12.34.

7266 Type 83E Titan School/PTM. Regd **G-EBYT** [CofR 1663] 15.6.28 to Bristol Aeroplane Co Ltd. CofA 1515 issued 17.7.28. Flown in round-Britain King's Cup Air Race 20-21.7.28; Racing number 20, entrant Herbert J. Thomas, MD of Bristol's and pilot Sqn Ldr Arthur G. Jones-Williams; race took place over 1,096.5 miles; 7th on the first day, then 14th overall, at an average speed of 123.43mph. CofA lapsed 16.7.29. Regn cld 12.30.

7350 Type 89A Advanced Trainer [Jupiter School]. Regd **G-AAGF** [CofR 1944] 11.4.29 to Bristol Aeroplane Co Ltd; operated by Bristol Reserve Flying School. CofA 2040 issued 16.5.29. Undershot landing, undercarriage hit stationery Bulldog and collapsed 30.4.31 (Fg Off A.L. Muir injured); repaired. Attempted to take-off too soon after third landing, undercarriage hit top of stationery Siskin, slight damage 4.5.31 (Plt Off L.G. Skinner unhurt); repaired. CofA lapsed 19.6.33. Regn cld 8.35.

7351 Type 89A Advanced Trainer [Jupiter School]. Regd **G-AALO** [CofR 2140] 29.8.29 to Bristol Aeroplane Co Ltd; operated by Bristol Reserve Flying School. CofA 2272 issued 24.10.29. Engine failure, forced-landed in small field, went into hedge 21.4.31 (Plt Off J.A.F. Sargeant unhurt); repaired. CofA lapsed 9.12.33. Regn cld 8.35.

7352 Type 89A Advanced Trainer [Jupiter School]. Regd **G-AAWJ** [CofR 2505] 9.4.30 to Bristol Aeroplane Co Ltd; operated by Bristol Reserve Flying School. CofA 2687 issued 22.8.30. Collided with Type 89A Trainer **G-EBOC** at 200ft while landing Filton 7.7.31 (Fg Off Charles H. Carter killed). Regn cld 8.31.

7711 Type 89A Advanced Trainer [Jupiter School]. Regd **G-ABPL** [CofR 3372] 2.9.31 to Bristol Aeroplane Co Ltd; operated by Bristol Reserve School. CofA No 3238 issued 23.10.31. Scrapped in 4.33 prior to CofA expiry on 23.10.33. Regn cld 12.34.

7712 Type 89A Advanced Trainer [Jupiter School]. Regd **G-ABPM** [CofR 3373] 2.9.31 to Bristol Aeroplane Co Ltd; operated by Bristol Reserve School. C of A 3256 issued 7.11.31. Used during .32 at Filton for trials of Dunlop 'doughnut' low-pressure tyres. CofA lapsed 6.11.32. Regn cld 8.35

Overseas civil:
Argentina
Long-distance flights
Buenos Aires-Rio

At 04:50 on 19 December 1920 civilian Anglo-Argentine pilot Eduardo Miguel Hearne and his mechanic, Camilo Brezzi, took off from El Palomar Aerodrome in an unidentified 300hp Bristol F.2B and headed north, for Rio. The first leg was covered in 4hr 5min, and they landed at Paso de los Libres (Province of Corrientes), 700km from Buenos Aires, to refuel. Departing at 10:40, Hearne then headed for Paso Fundo. He flew over Alegrete at 14:45, Santa Maria at 16:45, Cruz Alta at 17:50, Casa Singho at 18:50 and landed at Paso Fundo at 20:00, having covered 1,300km.

They resumed the flight the next day, but after flying for 3hr 20min they were forced to return to Paso Fundo owing to an engine failure. On completion of repairs, thanks to the labours of Brezzi, they set off again, but had to return owing to a heavy fog. On 21 December they reached Ponta Grossa, just 875km from Rio de Janeiro. The next day, Hearne took off at 06:30 and headed for Sao Paulo. At 12:25 he flew over Soracaba, to the south, and at 22:40 he landed in a field at Itatinga, 4.8km from Soracaba, due to an approaching storm. He took off later, but he had to make a forced landing because of an engine failure. In the process the aircraft apparently hit a mound of sand and was unfortunately damaged beyond repair.

On 28 January 1921 Hearne and his mechanic left Rio at 05:00 in an Ansaldo SVA-10. They landed at Santos at 08:00, and took off two hours later. Paranaguá was reached at 11:40, Florianopolis at 13:50, Laguna at 14:50 and Concepción del Arroy at 15:20, where Hearne had to land owing to a heavy storm. They had covered 1,400km in 8½hr, and there was just 950km to cover to complete the flight. Hearne continued on to Macarig, where engine failure forced the aircraft down. At this point Hearne disappeared and no one knew his whereabouts, but he continued the flight and had to land at San Feliciano, 150km from Porto Alegre. He finally arrived at El Palomar on 2 February. On arrival he received military and civil awards.

Later, in August 1921, Hearne carried out another long-range flight, sponsored by the Liga Patriotica Argentina and the Aero Club Argentino. On 3 August he set out for Mendoza in the same SVA-10 used for the previous raid. However, while he was flying over Córdoba, he had to land in a field owing to engine failure. He sent a telegraph to Buenos Aires, asking for his mechanic, Tomas Quesada, and following repairs Hearne took off and continued the trip. When he was close to reaching the Andes the engine failed again, and he had to make an emergency landing near Las Cuevas. The aircraft was destroyed during the landing, and some days later its remains were sent to Mendoza.

Buenos Aires-Lima

On 13 February 1922 Hearne and mechanic Tomas Quesada took off at 05:35 in another 300hp Hispano Suiza Bristol F.2B. After take-off he set off for Mendoza, but over Chivlicoy (Province of Buenos Aires) he had to land owing to engine failure. Following repairs he took off, but unfortunately he had to land again at Travesia (Province of San Luis), where he decided to abandon the flight.

Eduardo Miguel Hearne was born on 17 December 1895. During the First World War he saw action with the British Expeditionary Corps in Siberia. Early May 1920 he started learning to fly at the Handley Page Flying School at Hurlingham, Provincia de Buenos Aires. The school used de Havilland D.H.4s and D.H.6s, Martinsyde ADC.1s and a single Royal Aircraft Factory S.E.5a. On 24 July 1920 Hearne was awarded Brevet No.145. Like many 'Estancieros' (ranch owners) he saw the advantages of the use of aircraft. By train the journey from their Estancias to Buenos Aires took almost 24 hours, after which there was a four- or five-hour ride on horseback. By aeroplane, the whole distance could be covered in four or five hours. Eduardo Miguel Hearne died on 10 January 1962.

Australia

G-AUCA (c/n 6117) Type 28 Tourer Coupé Three-seater [Puma]. CofA 478 issued 8.5.21. Regd [CofR 46] 28.6.21 to Department of Defence, Civil Aviation Branch, Melbourne. Crashed Bourke, NSW, 16.3.23; en route Melbourne-Longreach. Regn cld. Rebuilt (reportedly using spare airframe c/n 6113) and regd **G-AUDX** [CofR 77] 1.3.23 to Western Australian Airways Ltd, Perth [note inconsistency of regn date but CofA 60 issued 12.8.23]. Regd 16.4.28 to F.T. O'Dea, Sydney. Sold 16.6.30 to H.R. Clarke, Sydney. Crashed in Queensland and regn cld 20.9.30.

G-AUDG (c/n 6111) Type 28 Tourer Coupé Three-seater [Puma]. CofA 520 issued 28.9.21. Regd [CofR 53] 28.11.21 to Western Australian Airways Ltd, Perth. Sold 1.8.28 to G.C. Wilson, t/a Wilson Air Service Ltd, Sydney. Dbr Wauchope, NSW 17.12.28.

G-AUDH (c/n 6115) Type 28 Tourer Coupé Three-seater [Puma]. CofA 518 issued 9.9.21. Regd [CofR 54] 28.11.21 to Western Australian Airways Ltd, Perth. Rocked after take-off, turned almost completely over then dived vertically into Port Hedland Creek, WA 15.7.24 (L. Taplin and George Wilson escaped but passenger drowned). Parts salvaged and rebuilt. Regd **G-AUDZ** [CofR 113] 12.11.24 to WA Airways Ltd, Perth. CofA 96 issued 13.8.25. Regd 2.28 to F.T. O'Dea, Sydney. Sold to H.R. Clarke, Sydney. Crashed Ceduna, SA 6.9.30 and dbf. Regn notionally changed to **VH-UDZ** prior to formal cancellation 26.2.31.

G-AUDI (c/n 6116) Type 28 Tourer Coupé Three-seater [Puma]. CofA 516 issued 9.9.21. Arrived Fremantle aboard SS *Surrey* 17.11.21. Regd [CofR 55] 28.11.21 to Western Australian Airways Ltd, Perth. Crashed nr Murchison River, WA 5.12.21 (R. Fawcett and E.W. Broad both killed)

G-AUDJ (c/n 6118) Type 28 Tourer Coupé Three-seater [Puma]. CofA 515 issued 9.9.21. Regd [CofR 56] 26.11.21 to Western Australian Airways Ltd, Perth. Sold 26.1.27 to Charles E. Kingsford Smith and Lt Keith V. Anderson, t/a Interstate Flying Services, Longueville, NSW; named *Old Pioneer*. Made round-Australia flight starting and finishing at Sydney 19-29.6.27. Crashed on landing nr Pine Creek, NT 11.9.28; en route Sydney-England. Regn cld 27.11.28.

G-AUDK (c/n 6119) Type 28 Tourer Coupé Three-seater [Puma]. CofA 517 issued 9.9.21. Regd [CofR 57] 26.11.21 to Australian

Airways Ltd, Perth. Crashed on take-off Port Hedland, WA 30.1.23; repaired. Crashed Roebourne, WA 16.6.24; repaired. Regd 27.1.27 to Charles E.Kingsford Smith and Lt Keith V. Anderson, t/a Interstate Flying Services, Longueville, NSW. Sold 21.12.27 to L. Shaw, Lae, New Guinea. Arrived aboard the schooner *Matubi* 4.2.28. Crashed on landing Lae 15.2.28 (pilot L. Shaw). Regn cld 13.8.28. Wreck sold to Ray Parer.

G-AUDF (Type 28 Tourer) see **G-EAXK**.

G-AUDX (Type 28 Tourer) see **G-AUCA**.

G-AUDZ (Type 28 Tourer) see **G-AUDH**.

G-AUEB (F.2B) c/n 4965 ex-**H1248**. Regd [CofR 80] 12.4.23 to Horace C. Miller, Port Melbourne. Sold 28.4.23 and regd 16.5.23 to QANTAS Ltd, Longreach. Crashed on landing Longreach 18.12.23 following engine failure (pilot A.W. Vigors). Rebuilt with 300hp Puma engine during 1924 for aerial medical service use, fitted with a stretcher and marked with red cross and re-flown 24.9.24. CofA renewed 28.10.24 but considered unsuccessful as not robust enough for bush work. Sold 20.7.27 and regd 3.11.27 to Kenneth Morton Frewin, Ascot, Qld. Possibly the machine christened *Stormbird* 20.8.27 for a proposed flight to New Zealand, but this was banned by the Australian Government as being unsafe. Sold 3.11.27 to Bulolo Goldfields Aeroplane Service Ltd, Wau, NG; arrived Port Moresby aboard SS *Morinda* 27.12.27. Assembled at Ela Beach, Port Moresby and tested 12.1.28. Crashed Wau 17.4.28 (pilot Basil Daish). Regn cld 11.9.28.

Reproductions:

VH-UDR Replica built originally as a Bristol Tourer for the Australian film *A Thousand Skies*. Extant as static exhibit with Flypast Museum of Australian Army Flying, Oakey, Queensland, marked '**C4623**' to represent an aircraft flown by the 1st Squadron, Australian Flying Corps (q.v.).

VH-IIZ In 2015 the Ed Storo replica (previously **N624**) with The Vintage Aviator in New Zealand, **ZK-JNU/B1112**, was sold to Australian owner Donal John McDonald, to whom it was registered on 19 June 2015. It is now operated by The Australian Vintage Aviation Society (TAVAS) at Caboolture in Queensland, and flies in the colours and markings of **B1229**, the aircraft flown by Capt Ross McPherson Smith of 1 Sqn AFC in Egypt.

Bulgaria

B-BEBA Type 88A Viper Tourer (c/n 6937). Delivered .26.

B-BECA Type 88 Bulgarian Tourer (c/n 6383). Delivered 4.24.

B-BEHA Type 88 Bulgarian Tourer (c/n 6384). Delivered 4.24.

B-BEKA Type 88A Viper Tourer (c/n 6939). Delivered .26.

B-BEPK Type 83B Lucifer School/PTM (c/n 6936). Delivered .26.

B-BETO Type 88A Viper Tourer (c/n 6938). Delivered .26.

Newfoundland

Type 29 Tourer Coupé Two-seater (c/n 6123). Ordered .22 by The Aerial Survey Co (Sidney Cotton) and reportedly shipped 5.23 to be flown on skis (but unconfirmed if order was actually fulfilled).

New Zealand

ZK-BRI Rebuild ex-**G-ACAA** (2), to New Zealand 2006 and initially located at Foxton. To Stuart Tantrum at the Omaka Aviation Heritage Centre for restoration for film maker Sir Peter Jackson. Marked '**D8084**' with individual letter 'S' with Old Stick and Rudder Company, Hood Aerodrome, Masterton, marked '**D8084**'.

ZK-JNU A replica built by Fedex DC-10 pilot Ed Storo of Memphis, Tennessee, over an eight-year period, this aircraft, c/n ERS-2, was registered as **N264** in 1992. Its fuselage and fin and rudder are steel-framed, but the wings and tailplane are built from spruce and are similar to the original F.2B wings. Equipped with First World War and modern instruments, it is powered by a 200hp six-cylinder in-line Ranger engine. Imported into New Zealand by Sir Peter Jackson, it was registered there as **ZK-JNU** on 8 May 2002. Storo's original RAF colour scheme represented **J7624** of 2 Sqn in 1919, the serial number fortuitously being a combination of Ed Storo's wife's and son's birthdays (June 7 and June 24). On 13 September 2005 ZK-JNU had a change of paint scheme, being finished to represent **B1112** 'F', the aircraft flown by Capt C. Jones of 22 Sqn RFC in 1918. Ownership was transferred to The Vintage Aviator on 11 September 2007 and it was based at mainly Omaka for its life in New Zealand, before being shipped to Australia in 2015, becoming **VH-IIZ** (q.v.).

Nicaragua
(Type 29 Open Tourer/PT2S) see **G-EANR** (c/n 5868).

Spain
Tourers delivered to Spain in 1921 for civil use:

M-AAAF (s/n 6109) Type 28 Tourer Three-seater. CofA 508 issued 16.7.21. Delivered ex Croydon 27.8.21 (pilot Larry Carter). Regd 9.21 to Compañía Española de Navegación Aérea; fate unknown.

M-AAEA (s/n 6114) Type 28 Tourer Coupé, see **G-EAWQ**.

M-AAFA (Identity not known) Type 29 Tourer. Regd 6.7.21 to Sociedad Funicular Archanda Bilbao. Current .30; regd to Aeronautica Militar Espanola.

M-AEAA (s/n 6112) Type 28 Open Tourer Three-seater, see **G-EAWR**.

M-AFFA (s/n 6121) Type 29 Tourer/PT2S Two-seater. CofA issued 23.8.21. Delivered to Croydon 31.8.21 and to Spain 1.9.21 (pilot Leslie Tait-Cox). Regd 10.21 to Compañía Española de Navegación Aérea. Regd [.30] to Sociedad Otie, San Sebastian; fate unknown.

M-AFFF (s/n 6110) Type 28 Open Tourer Three-seater. CofA 512 issued 23.8.21. Delivered ex Croydon 27.8.21 (pilot Carter). Regd 10.21 to Compañía Española de Navegación Aérea. Regd .30 to Sociedad Otie, San Sebastian; fate unknown.

Bristol Type 28 Open Tourer three-seater M-AFFF was delivered to Spain via Croydon on 27 August 1921 and was initially operated by the Compañía Española de Navegación Aérea. *(A.J. Jackson Collection at Brooklands Museum www.ajjcollection.co.uk)*

Six Bristol Fighter variants with 300hp Hispano-Suiza 8Fb engines were supplied to Spain by ADC Aircraft Ltd and were each given a UK CofA for delivery purposes:

M-CAAJ ex **E2301** CofA 1622 issued 25.9.28; fitted with 300hp Hispano 8Fb. Regd 30.1.30 to CEA Compañía Española de Aviación, Albacete. Regd **EC-AAJ** (CofR 58) 21.4.31 to same owner. Wfu .32. Regn cld 12.11.40.

M-CAJA ex **D2696** CofA 1624 issued 25.9.28; fitted with 300hp Hispano 8Fb. Regd 30.1.30 to CEA Compañía Española de Aviación, Albacete. Regd **EC-AJA** (CofR 59) 21.4.31 to same owner. Wfu .32. Regn cld 12.11.40.

M-CIAI ex **E1916** CofA 1619 issued 25.9.28; fitted with 300hp Hispano 8Fb. Regd 30.1.30 to CEA Compañía Española de Aviación, Albacete. Regd **EC-IAI** (CofR 56) 21.4.31 to same owner. Wfu .32. Regn cld 12.11.40.

M-CIIA ex **E2360** CofA 1623 issued 25.9.28; fitted with 300hp Hispano 8Fb. Regd 30.1.30 to CEA Compañía Española de Aviación, Albacete. Regd **EC-IIA** (CofR 55) 21.4.31 to same owner. Wfu .32. Regn cld 12.11.40.

M-CIII ex **E1962** CofA 1620 issued 25.9.28; fitted with 300hp Hispano 8Fb. Regd 30.1.30 to CEA Compañía Española de Aviación, Albacete. Regd **EC-III** (CofR 57) 21.4.31 to same owner. Wfu .32. Regn cld 12.11.40.

M-CJAA ex **E2199** CofA 1621 issued 25.9.28; fitted with 300hp Hispano 8Fb. Regd 30.1.30 to CEA Compañía Española de Aviación, Albacete. Regd **EC-JAA** (CofR 60) 21.4.31 to same owner. Wfu .32. Regn cld 12.11.40.

A Bristol Fighter reproduction in Spanish Air Force colours and serialled 'B.21' is on static display in the Museo del Aire at Cuatro Vientos Airfield, Madrid.

Sweden
SE-AEE (c/n 6380) Type 76A Jupiter Fighter. See **G-EBHG**.

USA
— (c/n 5873) Type 34 Open Seaplane Tourer Three-seater 1921.
— (c/n 5874) Type 34 Open Seaplane Tourer Three-seater 1921. [Only one of these two completed.]
— (c/n 5877) Type 28 Three-seat Tourer Coupé. (Also reported as Type 47)
— (c/n 5878) Type 28 Three-seat Tourer Coupé. (Also reported as Type 47)
— (c/n 5879) Type 28 Three-seat Tourer Coupé. (Also reported as Type 47)
— (c/n 5880) Type 28 Three-seat Tourer Coupé. (Also reported as Type 47)
— (c/n 5881) Type 28 Three-seat Tourer Coupé. (Also reported as Type 29 Two-seat Tourer)
— (c/n 5891) Type 28 Three-seat Tourer Coupé.

Civil registrations issued from 1926/7. Only these known:

NC826Y Listed in 1931 register as Allinio Bristol Cabin c/n 4, Puma engine, Three-seater.

NC1191 Listed as a Bristol Tourer and possibly one of the Curtiss-built USAO-1s.

This monstrosity is believed to be NC826Y, described in the 1931 US civil register as 'Allinio Bristol Cabin c/n 4, Puma engine, Three-seater'. *(Eric Harlin)*

Appendix 8
BRISTOL SEQUENCE NUMBERS

The following table is based on information extracted by the late Jim Oughton from various Bristol/BAC Inspection, Contracts and Certification documents and AID records.

Sequence number	Type	Quantity	Comments
1379-1380	T.9 R.2a (To T.12 F2a)	2	A3303-3304
1431-1480	T.12 F.2A	50	A3305-3354
2067-2068	T.13 MR.1 Metal Biplane	2	A5177-5178
2069-2268	T.14 F.2B Fighter	200	A7101-7300
2269-2518	T.14 F.2B Fighter	250	B1101-1350
2851-2950	T.14 F.2B Fighter	100	C4801-4900
2951-3150	T.14 F.2B Fighter	200	C4601-4800
3151-3450	T.14 F.2B Fighter	300	C751-1050
3451-3750	T.14 F.2B Fighter	300	D7801-8100
3754-4253	T.14 F.2B Fighter	500	E2151-2650
4257-4956	T.14 F.2B Fighter	700	F4271-4970
4957-5106	T.15 F.2B Fighter	150	H1240-1389. Arab engine
5107-5115	T.14 F.2B Fighter	9	H1390-1398. Falcon engine
5116-5117	T.15 F.2B Fighter	2	H1399-1400. Arab engine
5118-5123	T.14 F.2B Fighter	6	H1401-1406. Falcon engine
5124	T.15 F.2B Fighter	1	H1407. Arab engine
5125-5406	T.14 F.2B Fighter	282	H1408-1689. Falcon engine
5407-5424	T.14 F.2B Fighter	18	H1690-1707. Puma engine
5425-5456	T.14 F.2B Fighter	(32)	H1708-1739 Puma engine. Cancelled
5457-5656	T.14 F.2B Fighter	(200)	J1231-1430. Puma engine. Cancelled
5659-5664	T.14 F.2B Fighter	6	E5253-5258. Standard. To Puma engine
5665-5714	T.14 F.2B Fighter	50	E5259-5308. Puma engine
5867	T.29 F.2B Open Tourer/PT2S	1	G-EAIZ. Two-seat. Puma engine
5868	T.29 F.2B Open Tourer/PT2S	1	G-EANR Two-seat. Puma engine
5870	T.36 Seely Puma	1	G-EAUE To Jupiter engine/J7004
5873-5874	T.34 Open Seaplane Tourer	2	Three-seaters
5876	T.28 3-seat Tourer	1	G-EART. Open cockpits
5877-5880	T.28 3-seat Tourer	4	Coupé top. To USA
5881	T.28 3-seat Tourer	1	Coupé top. To USA
5891	T.28 3-seat Tourer	1	Coupé top. To USA
5892	T.29 2-seat Tourer	1	G-EAVU
5893	T.14 F.2B 'J' Type (Mk.II)	1	J6586. Prototype
5894-6107	T.14 F.2B Mk.II	214	J6587-6800
6108	T.28 3-seat Tourer Coupé	1	G-EAXK/G-AUDF
6109-6110	T.28 3-seat Tourer Open	2	M-AAAF & M-AFFF
6111	T.28 3-seat Tourer Coupé	1	G-AUDG
6112	T.28 3-seat Tourer Open	1	G-EAWR/M-AEAA
6113	T.28 3-seat Tourer Open	1	Not sold
6114	T.28 3-seat Tourer Coupé	1	G-EAWQ/M-AAEA
6115-6116	T.28 3-seat Tourer Coupé	2	G-AUDH & G-AUDI
6117	T.28 3-seat Tourer Coupé	1	G-AUCA

Sequence number	Type	Quantity	Comments
6118-6119	T.28 3-seat Tourer Coupé	1	G-AUDJ & G-AUDK
6120	T.29 2-seat Tourer/PT2S	1	G-EAXA
6121	T.29 2-seat Tourer/PT2S	1	M-AFFA
6122	T.29 2-seat Tourer/PT2S	1	G-EAWB
6123	T.29 2-seat Tourer/PT2S	1	To Canada/Newfoundland
6140-6144	T.17 F.2B (300hp Hispano-Suiza)	5	M-MRAZ, M-MRAY, M-MRAX, M-MRAI & M-MRCO [One source has these as being the five aircraft supplied, supposedly as new, to Norway in 1.21, which now seems unlikely. More puzzling is that 13 aircraft were supplied to Spain between 8.21 and 12,21, four of which were from ADC and nine from Filton to Spain via Croydon, precise delivery dates for the latter being known for M-MRAC, 'AG, 'AH, 'AI, 'AL, 'AM, 'AN, 'AO & 'AV, of which only M-MRAI seems to fit the five listed in Bristol records.]
6153-6155	T.73 L3S Taxiplane	3	G-EBEW, G-EBEY & G-EBFY
6156-6161	F.2B Fighter (reconditioned)	6	To Greece
6162-6221	F.2B Fighter (reconditioned)	60	To RAF. No serials recorded.
6223	T.17A (300hp Hispano-Suiza)	1	G-EBCN
6224-6238	T.17A (300hp Hispano-Suiza)	1	To Belgium (SABCA). No engines
6239-6242	T.81 Puma-School 'B'	4	G-EBFR, G-EBFS, G-EBFT & G-EBFU
6243-6372	F.2B Fighter (reconditioned)	130	To RAF. J' Type – Mk.II: F4755, F4952, F4749, F4745, F4742, C1042, F4953, F4756, F4727, F4729, F4731, F4968, F4735, F4744, F4732, F4743, F4741, F4748, F4751, F4320, F4753, F4734, F4746, F4726, F4870, F4733, F4758, H1565, F4747, F4760, F4589, F4896, F4902, F4567, F4507, F4569, F4904, F4568, F4484, F4542, F4591, F4485, F4326, F4903, F4500, F4570, F4541, F4566, F4463, F4592, F4584, F4658, F4716, F4496, F4551, F4491, F4497, F4547, F4607, F4561, F4495, F4487, F4621, F4464, F4599, F4723, F4514, F4510, F4704, F4624, F4490, F4506, F4623, F4489, F4513, F4884, F4712, F4508, F4481, F4505, F4465, F4905, F4548, F4454, F4565, F4549, F4574, F4504, F4587, F4546, F4517, F4586, F4492, F4581, F4596, F4588, F4515, F4571, F4706, F4610, F4519, F4550, F4518, F4606, F4486, F4882, F4554, F4553, F4516, F4572, F4590, F4543, F4737, F4598, F4714, F4600, F4583, F4544, F4720, F4606, F4713, F4881, F4602, F4555, F4702, F4703, F4719, F4563, F4601, F4883
6373-6378	T.83A Preliminary Training Machine	6	G-EBFZ to G-EBGE
6379	T.76 Jupiter Fighter	1	G-EBGF
6380	T.76A Jupiter Fighter	1	G-EBHG/Swedish 4300
6381	T.76B Jupiter Fighter	1	G-EBHH
6382	T.89 Jupiter School	1	G-EBIH
6383-6384	T.88 Bulgarian Tourer	2	B-BECA & B-BEHA
6385-6459	F.2B Fighter (Reconditioned)	75	To 'J' Type – Mk.II. 6429 to 6432 & 6439 to 6444 to dual controls: F4970, F4960, F4956, F4946, C799, F4964, C763, C4738, C765, F4338, F4954, F4969, C810, F4595, D7801, C798, D7851, F4962, F4949, F4339, F4948, C764, F4950, F4951, F4961, F4958, F4947, F4594, F4955, F4957, F4693, C801, C812, F4693, D8055, H1562, F4967, F4965, C4734, C4683, C1014, C4741, F4645, F4688, F4647, F4342, F4691, F4692, D7874, D7812, C4897, C4681, D7873, D7876, F4648, F4685, C4680, F4650, F4642, F4827, C802, C4682, F4349, D8031, C762, H1609, F4697, F4754, F4840, F4644, D7854, F4737, F4484, F4646, F4649
6460-6509	F.2B Fighter (Reconditioned)	50	To 'J' Type – Mk.II. 6476 to 6494 no engines, 6495 to 6509 dual controls: F4573, F4935, H1416, F4812, F4711, F4609, F4603, H1634, F4715, F4901, F4932, F4545, F4699, F4717, F4698, F4694, F4681, F4687, F4684, F4682, F4683, F4689, F4619, H1424, F4929, F4916, H1413, F4914, F4915, F4907, H1461, H1458, F4695, F4887, F4789, F4722, F4913, F4701, F4811, F4786, F4708, H1392, F4705, H1444, H1396, H1390, H1398, H1589, J6676, J6586

Sequence number	Type	Quantity	Comments
6510-6521	T.17 F.2B (300hp Hispano-Suiza)	12	To Spain
6522-6524	T.89 Jupiter School	1	G-EBJA to G-EBJC
6525	T.89 Jupiter School	1	Airframe for stock
6529-6628	F.2B Fighter (Reconditioned)	100	To 'J' Type – Mk.II: F4836, E2435, F4845, F4418, F4501, H1393, H1432, H1417, F4503, F4853, H1598, F4944, C4750, H1588, H1486, F4488, F4934, F4381, C4794, H1640, J6664, E2533, F4285, E2629, E2259, F4771, F4804, F4942, C1027, F4680, H1632, F4285, F4509, F4810, F4375, F4366, H1423, F4376, F4473, C1015, C4676, F4618, H1483, F4830, F4854, J6662, E2624, F4450, H1440, F4301, H1451, D8044, F4379, E2264, C903, F4898, E2257, H1601, F4908, H1428, J6678, F4643, C1032, H1686, C804, F4498, F4523, F5996, F4369, H1397, F4423, F4667, H1583, F4477, H7064, F4537, H1604, H1606, H1430, H1617, C1039, E2504, C923, F4819, H1457, E2501, F4670, D8009, F4494, F4665, C4766, F4839, F4396, H1581, F4857, F4921, J6700, F4660, E2552
6629-6708	F.2B Fighter (Reconditioned)	80	To 'J' Type – Mk.II: J6670, J6632, J6663, F4706, J6746, J6715, D7890, F4392, F4559, H1616, F4556, F4344, D7864, F4558, H1599, J6735, J6677, H1488, D8092, J6752, H1395, J6718, J6716, H1410, J6729, J6681, J6701, J6800, J6756, C4631, J6740, F4401, F4330, E2297, F4896, J6761, J6721, J6736, H1637, F4886, H1420 (new layout – Mk.III), J6711, F4813, C767, B1325, B1326, J6765, H1415, J6691, J6708, F4710, F4721, D7847, F4892, F4700, H1600, F4605, F4341, F4278, H1624, J6730, D7848, D7850, F4815, F4562, F4906, F4362, C4845, H1555, F4416, F4414, F4511, F4686, F4891, H1391, H1394, H1438, H1473, F4753, C766
6712-6717	T.81A Tourer/Trainer	6	To Greek Navy
6721-6804	F.2B Fighter (Reconditioned)	84	To 'J' Type – Mk.II: J7616-7699
6806-6855	F.2B Fighter (Reconditioned)	50	To 'J' Type – Mk.II. Dual controls from 6816: H1454, H1455, H1501, H1526, H1623, H1627, H1636, H1668, H1677, H1685, D7839, F4925, F4939, F4940, F4814, F4946, F4585, H1493, H1496, H1463, D8033, H1469, H1439, H1644, F4885, E2300, F4911, F4912, F4751, F4756, F4490, H1669, E2643, F4968, F4622, F4826, F4492, H1642, H1502, F4507, D8085, F4727, D8096, H1492, H1681, H1660, H1494, H1456, H1465, F4651
6856-6857	F.2B Fighter – New build	2	To New Zealand
6858-6863	F.2B Fighter – New build	6	To Irish Free State [Nos 17-21]
6864-6917	F.2B Fighter (Reconditioned)	54	To 'J' Type – Mk.II. Dual controls except 6917: C1049, F4434, E2624, C4740, F4423, F4548, J6791, F4385, J6708, F4369, F4721, F4418, H1468, F4584, F4510, J6790, F4956, F4705, F4960, J6661, F4715, H1614, F4970, J6589, J6685, D8100, J6702, F4607, J6600, J6658, F4963, J6677, J6734, J6602, D8045, F4882, J6793, F4588, F4934, F4375, F4586, D8083, F4564, F4515, F4497, E2432, H1634, E2434, F4561, F4610, J6697, J6738, F4757, J6696
6918-6919	T.89 Jupiter Trainer	2	G-EBML & G-EBMN
6922-6923	T.83 Lucifer School/PTM	2	G-EBNB & G-EBNC
6924-6935	T.83 Lucifer School/PTM	12	To Chile [Type 83B?]
6936	T.83 Lucifer School/PTM	1	To Bulgaria. B-BEPK
6937-6939	T.88A Viper Tourer	3	B-BEBA, B-BETO & B-BEKA
6940-6959	F.2B Fighter (Reconditioned)	20	To 'J' Type – Mk.II: F4744, F4567, D8056, J6622, D7818, D7815, F4732, F4591, J6798, F4745, C4794, J7658, D7812, F4903, J6747, D7801, F4845, F4571, F4500, F4465
6960-6962	T.83 Lucifer School/PTM	3	To Hungary
6963-6964	T.89 Jupiter Trainer	2	G-EBNZ & G-EBOA
6965-6967	T.89A Jupiter Trainer	3	G-EBOC, G-EBOD & G-EBQS
6968-6987	F.2B Fighter (Reconditioned)	20	To 'J' Type – Mk.II: C4676, J6701, H1415, H1451, F4902, J6680, J6775, J6695, F4965, F4624, J7685, J6694, F4836, F4603, F4812, F4698, H1424, F4486, J7620, F4684
6988-7017	T.96 F.2B Mk.III DC	30	J8429-8458. New build

Sequence number	Type	Quantity	Comments
7020-7039	T.96 F.2B Mk.III	20	Reconditioned and converted. Serial numbers not recorded.
7040-7059	T.96 F.2B Mk.III	30	J8242-8261. New build. No engines
7060-7070	T.96 F.2B Mk.III	11	J8262-8272. New build. Engines
7071-7089	T.96 F.2B Mk.III	19	J8273-8291. New build. No engines
7090-7119	T.96 F.2B Mk.III	30	Reconditioned and converted. Dual controls from 7110; H1417, F4366 (first with serial numbers under wings), J6749, F4952, F4590, H1562, J7621 (longerons strengthened), F4489 (new top and bottom fins), J7686 (wings set back 4in), F4496, J7616, F4618, F4967, J6662, F4412, J6719, F4741, J7689, J7657, J7636, F4516, H1396, H1644, F4811, J7618, F4810, F4721, F4701, F4492, E2630
7120-7122	T.96 F.2B Fighter Mk.III	3	RNZAF [NZPAF at that time. Per NZ sources, 7120 = Mk.IIIDC, 7121 & 7122 'J' Type, army co-operation]
7124	T.89A Jupiter School	1	G-EBQT
7125-7154	T.96 F.2B Mk.III	30	Reconditioned and converted. Dual controls to 7132: H1494, F4691, F4342, F4912, F4519, C4680, D8033, F4756, F4545, F4553, F4944, F4517, C4750, H1432, H1624, H1598, F5996, J6766, F4681, F4542, H1596, F4587, F4957, F4381, J7670, J7659, F4754, C767, F4569, F4565
7156-7157	T.89A Jupiter School	2	G-EBSB & G-EBSH
7158-7177	T.96 F.2B Mk.III	20	Reconditioned and converted; J6668, J6760, F4645, J7660, H1526, J6743, J7656, J7690, H1640, H1440, J6722, C4737, H1660, C763, F4588, H1642, F4946, E2643, H1493, F4913
7221	T.89A Jupiter School	1	For stock
7222-7231	T.17B F.2B (200hp Hispano-Suiza)	10	To Mexico
7234	T.89A Jupiter School	1	G-EBVR
7236-7247	T.96 F.2B Mk.III	12	Reconditioned and converted. Dual controls from 7245; B1326, J7638, C4683, J6742, J7640, J6776, C4655, H1560, F4329, F4610, F4970, H1398
7248-7264	T.96 F.2B Mk.IV	17	Reconditioned and converted; F4545, H1420, J8265, J8269, J8272, J8267, J8270, F4590, J7621, H1562, F4366, F4952, J8271, J6749, J6662, F4412, J8262
7265	T.89A Jupiter School	1	G-EBYL
7266	T.83 Titan School/PTM	1	G-EBYT
7301-7310	T.96 F.2B Mk.IV	10	Converted from Mk.III. 7301 fitted engine from F4545, remainder no engines: J8286, J8249, J8258, J8273, J8252, J8289, J8281, J8287, J8280, J8279
7312-7321	T.96 F.2B Mk.IV	10	Converted from Mk.III. No engines: J8275, J8246, J8283, J8274, J8284, J8291, J8276, J8244, J8248, J8247
7350-7352	T.89A Jupiter School	3	G-AAGF, G-AALO & G-AAWJ
7419-7428	T.96 F.2B Mk.IV	10	Reconditioned and converted from Mk.III: J7686, J7616, J8253, J7657, J8288, J8255, J8260, J8277, F4741, J8290
7429-7435	T.96 F.2B Mk.III DC	7	Converted to dual controls: J7689, J6719, J8285, J8282, J8259, F4516, J8245
7436-7438	T.96 F.2B Mk.III DC	(3)	Not taken up
7556	T.96 F.2B Mk.III DC	1	F4811 reconditioned
7557	T.96 F.2B Mk.IV DC	1	D8085 reconditioned
7558-7559	T.96 F.2B Mk.III DC	2	H1397 & F4721 reconditioned
7568-7581	T.96 F.2B Mks.III & IV	14	Reconditioned – dual controls: J8434, F4548, C4897, J8437, H1660, J8429, J8446, D8096, J6790, J8448, F4342, J8444, J8455, F4434
7711-7712	T.89A Jupiter School	2	G-ABPL & G-ABPM

Appendix 9

RFC AND RAF UNITS

2 Squadron

Re-formed 1.2.20 ex-105 Sqn at Oranmore (HQ & 1 Flt there throughout?) in 11th (Irish) Group (later Wing), Flts at Castlebar @6.3.20-@6.4.20 (but not 29.5.20), also Fermoy 1.2.20-13.2.22 (2 Flts there @29.5.20). One Flt moved from Castlebar to Oranmore 4.20. To Digby 13.2.22, then Aldergrove in 12th Wing 2.6.22 (or 31.5.22) until 26.7.22, then Farnborough (HQ & 2 Flts) from 28.9.22 leaving C Flt (four a/c) at Aldergrove until 7.2.23. To Andover 17.9.23, then Manston in No.22 Group 31.3.24. Left for China via Southampton 20.4.27. To HMS *Hermes* & SS *Neuralia* 26.4.27. Arrived Shanghai Racecourse 31.5.27. Left for UK in HMS *Hermes* 26.8.27. Arrived Manston 23.10.27; re-equipped there with Armstrong Whitworth Atlases 12.29-1.30.

Commanding Officers: Sqn Ldr B.F. Moore 1 Feb 1920; Sqn Ldr F.W. Stent MC 10 May 1920; Sqn Ldr H.J. Butler MC DFC 16 Aug 1920; Sqn Ldr L.E. Forbes MC 15 May 1922; Sqn Ldr R.E. Saul DFC 2 Mar 1925; Sqn Ldr W. Sowrey DFC 1 Oct 1926; Sqn Ldr H.M. Probyn DSO 17 Mar 1928 to 18 Dec 1931.

Squadron identification markings: three vertical coloured bands around the rear fuselage, the outer bands being red with the centre band in the relevant flight colour: 'A' Flt white, 'B' Flt yellow and 'C' Flt blue. They also carried a heart, club, diamond or spade motif on the fin. Around 1927/9 at least one aircraft (J6694) carried a white number '2' in a dark-coloured pyramid-shaped triangle, no bands on the fuselage.

Known serial numbers: B1325, B1326, B1329, C757, C767, C1014, C4741, C4750, D7865, D7880, D8025, E1925, E2546, F4321, F4322, F4354, F4366, F4369, F4388, F4412, F4428, F4484, F4489, F4490, F4500, F4537 V, F4542, F4545, F4546, F4563, F4567, F4585, F4590, F4603, F4624, F4646, F4699, F4714, F4717, F4722, F4737, F4767, F4767, F4769, F4779, F4795, F4797, F4798, F4812, F4825, F4837, F4854, F4895, F4908, F4956, F4965, F4967, F5996, H1391, H1441, H1445, H1448, H1455, H1485, H1486, H1487, H1490, H1526, H1562, H1570, H1571, H1590, H1595, H1603, H1610, H1615, H1620, H1621, H1640, J6592, J6595, J6623, J6662, J6663, J6668, J6669, J6671, J6673, J6674, J6678. J6679, J6688, J6691, J6692, J6693, J6694, J6695, J6696, J6700, J6701, J6703, J6705, J6708, J6711, J6712, J6714, J6716, J6717, J6722, J6728, J6730, J6732, J6735, J6736, J6743, J6745, J6748, J6749, J6756, J6763, J6775, J6795 G, J7642, J7651, J7652, J7656, J7657, J7659, J7664, J7665, J7666, J7667, J7683, J7685, J7686, J7699, J8245, J8252, J8253, J8255, J8265, J8267, J8269, J8270, J8432.

4 Squadron

(1) Basically equipped with R.E.8s in France, a single F.2B was attached between June and October 1918, the squadron being then at St Omer until moving to Ste-Marie Cappel 18.9.18.

(2) Re-established at Farnborough in No.7 Group with A & B Flts 30.4.20; C Flt formed at Stonehenge 8.3.20 [*sic*]. Came under HQ Inland Area 1.4.20. A Flt detached to Aldergrove 8.20, moved to Baldonnel 4.5.21. Returned to Farnborough 18.1.22. Sqn sailed for Turkey

22.8.22; in HMS *Argus* 18.9.22 to 26.9.22, then HMS *Ark Royal* 26.9.22 to 8.10.22. Arrived Kilia Bay in Constantinople Wing 11.10.22, to Kilid el Bahr 11.12.22. Left for UK in HMS *Ark Royal* 5.9.23. Arrived Farnborough in No.7 Group 18.9.23.

Commanding Officers:
(1) Maj R.E. Saul DFC
(2) Sqn Ldr C.H. Blount MC 31.3.20; Sqn Ldr J.C. Slessor MC 4.4.25; Sqn Ldr N.H. Bottomley 15.10.28; Sqn Ldr F.H.E. Reeve 14.12.29-6.1.30.

Squadron identification markings: in 1926 H1415 and H1526 carried a letter 'A' forward of the fuselage roundel and a number '2' aft of it.

Known serial numbers:
(1) C920, C1036, E2570.
(2) C1014, D8076, D7835, D8085, D8100 C4, E2624 A4, E2624, F4366, F4391, F4412, F4420, F4450, F4544, F4545, F4573, F4603, F4648, F4657, F4681, F4697, F4738, F4854, F4904, F4932, F4935, F4944, F4970, H1014, H1415 A2, H1420, H1452, H1468, H1485, H1486, H1488, H1526 A2, H1606, J6608, J6661, J6666, J6698, J6703, J6704, J6710, J6711, J6712, J6713 A4, J6761 C1, J6715 A1, J6719, J6720, J6721, J6727, J6752, J6760, J6764, J6784, J6787, J6788, J6793, J7619, J7619 A3, J7636, J7640, J7654, J7658, J7659, J7660, J7661, J7685, J7686, J7687, J7688, J8246, J8264, J8266, J8267, J8271, J8272, J8273, J8274, J8275, J8276, J8290.

5 Squadron

Re-equipped from R.E.8s at Hangelar, Germany, in 2nd Wing 2nd Brigade 3.19; Ret'd UK to Bicester and discarded aircraft 8.9.19, disbanding 20.1.20.

Re-formed ex-48 Sqn at Quetta, India, 1.2.20; Ambala 26.10.22; Dardoni 10.3.24; Kohat 22.1.25; Risalpur 15.10.25 (detachment at Tank 3.28-5.25. Flt at Miranshah 3.28); Quetta 12.12.28; Kohat (date not found); Quetta 15.5.30 (Flt to Miranshah 14.6.30); Re-equipped with Westland Wapiti IIA 10.31 in India.

Commanding Officers: Maj D.F. Stevenson 2.3.19; Unknown 8.9.19; Sqn disbanded 20.1.20; Sqn Ldr P.C. Maltby DSO DFC 1.2.20; Sqn Ldr A.J. Capel DSO DFC 12.1.24; Sqn Ldr O.C. Bryson MC DFC 9.11.28-13.10.31.

Squadron identification markings: around 1925 a horizontal [black?] band along the centre fuselage, with a large black '5' on the fin. By 1931 a single blue band around was carried the rear fuselage.

Known serial numbers: C801 A, C804, C1039 B, D7807, D7809, D7813, D7830 J, D8035 A also M and H, D8036 H, E2257, E2283, E2421 C, E2463, E2501 R, E9615 T, E9616, F1565 A and H, F4320 D, F4377, F4394 W, F4403 C, F4436, F4461, F4463, F4470, F4488, F4498, F4500, F4543 Y, F4544, F4555, F4566 M, F4568, F4592 D, F4593, F4597 U, F4598, F4607, F4611 D, F4614, F4616 M, F4621, F4625, F4627, F4630, F4634, F4635, F4636, F4637 A, F4644 F, F4658, F4660, F4670, F4689, F4693, F4706, F4707, F4730, F4734, F4735, F4746 B, F4766 H, F4825 X, F4861, F4870, F4878, F4881, F4896, F4924 V, F4929, F4947 G,

F4958, F4975 G, H1428, H1458, H1461, H1497, H1498 T, H1508, H1509, H1513, H1515, H1516, H1518 P, H1520, H1523, H1528, H1530 A, H1535, H1539 A, H1544, H1546 O, H1552, H1565 H, H1657, J6591, J6598, J6599, J6601 C, J6613 D and O, J6624, J6628 D, J6631 P, J6632, J6634 V, J6637, J6638, J6641, J6643, J6651 C, J6653, J6654 B, J6660, J6670, J6700 M, J6711, J6715 R, J6741 C, J6746, J6750 L, J6759 L, J6761, J6762, J6770 L, J6771 T, J6772, J6774 C and W, J6777, J6782 O, J7677 D.

6 Squadron

Some F.2Bs on strength in addition to R.E.8s from 2.19 at Gerpinnes, Belgium, in 15th Wing, 5th Brigade, moving to Sart 19.3.19, aircraft left behind when embarked for Iraq 14-15.4.19. Re-equipped with R.E.8s on arrival at Baghdad 18.7.19, but exchanged these for F.2Bs 7.20 at Baghdad West (Flt at Hillah 10.10.20-11.20); ('C' Flt at Bushire 6.20 to 20.12.20). Sqn to Hinaidi 9.10.22 and designated 6 (Army Co-operation) Sqn 27.3.24 (detachments at Kirkuk 1922-1925 and Kingerban 1924); squadron to Mosul 19.5.24, Hinaidi 20.10.26. In transit to Egypt 23.10.29, arrived Ismailia 25.10.29 (detachment at Ramleh from 4.31). Received F.2B Mk.IIIAs 4.31, then some Fairey Gordons 5.31. The last F.2B left 6.32.

Commanding Officers: Maj G.C. Pirie MC 3.7.18; Sqn Ldr W. Sowrey AFC 13.2.20; Sqn Ldr E.A.B. Rice MC 28.5.20; Sqn Ldr H.G. Smart 26.4.22; Sqn Ldr E.R. Manning DSO MC 21.6.22; Sqn Ldr D.S.K. Crosbie OBE 11.1.24; Sqn Ldr D.F. Stevenson DSO MC & Bar 15.11.25; Sqn Ldr C.N. Lowe MC DFC 26.11.26; Sqn Ldr C.H. Keith 10.1.28; Sqn Ldr C.R. Cox AFC 1.3.30; Sqn Ldr J.P. Coleman AFC 1.2.31 to 1 Feb 1934.

Known serial numbers: C766, C903, C923, C1048, CR4682, C4683, C9879, D7814, D7818, D7832, D7833, D7834, D7838, D7844, D7845, D7848, D7858, D7867, D7874, D7876, D8032, D8037, D8038, D8040, D8051, D8052, D8056, D8085, E2424, E2476, E2529, E2533, E2580, E2629, E2662, F4326, F4329, F4344, F4349, F4362, F4477, F4511, F4570, F4583, F4586, F4590, F4591, F4600, F4601, F4681, F4682, F4683, F4686, F4727, F4729, F4731, F4732, FR4744, F4746, F4752, F4753, F4756, F4760, F4771, F4782, F4783, F4785, F4787 C, F4788, F4790, F4856, F4860, F4868, F4877, F4880, F4888, F4890, F4893, F4897, F4903, F4911, F4923, F4925, F4928, F4936, F4937, F4938, F4958, F4961, F4968, F5997, H1394, H1424, H1438, H1450, H1453, H1454, H1462, H1464, H1493, H1500, H1560, H1627, H1630, H1631, H1632, H1640, H1645, H1663, H1665, H1668, H1671, H1674, H1675, H1677, J6614, J6617, J6622, J6627, J6635, J6658, J6659, J6684, J6699, J6742, J6781, J6785, J6798, J7623, J7638, J7647, J7676, J8244, J8247, J8274, J8277, J8280, J8281, J8284, J8285, JR9657, JR9806.

8 Squadron

Re-equipped from F.K.8s at Le Bellevue in 12th Wing 3rd Brigade 12.18. To 89th Wing 5th Brigade 17.1.19 and to 91st Wing 1st Brigade 3.19. To Sart, Belgium, in 2nd Wing 2nd Brigade 11.5.19 and to cadre there 7.19.

Commanding Officer: Maj T.L. Leigh-Mallory throughout this period.

Known serial numbers: B1167, C1010, C9837 B4, C9873, C9877, C9974, C9977, C9982, C9984, D7814, D7823, D7827, D7852, D7881, D7887, D7892, D7898, D7901, D7913, D7923, D7952, D7989, E2134, E2162, E2233, E2271, E2319, E2343, E2353, E2649, E2660, E9573, E9578, F4408, F5110, F5133, F5135.

9 Squadron

Mainly equipped with R.E.8s but some F.2B 7.18-10.18 and 2.19-7.19. Based Quevenvillers from 17.7.18, then Amiens 15.8.18, Proyart 7.9.18, Athies 15.9.18, Montigny Farm 6.10.18, Prémont 18.10.18, Tarcienne 29.11.18, Cognelée 11.12.18, Ludendorf 3.1.19; to UK as cadre 31.7.19.

Commanding Officer: Maj J.T. Rodwell throughout this period.

Known serial numbers: B1347, C836, C917, C924, C936, C9879, C9899, C9950, C9976, D2707, D2729, D2730, D2742, D2753, D7903, D7997, E1908, E2150, E2271, E2272, E2529, E9582, E9588, E9595, E9602, E9617, E9642, F5138, F5139, F5809.

10 Squadron

Mainly equipped with F.K.8s but establishment included two F.2B for corps work by 2.18-10.18. Based Abeele in 2nd Wing 2nd Brigade by 3.18, then Droglandt 12.4.18, Abeele 21.9.18, Menin 21.10.18.

Commanding Officer: Maj K.D.P. Murray MC throughout this period.

Known serial numbers: A7214, A7256, A7300, B1234, C967, C984, C4818, E2250, E2426, F4322.

11 Squadron

Re-equipped from F.E.2b to F.2A 5.17 in 13th Wing 3rd Brigade at La Bellevue, France, soon replaced by F.2B. Then Fienvillers 27.3.18, Remaisnil 16.4.18, Le Quesnoy 9.7.18, Vert Galand 19.9.18, Mory 15.10.18, Bettoncourt 1.11.18. To 90th Wing 3rd Brigade 10.11.18; Aulnoy in 51st Wing 9th Brigade 18.11.18, Nivelles 19.12.18, Spich, Germany, 20.5.19. Ret'd UK and discarded aircraft 3.9.19

Commanding Officers: Maj C.T. Maclean MC by 6.17, Capt R.R. Barker (temp) 6.17 or 7.17, Maj R.F.S. Morton 21.8.17, Maj H.P. Davey

17.5.18, Maj R.W. Heath 10.7.18, Maj M. Le Blanc-Smith 11.2.19, Maj E.A.B. Rice 18.3.19.

Squadron identification markings: from August 1917 until 22.3.18 inward sloping diagonal white stripes fore and aft of fuselage roundels. Wheel discs painted white ('A' Flight), red ('B' Flight) and blue ('C' Flight); 'A' Flight individual white numbers on rear fuselage, 'B' and 'C' Flights white letters. Squadron marking changed 22.3.18 to a single white vertical band aft of fuselage roundels.

Known serial numbers: A3312, A3315, A3325, A3327, A3329, A7113, A7114, A7121, A7124, A7125, A7126, A7127 U, A7128, A7129, A7130 3, A7131 5, A7132, A7134, A7138, A7139, A7140, A7141, A7142, A7143 Y, A7144, A7145, A7147 5, A7152, A7153, A7154, A7156, A7157, A7158, A7159, A7161, A7167 5, A7168, A7174 F, A7175, A7191, A7209, A7215, A7220, A7226, A7231 1, A7235, A7248, A7252, A7254, A7261, A7266, A7275, A7276, A7281, A7284, A7288 7, A7290, A7291, A7292 F, B1103, B1109 A, B1110, B1116, B1127, B1143, B1167, B1183, B1189, B1194, B1252, B1256, B1283, B1307, B1309, B1332, B1334, B8914, B8914, C775, C792, C794, C797, C807, C813, C845, C867, C869, C872, C878, C883, C898, C911, C925, C931, C934, C937, C946, C955, C957, C958, C1037, C4601 V, C4646, C4663, C4673 Y, C4745, C4753, C4814 D, C4819, C4839, C4842, C4843, C4844, C4845 1, C4846 16, C4847, C4848, C4849, C4852, C4868, C4861, C4862, C4882, C7906, D7911, D7912, D7978, D7981, D8088, D8089, E2215, E2363, E2364, E2365, E2366, E2421, 2424, E2428, E2476, E2537, E2554, E2555, E2557, E2565, E2569, E2586 6, E2587, E2591, E2600 4, E2602, E2605, F4397, F4399, F4437, F4477, F4795, F4870, F4873, F4894, F4896, F5814, F6131, F6207, F6217, H1579, H7061, H7066. Also, C765 on strength at Netheravon 1.26 to 9.26.

12 Squadron

Main equipment R.E.8s, but received one F.2B for corps work 3.18, re-equipping entirely with F.2Bs post war. In 3.18 at Soncamp, France, in 12th Wing 3rd Brigade, then Mory 17.9.18, Estourmel 17.9.18. To 15th Wing 5th Brigade 16.11.18, Gerpinnes, Belgium, 29.11.18, Clavier in 11th Wing 2nd Brigade 6.12.18, Düren, Germany, 19.12.18, by 3.19 in 2nd Wing 2nd Brigade, Heumar 5.5.19, to RAF Rhine 13.9.19,

to 91st Wing 1st Brigade 2.10.19, Bickendorf 17.11.20 until disbanded there 27.7.22, being the last RAF squadron to leave Germany.

Commanding Officers: Maj T.Q. Back by 12.18, Maj G.H.B. McCall 16.3.19, Maj J.G. Selby MC 20.4.19, Sqn Ldr R.E. Saul DFC 3.9.19, Sqn Ldr H.J.F. Hunter MC 1.3.21, Flt Lt P.F. Fullard DSO MC AFC 23.5.22 until disbanded.

Squadron identification markings on R.E.8s: horizontal white bar along bottom of fuselage just behind roundels to leading edge of tailplane. Post-war F.2Bs had flight/individual number combinations on rear fuselage.

Known serial numbers: B1182, B8914, C765, C1031 A2, C1037, C4663, C9609? A6, C9947, C9982 A1, D2146, D2167, D7923, D7937 A5, D7982, D8059 B5, E2220 C1, E2233 B4, E2476, E2506 A2, E2533 C6, E2608 18, E2630 A3, E2643 A5, E9578 B3, E9597 E3, E9609 A6, F4402 B3, F4412, F4413 A3 later A1, F4414 B2, F4425 B1, F4423 A3, F4428 A4, F4435 C2, F4445 B, F4465, F4529, F4661 B6, F4845, F4855 B4, F4856 C5, F4865 B3, F4875, F4877, F4879, F4891 N, F4893 C1, F4895 C3, F4898 C2, F4900, F4942 A6 also A, F5140 A5, F5142, H1514, H1566 B1, H1568 C6, H1569 8, H1571, H1574 C4, H1581 A1, H1587 A5, H1589 A5, H194, H1596, H1599, H1669, H7061, J6600, J7661, J8256.

13 Squadron

Re-formed 1.4.24 ex-Signal Co-operation Flight as 13 (Army Co-operation) Sqn at Kenley. To Andover 30.6.24. To No.1 Wing No.7 Group 5.25. To No.22 Group 12.4.26. Re-equipped with Armstrong Whitworth Atlas between 8.27 and 1.28.

Commanding Officers: Temp (unknown) 1.4.24, Sqn Ldr C.C. Durston 23.5.24, Sqn Ldr H.I. Hanmer DFC 1.10.26, Sqn Ldr G.R.A. Deacon 13.4.27, Sqn Ldr H.H.McL. Fraser 8.10.27.

Known serial numbers: C901, C1042, C4897, D7801, D7812, D7874, F4369, F4423, F4432, F4448, F4481, F4488, F4503, F4516, F4545, F4549, F4563, F4565, F4572, F4703, F4708, F4737, F4903, F4932, F4948, F4955, F4957, H1440, H1623, H1627, J6694, J6702, J6710, J6743, J6747, J6766, J6800, J7637, J7647, J7650, J7660, J7668, J7669, J7671, J7689, J7690, J8290.

14 Squadron

Re-formed 1.2.20 ex-111 Sqn in Palestine Brigade (later Group, then Wing then Command) at Ramleh, Palestine (Flts at Aleppo and Damascus c.3.20-5.20); Flts at Amman and Mafrak 7.22; Detachment at Amman from 1924; Flt detached Beersheba 17-19.1.25); Became 14 (Army Co-operation) Sqn 5.24 and partly re-equipped with D.H.9A 8.24. Squadron HQ moved to Amman mid-1926 and became 14 (Bomber) Sqn with flights detached periodically to Ramleh. Discarded F.2B 2.26.

Commanding Officers: Temp (unknown) 1.2.20, Sqn Ldr W.L. Welsh DSC AFC 9.4.20, Sqn Ldr J.S.T. Bradley CBE 21.4.22, Sqn Ldr W.H. Dolphin to 6.6.24, Sqn Ldr A.N. Gallehawk AFC 6.6.24.

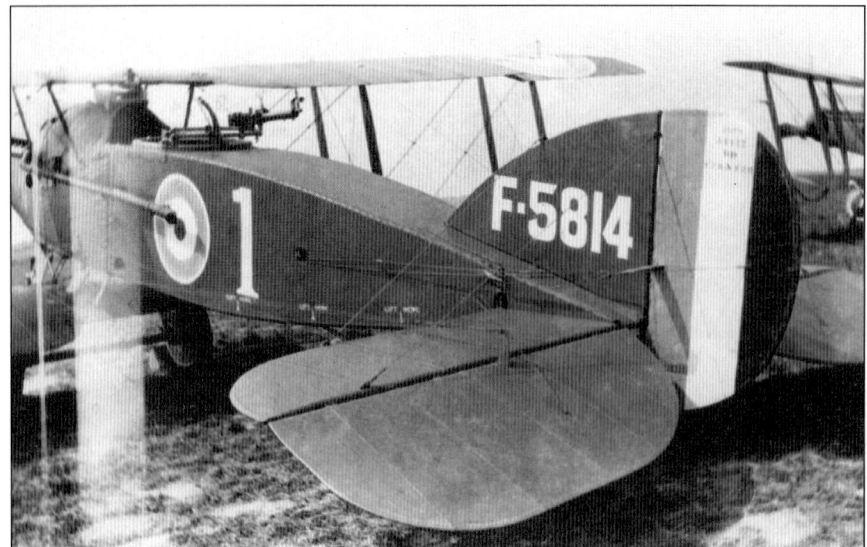

After F.2B A7151 caught fire on starting up on 23 March 1918, while with 20 Sqn, it was reconstructed and renumbered F5814, eventually becoming '1' of 11 Sqn. It was lost in action during an OP on 29 September 1918, 2nd Lt T.T. Smith and Lt J.L. Bromley both perishing. *(Eric Harlin)*

Squadron identification markings: H1651 had a chequered fin in 1922, and in 1924 at least two aircraft (H1502 and J6648) had a spade motif on the fin in a white circle.

Known serial numbers: B1147, B1198, C764, C802, C981, C1049, CR4651, D7815, D7839, D7924, D8058, E2288, E2290, E2293, F4285, F4349, F4459, F4488, F4512, FR4583, FR4600, F4612, F4651, F4709, F4712, F4889, F4910, F4912, F4919, FR4920, F4927, F4939, H1451, H1465, H1467, H1491, H1502, H1504, H1526, H1533, H1534, H1628, H1633, H1646, H1649, H1651, H1653, H1654, H1661, H1664, H1672, H1676, H1677, H1681, H1684, J6589, J6592, J6593, J6602, J6606, J6618, J6619, J6633, JR6635, J6648, JR6726, JR6767, J6798.

15 Squadron
One F.2B attached for corps work 2.18–4.18 at Lechelle, France, in 12th Wing 3rd Brigade, main equipment R.E.8. Two F.2B on strength from 5.24 at Martlesham Heath, main equipment D.H.9A.

Squadron identification markings on R.E.8s: A vertical white bar just in front of tailplane.

Commanding Officers: Maj H.V. Stammers DSFC in 3.18, Sqn Ldr P.C. Sherran MC 20.3.24, Sqn Ldr C.E.H. James MC 2.12.27, Wg Cdr J.K. Wells AFC 2.9.29, Sqn Ldr G.H. Martingell AFC 2.3.30.

Known serial numbers: (1918) A7129; (1924/30) F4724, F4725, F4745, J7643, J8242.

16 Squadron
Two F.2Bs on strength for corps work from 2.18 at Complain l'Abbé, France, in 1st Wing 1st Brigade, main equipment R.E.8s. To La Brayelle 21.10.18, Auchy 25.10.18, to UK at Fowlmere 12.2.19 until disbanded 31.12.19. Re-formed 4.24 as 16 (Army Co-operation) Sqn fully equipped with F.2B at Old Sarum, working with the School of Army Co-operation. Re-equipped with Armstrong Whitworth Atlas between 1.31 and 3.31.

Commanding Officers: Maj C.F.A. Portal DSO in 3.18, Maj A.W.C.V. Parr 5.6.18, Unknown 2.19, squadron disbanded 31.12.19. Sqn Ldr J.O. Archer CBE 1.4.24, Sqn Ldr W.A. Coryton MVO DFC 16.8.25, Sqn Ldr D.O. Mulholland AFC 25.9.28-1931.

Squadron identification markings on R.E.8s: Two vertical white bands, one either side of fuselage roundels.

Known serial numbers: (1918/9) A7259, B1112 F, C968, C986.
(1924/30) B1325, C4676, C4681, C4794, D7801, D7854, F4366, F4381, F4492, F4500, F4506, F4513, F4519, F4545, F4550, F4558, F4567, F4569, F4580, F4587, F4618, F4623, F4683, F4691, F4705, F4710, F4721, F4741, F4754, F4812, F4830, F4840, F4842, F4845, F4905, F4908, F4944, F4956, F4957, F4960, F5822, H1390, H1396, H1403, H1405, H1416, H1432, H1451, H1483, H1506, H1562, H1598, H1600, J6682, J6683, J6701, J6719, J6722, J6734, J6756, J7616, J7619, J7649, J7653, J7662, J7663, J7675, J7686, J7687, J7692, J7696, J7697, J8248, J8252, J8271, J8272, J8276, J8288, J8291.

19 Squadron
Two F.2Bs on strength c.5.24-6.24 at Duxford, main equipment Sopwith Snipe and Avro 504K.

Commanding Officer: Flt Lt T.V. West (temp).

Known serial numbers: H1415, J6713.

20 Squadron
Re-equipped from F.E.2d, received its first F.2B 10.8.17 at Ste Marie Cappel, France, in 11th Wing 2nd Brigade and was fully equipped 21.9.17. Boisdinghem 13.4.18, Vignacourt 26.8.18, Suzanne 16.9.18, Proyart 24.9.18, Moislains 7.10.18, Clary/Iris Farm in 89th Wing 5th Brigade 25.10.18, to 22nd Wing 5th Brigade 16.11.18, Ossogne 3.12.18, Left Marseilles for India 30.5.19, arrived Risalpur in 52nd Wing 16.6.19 and established as 20 (Army Co-operation) Sqn. To Parachinar 21.7.19, Bannu 22.9.19, Parachinar 18.7.20, Tank 5.11.20, Parachinar 11.4.21, Ambala 17.10.21, came under HQ RAF India 22.10.22, Quetta 24.10.22, Peshawar 5.1.25, Kohat 22.5.25, Peshawar 12 Oct 1925 until re-equipped with Westland Wapiti between 11.31 and 3.32.

Commanding Officers: Maj W.H.C. Mansfield DSO in 8.17, Maj E.H. Johnston OBE 15.10.17, Maj J.C. Russell 29.1.19, Flt Lt J.L. Vachell MC (temp) 1.20, Sqn Ldr (later Wg Cdr) J.H.S. Tyssen 27.4.20, Sqn Ldr R.T. Leather AFC 4.23, Sqn Ldr C.B. Cooke 25.1.24, Sqn Ldr J.B. Cole-Hamilton 8.10.25, Sqn Ldr J.C. Steele OBE 23.7.26, Sqn Ldr C.H. Nicholas DSC AFC 17.3.28, Sqn Ldr L.O. Brown DSC AFC 7.3.30 to .32.

Squadron identification markings: from August 1917 allotted two vertical white bands aft of fuselage roundels, but no evidence that this was actually applied. Then from October 1917 single white vertical band forward of fuselage roundels. By 1927 until 1931 a single wide red band carried around the rear fuselage.

Known serial numbers: A7112, A7118, A7123, A7129, A7141, A7144, A7151, A7164, A7193, A7203, A7210, A7211, A7214, A7215, A7223, A7228, A7234, A7240, A7241, A7245, A7246, A7248, A7250, A7253, A7255, A7256, A7269, A7270, A7271, A7285, A7287, A7294, A7298, A7299, B883, B1102, B1104, B1108, B1110, B1111, B1114, B1116, B1118, B1120, B1122, B1125, B1126, B1130, B1132, B1133, B1135, B1137, B1138, B1139, B1155, B1156, B1168, B1170, B1177, B1191, B1193, B1196, B1209, B1211, B1233, B1257, B1275, B1279, B1307 K, B1344, C762 B, C808, C811, C817, C819, C843 6, C850, C856, C859, C873, C874, C881, C889, C892, C904, C938, C951, C976, C979, C980, C987 O, C996, C1011, C4604, C4605, C4753, C4615, C4616, C4617, C4641, C4649, C4672, C4677, C4699, C4718, C4748, C4749, C4763, C4764, C4766, C4802, C4817, C4818, C4820, C4821, C4825, C4826, C4836, C4837, C4851, C4856, D2155, D2187, D2212, D2213, D2214, D2215, D2224, D2225, D2245, D2643, D2644, D2650, D7807 N, D7809, D7813, D7816, D7821, D7851 D, D7864, D7897, D7915, D7917, D7919, D7939 P, D7951, D7993, D8023, D8035 M, D8036, D8039, D8086, D8090, D8092, E1614, E2106 H, E2154, E2155, E2158, E2181, E2213, E2238, E2246, E2249, E2252, E2253, E2255, E2258, E2297, E2300, E2331, E2337, E2338, E2339, E2340, E2346, E2370, E2377, E2403, E2404, E2406, E2407, E2419, E2420, E2423, E2429, E2433, E2437, E2446, E2447, E2448 M, E2452, E2467, E2470, E2471, E2493, E2512, E2536, E2543, E2561, E2562, E2567, E2568, E2584, E2588, E2590, E2593, E2597, E2603, E2605, E2644, E2650, E9544, E9616, E9618, E9619, F4275, F4304, F4321, F4330 B, F4396 B, F4401,

F4414 N, F4415 N, F4421, F4427, F4436, F4446, F4447, F4463 L, F4487, F4494, F4544, F4555 E, F4562 C, F4592, F4597, F4598, F4599, F4602, F4603, F4604, F4608 H, F4614, F4621 K, F4626, F4628, F4629, F4633, F4643, F4658 H, F4663, F4665 K, F4668 H, F4689, F4693, F4700 N, F4706 H, F4720, F4730, F4766, F4789, F4809, F4839 E, F4862, F4867, F4881, F4905, F4908, F4914 F, F4915, F4916, F4921 F, F4927 G, F4929, F4953, F4958 A, F5816, F6116, F6121 S, F6195, F6208, F9616, H1428 K, H1462, H1507, H1508 P, H1518, H1520, H1521, H1524, H1529, H1535, H1548, H1549, H1553, H1601, H1657 G, H1658, H1686, J6588, J6594, J6601, J6613, J6616, J6621 H, J6622, J6623, J6631, J6634 L, J6638, J6641, J6643 G, J6644, J6645 K, J6647 F, J6650, J6651, J6654, J6655, J6656, J6660, J6663 B also M, J6668, J6700, J6711 F, J6730 M, J6736, J6741, J6752 K, J6771, J6774 C, J6781 B, J6782 M, J6783, J6792 A and E, J6794, J6796, J7644, J7645 A, J7677, J7680, J7681, J7682 C, J7684.

22 Squadron
Re-equipped from F.E.2b 7.17 at Izel-le-Hameau, France, in 9th Wing GHQ Brigade. Boisdinghem 14.8.17, Estrée Blanche 10.9.17, Auchel in 10th Wing 1st Brigade 22.1.18, Treizennes 2.2.18, Serny 21.3.18, Vert Galand in 13th Wing 3rd Brigade 23.3.18, Serny 10.4.18, Maisoncelle 30.7.18, Izel-le-Hameau 22.10.18, Aniche 26.10.18, Aulnoye in 51st Wing 9th Brigade 17.11.18, Witheries 22.11.18, Nivelles, Belgium, 20.12.18, Spich, Germany, 21.5.19, to England without aircraft 1.9.19. Re-formed 24.7.23 within A&AEE Martlesham Heath for testing aircraft types, with two F.2Bs on strength for a time. Disbanded 1.5.34.

Commanding Officers: Maj J.A. McKelvie at 7.17, Maj V.A.H. Robeson 10.2.19, Maj J.C. Quinnell 23.7.19.

Squadron identification markings: from August 1917 allotted a vertical white band each side of the fuselage roundels, but no evidence that this was actually applied. From December 1917 a single vertical white band forward of the fuselage roundels, another just behind and a third just in front of the tailplane. Wheel discs 'A' to 'C' Flights coloured red, white and blue respectively.

Known serial numbers: (1917/9) A7102, A7108, A7112, A7114, A7118, A7119, A7120, A7125, A7133, A7144, A7149, A7151, A7160, A7161, A7162, A7163, A7165, A7167, A7169, A7172, A7174 F, A7178, A7179, A7181 H, A7185, A7189, A7201, A7204, A7205, A7207, A7208, A7223 E, A7226, A7230, A7232, A7233 I, A7239, A7243, A7244, A7246, A7247, A7251, A7256, A7258, A7261, A7264, A7268, A7279, A7280, A7281, A7283, A7286, A7300 A, B1101, B1103, B1104, B1105, B1111, B1112 F, B1115, B1120, B1121, B1123, B1136, B1141, B1144, B1152 C, B1153, B1155, B1162, B1163, B1164 D, B1168, B1171, B1177, B1209, B1213, B1217 Z, B1253 E, B1314, B1330, B8914, C770, C776, C795, C797, C840 M, C842 K, C887, C901, C929, C961, C978 O, C989, C1003, C1035, C1038, C1040, C4631 T, C4706 Q, C4747, C4801, C4808, C4810 K, C4817 D, C4818, C4827, C4828, C4832, C4835 R, C4838, C4843, C4848, C4856 L, C4888 PC4894 L, D2676 B, D7894, D7896, D7908, D7986, D7990, D8089, E2203, E2243, E2247, E2263, E2266, E2269 Z, E2408, E2410 F, E2425, E2453, E2454,

E2466 I, E2477, E2491, E2499, E2500,
E2514 K, E2516, E2517, E2519, E2556,
E2560, E2566, E2575, E2576, E2578, E2601,
E2615, E2617, E2628, F4408, F4409, F4416,
F4425, F4430, F4445, F4448, F4673, F4847,
F4848, F4852, F4879, F4891, F4892, F4898,
F5820, F5823 Y, F5824, F5996, F6040,
H7061; (1923/7) F4743, H1436,

24 Squadron

Re-formed 1.2.20 from No.1 Communication
Squadron and Air Council Inspection Squadron
at Kenley in No.6 Group with some F.2B on
strength. To Fighting Area 20.5.26. To Northolt
1.2.27, last F.2B 6.28 on re-equipment with de
Havilland Moth.

Commanding Officers: Sqn Ldr E.H. Johnston
OBE 1.2.20, Sqn Ldr O.T. Boyd OBE MC AFC
23.10.22, Sqn Ldr E.R.L. Corballis DSO
12.2.23, Sqn Ldr R.S. Maxwell MC DFC AFC
22.10.23, Sqn Ldr W.H.L. O'Neill MC 27.8.25,
Sqn Ldr S.N. Cole 26.8.27.

Known serial numbers: B8947[?], C761,
C800, C1015, D7864, D8033, E2423, E2505,
F4341, F4342, F4385, F4420, F4423, F4478,
F4491, F4496, F4548, F4551, F4556, F4561,
F4571, F4584, F4586, F4645, F4646, F4649,
F4684, F4688, F4698, F4716, F4737, F4739,
F4744, F4748, F4751, F4757, F4823, F4829,
F4831, F4852, F4878, F4879, F4891, F4894,
F4898, F4913, F4941, F4943, F4966, F5996 P,
H1394, H1406, H1407, H1408, H1415,
H1417, H1424, H1426, H1453, H1456,
H1459, H1460, H1489, H1570, H1581,
H1589, H1604, H1617, H1624, H1688,
H1689, H7064, J6609, J6661, J6670, J6681,
J6688, J6692, J6704, J6718, J6722, J6730,
J6736, J6738, J6743, J6744, J6745, J6749,
J6800, J8249, J8258, J8262, J8265, J8273,
J8443, J8453.

28 Squadron

Re-formed 1.4.20 ex-114 Sqn with F.2Bs at
Ambala, India, under HQ RAF India, to No.3
(Indian) Wing when it was formed on 1.4.20
(renumbered No.1 (Indian) Wing 10.7.20). To
Kohat 15.10.21, Parachinar 15.4.22, Kohat
10.10.22, Dardoni 12.12.22, Tank 17.3.23,
Peshawar 19.4.23. Became 28 (Army Co-
operation) Sqn 27.3.24. To Quetta 5.1.25,
Ambala 15.12.26, Risalpur 13.8.30, Ambala
2.12.30. Re-equipped with Westland Wapiti
9.31.

Squadron identification markings: by 1931 a
single green band around was carried the rear
fuselage.

Commanding Officers: Sqn Ldr R.J.F. Barton
OBE 1.2.20, Sqn Ldr J.T. Whittaker MC 7.3.22,
Sqn Ldr A.W.F. Glenny MC DFC 1.8.22, Sqn
Ldr H.S. Powell MC 14.9.23, Wg Cdr A.A.
Walser MC DFC 2.5.24, Sqn Ldr C.S. Wynne-
Eyton DSO 23.9.24, Sqn Ldr A.W. Mylne
15.2.26, Sqn Ldr J.T. Whittaker MC 16.9.27,
Sqn Ldr A.F. Brooke 23.2.28 to 11.31.

Known serial numbers: B1185, B1212, B1214,
B1230, B1239, C1032, C1039 M, C4618,
C4622, C4700, D7851 E, D7809 J, D7871 E,
D8009, D8026, D8034, D8036, D8057,
D8063, E2248, E2283, E2284, E2442,
E2448 M, E2605 C, E2611, F4286, F4288,
F4498, F4543, F4614, F4630, F4634, F4636,
F4640, F4707 A, F4752, F4870, F4931,
H1413?, H1499, H1508, H1509, H1531,
H1512, H1514, H1520, H1521, H1529,
H1531, H1536, H1537, H1538, H1539,
H1541, H1548, H1549, H1554, J6588, J6591,
J6599, J6601, J6621 E, J6624, J6626, J6630,
J6638, J6639, J6641 T, J6646, J6650, J6651,
J6656 C, J6716 L?, J6740 L, J6761, J6762,
J6769, J6770, J6778, J6779 D, J6780, J6781 C,
J6781, J6782 H, J6783, J6792, J6794, J6795 B,
J6796, J6799, J7677, J7681.

31 Squadron

Re-equipped with F.2Bs 6.19 at Risalpur (India)
in 52nd Wing, which became No.3 (Indian)
Wing 1.4.20 (renumbered 1 (Indian) Wing
10.7.20). To Mhow 15.4.20, Cawnpore
26.11.20, Peshawar 19.10.21, Dardoni 17.4.23,
Ambala 13.3.24. Became 31 (Army Co-
operation) Sqn 27.3.24. Quetta 15.12.26. Re-
equipped with Westland Wapiti between 2.31
and 4.31.

Squadron identification markings: by 1931 a
single red black around was carried the rear
fuselage.

Commanding Officers: Maj E.L. Millar OBE in
6.19; Flt Lt D.H.M. Carberry MC DFC (temp)
10.8.19, Sqn Ldr A.L. Neale MC 22.1.20, Sqn
Ldr A.T. Harris AFC 26.1.21, Sqn Ldr A.C.
Maund CBE DSO 6.5.22, Sqn Ldr A.D. Walser
MC DFC 2.5.24, Sqn Ldr H.S. Powell MC
24.6.24, Sqn Ldr J.O. Archer CBE 18.1.25, Sqn
Ldr J.F. Gordon DFC 1.4.26, Sqn Ldr B. Ankers
DCM 25.3.31.

Known serial numbers: D7807 A, D7813,
D8034 A, D8049, D8097, E2139, E2189,
E2257 E, E2287, E2297, E2334, E2450,
E2501, F4315, F4320 D, F4375, F4390 R,
F4415, F4424, F4463 L, F4464, F4494 F,
F4495, F4542, F4555 E, F4593, F4594, F4604,

F4643 J also L, F4658, F4664, F4665,
F4689 B, F4693, F4707 A, F4713, F4758,
F4814 F, F4839 F, F4907, F4907, F4915 H,
F4942 H, F4951 J, F4958 L, H1428 L, H1457,
H1458 E, H1461 F, H1497, H1510 H,
H1519 B, H1554, H1586, H1659, H1686,
J6616 C, J6621, J6623, J6625, J6626, J6634,
J6639, J6640 K, J6641 E, J6642, J6643,
J6647 K, J6649, J6650, J6651 B, J6652 A,
J6654 O, J6657 P, J6663 C, J6674 K, J6675,
J6741, J6750, J6754, J6757, J6758, J6761 A,
J6771, J6774, J6776, J6781, J6782 C, J6783 L,
J6795, J6796, J7680, J7681, J7683 L.

33 Squadron

Home Defence squadron with some F.2Bs on
strength between 6.18 and 8.18 at Kirton-in-
Lindsey in 48th Wing 6th Brigade (A Flt at
Brattlesby/Scampton, B Flt at Kirton-in-Lindsey
and C Flt at Elsham).

Commanding Officer: Capt G.M. Turnbull

Known serial numbers: B1186, C4698, D8003.

34 Squadron

Received F.2Bs 3.18 to supplement R.E.8s at
Istrana, Italy. To Villaverla 30.3.18, Santa Luca
23.10.18, Villaverla 16.11.18, Caldiero 28.2.19.
Returned to UK 3.5.19 without aircraft.

Known serial numbers: B1185, B1212, B1214,
B1230, C913, C916, C990, C991, C992,
C993, C996, C997, C999, C4700, C4754,
C4755, C4756, C4757, C4758, C4759,
C4760, C4761, C4762, C4860, D7957,
D8063, D8066, D8078, E2185, E2187,
E2189, E2190, E2283, F4280.

35 Squadron

Two F.2Bs attached for corps work by 2.18 at
Chipilly, France, in 15th Wing 5th Brigade,
main equipment F.K.8. To Poulainville 24.3.18,
Abbeville 28.3.18, Poulainville 5.4.18, Villers
Bocage 2.5.18, Suzanne 7.9.18, Moislains
13.9.18, Longavesnes 6.10.18, Elincourt
17.10.18, Flaumont 10.11.18, Le Grand Fayt
11.11.18, Elincourt 13.11.18, to 12th Wing 3rd
Brigade 16.11.18, La Bellevue 29.11.18, Ste
Marie Cappel in 91st Wing 1st Brigade 19.1.19,
to England without aircraft 3.19.

Commanding Officers: Maj A.V. Holt DSO by
3.18, Maj K.F. Balmain 15.4.18, Maj D.F.
Stevenson DSO MC 8.9.18.

Squadron identification markings: a single
horizontal white line along the centre of the
fuselage sides.

Known serial numbers: A7221, B1134 19,
B1347, C917, C4849, D7903.

36 Squadron

Home Defence squadron partly equipped with
F.2Bs from 4.18 at Cramlington in 46th (HD)
Wing 6th Brigade. HQ to Newcastle 1.7.18 (A
Flt at Hylton/Usworth, B Flt at Ashington and C
Flt at Seaton Carew). HQ to Usworth (Hylton)
1.7.18, disbanded 13.6.19.

Commanding Officers: Maj S.W. Price MC
1.1.18, Maj W.J. Tempest DSO MC 26.7.18,
Unknown 16.1.19.

Known serial numbers: B1185?, C890, C4780,
C4896, C4897, C4898, D8004.

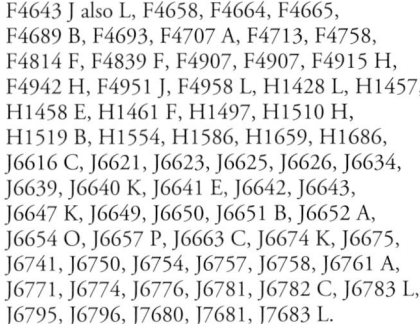

This C-serialled F.2B with a chequered nose was
serving with No.35 Training Squadron at Port
Meadow. (RAF Museum)

37 Squadron

Home Defence squadron with at least one F.2B 12.18 at Stow Maries in 50th (HD) Wing 6th Brigade.

Commanding Officer: Maj F.W. Honnett

Known serial number: E2361.

39 Squadron

Based as a Home Defence squadron with headquarters at Salway Lodge, Woodford Green, in 50th (HD) Wing 6th Brigade with a variety of aircraft, including F.2Bs. Disbanded 16.11.18.

Commanding Officers: Maj W.H.D. Acland MC 9.8.17. Maj G. Allen 20.11.17. Maj W.T.F. Holland 1.7.18.

Squadron identification markings: a horizontal white line along the centre of the rear fuselage extending from the rear of the roundel to the front of the tailplane.

Known serial numbers: A3314, A7249, A7265, A7267, B1145 5, B1157, B1184, B1186, B1252 8, B1260, B1261, B1262, B1263, B1264, B1266, B1308, B1316, B1331 2, B1350 3, B8936, C954, C964, C971, C4635, C4636 A-6, C4638, C4639, C4645 4, C4646, C4650 1, C4670, C4671, C4698, C4711, C4777, C4779, C4815, C4823, C4850, C4895, D2152, D2156, D2180, D8001, E2156, E2160, E2262, E2361, E2390, E2436?, E2462, E2577, E2581, F4485, F4536?.

48 Squadron

Began to re-equip from B.E.12 to F.2A 1.17 at Rendcomb. Flew to France 8.3.17 to be based at La Bellevue in 13th Wing 4th Brigade, F.2Bs arriving 5.17. To Frontier (Bray Dunes) in 14th Wing 4th Brigade 11.7.17, Leffrinckhoucke 15.9.17, Liettres 6.12.17, Villers-Bretonneux in 22nd Wing 5th Brigade 18.12.17, Flez 29.12.17, Champien 22.3.18, Bertangles 24.3.18, Boisdinghem 25.8.18, Ste Marie Cappel NW 30.9.18, Reckem North in 11th Wing 2nd Brigade 23.10.18, Nivelles, Belgium, 27.11.18, Bickendorf, Germany, 19.12.18. Left for India 26.5.19, arrived in India 22.6.19, Quetta in 52nd Wing 12.7.19, redesignated 5 Sqn 1.2.20.

Commanding Officers: Maj A.V. Bettington 3.17, Maj H.S. Shield MC 7.17, Maj K.R. Park MC 4.18, Maj F.W. Stent 11.18, Unknown 3.19, Sqn Ldr P.C. Maltby DSO AFC 27.11.19.

Squadron identification markings: from August 1917 two vertical white bands aft of the fuselage roundels; probably applied but no photographic evidence has come to light. From/by December 1917 a single vertical white band in front of tailplane. Later a horizontal white zig-zag aft of fuselage roundels. Individual white numbers, often placed either side of the fuselage roundel in the case of two-digit numbers. Wheel discs 'A' to 'C' Flights coloured red, white and blue respectively.

Known serial numbers: A3305, A3306, A3310, A3313, A3315, A3316, A3317, A3318, A3320, A3321, A3322 5, A3323, A3324 2, A3325 4, A3326, A3327, A3328, A3329, A3330, A3333, A3334 3, A3335, A3336 1, A3337, A3338, A3340, A3341, A3343 5, A3345, A3346, A3347, A3348, A3349, A3350, A3352, A3353, A3354, A7101, A7102, A7104, A7105, A7106, A7107, A7108, A7109, A7110, A7111, A7112, A7114, A7115, A7116, A7117, A7118, A7119, A7121, A7123, A7125, A7128, A7129, A7137, A7146, A7149, A7150, A7151, A7153, A7155, A7159, A7164, A7166, A7167, A7170, A7171, A7176, A7177, A7182, A7187, A7210, A7213, A7216, A7217, A7219, A7220, A7221, A7222, A7224, A7227, A7229, A7248, A7254, A7257, A7262, A7266, A7277, A7282, A7290, A7293, A7295, A7298, B1108, B1111, B1113, B1115, B1117, B1124, B1126, B1132, B1134, B1135, B1181, B1182, B1187, B1190, B1192, B1193, B1210, B1231, B1254, B1255, B1265, B1269, B1271 22, B1273, B1277, B1299, B1301, B1302, B1328, B1337, B1346, B1348, B1349, C786, C789, C791, C793, C805, C808, C814 12, C816, C818, C841 11, C846, C849, C855, C871, C876, C877, C883, C886, C914, C926, C928, C932, C935, C940, C941, C943, C944, C947, C950, C962, C974, C993, C4603, C4606, C4628, C4629, C4640, C4701, C4707, C4710, C4719, C4745, C4750, C4753, C4816, C4831, C4864, C4886, D2167, D7900, D7902, D7909, D7936, D7987 4, D8027, D8061, D9784, E2151, E2214, E2260, E2265, E2267, E2268, E2281, E2282, E2283, E2367, E2413, E2415, E2455, E2458 9, E2469, E2472, E2480, E2482, E2492, E2495, E2496, E2498, E2507, E2510, E2511, E2520, E2522, E2523, E2524, E2526, E2527, E2530, E2531, E2532, E2534, E2583, E2589, E2592, E2596, E2608 18, E2609, E2625, E2635, F4311 19, F4377, F4403 C, F4408, F4425 17, F4442, F4470, F4488, F4611 D, F4625, F4627, F4637 A, F4861, F4866, F4878, F5130, F5132, F5809, F5811, F5817 11, F6041, F6093, F6094, F6118, F6404, F9606, H1530, H1544, H1552.

51 Squadron

Home Defence squadron at Marham, proposed to re-equip with 24 F.2Bs in 6.18, but these did not materialise.

53 Squadron

At least one F.2B on strength 1.19 at Laneffe, Belgium, in 15th Wing 5th Brigade.

Commanding Officer: Capt G.B.A. Baker.

Known serial number: D7901.

59 Squadron

Several F.2Bs on strength c.4.18-2.19 initially at Vert Galand in 12th Wing 3rd Brigade, main equipment R.E.8. To Beugnatre 17.9.18, Caudry 14.10.18, to 15th Wing 5th Brigade 16.11.18, Gerpinnes 29.11.18.

Commanding Officers: Maj C.J. Mackay MC by 4.18; Maj A.P.D. Hill 26.12.18.

Squadron identification markings: two vertical white bands just behind fuselage roundels on R.E.8s.

Known serial numbers: A7129, C9853, C9877, C9897, C9973, D2660, D2672, D2708, D2755, D7860, D8087, E1978, E1992, E2014, E2015, E2016, E2028, E2030, E2050, E9606, F5117, F5118, F5130, F5132, F5815, F6115.

62 Squadron

Equipped with F.2Bs 5.17 at Filton, to Rendcomb 17.7.17. To France, sailed from Southampton to Le Havre 21.1.18. Arrived Liettres 22.1.18. Ground crew to St Omer 23.1.18, aircraft flew over 29.1.18 and to Serny in 9th Wing attached HQ RFC (later 9th Brigade) 30.1.18. Cachy 8.3.18, Remaisnil 24.3.18, Planques 29.3.18. Attached 81st Wing 9th Brigade 3.6.18, ret'd 9th Wing 9th Brigade 21.6.18. To 54th Wing 9th Brigade 17.7.18, Croisette 7.8.18, La Bellevue 26.9.18, Villers-lez-Cagnicourt 29.10.18, Aulnoye 18.11.18. To 51st Wing 9th Brigade 20.11.18, Bouge, Belgium, 14.12.18; Nivelles 20.12.18, Spich, Germany, 2.5.19. Squadron disbanded 31.7.19.

Commanding Officers: Maj R.G.D. Small 21.1.17; Maj F.W. Smith 18.10.17, Maj C.H. Hayward 14.2.19.

Squadron identification markings: from August 1917[?] three vertical white bands, one in front and two behind fuselage roundels. Individual white letters on nose. No known flight markings.

Known serial numbers: A3307, A3310, A3342, A7114, A7132, A7133, A7137, A7138, A7139, A7197, A7215, A7243, A7248, A7278, A7293, A7298, B1207, B1211, B1215, B1216, B1218, B1219, B1233, B1234, B1235, B1238, B1240, B1241, B1243, B1245, B1246, B1247, B1250, B1251, B1266, B1267, B1268, B1269, B1271, B1273, B1281, B1300, B1314, B1302, B1305, B1335, B1336, B1339, B1343, B1344, B1345, C769 A, C779, C788, C790, C791, C796, C866, C874, C886, C895, C919, C934, C944, C953, C959, C960, C965, C970, C973, C1002, C4602, C4609, C4610, C4613, C4614, C4619 R also C, C4620, C4621, C4629, C4630 J, C4632, C4633 B, C4637, C4659, C4703 7, C4709 8, C4744, C4746, C4750, C4751 T, C4783, C4811, C4812, C4818, C4824, C4845, C4859, C4887, D7899, D7945, D7948, D8024, D8028, E2182, E2152, E2217, E2218, E2244, E2256, E2408, E2409, E2416, E2417, E2422, E2456, E2457 7, E2468, E2475, E2479, E2494, E2497, E2508, E2509, E2513, E2515, E2518, E2525, E2528, E2559, E2580 C, E2595 K, E2598, F5810, F6517, F6158, H7065, H7293 3?

67 (Australian) Squadron/1st Sqn Australian Flying Corps from 14.1.18

Re-equipped from Elephant from 29.12.17 at Julis, Palestine, in 40th Wing, Palestine Wing; El Mejdel 6.2.18, Ramleh 23.4.18 (one flight to Haifa 25.9.18); Haifa 3.10.18 (det'd Homs, Syria, 15.10.18, to Hama 23.10.18 until 25.11.18) (ALG at Rinjaq); to Homs 15.10.18; Sqn to Ramleh 22.11.18 (det'd at Rayak 25.11.18 to 2.19), Kantara 2.19; Aircraft handed over to 111 Sqn 2.19. Sailed for Australia in SS *Port Sydney* 5.3.19.

Commanding Officer: Maj S.W. Addison.

Known serial numbers: A7184, A7188, A7190, A7192, A7194, A7196, A7198, A7200, A7202, A7236, A7237, A7273, B1128, B1129, B1146, B1147, B1148, B1149, B1150, B1198, B1199, B1205, B1222, B1223, B1225, B1229, B1276, B1278, B1280, B1284, B1285, B1286, B1287, B1295, B1298, C4623, C4624, C4625, C4626, C4627, C4730, C4840.

75 Squadron

Home Defence squadron at Elmswell. A small number of F.2Bs on strength around 5.18–11.18 in 50th (HD) Wing 6th Brigade.

Commanding Officer: Maj C.S. Ross.

Known serial number: E2248

76 Squadron

Home Defence squadron at Ripon in 46th (HD) Wing 6th Brigade with various detached flights. A small number of F.2Bs on strength from 8.18.

Commanding Officer: Maj A.C. Wilson.

Known serial numbers: none identified.

82 Squadron

Partly equipped with Bristol Fighters at Waddington from July 1917 until going to France on 17 November 1917 re-equipped with F.K.8s.

Captain A. Hepburn of 88 Sqn standing beside F.2B F4442 '1' shortly after the end of the First World War. In the background is the 'Lion of Waterloo' memorial monument on a mound at the site of the famous battlefield. It stands on the spot where the Prince of Orange was wounded, and was constructed in 1820 on the order of his father, King William I of the Netherlands, to commemorate his son's bravery.

A7200, A7202, A7236, A7237, A7260, A7288, B1127, B1129, B1146, B1147, B1198, B1199, B1223, B1229, B1284, B1287, B1293, B1295, B1296, B1298, B1317, C4623, C4626, C4627, C4652, C4725, C4726, C4727, C4730, C4731, C4732, C4840, C4899, D7918, D7992, E2286, E2287, E2288, E2289, E2290.

114 Squadron
Began re-equipping mainly with F.2Bs 10.19 at Ambala, India, in 52nd Wing. Redesignated 28 Sqn 1.4.20.

Commanding Officer: Maj D.E. Stodart DSO DFC.

Known serial numbers: E2248, E2543, F4630, F4634, F4636, F4640, H1499, H1509, H1512, H1514, H1520, H1541.

138 Squadron
Formed at Chingford in South Eastern Area with F.2Bs 30.9.18. Disbanded 1.2.19.

Commanding Officer: Not identified.

Known serial numbers: F4276, F4281 P, F4283, F4286, F4289, F4290, F4291, F4292, F4293, F4294, F4295, F4300, F4301, F4316, F4318, F4523, F4525, F4526, F4527, F4528, F4530, F4535, F4538, F4540, F4576, F4577, F4578, F4579, F4580, F4591.

139 Squadron
Formed 3.7.18 from 34 Sqn 'Z' Flight with F.2Bs at Villaverla, Italy, in 14th Wing, Grossa 10.10.18, San Luca 26.10.18, Arcade 8.11.18, Grossa 14.11.18, Caldiero 30.1.19 and to cadre. Left for UK and arrived Blandford 25.2.19 and disbanded 7.3.19.

Commanding Officers: Capt A.A. Harcourt-Vernon 3.7.18; Maj W.G. Barker DSO MC DFC 14.7.18; Capt S. Dalrymple DFC (temp) 30.9.18; Maj H.H. Kitchener 21.10.18.

Squadron identification markings: an increasing number of vertical white bands around the rear fuselage with black band between them, and two white band across the upper wings from roundel to roundel.

Known serial numbers: B1185, B1214, C916, C990, C991, C992, C994, C996, C997 K, C999, C4754 M, C4756, C4759, C4760, C4762, D2185, D7954, D7957, D7960, D7963, D7966, D7969, D7972, D7975, D7986, D8047, D8048, D8060, D8063 D, D8066, D8069, D8072, D8075, D8078, D8081, D8084 S, E2185 S, E2186, E2187 P, E2188 V, E2189 C, E2190, E2192, E2270, E2284, E2285 A, E2291, E2292.

141 Squadron
Re-equipped with F.2Bs at Biggin Hill in 49th (HD) Wing 6th Brigade 3.18. To Tallaght 1.3.19. Flt det'd to The Curragh 15.4.19 to 14.12.19. Det'd to Birr 1919-1920. Det'd at Gormanston 1919-1920. Sqn to Baldonnel 14.12.19. Disbanded into 100 Sqn 1.2.20.

Commanding Officer: Maj B.E. Baker DSO MC 9.2.18; Sqn Ldr The Hon L.J. Twistleton-Wykeham-Fiennes 12.19.

Commanding Officer: Maj A.H. Jackson.

Squadron identification markings in September 1917: believed two vertical narrow white lines just forward of the tail surfaces.

Known serial numbers: A3342, A3348, A7195, A7197, A7199, A7212, A7242.

87 Squadron
One Bristol Fighter on strength for testing while mobilising at Hounslow in April 1918, before going to France.

Commanding Officer: Maj J.C. Callaghan.

Known serial number: C795.

88 Squadron
Equipped with F.2B 7.17 at Gosport, moving to Harling Road 2.8.17, Kenley 2.4.18. To St Omer, France, 14-16.4.18, Bergues-Capelle in 65th Wing 7th Brigade 25.4.18, Petite Synthe 27.4.18, Drionville 19.7.18, Serny 2.8.18, Floringhem 21.10.18, Ascq 23.10.18, Gondecourt 26.10.18, Bersée 28.10.18, Aulnoye 18.11.18, Dour 13.12.18, Burdinne 14.12.18, Nivelles (Belgium) 18.12.18, Hangelar, Germany, in 51st Wing 9th Brigade 5.19. Squadron disbanded 10.8.19.

Commanding Officers: Unidentified 24.7.17; Maj R.T. Leather 27.3.18; Maj R.N. Montagu-Stuart-Wortley 9.18; Maj C.C. Darley 28.5.19.

Squadron identification markings: allocated single vertical white band in front of tailplane, but no photographic evidence of use has come to light. Wheel discs and radiator shells of 'A' to 'C' Flights coloured white, red and blue respectively. Large white individual numbers aft of the fuselage roundel: 'A' Flt 1 to 8, 'B' Flt 9 to 16, 'C' Flt 17 to 24.

Known serial numbers: B1187, B1231, B1337, B1341, B7947 5, C774, C775, C776, C777, C778, C780, C781, C782, C783, C785 JP C787, C788, C789, C790, C821, C825, C839, C852 22, C870, C879, C882, C922, C952, C983, C1000, C4601, C4713, C4718, C4720, C4867, C4869, C4880, D7905, D7914, D7942, D8022 23, D8026, D8044, D8062, D8064, D8065, E2153, E2183, E2216, E2220 22, E2239, E2263 Q, E2339, E2412, E2451, E2458 9, E2459 12, E2460, E2474, E2481, E2506, E2533, E2563, E2579, E2610 3, E2612 20, E2637, E2649, F4355, F4426, F4429, F4441?, F4442 1, F4474, F5997, F5999.

100 Squadron
Cadre from St Inglevert (France) to Baldonnel in 11th (Irish) Group (later Wing), restored there 1.2.20 with D.H.9As and some F.2Bs. 'A' Flight

at Castlebar by 29.5.20-@12.20. A Special Duties Flight was det'd to Oranmore 1.21, returning to Baldonnel 25.1.22. The squadron left for Spittlegate to 29.1.22 and the F.2Bs were replaced by Vimys 3.22.

Commanding Officers: Sqn Ldr The Hon J.E. Twistleton-Wykeham-Fiennes 31.1.20; Sqn Ldr J.V. Steel 30.11.20; Sqn Ldr F. Sowrey DSO MC AFC 19.2.21.

Known serial numbers: D7876, E2411, E2551, H1567, H1612, J6666, J6671, J6675, J6678, J6690, J6693, J6699, J6706, J6707.

105 Squadron
Went from Andover to Omagh 19.5.18 with R.E.8s, re-equipping with F.2Bs 12.18. To 11th (Irish) Group (later Wing) 22.8.18. 'A' Flt detached to Oranmore (to 7.19?) and 'B' Flt to Castlebar. 'A' Flt was at Gormanston by 3.19-5.19. Sqn to Oranmore 28.1.19. Flt at Fermoy 10.19-1.2.20 and det'd at Castlebar 8.19-1.2.20. Renumbered 2 Sqn 1.2.20.

Commanding Officers: Maj D.G. Joy 25.3.18; Maj H.J.F. Hunter 15.1.19.

Known serial numbers: F4330, F4332, F4334, F4380, F4616, F4651, F4669, F4678, F4679, F4680, F4769, F4796, F4801 15, H1441.

106 Squadron
Went from Ayr to Fermoy 30.5.18 in 11th (Irish) Group (later Wing) with R.E.8s, re-equipping with F.2Bs 1.19. Flt det'd Athlone 1.19-7.19. Flt det'd Birr 8.19-10.19. Det'd to Oranmore 1919. Sqn disbanded 8.10.19 (into 105 Sqn?).

Commanding Officers: Maj E.A.B. Rice.

Known serial numbers: E2553, F4352, F4373, F4380, F4479, F4796, H1441, H1442, H1590.

111 Squadron
Main equipment from 25.9.17 at Deir el Balah (Palestine), in 40th Wing, Palestine Brigade also ten S.E.5as and a small number of other types. To Julis 1.12.17. F.2Bs transferred to No.1 Sqn AFC 2.18. Received six more F.2B 1.19, at Kantara, To Ramleh 6.2.19 ('A' Flt at Aleppo 23.3.19 to 9.11.19; 'B' Flt at Damascus 24.3.19 to 18.11.19). Squadrons disbanded 1.2.20 on re-designation as 14 Sqn.

Commanding Officers: Maj A. Shekleton 1.8.17, Maj F.W. Stent 25.11.17. By 1.19 Maj S.H. Long DSO MC; Maj R.M. Drummond DSO MC 20.2.19; Maj C.E.H. Medhurst OBE MC 8.3.19.

Known serial numbers: A7184, A7186, A7188, A7190, A7192, A7194, A7196, A7198,

Known serial numbers: C819, C820, C823, C844, C847, C851, C853, C858, C863, C895, C880, C884, C887, C904, C923, C977, C981, C4631, C4713, C4715, C4777, C4778, C4822, C4823, C4834, D2157, D2159, D2211, D2244, D2246, D2247, D2248, D2262, D2362, D2368, D2411, D2478, D7987, E2212, E2245, E248, E2261, E2262, E2368, E2411, E2462, E2478, E2535, E2574, E2585, E2763, F4306, F4368, H1484, H1487.

208 Squadron
Re-equipped with F.2Bs at Ismailia, Egypt, in Palestine Group (later Wing) 10.20. To Turkey in SS *Podesta* and SS *Khartoum* 25.9.22, arrived San Stephano 30.9.22. Returned to Egypt, shipped from Moascar to Alexandria 23.9.23 and on to Ismailia 26.9.23. To Heliopolis 27.10.27. Re-equipped with Atlases 5.30.

Commanding Officers: Sqn Ldr W.J.Y. Guilfoyle OBE MC 1.2.20; Sqn Ldr A. ap Ellis 17.2.22; Sqn Ldr A.C. Winter 14.11.23; Sqn Ldr H.M. Probyn 8.3.24; Sqn Ldr A.S.C. MacLaren OBE MC DFC AFC 12.12.25; Sqn Ldr V.S.E. Lindop 14.3.27; Sqn Ldr M. Moore OBE 14.4.30.

Squadron identification markings: in Turkey in 1923 J6789 has a man's head wearing a top hat motif in a white circle on the fin.

Known serial numbers: C762, C802, C1015, C4651, CR4723, C4743, C4766, CR4723, D7802 11, D7819, D7838, D7839, D7930, D8056, D8096, D8098, D8099, E1930, E2287, E2294, E2295, E2298, E2299, E2438, E2533, F4329, F4349, F4410, FR4435, F4446, F4571, F4574, F4575, FR4582, FR4583, FR4588, F4589, FR4600, F4601, F4616, F4623, F4651, F4655, F4682, F4714, F4719, F4724, F4729, F4731, F4743, F4773, F4791, F4883, F4887, F4902, F4910, F4926, F4930, F4939, F4950, F4962, H1410, H1435, H1451, H1454, H1455, H1456, HR1463, H1468, H1469, H1490, H1491, H1492, H1494, H1496, H1501, H1583, H1623, H1628, HR1635, H1636, H1641, H1642, H1644, H1646, H1648, H1649, H1650, H1652, H1653, H1669, H1670, H1673, H1677, H1678, H1682, H1685, J6589, JR6592, J6595, J6596, JR6600, JR6604, J6617, J6648, J6676, J6686, J6758, JR6767, J6776, JR6785, JR6788, JR6789, J6794, J6798, J7640, J8247, J8274. (At one time the fins sported a Heart, Club, Diamond or Spade motif in a white circle outlined in black, of which the Spade motif was worn by 'A' Flight.)

1st Squadron, AFC: see 67 (AFC) Sqn

3rd Squadron, AFC
A few F.2Bs temporarily attached 9.18 to 1.11.18 while based at Proyart in 15th Wing; 21.9.18 Bouvincourt; 7.10.18 Bernes; 17.10.18 Prémont.

Commanding Officers: Maj D.V.J. Blake by 9.18; Maj W.H. Anderson DFC 26.10.18.

Known serial numbers: C917, C995, C9897, D7870, E2326, E2329, E2348, E2351, E2529, E2660.

Aden Defence Flight
Formed c.10.20 at Khormaksar (det'd Somaliland by 1925). Probably absorbed into 8 Sqn 1.1.28.

Known serial numbers: D8031, D8098, F4865, F4922, H1495, H1633, H1642, J6773.

No.1 School of Aerial Fighting
Formed 17.9.17 at Ayr. Disbanded into No.1 SoAF&G 10.5.18.

Known serial numbers: A7195, B1160, B1178, B1180 '3', B1272, C4685, C4687, C4688, C4689, C4690, C4691.

No.1 School of Aerial Fighting and Gunnery
Formed 10.5.18 from No.1 SoAF Ayr and No.2 (Aux) SoAG Turnberry at Ayr and Turnberry. Redesignated No.1 Fighting School 29.5.18.

Known serial numbers: B1178, C4685.

No.2 School of Aerial Fighting and Gunnery
Formed 6.5.18 at Marske. Redesignated No.2 Fighting School 29.5.18.

Known serial numbers: C770, C4693, C4694 16, C4695 76.

School of Aerial Gunnery and Bombing
Formed 4.20 at Eastchurch. Redesignated Armament & Gunnery School 1.4.22.

Known serial numbers: E2486, F4696, F4957, H1572.

Aeroplane & Armament Experimental Establishment
Formed 24.3.24 ex-Aeroplane Experimental Establishment at Martlesham Heath. Some F.2Bs up to at least 10.30.

Known serial numbers: C4654, F4545, F4587, F4618, F4631, F4724, F4725, F4743, F4745, F4864, F4949, F4967, H1436, H1490, H1614, J6689, J6790, J6797, J7643, J8242, J8251, J8252, J8263.

Aeroplane Experimental Establishment
Formed 16.3.20 ex-Aeroplane Experimental Station at Martlesham Heath; redesignated Aeroplane & Armament Experimental Establishment 24.3.24.

Known serial numbers: C4654, F4819, F4864, H1436, H1559, H1561, J6586, J6753, J6790, J6800.

Aeroplane Experimental Station
Formed 16.10.17 ex-Testing Squadron at Martlesham Heath; redesignated Aeroplane Experimental Establishment 16.3.20.

Known serial numbers: A7260, B1200, B1201, B1204, B1206, B8915, C5654, C9842, C9880, C9883, D7868, D7907, D7910, D7965, D7968, D7971, E2306, E2400, F4631, F4864.

Air Council Inspection Squadron
Formed 25.6.19 at Waddon; redesignated 24 Sqn at Kenley 1.2.20.

Known serial numbers: E2259, F4375, F4670, F4827, F6235, H1460.

No.2 (Hendon) Aircraft Acceptance Park Communications Flight
Formed 1917 at Hendon with at least one F.2B on strength. Redesignated The Communications Squadron 23.7.18.

Known serial numbers: B1206, C4885.

School of Air Pilotage
Formed 23.9.19 as the School of Air Pilotage from Nos. 1 & 2 Schools of Navigation & Bomb Dropping at Andover; 23.12.19 renamed Air Pilotage School; 1.4.20 reduced to cadre; Disbanded 15.1.23 and 11 Sqn formed on the basis of its cadre.

Known serial numbers: C4631, C4766, C4897, E2575, E2870, F4360, F4376, F4406, F4416, F4666, F4772, F4823, F4820, F4832, J6677, F4833, F4834, F4835, F4836, F4870, H1577, H1583, H1588, H1601, H1602, H1603, H1606, H1609, H1614, H1616, H1689, J6708, J6734, J6735, J6740, J6757, J6760.

Andover Communication Flight
Formed 28.3.27 from the Staff College Flight & Wessex Bombing Area Communication Flight at Andover with four dual F.2Bs and four Avro 504, to at least 2.32.

Known serial numbers: C763, D7874, D8033, E2597, F4553, F4743, H1494, J6708, J7692, J8245, J8256, J8257, J8262, J8267, J8289, J8430, J8440, J8448.

Armament Experimental Station Orfordness
Formed 13.10.17 ex-Armament Experimental Squadron at Orfordness; disbanded 16.3.20.

Known serial numbers: A3303, A7183, A7260, B1308, C4714, D7965, D8030, D8032, E2623.

Armament and Gunnery School
Formed 1.4.22 ex-School of Aerial Gunnery & Bombing at Eastchurch; Bristol Fighters replaced by Wapiti IIAs 11.31.

Known serial numbers: D7812, D7817, D7848, D7853, D7864, D7873, D8055, E2545, E2643, F4340, F4346, F4356, F4387, F4388, F4493, F4517, F4560, F4561, F4691, F4742, F4957, H1442, H1449, H1486, H1556, H1562, H1574, H1588, H1596, H1597, J6662, J6671, J6672, J6676, J6742, J6749, J7621, J7625, J7626, J7627, J7628, J7643, J7693, J7694, J8272, J8279, J8287, J8289.

School of Army Co-operation
Formed 23.12.19 at Worthy Down; disbanded 8.3.20; re-formed 8.3.20 at Stonehenge (detachment at Worthy Down) with F.2Bs; 9.2.21 Old Sarum; 9.29 re-equipped with Atlases.

Known serial numbers: B1323, C1014, C1018, C1037, C4631, C4644, C4676, C4681, C4697, C4737, D7801, D7835, D7847, D7874, D8092, E2533, F4330, F4366, F4376, F4381, F4455, F4456, F4473, F4492, F4506, F4513, F4518, F4519, F4542, F4550, F4565, F4567, F4590, F4600, F4603, F4606, F4618, F4622, F4631, F4646, F4679, F4754, F4779, F4786, F4812, F4813, F4830, F4836, F4840, F4842, F4845, F4851, F4901, F4905, F4917, F4933, F4944, F4950, F4952, F4956, F4960, H1390, H1395, H1396, H1416, H1420, H1432, H1437, H1438, H1440, H1444, H1451, H1455, H1483, H1506, H1562, H1598, H1599, H1600, H1603, H1608, H1640, H1668, J6682, J6683, J6696, J6716, J6719, J6722, J6724, J6726, J6728, J6734, J6754, J6756, J7616, J7618, J7619, J7634, J7649, J7653, J7659, J7662, J7663, J7668, J7671, J7675, J7686, J7687, J7689, J7690, J7692, J7697, J8248, J8257, J8260, J8271, J8272, J8288, J8290.

Artillery Flight
Formed by 1.7.18 in 1st Wing at Bruay; became 'L' Flight 9.7.18.

Known serial numbers: D7872, F5815, F6101.

Artillery & Infantry Co-operation Squadron

Formed 12.10.17 ex-Wireless and Observers School at Hursley Park, Winchester (flying elements at Worthy Down by 1.18); 31.5.18 HQ and ground training elements joined flying element at Worthy Down; redesignated RAF & Army Co-operation School 19.9.18.

Known serial numbers: C9840, C9841, C9842, C9843, C9844, C9847, C9856, C9857, C9858, C9859, C9860, C9861, C9862, F4292.

No.1 (Auxiliary) School of Aerial Gunnery

Formed 1.17 at Hythe (det'd at Lympne until 10.9.17); disbanded into No.1 (O)SoAG 9.3.18.

Known serial numbers: A7261, B1208, C4607, C4648.

No.2 (Auxiliary) School of Aerial Gunnery

Formed 1.17 at Turnberry; disbanded into No.1 SoAF&G 10.5.18.

Known serial numbers: C4691, C4841.

No.3 (Auxiliary) School of Aerial Gunnery

Formed 1.8.17 at New Romney; disbanded into No.1 (O)SoAG 9.3.18.

Known serial numbers: C4819 56, C4822.

No.4 (Auxiliary) School of Aerial Gunnery

Formed 1.11.17 at Marske; disbanded into No.2 SoAF&G 6.5.18.

Known serial numbers: B1179, B1195, B1226, B1227 79, B1321 36, C756, C4695 76.

School of Aerial Gunnery and Bombing

Formed 4.20 at Eastchurch. Redesignated Armament and Gunnery School 1.4.22.

Known serial numbers: E2486, F4696, F4957, H1572.

Central Flying School

F.2Bs on strength at Upavon by 1.20 to at least 10.30.

Known serial numbers: A3303, A3304, B1119, C1032, C4680, C4683, C4734, D7810, E2294, E2300, E2311, E2432, E2624, F4278, F4284, F4285, F4418, F4423, F4428, F4497, F4504, F4515, F4567, F4569, F4680, F4683, F4756, F4830, F4833, F4853, F4912, F4946, H1447, H1484, H1634, H1644, H1689, J6665, J6732, J6737, J8453.

No.1 Communication Squadron

Formed 23.7.18 from No.2 (Hendon) AAP Communications Flight as The Communications

Squadron at Hendon, 'B' Flt having one F.2B initially; 13.4.19 Kenley; redesignated 24 Sqn 1.2.20.

Known serial numbers: C4885, C9841, E2581.

No.3 Communication Squadron

Formed 2.19 at Hounslow. Four F.2B allotted 2.5.19. Disbanded 3.19 into No.1 Communication Squadron.

Known serial numbers: None.

Department of Chief of Air Staff Communication Flight

Based at both Northolt and Kenley c.1925/6.

Known serial numbers: F4387, F4491, F4496, F4913, J6729.

Development Squadron

Formed 17.8.18 at Gosport with F.2Bs on strength; disbanded 2.20.

Known serial numbers: C820, D7998, D7999, E2564, E2607, F4835, F4844.

HMS *Eagle* Trials Flight

Formed 4.20 at Gosport for service trials aboard HMS *Eagle*, initial establishment including three F.2Bs. Disbanded 11.20.

Known serial numbers: F4453, H1605.

Electrical and Wireless School

Formed 23.12.19 at Flowerdown, with flying from Worthy Down until 11.3.27; to Cranwell 8.29. F.2Bs until at least 11.30.

Known serial numbers: C767, C4897, D8096, E1630, F4484, F4454, F4488, F4609, F4711, F4903, H1390, H1466, H1624, H1637, J6586, J6685, J6694, J6727, J7617, J7629, J7630, J7633, J7650, J7696.

No.1 Fighting School

Formed 29.5.18 ex-1 SoAF&G at Turnberry (and Ayr) with F.2Bs on strength; disbanded 25.1.19.

Known serial numbers: B1161, B1270, C4684, C4685, E2464, E2465.

No.2 Fighting School

Formed 29.5.18 ex-No.2 SoAF&G at Marske with F.2Bs on strength; disbanded late 1919.

Known serial numbers: B1179, B1195, B1226, B1227 79, B8938 82, C752 75, C754, C755, C756, C822, C1008, C1009 85, C4692 43,

C4696 76, C4892 48, E2550, E2631 77, F4286 79, F4315, F4321 76, D4326, F4725.

No.3 Fighting School

Formed 29.5.18 ex-No.3 SoAF&G at Bircham Newton with at least one F.2B on strength; 21.9.18 Sedgeford. Redesignated No.7 Training School 14.3.19.

Known serial numbers: C9866 1, C9867 6, D8067, D8073, D8074.

No.5 Fighting School

Formed 5.3.18 ex-School of Aerial Fighting at Heliopolis; disbanded 22.7.19.

Known serial numbers: A7194, B1127, B1293, B1294, C4651, C4653.

Fleet School of Aerial Fighting & Gunnery

Formed 19.7.18 ex-No.208 TDS at East Fortune; 10.11.18 Leuchars to become Grand Fleet School of Aerial Fighting & Gunnery; disbanded 1920.

Known serial numbers: B8943, E1902, E1964, F4322, F4736.

'L' Flight

Formed 9.7.18 ex-Artillery Flight as a Long-Range Artillery Flight in 1st Wing at Bruay to at least 18.9.18; by 11.18 at Auberchicourt; late 11.18 to Aulnoy; disbanded in 1st Wing 6.2.19. Aircraft carried individual letters between A and F.

Known serial numbers: C968, C986, C1034, C4655, C9894, D2126, D2184, D7805, D7814, D7925, D7934 D, D7938, D8025, E2161, E2163, E2184, E2242, E2473, E2521, F4306, F5812 A, F5822.

'M' Flight

Formed 6.10.18 as a Long-Range Artillery Flight in 2nd Wing at St Omer/Longuenesse; 22.10.18 Menin; 15.11.18 Wevelghem; 24.11.18 in transit; 26.11.18 Cognelée; 6.12.18 in transit; 8.12.18 Elsenborn Camp; 13.12.18 Bickendorf; 27.12.18 Hangelar. Disbanded 4.8.19. Establishment two F.2Bs initially, later increased to six.

Known serial numbers: C927 'A1', D2362, D7878, E2162, E2193, E2362, E2426, E2570, E2594, E2599, E2641, F4274, F4297, F4305, F4435.

'N' Flight

Formed 9.18 [by 18.9.18] as a Long-Range Artillery Flight in 12th Wing at Vert Galand; 9.18 Beugnatre; by 15.11.18 at Estourmel. Disbanded 2.19.

Known serial numbers: C9896, C9948, D7863, D7872, D7913, D7919, D7946, F5815, F5819, F6101.

'O' Flight

Formed 1.11.18 as a Long-Range Artillery Flight in 15th Wing at Premont; by 9.11.18, Elincourt 29.11.18, Gerpinnes by 12.18, Stree 9.12.18, Laneffe by 2.19, Thy-le-Bauduin; fate unknown.

Known serial numbers: C917, C995, E2329, E2351, E2529, F4307.

'P' Flight

Formed 29.8.18 as a Long-Range Artillery Flight in 81st Wing at Serny; 18.10.18 Bruay; 26.10.18 Cysoing; 3.12.18 Reckem. Disbanded 20.1.19.

An anonymous Bristol Fighter with a four-bladed propeller with the CFS at Upavon. *(Philip Jarrett)*

Known serial numbers: C927, C1013, C9891, D2136, D2652, D7884, D7916, D7925, D7931, D7947, E2162, F4438, F4444, F4535, F4838.

'X' Flight

Formed 10.17 from Special Service Flight of 14 Sqn at Aqaba with three B.E.2c initially; 6.18 to El Guiera (two a/c det'd Azraq 9.18); Two F.2B 8.18 to 15.9.18. Disbanded sometime after 17.7.19.

Known serial numbers: A7184, A7188.

'Z' Flight

With another flight attached to 34 Sqn at Villaverla, Italy, 3.18 with F.2B until 7.18, when it became 139 Sqn.

Known serial numbers: B1185, B1212, B1214, B1230, C913, C916, C990, C991, C992, C993, C997, C999, C4700, C4755, C4756, C4757, C4758, C4759, C4760, C4761, C4762, C4860, D8079.

Flying Instructors School

Formed 23.12.19 ex-Central Flying School at Upavon with a few F.2Bs. Reverted to title Central Flying School 26.4.20.

Known serial numbers: None.

No.1 Flying Training School

Formed 23.12.19 in No.7 Group by retitling the Netheravon Flying School. Disbanded 1.2.31.

Known serial numbers: C1020, C4718, C4870, D7803, D7810, D7816, E2434, E2505, F4282, F4482, F4483, F4485, F4493, F4494, F4501, F4503, F4510, F4514, F4523, F4563, F4651, F4700, F4710, F4718, F4721, F4757, F4760, F4771, F4845, F4882, H1411, H1435, H1440, H1449, H1456, H1460, H1505, H1611, H1614, H1617, H1640, H1681, J6658, J6673, J6677, J6696, J6704, J6727, J6729, J6730, J6732, J6733, J6734, J6739, J6746, J6752, J6762, J6765, J6793, J8250.

No.2 Flying Training School

Formed 26.4.20 in No.3 Group at Duxford, 'C' Flt having F.2Bs; to Digby 30.6.24; F.2Bs replaced by Atlas Trainer 3.32.

Known serial numbers: C798, C1017, C1018, C4684, D7801, D8033, D8083, E2434, E2435, E2526, E2643, F4287, F4339, F4341, F4342, F4362, F4375, F4389, F4416, F4420, F4422, F4692, F4485, F4489, F4496, F4502, F4507, F4510, F4584, F4585, F4589, F4595, F4618, F4648, F4650, F4671, F4685, F4690, F4691, F4744, F4766, F4807, F4810, F4811, F4836, F4841, F4845, F4885, F4892, F4895, F4902, F4904, F4946, H1390, H1396, H1397, H1403, H1417, H1410, H1419, H1421, H1423, H1425, H1427, H1429, H1430, H1433, H1439, H1460, H1484, H1493, H1505, H1555, H1595, H1602, H1634, H1644, J6611, J6685, J6697, J6713, J6714, J6718, J6723, J6743, J6745, J6751, J6756, J8254, J8278, J8431, J8437, J8441, J8442, J8446, J8448, J8449, J8450, J8452, J8458.

No.3 Flying Training School

Formed 26.4.20 ex-No.59 Training School at Scopwick (Digby), with some F.2B. Disbanded 1.4.22.

Known serial numbers: F4681, H1428.

No.4 Flying Training School

Formed 1.4.21 at Abu Sueir, Egypt, 'A' and 'B' Flts having F.2Bs until 12.23; again received F.2Bs 8.27 until at least 10.30.

Known serial numbers: B1198, C4651, C4742, D7837, DR7839, D7921, D7933, E2290, E2299, E2647, F4435, F4455, F4651, F4695, F4883, F4887, F4889, F4920, F4922, F4927, H1398, H1463, H1470, H1493, H1496, H1501, H1505, H1626, H1635, H1642, H1644, H1647, H1652, H1666, H1669, H1677, J6590, J6600, J6604, J6605, J6606, J6615, J6617, J6758.

No.5 Flying Training School

Formed 26.4.20 from No.4 Training School at Shotwick (renamed Sealand 26.6.24); F.2Bs replaced by Atlas Trainers 7.31.

Known serial numbers: B1327, C763, C766, C767, C799, C806, C1046 7, C4735, C4750?, D7804, D7857, D7877, D8032, D8045, D8100, E2436, E2543, E2613, F4342, F4370, F4414, F4431, F4460, F4477, F4490, F4508, F4519 5, F4610, F4620, F4647, F4660, F4680, F4691, F4708, F4721, F4722, F4751, F4756, F4757, F4760, F4761, F4772, F4827, F4911, F4912, F4946, F4954, F4964, F4969, H1325, H1326, H1396 6, H1398, H1456, H1463, H1465, H1493, H1496, H1634 6, H1660, H1663, H1669, J6602, J6661, J6673?, J6679, J6685, J6695, J6696, J6698, J6702, J6706, J6708, J6762, J6791, J8282 4, J8429, J8430, J8433, J8434, J8442, J8445, J8446, J8447, J8449, J8451, J8453, J8457.

No.6 Flying Training School

Formed 26.4.20 from No.39 Training School at Spittlegate with some F.2Bs; 21.9.20 Manston; disbanded 1.4.22.

Known serial numbers: C761, F4345, F4418, F4478, H1404.

No.21 Group Communication Squadron

Formed 12.4.27 at Northolt and existed until at least 11.27.

Known serial number: J6714.

Home Aircraft Depot Station Flight

Depot formed 12.4.26 at Henlow, F.2Bs until at least 1.29.

Known serial numbers: F4504, F4534. F4965, J6727.

Home Communication Flight

Formed 1.2.27 ex-Inland Area Communication Flight at Northolt. To Hendon 16.4.28. Absorbed into 24 Sqn 10.7.33.

Known serial numbers: D8085, E2630, F4517, F4546, F4727, F4747, H1396, H1617, H1685, J8443.

HQ RAF India Communication Flight

Formed 16.10.28 at Lahore in summer and Willingdon in winter, with some F.2Bs to at least 2.31.

Known serial number: J7648.

Inland Area Aircraft Depot

Formed 16.3.20 ex-No.5 (E) ARD at Henlow with three F.2Bs on strength. Redesignated Home Aircraft Depot 12.4.26.

Known serial numbers: C1020, F4590, F4757, F4775, F4592, F9504, J6694, J6738.

Inland Area Communication Flight

Formed 1.4.20 at Northolt by redesignating the South Eastern Area Communication Flight; Replaced by the Home Communication Flight 1.2.27.

Known serial numbers: C4666, E4358, E4375, E4399, E4564, F4747, H1394, H1398, H1434, H1598, J6597, J6661, J6678, J6695, J6697, J6747.

Instrument Design Establishment

Formed 1.11.19 ex-W/T Experimental Establishment at Biggin Hill; 3.20 renamed Instrument Design Establishment (Home); disbanded 1.4.22.

Known serial numbers: B1201, C4875, F4724, F4875, H1415, H1433, H1450, H1533, J6612, J6689.

AHQ Iraq Command Communication Flight

Formed by 11.25 at Baghdad, to at least 5.28. Fate unknown.

Known serial numbers: F4341, F4558, F4573, F4605, F4687, F4753, F4857, H1438.

Iraq Command Training Flight

Formed by 1927 at Baghdad; redesignated Communication Flight Iraq and Persia 30.12.30.

Known serial numbers: C1028, E2477, F4344, F4362, F4744, H1027, H1632, J6659.

Irish Flight

Formed 18.1.22 at Baldonnel with four F.2Bs; 1.5.22 Collinstown; disbanded 31.10.22.

Known serial numbers: E2411, E2505, F4934, H1437, H1485?, H1489, J6623, J6688, J6692, J6704, J6732, J6744, J6748, J6756, J6762, J6763.

No.2 Marine Observers School

Formed 1.1.19 ex-No.1 Observers School at Eastchurch; disbanded 14.6.19.

Known serial number: C903.

Medical Flight

Formed by 4.18 at Hendon with one F.2B; redesignated No.29 TS 1.8.18.

Known serial number: C4889.

Meteor Flight (Meteorological Flight)

Existed by 14.12.18 under HQ 8th Brigade at Berck-sur-Mer; 1.4.19 to 91st Wing; 30.5.19 in transit; 5.6.19 Bickendorf. Disbanded 3.9.19.

Known serial numbers: F4442, F4849, F4865.

No.1 School of Navigation & Bomb Dropping

A few F.2Bs on strength at Stonehenge between 3.18 and 3.19.

Known serial numbers: C4631, F4631, H1577.

Netheravon Flying School

Formed 29.7.19 ex-No.8 TS at Netheravon; redesignated No.1 FTS 23.12.19.

Known serial number: F4579.

Night Flying Flight

Formed 1.7.23 at Biggin Hill with three Vimy and one F.2B; redesignated Anti-Aircraft Co-operation Flight 22.10.31.

Known serial numbers: C798, J6600, J6668, J6681, J6714.

North-Western Area Flying Instructors School

Formed 1.7.18 at Ayr with some F.2Bs. To Redcar 15.1.19. Disbanded 1919.

Known serial numbers: None.

No.1 (Observers) School of Aerial Gunnery

Formed 9.3.18 ex-Nos.1 & 3 (Auxiliary) Schools of Aerial Gunnery at Hythe, with a detachment at New Romney/Dymchurch. To New Romney 1.12.18. Returned Hythe early 1919. Disbanded 14.2.19.

Known serial numbers: A7262, A7276, B1104 11, B1208, B1282, C4607, B1288, B1320, C4648, C4703, C4704, C4705, C4766, C4781, C4791, C4797, C4798, C4799, C4822, C9854, D8009, D8010, D8016, D8020 23, D8067, E2484, E2485 5, E2487 24.

School of Photography Flight

Formed 23.12.19 ex-Photographic Park at South Farnborough, mainly with F.2Bs, which were replaced by Atlases 4.31.

Known serial numbers: F4284, F4391, F4428, F4486, F4492, F4517, F4561, F4587, F4645, F4691, F4697, F4701, F4838, F4845, F4853, F4884, H1415, H1451, J6702, J6708, J6712, J6754, J6787, J7656, J7670, J7672, J8270, J8275.

Pool of Pilots

Formed 1.4.18 at Manston. To Joyce Green 5.10.18. Disbanded 23.11.19.

Known serial numbers: C902, C905, C907, C910, D8094, F4308, F4328, F4366.

Royal Aircraft Factory

Formed 11.4.12 ex-Army Aircraft Factory at Farnborough; c.1.14 Experimental Squadron formed. Redesignated Royal Aircraft Establishment 1.4.18.

Known serial numbers: A7260, B1201.

Royal Aircraft Establishment

Formed 1.4.18 ex-Royal Aircraft Factory, Farnborough; F.2Bs until 3.37.

Known serial numbers: A7260, B1201, C810, C1025, C4654, C4655, C4776, D7835, D7860, E2069, F4329, F4360, F4365, F4411, F4491, F4567, F4586, F4587, F4675, F4728,

F4741, F4745, F4769, F4776, F4819, F4827, F4845, F4886, F4893, F4967, F6282, H1390, H1392, H1417, H1422, H1434, H1450, H1473, H1559, H1560, H1561, H1624, H1625, J6611, J6676, J6689, J6721, J6722, J6749, J6757, J6776, J6790, J6797, J7635, J7642, J7643, J8251, J8260, J8263, J8264, J8289, J8438, J8448.

Royal Air Force College

Formed 23.12.19 at Cranwell, 'B' and 'D' Flights with F.2Bs until 1930.

Known serial numbers: C767, C768, C903, C1049, C4740 D1, D8083 5, E1969, E1971, E2431, E2434 8, F4271, F4385, F4395, F4397, F4412, F4413, F4423, F4425, F4432, F4434, F4435, F4492, F4497, F4499, F4502 7 later B7, F4507, F4511 3 later B3, F4515, F4516, F4521 D2, F4526, F4546, F4547, F4548, F4549, F4552, F4564, F4571 4, F4584, F4588, F4607, F4610, F4619, F4622, F4705 B5, F4740 D1, F4747, F4751 B4, F4811, F4814 D4, F4822, F4823, F4826, F4845, F4870, F4884, F4893, F4898, F4912, F4938, F4939 B6, F4940, F4956, F4970, H1438, H1439, H1451, H1502, H1598, H1642, J6678, J6719, J6748, J6791, J7617, J7689, J8243, J8253, J8259, J8261, J8275, J8288.

RAF & Army Co-operation School

Formed 19.9.18 ex-Artillery & Infantry School at Worthy Down. Redesignated School of Army Co-operation 23.12.19.

Known serial numbers: E2756, E9529, F4281, F4283, F4286, F4289, F4291, F4292, F4293, F4294, F4295, F4301, F4316, F4318, F4523, F4525, F4526, F4527, F4530, F4538, F4577, F4578, F4579, F9638.

Royal Air Force Staff College Flight

Formed 1.4.22 at Andover with two F.2Bs and two D.H.9As; renamed Andover Communication Flight 28.3.27.

Known serial numbers: C763, C4677, D8033, D8083, F4388, F4440, F4667, F4677, F4643, F4840, F4882, F4884, H1459, H1624, H1689, J6677, J6697, J6740, J6742, J6743, J6760, J6775.

RAF Training Base Leuchars

Formed in 1925 at Leuchars; redesignated No.1 FTS 1.4.35.

Known serial number: H1458.

Signal Co-operation Flight

Formed 1.4.21 at Biggin Hill; 15.12.22 to Kenley; redesignated 13 Sqn 1.4.24.

Known serial numbers: F4745, J6612.

South Eastern Area Flying Instructors School

Formed 7.18 at Shoreham; disbanded 31.3.19.

Known serial number: D7981.

Special Duties Flight

Formed by 1926 at Old Sarum; 12.9.28 to Netheravon until at least 8.30. Establishment included one F.2B.

Known serial numbers: F4675, F4745.

No.1 School of Special Flying

Formed 2.8.17 as School of Special Flying at Gosport with a few F.2Bs on strength, becoming No.1 School of Special Flying on 18.5.18. Redesignated South Western Area Flying Instructors School 1.7.18.

Known serial numbers: A7263, C4687.

Special Instruction Flight

At Almaza by 1.20, with F.2Bs to at least 12.20.

Known serial numbers: A7192, D7927, E2290, H1470.

Station Flight Duxford

Existed at Duxford by 10.26 to at least 8.27.

Known serial numbers: F4366, F4738, F4893.

Station Flight North Coates

Existed at North Coates by 6.30.

Known serial number: J8256.

Station Flight Quetta

Existed at Quetta by 5.28 until at least 11.29.

Known serial numbers: C803, D7809, D7813, F4541, F4644, F4766, F4908, F4953, J6700, J6782.

(No.1) School of Technical Training

Formed 16.3.20 at Halton, with an establishment of four F.2Bs to at least 1925.

Known serial numbers: F4353, F4385, F4465, F4484, F4492, F4581, F4676, F4715, F4832, F4841, F4844 6, F4845 6, F4960, F4966, F4970, H1390, H1488, H1614, J6589, J6661, J6677, J6680 7 later 6, J6690, J8271, 540M.

No.3 School of Technical Training

Re-formed 16.3.20 at Manston with various ground instructional airframes initially, including F.2Bs.

Known serial numbers: H1015, H1572.

Testing Squadron

Martlesham Heath from 16.1.17. Redesignated Aeroplane Experimental Station 16.10.17.

Known serial number: A7183.

No.1 Torpedo Training Squadron

Formed 19.7.18 out of No.208 TDS at East Fortune, with at least one F.2B. Redesignated No.201 TDS 14.8.18.

Known serial number: B8937.

Bristol F.2B F4814 served as 'D1' at Cranwell in J Type DC form in the mid-late 1920s. The date of this crash is unknown. *(Philip Jarrett)*

No.2 Training Depot Station
Formed 14.4.18 at West Fenton (Gullane) (30th Wing). Disbanded 21.11.19.

Known serial numbers: C4658, C4805.

No.3 Training Depot Station
Formed 5.9.17 at Lopcombe Corner (34th Wing), had at least one F.2B on strength. Redesignated No.3 TS 15.5.19.

Known serial number: A7106.

No.4 Training Depot Station
Formed 19.9.17 at Hooton Park (37th Wing), had at least one F.2B on strength. Redesignated No.4 TS 14.3.19.

Known serial number: E2313.

No.5 Training Depot Station
Formed 24.9.17 at Easton-on-the-Hill (Stamford) (35th Wing), had at least two F.2Bs on strength. Redesignated No.5 TS 14.3.19.

Known serial numbers: C988, E2166.

No.16 Training Depot Station
Formed 21.7.18 ex-No.194 TS at Amriya, Egypt (20th Wing), moving to Abu Sueir 11.18 and to Heliopolis 6.7.19. Disbanded 8.20.

Known serial numbers: A7192, B1127, B1205, C4653, D7927, D7933, E2294, E2295.

No.17 Training Depot Station
Formed 21.7.18 ex-No.57 TS at El Firdan, Egypt (32nd Wing later 69th Wing) mainly with B.E.2 variants, R.E.8s and F.K.8s, but also some F.2Bs. Moved to Abu Sueir 11.28 (69th Wing), then Shallufa 5.19. Disbanded 25.7.19.

Known serial numbers: D7933, E2293, E2294, E2295.

No.19 Training Depot Station
Formed 21.7.18 ex-No.195 TS at El Rimal, Egypt (32nd Wing later 69th Wing) mainly with Avro 504s and Sopwith Pups, but at least one F.2B. Disbanded 25.7.19.

Known serial number: B1147.

No.21 Training Depot Station
Formed 15.7.18 at Driffield (19th Wing later 8th Wing) mainly with S.E.5as and D.H.6s, but at least one F.2B. Redesignated No.21 TS 7.19.

Known serial number: C902.

No.27 Training Depot Station
Formed 15.8.18 at Crail (No.20 Group); disbanded 31.3.19.

Known serial numbers: B1270, C4684, E2465, E2611, E2614, F9395, F9397.

No.33 Training Depot Station
Formed 15.8.18 ex-Nos.7 and 8 TS at Witney (21st Wing). Disbanded 6.9.19.

Known serial numbers: A7170, B1169, B1242, B1329, B1342, B8927, B8928, B8931, C828, C829, C836, C837, C902, C908, C4646, C4666, C4667, C4771, C4772, C4773, C4789, C4879, D2646, D7822, D7824, E2624, E2640, E2642, E9611, E9612, F4323, F4479, F4524, F9401, F9403, F9404.

No.36 Training Depot Station
Formed 15.7.18 from Nos.13 and 66 TS at Yatesbury (28th Wing). Disbanded into new No.36 TS 25.3.19.

Known serial numbers: D2629, E2221 C, E2223 G, E2224.

No.37 Training Depot Station
Formed 15.7.18 from Nos.16 and 17 TS at Yatesbury (28th Wing). Disbanded into No.36 TS 15.5.19.

Known serial numbers: C918, C1001, C1038, C1044, C9886, C9887, C9890, D2128, D2131, D2221, D2222, D2627, D7852, D7959, D7973, E2126, F5096.

No.39 Training Depot Station
Formed 15.8.18 from Nos.15 and 37 TS at Spittlegate (24th Wing). Redesignated No.39 TS 1919. Disbanded 14.3.19.

Known serial numbers: C4878, D2169, D7904, E1911.

No.44 Training Depot Station
Formed 15.8.18 from Nos.35 and 71 TS at Port Meadow (Oxford) (21st Wing), moving to Bicester 1.10.18. Disbanded into No.44 TS 8.19.

Known serial numbers: A7238, B826, C751, C784, C759, C826, C833, C854, C897, C1021, C1024, C1026, C4674, C4675, C4779, C4784, C4788, D7987, D8012, E2622, F4313, H1284.

No.45 Training Depot Station
Formed 15.8.18 ex-Nos.38 and 71 TS at Rendcomb (21st Wing). Redesignated No.45 TS 6.19.

Known serial numbers: A7238, B1030, B1160, B1182, B1242, B1259, B8923, B8946, B8948, B8949, B8950, C834, C903, C1030, C4669, C4676, C4677, C4678, C4716, C4774, C4847, C4858, C4874, C4878, D2626, F4287.

No.50 Training Depot Station
Formed 15.7.18 from No.54 TS at Eastbourne (60th Wing later 6th Wing), moving to Manston, where it disbanded 24.10.19.

Known serial number: C903.

No.56 Training Depot Station
Formed 27.7.18 ex-No.201 TDS at Cranwell (59th Wing), with at least one F.2B; disbanded 13.3.19.

Known serial numbers: C4876, D2208, D2743, E1971, E2001, F4762.

No.59 Training Depot Station
Formed 8.7.18 at Portholme Meadow (26th Wing), moving to Scopwick (59th Wing) 15.10.18. Redesignated No.59 TS 14.3.19.

Known serial numbers: B1172, E1975, F4880.

No.61 Training Depot Station
Formed 15.12.18 at Tangmere (No.2 Group). Redesignated No.61 TS 20.6.19.

Known serial numbers: F4767, F4777, F4779, F4793.

No.201 Training Depot Station
Re-formed 14.8.18 ex-No.1 Torpedo Training Sqn at East Fortune; redesignated Torpedo Training Sqn 30.4.19.

Known serial number: B8942.

No.204 Training Depot Station
Formed 1.4.18 from Naval Flying School at Eastchurch, with at least two F.2Bs. Disbanded 3.19.

Known serial numbers: E2141, E2142.

No.4 Training Squadron
Formed 31.5.19 ex-No.51 TS at North Shotwick (7th Wing) with at least one F.2B. Disbanded into No.5 FTS 26.4.20.

Known serial number: C1023.

No.7 Training Squadron
At Netheravon (4th Wing), with some F.2Bs by 2.18. To Witney (21st Wing) 30.4.18. Disbanded into No.33 TDS 15.8.18.

Known serial numbers: B857, B1244, B1310, B8930, C4634, C4642, C4666.

No.8 Training Squadron
At Netheravon (4th Wing), with some F.2Bs from 1.18. To Witney (21st Wing) 1.4.18. Disbanded into No.33 TDS 15.8.18.

Known serial numbers: A7170, A7296, A7297, B857, B1169, B1244, B1249, B1313, B8918, B8928, C836, C837, C4644, C4687, C4702, C4717, C4806, C4809, C4854, C4865.

No.10 Training Squadron
Re-formed 14.3.19 ex-No.10 TDS at Harling Road. Disbanded 3.20.

Known serial numbers: E2005, E2014.

No.15 Training Squadron
At Spittlegate by 5.18. Disbanded into No.39 TDS 15.8.18.

Known serial numbers: B1329, C885, C888, C4708, C4712, C4769, C4770, C4786, D8017.

No.24 Training Squadron
By 2.18 at Netheravon (4th Wing). To Witney (21st Wing) 30.3.18. Disbanded into No.24 TDS at Collinstown 15.8.18.

Known serial numbers: A3319 2, B1242, B1249, B1313, B1338, B8927, B8931, B8932, C784, C908, C4702, C4771, C4866, C4881.

No.29 Training Squadron
At Stag Lane from 6.8.18 with various types including at least one F.2B. To Croydon (18th Wing) 14.12.18. Disbanded into No.8 TDS 14.7.19.

Known serial number: F4335.

No.30 Training Squadron
Re-formed 5.19 ex-No.30 TDS at Northolt. Disbanded 15.3.20.

Known serial number: F4824.

No.31 Training Squadron
At Wyton (26th Wing) with at least one F.2B. Disbanded into No.23 TDS Baldonnel 2.9.18.

Known serial number: A7199.

No.34 Training Squadron
Equipped with various types including F.2B by 5.18 at Chattis Hill (34th Wing), where it disbanded into No.43 TDS on 15.7.18.

Known serial number: C813.

No.35 Training Squadron
At Northolt (18th Wing) as No.35 Reserve Squadron, with F.2Bs from 28.4.17, becoming No.35 TS 31.5.17; to Port Meadow (21st Wing) 16.12.17. Disbanded into No.44 TDS 15.8.18.

Known serial numbers: A3314, A3325, A3332, A3344, A3351, A7103, A7122, A7135,

A7136, A7173, A7180, A7212, A7218, A7229, A7238, A7249, A7263, A7265, A7267, A7273, B1140, B1159, B1160, B1172, B8919, B8921, C830, C831, C891, C4647, C4660, C4804, C4805, C4812, C4813, C4830, C4833.

No.38 Training Squadron (ex-38 Reserve Squadron to 31.5.17)
At Rendcomb (21st Wing), with F.2Bs from 20.12.16. Disbanded into No.45 TDS 15.8.18.

Known serial numbers: A3305, A3306, A3307, A3308, A3309, A3310, A3311, A3313, A3316, A3319, A3328, A3329, A3331, A3350, A7148 6, A7274, B1103, B1107, B1218, B1259, C752, C754, C848, C912, C915, C4716, C4774, C4779, C4792, C9940.

No.44 Training Squadron
At Waddington (27th Wing), with F.2Bs by 5.18. Disbanded into No.48 TS 14.3.19.

Known serial number: C4858.

No.50 Training Squadron
At Spittlegate (24th Wing), with some F.2Bs by 3.18. Disbanded into No.27 TDS 15.8.18.

Known serial numbers: B1329, C4712.

No.59 Training Squadron
At Yatesbury (28th Wing) with F.2Bs by 8.17. To Beaulieu (17th Wing) 30.10.17. To Netheravon (4th Wing) 20.11.17. To Lilbourne (25th Wing) 6.12.17. To Rendcomb (21st Wing) 1.2.18. Disbanded into No.24 TDS 15.8.18.

Known serial numbers (bore individual numbers up to at least 18): A7102, A7229, A7218 1 *PANTHER*, A7238 6 *TIGER*, A7278

11, B1106, B1107, B1159, B1160 8, B1236, B1258, B8917, B8925 18, B8926 13, C775 20, C854, C891 21, C903, C4612, C4775 19.

No.71 Training Squadron
At Port Meadow (21st Wing), with F.2Bs by 5.18; disbanded into No.44 TDS 15.8.18.

Known serial numbers: B8933, C759, C784, C831, C835, C897, C903, C4724, C4858.

No.189 (Night) Training Squadron
At Sutton's Farm (49th Wing), with some F.2Bs from 1.4.18. Disbanded 1.3.19.

Known serial number: C4777.

No.201 Training Squadron
Formed 14.8.18 ex-No.1 Torpedo Training Squadron at East Fortune (No.22 Group); disbanded 3.4.19.

Known serial numbers: B8942, B8945.

7th (Training) Squadron, Australian Flying Corps
Formed 14.1.18 ex-No.32 TS (AFC) at Yatesbury (28th Wing). To Leighterton (1st Wing AFC) 23.2.18; disbanded 5.19.

Known serial numbers: C998, C9844, C9850, C9853, C9858, C9859, C9869, D2691, D2607, D2629, D2687, D2691, D2697, D7955, D7970.

Cambridge University Air Squadron
Flying facilities from 1.5.26 at Duxford. To at least 7.30.

Known serial numbers: C4740, F4542, F4548, F4644, F4645, J6602, J7689, J8286, J8434, J8438, J8443.

Oxford University Air Squadron
Flying facilities from 10.1.28 at Upper Heyford. To 2.32.

Known serial numbers: J6685, J7636 Y, J8249, J8250 X, J8257 Z.

18th Wing Fighting School
At London Colney with some Pups in 9.17. Later a few F.2Bs.

Known serial numbers: A7311, B1847.

Wireless Experimental Establishment
Formed 14.12.17 ex-Wireless Testing Park at Biggin Hill; became W/T Establishment 2.4.18, then Instrument Design Establishment 1.11.19.

Known serial numbers: A7107 6, B1220, C4611 1, C4686, C4778, D8029 5, F4659.

No.1 (T) Wireless School
Formed 8.11.17 at South Farnborough, with at least one F.2B by 6.18. To Flowerdown 8.3.19. Redesignated Electrical and Wireless School 23.12.19.

Known serial number: C4696.

No.2 Wireless School
Formed 8.11.17 at Penshurst, with at least one F.2B. Disbanded 23.3.19.

Known serial number: C4803.

Wireless Telephony School
Formed 2.4.18 at Biggin Hill. To Chattis Hill 16.4.18, then Winton 21.11.18, Beaulieu 5.19. Disbanded 1.9.19.

Known serial numbers: B1291, C9863, C9864, C9865, D8013, D8016.

No.2 School of Wireless Telephony
Formed ex-21st Wing Wireless Telegraphy Flight at Port Meadow; redesignated Wireless Telephony Flight?

Known serial numbers: B8916, B8933, C4774, F4579.

Wireless Testing Park
Formed 21.10.16 at Port Meadow. To Biggin Hill 1.1.17, with at least one F.2B. Became the Wireless Experimental Establishment 14.12.17.

Known serial number: A7146.

Anonymous J-Type F.2B 'R' of one of the RAF squadrons in India approaching the stall, with the autoslots in the upper wing leading edges deployed. The aircraft is equipped for night flying, with Holt flare brackets beneath the lower wingtips and lights above the upper wingtips. *(Philip Jarrett)*

Following its complete refurbishment, the Shuttleworth Collection's Bristol F.2b has been finished to represent B1162, flown by Sgt Ernest John Elton DCM, MM of 22 Sqn, the RFC's most successful NCO pilot, who in a combat on 29 March 1918 destroyed three enemy aircraft. In the space of 32 days Elton and his crewmen amassed a tally of 14 destroyed plus two out of control; ten with the front gun and six with the rear gun. This picture was taken on 28 August 2020. *(Bill Grigg)*

Appendix 10

SURVIVORS AND REPRODUCTIONS

A small number of Bristol Fighters still survive and all are being preserved for posterity. A number have been built by Skysport Engineering, based on six fuselages and a lot of components recovered from a barn at Weston-on-the-Green, Oxfordshire, in the 1960s and incorporating 'loads of bits and pieces from all over the place. Wings, hundreds of parts, tail ends, bits, all sorts', to quote Skysport founder Tim Moore.

During the First World War Weston-on-the-Green was the location of No.28 TDS, though no Bristol Fighters are known to have flown from there. In 1919 H.F.V. Battle was assigned to the Depot at Uxbridge and appointed to one of the Recruits Training Squadrons, a non-flying duty. However, the pilots at the Depot were encouraged to keep in practice by flying the aircraft of the Communications Flight at Northolt, and by undertaking the odd

ferrying trip. In the latter part of the year Battle and some other pilots were detailed to collect Bristol Fighters from Weston-on-the-Green and fly them to Kenley, near Croydon. A few days later six pilots set off to repeat the exercise, but this time things went awry and most of the aircraft temporarily ended up at Northolt. This story is mentioned merely to illustrate the point that there were evidently a lot of F.2Bs at

Weston-on-the-Green at this time. It seems that a number were eventually sold off as surplus.

The relics comprised six uncovered wire-braced F.2B fuselage frames which were purchased in 1919, along with other components, including tailplane parts, by a wheelwright named Mr Boddington, who used them as trusses to support the roof of his nearby barn at Weston-on-the-Green.

Taken by the late John Bagley on 21 August 1950, this rare shot shows D8096 at Old Warden shortly after acquisition and before it went to Bristol's for restoration. The aircraft was purchased at a disposal sale in 1933/34 by Capt. C.P.B Ogilvie and languished in his Primrose Garage at Watford, its civil conversion never being carried out. It can be seen that its pre-war civil registration, G-AEPH, was never applied, and that it retained its Mk.IV fin and **rudder.** *(Philip Jarrett)*

Left: **Bristol test pilot A.J. Pegg aloft in D8096 after its restoration to flying condition. The first post-restoration test flight took place on 14 February 1951.** *(Bristol)*

to the Science Museum from 1923 to 1931. It returned to the Imperial War Museum at Lambeth in London in 1936, where it was displayed until it was moved to Duxford in March 1984.

D8096 is maintained in airworthy condition and flown on suitable occasions by the Shuttleworth Trust at Old Warden, Bedfordshire, its civil registration (which it has never carried) being **G-AEPH**. When the collection acquired it in 1950 it retained its J-Type configuration, but was restored to its earlier form.

Following its complete refurbishment during 2019–2020, the Shuttleworth Bristol F.2B has been finished to represent B1162, flown by Sgt Ernest John Elton DCM, MM of 22 Sqn, the RFC's most successful NCO pilot, who in a combat on 29 March 1918 destroyed three enemy aircraft. In the space of 32 days Elton and his crewmen amassed a tally of 14 destroyed plus two out of control; ten with the front gun and six with the rear gun.

Above: **In more recent years D8096 has had its interwar aluminium and grey finish replaced by a First World War PC10 and battleship-grey scheme.** *(Philip Jarrett)*

Initially, the barn doors were fashioned from F.2B wing panels, but these were replaced in 1962. No clues as to the individual identities of the fuselage frames could be found.

Around 1965 four of the frames were recovered for the RAF Museum and stored first at No.71 MU at Bicester and then at RAF Henlow. Two of these were accessioned by the museum and then disposed of in 1988 in exchange for Lockheed Hudson turret components. At least one fuselage went to an Australian dealer via Skysport Engineering, and this ended up as **D8084**

with Sir Peter Jackson in New Zealand. In late 1972 another fuselage frame was restored by technicians at Henlow for display at the RAF Museum at Hendon in a 'hangar workshop' setting, eventually becoming BAPC.165 (see below).

E2581, belonging to the Imperial War Museum, is displayed at its Duxford Airfield site. Built by the British & Colonial Aeroplane Co in September 1918, it went to 39 (HD) Sqn at North Weald, Essex. In March 1921 it was transferred to the Imperial War Museum, and it was on loan

BAPC.165, incorporating one of six fuselage frames recovered from Weston-on-the-Green, is currently displayed in the RAF Museum at Hendon. In 1979 this frame was removed and transferred to Cardington for rebuilding, much of the fuselage framework being replaced in the process. By the autumn of 1981 reconstruction of a complete F.2B was under way, and a replica Falcon engine incorporating original cylinders, magnetos and exhaust manifolds was also in production. The engine, along with a replica radiator, was installed in the fuselage. The Shuttleworth Collection provided an original tailplane and an original lower starboard wing panel; the other three wing panels came from a batch of five panels and six wing spars which the RAF Museum had acquired in 1971 from the factory of Thomas Thompson & Co Ltd of Carlow, Eire, where they had been built under subcontract in 1918 but were never

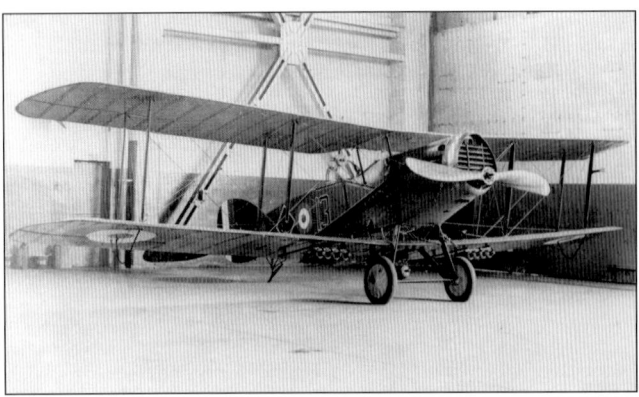

The Imperial War Museum officially received its F.2B, E2581, in December 1922. During the First World War the aircraft had served with 39 Home Defence Sqn at Hounslow. In 1953 it was rebuilt for the museum by No.58 MU at RAF Honington, where these pictures were taken. *(via Philip Jarrett)*

Above: **For many years E2581 was suspended in the Imperial War Museum at Lambeth in London, as seen here. In 1984 it was re-covered by Skysport Engineering, and it is now displayed in the museum's site at Duxford Airfield, Cambridge.** *(via Philip Jarrett)*

delivered. During the work at Cardington the original spars were retained but all the ribs were replaced. The fuselage is now mostly of new wood but has the original metal engine bearers and fittings. The propeller and machine guns came from the museum's stock, and two original wheels were purchased. Final assembly took place in 1986, the aircraft being only half covered, enabling the aircraft's structure to be displayed. It went on display at Hendon in July 1986 and has been there ever since, apart from a brief period at RAF Marham in 1993 during the celebrations for the RAF's 75th Anniversary. It is marked as **E2466**, an aircraft flown from Maisonelle by Capt W.F.J. Harvey and Capt D.E. Waight of 22 Sqn during the First World War, Harvey being 'B' Flight Commander.

Registration **G-ACAA** was reissued on 25 October 1991 for a Skysport rebuild. Incorporating an ex-RAF Museum fuselage, c/n 7434, built in 1917 as **F4516**, plus ex-

Right: **The RAF Museum's Bristol Fighter, 'E2466', completed in 1986, is a reproduction incorporating original components including a fuselage frame and wings. The engine is an 'external replica'. While the fuselage and wings have been covered on the port side (as shown in the upper photo,** *via Philip Jarrett***), they are uncovered on the starboard side to reveal the type's internal details.** *(Mark Tuffield)*

RAF Museum struts, seat, and wing and tail components. it was first flown in the summer of 2006 by The Fighter Collection, founded by Stephen Grey, marked as **D8084**, and has since been sold to New Zealand film director Peter Jackson at Omaka, New Zealand. It flies from Hood Aerodrome, In Masterton, New Zealand. Jackson already owned a Ranger-powered replica F.2B and had another under restoration.

The Aviation Heritage Centre, In Omaka, New Zealand, holds a second, original fuselage.

Another restoration/rebuild was **G-AANM** (**BAPC.166**), which belonged to Guy Black's Aero Vintage Ltd at St Leonards-on-Sea, Sussex. It was based upon a 'very derelict' fuselage frame and various components from Falcon-engined **D7889**, which Guy purchased from Neville Franklin (one of the original founders of the Newark Air Museum) in the late 1980s, along with the 'even worse' remains of an Hispano-engined F.2B. In addition to what remained of D7889's fuselage and wing structures, there were its original cowlings, seat,

tanks and much more, the aircraft's original identity being found stencilled on the cowlings. In 1982 an exchange was agreed with the Shuttleworth Collection whereby a huge quantity of original F.2B parts were acquired, including an ex-Weston-on-the-Green fuselage, a set of the original wings from Shuttleworth's D8096, struts, and a complete empennage, all in amazing condition. Although the wings and tail surfaces were still fabric-covered, the uncovered fuselage was more degraded, but it came with a large quantity of unused original spare parts. In addition, Guy purchased another Weston-on-the-Green fuselage to enable the Hispano-engined F.2B to be completed as a static exhibit, now displayed in the Musée Royal de l'Armée in Brussels (see below). The search then continued for more parts and information and a Falcon engine, and eventually a damaged Falcon was acquired from the Musée Royal de l'Armée in Brussels in exchange for a Gnome rotary engine and a supercharged Rolls-Royce Kestrel.

Skysport Engineering, near Sandy in Bedfordshire, was tasked with restoring the airframe components, while Aero Vintage restored the sheet metal items and the

radiator, and the wings were restored by the Shuttleworth Collection. It proved possible to use just about all the metal components apart from the cowlings, which were too corroded, although their brass latches were reused. The cowlings were kept, however, because they contained the evidence of the airframe's identity. The wings were in perfect condition, but most of the critical wooden joints were re-glued. In 1999 the airframe restoration was completed, but it took another seven years for the damaged Falcon III engine to be restored by Aero Vintage (the bottom end being done by Vintec). It was then installed by Skysport Engineering. The aircraft first flew on 25 May 2006, piloted by Stuart Goldspink. Several air tests were made at Henlow, after which it was flown to Duxford. Early in December 2006 D7889 went to the Canadian Aviation and Space Museum at Rockcliffe, Ontario, in exchange for Heinkel He 162 Wk Nr 120076 (Air Min 59, RAF serial VH523) and a collection of aero engines, including the Siddeley Puma that now powers D.H.9 D8894.

The Musée Royal de l'Armée, Brussels, Belgium, has a Hispano-engined reconstruction based on a Weston-on-the-Green fuselage frame (see the history of D7889, above). It was built by Skysport Engineering at Hatch for Aero Vintage, as BAPC.19, then exchanged in June 1989 for a Spitfire Mk.IX.

In September 2014 a Bristol F.2B with a 300hp Hispano-Suiza engine went on temporary display for several months in the Polish Aviation Museum at Kraków. This aircraft had been rebuilt by Skysport and The Vintage Aviator Ltd in New Zealand for Rob Greinert, incorporating some 60 per cent of original parts. For this display it was painted to represent aircraft **20.48** (**H1279**) of 1 Eskadra Wywiadowcza at the time of the Polish-Bolshevik War. It then went to Sydney, Australia.

An original fuselage, said to be that of **D2751** and probably one of the Weston-on-the-Green fuselage frames, was purchased from one Roger Freeman and is being rebuilt into a flyable aircraft for the Ross Walton Family Collection at Bardstown, Kentucky, in the USA. It will have a 1921 Wright-built 300hp Hispano and 'original instruments and hardware'. An authentic set of wings has been built, incorporating fittings provided by The Vintage Aviator Ltd of New Zealand. The fuselage and completed wings were

Bristol F.2B replica (HR2C) N29HC, seen here on display at Oshkosh in the USA, is now with the New Zealand Warbirds Association in New Zealand. *(J.M Gradidge)*

turned over to Fred Murrin, who is seeing the project through to completion, using original drawings. The aircraft is to be finished to represent the F.2B flown by American pilot Capt George Bulmer of 22 Sqn RFC.

The Aerospace Bristol museum has purchased an 'original' Bristol Fighter in the USA, where it is being rebuilt. At the time of writing its wings, tailplane and fin sections were in Andy Crumpholt's home in Gardner, Massachusetts, while the fuselage (one of those rescued from Weston-on-the Green and subsequently sold to an American), and fittings were at Lawrence Airport, north of Boston. Many original components are included. The engine bearers and certain other parts are to be made in the UK.

Reproductions
F.2Bs for the film *A High Road to China*
In the late 1970s ambitious plans were made in the USA to shoot a film based on the 1977 novel *A High Road to China* by Australian author Jon Cleary, which featured three war-surplus Bristol Fighters. As the film was to be shot in two different locations, no fewer than six airworthy F.2B reproductions ('HR2Cs') were required, plus another one or two static lookalikes for destruction or studio filming. The six flyers were to be made by Vernon Ohmert of Ypsilanti, Michigan, for production company Golden Harvest of Hong Kong at a cost of some $750,000. They had steel-tube fuselage frames, and, as no Rolls-Royce Falcons were available, they were powered

This study of D8084 on display in a partly completed state provides a good view of the engine bearers, radiator, oil tank, firewall and the aerofoil section of the wings' centre-section panels. *(via Philip Jarrett)*

by 200hp Fairchild Ranger six-cylinder in-line engines, converted to run upright. Production of the Bristols was begun in 1979, and in 1980 several were trucked from Ann Arbor, Michigan, to Palomar Airport in California, where they were to be modified, reassembled and flight-tested. Unfortunately, the plans went awry and construction of the F.2Bs was stopped, a lower-budget version of the film being shot using 'restyled' Stampe S.V.4s. It was released in 1983. Meanwhile, one of the four completed airworthy reproduction F.2Bs had featured the 1981 movie *Death Hunt*, with its fuselage and tail painted brick red, blue-grey cowlings and cream wings with roundels.

Eventually one of the F.2Bs, N36HC, went on display at the Planes of Fame Museum at Valle, Arizona. A second one, *sans* engine, is suspended from the roof of the other Planes of Fame Museum at Chino, California. This one, referred to as the 'Brown Bristol', is believed to be made up one of the two non-airworthy airframe sets combined with some good airworthy airframe components, such as struts and flying wires.

Five of the F.2Bs, however, were stored in shipping containers at Chino in the early 1980s, until they were acquired in 2017 by American vintage aircraft operator Chris Prevost and Graham Orphan of Omaka, New Zealand, editor of *Classic Wings* magazine. Three of them had been flown previously, but the other two were uncompleted. Apart from VO.4 (N47HC), they were missing all of the lower centre-

On 15 July 2006, during a Shuttleworth Collection evening display at Old Warden, enthusiasts were treated to the rare sight of no fewer than three Bristol Fighters flying in formation. This photograph, taken on that occasion, shows, front to rear: D8084/G-ACAA, then with The Fighter Collection; Shuttleworth's own D8096/G-AEPH; and D7889/G-AANM, at that time belonging to Guy Black's Aero Vintage but soon to depart for New Zealand. *(Richard Paver)*

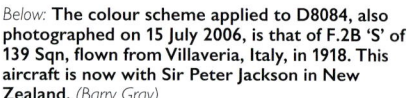

Above: **A three-quarter port side view of D7889 at Old Warden on 15 July 2006. Its twenty-year restoration by the Historic Aircraft Collection and Skysport had culminated in a first flight on 25 May that year. Its Falcon engine is the oldest flying Rolls-Royce aero engine in the world.** *(Barry Gray)*

Left: **The Shuttleworth Collection's own F.2B, D8096, which had served in India during the interwar era, at Old Warden on 15 July 2006.** *(Barry Gray)*

Below: **The colour scheme applied to D8084, also photographed on 15 July 2006, is that of F.2B 'S' of 139 Sqn, flown from Villaveria, Italy, in 1918. This aircraft is now with Sir Peter Jackson in New Zealand.** *(Barry Gray)*

section struts and almost all of the upper centre-section struts, so a programme was undertaken to remanufacture these as a batch production to support all of the Bristols. In addition, on each aircraft the undercarriage incorporated Ford Model 'A' wheels as supplied for the movie role, but only VO.4 came with wheel hubs. Several components, such as flying wires, anything at all in the rear cockpit including seat bases, etc., propeller hubs, interplane struts, etc. were also absent from the storage location, but every effort is being made to ensure that all of the Bristols go to new homes fully equipped with the key items they need to be made complete and airworthy.

Individual histories
C/n VO.1 N29HC *Eva*, ZK-PRK
The first of the HR2C Bristols, it differed very slightly from the rest, having some additional details in some areas. Last flown during the early 1980s, it was sold to the NZ Warbirds Association, and has undergone a major overhaul and significant upgrade by JEM Aviation (to include radio, intercom, transponder, brakes etc). The recommissioning of this machine turned into more of a restoration, and the resultant aircraft is a very high quality reproduction. It has been completed to represent the aircraft flown by Kiwi First World War ace Sir Keith Park, and has lost its *Eva* name to become simply C814. It flew again on 17 November 2019 from Omaka Airfield, powered by a 200 h.p. Ranger engine and piloted by Ryan Southam for the 15min test flight. Ryan reported that the aircraft handled well; slow and heavy, but enjoyable. Owned by the NZ Warbirds Association, based at Ardmore, Auckland, the aircraft was flown up to join the Association by Ryan on 27 February 2020.

C/n VO.2 N34HC *Huntress*
This aircraft is the best known of the group, having appeared in the 1981 movie *Death Hunt*, in which it operated on skis in some memorable cinematic footage. Now located at Omaka, New Zealand, this aircraft requires assembly and some remedial work, but is complete and in sound condition. It is being retained as a 'keeper' by *Classic Wings*, to be based permanently at the historic Omaka Airfield, in recognition of the fact that the first aircraft to alight on this hallowed ground was a Brisfit in 1928.

C/n VO.3 N36HC
In the Planes of Fame Museum at Valle, Arizona.

C/n VO.4 N47HC
Graham Orphan's aircraft. This is complete as a basic flyable aircraft with everything apart from the rear gunner's Scarff ring. It has been reassembled and is being prepared to fly again at his private base, Schellville

Although the new F.2B at the Aerospace Bristol museum is not a reproduction in the true sense of the word, it still looks very convincing. It bears the identity and markings of A7288 of 11 Sqn. *(Aerospace Bristol)*

The replica Hispano-engined F.2B in the Museo del Aire at Cuatro Vientos, Madrid, Spain. *(Ken Smy via SAAF Museum)*

One of the ex-*A High Road to China* F.2B replicas, N36HC, on display in the Planes of Fame Museum (Arizona Branch) at Valle Airport in April 2013. *(Barry Dowsett)*

Bristol F.2B reproduction ZK-PRK airborne with Ryan Southam at the controls during an air-to-air photographic sortie for *Classic Wings* magazine. *Classic Wings*' own 450hp Stearman, flown by Aaron Patchett, served as the camera ship. *(Gavin Conroy via Graham Orphan)*

Airport, near Sonoma, northern California, USA. The engine has been started and runs beautifully. The aircraft has some 30hr total time since new and since the engine was overhauled and 'uprighted'. In July 2019 it was again for sale, with the strongest interest coming from Australia.

C/n VO.5 N65HC
This aircraft is structurally complete. It includes four wings and two centre-sections complete and covered. It includes a full set of tail surfaces, complete and covered and including stainless-steel bracing wires. The fuselage has been structurally completed and covered, the covering incorporating removable lace-up side-panels as per the original F.2Bs. Upper and lower cabane struts are included to mount the centre-sections. The undercarriage structure is included, along with wheels and tyres (Ford Model A), as well as a partly complete tailskid assembly.

The project includes cockpit controls and an instrument panel with most instruments present, and the engine mount and 200hp Ranger engine. The engine was overhauled and 'uprighted' by H&S Aircraft in the USA in the late 1970s but, alas, no logbooks have survived with the aircraft. Primary and secondary fuel tanks are included. Although it has the distinctive nose cowling with louvred radiator, a functioning radiator is not required for the air-cooled Ranger. A full set of exhaust pipes (functional port side, decorative starboard side) is included in the package. The aircraft still requires interplane struts, flying and landing wires, some external wing fittings, cables, propeller and hub.

At the time of writing, this aircraft remained 'in stock' with *Classic Wings* magazine/CAS Ltd. There is no urgent imperative to sell it, and, ideally, the present owners would like to see it remain at Omaka and return to service there, perhaps as a syndicate-owned machine.

C/n VO.6 N75HC
This aircraft is structurally complete. It includes four wings and two centre-sections,

complete and covered. There is a full set of tail surfaces, complete and covered and including stainless-steel bracing wires. The fuselage has been structurally completed and covered, the covering incorporating removable laced-up side panels as per original F2Bs. Cabane struts, upper and lower, are included to mount the centre-sections. The undercarriage structure is also included, along with Ford Model A wheels and tyres, plus a partly complete tailskid assembly. In most ways it is identical to c/n VO.5, above.

This aircraft was sold to Philip Cooper of Queensland, Australia, in the second half of 2017. He negotiated a price without engine, determining that he would prefer to adapt a de Havilland Gipsy Queen for his aircraft. He has moved the aeroplane to Luskintyre Aircraft Restorations of Sydney, New South Wales for completion.

Plus one non-airworthy structure in the Planes of Fame Museum at Chino, California, and another set of non-airworthy components now in New Zealand, possibly to be made into a static exhibit for the Omaka Aviation Heritage Centre.

VH-UDR Built originally as a Bristol Tourer for the Australian film *A Thousand Skies*. Extant as static exhibit with Flypast Museum of Australian Army Flying, Oakey, Queensland, marked 'C4623' to represent an aircraft flown by the 1st Squadron, Australian Flying Corps (q.v.).

VH-IIZ, ex-N624 and ZK-JNU Built between 1986 and 1993 at Memphis, Tennessee, USA, by Ed Storo, powered by a 200hp Ranger 440-5 engine, registered **N624** and painted in RAF colours marked '**J7624**'. To Sir Peter Jackson in New Zealand May 2002 as **ZK-JNU**, painted in RFC colours as '**B1112**', with 22 Sqn markings and coded 'F'. In 2015 it was acquired by The Australian Vintage Aviation Society (TAVAS) at Caboolture in Queensland. Registered **VH-IIZ** in the name of Donal John McDonald on 19 June 2015, it now flies in the colours and markings of **B1229**, the aircraft flown by

Capt Ross McPherson Smith of 1 Sqn AFC in Egypt.

The Museo del Aire, Cuatro Vientos, Madrid, Spain, has a replica marked as '**B21**'.

The new Aerospace Bristol museum has on display a very presentable static 'lookalike' Bristol Fighter built by Rolls-Royce and Airbus apprentices using original plans and a 'mix of traditional and modern materials and methods', in celebration of 100 years of aircraft manufacture at Filton Bristol, where the original fighters were designed and built. It is finished to represent **A7288** of 11 Sqn, flown by Capt A.E. McKeever.

Tailpiece
The Shuttleworth Collection also has the rudder from F.2B Mk.III J6790/ G-ACCG, and this was displayed in one of the Old Warden hangars at the time of writing.

The rudder of F.2B Mk.III DC J6790 at Old Warden in July 2019. This must have been replaced by another rudder when the aeroplane went on to the civil register as G-ACCG, as the rudder then fitted was plain-doped. *(Philip Jarrett)*

A complete skeletal Bristol F.2B Fighter airframe, probably at Filton, with a Bristol Scout fuselage in the background on the right. *(Philip Jarrett)*

Appendix 11

THE F.2B IN DETAIL

Bristol Fighters under construction at Filton, with F4712 prominent. This machine was one of a batch of 700 F.2Bs built by the British & Colonial Aeroplane Company under Contract No.35A/779/C658 dated 5 June 1918. In the 1920s it was reconditioned to J Type. *(Bristol)*

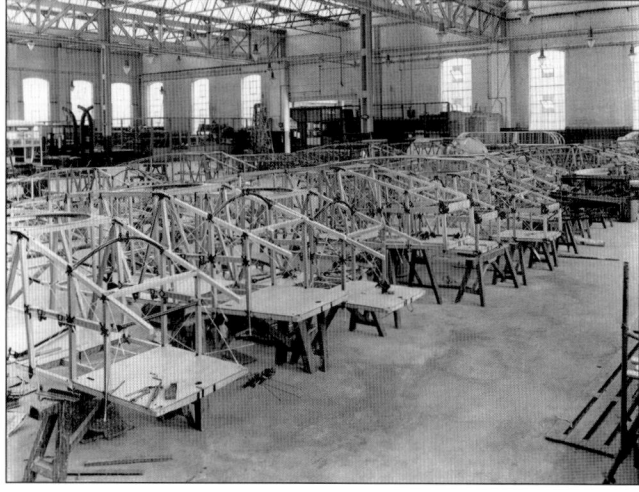

Factory-fresh fuselages at Filton. *(Bristol)*

Bristol Fighter fuselages in various stages of assembly at Filton in 1918. Visible serial numbers are F4890-F4899, F4911 and F4912. *(Bristol)*

The control cables and tail bracing wires of F.2B H907, a Gloster-built aircraft which probably had an Arab engine. *(Philip Jarrett)*

The fuselage frame of an F.2B, complete with engine bearers. *(Philip Jarrett)*

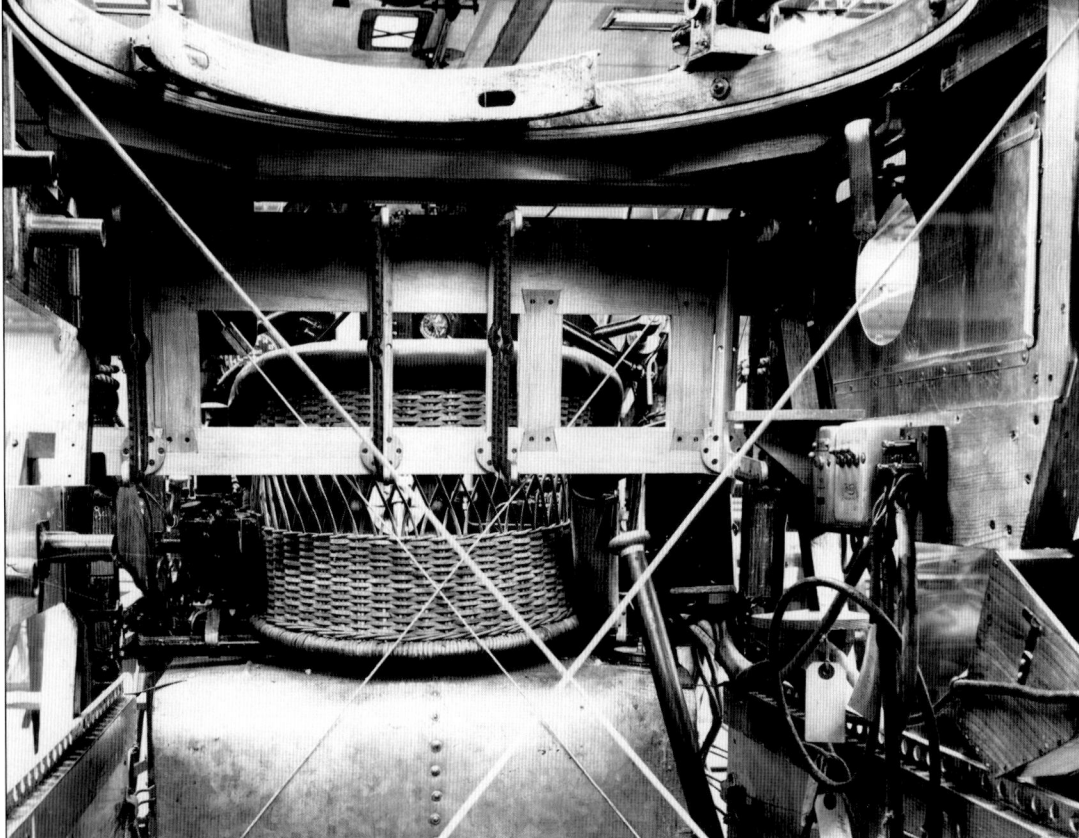

Left: The view inside an F.2B fuselage, looking forward from the rear cockpit. On the right in the foreground can be seen the emergency control column in the gunner's cockpit. When not in use this was normally carried in a pair of spring-steel clips at the starboard side of the floor. The 19gal fuel tank beneath the wicker pilot's seat is also well shown.

The forward fuselage of an Hispano-engined F.2B, 1918. Note the wicker pilot's seat. *(Philip Jarrett)*

The upper cockpit area of an Hispano-engined F.2B, 1918, showing the mounting for the Vickers gun at the top and the fuel tank selector switch at the bottom. *(Philip Jarrett)*

This F.2B displays some typical interwar features of the type. There is a semi-retractable electrical generator in the fuselage side beneath the gunner's Scarff ring. A High Altitude Mk.1A bombsight is just in front it, alongside the pilot's cockpit, and the bomb-sighting gap in the lower wing root is evident. The petrol pump impeller is attached to the starboard front undercarriage leg. Although the fittings to take the pilot's Aldis sight can be seen beneath the upper centre section, the sight has been removed. *(Philip Jarrett)*

The observer/gunner in this F.2B of 48 Sqn in the latter part of 1918 is tending to the downward-pointing Thornton-Pickard camera immediately aft of his cockpit. At his shoulder level on either side are three Lewis gun magazines, and the tubular objects in the rack at his seat level are signal flare cartridges. Just aft of these is the small demolition charge that was to be used to destroy the aeroplane if it was forced down in hostile territory. The aircraft's long exhaust pipes have been cut short. *(C&C)*

The front cockpit of an F.2B Mk.IV. The pilot now has an aluminium bucket seat with a squab. The breech of the Vickers gun protrudes into the cockpit at the top of the instrument panel. A Morse key and the hand air-pressure pump for the fuel system are at the pilot's right hand. *(Philip Jarrett)*

The mid-fuselage section of an Hispano-engined F.2B, 1918, showing the gunner's position. *(Philip Jarrett)*

The uncovered fuselage of an F.2B undergoing overhaul. *(Philip Jarrett)*

The crew area of an F.2B Mk.IV. On the right can be seen the ammunition belt box for the Vickers gun, sandwiched between the front upper 26gal fuel tank and the pilot's instrument panel. The rear fuel tank, holding 19gal, is beneath the pilot's seat. A High Altitude Mk.1A bombsight is attached to the cockpit side, and there is a bomb-sighting gap in the lower starboard wing root. Beside the rear cockpit is the impeller-driven semi-retractable generator to power the electrical services. On some aircraft the generator was non-retractable. *(Philip Jarrett)*

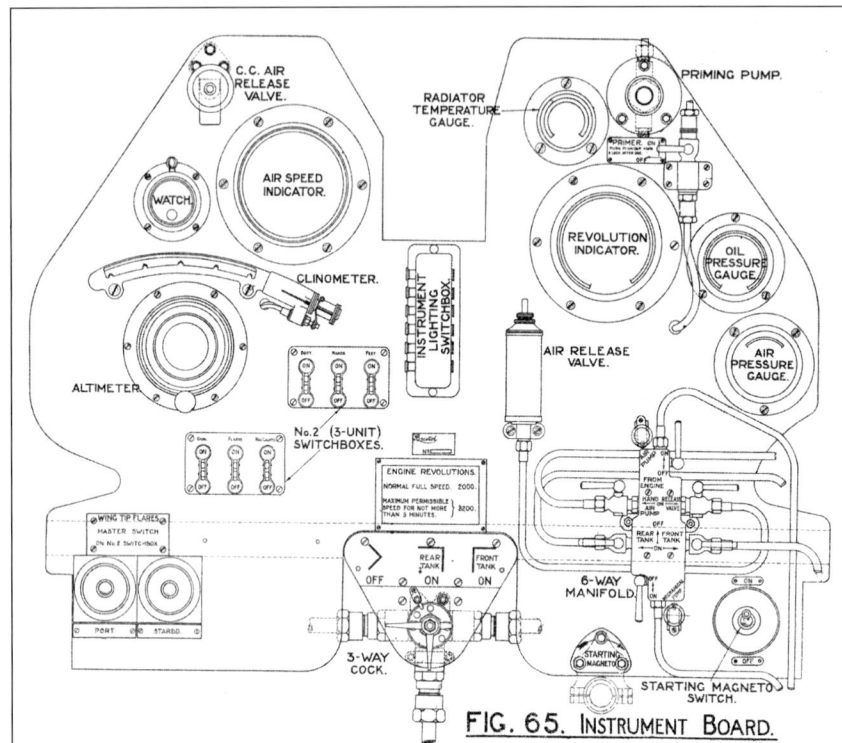

FIG. 65. INSTRUMENT BOARD.

Left: **The instrument arrangement on the board in the Mk.IV cockpit.** *(via Philip Jarrett)*

Below: **The mounting for the auxiliary radiator fitted to F.2B Mk.IVs for tropical use. The front of the aircraft is to the left.**

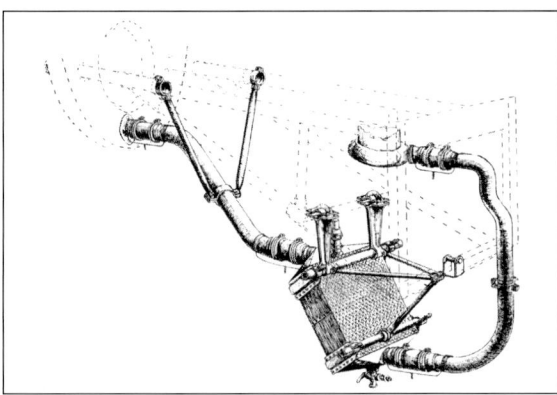

Below: **The auto slots on the upper wingtips of later F.2Bs were attached to the wing leading edge at three points, and moved upward and forward to create the slot. Port and starboard auto slots were interchangeable.** *(Philip Jarrett)*

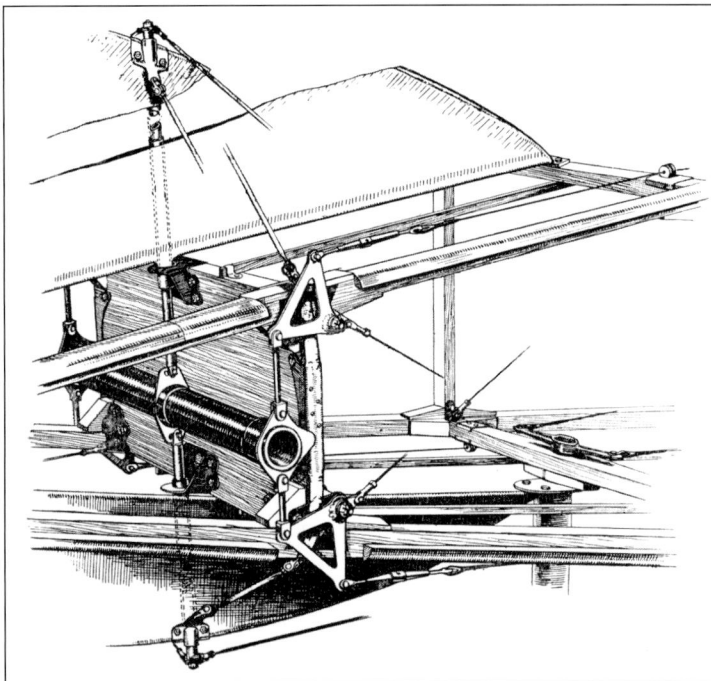

Above: **The tailplane variable-incidence gear was operated from the pilot's cockpit by means of a large lever low on the starboard side of the pilot's seat, which was connected by cables to bell-cranks linked to a central tube to which the tailplanes' front spars were connected. This detail drawing shows the linkages at the rear fuselage.**

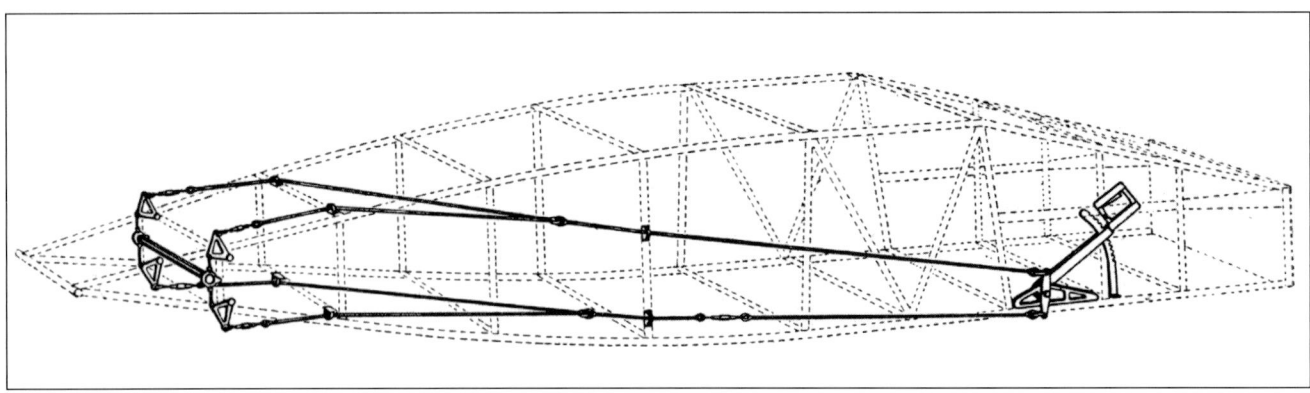

A diagram showing the means of operating the variable-incidence tailplane from the pilot's cockpit.

Engines

A Rolls-Royce Falcon engine awaiting installation in a Bristol Fighter of 5 Sqn in India in the 1920s. *(Philip Jarrett)*

An F.2B's Falcon engine undergoes maintenance in 1918. *(Philip Jarrett)*

The ungeared 300hp Hispano-Suiza engine. *(Philip Jarrett)*

The 200hp Sunbeam Arab I engine. *(Philip Jarrett)*

An F.2B's Falcon engine undergoes a test run in the Middle East in the 1920s. *(Philip Jarrett)*

A 1920's F.2B cockpit, with a white rubber watch holder on the extreme left. It was evidently common practice to have the instrument dials installed out of vertical. *(Philip Jarrett)*

Left: **The cockpit of an F.2B attached to a wartime training unit in the Bournemouth area.** *(Philip Jarrett)*

Above: **The pilot's cockpit of an F.2B in the Middle East in the 1920s.** *(Philip Jarrett)*

A close-up of the radiator for the Sunbeam Arab-engined F.2B. *(Philip Jarrett)*

The forward fuselage and engine installation for an F.2B powered by the 300hp Hispano-Suiza engine

Detail views of the Hispano-engined F.2B rebuild in the Musée Royal de l'Armée et d'Histoire Militaire in Brussels.
(All by Geoffrey Bussey)

Propeller and radiator.

Port interplane struts, with pitot head on outer front strut.

Impeller-driven fuel pump on port front undercarriage leg.

The underside of the engine cowling.

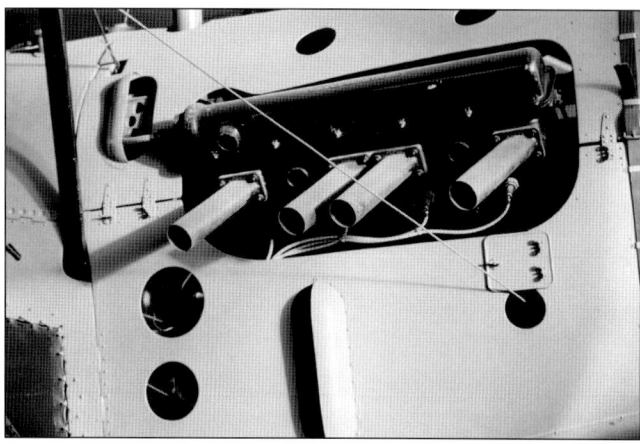

The engine and exhaust stubs, starboard side.

Elevator control lever, port side.

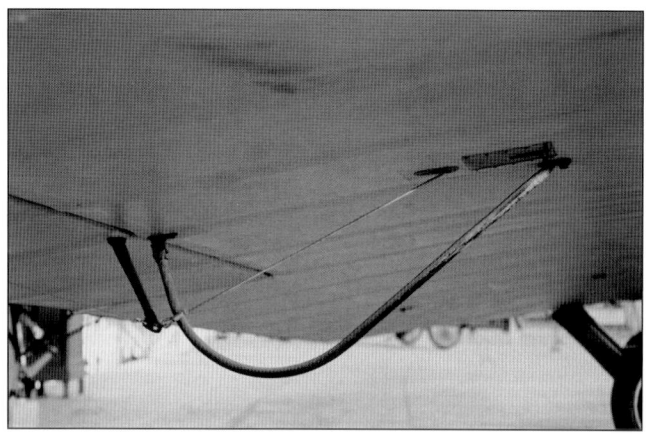

Bamboo wingtip skid and aileron control lever, starboard side.

Struts and bracing at junction of port upper wing panel and upper centre section, and Aldis sight attached to underside of centre section

Gunner's Lewis machine gun with ring-and-bead sights and 97-round ammunition drum, mounted on Scarff ring.

Tailplane and elevator, port side.

Elevator and aileron control cables and foot step, starboard side.

Fin and rudder and tailplane, starboard side.

Pilot's windscreen, compass in centre-section trailing edge, Aldis sight for Vickers gun, and access panel to ammunition belt box.

Tailskid from starboard side.

Main undercarriage wheel and struts, port side.

Two close-up views of the fuselage centre-section and lower wing attachment of the Imperial War Museum's F.2B, E2581, taken when it was displayed in the museum's building in Lambeth, London. *(Philip Jarrett)*

Internal details of the Shuttleworth Collection's F.2B, D8096, taken on 5 May 2019, when the aircraft was in the process of being re-covered.

(All by Philip Jarrett)

The uncovered fuselage and port upper wing panel.

The forward fuselage, port side.

The rear fuselage.

The front cockpit area, starboard side, showing the bucket seat typical of the later marks.

The cockpit area, port side.

In this low view of the front cockpit area, the lever handle of the variable-incidence tailplane gear is visible by the far side of the under-seat fuel tank.

The instrument panel is typical of an F.2B Mk.IV.

The cockpit area, with the engine control levers and rods on the port side.

The port upper wing panel.

Above: **Four studies of the RAF Museum's half-uncovered Bristol Fighter reconstruction, 'E2466', displayed in a rather dark and cluttered corner of the Grahame-White hangar in April 2019.** *(Mark Tuffield)*

The uncovered starboard side of 'E2466'.   An overhead view. This F.2B has the earlier wicker pilot's seat.

Appendix 12

LINE DRAWINGS AND COLOUR PROFILES

**The following series of general-arrangement drawings
are the work of Mick Davis of Cross and Cockade International.**

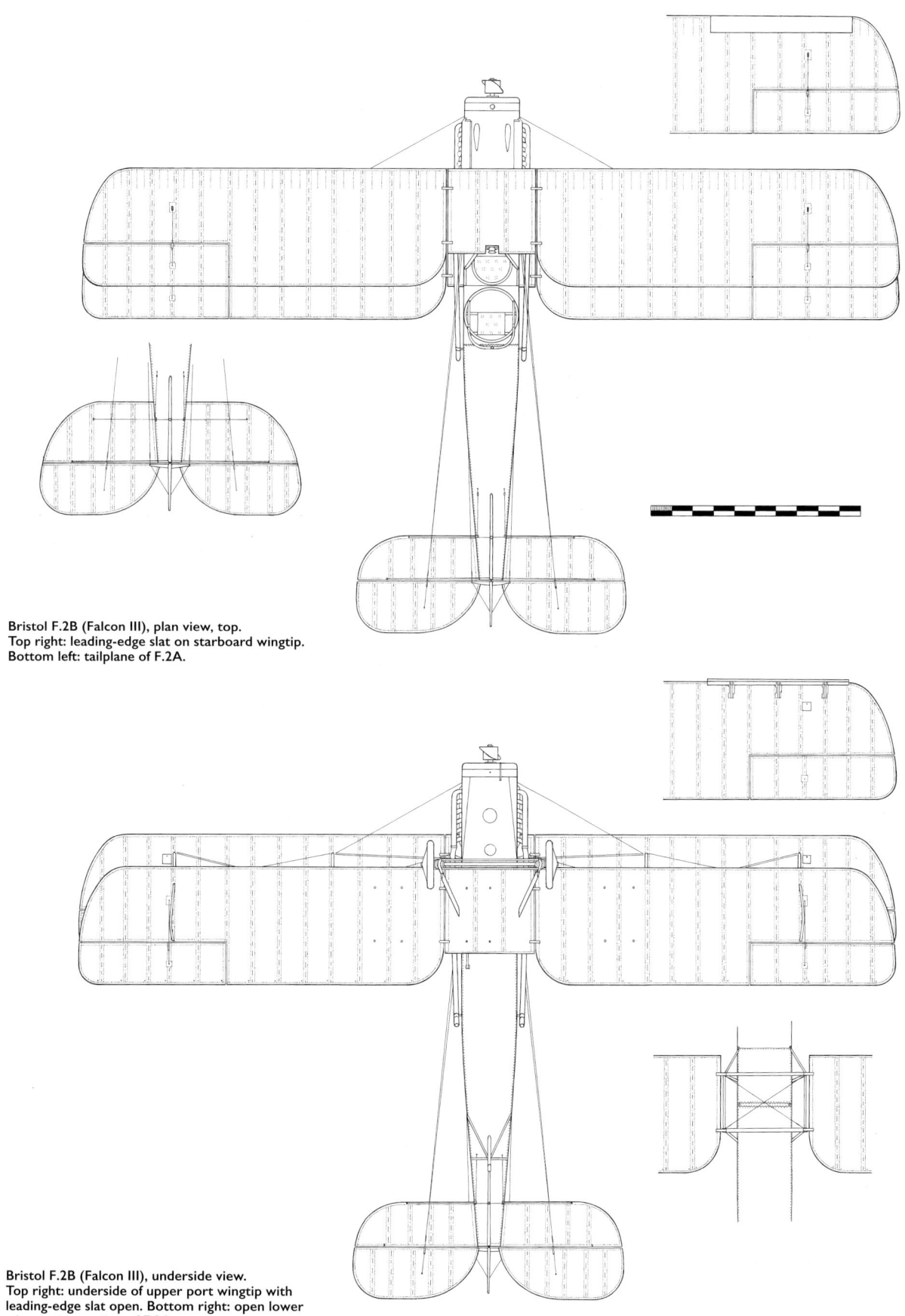

Bristol F.2B (Falcon III), plan view, top.
Top right: leading-edge slat on starboard wingtip.
Bottom left: tailplane of F.2A.

Bristol F.2B (Falcon III), underside view.
Top right: underside of upper port wingtip with
leading-edge slat open. Bottom right: open lower
wing centre-section of F.2A.

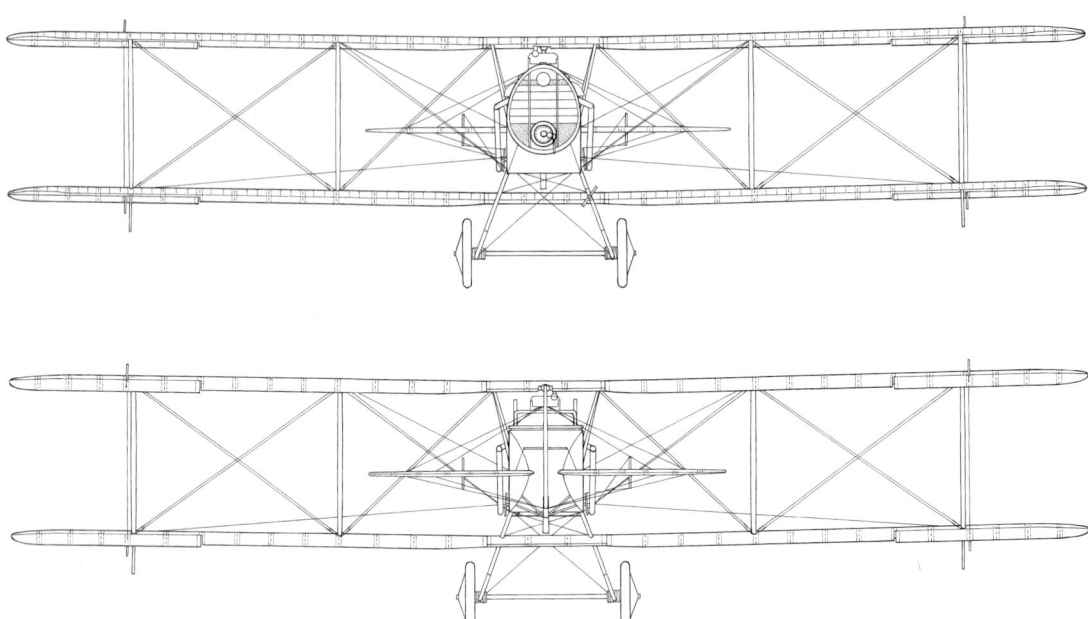

Bristol F.2B (Falcon III), front and rear views.

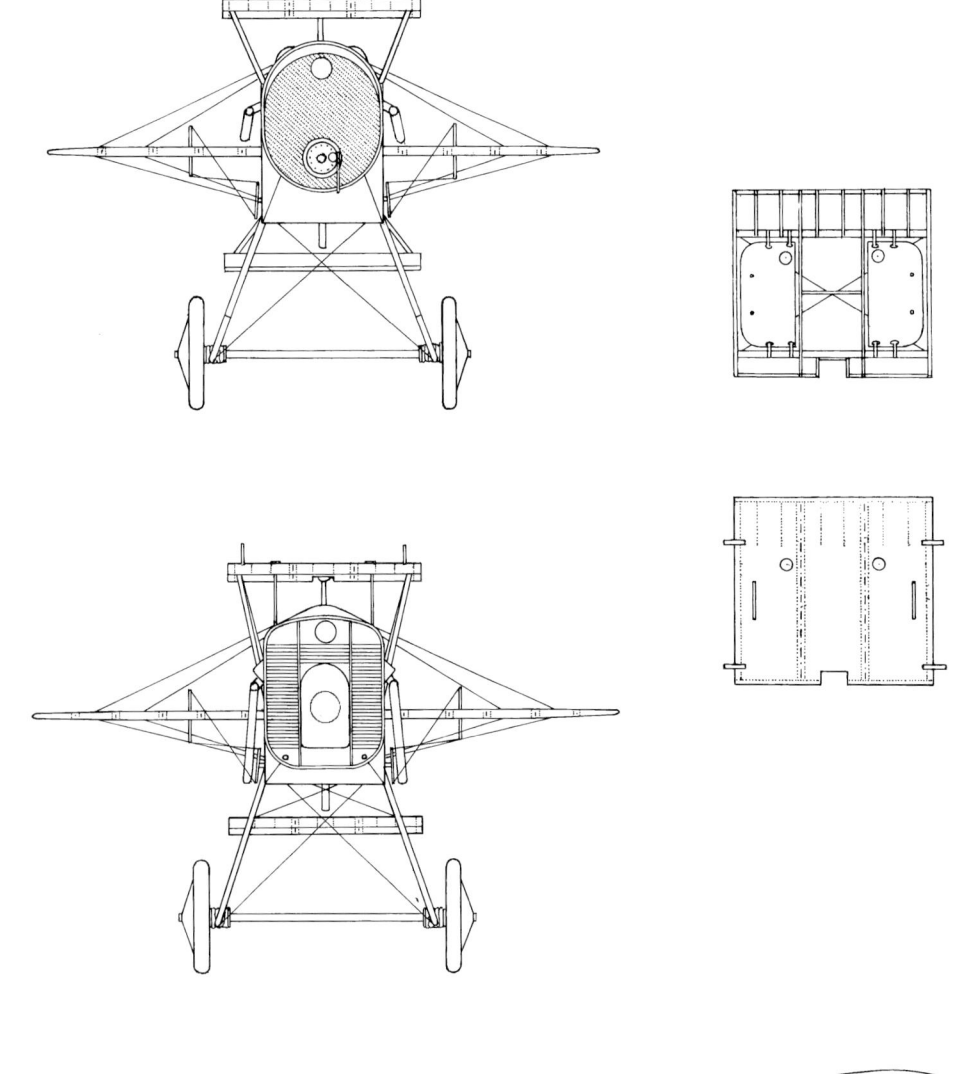

Top left: F.2A front view. Bottom left: F.2B
(Arab) front view. Top right and centre: F.2B
(Arab) upper centre section with gravity tanks.
Bottom right: propeller.

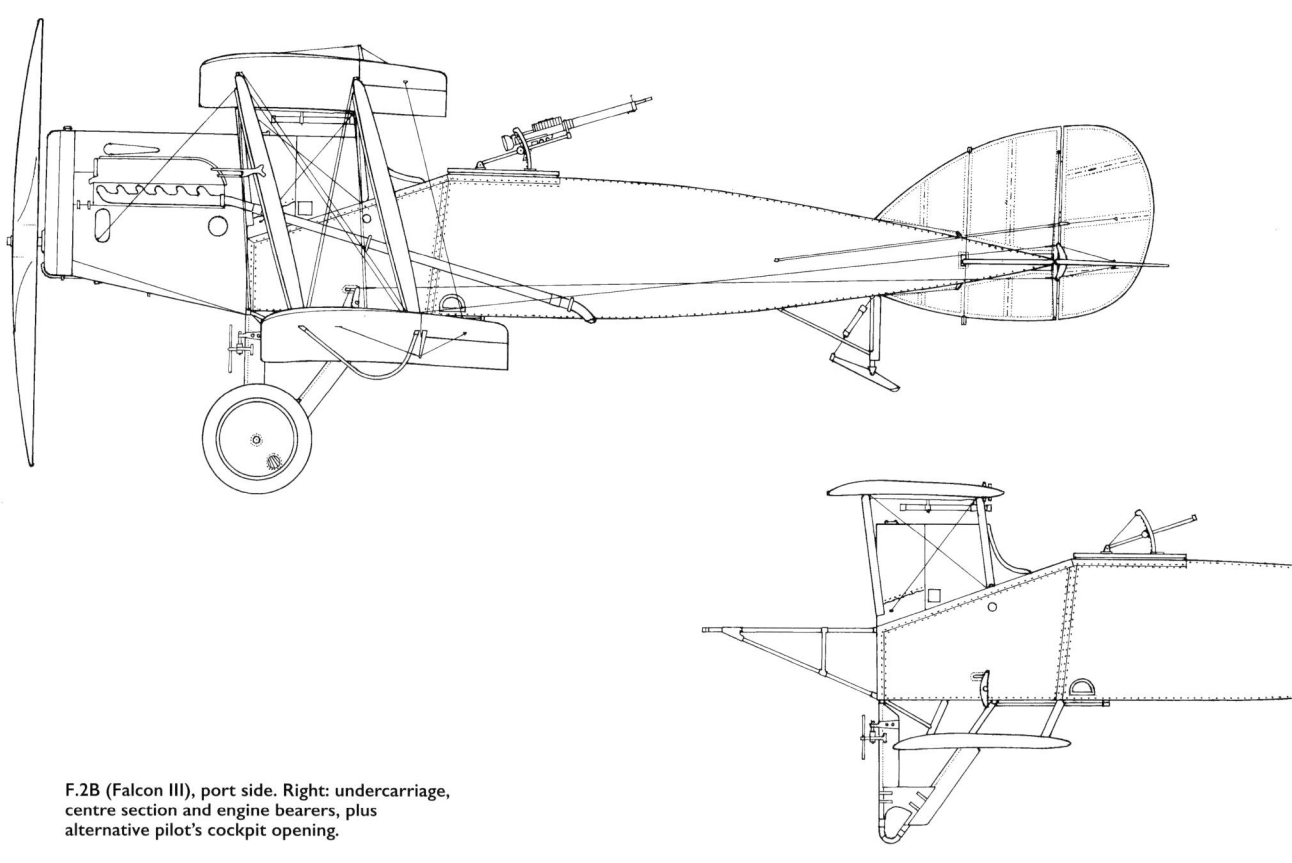

F.2B (Falcon III), port side. Right: undercarriage, centre section and engine bearers, plus alternative pilot's cockpit opening.

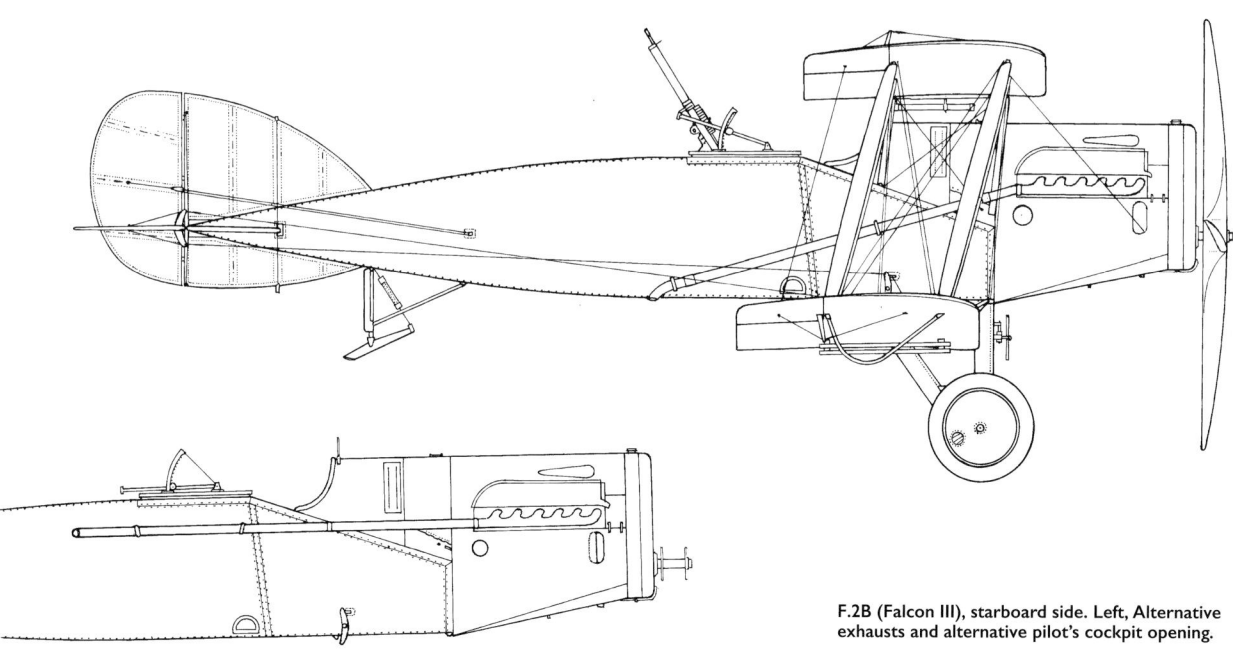

F.2B (Falcon III), starboard side. Left, Alternative exhausts and alternative pilot's cockpit opening.

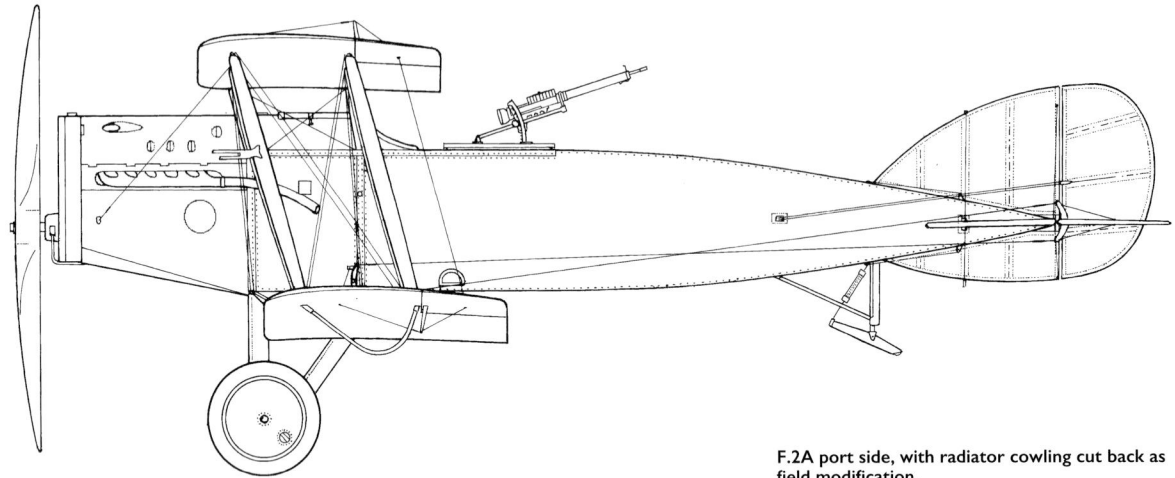

F.2A port side, with radiator cowling cut back as
field modification.

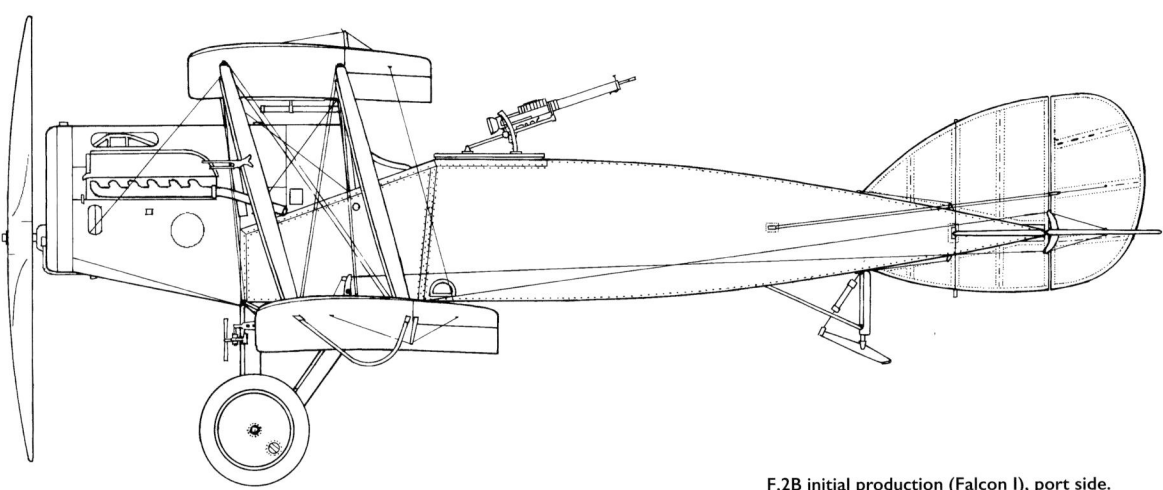

F.2B initial production (Falcon I), port side.

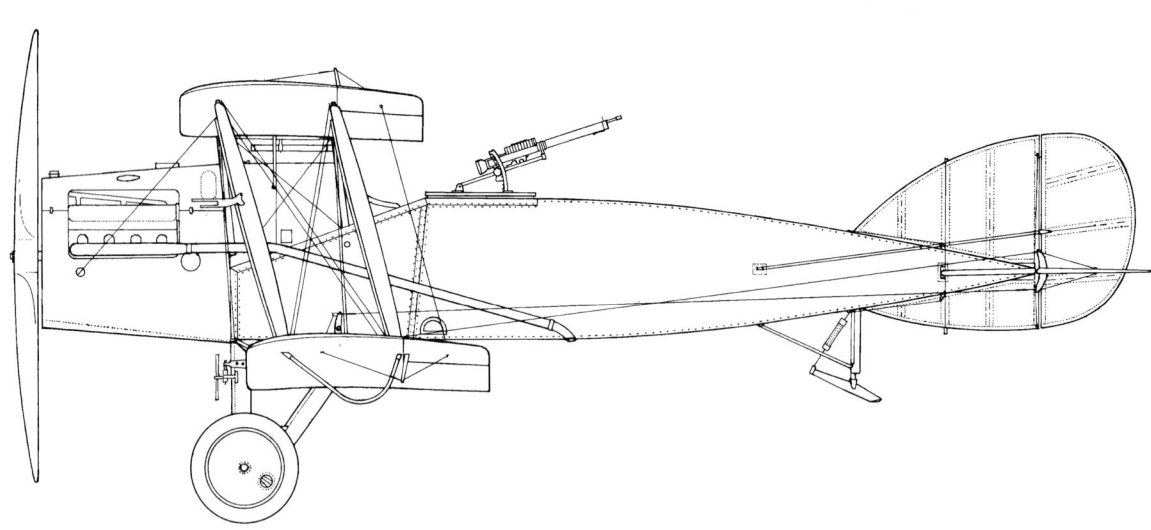

F.2B (Arab), port side.

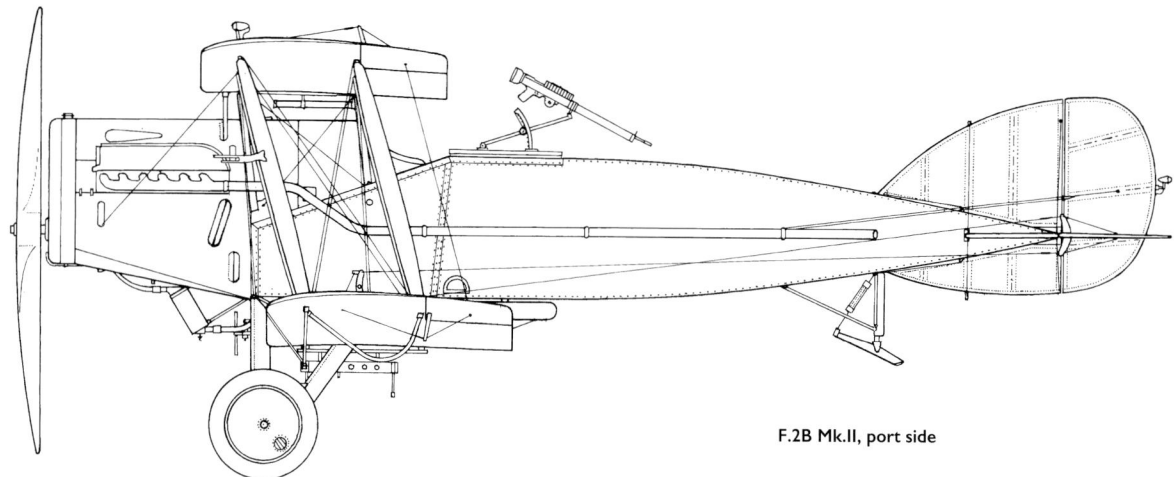

F.2B Mk.II, port side

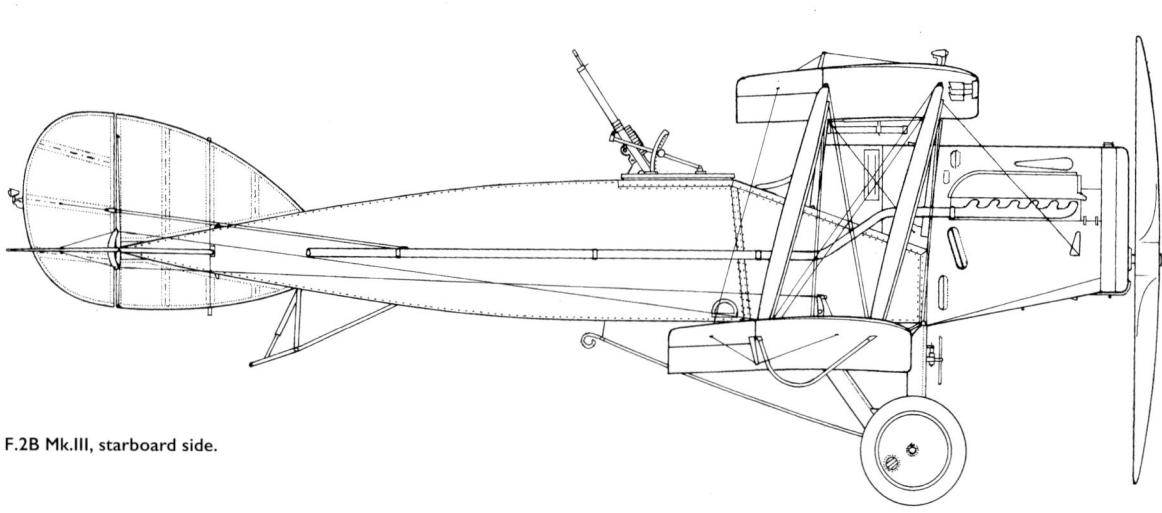

F.2B Mk.III, starboard side.

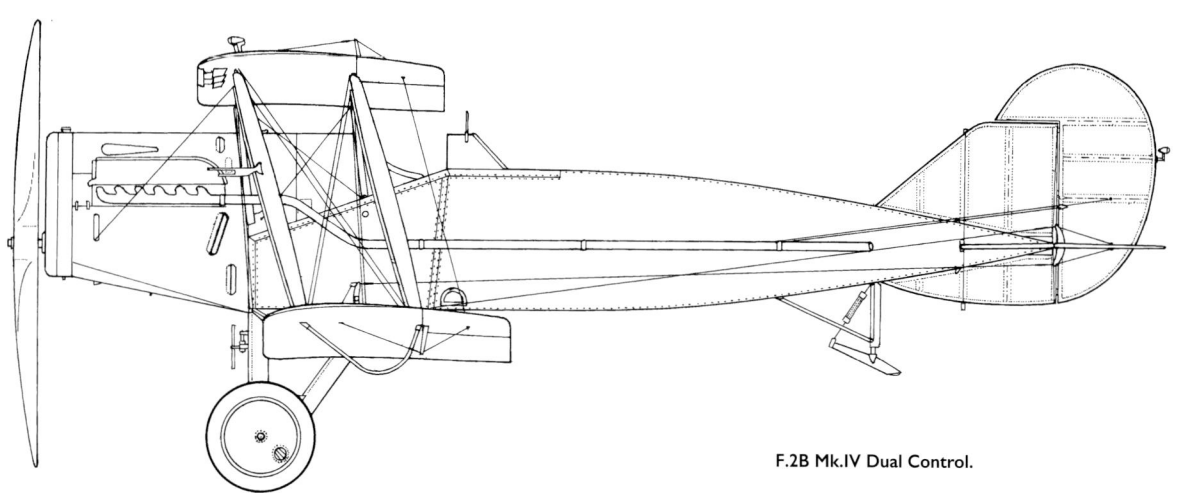

F.2B Mk.IV Dual Control.

Above: This masterly detailed cutaway of a standard Bristol F.2B Fighter was drawn by the late Frank Munger, AMRAeS.

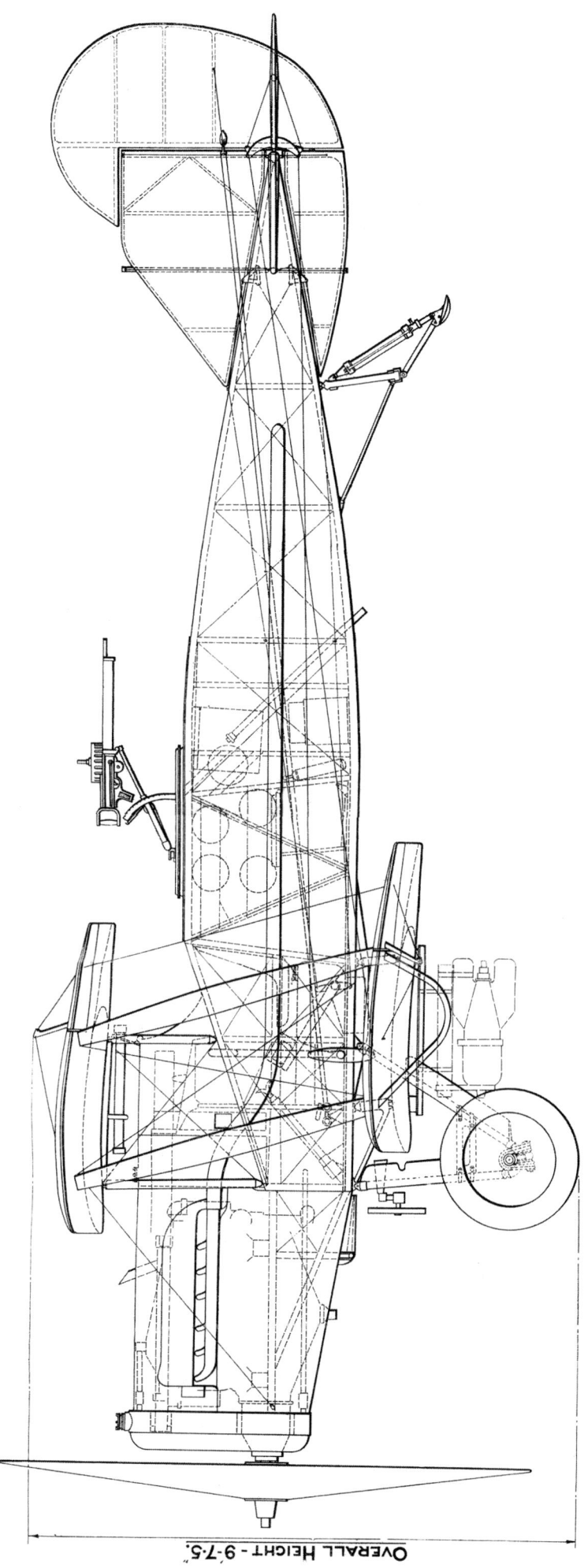

OVERALL HEIGHT – 9'·7·5.˝

Above: **This open side elevation of the Bristol F.2B Mk.IV showing internal details and fittings, is taken from** *Air Ministry Air Publication 866,* **the descriptive handbook for this variant.**

The following colour profiles are the work of Juanita Franzi.

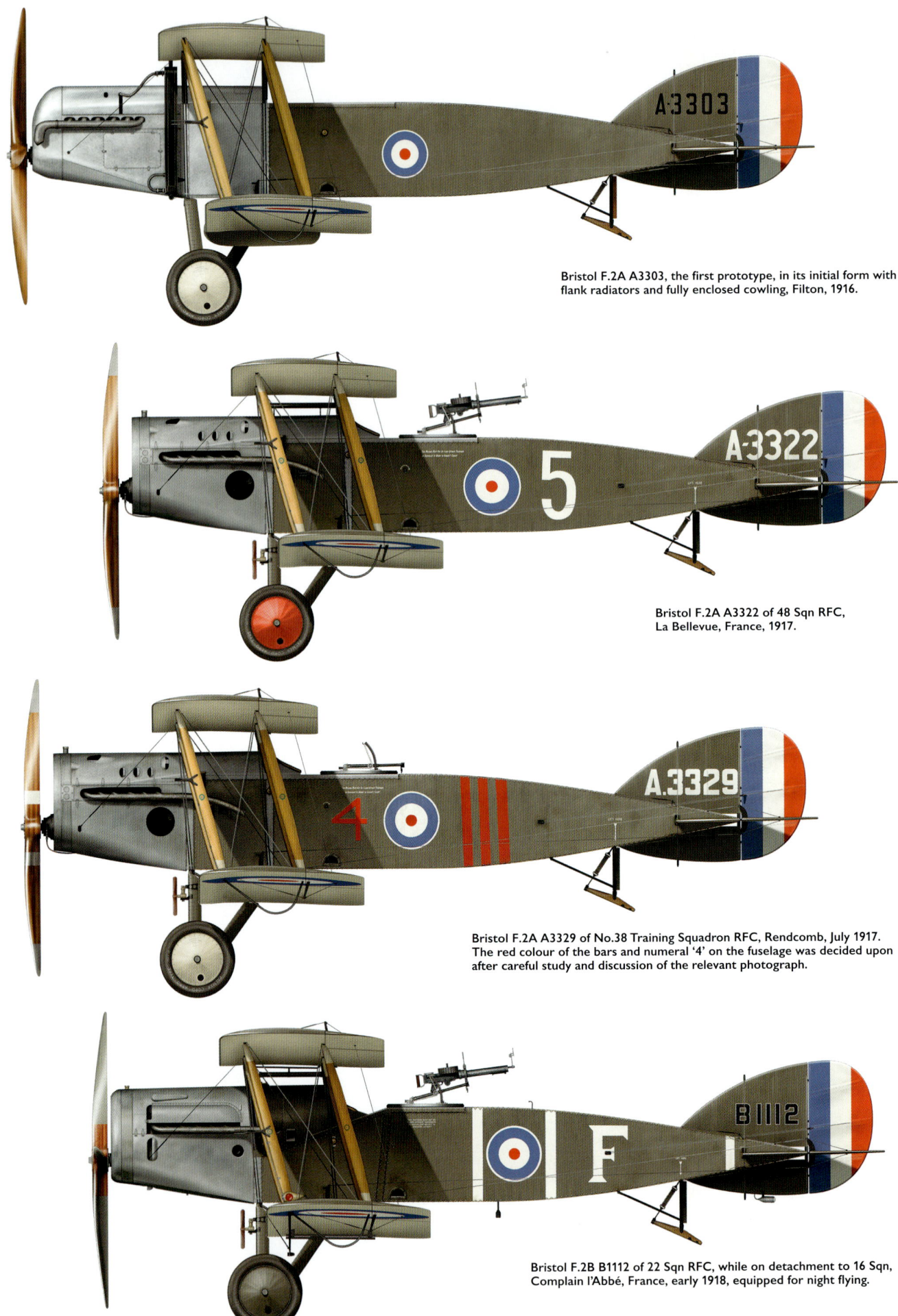

Bristol F.2A A3303, the first prototype, in its initial form with flank radiators and fully enclosed cowling, Filton, 1916.

Bristol F.2A A3322 of 48 Sqn RFC, La Bellevue, France, 1917.

Bristol F.2A A3329 of No.38 Training Squadron RFC, Rendcomb, July 1917. The red colour of the bars and numeral '4' on the fuselage was decided upon after careful study and discussion of the relevant photograph.

Bristol F.2B B1112 of 22 Sqn RFC, while on detachment to 16 Sqn, Complain l'Abbé, France, early 1918, equipped for night flying.

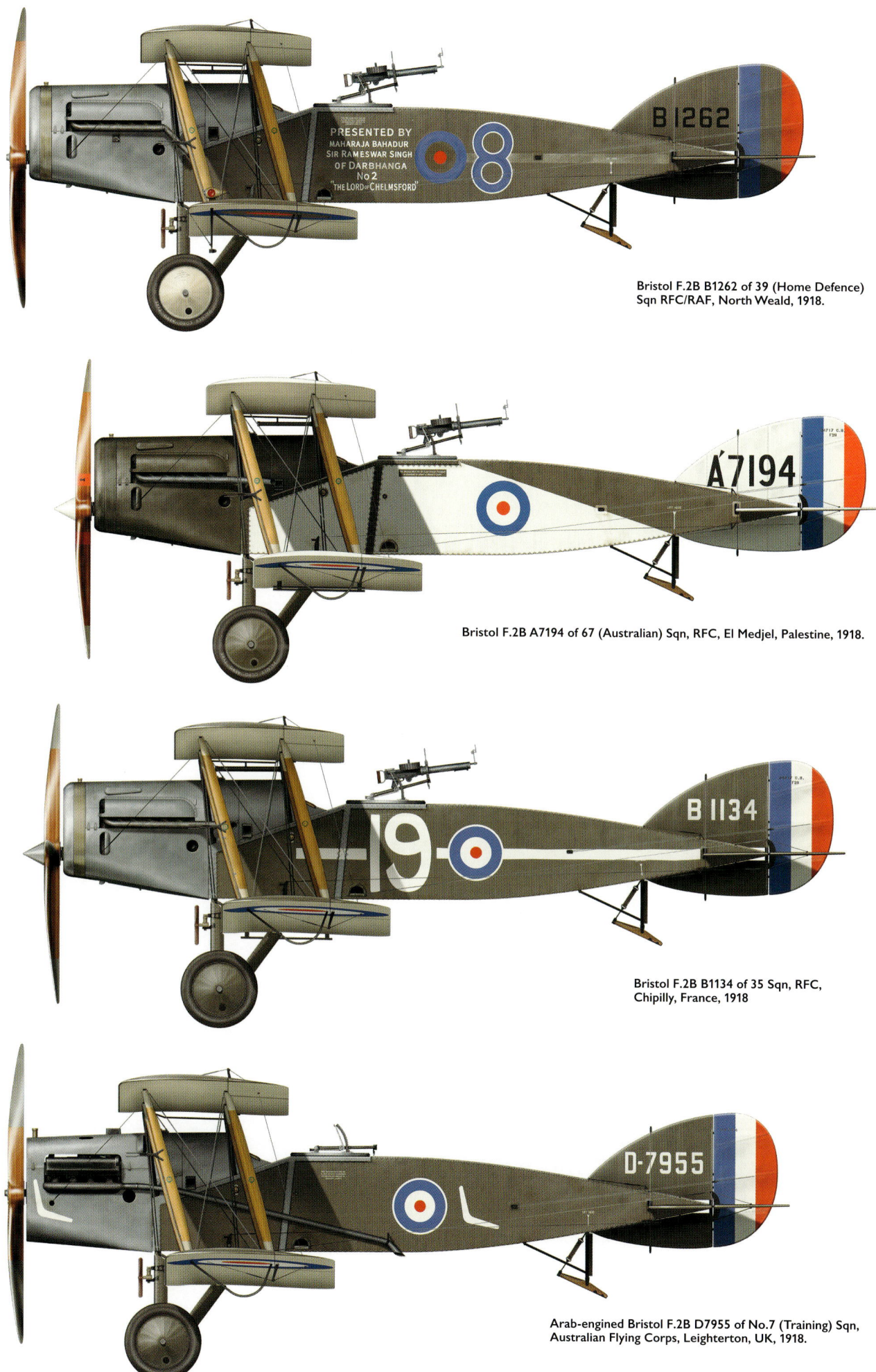

Bristol F.2B B1262 of 39 (Home Defence) Sqn RFC/RAF, North Weald, 1918.

Bristol F.2B A7194 of 67 (Australian) Sqn, RFC, El Medjel, Palestine, 1918.

Bristol F.2B B1134 of 35 Sqn, RFC, Chipilly, France, 1918

Arab-engined Bristol F.2B D7955 of No.7 (Training) Sqn, Australian Flying Corps, Leighterton, UK, 1918.

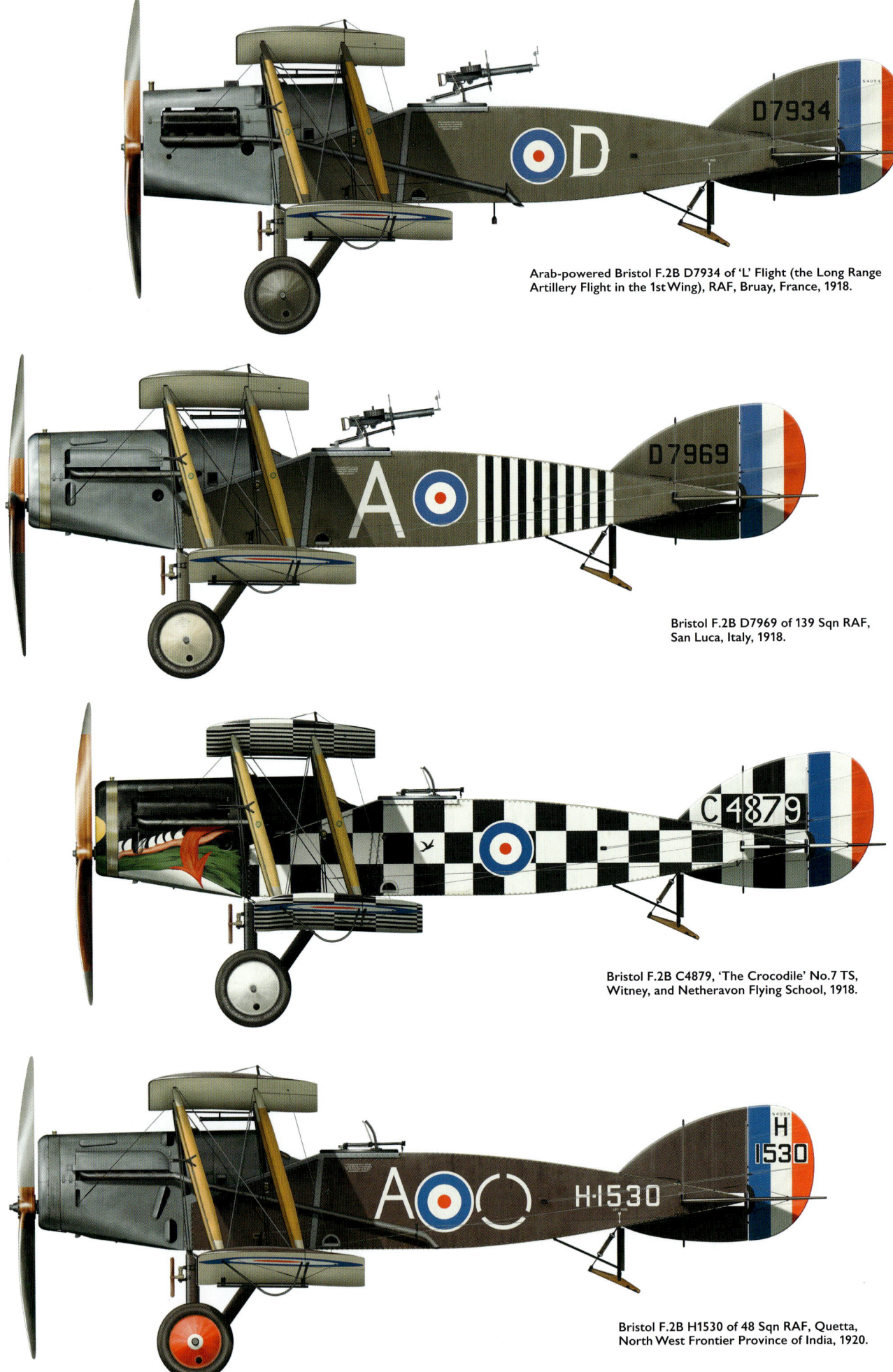

Arab-powered Bristol F.2B D7934 of 'L' Flight (the Long Range
Artillery Flight in the 1st Wing), RAF, Bruay, France, 1918.

Bristol F.2B D7969 of 139 Sqn RAF,
San Luca, Italy, 1918.

Bristol F.2B C4879, 'The Crocodile' No.7 TS,
Witney, and Netheravon Flying School, 1918.

Bristol F.2B H1530 of 48 Sqn RAF, Quetta,
North West Frontier Province of India, 1920.

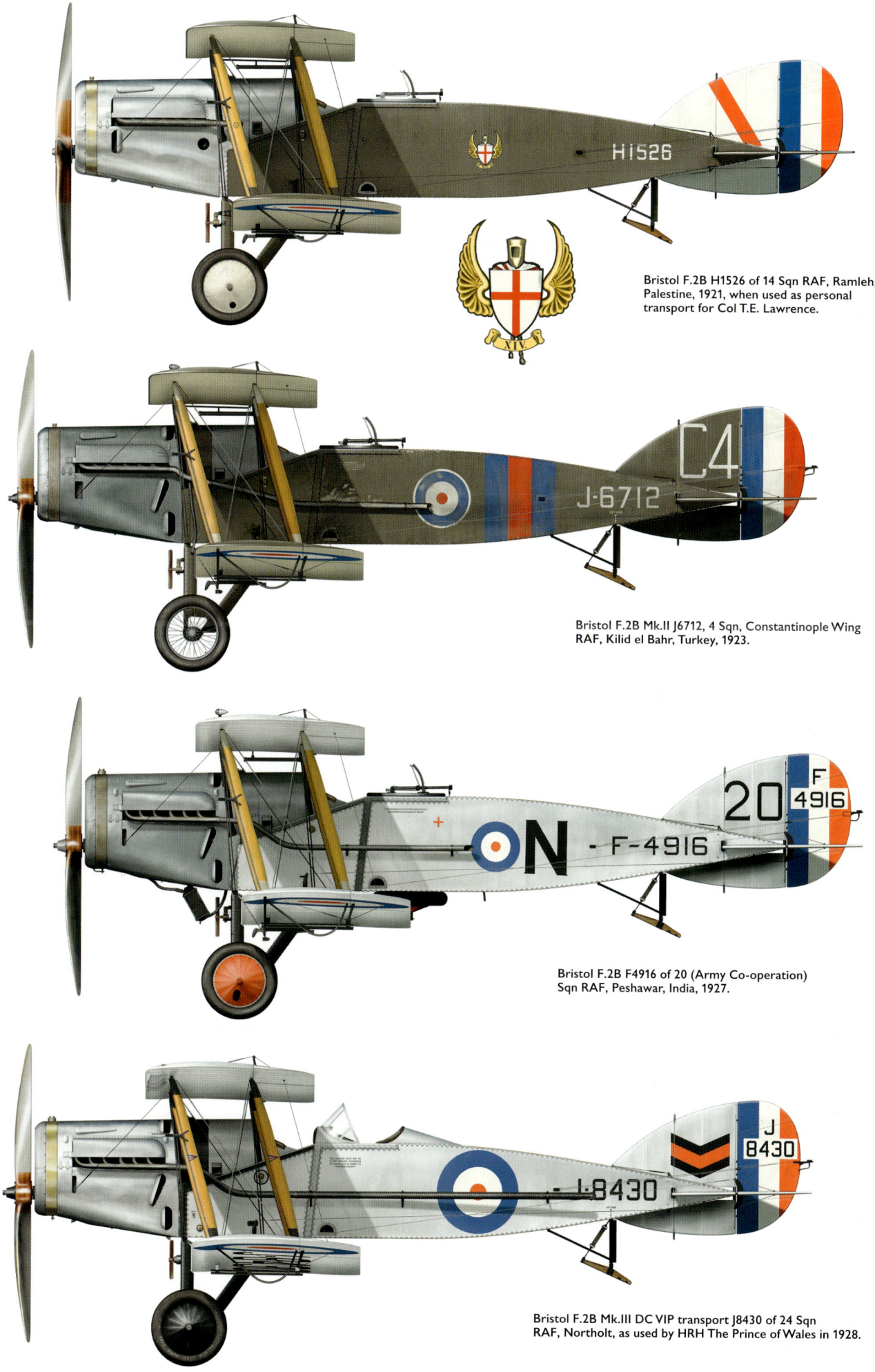

Bristol F.2B H1526 of 14 Sqn RAF, Ramleh, Palestine, 1921, when used as personal transport for Col T.E. Lawrence.

Bristol F.2B Mk.II J6712, 4 Sqn, Constantinople Wing RAF, Kilid el Bahr, Turkey, 1923.

Bristol F.2B F4916 of 20 (Army Co-operation) Sqn RAF, Peshawar, India, 1927.

Bristol F.2B Mk.III DC VIP transport J8430 of 24 Sqn RAF, Northolt, as used by HRH The Prince of Wales in 1928.

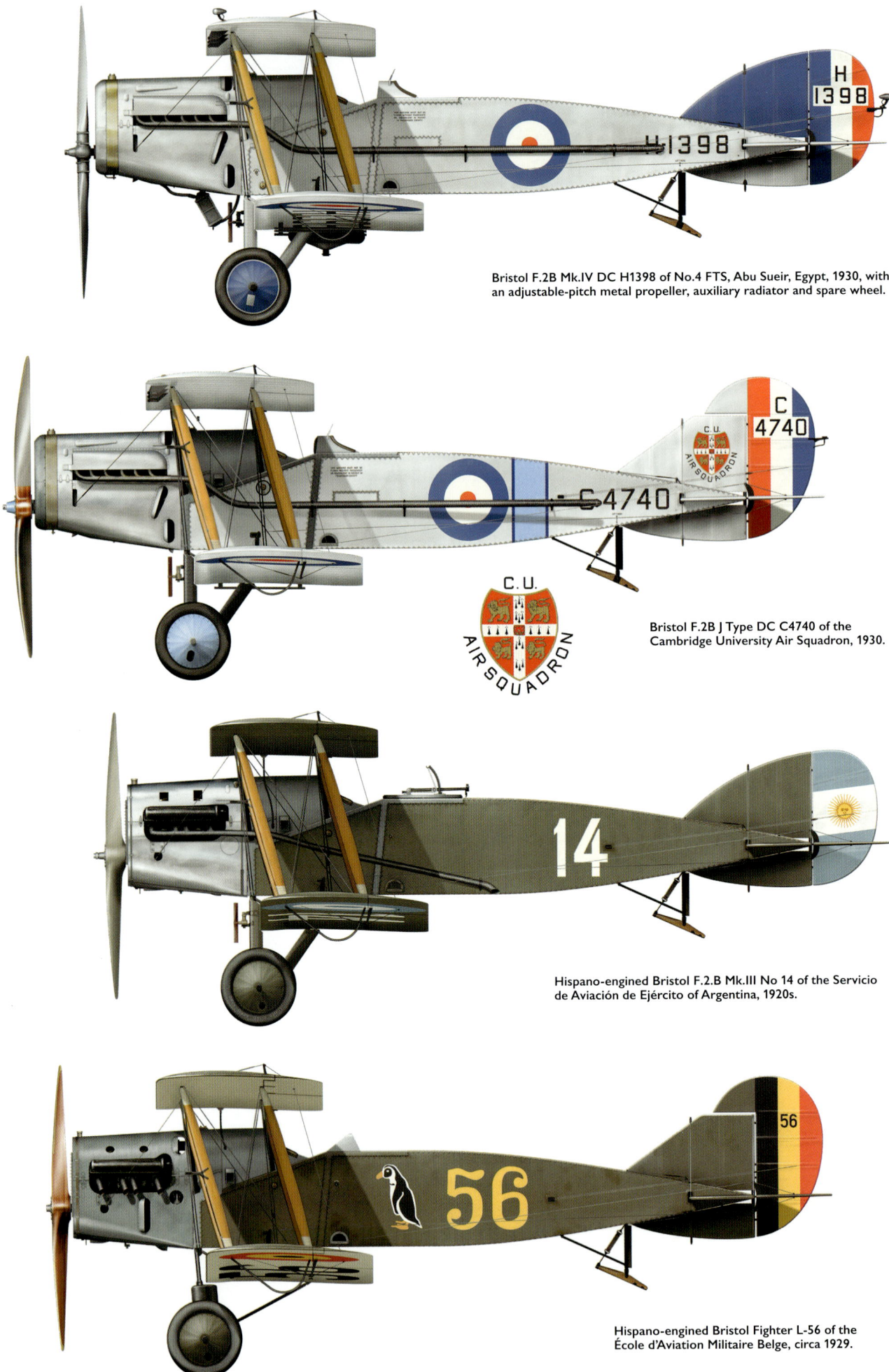

Bristol F.2B Mk.IV DC H1398 of No.4 FTS, Abu Sueir, Egypt, 1930, with an adjustable-pitch metal propeller, auxiliary radiator and spare wheel.

Bristol F.2B J Type DC C4740 of the Cambridge University Air Squadron, 1930.

Hispano-engined Bristol F.2.B Mk.III No 14 of the Servicio de Aviación de Ejército of Argentina, 1920s.

Hispano-engined Bristol Fighter L-56 of the École d'Aviation Militaire Belge, circa 1929.

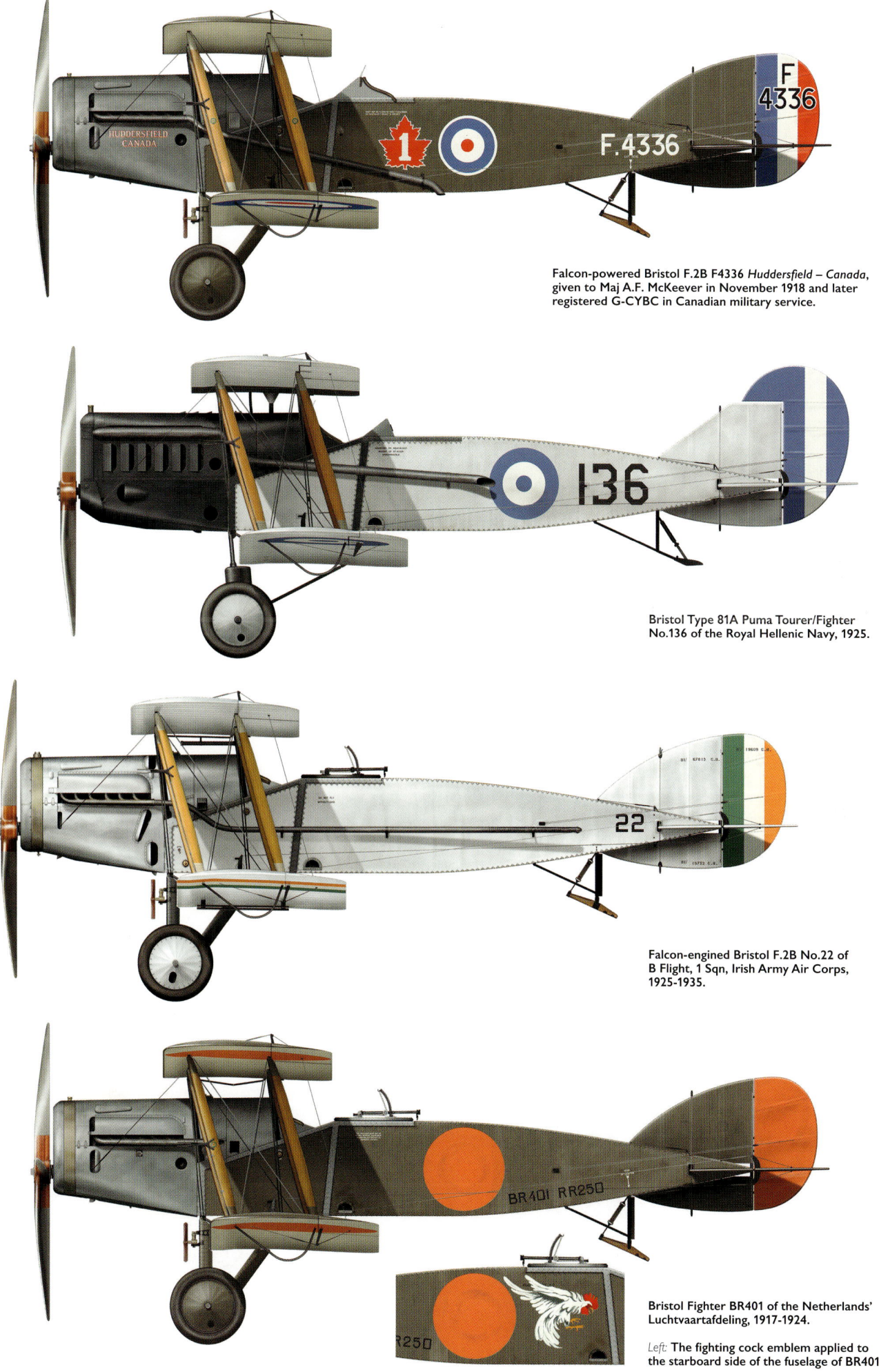

Falcon-powered Bristol F.2B F4336 *Huddersfield – Canada*, given to Maj A.F. McKeever in November 1918 and later registered G-CYBC in Canadian military service.

Bristol Type 81A Puma Tourer/Fighter No.136 of the Royal Hellenic Navy, 1925.

Falcon-engined Bristol F.2B No.22 of B Flight, 1 Sqn, Irish Army Air Corps, 1925-1935.

Bristol Fighter BR401 of the Netherlands' Luchtvaartafdeling, 1917-1924.

Left: The fighting cock emblem applied to the starboard side of the fuselage of BR401.

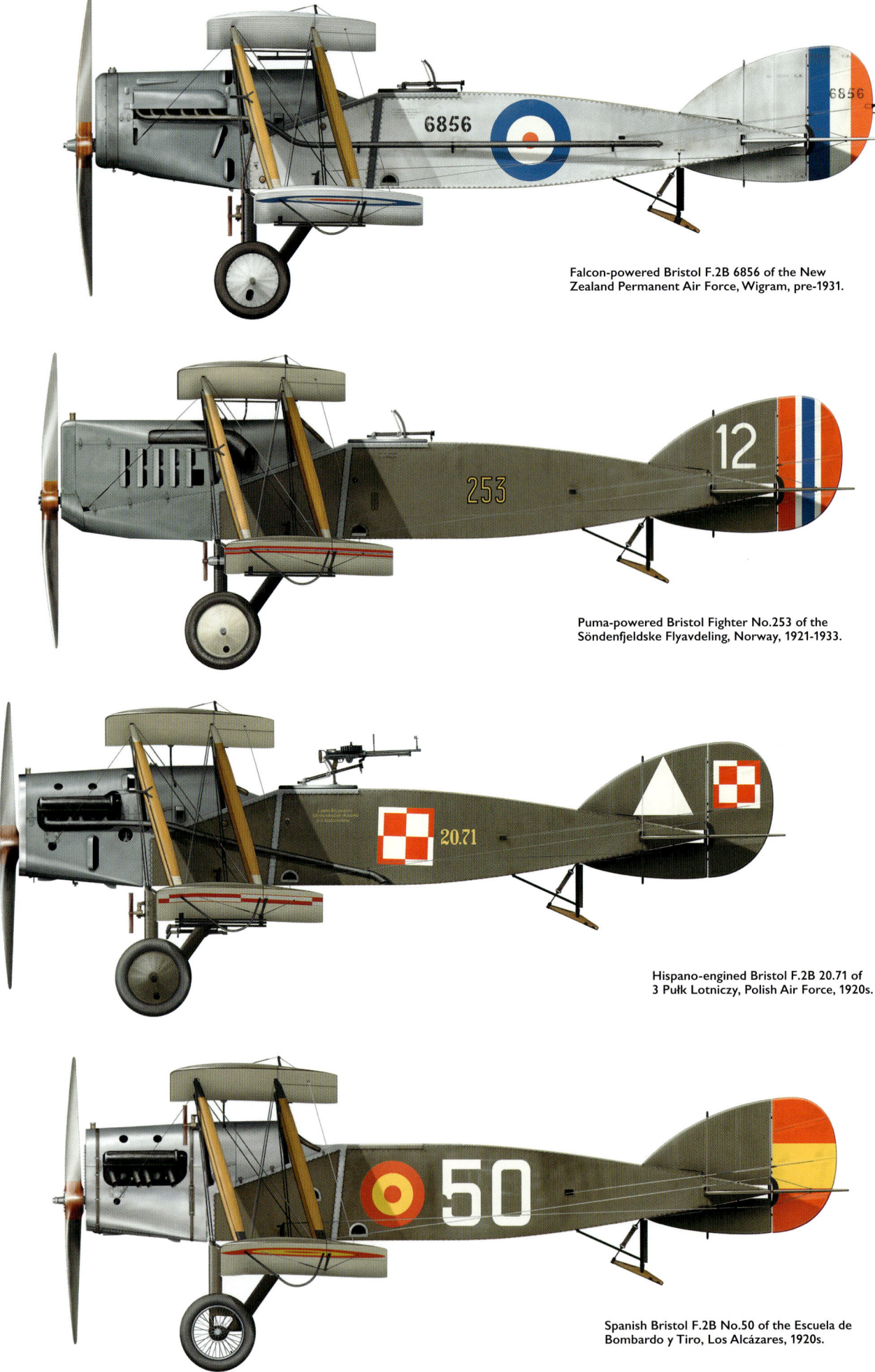

Falcon-powered Bristol F.2B 6856 of the New Zealand Permanent Air Force, Wigram, pre-1931.

Puma-powered Bristol Fighter No.253 of the Söndenfjeldske Flyavdeling, Norway, 1921-1933.

Hispano-engined Bristol F.2B 20.71 of 3 Pułk Lotniczy, Polish Air Force, 1920s.

Spanish Bristol F.2B No.50 of the Escuela de Bombardo y Tiro, Los Alcázares, 1920s.

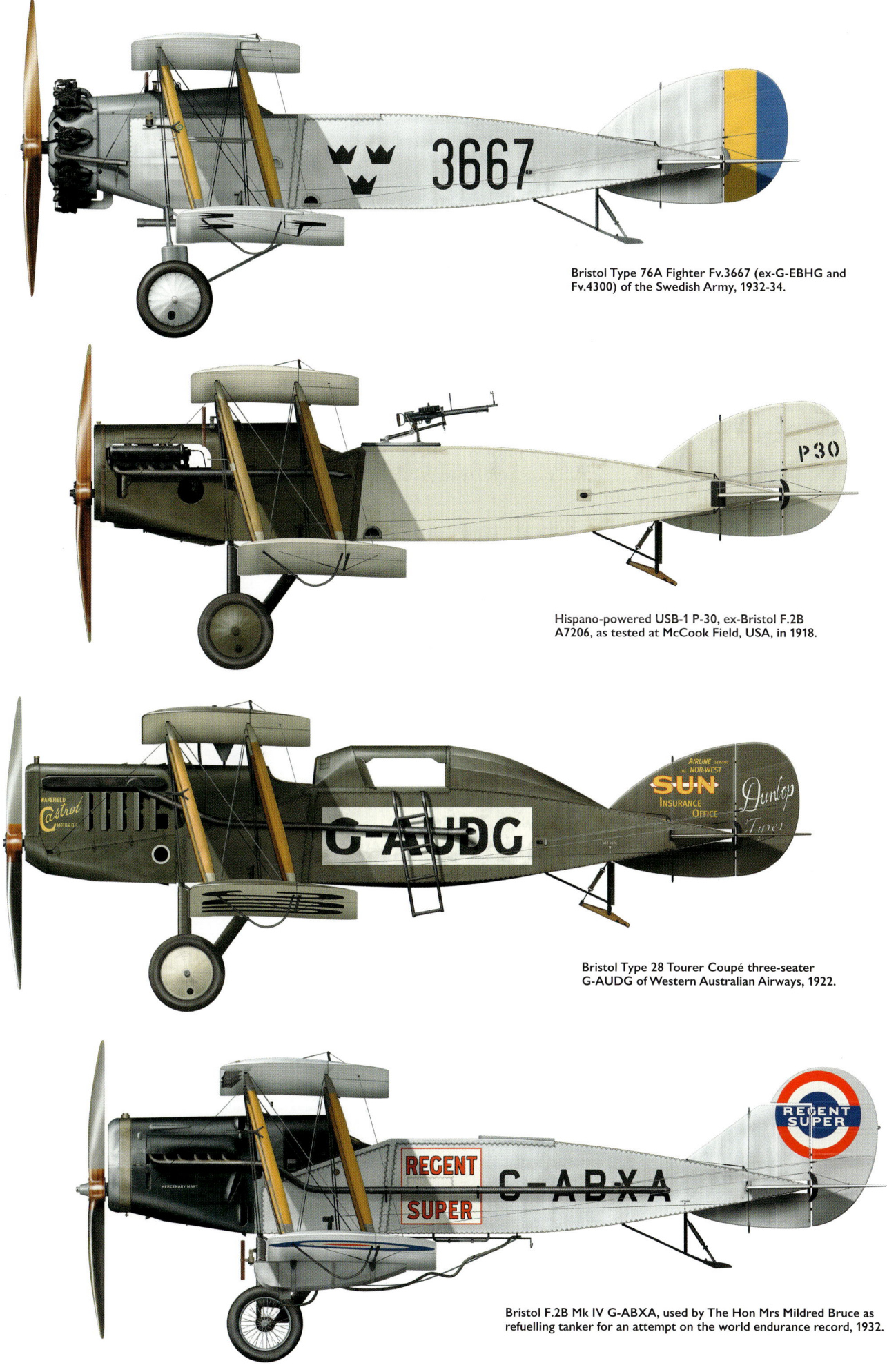

Bristol Type 76A Fighter Fv.3667 (ex-G-EBHG and Fv.4300) of the Swedish Army, 1932-34.

Hispano-powered USB-1 P-30, ex-Bristol F.2B A7206, as tested at McCook Field, USA, in 1918.

Bristol Type 28 Tourer Coupé three-seater G-AUDG of Western Australian Airways, 1922.

Bristol F.2B Mk IV G-ABXA, used by The Hon Mrs Mildred Bruce as refuelling tanker for an attempt on the world endurance record, 1932.

BIBLIOGRAPHY

The greater part of this book's factual content is derived from many of the official files (mainly those in the AIR.1 series) in the National Archives, Kew, from early volumes of the weekly magazines *Flight* and *The Aeroplane*, articles in the quarterly journal of *Cross & Cockade International*, and from logbooks and other documents in the Royal Air Force Museum, Hendon, and the Fleet Air Arm Museum, Yeovilton. Relevant matter, much of it substantial, has also come from the following publications.

Aeronautical Research Committee Reports and Memoranda (Rs & M):
R & M No.849, Aerodynamics staff of the RAE, *The Effect Upon the Control of an Aeroplane of Carrying Load Distributed Along the Planes*, HMSO, 1922.
R & M No.859, Aerodynamics staff of the RAE, *Lift and Drag of the Bristol Fighter with Wings of Three Aspect Ratios*, HMSO, 1923.
R & M No.966, Garner, H.M., and Jones, E.T., *Full Scale Tests of Different Ailerons on Bristol Fighter Aeroplane*, HMSO, 1925.
R & M No.972, Stevens, H.L., *Full Scale Tests of a Bristol Fighter with Increased Rudder Control*, HMSO, 1925.
Air Ministry, *Air Publication 125, A Short History of the Royal Air Force*, 2nd revised edition, HMSO, 1936.
————, *Air Publication 129, Royal Air Force Flying Training Manual, Part 1, Flying Instruction*, HMSO, 1923.
————, *Air Publication 866, The Bristol Fighter Mark IV*, 2nd edition, HMSO, 1928.
Barnes, C.H., *Bristol Aircraft since 1910,* 3rd edition, Putnam, London, 1988.
Battle, Air Cdre H.F.V., *Line! The Reminiscences of a Royal Air Force Pilot*, Nicholas Battle/Countryside Books, 1984.
Bowers, Peter M., *Curtiss Aircraft 1907-1947*, Putnam, London, 1979.
Bowyer, Chaz, *Bristol F.2B Fighter, King of Two-seaters*, Ian Allan, London, 1985.
————, *RAF Operations 1918-1938*, William Kimber, London, 1988.
————, *Aircraft Profile No.237: Bristol F.2B Fighters: RAF 1918-32*, Profile Publications, Windsor, Berks, 1972.
Bridgeman, Brian, *The Flyers*, self-published by Brian Bridgeman, Swindon, Wiltshire, 1989.
Bridgman, Leonard (text by Oliver Stewart), *The Clouds Remember*, Gale & Polden, Aldershot, 1934.
Bruce, J.M., *British Military Aeroplanes 1914-18*, Putnam, London, 1957.
————, *The Aeroplanes of the Royal Flying Corps (Military Wing)*, 2nd revised edition, Putnam, London, 1992.
————, *Vintage Warbirds No.4, The Bristol Fighter*, Arms and Armour Press, London, 1985.
————, *Profile Publications No.21 The Bristol Fighter*, Profile Publications, Leatherhead, Surrey, 1965.
————, *War Planes of the First World War; Fighters*, Vol 1, 2nd fully revised impression, Macdonald, London, 1970.

————, *Windsock Datafile No.4, Bristol Fighter*, Albatros Productions, Berkhamsted, Herts, 1987.
————, *Bristol Fighter* Vols 1 and 2, Windsock Datafile Specials, Albatros Productions, Berkhamsted, Herts, 1997 and 1998.
Butler, Phil, *Liverpool Airport History*.
Casari, Robert B., *American Military Aircraft 1908-1919*, Aeronaut Books, Reno, Nevada, USA, 2014.
Cole, C., and Cheesman, E.F., *The Air Defence of Britain 1914-1918*, Putnam, London, 1984.
Cooksley, Peter, *Bristol Fighter in Action, Aircraft No.137*, Squadron/Signal Publications, Carrollton, Texas, USA, 1993.
Cross & Cockade International (various contributing authors), *Lawrence of Arabia & Middle East Air Power*, Cross & Cockade International, Woodhall Spa, Lincolnshire, 2016.
Cutlack, F.M., *The Australian Flying Corps in the Western and Eastern Theatres of War 1914-1918*, Vol. VIII of *The Official History of Australia in the War of 1914-18*, 9th edition, Angus and Robertson, Sydney, Australia, 1940.
Dousek, Petr, et al, *Bristol Fighter F.2B in Detail*, Wings & Wheels Publications, Prague, Czech Republic, 2008.
Franks, Norman, Bailey, Frank, and Duiven, Rick, *The Jasta War Chronology*, Grub Street, London, 1998.
————,————, ————, *Casualties of the German Air Service 1914-1920*, Grub Street, London, 1999.
Gardner, Brian, *Aerial Refuelling at Farnborough*, Air-Britain, Tunbridge Wells, Kent, 1999.
Grey, C.G. (Ed.) *Jane's All the World's Aircraft*, various editions.
Gurdon, John E., *Over and Above*, 1919; new edition with additional material, Grub Street, London, 2018.
Guttman, John, *Bristol F.2 Fighter Aces of World War 1*, Osprey Aircraft of the Aces series, No.79, Osprey, Oxford, 2007.
Halley, J.J., *The Squadrons of the Royal Air Force and Commonwealth 1918-1988*, Air-Britain, Tonbridge Wells, Kent, 1988.
Harvey, W.F.J., *'Pi' in the Sky: A History of No 22 Squadron Royal Flying Corps & RAF in the War of 1914-1918*, Colin Huston, 1971.
Hayes, Karl E., *A History of the Royal Air Force and United States Naval Air Service in Ireland 1913-1923*, Irish Air Letter, 1988.
Heazell, P., *Most Secret: The Hidden History of Orford Ness*, The History Press, Stroud, Gloucestershire, 2010.
Henshaw, Trevor, *The Sky their Battlefield II*, 2nd revised edition, Fetubi Books, 2014.
Howson, Gerald, *Aircraft of the Spanish Civil War 1936-1939*, Putnam, London, 1990.
Jackson, A.J., *De Havilland Aircraft since 1909*, Putnam, London, 1987.
————, *British Civil Aircraft since 1919, vols 1, 2 & 3*, Putnam, London, 1973 and 1974.
Jones, Lorraine Colvill, *Your Ever Loving Son: the Story of the First Argentine 'Ace' of the First World War*, Grupo Abierto Communicationes, Buenos Aires, Argentina, 2008.
Keith, C.H., *Flying Years*, John Hamilton, London, 1937.

King, H.F. *Armament of British Aircraft 1909-1939*, Putnam, London, 1971.
Kopanski, Tomasz J., *British WW1 Aircraft in the Polish Air Force*, Mushroom Model Publication, Redborn, 1999.
————, *Polish Wings 22; Bristol F.2B Fighter, RAF SE5a, Sopwith 1F.1 Camel, Sopwith 5F.1 Dolphin, Martinsyde F.4 Buzzard*, Stratus, Poland, 2017.
Lewis, Cecil, *Farewell to Wings*, Temple Press, London, 1964.
Macmillan, Norman, *Freelance Pilot*, William Heinemann, London, 1937.
————, *Wings of Fate*, G. Bell and Sons, London, 1967.
Napier, Michael, *Winged Crusaders: The Exploits of 14 Squadron RFC & RAF 1915-1945*, Pen & Sword, Barnsley, South Yorkshire, 2012.
Nesbitt-Dufort, John, *Open Cockpit: Flying Pre-war Fighting and Training Aircraft*, Speed and Sports Publications, London, 1970.
Noble, Walter, *With a Bristol Fighter Squadron*, Andrew Melrose, 1920 (large print edition Cedric Chivers, Bath, 1977).
Parnell, Neville, and Boughton, Trevor, *Flypast – A Record of Aviation in Australia*, Australian Government Publishing Service, 1988.
Raleigh, Sir Walter, and Jones, H.A., *The War in the Air* (6 vols plus maps and appendices), Oxford University Press, 1922-1937.
Rogers, L.A., *Windsock Datafile No.115, Bristol Fighter*, Albatros Productions, Berkhamsted, Herts, 2006.
Royal Aircraft Establishment Report No.B.A.368, *Lateral Control of Bristol Fighter with Puma Engine*, 8 October 1920.
Royal Aircraft Establishment Report No.B.A.369, *The Nose Heaviness of Puma Bristol Fighters*, 11 October 1920.
Sellwood, Robert A., *Winged Sabres: One of the RFC's Most Decorated Squadrons* (20 Sqn), Pen & Sword, Yorkshire, 2018.
Shores, Christopher, Franks, Norman, and Guest, Russell, *Above the Trenches*, Grub Street, London, 1990.
————, ————, ————, *Above the Trenches Supplement*, Grub Street, London, 1996.
Simpson, Alan, *Loughton Air Park – Abridge Aerodrome*, The Alderton Press, Loughton, Essex, 2018.
Smiddy, Paul, *A Passion for Speed: The Daring Life of Mildred, The Honourable Mrs Victor Bruce*, History Press, Stroud, Gloucestershire, 2017.
Swanborough, Gordon, and Bowers, Peter M., *United States Military Aircraft since 1918*, Putnam. London, 1971.
Voss, Vivian ('Roger Vee'), *Flying Minnows*, John Hamilton, London, 1935. Reprint with amendments and additions by Arms & Armour Press, London, 1977.
Wheeler, Allen, *Flying Between the Wars*, G.T. Foulis, Henley-on-Thames, 1972.

Ledger listing Bristol Aeroplane Company production contracts. From the collection of the late C.H. Barnes, ex-Technical Librarian of Bristol Aircraft and author of *Bristol Aircraft since 1910* (see above). Now in Philip Jarrett's collection.

INDEX